# THE OXFORD HANDBOOK OF

# ASIAN BUSINESS SYSTEMS

# THE OXFORD HANDBOOK OF

# ASIAN BUSINESS SYSTEMS

*Edited by*

MICHAEL A. WITT

*and*

GORDON REDDING

OXFORD
UNIVERSITY PRESS

# OXFORD
### UNIVERSITY PRESS

Great Clarendon Street, Oxford, OX2 6DP,
United Kingdom

Oxford University Press is a department of the University of Oxford.
It furthers the University's objective of excellence in research, scholarship,
and education by publishing worldwide. Oxford is a registered trade mark of
Oxford University Press in the UK and in certain other countries

© Oxford University Press 2014

The moral rights of the authors have been asserted

First published 2014
First published in paperback 2015

Published in the United States of America by Oxford University Press
198 Madison Avenue, New York, NY 10016, United States of America

British Library Cataloguing in Publication Data
Data available

Library of Congress Cataloging in Publication Data
Data available

ISBN 978-0-19-965492-5 (Hbk.)
ISBN 978-0-19-874542-6 (Pbk.)

Links to third party websites are provided by Oxford in good faith and
for information only. Oxford disclaims any responsibility for the materials
contained in any third party website referenced in this work.

# Preface and Acknowledgements

THE origins of this handbook lay in the observation that growing interest in Asia, both in the field of socio-economics and among practitioners, was not matched with ready availability of up-to-date empirics. In late 2010, we thus approached David Musson of Oxford University Press with a proposal for an edited volume comprising what has become Part I of this handbook. With David's encouragement, we subsequently widened our scope to the present *Oxford Handbook*. We would like to express our sincere thanks to David and his team at Oxford University Press for their consequent backing and support.

The result is the present handbook. It comprises thirty chapters produced by thirty leading scholars and ourselves. As it turned out, finding a team of experts who could write the kinds of chapters this handbook calls for was extremely challenging. For Part I chapters, we needed scholars capable of analysing an entire business system, not just individual components such as corporate governance or employment relations. For Part II chapters, we needed scholars capable of exploring individual components of business systems across the entire region, from India to Japan, rather than in one or a handful of economies. We are very fortunate to have been able to assemble such a team. We are also conscious of many distinguished scholars who might also have been included in the list of writers, but whose work nevertheless still permeates many chapters. We would like to thank all of our fellow authors for their willingness to contribute to this endeavour. Clearly the book rests largely on their scholarship.

Essential to this effort has also been the copy-editing provided by John Billingsley. We are very grateful for his tireless work to ensure that each chapter adheres to the same style, has complete references, and in particular, is written in a form accessible to a wide readership. We would also like to thank the librarians at INSEAD's Tanoto library for helping us gain access to all the information we needed, no matter how difficult to obtain. Our earlier experience at INSEAD's Euro-Asia Centre, now transmuted into the Singapore Campus, and at the Universities of Hong Kong, Manchester, Stanford, and Harvard, laid much-appreciated foundations. Avegail Villaneuva at INSEAD and Leah Chan at the HEAD Foundation Singapore provided editorial assistance of a high order, for which we record our grateful thanks.

Part of the editorial work of this handbook happened at the Free University Berlin, where Michael Witt spent the summers of 2011 and 2012 as a Humboldt Fellow. He thanks Gregory Jackson for hosting him and the Humboldt Foundation for its generous financial support. Gordon Redding was kindly supported at the HEAD Foundation,

Singapore, while working on this handbook. He also benefited greatly from the years of regional excursions with the Wharton International Forum, led by Michael Alexander.

For a topic as large, varied, and complex as the one addressed here, the audacity of the attempt to rein it in can only be partially counterbalanced by years of study, of teaching, and of practical immersion. Crucial in this learning process have been the influences of other scholars, and the editors wish to record their gratitude for the large number of shapers of their thinking. They cannot all be listed, but at least certain key debts are now gratefully acknowledged. For Gordon Redding these are: Peter Berger, the late Max Boisot, Michael Harris Bond, John Child, Derek Pugh, and particularly Richard Whitley. For Michael Witt these are: Henri-Claude de Bettignies, Peter A. Hall, Arie Y. Lewin, Susan J. Pharr, Gordon Redding, and Steven K. Vogel.

Last but not least, we would like to thank our patient families for letting us indulge in this endeavour.

Singapore, 5 February 2013
Michael A. Witt and Gordon Redding

# Contents

## PART II  THEMES IN COMPARATIVE PERSPECTIVE

## PART III  EVOLUTIONARY TRAJECTORIES

## PART IV  CONCLUSIONS

# LIST OF FIGURES

# List of Tables

# Contributors

**Regina M. Abrami** is a Senior Lecturer at the Political Science Department, Senior Fellow in the Management Department of the Wharton School of Business, and Director of the Global Program of the Lauder Institute of Management and International Studies, University of Pennsylvania, US.

**Christina L. Ahmadjian** is Professor of Management at the Graduate School of Commerce and Management, Hitotsubashi University, Tokyo, Japan.

**Edo Andriesse** is Assistant Professor at the Department of Geography, Seoul National University, Korea.

**Michael Harris Bond** is Visiting Chair Professor of Psychology at the Department of Management and Marketing, Hong Kong Polytechnic University, Hong Kong.

**Michael Carney** is Professor in the Department of Management at the John Molson School of Business, Concordia University, Montreal, Canada.

**Richard W. Carney** is a Fellow at the Australian National University, Australia.

**Arnoud De Meyer** is President at Singapore Management University, Singapore.

**Stephen J. Frenkel** is Professor of Organisation and Employment Relations at the Australian School of Business, University of New South Wales, Australia.

**Axèle Giroud** is Reader in International Business at Manchester Business School, University of Manchester, Manchester, UK.

**Gary G. Hamilton** is Professor at the Department of Sociology and The Jackson School of International Studies, University of Washington, US.

**Hsin-Huang Michael Hsiao** is Distinguished Research Fellow and Director of the Institute of Sociology, Academia Sinica, Taipei, Taiwan.

**Mari Kondo** is Professor at the Graduate School of Business, Doshisha University, Kyoto, Japan.

**Zong-Rong Lee** is Associate Research Fellow at Academia Sinica, Institute of Sociology, Taipei, Taiwan.

**William K. W. Leung** is the Founding Partner of William KW Leung & Co., Solicitors, Hong Kong.

**Arie Y. Lewin** is Professor of Strategy and International Business at the Fuqua School of Business, Duke University, US.

**Peter Ping Li** is Professor of Chinese Business Studies at Copenhagen Business School, Denmark.

**Shige Makino** is Professor and Chairman of the Department of Management at the Chinese University of Hong Kong, Hong Kong.

**Gordon Redding** is a professor of Asian Business and Comparative Management at INSEAD, Singapore, Professor Emeritus of Management Studies, University of Hong Kong and the Secretary General of the Head Foundation, Singapore.

**Andrew James Rosser** is Australian Research Council Future Fellow at the University of Adelaide, Australia.

**Chris Rowley** is Professor at Cass Business School, City University, London, UK, and Director, Research and Publications, at HEAD Foundation, Singapore.

**Lawrence Saez** is Professor in the Political Economy of Asia at the Department of Politics, School of Oriental and African Studies (SOAS), University of London, UK.

**Solee I. Shin** is a Ph.D. Candidate in Sociology at the University of Washington, US.

**Akira Suehiro** is Professor at the Institute of Social Science at the University of Tokyo, Japan.

**Quang Truong** is Emeritus Professor at the Maastricht School of Management, the Netherlands.

**Natenapha Wailerdsak Yabushita** is Lecturer at Thammasat Business School, Bangkok, Thailand.

**Richard Whitley** is Emeritus Professor of Organizational Sociology at Manchester Business School, University of Manchester, UK.

**Michael A. Witt** is a professor of Asian Business and Comparative Management at INSEAD, Singapore, and an Associate in Research at the Reischauer Institute, Harvard University, US.

**Gilbert Y. Y. Wong** is an Associate Professor at the School of Business at the University of Hong Kong, Hong Kong.

**Daphne W. Yiu** is an Associate Professor at the Department of Management at the Chinese University of Hong Kong, Hong Kong.

**Leslie Young** is Wei Lun Professor of Finance at the Chinese University of Hong Kong, Hong Kong.

**Kyoung-Hee Yu** is Lecturer at the Australian School of Business at the University of New South Wales, Australia.

**Xing Zhong** is a Research Associate at the Fuqua School of Business, Duke University, US.

# CHAPTER 1

## INTRODUCTION

### MICHAEL A. WITT AND GORDON REDDING

THE exploration of Asian business systems can look back on a long and somewhat adventurous history. Among its earlier classics are works such as Dore's (1973) comparison of British and Japanese factory organization; Aoki's (1988) research on the workings of the Japanese economy; Redding's (1990) exposition of ethnic Chinese capitalism in South East Asia; Whitley's (1992) work on East Asian business systems, which helped lay the foundation for one of the key works of the field, Whitley's (1999) elaboration of business systems theory; and Orrù, Biggart, and Hamilton's (1997) explorations of economic organization in East Asia.

Recent years have seen a surge of works seeking to expand the boundaries of our knowledge of Asian business systems and of extant theories and models in the field. The case of Japan has continued to attract much attention. A series of works has explored topics such as how the Japanese business system compares with those of other advanced industrialized economies (e.g. Berger and Dore 1996; Dore 2000; Streeck and Yamamura 2001) and how it evolves over time (e.g. Dore 2000; Yamamura and Streeck 2003; Anchordoguy 2005; Vogel 2006; Westney 2006; Witt 2006; Aoki, Jackson, and Miyajima 2007; Lechevalier 2007; Sako 2008).

Research on other Asian economies, as well as wider comparative work, has likewise built up steam. There has been a proliferation of focused studies, especially of China (e.g. Huang 2008; Witt and Redding 2009; Robins 2010), but also of other Asian economies, individually (e.g. Andriesse and van Westen 2009; Ritchie 2009) or viewed as a cluster (e.g. Loveridge 2006; Heugens, van Essen, and van Oosterhout 2009; Steier 2009; Tipton 2009). A number of works undertaking broad intra-Asian comparisons and surveys have emerged, including volumes by Redding and Witt (2007) (China, Japan, Korea, ethnic Chinese business in South East Asia); Pascha, Storz, and Taube (2011) (China, Japan, Korea); Storz and Schäfer (2011) (China and Japan); and Boyer, Uemura, and Isogai (2012) (China, Japan, Korea, East Asia).

Yet much work remains to be done. The progress of science depends on the constant interplay of idiographic description and nomothetic theorizing, and thus less on logical procedures of deduction than on the inventing of testable explanations based on immersion in empirical reality (Popper 1963; Tsoukas 1989; Runciman 2005; Babble 2012). These can then be tested and possibly destroyed, but they must be conjectured first, and a way forward in this is describing and categorizing.

At the point of this writing, the literature lacks a comprehensive, up-to-date, and detailed overview of the institutional features of Asian economies in comparative perspective. In general, the further away one moves from Japan, the less well understood the institutional structures and dynamics of business systems in Asia become. South East Asian economies, for instance, are usually clustered together, sometimes jointly with Hong Kong and Taiwan (e.g. Whitley 1992, 1999; Redding and Witt 2007). There is some justification for this, in the sense that ethnic Chinese businesses produce much of the economic value in these countries. At the same time, institutional variations that are important for understanding these economies are unaccounted for. India, now Asia's third-largest economy, is virtually terra incognita from a business-systems perspective. We also do not know how the institutional structures of Asian economies compare and may form clusters of similar Asian varieties of business systems.

The scarcity of systematic and detailed comparative data means that we have been unable to leverage the full institutional diversity that Asia affords for testing and amending extant theory of institutional variations—lack of idiographic detail means foregone nomothetic progress.

The objective of this handbook is to help address this issue. In the twenty-nine chapters that follow, it presents detailed institutional analyses of each of the major Asian business systems; comparative analyses of important themes across these business systems; perspectives on the impact of history and institutional change; and summary conclusions for business-systems research and business practitioners.

In the following pages, we begin with definitions. We then briefly discuss the structure of this book and, where appropriate, its methodological and epistemological foundations. We deliberately abstain from summarizing each chapter here, leaving this task to Part IV. We further do not engage in an extensive review of business-systems theory, but assume that our scholarly readership is familiar with the key foundational works, especially those by Whitley (1992; 1999); Hall and Soskice (2001), augmented by the critical evaluation of Hancké, Rhodes, and Thatcher (2007); Amable (2003); and Redding (2005).

# DEFINITIONS

In this handbook, we define 'Asia' to mean the land-mass from India to Japan, excluding the territory of Russia as well as the Antipodes.

We use the term 'business system' to refer to the institutions—the 'humanly devised constraints that shape human interaction' (North, 1990:3)—governing economic activity inside and outside firms, as identified in the models of Whitley

(1999), Hall and Soskice (2001), Amable (2003), Redding (2005), and Hancké et al. (2007) and summarized in Table 1.1. Our definition of business system deviates from the original meaning proposed by Whitley (1999), who used the term for the institutional structure of firms, which in turn is derived from the societal institutional structure in which firms are embedded. However, in subsequent use, the focus of the term has widened to include institutions both at firm and societal level (e.g. Edwards et al. 2005; Redding 2005; Redding and Witt 2007), and even Whitley's own usage has been ambiguous (e.g. Casper and Whitley 2004). We stay consistent with this evolved meaning.

Throughout this book, 'Korea' refers to the Republic of Korea, that is, South Korea. We note that this usage is consistent with that employed by South Koreans themselves.

## Structure of this Book

This handbook contains twenty-nine chapters (in addition to this one) divided into four major parts. Part I comprises thirteen chapters, each of which presents a detailed institutional analysis of one major Asian business system. Part II has eleven chapters. Each analyses one particular topic of interest, across as many of the thirteen business systems described in Part I as possible. Part III consists of three chapters, which offer perspectives on the impact of history on Asian business systems and on the dynamics of institutional change. Part IV presents two summary chapters bringing together the results emerging from the preceding parts. One of these is written for scholars, the other for business practitioners.

*Part I.* The goal of the chapters in this part was to present up-to-date, in-depth institutional descriptions and analyses of the major Asian business systems as they are today. The authors deliberately abstained from recounting the historical trajectories of these systems in any detail beyond that needed to contextualize the status quo. This design choice was based on the editors' assessment that, while there is an abundance of historical accounts of what once was or happened in many Asian business systems, there is great scarcity of truly contemporary analyses of what currently is. The story of economic reforms in China, for instance, has already been told thousands of times, and the probability of any additional account adding actual value to science is slim at best. The same goes for topics such as the developmental state (and attendant business systems) of Japan, Korea, or Taiwan, to name a few examples.

There are two basic approaches to structuring an institutional analysis. One is to let dimensions of variation emerge from cross-sectional data, as Amable (2003) did for the advanced industrialized countries. The other is to draw on existing models to identify key dimensions of different types of business systems and to search for data relevant to these dimensions. We chose the latter approach, for two reasons. First, given all the efforts at theory-building and empirical research in the field and the elaborate models that have resulted, it seemed prudent to draw on this existing theoretical and empirical basis rather than to start from scratch—not least also given that two major models, Whitley (1992; 1999) and Redding (2005), were built with Asia in mind. Second, keeping dimensions consistent with existing models facilitates the drawing of conclusions about the utility of existing models for understanding Asia, and about the possible directions of further theory-building. By engaging existing theory, it is easier for idiographic description to facilitate nomothetic progress.

We structured our comparison around the key dimensions suggested in four major models of comparative institutional analysis: Whitley (1992; 1999); Hall and Soskice (2001), augmented by the critical evaluation by Hancké et al. (2007); Amable (2003); and Redding (2005). Table 1.1 summarizes these dimensions. As indicated in the left-most column, we selected for our comparative analysis all eight institutional dimensions mentioned by at least two of these five works.

The resulting range of dimensions is consistent with the themes in the 2010 *Oxford Handbook of Comparative Institutional Analysis* (Morgan et al. 2010), which is a survey of the state of the art. The one additional dimension the 2010 *Handbook* discusses is the nature of the national innovation system, which is not included in any of the other models (but will be covered, in comparative perspective, in Part II). The 2010 *Handbook* also shares with Amable (2003) a concern for social protection and social welfare. We chose not to pursue this dimension separately, as a survey of the role of state in society will subsume it.

**Table 1.1  Institutional dimensions of leading models of comparative institutional analysis**

| Selected | Dimension | Whitley, 1999 | Hall and Soskice, 2001 | Amable, 2003 | Redding, 2005 | Hancké et al., 2007 |
|---|---|---|---|---|---|---|
| | Civil Society Role | | | | y | |
| y | Education and Skills Formation | y | y | y | y | y |
| y | Employment Relations | y | y | y | y | y |
| y | Financial System | y | y | y | y | y |
| y | Inter-firm Networks | y | y | | y | y |
| y | Internal Dynamics of the Firm | y | y | | y | y |
| y | Ownership and Corporate Governance | y | y | | y | y |
| | Product Markets | | | y | | |
| y | Social Capital (Trust) | y | | | y | |
| | Social Protection | | | y | | |
| y | State Role | y | | | y | y |

With the above in mind, each of the Part I chapters follows this standardized outline:

1. Introduction
2. Brief context (if needed)
3. The role of the state
4. Financial system
5. Ownership and corporate governance
6. Internal structure of the firm
7. Employment relations
8. Education and skills formation
9. Inter-company relations
10. Social capital
11. Conclusion

A number of Part I chapters further identify salient institutional complementarities (cf. Hall and Soskice, 2001) and discuss the state of knowledge about the dynamics of institutional change in the respective business system.

*Part II.* The objective of the chapters in this part was to present comprehensive analyses of important themes across the region. These themes generally fall into three categories: major institutional aspects of business systems viewed in comparative perspective; factors influencing the evolution of these systems; and variations in outcomes produced by them.

The chapters in the first of these categories leverage the empirical data on the given topic contained in the Part I chapters, paired with suitable additional comparative data, to identify overall patterns across the region and draw conclusions for business-systems theory and social-science theory more generally. Topics covered include, in alphabetical order: business groups, corporate governance, employment relations and human-resource management, finance, social capital, and the role of the state.

The chapters in the second and third categories open up additional avenues of idiographic exploration and nomothetic theorizing. Major factors influencing the evolution of Asian business systems include, in particular, culture, but also the role of multinational enterprises (MNEs) and of offshoring, outsourcing, and supply chains in the region. Given the concern of the business-systems literature with outcomes such as innovation and economic performance (e.g., Hall and Soskice 2001; Whitley 2007), chapters in the third category cover national innovation systems as well as firm strategy and performance patterns in the region.

Part II chapters follow this generic outline, with deviations as required by the topic:

1. Introduction
2. Literature review: relevant theory and empirical findings in
   a. the business-systems literature
   b. the social sciences more generally
3. Empirical patterns visible in the region
4. Implications for existing theory
5. Conclusion

*Part III*. This set of three chapters examines patterns in the evolutionary trajectories of Asian business systems. One of them explores the long-term key historical influences underlying the institutional diversity visible in Asia today. The other two focus on recent institutional change, one with respect to retail markets, the other with respect to organizational forms. There is no standard outline for these chapters.

*Part IV*. The two concluding chapters in this section provide synopses and spell out implications for scholars and business practitioners. The former summarizes the key institutional data from Parts I and II. It identifies five major clusters, or types of business systems, in Asia, and it draws conclusions about the utility of extant business-systems theory for understanding Asian business systems today. It also proposes a range of additional variables the field needs to incorporate in its analytical toolset to come to terms with empirical diversity and institutional change in Asia.

The chapter for business practitioners identifies salient themes relevant to managers in the region and possible responses to some of the main challenges.

In preparing this handbook, the aim of the editors has been to gather together conveniently the work of the leading writers in this rapidly expanding field, and to locate their work against the backdrop of a massive global shift towards a new centre of gravity for world trade and industry. It is necessary for people from many parts of the world, and from industry as well as academe, to be able to grasp the dynamics of that shift. More especially is it necessary for them to be able to judge for themselves the likely future patterns as such shapes appear out of the often puzzling detail. Such patterns have increasing relevance in many aspects of international life and work.

In doing so, we enter two important caveats. The first is that the volume of research work out there is now such as to force selection, and we are more aware than most of how much scholarship could have been added. In these circumstances we have paid special attention to judging our options and choices. Second, the scene is shifting rapidly, as regional growth continues apace. We have deliberately addressed change where it has been feasible to do so, but we invite all readers to accept the intellectual adventure of themselves carrying their own particular questions forward in time, using the resources given here to this date.

# Acknowledgements

Parts of the text of this chapter were previously published in Witt and Redding (2013). We thank Oxford University Press for permission to use them for this chapter.

# References

Amable, B. (2003). *The Diversity of Modern Capitalism*. Oxford, Oxford University Press.
Anchordoguy, M. (2005). *Reprogramming Japan: The High Tech Crisis under Communitarian Capitalism*. Ithaca, Cornell University Press.

Andriesse, E. and G. van Westen (2009). 'Unsustainable Varieties of Capitalism along the Thailand–Malaysia Border? The Role of Institutional Complementarities in Regional Development'. *Asia Pacific Journal of Management 26*(3): 459–479.

Aoki, M. (1988). *Information, Incentives, and Bargaining in the Japanese Economy*. Cambridge, Cambridge University Press.

Aoki, M., G. Jackson, and H. Miyajima, Eds. (2007). *Corporate Governance in Japan: Institutional Change and Organizational Diversity*. Oxford, Oxford University Press.

Babble, E. R. (2012). *The Practice of Social Research*. Belmont, Wadsworth.

Berger, S. and R. P. Dore, Eds. (1996). *National Diversity and Global Capitalism*. Ithaca, Cornell University Press.

Boyer, R., H. Uemura, and A. Isogai, Eds. (2012). *Diversity and Transformations of Asian Capitalisms*. Abingdon, Routledge.

Casper, S. and R. Whitley (2004). 'Managing Competences in Entrepreneurial Technology Firms: A Comparative Institutional Analysis of German, Sweden and the UK'. *Research Policy 33*(2004): 89–106.

Dore, R. P. (1973). *British Factory, Japanese Factory: The Origins of National Diversity in Industrial Relations*. Berkeley, University of California Press.

—— (2000). *Stock Market Capitalism: Welfare Capitalism: Japan and Germany Versus the Anglo-Saxons*. Oxford, Oxford University Press.

Edwards, T., P. Almond, I. Clark, T. Colling, and A. Ferner (2005). 'Reverse Diffusion in US Multinationals: Barriers from the American Business System'. *Journal of Management Studies 42*(6): 1261–1286.

Hall, P. A. and D. Soskice (2001). 'An Introduction to Varieties of Capitalism'. In P. A. Hall and D. Soskice, Eds., *Varieties of Capitalism: The Institutional Foundations of Comparative Advantage*: 1–68. Oxford, Oxford University Press.

Hancké, B., M. Rhodes, and M. Thatcher (2007). 'Introduction: Beyond Varieties of Capitalism'. In B. Hancké, M. Rhodes, and M. Thatcher, Eds., *Beyond Varieties of Capitalism: Conflict, Contradictions, and Complementarities in the European Economy*: 3–38. Oxford, Oxford University Press.

Heugens, P. P., M. van Essen, and J. H. van Oosterhout (2009). 'Meta-Analyzing Ownership Concentration and Firm Performance in Asia: Towards a More Fine-Grained Understanding'. *Asia-Pacific Journal of Management 26*(3): 481–512.

Huang, Y. (2008). *Capitalism with Chinese Characteristics: Entrepreneurship and the State*. Cambridge, Cambridge University Press.

Lechevalier, S. (2007). 'The Diversity of Capitalism and Heterogeneity of Firms: A Case Study of Japan During the Lost Decade'. *Evolutionary and Institutional Economics Review 4*(1): 113–142.

Loveridge, R. (2006). 'Developing Institutions—"Crony Capitalism" and National Capabilities: A European Perspective'. *Asian Business & Management 5*(1): 113–136.

Morgan, G., J. H. Campbell, C. Crouch, O. K. Pedersen, and R. Whitley, Eds. (2010). *The Oxford Handbook of Comparative Institutional Analysis*. Oxford, Oxford University Press.

North, D. C. (1990). *Institutions, Institutional Change and Economic Performance*. Cambridge, Cambridge University Press.

Orrù, M., N. W. Biggart, and G. G. Hamilton (1997). *The Economic Organization of East Asian Capitalism*. London, Sage.

Pascha, W., C. Storz, and M. Taube, Eds. (2011). *Institutional Variety in East Asia: Formal and Informal Patterns of Coordination*. Cheltenham, Edward Elgar.

Popper, K. R. (1963). *Conjectures and Refutations: The Growth of Scientific Knowledge*. London, Routledge and Kegan Paul.

Redding, G. (2005). 'The Thick Description and Comparison of Societal Systems of Capitalism'. *Journal of International Business Studies* 36(2): 123–155.

—— and M. A. Witt (2007). *The Future of Chinese Capitalism: Choices and Chances*. Oxford, Oxford University Press.

Redding, S. G. (1990). *The Spirit of Chinese Capitalism*. Berlin, Walter de Gruyter.

Ritchie, B. K. (2009). 'Economic Upgrading in a State-Coordinated, Liberal Market Economy'. *Asia Pacific Journal of Management* 26(3): 435–457.

Robins, F. (2010). 'China: A New Kind of "Mixed" Economy?'. *Asian Business & Management* 9(1): 23–46.

Runciman, W. G. (2005). 'Culture Does Evolve'. *History and Theory* 44(1): 1–13.

Sako, M. (2008). *Shifting Boundaries of the Firm: Japanese Company—Japanese Labour*. Oxford, Oxford University Press.

Steier, L. P. (2009). 'Familial Capitalism in Global Institutional Contexts: Implications for Corporate Governance and Entrepreneurship in East Asia'. *Asia Pacific Journal of Management* 26(3): 513–535.

Storz, C. and S. Schäfer (2011). *Institutional Diversity and Innovation: Continuing and Emerging Patterns in Japan and China*. Abingdon, Routledge.

Streeck, W. and K. Yamamura, Eds. (2001). *The Origins of Nonliberal Capitalism: Germany and Japan in Comparison*. Ithaca, Cornell University Press.

Tipton, F. B. (2009). 'Southeast Asian Capitalism: History, Institutions, States, and Firms'. *Asia Pacific Journal of Management* 26(3): 401–434.

Tsoukas, H. (1989). 'The Validity of Idiographic Research Explanations'. *Academy of Management Review* 14(4): 551–561.

Vogel, S. K. (2006). *Japan Remodeled: How Government and Industry Are Reforming Japanese Capitalism*. Ithaca, Cornell University Press.

Westney, D. E. (2006). 'The "Lost Decade" and Japanese Business Studies'. *Asian Business & Management* 5(2): 167–185.

Whitley, R. (1992). *Business Systems in East Asia: Firms, Markets and Societies*. London, Sage.

—— (1999). *Divergent Capitalisms: The Social Structuring and Change of Business Systems*. Oxford, Oxford University Press.

—— (2007). *Business Systems and Organizational Capabilities*. Oxford, Oxford University Press.

Witt, M. A. (2006). *Changing Japanese Capitalism: Societal Coordination and Institutional Adjustment*. Cambridge, Cambridge University Press.

—— and G. Redding (2009). 'Culture, Meaning, and Institutions: Executive Rationale in Germany and Japan'. *Journal of International Business Studies* 40(5): 859–895.

—— (2013). 'Asian Business Systems: Institutional Comparison, Clusters, and Implications for Varieties of Capitalism and Business Systems Theory'. *Socio-Economic Review* 11(2): 265–300.

Yamamura, K. and W. Streeck, Eds. (2003). *The End of Diversity? Prospects for German and Japanese Capitalism*. Ithaca, Cornell University Press.

# PART I

## ASIAN BUSINESS SYSTEMS

CHAPTER 2

........................................................................................................

# CHINA

## *Authoritarian Capitalism*

........................................................................................................

## MICHAEL A. WITT AND GORDON REDDING

By any measure, China has re-emerged as a major player in the world economy. By the latest reckoning, it now has the world's second-largest GDP, whether measured at nominal or purchasing-power parity exchange rates; produces the world's largest trade surplus; holds the world's largest foreign-currency reserves; attracts more foreign direct investment than any other country except the United States; and is now the world's largest market for a range of products, including automobiles. While there is some discussion about the eventual end-point of China's economic rise in terms of per capita GDP (Redding and Witt 2007), most observers consider it likely that the country will within the next decades overtake the United States in terms of overall GDP.

The shape of the Chinese business system is more set in its evolutionary trajectory than is commonly appreciated (cf. also Walter and Howie 2012). A widespread fallacy is to equate high economic growth with fast and especially discontinuous institutional change. While the Chinese business system is more in flux than those in most advanced industrialized economies, recent years have seen relatively limited institutional change compared with the far-reaching adjustments between the start of economic reforms in 1978 and the early 2000s. Three decades of rapid economic growth, and relative stability in the face of the 2008 financial crisis, have given rise to confidence in Beijing and elsewhere that the Chinese business system may in many respects be at least equal, if not superior, to those of the advanced industrialized nations. Accordingly, China in recent years has produced more incremental than discontinuous institutional change, with an emphasis on adjustments to, and deepening of, the current institutional structure rather than changes to the basic architecture. On recent form, it appears likely to congeal as a modern form of state-dependent mercantilism, rather than a version of the free-market democratic capitalism that once appeared to have been 'the end of history' (Fukuyama 1992; Fingleton 2008). Whether such a configuration would be conducive to long-term economic performance is open to question.

Our business-systems analysis reveals a complex picture that suggests that much institution-building is still to be done within the basic architecture now in place. This is clearly evident in the provision of education and skills training, which does not yet match firms' needs. It is also visible in the lack of institutionalized trust in the system, which in turn leads to high levels of centralization and low delegation inside firms. Deviance of actual practice from formal rules is common and especially salient in the financial system (formally bank led, but not providing loans to most of the economy) and the employment relations area (formally tripartite, but in reality dominated by the Communist Party). Throughout the system, the influence of the Communist Party of China is pervasive (Malesky, Abrami, and Zheng 2011).

# CONTEXT

Like many large countries, China is home to multiple business systems. Firms with different types of ownership—state, private, or hybrid, as explained below—are subject to different rules of the game. Similarly, there are regional institutional variations. The presence of such diversity naturally complicates the task for this chapter. At the same time, the fundamental challenge is qualitatively identical to analysing, for instance, the United States, which has a mixture of publicly-listed, family-owned, and non-profit enterprises operating within institutional contexts that vary, at the very least, by region. Guangzhou and Shanghai may be quite different, but so are Silicon Valley and Main Street.

Within the constraints of this chapter, we will reduce complexity by focusing on ownership patterns, which we see as the main dimension of variation. Specifically, we will contrast private and state-owned firms, with hybrid firms falling somewhere in between. We acknowledge the presence of geographic variations, though evidence suggests that their impact may be diminishing over time (Witt and Lewin 2004). We can give spatial differences only limited treatment, specifically in the context of political and evolutionary dynamics.

# ROLE OF THE STATE

Viewed from a Western perspective, China's political system is unusual in that ultimate political power rests, not with the government, but with a political party, the Communist Party of China (CPC). Government structure overall mirrors that of the CPC, with the same personnel often occupying equivalent positions in both organizations, so we will use the terms 'CPC' and 'state' interchangeably. While formally subject to the Constitution of the People's Republic of China, the CPC is effectively above the law, and individual cadres often escape legal punishment for transgressions (though they may be sanctioned by the party). The main constraint on the CPC is the concern that it could fall from power if it loses popular legitimacy. Maintaining this legitimacy is seen to require the maintenance of a stable political order, which in turn implies a need to suppress open protest and improve material living conditions through economic growth.

Accordingly, China today is a developmental state with distinct predatory admixtures. The developmental objective is based, not only on the desire of the CPC to remain in power, but also on a sense of historical humiliation and decline, and an attendant desire to restore China to what is seen as its rightful place in the world. China in 1800 produced about one-third of world industrial output; by 1978, its share of world GDP was less than 1.8 per cent (World Bank 2010), and China had become one of the world's poorest societies. Economic reforms aimed at rectifying this situation began in 1978. A key component in these efforts was the gradual strengthening of market mechanisms (Naughton 1996) and material incentives for engaging in economic activities.

The developmental dimension of Chinese economic policy is visible in its adoption and adaptation of Japanese-inspired industrial policy (Nolan 2002). Targeted firms are in particular the present 117 core state-owned enterprises (SOEs) (SASAC 2012) under the auspices of the central government State-Owned Assets Supervision and Administration Commission (SASAC), which comprise firms in industries considered essential and thus too important to be left to market forces alone, as well as firms intended to develop into world-competitive multinational enterprises (MNEs). Lower levels of government often have their own SASACs and industrial champions.

Industrial policy tools have included oversight and protection by government, the allocation of capital at subsidized rates, and export promotion. Unlike Japan, China has permitted foreign competition into the country through imports and inward foreign direct investment (IFDI), the latter providing a basis for learning best practices through joint ventures. Also unlike Japan, China has so far had limited success at coordinating technology diffusion and joint research and development involving competing firms. Arguably, the state facilitates diffusion of technology through relatively lax enforcement of intellectual property rights.

Predatory elements are visible in personal enrichment by party officials and their families and friends. Common manifestations include corruption and the illegal appropriation of communal land or state property for private benefit (Ong 2012). While senior leaders are generally perceived to be clean, their children, known as 'princelings', and extended families tend to do remarkably well in business, presumably helped by their connections. For instance, relatives of Xi Jinping, the current CPC Chairman, allegedly have amassed a fortune exceeding US$700 million (Bloomberg 2012), and relatives of the disgraced Politburo member Bo Xilai, more than US$160 million (Barboza and LaFraniere 2012). While there is no evidence that these and similar fortunes were unfairly gained, they do represent a public-relations challenge for a party supposed to represent the interests of the proletariat. Efforts to stamp out corruption have so far been only mildly successful.

China at first seems like a statist environment, with top-down decision-making. Corporatism-style tripartite structures exist, but as we will discuss later, these are under effective CPC control. While they do permit for some voice and accountability (Kennedy 2005; Malesky, Abrami, and Zheng 2011), their consultative and participatory functions are limited compared with Western democratic corporatism.

However, China's highly decentralized quasi-federalist structure facilitates the emergence of bottom-up economic policy initiatives (Cao, Qian, and Weingast 1999; Naughton 2007; Redding and Witt 2007; Carney, Shapiro, and Tang 2009). Counter to conventional wisdom, which sees the central government as all-powerful and fully in control, much policy-making and implementation is devolved to lower levels of government, including revenues and outlays (OECD 2005). This decentralization is partially an inadvertent consequence of the country's size, with more remote areas having historically enjoyed higher degrees of autonomy. It is also the result of deliberate policy intended to provide room for local competition and experimentation, so as to evolve information about the feasibility of specific institutional reforms for China's transition towards a modern economy—hence Deng's notion that China would develop by 'groping for stones while crossing the river'. We will explore this aspect in more detail below.

Implementation of government policy as expressed in laws is relatively weak. While government effectiveness in 2010 was passable, at about the 60th percentile among all countries worldwide (par with Thailand, but far behind other North-East Asian economies), the rule of law remained weak, at the 45th percentile (World Bank 2012b). Among the economies explored in this handbook, only Vietnam, the Philippines, and Laos performed worse on this measure. Part of the explanation for this was corruption, with China scoring 3.6 out of 10 (10 = cleanest) in the 2011 Corruption Perception Index (Transparency International 2011). At the same time, the local experimentation already noted has by necessity involved breaches of existing laws, and local officials' prospects for promotion depend much more on producing growth than on remaining within the law (*Economist* 2012; World Bank 2012a). Though laws may in due course be updated to reflect new realities, the implication is that there is usually divergence between published laws and actual practice.

The CPC remains highly interventionist. The Economic Freedom index score for China in 2011 was 51.2 out of 100, earning China a rank of 138 out of 179 countries, behind all other Asian economies from India eastwards except Laos (50.0) (Heritage Foundation 2012). Likewise, the OECD (2012) found that Chinese product markets in 2008, the latest year for which data are available, were more heavily regulated than those of all OECD countries and the BRIICS,[1] especially with respect to state control and barriers to entrepreneurship.

# FINANCIAL SYSTEM

China's financial system, at first glance, is clearly bank led, relying heavily on state-owned banks to provide access to finance. In 2010, 82.9 per cent of corporate funds raised in the Chinese domestic market came from banks (Walter and Howie

2012). Corporate bonds accounted for 9.1 per cent, and stock issues for the remainder (Walter and Howie 2012). This situation is unlikely to change much, as policy-makers see bank dominance as a means of maintaining control over the financial system (Naughton 2007).

Further exploration reveals a more complex picture. In particular, system characteristics vary greatly depending on ownership. Private businesses have had very limited access to official bank loans, not to mention capital markets (Tsai 2002; Rothman 2005; Herd, Piggot, and Hill 2010). The latest published statistics show that in 2009 loans to private enterprises and self-employed individuals were RMB711 billion, out of a total loan volume of RMB68.2 trillion (National Bureau of Statistics of China 2011)—in other words, 1.0 per cent. Even if we assume that the number given only refers to short-term loans (the statistics are unclear on this), the private-sector loan share in that segment would amount to only about 4.9 per cent (National Bureau of Statistics of China 2011). It is possible that the actual number is somewhat higher, as entrepreneurs have been known to find creative ways to pose as a state-owned business or may leverage political connections in order to obtain access to finance (Tsai 2002). Overall, however, private business is relatively starved of official capital, and its predominant mode of funding is savings, loans from family and friends, and unofficial financial operations, such as loan sharks and unlicensed banks (Tsai 2002; Rothman 2005; OECD 2010). Estimates put the volume of underground bank loans at about 30 per cent of the total (Yao 2011). The unofficial benchmark rate for such loans, the so-called 'Wenzhou rate', is usually a multiple of the official lending rate. In spring 2011, it reached 6–8 per cent per month (*Economist* 2011), implying that such finance is usually short term.

By contrast, SOEs and well-connected firms tend to enjoy ready access to long-term finance. State-owned banks, including the China Development Bank and the China Export-Import Bank, represent their main source of funding, often at favourable interest rates and for the long term. For instance, Huawei, a well-connected leading producer of telecommunications equipment, disclosed in its 2010 Annual Report that it had annual borrowing costs below 1.7 per cent for more than half of its outstanding loans, with some rates as low as 0.94 per cent. Stock-market listings for these companies serve as a complementary source of external finance. Where such listings involve SOEs, the state often retains a controlling stake (Naughton 2007; Tian and Estrin 2008).

# OWNERSHIP AND CORPORATE GOVERNANCE

Ownership is the key differentiator of domestic firms in China. In simplified terms, firms can be sorted into three buckets (Redding and Witt 2007): private, state owned, and hybrid. Private firms are usually privately held family businesses or partnerships. It is these firms that have been driving China's high growth rates. In 2007, they accounted for 75 per cent of all firms in China (cf. 1998: 24%), 50 per cent of total employment (1998: 13%), 32 per cent of fixed assets (1998: 10%), and 45 per cent of value added (1998: 15%) (OECD 2010).

Recent developments in the wake of the 2008 financial crisis suggest some efforts to pare back this private predominance, under the unofficial slogan 'guo jin, min tui' ('the country/government moves in; the private sector retreats'). It remains unclear whether these efforts represent a new pattern or another ephemeral policy initiative; the most recent available systematic evidence on the private sector, where much of this experimentation happens, suggests continued vibrancy (OECD 2010).

Firms under state ownership come in various guises. The best-known type is the so-called state-owned enterprise (SOE). SOEs in industries considered strategic to China's development and security tend to be fully state held (Naughton 2007). Many other SOEs have been listed on stock exchanges inside and outside China. Though Chinese official statistics no longer classify them as SOEs, the state usually retains a direct or indirect controlling stake (Naughton 2007), and more than half of China's listed firms in 2009 were ultimately state owned (Yang, Chi, and Young 2011). In 2007, SOEs under direct or indirect state ownership accounted for 6 per cent of all firms in China (1998: 38%), 22 per cent of total employment (1998: 62%), 47 per cent of fixed assets (1998: 69%), and 31 per cent of value added (1998: 55%) (OECD 2010). As these statistics suggest, SOEs tend to be considerably more capital-intensive than private firms.

The 'state-owned' category arguably also includes collective enterprises. These differ from SOEs mostly in terms of the government level that exerts control: collectives are usually under the authority of a lower level of government, such as a township or village, while SOEs are the domain of higher levels, such as provinces or central government. Collectives are by now virtually insignificant in the economy, with a share of less than 5 per cent across measures (OECD 2010). We consequently exclude them from the discussion.

Hybrid firms are, as the name implies, in between. They often look and behave like private enterprises, but their ownership pattern may involve a considerable government stake. To complicate matters further, in official statistics they may be counted in either the state-owned or private sector, depending on their evolutionary trajectory. They are commonly referred to as 'local corporates', a term suggesting a local branch of state administration in alliance with indigenous entrepreneurs and possibly foreign investors, who may bring in technology and international market access. In our analysis, we consequently focus on private and state-owned firms, the two extremes between which hybrid firms will fall.

Of further importance are foreign private firms operating in China. These firms are both economically significant and, as conveyors of foreign expertise, an important source of social and technological innovation. They are usually hybrids combining some characteristics of their home countries with adaptation, successful or otherwise, to the Chinese environment. The need for adaptation is perhaps smallest in the financial sphere, as foreign firms may source capital at home or elsewhere. In other spheres of the political economy, however, pressures for local adaptation are stronger. For instance, even in the area most directly under control of the firm, internal structure, a long stream of studies in the field of international HR suggests a need for local adaptation of HR practices (Kostova 1999). Given their hybrid status, we will exclude these firms from analysis here.

Corporate governance in China is still weakly developed. In 2010, the Asian Corporate Governance Association (Gill, Allen, and Powell 2010) rated Chinese corporate governance seventh among eleven Asian countries, par with India and up from ninth place in 2007. Of various factors affecting the overall score, only its implementation of the International Generally Accepted Accounting Principles was close to world-class standards. By contrast, the report identified corporate governance culture and enforcement as the weakest links in the corporate governance system, scoring 30 and 36 out of 100 points, 50 and 44 points below the world-class benchmark.

Corporate governance in private-sector firms usually involves direct managerial control by their individual or family owners. There is considerable reluctance to separate ownership from control, mostly because owners do not trust professional managers to run the firm faithfully on their behalf. This mistrust is related to the lack of institutionalized trust in the business system, discussed later.

Given the role of the state as owner of SOEs as well as their primary source of funding, one might expect the state to keep close control over SOE activities and use of financial resources. In reality, this is not the case, because the Chinese state is everything but a unitary actor, as already explained. Similarly, banks do not enjoy much control over SOEs. They are not allowed to own stock and must extend many of their loans following government direction (Naughton 2007). In addition, the leaders of about half of the core SOEs outrank those of the major banks, with the former holding the rank of minister and the latter of vice minister (Walter and Howie 2012). As a result, the state-owned sector has neither a bank-based nor a market-based system of corporate governance. As Naughton (2007: 320–1) summarizes,

> To the extent that China has a control-based system [of governance], the control is fragmented among state-owned industrial holding companies, SASACs[2] at various levels, and government and Communist party bodies. These agencies do not share consistent interests in firm performance or managerial incentives.

The result of this fragmentation is that managers of Chinese state firms are highly independent from markets, banks, and the state. Abuse of investors continues to be prevalent, especially with respect to minority shareholders, who possess neither strong legal protection nor much leverage over management through market mechanisms. For instance, some 70 per cent of listed SOEs are reported to have built pyramidal structures, whose purpose is usually to enable the expropriation of investors through 'tunnelling', that is, the clandestine transfer of assets from one organization to another (Carney 2012).

# INTERNAL STRUCTURE OF THE FIRM

The available evidence on the internal structure of Chinese firms suggests that decision-making is in essence the exclusive prerogative of the very top of the pyramid. In prior research, Lieberthal and Lieberthal (2003) criticized Chinese firms for their weak integration and their tendency to be structured in silos, each with top-down control, and lacking in managers able to exercise integrating roles or envision entire value-chains. An autocratic tendency is evident in the finding that human resource management—that is, hiring, managing, and dismissing employees—is not being strategically devolved to line managers (Zhu et al. 2008). The same hierarchical sense pervades managerial ideology (Cheng, Chou, and Farh 2006; Kong 2006). Ideals of discipline, control, and paternalism are key organizational norms (Kong, 2006), and managers tend to be reluctant to delegate to people not personally trusted (cf. Chen, Peng, and Saparito 2002). These patterns are evident in both state-owned and privately owned firms (Redding and Witt 2007).

Recent comparative evidence from the Global Competitiveness Report (Schwab 2010) paints a consistent picture. Asked to report the extent of delegation within firms in their specific national contexts, executives from northern European countries report an average score of 5.31 out of 7, with 7 being highest. The score for Anglo-Saxon countries is 4.87, that for China, 3.60. The same basic pattern is visible in the choice between selecting senior executives on the basis of merit and qualifications or on the basis of friendship and family relationships. Here, the northern European countries report an average score of 5.83, Anglo-Saxon societies 5.95, and China 4.70. Connections and trust are thus considerably more important for gaining promotions in Chinese firms than in the West.

It seems unlikely that the situation will change much in the near future. First, the high labour turnover noted below is inimical especially to collaborative decision-making, as employees rarely have deep knowledge of, or much commitment to, the firm. Second, lack of institutionalized trust, as discussed below, hinders large-scale delegation as occurs in Western societies and Japan (Redding and Witt 2007). In particular, the absence of a reliable legal system means that it remains very difficult to hold others accountable if they abuse the trust implicit in delegation. Third, in SOEs, the custom of political state appointments for top managerial positions (Naughton 2007; Walter and Howie 2012), often from outside, virtually assures a disconnect between top management and the rest of the firm, both in terms of working relationships and of objectives.

In sum, the available evidence suggests that the internal structure of Chinese firms is relatively top heavy and centralized, and that interdependence between managers and employees is generally weak. The implied stress on vertical discipline and control is unlikely to foster organizational competences in industries requiring extensive creativity or complex coordination.

# EMPLOYMENT RELATIONS

Formally, China has many trappings of northern European social democracies in this area. Industrial relations have been under a tripartite framework since 2001 (Lee, Sheldon, and Li 2011); the All-China Federation of Trade Unions (ACFTU) in 2008 had a union density of 48.3 per cent and a collective bargaining coverage of 34.1 per cent (Liu, Li, and Kim 2011); and employers organize in the China Enterprise Confederation (CEC), the All-China Federation of Industry and Commerce (ACFIC), and numerous local associations (Lee, Sheldon, and Li 2011).

The reality is more complex. For one thing, the tripartite process is highly fragmented among '10,702 tripartite bodies across national, provincial, municipal, county, district, and even street levels' (Lee, Sheldon, and Li 2011: 311). Second, the ACFTU is not really a union *qua* independent representative body of employee interests, but an organ of political control for the CPC (Taylor and Li 2007; OECD 2010; Liu, Li, and Kim 2011). This is logical if one considers that in a communist political system, there can be no independent unions, as the party already represents the interests of the proletariat. Accordingly, CPC endorsement is needed for new ACFTU initiatives, and the chair of the ACFTU is a member of the Politburo Standing Committee of the CPC and holds a government position senior to that of the head of the Ministry of Labor and Social Security (Taylor and Li 2007).

This has perverse implications in terms of interest representation, because in many cases CPC interests are closely aligned with those of business. Government owns many firms, and even where ownership is formally private, party officials often hold a personal stake. In addition, local government depends on tax receipts from local enterprises and income from their land use, and local cadres need good business performance and high investments if they want to be promoted. As a result, the ACFTU tends to fail to promote labour's interests and shows a pattern of siding with management against striking workers (Taylor and Li 2007).[3]

The situation on the employers' side is more complicated (Kennedy 2005). A recent survey (Lee, Sheldon, and Li 2011) suggests broadly the following picture. The CEC and ACFIC are top-down, state-controlled associations. As such, they are the counterparts of the ACFTU, with CEC having stronger standing with SOEs, and ACFIC with private firms. One implication is that for SOEs, all three parties to the tripartite process are controlled by the CPC.

Private business does show some signs of independent representation, though its future direction is unclear. Until 2008, only the CEC was involved in industrial relations issues, and since its organizational structure did not extend much downwards, it left a vacuum in tripartite negotiations at lower levels of administration. Local employer associations arose to fill this opening, some of them under the control of local governments, but others apparently genuinely free to represent employers' interests (see also Zhang 2007). With the entry of the ACFIC into the industrial-relations arena, a number of these local associations seem to have become affiliated with the ACFIC; only time will tell whether this signals a shift of the ACFIC towards civil society or the subordination of previously relatively free bottom-up employer associations under state control.

Employment protection shows a similar divergence between outward appearance and actual practice. *De jure*, following the tightening of labour regulations in 2007, China features levels of employment protection that exceed those in the CMEs mentioned in Hall and Soskice (2001) (OECD 2010). *De facto*, however, 'employment protection is far less than *de jure*, with an enduring preponderance of fixed-term contracts involving few restrictions' (OECD 2010: 153). This is consistent with survey responses contained in the Global Competitiveness Report 2010 (Schwab 2010) about the ease of hiring and firing. On a scale from 1 to 7 (1 = impeded by regulations, 7 = flexibly determined by employers), China scores 4.10, about the same as the UK. This compares with average scores of 3.81 for northern European countries and 4.25 for Anglo-Saxon countries (note that the average for the former is pulled up considerably by free employment regimes in Denmark, Switzerland, and Iceland; the median score for northern European societies is 3.20, that for Anglo-Saxon ones, 4.0).

Unsurprisingly, employment tenures tend to be short. Li and Sheldon (2011), for instance, found annual turnover levels of up to 30 per cent. Smyth, Zhai, and Li (2009) present a case study exhibiting monthly (!) turnover rates of 10 per cent, with one-third of the workforce actively looking for a different job and 40 per cent ready to leave without hesitation.

Overall, while China from the outside looks like a European-style social democracy in this sphere, actual practice deviates considerably. In terms of interest representation, collective bargaining along northern European lines is impossible, foremost because there is no organization truly representing labour interests. In terms of employment protection, actual practice in China is in line with that in Anglo-Saxon countries. Given the vested interest party officials have in business, as already mentioned, it also seems unlikely that a true tripartite structure will emerge soon.

# EDUCATION AND SKILLS FORMATION

In exploring the Chinese education and skills formation system, it first bears emphasizing the relative weakness of the Chinese education system, despite many advances in recent years. UNDP publishes an education attainment index, which presents a composite score of literacy and school enrolment rates at all levels (UNDP 2009). In this, the lowest scorer among the countries considered in Hall and Soskice (2001) is Switzerland, with a score of 0.936 (out of 1 possible). China scores 0.851, par with Malaysia, just ahead of Suriname and just behind Lebanon. While the literacy rate in China was relatively high at 93.7 per cent in 2008 (World Bank 2010), enrolment rates were still comparatively low, especially at the upper secondary and tertiary level (UNDP 2009).

In the economic context, China has faced a shortage of usable skills and a skills mismatch. Li and Sheldon (2011) reported that since 2002, demand for technical employees had exceeded supply. By 2009, demand-to-supply ratios had reached 1.43 at the most junior level, 2.24 for senior technicians, and 2.28 for senior engineers. The World Bank found that of 4.95 million students graduating in China in June 2007, 1.4 million were unfit for finding a job (World Bank 2007). Moreover, a 2005 McKinsey study found that of 1.6 million engineers in the Chinese labour market, only 160,000, about the same as in the UK, had the requisite skills to work at the level required in multinational corporations (Farrell and Grant 2005).

Part of the problem is that the build-up of the modern Chinese education system has emphasized general skills over vocational training (Li, Sheldon, and Sun 2011). From 1990 to 2008, enrolment in regular secondary schools grew from about 4.6 million to 80.5 million, a factor of 17.5, while the number of schools has fallen from 87,631 to 72,907 (Li, Sheldon, and Sun 2011). During the same period, enrolment in vocational secondary schools has increased only from 3 million to 7.7 million, a factor of 2.6, and the number of schools has fallen from 9,164 to 6,128 (Li, Sheldon, and Sun 2011). Not only are vocational training opportunities insufficient, educational contents are often misaligned with corporate needs, as linkages between educational organizations and companies are generally absent (Li and Sheldon 2011).

In principle, companies could make up for this failure of the public education system through in-house training. In practice, the high levels of employee turnover already noted are a strong deterrent against this approach (Li and Sheldon 2011). Recent labour shortages have if anything increased the incentives for firms to poach from one another and for employees to follow the call of higher salaries. These conditions do not allow the emergence of a strong in-house training system.

It seems likely that at least some of these problems will persist into the foreseeable future. In particular, there seems to be a strong disinclination against vocational training for cultural reasons:[4] Classical Chinese education tended to emphasize general intellectual skills, not unlike a liberal arts education in the West. By contrast, vocational training is associated with manual labour, which is not prestigious (Brabasch, Huang, and Lawson 2009). Even in Singapore, which is far more advanced in terms of GDP but retains many aspects of 'Chinese' ways of business, vocational training is seen as a sign of failure in school.

Overall, China's education and training system is not yet up to the levels of the advanced industrialized nations. The education system that is in place leans towards general education, while skills training is weak.

## INTER-COMPANY RELATIONS

The Chinese context features a high number of inter-firm alliances aiming at technology transfer in the shape of joint ventures (JV) between a local and a foreign firm. However, while such alliances tend to be voluntary in nature in advanced industrialized countries, in China they tend to be the result of legislation providing for market access in exchange for technology (Naughton 2007). Following the entry of China into the World Trade Organization in 2001, these requirements were successively relaxed. To the extent possible, new entrants have been forming wholly foreign-owned enterprises (WFOEs), and numerous JVs have undergone conversion to WFOEs (Puck, Holtbrügge, and Mohr 2009). In 2000, 53.3 per cent of IFDI in China involved JVs, and 47.4 per cent WFOEs; by 2009, the proportions were 20.9 per cent and 74.8 per cent, respectively (Walter and Howie 2012). As China further deregulates market access, JVs are likely to disappear almost completely as an entry mode.

Among domestic firms, there is limited need to form similar alliances for technology diffusion. China's system of intellectual property protection suffers from weak enforcement (Keupp, Beckenbauer, and Gassman 2010), so Chinese firms are free to copy what they need. In addition, skilled workers freely move among competing companies, taking knowledge with them, and poaching is common (Li and Sheldon 2011).

A series of other forms of network exist, for various purposes. Business associations, as already discussed, seem to have evolved mostly in response to employment relations needs. Such associations, and also private ties among firms in the same industries, may also serve as a coordination device to help deflect price pressures from customers, especially those from abroad (Kennedy 2005; Lee, Sheldon, and Li 2011). Private ties with other managers and government officials have also been shown to affect firm performance (Peng and Luo 2000). At the same time, the depth of these networks does not appear to extend to areas such as standards and technology diffusion, which differentiates them from other Asian contexts such as Japan (Witt 2006).

Private-sector firms are frequently embedded in local production networks (Zeng and Williamson 2007). In these, a number of small firms collaborate in the production of a given product, similar to the pattern seen in European industrial districts (Whitley 1999). This form of collaboration can be highly efficient and effective; for instance, in the early 2000s, such networks, which are usually highly localized, accounted for 70 per cent of the world market in cigarette lighters, 50 per cent in shoes, 26 per cent in toys, and 20 per cent in neckties (Zeng and Williamson 2007).

SOEs and, to a much lesser extent, some private firms have also banded together to form business groups (qiye jituan). However, since most of these groups are actually dominated by a large SOE (Ma and Lu 2005; Keister 2009), including through ownership ties, these groups are perhaps best thought of as hierarchical conglomerates, rather than as networked business groups without a dominant member, as one would find in Japan (Gerlach 1992).[5] Earlier studies indicated that banding together in business groups, as expressed in interlocking directorates, improved performance and productivity in member firms (Keister 1998). On the other hand, more recent work has found that business-group membership has been declining in value (Carney, Shapiro, and Tang 2009), which may suggest that groups may disappear over time.

In summary, in terms of networking among firms, China is relatively well endowed, especially if we relax the definition of 'social networks' to include Chinese-style business groups.

# Social Capital

Chinese society is noted for its reliance on interpersonal trust as expressed in instrumental personal ties *(guanxi)* (Walder 1986; Chan 2009). These ties usually extend to family members and friends, with trust diminishing with decreasing closeness as expressed in degree of family relationship and closeness of reciprocal friendship ties. Within the resultant concentric circles of trust, win-win cooperation is possible and common. Individuals outside these circles tend to be ignored or seen as rivals in a zero-sum competition.

Institutionalized trust is weak. The Civicus Civil Society Survey (Civicus 2006) identified trust levels in Chinese society as scoring 1 out of 3 (higher = more trust). Since this assessment includes the positive effect on trust of *guanxi*, actual levels of institutionalized trust are likely to be lower still. Similarly, results from the World Values Survey (2009) show that 89 per cent of Chinese do not trust strangers. This mistrust is higher than in most of the advanced industrialized world; for example, the corresponding percentages were 49 per cent for Canada, 74 per cent for Germany,[6] 31 per cent for Sweden, and 60 per cent for the United States. As a result, cooperation in business and elsewhere usually requires patient building of interpersonal trust.

The main avenue for building institutionalized trust in much of the West, especially the Anglo-Saxon economies, is a strong rule of law, which despite recent improvements remains elusive in China. Shortcomings in this respect include the lack of checks and balances in government, absence of legal accountability of the CPC and its organs and higher officials, CPC interference in court cases, a constitution whose provisions for individual rights are mostly honoured in the breach, and poor training and corruption of judges, prosecutors, and lawyers (Bertelsmann Stiftung 2009).

Similarly, civil society overall remains relatively weak. The Civicus Civil Society Survey (Civicus 2006) attested an average score of 1.40 for Chinese civil society (out of 3, higher = better), slightly ahead of Russia (1.23), but considerably behind the advanced industrialized societies for which the survey provided data (Germany: 2.35, Netherlands: 2.08, Northern Ireland: 2.1, Wales: 2.35). Key issues in the further development of Chinese civil society are a lack of funding and continued political control (Chan 2009). Ironically, the question of resources is related to the lack of institutionalized trust, as Chinese individuals have no confidence that civil society organizations will handle their money properly (Chan 2009).

# Institutional Complementarities

The Chinese business system features a number of institutional complementarities, with important implications for comparative advantages of the Chinese economy. The main complementarities among the elements laid out earlier can be summarized as follows:

1. Bank-led finance and long-term availability of financial capital to SOEs based on government allocation are linked. Having bank-led finance does not in itself guarantee patient capital, but given state ownership and control, banks are a suitable tool for long-term capital provision. The same cannot be said of present-day financial markets, which tend to focus on the short term.

2. For SOEs, the combination of bank-led finance and majority or substantial state ownership is linked to weak corporate governance, as viewed from the perspective of minority shareholders. Since companies are not dependent on markets for financing, and state ownership effectively eliminates the threat of a hostile takeover, minority shareholders have little leverage on management.

3. For SOEs, the combination of weak corporate governance and long-term finance in principle should enable long-term employment by offering protection against shareholder demands to improve profitability through lay-offs. This linkage fails, of course, in cases where the state decides to restructure the firm. It also seems to fail with respect to talented staff, who may leave voluntarily to enjoy higher pay in the private sector.

4. For private enterprises, government industrial policy targeting SOEs and the difficulty of obtaining official bank finance are linked. The financing needs of SOEs are such that the amounts available to the private sector are relatively small.

5. The relative lack of institutionalized trust is linked to the pervasive role of the state in the economy and attendant absence of the rule of law, as discussed.

6. Access to bank credit for private firms is further hindered by the lack of institutionalized trust. Even though they are part of the state apparatus, banks will be concerned that they will be unable to recover loans from private firms. While the same risk is in principle present for loans to SOEs, these are politically safe for banks as they extend these loans to other branches of the state apparatus, usually at the behest of other state agencies.

7. In the private sector, the lack of official bank finance and a more short-term view of finance are linked. The shadow banking system in China charges high interest rates to compensate for the risks associated with its activities. This makes unofficial bank loans a very expensive source of capital and provides a disincentive for relying on loans from these sources for the long term.

8. For private firms, state rules and practices preventing listings on the stock exchange are linked to a strong pattern of closely held private ownership, often by families.

9. For private firms, family ownership and lack of institutionalized trust imply a tendency not to separate ownership and control. Instead, owners exert full managerial control.

10. For private firms, management by owners for the benefit of owners tends to be linked to short-term employment. Neither owners nor employees see each other in a reciprocal collaborative relationship.

11. Short-term employment and a relatively poor skills training system combine to produce a skills shortage. There is no well-functioning public training system to equip workers with needed skills, and firms have a disincentive to train employees because the short time-horizon of employment makes it unlikely that investments on training can be recouped. This is likely to reduce the ability of the Chinese economy to compete in areas requiring high levels of labour skills.

12. For all firms, low institutionalized trust prevents delegation outside the concentric circles of confidantes. This in turn is inimical to participatory decision-making and thus reinforces the top-down nature of management processes. As a result, management and production processes requiring an ability to handle high levels of complexity are likely to be difficult to implement successfully.

13. Interpersonal trust and the inter-organizational networks in the business system, including production networks and business associations, are linked. Their relationship is in part endogenous, with personal contact at associations enabling the building of interpersonal trust, which in turn enables further cooperation in the association and possibly in business.

14. The CPC monopoly on the representation of workers prevents the evolution of a strong union movement representing the interests of workers, rather than those of the CPC and its corporate interests.

# EVOLUTIONARY DYNAMICS

China's evolutionary trajectory is remarkable in that it has undergone fundamental institutional reforms in the economy without attendant regime change, a feat that eluded the Eastern European countries in general and the Soviet Union in particular. Five factors in particular seem to be key in this context (Xu 2011). First, as already noted, the governance structure of China is highly decentralized, and regional leaders are effectively in control of economic policy within their territories. Second, the CPC retains tight control of the reins of power and of promotions and punishment within its ranks. China thus achieves the elusive benefits of simultaneous loose-tight properties. Third, party officials in the regions compete with their peers for rewards and promotion on their ability to meet a range of targets that prominently include economic performance. This gives lower-level officials an incentive to create and maintain an environment conducive to economic performance (though it also may induce officials to embellish statistics, and for those whose performance is too weak for promotion to use their office to line their pockets).

Fourth, many regions in China resemble one another in terms of economic structure. On the one hand, this creates a very difficult environment for firms to generate profits, as many industries have large numbers of firms that are protected by local government and fight over a limited market. On the other hand, it has the effect of making the performance of officials in different parts of the country comparable, as conditions are roughly similar. And fifth, the exercise of political power is pragmatic in the sense that the contravention of existing formal institutions is tolerated as long as it serves the accepted ends and does not challenge or jeopardize the rule of the CPC.

In combination, these factors help reduce institutional inertia, at least with respect to the economy. The fragmentation of the institutional change process increases the difficulty for vested interests to prevent changes across the entire country. Competition facilitates diversity in experiments, which in turn evolves information about the feasibility of each solution and reduces the risk of instituting an unsuitable reform. China is, then, a vast laboratory full of experiments.

Among the drawbacks of this system is a high fragmentation of the rules of the game in Chinese business and attendant efficiency losses through increased transaction costs and competitive barriers. More importantly, however, it hinders the evolution of institutionalized trust by treating established institutions, including written laws, as expendable when expedient. In the long term, this is likely to have a detrimental impact on economic development prospects.

# CONCLUSION

In summary, the Chinese state, dominated by the CPC, mixes developmental with predatory elements and remains highly interventionist. The Chinese financial system continues to be state-dominated, with funds flowing mostly to SOEs. Corporate governance of listed firms, especially the majority that are SOEs, seems to be weak, while private firms are usually directly controlled by their owners. Management style is top-down, with decision power concentrated at the very top. Employment relations look tripartite but are dominated by state actors on three sides, so independent representation of interests is rare. The education system tends to produce general skills, and overall, the economy continues to suffer a skills shortage. Various forms of inter-company relations exist. Social capital is strong in terms of interpersonal trust, but institutionalized trust remains weak. The decentralized and competitive nature of institutional change renders the system resilient against deadlock, though at the expense of efficiency and institutionalized trust.

The very strong role of government is perhaps the most significant key to what may follow, and given the clear economic need for a vibrant entrepreneurial base, it is not beyond China, with its tradition of pragmatism, to forge an alloy that mixes the private drive to accumulate wealth with the legitimate public duty to preserve order. Chinese ideals have always contained those two strands, and arguably they will remain in effect beneath the continuing experimentation.

It is worth noting that the state's ownership of all land reinforces its power. There is no freehold in China, and the handicap this introduces to the progression of the economy at a future stage could be challenging, as it locks up much of the collateral that other societies have learned to permit their people to use (de Soto 2000). A similar restraint, tangentially related to the ownership of assets, and also crucial in other trajectories of economic progress, is the role of a bourgeoisie. For China, with its clearly vibrant private sector, it would appear at first glance that a strong bourgeoisie would be forming and might well exert the kind of 'reforming' pressure historically found in civil-society activism elsewhere. Several Western forms of capitalism have evolved with the strong participation of this force, as it has carried both professionalism and self-regulation into many areas of economic life. In a comment on this process, Bergère (2007) points out that the Chinese state has kept docile the business people under its monopoly and has so arranged matters that in accepting entrepreneurs but refusing a bourgeoisie, it has created a system of capitalism without capitalists. Its mechanisms of producing this docility include two main interventions: the co-option of key players into the CPC as they emerge, and the persistent restraining of property rights.

Although in a classic mercantilist state, the government that drives the economic nationalism is pushed to do so by the business and industrial elite, it is feasible for China, without such overt business interests being exerted, to still adopt mercantilist practices in the interests of national re-assertion. Pride is very important to China, and its significance is enhanced by the history from which it is now escaping. It is also arguable that government interest in the Chinese economy remains high by both direct and indirect means, and that this removes the need for it to be pushed by a *bourgeoisie* seeking freedom to act. So, too, does the Chinese government know that its legitimacy remains based on its capacity to keep delivering not just order, but prosperity.

This assessment is of course not the final word. The Chinese economy is still far from the living standards prevalent in advanced industrialized countries, and its institutional structure, both formal and informal, is likely to require further refinement. As for any other economy, continued economic success will be contingent on the ability of the Chinese business system to meet three interrelated requirements (cf. Beinhocker 2005): innovativeness, adaptiveness, and efficiency. So far, just as Japan may be praised for innovativeness and efficiency, but criticized for weak adaptiveness, China may be praised for adaptiveness and efficiency, but criticized for weaknesses in innovation (Redding and Witt 2009).

Progress on all three dimensions is needed for China to become truly rich on a per capita basis. As we have already seen, further adaptability may be hamstrung by cultural factors and the presence of vested interests. Efficiency improvements will likely require the country to face core societal issues, including fostering individual initiative, creativity, and commitment, and, in parallel, building the quality of institutionalized trust to raise the density of economic exchange. This latter issue does not just relate to trade in goods and services, but also to trading cooperation in a boss–subordinate relationship. Most societies that have successfully trodden this path have done so in the context of the emergence of civil society and decentralization of political power, and eventually the emergence of individual voting rights over national issues. While it is possible that China will discover a new path towards the same end, it is still legitimate to wonder how it might face these universally applicable issues in its own way. Unless it does so successfully, it runs the risk of becoming stuck in what is known as the 'middle-income trap', which denotes the difficulty of producing a PPP per capita GDP higher than about USD16,000 (Redding and Witt 2007; Eichengreen, Park, and Shin 2011). Given current growth rates, the moment of truth is likely to arrive around 2020.

Untested as yet is also the ability of modern China to produce world-class innovativeness. Evidence to date suggests that innovation will remain a serious point of weakness that can only be counterbalanced by continued technical borrowing. There are several immediate sources of that weakness, including inadequate legal infrastructure, which relates to institutionalized trust and the property rights it implies; organizational traditions of autocracy and tight control that stifle close manager–worker interdependence; scale limitations in small enterprise that stem from mistrust; and limited availability of venture capital (Kenney, Haemmig, and Goe 2008; Redding and Witt 2009).

Turning to the implications of this chapter for the conceptual development of the business systems literature, two aspects stand out. First, unlike in most of the advanced industrialized countries studied in the literature, formal structure and actual practice in China diverge fundamentally. This is logical if one considers the reliance of the Chinese political economy on local experimentation and thus local variation in institutions, much of it in contravention of existing national laws and thus running counter to the formal coordinating structure. To the extent this evolutionary mechanism remains in place, as it is likely to, efforts to make sense of China on the basis of formal institutions are likely to reach conclusions of limited validity.

Second, our analysis raises the question of how to accommodate the possibility of multiple varieties of capitalism within the same national boundaries. At least in some spheres, private and state-owned Chinese firms play by different rules of the game. One possible interpretation is that this phenomenon is a temporary artefact of China's transition from central planning to a market orientation. The shrinking of the state-owned sector as well as the emergence of a hybrid sector amalgamating elements of both can be interpreted as a harbinger of eventual convergence on a single model (though this may be so far off in time as to raise the question of when a transitory state stops being transitory). However, there is also the possibility that private and state-owned firms may represent two distinct sustainable punctuated equilibria. In this view, hybrid firms may either be a third equilibrium in-between the others (Redding and Witt 2007), or just the tails of the statistical distributions centred on these equilibria.

# ACKNOWLEDGEMENTS

We thank Regina Abrami and Mike W. Peng for very helpful comments. All errors that remain are our sole responsibility.

# NOTES

1. BRICS and Indonesia
2. State-owned Assets Supervision and Administration Commissions, agencies put in place at each level of government (centre, provinces, etc.) to oversee SOEs owned at that level of government.
3. This makes perfect sense in a Marxist worldview, because workers opposing the interests of the party must obviously be confused.
4. On the connection between culture and institutions in general, see Redding (2005) and Witt and Redding (2009); in China, see Redding and Witt (2007).
5. Networks are customarily defined as 'any collection of actors (N2) that pursue repeated, enduring exchange relations with one another and, at the same time, lack a legitimate organizational authority to arbitrate and resolve disputes that may arise during the exchange' (Podolny and Page 1998: 59).
6. Distrust in Germany would presumably be lower if only residents of the former West Germany (i.e. without experience of Communist authoritarianism and subsequent system collapse) were polled.

# REFERENCES

Barboza, D. and S. LaFraniere (2012). '"Princelings" in China Use Family Ties to Gain Riches'. Retrieved 31 August 2012 from <http://www.nytimes.com/2012/05/18/world/asia/china-princelings-using-family-ties-to-gain-riches.htm>.

Beinhocker, E. D. (2005). *The Origin of Wealth: Evolution, Complexity, and the Radical Remaking of Economics*. London, Random House.

Bergère, M.-C. (2007). *Capitalismes et Capitalistes en Chine: XIXe–XXIe Siècle*. Paris, Perrin.

Bertelsmann Stiftung (2009). *Bti 2010: China Country Report*. Gütersloh, Bertelsmann Stiftung.

Bloomberg (2012). 'Xi Jinping Millionaire Relations Reveal Fortunes of Elite'. Retrieved 31 August 2012 from <http://www.bloomberg.com/news/print/2012-06-29/xi-jinping-millionaire-relations-reveal-fortunes-of-elite.html>.

Brabasch, A., S. Huang, and R. Lawson (2009). 'Planned Policy Transfer: The Impact of the German Model on Chinese Vocational Education'. *Compare* 39(1): 5–20.

Cao, Y., Y. Qian and B. R. Weingast (1999). 'From Federalism, Chinese Style to Privatization, Chinese Style'. *Economics of Transition* 7(1): 103–131.

Carney, M., D. Shapiro, and Y. Tang (2009). 'Business Group Performance in China: Ownership and Temporal Considerations'. *Management and Organization Review* 5(2): 167–193.

Carney, R. W. (2012). 'Political Hierarchy and Finance: The Politics of China's Financial Development since 1978'. In A. Walter and X. Zhang, Eds., *East Asian Capitalism: Diversity, Change and Continuity*: 159–178. Oxford, Oxford University Press.

Chan, K.-M. (2009). 'Civil Society and Social Capital in China'. In H. Anheier and S. Toepler, Eds., *International Encyclopedia of Civil Society*: 242–247. New York, Springer.

Chen, C. C., M. W. Peng, and P. A. Saparito (2002). 'Individualism, Collectivism, and Opportunism: A Cultural Perspective on Transaction Cost Economics'. *Journal of Management* 28(4): 567–583.

Cheng, B.-S., L.-F. Chou, and J.-L. L. Farh (2006). *Do Employees' Authoritarian Values Matter? Effectiveness of People vs. Task-Oriented Authoritarian Leadership in China and Taiwan*

*Private Business.* 2006 International Association of Chinese Management Research Conference, Nanjing.

Civicus (2006). 'Civil Society Survey'. Retrieved 13 December 2010 from <http://www.civicus.org/csi-phase1/index.php?option=com_csidata&Itemid=27>.

de Soto, H. (2000). *The Mystery of Capital.* New York, Basic Books.

Economist (2011). 'The China Price'. Retrieved 28 April 2011 from <http://www.economist.com/node/18620804>.

Economist (2012). 'The Emperor Does Know: How the System Rewards Repression, in the Name of Maintaining Stability'. Retrieved 23 May 2012 from <http://www.economist.com/node/21554561/print>.

Eichengreen, B., D. Park, and K. Shin (2011). *When Fast-Growing Economies Slow Down: International Evidence and Implications for China.* NBER Working Paper Series. Cambridge, MA, NBER.

Farrell, D. and A. Grant (2005). *Addressing China's Looming Talent Shortage.* New York, McKinsey Global Institute.

Fingleton, E. (2008). *In the Jaws of the Dragon: America's Fate in the Coming Era of Chinese Dominance.* London, St. Martin's Press.

Fukuyama, F. (1992). *The End of History and the Last Man.* New York, Free Press.

Gerlach, M. L. (1992). *Alliance Capitalism: The Social Organization of Japanese Business.* Berkeley, University of California Press.

Gill, A., J. Allen, and S. Powell (2010). 'CG Watch 2010: Corporate Governance in Asia', CLSA. Retrieved 1 September 2012 from <http://www.clsa.com/assets/files/reports/CLSA-CG-Watch-2010.pdf?disclaimer=on&accept=+Yes%2C+I+Agree>

Hall, P. A. and D. W. Soskice (2001). *Varieties of Capitalism.* Oxford, Oxford University Press.

Herd, R., C. Piggot, and S. Hill (2010). *China's Financial Sector Reforms.* Economics Department Working Papers. Paris, OECD.

Heritage Foundation (2012). '2012 Index of Economic Freedom'. Retrieved 31 August 2012 from <http://www.heritage.org/index/ranking>.

Keister, L. A. (1998). 'Engineering Growth: Business Group Structure and Firm Performance in China's Transition Economy'. *American Journal of Sociology 104*(2): 404–440.

Keister, L. A.(2009). 'Inter-firm Relations in China: Group Structure and Firm Performance in Business Groups'. *American Behavioral Scientist 52*(12): 1709–1730.

Kennedy, S. (2005). *The Business of Lobbying in China.* Cambridge, MA, Harvard University Press.

Kenney, M., M. Haemmig, and W. R. Goe (2008). 'Venture Capital'. In J. T. Macher and D. C. Mowery, Eds., *Innovation in Global Industries: US Firms Competing in a New World*: 313–340. Washington, DC, National Academy Press.

Keupp, M. M., A. Beckenbauer, and O. Gassmann (2010). 'Enforcing Intellectual Property Rights in Weak Appropriability Regimes'. *Management International Review 50*(1): 109–130.

Kong, S.-H. (2006). 'An Empirical Investigation of Mainland Chinese Organizational Ideology'. *Asian Business and Management 5*(3): 357–378.

Kostova, T. (1999). 'Transnational Transfer of Strategic Organizational Practices: A Contextual Perspective'. *Academy of Management Review 24*(2): 308–324.

Lee, C.-H., P. Sheldon, and Y. Li (2011). 'Employer Coordination and Employer Associations'. In P. Sheldon, S. Kim, Y. Li, and M. Warner, Eds., *China's Changing Workplace: Dynamism, Diversity and Disparity*: 301–320. London, Routledge.

Li, Y. and P. Sheldon (2011). 'Skill Shortages: Where Labour Supply Problems Meet Employee Poaching'. In P. Sheldon, S. Kim, Y. Li, and M. Warner, Eds., *China's Changing Workplace: Dynamism, Diversity and Disparity*: 129–143. London, Routledge.

Li, Y., P. Sheldon, and J.-M. Sun (2011). 'Education, Training and Skills'. In P. Sheldon, S. Kim, Y. Li, and M. Warner, Eds., *China's Changing Workplace: Dynamism, Diversity and Disparity*: 111–128. London, Routledge.

Lieberthal, K. and G. Lieberthal (2003). 'The Great Transition'. *Harvard Business Review* 81(10): 70–81.

Liu, M., C. Li, and S. Kim (2011). 'Changing Chinese Trade Unions: A Three-Level Analysis'. In P. Sheldon, S. Kim, Y. Li, and M. Warner, Eds., *China's Changing Workplace: Dynamism, Diversity and Disparity*: 277–300. London, Routledge.

Ma, X. and J. W. Lu (2005). 'The Critical Role of Business Groups in China'. *Ivey Business Journal* 69(5): 1–12.

Malesky, E., R. Abrami, and Y. Zheng (2011). 'Institutions and Inequality in Single-Party Regimes'. *Comparative Politics* 43(4): 401–419.

National Bureau of Statistics of China (2011). 'China Statistical Yearbook 2011'. Retrieved 31 August 2012 from <http://www.stats.gov.cn/tjsj/ndsj/2011/indexeh.htm>.

Naughton, B. (1996). *Growing out of the Plan: Chinese Economic Reform, 1978–1993*. Cambridge, Cambridge University Press.

—— (2007). *The Chinese Economy: Transitions and Growth*. Cambridge, MA, MIT Press.

Nolan, P. (2002). 'China and the Global Business Revolution'. *Cambridge Journal of Economics* 26: 119–137.

—— (2005). *OECD Economic Surveys: China*. Paris, OECD.

—— (2010). *OECD Economic Surveys: China*. Paris, OECD.

OECD (2012). 'OECD.Stat'. Retrieved 31 August 2012 from <http://stats.oecd.org>.

Ong, L. H. (2012). 'Between Developmental and Clientilist State: Local State-Business Relationships in China'. *Comparative Politics* 44(2): 191–209.

Peng, M. W. and Y. Luo (2000). 'Managerial Ties and Firm Performance in a Transition Economy: The Nature of a Micro-Macro Link'. *Academy of Management Journal* 43(4): 486–501.

Podolny, J. M. and K. L. Page (1998). 'Network Forms of Organization'. *Annual Review of Sociology* 24: 57–76.

Puck, J. F., D. Holtbrügge, and A. T. Mohr (2009). 'Beyond Entry Mode Choice: Explaining the Conversion of Joint Ventures into Wholly-Owned Subsidiaries in the People's Republic of China'. *Journal of International Business Studies* 40(3): 388–404.

Redding, G. (2005). 'The Thick Description and Comparison of Societal Systems of Capitalism'. *Journal of International Business Studies* 36(2): 123–155.

—— and M. A. Witt (2007). *The Future of Chinese Capitalism: Choices and Chances*. Oxford, Oxford University Press.

—— (2009). 'China's Business System and Its Future Trajectory'. *Asia Pacific Journal of Management* 26(3): 381–399.

Rothman, A. (2005). *China's Capitalists*. Shanghai, CLSA.

SASAC (2012). 'Core SOEs'. Retrieved 31 August 2012 from <http://www.sasac.gov.cn/n1180/n1226/n2425/index.html>.

Schwab, K., Ed. (2010). *The Global Competitiveness Report 2010–2011*. Geneva, World Economic Forum.

Smyth, R., Q. Zhai, and X. Li (2009). 'Determinants of Turnover Intentions among Chinese Off-Farm Migrants'. *Economic Change & Restructuring* 42(3): 189–209.

Taylor, B. and Q. Li (2007). 'Is the ACFTU a Union and Does It Matter?' *Journal of Industrial Relations* 49(5): 701–715.

Tian, L. and S. Estrin (2008). 'Retained State Shareholding in Chinese plcs: Does Government Ownership Always Reduce Corporate Value?' *Journal of Comparative Economics* 36(1): 74–89.

Transparency International (2011). 'Corruption Perception Index'. Retrieved 31 August 2012 from <http://www.transparency.org/policy_research/surveys_indices/cpi/2010>.

Tsai, K. S. (2002). *Back-Alley Banking: Private Entrepreneurs in China*. Ithaca, Cornell University Press.

UNDP (United Nations Development Programme) (2009). *Human Development Report 2009*. New York, UNDP.

Walder, A. G. (1986). *Communist Neo-Traditionalism*. Berkeley, University of California Press.

Walter, C. E. and F. J. T. Howie (2012). *Red Capitalism: The Fragile Financial Foundation of China's Extraordinary Rise*. Singapore, John Wiley & Sons.

Whitley, R. (1999). *Divergent Capitalisms: The Social Structuring and Change of Business Systems*. Oxford, Oxford University Press.

Witt, M. A. (2006). *Changing Japanese Capitalism: Societal Coordination and Institutional Adjustment*. Cambridge, Cambridge University Press.

—— and A. Y. Lewin (2004). 'Dynamics of Institutional Change: Institutional Stickiness and the Logic of Individual Action'. *Euro-Asia Centre Working Paper Series*. Fontainebleau, INSEAD.

Witt, M. A. and G. Redding (2009). 'Culture, Meaning, and Institutions: Executive Rationale in Germany and Japan'. *Journal of International Business Studies* 40(5): 859–895.

World Bank (2007). *Enhancing China's Competitiveness through Lifelong Learning*. Washington, DC, World Bank.

—— (2010). 'World Development Indicators'. Retrieved 10 September 2010 from <http://data.worldbank.org/data-catalog/world-development-indicators>.

—— (2012a). *China 2030*. Washington, DC, World Bank.

—— (2012b). 'Worldwide Governance Indicators'. Retrieved 21 July 2012 from <http://info.worldbank.org/governance/wgi/>.

World Values Survey (2009). 'World Values Survey 2005 Official Data File V. 20090901'. Retrieved 31 August 2012 from <http://www.worldvaluessurvey.org>.

Xu, C. (2011). 'The Fundamental Institutions of China's Reforms and Development'. *Journal of Economic Literature* 49(4): 1076–1151.

Yang, J., J. Chi, and M. Young (2011). 'A Review of Corporate Governance in China'. *Asian-Pacific Economic Literature* 25(1): 15–28.

Yao, W. (2011). 'China's Shadow Banking Needs a Rescue'. *The economic news*, Societé Generale.

Zeng, M. and P. Williamson (2007). *Dragons at Your Door: How Chinese Cost Innovation Is Disrupting Global Competition*. Boston, Harvard Business School Press.

Zhang, J. (2007). 'Business Associations in China: Two Regional Experiences'. *Journal of Contemporary Asia* 37(2): 209–231.

Zhu, C. J., B. Cooper, H. De Cieri, S. B. Thomson, and S. Zhao (2008). 'Development of HR Practices in Transitional Economies: Evidence from China'. *International Journal of Human Resource Management* 19(5): 840–855.

CHAPTER 3

# HONG KONG

*Hybrid Capitalism as Catalyst*

GORDON REDDING, GILBERT Y. Y. WONG, AND
WILLIAM K. W. LEUNG

## INTRODUCTION

In a World Bank (2012) survey of the best places to conduct business, what is now termed 'Hong Kong, China' fared very well among 178 countries: second in ease of doing business, and trading across borders; third in protecting investors; fourth in getting credit and paying taxes; and tenth in enforcing contracts. The Heritage Foundation's (2012) annual rating of economic freedom placed Hong Kong first for eighteen years straight. This chapter provides background for this performance.

Hong Kong's character was set when it was first settled by international merchants in 1841. It was and remains a place to trade globally. In the eighteenth and nineteenth centuries, British foreign direct investment expanded hugely from state-licensed 'merchant-venturer' corporations dating from the early 1600s to the full Victorian free-trade imperial colossus. By 1914, Britain accounted for 45 per cent of world FDI (Jones and Wale 1998). Hong Kong, for most of its existence as a political entity, was a component of this vast colonial business system. Hong Kong today has developed in a post-colonial context, essentially as a gateway to mainland China, whose GDP is now five times greater than at the handover in 1997.

## HISTORICAL CONTEXT

The coast of China was long a magnet for international traders, even though several dynasties severely restricted access to the China market. Under a gunboat-enforced agreement in which British merchants in Canton were able to evade restrictions on their dealings, in 1841 they were permitted to occupy nearby Hong Kong island, then home only to fishing villages. Further treaties in 1858 and 1898 expanded the colonial territory onto the mainland, to a total of 1100 sq km. It is this total territory that was returned to China in 1997, under an agreement that defined it as a Special Administrative Region of China, using an agreed 'Basic Law' for the ensuing fifty years. Under this system, the HKSAR exercises executive, legislative, and judicial power, including that of final adjudication.

This far-sighted agreement enshrined the *realpolitik* of Britain's wish to move on from its colonial past, without abandoning the people of Hong Kong to a potentially threatening future, while for Mainland China, as dogma gave way to pragmatism, there were economic benefits from incorporating a controlled experiment in advanced modernization. The ending of a perceived historical outrage added deeper satisfaction to the process for the Chinese people. It also coincided with parallel trends inside China to encourage the decentralization of societal decision-making in the economy, a movement that has led to unusually high levels of local autonomy compared to OECD countries as a whole (OECD 2005). It should be noted that the nearby province of Guangzhou has a history of relative independence from control by Beijing, and of entrepreneurship. A study of attitudes to management in China concluded that the 'Hong Kong model' was clearly favoured by practitioners across much of the country (Ralston et al. 2006), although in policy circles the alternative 'Shanghai model' appeals to many in the Party for its emphasis on government control.

There is evidence that, in formulating the handover, China saw Hong Kong as a valuable conduit for knowledge, technology, and capital between the globalizing world and its own internal economy. PRC officials carefully studied Hong Kong's societal infrastructure, and adopted substantial portions, such as its stock market regulation (HK Stock Exchange 1992).

Hong Kong's recent economic history may be seen as a series of discernible but overlapping phases. With a population of only half a million in 1945, the flow of refugees from China became almost overpowering by the 1960s, but offered a large pool of labour, which meant that from around 1960 to 1980 Hong Kong grew as a major industrial city, making or assembling light-industrial and consumer goods for the world market. In the second phase, from around 1980, as China slowly opened up, Hong Kong's manufacturing industry was in effect sucked into the southern China provinces by their cost advantages, and its industrial reach grew significantly. This led to a third phase, from about 1990, as Hong Kong itself had to adjust, and it became a centre for the management (and ownership) of much of that industry, plus a centre for the professional servicing needed to link that industry with world markets. In effect, over the last two phases, Hong Kong's economic hinterland expanded greatly beyond its territory back into the mother country. Since then, carefully consolidating its position with the mainland, it has become one of the world's leading commercial cities in both volume and efficiency.

Since 1978, visible trade between Hong Kong and mainland China expanded 231-fold, at an annual average rate of 19 per cent in value terms, making the two respectively now the eleventh and second largest trading entities in the world.[1] Half of Hong Kong's trade goes to the Mainland, and 90 per cent of its re-exports. By the end of 2011 the cumulative value of Hong Kong's realized direct investments in the mainland was US$527bn, or 45 per cent of China's national FDI. The composition of this has shifted gradually from industrial processing to a wider spectrum, now including hotels, tourism, real estate, retail, construction of infrastructure, ports and terminals, business services, and communications. It is essential to acknowledge that for much of this, Hong Kong's role, like that of *entrepot* cities such as Venice, Constantinople, and London, is that of conduit.

A natural bias tends towards the neighbouring province of Guangdong in the pattern of Hong Kong's mainland investment, with US$170bn of Hong Kong's accumulated FDI in that province. Many companies have their operations in the Mainland and management in Hong Kong. By 2011 local primary and secondary manufacturing had fallen, engaging only 3.2 per cent of Hong Kong employment, from 40 per cent in 1989. This change has been accompanied during the third stage by major societal shifts in Hong Kong, especially those orchestrated by the SAR and preceding government in such fields as education, research, and telecoms infrastructure, as Hong Kong re-skilled its workforce for the service and knowledge industries.

In that third stage, during the 1990s, integration began to take place on a much wider front, as the economies of Hong Kong and Guangzhou (and China more broadly) started knitting together (Enright, Scott, and Chang 2005; Yeung 2011). This shift was accompanied by growing trust, as the fear of interference by mainland China slowly subsided (though it has not disappeared).

The combination of the two economies is clearly visible in the patterns of enterprise listing and capital flows. Hong Kong had become a regional hub during the earlier Asian 'little dragons' phase. By 2011 it hosted 6,948 overseas companies, with 3,752 of those defined as regional headquarters or regional offices, an indication of confidence in its legal, professional, and regulatory systems. China-based firms followed and poured in money. At the end of 2010, cumulative Mainland FDI in Hong Kong was US$402bn, or 37 per cent of Hong Kong's total received FDI. By mid-2011, 248 mainland companies had established regional headquarters there, and 557 had established local offices. By then 640 mainland companies were listed on the Hong Kong stock market. During 2011 mainland enterprises raised equity funding of US$226bn in Hong Kong. Capital-sourcing for mainland China was also enhanced by the growth of *renminbi* trading, with sixty Hong Kong banks licensed, RMB590bn deposited, and RMB182bn in bonds issued. This role has now been expanded with official mainland support for Hong Kong and London as world centres for *renminbi* trading.

Two further features relate to this continuing integration. First, in 2009 the two governments agreed on a Closer Economic Partnership Arrangement (CEPA) in which further liberalization measures were agreed over forty-two service areas. The fence between Hong Kong and its hinterland continues to be lowered as the administrative systems of the two jurisdictions slowly converge, although this does not include the agreed political structures guarded by a vociferous Hong Kong minority.

Second, and at the level of practicality, the cross-boundary infrastructure grows daily. The new Hong Kong–Zhuhai–Macao Bridge, 50km in length, and scheduled to open in 2015, will facilitate flows of people and goods between Hong Kong and the Western Pearl River Delta region—into the still relatively undeveloped Zhuhai and beyond. In the north–south direction of the delta, an express rail link now connects Hong Kong with Shenzhen and Guangzhou, and is also stimulating similar expanded flows. The Pearl River Delta, a region of 120 million people distinct for its Cantonese dialect and sub-culture, may yet host the world's largest mega-region, an agglomeration of conjoined cities reaching in this case a population of 100 million (UN Human Settlements Programme 2011).

To consider Hong Kong inside its geographical border alone is therefore to limit understanding. It is already 'Hong Kong, China', with interdependencies running across politics, economic and social issues, culture, and history. We propose here to describe Hong Kong in its interaction with China, while trying to capture the features that allow it to retain its own distinct character and independent trading traditions and power. Accidents of location and history make Hong Kong now the world's largest container port. Along with its immediately adjacent neighbour, Shenzhen, over whose port systems it has much influence through Hong Kong-led joint ventures, it shipped 46 million TEUs[2] of containers in 2010 (24mn HK and 22mn Shenzen), compared to 29 million for its nearest rival, Shanghai (World Shipping Council 2012). Since 1996, its airport has had the world's highest export-freight volume, currently at over 4mn metric tonnes p.a. (Airports Council International 2011). This figure conceals the high value of goods shipped by air—30 per cent of domestic exports and 38 per cent of imports by value (Chen 2010). Hong Kong is also the world's biggest issuer of IPOs, and home to the world's third largest bank, as well as globally significant trading companies, a global airline, large property empires, and large telecoms companies, that is, it punches far above its population weight of seven million.

The process of hybridization with the mainland is fraught with challenges each way (Tang 1999; Loh 2006; Wu 2008). Put simply, Hong Kong has developed to a high point of modernity and individual prosperity, but mainland China, despite its recent explosive growth, remains essentially pre-modern, in the technical sense of not being able or willing to decentralize power to individual citizens without serious instability. Given the scale of China's challenges, and the dramas of its recent history, this is perhaps unsurprising, but the end-result is that authority is exercised in very different ways each side of the border. Any meeting in the middle would risk China absorbing what some mainland observers see as a revolutionary cell. Hong Kong's pluralism and free press, openness of information, and traditions of rational accountability, do not fit comfortably with a one-party structure dedicated to the preservation of order. Hong Kong's defenders, on the other hand, see it as a transforming catalyst. Nonetheless, almost all the power lies with China, and that could undermine Hong Kong's freedoms, and the civil structures of professional administration that it has come to rely on. As China becomes increasingly mercantilist, with government now moving strongly into the economy, the contrasts increase.

# THE ROLE OF THE STATE

The policy of the Hong Kong government after 1970, when trading was joined by manufacturing, was officially termed 'positive non-intervention', meaning that the government would provide social order and infrastructure, while the economy was largely left to be managed by business itself. Thus, Hong Kong became a bastion of laissez-faire economic doctrine (Friedman 1998). At the same time, there being a long tradition of civic duty, business leaders were influential in key government committees (Carroll 2005).

As an aside to illustrate such civic-duty conventions, it is worth mentioning a remarkable Hong Kong phenomenon involving committed business leaders. The Hong Kong Jockey Club has a granted monopoly on gambling, and two of the world's greatest horse-racing venues. It also channels large volumes of local money into charitable use and into supporting key infrastructure such as hospitals and universities. With gambling revenue per race at fifty times the US average, 72 per cent of revenues go to the government, accounting for 7 per cent of the territory's tax revenue.

Positive non-intervention meant that if companies failed, they went bankrupt; if they succeeded, they remained taxed at low levels. This fostered prosperity, not just for owners, but for the population, who benefitted from the growth. Financial crises were handled largely by the banking sector's standing committee, in close touch with the Financial Secretary. Labour laws allowed employees only limited power, and entrepreneurship flourished. This regime gradually adopted more formal regulation as its scale increased, but the ideal of a capitalist paradise has not entirely disappeared, even with government intervention and regulation.

It was never true, however, that the Hong Kong government really stood back. Throughout the 'miracle' years from 1970, it always retained strong influence over several key sectors. Property prices are greatly influenced by a restricted property market in which the government owns all land and releases parcels at auction on long leases. The government continues to depend heavily on land as a source of revenue. Of 2011 revenue, 31 per cent came from the Land Fund, stamp duties, and the land premium. This ensures that the market price of land remains controlled at a high level and counterbalances the light taxes on salaries and profits of what is widely seen by outsiders as a low-tax regime. For those not in public housing, high property expenses are a displaced form of taxation.

Government intervention in the economy through schemes of control occurs in the pricing of fresh food supplies, in the control of transport prices, power costs, and the provision of extensive subsidized healthcare and education. Thirty per cent of people live in public housing, with a further 17 per cent in subsidized home-ownership flats. Private-sector housing follows government guidance. It is therefore deceptive to see Hong Kong as fully laissez-faire, but in the world of most day-to-day business practice, it is.

There is therefore considerable space in the business system for bottom-up institutional innovations. What regulations the government issues have normally flowed from extensive consultation with the business world and are generally well-enforced, as indicated by the low corruption levels (Transparency International 2011) and the presence of the rule of law (Kaufmann, Kraay, and Mastruzzi 2012). Hong Kong is not a full democracy, but it has two features that leave it with a degree of political openness: one is grass-roots participation in local government, long encouraged and well supported, and the other is a lively legislature, albeit of limited enfranchisement, in which debate is often now furiously confrontational. However, the previously high level of press freedom cannot be reported as maintained (Cheung 2003).

# Financial System

Although business financing in Hong Kong is not directed or planned by the administration, the government has nonetheless been instrumental in building strong regulatory frameworks for the conduct of investment. With unrestricted flows of money in or out, it works rather like London in relation to Europe—a clearing-house for much continental and global financial action. It has thus become one of the world's top financial centres, seventh in terms of market capitalization, sixth in foreign exchange trading, recently third in raising equity funds, and first in IPOs. Of its 152 licensed banks, 142 are foreign-owned and 73 of the world's top 100 banks are present. For Tier-1 capital it is third in the world (*Economist* June 30 2011: <http://www.economist.com/node/18895150>). As far as capital availability is concerned, this environment is unusually favourable and highly liquid. As noted earlier, in the World Bank 'Ease of Doing Business' scores, it ranks fourth in the world for getting credit. In the field of finance, it scores ten out of ten for legal rights and disclosure, and nine out of ten for investor protection (World Bank 2012), even though such protection mostly serves dominant owner interests.

For firms relying on sourcing finance in Hong Kong, two main patterns may be discerned. At the base of the pyramid are large numbers of small and medium-sized enterprises (SMEs). These are usually closely held and owned in tight social networks such as families, drawing their funding mainly from retained earnings. Many, however, have also cultivated strong and long-standing relations with local banks to obtain working and investment capital for expansion, local banks being permitted to take equity. This process has often brought with it a great deal of managerial standard-setting, control, and advice as conditions of such funding. The banks have then played an important part in raising local standards of organizing and managing business (Jao 1983). In such a highly liquid market for finance, apart from retained earnings, the main source of funding is banks, and the main basis of such funding is relationships; because of this, capital is normally patient.

At larger organizational scales, a number of local enterprises have attained significant size and global reach, such as the Cheung Kong group. Such conglomerates, as they grew, usually incorporated highly professional finance functions able to interact fruitfully, not just with local, but with global sources of capital. Many incorporated banks into their structures, or cooperated closely with global banks. For instance, Li Ka Shing was for a period Deputy Chairman of HSBC; his conglomerate included the merchant bank Peregrine and the Royal Bank of Canada. The consequent exposure to full international scrutiny required conformity to global standards of accounting and conduct, all of which could be provided in Hong Kong itself. This ability to live in the two worlds of (a) local entrepreneurship and networks and (b) global capital-sourcing has been a powerful formula, giving rise to a number of globally significant business empires. Into this mixture can be added an instinct for alliance-building, and cultural compatibility with the mainland (Mathews 2006).

What is not found here, compared to many other Asian environments like Singapore, South Korea, Japan, and Taiwan, is a strong government-controlled central source of investment capital, or a central bank used by the government to manage the economy, although there does now exist a fund of approximately US$50bn stemming from a mandatory provident fund set up in 2000. Instead, a series of autonomous commissions regulate the operation of finance laws. The success of Hong Kong and its differences from Singapore show that there are several ways for a city-state to build prosperity, and that such options are shaped by heritage. In this case, strong private banking has taken over the role of a central bank. This would not have worked for so long without close collaboration between the highest levels of government and business.

## Ownership and Corporate Governance

There are four main categories of enterprise in Hong Kong. First are the large, long-established organizations that were originally colonial and have evolved into global players, still with a Western flavour, though several have been acquired by Chinese capitalists. They are known locally as the *hongs*. Examples of the originally colonial are the Jardine and Swire groups, and HSBC, while Cheung Kong/Hutchison and the Worldwide group are among the acquired entities. The second category is that of global arrivals establishing branches of large companies based elsewhere, such as Citibank, whose Hong Kong branch was established in 1908. The third and numerically largest group is that of local SMEs, usually displaying the flexibility needed to adapt to the shifting industrial structure, but with many members retaining their industrial roots by managing operations transferred to China or acquired. Fourth are the organizations arriving from China, usually with a view to engaging directly in global business, an early example being CITIC.

Mainland enterprises in Hong Kong come in three categories: H-share companies, incorporated in China and controlled by either government entities or individuals; Red Chip companies, incorporated outside China, but controlled by Chinese government entities; and Non-H Share mainland private enterprises, incorporated outside China, but controlled by Chinese individuals (although listed in Hong Kong, they normally register elsewhere, popular bases being Bermuda, the Cayman Islands, and more recently British Virgin Islands). China-related companies at the end of 2010 numbered

163 H-Share, 102 Red Chips, and 327 Non-H. This total of 592 grew to 640 during 2011 and accounted for 57 per cent of Hong Kong's market capitalization.

Hong Kong is attractive for regional headquarters; in 2010 it had 288 American, 224 Japanese, 113 British, 99 PRC, and 72 German bases. The focus of their work tends to be principally China, but sometimes extends further.

It cannot be said that full transparency is the norm for most companies, and the protection of minority-shareholder rights has long been contentious. Tracking ownership patterns in the largest 200 publicly-traded firms in Hong Kong, Carney and Child (2012) found that 60 per cent remained under family control in 2008, compared to 65 per cent in 1996. The new feature in the Hong Kong pattern was the growth of state ownership from 4 to 28 per cent over that period. Two forces have had opposing impacts on the possible bias stemming from family control. One is the flow of international influence reforming governance behaviour, but countering this has been an increasing tendency for financial manipulation to be conducted across the mainland border, and for miscreants to be unreachable (Cheung, Rau, and Stouraitis 2004).

Therefore, compared with Western systems of administration, the governance of most companies in Hong Kong remains relatively closed. Shares tend to be closely held, in family groupings or through nominees. There is also a strong tendency for owners in their governance behaviours to co-opt political support, especially in larger enterprises (Wong 2010). This has long been a standard feature of companies throughout the region and is a rational response to the regional environment of high volatility, opaque information, and strong government influence (Redding 1990). In Hong Kong, government committees tend to be quite heavily occupied by business representatives, perhaps not unlike old Venice's business-dominated oligarchy, in which public duty was an honour as well as a convenience. Despite the implied honour, this leads to sporadic charges of collusion in industries such as property development, where government land policies are clearly of strategic relevance (Goodstadt 2005). During the handover transition, Scott (2000) reported a wave of defections from the British political camp to that of Beijing, and a breakdown of the earlier informal coordination and balancing between interest groups that had underpinned much of the society's political functioning. In practice, recent co-option of this sort involves executives sitting on key committees such as the Election Committee, which chooses the Hong Kong contenders for senior government positions, or in more favoured cases joining one of China's People's Political Consultative Committees.

An outcome of patrimonial domination by ownership is a downplaying of the role of shareholders in financial markets and firm strategy-making, and the retention of the connection between ownership and control. At small scale, this is quite normal, but at large scale it reaches levels that make Hong Kong symbolize what some see as a pre-industrial form of mercantile capitalism (Whitley 1992). It may equally be seen as a very well-judged response to potential hybridization, whereby Chinese and Western skills and attributes combine. Typical contributions to this mixture from the Chinese side would be political connections co-opted across the region by major players, and especially in China and Hong Kong; extensive private networks of information-sharing and deal-making; and the ability to pull together at low transaction cost syndicates of investors tied by bonds of trust, risk-sharing, and rapid response to opportunities (Redding 1995). From the Western side, the contributions have tended to be capital itself, from banks tapping global capital markets; managerial and professional skills in the handling of complex, technical, or large-scale organization; and means of access to global markets.

Hong Kong's largest indigenous companies have tended to be built on certain distinct foundations: a patrimonial leadership based on original ownership; reliance on property investment; heavy early investment in cash-cow industries related to development (e.g. trading, construction materials, retailing, food refining, and distribution); and high entry-barrier industries yielding steady cash-flow (e.g. container ports and terminals, airlines, power generation and distribution, telecommunications) (Ko 1998; Elvis 1999; Yeung 2006). Absent from this list are complex manufacturing industry; the creation of global consumer-goods brands; and direct dependence on high-technology specialists. Reasons for this mainly reflect how managerial authority is exercised.

## Internal Structure of the Firm

The Chinese family firm, large or small, has a management structure reflecting its origins in Chinese social history (Redding 1990; Faure 2006). Until 1949, entrepreneurs in China had to survive revolution, invasion, civil wars, and two world wars; after that, family business was banned under Maoism for thirty years, and then re-emerged slowly. Hong Kong thus became a twentieth-century refuge for this family business formula, a role it shared with Singapore and countries around the South China Sea, where ethnic Chinese have been trading for over a thousand years.

The resulting organizations tend to be run by dominant owners who take all key decisions. They are likely to be assisted by family members and trusted subordinates or specialists. A spirit of paternalism is common and conveys the Confucian ideals of responsibility downwards in exchange for disciplined obedience upwards (Westwood, Sparrow, and Leung 2001). When well used, it can release 'the efficiency of benevolence' (Pye 1985). Control is usually tight. External relations are usually managed personalistically if strategic, on networks of reciprocal obligation from the owner outwards. Such networks may also be used to carry information and share investment risks. At larger scales, networks may entail co-opting political support.

Social respect is accorded to owners, not employees. Owners strive to fulfil the duty of building or enhancing the family 'name'. In most environments, officialdom is seen as potentially threatening, with unpredictable demands. A norm of secrecy thus builds and typifies action, as do norms of hard work, discipline, and control (Man and Lau 2005; Anderson and Lee 2008; Cheung and Chan 2008).

In structures of this nature, trust, though perhaps intense, is limited, so delegation and organizational growth have limits. The depersonalization of power is difficult, and organizations only attain large scale if they evolve out of the basic patrimonial formula. This can be done by professionalizing management, but tends to be rare. The risks of not evolving away from personalism are high. A study of 127 such large organizations in Hong Kong, Singapore, and Taiwan (Fan, Jian, and Yeh 2008; Fan, Wong, and Zhang 2012) examined market-adjusted stock returns over the five-year period during which owners pass control to successors. They reported an average loss in value of 56 per cent, attributed to the specialized assets of the owner being in the form of non-transferable connections, and to slow responses to declining values.

Even so, some firms adjust and incorporate professionalism, producing hybrid large firms able to deploy networking and alliance skills to counter the uncertainties of foreign markets and industries (Mathews 2006). Hong Kong is a natural centre for such new forms. Of the top 50 MNEs from developing countries classified by UNCTAD, 26 derive from Pacific Asia. Of these, 15 are unequivocally from the private sector, rather than being extensions of government funding. Of these, half come from Hong Kong.

Few societies display more clearly the constant work of creative destruction that typifies successful entrepreneurial economies (Yu 1997). There is a tendency for these organizations to stay focussed in one main business field. The sense of hierarchy also limits manager–worker interdependence, except for bonds where key loyal employees hold technical competence—that is, an accountant or production manager might over time be treated like an honorary family member. Social distancing between management and workers would have emerged in earlier periods in conditions of relatively straightforward work, where control was not complex. It will predictably give way to greater interdependence—and some change towards more participative style—as industry is redesigned around the more technical skills of workers in the new service industries. Influencing this also is the influx of Western and Japanese employers using more open styles of control and motivation, usually preferred by workers (Ngo et al 1998; Fields, Chau, and Akhtar 2000).

Change towards less personalistic structures is clearly affected by the absence (or at least weakness) of a market for corporate control in the larger system of share ownership and finance (Cheung 2008). The inroads of new corporate-governance regulations and practices have had little effect so far, possibly because of their embeddedness in Western assumptions (Redding 2004; Tan 2010). It is as if Hong Kong's business owners are responding to their social history, and perhaps to an anticipated destination, and so maintain their trusted beliefs and institutions.

The ex-colonial companies have remained prosperous and still reflect their trading origins in such industries as air transport and services, shipping, sugar-refining, drinks-bottling and distribution, insurance, and engineering services, with solid reserves of property investment in the background. So too have the once-colonial banks flourished on the global stage as the world's centre of business gravity moved in their favour and they were flexible enough to take advantage.

# Employment Relations

Hong Kong has one of the world's lowest average loss of working days per 1000 employees (Hong Kong Yearbook 2011: 135). Labour relations are comparatively quiescent, maintaining a long-standing feature of a society unused to active labour defence of its status. Too much overt democracy would have disturbed the peace with China, where unions are essentially instruments of the Party, involved only in communication and limited welfare. In any case, most Hong Kong workers were never exposed to the ideals of socialism in its Western forms. The majority were from refugee families escaping the ravages of the Great Leap Forward (Dikotter 2010), the hounding of landlords and 'capitalist-roaders', and the extreme cruelties of the Cultural Revolution (Chang and Halliday 2005; MacFarquhar and Schoenhals 2008). Their tolerance of left-wing ideology is unlikely to have been enhanced.

Confucian paternalism is an alternative, with its own moral force, and lies deeper in the Chinese psyche (Bond 1986; Tu 1996). The metaphor of the iron rice bowl has real meaning. One might also note that the market itself, when as fluid as Hong Kong's, and all in one city, affects employment conditions directly. When growth is good, employees can leave, and this protects them from abuse.

The government has shaped most labour legislation along ILO guidelines, mainly following British institutional practices, without granting the kind of collective bargaining rights usual in Europe (Chiu 2002; Ng 2010). Unionization has risen slowly in the early 2000s from about 20 per cent to about 23 per cent, partly through a rise in China-supported left-wing activism. Within that proportion, membership of the pro-Beijing HK Federation of Trade Unions now accounts for 48 per cent. However, union membership tends to cluster around the large public institutions and big firms that depend on labour, such as airlines and major utilities. Ninety-eight per cent of union membership is defined by craft or occupation (Labour Dept. 2012).

In most of the 303,000 SMEs, labour relations are personalistic rather than formally institutionalized, and strikes are rare. In most firms, matters such as pay and conditions are dealt with by owners against a backdrop of a highly fluid labour market. Union representatives are only involved in negotiations with the few large and relatively visible organizations where employer negotiations are conducted by professionals, not owners. Even in those cases, strikes are very rare. Significant here have been government actions such as (a) a statutory minimum wage of HK$28 p.h., introduced in May 2011, and (b) a mandatory provident fund brought in ten years earlier.

For the vast majority of employees not connected personally with employers, there is a tendency to move jobs readily and easily, often for quite small advantage in pay. Voluntary turnover runs at 14.5 per cent (Hong Kong Institute of Human Resource Management 2012). What does hold employees is the availability of training, and the fact that many foreign companies offer this makes them preferred employers for a workforce driven by ideals of self-improvement.

## EDUCATION AND SKILLS FORMATION

We have noted earlier how the radical transition of the Hong Kong economy from manufacturing towards services, including the addition of extensive managerial intervention in the mainland, has caused a shift in the nature of work. The government had planned for this by giving early priority to expanding education and skills training. Consequently, Hong Kong now competes with Singapore as a regional hub in education, invests heavily in it, and responds to global education trends such as e-learning, advanced scientific research, and the self-financing of higher education. Its oldest university, the University of Hong Kong, was ranked top among Asian universities in both the recent Quacquarelli Symonds (QS) and 2012 *Economist* rankings (*Economist* 2012; QS 2012). QS placed six of the twelve local universities in the world's top 100.

The educational structure consists of competent and accessible primary and secondary education over a wide spectrum of types, subsidized extensively by government; standards are above average, ranking third among seventy-four countries in maths, third in science, and fourth in reading (OECD 2009). Higher levels comprise two sets of institutions, universities and vocational training institutions, also supported by government funding, as well as local philanthropy. Under mainland influence, its universities are now changing from three- to four-year degrees.

Holders of tertiary-level degrees in Hong Kong have increased from 3 per cent of the population in 1986 to 16 per cent in 2010; numerically, from 164,000 to 1,107,000, with an equal gender balance. In management education, Hong Kong has Asia's top-ranked MBA programme and a cluster of close followers; its business schools receive 17 per cent of the region's GMAT applications, despite Hong Kong having 0.2 per cent of the population (GMAC 2011), a statistic that illustrates Hong Kong's business character.

In addition to formal full-time education, workforce skilling is boosted by high popular interest in self-improvement, supported by an array of institutions offering part-time education. Much technical training is coordinated by the Vocational Training Council, itself with ten campuses and strong links with industry, although on-the-job training is uncommon. Professional education runs parallel with degree teaching, often sponsored by the professions themselves. There is also a wide choice of foreign qualifications available, either online or locally; quality is monitored where possible by the Hong Kong Council for Academic Accreditation.

# INTER-COMPANY RELATIONS

There are two scales at which networking operates in the Hong Kong economy. The first is small-business networking, often to construct a flexible value or supply chain, the components of which are separately owned, but whose effectiveness depends on maintaining and operating connections personally, and thus at low transaction cost. This partly explains the large number of small companies, as the coordination of scale is generally handled by networking across still-autonomous units rather than by managerial integration under one firm. It results in the retention of owner-inspired responsibility in each sub-unit—the source of the 'strength of weak ties' that gives flexibility to the business system as a whole.

The second applies on a larger scale, where collaboration lies mainly in capital invest-ment, and where necessary political lobbying. This often entails sharing opportunity and risk. Personal ties are also active here, strongest where they link people originat-ing from the same region, and so speaking the same dialect and having similar trust networks. The main dialect subgroups of this nature in Hong Kong are the majority Cantonese from the Pearl River Delta, Hokkienese from southern Fujian, and Teochew from eastern Guangdong. To these may be added smaller groups from Fujian, Shanghai, and the Hakka, from a wide area of south China (McKeown 2005).

Like the other *entrepot* cities noted earlier, Hong Kong has the virtue of smallness, or at least human scale, when it comes to inter-company relations. People tend to know each other, or are able to find out about someone, especially within an industry or pro-fession. Sometimes like a large village, connections run through the fabric of business dealings, meetings, and boards, as well as the social institutions that maintain net-works: the dining clubs and restaurant hospitality, interlocking directorships, hospital charities, the Jockey Club (where stewardship status is especially coveted), and the gov-ernment advisory committees that knit together the worlds of business and adminis-tration. As in the City of London, or Wall Street, most senior business meetings can be reached on foot, and on the way you are likely to bump into a number of your network of several hundred.

At the scale of small-firm networking, efficient and flexible supply chains grow nat-urally, and Hong Kong companies regularly find themselves intermediating between, or occupying parts of, supply webs in China and distribution webs in global markets. The 'workshop of the world' with its price competitiveness owes much to these network structures and the psychological cement that holds them stable but not rigid.

The fierceness of competition in most markets has kept Hong Kong mainly free of car-tels. In industries with high entry barriers, such as power generation, or cross-harbour tunnels, the government has prevented the possible abuse of monopoly by imposing licensing, and collusion with government over such matters was more or less elimi-nated by the work of the Independent Commission Against Corruption, launched in 1974. There is nonetheless always a sense of uncertainty over the property industry, and abuses were regularly reported into the 1990s (Lo 1993). More recent studies of cor-ruption suggest that this issue is also now under control (Manion 2004), and in 2011 Hong Kong scored twelfth of 182 countries on Transparency International's Corruption Perceptions Index (with China at 75th).

# Institutional Complementarities

In the literature on comparative capitalism, the commonly accepted unit of analysis so far has tended to be the nation-state with its own cultural heritage, or clusters of countries with similar heritages, such as liberal market economies. In Asia we find a set of coun-tries with similar distinctions, such as China or Japan, but many are hybrids, tending to emerge from colonial histories. They vary in economic success from struggling, such as the Philippines (Kondo 2014), to successful, such as Taiwan (Lee and Hsiao 2014). It may be that success stories coincide with the coming together of two strong cultures robust enough to interact fruitfully without loss to one side. In weak outcomes it is often a local culture that is not yet fully formed at a level of national identity at the onset of colonialism that is subsumed and can only play a weak part. Hong Kong and Singapore are hybrids of Chinese and British culture, both strong, and their different routes to similar results illustrates how complex adaptive systems evolve on different trajectories. We now briefly note complementarities in Hong Kong, visible in the connections between forms of enterprise and economic coordination, and the institutions that emerged from the hybridizing of cultures.

## Forms of Enterprise Management

The confluence of British and Chinese institutions is perhaps best seen in company ownership and management, especially in the vibrant SME base, from which larger structures are constantly emerging. The institutions that interact here largely stem from laissez-faire political philosophy. There are simple, clear, and well-organized administrative regulations of commercial law and accounting based on Western company law and strong professions, efficient and business-friendly commercial banking, a fluid labour market capable of skilling itself, agencies to connect with world markets, available business services, and local traditions of private family ownership and partnership that have their own long history. To exercise the last with the support of the former makes for a fruitful combination and self-reinforcement of elements.

## Acquiring Organizational Scale

An important follow-on from Hong Kong's entrepreneurship appears in the evolution of large conglomerates moving onto the world stage (Peng and Delios 2006). These new players exhibit two features: the habits of entrepreneurship and alliance networking at large scale that were culturally instinctive at small scale, and the ability to absorb into the same structures the most modern professional standards in the managing and financing of operations. It is arguable that the institutional environment of Hong Kong acted as a test bed and facilitator for much of this new organization skill, as it did historically to foster fruitful interaction between the two cultures as the industrial terrain came to be shared. An early form of this was the incorporation of Chinese (or Eurasian) interface specialists, or *compradors*, often of very high status, into the managing of complex Western organizations such as banks or trading houses, to handle key issues in the local environment. In the other direction was the employment of Western technical specialists such as engineers into local organizations.

The Hong Kong institutions in this configuration for large international firms might be summarized as (1) systems of bureaucratic government administration, (2) autonomous commissions regulating financial markets, (3) training and education systems that input appropriate talent (e.g. access to employment in the administrative grade of the civil service is seen as entry to an elite by an intellectual subset), (4) autonomous professions regulating much of the behaviour of lawyers, accountants, engineers, doctors, etc., (5) a legal system based on common law and an independent judiciary, backed by an effective corruption-prevention force. All these institutions can be traced back to colonial and post-colonial flows of influence and example, connections that have not yet disappeared. They are also in accord with Chinese traditions of bureaucracy and order.

## A Business-Friendly Infrastructure

Hong Kong has been a world leader in public transport, telecoms connectivity, corruption prevention, tax administration, free and sophisticated advisory systems to encourage the finding of suppliers or customers, and keeping systems simple and accessible. Such determined pursuit of an ideal business context would not have arisen without a special feature of public administration in Hong Kong—politically disinterested rationality, visible in the institutions of long-range planning for infrastructure, in the clearly visible public management of societal finances, and in an elite civil-service cadre selected for educational quality, reminiscent of the traditional mandarinate of China and the Whitehall 'mandarins' of London. A contribution has also been made to the workings of this configuration by the tradition of direct accountability to the public of all departments of government, and openness to criticism and suggestion.

The main outcome of such a business-friendly environment is the high level of entrepreneurship. Start-up is simple, and expansion is facilitated by the availability from banks, not just of loans, but of managerial guidance. Also, the sheer size of the opportunity space provided by the China access and global connections adds much to the mixture. On top of this is a skilled and mobile labour force.

## Strong Human Capital

Human capital is essentially the availability of skills and knowledge. In Hong Kong, its development has been zealous at several levels. With many families fleeing China as refugees, survival through to prosperity was mostly achieved through hard work, self-denial, and discipline, as well as through family support for individuals. For individual members, in response, familial duty is dominant and powerfully moral. This bestows a strong sense of responsibility to enhance the 'family name'. The dedication to education and level of attainment attest to this. These aspects of traditional Chinese familism have stabilized as institutions, rendering a predictability to behaviour patterns.

Familism alone, however, is insufficient to explain the development of such high levels of human capital. Other contributions in that configuration have been the accessible and subsidized educational system, the breadth of education, vocational as well as basic, the quality attained through inspection and regulation, the fluidity of the labour market and career opportunities, the wealth that permits access to foreign education for many, and lastly the institutionalized respect for education as a basis for status, so central to Chinese society.

## Preserving Freedoms

The commonly agreed keys to economic progress include property rights, freedom from government interference, a context of high and reliable information flow, and the liberty to express individual initiative and creativity. These do not accord with autocracy. Although Hong Kong has never been a full democracy, much had been done to encourage political participation at local levels. There was and remains a high degree of civil rights, rule of law, an independent judiciary, and a well-developed civil society that included until recently a vigorous free press.

Appearing now are fears of 'growing authoritarian Chinese clouds above Hong Kong' (Wu 2008: 279), as local politicians are either co-opted or go quiet. As Ghai (1999) concludes, it is in the nature of state-dominated capitalism to use official patronage as a lever of control over business behaviour. As So (2000: 379) puts it, an 'unholy alliance developed between Beijing and big business in Hong Kong' and 'integration with the mainland generated both conservative forces to obstruct democratization and popular forces to promote it'. This tension continues, but has been greatly eased by China's promise that elections to the Legislative Council will be on the basis of universal suffrage by 2020. Questions remain as to whether and how the large firms and professions will respond to this promised easing, and whether the political system will remain sufficiently sophisticated and robust to handle the extra demands of a much more complex set of interests.

In all this, it must be remembered that Hong Kong is also exerting countervailing pressures on China by virtue of its capacity to perform at global standards of efficiency. The per capita income gap—US$46,000 in Hong Kong, against US$7500 in China—suggests that the game will be played out over a long period, and will be full of twists and turns.

## Evolutionary Dynamics

Hong Kong's business system is evolving in quite dramatic circumstances due to the scale of the issues affecting it. As one of the world's most successful interpreters of laissez-faire capitalism, dedicated to the dominance of market logics, it is being absorbed into a society whose own future direction is a matter of experiment, but whose tradition of controlling government is deeply entrenched. Hong Kong has demonstrated how a society of Chinese people can grow prosperous and acquire most of the trappings of modernity with which to continue stable progress. But Hong Kong is a hybrid and China is not; and China's gigantic scale, together with its own political legacy, mean that what is possible in a city of seven million is unlikely to be possible in a continent-sized country with a fifth of the world's population. The stage is therefore set for some decades of finding a workable balance between alternatives.

A related feature of importance to Hong Kong is the unpredictability of socio-economic policy in China. Only two aspects may be proposed with any confidence as likely: (1) the priority given by the mainland government to maintaining social order, and (2) the concern of that government to legitimize its retention of power by delivering continued prosperity. For Hong Kong, the spectrum of judgement as to what will happen is wide. In lay terms, at one end there were people describing 1997 as 'the great Chinese take-away'; at the other end were Hong Kong business leaders who, when asked 'What happens when China takes over Hong Kong?', would say 'Hong Kong takes over China'.

Against this uncertain background, Hong Kong's business system has evolved in two main ways: it has become much more closely intertwined with China, and at the same time has strengthened its global reputation as a city for business. The latter feeds off the former. Hong Kong is now a global city to the extent that China is a global economy, but it would be hard to demonstrate that China is a global economy to the extent that Hong Kong is a global city, as China has alternatives.

The success of the first stage of transition, visible in economic growth, may well owe much to the high level of cooperation with Chinese provincial governments. Examples of the transfer of crucial 'soft skills' from Hong Kong to China are the work of the Hutchison Whampoa group in establishing the container ports of Yantian and Shanghai, the hundred plus China joint-ventures of Hong Kong Towngas, and the role of Hong Kong's Mass Transit Railway engineers in the new city rail systems of Shenzhen and Beijing.

The second evolutionary dynamic has been Hong Kong's dramatic progress as a world business city, an evolution that continues a long trajectory, but has perhaps speeded up greatly with the weight of the mainland economy. Between 1997 and 2010, China's GNP, in PPP terms, grew from US$2.23 trillion to US$10.13 tr. Symbolic of the impact of this was the return of the HSBC headquarters from London to Hong Kong in 2010. Equally emblematic was Beijing's preferment of Hong Kong over Shanghai as its base for global *renminbi* trading. Much of this evolution has been due to the deliberate incorporation of global standards into higher definitions of best practice among Hong Kong professionals, regulators, and administrators; also contributory has been bottom-up institutional innovation, facilitated by light regulation.

# CONCLUSION

Hong Kong is often compared to Singapore. They are roughly the same size, with a similar colonial heritage, and they now enjoy similar levels of economic success per capita.

They are both modern societies. Even though neither is a fully functioning democracy, they have tried in their own ways to establish government legitimacy by the delivery of wealth, opportunity, and stability, and could not be called autocracies. But, apart from having different industrial bases, their trajectories have diverged in one major respect. Singapore is a developmental state, with direct strong government intervention in the economy, including complex planning. Hong Kong remains a bastion of laissez-faire capitalism. One outcome of this divergence is that Singapore is heavily dependent on multinationals and has a relatively weak indigenous business sector, whereas Hong Kong has ethnic-Chinese control of the economy and a relatively weak foreign sector. Its government is light and positively non-interventionist. We have noted certain imperfections in some markets in Hong Kong, but this does not prevent the overall balance being strongly towards competitive discipline, as opposed to government policy, as the decider of events.

Such contrasts bring out the way in which business systems vary and reflect their geographical context, histories, and cultures; and so too the consequent evolutions of their forms of order are distinct. The level of measured success in Hong Kong and Singapore may be similar, but the subtle differences that are not always visible will continue to work in shaping and adjusting them. The impact of this on both policy-makers and practitioners can be significant.

Almost all Asian state governments are 'stronger' in the political economy sense than Hong Kong (Wade 1990). The explanation for this may lie in two factors. In many other Asian states, their histories have brought into the modern age the vested interests of dominant elites which have either been traditional or historical, as occurs with landowners, or opportunistic, as with military power groups. Partly as a result, many other states in the region have been hampered by corruption and cronyism, unable to release the positive power of advanced social capital, and have only managed to stage 'ersatz' (Yoshihara 1985) or mercantile capitalism (Whitley 1992), instead of the free-market liberal form that has underpinned Hong Kong. This is arguably historical accident: British Victorian zeal met equally zealous, different but complementary Chinese partners, and once set in motion, the combined system became self-perpetuating.

How far Hong Kong can continue, and in what way, has arguably the largest potential import for the world's economies. China's dominance in solving the equation is balanced by its dependence on the managerial and societal technology that Hong Kong expresses at such a high level. At one time that would have been a challenge to national face. It no longer is, as learning, adaptiveness, and progress are slowly becoming entirely internal.

# ACKNOWLEDGEMENTS

The authors are most grateful for comments and suggestions made by Dr Philip Chen, Dr Kenneth Tse, David O'Rear, Simon Tam, and Prof. Ng Sek Hong

# NOTES

1. Unless otherwise stated, all figures in this chapter derive from the Hong Kong Yearbook 2011 published by the Hong Kong Government, Information Services Department.
2. TEU = Twenty-foot equivalent units, the standard measurement in the container industry.

# REFERENCES

Airports Council International (2011). *Annual Report*. Geneva, ACI.

Anderson, A. R. and E. Y. C. Lee (2008). 'From Traditional to Modern: Attitudes and Applications of Guanxi in Chinese Entrepreneurship'. *Journal of Small Business and Enterprise Development* 15(4): 775–787.

Bond, M. H., Ed. (1986). *The Psychology of the Chinese People*. New York, Oxford University Press.

Carney, R. W. and T. B. Child (2012). 'Changes to Ownership and Control of East Asian Corporations between 1996 and 2008: The Primacy of Politics'. *Journal of Financial Economics*. doi: 10.1016/j.jfineco.2012.08.013.

Carroll, J. (2005). *Edge of Empires: Chinese Elites and British Colonials in Hong Kong*. Cambridge, Harvard University Press.

Chang, J. and J. Halliday (2005). *Mao: The Unknown Story*. London: Jonathan Cape.

Chen, P. N. L. (2010). *Great Cities of the World*. Centre of Asian Studies Monograph 162. Hong Kong, University of Hong Kong.

Cheung, A. S. Y. (2003). *Self-Censorship and the Struggle for Press Freedom in Hong Kong*. New York, Kluwer.

Cheung, C.-K. and A. C. F. Chan (2008). 'Benefits of Hong Kong Chinese CEOs' Confucian and Daoist Leadership Styles'. *Leadership and Organization Development Journal* 29(6): 474–503.

Cheung, R. (2008). 'Corporate Governance in Hong Kong'. *International Company and Commercial Law Review* 19(6): 181–191.

Cheung, Y. C., P. R. Rau, and A. Stouraitis (2004). 'Tunnelling, Propping and Expropriation: Evidence from Connected-Party Transactions in Hong Kong'. Working Paper, Dept of Economics, City University of Hong Kong.

Chiu, C. C. H. (2002). 'Labour Relations and Regulation in Hong Kong: Theory and Practice'. Working Paper No.37, Southeast Asia Research Centre, City University of Hong Kong.

Dikotter, F. (2010). *Mao's Great Famine*. London, Bloomsbury.

Economist (2011) 'Some like it hot'. Retrieved 30 June 2011 from <http://www.economist.com/node/18895150>

——— (2012). 'Which MBA: 2012 Full-Time MBA Rankings'. Retrieved 29 July 2012 from <http://www.economist.com/whichmba/full-time-mba-ranking>.

Elvis, P. J. (1999). 'The Strategy and Structure of the Large, Diversified, Ethnic Chinese Organizations of Southeast Asia'. Unpub. doctoral thesis, University of Hong Kong.

Enright, M. J., E. E. Scott, and K. M. Chang (2005). *Regional Powerhouse: The Greater Pearl River Delta and the Rise of China*. Singapore, John Wiley.

Fan, J. P. H., M. Jian, and Y.-H. Yeh (2008). 'Family Firm Succession: The Roles of Specialized Assets and Transfer Costs'. Working Paper, Faculty of Business Administration, Chinese University of Hong Kong.

Fan, J. P. H., T. J. Wong, and T. Zhang (2012). 'Founder Succession and Accounting Properties'. *Contemporary Accounting Research* 29(1): 283–311.

Faure, D. (2006). *China and Capitalism*. Hong Kong, Hong Kong University Press.

Fields, D., A. Chau, and S. Akhtar (2000). 'Organizational Context and Human Resources Management Strategy: A Structural Equation Analysis of Hong Kong Firms'. *International Journal of Human Resources Management* 11(2): 264–277.

Friedman, M. (1998). 'The Hong Kong Experiment'. *Hoover Digest* No.3. Stanford, Hoover Institution.

Ghai, Y. (1999). *Hong Kong's New Constitutional Order*. Hong Kong, Hong Kong University Press,

GMAC (Graduate Management Admissions Council) (2011). *Annual Report*. Reston, GMAC.

Goodstadt, L. F. (2005). *Uneasy Partners: The Conflict between Public Interest and Private Profit in Hong Kong*. Hong Kong, Hong Kong University Press.

Heritage Foundation (2012). *2012 Index of Economic Freedom*. Washington, DC, Heritage Foundation.

Hong Kong Govt. Census and Statistics Dept. (2010). *Report on 2010 Annual Survey of Companies in Hong Kong Representing Parent Companies Located outside* Hong Kong. Retrieved 29 July 2012 from <http://www.statistics.gov.hk/pub/B11100042010AN10B0100.pdf>.

Hong Kong Institute of Human Resource Management (2012). 'Employers' Intentions to Hire remain steady for Q3 2012'. Retrieved 29 July 2012 from <http://www.hkihrm.org/ihrm_eng/ih_pre_01.asp?id=158>.

Hong Kong Stock Exchange and China Securities Regulatory Commission (1992). *A Practical Guide to Listing: Papers Presented at the Share-Issuing Seminar*. Beijing, China Securities Regulatory Commission.

Hong Kong Yearbook (2011). *Hong Kong Yearbook*. Hong Kong, Information Services Department.

Jao, Y. C. (1983). 'Financing Hong Kong's Early Post-War Industrialization: The Role of the Hongkong and Shanghai Banking Corporation'. In F. H. H.King, Ed., *Eastern Banking*: 545–574. London, Athlone Press.

Jones, G. and J. Wale (1998). 'Merchants as Business Groups: British Trading Companies in Asia before 1945'. *Business History Review* 72(3): 367–408.

Kaufmann, D., A. Kraay, and M. Mastruzzi (2012). 'Worldwide Governance Indicators'. Retrieved 29 July 2012 from <http://info.worldbank.org/governance/wgi/index.asp>.

Ko, A. C. K. (1998). 'Strategy and Performance of Listed Firms in Hong Kong'. Unpub. doctoral thesis, University of Hong Kong.

Kondo, M. (2014) 'The Philippines: Inequality-Trapped Capitalism'. In M. A. Witt and G. Redding, Eds., *The Oxford Handbook of Asian Business Systems*: 169–191. Oxford, Oxford University Press.

Labour Dept. (2012). *Annual Statistical Report of Trade Unions in Hong Kong 2011*. Hong Kong Govt.

Lee, Z.-R. and H.-H. M. Hsiao. (2014) 'Taiwan: SME-Oriented Capitalism in Transition'. In M. A. Witt and G. Redding, Eds., *The Oxford Handbook of Asian Business Systems*: 238–259. Oxford, Oxford University Press.

Lo, T. W. (1993). *Corruption and Politics in Hong Kong and China*. Buckingham, Open University.

Loh, C. (2006). 'Hong Kong's Relations with China: The Future of 'One Country, Two Systems'. *Social Research* 73(1): 293–316.

MacFarquhar, R. and M. Schoenhals (2008). *Mao's Last Revolution*. Cambridge MA, Harvard University Press.

McKeown, A. (2005). 'Chinese Diaspora'. In M. Ember, C. R. Ember, and A. Skoggard, Eds., *Encyclopaedia of Diasporas*: 65–76. New York, Springer.

Man, T. W. Y. and T. Lau (2005). 'The Context of Entrepreneurship in Hong Kong'. *Journal of Small Business and Enterprise Development* 12(4): 464–481.

Manion, M. (2004). *Corruption by Design: Building Clean Government in Mainland China and Hong Kong.* Cambridge, Harvard University Press.

Mathews, J. A. (2006). 'Dragon Multinationals: New players in 21st-century globalization'. *Asia-Pacific Journal of Management* 23: 5–27.

Ng, S. H. (2010). *Labour Law in Hong Kong.* Leiden, Kluwer Law.

Ngo, H.-Y, D. Turban, C.-M. Lau, and S.-Y. Lui (1998). 'Human Resources Practices and Firm Performance of Multinational Corporations: Influences of Country of Origin'. *International Journal of Human Resources Management* 9(4): 632–652.

OECD (2005). *China.* Paris: OECD.

OECD (2009). *Pisa 2009 Results: What Students Know and Can Do.* Paris, OECD.

Peng, M. W. and A. Delios (2006). 'What Determines the Scope of the Firm Over Time and Around the World: An Asia-Pacific Perspective'. *Asia-Pacific Journal of Management* 23(4): 385–405.

Pye, L. (1985). *Asian Power and Politics.* Cambridge, Harvard University Press.

QS (Quacquarelli Symonds) (2012) 'QS Asian University Rankings: Overall in 2012'. Retrieved 29 July 2012 from <http://www.topuniversities.com/university-rankings/asian-university-rankings/2012>.

Ralston, D., J. Pounder, C. W. H. Lo, Y. Y. Wong, C. P Egri, and J. Stouffer (2006). 'Stability and Change in Managerial Work Values: A Longitudinal Study of China, Hong Kong, and the US'. *Management and Organization Review* 2(1): 67–94.

Redding, G. (1990). *The Spirit of Chinese Capitalism.* New York, de Gruyter.

—— (1995). 'Overseas Chinese Networks: Understanding the Enigma'. *Long Range Planning* 28(1): 61–69.

—— (2004). 'The Conditional Relevance of Corporate Governance Advice in the Context of Asian Business Systems'. *Asia-Pacific Business Review* 10(3–4): 272–291.

Scott, I. (2000). 'The Disarticulation of Hong Kong's Post-Handover Political System', *China Journal* 43: 29–53.

So, A. Y. (2000). 'Hong Kong's Problematic Democratic Transition: Power Dependency or Business Hegemony?'. *Journal of Asian Studies* 59(2): 359–381.

Tan, K. (2010). 'The Public's Advocate: "Reformed" Investment Banker Revels in Role as Corporate Governance Watchdog'. *INSEAD Knowledge,* 6 May. Retrieved 29 July 2012 from <http://knowledge.insead.edu/csr/corporate-governance/the-publics-advocate-2303>.

Tang, J. T. H. (1999). 'Business as Usual: The Dynamics of Government-Business Relations in the Hong Kong Special Administrative Region'. *Journal of Contemporary China* 8(21): 275–295.

Transparency International (2011). 'Corruption Perceptions Index 2011'. Retrieved 29 July 2012 from <http://files.transparency.org/content/download/101/407/file/2011_CPI_EN.pdf>.

Tu, W.-M., Ed. (1996). *Confucian Traditions in East Asian Modernity.* Cambridge, Harvard University Press.

UN Human Settlements Program (2011). *State of the World Cities Report: Bridging the Urban Divide.* New York, UN.

Wade, R. (1990). *Governing the Market.* Princeton, Princeton University Press.

Westwood R., P. Sparrow, and A. Leung (2001). 'Challenges to the Psychological Contract in Hong Kong'. *International Journal of Human Resources Management* 12(4): 621–651.

Whitley, R. (1992). *Business Systems in East Asia.* London, Sage.

Wong, S. H. (2010). 'Political Connections and Firm Performance: The Case of Hong Kong'. *Journal of East Asian Studies* 10(2): 275–313.

World Bank (2012). 'World Development Indicators 2012'. Retrieved 29 July 2012 from <http://data.worldbank.org/sites/default/files/wdi-2012-ebook.pdf>.

World Shipping Council (2012). 'The Top 50 World Container Ports'. Retrieved 29 July 2012 from <http://www.worldshipping.org/about-the-industry/global-trade/top-50-world- container-ports>.

Wu, G. (2008). 'Hong Kong's Political Influence over China: Institutional, Informative, and Interactive Dynamics of Sovereignty'. *Pacific Review* 21(3): 279–302.

Yeung, H. W. C. (2006). 'Change and Continuity in Southeast Asian Ethnic Chinese Business'. *Asia-Pacific Journal of Management* 23(3): 229–254.

Yeung, Y-M. (2011). 'The Pearl River Delta: Governance Issues and Implications'. In B. K. Won, Y-M. Yeung, and S-C. Choe, Eds., *Collaborative Regional Development in Northeast Asia*: 309–328. Hong Kong, Chinese University Press.

Yoshihara, K. (1985). *The Rise of Ersatz Capitalism in Southeast Asia*, Kuala Lumpur, Oxford University Press.

Yu, A. F.-L. (1997). *Entrepreneurship and Economic Development in Hong Kong*, London, Routledge.

# CHAPTER 4

..................................................................................................

# INDIA

## *From Failed Developmental State Towards Hybrid Market Capitalism*

..................................................................................................

LAWRENCE SAEZ[1]

An extensive literature exists on the political economy of government and industrial relations in India (Bardhan 1984; Rudolph and Rudolph 1987). Most works on the development of capitalism in India have focused on the role of the state as an autonomous actor and on the emergence of dominant proprietary classes. However, any analysis of comparative business systems in Asia must contend with the fact that the Indian economy has undergone significant transformation since the country adopted economic liberalization measures after 1991. In response to a balance of payments crisis in the early 1990s, the government opened up India's economy to trade and investment, introduced some tax reforms and deregulation, and explored the idea of privatizing strategic sectors. Although there is intense debate about the developmental costs and benefits of India's economic liberalization policies, it is clear that they have enabled new sectors of the economy to flourish and compete internationally, particularly in the computer software, pharmaceuticals, and financial services sectors. At a macroeconomic level, India's economic growth has been more stable than during the pre-liberalization period.

The objective of this chapter is to provide an overview of the institutional structure of the Indian business system—a challenging task for various reasons. First, because India is a federal country with very distinctive regional orientations to economic development, industrialization, and openness to foreign direct investment since the economic liberalization period that started in 1991 (Saez 2001). The diversity in adoption of economic liberalization measures and responses to globalization have resulted in the development of business clusters in different regions. Some authors, notably Sinha (2005), have shown that the sub-national variation in India's political economy has given rise to divergent developmental models of business–government relations. Drawing on case studies of some of India's most prominent states (West Bengal, Gujarat, Tamil Nadu), Sinha has shown a wide variation in state–business relations, business responses to licensing regimes, and the state's developmental pathways. She argues, for instance, that the state of Gujarat is a model of competitive capitalism, whereas the state of West Bengal is a model of vertical confrontation. Thus, when viewing India as a model of capitalism, one is likely to overlook significant cross-sectional variations in capitalist development occurring at sub-national or regional level. Drawing on the importance of regional variation, other authors (like Besley and Burgess 2004) have also shown important differences in the adoption and enforcement of labour regulations across India.

Bearing this in mind, this chapter seeks to offer a stylized overview of the Indian business system. The basic premise is that institutional mechanisms have a temporal dimension, hence it is important to understand the influence of British colonial rule and the role of the state (as envisioned by Jawaharlal Nehru) in Indian political life. We will then show the relationship between development in India's financial system, ownership, and corporate governance, and the internal structure of the firm. We go on to examine employment relations, education and skills formation, and inter-company relations. The second section of the chapter will concentrate on peculiarities of India's industrial-relations regime. In this setting, particular attention will be given to labour unions and recent trends in industrial action. The third section will look at social capital in India.

# The Role of the State

Any analysis of the contemporary patterns of capitalism in India needs to take into account two overlapping historical trends: the influence of British colonial power in the Indian subcontinent since the 1850s and the establishment of post-independence state institutions since the 1950s. Prior to India's independence in 1947 (Saez 2004), British colonial power enabled the development of indigenous financial and banking institutions: the Bombay Stock Exchange (BSE) was founded in 1875, and, by 1881, the Oudh Commercial Bank became the first Indian banking institution of limited liability not managed directly by the British. British colonial power also had a lasting impact on the post-independence regulatory structure, such as the creation in 1935 of the Reserve Bank of India (RBI), India's central bank. After independence, most of the existing financial services industry formed the backbone of India's contemporary financial services system.

In addition to the influence of British colonial rule on institutionalizing capitalism in India, the first three decades of post-independence India have been influential. The political economy in India's post-independence period was a classic form of state capitalism. Jawaharlal Nehru, India's first prime minister (1947–1964), provided the framework for the economic structure of post-independence India. Although a believer in Soviet-style planning and centralization, Nehru fomented a mixed economic system where the means of production continued to be privately owned, but the state exerted considerable control over the allocation of credit and investment (Sandesara 1992). One core institution of the Nehruvian economic model was a central planning body, the Planning Commission. Under its guidance, the Indian developmental model emphasized state-led industrialization and import substitution (Chakravarty 1987). Most importantly, there was an increasing amount of regulatory density, particularly through the imposition of onerous licensing requirements to private business transactions. This regulatory regime—pejoratively referred to as license *raj* (rule)—handicapped private-sector entrepreneurship and provided incentives for rent-seeking activity. In effect, Nehru was attempting to establish a local variant of a developmental state, an effort that failed because of poor implementation of centralized planning schemes. Eventually, the successor to Nehru's policy-making strategy, Indira Gandhi, steered the Indian economy on a more distinctive socialist footing, with increasing reliance on top-down policy decision-making, nationalizing most of the banks operating in India in 1969.

Although India's economic liberalization policies from 1991 onwards were gradual, the economy has been dramatically transformed. Prior to liberalization, the economy had many features of a 'command-and-control' *dirigiste* economy, and has often been depicted as a failed developmental state (Sinha 2003). The state remains a critical actor in India's political economy, and important features of the centralized mixed-economic model remain in place. In many instances, the state owns a controlling share of publicly listed firms, thus acting as a capitalist actor itself. In this sense, India can still be portrayed as a classic case of state capitalism, namely an economic system where the means of production are privately owned and the state exerts considerable control over the allocation of credit and investment. Some authors (e.g. Mazumdar 2010) have argued that the contemporary political economy of Indian capitalism is deeply embedded within pre-existing forms of colonial-era capitalism, but contend that as the Indian state has not enacted agrarian reform, there is no fully developed model of capitalism in India that would fit well within the framework of a liberal market economy. Basing their analysis on the emergence of global business firms and multinationals from India, Saez and Chang (2010:267) have argued that the existing framework of capitalism in India appears to be a hybrid, and assert that the 'final direction of change depends strongly on the strategies of powerful internal actors', namely regional governments.

Observers of post-reform India (Jenkins 2004; Kennedy 2007; Palit and Bhattacharjee 2007; Mukherji 2008) have further drawn attention to regional industrial policies and the challenges of second-generation economic reforms, and have focused on the transformation of corporatized government agencies, parastatals (companies wholly or largely owned by the government, known in India as public-sector undertakings or PSUs), and special economic zones (SEZs). Present-day Indian political governance thus incorporates a considerable bottom-up element in which different states produce different responses to institutional challenges. Although corruption levels are high, there is wide variation across different states.

# FINANCIAL SYSTEM

Like other transition economies, India's economic system has been heavily influenced by the structure of its financial system and its financial services sector. India's basic infrastructure for capital markets transactions is solid, and its banks and other forms of financial intermediation provide significant avenues for indirect financial allocation.

The principal actors in India's contemporary financial system are the stock exchanges. At present, India has twenty-three regional stock exchanges, including Asia's oldest, the Bombay Stock Exchange (BSE). The stock exchanges in Delhi and Calcutta were also established during the colonial period. Following economic liberalization, new capital-market institutions were created to become nationwide trading platforms, including the National Stock Exchange (NSE), the Over-the-Counter Exchange of India (OTCEI), and the newly created commodities futures exchange, the Multi-Commodity Exchange of India (MCX).

Other critical actors in India's financial system include the financial services industry, which incorporates both depository institutions (primarily banks) and non-depository institutions (primarily insurance companies). As discussed above, both sectors were severely affected by nationalization policies. Following nationalization, the State Bank of India (SBI) and its associate banks became the dominant players in the banking sector, overshadowing competitors in terms of the percentage of public banking assets held and the number of bank branches. A similar process of state-enforced consolidation of the insurance sector also took place under Indira Gandhi's direction. New entrants in the 1990s have increasingly challenged this level of dominance.

There has been a dramatic transformation of the financial system since the economic liberalization measures. In 1991, for instance, the market capitalization of all stock exchanges was US$47 billion, approximately equivalent to 19 per cent of gross domestic product (GDP) (Saez 2004: 92). In a 1993 survey of the world's emerging stock markets, India was not included, because it was 'long virtually closed to foreign portfolio investment' (van Agtmael 1993: 37). Until the 1990s, equity markets were not important sources of funding for non-state actors. However, the gradual opening of the economy prompted gradual inflows of portfolio equity investment and foreign direct investment. By 1995, the capitalization of India's stock markets had tripled since 1991. Twenty years after liberalization, the BSE is the ninth largest stock exchange in the world, closely behind Deutsche Börse (World Federation of Exchanges 2011), while the NSE is the tenth largest. According to data from the World Federation of Exchanges, the BSE has the highest number of listed companies (5,034 companies), twice as many as the New York Stock exchange (2,238). However, even though India's stock markets have increased in size, the banking sector remains the dominant player in capital markets, both in size and in its role in allocating resources.

There are two broad types of banks in India: public-sector and private-sector banks. Within public-sector banks, there are three main sub-categories: the SBI and its associates, nationalized banks, and general public-sector banks. The sector is dominated by the SBI and seven associate institutions. There are also smaller public-sector banks, namely regional rural banks. In conjunction with the nationalized banks and the general public-sector banks, the aggregate public-sector group accounts for nearly 76 per cent of total banking assets and around 90 per cent of bank branches in India (RBI 2011). Insofar as the allocation of capital is dominated by state financial institutions and most firms are state controlled, most capital investment is long term. However, credit allocation on non-market-based criteria has resulted in the inefficient allocation of capital into money-losing public-sector enterprises.

Although there is no functional distinction between different types of private-sector banks, India's central bank has devised a confusing array of private-sector bank sub-categories. These include old private-sector banks, new private-sector banks, private-sector banks, and foreign banks. Old private-sector banks are those that existed prior to independence; private banks and new private-sector banks are those established since the 1991 reforms. Given the significance of the state in India's economy, capital allocation is predominantly state controlled, though economic liberalization measures and the growing presence of private-sector banks have enabled the introduction of market criteria as a determinant of capital allocation. At present, domestic private-sector banks account for 21 per cent, and foreign banks 4 per cent, of total banking assets (RBI 2011).

# OWNERSHIP AND CORPORATE GOVERNANCE

There are two types of ownership patterns in India: government and non-government companies. Government companies are state-owned enterprises or firms with state institutions as majority shareholders. They tend to be concentrated in labour-intensive industries, and profit maximization is usually not their objective. By contrast, non-government companies are private-sector firms, with a primary objective of profit maximization. These tend to be concentrated in financial services, real estate, and business services. According to data provided by the Ministry of Corporate Affairs, there were 1,624 government companies and 834,218 non-government companies at the end of 2010. However, although government companies represent about 0.19 per cent of total companies, they account for 25 per cent of paid-up capital. In terms of paid-up capital, government firms are equivalent to 15 per cent of India's GDP, while non-government firms represent 53.9 per cent. By virtue of their size, individual state-owned firms are dominant in terms of aggregate assets and market share. However, private-sector firms are fast gaining ground, largely by pursuing much more effective outward-investment strategies.

State-owned firms (or public-sector undertakings, PSUs) are split between central and state-controlled firms. About 30 per cent of India's government companies, known as central public-sector enterprises (CPSEs), operate under the administrative control of a central government ministry or department. The central government holds the majority share in CPSEs. Some of India's largest corporations are CPSEs and include companies like Indian Oil, National Thermal Power Corporation Limited, Oil and Natural Gas Corporation Limited, and the Steel Authority of India. These CPSEs receive special protection from the state and have been granted enhanced financial and operational powers to expand their operations in domestic and foreign markets. The state, whether the central or state governments, has reduced its stake in PSUs through a process of gradual corporatization.

As a result of state patronage during the Nehru era of managed state capitalism and Indira Gandhi's failed neo-corporatism, there are different varieties of private-sector enterprises: business houses and private-sector firms. Business houses account for most private business activity. These enterprises are family-owned conglomerates, a feature connected to the impact of Nehru-style policies on the country's private-sector corporate governance structure, particularly in the promotion of selected family-owned conglomerates. Prior to independence, two of India's most prominent family-owned business houses were Birla and Tata. In the 1980s, these two business houses controlled 115 companies and accounted for nearly 40 per cent of all sales of the top business houses (Bardhan 1984). These were joined by other favoured family-owned firms, led by the Ambani, Modi, and Nanda families. On the basis of their overwhelming corporate strength, some authors (Ghosh 1974; Ito 1984) have drawn apt comparisons between India's large family-controlled vertical oligopolies and Japanese *zaibatsu*.

Business houses have continued to form the core of India's contemporary industrial capitalist class, enjoying close engagement with the state. Nevertheless, these family-owned firms have proven resilient to new market entrants. In most cases, these firms have experienced rapid growth that has led to extensive diversification of core competencies. Although there is some debate about the impact of diversification on firm performance in developing countries (Nachum 1999; Mishra and Akbar 2007), firms like Reliance Industries and Reliance ADAG (owned by the Ambani brothers), for instance, have developed into modern-day horizontally diversified business conglomerates, with industrial capabilities ranging from textiles to chemicals and oil exploration. Despite the high level of internal diversification of these business houses, they remain firms where family members are large controlling shareholders (Kohli 2012). Generally, the most prominent Indian conglomerates are family-owned enterprises based on concentrated ownership by financial institutions and long-term debt-based financing. Through their close engagement with state institutions and state-owned banks, business houses in India represent the most obvious strand of crony capitalism.

Since the 1990s, privately owned enterprises with dispersed ownership and market-based equity financing and private firms with a significant presence of foreign corporate shareholders have emerged. Privately owned enterprises tend to be concentrated in the financial services and information and business process outsourcing (IT/BPO) sectors. Private-sector firms—those that are not business houses—represent a new strand of capitalism in India, which could be labelled entrepreneurial capitalism.

One distinctive feature of the Indian corporate landscape is the ownership structure of some leading firms. Forbes magazine's Global 2000 ranking of the world's leading firms lists 56 Indian companies (Forbes 2010). The state is the dominant player in industries engaged in oil and gas operations (e.g. Oil and Natural Gas, Bharat Petroleum, Oil India), materials and natural resource extraction (e.g. Steel Authority of India, National Aluminium), utilities (Power Grid of India), and banking (State Bank of India Group) (Saez and Chang 2010). However, equally powerful corporate players can be found in the private sector. The list of leading Indian private-sector corporations operating under a business house umbrella includes Reliance Industries (oil and gas operations), Reliance Telecommunications (telecommunications services), Tata Steel (materials and natural resource extraction), and Tata Motors (consumer durables). Leading privately owned firms include ICICI Bank (banking), Bharti Airtel (telecommunications services), Infosys Technologies, and Wipro (software).

The tremendous growth in capital-market development since 1991 has refocused the contemporary legal arrangements dealing with corporate governance. India's principal regulator of capital markets is the Securities and Exchange Board of India (SEBI). SEBI has a direct impact on companies listed in the stock exchanges, although the level of this impact is evolving. For instance, listed companies are required to maintain a substantial presence of independent directors on company boards and stringent internal controls, implementation remediation processes, and detailed compliance-report disclosure. The underlying rule became operational only in 2005, so the exact impact of this governance arrangement remains to be seen (see Kohli 2012).

The example set by some large publicly traded companies should be interpreted as being ideal-types, not necessarily representative of the bulk of Indian enterprises. Even companies appearing to be models of corporate probity can become embroiled in accounting fraud investigations. For non-listed companies, the level of corporate governance is well below international standards. In the 2011 Doing Business survey, Indian firms ranked 32nd in the world in terms of getting credit and 44th in protecting investors (World Bank 2011). This ranking shows the relative strength of banking as a source of funding and regulatory protection of investors.

Although family-owned business have been successful in a period of liberalization, it is unclear whether these firms have been successful on account of the optimization of their core competencies, the strategic vision of their leaders, or ongoing political connections to state patrons. Beyond the realm of family-owned firms, though, country-level empirical evidence for Indian companies offers mixed lessons on the causal mechanisms relating to the impact of corporate board structure on firm performance. Some studies have suggested that large corporate boards in India have a dampening effect on performance (Ghosh 2006). In contrast, rather than corporate board size or its degree of independence, other studies have suggested that corporate board quality, often with the presence of a foreign representative, is the primary determinant of corporate performance and reduced management earnings (Sarkar, Sarkar, and Sen 2008).

# INTERNAL STRUCTURE OF THE FIRM

The comparative political economy literature on Asian business systems places the analysis of the firm as a centrepiece of the strategic interactions that are central to the behaviour of economic actors. To discuss the internal structure of the firm in India, we must initially make a clear distinction between the principal types of corporate structure typically found there, namely business houses, privately owned enterprises, and state-owned enterprises. It is also important to differentiate the internal structure of the firm on the basis of the level of its industry portfolio diversification. For instance, family-owned conglomerates have horizontal integration across sectors. However, as a result of the distribution of authority to a small number of shareholders, these horizontally bound conglomerates are bundled within a loosely flat pyramidal firm structure, often combining services and manufacturing sector outlets.

Privately owned enterprises, particularly in industries with a high degree of intra-firm specialization (e.g. consulting, information technology, business process outsourcing or BPO, engineering services and R&D, and software development sectors), are relatively flat and less hierarchical than other forms of enterprise in India (D'Costa 2004). The relatively flat internal structure reflects the narrow gap in skill set between managers and workers. In some instances, applicants to entry-level jobs hold advanced postgraduate degrees, a situation enabling firms to delegate some decision-making functions to employees. Correspondingly, since many operate in industrial sectors for which there is a high degree of demand for a specialized skill set, there is a high level of voluntary employee turnover to competing firms (D'Costa 2004). Indian IT firms have an employee turnover rate of 25 per cent per year, something which imposes a heavy burden on them to retrain new workers (Basi 2009). In order to respond to these market pressures, these enterprises have introduced innovative management characteristics, such as teamwork and horizontal monitoring of worker productivity.

State-owned enterprises, particularly since they function in heavy manufacturing and extractive industries, tend to follow a rigid top-down tall hierarchical structure. In state-owned enterprises, there is little delegation of decision-making to employees and correspondingly minimal employee participation in decision-making. Moreover, the output prices from the products generated by these industries tends to be protected (e.g. by regulation), a factor which discourages innovation (Mukherji 1985; Morris and Basant 2008). As there is there is no hard budget constraint for these firms to be profitable, state-owned enterprises tend to be staffed well above levels that would be considered prudent to remain profitable. The Ministry of Heavy Industries and Public Enterprises (2011) estimated that 59 of 217 CPSEs operate at a loss. CPSEs are, in effect, civil service jobs where the internal promotion structure is built on the notion of seniority, rather than talent. In addition, as a result of India's rigid labour laws, employee turnover ratios are very low. In combination, these factors account for low worker productivity. Moreover, in an increasingly liberalized economy, CPSEs do not attract the best talent, so there is an increasing skill gap between the management of CPSEs and private-sector firms.

# EMPLOYMENT RELATIONS

An evaluation of employment relations in India must first take into account the substantial discrepancy between available data on the formal and informal sectors of the economy. If we exclude children under 15 and adults over 60 years old, India has a potential working-age population of approximately 671 million (UN 2011). The World Bank (2011: 41) estimates the labour force at 457 million. However, according to the labour statistics dataset compiled by the International Labour Organization (ILO), India has an aggregate labour force of 286 million, a figure that would appear rather small for a population that exceeds one billion. The ILO figure corresponds to the Indian government's own estimates for the organized sector (Ministry of Finance 2011). As such, a broad estimate of India's labour force suggests that roughly two-fifths work in the informal sector. Some independent scholarly assessments have provided a much larger allocation. For instance, Harriss-White (2003: 17) makes the case that in India's total labour force, 'only 7% are in the organized sector (that is, are workers on regular wages and salaries) in registered firms and with access to the State's social security system and its framework of labour law'. Hence, a holistic analysis of industrial relations in India is hampered because there is no accurate assessment as to how many people work in the informal sector, though the proportion is significant. Furthermore, government data on the organized sector are derived from national census data, so are often outdated by almost a decade by the time they are officially released.

According to the ILO (2011), of India's aggregate organized-sector labour force total, approximately 67 per cent works in rural employment, and the remaining 22 per cent in the urban sector. Female participation is higher in rural employment (comprising approximately 25 per cent of total rural employment) than in the urban setting (13 per cent of total urban employment).

The state remains India's largest provider of employment in the organized sector. Regional and municipal governments also account for an important share of employment in this sector, though the private sector proportion has been growing in recent years. The Indian government measures employment in the private sector as relating to non-agricultural employment in a private-sector enterprise that employs ten or more people. Employment in the agricultural sector is primarily informal.

Figure 4.1 shows that public employees account for nearly 70 per cent of India's total labour force, primarily in public administration and defence-related services. However, the proportion in the private sector increased dramatically from 1985 to 2005.

India's Ministry of Labour officially recognizes a core number of trade unions as central trade union organizations (CTUO). In order to be recognized as such, a union needs to have a minimum membership of 500,000, with a presence in at least four states in India and across four industrial sectors. Using these criteria, the Ministry of Labour conducts periodic, but irregular, verifications of union membership. Based on the latest Ministry membership survey in 2001, the ten largest unions in India had an aggregate membership of 22 million, roughly equivalent to 10 per cent of the aggregate organized

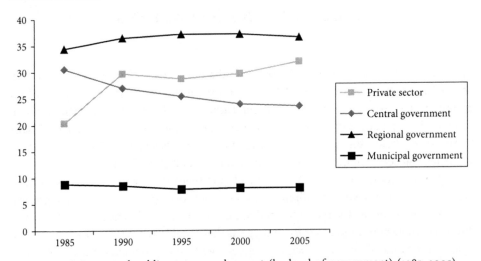

FIGURE 4.1 Private- and public-sector employment (by level of government) (1985–2005)

*Note*: Figures represent percentages as a proportion of the total labour force in the organized sector.

*Source*: ILO.

labour force.[2] The Ministry collects membership data including and excluding agricultural and rural workers (A&RW). Table 4.1 shows the strength of the ten principal unions, based on membership size.

India's leading four labour unions are the Bharatiya Mazdoor Sangh (BMS), the Indian National Trade Union Congress (INTUC), the Hind Mazdoor Sabha (HMS), and the Centre for Indian Trade Unions (CITU). The membership of these four unions constitutes about two-thirds of India's entire officially recognized union membership. Although nearly 30 per cent of total union membership is classified as A&RW, there are no significant variations in the relative strength of the top four, whether including or excluding membership data on A&RWs.

Unions in India have strong identification with leading political parties. The largest, the BMS, forms part of a loose confederation of Hindu nationalist organizations (*sangh parivar*) affiliated to the Bharatiya Janata Party (BJP). On most economic matters, the BJP has a centre-right ideological focus favouring free-market policies, although sectors of the BJP also support protectionist trade measures. The second largest union, the INTUC, is closely affiliated to the Indian National Congress, arguably India's most important national political party, strongly identified with the policies of Jawaharlal Nehru and Indira Gandhi.

As a consequence of the variety and ideological distinctiveness of the principal labour unions, there is little inter-union cohesiveness, even among those divided by what would appear to be trivial ideological differences. Datta-Chaudhuri (2000: 456) estimated that between 1950 and 1975, 'almost 30 per cent of the industrial disputes in India could be attributed the problems of union recognition and inter-union rivalry'. As such, he concludes that 'the large number of trade unions has led to inter-union rivalry for members'.

Table 4.1    Membership of the top ten labour unions in India (2002)

| Name of union | Membership excluding A&RW | Membership including A&RW |
|---|---|---|
| BMS | 4,879,480 | 6,215,797 |
| INTUC | 2,947,205 | 3,892,011 |
| HMS | 2,641,988 | 3,342,213 |
| CITU | 2,567,010 | 3,222,532 |
| AITUC | 1,971,907 | 2,677,979 |
| UTUC (LS) | 622,861 | 1,368,535 |
| SEWA | 383,946 | 606,935 |
| UTUC | 274,846 | 383,946 |
| TUCC | 183,553 | 732,760 |
| AICCTU | 135,023 | 639,962 |
| **Total top ten unions** | 16,607,819 | 22,775,358 |
| **Total all unions** | 17,131,529 | 24,601,589 |

*Abbreviations*: AITUC: All-India Trade Union Congress; UTUC (LS): United Trade Union Congress (Lenin Sarani faction); SEWA: Self Employed Women's Association; UTUC: United Trade Union Congress; TUCC: Trade Union Coordination Committee; AICCTU: All-India Central Council of Trade Unions.
*Source*: Ministry of Labour, Government of India.

Given the peculiarities of India's capitalist system, with a large unorganized sector and highly fragmented labour unions, the industrial relations regime does not feature the comprehensive and identifiable forms of competitive pluralism found elsewhere, including union–employer relations across different industrial sectors. Union penetration of India's burgeoning private sector, particularly in IT-enabled services (ITES), telecommunications, and BPO sectors, has been negligible.[3] Noronha and D'Cruz (2001: 2115) have argued that a new relationship between employers and workers in the ITES–BPO sectors 'marginalises the role of unions in the workplace or emphasises overt union avoidance'. There is also little unionization in privately owned small and medium enterprises, sectors characterized by the use of casual labour and where the enforcement of employment practices is fluid. In those areas where economic activity is organized, the relationship between the state, employers, workers, and unions has been one of uneasy coexistence.

A macro-level analysis of industrial action in India suggests a steady decline of strikes and lockouts across all industrial sectors since the 1970s. Most such strike and lockout activity in India involves the manufacturing sector, followed by mining and agriculture. Using ILO data on strikes and lockouts by economic activity in India, we find that they peaked in 1975, experienced sharp decline in 1975–1977, and declined steadily from the 1980s (see Figure 4.2).

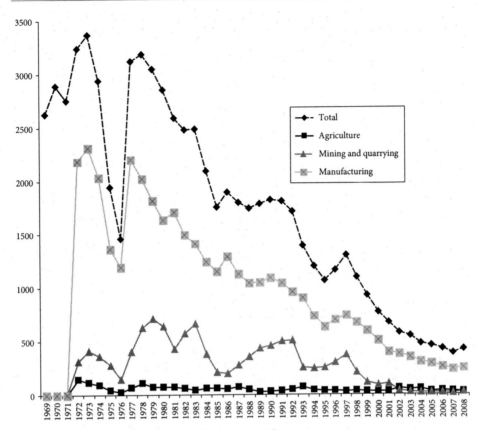

FIGURE 4.2  Strikes and lockout in India (1968–2008)

Note: ILO data do not include a sectoral breakdown for 1968–1970, hence the data for those years is zero.

Source: ILO.

An analysis of the data in Figure 4.2 suggests that industrial action was strongest in the early 1970s, largely as a result of a number of compounding factors, such as industrial stagnation, oil price shocks, and labour union opposition to Indira Gandhi's policies (Bhattacherjee 1999: 8). The rapid decline in the 1975–1977 period coincides with Gandhi's declaration of a state of emergency, which made strikes illegal. During this period, many opposition leaders were jailed, including prominent trade unionists. As Figure 4.2 also shows, there was a brief resurgence of industrial action during 1977–1979, during a period of coalition rule by opponents of Indira Gandhi.

In an atmosphere of intense union competition for membership, there are some unusual outcomes. In terms of collective action, the BMS, representing public-sector workers, has been the most effective at challenging proposed policies for reforming public-sector employment. White-collar strikes have become an emerging feature of the post-1991 economic liberalization period. ILO data (2011) show a rapid growth in the number of workers affected by strikes in the financial intermediation industry. For instance, in 2000, 12,803 were affected by 14 financial intermediation-related strikes.

**Table 4.2 Number of strikes and lockouts (2002–2005, 2008–2009)**

| Year | 2002 | 2003 | 2004 | 2005 | 2008 | 2009 |
|---|---|---|---|---|---|---|
| Strikes | 295 | 255 | 236 | 227 | 240 | 204 |
| Workers affected (thousands) | 900 | 1,010 | 1,903 | 2,722 | 1,513 | 1,539 |
| Lockouts | 284 | 297 | 241 | 229 | 181 | 187 |
| Workers affected (thousands) | 179 | 804 | 169 | 190 | 65 | 91 |

*Source*: Ministry of Labour, Government of India.

In 2008, 854,134 workers were affected by 42 financial intermediation-related strikes (exceeding the number of workers affected by strikes in manufacturing, mining, agriculture, and transport combined).

The Ministry of Labour's statistical division, the Labour Bureau, disaggregates strike and lockout data for recent years. Although there is an overall decline in the total number of strikes and lockouts, at first glance there also appeared to be a trend away from strikes and in favour of lockouts from 2001 to 2005. In 2003, for instance, lockouts exceeded strikes. However, as Table 4.2 shows, the trend (based on provisional estimates for 2008 and 2009) appears to have reversed again in recent years.

The data in Table 4.2 suggest that despite a decline in the overall number of strikes, the number of workers affected by these actions has increased.

## EDUCATION AND SKILLS FORMATION

Education and skills formation are an important component of India's industrial regime. Any discussion of this topic in India, though, first requires an understanding of the fundamental facets of the educational system. According to the most recent available data provided by UNESCO (2010: 226), India's overall adult literacy rates are 62.8 per cent of the population.[4] UNESCO estimates that over 65 per cent of the female adult population in India is illiterate. On the other hand, there appears to be an important improvement in youth literacy rates. Overall youth literacy rates in India are 81.1 per cent, nearly 20 percentage points higher than for the overall adult population.[5] However, female youth illiteracy rates are 67 per cent, two percentage points higher than the overall illiteracy rate for all adults.

An assessment of the likelihood of educational quality in India needs to take into account the great deal of asymmetry in the levels of illiteracy across different states.

For instance, the states of Kerala, Mizoram, and Goa have above-average literacy rates of 90.92, 88.49, and 82.32 per cent respectively.[6] On the other hand, the states of Bihar, Jammu and Kashmir, and Arunachal Pradesh have below-average literacy rates of 47.53, 54.13, and 54.74 per cent respectively. It is worth stressing that there is approximately a 20 per cent differential in literacy rates between men and women within states; in some instances, the differential is higher. For instance, in Bihar, the male literacy rate is 60.32 per cent, but for females it is 33.57 per cent. In general, female literacy rates in India are alarmingly low. Bihar's rate for female literacy compares unfavourably with those of some low-income countries in sub-Saharan Africa.[7]

An overview of the number of educational institutions at all levels in India is staggering. According to the Ministry, there were 772,568 primary schools, 288,493 upper primary schools, 159,667 junior colleges, 11,698 colleges for general education, and 5,284 colleges for professional education in 2005–2011 (Ministry of Human Development and Resource Development 2011). In addition, India's Ministry of Labour has an elaborate network of educational training and skills formation, though for all intents and purposes, these facilities are not widely used, relative to other forms of training.

Given India's poor performance on basic literacy skills, the abundance of educational institutions should not be interpreted as a representation of participation or quality. For instance, India's primary education completion rate—the percentage success rate to the last grade of primary school—is 65 per cent, lower than sub-Saharan Africa (UNESCO 2011: 315). At the same time, a thorough assessment of India's education and training systems is difficult to obtain, because it does not participate in international measures of educational excellence, such as the Trends in International Mathematics and Science Study (TIMMS) or the Programme for International Student Assessment (PISA). Curiously, the states of Himachal Pradesh and Tamil Nadu participated in an extended version of the PISA 2009 assessment, but the results from that limited exercise had not been released at the time of writing in 2013.

As can be gathered from data available from the University Grants Commission (UGC), India's principal education regulator, there is a pyramidal structure of university-level institutions. Altogether India has 600 universities, comparatively few relative to population. The shortage is even more acute than these numbers suggest, because of these 600, there are important sub-groups with sharply different levels of quality. The UGC enumerates different categories of universities. At present, there are 42 central universities (established through an Act of Parliament by the Department of Higher Education) and 274 state universities (established by state governments) (University Grants Commission 2011a, 2011b). The central universities have massive enrolment figures; for instance, the University of Delhi has 220,000 students. There are also 85 private universities, generally perceived to be of very poor quality. The UGC also enumerates a special category of university-like institutions. These include high-performing research institutions that are labelled 'deemed universities' and 'institutions of national importance' (University Grants Commission, 2011c). 'Deemed universities' are prominent research institutions granted degree-award powers for courses approved by the UGC. Some prominent 'deemed universities' include the Homi Bhabha

National Institute and the Indira Gandhi Institute of Development Research. 'Institutes of national importance' incorporate all Indian Institutes of Technology (IITs), as well as a plethora of other elite educational institutions, such as the Indian Institutes of Information Technology (IIITs), National Institutes of Technology (NITs), the National Institutes of Pharmaceutical Education and Research (NIPERs), Indian Institutes of Science Education and Research (IISERs), and Indian Institutes of Managements (IIMs). Enrolment figures for these university-like institutions are comparatively small. For instance, all IITs combined have an enrolment of roughly 15,000 undergraduate and 12,000 postgraduate students.

In international rankings of educational quality for university education, Indian institutions do not fare competitively. For instance, in the QS ranking of the world's top universities, only five Indian institutions rank among the top 400. In that particular league table, the highest-ranked Indian educational institution is the IIT-Bombay, ranked 137th, behind the Université Paris Sorbonne, Paris IV, and ahead of the University of Iowa (QS 2011). The other Indian educational institutions ranked among the top 400 were the IIT-Delhi (202nd), IIT-Kanpur (249th), IIT-Madras (262nd), and IIT-Kharagpur (311th). Altogether, of the seven IITs in India, five feature in the QS rankings. India's largest public universities (e.g. Universities of Mumbai, Delhi, Calcutta, Pune) rank in the bottom third.

In view of the domestic success of IITs, the government has decided to expand their number to 15. What is distinctive about IITs is that they are engineering and technology institutes that have a governance structure enabling them to operate with a high degree of autonomy from government interference in curriculum design and academic content. By contrast, most public universities are crippled by an excessively anachronistic and bureaucratic regulatory environment fostered by the UGC. Moreover, in a country struggling to enact ambitious affirmative-action programmes for traditionally disadvantaged lower-caste groups, IITs have an advantage in that they have a largely meritocratic admissions policy, considered among the most competitive in the country. There is no doubt that IITs are viewed as elite institutions within India, but they have yet to be viewed elsewhere as international leaders. For instance, the *Times Higher Education* (THE) ranking of the world's top 200 universities does not include any Indian institution, nor does its ranking for the top 25 universities in Asia. Likewise, the Academic Ranking of World Universities (ARWU), commonly known as the Shanghai Jiao Tong ranking, only ranks one Indian university among its top 500 universities in the world (Academic Ranking of World Universities, 2011).

In order to address the weaknesses in the provision of training from different layers of the state-funded educational system, some of India's largest private companies are also some of the largest training providers. Among the largest private-sector employers, particularly in the ITES sector, there are well-developed workforce development practices. These educational and training systems are geared towards the formation and development of firm-specific skills. Although Indian universities produce hundreds of thousands of graduates in engineering and other technical skills, there is a distinct chasm between elite educational institutions and mainstream universities. In response to this skills gap, some private firms have developed ambitious educational programmes. For instance, Infosys, one of the most respected ITES firms in India, opened the Infosys Global Education Centre in Mysore, to train thousands of new employees a year. The centre offers a residential foundation programme with the capacity to train up to 24,000 individuals, with residential facilities for 8,000 people. Infosys is not unique among ITES-sector industries, but it is the most renowned. In recognition of efforts by leading Indian private firms, the American Society for Training and Development (ASTD) has consistently rated Infosys, Wipro Technologies, ICICI Bank, and Tata Consulting Services as among the world's best in employee training and development (ASTD 2011). Thus, private-sector provision of employee training is geared towards new employees, rather than enhancing the human capital development of existing employees or providing effective vocational training schemes to discourage poaching.

As a means of harnessing the involvement of its members, some labour unions also provide education and skills formation training. For instance, SEWA, the union representing self-employed women, negotiates with private firms to provide training to its members (particularly in the construction sector). According to Jhabvala and Kanbur (2004: 305), 'existing employment exchanges only cater to formal-sector jobs'. In order to address this gap in education and training, SEWA 'has set up its own employment centre, where SEWA members register themselves, their qualifications and skills, and the kind of work they are willing to do'. Jhabvala and Kanbur report that SEWA then contacts employers to find work for women suitable to their skills. At the same time, SEWA runs courses, particularly in garment-making, to diversify the existing skills of its members. SEWA operates the SEWA Academy, an informal university that provides leadership training and education in small groups, based on the principle of learning through mutual sharing. According to SEWA, nearly 20,000 women have participated in their educational programmes.

## INTER-COMPANY RELATIONS

Inter-company relations refer to the type of linkages that enable the diffusion of technology across the economy. In other country contexts, business networks, in particular, lie at the core of inter-company relations and are supported by a number of institutions and public officials. In the context of India's highly fragmented and dysfunctional industrial-relations system—further characterized by a substantial proportion of unorganized labour in the overall composition of the labour force—it is fanciful to anticipate a well-cultivated inter-company relations framework.

At national level, we find business groups loosely organized around the principal family-owned conglomerates (e.g. Tata, Birla, Ambani), which, as discussed, are diversified groups with interests across a wide range of industry sub-sectors. Although these business groups historically have strong ties to state institutions, they do not necessarily cooperate with public officials to determine how firm competencies can be improved or how publicly subsidized programmes can be orchestrated. These conglomerates also have not shown any intention to collude with each other to enhance their market share vis-à-vis state-owned enterprises.

At regional level, we can identify specific business networks, often mediated by common caste or religious linkages. Some regions have developed specialisms. For instance, the town of Surat, in Gujarat, has been a centre of diamond-cutting for centuries. With the rise of globalization, the diamond-cutting business network from this area has become trans-national, expanding into Mumbai, South Africa, and the Gulf. Such networks based on caste or religious linkages, though, are founded on traditional forms of relational contracting for specialized trades (e.g. diamond-cutting, money-lending), but do not act as effective transmitters of technology transfer.

Western-style inter-company relations in India can be identified in a number of business organization and industry promotion lobby groups. At a pan-industry level, the most prominent are the Confederation of Indian Industry (CII) and the Federation of Indian Chambers of Commerce and Industry (FICCI). Within the IT-enabled services industry, the most prominent business group has been the National Association of Software and Services Companies (NASSCOM). Since the IT-enabled services industry is clustered regionally, it may be fair to classify this as a regional business group.

## SOCIAL CAPITAL

India is a highly heterogeneous country with a multitude of social cleavages, including kinship, caste, language, religion, and other ascriptive traits. In such a context, it is crucial to understand social capital. The concept of social capital is an important ingredient in the varieties of capitalism literature, because it is viewed as a resource that can be utilized by groups to act collectively. Using India as the source of their exploration, a basic definition of social capital (Blomkvist and Swain 2001: 639) defined it as 'trust, networks and norms shared by a group of actors that enable them together more effectively to pursue shared objectives'.

Owing to the difficulties of collecting survey data in a country like India, it is difficult to obtain a comprehensive measure of interpersonal trust. To date, the World Values Survey (2009) has undertaken just one survey of interpersonal trust in India. The survey, undertaken during Wave 2 (1990), shows that Hindus have a substantially higher level of interpersonal trust than non-Hindus; Hindus' average score was 1.63, compared to 2.21 for non-Hindus. Other all-India surveys also suggest a low level of interpersonal trust across communities. For instance, the CSDS/Lokniti's State of the Nation Survey (2001) shows that there is reluctance among some communities to engage with other communities in fairly elementary societal transactions (e.g. attending a social event, eating together in a restaurant). This reluctance to engage with communities other than one's own becomes more problematic for an individual's most important life decisions. For instance, traditional values relating to marriage prompt many Indians to consent to arranged marriages, often with a dowry. Within this context, finding a marriage partner matching specific caste and religious specifications can be a source of great anxiety for families. Survey data shows that religious affiliation is an important variable in identifying in-groups. For instance, a CSDS/Lokiniti survey shows that different religious groups tend to have a negative view of marriage outside one's own caste or religious community (see Table 4.3).

The evidence in Table 4.3 suggests that India has high levels of interpersonal trust within members of a community, however it is defined, but little interpersonal trust with members of other communities. Hence, we can conclude that interpersonal trust relationships are mediated by an individual's religious and caste identities. This is not to suggest that such identities are immutable or unchanging—Indian society appears to be in transition away from traditional values. Nevertheless, one should be aware that prevailing prejudices against other communities has a deep impact in most day-to-day social and commercial transactions, particularly in rural areas.

Similarly, there is strong evidence that institutionalized trust is in short supply. Innumerable surveys of trust in political and legal institutions show that Indians have little trust in most formal institutions. The lack of interpersonal trust towards persons outside one's community tends to translate into more negative outcomes on institutionalised trust. For instance, India consistently ranks low on international comparisons of corruption and transparency. On a global ranking of 178 countries, Transparency International's 2010 Corruption Perceptions Index ranks India 87th (with a score of 3.3 on a 0–10 scale, with 0 being highly corrupt and 10 being very clean). India's global placement is one above Jamaica and Liberia and one below Albania. Similarly, India does not score highly in World Bank surveys of corruption. The World Bank maintains six principal global rankings of corruption—in most of these, India's performance is very poor (see Table 4.4).

India's highest score in the World Bank's corruption indices is in the judicial/legal effectiveness index (JLEI). If one views other surveys on the level of trust in the legal system in India, one finds a generally favourable opinion of the legal system. For instance, an AsiaBarometer survey shows that a majority of respondents placed a degree of trust in the system; asked to indicate to what extent individuals trusted the legal system to operate in the best interests of society, 18 per cent of respondents claimed that they trusted the system a lot and an additional 47 per cent claimed that they trusted it to a great degree (Asia Barometer 2001).

On account of the importance of legal proceduralism during India's independence movement, one would be tempted to conclude that India is a country that continues to take the legal process seriously. However, its trustworthiness is under threat, because it is unable to cope with the large number of legal disputes. India's Supreme Court has a backlog of over 40,000 cases and it is estimated that there are 30 million cases awaiting adjudication in lower courts. In a global report on corruption and legal systems, Transparency International (2007: 216) noted chronic vacancies and the low number of judges available to adjudicate cases. For that reason, some prominent cases can take decades—for instance, the Allahabad High Court has yet to offer a judgement on five cases relating to the controversial Babri Masjid site, brought to court in the 1950s. Another

## Table 4.3 Attitudes towards marriage within one's own caste or religious group

| | Question 1. Marriage must take place within one's own caste-community<br>Question 2. There is nothing wrong if boys and girls of different caste/religion marry | | | |
| --- | --- | --- | --- | --- |
| | Agree with question 1 | Agree with question 2 | No opinion | Total |
| Hindu | 1,572 | 633 | 431 | 2,636 |
| | 59.6% | 24.1% | 16.4% | 100% |
| | 81% | 84.1% | 74.3% | 80.7% |
| Muslim | 244 | 70 | 58 | 372 |
| | 65.6% | 18.8% | 15.6% | 100% |
| | 12.6% | 9.3% | 100% | 11.4% |
| Christian | 35 | 22 | 23 | 80 |
| | 43.8% | 27.5% | 28.8% | 100% |
| | 1.8% | 2.9% | 4.0% | 2.5% |
| Sikh | 36 | 9 | 24 | 69 |
| | 52% | 13.0% | 34.8% | 100% |
| | 1.9% | 1.2% | 4.1% | 2.1% |
| Buddhist | 14 | 5 | 12 | 31 |
| | 45.2% | 16.1% | 38.7% | 100% |
| | 0.7% | 0.7% | 2.1% | 0.9% |
| Jain | 6 | 3 | 1 | 10 |
| | 60% | 30.0% | 10.0% | 100% |
| | 0.3% | 0.4% | 0.2% | 0.3% |
| Others | 25 | 11 | 31 | 67 |
| | 37.3% | 16.4% | 46.3% | 100% |
| | 1.3% | 1.5% | 5.3% | 2.1% |
| Total | 1,932 | 753 | 580 | 3,265 |
| | 59.2% | 23.1% | 17.8% | 100% |
| | 100% | 100% | 100% | 100% |

*Note*: Data in the cells organised as follows: first line represents number of respondents, second line represents row percentage, and third line represents column percentage.
*Source*: CSDS/Lokniti, State of the Nation Survey (SONS), 2006.

**Table 4.4  India's ranking in World Bank indices**

| Index | Acronym | India 2010 |
|---|---|---|
| Corporate illegal corruption index | CICI | 39.4 |
| Corporate legal corruption component | CLCC | 29.8 |
| Business ethics index | BEI | 34.6 |
| Public sector ethics index | PSEI | 31.7 |
| Judicial/legal effectiveness index | JLEI | 59.9 |
| Corporate governance index | CGI | 55.4 |

*Note*: Indices ranked from 0 (lowest) to 100 (highest).
*Source*: Kaufmann (2004).

high-profile case, involving allegations of kickbacks from a Swedish military contractor, was initiated in the late 1980s, and eventually dismissed in the Delhi High Court in 2011.

Although Indians have a high regard for the legal profession and for legal processes (at least in an abstract sense), the slow pace of dispute resolution and the absence of forums to arbitrate disputes results in the emergence of 'middlemen' to act as intermediaries. Manor's seminal work on provincial-level corruption in India showed that 'middlemen' served as 'crucial political intermediaries between the localities and powerful figures (bureaucrats and, especially, politicians) at higher levels' (Manor 2000: 817). Although the legal system has typically been immune from such intermediaries, there is growing evidence that 'middlemen' are also a growing force in the legal system. As a result of the length of time that it takes to adjudicate cases, such 'middlemen' are in effect agents involved in low-level corruption, mostly to speed up the time taken to adjudicate cases. According to a study undertaken by the Centre for Media Studies, the estimated amount paid in bribes over a 12-month period was US$580 million, out of which 61 per cent was paid to lawyers, 29 per cent to court officials, and 5 per cent to middlemen (Transparency International 2007: 215).

The low level of institutional trust is likely to have a direct impact on long-term productivity in the services sector and on the sustainability of high levels of economic performance. Despite significant measures to liberalize the economy, there are important domestic lobbies that have prevented the establishment of a market-based capitalist system. For instance, despite the inefficiency of the legal system, foreign law firms are prevented from practising law. A similar pattern of barriers to entry is found in education and the financial services industry (Saez 2009). In the absence of new entrants, the development of the capitalist system is likely to entail elements of predatory capitalism and corruption.

# CONCLUSION

According to the IMF's World Economic Outlook database (2011), India is one of the leading economies in Asia and the world. Viewed in terms of nominal GDP, it is the world's tenth largest economy; in terms of purchasing power parity (PPP) valuation of country GDP, it is the fourth largest. Therefore, an analysis of the trajectory of India's capitalist system is essential for a comprehensive understanding of the varieties of capitalism literature.

At the same time, we must offer a nuanced understanding of the development of capitalism. India remains a country with endemic levels of poverty. Nearly 41.6 per cent of the population are income-poor, living on US$1.25 or less a day (Alkire and Santos 2010). The paradox of India's emergence as a global economic power and the serious developmental challenges that the country faces should moderate the wholesale applicability of the varieties of capitalism model to India. In many parts of India, capitalism is poorly and unevenly developed or encompasses the worst features of primitive accumulation.

In this chapter I have attempted to provide a summary description and analysis of the principal features of India's economy, structured within the dimensions of the varieties of capitalism framework. As discussed eloquently by Harriss-White (2003: 19), Indian capitalism 'has developed in distinctive eras, strata, sectors, and regional blocks'. In this sense, I have outlined some of the main historical drivers in the development of India's unique form of capitalism. In a country with a wide range of regional industrial regimes and individual regional units with a population larger than most European countries (e.g. the state of Uttar Pradesh has a population of 190 million), one can speak of varieties of capitalism. Viewed through the prism of the internal structure of the firm and employment relations, India offers evidence of being a hybrid form of capitalist development.

Although India has a fairly sophisticated infrastructure for the intermediation of capital and financial market transactions, one can foresee important obstacles that will inhibit a more optimal development of core strengths. Education and skills formation are, contrary to expectations, deplorable, even among higher-level institutions. Moreover, the country suffers from a debilitating level of social capital and institutional trust. Although India is booming economically, it is apparent that the future trajectory of its capitalism will be sapped by an inadequate level of educational infrastructure and corruption.

## NOTES

1. The author is grateful for research assistance provided by Katharina Huhn.
2. Note that one cannot obtain union density data from the statistics provided by India's Ministry of Labour, because not all unionized workers belong to a CTUO.
3. The Union of IT-Enabled Services Professionals (UNITES Professionals), formed in 2005, is India's first union representing the interests of workers in IT manufacturing and call centres.
4. Unless otherwise noted, literacy data for India is derived from UNESCO, whose reference year, based on Indian census statistics from the 2001 census, is 2006. Data for the adult population encompasses people who are 15 years or older.
5. Youth encompasses individuals between 15 and 24 years old.

6. State literacy rates in India have been derived from data released by the Rajya Sabha (2001: 111). The data reported herein includes people of 7 years or older. It is interesting to note that the states with the highest literacy rates have a large Christian population.

7. For instance, female literacy rates in Burundi, Malawi, and Gabon are 39.2, 35.7, and 34.8 per cent respectively. See UNESCO (2010: 226).

## References

Academic Ranking of World Universities (2011). 'Academic Ranking of World Universities 2010'. Retrieved 20 October 2011 from <http://www.arwu.org/ARWU2010.jsp>.

Alkire, S. and M. E. Santos (2010). *Multidimensional Poverty Index: 2010 Data*. Oxford Poverty and Human Development Initiative. Retrieved 29 August 2011 from www.ophi.org.uk/policy/multidimensional-poverty-index.

American Society for Training and Development (ASTD) (2011). 'Best Awards'. Retrieved 19 November 2011 from http://www.astd.org/ASTD/aboutus/AwardsandBestPractices/bestAwards/bestWinners.htm.

Asia Barometer (2001). Asia Barometer Survey – India. Retrieved 23 November 2011 from http://www.asianbarometer.org/newenglish/surveys/.

Bardhan, P. (1984). *The Political Economy of Development in India*. Delhi, Oxford University Press.

Basi, T. (2009). *Women, Identity, and India's Call Centre Industry*. London, Routledge.

Besley, T. and R. Burgess (2004). 'Can Labour Regulation Hinder Economic Performance? Evidence from India'. *Quarterly Journal of Economics* 19(1): 91–134.

Bhattacherjee, D. (1999). *Organized Labour and Economic Liberalization in India: Past, Present, and Future*. International Institute for Labour Studies Discussion Paper DP/105/1999. Geneva, ILO.

Blomkvist, H. and A. Swain (2001). 'Investigating Democracy and Social Capital in India', *Economic and Political Weekly* 36(8): 639–643.

Chakravarty, S. (1987). *Development Planning: The Indian Experience*. Oxford, Clarendon Press.

CSDS/Lokniti. (2001). *State of the Nation Survey 2001*. Retrieved 14 February 2012 from http://www.lokniti.org/state_of_the_nation.html

Datta-Chaudhuri, M. (2000). 'Labour Markets as Social Institutions in India'. In S. Kähkönen and A. Lanyi, Eds., *Institutions, Incentives and Economic Reforms in India*: 449–468. New Delhi, Sage.

D'Costa, A. P. (2004). 'The Indian Software Industry in the Global Division of Labour'. In A. P. D'Costa and E. Sridharan, Eds., *India in the Global Software Industry: Innovation, Firm Strategies and Development*: 1–26. Basingstoke, Palgrave Macmillan.

*Forbes magazine* (2010). 'The Global 2000'. Retrieved 15 January 2011 from http://www.forbes.com/lists/2010/18/global-2000-10_The-Global-2000_Counrty_6.html.

Ghosh, A. (1974). 'Japanese Zaibatsus and Indian Industrial Houses: An International Comparison'. *American Journal of Economics and Sociology* 33(3): 317–326.

Ghosh, S. (2006). 'Do Board Characteristics Affect Corporate Performance? Firm-Level Evidence for India'. *Applied Economics Letters* 13(7): 435–443.

Harriss-White, B. (2003). *India Working: Essays on Society and Economy*. Cambridge, Cambridge University Press.

International Labour Organization (2011). 'Laboursta'. Retrieved 12 September 2011 from http://laboursta.ilo.org.

Ito, S. (1984). 'Ownership and Management of Indian *Zaibatsu*'. In A. Okochi and S. Yasuoka, Eds., *Family Business in the Era of Industrial Growth*: 147–166. Tokyo, University of Tokyo Press.

Jenkins, R. (2004). 'Labour Policy and the Second Generation of Economic Reform in India'. *India Review 3*(4): 333–363.

Jhabvala, R. and R. Kanbur (2004). 'Globalisation and Economic Reform as seen from the Ground: SEWA's Experience in India'. In K. Basu Ed., *India's Emerging Economy: Performance and Prospects in the 1990s and Beyond*: 293–312. New Delhi, Oxford University Press.

Kaufmann, D. (2004). 'Corruption, Governance and Security: Challenges for the Rich Countries and the World'. *Global Competitiveness Report 2004/2005*. Washington, DC, World Bank.

Kennedy, L. (2007). 'Regional Industrial Policies Driving Peri-Urban Dynamics in Hyderabad, India'. *Cities 24*(2): 95–109.

Kohli, N. (2012). 'Corporate Governance and Initial Public Offerings in India'. In A. Zattoni and W. Judge, Eds., *Global Perspectives on Corporate Governance and Initial Public Offerings*: 167–189. Cambridge: Cambridge University Press.

Manor, J. (2000). 'Small-Time Political Fixers in India's States: "Towel Over Armpit"'. *Asian Survey 40*(5): 816–835.

Mazumdar, S. (2010). *Industry and Services in Growth and Structural Change in India*. Working Paper 2010/02. New Delhi, Institute for Studies in Industrial Development.

Ministry of Finance (2011). *Economic Survey 2010-11*. New Delhi, Oxford University Press.

Ministry of Heavy Industries and Public Enterprises (2011). *Annual Report on the Performance of Central Public Enterprises, 2009–2010*, Vol. I. New Delhi, Government of India.

Ministry of Human Development and Resource Development (2011). 'Time Series Data'. Retrieved 23 December 2011 from http://education.nic.in/stats/Timeseries0506.pdf.

Mishra, A. and M. Akbar (2007). 'Empirical Examination of Diversification Strategies in Business Groups: Evidence from Emerging Markets'. *International Journal of Emerging Markets 2*(1): 22–38.

Morris, S. and R. Basant (2008). 'Small and Medium Enterprises in India Today: Overcoming Policy Constraints to Achieving Rapid Growth in a Globalized Economy'. In Asian Development Bank Ed., *Trade Policy, Industrial Performance, and Private Sector Development in India*: 246–326. New Delhi, Oxford University Press.

Mukherji, A. K. (1985). *Economics of Indian Industry*. New Delhi, S. Chand.

Mukherji, R. (2008). 'The Political Economy of India's Economic Reforms'. *Asian Economic Policy Review 3*: 315–331.

Nachum, L. (1999). 'Diversification Strategies of Developing Country Firms'. *Journal of International Management 5*(2): 115–140.

Noronha, E. and P. D'Cruz (2001). 'Organising Call-Centre Agents: Emerging Issues'. *Economic and Political Weekly 41*(21): 2115–2121.

Palit, A. and S. Bhattacharjee (2007). *Special Economic Zones in India: Myths and Realities*. New Delhi, Anthem.

QS (2011). 'World University Rankings 2010/2011'. Retrieved 24 October 2011 from http://www.topuniversities.com/university-rankings/world-university-rankings.

Rajya Sabha (2001). '*Rajya Sabha Official Debates. Rajya Sabha Unstarred Question No. 660*', dated 23 November 2001. New Delhi: Rajya Sabha Secretariat.

Reserve Bank of India (2011). *Statistical Tables Relating to Banks in India, 2010–11*. Mumbai, Reserve Bank of India.

Rudolph, L. and S. Rudolph (1987). *In Pursuit of Lakshmi: The Political Economy of the Indian State*. Chicago, University of Chicago Press.

Saez, L. (2001). *Federalism Without a Centre, The Impact of Political and Economic Reforms on India's Federal System*. New Delhi: Sage.

—— (2004). *Banking Reform in India and China*. New York, Palgrave Macmillan.

—— (2009). 'The Political Economy of Financial Services Reform in India: Explaining Variations in Political Opposition and Barriers to Entry'. *Journal of Asian Studies* 68(4): 1137–1162.

—— and C. Chang (2010). 'The Political Economy of Global Business Firms from India and China'. *Contemporary Politics* 15(3): 265–286.

Sandesara, J. C. (1992). *Industrial Policy and Planning, 1947-91*. New Delhi, Sage.

Sarkar, J., S. Sarkar, and K. Sen (2008). 'Board of Directors and Opportunistic Earnings Management: Evidence from India'. *Journal of Accounting, Auditing, and Finance* 23(4): 517–551.

Sinha, A. (2003). 'Rethinking the Developmental State Model: Divided Leviathan and Sub-national Comparisons in India'. *Comparative Politics* 35(4): 459–476.

—— (2005). *The Regional Roots of Developmental Politics in India*. Bloomington, Indiana University Press.

Times Higher Education (2011). 'Times Higher Education World University Rankings'. Retrieved 19 October 2011 from http://www.timeshighereducation.co.uk/world-university-rankings/2010-2011/top-200.html.

Transparency International (2007). *Global Corruption Report 2007*. Berlin, Transparency International Secretariat.

United Nations (2011). 'Statistical Databases'. Retrieved 15 December 2011 from http://unstats.un.org/unsd/demographic/products/socind/youth.htm.

UNESCO (2010). *Global Education Digest*. New York, UNESCO.

—— *EFA Global Country Report*. New York, UNESCO.

University Grants Commission (2011a). 'Central Universities'. Retrieved 22 October 2011 from http://www.ugc.ac.in/inside/centraluni.html.

—— (2011b). 'State Universities'. Retrieved 22 October 2011 from http://www.ugc.ac.in/inside/StateUniv_total.pdf.

—— (2011c). 'Deemed Universities'. Retrieved 22 October 2011 from http://www.ugc.ac.in/inside/deemeduniv.html.

Van Agtmael, A. (1993). 'Investing in Emerging Markets'. In K. Park and A. van Agtmael, Eds., *The World's Emerging Stock Markets*: 17–45. Chicago, Probus.

World Bank (2011). 'World Development Indicators'. Retrieved 20 November 2011 from http://databank.worldbank.org/ddp/home.do?Step=12&id=4&CNO=2.

World Federation of Exchanges (2011). Retrieved 26 November 2011 from www.world-exchanges.org/statistics.

World Values Survey (2009). 'World Values Survey 1981–2008, Official Aggregate v.20090901'. Retrieved 19 November 2011 from http://www.worldvaluessurvey.org.

# CHAPTER 5

...........................................................................................

# INDONESIA

## *Oligarchic Capitalism*

...........................................................................................

ANDREW JAMES ROSSER

THIS chapter examines the nature of capitalism in contemporary Indonesia. It suggests that notwithstanding extensive neo-liberal economic policy and institutional reform since the mid-1980s and, in particular, since the onset of the Asian economic crisis in 1997–1998, Indonesian capitalism has yet to evolve into a fully fledged liberal market system. Rather, it is characterized by a combination of market-based policies and institutions, direct forms of state intervention, and coordination based on the predatory interests of powerful politico-business families, giving it overall a unique and hybrid character. Further, this chapter suggests that the emergence of this model of capitalism reflects two aspects of Indonesia's political economy: (i) the continued political and social dominance of politico-bureaucratic and corporate elements that were nurtured under the 'New Order', the government that ruled Indonesia from the mid-1960s to the late 1990s; and (ii) the opportunities that the post-New Order period has opened up for elements previously excluded from the policy-making process (for instance, peasants, labour, and progressive NGOs) to participate in this process and, in doing so, influence the nature of economic policy and institutions. Combined, it is argued, these factors have served to ensure that non-market variables continue to play a key role in shaping how Indonesian capitalism operates and, in particular, how resources are allocated.

In presenting this argument, I proceed by examining the types of firms that operate in the Indonesian context and then exploring the nature of contemporary Indonesian capitalism in eight key spheres of political economy—(i) the role of the state, (ii) the financial system, (iii) ownership and corporate governance, (iv) the internal structure of the firm, (v) employment relations, (vi) education and skills formation, (vii) inter-company relations, and (viii) social capital. In the penultimate section, I then examine the dynamics that have shaped the evolution of Indonesian capitalism over time and, in particular, how they have constrained market-oriented development. I conclude with a summary of the analysis and a brief discussion of the likely trajectory of Indonesian capitalism in the foreseeable future.

# TYPES OF FIRMS

In broad terms, three main types of firm operate in the Indonesian context: (i) large, highly diversified, and politically connected family-owned private conglomerates (which in turn can be divided into those owned by ethnic Chinese families and those owned by *pribumi*—or indigenous—families), (ii) state-owned enterprises (SOEs), and (iii) foreign joint ventures/multinational corporations (MNCs). Of these, the first (especially conglomerates owned by ethnic Chinese families) currently dominate the Indonesian economy, although the role of SOEs has increased significantly since the Asian economic crisis in 1997–1998, as has that of foreign capital.

Private conglomerates became the key actors in the Indonesian economy during the New Order period as a result of their ability to leverage their political connections for privileged access to state licences, finance, and facilities and opportunities opened up by deregulation and privatization during the 1980s and 1990s. The Asian economic crisis led to widespread insolvency among these conglomerates and the nationalization or closure of numerous private domestic banks. At the same time, conglomerate owners were forced to surrender many of their corporate assets to the Indonesian Bank Restructuring Agency (IBRA), a government agency tasked with sorting out the banking system in the wake of the crisis, to settle their banks' debts. While IBRA subsequently sold most of these assets back to the private sector, the result was a significant increase in state ownership of corporate equity and the role of state-owned enterprises (SOEs) in the economy (Sato 2004: 161–163). According to the current Minister for SOEs, Mustafa Abubakar (2010), SOEs now account for around 30 per cent of the market capitalization of the Indonesian Stock Exchange (IDX).[1] Post-New Order governments have sought to reduce the role of SOEs in the economy as well as generate income for the national budget through privatization, but progress has been slow, reflecting strong political opposition (Abeng 2001; Wicaksono 2008). Foreign ownership of corporate assets also increased substantially as foreign investors moved to purchase assets sold by IBRA and negotiated equity-for-debt swaps with indebted conglomerates. Foreign investors now account for an estimated two-thirds of share ownership in companies listed on the IDX, although it is important to note that much 'foreign' investment in these companies is widely believed to be offshore Indonesian capital coming back into the country (World Bank 2010a: 8).

Despite these changes, however, many of the conglomerates and their owners survived the crisis and remain active in business. Most companies listed on the IDX remain controlled by families or family-owned company groups, despite growing foreign and state ownership of corporate assets (Sato 2004). At the same time, lists of the country's wealthiest business people remain dominated by individuals who made their fortunes during the New Order, including several who had strong connections to former President Suharto. *Globe Asia* magazine's list of the 150 richest Indonesians in 2009, for instance, included ethnic Chinese entrepreneurs such as Sudono Salim (one of Suharto's closest friends and Indonesia's richest businessperson for much of the New Order period), Prajogo Pangestu (another former Suharto crony), Sofyan Wanandi (an entrepreneur who benefited from close connections to the Indonesian military during the New Order), and Eka Tjipta Widjaja (another former Suharto crony); a group of indigenous entrepreneurs linked to Pertamina (the state-owned oil company), the Ministry for Research and Technology, the state secretariat and/or other bastions of economic nationalism during the New Order, such as Pontjo Sutowo, Aburizal Bakrie, Jusuf Kalla, Siswono Yudohusodo, and Ilham and Tareq Habibie; and Suharto family members, such as Bambang Trihatmojo, Sudwikatmono, Siti Hardijanti Rukmana, Sigit Hardjojudanto, Hutomo Mandala Putra, and Sukamdani Gitosardjono (Globe Asia 2009). As during the New Order, companies owned by ethnic Chinese entrepreneurs remain the largest private corporate players in contemporary Indonesia, with indigenous entrepreneurs a distant second.

# Role of the State

Over the past three decades, the Indonesian state has come increasingly to resemble a regulatory state, at least in terms of broad economic policy settings. During the 1970s and early 1980s, when the country was awash with petrodollars, the New Order government pursued a nationalist economic strategy involving heavy and direct state intervention in the economy. Rather than attempting to industrialize through the promotion of internationally competitive export-oriented industries as in countries such as South Korea and Taiwan, it focused instead on import substitution industrialization aimed at increasing domestic (and, in particular, indigenous) control over the economy. In practice, this meant high levels of state ownership and investment and the allocation of monopolies, subsidies, and facilities to SOEs and well-connected private business conglomerates. Since the collapse of international oil prices in the early to mid-1980s and, in particular, the 1997–1998 economic crisis, however, the Indonesian government's economic policies have shifted in a much more market-oriented direction. During the late 1980s and early 1990s, it deregulated sectors such as banking, the capital market, television, telecommunications, and airlines; initiated a selective process of privatization; and introduced regulatory reforms such as new prudential regulations for the financial sector and intellectual property laws (Rosser 2002). Following the 1997–1998 crisis, it introduced further market-oriented reforms, including the elimination of monopolies, the closure of insolvent banks, further privatization of SOEs, decentralization, and the introduction of new laws and institutions aimed at combatting corruption, promoting competition, and facilitating bankruptcy, with many of these changes occurring within the context of an IMF bailout programme between 1997 and 2003 (Robison and Hadiz 2004; Hill and Shiraishi 2007).

But Indonesia has failed to develop a fully fledged regulatory state, because state capacity to supervise and regulate the economy in accordance with market principles has remained weak, reflecting the continued influence of corruption over government decision-making. Notwithstanding the introduction of new anti-corruption laws, the establishment of an anti-corruption commission, the exposure of numerous corruption cases, and the introduction of various measures aimed at improving judicial independence since the fall of President Suharto in 1998, post-New Order governments have made only modest progress in combating corruption. As Crouch (2009: 228) explains:

> During the Reformasi period, dozens of political figures, bureaucrats, and businesspeople found themselves targets of corruption investigations by the police or prosecutors, but few were eventually brought to court and even fewer convicted. In the case of former President Soeharto, the investigations were not only ineffective, but not even intended to succeed…Under strong pressure to 'do something about corruption', successive governments established a series of anti-corruption bodies, but showed little determination to ensure that they worked effectively.

Since his election as President in 2004, Susilo Bambang Yudhoyono has launched an anti-corruption campaign that has resulted in the successful prosecution of numerous senior political figures, including parliamentarians, former ministers, and regional governors. But the judiciary has remained riddled with corruption, limiting the scope for successful prosecutions and making it difficult for regulatory agencies to enforce government regulations (Crouch 2009: 229). At the same time, the parliament and national police have joined forces in an effort to dramatically reduce the power of the anti-corruption commission and, in particular, its power to prosecute. Despite Yudhoyono's successes, therefore, corruption remains an endemic problem that has stymied the development of the regulatory and supervisory capacities characteristic of the regulatory state. For this reason, some commentators have suggested that the post-New Order state is better viewed as a predatory state and have emphasized the way in which, like the New Order, it has served oligarchic interests rather than those of workers, peasants, and progressive elements in the middle class (Robison and Hadiz 2004; Hadiz 2010).

# Financial System

Prior to the 1997–1998 economic crisis, Indonesia's financial system was dominated by the banking sector and, in particular, state banks and private domestic banks. During the oil boom years, the New Order used the state banks as a key conduit for investing the country's new-found oil wealth and encouraging the growth of SOEs and well-connected conglomerates. Then, following the collapse of international oil prices in the 1980s, when the country desperately needed to mobilize new sources of investment funds, it deregulated the banking system, producing a massive increase in the number of private domestic banks and foreign banks, as the conglomerates and foreign investors rushed to enter a market that had previously been closed to them (Rosser 2002: 51–83).

By contrast, the New Order did relatively little for much of its rule to promote the development of a capital market in Indonesia. It re-established the Jakarta Stock Exchange (JSX) in the late 1970s, but did so primarily to provide a mechanism by which wealth could be seen to be redistributed to indigenous Indonesians, rather than facilitate inflows of portfolio capital. It was only after deregulation in the late 1980s that its role in corporate finance grew significantly: between 1987 and 1996, the number of listed companies increased from 24 to 267 and the JSX's market capitalization increased to Rp193 trillion. But having started from a relatively low base, the capital market remained small compared to the banking system: whereas outstanding bank loans amounted to 55 per cent of GDP in 1996, the market capitalization of the JSX amounted to only 36 per cent of GDP (Rosser 2002: 85–121; Kung, Caverhill, and McLeod 2010). With the conglomerates and SOEs also borrowing large amounts offshore in the wake of deregulation, corporate financial structures were thus characterized by high levels of indebtedness.[2]

The period since the 1997–1998 economic crisis has seen substantial changes in the nature of Indonesia's financial sector and the structure of corporate finance. First, it has led to a marked shift in the relative importance of the banking system and capital market in the Indonesian economy. The crisis produced a massive contraction in bank lending as bank capital adequacy problems and rising non-performing loans made it increasingly difficult for banks to lend (Bank Indonesia 2001): between 1996 and 2001, total outstanding bank credit fell from 55 per cent of GDP to 22 per cent, and by 2007 it had only recovered to 26 per cent. At the same time, the role of the stock market has increased significantly as investors have regained confidence in the Indonesian economy and more Indonesian companies have gone public. Between 2001 and 2007, the market capitalization of the IDX increased from 14 to a whopping 50 per cent of GDP, although it then fell sharply as a result of the global financial crisis in 2008, before recovering in 2009 to almost 40 per cent, a few percentage points higher than its peak before the 1997–1998 crisis (Kung, Caverhill, and McLeod 2010: 333; Economist Intelligence Unit 2010).

Second, consistent with this shift in the financial sector, Indonesian companies have undergone a process of de-leveraging as they have repaid or renegotiated debt and turned increasingly to the stock market to finance their activities. Foreign and domestic credit continues to be by far the largest source of capital for Indonesian companies. According to the IMF (2008: 41), foreign loans combined with offshore corporate bonds and domestic bank credit accounted for 47 and 40 per cent respectively of non-financial companies' total financing in 2007. Similarly, Okuda and Take (2009: 21) report that the ratio of total debt to total assets at companies listed on the JSX in 2005 was 42 per cent for government-controlled companies, 48 per cent for ethnic Chinese-owned companies, 47 per cent for indigenously owned companies, and 46 per cent for foreign joint venture companies. But these levels are all several percentage points lower than they were prior to the crisis, indicating that these companies have deleveraged. At the same time, cumulative equity issuance by non-financial Indonesian companies has increased sharply in recent years to the point that it reached 10 per cent of these companies' total financing in 2007 (IMF 2008: 41).

There have nevertheless been important continuities in the nature of Indonesia's financial system, particularly with regard to the influence of non-market factors on the way in which lending decisions are made. Private domestic banks did not lend on a strictly commercial basis during the New Order, but rather acted as mechanisms for financing the activities of companies within their own groups, leading to a highly concentrated pattern of lending that became a key vulnerability during the 1997–1998 crisis. With the collapse of many group-affiliated banks as a result of the crisis, this pattern of lending has probably become less common. But lending practices at state banks appear to have changed little. During the New Order, well-connected borrowers were able to raise state bank loans through collusion with state bank officials, despite being involved in questionable projects or lacking sufficient collateral. In addition, senior politico-bureaucrats within the government would often 'command' state banks to make loans to favoured individuals (MacIntyre 1993: 151). In both cases, well-connected borrowers were able to avoid repaying loans, leading to serious problems with non-performing loans at many state banks (Rosser 2002: 76–82).

According to Hill and Shiraishi (2007: 138), little has changed in these respects since the fall of the New Order. State banks, which currently dominate the banking system, continue to receive 'commands' from senior officials to lend to favoured clients, make loans on the basis of corrupt dealings with borrowers, and be afflicted by high levels of non-performing loans (NPLs). The case of Bank Mandiri, the largest of the state-owned banks, illustrates the way in which these practices have endured. In 2005, it was revealed that the bank's NPLs had blown out to 25 per cent of its total loan portfolio, leading to an Attorney-General's Department investigation into loans to twenty-eight companies and the arrest of three senior bank officials and a number of corporate executives on corruption charges. Among the companies under investigation were ones linked to senior political figures, including Jusuf Kalla (then Vice President), Aburizal Bakrie (then Coordinating Minister for the Economy), Surya Paloh (then a member of the Golkar party executive), Sutrisno Bachir (then the Chairman of the National Mandate Party), and Prabowo Subianto (Suharto's former son-in-law). With a change in Bank Mandiri's leadership in the wake of this scandal, the bank appears to have reined in its NPL problem. However, a number of subsequent corruption cases at the bank raise doubts about the extent to which its lending and management practices have really changed since 2005 (Donnan 2005a, 2005b; Donnan and Hidayat 2005; Hotland 2005; Komandjaja 2005a, 2005b; *Jakarta Post* 2009; *Vivanews.Com* 2011).

# OWNERSHIP AND CORPORATE GOVERNANCE

The ownership and corporate governance structure of firms in Indonesia—whether state-owned or private—is characterized by strong majority shareholder control. Although private Indonesian conglomerates are large-scale enterprises and are involved in a diverse range of businesses, most are run as family businesses, with positions on the

Board of Commissioners and Board of Directors (Indonesian companies have a two-tier board structure) generally being given to family members or close relatives, rather than professional managers (Robison 1986; Sato 2004; World Bank 2010a). Stakeholders such as workers or creditors are generally not incorporated into corporate board structures in contrast to, say, German enterprises, where supervisory boards commonly include worker representatives. Following the 1997–1998 economic crisis, the Indonesian government introduced requirements for public companies to reserve 30 per cent of positions on the Board of Commissioners for independent commissioners, in an attempt to improve protection of minority shareholders. At the same time, changes in the ownership structure of many conglomerates brought about by increasing state and foreign ownership has led to some dilution of controlling family presence on many corporate boards (Sato 2004: 163). But company boards reportedly continue to be dominated by members with close links to controlling shareholders. In a recent report on corporate governance practices in Indonesia, for instance, the World Bank (2010a: 20) notes that, notwithstanding the presence of independent commissioners, there remain strong concerns 'that too many board members continue to act in the interest of controlling shareholders, and not other shareholders or the company'—or, one might add, stakeholders such as workers and creditors.

Similarly, SOEs have long been subject to heavy influence from the government departments and agencies that control them, with the appointment of SOE commissioners and directors based much less on skills and experience than political criteria. During the New Order, for instance, Suharto exercised significant influence over the appointment of SOE board members, appointing individuals who could be relied upon to direct SOE contracts towards the businesses of his sons and daughters (Abeng 2001: 33, 74). Since the end of the New Order, SOE appointments have been influenced much more by the interests of political parties which have seen them as potential cash cows and, in particular, a potential source of funding for election campaigns (Wicaksono 2008: 149; Aswicahyono, Bird, and Hill 2009: 360). To improve the performance of SOEs, the government has recently embarked upon a programme of enhancing corporate governance at SOEs, the main components of which have been attempts to recruit individuals with high levels of integrity and technical competence, often from private-sector backgrounds, into senior positions, and hold them accountable for their performance (McLeod 2008: 206–207; World Bank 2010a: 22). However, it is not yet clear if these efforts have been effective in reducing political influence over the composition of SOE boards.

## INTERNAL STRUCTURE OF THE FIRM

Very little has been written about the nature of internal decision processes within Indonesian firms. To the extent that scholars have explored these processes, the evidence suggests that they are top-down rather than participatory in nature. Harianto and Pangestu (2002: 178), for instance, suggest that ethnic Chinese conglomerates, *pribumi* conglomerates, and SOEs have all been characterized by paternalistic approaches to management, with power being concentrated in the hands of a few individuals, particularly members of the boards of directors, and direct inclusion of workers in decision-making processes being rare (see also Abeng 2001: 32). Habir and Larasati (1999) report that PT Rekayasa Industri, a state-owned engineering, procurement, and construction firm, has sought to improve corporate learning by organizing regular sessions at which employees are given the opportunity to share their experiences and disseminate insights from outside seminars and workshops they have attended. But they also indicate that this company is something of an exception in this respect. Similarly, Rudnyckyj's (2009) analysis of the role of spiritual training sessions known as 'Emotional and Spiritual Quotient (ESQ)' training within PT Krakatau Steel, a state-owned steel company, suggests that relationships between management and workers are hierarchical and controlling in nature. The purpose of these sessions, he suggests, has been to 'make participants more amenable to managerial norms', while also making them 'more effective at self-management by transforming their work into a matter of religious piety'. In other words, they have served to control labour in a way that serves corporate profitability.

Indonesian companies have become increasingly meritocratic in their recruitment and promotion practices, even in the state sector, where appointments have historically been a key form of patronage, as increased competition has made it increasingly important for them to recruit qualified and capable staff (Sutiyono 2007). However, it remains to be seen whether this will lead to less paternalistic and more inclusive internal decision-making.

# Employment Relations

During the New Order period, the Indonesian government pursued an approach to employment relations that was simultaneously repressive and protective (Caraway 2004). On the one hand, it imposed severe restrictions on unionization, prohibiting the establishment and operation of any trade unions other than the state-sanctioned All Indonesia Workers Union (SPSI), and employed the military to quell worker unrest (Manning 1993; Hadiz 1997). On the other hand, it intervened extensively in labour markets to provide formal protections for workers. As Quinn (2003: 5–6) has noted, 'minimum wage legislation, a tight regulatory framework on dismissals, and a large number of protective regulations were all developed during this period, and the Ministry of Manpower had a direct role in management and enforcement' of these regulations, even if it did not perform this role particularly well. Another feature of the New Order's approach to industrial relations was a limited role for collective bargaining. Indeed, the New Order actively discouraged collective bargaining by specifying a standard format for collective labour agreements (CLAs) and recognizing CLAs prepared by companies without worker input, particularly during the years that former security chief Sudomo was Minister for Manpower (Manning 1993: 75). Consistent with these practices, the New Order emphasized a need for partnership between employers, employees, and the government in accordance with *Pancasila*, the organicist state ideology (Quinn 2003: 13).

With the fall of the New Order, the government's employment relations system has become significantly less repressive, reflecting the broader process of political reform that has occurred since then. In June 1998, the government ratified Convention No. 87 on Freedom of Association and Protection of the Right to Organize, and in 2001 it enacted a new trade union law that permitted small groups of workers to form trade unions, leading to a massive increase in the number of officially registered trades unions: in 2009, the country had an estimated 11,852 unions, including all the major types—that is, craft, company, and industry[3]—and three national confederations (International Labour Organization 2011: 66).[4] At the same time, military intervention in labour disputes has become much less common, although clashes between workers and the military and police continue to be reported. However, the employment relations system has remained highly interventionist. For instance, until 2001, the Ministry of Manpower and Transmigration (MMT) continued to set minimum wages, after which this responsibility was transferred to regional governments in accordance with decentralization, with the result that minimum wages now vary from region to region. Likewise, the regulatory framework governing dismissals has continued to be tight, with the 2003 Manpower Law requiring employers to go through potentially lengthy negotiations and legal processes and make substantial severance payments in order to terminate employees (Quinn 2003; Palmer 2008). The Indonesian Employers Association (APINDO) has lobbied hard to liberalize this framework, but thus far to little effect. The OECD, which assesses employment protection levels in OECD and selected emerging economies on a regular basis, has rated Indonesia as the most protective of the forty countries included in its survey in terms of protection of permanent workers against individual dismissal.[5]

Within this context, collective bargaining has spread very slowly. The Manpower Law provides for enterprise-level CLAs and defines them as being negotiated between employers and employees, rather than simply handed down by the company. But the vast majority of companies have not negotiated CLAs with their workforces or even prepared company regulations as a substitute, notwithstanding a requirement for all companies with more than ten employees to do so. The key barrier to collective bargaining has been that central regulation of terms and conditions of employment has weakened unions' ability to negotiate, because they have had little scope to offer attractive trade-offs to employers. The government's interventionist approach has also contributed to a growth in contract work and outsourcing, both of which are permitted under the Manpower Law under certain conditions, as companies have sought to avoid the restrictions imposed by permanent employment, in particular those related to severance pay (Palmer 2008: 7, 14–15; Juliawan 2010). Combined with the fact that many Indonesians work in the informal sector[6] and hence outside the scope of the Manpower Law and its protections, and that many companies successfully avoid paying permanent workers the severance pay to which they are entitled,[7] the result has been to expose the vast majority of Indonesian workers and their livelihoods to the vagaries of market forces, notwithstanding the continued interventionist and protective character of industrial relations legislation. Contract, outsourced, and informal-sector workers have all been much easier to dismiss when no longer required than permanent workers subject to the provisions of the Manpower Law, while severance pay obligations have often been circumvented.[8]

# EDUCATION AND SKILLS FORMATION

Until fairly recently, Indonesian governments gave education and training relatively low priority as an area of policy. Although the New Order invested heavily in expanding the school system during the oil-boom years when it had substantial discretionary investment resources at its disposal, it wound back education spending significantly following the collapse of international oil prices in the mid-1980s (World Bank 1998: 148). Post-New Order governments have been more favourably disposed towards education. In 2000, the members of the People's Consultative Assembly (MPR) amended the 1945 Constitution to provide all Indonesian citizens with (among other rights) the right to obtain an education, and in 2002 they introduced requirements for citizens to pursue a basic education, for the government to fund this, and for central and regional governments to spend at least 20 per cent of their budgets on education. In the wake of this, central government spending on education has increased significantly, particularly following the election of the Yudhoyono government in 2004 (Rosser, Joshi, and Edwin 2011).

To the extent that Indonesian governments have been concerned about education outcomes, their main priority has been to improve citizens' access to education, particularly basic education (which in the Indonesian context means the primary and junior secondary levels of schooling). During the New Order period, enrolment rates at both primary and junior secondary schools improved dramatically as the economy grew, poverty rates declined, and the school system expanded during the 1970s and 1980s, with the country almost achieving universal primary enrolment by the mid-1980s (Hull and Jones 1994: 161). Post-New Order governments have also tried to improve citizens' access to basic education by introducing legal and regulatory changes prohibiting the charging of user fees at most public primary and junior secondary schools and introducing schemes such as 'school operational assistance' (BOS) (2005), which aims to free students at public and private schools that receive BOS funds from paying the operational costs of schooling. According to official statistics, 99 per cent of primary-school age students and 85 per cent of junior-secondary-school age students currently attend school, indicating that these efforts have been broadly successful (Rosser, Joshi, and Edwin 2011).[9]

By contrast, Indonesian governments have given relatively little attention to ensuring that school curricula and the quality of education in general are such that students emerge from their education with skills that make them employable. Indeed, the quality of education in Indonesia is widely regarded as low by international standards (Leigh 1999). For instance, the country's results in the 2009 OECD Programme for International Student Assessment (PISA) were statistically significantly below the OECD average on all three of the key assessment scales: reading, mathematics, and science. Similarly, the country's results on the Trends in International Mathematics and Science Study (TIMSS) mathematics test have consistently been lower than neighbouring countries such as Singapore, Thailand, and Malaysia over the past decade (Suryadarma 2011).

Most importantly for our purposes, Indonesian governments have also given little attention to producing graduates with skills that fit the specific needs of particular industries and firms. At both junior and upper secondary school, students are able to pursue a vocationally oriented curriculum by enrolling in specialist vocational schools. But, historically, relatively few students have taken this path, apparently seeing it as having lower pay-offs in career terms than the traditional academic path (Wilson 1991; World Bank 2010b). In addition, the vocational curriculum has not been well aligned with the needs of industries and firms. In a recent study of the Indonesian education system and its role vis-a-vis the country's labour market, the World Bank (2010b: 120–1) found that, while the upper secondary vocational school curriculum is *generally* aligned with the needs of the services and, to a lesser extent, manufacturing sector' (italics added), the *specific* part of the curriculum—that is, the part related to schools' industry specializations—is driven by the Ministry of National Education, with little coordination from the Ministry of Industry or input from firms operating in the industry. Internship programmes have been used as one way of enhancing training of students in industry- and firm-specific skills, but linkages between schools and industries are unsystematic, and firm participation in internship programmes is weak. The World Bank has presented evidence to suggest that industry linkages at the tertiary level are no better (World Bank 2010b: 121, 141).

In its 2005–2009 strategic plan, the Ministry of National Education announced plans to dramatically increase the proportion of upper secondary school students attending vocational schools. However, this new focus on vocational education does not appear, at this stage at least, to entail a shift away from producing graduates with general skills to ones with industry- or firm-specific skills.

## INTER-COMPANY RELATIONS

Studies of inter-company relationships in Indonesia suggest that these relationships tend to be predominantly short term and non-cooperative in nature. While intermediary organizations such as business associations exist, they generally play little role in coordinating the activities of firms. There is also little coordination within conglomerates, notwithstanding the fact that firms within each conglomerate are owned by the same shareholders, reflecting the fact that these firms tend to operate in unrelated sectors and activities. Rademakers (1998: 1022) argues that inter-company relationships in Indonesia are often characterized by paternalism: companies, he suggests, often 'take care of' suppliers and customers to which they are linked. While such paternalism sometimes goes hand-in-hand with long-term relationships between companies and their suppliers and customers, it does not amount to coordination—relationships between these entities, he says, remain 'rather loose' (Rademakers 1998: 1022). Most importantly for our purposes, there is little evidence that Indonesian companies coordinate with one another to promote the dissemination of technology across the economy (Rademakers 1998; Rademakers and van Valkengoed 2001; Adam and Tisdell 2008). Rather, firms tend to focus on cultivating strong personal relationships to powerful political patrons to gain competitive advantage. As Rademakers (1998: 1010) notes: 'Good relationships with state officials are regarded as more important for business success than cooperative inter-firm linkages.'

At the same time, linkages between Indonesian companies are not based on 'standard market relationships and enforceable formal contracts' (Hall and Soskice 2001: 30). Indonesia's legal system has long been characterized by high levels of corruption and inefficiency rather than the rule of law.[10] In this context, contracts between companies have in many cases effectively been unenforceable. For instance, as Hill and Tandon (2010: 10) note, Indonesian companies in dispute with their foreign creditors in the wake of the 1997–1998 economic crisis successfully used the legal system to defeat the latter's contractual claims. Rather, it has been personalistic linkages between firms and to powerful political patrons that have provided firms with the certainty and security to transact. In a survey of firms operating in the garment industry in Bandung, Adam and Tisdell (2008: 3), for instance, found that family connections were one of the most important factors in fostering subcontracting and other forms of trading arrangements between companies (see also Rademakers 1998). Likewise, numerous commentators have pointed to the way in which links to powerful political figures have served to provide the property rights protection required to facilitate private-sector investment in multi-billion dollar industrial projects (see, for instance, MacIntyre 2001).

Finally, it is important to note here that technological innovation has not been a key source of competitive advantage for Indonesian companies. As Hill and Tandon (2010: 10) have noted:

> Total R&D expenditure as a percentage of GDP has never exceeded 0.2%. Most of it has occurred in the public sector, as domestic firms have never made any significant commitment to R&D. Moreover, MNEs do not regard the country as a suitable base for R&D activity, owing to the weak skill base, the limited protection of intellectual property rights, and the absence of any significant public support for R&D.

Within this context, it has not been functionally necessary for Indonesian firms to devise institutionalized mechanisms, whether market-based or coordinated/cooperative in nature, to facilitate the dissemination of technology across the economy. To be sure, Indonesian companies active in industries such as automobile manufacture and mining have required access to foreign technology in order to produce their respective products. But they have been able to acquire this through joint ventures with foreign firms, avoiding the need to develop it independently.

# SOCIAL CAPITAL

Consistent with this pattern of inter-company relations, social capital in Indonesia is generally regarded as low. Institutionalized trust is more or less absent: without a properly functioning legal system, business actors have little faith that other actors will act in accordance with written and verbal agreements, even if they are formally legally enforceable. In this context, as noted above, they have had to rely heavily on family and ethnic ties, personal reputation, and close personal relationships with powerful political patrons—that is, interpersonal forms of trust—to reduce the uncertainties involved in carrying on a business (Rademakers 1998; Turner 2007; Carney, Dieleman, and Sachs 2008). For instance, in a recent study of one of Indonesia's largest business conglomerates, the Salim group, Carney, Dieleman, and Sachs (2008) argue that this group's success has been based on its ability to mobilize and maintain bonding social capital (in particular, linkages to ethnic Chinese business networks in Asia, domestic *Hokchia* dialect groups, and other family and clan members) and bridging social capital—in particular, linkages to former President Suharto and other senior political figures, Japanese and Western multinational companies, and key domestic businesses. Of course, as Turner's (2007) analysis of social capital among small-scale entrepreneurs in Makassar, South Sulawesi, indicates, such social capital is unevenly distributed in Indonesia, meaning that some business actors have much greater opportunity to realize business opportunities than others. Bonding capital, she notes, is prevalent among small-scale entrepreneurs in Makassar, but bridging capital is much less prevalent, and linking capital—that is, the capital associated with linkages across social and economic boundaries—is virtually absent (2007: 415). In contrast to the members of the Salim family, then, these small-scale entrepreneurs have few opportunities to advance beyond small-scale activities to build major business empires.

# EVOLUTIONARY DYNAMICS

Despite the fact that Indonesia's political economy has undergone significant change between the New Order and post-New Order periods, there has been considerable continuity in the forces that have shaped the nature of capitalism in the country during these periods. The New Order was dominated by the 'politico-bureaucrats' who occupied the state apparatus and the domestic business conglomerates. After taking power in 1965, the politico-bureaucrats in the Indonesian military reduced the national parliament to a rubber stamp, ensuring that real political authority remained within the bureaucracy and executive, and exercised strict control over the judiciary, enormously limiting its independence. Unconstrained by either parliament or the rule of law, the politico-bureaucrats transformed the state apparatus into a franchise-like operation, the key feature of which was the purchase of government positions in exchange for access to the rents they could generate (McLeod 2000). As we have seen, this situation allowed business people who had strong connections to senior political figures to gain privileged access to state facilities, licences, and concessions and, in doing so, transform their enterprises into large diversified conglomerates. The result was that both forces developed a strong interest in the pursuit of a *dirigiste* economic strategy, except to the extent that economic deregulation and privatisation opened up lucrative opportunities for the conglomerates.

While the 1997–1998 economic crisis weakened the politico-bureaucrats and conglomerates by precipitating democratization, decentralization, and widespread corporate insolvency, they have successfully reconstituted themselves in the post-New Order period through new alliances and vehicles such as political parties and mass organizations (Hadiz 2003; Robison and Hadiz 2004), and thus retained considerable influence over the state. This is most apparent in the fact that many leading New Order military officials and business figures have held senior government positions in major political parties and post-New Order governments—for instance, Susilo Bambang Yudhoyono (SBY), Wiranto, Aburizal Bakrie, Fahmi Idris, Fadel Muhammad, and Jusuf Kalla— and the fact that many of the conglomerates and their owners appear to have survived the crisis and remain active in business. The continued importance of patrimonial and predatory linkages to senior government officials for business success in the post-New Order period has meant that many of these conglomerates have maintained their competitive advantage in the domestic marketplace, notwithstanding the continued trend towards economic liberalization (Davidson 2010).

The continued political dominance of the politico-bureaucrats and conglomerates has been readily apparent in the policy-making process. Despite the much greater authority invested in national and regional parliaments as a result of democratization and decentralization, national laws and regional regulations still tend to originate from within the bureaucracy, while parliamentary endorsement of these laws and regulations is frequently purchased by predatory elements within the bureaucracy and/or business communities (Rosser, Roesad, and Edwin 2005; Buehler 2009). In addition, when specific legal provisions have potentially threatened the interests of the politico-bureaucrats and conglomerates, they have been able to prevent the issuance of the subordinate regulations required to implement them. In the late 2000s, for instance, a group of business representative organizations, including the Indonesian Chamber of Commerce and Indonesia Business Links, launched a successful effort to stop the national government issuing a regulation to implement provisions in the 2007 Companies Code that would have introduced a mandatory requirement for natural-resource companies to carry out corporate social responsibility, a provision that raised the prospect of new corporate taxes and opportunities for bureaucratic rent-seeking (Rosser and Edwin 2010).

Another point of continuity has been the continued structural power of controllers of mobile capital, such as portfolio investors, international banks, footloose manufacturers, and international donors. During the New Order, these elements were able to exploit their control over much-needed investment resources to push for market-oriented economic reforms, particularly at times of economic crisis such as the mid-1980s. The main exception in this respect was the oil-boom period (1974–1982), when the government was awash with petrodollars and hence relatively unresponsive to their needs (Winters 1996). The Asian economic crisis, which resulted in massive capital flight, strengthened the hand of these elements considerably, particularly following the government's negotiation of a bail-out package with the IMF. On a number of occasions, the IMF withheld or delayed promised financial support in order to force the government to adopt or implement market-oriented reforms. With the Indonesian economy having largely recovered by the mid-2000s, the Yudhoyono government brought an end to the IMF programme in 2006, reducing the influence of this particular organization. It also shut down the Consultative Group on Indonesia (CGI), a key government-donor forum. But the interests of mobile-capital controllers have remained a powerful influence nevertheless, because of the country's lack of access to alternative investment resources[11] and consequent need to provide an investment climate that is attractive to private investors.

The main point of difference between the New Order and post-New Order periods in terms of the forces that have shaped the nature of Indonesian capitalism has been that peasants, workers, small businesses, and NGO activists, all of whom were strictly excluded from the policy-making process during the New Order, have been able to exercise slightly greater influence over policy-making. Democratization of Indonesia's political system has removed key obstacles to organization by these elements, making it easier for them to engage in collective action aimed at producing policy change. It also created an incentive for politicians and political parties to promote policies that favour these groups, because they represent such a large section of the electorate. At the same time, decentralization strengthened the ability of NGOs and other previously excluded groups to access and monitor policy-making and implementation by bringing it closer to them. The result has been to inject into policy discussions, calls for direct forms of state intervention to promote the realization of citizens' rights to free basic education and health care, protect workers' rights, protect the environment, ensure corporate social responsibility, and combat corruption, although resistance from politico-bureaucratic, corporate, and mobile-capital forces has meant that these calls have often been ineffective (Antlov 2003; Rosser, Roesad, and Edwin 2005; Carnegie 2008; Rosser and Edwin 2010; Rosser, Joshi, and Edwin 2011). Finally, the establishment of a Constitutional Court with powers of judicial review has provided previously excluded groups with a mechanism for contesting laws that they oppose on the grounds of their constitutionality, one they have used on issues such as international-standard schools, water privatization, and the size of the education budget.

In sum, then, the nature of capitalism in Indonesia during the post-New Order period has been shaped by three contradictory agendas—(i) the predatory, rent-seeking agenda pursued by the politico-bureaucrats and their corporate clients; (ii) the market-oriented agenda pursued by controllers of mobile capital (and conglomerates when it works to their favour); and (iii) the social justice/redistributive agenda pursued by peasants, workers, and small businesses and their allies in the NGO community. Of these, the first two have been the most influential in shaping Indonesian capitalism, reflecting the politico-bureaucrats and conglomerates' instrumental control over the state apparatus and mobile capital controllers' structural power. The result of this political context has been to produce a form of capitalism in Indonesia that is in effect a compromise between these competing agendas—in particular, one that favours the politico-bureaucrats and the conglomerates, while accommodating mobile-capital controllers and incorporating concessions to peasants, workers, and other marginalized elements.

# CONCLUSION

On the whole, then, how should one characterize the nature of capitalism in contemporary Indonesia? In this respect, it is useful to draw on Hall and Soskice's (2001) distinction between liberal market economies (LMEs) and coordinated market economies (CMEs). Does Indonesian capitalism constitute a LME, a CME model, or something else?

The internal structure of Indonesian firms and the nature of the country's education and training system are broadly consistent with the LME model, reflecting strong majority shareholder control of Indonesian companies, the top-down nature of Indonesian corporate management, and the country's educational focus on producing school graduates with generalist rather than sector or firm-specific skills. Likewise, the country's industrial relations system fits the LME model better than the CME model because, while it is highly interventionist in formal terms, in practice most workers' fates hinge on market forces, given the pervasive role of short-term labour contracts and the fact that many workers operate in the informal sector. But the country's financial system and corporate financial structure fit the CME model better than the LME model. Indonesian companies have de-leveraged in recent years and the stock market is playing an increasingly important role *vis-à-vis* corporate finance, trends that are consistent with a shift away from a CME towards a LME. But debt remains an important, indeed, the main source of finance for Indonesian companies, while non-market factors, especially political connections, continue to shape the allocation of state bank credit. The fact that in the realm of social capital, institutionalized trust is low and firms rely on interpersonal mechanisms to reduce uncertainties involved in carrying on a business also fits with the CME model. Finally, inter-company relations in Indonesia do not fit either model well: they are neither coordinated on a cooperative basis as per the CME model, nor driven by standard market relationships and enforceable contracts as per the LME model.

On the whole, then, Indonesian capitalism fits better with the LME than the CME model, but clearly does not constitute a pure exemplar of the former, notwithstanding three decades of neo-liberal economic policy and institutional reform. In essence, it represents a unique combination of market-based policies and institutions, direct forms of state intervention, and coordination based on the predatory interests of powerful politico-business families.

However one characterizes Indonesian capitalism, of course, it is unlikely to change dramatically over the short to medium term. While the structural power of mobile capital controllers means that there will be sustained pressure on the Indonesian government to adopt market-oriented policies in the future, the continued political dominance of the politico-bureaucrats and their corporate clients, and the pressure for populist policies created by democratization, will continue to work against the emergence of a LME. In particular, these factors will ensure that political connections and state intervention continue to influence the allocation of economic resources, even in contexts where formally market-based policies and institutions prevail.

## Notes

1. The IDX was formed in 2008, when the Jakarta Stock Exchange and the Surabaya Stock Exchange were merged.
2. According to Okuda and Take (2009: 21), the ratio of total debt to total assets at companies listed on the JSX in 1996 was 45% for government-controlled companies, 53% for ethnic Chinese-owned companies, 54% for *pribumi* companies, and 53% for foreign joint venture companies. At the same time, much of this debt was short term in nature and denominated in foreign currencies, leaving these companies vulnerable to a sharp fall in the value of the rupiah, as happened in 1997—1998. According to Okuda and Take, the ratio of short-term debt to total assets at companies listed on the JSX in 1996 was 23% for government-controlled companies, 33% for ethnic Chinese-owned companies, 31% for indigenously owned companies, and 42% for foreign joint venture companies.
3. I wish to thank Vedi Hadiz for his advice on this point.
4. Indeed, labour activists see union fragmentation as being a key weakness of the labour movement (see Silaban 2009), while business groups are clearly frustrated by the potential need to negotiate with several different unions at the company level.
5. See the results for 2008. Retrieved 26 June 2013 from at <http://www.oecd.org/document /11/0,3746,en_2649_37457_42695243_1_1_1_37457,00.html#data>.
6. Official estimates suggest that approximately 60% of Indonesian workers are employed in the informal sector and 40% in the formal sector. Of the latter, around three-quarters are classified by the Central Bureau of Statistics as 'regular employees'—that is, employees who work for another institution or person permanently for payment in cash or in kind (International Labour Organization 2011: 13—14).
7. According to Brusentsev, Newhouse, and Vromen (2012), only one-third of workers entitled to severance pay receive it, and those who do receive it get on average only 40% of their entitlement.
8. Little is known about how these factors translate into patterns of long-term versus short-term employment in the formal sector. It is possible, for instance, that casual and contract employees may remain with a single employer for the long term, notwithstanding their relatively precarious terms of employment. Likewise, permanent staff may regularly

job-hop to take advantage of new opportunities, rather than remain loyal to a single employer. Bennington and Habir (2003) assert that job-hopping is common among highly skilled employees in Indonesia. But, to the best of my knowledge, no-one has tested these phenomena empirically at a national level.

9. The enrolment rate at upper secondary school level, which has not been included in the government's free education programme, is much lower, at 57%.

10. The World Justice Project's (2011) Rule of Law Index, arguably the most comprehensive global index measuring the rule of law, scores Indonesia highly (compared to both other countries in East Asia and the Pacific and other lower-middle-income countries) on criteria such as limited government powers, government openness, and fundamental rights, but poorly on criteria such as corruption and access to civil justice.

11. Over the past decade or so, Indonesia has gone from being a net exporter to a net importer of oil.

## References

Abeng, T. (2001). *Indonesia Inc: Privatising State-owned Enterprises*. Singapore, Times Academic Press.

Abubakar, M. (2010). 'Towards World-Class Corporations'. Retrieved 1 June 2011 from <www.euromoneyconferences.com/downloads/Asia/2010/Indonesia10/SOE.pdf>.

Adam, L. and C. Tisdell (2008). *Interfirm Networks in the Indonesian Garment Industry: Trust and other Factors in their Formation and Duration and their Marketing Consequences*. University of Queensland Economic Theory, Applications and Issues Working Paper No. 47. Brisbane, University of Queensland.

Antlov, H. (2003). 'Not Enough Politics! Power, Participation, and the New Democratic Polity in Indonesia'. In E. Aspinall and G. Fealy, Eds., *Local Power and Politics in Indonesia: Decentralisation and Democratisation*: 72–86. Singapore, Institute of Southeast Asian Studies.

Aswicahyono, H., K. Bird, and H. Hill (2009). 'Making Economic Policy in Weak, Democratic, Post-Crisis States: An Indonesian Case Study'. *World Development* 37(2): 354–370.

Bank Indonesia (2001). *Credit Crunch in Indonesia in the Aftermath of the Crisis: Facts, Causes and Policy Implications*. Jakarta, Bank Indonesia.

Bennington, L. and A. Habir (2003). 'Human Resource Management in Indonesia'. *Human Resource Management Review* 13: 373–392.

Brusentsev, V., D. Newhouse, and W. Vromen (2012). *Severance Compliance in Indonesia*. World Bank Policy Research Working Paper 5933. Washington DC, World Bank.

Buehler, M. (2009). 'Decentralisation and Local Democracy in Indonesia: The Marginalisation of the Public Sphere'. In E. Aspinall and M. Mietzner, Eds., *Problems of Democratization in Indonesia: Elections, Institutions, and Society*: 267–285. Singapore, Institute of Southeast Asian Studies.

Caraway, T. (2004). 'Protective Repression, International Pressure, and Institutional Design: Explaining Labour Reform in Indonesia'. *Studies in Comparative International Development* 39(3): 28–49.

Carnegie, P. (2008). 'Democratization and Decentralization in Post-Soeharto Indonesia: Understanding Transition Dynamics'. *Pacific Affairs* 81(4): 515–525.

Carney, M., M. Dieleman, and W. Sachs (2008). 'The Value of Social Capital to Family Enterprises in Indonesia'. In P. Phan, S. Venkataraman, and S. Velamiuri, Eds., *Entrepreneurship in Emerging Regions Around the World: Theory, Evidence and Implications*: 297–323. Cheltenham, UK, and Northampton, USA, Edward Elgar.

Crouch, H. (2009). *Political Reform in Indonesia after Soeharto*. Singapore, Institute of Southeast Asian Studies.

Davidson, J. (2010). 'How to Harness the Positive Potential of KKN: Explaining Variation in the Private Sector Provision of Public Goods in Indonesia'. *Journal of Development Studies* 46(10): 1729–1748.

Donnan, S. (2005a). 'Probe Launched into Bank Mandiri Loans'. *Financial Times* 13 April: 30.

—— (2005b). 'Mandiri Searches for Right Values'. *Financial Times* 2 August: 21.

—— and T. Hidayat (2005). 'Neloe Trial Seen as Test Case'. *Financial Times* 11 October: 28.

Economist Intelligence Unit (2010). 'Indonesia: Financial Services Report'. Retrieved 29 June 2013 from <http://www.eiu.com/index.asp?layout=ib3Article&article_id=127482997&pubtype id=1132462498&category_id=775133077&country_id=1810000181&page_title=Forecast>.

Globe Asia (2009). '150 Wealthiest Indonesians'. *Globe Asia* June: 32–37.

Habir, A. D. and A. Larasati (1999). 'Human Resource Management as Competitive Advantage in the New Millennium'. *International Journal of Manpower* 20(8): 548–562.

Hadiz, V. (1997). *Workers and the State in New-Order Indonesia*. London, Routledge.

—— (2003). 'Reorganizing Political Power in Indonesia: A Reconsideration of So-Called "Democratic Transitions"'. *Pacific Review* 16(4): 591–611.

—— (2010). *Localising Power in Post-Authoritarian Indonesia: A Southeast Asia Perspective*. Stanford, Stanford University Press.

Hall, P. and D. Soskice (2001). 'An Introduction to Varieties of Capitalism'. In P. Hall and D. Soskice, Eds., *Varieties of Capitalism: the Institutional Foundations of Comparative Advantage*: 1–68. Oxford, Oxford University Press.

Harianto, F. and M. Pangestu (2002). 'Changes in Corporate Governance Structure in Indonesia'. In G. de Brouwer and W. Pupphavesa, Eds., *Asia-Pacific Financial Deregulation*: 73–82. London, Routledge.

Hill, H. and T. Shiraishi (2007). 'Indonesia After the Asian Crisis'. *Asian Economic Policy Review* 2(1): 123–141.

Hill, H. and P. Tandon (2010). 'Innovation and Technological Capability in Indonesia'. Retrieved 16 June 2011 from <http://docs.google.com/viewer?a=v&q=cache:HqYcfR1YECcJ:siter esources.worldbank.org/EASTASIAPACIFICEXT/Resources/226300-1279680449418/ HigherEd_InnovationandTechnologicalCapabilityinIndonesia.pdf+hill+tandon +technology+indonesia&hl=en&gl=au&pid=bl&srcid=ADGEESicj5eb2J3GlSqh s4UXFqDyr5umHGJWjOGV7Hrly5Dj          IWCLk8e8M8FQNWSG3MnJCLpbiuin JaXRwHr1u6UMArEjf5Wqg48p8-  K69wxVYydqg_Is4x2Q9weo-Soqtp_Yl_8K16-T&sig= AHIEtbR2dByEib-hQwnD0-XrRKIuJAMb1Q>.

Hotland, T. (2005). 'Bosowa, Bakrie Companies Clean, Says AGO Chief'. *Jakarta Post* 27 May: 8.

Hull, T. and G. Jones (1994). 'Demographic Perspectives'. In H. Hill, Ed., *Indonesia's New Order: The Dynamics of Socio-Economic Transformation*: 123–178. St. Leonards, Australia, Allen and Unwin.

International Labour Organization (2011). *Decent Work Country Profile: Indonesia*. Geneva, ILO.

International Monetary Fund (2008). *Indonesia: Selected Issues*. IMF Country Report No. 08/298. Washington, DC, IMF.

*Jakarta Post* (2009). 'Mandiri Stays Confident Despite "Bad" Debts', 2 November: 14.

Juliawan, B. (2010). 'Extracting Labor From its Owner'. *Critical Asian Studies* 42(1): 25–52.

Komandjaja, E. (2005a). 'Bank Mandiri Officials Quizzed Over Lending Scam'. *Jakarta Post* 16 April: 4.

—— (2005b). 'Detention Urged for Charged Bankers'. *Jakarta Post* 14 May: 4.

Kung, J., A. Caverhill, and R. McLeod (2010). 'Indonesia's Stock Market: Evolving Role, Growing Efficiency'. *Bulletin of Indonesian Economic Studies* 46(3): 329–346.

Leigh, B. (1999). 'Learning and Knowing Boundaries: Schooling in New-Order Indonesia'. *Sojourn* 14(1): 34–56.

MacIntyre, A. (1993). 'The Politics of Finance in Indonesia: Command, Confusion, and Competition'. In S. Haggard, C. Lee, and S. Maxfield, Eds., *The Politics of Finance in Developing Countries*: 123–164. Ithaca, Cornell University Press.

—— (2001). 'Investment, Property Rights, and Corruption in Indonesia'. In J. Campos, Ed., *Corruption: The Boom and Bust of East Asia*: 25–44. Manila, Ateneo de Manila University Press.

McLeod, R. (2000). 'Soeharto's Indonesia: A Better Class of Corruption'. *Agenda* 7(2): 99–112.

—— (2008). 'Survey of Recent Developments'. *Bulletin of Indonesian Economic Studies* 44(2): 183–208.

Manning, C. (1993). 'Structural Change and Industrial Relations during the Soeharto Period: An Approaching Crisis?' *Bulletin of Indonesian Economic Studies* 29(2): 59–95.

Okuda, H. and Y. Take (2009). *Institutional Change and Corporate Financing in Indonesia: Estimating the Effects of Social and Political Factors on Capital Structure*. Global COE Hi-State Discussion Paper no. 108. Tokyo, Institute of Economic Research, Hitotsubashi University.

Palmer, S. (2008). *Freedom of Association and Collective Bargaining: Indonesian Experience 2003-2008*. ILO Working Paper. Geneva, ILO.

Quinn, P. (2003). *Freedom of Association and Collective Bargaining: A Study of Indonesian Experience 1998-2003*. ILO Working Paper. Geneva, ILO.

Rademakers, M. (1998). 'Market Organization in Indonesia: Javanese and Chinese Family Business in the Jamu Industry'. *Organization Studies* 19(6): 1005–1027.

—— and J. R. van Valkengoed (2001). 'The Institutional Embeddedness of Inter-firm Relations in Indonesia'. In G. Jakobsen and J. Torp, Eds., *Understanding Business Systems in Developing Countries*: 65–86. London, Sage.

Robison, R. (1986). *Indonesia: The Rise of Capital*. Sydney, Allen and Unwin.

Robison, R. and V. Hadiz (2004). *Reorganizing Power in Indonesia: The Politics of Oligarchy in an Age of Markets*. London, Routledge.

Rosser, A. (2002). *The Politics of Economic Liberalisation in Indonesia: State, Market and Power*. Richmond, Curzon.

Rosser, A. and D. Edwin (2010). 'The Politics of Corporate Social Responsibility in Indonesia'. *Pacific Review* 23(1): 1–22.

Rosser, A., A. Joshi, and D. Edwin (2011). *Power, Politics, and Political Entrepreneurs: Realising Universal Free Basic Education*. IDS Working Paper 358. Brighton, Institute of Development Studies.

Rosser, A., K. Roesad, and D. Edwin (2005). 'Indonesia: The Politics of Inclusion'. *Journal of Contemporary Asia* 35(1): 53–77.

Rudnyckyj, D. (2009). 'Spiritual Economies: Islam and Neoliberalism in Contemporary Indonesia'. *Cultural Anthropology* 24(1): 104–141.

Sato, Y. (2004). 'Corporate Ownership and Management in Indonesia: Does it Change?' In M. Chatib Basri and P. van der Eng, Eds., *Business in Indonesia: New Problems, Old Challenges*: 158–177. Singapore, Institute of Southeast Asian Studies.

Silaban, R. (2009). *Repositioning of the Labour Movement: Road Map for the Indonesian Labour Movement After Reformasi*. Rekson Silaban, Friedrich Ebert.

Suryadarma, D. (2011). 'The Quality of Education in Indonesia: Weighed, Measured, and Found Wanting'. Retrieved 3 August 2012 from <http://www.crawford.anu.edu.au/acde/ip/pdf/lpem/2011/Daniel_2011a.pdf>.

Sutiyono, W. (2007). 'Human Resource Management in State-Owned and Private Enterprises in Indonesia'. *Bulletin of Indonesian Economic Studies, 43*(3): 377–394.

Turner, S. (2007). 'Small-Scale Enterprise Livelihoods and Social Capital in Eastern Indonesia: Ethnic Embeddedness and Exclusion'. *Professional Geographer 59*(4): 407–420.

Vivanews.Com (2011). 'Pejabat Bank Mandiri Didakwa Korupsi'. Retrieved 1 June 2011 from <http://us.nasional.vivanews.com/news/read/208307-pejabat-bank-mandiri-didakwa-korupsi>.

Wicaksono, A. (2008). 'Indonesian State-Owned Enterprises: The Challenge of Reform'. *Southeast Asian Affairs* 2008: 146–167.

Wilson, D. (1991). 'Reform of Technical-Vocational Education in Indonesia and Malaysia'. *Comparative Education 27*(2): 207–221.

Winters, J. (1996). *Power in Motion: Capital Mobility and the Indonesian State*. Ithaca, Cornell University Press.

World Bank (1998). *Education in Indonesia: From Crisis to Recovery*. Washington, DC, World Bank.

—— (2010a). *Report on the Observance of Standards and Codes (ROSC): Corporate Governance Country Assessment: Indonesia*. Washington, DC, World Bank.

—— (2010b). *Indonesia Skills Report: Trends in Skills Demand, Gaps, and Supply in Indonesia*. Washington, DC, World Bank.

World Justice Project (2011). *Rule of Law Index 2011*. Washington, DC, World Justice Project.

# CHAPTER 6

# JAPAN

## *Coordinated Capitalism Between Institutional Change and Structural Inertia*

### MICHAEL A. WITT

JAPAN was the first country in East Asia to industrialize, and is still the region's second-largest economy. Its meteoric rise from the ashes of World War II inspired many of the Asian miracles that followed. Japanese-style industrial policy (Johnson 1982) featured prominently in South Korea and Taiwan, and later also in China. By the 1980s, Japan had become a source of learning and even awe for Western nations.

Then came the burst of the Japanese bubble economy of the 1980s. With Japan unable to extricate itself from its sea of troubles, awe initially turned to relief—Japan was not going to take over the world after all—then to concern and resignation. Public attention turned to dynamic China, and Japan was mentally written off. Perhaps as a result, few seem to have realized that Japan registered higher GDP growth on a per capita basis in the first decade of this century than the United States. It has also remained one of the leading sources of profits for foreign firms in the Asia-Pacific region.

An open question in this context is how the business system has evolved during the past two decades of trials and tribulations. The objective of this chapter is to draw on the latest available data to shed some light on this question.

## THE ROLE OF THE STATE

From the end of World War II through about the 1980s, Japan was the paradigmatic developmental state (Johnson 1982). Its approach to economic development became the model for much of Asia (e.g. Amsden 1989; Woo-Cummings 1999), and it is arguably impossible to understand the economic trajectory of Asia-Pacific without some appreciation of the Japanese model.

The Japanese developmental model has received considerable attention in the literature (Johnson 1982; Samuels 1987; Okimoto 1989; Pekkanen 2003). In simple terms, the objective of Japanese post-war industrial policy was to accelerate economic development by speeding up the transition from labour-intensive to capital-intensive and later to knowledge-intensive industries. Based on observation of Western nations' development, Japan knew what industries would follow one another. A capable and clean bureaucracy—especially the Ministry of International Trade and Industry (MITI)—judged when it was time to start developing a given industry and then used a combination of tools to help the fledgling industry grow and become internationally competitive. Firms engaged in new industries typically received preferential access to capital, then a scarce resource, often at depressed interest rates. Capital controls ensured that the money was used within the country. Strict barriers on imports and inward foreign direct investment prevented established international firms from out-competing infant Japanese industries. At the same time, the drive to export Japanese products brought in foreign currency and, more importantly, exposed Japanese companies to international competition, pushing them to improve their exported products. Through licensing and R&D consortia, the Japanese state also fostered the acquisition and diffusion of knowledge from the West. While all this sounds straightforward today, it was revolutionary in its day. South Korea and Taiwan in particular drew inspiration from it, and China's management of its state-owned sector shows intriguing parallels.

In initial accounts, the policy- and decision-making process looked top down: the bureaucracy decided, and industry obeyed (Johnson 1982). Later accounts (Samuels 1987; Okimoto 1989; Tsuru 1993) found that the process was coordinated rather than top down, or in Samuels's expression, characterized by 'reciprocal consent' between government and business. Most observers also argued that while politicians may have had the formal trappings of power, the bureaucracy really ran the country. This may be an overstatement (see Ramseyer and Rosenbluth 1993), but given that the general direction of the country was clear during the decades following the war—focus on economic recovery and further development—the country effectively ran on autopilot for most of this period.

This point is important, because it partly accounts for the far less impressive state of Japanese politics today. As Japan caught up with the West technologically and economically, the developmental model had run its course, raising the question of where to take Japan next. The burst of the 1980s bubble economy and the subsequent 'lost decade' of the 1990s added pressure for political leadership, which neither the bureaucracy nor the politicians have been able to provide. The former lacks legitimacy, while the latter seem to have neither the will nor the skill. Prime Minister Junichiro Koizumi (2001–2006) was the exception that proves the rule, but the drive for structural reforms he initiated has proved ephemeral. Since then, Japan has had six prime ministers[1] and is effectively directionless, with the bureaucracy administering the status quo and institutional change proceeding slowly, as discussed in the section 'Evolutionary Dynamics'.

One important shift in recent years has been a reduction in the extent of state intervention in the economy. The OECD's product-market regulation index (OECD 2011) shows a steady decline in regulatory burden, from around the OECD average in 1998 to somewhat below the average in 2008, remaining somewhat higher than the average for Anglo-Saxon countries, but lower than that for the Northern Europeans. However, this probably understates the extent of state intervention, as much intervention has traditionally occurred informally ('administrative guidance') (Johnson 1982). There is also evidence that deregulation, at least in some sectors, actually amounted to a process of re-regulation with more rules (Vogel 1996). Finally, it is worth noting that even among the business community, there is no desire for free-market competition: while deregulation *(kisei kanwa,* lit. a softening of regulations) is high on the wish list of senior executives, liberalization *(jiyuka,* denoting the abolition of regulations) is perceived as undesirable (Witt and Redding 2009).

# Financial System

Japan's present-day financial system is best understood in the context of its classical post-war configuration as a bank-led system. Firms obtained most of their funding through a long-term business relationship with a single 'main bank'. In particular, business groups, also known as *keiretsu* (discussed below), all centred on a major bank that represented the main source of funding for group members. In the early days of post-war recovery, the state controlled the allocation of financial capital through directed lending to firms targeted by industrial policy (cf. Johnson 1982). As Japan caught up with the West and firms grew larger and richer, this state role faded into the background, and market criteria such as credit-worthiness attained greater importance. Throughout, however, the nature and strength of the 'main bank' relationship continued to matter. Bank loans remained available for the long term, as shown in the proliferation of so-called 'zombie' companies in the late 1990s and early 2000s: while practically insolvent, these companies were kept afloat by the willingness of their banks to roll over existing credit and extend new loans as needed (Caballero, Hoshi, and Kashyap 2008).

Recent evidence suggests that while the importance of bank lending has declined and markets have become more important (Witt 2006; Yoshikawa and McGuire 2008; McGuire and Dow 2009; BIS 2010), Japan's financial system remains bank led. The ratio of bank credits over GDP in Japan fell from about 1.25 in 1980 to about 1.05 in 2009 (BIS 2010). During the same period, the ratio of stock market valuation over GDP increased from about 0.2 to about 0.55 (BIS 2010). For comparison, the respective ratios for the United States in 2009, which is clearly a market-led system (Witt 2006), were about 0.6 for credit and 0.6 for stock valuation (BIS 2010). Germany, where banks play an even stronger role than in Japan (Witt 2006), had 2009 ratios of about 1.15 and 0.3 (BIS 2010).

# OWNERSHIP AND GOVERNANCE

Most outstanding shares of listed firms used to be owned by the main bank and other friendly firms, such as other members of the same business groups. In 1980, 64.4 per cent of the value of outstanding stock of listed corporations was in the hands of financial institutions and business corporations (TSE 2010). These shareholdings would often be reciprocal, leading to high levels of cross-shareholdings in the Japanese economy. Monitoring by the main bank and other business group members represented the main mechanism of corporate governance (Dore 2000). Boards were typically large collections of insiders; Sony, for instance, had a board of thirty-eight (Yoshikawa and McGuire 2008). A market for corporate governance involving hostile takeover bids was practically non-existent; indeed, firms had begun to adopt cross-shareholdings in the 1960s to counter the threat of such takeovers (Witt 2006).

Shareholding patterns began to shift during the 'lost decade' of the 1990s, as corporations and financial institutions sold off shares to recapitalize themselves. In 2000, the combined holdings of financial institutions and corporations were 60.9 per cent of market valuation. In 2009, their holdings were down to 51.9 per cent, though this marks a slight recovery from a 2006 low of 51.5 per cent (TSE 2010). As firms and, to a lesser extent, individuals in Japan sold shares, foreigners increased their share from 5.8 per cent in 1980 to 18.8 per cent in 2000 and 26.0 per cent in 2009 (TSE 2010).

Increased foreign shareholdings have meant pressure for changes in corporate governance towards more attention to shareholders' interests. Traditionally, shareholders mattered little to Japanese corporations. Instead, firms focused on fulfilling their obligations to a range of stakeholders, including employees, society, and customers (Dore 2000), an attitude that had little changed by the early 2000s (Witt and Redding 2010). Firms, especially those with large foreign shareholdings, have started to yield to the pressure. Legal reforms starting in 1997 facilitated this development, culminating in a 2002 change of the Company Law to permit the formation of US-style boards of directors (Shishido 2007). Notable changes visible in practice include reductions in board sizes (Sony cut its board to ten members), the introduction of the executive-officer system, the appointment of outside directors, and increases in disclosure and transparency (Ahmadjian and Okumura 2011).

The practical significance of most of these changes is unclear. Perhaps the greatest progress has been made in terms of disclosure and transparency (Ahmadjian and Okumura 2011). Other reforms have been less successful. For instance, as of July 2012, only 58 of Japan's nearly 4000 listed firms had introduced a US-style committee system (Japan Association of Corporate Directors 2012; World Bank 2012a). Even where structural reforms have occurred, this may matter little in reality. Dore (2007), for instance, explained how the same senior directors now making up reformed smaller boards used to form a sub-committee of the old board—the *jomukai*—to drive many of its decisions.

Meanwhile, the old board continues to exist and meet in the guise of joint meetings of the new board and the newly created executive-officer group (who under the old system would have been board members).

In addition, outside directors continue to be a great rarity. In 2009, 44.1 per cent of firms had at least one outside director, with the average number of such outsiders at 1.76 (Ahmadjian and Okumura 2011). The effect thus seems to be one of insiders monitoring insiders, as before (Ahmadjian and Okumura 2011; Aman and Nguyen 2012). In addition, the loose definition of 'outsider' has in effect enabled parent companies to take even tighter control of their formally independent subsidiaries, thus defeating the intended goal of openness and transparency (Dore 2007).

At the same time, takeover defences continue to deprive shareholders of their ultimate recourse: selling to the highest bidder. Cross-shareholdings seem to have started to strengthen again from 2005 onward (Nakamura 2011). In addition, by 2008, 23.8 per cent of first-section TSE firms had takeover defences such as poison pills, and hostile takeover bids, whether by Japanese or foreign investors, have generally failed (Ahmadjian and Okumura 2011). A further deterrent, at least for insiders, is likely to be found in the fate of the two leading Japanese activists for shareholder rights, Takafumi Horie and Yoshiaki Murakami. After a public hostile takeover bid for Fuji Television in 2005, both were found guilty of securities fraud and handed prison sentences.

# INTERNAL STRUCTURE

Japanese firms tend to be hierarchical. Within general management grades, five to eight layers seem to have been the norm, compared with about the same number in the UK and up to thirteen layers in US firms (Morris, Hassard, and McCann 2008; McCann, Hassard, and Morris 2010). In the past decade, Japanese firms seem to have sought to streamline operations by de-layering, roughly halving the number of managerial grades (Inagami and Whittaker 2005; Morris, Hassard, and McCann 2008; McCann, Hassard, and Morris 2010). However, studies documenting such de-layering are based on relatively few cases, so it remains open how widespread this really is. The evidence is also contradictory. For instance, in two separate studies involving the same author, one found de-layering to be common (Morris, Hassard, and McCann 2008), the other found the opposite (Iida and Morris 2008). It is also unclear whether the reduction of formal managerial grades has led to a reduced hierarchy in actual practice. Given the hierarchical nature of Japanese society, it is possible that informal determinants of hierarchy, such as seniority, may have substituted for abolished formal titles.

Despite the hierarchical structure, decision-making in Japanese firms has had a consensual and participatory element in non-routine decision-making (Dore 1973; Aoki 1988). Major decisions usually involve informal consensus-building among the main internal stakeholders before formal steps are taken, a process known as *nemawashi* (preparing the roots). Once consensus has been reached, the proposal is put on the agenda of the appropriate forum, such as the board, where it usually passes without further discussion. Middle-management in this context is an important source of initiatives and factual input.

In contrast with much of the rest of Asia, improving a company's workings is the responsibility of all (regular) employees. The principle of *kaizen* (continuous improvement), for instance, calls on all echelons of the firm to keep looking for ways to increase productivity. Suggestion boxes and teams such as quality circles are conduits by which individual workers can contribute to this process. The *ringi* system enables non-executive managers to feed proposals into the decision-making system. The process involves writing up a proposal for a change, which is then circulated for peer review before being submitted to higher-level management for a decision. Usually, authors of a *ringi* proposal will seek to build an informal consensus before drafting a formal proposal. Accordingly, comparative statistics suggest that Japan has the highest level of delegation among the economies, scoring 4.8 out for 7, with higher numbers indicating more delegation (Schwab 2010). This is about par with the average for Anglo-Saxon countries, 4.87, though lower than the average score in northern European countries, 5.31 (Schwab 2010).

Recent developments seem to have not so much abolished these processes as streamlined them, to speed up decision-making and improve efficiency. De-layering, for instance, should in principle speed up information flow through the hierarchy. At the same time, there is evidence that companies have devolved more decisions to lower management levels, emphasized the need to make more decisions without lengthy consensus-building, and increased the control spans of individual managers (Inagami and Whittaker 2005; McCann, Hassard, and Morris 2010). As with de-layering and for the same reasons, it is unclear to what extent these other changes have diffused through the Japanese economy. In addition, as discussed, some firms have also shrunk their boards and brought them structurally in line with the US model, though this may in effect amount to no more than a renaming exercise (Dore 2007).

## EMPLOYMENT RELATIONS

Japanese post-war employment relations have rested on three main pillars, or 'sacred treasures': lifetime employment *(shushin koyo)*, seniority system *(nenko joretsu)*, and enterprise unions. All three came under considerable pressure from the 1990s onward (Dore 2000; Jacoby 2005; Vogel 2006), raising the possibility of possible convergence, partial or total, on the Anglo-Saxon model. The most recent evidence on the question suggests that practices in all three areas have changed, though not necessarily as much as earlier studies had anticipated.

Lifetime employment refers to the promise, usually implicit rather than spelled out in contracts, to keep regular male employees *(seishain)* until retirement age (initially 55, now usually around 60). Even though only about a quarter of private-sector firms offered 'lifetime employment' (Iida and Morris 2008), it became a normative model for society (Dore 1973). As a result, most small and medium-sized enterprises tended to follow the same basic norm of long-term employment (Iida and Morris 2008).

Counter to earlier expectations, lifetime or long-term employment seems still the norm. Following a review of the literature of the past two decades, Iida and Morris conclude that 'the lifetime employment system thus appears to be fairly robust' (Iida and Morris 2008: 1075), though they also note the rise of non-regular employees without such guarantees and a possible shortening of the age bracket during which it applies. Keizer (2011: 579) paints a consistent picture, noting, among others, a 2007 survey by the Japan Institute for Labour Policy and Training, which found that almost 90 per cent of companies 'aimed to maintain lifetime employment policies in their current or partially adjusted form'. The same survey reported that 78 per cent of employees preferred the practice. Similarly, a 2010 survey of new recruits shows that almost 60 per cent preferred to stay working for the same company (Japan Productivity Centre 2010).

Even if companies want to reduce their workforce, regulations make this fairly difficult. The Global Competitiveness Report rates the ease of hiring and firing on a scale from 1 to 7 (1 = impeded by regulations, 7 = flexibly determined by employers). Japan scores 3.0, the lowest value for all Asian countries in the survey (Schwab 2010), putting Japan roughly par with continental European countries such as Belgium, France, Norway, and Sweden. Similarly, the OECD rates Japanese employment protection for regular employees at 1.87—lower than for northern European countries, but considerably higher than the Anglo-Saxon nations (OECD 2012).

This all suggests little change in actual employment practice. The statistics on duration of employment present a consistent picture. According to the Basic Survey on Wage Structure by the Ministry of Health, Labour and Welfare, in 2010, the average tenure of regular male employees was 18.4 years for middle-school graduates, 14.8 years for high-school graduates, 11.7 years for graduates from junior colleges and colleges of technology, and 12.8 years for college and university graduates (Ministry of Health 2011b). Breakdown by company size shows a positive correlation between firm size and tenure, especially for middle-school and high-school graduates. However, even for small firms, the numbers are only just below average. Importantly, tenure lengths have actually increased over the past decade. In 1998, the earliest date for which the survey contains them, tenure durations were 17.6, 13.4, 9.2, and 11.9 years, respectively (Ministry of Health 2011b). Increases in the pension age may be part of the explanation. Overall, while there is no doubt that some individual firms may have moved away from the norm of lifetime or long-term employment, it is also clear that at the level of the business system, the practice seems to persist.

'Seniority system' describes the practice of increasing wages or salaries with tenure inside the firm (which correlates with age, as most recruits of a given background join at the same age). One rationale for this practice is that length of tenure is an indicator of experience in the company, and thus of knowledge or ability. In addition, the system has historically differentiated on the basis of educational attainment, with holders of higher degrees receiving higher pay.

In recent years, a third element has entered the scene: performance-based pay. By 2010, 45.1 per cent of companies had introduced a performance-evaluation system. Among large firms with 1,000 employees of more, the proportion was 83.3 per cent (Ministry of Health, Labour and Welfare 2011c). While several authors initially suggested that this development could lead to the breakdown of the seniority system (e.g. Keizer 2011), this does not seem to have happened. In particular, the 2010 Basic Survey on Wage Structure by the Ministry of Health, Labour and Welfare (2011b) shows that across education levels and industry sizes and up to the usual retirement age of 60 years, salaries still increase with age, peaking around age 55. What seems to have changed is the relative height of the peak. For instance, for male university graduates, Inagami and Whittaker (2005) find a peak of about 2.7 times the pay of fresh recruits in 2000, while the 2010 multiple was 2.23. This continues a gradual trend visible since the 1970s (Inagami and Whittaker 2005). One interpretation is that, unlike firms elsewhere, especially in the United States, Japanese firms are restraining wages at the top rather than bottom.

Case studies exploring the details of the introduction of performance-based pay similarly suggest that in general, its impact on the seniority system has been limited. For instance, Keizer (2011: 590) found performance-based pay to be 'usually limited to more senior employees and predominantly impact[ing] bonus payments'. Iida and Morris (2008: 1076) suggested that 'while pay is increasingly individualized, promotion remains seniority-based', which implies a de facto continuation of the seniority system augmented by increased variance around the mean pay for the respective age group. The overall result is thus that 'changes have not been as revolutionary as suggested in the early years of the debate' (Keizer 2011: 590).

The third pillar, enterprise unions, seems to have stabilized in the second half of the 2000s, after years of decline. According to the Ministry of Health, Labour and Welfare's Basic Survey on Labour Unions (reported by Japan Institute for Labour Policy and Training 2011), union density has fallen from 25.2 per cent in 1990 to 18.5 per cent in 2010, though it is showing some signs of recovery from its low of 18.1 per cent in 2007/08. In large companies with more than 1000 employees, density fell from 61.0 per cent in 1990 to 46.6 per cent in 2010, recovering from a low of 45.3 per cent in 2008.

The overall downward trend in Japan started in the 1970s and is consistent with the decline of labour unions worldwide (cf. Witt 2006), stemming from factors such as globalization and sectoral shifts away from manufacturing. Specific to Japan are two further challenges: first, non-regular workers, traditionally ineligible for membership, make up a much larger proportion of the working population today. And second, the need for unions as interest representatives is limited, at least for regular employees, given that most Japanese business-leaders consider the provision of benefits to employees a prime reason for the existence of their firms and see unions as partners in running the firm (Witt and Redding 2010). As a result, the interests of regular employees and their firms are generally well aligned, as expressed in the fact that Japan has the lowest number of strike days among any OECD country, regardless of population size (OECD 2012).

Japanese unions have sought to respond by re-inventing themselves, changing their organizational boundaries together with their enterprises (Sako 2006) and starting their own welfare programmes (Akimoto and Sonoda 2009). They have also begun to admit part-time workers, achieving a unionization rate of 5.6 per cent among this group in 2010. Whether these changes will lead to a sustainable stabilization or even a recovery remains to be seen.

A development informing much of the recent debate on industrial relations is the increase of non-regular employees (e.g. Inagami and Whittaker 2005; Vogel 2006; Schaede 2008). This is of potential significance, because the three pillars of employment relations have traditionally only applied to regular employees. A proliferation of non-regular employees would thus be indicative of major changes to the Japanese way of handling human resources.

On the surface, such a proliferation is precisely what has occurred over recent decades. In 1984, the first year of the historical time-series offered by the Japan Statistics Bureau (Ministry of Internal Affairs and Communications 2011), 15.3 per cent of employees were in non-regular employment. This proportion rose to 20.2 per cent in 1990, 26.0 per cent in 2000, and reached 34.4 per cent in 2010. It is tempting to see this as evidence of a breakdown in traditional employment relations.

A more careful analysis suggests a different picture. The numbers on the rise of non-regular employment usually cited include all workers in the economy, male and female, of all ages. However, being a 'regular' employee has traditionally meant being male and between about 25 and 55 years of age—in other words, out of school and before retirement. To avoid comparing apples with oranges, one needs to look exclusively at this group of employees. There, the data (Ministry of Internal Affairs and Communications 2011) show that between 1990 and 2010, the proportion of non-regular workers increased from 3.6 per cent to 10.1 per cent. Most of this growth comes from the age-group 25–34, which rose from 3.2 per cent to 14.0 per cent during this period. Part of the explanation for this latter trend is a higher propensity to stay in tertiary education and engage in part-time work while doing so (see the section 'Education and Skills Formation'). In addition, some younger workers probably permanently lost out on the chance to become a regular employee as a result of reduced hiring during the recessionary years of the 1990s and 2000s (Ahmadjian and Robinson 2001; Morris, Hassard, and McCann 2008).

Much of the growth in the total proportion of non-regular employees is explained by a rising propensity of women to work. Between 1984 and 2010, the overall number of male employees in the economy grew by 14.4 per cent; that of female employees, by 61.0 per cent. Since women are approximately three times as likely to work in non-regular employment, this has served to inflate the overall proportion of non-regular workers in the economy. Furthermore, much of the rise in female employment seems to involve areas not covered by regular employees. For instance, in the 2000s, the industry with by far the greatest increase in female employment was medical, healthcare, and welfare, which seems to be related to newly created lines of employment such as home-care.

Similarly, the number of employees above the age of 55 has more than doubled since 1984. The increase in the retirement age from 55 to 60 years is part of the explanation, but so is improved health and life expectancy. Increasing the proportion of young Japanese in tertiary education has likewise had the effect of driving up non-regular employment within the 15–24 age bracket; in fact, students in 2010 accounted for half of non-regular employment in this group.

Overall, while there is no doubt that the proportion of non-regular employment has increased and that some firms are substituting cheaper non-regular workers for some of their regular workers, the picture does not suggest a breakdown of the traditional employment system. It does suggest the rise of a second major form of employment practice in the Japanese political economy. On present evidence, it seems that this represents more of a complement to, than a substitute for, the traditional regular employment system.

# EDUCATION AND SKILLS FORMATION

The present education system was put in place after World War II on the basis of the US model. Students go through six years of primary school, three years of junior high school, and three years of high school before moving on to two-year or four-year college, which in turn may be followed by graduate degree programmes. Schooling is essentially universal through high school, and Japan's 2010 secondary gross enrolment rate of 102 per cent[2] was the highest in Asia except for Brunei (World Bank 2012a). The proportion of students attending college is similarly high, with a 2010 tertiary gross enrolment rate of 60 per cent, third in Asia after South Korea and Macau (World Bank 2012a).

The output of this system is generally good. In the 2011 UNDP education attainment index, which presents a composite score of mean years of schooling of adults and expected years of schooling of children, Japan scores 0.883 (United Nations Development Programme 2011). Among world nations, this places Japan eighteenth, approximately par with Belgium and ahead of all Asian economies east of India except South Korea. In comparative studies of student attainment, Japan similarly tends to perform well. In the 2009 PISA studies comparing students' ability in reading, mathematics, and sciences, Japan overall came fifth among sixty-five economies, beaten only by Hong Kong, Finland, Singapore, and South Korea (OECD 2010). In the 2007 Trends in Mathematics and Science Study, Japan ranked fourth among thirty-six economies, behind Taiwan, Singapore, and South Korea (National Center for Education Statistics 2009).

Relatively underdeveloped are public[3] vocational training schemes. The main avenues are specialized training colleges *(senmon gakko)* and colleges of technology *(kosen)*. Relative to other educational tracks, student numbers are fairly small. In 2009, these two types of school enrolled a total of 684,261 students, compared with a junior college and college population of about 3,006,884 students (Ministry of Education 2011). The gap between vocational and generalist education has been growing. College enrolment rose by 15.1 per cent between 1990 and 2009, while vocational student numbers fell by 19.0 per cent during the same period (Ministry of Education 2011). Part of the reason for this decline is that, as a result of Japan's low birthrate, universities are facing a shortfall of students, which at least some of them are working to compensate for by recruiting students from the traditional catchment area of vocational schools.

Specialized training colleges have borne the brunt of this shift, suffering a 21.0 per cent decline from 791,431 in 1990 to 624,875 in 2009 (Ministry of Education 2011). By contrast, colleges of technology have been holding up fairly well, with an increase of 12.3 per cent during the same period, but even so they enrolled only 59,386 students in 2009 (Ministry of Education 2011). The Japanese vocational training system also looks weak in international comparison. For 2009, OECD (2012) statistics show 279,434 graduates from vocational and technical programmes at the upper secondary level,[4] less than two-thirds the number for Germany (441,522), a country with about two-thirds the population of Japan. The number has seen a precipitous decline since the beginning of the time-series in 1998, when Japan reported 1,580,988 graduates (OECD 2012).

As in most other East Asian nations, entrance examinations are an integral part of the education system. Most colleges have such exams, and since leading firms tend to hire only from leading schools, competition for top schools is stiff. Entrance examinations further exist for the more prestigious primary and secondary schools as well as for Japan's leading kindergartens. These examinations, which have their origins in the Confucian examination system for civil servants, give the system a strong meritocratic element. In the Japanese case, family wealth seems to temper this element only moderately, as most Japanese families seem to have the means for private tutoring in cram schools (juku).

At the same time, the examination system has drawbacks. Pressure on students is tremendous, and it is not rare for school, cram school, and homework to keep students busy until the late evening hours. Rote rehearsal and recall are emphasized over application and creativity (Schoppa 1993). Since graduation is virtually assured once students have passed their college entrance examinations, tertiary education for many amounts to a four-year vacation. The result is that the average Japanese college student is likely to know less at the time of graduation than when s/he entered.

This latter point, in combination with the fairly weak public vocational training system and the highly firm-specific nature of skills in the Japanese workplace (Dore 2000), implies a need for extensive training of employees. This was traditionally accomplished through extensive on-the-job training (OJT) involving, among other things, rotations through various departments of the firm for new recruits (Dore 1973). While recent years have seen the rise of off-the-job training (off-JT) programmes (Dalton and Benson 2002), OJT seems to remain the norm. According to a 2010 survey by the Ministry of Health, Labour, and Welfare asking firms to choose which they consider more important, OJT or off-JT, 70.5 per cent emphasized OJT training for regular employees (non-regular: 76.9%) (Ministry of Health 2011a). Some OJT seems to occur informally, as only 57.8 per cent of firms reported the implementation of deliberately planned OJT for regular employees (non-regular: 27.7%). At the same time, 67.1 per cent of firms reported implementing off-JT for regular employees (non-regular: 31.4%), and 41.7 per cent of firms supported self-training programmes for regular employees (non-regular: 18.4%). While OJT proportions remained basically stable over the preceding three years, off-the-job training and self-improvement programmes showed a decline of 10 and 16.4 percentage points for regular employees (non-regular: 8.2 and 18.9 percentage points).

In general, employers and employees are willing to invest in these training schemes because the persistence of long-term or 'lifetime' employment, as explained earlier, gives both sides reasonable assurance that their investments will pay off. This is clearly visible in the willingness of employers to pay for off-JT and self-improvement programmes, which is considerably higher for long-term, regular employees than for shorter-term, non-regular employees, as the previous paragraph suggested. In addition, the quality and intensity of OJT offered to regular employees is higher than that of OJT for non-regular employees (Morishima and Shimanuki 2005; Jones 2007).

# INTER-COMPANY RELATIONS

Inter-company relations in the post-war Japanese economy reached such levels of density that observers dubbed it a 'network economy' (Lincoln 1990; Kumon 1992). In reviewing the literature on social networks in the Japanese political economy, Witt (2006) summarized four general types: business groups (also known as horizontal *keiretsu*), vertical *keiretsu*, R&D consortia, and a government–association–industry nexus that includes cartels and, more commonly, intra-industry loops.

Business groups developed in two basic types: former *zaibatsu*, and bank-led groups. The *zaibatsu* type, comprising the Mitsubishi, Mitsui, and Sumitomo groups, has its origin in pre-war and wartime *zaibatsu*, family-controlled holding companies owning vast conglomerates of firms in unrelated industries. US occupation forces dissolved holding firms in 1947 (Hirschmeier and Yui 1981). However, *zaibatsu* member firms maintained informal links reinforced by business and equity ties, and the banks in each group informally replaced the abolished holding companies as the centre of group coordination (Ito 1992; Nakamura 1995). Bank-led business groups—Fuyo, Ikkan, Sanwa, plus some smaller groups—coalesced around banks only after the war. Partially forced together by what was then the Ministry of International Trade and Industry (MITI) (Johnson 1982), they were less closely knit than the former *zaibatsu*.

Evidence on the current state of Japanese business groups is mixed and complicated by cross-group mergers and reconfigurations (McGuire and Dow 2009). In particular, bank mergers in 2000 and 2001 effectively reduced the number of business groups to four, bringing together the Sumitomo and Mitsui groups and the Mitsubishi and Sanwa groups (McGuire and Dow 2009). Within these changing contexts, lower bank-lending to group members, a decline of cross-shareholdings in most groups, and reduced exchanges of personnel seem to indicate a reduction of the significance of business groups (Witt 2006; McGuire and Dow 2009), with some authors going so far as to suggest that they effectively no longer exist (Lincoln and Shimotani 2010). However, other data suggest a stabilization or even revival of some features. For instance, Nakamura (2011) shows evidence suggesting a strengthening of cross-shareholdings from 2005 onwards.

Vertical *keiretsu* have assumed three general types: production *keiretsu*, which are supply chain networks; distribution *keiretsu*, which are distribution networks; and capital *keiretsu*, which build on capital flows from a parent company to a subsidiary (Gerlach 1992). Of these, production networks have received most attention, in particular in the context of the competitive strength of the Japanese automobile industry (e.g. Dyer 1996). Recent evidence on vertical *keiretsu* is relatively scarce. What evidence is available suggests a weakening of ties starting as early as the 1980s, but also some trend towards ownership integration of key suppliers in order to prevent them falling into the hands of competitors (Ahmadjian and Lincoln 2001; Lincoln and Gerlach 2004; McGuire and Dow 2009).

R&D consortia link large firms in the same or related industry for the duration of a research and development project—typically, five to ten years. Often, these projects receive government funding, though the amounts involved are usually relatively small (Sakakibara 1997). More important seems to be the signalling effect on firms and banks, as government decisions to support a project are usually taken on the basis of thorough reviews of the project's success potential (Witt 2006). In the decades following World War II, R&D consortia were geared mostly towards helping firms catch up with Western competitors. In recent decades, their character has shifted towards promoting basic research (Witt 2006).

Japanese firms are further embedded in a nexus connecting them to industry associations and the state. Large firms especially tend to belong to one or several peak-level associations, such as Keidanren (Schaede 2000). In addition, virtually all Japanese industries are organized in government-approved industry associations, which in turn count on average 90 per cent of firms in the respective industries as members (Schaede 2000). These associations permit government to remain informed about the goings-on in industry, but they also provide firms with a pipeline to state bureaucracy and a means of coordination and information-sharing within the industry (Schaede 2000; Witt 2006). In addition, they become the main forum for the formation of intra-industry loops, that is, informal connections that firms in the same industries use to trade market and technological information with one another (Witt 2006). Recent research suggests that industry associations and the intra-industry loops around them persist when they successfully adjust to the forces of globalization and technological change (Nelson 2010).

# SOCIAL CAPITAL

Japanese society is a high-trust society (Sako 1992; Fukuyama 1995). Prior research suggests that levels of interpersonal trust—that among family and friends—in Japan are high, at least in comparison with Anglo-Saxon nations such as the United States (Yamagishi and Yamagishi 1994; Yamagishi, Cook, and Watabe 1998) or UK (Dore 1973; Sako 1992). It is not clear how Japanese interpersonal trust levels have developed in recent years. However, there has been strong growth in voluntary non-governmental organizations (Ogawa 2009). Such NGOs have been shown to foster interpersonal trust in other contexts (Anheier and Kendall 2002), and as far as this mechanism holds for Japan as well, trust levels may well have risen in recent years.

Institutionalized trust levels are also relatively high (Fukuyama 1995). The 2010 Corruption Perception Index score for Japan was 8.0, with Japan ranking 14th of 182 nations and beating a number of Western nations, including the UK (7.8) and United States (7.1) (Transparency International 2012). Among the societies considered in this handbook, only Singapore and Hong Kong score higher, suggesting that, in general, the rule of law applies. Similarly, Japan's 2009 governance indicators for voice and account-ability, political stability, government effectiveness, regulatory quality, and rule of law fall between the 75th and 90th percentile among 213 economies in the world, while the control of corruption scores above the 90th percentile (World Bank 2012b). Viewing the average of all indicators, most Anglo-Saxon and northern European nations score higher, as do Hong Kong and Singapore within the region studied for this handbook. To the extent that these statistics are indicative of institutionalized trust, they indicate high levels relative to most of the rest of Asia, though somewhat lower levels relative to Anglo-Saxon and north-ern European nations. In direct comparison of Japan vs. the United States, research at the level of the individual affirms this picture (Yamagishi, Cook, and Watabe 1998).

Unlike most advanced industrialized countries, the main mechanism for maintaining institutionalized trust is not the legal system, but social pressure. In international com-parison, the Japanese legal infrastructure is weakly developed. For instance, the num-ber of lawyers registered in bar associations in Japan on 1 June 2011 was 30,488 (Japan Federation of Bar Associations 2011), while the respective 2010 numbers for Germany and the United States stood at 153,251 and 1,225,452 (American Bar Association 2011; Council of Bars and Law Societies of Europe 2011). Lawsuits are thus relatively rare. Instead, the networked nature of Japanese society facilitates the flow of information about breaches of trust, which in turn can trigger sanctions such as ostracism or the withholding of contracts or information (Hagen and Choe 1998; Witt 2006).

# COMPLEMENTARITIES

The Japanese business system is rich in institutional complementarities. This has impor-tant implications for comparative advantages of the Japanese economy, but also for its evolutionary dynamics, as discussed later in this chapter.

The main complementarities among the elements laid out earlier can be summarized as follows:

1. Bank-led finance and the long-term availability of financial capital are linked. Having bank-led finance does not in itself guarantee patient capital, but given sufficient institutional and monetary support from authorities, banks are a

suitable tool for long-term capital provision. The same cannot be said about markets, at least not in the institutional structuring of capital markets today. While individual investors may be long-term oriented, markets as we know them tend to focus on the short term.

2. Bank-led finance is linked to relatively weak corporate governance, in the sense of weak shareholder control over the company's fate. De facto, Japanese firms remain mostly under the control of insiders, and thus ultimately of employees. They can afford to do so because their ability to obtain funding from banks, instead of capital markets, deprives shareholders of an important source of leverage.

3. Weak corporate governance is linked to cross-shareholdings and takeover defences such as poison pills. They further help insulate management from shareholder pressure in the form of the threat of selling to the highest bidder in the context of a hostile takeover.

4. The combination of weak corporate governance and long-term finance enables long-term employment. Jointly, they offer at least partial protection against shareholder demands to improve profitability through lay-offs.

5. Long-term employment is a prerequisite for the seniority system. Since tenure is an important determinant of rank and pay, the current hierarchical structure of the firm would be impossible to maintain if employees frequently changed firms.

6. Long-term employment is linked to collective decision-making in the firm. Long-term employment facilitates a sense that the firm is a community, and thus increases the probability that employees take an active interest in its concerns (Dore 1973; Inagami and Whittaker 2005). This, in turn, fosters a willingness to contribute to decision-making and to find a consensus.

7. Long-term employment is connected to OJT. Japanese-style OJT, such as training and job rotations especially during the first years of employment, is expensive. Firms can only afford to engage in it if they can be reasonably certain that employees will stay with the firm long enough for there to be a positive return on the training investment.

8. Insider corporate governance is connected to peaceful labour relations. In effect, Japanese firms tend to be run by employees for employees. This means that in the inherent conflict over the distribution of value created in the firm, employees tend to have the upper hand over shareholders.

9. Consensual decision-making contributes to peaceful labour relations. Because of the flow of information in decision-making processes, transparency inside the firm is fairly high. It is therefore easy for employees and their unions to verify that the information they receive from management—for example in the context of pay negotiations—is accurate.

10. Consensual decision-making is further linked to social capital. The transparency already noted fosters institutionalized trust, that is, a willingness to believe that the company will act appropriately and fairly. Among personnel involved in direct communications, it is further likely to help build interpersonal trust.

11. Institutionalized and interpersonal trust enable the high levels of social networking in Japanese society—people usually do not network with those they do not trust.

12. Conversely, the presence of these social networks is a prerequisite for the Japanese variant of institutionalized trust. Networks provide a conduit for reputational information, which makes them a useful tool for collective social punishment.

# EVOLUTIONARY DYNAMICS

The evolutionary dynamics of the Japanese business system have attracted considerable attention in recent years. One can broadly distinguish two types of works in this vein: those exploring institutional stickiness, or inertia (e.g. Anchordoguy 2005; Schoppa 2006; Witt 2006), and those examining institutional changes (e.g. Vogel 2006; Aoki, Jackson, and Miyajima 2007; Schaede 2008; Söderberg and Nelson 2010). Though this is not immediately obvious, the pictures they present are more complementary than contradictory. The former type of work tends to focus on the state and conditions of the business system as a whole. There, aggregate statistics suggest that considerable pressure has produced only limited change, and these works seek to establish the causes of this phenomenon. The latter kind of work tends to explore how institutions are changing within limited contexts, such as individual firms or sets of them. They usually draw on case studies to identify changes and the mechanisms permitting or driving them. In other words, the first collection of works tends to examine slow change in the mean of the distribution of institutional characteristics in the business system, while the second group tends to explore how the progressive tail moves forward.

Among the sources of inertia identified in the literature, four stand out. First, the existing system has enjoyed a great deal of legitimacy, and the will to effect major changes seems to be weak, not only among people in general, but also among top managers (Vogel 2006; Witt and Redding 2009; Witt and Redding 2010). Second, the high levels of complementarities in the business systems constrain the extent of possible changes (Witt 2006). For instance, while change in a given element may be desirable, it may be difficult to implement, as doing so may require attendant changes in other elements that decision-makers would, for whatever reasons, prefer to maintain.

Third, the coordinated and consensual nature of decision-making in the Japanese political economy is prone to deadlock (Witt 2006). Factors contributing to this problem are manifold (Witt 2006). For instance, Japan needs to devise new institutional configurations mostly on the basis of conjecture and deliberation, as the unitary nature of the Japanese political economy does not provide for prior experimentation using local institutional variations, as in China or in the United States. Given the inherent uncertainty in institutional reforms and the costs of getting things wrong, the process requires extensive deliberations. Compounding this issue is the high level of institutional complementarities in the business system, as every change to a single component of the system may have knock-on effects on others. This increases complexity and thus time-intensity in decision-making. Furthermore, the consensual nature of decision-making, not just in the firm, but also in the political economy more generally, gives vested interests the power to block changes they disapprove of, even if changes are in the general interest of the nation.

A fourth major source of inertia is the low level of institutional deviance in the Japanese political economy (Anchordoguy 2005; Schoppa 2006; Witt 2006). Usually, lack of change in the formal institutional structure prompts individual actors to adjust locally by working around formal constraints. In Japan, such deviant behaviour happens at relatively low levels, which means that they cannot build up sufficient pressure on policy-makers to change the formal institutional structure. Ironically, the same social networks that enable institutionalized trust in Japan make institutional entrepreneurship difficult (Witt 2006).

While these factors contribute to slowing down institutional change processes in Japan, they do not make them impossible. In some cases, amendments to formal institutions, such as the legal changes in the area of corporate governance already discussed, enable a series of formal structural changes (though, as also mentioned, not necessarily change in actual practice) (Aoki, Jackson, and Miyajima 2007). Institutional entrepreneurship, especially by large firms with high levels of legitimacy and under pressure from foreign shareholders, may provide the impetus for legal changes, which in turn may enable further institutional entrepreneurship, and so forth (Vogel 2006).

It seems likely that these patterns of inertia and incremental change will continue into the future. At the same time, a confluence of factors is building pressure for more fundamental institutional adjustments. These include the aftermath of the 2008 financial crisis; the consequences of the 2011 earthquake, tsunami, and nuclear meltdown; the continued inability of Japan to reap the full benefits of the IT revolution (cf. Vogel forthcoming); strong competition from Korea in core areas of Japanese industrial strength; a shrinking and rapidly ageing population; and the rise of an increasingly assertive China.

# CONCLUSION

In summary, the financial system continues to be bank led, though markets have attained greater importance over the years. Corporate governance of listed firms has undergone structural changes towards the US model, but actual practice suggests continued insider control over the firm. Internal dynamics blend a hierarchical structure with a consensual decision-making process for non-routine issues, and a number of mechanisms enable lower echelons to contribute to and shape this decision-making process. Recent reforms in employment relations seem to have fine-tuned rather than destroyed lifetime/long-term employment and the seniority principle. The much-discussed rise of non-regular workers in the Japanese economy is, on closer inspection, not a sign of large-scale decline in long-term employment, but seems to signify the emergence of a new, possibly complementary, system. Labour relations are exceedingly cordial, with unions seeming to have arrested their decline and reorganizing in response to changed realities. Public education continues to excel at the general level, but is weak in vocational training, with firms filling this gap through a combination of OJT and off-JT. Inter-company relations in Japan include business groups, supplier networks, R&D consortia, and intra-industry loops. Overall, most of these networks seem to have weakened in recent years. Social capital is high on both the interpersonal and institutionalized level, with the latter maintained more through reputational mechanism than through the legal system. Complementarities among elements of the Japanese business system are strong and numerous.

Interpreted in the context of the Hall and Soskice (2001) model, Japan clearly represents a coordinated market economy (CME). Developments over previous decades seem to have pushed Japan closer to the Anglo-Saxon liberal market economy (LME) model. At the same time, it seems that the resulting partial convergence in structures—for example in the context of corporate governance—was not accompanied by a concomitant degree of convergence where it really mattered (Aoki 2007): in actual practice. Rather, Japan seems to have adapted these structures to its own liking and needs, thus providing a good example of selective adaptation and institutional hybridization (Pieterse 1994; Djelic 1998).

For the literature on comparative business systems, the present case thus suggests a need to pay more attention to practice than structure. The focus of most of the literature to date has been on formal structures. For instance, Streeck and Thelen (2005) explicitly bracket informal institutions, and the bulk of the edited volume by Aoki et al. (2007) explores changes in the formal structure of Japanese corporate governance. At some level, this emphasis on formal structure is justifiable, because economic actors in most of the advanced industrialized countries do play by the official rules of the game. However, once we move to Japan—or indeed, outside the Anglo-Saxon and northern European countries—this alignment of practice and formal structure starts to deteriorate. This suggests a need to acknowledge to a much greater extent that, in the words of Aoki (2007: 434), 'the law defines the formal rules, but [what] we should ultimately be concerned with are the "ways by which the game is actually played"'.

# ACKNOWLEDGEMENTS

I thank Harukiyo Hasegawa, Patricia A. Nelson, and Steven K. Vogel for very helpful comments. Any errors that remain are my sole responsibility.

## NOTES

1. As of late fall 2012, when this chapter was finalized.
2. The gross enrolment rate is the number of students in certain grades over the number of youths in the applicable age bracket. As a result, enrolment rates larger than 100 per cent are possible.

3. In the sense of publicly accessible.
4. Data for post-secondary non-tertiary vocational and technical programmes for Japan are unavailable.

## REFERENCES

Ahmadjian, C. L. and J. R. Lincoln (2001). '*Keiretsu*, Governance, and Learning: Case Studies in Change from the Japanese Automotive Industry'. *Organization Science* 12(6): 683–701.

——and A. Okumura (2011). 'Corporate Governance in Japan'. In C. A. Mallin, Ed., *Handbook on International Corporate Governance: Country Analyses*: 247–268. Cheltenham, Edward Elgar.

——and P. Robinson (2001). 'Safety in Numbers: Downsizing and the Deinstitutionalization of Permanent Employment in Japan'. *Administrative Science Quarterly* 46: 622–654.

Akimoto, T. and Y. Sonoda (2009). 'Labor Welfare in Japan: Social Change and Enterprise Unionism'. *Journal of Workplace Behavioral Health* 24: 243–264.

Aman, H. and P. Nguyen (2012). 'The Size and Composition of Corporate Boards in Japan'. *Asian Business and Management* 11(4): 425–444.

American Bar Association (2011). 'National Lawyer Population by State'. Retrieved 7 June 2011, from <http://www.americanbar.org/content/dam/aba/administrative/market_research/2011_national_lawyer_by_state.authcheckdam.pdf>.

Amsden, A. H. (1989). *Asia's Next Giant: South Korea and Late Industrialization*. Oxford, Oxford University Press.

Anchordoguy, M. (2005). *Reprogramming Japan: The High Tech Crisis under Communitarian Capitalism*. Ithaca, Cornell University Press.

Anheier, H. and J. Kendall (2002). 'Interpersonal Trust and Voluntary Associations: Examining Three Approaches'. *British Journal of Sociology* 53(3): 343–362.

Aoki, M. (1988). *Information, Incentives, and Bargaining in the Japanese Economy*. Cambridge, Cambridge University Press.

Aoki, M. (2007). 'Conclusion: Whither Japan's Corporate Governance?'. In M. Aoki, G. Jackson, and H. Miyajima, Eds., *Corporate Governance in Japan: Institutional Change and Organizational Diversity*: 427–448. Oxford, Oxford University Press.

Aoki, M., G. Jackson, and H. Miyajima, Eds. (2007). *Corporate Governance in Japan: Institutional Change and Organizational Diversity*. Oxford, Oxford University Press.

BIS (Bank for International Settlements) (2010). *Long-Term Issues in International Banking*. Committee on the Global Financial System Working Paper 41. Basel, Bank for International Settlements.

Caballero, R. J., T. Hoshi, and A. K. Kashyap (2008). 'Zombie Lending and Depressed Restructuring in Japan'. *American Economic Review* 98(5): 1943–1977.

Council of Bars and Law Societies of Europe (2011). 'Number of Lawyers in European Countries—2009'. Retrieved 7 June 2011 from <http://www.ccbe.eu/fileadmin/user_upload/NTCdocument/2010_Table_of_Lawyer1_1297251018.doc>.

Dalton, N. and J. Benson (2002). 'Innovation and Change in Japanese Human Resource Management'. *Asia Pacific Journal of Human Resources* 40(3): 345–362.

Djelic, M.-L. (1998). *Exporting the American Model: The Postwar Transformation of European Business*. Oxford, Oxford University Press.

Dore, R. P. (1973). *British Factory, Japanese Factory: The Origins of National Diversity in Industrial Relations*. Berkeley, University of California Press.

—— (2000). *Stock Market Capitalism: Welfare Capitalism—Japan and Germany Versus the Anglo-Saxons*. Oxford, Oxford University Press.

—— (2007). 'Insider Management and Board Reform: For Whose Benefit?'. In M. Aoki, G. Jackson, and H. Miyajima, Eds., *Corporate Governance in Japan: Institutional Change and Organizational Diversity*: 370–398. Oxford, Oxford University Press.

Dyer, J. H. (1996). 'Does Governance Matter? *Keiretsu* Alliances and Asset Specificity as Sources of Japanese Competitive Advantage'. *Organization Science* 7(6): 649–666.

Fukuyama, F. (1995). *Trust: The Social Virtues and the Creation of Prosperity*. New York, Free Press.

Gerlach, M. L. (1992). *Alliance Capitalism: The Social Organization of Japanese Business*. Berkeley, University of California Press.

Hagen, J. M. and S. Choe (1998). 'Trust in Japanese Interfirm Relations: Institutional Sanctions Matter'. *Academy of Management Review* 23(3): 589–600.

Hall, P. A. and D. Soskice (2001). 'An Introduction to Varieties of Capitalism'. In P. A. Hall and D. Soskice, Eds., *Varieties of Capitalism*: 1–68. Oxford, Oxford University Press.

Hirschmeier, J. and T. Yui (1981). *The Development of Japanese Business, 1600–1980*. London, Allen & Unwin.

Iida, T. and J. Morris (2008). 'Farewell to the Salaryman? The Changing Roles and Work of Middle Managers in Japan'. *International Journal of Human Resource Management* 19(6): 1072–1087.

Inagami, T. and D. H. Whittaker (2005). *The New Community Firm: Employment, Governance and Management Reform in Japan*. Cambridge, Cambridge University Press.

Ito, T. (1992). *The Japanese Economy*. Cambridge, MA, MIT Press.

Jacoby, S. M. (2005). *The Embedded Corporation: Corporate Governance and Employment Relations in Japan and the United States*, Princeton, Princeton University Press.

Japan Association of Corporate Directors (2012). '委員会設置会社リスト（上場企業) [List of Companies That Have Established Committees (Listed Enterprises)]'. Tokyo, Japan Association of Corporate Directors. Retrieved 14 August 2012 from <http://www.jacd.jp/news/gov/120720_02report.pdf>.

Japan Federation of Bar Associations (2011). '日弁連の会員 [Members of the Japanese Federation of Bar Associations]'. Retrieved 7 June 2011 from <http://www.nichibenren.or.jp/ja/jfba_info/membership/index.html>.

Japan Institute for Labour Policy and Training (2011). 'Industrial Relations'. Retrieved 3 June 2011 from <http://www.jil.go.jp/english/estatis/eshuyo/201106/e0701.htm>.

Japan Productivity Center (2010). '平成22年度新入社員 (2,663人) の「働くことの意識」調査結果 [Results of the 2010 Survey of New Recruits (2,663 Individuals) About "Thinking About Work"]'. Tokyo, Japan Productivity Center.

Johnson, C. (1982). *MITI and the Japanese Miracle: The Growth of Industrial Policy 1925–1975*. Stanford, Stanford University Press.

Jones, R. S. (2007). 'Income Inequality, Poverty and Social Spending in Japan'. *OECD Economics Department Working Papers*. Paris, OECD.

Keizer, A. B. (2011). 'Flexibility in Japanese Internal Labour Markets: The Introduction of Performance-Related Pay'. *Asia Pacific Journal of Human Resources* 28(3): 573–594.

Kumon, S. (1992). 'Japan as a Network Society'. In S. Kumon and H. Rosovsky, Eds., *The Political Economy of Japan, Volume 3: Cultural and Social Dynamics*: 109–141. Stanford, Stanford University Press.

Lincoln, J. R. (1990). 'Japanese Organization and Organization Theory'. *Research in Organizational Behavior* 12: 255–294.

—— and M. L. Gerlach (2004). *Japan's Network Economy: Structure, Persistence, and Change.* Cambridge, Cambridge University Press.

—— and M. Shimotani (2010). 'Business Networks in Postwar Japan: Whither the *Keiretsu*?' In A. M. Colpan, T. Hikino, and J. R. Lincoln, Eds., *The Oxford Handbook of Business Groups*: 127–156. Oxford, Oxford University Press.

McCann, L., J. Hassard, and J. Morris (2010). 'Restructuring Managerial Labour in the USA, UK and Japan: Challenging the Salience of "Varieties of Capitalism"'. *British Journal of Industrial Relations* 48(2): 347–374.

McGuire, J. and S. Dow (2009). 'Japanese *Keiretsu*: Past, Present, Future'. *Asia Pacific Journal of Management* 26(2): 333–351.

Ministry of Education, Culture, Sports, Science and Technology (2011). 'Statistics'. Retrieved 4 June 2011 from <http://www.mext.go.jp/english/statistics/index.htm>.

Ministry of Health, Labour and Welfare (2011a). '平成22年度「能力開発基本調査」結果 の概要 *(Summary of the Results of the 2010 Basic Survey on Development of Skills)*'. Retrieved 3 June 2011 from <http://www.mhlw.go.jp/stf/houdou/2r985200000135nu.html>.

—— (2011b). '賃金構造基本統計調査 *(Basic Survey on Wage Structure)*'. Tokyo, Ministry of Health, Labour, and Welfare.

—— (2011c). '平成22年就労条件総合調査結果の概況 *(Overview of the Results of the 2010 Comprehensive Survey on Labor Conditions)*'. Retrieved 31 May 2011 from <http://www. mhlw.go.jp/toukei/itiran/roudou/jikan/syurou/10/dl/gaiyou03.pdf>.

Ministry of Internal Affairs and Communications, Statistics Bureau (2011). 'Employees by Type of Employment'. Retrieved 10 June 2011 from <http://www.stat.go.jp/data/roudou/long-time/zuhyou/lt51.xls>.

Morishima, M. and T. Shimanuki (2005). 'Managing Temporary Workers in Japan'. *Diversification of Employment and Human Resource and Personnel Management Issues* 2(2): 78–103.

Morris, J., J. Hassard, and L. McCann (2008). 'The Resiliance of "Institutionalized Capitalism": Managing Managers under "Shareholder Capitalism" and "Managerial Capitalism"'. *Human Relations* 61(5): 687–710.

Nakamura, M. (2011). 'Adoption and Policy Implications of Japan's New Corporate Governance Practices after the Reform'. *Asia Pacific Journal of Human Resources* 28: 187–213.

Nakamura, T. (1995). *The Postwar Japanese Economy: Its Development and Structure, 1937–1994* (2nd Ed.). Tokyo, University of Tokyo Press.

National Center for Education Statistics (2009). *Highlights from Timms 2007: Mathematics and Science Achievement of US Fourth- and Eighth-Grade Students in an International Context.* Washington, DC, National Center for Education Statistics.

Nelson, P. A. (2010). 'Stability and the Status Quo: Changing Power Structures in the Optics Industry'. In M. Söderberg and P. A. Nelson, Eds., *Japan's Politics and Economy: Perspectives on Change*: 161–181. London, Routledge.

OECD (2008). 'Integrated PMR Indicator 2008'. Retrieved 13 June 2011 from <http://www.oecd. org/dataoecd/33/12/42136008.xls>.

—— (2010). *Pisa 2009 Results: What Students Know and Can Do—Student Performance in Reading, Mathematics and Science (Volume I)*. Paris, OECD.

—— (2012). '*OECD.Stat*', Paris, OECD.

Ogawa, A. (2009). *The Failure of Civil Society? The Third Sector and the State in Contemporary Japan*. Albany, SUNY Press.

Okimoto, D. I. (1989). *Between MITI and the Market: Japanese Industrial Policy for High Technology*. Stanford, Stanford University Press.

Pekkanen, S. M. (2003). *Picking Winners? From Technology Catch-up to the Space Race in Japan*. Stanford, Stanford University Press.

Pieterse, J. N. (1994). 'Globalization as Hybridization'. *International Sociology* 9(2): 161–184.

Ramseyer, J. M. and F. M. Rosenbluth (1993). *Japan's Political Marketplace*. Cambridge, Harvard University Press.

Sakakibara, M. (1997). 'Evaluating Government-Sponsored R&D Cooperatives in Japan: Who Benefits and How?' *Research Policy* 26: 447–473.

Sako, M. (1992). *Price, Quality and Trust: Inter-Firm Relations in Britain and Japan*. Cambridge, Cambridge University Press.

—— (2006). *Shifting Boundaries of the Firm: Japanese Company—Japanese Labor*. Oxford, Oxford University Press.

Samuels, R. J. (1987). *The Business of the Japanese State: Energy Markets in Comparative and Historical Perspective*. Ithaca, Cornell University Press.

Schaede, U. (2000). *Cooperative Capitalism: Self-Regulation, Trade Associations, and the Anti-Monopoly Law in Japan*. Oxford, Oxford University Press.

—— (2008). *Choose and Focus: Japan's Business Strategies for the 21st Century*. Ithaca, Cornell University Press.

Schoppa, L. J. (1993). *Education Reform in Japan: A Case of Immobilist Politics*. London, Routledge.

—— (2006). *Race for the Exits: The Unravelling of Japan's System of Social Protection*. Ithaca, Cornell University Press.

Schwab, K., Ed. (2010). *The Global Competitiveness Report 2010–2011*. Geneva, World Economic Forum.

Shishido, Z. (2007). 'The Turnaround of 1997: Changes in Japanese Corporate Law and Governance'. In M. Aoki, G. Jackson, and H. Miyajima, Eds., *Corporate Governance in Japan: Institutional Change and Organizational Diversity*: 310–329. Oxford, Oxford University Press.

Söderberg, M. and P. A. Nelson, Eds. (2010). *Japan's Politics and Economy: Perspectives on Change*. London, Routledge.

Streeck, W. and K. Thelen (2005). 'Introduction: Institutional Change in Advanced Political Economies'. In W. Streeck and K. Thelen, Eds., *Beyond Continuity: Institutional Change in Advanced Political Economies*: 1–39. Oxford, Oxford University Press.

Transparency International (2012). 'Corruption Perception Index 2011'. Retrieved 21 July 2012 from <http://www.transparency.org/policy_research/surveys_indices/cpi/2011/results>.

TSE (Tokyo Stock Exchange) (2010). '2009 Shareholdership Survey'. Tokyo, Tokyo Stock Exchange.

Tsuru, S. (1993). *Japan's Capitalism: Creative Defeat and Beyond*. Cambridge, Cambridge University Press.

United Nations Development Programme (2011). 'Education Index'. Retrieved 20 July 2012 from <http://hdrstats.undp.org/en/indicators/103706.html>.

Vogel, S. K. (1996). *Freer Markets, More Rules: Regulatory Reform in Advanced Industrial Countries*. Ithaca, Cornell University Press.

—— (2006). *Japan Remodeled: How Government and Industry Are Reforming Japanese Capitalism*. Ithaca, Cornell University Press.

—— (2013). 'Japan's Information Technology Challenge'. In D. Breznitz and J. Zysman, Eds., *Can Wealthy Nations Stay Rich?*: 350–372. Oxford, Oxford University Press.

Witt, M. A. (2006). *Changing Japanese Capitalism: Societal Coordination and Institutional Adjustment*. Cambridge, Cambridge University Press.

—— and G. Redding (2009). 'Culture, Meaning, and Institutions: Executive Rationale in Germany and Japan'. *Journal of International Business Studies* 40(5): 859–895.

—— (2010). *The Spirits of Capitalism: German, Japanese, and US Senior Executive Perceptions of Why Firms Exist*. INSEAD Working Papers. Fontainebleau and Singapore, INSEAD.

Woo-Cummings, M., Ed. (1999). *The Developmental State*. Ithaca, Cornell University Press.

World Bank (2012a). 'World Development Indicators', World Bank. Retrieved 20 July 2012 from <http://data.worldbank.org/indicator/all>.

—— (2012b). 'Worldwide Governance Indicators'. Washington, DC, World Bank. Retrieved 21 July 2012 from <http://info.worldbank.org/governance/wgi/>.

Yamagishi, T., K. S. Cook, and M. Watabe (1998). 'Uncertainty, Trust, and Commitment Formation in the United States and Japan'. *American Journal of Sociology* 104(1): 165–194.

—— and M. Yamagishi (1994). 'Trust and Commitment in the United States and Japan'. *Motivation and Emotion* 18(2): 129–166.

Yoshikawa, T. and J. McGuire (2008). 'Change and Continuity in Japanese Corporate Governance'. *Asia Pacific Journal of Management* 25: 5–24.

# CHAPTER 7

## LAOS

### *Frontier Capitalism*

### EDO ANDRIESSE

THIS chapter focuses on the second smallest economy in South East Asia, after Timor-Leste, Lao People's Democratic Republic, hereafter referred to as Laos. Laos as a territorial entity is a product of the colonial era, in which the French sought to disconnect the area east of the Mekong River from the economy and culture of Siam (contemporary Thailand) (Ivarsson 2008). In addition, the Vietnam War caused enormous havoc in Laos, with communists and pro-North Vietnamese forces fighting non-communists, largely made up of ethnic minorities such as the Hmong people. In 1975, the Lao People's Revolutionary Party (hereafter referred to as the Party) claimed victory and has ruled the country ever since.

Laos, however, remained a purely communist country for only eleven years. The Party, facing external debts and an economy in shambles and in the light of economic reforms in the USSR and China announced the New Economic Mechanism (NEM) in 1986, similar to Vietnam's Doi Moi reforms and associated economic opening-up (Stuart-Fox 1997: 195–201). The NEM has been responsible for the entry of capitalist institutions, privatization, a remarkable opening up of markets and the influx of foreign direct investment (FDI). Nevertheless, the political system has remained strictly authoritarian. The Politburo of the Communist Party is in firm control of all political activities and the Secretary-General of the Party is also President of the Republic.

This chapter assesses the current business system in Laos. Given the socio-economic poverty in the country and the transitory nature of capitalist institutions, it is no surprise that Laos does not fit into any established Asian business system (Carney, Gedajlovic, and Yang 2009). Instead, this chapter will conclude that at this stage the business system can be characterized as a state-coordinated *frontier* economy, as compared to Singapore, which is a state-coordinated *liberal market* economy. The Singaporean state has been highly instrumental in fostering certain industries, upgrading technological capabilities and levels of education and advanced skills, while maintaining a liberal market environment (Ritchie 2009). The narrative for Laos is obviously markedly different. The following sections discuss the interactions between the public and (foreign) private sectors and justify the choice of description as a frontier economy. It should also be noted that relatively few academics have written on capitalist institutions in Laos, especially on ownership and corporate governance, internal structure of firms' employment relations, and state-owned enterprises (SOEs); fortunately, however, the development community has prepared a number of excellent reports (notably UNDP 2006, 2009; Ngongvongsithi and Keola 2009). This is particularly so with the clothing industry, which is the leading factory-based industry in the country, and can thus in certain circumstances provide a useful illustration of the current business system in Laos.

# FRONTIER CAPITALISM

As Laos is generally less well known as a country, this section starts with a brief overview of its socio-economic situation. The population of just over 6 million is small in the South East Asian context, as is the economy; moreover, 76 per cent of the labour force works in agriculture (ADB 2011a). Important agricultural produce includes rice and sugar from the lowlands and timber, rubber, and coffee from the hills. In the latest UNDP Human Development Report, Laos is ranked 122 in the human development index (HDI), with a value of 0.497. Timor-Leste is ranked above Laos (120), whereas Cambodia (124) and Burma/Myanmar (132) are somewhat lower (UNDP 2010: 145). The high reliance on development aid also reflects the relatively low level of human development. Official development assistance accounts for 10 per cent of the gross national income (UNDP 2010: 204).

According to the International Monetary Fund, the top three exports in 2008 were copper, clothing, and timber (IMF 2009). The top three export destinations are Thailand, Vietnam, and China. Another important export 'item' is labour, as wages in Thailand and other countries are much higher. It is estimated that around 300,000 legal and irregular Lao labourers work in Thailand (UNDP 2009: 157). Clothing, wood products, and processed foods have a high potential for export and thus are useful from a human development perspective (generating employment and limiting environmental pollution, if managed well), but in the contemporary Lao political economy, the booming industries are copper- and gold-mining and hydropower, industries that generate little employment and degrade the natural environment (UNDP 2006; DIE 2009). Ten years ago there were no copper exports; in 2008 the export value totalled US$620.3 million (IMF 2009). Another example is the development of new bauxite mines in Southern Laos (Lao Voices 2011). Laos aims to be a kind of *battery*, as it were, for neighbouring countries. At the end of 2010 the completed Nam Theun 2 dam (NT2) and hydropower facility began selling electricity to Thailand (Bangkok Post 2010a).

The current trends in Lao mining and hydropower are part of a wider economic geographical phenomenon which can be described as a resource frontier, that is, a process of change which involves three interlocking elements: population dynamics (notably migration), land use, and the geography of economic activities. As Armstrong (1991) states, the frontier is a dynamic process of spatial interaction, where resource-rich regions can be incorporated into national economic space. In fact, in the Lao case it is more appropriate to think of international economic spaces, as foreign companies have had a high impact on unoccupied resource-rich regions (see also Hayter, Barnes, and Bradshaw 2003 for a more theoretical exposition of resource peripheries). Thai companies, for example, have invested in sugarcane plantations in Southern Laos, the Chinese state-owned copper importer Minmetals owns a copper and gold mine in Savannakhet province, Chinese and Vietnamese are involved in rubber plantations in the northern and southern provinces respectively, and the NT2 dam is a complex project involving direct investment by Thailand and France (Cohen 2009; Baird 2010; Bangkok Post 2010a; International Rivers 2010; Shrestha 2010). The resource frontier 'captures empirical reality concerning the political economy of rapid and uneven development in the country' (Barney 2009: 150). It should be noted, however, that foreign investors have not only made inroads in resource frontiers, but also in manufacturing industries such as clothing and motorcycle assembly (Ngongvongsithi and Keola 2009). Between 2000 and 2005, net average FDI inflow as a percentage of gross domestic product (GDP) was only 1.3 per cent, but between 2006 and 2009 it rose to 5.8 per cent (ADB 2011a).

For the purpose of this chapter, we need to zoom in on the manufacturing sector (including power generation and mining), as this sector displays most clearly the emergence of certain capitalist institutions in Lao's development trajectory. Table 7.1 shows that a relatively large number of people work in the construction material business and that food and agro-processing firms generally employ few workers, whereas each hydropower facility and mining site employs a reasonable number of workers, but does not contribute much to employment generation for the Lao economy in general.

# ROLE OF THE STATE

Although the power of the state has somewhat diminished since the economic reforms instigated in 1986, it remains a very important economic actor. The Party portrays itself as the ultimate mentor of society. The government allows the private sector to start and conduct businesses, and foreign investors are welcomed, but there are no signs whatsoever of a gradual shift towards a multi-party democracy. The Party is responsible for all major political appointments at all government layers inside and outside Vientiane: 'the government is merely the executive arm of the Party' and 'there is no distinction between the Party and the judiciary' (Stuart-Fox 2006: 65, 70). The government-controlled *Vientiane Times* frequently publishes articles on successes and achievements in terms of poverty reduction, as if the government has become a truly developmental state. In reality, however, high economic growth rates since the 1990s have not led to sufficiently corresponding levels of poverty reduction (as occurred in Malaysia, Thailand,

Table 7.1 The manufacturing sector in Laos, 2006

| Industry | Number of establishments | Number of employees |
|---|---|---|
| Construction materials | 10,300 | 100,720 |
| Food and agro-processing | 18,855 | 35,000 |
| Clothing | 82 | 25,000 |
| Wood products | 2,200 | 25,000 |
| (Hydro)power generation | 10 | 7,000 |
| Mining | 30 | 6,000 |
| Others | 119 | 10,500 |
| Total | 31,596 | 209,220 |

Source: Ngongvongsithi and Keola 2009.

and Indonesia in the 1980s and 1990s and is happening now in China and Vietnam) and there have been increasing signs of the predatory nature of the state. The government does not seem to focus much on citizens displaced to make way for dams and reservoirs for hydropower, mining sites, and special economic zones, corruption is pervasive (see also the section 'Social Capital'), and the distribution of 'frontier revenues' to disadvantaged groups in society has been very limited (Shrestha 2010; Smith 2011). In four provinces, the percentage of people living below the national poverty line increased between 2002/03 and 2007/08; in the case of Vientiane Province this was probably a result of in-migration from more remote provinces (UNDP 2009: 215). It seems that Laos is governed in a more top-down fashion than China and Vietnam (Flint 2011; Witt 2014). There are in fact no incentives to implement any form of bottom-up decision structures.

Doing business in Laos is hampered by a heavy regulatory burden. Laos was ranked 165 out of 183 countries in the World Bank's 'ease of doing business' 2012 table; a year earlier it ranked 163. This makes Laos the worst South East Asian country in which to do business, after Timor-Leste. Cambodia is ranked 138, Vietnam 98, and Thailand 17 (World Bank 2012: 6). It takes 93 days to start a business, and the country ranks 182 in terms of investor protection (World Bank 2012: 107). A large number of protected state-owned enterprises further limit growth opportunities for small and medium-sized enterprises (SMEs). In subsequent sections it will be revealed how the regulatory burden and strong direct state intervention affect major institutional economic arrangements.

# FINANCIAL SYSTEM

The financial system is still in its infancy. Many transactions, especially in the tourism industry and in provinces bordering on Vietnam and Thailand, take place in foreign currencies, such as the Thai baht, the Vietnamese dong, or the US dollar, rather than Lao's own currency, the kip. Although the government is trying to institutionalize the Lao kip, there has been little success so far.

The financial industry has just celebrated a milestone. At the end of 2010 the Lao Stock Exchange started operating, with the initial public offering of two companies: Électricité du Laos (EDL), a spin-off from a state-owned company, and the partly state-owned Banque Pour Le Commerce Exterieur (BCEL) (New Straits Times 2010). The aim of this Exchange in the near future is to offer share trading in around twenty state-owned companies (People's Daily Online 2009; Vientiane Times 2011). Nevertheless, it remains to be seen to what extent the Lao Stock Exchange turns out to be a real success.

Banks are important for Laos, particularly for state-owned and foreign firms. Four groups characterize the banking industry: four state-owned commercial banks (controlling around 60 per cent of total banking sector assets), three joint ventures, two privately owned banks and fourteen foreign branches (World Bank 2011a: 17). At least five major Thai banks have opened branches in Vientiane, mainly catering to the many Thai investors in the country. Capital is patient for large companies who can easily borrow money from state-owned banks, but for small and medium-sized companies it has been difficult to obtain access to finance from banks and the interest rate is high (Ngongvongsithi and Keola 2009). The situation is as follows:

> The state banking system is still weak and burdened by non-performing loans to state-owned enterprises (SOEs)...Many Lao private firms without any FDI have limited or no access to credit. As a result, some of these firms are unable to invest enough and remain too small, unable to take advantage of economies of scale, less able to compete with imports, and less able to make investments to protect the environment. (UNDP 2006: 10)

These comments also hold for smaller firms in the clothing industry. There is a lack of working capital, and borrowing money is a cumbersome process. For certain companies the financial system is 'simply not at all accessible' (UNDP 2006: 47). On the other hand, companies that have teamed up with foreign investors, often former SOEs, have had much easier access to finance, notably in the fields of power generation, rubber, and sugarcane production, mining and industry, and handicrafts. Companies from neighbouring countries have been particularly involved (Table 7.2). Foreign capital in the hydropower industry is patient, mainly due to the huge demand for energy in neighbouring Thailand. Yet investors in other industries seek shorter-term gains and can divest easily should the international economic landscape change. Laos Microfinance is a relatively new industry that could have benefits for small enterprises in the future, but there is a need for a regulatory framework to enable and facilitate long-term access to this type of finance (Badiola 2008). International donors have been active in the starting-up of microfinance, but their long-term commitment is not guaranteed because of changing interests and the increasing political and financial constraints of donor countries.

In sum, the financial system is state-mediated. Access to finance still depends on the relationship a company has with the government. For instance, EDL Generation and

**Table 7.2 Approved FDI in percentages 2003–2008**

| By country* | | By sector | |
|---|---|---|---|
| Thailand | 23.7 | Power generation | 53.9 |
| China | 16.9 | Agriculture | 11.4 |
| Vietnam | 9.3 | Mining | 9.8 |
| Japan | 5.8 | Industry and Handicraft | 7.5 |
| France | 5.7 | Services | 4.3 |
| India | 4.8 | Trading | 3.8 |
| South Korea | 4.7 | Construction | 2.9 |
| Australia | 4.6 | Hotel and Restaurant | 2.6 |
| Malaysia | 1.8 | Other activities | 3.7 |
| Singapore | 1.4 | | |
| Others | 21.3 | | |

\* Preliminary 2011 data based on cumulative FDI between 2000 and 2010 suggest Vietnam ranks No. 1, closely followed by China and Thailand (Business in Asia 2011).
*Source*: IMF 2009.

BCEL are clearly very well connected to the public sector. BCEL frequently finances the investments of SOEs such as Lao Airlines. Also, many of the firms currently operating joint ventures with foreign companies are in effect direct or indirect SOEs.

# OWNERSHIP AND CORPORATE GOVERNANCE

Entrepreneurial activity in general has experienced a boost since the 1990s. The proportion of agriculture in terms of GDP declined from 61 per cent in 1990 to 31 per cent in 2010 (ADB 2011a), while many mining and manufacturing firms have opened their doors. At present several types of firm operate in Laos: small and medium-sized firms, joint ventures between the Lao government and foreign firms, joint ventures between private Lao and foreign firms, between 160 and 200 traditional SOEs, and an unknown number of unregistered firms operating in the informal economy. Lao citizens own informal, micro- and small firms, whereas foreigners and the government are strong and active among medium-sized and large firms (Onphanhdala and Suruga 2010).

In the 1990s, the government privatized many SOEs, notably in the agricultural sector, yet owing to a lack of openness the precise size and boundaries of SOEs are not entirely clear (Bertelsmann Stiftung 2009). In 1989, at the beginning of the economic reforms, Laos had 640 SOEs (Quang and Thavisay 1999). Stuart-Fox (2006) mentioned a total of 158 SOEs using World Bank data (of which 50 were owned by line ministries within central government and the remainder by provincial governments), but the Lao media generally put the figure closer to 200 (see, for example, Vientiane Times 2011). SOEs are particularly strong in the transportation, telecommunications, electricity, insurance, and banking industries (Leung, Thanh, and Viseth 2005). Indeed, trade in services is a major topic in current negotiations concerning Laos's accession to the World Trade Organization (WTO). The Ministry of Finance influences the financial management of SOEs, has the right to inspect state-owned entities, and its State Assets Department has a coordinating role in all state-owned entities and assets at the national and local level. In addition, despite privatization and the influx of FDI into former SOEs the government has retained considerable corporate influence through networks of political patronage (see section 'Social Capital') and mediation through the state-owned commercial banks (see section 'Ownership and Corporate Governance').

A detailed study on industrial upgrading estimated that there were 31,596 manufacturing establishments in 2006 and 81,780 wholesale, retail trade, and repairing establishments. With 20,820 establishments in an array of other sectors, Laos has a total of 134,196 establishments (Ngongvongsithi and Keola 2009). Within the private sector, domestic shareholders play a relatively minor role, which makes the Lao economy highly dependent on the strategies and financial capabilities of foreign companies (UNDP 2009: 95). This is especially a problem in key sectors such as mining and clothing. Virtually all mining companies have foreign involvement, and about 75 per cent of the export-oriented clothing factories are foreign-owned.

The concepts of accounting, auditing, and corporate governance are in effect new to Laos. Foreign companies operating in Laos use the services of international firms such as Pricewaterhouse Coopers, but financial reporting among Laos-owned companies is often limited. Until 2009 no university offered an accounting programme, but the National University of Laos now has a faculty of economics and business administration and the Laos–Japan Human Development Institute offers courses on business management. Meanwhile, Laos is working on improvements over a range of issues, including the setting-up of training facilities, standardization, adoption of international best practices, improving governance of microfinance and rural finance, and specific financial reporting requirements for SMEs (World Bank 2009; ADB 2011b).

## INTERNAL STRUCTURE OF THE FIRM

Few studies deal explicitly with the internal structure of firms. Doing objective research within SOEs or companies somehow connected to the state is not easy, owing to the lack of openness and transparency (Bertelsmann Stiftung 2009). Only one study has explicitly scrutinized SOE operations, mostly, however, focusing on human resource development (see section 'Inter-Company Relations'). It detected the following managerial problems: 'Constant conflicts in control among line ministries, the Ministry of Finance and the Prime Minister's Office; lack of corporate strategy and well-defined autonomy, and unclear and slow decisions from policy-makers hinder SOEs' efforts to improve effectiveness and efficiency level' (Quang and Thavisay 1999: 105). The efficiency of SOEs is further hampered by their reliance on patronage, often linked to the Party. Employees who are well-connected are promoted irrespective of their skills and capabilities (Bertelsmann Stiftung 2009).

There are more recent data on SMEs. A study reporting results of interviews with fifty-two SMEs in Vientiane, Luang Prabang, and Savannakhet focuses somewhat more on the relationships between SMEs and the external competitive environment, but does provide some insights into internal affairs. Most SMEs are family-run businesses focusing more on day-to-day operations than on longer-term strategic planning. Business owners manage their firms in a top-down fashion, with little input from employees who are not relatives, neighbours, or friends, and learn more from their parents than from their time in education or training facilities. Family membership has frequently been one of the most important criteria for employee promotion. The interviewed SMEs in Luang Prabang, active in the hotel and tourism industry, have a somewhat more liberal attitude towards employees. Competition is stiff, and managers of hotels, restaurants, and travel agencies need to make sure that employees do their best to attract customers. On average, however, entrepreneurs do little to motivate employees (see section 'Ownership and Corporate Governance'). In sum, there is in general limited entrepreneurial experience and a lack of professional business administration and managerial skills and external networking (Southiseng and Walsh 2010a). These results resemble the observation that SMEs employ relatives and friends, rather than professional employees without any prior connection to the employer (Rehbein 2007: 67). On the one hand, these results are logical, as the private sector itself, as a phenomenon, is only around twenty-five years old. On the other hand, it seems that the government pays insufficient attention to the development of SMEs, particularly with respect to professionalizing internal structures. Many employees are forced to fend for themselves and participate little in decision-making processes (Onphanhdala and Suruga 2010).

## EMPLOYMENT RELATIONS

Working conditions among waged workers are still harsh; the judiciary rarely enforces the 2006 labour law and workers are insecure and vulnerable. It is possible to identify four phases in Laos's employment relations: the colonial era; the Royal Lao Government era, between 1947 and 1975 (very much affected by the Vietnam War, of course); the communist era, between 1975 and 1986; and the post-1986 era, in which formal and informal capitalist institutions have made serious inroads into the Lao development trajectory (Fry 2008). For the purpose of this chapter, the last era is the most instructive.

The continuing autocratic nature of political institutions has led to a vulnerable situation for employees, who are not allowed to strike and have limited possibilities for associations, trades unions, and collective bargaining. According to the law, unions can present claims and negotiate, but lack collective bargaining rights (Fry 2008). However, although the law allows for independent unions, the only active union accepted by the government so far has been the Lao Federation of Trade Unions (LFTU), which is very closely linked to the Party (ITUC 2011). The LFTU manages and controls all branches, organized at government office, company, and provincial level. Moreover, wages in Laos are very low, putting the majority of workers in a difficult position. Labour laws and the Constitution adopted in 1991 have not been helpful for employees. In a report by UNIDO in 2003, the only item (out of nineteen) for which Laos scored ten out of ten for being 'market-based' was wages (Fry 2008). One can conclude that business owners perceive labour as an input factor which can be exploited. There is more room for manoeuvre for employers. Employer associations, such as Lao National Chamber of Commerce and Industry (LNCCI) and the Association of the Lao Garment Industry (ALGI), are relatively free to promote their industries (see also section 'Internal Structure of the Firm').

In a large survey among 800 urban workers in four cities, 34 per cent of clothing factory workers had signed contracts, and only 6 per cent of hotel and tourism workers (UNDP 2009: 141–158). This, combined with a top-down internal firm structure, implies that the majority of workers are highly dependent on the will of employers. The survey also found the average working time of waged workers to be around 55 hours per week, whereas the government has set a limit of 48 hours; moreover, 50 per cent of labourers working with machines, chemicals, and electrical equipment appear to be insufficiently protected. Consequently, employment is generally short term. Many switch between waged work and (self-employed) activities in the informal sector, occasionally returning to their villages in rural areas or seeking work as irregular migrants abroad. The weak institutional position of labour in Laos's political economy has not culminated in a decisive comparative advantage, as happened in Indonesia, Thailand, and Malaysia in the 1980s and 1990s, since other production and transaction costs remain high (UNDP 2006; World Bank 2012: 107). More generally, the harsh working conditions, low wages, and poor employee protection have contributed to labour migration to Thailand (see section 'Role of the State'). The UNDP has lobbied for institutional mechanisms for labour market information, particularly for workers in the more vulnerable so-called 'lower circuit'.

## EDUCATION AND SKILLS FORMATION

Primary education in Laos has improved remarkably and in general has a reasonably good geographical coverage. The literacy rate among over-15s was 60 per cent in 1995, but improved to 73 per cent in 2005, and for a few years now almost everybody aged between 15 and 25 years has been able to read and write (UNDP 2009: 23). Nevertheless, there is a pressing need to expand and improve secondary education (UNESCO 2000). In some parts of the country, children need to travel great distances to high schools. Another critical issue is the quality of education. A shift in national budget priorities would be welcome in this respect. According to the UNDP (2010: 204), Laos spent 2.3 per cent of its GDP on education between 2000 and 2007. This percentage is quite low, considering that Thailand spent 4.9 per cent and Vietnam, also a country in transition, 5.3 per cent. Higher education has expanded since the start of the new economic mechanism (NEM) in 1986. The only comprehensive university in the country is the National University of Laos in Vientiane, but several other small universities and many private colleges and institutes were set up after 2000 (Ogawa 2008).

Despite the improvements, education and skills formation pose a great challenge in contemporary Laos. Only 37 per cent of men aged over 25 and 23 per cent of women have completed secondary education, a sign of serious gender inequality (UNDP 2010: 158). Many commentators on Laos have said that the country does not suffer from a shortage of labour, but from a shortage of *skilled* labour (see, for example, UNDP 2006: 47; Cornford 2006; Rasiah 2009). The educational system is still in transition and clearly needs massive improvements, but two interrelated complex problems arise. First, owing to the extremely low salaries of teachers and university lecturers, it is not easy to attract motivated and skilled educators (Rehbein 2007: 106). To make a reasonable living, most teachers and lecturers need second jobs. Second, around 50 per cent of the Lao population, mainly living in peripheral upland areas, have grown up using languages other than Lao, such as Mon-Khmer, Tibeto-Burman, Miao-Yao, or Viet-Muong (Rehbein 2007: 96). This makes them hard to integrate into mainstream society. Therefore, encouraging unemployed men and women to migrate to places where work is available is not always advisable, although improvements are likely in future, owing to the much higher literacy rates among younger people (Cornford 2006; Cohen 2009).

The available sources on skills formation and training in the private sector paint a bleak picture. In the 1990s, SOEs undertook annual performance appraisals and increased efforts to enhance skill levels among employees, but managers rarely had a modern perspective on human resources management. It has been a process on the sidelines rather than integrated in corporate plans and viewed as a key ingredient for growth. Moreover, each line ministry had different ideas on human resources management, leading to an absence of standardization among the various SOEs (Quang and Thavisay 1999). The current situation is not known, but the combined insights into employment relations and the remainder of this section suggest that few SOEs have made much progress.

Research among SMEs indicates that they value honesty, good manners, ability to speak Vietnamese, Chinese, and English, and experience over educational level (Southiseng and Walsh 2010a). Obviously, experience is a source of skills, but entrepreneurs view it as something that employees acquire naturally, instead of an asset that can be strategically nurtured through guidance and training. And with respect to entrepreneurs themselves, small urban entrepreneurs who have completed secondary education and small rural entrepreneurs who have completed primary education perform significantly better than those who did not (Onphanhdala and Suruga 2010). In addition, a comparative analysis of human resource development practices in the Thai and Lao telecommunications industry reveals that Thai telecommunications companies are doing much more to improve their employees' capabilities (Southiseng and Walsh 2010b). Insights from the relatively well-studied clothing industry confirm the lack of proactive human resources development. Major obstacles to further growth are a lack of skilled labour, high turnover, and the lack of efficiency wages—'paying above-market wages to retain the best workers, increase productivity and reduce training costs' (UNDP 2006: 47). Those obstacles might may become a serious threat to the survival of the clothing industry in the event of the removal of preferential trading regimes by developed import and trading blocs/countries, such as the European Union and USA (Rasiah 2009). In that case, clothing factory owners, particularly foreign ones, could opt for relocation to cheaper areas near seaports, such as in Cambodia or Vietnam. The end of the WTO-led Multi-Fibre Arrangement and associated quotas in 2005 has already led to problems for the industry. Note that high transportation costs remain a burden for any industry in Laos (Ngongvongsithi and Keola 2009; National Statistics Centre n.d.). Although the education and skills formation system will probably be in transition until 2030 or so, it is fair to conclude that Laos as of now is leaning towards a model in which the government and entrepreneurs value labour more as an exploitable input factor than as human capital.

## Inter-Company Relations

No study has dealt explicitly with inter-company relations among SOEs and in the mining, hydropower generation, and plantation industries, three activities operating in Laos's resource frontiers. Nevertheless, it is possible to infer inter-company relations from authors who have studied socio-economic changes in the frontiers. Frontier industries need approval and licences from the Lao government before resource extraction or the development of plantations can be embarked upon, and as in all frontiers there is a tendency to 'first come, first served'. Therefore, companies interested in beginning operations tend to cultivate good relations with the government and consider other companies as competitors who should be kept at bay rather than as possible partners for cooperation. For example, the Japanese company Oji Paper purchased BGA Forestry in 2005, a company which held the original concession to start commercial eucalyptus plantations in Khammouane province totalling 150,000 hectares (Barney 2009). In 2008, seventeen large, mostly foreign, companies obtained concessions to start large-scale rubber plantations (Baird 2010) and even the military granted a rubber plantation concession to a Chinese company (Cohen 2009).

Furthermore, the new Lao Holding State Enterprise increasingly engages in joint ventures with foreign companies, an indication of the continuing relevance of state mediation, as in France between the 1950s and 1980s and in Malaysia (Schmidt 2003;

Andriesse and van Westen 2009). This state enterprise is part of the Ministry of Finance and mainly operates in hydropower generation, but will presumably venture into other industries as well. Currently, it has a 25 per cent stake in the NT2 dam; Électricité de France International has 40 per cent and the Electricity Generating Company of Thailand 35 per cent (International Rivers 2010). As the tax base in Laos is very narrow, the government is eager to find ways of boosting revenues. Frontier industries provide an excellent opportunity for generating royalties, export duties and other revenues. For instance, the export duty for electricity is 20 per cent of the invoice value (IMF 2009), which means that NT2 will become a huge contributor to the Lao state coffers. The government privatized many companies in the 1990s, but new entities such as the Lao Holding State Enterprise will ensure the continuing influence of the Party on domestic inter-company relations and relations with foreign direct investors in the medium term.

Once again, a look at the clothing industry brings more in-depth insights into current inter-company relations, particularly among SMEs. In a case study on SME development, twenty clothing manufacturers were surveyed. External networking seems non-existent. Out of twenty SMEs, only one was in touch with the Small and Medium-Sized Enterprise Promotion and Development Office (SMEPDO), and none with ALGI. Furthermore, company owners have insufficient market information, for instance about industry trends, the ASEAN Economic Community, and the implications of the ASEAN–China free trade area (UNDP 2006: 48; Kyophilavong 2009). Several shortcomings exist:

> Small and medium companies tend to operate on their own, a risky policy in an increasingly competitive market, and the team points to strengthened networks within the garment industry, where larger companies, ALGI and the government should develop mechanisms to assist small and medium companies in the sector. (National Statistics Centre n.d.)

Indeed, ALGI and the Lao National Chamber of Commerce seem to be vehicles for large enterprises, joint ventures, and SOEs than for SMEs. Another problem for SMEs is the supply side. Most inputs for clothing manufacturing come from abroad (IMF 2009; Rasiah 2009) and SMEs find it difficult to foster good relations with foreign suppliers.

Besides clothing, food and agro-processing is a suitable export industry (UNDP 2006; DIE 2009). An analysis of the coffee industry in Southern Laos confirms this. The value of coffee exports has increased steadily since the inception of the NEM, from US$10 million in 1986 to US$29 million in 2008 (FAO 2011). Another positive factor is that two larger firms have been able to capture part of the high value-added activities from foreign actors. Value addition such as roasting and packaging used to be carried out abroad, but Lao companies are increasingly taking over such activities. Furthermore, the Lao Coffee Export Association has been instrumental in providing access to foreign buyers and foreign coffee experts. Nowadays, Germany, France, and Japan are the top three destinations for Lao coffee and in Bangkok's supermarkets it is sold as a fashionable gourmet product (Andersson, Engvall, and Kokko 2007). Nevertheless, in order to become a truly viable industry in an eventual trading regime under WTO rules, stakeholders will need to address many issues, including the enhancement of inter-company relations (DIE 2009: 104–115).

Overall, inter-company relations are virtually absent among SMEs. While medium and large companies foster ties with the state, micro- and small companies operate in isolation without the involvement of business associations and other forms of inter-company relations (Onphanhdala and Suruga 2010). The Lao government is not only a facilitator of the booming mining, hydropower, and plantation industries, but is also a genuine *interventionist*. This is most obvious in the strong inter-company relations between SOEs and state-owned commercial banks (Leung, Thang, and Viseth 2005; World Bank 2011a). The latter directs cheap credit to the former—a phenomenon that is politically motivated and often lacks an economic rationale.

# Social Capital

As in many other South East Asian countries, levels of interpersonalized trust in Laos are higher than institutionalized trust. Probably the only institutionalized form of trust is Party membership, which opens doors and guarantees easier access to economic opportunities. Corruption is a strong glue for cultivating and maintaining interpersonalized trust in the country (Lintner 2008; Bertelsmann Stiftung 2009). Transparency International (2011) ranks Laos at 154 in terms of corruption perception, equal with Cambodia and several other countries. In South East Asia, only Burma/Myanmar ranks lower. Furthermore, the World Bank's (2011b) world governance indicators put Laos between the zero and 10th percentiles for voice and accountability, between the 10th and 20th percentiles for government effectiveness and regulatory quality, and between the 40th and 50th percentiles for political stability and absence of violence. Laos also ranks at 110 in terms of contract enforcement (World Bank 2012: 107). These data indicate that institutionalized trust is very low.

Stuart-Fox (2006: 67) wrote an insightful qualitative account of corruption in Laos. He argues that in the last thirty years or so, the Party has become an organization in which the role of patronage has increased:

> After 1975, senior Party members soon began to dispense patronage in the traditional Lao way, rewarding extended family members and loyal retainers with jobs for which they were often poorly qualified, in order to build a political support base.... With no tradition of bureaucratic administration (as in China and Vietnam), politics in Laos reverted to competition between networks of influence and patronage cohering around senior Party officials, leading to what might be described as clientelism.

The phenomena of patronage and clientelism somewhat resemble the personal capitalism of Malaysia (Carney and Andriesse 2014). These phenomena could strengthen further if in the future the power of the Party erodes and membership ceases to be an overarching requirement. The problem with the prevailing arrangements is that hard evidence is difficult to obtain. There is no distinction between the Party, government, and judiciary; Party finances are secretive and the media are censored (Bertelsmann Stiftung 2009). At the end of 2010, the National Assembly appointed a new prime minister; the previous one had wished to crack down on corruption, but the Party did not back him (*Bangkok Post* 2010b).

For the majority of the population, nevertheless, the Party is something rather abstract and the people need to cultivate interpersonalized trust in their communities. Kinship, friendship, ethnicity, and village origin play very important roles. Such social identities often 'regulate' job-seeking in the clothing industry in Vientiane, initiating migration (irregularly) to Thailand and many other forms of economic survival. In the communist era of 1975–1986, hierarchy, reciprocity, and village patronage structured social life, but nowadays many find it difficult to cope with the capitalist features of urban individualism and competition. Migrants arriving in Vientiane without connections in the city have considerably higher chances of becoming beggars, prostitutes, criminals, or drug addicts (Rehbein 2007). In addition, ethnic Lao people look down upon ethnic minorities, and the country is geographically fragmented. In socio-economic, ethnic, and linguistic terms, Southern Laos is better connected to Vietnam and Thailand than with the rest of Laos—Vientiane has many linkages with Thailand—and Northern Laos is increasingly more connected to China than with the rest of Laos. Therefore, it cannot be expected that nationwide more neutral forms of social capital will emerge anytime soon (Andriesse 2011).

## INSTITUTIONAL COMPLEMENTARITIES

On the basis of the institutional arrangements discussed above, it is possible to identify three institutional complementarities:

1. The strong interventionist role of the state in the general political economy as discussed in section 'Role of the State', a state-mediated financial system, state-mediated inter-company relations, and the suppression of trades unions have jointly led to a business system in which large companies that are somehow connected to the Party, either through patronage or partial government ownership, can flourish (see Whitley 1999; Schmidt 2003; Tipton 2009; Andriesse and van Westen 2009 for state mediation in South Korea, France, South East Asia in general, and Malaysia respectively). On the other hand, it has resulted in disabling arrangements for SMEs. Ordinary entrepreneurs find it very difficult to obtain access to finance; the LNCCI, SMEPDO, and other business

organizations do not support SMEs, and consortia of SOEs and foreign companies are the main beneficiaries of this model. In this respect, Laos could take Thailand as an example, where state-owned banks such as the Krung Thai Bank, SME Bank and Export–Import Bank provide easy access to finance and other services to small entrepreneurs.

2. The absence of inclusive employment relations, improved but still low levels of educational attainment, low wages, insufficient levels of social capital, and the government's approval of exploiting natural resources have resulted in a frontier mentality. A 'first come, first served' arrangement steers a considerable part of the frontier economy, whereby business interests force farmers, fishermen, smallholders, and villagers to relocate to make way for large-scale frontier operations in hydropower, mining, and plantations (see, for example, International Rivers 2010 and Hirsch 2010). The lack of education and a narrow base of civil society make protesting difficult, if not impossible. This complementarity explains the current trajectory of rapid but uneven growth. The danger in the long term is increasing socio-economic inequality.

3. A virtual absence of corporate governance and on-the-job skills formation, a hierarchical internal firm structure, and the lack of trust-based inter-company relations within industries have created an institutional vacuum. Instead of industries endowed with 'institutional thickness' (Amin and Thrift 1994: 15), institutional thinness prevails, and firms in Laos's major industries are not embedded in well-organized global value chains (except for mining), industrial districts, or collaborative business systems (Whitley 1999: 43–44; Andriesse et al. 2011). Consider the clothing industry. Many actors, including the government, knew that the industry would see the end of the Multi-Fibre Arrangement and was likely to experience difficulties once preferential trading regimes for the least developed countries were toned down, but relevant stakeholders have conducted few concerted efforts to enhance the capabilities of the industry (Rasiah 2009).

# EVOLUTIONARY DYNAMICS

Twenty-five years after the birth of capitalist institutions in Laos, the country is still in a transitory phase and it is difficult to predict what kind of stable business system it will eventually attain. Cohen (2009) has concluded that the economic activities in Northern Laos are a form of *unregulated* frontier capitalism. The available evidence presented in this chapter provides a different picture. In fact the Lao government has enabled frontier capitalism through deliberate intervention in markets, notably the financial market, as well as mediation of inter-company relations. Consider the regulatory burden of doing business, the ban on the active participation of employees in decision-making processes, and the poor investment in the educational system and skills formation: it is argued here that limited deregulation in economic frontiers is an outcome (for the time being) of overarching state coordination. Laos can thus be categorized as a *state-coordinated frontier economy*. Even the clothing industry based in and around Vientiane displays frontier characteristics. Clothing factory owners seek to take advantage of low wages and preferential trading access to the USA and the EU, but could easily leave for other short-term frontiers once those advantages vanish.

Since the 1990s, the role of the market has undoubtedly increased. Privatization of SOEs, Lao's membership of ASEAN since 1997 and the influx of FDI have transformed institutional economic arrangements. This internationalization process is continuing. Laos is preparing to become a member of the WTO, and the forthcoming ASEAN Economic Community and ASEAN–China free trade area, both scheduled for 2015, necessitate major improvements in most of the institutional arrangements discussed in this chapter. The World Bank, Asian Development Bank and wider development community are supporting Laos in preparing for this economic future, but few indicators suggest that Laos's business system is improving fast enough to be able to face more competition from the neighbouring countries of Thailand, Vietnam, and Cambodia. For instance, between 2005 and 2011 Cambodia improved faster in terms of the ease of doing business than Laos (World Bank 2012: 10). Also worrying is the limited effort to foster more effective and inclusive forms of social capital that could result in a more balanced socio-economic development trajectory. The dangers of weak preparation are greater exploitation of resource frontiers and more out-migration, which would further reduce socio-economic cohesiveness.

While Laos's political economy is not changing fast and top-down state coordination is not shrinking significantly, economic frontier opportunities will remain vibrant in the coming decade. Continued internationalization as mentioned above could transform Laos into a country with some political economy features similar in the medium term to Cambodia. There, strongman Prime Minister Hun Sen at the time of writing presides over a business system known as cowboy capitalism. Rapid economic growth, improvements in the ease of doing business and quick profits for a small well-connected business elite characterize this system, but high socio-economic inequality and slow rates of poverty reduction make it rather unsustainable (Crispin 2007; Stuart-Fox 2008; Hill and Menon 2011; Kerbo 2011).

# CONCLUSION

This chapter has shown that the various institutional economic arrangements in Laos, together with political institutions and social capital, have produced a unique business system that fits neither into any major system existing in Asia (Carney, Gedajlovic, and Yang 2009) nor in the variety of capitalism literature described by Hall and Soskice (2001) and Schmidt (2003), and nor in Whitley's (1999: 43) distinctive business systems. One could argue that the strong interventionist nature of the Lao government places Laos in Whitley's *state-organized business system*, but it would be wrong to give it the same classification as his more effective and inclusive examples of South Korea and Taiwan.

Instead, it is appropriate here to give Laos the label of a *state-coordinated frontier economy*. This implies a strong role for the state, coupled with a frontier mentality in which large companies, especially those that are well connected to the Party, can thrive, owing to (1) easy access to finance through state-owned banks and foreign companies, (2) exploitation of labour as a result of a hierarchical internal firm structure, absence of measures to guarantee fundamental labour rights (maximum working hours, job safety, collective bargaining), and insufficient commitment to skills formation, and (3) a lack of social capital through which civil society can address the practices of large companies towards labour and the natural environment. The Lao business and political elite benefit from this business system, whereas SMEs, labourers, smallholders, and villagers essentially need to fend for themselves. This is in stark contrast to Singapore, an effective state-coordinated *liberal market* economy where entrepreneurs in the manufacturing and services sectors set up businesses for the long term, rather than seeking shorter-term frontier gains, and where employment generation and strong focus on education and skills formation have led to a substantial increase in the average standard of living (Ritchie 2009).

Given the extremely different circumstances of Laos from those of Singapore, simply copying the Singaporean model will not work. The task for Laos now is to incorporate appropriate pockets of Singaporean effectiveness, balanced with ameliorative policy initiatives catering to ordinary employees, displaced villagers, and the natural environment. A carefully relation-based rather than rule-based growth strategy, linking institutional arrangements to both economic growth and the plight of disadvantaged socio-economic groups, could bring the country closer to the countries of the middle-income group (Bardhan 2005: 30; Cornford 2006; Ochieng 2008; Rigg and Wittayapak 2009; Andriesse and van Westen 2009; UNDP 2010; Andriesse 2011). Too much attention to economic growth alone might lead to excessive forms of inequality such as Cambodia now faces. Nevertheless, integrating the Lao population into a capitalist system, even a modest and inclusive one, will be a difficult endeavour, as there is still a profound mismatch between the prevailing institutional economic complementarities and cultural institutions, as Rehbein (2007: 72–73) eloquently observed:

> While the habitus of most Lao is still firmly rooted in the rural past, it is now being exposed to radical changes and is under pressure to adapt to the market economy…And even if they succeed in adapting to the market economy, Lao often adhere to traditional conceptions of time, work, happiness, and behaviour that are hardly compatible with the 'spirit of capitalism'.

## REFERENCES

ADB (2011a). *Key Indicators for Asia and the Pacific 2011*. Manila, Asian Development Bank.
ADB (2011b). *Rural and Microfinance in the Lower Mekong Region: Policies, Institutions and Market Outcomes*. Manila, Asian Development Bank.
Amin, A. and N. Thrift (1994). 'Living in the Global'. In A. Amin and N. Thrift, Eds., *Globalization, Institutions and Regional Development in Europe*: 1–22. Oxford, Oxford University Press.

Andersson, M., A. Engvall, and A. Kokko (2007). *Regional Development in Lao PDR: Growth Patterns and Market Integration*. Working Paper 234. Stockholm, Stockholm School of Economics.

Andriesse, E. (2011). 'Introducing the Regional Varieties of Capitalism Approach to Lao PDR'. *ASEAN Economic Bulletin 28*(1):61–67.

——— N. Beerepoot, B. van Helvoirt, and G. van Westen (2011). 'Regional Business Systems and Inclusive/Exclusive Development in South East Asia'. In B. Helmsing and S. Vellema, Eds., *Value Chains, Inclusion and Endogenous Development: Contrasting Theories and Realities*: 151–178. Abingdon, Routledge.

——— and G. van Westen (2009). 'Unsustainable Varieties of Capitalism along the Thailand-Malaysia Border? The Role of Institutional Complementarities in Regional Development'. *Asia Pacific Journal of Management 26*(3): 459–479.

Armstrong, A. (1991). 'Resource Frontier and Regional Development: The Role of Refugee Settlement in Tanzania'. *Habitat International 15*(1/2): 69–85.

Badiola, J. (2008). 'Creating a Conducive Rural Finance and Microfinance Policy Environment in Lao PDR'. Microfinance Working Group for the Lao PDR. Retrieved 25 August 2011 from <http://www.mfwglaopdr.org/wp-content/uploads/2008/02/national-study.pdf>.

Baird, I. (2010). 'Land, Rubber, and People: Rapid Agrarian Changes in Southern Laos'. *Journal of Lao Studies 1*(1): 1–47.

*Bangkok Post* (2010a). 'PM Abhisit Leaves for Laos'. 9 December.

——— (2010b). 'Laos ex-PM Lacked Strong Support'. 24 December.

Bardhan, P. (2005) *Scarcity, Conflicts and Cooperation: Essays in the Political and Institutional Economics of Development*. Cambridge, MIT Press.

Barney, K. (2009). 'Laos: the Making of a "Relational Resource Frontier"'. *Geographical Journal 175*(2): 146–159.

Bertelsmann Stiftung (2009). *BTI 2010-Laos Country Report*. Gütersloh, Bertelsmann Stiftung.

Business in Asia (2011). 'Vietnam Leads Foreign Investment in Laos, followed by China and Thailand'. Retrieved 22 January 2012 from <http://www.business-in-asia.com/laos/fdi_in_laos.html>.

Carney, M. and E. Andriesse (2014). 'Malaysia: Personal Capitalism'. In M. A. Witt and G. Redding, Eds., *The Oxford Handbook of Asian Business Systems*: 144–168. Oxford, Oxford University Press.

——— E. Gedajlovic, and X. Yang, (2009). 'Varieties of Asian Capitalism: Toward an Institutional Theory of Asian Enterprise'. *Asia Pacific Journal of Management 26*(3): 361–380.

Cohen, P. (2009). 'The Post-Opium Scenario in Northern Laos: Alternative and Chinese Models of Development'. *International Journal of Drug Policy 20*(5): 424–430.

Cornford, J. (2006). *Globalisation and Change in Southern Laos*. Bangkok: Focus on the Global South Occasional papers 1. Retrieved from <http://www.focusweb.org/node/855>.

Crispin, S. (2007). 'Cambodia's Cowboy's Capitalism'. *Asia Times* 13 July. Retrieved 23 August 2011 from <http://www.atimes.com/atimes/Southeast_Asia/IG13Ae01.html>.

DIE (2009). *Laos on its Way to WTO Membership: Challenges and Opportunities for Developing High-Value Agricultural Exports*, Studies No. 51. Bonn, Deutsches Institut für Entwicklungspolitik.

FAO (2011). FAOstat online database. Rome: Food and Agricultural Organisation. Retrieved 27 August 2011 from <http://faostat.fao.org/site/342/default.aspx>.

Flint, Y. (2011). 'Capitalism Vietnamese-style: Combining Top-down with Bottom-up'. Paper presented at EADI-DSA conference, York, UK, 19–22 September 2011. Retrieved 9 September 2011 from <http://www.eadi.org/index.php?id=1519>.

Fry, S. (2008). 'Three Transformations of Industrial Relations in Laos'. *Journal of Industrial Relations* 50(5): 779–795.

Hall, P. and D. Soskice (2001). 'An Introduction to Varieties of Capitalism'. In P.A. Hall and D. Soskice, Eds., *Varieties of Capitalism*: 1–68. Oxford, Oxford University Press.

Hayter, R., T. Barnes, and M. Bradshaw (2003). 'Relocating Resource Peripheries to the Core of Economic Geography's Theorizing: Rationale and Agenda'. *Area* 35(1): 15–23.

Hill, H. and J. Menon (2011). 'Reducing Vulnerability in Transition Economies: Crises and Adjustment in Cambodia'. *ASEAN Economic Bulletin* 28(2): 134–159.

Hirsch, P. (2010). 'The Changing Political Dynamics of Dam-Building on the Mekong'. *Water Alternatives* 3(2): 312–323.

IMF (2009). 'Lao People's Democratic Republic: Statistical Appendix, September 2009'. IMF country report No.09/285. Retrieved 5 January 2011 from <http://www.imf.org/external/pubs/ft/scr/2009/cr09285.pdf>.

International Rivers (2010). 'Nam Theun 2 Hydropower Project: The Real Costs of a Controversial Dam'. Retrieved 6 January 2011 from <http://www.internationalrivers.org/files/NT2_factsheet_Dec10.pdf>.

ITUC (2011). 'Annual Survey of Violations of Trade Union Rights'. Retrieved 9 January 2012 from <http://survey.ituc-csi.org/>.

Ivarsson, S. (2008). *Creating Laos: The Making of a Lao Space between IndoChina and Siam, 1860–1945*. Copenhagen, Nias Press.

Kerbo, H. (2011). *The Persistence of Cambodian Poverty: From Killing Fields to Today*. Jefferson, McFarland.

Kyophilavong, P. (2009). 'SME Development in Lao PDR'. In R. Banomyong and M. Ishida, Eds., *A Study on Upgrading the Industrial Structure of CLMV Countries*, ERIA Research project 2009-7-3. Retrieved 19 December 2010 from <http://www.eria.org/publications/research_project_reports/a-study-on-upgrading-industrial-structure-of-clmv-countries.html>.

Lao Voices (2011). 'Lao Bauxite Mine Development Reaches Milestone'. Retrieved 30 October 2011 from <http://laovoices.com/2011/08/10/lao-bauxite-mine-development-reaches-new-milestone/>.

Leung, S., V. T. Thanh, and K. R. Viseth (2005). *Integration and Transition: Vietnam, Cambodia, and Lao PDR*. International and Development Economics Working Paper 05-1. Canberra, Asia Pacific School of Economics and Government.

Lintner, B. (2008). 'Laos: At the Crossroads'. *Southeast Asian Affairs 2008*. D. Singh. Singapore, ISEAS: 171–183.

National Statistics Centre (n.d.). 'Assessing the Impact of Phasing Out of Textiles and Clothing Quotas in Lao PDR'. Policy Brief. Retrieved 4 January 2011 from <http://www.nsc.gov.la/Products/Post%20ATC/Policy%20Brief%20ATC/PolicyBrief_1_Eng.pdf>.

*New Straits Times* (2010). 'Investors Line up for First IPOs in Laos', 28 December, p. B6.

Ngongvongsithi, L. and S. Keola (2009). 'Upgrading and Diversification of Industrial Structure in Lao PDR: Prospect and Challenges'. In R. Banomyong and M. Ishida Eds., *A Study on Upgrading the Industrial Structure of CLMV Countries*. ERIA research project 2009-7-3. Retrieved 19 December 2010 from <http://www.eria.org/publications/research_project_reports/a-study-on-upgrading-industrial-structure-of-clmv-countries.html>.

Ochieng, C. (2008). 'Comparative Capitalism and Sustainable Development: Stakeholder Capitalism and Co-Management in the Kenyan Fisheries Sub-Sector'. *Natural Resources Forum* 32: 64–76.

Ogawa, K. (2008). 'Higher Education in Lao People's Democratic Republic: Historical Perspective'. *Journal of International Cooperation Studies* 16(1): 105–129.

Onphanhdala, P. and T. Suruga (2010) 'Entrepreneurial Human Capital and Micro and Small Business in Lao PDR'. *Developing Economies* 48(2): 181–202.

*People's Daily* Online (2009). 'Laos to Shortlist 20 Companies for Listing in its 1st Stock Market', 25 February. Retrieved 23 November 2010 from <http://english.peopledaily.com.cn/90001/90778/90858/90863/6601060.html>.

Quang, T. and C. Thavisay (1999). 'Privatizatio and Human Resource Development Issues: A Preliminary Study of State-Owned Enterprises in the Lao People's Democratic Republic'. *Research and Practice in Human Resource Management* 7(1): 101–123.

Rasiah, R. (2009). 'Can Garment Exports from Cambodia, Laos and Burma be Sustained?'. *Journal of Contemporary Asia* 39(4): 619–637.

Rehbein, B. (2007). *Globalization, Culture and Society in Laos*. Abingdon, Routledge.

Rigg, J. and C. Wittayapak (2009). 'Spatial Integration and Human Transformations in the Greater Mekong Sub-region'. In Y. Huang and A. Bocchi, Eds., *Reshaping Economic Geography in East Asia*: 79–99. Washington, DC, World Bank.

Ritchie, B. (2009). 'Economic Upgrading in a State-Coordinated Liberal Market Economy'. *Asia Pacific Journal of Management* 26(3): 435–457.

Schmidt, V. (2003). 'French Capitalism Transformed, yet still a Third Variety of Capitalism'. *Economy and Society* 32(4): 526–554.

Shrestha, O. (2010). 'Laos: Lao People's Democratic Republic in 2009: Economic Performance, Prospects, and Challenges'. In D. Singh, Ed., *Southeast Asian Affairs 2010*: 145–152. Singapore, ISEAS.

Smith, B. (2011). 'Local Losers in Lao Casino Capitalism'. *Asia Times Online* 2 August. Retrieved 23 August 2011 from <http://www.atimes.com/atimes/Southeast_Asia/MH02Ae01.html>.

Southiseng, N. and J. Walsh (2010a). 'Competition and Management Issues of SME Entrepreneurs in Laos: Evidence from Empirical Studies in Vientiane Municipality, Savannakhet and Luang Prabang'. *Asian Journal of Business Management* 2(3): 57–72.

—— (2010b). 'A Comparison of Human Resource Development in Telecommunications Business of Thailand and Laos'. *NIDA Development Journal* 50(2): 89–127.

Stuart-Fox, M. (1997). *A History of Laos*. Cambridge, Cambridge University Press.

—— (2006). 'The Political Culture of Corruption in the Lao PDR'. *Asian Studies Review* 30: 59–75.

—— (2008). 'The Persistence of Political Culture in Laos and Cambodia'. *Journal of Current Southeast Asian Affairs* 27(3): 34–58.

Tipton, F. (2009). 'Southeast Asian Capitalism: History, Institutions, States and Firms'. *Asia Pacific Journal of Management* 26(3): 401–434.

Transparency International (2011). 'Corruption Perception Index 2010'. Berlin, Transparency International Secretariat. Retrieved 9 January 2012 from <http://www.transparency.org/policy_research/surveys_indices/cpi>.

UNDP (2006). *International Trade and Human Development: Lao PDR 2006*. Vientiane, United Nations Development Programme.

—— (2009). *4th National Development Report Lao PDR 2009: Employment and Livelihoods*. Vientiane, United Nations Development Programme.

—— (2010). *Human Development Report 2010: 20th Anniversary Edition*. New York, Palgrave Macmillan.

UNESCO (2000). 'Educational Financing and Budgeting in Lao PDR'. International Institute for Educational Planning. Retrieved 1 March 2011 from <http://www.iiep.unesco.org>.

*Vientiane Times* (2011). 'Govt to List More State Enterprises on Stock Market', 29 January: 1.

Whitley, R. (1999). *Divergent Capitalisms*. New York, Oxford University Press.

Witt, M. A. (2014). 'China: Authoritarian Capitalism'. In M. A. Witt and G. Redding, Eds., *The Oxford Handbook of Asian Business Systems*: 11–32. Oxford, Oxford University Press.

World Bank (2009). *Report on the Observance and Standards and Codes (ROSC). Lao PDR*. Washington, DC, World Bank.

—— (2011a). *Lao PDR Economic Monitor May 2011*. Vientiane, World Bank/Lao PDR Country Office.

—— (2011b). *Worldwide Governance Indicators*. Washington, DC, World Bank

—— (2012). *Doing Business 2012: Doing Business in a More Transparent World*. Washington, DC, World Bank.

# CHAPTER 8

## MALAYSIA

*Personal Capitalism*

MICHAEL CARNEY AND EDO ANDRIESSE

SINCE the implementation of the New Economic Policy (NEP) in 1971, Malaysia has attained several notable social achievements, including the virtual eradication of poverty, relatively low levels of income inequality, and significant improvements in a variety of quality-of-life indicators, including life expectancy, infant mortality, and primary school enrolment (Roslan 2003). In doing so, the state has also maintained enduring social peace among an ethnically diverse population, made up of ethnic Malays (65%), ethnic Chinese (25%), ethnic Indians (8%), and others (2%). The NEP has also been accompanied by an impressive economic performance, resulting in high levels of economic growth, low unemployment, and the construction of a world-class infrastructure, and Malaysia has become a major exporter, based on the production of high-quality electronics (Asian Development Bank 2011).

Despite these achievements, signs of economic inertia have become apparent over the past decade. Private investment as a percentage of gross domestic product (GDP) has declined to very low levels, and the country is losing its attractiveness as a destination for foreign investment. Malaysia has seen its ranking in the Global Competitiveness Index fall from 18th in 2006 to 26th in 2010 (Schwab 2010). Analysts suggest that Malaysia's economic development has 'stalled' (Henderson and Phillips 2007) and hit a 'glass ceiling' (Ohno 2009). Others suggest that Malaysia is enmeshed in a 'middle-income trap' characterized by continuing dependence upon exports of low value-added primary commodities and low-wage, low-skill manufacturing (Woo 2009; World Bank 2009, 2010). Statistics show stagnant labour productivity, as well as growing inequality between the wealthy capital city region and Penang on the one hand and a lagging periphery on the other (Woo 2009; World Bank 2010).

Successive governments have recognized the structural nature of these interrelated problems and have launched bold initiatives, such as a national information technology agenda to promote the development of information and communications technology (ICT) and the establishment of the Multi-Media Super-Corridor. There are also plans to establish a biotechnology industry (Ahn and York 2011) and a financial services hub focusing on Islamic banking (Elgindi, Said, and Salevarukis 2009). Unfortunately, there are few indications that these initiatives are meeting their primary objective of driving Malaysian industry up the value-added ladder. In this chapter we trace the origins of this incipient economic inertia to the institutionalization of state–business relations that we describe as *personal capitalism*.

Personal capitalism is characterized by concentrated enterprise ownership and the use of corporate control devices such as pyramids, dual class shares, restricted voting, and other arrangements that place significant discretion in the hands of an owner-entrepreneur (Morck, Wofenzen, and Yeung 2005). This discretion is exercised in a preference for relational contracting in which relationships with politicians and gatekeepers to financial and material resources are predicated upon patronage and the expectation of reciprocity. Owner-entrepreneurs exercise little managerial control over their subsidiaries (Tipton 2009) and rarely manage their enterprises according to a strategic plan, preferring instead to engage in opportunistic investments to buy and sell business units according to purely financial criteria (Gomez 2006, 2009). Owner-entrepreneurs are often reluctant to delegate authority and rarely dedicate resources to the development of a cadre of professional management. Personalism in the corporation is nurtured and sustained by personalism in the political domain. Politicians and other senior officials in political parties and the public bureaucracy operate a patronage-driven system in which leaders rely upon their capacity to distribute economic rents to secure political support and advance their own private business interests (Siddiquee 2010).

## ROLE OF THE STATE

The socio-political objectives of the NEP were joined with a developmental state model aimed at creating a population of Malay-owned competitive and self-sustaining corporate enterprises. Part of the developmental state model embodied a 'Look East' policy intended to imitate Japan and Korea's diversified business groups, which had pioneered technology development and the establishment of large-scale managerial enterprise (Jomo 2003). However, Malaysia's version of the developmental state differed in three key respects from the Japanese and Korean approach. First, Japan and Korea were unfriendly towards foreign investment by multinational enterprises (MNEs). As a condition for entering into relationships with domestic firms, both Japan and Korea required significant transfers of technology by foreign partners (Amsden 2009). Second, the governments of Japan and Korea rationed state credit and made its allocation conditional upon the attainment of specific export goals and organizational development. Third, to assure monopoly control over credit, both governments suppressed the development of public equity markets, which made domestic growth-oriented firms dependent upon state credit. Together, these mechanisms fostered the development of infant industries, because they provided protection, resources, and discipline for firms to develop strong organizational and technological capabilities to compete effectively with the established international competition (Amsden and Hikino 1994).

While the Malaysian state adopted an ambitious economic development agenda, several basic tenets of the Japanese/Korean developmental state model were not fully applied (Gomez 2009). First, Malaysia adopted highly liberal policies towards foreign direct investment, which resulted in substantial investment in the country, but not the transfer of technology and organizational know-how to local firms. Moreover, while the state generously allocated credit to state-owned enterprises (SOEs) and government-linked companies (GLCs), it did not make credit conditional upon the attainment of specific performance goals, nor did the state effectively monitor these loans. Third, the state also encouraged the development of public equity markets, which provided domestic firms with an alternative source of working capital. In these three respects, Malaysia simultaneously adopted a combination of the developmental state and liberal market models of development. We propose that this combination produced personal capitalism, which we survey in the following sections.

The personal nature of Malaysian capitalism also dictates that the identity of an enterprise's owner will determine his or her treatment at the hands of the state. Since gaining independence in 1957, the Malaysian state has effected four major movements against or in favour of specific types of owners. The first movement, in the immediate post-independence period, was a drive to displace the colonial-era business groups that owned and controlled large sectors of the agricultural and resource economy (Drabble and Drake 1981). The second movement consists of continuing efforts to contain ownership and control over capital by ethnic Chinese entrepreneurs. This largely self-made entrepreneurial class quickly filled the vacuum left by departing colonial owners. As ethnic Chinese business groups consolidated their position as the dominant capitalist class in Malaysia, the state engaged in countervailing action to provide space for ethnic Malay entrepreneurs. Hence, the third movement consists of long-standing efforts to create an indigenous Malay entrepreneurial class. Affirmative action programmes are intended to place 30 per cent of the ownership of the corporate sector into the hands of Muslim Malays, known as the Bumiputra (literally, sons of the soil). These programmes have engendered a variety of new government agencies, including federal and provincial investment holding companies (e.g. Khazanah Nasional), trusteeships (e.g. Amanah Raya), which nominally hold corporate assets in trust for the benefit of the ethnic Malays (Tam and Tan 2007), and government-controlled pension funds (e.g. the Employment Provident Fund). Also included in this category are GLCs, which are business groups and holding companies that are closely connected to government elites. Nevertheless, whereas the Bumiputra population represents around 65 per cent of total households in Malaysia, in 2008 it controlled 21.9 per cent of the share capital of limited companies and only 14 per cent of commercial buildings and premises (Economic Planning Unit 2010: 166). Correspondingly, ethnic Chinese and foreigners control a disproportionately large amount of share capital. The fourth movement is the product of a policy designed to attract foreign direct investment, which produced an export-oriented electronics manufacturing industry largely owned and controlled by Japanese, American, and Korean multinational enterprises.

While the state has orchestrated the cultivation and containment of specific types of owners, it has not developed an administrative capacity sufficient to coordinate and monitor the achievement of its ambitious economic developmental goals (Tipton 2009; Siddiquee 2010). Constitutionally, each of Malaysia's states has substantial policy responsibility, but in practice the states are economically dependent upon federal government. Fiscal controls and responsibilities are highly concentrated in the hands of the federal government and centralized in the capital, and the economic policy-making process can be best described as top-down. The Prime Minister's office houses an Economic Planning Unit, which has the key responsibility for drafting the five-year economic plans. At the heart of our analysis is the idea that Malaysia's capitalist institutions have been indelibly marked by personalized relationships in the political and corporate domains.

# FINANCIAL SYSTEM

The financial system is very much an equity–credit hybrid with both a stock market (Bursa Malaysia) for publicly listed firms and a substantial banking system. The former appears to serve as a mechanism for politically connected entrepreneurs to capitalize on the value of their connections by means of financial manipulation and speculation (see also the next section) (Gomez 2009) and is not considered a source of patient capital. The banking system has gradually been brought under either direct state ownership or indirect state control. The banking and credit system, including a variety of state credit allocation agencies, such as the MARA, part of the Ministry of Entrepreneur and Co-operative Development and the Co-operative Development Department (JPS), has engendered criticism for systematic discrimination in favouring Bumiputra firms with soft loans (Saleh and Ndubisi 2006). Recently, the government has taken steps to strengthen Malaysia's position as a global hub of Islamic finance, which some expect will encourage higher levels of social equity and economic stability (Elgindi, Said, and Salevarukis 2009). However, Islamic finance does little to fund small ethnic Chinese and ethnic Indian firms. One study investigating the activities of small ethnic Chinese firms in a rural setting finds that they obtained capital mainly from their owners and extended families, rather than from banks or governmental authorities (Rutten 2003).

However, capital originating from the central government is probably the only source of patient capital for the economy. Agencies such as the Khazanah Nasional and the Employment Provident Fund own substantial equity stakes in many of the country's largest firms (Table 8.1), but these investments appear to sustain employment in underperforming firms rather than cultivate profitability and competitive development. The major beneficiaries of government credit are large SOE trusteeships and other government agencies. These include state government-owned firms, through their respective

**Table 8.1** Ownership of top 30 Malaysian public listed firms by market capitalization

| Rank | Company | Owner identity | Shareholder 1 | % | Shareholder 2 | % |
|---|---|---|---|---|---|---|
| 1 | CIMB Group | Complex ethnic Chinese/Bumiputera group | Khazanah Nasional Bhd | 28.61 | Employ. Provident Fund Board | 12.93 |
| 2 | Public Bank | Ethnic Chinese | Tan Sri Dr. Teh Hong Piow | 24.08 | Employ. Provident Fund Board | 12.77 |
| 3 | Malayan Banking | Founded by ethnic Chinese, now Bumiputera | AmanahRaya Trustees Bhd | 44.81 | Employ. Provident Fund Board | 10.90 |
| 4 | Sime Darby | Founded by British, now Bumiputera | AmanahRaya Trustees Bhd | 37.40 | Employ. Provident Fund Board | 14.09 |
| 5 | IOI Corporation | Ethnic Chinese | Progressive Holdings Sdn Bhd | 19.38 | Progressive Holdings Sdn Bhd | 16.00 |
| 6 | Tenaga Nasional | Listed SOE | Khazanah Nasional Bhd | 35.63 | Employ. Provident Fund Board | 11.84 |
| 7 | Axiata Group | Listed SOE | Khazanah Nasional Bhd | 38.30 | Employ. Provident Fund Board | 13.28 |
| 8 | Genting | Ethnic Chinese | Kien Huat Realty Sdn Bhd | 20.85 | CIMB Group Nominees Sdn Bhd | 6.75 |
| 9 | MISC | Subsidiary of Petronas | Cartaban Nominees Sdn.Bhd. | 62.67 | Employ. Provident Fund Board | 9.91 |
| 10 | AMMB Holdings | Foreign/Bumiputera joint venture | ANZ Funds Pty Ltd | 23.78 | Employ. Provident Fund Board | 11.35 |
| 11 | Maxis | Ethnic Indian | Maxis Communications Bhd | 70.00 | Employ. Provident Fund Board | 4.78 |
| 12 | PPB Group | Ethnic Chinese | Kuok Brothers Sdn Bhd | 50.76 | Employ. Provident Fund Board | 9.71 |
| 13 | Telekom Malaysia | Listed SOE | Khazanah Nasional Bhd | 27.96 | AmanahRaya Trustees Bhd | 11.21 |
| 14 | Kuala Lumpur Kepong | Founded by British, now Ethnic Chinese | Batu Kawan Bhd | 45.65 | Employ. Provident Fund Board | 10.66 |
| 15 | Genting Malaysia | Ethnic Chinese | Genting Bhd | 49.36 | | ? |
| 16 | YTL Corporation | Ethnic Chinese | Yeoh Tiong Lay&Sons | 40.04 | Employ. Provident Fund Board | 10.37 |
| 17 | YTL Power International | Ethnic Chinese | YTL Corporation Bhd | 39.92 | Employ. Provident Fund Board | 10.02 |

*(Continued)*

**Table 8.1** Continued

| Rank | Company | Owner identity | Shareholder 1 | % | Shareholder 2 | % |
|------|---------|----------------|---------------|---|---------------|---|
| 18 | Digi.com | Foreign/Bumiputera joint venture | Telenor Asia | 49.00 | Employ. Provident Fund Board | 15.57 |
| 19 | Plus Expressways | Bumiputera | UEM Group Bhd | 38.48 | Khazanah Nasional Bhd | 13.81 |
| 20 | British American Tobacco | Foreign/Bumiputera joint venture | British American Tobacco | 50.00 | AmanahRaya Trustees Bhd | 6.05 |
| 21 | Hong Leong Bank | Ethnic Chinese | Hong Leong Company | 29.41 | Guoco Assets | 25.37 |
| 22 | Petronas Gas | Listed SOE | Cartaban Nominees Sdn Bhd | 60.63 | Employ. Provident Fund Board | 14.87 |
| 23 | UMW Holdings | Founded by Ethnic Chinese, now Bumiputera | AmanahRaya Trustees Bhd | 42.24 | Employ. Provident Fund Board | 9.70 |
| 24 | Berjaya Sports | Ethnic Chinese | HSBC Nominees Sdn Bhd | 18.12 | Cartaban Nominees Sdn Bhd | 3.07 |
| 25 | Tanjong PLC | Ethnic Indian | Usaha Tegas Sdn Bhd | 17.61 | Usaha Tegas Resources | 13.31 |
| 26 | Astro All Asia Networks | Privatised company | Khazanah Nasional Bhd | 21.40 | All Asia Media Equities Ltd | 20.12 |
| 27 | MMC Corp. | Listed SOE | Seaport Terminal Sdn.Bhd. | 49.03 | AmanahRaya Trustees Bhd | 16.67 |
| 28 | Petronas Dagangan | Listed SOE | Cartaban Nominees Sdn. Bhd. | 69.86 | Employ. Provident Fund Board | 6.40 |
| 29 | RHB Capital | Complex ethnic Chinese/ Bumiputera group | Employ. Provident Fund Board | 46.03 | RHB NOMINEES SDN Bhd | 25.00 |
| 30 | Nestle Malaysia | Foreign | Parent | 72.61 | Employ. Provident Fund Board | 7.65 |

*Source*: Authors, compilation from 2010 annual reports and/or company websites.

State Economic Development Corporations. Some, such as those in Johor and Sarawak, have become substantial owners of publicly listed firms through their investment arms. Affirmative action programmes entailed the creation of trust agencies, such as the Permodalan Nasional Berhad (PNB) and the Employees Provident Fund (EPF), Perbadanan Nasional Berhad (Pernas), whose social purpose is to accumulate capital on behalf of Malays. SOEs and trusts are the most stable Malaysian business organizations, but are not particularly dynamic. Their relative stability is in part attributable to state protection and easy access to capital. Malaysian SOEs, state investment funds, and trust agencies are typically connected to senior politicians such as former Prime Minister Mahathir, former Finance Ministers Daim and Anwar, or leading members of the ruling UMNO party (Gomez 2006). In contrast, they tend to be an ephemeral form of enterprise, because their success and survival are tied closely to the political fortunes of their patron. The typical trajectory of these enterprises is captured by the following anecdote (Gomez 2006):

> Mahathir appointed Daim as finance minister in 1984 and depended heavily on him to create privately owned Malay conglomerates. Daim approved of Mahathir's promotion of Malay capital, but did not appear supportive of Mahathir's use of state enterprises to develop heavy industries... Daim soon came to be seen as the most powerful figure in the corporate scene as his business associates rapidly secured leading privatisations. For example, in 1990, Daim's protégé Halim Saad obtained control of a multi-billion ringgit privatised North-South highway project, and swapped it for majority ownership of Renong, a moribund but quoted firm. In just five years, Renong would become the leading Malay-owned conglomerate, with a place among the top ten publicly-listed companies.... Renong became the symbol of Mahathir's success in creating a class of Malay 'new rich' through selective government patronage... Daim's total wealth reportedly amounted to a billion ringgit, including assets in foreign countries.... When Daim fell out of favour with Mahathir in 2001, the corporate assets owned by his business allies and proxies were taken over by GLCs.... In July 2001, the government announced a takeover of Renong.

Gomez (2009: 24) concludes that 'the so-called captains of industry of the 1990s [have] fallen away; and none of the Malays groomed by Mahathir, Anwar and Daim retain control of any major enterprise'. Ethnic Malay-owned firms focusing upon sectors such as finance and telecommunications are protected from international competition. No major ethnic Malay firms have appeared in manufacturing sectors that are exposed to international competition.

In sum, the financial system encourages rent-seeking behaviour by entrepreneurs and the misallocation of capital to unproductive ends and facilitates the expropriation of minority shareholders. The allocation of bank credit favours Bumiputra firms and hampers the development of a healthy small and medium-sized enterprise (SME) sector. It is therefore hardly surprising that Schwab (2010) finds that access to finance is the second most problematic factor in conducting business in Malaysia. A recent World Bank report concludes that 'private investment collapsed after the Asian crisis and never recovered, and remains an impediment to the goal of becoming a high-income economy' (2009: 53).

# OWNERSHIP AND CORPORATE GOVERNANCE

Before we discuss corporate governance, we outline the main characteristics of three types of firms that appear in Malaysia's political economy. These are (1) firms owned and controlled by ethnic Malays (the so-called Bumiputra firms); (2) firms owned and controlled by ethnic minorities, mainly those of Chinese and Indian origin; and (3) foreign-owned subsidiaries of multinational enterprises. We also briefly describe the status of SMEs, as this sector is singled out for attention as a focus for future development in Malaysia's tenth economic development plan. Table 8.1 details the thirty largest publicly listed Malaysian firms, ranked by market capitalization, and identifies the two largest shareholders, as well as their percentage shares where available.

Firms owned and controlled by ethnic Malays, SOEs, trusteeships, and GLCs constitute a major feature of Malaysia's corporate landscape. Controlling state ownership of Malaysian enterprises is extensive. Table 8.1 demonstrates that a state agency was the largest shareholder of twelve of the thirty largest companies in Malaysia, including six of the top ten companies. Several of these were recently privatized corporations that had failed under private ownership and were taken back into public ownership. The largest and most important SOEs are in strategically important industries targeted by the government for national development, including banking (e.g. the CIMB Group, Malayan Banking), telecommunications (e.g. Telekom Malaysia), and energy (Misc/Petronas).

## Ethnic Chinese-and Indian-Owned Firms

In the pre-colonial and colonial eras, there was significant immigration into Malaysia by ethnic Chinese and Indians. Several ethnic Chinese entrepreneurs amassed large fortunes in a range of industries; luminous examples include enterprises such as the Overseas Chinese Banking Corp. (OCBC), Oriental Holdings, Lion Group, and Cycle and Carriage. However, in the post-colonial period many of these enterprises became enmeshed in patrimonial politics and absorbed 'political-bureaucratic figures' into their management (Ling 1992). Gomez highlights the instability of these businesses and concludes that 'What is obvious is that the companies established by a number of the foremost businessmen of the colonial period were not sustained into the modern period' (2009: 7).

After the implementation of the NEP a new generation of ethnic Chinese entrepreneurs appeared and entered into partnerships with Malays in nominal leadership and ownership positions. These became known as Ali-Baba networks: partnerships between a Bumiputra (Ali) with access to tenders, the public sector, and politicians, and an ethnic Chinese entrepreneur (Baba) who provides financial capital and workers able to carry out the actual job. Some entered into partnerships with state governments seeking to develop their local economies. However, the fortunes of these enterprises remained subject to the inexorable contingencies of patrimonial relationships. Koon (1992) documents in detail the rise of ethnic Chinese business groups, such as the MUI Group, Multi-Purpose Holdings, and the Development and Commercial Bank, which flourished in the early days of the NEP, only to decline with the demise of their patrons. Gomez (2009) identifies a new cohort of entrepreneurs, noting that they are typically focused on real estate and property development infrastructure, vehicle distribution, and casinos and other leisure industries (e.g. the Genteng, YTL, and Hong Leong Groups). Few have developed international brand names or technology/innovation-based enterprises. Like their Malay-owned counterparts, ethnic Chinese and Indian firms have little or no presence in internationally competitive manufacturing sectors.

## Foreign-Owned Firms

Almost all the major foreign-owned firms established in the colonial era have been brought under the ownership of either state or ethnic Malay ownership. Since independence, a new wave of foreign-owned firms has appeared in the form of branch plants and subsidiaries of multinational enterprises. Their contribution to private investment is significant. The stock of foreign direct investment in the Malaysian economy reached some US$74.6 billion in 2009 (UNCTAD 2010): less than Singapore and Thailand, but more than Indonesia, the Philippines, and Vietnam. Much of this investment is concentrated in electronics and related industries and operates in export processing zones, such as those in Penang, where they are exempt from NEP ownership requirements. The typical operation is integrated into a global commodity chain in which strategic planning and global coordination are performed in the headquarters of multinational enterprises located in North America and Japan. Beyond the creation of relatively well-paid manufacturing jobs, foreign-owned firms contribute little to economic development, since they typically transfer to their Malaysian plants only the technology and know-how required to meet their manufacturing quality standards.

## Small and Medium-Sized Enterprises

The SME sector is relatively modest. Although the contribution of SMEs to GDP has increased, it was still not more than 31 per cent in 2008, compared with 55 per cent and 49 per cent, respectively, in Japan and Korea (Economic Planning Unit 2010: 95). Much of the SME activity is concentrated in the informal economy in agriculture and service activities and is characterized by low levels of investment, technological capability, and external linkages to other firms (World Bank 2009). Except in Penang, where regional state agencies have intervened to encourage SME upgrading, generally few SMEs have developed linkages with or benefitted from the presence of MNEs (Henderson and

Phillips 2007). Bumiputra owners of SMEs often seek to win tenders from state governments, cultivate close links with State Economic Development Corporations and the Council of Trust for the Indigenous People (MARA), and are members of the Malay Chamber of Commerce (Andriesse 2008: 68–69). In a pessimistic assessment of the ethnic Chinese SME sector, Koon suggests that the pervasive penetration of Malay-owned capital in the main sectors of the economy appears increasingly likely to 'marginalize the role of Chinese capital, especially medium- and small-scale capital, and push it towards the traditional ghetto specialization' (1992: 131).

Malaysia's formal system of corporate governance, as reflected in 'law on the books', provides an impression of a model system with high international standards of corporate governance. Tam and Tan (2007) suggest that compared with neighbouring countries Malaysia is a forerunner in developing and promoting a comprehensive system of corporate governance. Indeed, government leaders have long harboured hopes of establishing Kuala Lumpur as a regional finance centre to rival Hong Kong and Singapore. On the surface, Malaysia's governance institutions resemble those of the UK; many statutes are direct transplants from the UK. For example, the Companies Act of 1965 was modelled on the British Companies Act of 1948 and many rules follow an Anglo-American approach to corporate governance (Salim 2011).

Despite the establishment of an elaborate system of formal corporate governance, there is a significant gap between de jure and de facto corporate governance practice. Scholars have documented a wide range of systemic and firm-level problems in the financing of corporations. At the firm level, Salim (2011: 277) questions whether or not it is really possible to have 'an island of good corporate governance in a sea of poor public governance?'

A distinguishing empirical feature of corporate governance at the level of the firm is ownership concentration in both GLCs and ethnically controlled family business groups (Tam and Tan 2007). Ownership concentration can have both positive and negative outcomes. On the one hand, concentrated ownership by block-holders allows for the effective monitoring and disciplining of firm management. On the other hand, concentrated ownership provides opportunities for block-holders to entrench their control and expropriate wealth from minority shareholders. Research suggests that whether the positive or negative aspects of ownership concentration are available depends upon the quality of the country's corporate governance institutions (Van Essen et al. 2011). The consensus of empirical research finds that in Malaysia the negative effects of ownership concentration tend to prevail (Salim 2011). For instance, Tam and Tan (2007) provide evidence of the expropriation of minority shareholders by majority block-holders, and capital markets fail to act as a disciplinary mechanism for underperforming firms.

## INTERNAL STRUCTURE OF THE FIRM

The literature on organizational and management processes in Malay-owned firms is sparse. A common perspective focuses upon a culture emphasizing Islamic values, the importance of maintaining face, obedience to leaders, and a preference for harmony, cooperation, and conflict avoidance. Leadership is hierarchical, but accepting of patriarchal responsibility for employees and their families (Rowley and Abdul-Rahman 2007). Others suggest that a Malaysian management style reflects a composite influence of the former British colonial powers, joined in the 1970s by American notions of organization and a more explicit encouragement of Japanese management style and values, resulting from the state's 'Look East' policy in the 1980s (Rowley and Abdul-Rahman 2007). However, research on the transfer of American and Japanese management styles suggests only minimal foreign influence (Abdullah and Keenoy 1995).

Many large firms are highly diversified and they typically adopt a business group structure superficially resembling *keiretsu* and *chaebol*. However, for several reasons the majority of Malaysia's business groups have not yet developed comparable organizational and technological capabilities. First, by facilitating the entry of multinational enterprises into manufacturing, the Malaysian developmental state normally required MNEs to transfer know-how and technology to domestic firms, as was the case for partners in Korea and Japan. Consequently, domestic Malaysian firms rarely developed any organizational mechanisms to receive and customize foreign firm know-how to their own purposes. Second, because state credit allocation was made on the basis of favouritism and personal contact, with few external requirements for reporting and accountability, beneficiaries had little incentive to develop internal financial controls or the auditing capability necessary for accurate accounting of capital allocations within the firm. For both these reasons, business groups had little need for the services of professionally qualified engineers, scientific personnel, accountants, or a cadre of professional managers to integrate them into a meritocratic system of administration. Third, the readily available state credit (for some) and the development of (imperfectly regulated) public equity markets enabled business groups to engage in rapid growth through mergers, acquisitions, and corporate restructurings. The incentives and mechanisms driving corporate growth are not based on careful accounting of cost savings and rationalization or on the leveraging of managerial know-how of a particular industry, but on speculation, inside information, and the perceived opportunity for fast profits. The combination of these factors has resulted in a population of business groups organized as holding company structures that do not easily survive the loss of patronage.

Compared with the sparse literature on ethnic Malay-owned corporations, much has been written about the internal structure and management processes of ethnic Chinese family firms in SouthEast Asia. Leading accounts suggest that firms will adopt simple organization structures with centralized decision-making reliant upon the exercise of personal authority of an owner-entrepreneur (Redding 1990; Whitley 1992). The prevailing organizational culture will be paternalistic and mistrusting of outsiders, factors that limit firms' capacity to manage internationally diverse and technologically complex forms of organization (Redding 1990; Carney 1998).

Recent work suggests that these firms are hybridizing, adopting Western standards of corporate governance, and developing professional management structures and more open and cosmopolitan relational networks (Yeung 2004, 2006). Notwithstanding these developments, the archetypal Chinese family firm remains personally managed, since primary authority and control are retained within the family coalition (Tsui-Auch 2004). This literature suggests that these family-owned enterprises are subject to severe fragmentation tendencies once the founder retires. One recent study finds that publicly listed ethnic Chinese family firms in Hong Kong and Singapore lose an average of 60 per cent of their market value during the succession process (Fan, Jian, and Yeh 2009). Gomez (2009) sees similar consequences in Malaysia, suggesting that conflict, family feuds, and dismantling follow in the wake of a founder's succession.

To the extent that ethnic Chinese business groups are able to secure state patronage either through direct linkages or through the construction of 'Ali-Baba networks', these firms are likely to be subject to similar problems of overdiversification and instability evinced by large Malaysian-owned firms. However, large ethnic Chinese family-controlled business groups are differentiated from their Malay counterparts in that many have access to international networks and secure channels to export capital to safer havens, such as Singapore and Hong Kong (Yeung 2004).

# Employment Relations

Malaysia's system of employment relations is a hybrid of institutions inherited from the colonial era and those emerging from the developmental state in the 1980s. A legacy of centralized trade unions dates to after the Second World War and consists of efforts by the returning and colonial authority to install a British-style reformist labour movement consisting of institutions resembling the British Labour Party's industrial unions (Wad 2001). In the immediate post-colonial period, the government attempted to neutralize the 'political unionism' implicit in industry-wide unions by containing the existing unions and suppressing the formation of new ones. Later, Mahathir recognized the potential role of the union movement and made preliminary efforts to establish a Japanese model of enterprise unionism that he believed would facilitate employee loyalty to the firm and productivity-oriented management–labour collaboration. Consequently, in the modern era, the central trade union organization, the Malaysian Trades Union Congress (MUTC), remains dominated by large national unions, but the employment relations landscape is characterized by pluralistic and competing union organizations engaged in enterprise-based collective bargaining with individual employers (Wad 2001). However, union power is weak, because unions are poorly resourced and severely restricted by government limits on their capacity for industrial action (Bhopal and Todd 2000).

The development of the employment relations system in the post-colonial era was shaped by the twin objectives of providing a package of favourable labour policies to attract foreign multinationals and affirmative action towards indigenous Malays. As an industrial strategy, export-led development is dependent upon the existence of an obedient low-cost workforce and the preservation of managerial prerogative in the workplace (Todd and Peetz 2001). So, while the government was keen to furnish foreign investors with a peaceful employment relations climate, it was also concerned with enhancing its legitimacy as a champion of Bumiputra rights and opportunity (Frenkel and Kuruvilla 2002). Accordingly, state intervention in employment relations is pervasive (Todd and Peetz 2001). Two examples illustrate the nature of intervention. Organising legal strikes is virtually impossible, because of very restrictive and cumbersome pre-strike regulations, and participants in illegal strikes risk severe penalties. Furthermore, the state has attempted to legislate employment protection measures, yet does not intervene when private-sector employers circumvent employee protection regulations by hiring part-time, temporary, and contract workers. The mantra of the Malaysian Employers Federation (MEF) is a call for numerical flexibility in the labour force, based on the argument that labour-market flexibility is the major generator of high-growth rates in economies such as the UK and USA (Ramasamy and Rowley 2011).

The tension between the state's economic development strategy and its goal of protecting employment rights for its Bumiputra constituency is an ongoing feature of Malaysian employment relations. On the one hand, there is continuing commitment to supplying low-cost and obedient labour for export-oriented manufacturing, notably in the electronics industry located in export processing zones (TUAC 1997). The government continues to facilitate the importation of low-cost labour on temporary immigration permits from Indonesia and Bangladesh. In addition, there are around 1.8 million illegal immigrants from countries such as Indonesia, the Philippines, Burma, and Bangladesh, who have a vulnerable position and receive low wages (Associated Press 2011). Research suggests that Malaysia's ratio of one foreign worker to every five local workers is one of the highest in the world (Ramasamy and Rowley 2011). Moreover, tight legislative restrictions on labour's freedom to engage in collective bargaining have been maintained and there is little commitment to raising the real wage levels of unskilled labour.

On the other hand, Mahathir adopted 'Vision to 2020', recognizing the growing regional competition for FDI and that Malaysia would need to migrate towards more value-added competitiveness, which implies higher levels of skills and enterprise capabilities. Mahathir recognized that greater value-added called for the transformation of the country's employment relations system, and the Japanese enterprise model of employment relations was singled out for praise and imitation. Despite Mahathir's admiration for Japanese-style employment relations, Japanese multinationals with plants and facilities located in Malaysia have made very little effort to transfer their domestically based cooperative labour relations practices to their Malaysian facilities. Indeed, Japanese electronics firms appear to resist the establishment of enterprise unions. According to Abdullah and Keenoy (1995), attempts to transfer key human resource policies are 'lost in transit'; policies such as lifetime employment and quality circles are rarely attempted. Instead, Japanese firms generally adopt a paternalistic stance in their employment relations: they seek to instil a belief that the company cares about its employees, but the thrust of Japanese employment relations in Malaysia has been to co-opt the 'union into a supplementary source of managerial authority and legitimacy' (Abdullah and Keenoy 1995: 760).

Tentative efforts to implement a consultative employment relations strategy, which could facilitate labour participation in skills upgrading, have produced disappointing results. The prevailing government policy preserves 'old-style employment relations', with management-dominated employment relations. This has impeded the movement towards a new mode of cooperative employment relations based on employee participation in decision-making, multi-skilling, autonomous work teams, and mutual commitment between management, reflected in greater employment security. Todd and Peetz summarize the state policy toward employment relations as 'ambivalent and contradictory' (2001: 138).

# EDUCATION AND SKILLS FORMATION

Malaysia's labour force has attained high levels of literacy and is amenable to training (Ramasamy and Rowley 2011). The overall skill level, as manifested in labour productivity statistics, shows Malaysia in the middle of the pack of Asian countries. Table 8.2 indicates that Malaysia outperforms countries such as China and India, but lags significantly behind neighbouring Singapore and other newly industrialized Asian economies. Public expenditure on education is consistently high; Malaysia has a well-developed system of primary and secondary education, and a similarly well-developed physical infrastructure of technical colleges and universities. The government promoted 'training and multiskilling' in the workforce in the 1990s (Todd and Peetz 2001). More recently, the Ninth Malaysia Plan (2006–2010) contained a range of initiatives to boost training, emphasizing franchising, SME skills, and 'technopreneur' development. The government also aims to sustain affirmative action to ensure the private sector employs Bumiputra and other minorities at professional and managerial levels.

Notwithstanding the attention and abundant resources allocated to education and skills formation, Malaysia has a chronic skills shortage. A variety of official reports suggests that the current situation in education and skills formation is probably insufficient to break out from this mid-level productivity performance. For example, a recent World Bank report on Malaysia's investment climate finds that some 40 per cent of 1,400 firms sampled in a recent survey reported the skills issue as a top investment climate obstacle (World Bank 2010: 89). Despite heavy investment, there is concern that the education system is producing the wrong mix of skills for the economic needs (World Bank 2009). The aggregate participation levels in tertiary education are low, compared with countries at similar levels of economic development. Entry requirements based on ethnicity have led to large numbers of Chinese students travelling abroad for their education and there are pressing calls for meritocracy in the selection of students, faculty, and university leadership (World Bank 2009). The state has invested heavily in vocational training, but enrolment is low, since vocational education is widely seen as inferior to university education. Moreover, there is low industry utilization of these programmes, because firms have little need for the skills being developed. In terms of advanced technology training, Malaysia currently lacks some critical elements to support the knowledge economy, such as adequately skilled people, supportive education and training systems, R&D capability, and the foundation of a science and technology base (Ramasamy and Rowley 2008). In general, there are few institutions in place to support the development of high-quality generic and specialized skills comparable to those found in neighbouring Singapore (Ritchie 2009).

Wage rates and fringe benefits are largely determined by legislation, and there is little that employers can do to differentiate themselves. Ethnic Malays engage in frequent job-hopping, as quotas and affirmative action programmes assure constant employment. The lack of loyalty shown by domestic employees is reciprocated by their employers, who generally invest little in their workers. Employers address shortages of domestic employees by hiring foreign workers; however, the majority are only given two-year contracts. Consequently, turnover remains very high, which in turn discourages employer investment in training. Training is limited to on-the-job task-related familiarization, and there is virtually no career planning. Human resource development is considered expensive and not worthwhile, given the high turnover. Human resource management is practised as old-style personnel management, based on autocratic management and top-down communication (Rowley and Abdul-Rahman 2007).

Neither have Malaysian firms developed internal labour markets to compensate for the institutional voids in the external labour markets. The absence of an efficient skills formation infrastructure has long plagued Asian economies, and this has put their firms at a disadvantage in their efforts to catch up with their more technologically advanced rivals (Hobday 1995). The Japanese enterprise system responded to external deficiencies by establishing internal labour markets (Keizer 2011). By offering workers greater

Table 8.2   Labour productivity, in US$1000 per worker in 2009

| | |
|---|---|
| Singapore | 45.3 |
| Taiwan | 39.2 |
| South Korea | 32.1 |
| Malaysia | 12.8 |
| Thailand | 4.6 |
| China | 3.7 |
| Indonesia | 3.2 |
| Philippines | 2.4 |
| India | 2.1 |

*Source*: Economic Planning Unit (2010: 5).

employment security and supplying them with dedicated training, Japanese firms lowered the barriers to workers' investment in specialized skills. Furthermore, by rotating managers across the various businesses of their diversified enterprises, concentrated owners may develop scarce managerial talent and increase allocational efficiency by shifting these managers to the businesses that most need them (Khanna and Palepu 1999). However, these practices have not been much adopted in Malaysia. For example, Rowley and Abdul-Rahman (2007) report that Malaysian managers encounter promotion ceilings and a lack of delegation from Japanese managers to local offices.

Malaysia's firms have few mechanisms to support systematic firm or industry-specific skills creation, such as an apprenticeship tradition or a participative labour regime in its employment relations, nor do they have a strong tradition of industry associations to generate and monitor labour standards. Because employers find it relatively easy to circumvent labour protection regulations, employees have little incentive to invest in firm-specific skills. High levels of turnover and the poor development of firm-specific skills means that employers can offer their employees very limited promotion or job rotation opportunities. Ramasamy and Rowley (2011) contend that human resource development is not a strategic priority in the vast majority of Malaysian firms.

While the state has set ambitious industrial development goals to establish a knowledge-based economy, we suggest that there are significant policy contradictions and gaps in the production of needed skills. High levels of government expenditure appear to be weakened by affirmative action policies that systematically undermine the meritocratic allocation of talent to the available opportunities, yet a meritocratic institutional environment is essential for the cultivation of 'star scientists', knowledge workers, and high-quality generic skills. Similarly, domestic firms individually and collectively lack the mechanisms to develop either industry-specific or firm-specific vocational and craft skills.

## INTER-COMPANY RELATIONS

Neither contractual inter-company agreements, such as joint ventures or strategic alliances, nor membership of collective groups, such as trade associations or peak organizations, are vital features of personal capitalism. Much greater faith is placed in personal contacts and relational contracting. With the exception of ethnic Chinese businesses, inter-company relations in Malaysia are in general state-led and state-mediated (Gomez 1994; Rasiah 1997), but are heavily influenced by racial politics. The hubs of state-mediated networks are situated in centralized federal government agencies radiating outwards from Kuala Lumpur to the regional state governments. The federal government has monopolized revenue collection and disbursement has made regional development highly dependent upon federal allocations (Woo 2009).

Many networks are based on direct government ownership of enterprises. One of the most important organizations is Khazanah Nasional, the investment holding arm of the federal government that has invested in more than fifty companies. For example, it owns 43 per cent of the car manufacturer Proton, 30 per cent of Bank Muamalat, 29 per cent of the CIMB group, 100 per cent of UEM Builders, and 33 per cent of Telekom Malaysia (Khazanah Nasional 2011). Government ownership provides a framework for Bumiputra firms to obtain public-sector contracts in a variety of industry sectors. Because public investment is increasingly the most important component of total investment, these government business relationships are typically more important than inter-company relationships among private-sector actors. There are some notable exceptions to this pattern. Rasiah (2002) finds that the Penang State Government, through the Penang Development Corporation, had a strong impact on the success of the machine-tool industry. Foreign direct investment by Japanese and US electronic firms is important in Penang and the local state has established links to them.

Intra-ethnic ties involving Chinese entrepreneurs who retain Malays as nominal owners or in senior managerial positions (Ali-Baba networks) have been historically important as a means of integrating ethnic Chinese people into the domestic economy. Owing to the large government share of investment spending, inter-ethnic ties were an important means through which Chinese entrepreneurs could win contracts. Since few of the Malay partners were themselves prominent entrepreneurs, the necessity of employing a politically acceptable front person only highlighted the vulnerability of ethnic Chinese capital within this system (Koon 1992). Intra-ethnic relationships were rarely founded upon deep interpersonal trust, since both parties attempted to minimize their dependence upon one another. The Malayan partner often maintained multiple relationships and the Chinese partner, 'well aware his protectors can easily be swept aside by the shifting political tides' (Koon 1992: 142), sought to diversify risk by shifting capital overseas. Gomez (2009) notes in recent years the growth in inter-ethnic relationships that are not reliant upon government patronage. He suggests that this represents an important social change, indicated by the emergence of an independent and dynamic Bumiputra middle class with a commitment to new types of business strategies and management styles and more open to inter-ethnic cooperation for mutual benefit. This indeed may well be the case. The growing importance of China's trade and investment in the region provides ethnic Chinese people, especially those with links to the mainland, with a growing currency in cultivating domestic networks.

Moreover, inter-ethnic networks are more common in globalized enclaves such as greater Kuala Lumpur, Penang, and Johor Bahru, where most of the GDP is generated, but such linkages are less frequent beyond these core areas (Andriesse and Van Westen 2009). In peripheral regions, intra-ethnic interpersonal relationships among socially segregated minorities remain important, especially among small firms that have not become dependent on the public sector. Gomez, Loh, and Lee (2003: 69) state that 'small-sized Chinese companies probably still adhere to the notion of intra-ethnic business cooperation as a means to counter the growing influence of well-connected Malays over the corporate sector'. Regional differences in the prevalence of inter- and intra-ethnic ties point to the existence of a dual political economy. Large ethnic Chinese firms located in the core regions, that are more active as exporters and as suppliers to foreign subsidiaries, frequently establish domestic inter-ethnic ties with Malay-owned businesses. These linkages provide a bridge to the international economy for Malay-owned firms. Peripheral regions continue to be racially stratified and domestically oriented sectors. The firms in these regions are linked to politics and dependent upon the central government for the allocation of developmental resources. Andriesse and Van Westen (2009) characterize the peripheral regions in this scenario as an unsustainable variety of capitalism, since a great deal of investment is allocated to unnecessary infrastructure projects. The absence of sustainable entrepreneurship and regional autonomy has led to calls for significant decentralization of economic and political power to state governments (Woo 2009).

# Social Capital

We refer to social capital in this section in the sense of generalized trust in the efficacy of a society's institutions (Fukuyama 1995). Historically, there is broad popular and electoral support for the governing regime, which is elected repeatedly and by a wide margin. Consistent with the idea of 'Asian values', the survey data reveal that the majority of Malaysians are willing to limit their democratic rights, particularly when the social order is threatened (Welsh 1996). More recently, however, the government has come to face serious popular opposition, including a series of mass protests; moreover, there are increasing power struggles within the ruling UNMO party. At the time of writing, there is growing political uncertainty and speculation about the future stability of the existing regime.

Malaysia's performance on indicators regarding the quality of governance is mixed. Measures for voice and accountability, political stability, and regulatory quality are typically poor, falling between the 30th and the 60th intermediate percentile among 213 economies in the world (World Bank 2011). In contrast, the performance on rule of law and government effectiveness ranks between the 60th and the 80th percentile, suggesting a high level of institutionalized trust. However, one analyst suggests that the rule of law in Malaysia is 'heavily politicized... at least in a narrow range of cases' and states that 'critics complain that the ruling party uses the legal system to harass political opponents and undermine democracy' (Peerenboom 2004: 16).

Moreover, corruption is a continuing problem and the situation is deteriorating. Transparency International's annual ranking of national perceived corruption levels shows that Malaysia declined from 23rd to 45th between 1996 and 2008. Siddiquee (2010: 166) suggests that Malaysia represents a case in which 'some of the basic conditions of good governance, like access to information, accountability, and transparency in public administration and independent media, are either absent or very weak'. There is a large amount of literature that attributes corrupt corporate governance to the NEP affirmative action policy, which accords special rights including an ethnic quota for bank loans and a target of 30 per cent corporate ownership to indigenous Malays. The NEP distorts incentives and provides systematic opportunities for rent-seeking by Malaysian entrepreneurs (Ling 1992; Woo 2009). Others attribute governance failure to the personal hegemony of the Prime Minister over the instruments of state. Gomez (2006) argues that the effectiveness of governance institutions such as the Securities Commission depends on the will of government leaders to enforce them, but too often politicians are unwilling to act even when there is evidence of corruption. Instead, 'corporate governance mechanisms are often used as tools by powerful politicians for their vested interests' (Gomez 2006: 106). Taken together, recent political disturbances, measures of governance performance, and evidence of endemic corruption are indicative of relatively low levels of institutionalized trust.

One consequence of low institutional trust is actors' reluctance to rely upon fiduciary relationships. A fundamental relationship in capitalist economies is the fiduciary responsibility of an agent to a principal. The fiduciary duty is literally a 'holding in trust' and is attached to a wide range of specific relationships, such as that between the corporate directors and officers of the company and its stockholders, estate administrators, and legatees and heirs, and between stockbrokers and their clients. The fiduciary relationship has both a legal and a moral connotation. In its legal form, the fiduciary has a duty of skill and care to employ best professional judgement for the benefit of the principal. In its moral form, the fiduciary responsibility is more akin to stewardship for multiple stakeholders or communities and the belief is that the agent will uphold the expectation of trust, act honestly, and put the communal needs ahead of his or her own needs. We propose that weak fiduciary relationships are evident in three aspects of the Malaysian business system: the dearth of professional managers, self-serving behaviour of public officials in their capacity as directors of trusts and government enterprises, and the fragmentation and short lifespans of family firms. We briefly discuss how undeveloped social capital undermines the formation of fiduciary responsibility and inhibits the development of more complex forms of capitalist organization.

A range of factors interact to impede the development of a class of professional managers. As noted above, large enterprises pay scant attention to human resource development in general, and management development in particular. This neglect is in part because Malaysian business groups are structured as financial holding companies with little need for professional managers (Amsden 2009). The shortage of qualified professional managers provides an advantage to senior civil servants, who are frequently appointed to senior positions in Malaysian business groups. Senior civil servants are sought after because they typically possess the requisite understanding of the bureaucracy and skill in navigating its abundant red tape (Ling 1992). The prevalence of family firms, in which managerial advancement is often based on nepotism, and GLCs, in which selection is based upon ethnic quotas and advancement upon favouritism or connections, does not result in a fertile environment for the emergence of meritocratic and competitive markets for executive talent. These organizations have little need for a class of fiduciary agents to serve in senior corporate roles, and it is unsurprising that few individuals are willing to invest in acquiring the skills needed to perform them. Second, the expected standards of stewardship in public service normally embody a fiduciary relationship in which public servants are expected to uphold the public interest, yet a strong public service ethos has not fully developed in Malaysia (Siddiquee 2010). This is problematic, because the common practice of seconding civil servants to government-owned companies and trusts has created a cadre of 'bureaucratic entrepreneurs' that straddles both business and government (Ling 1992). This cadre shows little capacity for self-regulation, because there is, according to Ling, 'little consensus on standards of behaviour...relevant business knowledge has been seen in terms of command over information and the ability to turn a profit to the exclusion of ethics, social obligation, and responsible administration' (1992: 125). There is little oversight of these leaders except for the personal control of the prime minister. Gomez (2009) describes Prime Minister Mahathir's growing personal hegemony over the state, which ensured that bureaucrats adopted and pursued his conception of the development model. Personal control continues to the present day, with a recently established office, the Anti-Corruption Agency (ACA), directly located in the Prime Minister's Department. Siddiquee (2010: 165) reports that 'evidence suggests that instead of acting as an independent agency, the ACA remained beholden to the wishes of the Prime Minister's Department'. On the question of regulating government-connected business, Ling (1992) concludes that legal regulation offers little promise, because 'In Malaysia the lawmakers have gotten too involved in the game themselves, and few officials have the courage and independence to enforce the controls that do exist' (1992: 125).

Personal capitalism is defined by the absence of fiduciaries, a class of agents including corporate officers, professional managers, and disinterested public servants, who can be trusted to act in the interests of principals. The fiduciary relationship is easily corruptible and the development of faithful fiduciaries requires attention to their regulation, qualification, incentives, and oversight, but these institutions are underdeveloped in Malaysia. Trust is the essence of the fiduciary relationship, and 'social capital is a capability that arises from the prevalence of trust in society or in certain parts of it' (Fukuyama 1995: 26). An important capability enabled by social capital is the creation and development of complex forms of business organization that are necessary for the development of high value-added economic activity. A corollary of the low levels of social capital is the prevalence of the simple and personalized organizational structures we find at the heart of Malaysian capitalism.

# Institutional Complementarities

Since 1971, Malaysia's political leaders have consistently put the capitalist economy to the service of greater equality between ethnic groups, the reduction of poverty, and maintaining social peace. To achieve these, they have combined the institutions of the developmental state with those found in liberal market economies and infused both with personalized patron–client relationships. The interaction of these institutional spheres has produced a succession of largely ephemeral business groups with weak holding-company structures and a managerial ethos that provides few incentives to develop sustainable forms of competitive advantage in the international marketplace. Those institutional spheres reinforced a system of corporate political complementarities and produced an institutional lock-in that is difficult to break. Political institutions distribute a reliable stream of rents to an increasingly self-confident Malay business elite and middle class, members of the ruling political party UMNO, and ethnic Chinese-controlled business groups linked to the wider Asian economy. Collectively, these interests form a political and corporate coalition that has a strong vested interest in the status quo.

Our perspective suggests that these political complementarities are bought at the cost of contradictions in several institutional spheres. Successive governments have pursued a developmental state model, but have not shielded their domestic manufacturing sector from competition from foreign multinational enterprises, as Japan and Korea did. The state encouraged the formation of bank-led financing, but also supported the emergence of a poorly regulated equity market that undermined the discipline of the state monopoly on credit. In the employment relations system, the government protected Bumiputra employment rights, but by accepting employers' appetite for numerical flexibility and imported labour it created no incentives for employees to cultivate skills. Capital markets that allowed large firms to buy, sell, and restructure enterprises relieved them of the responsibility for developing their productivity or competitive capabilities. Similarly, the growing dominance of public-sector investment over private investment has established government-dependent inter-company networks. The resulting system is neither a pure liberal market nor a developmental state model reflecting the discipline and mechanisms found at the heart of a developmental state model. In line with institutional complementarity hypotheses, the absence of coherence or 'strategic fit' among the institutional spheres suggests that Malaysian capitalism is underperforming compared with what might be attained under a purely liberal market or Asian developmental state models. Figure 8.1 graphically depicts the relationship.

# CONCLUSION

In this chapter we have argued that personal capitalism and its archetypal form, the personally managed firm, constitute a stable institutional matrix that has locked Malaysia into a middle-income trap. One of the main hypotheses in the literature on the diversity of capitalist systems is based on the principle of isomorphism and predicts that firms will adjust their strategies and organizational practices to take advantage of institutional opportunities in their local environment (Carney, Gedajlovic, and Yang 2009). In Malaysia, personally managed business groups have become isomorphic with the personalized institutional environments in which they operate. Unfortunately, these

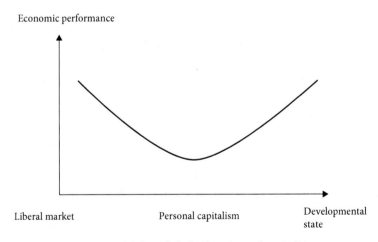

Economic performance

Liberal market                    Personal capitalism            Developmental
                                                                  state

FIGURE 8.1  Malaysia's hybrid variety of capitalism

institutions are undermined by contradictions that weaken the principal–agent relationships on which advanced capitalist societies depend. The challenge for the Malaysian state is to maintain and enhance its social–political achievements, while establishing institutional environments in which responsible fiduciary relationships may emerge and flourish.

## REFERENCES

Abdullah, S. and T. Keenoy (1995). 'Japanese Managerial Practices in the Malaysian Electronics Industry: Two Case Studies'. *Journal of Management Studies* 32(6): 747–766.

Ahn, M. and A. York (2011). 'Resource-based and Institution-based Approaches to Biotechnology Industry Development in Malaysia'. *Asia Pacific Journal of Management* 28(2): 257–275.

Amsden, A. (2009). 'Does Firm Ownership Matter? POEs vs FOEs in the Developing World'. In R. Ramamurti and J.V. Singh, Eds., *Emerging Multinationals in Emerging Markets*: 64–78. Cambridge, Cambridge University Press.

Amsden, A. H. and T. Hikino (1994). 'Project Execution Capability, Organizational Know-How and Conglomerate Corporate Growth in Late Industrialization'. *Industrial and Corporate Change* 3: 111–147.

Andriesse, E. (2008). 'Institutions and Regional Development in Southeast Asia. A Comparative Analysis of Satun (Thailand) and Perlis (Malaysia)'. Netherlands Geographical Studies No. 374, Utrecht, Royal Netherlands Geographical Society. Retrieved 4 June 2008 from <http://igitur-archive.library.uu.nl/dissertations/2008-0604-200854/UUindex.html>.

—— and G. van Westen (2009). 'Unsustainable Varieties of Capitalism Along the Thailand–Malaysia Border? The Role of Institutional Complementarities in Regional Development'. *Asia Pacific Journal of Management* 26(3): 459–479.

Asian Development Bank (2011). *Asian Development Outlook 2011: South-South Economic Links*. Manila, Asian Development Bank.

Associated Press (2011). '109 Detainees escape Malaysia Immigration Centre', April 5. Retrieved 6 April 2011 from <http://hosted.ap.org/dynamic/stories/A/AS_MALAYSIA_ IMMIGRATION_BREAKOUT?SITE=NCAGW&SECTION=HOME&TEMPLATE=DEF AULT>.

Bhopal, M. and P. Todd (2000). 'Multinational Corporations and Trade Union Development in Malaysia'. *Asia Pacific Business Review* 6(3–4): 193–213.

Carney, M. (1998). 'A Management Capacity Constraint? Obstacles to the Development of the Chinese Family Business'. *Asia-Pacific Journal of Management* 15: 1–25.

—— E. Gedajlovic, and X. Yang (2009). 'Varieties of Asian Capitalism: Toward an Institutional Theory of Asian Enterprise'. *Asia Pacific Journal of Management* 26(3): 361–380.

Drabble, J. H. and P. Drake (1981). 'The British Agency Houses in Malaysia: Survival in a Changing World'. *Journal of South East Asian Studies* 12: 297–328.

Economic Planning Unit (2010). Tenth Malaysia Plan 2011–2015. Putrajaya, Economic Planning Unit. Retrieved 29 March 2011 from <http://www.epu.gov.my/html/themes/epu/html/ RMKE10/rmke10_english.html>.

Elgindi, T., M. Said, and J. Salevarukis (2009). 'Islamic Alternatives to Purely Capitalist Modes of Finance: A Study of Malaysian Banks Between 1999 and 2006'. *Review of Radical Political Economics* 41(4): 516–538.

Fan, J., M. Jian, and Y. Yeh (2009). *Succession: The Roles of Specialized Assets and Transfer Costs.* IEF Working Paper. Hong Kong, Chinese University of Hong Kong.

Frenkel, S. and S. Kuruvilla (2002). 'Logics of Action: Globalization and Changing Employment Relations in China, Malaysia, India and the Philippines'. *Industrial Relations and Labor Review* 55(3): 387–412.

Fukuyama, F. (1995). *Trust: The Social Virtues and the Creation of Prosperity.* New York, Free Press.

Gomez, E. T. (1994). *Political Business: Corporate Involvement of Malaysian Political Parties.* Cairns, James Cook University of North Queensland.

—— (2006). 'Malaysian Business Groups: The State and Capital Development in the Post-Currency Crisis Period'. In Chang Sea-Jin, Ed., *Business Groups in East Asia: Financial Crisis, Restructuring, and New Growth*: 119–146. Oxford, Oxford University Press.

—— (2009). 'The Rise and Fall of Capital: Corporate Malaysia in Historical Perspective'. *Journal of Contemporary Asia* 39(3): 345–381.

—— W. Loh, and K. Lee (2003). 'Malaysia'. In E. T. Gomez and H. Hsiao, Eds., *Chinese Business in Southeast Asia: Contesting Cultural Explanations, Researching Entrepreneurship*: 62–84. London, Routledge Curzon.

Henderson, J. and R. Phillips (2007). 'Unintended Consequences: Social Policy, State Institutions and the "Stalling" of the Malaysian Industrialization Project'. *Economy and Society* 36(1): 78–102.

Hobday, M. (1995). 'East Asian Latecomer Firms: Learning the Technology of Electronics'. *World Development* 23: 1171–1193.

Jomo, K. S. (2003). *M Way: Mahathir's Economic Legacy.* Kuala Lumpur, Forum.

Keizer, A. (2011). 'Flexibility in Japanese Internal Labour Markets: The Introduction of Performance-related Pay'. *Asia Pacific Journal of Management* 28(3): 573–594.

Khanna, T. and K. Palepu (1999). 'The Right Way to Restructure Conglomerates in Emerging Markets'. *Harvard Business Review* 77(July–August): 125–134.

Khazanah Nasional (2011). 'Investment: Portfolio Companies'. Retrieved 2 April 2011 from <http://www.khazanah.com.my/index.htm>.

Koon, H. P. (1992). 'The Chinese Business Elite of Malaysia'. In R. McVey, *Southeast Asian Capitalism*: 127–144. New York, Cornell University.

Ling, S. L. M. (1992). 'The Transformation of Malaysian Business Groups'. In R. McVey, *Southeast Asian Capitalism*: 103–126. New York, Cornell University.

Morck, R., D. Wolfenzon and B. Yeung (2005). 'Corporate Governance, Economic Entrenchment, and Growth'. *Journal of Economic Literature 43*: 655–720.

Ohno, K. (2009). 'Avoiding the Middle-Income Trap: Renovating Industrial Policy Formulation in Vietnam'. *ASEAN Economic Bulletin 26*(1): 25–43.

Peerenboom, R. (2004). 'Varieties of Rule of Law: An Introduction and Provisional Conclusion'. In R. Peerenboom, Ed., *Asian Discourses of the Rule of Law: Theories and Implementation of Rule of Law in Twelve Countries: France and the USA*: 1–55. London, Routledge Curzon.

Ramasamy, N. and C. Rowley (2008). 'Trade Unions in Malaysia: Complexity of a State Employer System'. In J. Benson and Y. Zhu, Eds., *Trade Unions in Asia: An Economic and Sociological Analysis*: 121–139. Abingdon and New York, Routledge.

—— (2011). 'Labour Markets in Malaysia: Evolution to a Knowledge-Based Economy?'. In J. Benson and Y. Zhu, Eds., *The Dynamics of Asian Labour Markets: Balancing Control and Flexibility*: 191–223. Abingdon and New York, Routledge.

Rasiah, R. (1997). 'Class, Ethnicity and Economic Development in Malaysia'. In G. Rodan, K. Hewison, and R. Robison, Eds., *The Political Economy of South-East Asia*: 121–147. Melbourne, Oxford University Press.

—— (2002). 'Government-Business Coordination and Small-Enterprise Performance in the Machine-tool Sector in Malaysia'. *Small Business Economics 18*(3): 177–194.

Redding, G. (1990). *The Spirit of Chinese Capitalism*. New York, De Gruyter.

Ritchie, B. K. (2009). 'Economic Upgrading in a State-coordinated Liberal Market Economy'. *Asia-Pacific Journal of Management 26*(3): 435–458.

Roslan, A. (2003). 'Income Inequality, Poverty and Redistribution Policy in Malaysia'. *Asian Profile 31*(3): 217–238.

Rowley, C. and S. Abdul-Rahman (2007). 'The Management of Human Resources in Malaysia: Locally-owned Companies and Multinational Companies'. *Management Revue 18*(4): 427–453.

Rutten, M. (2003). *Rural Capitalists in Asia: A Comparative Analysis of India, Indonesia and Malaysia*. London, Routledge Curzon.

Saleh, A. and N. Ndubisi (2006). 'An Evaluation of SME Development in Malaysia'. *International Review of Business Research Papers 2*(1): 1–14.

Salim, M. R. (2011). 'Corporate Governance in Malaysia: The Macro and Micro Issues'. In C. Mallin, Ed., *Handbook of International Corporate Governance: Country Analysis*, 2nd ed.: 269–293. Cheltenham, Edward Elgar.

Schwab, K. (2010). *The Global Competitiveness Report 2010-2011*. Geneva, World Economic Forum.

Siddiquee, N. (2010). 'Combating Corruption and Managing Integrity in Malaysia: A Critical Overview of Recent Strategies and Initiatives'. *Public Organization Review 10*(1): 153–171.

Tam, O. and M. Tan (2007). 'Ownership, Firm Performance and Governance in Malaysia'. *Corporate Governance 15*(2): 208–222.

Tipton, F. (2009). 'Southeast Asian Capitalism: History, Institutions, States, and Firms'. *Asia Pacific Journal of Management 26*(3): 401–434.

Todd, P. and D. Peetz (2001). 'Malaysian Industrial Relations at Century's Turn: Vision 2020 or a Spectre of the Past?' *International Journal of Human Resource Management 12*(8): 1365–1382.

Tsui-Auch, L. S. (2004). 'The Professionally-managed Family-ruled Enterprise: Ethnic Chinese Business in Singapore'. *Journal of Management Studies 41*(4): 693–723.

TUAC (1997). 'Foreign Direct Investment and Labour Standards'. Discussion Paper. Retrieved 25 April 2011 from <http://old.tuac.org/statemen/communiq/fdicim.htm>.

UNCTAD (2010). *World Investment Report 2010: Investing in a Low-Carbon Economy*. Geneva, United Nations Conference for Trade and Development.

Van Essen, M., P. Huegens, J. H. van Oosterhout, E. Gedajlovic, and M. Carney (2011). *The Ownership and Performance of Asian Firms: A Meta-Analytic Test of Institutional Voids and Owner Identity*. Working Paper, University of Utrecht.

Wad, P. (2001). *Transforming Industrial Relations: The Case of the Malaysian Auto Industry*. Clara Working Paper 12. Amsterdam, IISG.

Welsh, B. (1996). 'Attitudes toward Democracy in Malaysia: Challenges to the Regime?'. *Asian Survey 36*(9): 882–903.

Whitley, R. D. (1992). *Business Systems in East Asia: Firms, Markets and Societies*. London, Sage.

Woo, W. (2009). 'Getting Malaysia out of the Middle-Income-Trap'. Retrieved 6 April from <http://www.econ.ucdavis.edu/faculty/woo/woo.html>.

World Bank (2009). *Malaysia Economic Monitor: Repositioning for Growth*. Bangkok, World Bank.

—— (2010). *Malaysia Economic Monitor: Growth through Innovation*. Bangkok, World Bank.

—— (2011). Worldwide Governance Indicators. Available at <http://data.worldbank.org/data-catalog/worldwide-governance-indicators>.

Yeung, H. (2004). *Chinese Capitalism in a Global Era: Toward Hybrid Capitalism*. London, Routledge.

—— (2006). 'Change and Continuity in Southeast Asia Ethnic Chinese Business'. *Asia Pacific Journal of Management 23*(3): 229–254.

# CHAPTER 9

## THE PHILIPPINES

*Inequality–Trapped Capitalism*

### MARI KONDO

THE Philippines, with its 92.3 million people (NSO 2012), is presently the world's twelfth most populous country (CIA 2012). Of the total, about 5 million Filipinos, who are known to be cheerful and capable English-speaking workers, are dispersed across more than 190 countries and territories (Tyner 2009). Strategically situated geographically, the Philippines is considered one of the Pacific gateways to Asia.

In the management literature, however, despite these advantages in terms of people and location, the Philippines is mentioned much less frequently than most other Asian societies. This is because the Philippine economic performance has been consistently poorer than that of its neighbours—and these days, the gap is widening.

While many of its neighbour countries have experienced an 'economic miracle' at one time or another, the Philippines has not. Even vis-à-vis its South East Asian neighbours with relatively slower growth, its performance has been lagging. For example, while its per capita GDP was roughly twice Thailand's and three times that of Indonesia in 1960, in 2006 it was less than half of Thailand's and almost the same as Indonesia's (Canlas, Cham, and Zhuang 2011). At this point it is apparent that the Philippine business system manifests certain systemic problems leading to the perpetual deterioration of its economy. Given the belief that one can learn more from failure than from success, the overarching objective of this chapter is to shed light on the Philippine phenomenon by describing its business system. Three particular questions come to mind:

1. What characteristics of the Philippine business system lie behind the persistent underperformance of the country's economy?
2. How is the Philippine business system evolving while global markets and economies—that is, global business systems—are further integrating?
3. What insights can the Philippine experience provide?

# Philippine Economy and Society

Vis-à-vis other Asian countries, Philippine history is unique because it is the only country to experience both Spanish colonization and American rule, earning it a nickname as the 'Latin America of Asia'. The Philippine economy and society have five distinct characteristics:

1. A historically high level of inequality, and slow poverty eradication even when the economy is growing.
2. An economy driven by private consumption, with industries that are not very competitive and do not provide enough jobs, but lean towards business process outsourcing, that is, 'skill export', instead.
3. An economy financed by remittances from overseas by 'exported' workers.
4. Fragmentation and extreme family-centredness, reinforced by folkloric Catholicism.
5. Fast population growth (or an economy that is 'growing people for export' (Kaye 2010: 30)).

The Philippines is a highly unequal society. Its Gini coefficient of 0.458 in 2006 ranked it 36th of 136 countries (CIA 2012). The economy has been basically run by and made for big elite business families, some of them descendants of landowners with huge land-holdings during Spanish rule. The IBON Foundation (2011: 2) reported that 'in 2009, the poorest half (50%) of Filipino families accounted for just 19.8 per cent of total income compared to the richest fifth (20%) which accounted for 51.9 per cent; the income of the richest 10 per cent of households is eighteen times that of the poorest 10 per cent of households'. The Asian Development Bank (ADB 2007a) reported a similar trend.

Because the distribution of the fruits of growth is skewed, poverty eradication has been much slower in the Philippines than in its neighbours, notwithstanding an increase in per capita income (Canlas, Khan, and Zhuang 2011). Between 2005 and 2006, about one-third of the population fell below the government-set poverty line, and more than 10 per cent fell under the $1-a-day absolute poverty line. More than 40 per cent of children belonged to poor households, and more than 20 per cent were part of subsistence-poor households (ADB 2007a; PIDS 2012).

The Philippine economy is not competitive, ranking 75th of 142 countries in the Global Competitiveness Report, almost at the bottom of the Asian countries listed (Schwab 2010). Similarly, in the World Bank's Doing Business report, the Philippines ranked 136th of 183 economies studied (World Bank 2011).

The Philippine industrial sector has been stagnating, accounting for only 31.3 per cent of GDP in 2010 (NSO 2012). This is low compared to the industrial shares of neighbouring South East Asian countries, particularly Indonesia (47%), Malaysia (50%), Thailand (45%), and Vietnam (42%) (World Bank 2008). The small Philippine industrial sector absorbed only about 10 per cent of employment in the last fifty years, a fact that may well be a major consideration in explaining the country's continuing poverty.

Low-productivity goods, such as food, beverages, textile, clothing, footwear, and similar items not requiring much inter-firm or intra-firm coordination (13.3% of GDP in 2005) dominate the domestic manufacturing sector (Canlas, Khan, and Zhuang 2011). Lack of scale, innovation and technologies are among the weaknesses affecting competitiveness—'innovation' ranked 108th, while 'technological readiness' ranked 83rd in the Global Competitiveness Report (Canlas, Khan, and Zhuang 2011; Schwab 2010; Canlas, Khan, and Zhuang 2011).

Meanwhile, the service-sector share has increased to 54.8 per cent of GDP, generating 52 per cent of employment (NSO 2012). A remarkable increase in the Business Process Outsourcing (BPO) industry, which includes call-centres, back-office operations, software development, and the like, has recently been noted. The economy is leaning towards exporting people's skills.

Third, the Philippines is one of the top suppliers of migrant labour worldwide, such that the remittances of such workers to their families are keeping the Philippine economy afloat. Estimated at $18.3 billion in 2008, these remittances were the second largest source of export revenue (Bangko Sentral ng Pilipinas 2011). The actual contribution would be bigger if informal remittances were included. The Philippines is considered competitive in 'exporting people'.

Fourth, being geographically and linguistically diverse, the Philippine society is fragmented. Its lack of a sense of unity has been always an issue in incidents requiring a certain level of coordination among players. Whether these involve labour unions, elite business, politicians, or others, they manifest a repeated pattern: Filipino groups easily break up.

What constitutes the backbone of Philippines society is the 'family-centredness' of individual Filipinos that comes partly from the Filipinos' particular kinship system. Filipinos tend to put family before others. For example, business is primarily for the family, an idea that can be carried to extremes, such that public service is also considered to be for the sake of family wealth. Philippine Catholicism, which counts 80 per cent of the population among its affiliates, reinforces the social norms of family-centrism (Abinales and Amoroso 2005), as I will elaborate later.

Fifth, between 1950 and 2010, the Philippine population increased almost fivefold (Canlas, Cham, and Zhuang 2011; NSO 2012). Its population growth rate of 1.87 per cent remains Asia's highest (CIA 2012). The combination of kinship system, influence of the Catholic Church, and the government's weak commitment to population control are acknowledged reasons behind this growth, but some pundits suggest the Philippines is, in fact, growing people for export (Tyner 2004, 2009; Kaye 2010).

# ROLE OF THE STATE

In the Failed State Index of 2012, the Philippines is considered 'critical', ranking 56th among the fifty-nine states studied and one of the worst in South East Asia (Freedom House 2012).

Why is it failing? Scholars have tried to describe Philippine capitalism as the embodiment of 'ersatz capitalism' (Yoshihara 1988), the 'anarchy of families' (McCoy 1993), 'booty capitalism' (Hutchcroft 1998), 'rent capitalism' (Sidel 1999), and 'crony capitalism' (Kang 2002); and the Philippine state as being an 'anti-developmental state' (Bello et al. 2006).

At first glance, the Philippine state appears to be 'anti-development', with the state preying on its citizenry, making it fit to be referred to as a 'predatory state', as defined by Evans (1995). However, there is debate among scholars as to whether the Philippine state is strong enough to be called 'predatory'. On closer investigation, the state is weak in relation to the overwhelming power of big business and/or landed families. These families wield considerable influence over almost all aspects of state functions, thereby enhancing the cause of private accumulation (McCoy 1993). Perhaps this explains why Hutchcroft (1998) categorized the Philippine state as a 'patrimonial oligarchic state': while the weak citizens are preyed on by the state, the state itself is weak and preyed upon by powerful oligarchic elite families whose economic bases are outside the state. In short, the state is weak in relation to the oligarchic elites, but sufficiently strong in relation to the people to function as a 'predatory state' (Quimpo 2009). This designation calls for a closer look.

Since the Spanish period, Philippine public service has become widely known to provide opportunities for plunder to families in power (World Bank 2000). Philippine bureaucracies have been less developed (De Dios 2011). The number of politically appointed positions in the Philippines is double that in the USA (World Bank 2000). Further, if one were elected to power in the country, one's family and friends would likely occupy positions for political appointees (World Bank 2001). Corruption remains rampant—the Corruption Perception Index is 2.6 out of ten, one of the worst in South East Asia (Transparency International 2011). In terms of the division of public funds, the Philippines ranked 127th of the 142 countries in the Global Competitiveness Report (Schwab 2010).

Because the potential returns from holding power are great, Philippine elections have become expensive investment exercises characterized by the '3Gs'—guns, gold, and goons. Global Integrity scored the political financing of elections extremely low, at 16 out of 100 (Global Integrity 2011). Philippine democracy is yet far from perfect.

The Philippines is known for its active NGO sector (Quimpo 2005). However, Philippine civil society does not necessarily function as checks and balances for business and the state (Abinales and Amoroso 2005). NGOs frequently function as cogs of government (Silliman and Noble 1998). Also, some businesses have created NGOs to ensure protection for elite interests, and even use these organizations to mobilize the masses, as evident in the ousting of two of the country's presidents as a result of the emergence of popular movements (Hedman 2006).

The legislature is controlled by the elite through pork barrel politics. Legislation usually reflects their interest, which is a major reason why Philippine land reform, given its legal loopholes, has been unsuccessful (Abinales and Amoroso 2005). Likewise, the legislature has been resisting the introduction of progressive taxation and/or inheritance tax systems (World Bank 2000). With the wealthy not properly taxed, the government suffers from chronic budget deficits: it has had to keep borrowing and dealing with large debt-service payments. The public trust that politicians enjoy is extremely low, ranking 128th among 142 countries (Schwab 2010).

With the national coffers empty, the government cannot provide adequate basic services, such as education and health. It also cannot invest in public works, including infrastructure (World Bank 2008). Philippine infrastructure is ranked 105th of 142 countries in the Global Competitiveness Report (Schwab 2010). As Filipinos do not trust their government, the delegitimization score of the state is extremely high (7.9 out of 10) in the Failed State Index (Freedom House 2012).

With the people not well served, the Philippines suffers from insurgencies, and it has South East Asia's longest experience of communist guerrilla activity and a Muslim separatist movement (Schiavo-Campo and Judd 2005). Its high scores in the categories of security apparatus (8.4) and group grievance (7.6) in the Failed State Index reflect these problems (Freedom House 2012).

The government cannot exercise much power to regulate business. Usually, key business sectors, such as transportation, energy, telecommunications, other utilities, the financial sector, and the like, are controlled by a limited number of corporations that are part of conglomerates owned by big business families (World Bank 2008). These families can easily influence the government, such that they are able to enjoy their rents, protect their business through setting up high entry barriers, and lessen competition. As a result, the cost of inputs for industries and the economy tends to be high. For example, the cost of power in the Philippines is considerable, just as the cost of financial intermediation is high (ADB 2007b). Reflecting these problems are the notably high score for factionalized elites (8.0) in the Failed State Index (Freedom House 2012) and the low rankings for goods market efficiency and market dominance, ranked 88th and 117th among the 142 countries in the Global Competitiveness Index (Schwab 2010).

Perceived as among the weakest institutions in the Philippine state system are the judiciary and law enforcement systems, which are seen as partial and ineffective, respectively. Some judges can allegedly be bought, just as members of the police are sometimes linked to criminal activities (World Bank 2000, 2001). In the Global Integrity Report, the Philippines' overall rating is 'Very Weak'. Indicative of this is the large gap between a legal framework score of 84 out of 100 and an actual implementation score of 31 (Transparency International 2011).

One area where the Philippine state functions well enough to be regarded as world-class is in its orchestration of the export of its people through various agencies. This will be further discussed in the 'Employment Relations' section.

# FINANCIAL SYSTEM

In 2004, the Philippine banking sector controlled 64 per cent of the financial sector's assets, while the market capitalization of the Philippine Stock Exchange was only 22 per cent, and non-bank financial institutions shared 14 per cent (ADB 2005). The banking sector has dominated the Philippine financial system over the years, with domestic private banks serving as the key players of the highly concentrated sector (IMF 2010).

In 2009, seven of the ten biggest banks belonged to conglomerates owned by elite families, and these seven owned about 60 per cent of bank assets (IMF 2010). The banking sector has historically been known for its oligopolistic behaviour and its strong influence on the Bangko Sentral ng Pilipinas (BSP), the Philippines central bank, which is supposed to have regulatory powers over the sector (Hutchcroft 1998; Krinks 2002).

Bank ownership provides various advantages to elite families. First, it is a great money-making apparatus. As the Philippine banking sector is oligopolistic and not rigorously regulated, deposit rates are relatively low, while lending rates are relatively high. The banks enjoy high spreads.

The second advantage comes from the banks' investment in bonds issued by the government, which suffers from budget deficits. Government bonds constitute risk-free investments, and are thus easy money. They make up about a quarter of the banks' assets, while loans comprise half (IMF 2010).

Third, banks within conglomerates facilitate the extension of long-term, low-cost financing, even to some questionable projects within the groups, through the utilization of domestic deposits under depressed rates. Besides, these banks are able to access funding from the international market, often at relatively low cost. Further, although the central bank can check the soundness of lending, their regulatory power is limited (Echanis 2006).

Fourth, easy access to bank financing allows owner-families to reduce their reliance on the capital market (ADB 2005). Relative to the markets of other Asian countries, the Philippine Stock Exchange is very small, largely because many Philippine private corporations are virtually family owned and these families are not interested in losing their control by going public. In 2005, some 500 to 1,000 companies were believed to be qualified to list (ADB 2005); by 2008, however, there were only 246 listed companies in the Philippines (IMF 2010).

Non-bank financial institutions are also small in the Philippines. While there are more than 150 insurance companies (ADB 2005), premiums collected in 2008 made up only about 1 per cent of GDP (IMF 2010). Philippine mutual funds are among the smallest in Asia, to the point that they were only 1.8 per cent of Thailand's (ADB 2005). In the absence of stronger state regulatory power, information on mutual funds is not sufficiently transparent or well disseminated; the funds are frequently hounded by scandals (IMF 2010).

While the Philippine financial market remains minuscule and underdeveloped, capital flight has been observed to occur cyclically, or whenever a domestic economic crisis or political instability occur (Baja 2006). In sum, the financial sector in the Philippines is notably small and underdeveloped. What exists is a system that caters to a very limited number of big business families and centres on their big banks, which provide patient capital.

It should also be noted that relatively depressed deposit rates discourage bank savings. The stock of net loans in the Philippines is equivalent to 35 per cent of GDP, rather low compared to other Asian countries (IMF 2010). Naturally, the overall contribution of the Philippine financial sector to the country's ordinary entrepreneurs is quite limited.

To further illustrate, only about 15 per cent of firms in the Philippines obtain financing for their working and investment capital needs from banks, while about 5 per cent use equity. The rest simply use their own funds or retained earnings (World Bank 2006b). In 2004, ADB (2005) surveyed 700 manufacturing firms and reported similar trends. More than half the working capital of these entities was funded internally, while only 20 per cent obtained bank or trade financing. A majority of Philippine firms do not use financing either from banks or the capital market. Instead, they maintain the status quo or try to grow within the constraints of internal financing.

## OWNERSHIP AND CORPORATE GOVERNANCE

The ownership pattern of Philippine corporations can be divided into four categories: publicly listed, foreign owned, government owned, and privately owned. Privately owned firms are most numerous and usually family owned; even some publicly listed corporations are, in reality, family owned (Saldaña 2001). Conglomerates of big business families are the main players in the Philippine economy, out-performing independent companies. These conglomerates hold 60 per cent of bank assets and 75 per cent of effective market capitalization (Saldaña 2001; IMF 2010).

Conglomerates provide a significant challenge in terms of corporate governance. Banks and creditors cannot control them, because the banks themselves are owned by the families, and are being crowded out by public debt, which accounts for about 90 per cent (Guinigundo 2005). Private debts are almost non-existent, constituting only 4 per cent of GDP (ADB 2005; IMF 2010).

The market cannot control conglomerates either. As mentioned earlier, only a small number of qualified companies in the Philippines are listed on the Philippine Stock Exchange. Even fewer are actively traded. In 2004, the top twenty equities accounted for 80 per cent of trading volumes. The participation of foreign investors in the stock market is restricted.

Furthermore, publicly listed corporations may trade only 10–20 per cent of their stocks, the exact percentage being determined by the firm's size (Saldaña 2001). Usually, families do not want to lose control, so they circulate a minimum and continue to hold large blocks of shares. Since minority shareholders cannot influence corporate decisions, their rights can be easily ignored.

The structure of family conglomerates is complicated by the regulations to protect minority shareholding rights. Family-owned conglomerates often assume pyramidal structures, comprising holding companies, some publicly listed companies, and many privately owned companies. These holding companies are privately owned, with families usually holding more than 50 per cent. Moreover, through their holding companies and, sometimes, in a combination of these and cross-shareholdings within the conglomerates, families are usually able to control their publicly listed corporations (Saldaña 2001; Echanis 2009). In 2009, among the top 100 listed companies, 74 companies each had a private company, most likely a holding company, as their largest shareholder. Meanwhile, 77 companies had a chief executive or chairman concurrently serving either as the chairman or as an executive officer of their largest shareholding (AIM Hills Governance Center 2011). This structure has has allowed funds to be easily transferred from one to another and has made it difficult for minority shareholder rights to be protected.

Quality auditing can play a key role in corporate governance. With the Philippine business sector being small, one particular accounting firm dominates, and its audits are sometimes known to be weak (World Bank 2006a). Setting up an independent board of directors can prove difficult because the community of the business elite in the Philippines is small, just as the number of individuals who have the qualifications and experience to serve as independent directors is limited. About 25 per cent of these directors are former executives of corporations (AIM Hills Governance Center 2011) and tend to hold several board seats. Most likely, they are friends of the owner-families, so are unlikely to act against these families.

Unsurprisingly, corporate governance in the Philippines is ranked worst among eleven Asian economies. At 37 out of 100, the Philippine score is lower than that of Indonesia (40) and much below that of Singapore (67), which is in first position. The Philippines had particularly low scores in four of five categories: enforcement (15, Singapore: 60), corporate government culture (25, Singapore: 53), CG rules and practices (35 versus Singapore's 65), and political and regulatory (37 versus Singapore's 69) (CLSA 2010). The World Bank's Doing Business report ranked the Philippines 132nd among 183 economies in terms of Protecting Investors, equal to Timor-Leste (132nd), but far below Malaysia (4th), Thailand (12th), and Indonesia (44th) (World Bank 2011).

After the Asian currency crisis, many mechanisms to improve corporate governance systems were rapidly installed in the Philippines throughout the 2000s (Wong 2010). For example, the Code of Corporate Governance introduced in 2002 was further revised in 2009. However, various reports point out that the absence of effective enforcement systems, such as the imposition of serious penalties for offences associated with fraud, hinders further improvements in corporate governance (Echanis 2006, 2009; Wong 2009). It seems that the country faces the same constraints again and again. Without a functioning enforcement system of laws and regulations, nothing much can be done, particularly in the face of concentration of ownership and power in business.

## INTERNAL STRUCTURE OF THE FIRM

Philippine businesses are largely family owned and were set up in the first place for families. Property rights are not well protected, and corporate governance mechanisms do not function well. In such an environment, family-business owners need to involve themselves directly in the management of their businesses.

In some cases, such as those involving conglomerates, families form family councils and meet once a week to make management decisions. Often, after the family council meetings, selected 'confidante managers' are called in to discuss further how to operationalize the decisions already made by the families. These executives are highly paid by the owners so that they are not tempted to exploit corporate wealth. Some corporations even have two separate HR sections, one directly relating to the owner CEOs and intended to handle confidante managers, and the other to handle the rest of the employees.

Beyond the inner circle executives, delegating responsibilities and coordinating tasks and information are little practised in Philippine corporations due to the difficulties inherent in the business context.

The internal structure of most corporations is hierarchical, a reflection of the very high power-distance in society. Pay and status are highly differentiated among managers and various layers of employees. Different groups eat different food in different places, wear different uniforms and clothing, commute via different types of vehicle, and reside in different kinds of place. What is more, the Labour Code and mode of communication differentiate supervisors from the rank and file. English tends to be used by those holding supervisory positions, while rank-and-file workers use Filipino and local dialects.

The socio-economic gap between regularized rank-and-file workers and casual workers is pronounced. Regularized rank-and-file workers, especially union members, are essentially labour aristocrats who enjoy job and income security by virtue of the Philippine Labour Code. On the other hand, casual workers, who are only allowed to work in the same company for less than six months, are extensively used and largely exploited: they are often paid less than minimum wages. Given the brief employment of casuals, combined with socio-economic gaps, delegation and coordination are even more difficult among the lower ranks.

Meanwhile, Philippine society is fragmented and full of mistrust. When a business is understood to have been set up for the benefit of the owner families, employees tend to feel exploited. In combination with weak property rights protection, this leads to low motivation and moral hazard. Many Filipino corporations suffer from corruption and moral hazards within. In an AIM survey (AIM Hills Governance Center 2005), 24 of 100 executives indicated that the 'manipulation of corporate documents was acceptable under certain circumstances', while 40 executives saw 'nothing wrong with interfering with their firms' bidding procedures'. They were averse to whistle-blowers, however. Given these tendencies, delegating responsibilities and tasks appears difficult.

Beneath the rhetoric of meritocracy, clientelism quietly but strongly affects every aspect of people management. Hierarchies of patron–client networks are evident from the top (i.e. owner) to the bottom (i.e. casuals), but especially among managers and supervisors, who are eligible to climb the corporate ladder whereas rank-and-file employees are rarely promoted (Kondo 2008).

In organizations with large power-distance, clients function as the 'eyes and ears' of the patron: they monitor those holding subordinate positions. As clients are also expected to work hard to stay in the organization, they are subject to training to avert the possibility of a brain or skills drain in the company, in the event that some other employees are poached by another company, whether in the Philippines or abroad, as has frequently been the case. As a consequence, clients are likely to be promoted (Kondo 2008).

However, most workers who do not have powerful patrons tend to become alienated. They are discouraged from investing in any new or additional skills specifically required for their jobs. Rather, in the hope of working overseas, some try to invest in the acquisition of more general skills and experiences usable in the international labour market.

Corporations also subscribe to paternalism, which targets all, but more so lower-ranked employees. To this end, management and business organizations try to convey the sense of a benevolent father-figure in one large happy family to their employees, for example by providing a 50kg sack of rice to each employee every month, or by providing stylish uniforms that can be worn outside work. Culturally selected images and practices of Roman Catholicism are frequently used to enhance the 'benevolent father' image.

Firms even extend paternalistic acts to neighbouring communities, especially when insurgency groups prevail. They also provide generous support to community activities, including the construction of chapels and daycare centres for kindergarten students (PBSP 2000).

## EMPLOYMENT RELATIONS

With the country's rapid population growth, the Philippine labour force is large, growing, and young. The population of individuals 15 years and above was 62.6 million in January 2012, a 1.15 million increase from the previous year (DOLE 2012). With its industries uncompetitive, the Philippines has been suffering from high unemployment and underemployment rates, of 6.4 per cent and 19.1 per cent, respectively. Another 30 per cent or so are semi-unemployed (NSO 2012).

Employees can be categorized as regular, probationary, casual, contractual, or project-based. Insofar as regular employees are concerned, labour law protects both workers' wage rights and their right to tenure. If terminated, workers frequently file cases, which can go up to the Supreme Court. To save time and expense, corporations often offer a payment so that employees will voluntarily leave their jobs—such as paying voluntary retirement benefits to an employee who has committed theft within the company, instead of firing the individual. Hiring and firing practices in the Philippines are ranked 113th and redundancy costs 118th among 142 countries in the Global Competitiveness Index (Schwab 2010).

In terms of wages, the regional statutory minimum wage in the Philippines is always set by tripartite representation, with employers represented by the Employers

Confederation of the Philippines. The minimum wage functions as a reference wage, especially for unskilled and semi-skilled labour (Ofreneo 2003).

The Philippine Constitution guarantees the right of employees to form unions in order for them to be able to undertake collective bargaining. Workers may form rank-and-file unions or supervisory unions at the enterprise level. Collective Bargaining Agreements (CBAs) can be negotiated every five years, but the economic terms in CBAs, including wages and benefits, are initially good for three years and are renegotiated for the remaining two years. Thus, unionized corporations' HR costs are fixed over multiple years.

A decreasing trend in unionization has been noted in the Philippines. In 2008, of the 38.9 million employed, only 1.7 million were unionized, and only 0.2 million workers were covered by collective bargaining agreements (DOLE 2011). Fragmentation of unions, increase in flexible work arrangements, expanding service sectors, and massive labour migration are possible causes of the decline.

Likewise, in recent years, industrial relations have been peaceful. Days lost from actual strikes and lockouts significantly declined to 34,000 by 2010 (DOLE 2011). Many corporations avoid unionization or promote industrial relations even with unions through the establishment of labour–management councils, which management uses to communicate with employees and hear their concerns (Ofreneo 2003).

The highly protective labour regulations are rooted in the long history of the Philippine labour movement. Along the way, various types of union were created, including some close to the militant communist insurgency groups demanding social fairness.

When inequality is highly pronounced, elites need to subdue the poor to avert social conflict. Taming organized labour was an easy avenue towards this, eventually resulting in the creation of labour-protective laws. Most extant unionized firms were established when the Philippines adopted import-substitution industrialization policies after independence (Ofreneo 2003). They were mostly in capital-intensive industries run by elite families that enjoyed protected rents. Since capital-intensive industries do not require many workers to begin with, it was easy to transfer some of the rents to their workers.

Currently, many Filipinos are unemployed, and millions leave the country to work abroad. For most Filipinos today, the labour market is not domestic, but overseas. This labour-force migration has been orchestrated by the state since the 1970s, with a very clear political view towards diffusing social unrest fuelled by unemployment, poverty, and the foreign exchange crisis. Even the 1974 Labour Code had provisions for this purpose (Tyner 2004).

The main state apparatus for migration is the Philippine Overseas Employment Administration (POEA), which many governments overseas recognize as a 'model'. Today, POEA processes more than 1.6 million workers a year (POEA 2011). It has the power to formulate rules and regulations governing recruitment and to adjudicate on violations of these regulations.

POEA works closely with the National Labour Relations Commission, a quasi-judicial agency that resolves labour compensation disputes; with the Overseas Worker Welfare Administration, which is a financial agency managing overseas workers' welfare funds;

and with the Technical Education and Skills Development Authority, which is responsible for developing skills (Agunias 2008; Ruiz 2008).

In order to promote migrant workers, the Philippine state refers to them as 'heroes' saving the country. Given that the policy—which seems to have been institutionalized by the massive number of people migrating, remitting money to make their families notably well off in their respective neighbourhoods, and coming back as 'heroes'—it is not surprising that Filipino children now dream of working abroad, rather than in their own country. The entire society is now leaning towards the exportation of its labour force as a national industry.

## EDUCATION AND SKILLS FORMATION

Social interest in education has been very high in the Philippines, unlike in other developing countries (Son 2011), because education is seen as having a good return on investment. According to the ADB (2009), half of households whose heads never completed elementary education are poor. The attainment of higher education is deemed key to getting a decent job.

While education can be a great equalizer, it can also a great divider. Basic education in the Philippines can be categorized as either private or public. Basic private education entails 11–14 years of schooling prior to college, inclusive of pre-school. It caters mostly to children of wealthy families and offers better school facilities than public education. Basic public education is one of the shortest in the world, at ten years. Attended by the majority of the population, it offers little or no extracurricular activities and limited facilities (Luz 2007). The drop-out rate of students in basic education is high, with fewer than 50 per cent of those entering Grade 1 completing Grade 10 or its equivalent (World Bank 2004; Son and Jose 2011).

Reflecting government budget constraints, education spending was just 2.4 per cent of GDP in 2005, far less than in other South East Asian countries such as Malaysia (8.1%), Vietnam (4.4%), and Thailand (4.2%) (Son and Jose 2011). Teachers' salaries take up around 90 per cent of the education budget, so little remains for other expenses. Classrooms, textbooks, laboratory equipment, desks, etc. are all in short supply. Moreover, good-quality female teachers tend to go abroad to work as maids, for which they earn more, depriving the public school system of good educators (World Bank 2004; Son and Jose 2011).

Perhaps the most serious problem in Philippine education is its weakness in the field of science and technology, quality- and quantity-wise. Students' proficiency in mathematics and science ranks among the lowest internationally. For instance, in the Global Competitiveness Index, the Philippines ranked 115th among 142 countries in quality of maths and science education (Schwab 2010). In the Philippines, students are not encouraged to study technology-related disciplines, nor do they wish to do so. In the 2002–2003 school year, only six students received a doctorate in engineering and technology, and only thirteen in computer science, whereas 295,000 students got bachelor degrees (Canlas, Khan, and Zhuang 2011). Thus, the Philippines has been unable to produce enough science and technology personnel to support industrial growth.

At the same time, the problem can be seen as a reflection of industry's lack of interest in innovation. Most corporations rely on technological improvements by purchasing new equipment and machinery or by hiring trained or skilled personnel: they do not bother to undertake their own research and development (Canlas, Khan, and Zhuang 2011). The number of full–time researchers in the Philippines is 81 per million people, far below Singapore (6,088), Korea (4,627), China (1,071), Thailand (311), Indonesia (205), and Vietnam (115) (Posadas 2009). Moreover, in 2006, the Philippines spent only 0.11 per cent of GDP on R&D, while Thailand spent 0.26 per cent and Malaysia, 0.69 per cent (Canlas, Khan, and Zhuang 2011).

The state cannot take care of tertiary education because of budget constraints. Instead, it relies on private institutions, which have mushroomed. In 2011, of the 2,247 higher education institutions, 1,604 were private (CHED 2011). Unfortunately, a number have become diploma mills, seeking profit instead of providing quality education (Abrenica and Tecson 2003).

It should be noted that there are many private training institutions that prepare Filipinos for overseas labour markets, and they respond quickly to the needs of international markets. For example, a large number of workers obtain maritime and nursing education so they can work as seamen, or as nurses or caregivers overseas (Alburo and Abella 2002; Ramirez 2002; Tyner 2004).

In contrast, Philippine corporations provide on-the-job training to regularized employees, especially those at supervisory and managerial levels. Big firms usually have a training department, and their professional HR officers organize various up-to-date Western-style managerial and technical training. Usually, they benchmark against practices prevalent in the USA (Ofreneo 2003).

Although Philippine corporations train well, they face skills shortages and encounter difficulty in finding managers, professionals, and administrative staff with the right skills. Among the reasons cited for the skills shortage are high turnover, lack of quality educational training, emigration of skilled workers, and low starting pay (Di Gropello 2010). Talented and experienced staff tend to take on international job assignments, particularly in developed countries that import professionals and block non-professional labour. This explains the drain in knowledge workers from the Philippines (Alburo and Abella 2002).

## INTER–COMPANY RELATIONS

Major elite families tend to have highly diversified conglomerates. However, there is no particular term for these conglomerates, and hardly any specialization can be seen within them (Saldaña 2001). There have been exceptions whereby conglomerates forge linkages with foreign companies in order to tap into the latter's resources, effectively gaining access to technologies (Batalla 1999). However, finding any type of production network among Philippine corporations remains difficult. Because different conglomerates show high concentrations within each sector, the different families compete over a small pie rather than foster productive collaboration. It becomes a zero-sum game, and inter-elite rivalry is fierce.

The only exception reflects rent-seeking and risk-avoidance investment patterns, with elite families additionally forging ad hoc alliances to influence the sector's regulatory agencies. Because of uncertainties associated with this regulatory capture, other firms, including SMEs and foreign entities, are hesitant to invest in these sectors in the Philippines (World Bank 2007).

Big-business families in the Philippines tend to fall into one of the following categories: (i) they have roots in the colonial past, (ii) they have been protected by policies imposed by the government after independence, or (iii) they have only recently emerged. The traditional elite families are likely to have belonged to the landed class during the Spanish period, before being transformed into industrialists during the American period; they grew even bigger after World War II. For their part, overseas-Chinese Filipinos experienced various incidents of discrimination, but have gained prominence over the last two decades (Krinks 2002). Among them, some collaboration has come about, sometimes with other overseas Chinese in South East and East Asia.

Regardless of the origins of these corporations, there are differences between the Philippine elite and elite leaders in other Asian countries in terms of intra-elite collaboration and rivalry. The Philippine elite is fragmented and lacks 'a clear articulation of common goals and convergence of ideas regarding the state' (Kang 2002; De Dios 2011: 3).

One hypothesis in this regard is that countries like India and Vietnam had to struggle for independence, whereas South Korea had to face threats from its neighbour. Therefore, elite leaders were forced to collaborate for the sake of broader goals. Philippine independence was guaranteed by the USA, and both country and elite leaders were under US protection, even after independence. The Philippine elite did not have to consider broader directions for the Philippines: all they needed to do was focus on narrow agendas dedicated to their personal or clans' benefit (De Dios 2011).

# SOCIAL CAPITAL

Family and religion are backbones of Philippine society. Filipino kinship is cognatic, putting equal emphasis on the male and female lines (Wolters 1999; Abinales and Amoroso 2005). A characteristic of this system is a vast spread of kin and trust around an individual: extended family members can easily number hundreds.

Since an individual can have numerous family members, when that individual suffers, there are many on whom he or she can depend. For example, it is common practice for an unemployed person to stay with a faraway relative for many months until he or she finds a job. Reciprocity is also heavily emphasized, so that this extended family system serves as a mutual help and security system.

More than 80 per cent of Filipinos are affiliated with the Roman Catholic Church (CIA 2012), whose rituals and teachings reinforce strong family loyalty. The Church also provides people with a certain degree of social capital. Many Filipinos tend to hold a certain trust in God, believing themselves to be God's created sons and daughters who appear equal before Him, regardless of wealth or poverty. They believe that God will destroy whoever destroys their trust in Him. Among the institutions studied in 2001, the Church enjoyed the highest trust score (Abad 2006); consequently, it has substantial power, be it socially, economically, or politically.

However, beyond families and the Church, social capital in the Philippines is weak in terms of both interpersonal and institutional trust. The effects of the high level of inequality over a long period on Philippine society are worth noting. Societies thus characterized exhibit similar symptoms: the erosion of social cohesion, high frequency of social conflict, and insufficient protection of property rights (Cornia and Court 2001). The Philippines suffers from this malaise (Labonne, Biller, and Chase 2007). The mistrust prevailing in society is extremely taxing in almost all aspects of the Philippine business system.

As for interpersonal relations, beyond family and kin, Philippine society is characterized by fragmentation and mistrust. The general level of interpersonal trust among Filipinos is much lower than international levels, according to the World Value Survey of 2001 (European Values Study Group and World Values Survey Association 2006). In this survey, Filipinos indicated that there were only a few they could trust completely (76%), expecting others to intend to take advantage (77%).

As for institutional trust, the country's public sector is perceived to be highly corrupt, and people in general do not trust public authorities. The Philippine judiciary and law-enforcement agencies have been said to be the least trusted. The Philippines is a litigious society with comprehensive laws and regulations, but some lawyers, judges, and police officers can be bought. Birth certificates, licences, and other documents are easily forged. Crime and murder rates are high, and guns are also easily available. As discussed earlier, both communist and Muslim insurgent activities persist. Institutional trust is weak, as with property rights protection.

# INSTITUTIONAL COMPLEMENTARITIES

Similar to the business systems of advanced industrialized economies, such as the USA or Germany (Hall and Soskice 2001), the Philippine business system is high in complementarities. However, in the Philippine case, these complementarities are such as to degrade its economy and competitiveness.

This chapter started with the question, 'What is the root cause of the persistent under-performance of the country's economy?' To understand the root cause, the concept of the 'inequality trap' highlighted by the World Bank in its *World Development Report of 2006* appears helpful (World Bank 2005).

An inequality trap is a phenomenon whereby inequalities instigate more inequalities. When large power differences exist as an initial condition, they tend to shape political, economic, and socio-cultural institutions in directions that allow the current power structure to flourish or be maintained. Therefore, a society experiencing persistent and severe inequalities can more easily be trapped. Once trapped, inequalities persist even when the economy grows. Eventually that society's capacity to be competitive will be eroded (World Bank 2005).

As the Philippines is a patrimonial oligarchic state, its economy is characterized by a concentration of wealth among a small group of elite families, sometimes dating back to the Spanish or American period. Over time, even as the Philippine economy grew, poverty did not diminish. It is easy to imagine how the Philippines' economic, political, and socio-cultural mores and institutions were historically shaped to allow these elite families to retain their power.

The Philippine business system can be seen as exemplifying 'inequality-trapped capitalism' as follows:

1. State: The power of elite families overwhelms the state. Insufficient tax collection, corruption, lack of fair competition, deviation of funds, and inefficient resource allocation generally favour the elite and big business. However, this makes it difficult for the state to invest in infrastructure and basic services, including education, which are key to raising people's standards of living. Higher input prices from regulatory capture, such as those seen in electric power, cause public and business entrepreneurs to suffer.

2. Finance: Banking businesses provide wealth to big business families, while also meeting the financial needs of their conglomerates. But lower deposit rates do not mobilize people's savings, and high finance costs hinder the growth of SMEs.

3. Corporate governance: Corporate governance measures through banks, stock market, and directors are ineffective, enabling big families to take advantage of minority shareholders. The stock market remains small and does not help entrepreneurs. The financial sector does not promote efficient resource allocation; instead, it further widens the financial gap among people.

4. The internal structure of the firm: The hierarchically divided structure of firms reflects and reinforces socio-economic divisions. Essentially nepotism, the patron-client system generally discourages workers from engaging and investing in upgrading their skills.

5. Employment relations: The heavy protection accorded to regular workers reflects an effort to buy industrial peace by channelling part of rents to regularized workers only when socio-economic inequalities are high. It increases the gap between regularized and non-regularized workers.

6. Education and skills formation: In spite of the social preference for education, the lack of public funds in support of education widens the socio-economic gaps.
7. Inter-company relations: Lack of inter-elite collaborations, except for lobbying and regulatory capture, prevent coordination that would help promote the country's broad objectives, including the competitiveness of its industries.
8. Social capital: Prolonged high inequality weakens interpersonal and institutional social capital. The weak trust among people and social systems, especially in the judiciary and law enforcement, directly hampers the development of the financial system (e.g. from trust to mutual funds), corporate governance (e.g. from trust to auditing), internal firm structure (e.g. from trust, to people, to delegation and coordination), employment relations (e.g. firing), education and skills formation (e.g. meritocratic HR practices so workers will be motivated to invest in skills acquisition), and inter-company relations (e.g. inter-elite rivalry).

# EVOLUTIONARY DYNAMICS

Responding to the ageing and decreasing populations of the developed world, among other factors, more than 250 million people around the globe hold, in one way or another, the status of migrant (Kaye 2010). Amidst globalization, the Philippines business system, which exemplifies 'inequality-trapped capitalism', is integrated into global markets and economies. The Philippines is one of the top sourcing countries of migrant labour in the world, and a dawning of 'exodus capitalism' or 'migration-trapped capitalism' can be observed in the country.

We can further explain the trajectory from 'inequality-trapped' to 'exodus' or 'migration-trapped' capitalism in the Philippines. While inequalities persist, industries cannot be competitive, and uncompetitive industries cannot provide jobs nor realize earnings in foreign currencies. This has created an exodus tendency, and systems and institutions have developed to formalize it, to the extent that exporting people has become a 'national industry', involving almost every part of society. This has also created a 'brain drain', such that it is hard for the country to gain and maintain competitiveness. Once a country reaches this stage, it will need to keep exporting a proportion of its citizens just to stay afloat. This phenomenon is not restricted to the Philippines. However, among sourcing countries, Philippine migration institutions and systems are recognized as among the most sophisticated and influential in the world, with even the World Bank trying to facilitate the adoption of the Philippine model in other sourcing countries. Hence, the dawning of 'exodus capitalism' in the Philippines can be considered a sophisticated variant at this time. Its features can be summarized as follows:

1. State: The state orchestrates the exportation of its people through POEA and other agencies. The state works hard to develop labour markets by diplomacy.
2. Finance Institutions: Institutions for remittances are well developed.

3. Ownership and corporate governance: These are not directly related. (Consumption-oriented and domestic-oriented industries grow, without competitiveness getting in the way, thanks to the remittances.)

4. Internal structure of firms: Firms expect that they can source employees with overseas experience. Also, firms are prepared for the eventuality that employees may leave for overseas positions.

5. Employment relations: The Labour Code provides legitimacy for the state to orchestrate personnel export. POEA and other agencies regulate private recruitment agencies, and provide a certain level of protection to migrant workers.

6. Education: Many education institutions provide skills training, catering to overseas labour markets. English education is now valued.

7. Inter-company Relations: The state tries to collaborate with NGOs, educational institutions, and other sectors of society to ensure the success of 'exporting people' as an industry. It collaborates with media and mounts campaigns to educate people about how migrant workers are the 'heroes' of the Philippines. BPO industries as skills exporters proliferate. For some individuals, like IT engineers, working for a BPO facility prepares them well for overseas assignments.

8. Social Capital: Civil-society NGOs try to protect migrant workers. Families provide extended networks lending support at home and abroad. The Church provides support to overseas communities. The Church also maintains and promotes its anti-birth control stance.

# CONCLUSION

The Philippine business system can be characterized as follows. The government is unable to do the following properly: regulate business, enforce laws, collect taxes, invest in infrastructure, or provide services to the people. The financial system is small and dominated by a limited number of banks belonging to conglomerates owned by big business families. Most Philippine corporations are family owned, with the more important ones being part of conglomerates owned by elite business families. Corporate governance is weak and not very relevant in such entities. The internal structure of corporations is hierarchical, a reflection of the very high power distance in Philippine society.

Patron–client relationships are heavily relied upon in almost all aspects of HR practice. Employment relations are rigid insofar as regular employees are concerned. The formerly militant labour unions are now less restive and industry relations more peaceful. Meanwhile, many Filipinos are unemployed and millions leave the country to work abroad.

Foreign observers of the Philippines note a deterioration in public education. Philippine education is particularly weak in science and technology, but industries themselves also show a lack of interest in R&D. Brain-drain is the issue here.

The conglomerates of major elite families are highly diversified rather than special-ized, as manifested in their rather ad hoc responses to rent-seeking opportunities. These elites' lack of initiative to move beyond the rather protected domestic market, combined with intra-elite rivalries, prevents them from cooperating towards coming up with innovations and enhancing efficiencies to create internationally competitive industries.

Social capital is very weak in the Philippines in terms of institutional and interper-sonal trust. Filipinos rely on large extended families, a phenomenon leading to excessive family-centredness.

What insights can the Philippine experience provide? There are three. The first relates to 'inequality-trapped capitalism'. Under ongoing globalization, many developed and developing countries have been experiencing increasing and persistent inequalities within their societies, as exemplified in the wide and rapid spread of the 2011 Occupy Wall Street demonstrations across the world. The Philippine experience points to the possibility of an undesirable trajectory of capitalism in the future, and it should be a warning to initiate serious efforts to make development as inclusive as possible.

The second insight relates to 'exodus' or 'migration-trapped' capitalism, which may be emerging quietly but steadily under twenty-first-century globalization. This is a form of capitalism characterized by mass migration and the convergence of domestic and international labour markets. Will this type of capitalism solve issues of inequality in the world at large? The answer has yet to be seen.

The third insight is the importance of studying failed or uncompetitive business sys-tems. Management scholars have focused research on successful and competitive state cases for many years because of their impression that competition ultimately success-fully solves many social issues. However, the global world today is not as successful or competitive as we would wish, experiencing frequent financial crisis and the deepening of certain social issues.

Management scholars may need to shed light on failed or uncompetitive capitalisms. This may be the right time to appreciate the rich lessons that unsuccessful state cases can provide for the future global world.

## REFERENCES

Abad, Ricardo, G. (2006). *Aspects of Social Capital in the Philippines: Findings from a National Survey*. Manila, Social Weather Stations.

Abinales, P. and D. Amoroso (2005). *State and Society in the Philippines*. Lanham, Rowman and Littlefield.

Abrenica, J. V. and G. R. Tecson (2003). 'Can the Philippines Ever Catch Up?' In S. Lall and S. Urata, Eds., *Competitiveness, FDI and Technological Activity in East Asia*: 268–304. Cheltenham, Edward Elgar.

ADB (2005). *Private Sector Assessment Philippines*. Manila, Asian Development Bank.

—— (2007a). *Key Indicators 2007: Inequality in Asia*. Manila, Asian Development Bank.

—— (2007b). *Philippines: Critical Development Constraints*. Manila, Asian Development Bank.

—— (2009). *Poverty in the Philippines: Causes, Constraints, and Opportunities.* Manila, Asian Development Bank.

Agunias, D. (2008). *Managing Temporary Migration: Lessons from the Philippine Model.* Washington, DC, Migration Policy Institute.

AIM Hills Governance Center (2005). *Towards Improved Corporate Governance: A Handbook on Developing Anti-Corruption Programs.* Manila, Asian Institute of Management.

—— (2011). *2009 Corporate Governance Trends in the 100 Largest Publicly Listed Companies in the Philippines.* Manila, Asian Institute of Management.

Alburo, F. A. and D. I. Abella (2002). *Skilled Labour Migration from Developing Countries: Study on the Philippines.* International Migration Papers 51. Geneva, ILO.

Baja, E. L (2006). 'Was Capital Fleeing Southeast Asia? Estimates from Indonesia, Malaysia, the Philippines, and Thailand'. *Asia Pacific Business Review* 12(3): 261–283.

Bangko Sentral ng Pilipinas (2011). 'Overseas Filipinos Remittances'. Retrieved 4 March 2011 from <http://www.bsp.archgov.ph/statistics/2010.keystat/ofw.htm>.

Batalla, E. (1999). 'Zaibatsu Development in the Philippines: The Ayala Model'. *Southeast Asian Studies* 37(1): 18–49.

Bello, W., H. Docena, M. de Guzman, and M. L. Malig (2006) *The Anti-Development State: The Political Economy of Permanent Crisis in the Philippines.* London, Zed Books.

Canlas, D., M. Cham, and J. Zhuang (2011). 'Development Performance and Policy'. In D. Canlas, M. E. Khan, and J. Zhuang, Eds., *Diagnosing the Philippine Economy*: 13–31. London, Anthem Press and Manila, Asian Development Bank.

—— M. E. Khan, and J. Zhuang (2011). 'Critical Constraints to Growth and Poverty Reduction'. In D. Canlas, M. E. Khan, and J. Zhuang, Eds., *Diagnosing the Philippine Economy*: 33–97. London, Anthem Press and Manila, Asian Development Bank.

CHED (Commission on Higher Education) (2011). 'Information on Higher Education System' (as of April 2011). Retrieved 30 July 2012 from <http://www.ched.gov.ph/chedwww/index.php/eng/Information>

CIA (Central Intelligence Agency) (2012). 'The World Factbook'. Retrieved 18 July 2012 from <https://www.cia.gov/library/publications/the-world-factbook/geos/rp.html>; <https://www.cia.gov/library/publications/the-world-factbook/rankorder/2119rank.html>. CLSA Asia-Pacific Markets (2010). *CG Watch 2010.* Hong Kong, CLSA.

Cornia, G. A. and J. Court (2001). *Inequality, Growth and Poverty in the Era of Liberalization and Globalization. Policy Brief.* Helsinki, UNU/WIDER.

De Dios, E. J. (2011). 'Governance, Institutions, and Political Economy'. In D. Canlas, M. E. Khan, and J. Zhuang, Eds., *Diagnosing the Philippine Economy*: 295–336. London, Anthem Press and Manila, Asian Development Bank.

Di Gropello, E. (2010). *Skills for the Labor Market in the Philippines.* Washington, DC, World Bank.

DOLE (Department of Labour and Employment Statistics, Bureau of Labour and Employment Statistics) (2011). LABSTAT Update 15(9): 1–9.

—— (2012) LABSTAT Update 16(12): 1–9.

Echanis, E. S. (2006). 'Philippine Corporate Governance: Issues and Reforms'. *Philippine Management Review* 13: 21–41.

—— (2009). 'Holding Companies: A Structure for Managing Diversification'. *Philippine Management Review* 16: 1–12.

European Values Study Group and World Values Survey Association (2006). 'European and World Values Surveys Four-Wave Integrated Data File, 1981–2004, V. 20060423, 2006'.

*Inter-University Consortium for Political and Social Research.* Retrieved 30 July 2012 from <http://www.icpsr.umich.edu/icpsrweb/ICPSR/studies/4531>.

Evans, P. (1995) *Embedded Autonomy: States and Industrial Transformation*. Princeton, Princeton University Press.

Freedom House (2012). *Failed State Index 2012: Fund for Peace and the Carnegie Endowment for International Peace*. Retrieved 30 July 2012 from <http://www.foreignpolicy.com/failed_states_index_2012_interactive>.

Global Integrity (2011). *Global Integrity Report 2010*. Retrieved 30 July 2012 from <http://www.globalintegrity.org/report/Philippines/2010>.

Guinigundo, Diwa C. (2005). 'The Philippine Financial System: Issues and Challenges'. BIS Paper No.28. Retrieved 30 July 2012 from <http://www.bis.org/publ/bppdf/bispap28t.pdf>.

Hall, P. A. and D. Soskice (2001). *Varieties of Capitalism: The Institutional Foundations of Comparative Advantage*. Oxford, Oxford University Press.

Hedman, E. E. (2006). *In the Name of Civil Society: Contesting Free Elections in the Post-Colonial Philippines*. Honolulu, University of Hawaii Press.

Hutchcroft, P. D. (1998). *Booty Capitalism: The Politics of Banking in the Philippines*. Quezon, Ateneo de Manila University Press.

IBON Foundation (2011). 'Submission by IBON Foundation, a Philippine NGO, to UN Human Rights Council (UNHRC) for Universal Periodic Review (UPR) of the Philippines during the 13th UPR Session (21 May–1 June 2012)'. Retrieved 18 July 2012 from <http://lib.ohchr.org/HRBodies/UPR/Documents/session13/PH/IF_UPR_PHL_S13_2012_IBONFoundation_E.pdf>.

IMF (2010). '*Philippines: Financial System Stability Assessment Update*'. IMF Country Report 10/90. Washington DC, IMF.

Kang, D. (2002). *Crony Capitalism: Corruption and Development in South Korea and the Philippines*. Cambridge, Cambridge University Press.

Kaye, J. (2010). *Moving Millions: How Coyote Capitalism Fuels Global Immigration*. Hoboken, NJ, Wiley.

Kondo, M. (2008). 'Twilling bata-bata into Meritocracy: Merito-Patronage Management System in a Modern Filipino Corporation'. *Philippine Studies* 56: 251–284.

Krinks, P. (2002). *The Economy of the Philippines: Elites, Inequalities and Economic Restructuring*. London, Routledge.

Labonne, J., D. Biller, and R. Chase (2007). *Inequality and Relative Wealth: Do They Matter for Trust? Social Development Paper Series 103*, Washington, DC, World Bank.

Luz, J. M. (2007). 'Are We (The Philippines) Educating for Competitiveness?'. International Institute of Rural Reconstruction. Retrieved 18 July 2012 from <http://www.fnf.org.ph/downloadables/Mike%20Luz.pdf>.

McCoy, A. W. (1993). 'An Anarchy of Families: A Historiography of the State and the Family in the Philippines'. In A. W. McCoy, Ed., *An Anarchy of Families: State and Family in the Philippines*: 1–32. Madison, University of Wisconsin Press.

NSO (National Statistics Office) (2012). 'Statistics'. Retrieved 18 July 2012 from <http://www.census.gov.ph/index.html>.

Ofreneo, R. E. (2003). 'Philippines'. In M. Zanko and M. Ngui, Eds., *Handbook of Human Resource Management Policies and Practices in Asia-Pacific Economics*: 390–445. Cheltenham, Edward Elgar.

PBSP (Philippine Business for Social Progress) (2000). *Our Legacy*. Manila, Philippines, PBSP.

PIDS (Philippine Institute for Development Studies) (2012). 'Economic and Social Database'. Retrieved 18 July 2012 from <http://econdb.pids.gov.ph/tablelists/table/303. http://econdb.pids.gov.ph/tablelists/table/305>.

POEA (2011). 'Overseas Employment Statistics'. Retrieved 30 July 2012 from <http://www.poea.gov.ph/stats/2010_Stats.pdf>.

Posadas, R. D. (2009). 'Scientific and Technological Capabilities and Economic Catch-up'. *Philippine Management Review* 16: 131–153.

Quimpo, N. G. (2005). 'Oligarchic Patrimonialism, Bossism, Electoral Clientelism, and Contested Democracy in the Philippines'. *Comparative Politics* 37(2): 229–250.

—— (2009). 'The Philippines: Predatory Regime, Growing Authoritarian Features'. *Pacific Review* 22(3): 335–353.

Ramirez, V. E. (2002). *Philippine Maritime and Nursing Education: Benchmarking with APEC Best Practices. Policy Note 2002–05*. Manila, Philippine Institute for Development Studies.

Ruiz, N. G. (2008). *Managing Migration: Lessons from the Philippines. Migration and Remittance Brief 6*. Washington, DC, World Bank.

Saldaña, C. G. (2001). 'Philippines'. In M. Capulong, D. Edwards, D. Webb, and J. Zhuang, Eds., *Corporate Governance and Finance in East Asia*: 155–228. Manila, Asian Development Bank.

Schiavo-Campo, S. and M. Judd (2005). *The Mindanao Conflict in the Philippines: Roots, Costs, and Potential Peace Dividend*. Washington, DC, World Bank.

Schwab, K. (2010). *Global Competitiveness Report 2010–2011*. Geneva, World Economic Forum.

Sidel, J. T. (1999) *Capital, Coercion, and Crime: Bossism in the Philippines*. Palo Alto, Stanford University Press.

Silliman, G. S. and L. G. Noble (1998). 'Citizen Movements and Philippine Democracy'. In G. S. Silliman and L. G. Noble, Eds., *Organizing For Democracy: NGOs, Civil Society, and the Philippine State*: 280–310. Honolulu, University of Hawaii Press.

Son, H. H. (2011). 'Human Capital'. In D. Canlas, M. E. Khan and J. Zhuang, Eds., *Diagnosing the Philippine Economy*: 193–208. London, Anthem Press and Manila, Asian Development Bank.

—— and J. C. Jose (2011). 'Equity and Social Sector'. In D. Canlas, M. E. Khan and J. Zhuang, Eds., *Diagnosing the Philippine Economy*: 208–259. London, Anthem Press and Manila, Asian Development Bank.

Transparency International (2011). 'Corruption Perception Index 2011'. Retrieved 30 July 2012 from <http://cpi.transparency.org/cpi2011/>.

Tyner, J. A. (2004). *Made in the Philippines: Gendered Discourse and the Making of Migrants*. London and New York, Routledge Curzon.

—— (2009). *The Philippines*. New York, Routledge.

Wolters, O. W. (1999). *History, Culture, and Region in Southeast Asian Perspectives* (Revised ed.). Ithaca, SEAP.

Wong, D. C. (2009). 'An Assessment of Corporate Governance Reforms in the Philippines: 2002–2009'. *Philippine Management Review* 16: 24–57.

World Bank (2000). *Combating Corruption in the Philippines*. Washington, DC, World Bank.

—— (2001). *Combating Corruption in the Philippines—Updates*. Washington, DC, World Bank.

—— (2004). *Philippines Education Policy Reforms in Action: A Review of Progress Since PESS and PCER*. Washington, DC, World Bank.

—— (2005). *World Development Report 2006: Equity and Development*. Washington, DC, World Bank.

—— (2006a). *Philippines—Report on the Observance of Standards and Codes (ROSC): Accounting and Auditing Update*. Washington, DC, World Bank.

—— (2006b). *Philippines—Report on the Observance of Standards and Codes (ROSC): Corporate Governance Country Assessment*. Washington, DC, World Bank.

—— (2007). *Philippines—Invigorating Growth, Enhancing its Impact*. Washington, DC, World Bank.

—— (2008). *Rising Growth, Declining Investment: The Puzzle of the Philippines Breaking the 'Low-Capital-Stock' Equilibrium*. Washington, DC, World Bank.

—— (2011). 'Doing Business in 2012'. Retrieved 30 July 2012 from <http://www.doingbusiness. org/data/exploreeconomies/philippines>.

Yoshihara, K. (1988). *The Rise of Ersatz Capitalism in Southeast Asia*. Singapore and New York, Oxford University Press.

# CHAPTER 10

........................................

# SINGAPORE

*Open State-Led Capitalism*

........................................

## RICHARD W. CARNEY[1]

FROM the perspective of capitalist theories, Singapore is a fascinating case. According to the World Bank's Ease of Doing Business Index, Singapore has ranked first in the world since 2007.[2] With respect to gross domestic product (GDP) per capita (on a purchasing power parity basis), Singapore ranked 5th out of 180 nations in 2010, according to the World Bank;[3] in 1965, it ranked 42nd out of 114 nations.

On the face of it, the small city-state is a glowing example of how to do things right. Yet there are reasons to be cautious about predicting future success on the basis of its past performance. One area of concern is its capacity to develop and sustain a durable base of innovative activity in the private sector. Once an economy ascends to the highest income levels, future growth increasingly depends on productivity improvements, and these in turn depend on innovation. That Singapore may face difficulties in this arena is an implication that emerges naturally by considering whether its capitalist arrangements—including financial system, corporate ownership and governance, internal firm structure, employment relations, educational and skills training systems, inter-firm relations, and social capital—generate complementary or conflicting innovation incentives. The structure of these institutions is heavily influenced by two key features: (1) the city-state's deep links to the international economy; and (2) its political system. So long as these persist in their present form, which seems highly likely, existing institutional arrangements and the attendant implications for innovation are likely to continue.

This chapter proceeds first with an overview of Singapore's political system and how it, in combination with its highly open economy, has influenced the capitalist arrangements mentioned earlier. The penultimate section discusses the extent to which these capitalist spheres complement one another, and their implications for innovation. The conclusion draws lessons for theories about modern capitalism, as well as implications for policy-makers and managers.

# ROLE OF THE STATE

After independence in 1965, the People's Action Party (PAP) dominated government and implemented export-oriented developmental state policies similar to those of Taiwan and South Korea (Woo-Cumings 1999). Part of this strategy involved shifting the country away from a sole dependence on *entrepôt* trade and towards industrialization (Chiu, Ho, and Lui 1997). To speed up economic modernization and to deal with unemployment, the state nurtured large state-owned enterprises and enticed multinational corporations to invest in Singapore. Adopting a foreign capital-dependent development strategy, the state imposed mandatory requirements on reporting and auditing to enhance financial transparency in publicly listed companies and strengthened both technological and business education to nurture local professionals (Tan, Leong, and Pang 1999).

This reliance on foreign capital, multinational businesses, and *entrepôt* trade remains vital to the structure of the economy, and has fundamentally shaped the composition of the city-state's capitalist institutions. These institutional outcomes received early political support from local Chinese business interests, who strongly supported the PAP following independence—particularly in contrast to those institutional arrangements favoured by a nascent Communist movement (Tan and Jomo 2001; Mauzy and Milne 2002).

Today, Singapore's political system is a hybrid regime between authoritarianism and democracy, according to the Economist Intelligence Unit's Democracy Index. It retains the hallmarks of what Deyo (1981: 107) has labelled a 'corporate paternalistic political order', with the business sector and broader economy firmly guided by the state, although it has evolved beyond playing 'catch-up' to other economies as a traditional developmental state. Table 10.1 illustrates that, compared with other high-income countries, Singapore is far less democratic, with the exception of Hong Kong. Germany and the USA are listed because they are commonly regarded as two contrasting ideal-types of how market economies are structured. It will be useful to compare Singapore to these nations along the capitalist dimensions in particular. Sweden and Switzerland are, like Singapore, small open economies (though with Sweden tending to privilege more social-welfare outcomes), while Switzerland's position as a centre for banking resembles that of Singapore's. Hong Kong, Taiwan, and South Korea are also listed, since they have also recently achieved high-income status as small open economies in the East Asian context.

The political indicators listed in Table 10.1 illustrate that the political arrangements are geared towards political stability and reflect the dominance of the PAP and its pro-business policies. Compared with the other countries listed, Singapore stands out for its low level of political participation. This is partly due to the lack of an independent media to foster political awareness among its citizens—all the papers and broadcast stations are controlled by the ruling party. Also, it is illegal for citizens to take part in any 'cause-related activity', no matter how many people are involved (a 'cause-related activity' is defined as a show of support for or against a position, person, group, or government). For 'major' events, the 2009 Public Order Act permits police to issue 'move-on' orders and to prohibit filming of their own activities. The use of defamation and bankruptcy actions against government critics has further contributed to an environment lacking in free and open political debate (Bryan 2007). Its electoral process is also relatively low, which is partly attributable to the lack of open political competition for opposition parties, and the difficulty of forming political and civic organizations that are free of state interference and surveillance (Bryan 2007).

However, the functioning of government is relatively high, because of the quality of its civil service. Once the government identifies talented individuals at an early age, it continually invests in them with scholarships and other opportunities. At the same time, talented individuals from the private sector are recruited into the civil service—the current education minister, for example, used to be a surgeon. Public-sector wages are kept closely in line with the pay structure in the private sector to attract capable people and maintain high standards of integrity. Pay is also linked to performance. Higher increments are given to more efficient staff and the principles of a meritocracy reign throughout all areas of public service. Teachers, for instance, need to have finished in the top third of their class. Headmasters are often appointed in their 30s and rewarded with merit pay if they do well, but moved on quickly if their schools underperform. Tests and performance assessments are ubiquitous. All this helps to ensure that government services are implemented effectively and efficiently, that corruption is kept low, and that loyalty to the government is assured. At the same time, the lack of effective checks and balances across government institutions, combined with a lack of transparency, keeps the functioning of government score lower than other developed democracies.

Political culture is also relatively high, because of popular support for technocrats/experts (in contrast to a democratically elected government) who have successfully delivered economic growth over a long period of time, as well as low levels of crime, corruption, and pollution. It is lower than other democracies because of the relatively lower proportion of people who believe that democracy benefits economic performance, and those who consider democracy better than any other form of government.

Finally, civil liberties are bolstered by the freedom of electronic media, religious tolerance, and the protection of private property from government influence, as well as high levels of basic security. It is relatively lower than other democracies because of the lack of freedom of expression, a free print media without state influence, restrictions on the freedom to form professional organizations and trades unions, and because of the extent to which the government invokes new risks and threats as an excuse for curbing civil liberties.

Since independence, key decision-making power has remained concentrated in the hands of the PAP, which has ensured the adoption and enforcement of business-oriented policies. For example, the economy's strong reliance on foreign business and investment has led the PAP to enforce compliance with global financial standards, strong protections for shareholders/investors while simultaneously retaining dominant ownership by local families or the state, English-language education modelled on Western systems,

**Table 10.1 Political system attributes**

| Country | Regime type | Overall score and rank (out of 167) | Electoral process and pluralism | Functioning of government | Political participation | Political culture | Civil liberties |
|---|---|---|---|---|---|---|---|
| Singapore | Hybrid regime | 5.89 #82 | 4.33 | 7.50 | 2.78 | 7.50 | 7.35 |
| *Capitalist Ideal-Types* | | | | | | | |
| USA | Full democracy | 8.18 #17 | 9.17 | 7.86 | 7.22 | 8.13 | 9.12 |
| Germany | Full democracy | 8.38 #14 | 9.58 | 7.86 | 7.22 | 8.13 | 9.12 |
| *Small, Open European States* | | | | | | | |
| Sweden | Full democracy | 9.50 #4 | 9.58 | 9.64 | 8.89 | 9.38 | 10.00 |
| Switzerland | Full democracy | 9.09 #9 | 9.58 | 9.29 | 7.78 | 9.38 | 9.41 |
| *Small, Open East Asian States* | | | | | | | |
| Hong Kong | Hybrid regime | 5.92 #80 | 3.50 | 5.36 | 4.44 | 6.88 | 9.41 |
| South Korea | Full democracy | 8.11 #20 | 9.17 | 7.86 | 7.22 | 7.50 | 8.82 |
| Taiwan | Flawed democracy | 7.52 #36 | 9.58 | 7.14 | 5.56 | 5.63 | 9.71 |

*Source*: Economist Intelligence Unit Democracy Index, 2010.

and the privileging of business interests over labour with a variety of laws and practices, including the current ease of hiring and firing employees. This last-cited element has contributed to the valuing of general skills in education. The efficient legal system, modelled on the British system and further strengthened by the need to appeal to foreign business, has contributed to arm's-length inter-firm relations and generates high levels of institutionalized trust. Indeed, the capitalist spheres examined here fundamentally owe their particular characteristics to the state's deep ties to and reliance on foreign capital and business.

# Financial System

Since independence in 1965, domestic financial activities have been kept largely separate from offshore activities, to insulate the domestic economy from both overcrowding by foreign participation and external shocks. This separation became all the more important when Singapore pioneered offshore currency markets in Asia with the establishment of the Asian dollar market in 1968, the counterpart of the Eurodollar market. While rigid guidelines have separated offshore banking services from the domestic financial sector,[4] the government has encouraged foreign participation through minimal regulations for offshore banking activities. As a result, assets in the offshore banking sector relative to domestic bank assets have increased from 27 per cent in 1970 to about 124 per cent in 2010 (Giap and Kang 1999; Dept of Statistics 2011).

Maintaining a separation between domestic and international segments of the financial sector allows for the non-internationalization of the Singapore dollar. Such a policy is seen as indispensable to the objective of 'throwing sand into the wheels' of perfect capital mobility and makes it harder to mount a speculative attack. For example, the only known major speculative attack on the Singapore dollar occurred in September 1985. The Singapore dollar was sold short against the US dollar in the foreign-exchange market, resulting in a 5 per cent depreciation of the local currency in just a few weeks. The Monetary Authority of Singapore successfully fended off the attacks by raising the overnight interest rate above 120 per cent, which tightened liquidity in the short-term money market in the domestic banking sector. This hurt speculators who needed short cover for their exchange positions from the local money market (*Straits Times* 1985). The effectiveness of this strategy depended on the lack of a matching pool of offshore Singapore dollars which could neutralize the tightening of liquidity in the local money market. To Singaporean leaders, the success of the interest rate hike demonstrated the benefits of the non-internationalization policy.

However, this policy has hindered the development of the capital markets. For example, not until November 1996 were foreign companies permitted to list Singapore dollar-denominated shares on the Stock Exchange of Singapore, and then only if they had operating headquarters status and at least 35 per cent of their revenue, profits, or expenses attributable to Singapore.[5] Under such stringent requirements, only two companies qualified. The guidelines have since been relaxed and current listing requirements do not stipulate any of these preconditions. As a result, as of the end of November 2009, 43 per cent of market capitalization was accounted for by non-Singaporean companies (Witt 2011).

The impact of non-internationalizing the Singapore dollar has been greater on the development of bond markets, which are further hindered by the government's budget surpluses for government bonds, as well as by ample liquidity from the domestic banking system with respect to corporate bonds. However, as part of the effort to develop this area of its financial services sector, (1) the government has steadily increased its issuance of debt securities to promote the development of bond markets; (2) the government has conducted experiments with the 'freer use' of Singapore-denominated bonds both by non-residents and by residents planning to use the proceeds outside Singapore; and (3) statutory boards and government-linked companies are encouraged to raise funds directly by issuing bonds in the market, instead of relying on government funding (Wu 2009).

The Asian Financial Crisis of 1997 revealed potential problems with existing arrangements and led to significant financial sector reforms designed to diversify and deepen its financial markets, as well as develop the country's role as a regional financial centre. These reforms have included (1) opening the domestic financial industry to greater foreign competition; (2) bringing regulatory and supervisory arrangements closer in line with international best practices; (3) developing deeper and more liquid fixed-income and equity markets; (4) promoting the asset-management industry; and (5) gradually liberalizing restrictions on the international use of the Singapore dollar. According to the IMF (2004), Singapore has become highly compliant with Banking Core Principles for effective banking supervision, and rules and standards advocated by the International Association of Insurance Supervisors, the International Organization of Securities Commissions (IOSCO), and the core principles for systemically important payment systems (CPSS) and CPSS–IOSCO Recommendations for Securities Settlement Systems. Key initiatives, discussed later, have also been taken to improve corporate governance.

Reflecting these efforts to bolster its financial markets, the first two columns in Table 10.2 demonstrate that, with respect to GDP, Singapore's equities markets appear to be well developed. Two dates are chosen, because of the financial crisis of 2008, which may lead to biased numbers for 2009. Data for both stock-market capitalization and deposit bank assets (representing the domestic banking sector) are listed, since they are indicative of the financial sector's orientation towards an arms-length versus a more coordinated/organized form of capitalism. The ratio of the two is particularly helpful in this regard. For example, it is clear that the USA exhibits a stronger reliance on stock markets, while Germany depends more heavily on banking. However, the Singapore numbers are inflated, because of the heavy representation of foreign companies on the stock exchange; the second number for 2009 indicates the adjusted value, which is 0.84. As a result, Singapore is more oriented towards bank lending when considering the adjusted value, which is consistent with the state's 'paternalistic' guidance of the local

**Table 10.2 Financial system indicators**

| | Stock Market Capitalization/GDP | | Deposit Bank Assets/GDP | | Ratio of Market Cap/Bank Assets | | Private Bond Market Capitalization/GDP | |
|---|---|---|---|---|---|---|---|---|
| | 2005 | 2009 | 2005 | 2009 | 2005 | 2009 | 2005 | 2009 |
| Singapore | 2.49 | 1.48/0.84[a] | 1.16 | 1.16 | 2.14 | 1.34/0.72[a] | 0.18 | 0.13 |
| *Capitalist Ideal-Types* | | | | | | | | |
| USA | 1.35 | 1.52 | 0.60 | 0.60 | 2.25 | 2.17 | 1.15 | 1.35 |
| Germany | 0.43 | 0.74 | 1.37 | 1.15 | 0.31 | 0.64 | 0.34 | 0.37 |
| *Small, Open European States* | | | | | | | | |
| Sweden | 1.10 | 1.47 | 1.10 | 1.10 | 1.05 | 1.05 | 0.42 | 0.60 |
| Switzerland | 2.43 | 3.40 | 1.71 | 1.88 | 1.42 | 1.80 | 0.32 | 0.29 |
| *Small, Open East Asian States* | | | | | | | | |
| Hong Kong | 3.85 | 7.40 | 1.60 | 1.30 | 2.40 | 5.60 | 0.17 | 0.13 |
| South Korea | 0.72 | 1.30 | 0.94 | 1.20 | 0.76 | 1.08 | 0.53 | 0.69 |
| Taiwan | 1.35 | 2.20 | n/a | n/a | n/a | n/a | 0.27 | 0.20 |

[a] The lower number excludes non-Singaporean companies listed on the Singapore Stock Exchange.
*Source:* Beck, Demirguc-Kunt, and Levine (2000), updated in 2010.

business sector. This orientation towards longer-term capital allocation suggests that we look more closely at the internal structure of firms to understand whether Singaporean managers face the same incentive structure as their American counterparts. Specifically, US managers are incentivized to pursue strategies that are in shareholders' best interests and quarterly earnings reports lead them to weight the near-term more heavily than managers from firms with one or a few dominants owners.

# OWNERSHIP AND CORPORATE GOVERNANCE

Ownership of Singapore's firms is predominantly in the hands of families or the state, as opposed to the widely held firms in the USA and UK (La Porta, Lopez-de-Silanes, and Shleifer 1999; Claessens, Djankov, and Lang 2000; Carney and Child 2013). The state maintains substantial ownership of corporatized state-owned enterprises, as well as a list of wholly owned subsidiaries through its holding companies—Temasek Holdings, MND Holdings and Health Corporation of Singapore—and statutory boards (Low 2006: 220). Owners of major local firms retain substantial power over the firms, mainly through pyramidal cascades of companies which accord the ultimate owners the benefits of diversification, while retaining control over a large sweep of the economy or through direct participation in management.

Contests for corporate takeovers are rare in Singapore, much like Japan and Continental Europe, but in contrast to the USA and UK (Wong et al. 2006; *Financial Times* 2007). The difference from Japan and Europe is that poison-pill and dual-class shares are not used in Singapore—its company law provides for and enforces a one-share, one-vote rule. Nonetheless, the pyramidal structure of ownership achieves the same end in the control of firms as dual-class shares (La Porta, Lopez-de-Silanes, and Shleifer 1999; Economist 17 March 2007). Moreover, the state's practice of informal guidance over mergers and acquisitions transactions has likely dented the frequency of takeovers (Economist Intelligence Unit 2006: 18–19).

To bolster its financial services activities and its reputation as a safe environment for foreign investors, relatively strong shareholder protections are in place. Indeed, Singapore's shareholder protections are often ranked among the strongest in Asia (e.g. CG Watch Reports 2001–2010). However, the persistence of concentrated ownership among families and the state is a key reason why its corporate governance regulations lag behind those of other high-income economies with a British heritage (e.g. UK, USA, Australia, Canada). One weakness regards non-financial reporting standards and practices, which tend to be formulaic and of limited value to investors. For example, corporate governance statements commonly dwell more on corporate policy than practice.

A second reason for underperformance is that, unlike most developed markets in Asia and elsewhere, Singapore does not require independent directors of listed non-financial companies to be independent of controlling shareholders *as well as* management. Its

Code of Corporate Governance—first issued in 2001 and updated in 2005—only states that an independent director should have 'no relationship with the company, its related companies or its officers'.

A third area of concern regards the number of independent directors. While Singapore's Code encourages listed companies to have at least one-third of their board made up of independent directors, the listing rule only requires two. In strict rule terms, this puts Singapore behind Hong Kong, China, India, Korea, and Thailand, slightly behind Malaysia and on a par with the Philippines.

However, since the financial crisis of 2008 Singapore has exhibited clear improvements with regard to enforcement, according to a survey conducted by CLSA (2010). This is likely due to the heightened activism of the Singapore Stock Exchange in enforcing its rules since the global financial crisis compared to before. New corporate governance guidelines are also expected to be implemented imminently, which will further strengthen minority shareholder protections (Monetary Authority of Singapore 2011).

## Internal Structure of the Firm

Because a large fraction of Singaporean firms belong to business groups owned either by families or the government, decision-making power has traditionally remained under these actors' tight control; however, this is slowly changing.

The largest non-government-owned groups belong primarily to ethnic Chinese families. Historically, the lack of a codified law, the weakness of guilds, and the inaccessibility of political power have led to differences in the organization and practice of firms located in China and South East Asia, compared to those of Western firms. Personal relations hence became important for constructing networks of interdependent relationships among firms, while the firm itself would remain under family control, with key positions occupied by those whom the owner could trust (Wong 1985; Redding 1990; Redding and Hsiao 1990; Whitley 1992; Fukuyama 1995). To maximize revenues, reduce risks, and penetrate new markets, ethnic Chinese firms would diversify substantially. The resulting structure resembles a web rather than a unitary organization, with numerous independent firms linked to a core company. However, as a result, networking between different firms is fluid and loose.

To facilitate coordination among firms, business families tend to rely on one or several holding companies. The founder's authority pervades the entire group through control over decisions on finance, investment, market expansion, personnel, and so on. Through interlocking directorates, the founding families are able to control and coordinate the strategies of subsidiaries and affiliates (Tsui-Auch and Yoshikawa 2010).

At the same time, economic modernization has contributed to increases in firm size and growing complexities of doing business, leading many owners to professionalize management to gain legitimacy in the eyes of the local regulatory authority and their foreign customers. Singapore's business schools—National University of Singapore, Nanyang Technological University, and Singapore Management University—have also recruited Western-educated professors and adopted Anglo-American text-books, leading to the import of Western (especially American) management models (Tan et al. 1999). The principle of professional management and the recruitment of non-family managers have taken on a greater degree of legitimacy and become insti-tutionalized as they were endorsed by the state, multinational corporations, and busi-ness schools.

In response to pressures to professionalize the management of their enterprises, family owners have opted to develop a hybrid model—a combination of professional management and family rule. However, career advancement for non-family managers is likely to be limited unless they demonstrate both exceptional ability and absolute loy-alty to the business family. Because the labour market is rather open (unlike the rigid Japanese labour market, for example), these managers often acquire the desired skills and move on. By contrast, family managers who hold top management positions are not bound by limited tenures (Tsui-Auch 2004). The retention of family rule offers the advantage of long-term commitment and fast decision-making, since control is concen-trated disproportionately at the top. According to the World Economic Forum's Global Competitiveness Report, 2010–11, Singapore falls between its East Asian and Western counterparts in terms of willingness to delegate authority to subordinates: On a scale of 1 to 7, where a higher number indicates a greater willingness to delegate authority to sub-ordinates, Singapore scores 4.5; Germany and the USA score 5.0 and 5.1, respectively; Switzerland and Sweden score 5.2 and 6.5, respectively; South Korea scores 3.3, Taiwan scores 3.9, and Hong Kong scores 4.1.

Compared with family-owned firms, government-linked corporations (GLCs) have more quickly moved towards the professionalization of management and recruitment of independent directors (i.e. not from the civil service). These changes are due to the stronger pressures to comply with international standards of best practice for GLCs compared with family-owned firms, as well as the increasing number of joint ventures with private-sector firms (Yeung 2006).

While the ratio of outside directors has increased in many GLCs, a high level of state control continues to pervade much of the private sector. The government's sub-stantial influence is clearly seen through its ownership of Temasek Holdings, a wholly government-owned company which is the largest shareholder of many GLCs. In 2006, its ownership stakes accounted for one-third of the Singapore Stock Exchange's mar-ket capitalization (Goldstein and Pananond 2008). The fundamental belief that GLCs are instruments for nation-building and safeguards of national security means that the government can ignore market pressures from institutional investors to divest its equity in these corporations. Even among those that shed non-core assets, such divestment may not be genuine, as the asset could be sold to another GLC under the state's own-ership control, as occurred with DBS's sale of DBS Land to a subsidiary of Singapore Technologies (Tsui-Auch and Yoshikawa 2010). Thus, while independent directors have increased in number for GLCs, few board chairs, presidents, CEOs, and managing directors come from the private sector.

# EMPLOYMENT RELATIONS

One of the keys to Singapore's economic success has been the management of its labour market. As Coe and Kelly (2000: 414) note, 'There can be few other places in the world where the social regulation of the labour market has been so consistently and explicitly a central component of national development strategy as it has been in Singapore'.

The management of employment relations is advertised as tripartite, with employers, employees, and the government as the key actors. Employers and managers are highly institutionalized in a variety of professional associations and consulted regularly on a range of issues. The main employers' association is the Singapore National Employers Federation (SNEF). Its policy is made by its Council, mainly comprising senior executives, after being drafted by an Industrial Relations Panel made up of human resource practitioners and the chairpersons of industry groups (Leggett 2011).

Trade union movements are brought under the aegis of the National Trades Union Congress (NTUC), led by a technocratic elite co-opted by the government with a cabinet post (Khong 1995: 122). 'The NTUC's purpose appears to be to explain government policy to union members and mobilize their support behind government initiatives. The wage-negotiating function...has been appropriated by the National Wages Council, which meets in closed-door sessions with employers and government' and releases recommendations on wage changes (Alagappa 1995: 122). But the NTUC's function of maintaining workforce compliance with national manpower imperatives has created critical challenges for maintaining a credible level of membership.

Employers' long-term strategies in Singapore were originally dependent on the competitive advantage presented by relatively low labour costs, in addition to infrastructure, fiscal incentives, strategic location, and the regulated, strike-free industrial-relations environment (Acharya and Ramesh 1993: 193). Industrial relations were characterized by stable employment, company loyalty, and discipline (Leggett 2007).

Partly to bolster union membership and enhance the NTUC's effectiveness, a 1983 amendment to the Trade Unions Act fragmented large unions into industry-based unions, and then into smaller in-house unions with management participation. In another effort to reinvigorate its effectiveness, the NTUC restructured again after 1997, and the former preference for house unions gave way to amalgamation and merger (Lee 2000: 113). In 2003, of the 68 registered trade unions, 13 had more than 10,000 members, compared with five in 1993 (Ministry of Manpower 2004: 131). Likewise, the 272,769 members of NTUC affiliates in 1998 rose to 417,166 in 2003 (Ministry of Manpower 2003: 5, 139–41).

Labour's position as a subservient partner to government—hence the employer-favoured policies—was further clarified in the wake of an attempt by the

Airline Pilots' Association of Singapore to vote out its entire executive board for allegedly siding too much with management in negotiation agreements in 2003. A new union rule was instituted which 'remove[s] the need for its elected leaders to seek members' approval before concluding collective agreements or settling disputes with management' (*Financial Times* 2003; Straits Times 2004; Rodan 2006: 157). The government later revoked a pilot's 26-year permanent residency status as punishment for instigating the campaign and as a reminder of the consequences for other union militants.

Clearly, labour in Singapore has a weaker voice than those in other high-income countries (with the exception of Hong Kong). Thus, the tripartism in Singapore, much-lauded by its leaders despite the conspicuous top-down features (Ministry of Finance 2006: 2; Straits Times 2007), differs markedly from the tripartism in other small and corporatist OECD countries such as Switzerland and Austria (Katzenstein 1984).

Further exacerbating labour's weak bargaining power is the fact that a Citigroup report on the dual economy found that foreigners constitute a higher proportion of the labour force in the high-growth external demand sectors in Singapore (Chua 2006: 3). Moreover, expatriate managers, engineers, and scientists are generally expected to stay in Singapore for a short period of time.

Today, the labour market in Singapore is highly fluid. The Asian financial crisis spurred a transformation already underway towards services and a knowledge-based economy with an increasingly flexible and mobile workforce to ensure employability, as global competition intensified and technologies advanced. There is no law prohibiting the firing of workers and no minimum wage (Lopez-Claros et al. 2006: 485). These conditions are hailed as critical for attracting foreign direct investment. The government holds considerable discretion in determining the supply and costs of labour, for example through setting the Central Provident Fund contribution rate or adjusting the quota of foreign workers, which is kept secret from the people and from labour (Bhaskaran 2003; Low 2006: 376). The Central Provident Fund is a compulsory savings scheme that allows workers to save for their retirement. As a result, Singapore has one of the least rigid labour markets in the world. According to the Global Competitiveness Report 2010–2011, Singapore's score on a Rigidity of Employment Index is 0, where the index ranges from 0 to 100 and higher is more rigid. In comparison, the USA and Hong Kong also score 0, Switzerland scores 7, Sweden and South Korea both score 38, Germany scores 42, and Taiwan scores 46.

# EDUCATION AND SKILLS FORMATION

Education and skills training have been integral to Singapore's economic development since the 1960s (Osman-Gani and Tan 2010). Occasional reforms to the educational system have primarily occurred as a way to retool the productive capacity of the economy (Gopinathan 2007). As in other rapidly modernizing, export-oriented economies, such as Hong Kong and Taiwan, Singapore emphasized Western education over classical or religious doctrines following independence. In 1979, the Ministry of Education revised the school system to focus on mathematics, science, and English at the primary level, and stream pupils into arts, commerce, science, and technical education at the second-ary level, followed by junior college for university entrance or vocational training for the less academic. To be competitive in the emerging new economy, the Government began a review of the entire system from pre-school education to university admission criteria and curriculum in 1997. As Brown and Lauder (2001: 114) explain, 'the learning model of the mass production of goods and services [had] become a source of "trained incapac-ity" in a knowledge-driven economy'. The growth of the service sector and a speeding up of market liberalization for banking and telecommunication and the emerging oppor-tunities in a technology-driven economic environment put a high premium on inno-vation, flexibility, entrepreneurship, creativity, and a commitment to lifelong learning. It was recognized that Singapore schools needed a much higher threshold for experi-mentation, innovation, and uncertainty, where output would not always be guaranteed (Osman-Gani 2004).

University curricula were also modified and the range of higher education institu-tions increased to meet the needs of more knowledge-intensive jobs in the private sec-tor. The National University of Singapore and Nanyang Technological University were complemented by the Singapore Management University in 2000, and subsequently by eight private universities, seven of them offshore wings of overseas universities offering specialist graduate courses in management, software engineering, chemical engineer-ing, and hospitality management. For the past decade, Singaporeans have been able to study—partly online—as undergraduates at universities, mainly from North America, the UK, and Australia. Singapore's five polytechnics also train middle-level profession-als, and provide continuing education and post-employment professional development programmes and services.

While the Singapore education system is often lauded for delivering excellent results at primary and secondary school levels, according to international comparisons of edu-cational quality, learning remains heavily geared towards test preparation. This form of education is often criticized as producing students who learn material appropriate for exams, but not encouraging students to think creatively, foster a sense of curiosity, make connections among different subject areas, or question prevailing theories or ways of doing things. This latter critique is often lobbed at Eastern forms of education, which tend to be hierarchical and do not encourage students to question teachers or to think independently.

With regard to vocational skills training, employers in Singapore have been encour-aged to provide approved skills training through government programmes or, alter-natively, by paying a payroll levy to the Skills Development Fund since 1984. By 1996, roughly 33 per cent of the workforce was receiving training, and corporations were spending 3.6 per cent of their payroll on training (Leggett 2011). However, these pro-grammes are directed more towards Singaporean companies than multinational cor-porations, which for the most part have a broader Human Resources Development perspective than local enterprises.

The Singapore government also encourages company-based training centres for both multinational corporations and Singaporean firms. The Productivity Standards Board identifies opportunities for productivity improvements in different industries, and points firms to the appropriate skills training institutions. For some multinational corporations, the centres provide training for their employees both in Singapore and in the wider region.[6] The NTUC also provides a range of programmes including information technology skills through the NTUC LearningHub. Finally, there is an array of basic skills training programmes offered in cooperation with the NTUC and/or SNEF.[7]

In terms of the types of skills and knowledge that are taught—general or specific—Singapore's educational system places greater emphasis on general knowledge. This emphasis is appropriate for a job market in which employees switch jobs frequently. While the workforce is highly educated, the nature of the local economy, with a heavy reliance on multinational corporations who can easily hire and fire employees, means that there is little incentive to acquire specialized skills. This is reflected in a survey which assessed the Human Resources Development practices of multinational corporations and large Singaporean companies. The survey found that local companies did not rate the level of importance of their human resources as highly as did the multinational corporations (Huang et al. 2002), which is consistent with the fact that the managers, engineers, and scientists working in Singapore's high-growth sectors—those with highly specialized knowledge and skills—are commonly expatriates.

## INTER-COMPANY RELATIONS

Because family-owned corporate groups commonly pursue unrelated diversification, the corporate network of a single group is not cohesive and complementary; rather, inter-firm relations tend to be at arm's-length. The group is held together by the controlling family via one or several holding companies and the founding families maintain control and coordinate the strategies of firms via cross-holding and interlocking directorates (Hamilton 1997; Tong and Yong 1998; Brown 2000; Tsui-Auch and Yoshikawa 2010). The demise of the founding patriarch often leads to the rise of several family business lines, further loosening ties among the group's firms (Tong and Yong 1998).

The organization of GLCs resembles that of family groups with regard to a loose network held together via interlocking boards and centralized control. For example, Temasek Holdings owns more than 200 government-linked corporations covering a wide spectrum of industries, including transportation and logistics, ship repair and engineering, power and gas, telecommunications, media, financial services, manufacturing, and properties. It does not conduct trade or business, but instead holds investments, thus deriving income from dividends, interest, and rentals. Its sole shareholder, the Ministry of Finance Inc., can veto its decisions. GLCs are owned through other holding companies, including MND Holdings and Health Corporation of Singapore, as well as statutory boards (Low 2006: 220).

Because of the weak ties between firms within a business group, Singaporean firms tend to deal with each other at arm's length, and their relationships are largely dictated by price signal, as in the USA and UK. A survey conducted by the Institute of Policy Studies and the Monitor Group finds that even where inter-firm partnerships exist, they are predominantly transactional in nature, mainly to fill competency gaps (Patel 2006: 49). Singapore's similar contract laws and legal environment with the US and UK tend to discourage deep and meaningful inter-firm collaboration as well. The same survey reveals that companies working on the same project do not actively 'share information and expertise beyond what is necessary for a particular project' (Patel 2006: 53). This is not unexpected. Technological diffusion in the US and UK is usually in the form of licensing, staff movements, or through M&A activities. This market-based environment renders employees' movements between firms easier and more acceptable than the industrial associations in Germany and rival group firms in Japan. In the relationship-based settings of Japan and Germany, parties to an agreement have the capacity to sanction any defection from cooperative behaviour.

# SOCIAL CAPITAL

For much of its history, Singapore was drug-ridden and corrupt. But since independence, the PAP has sought to develop the economy by building on its advantageous position as an *entrepôt* state. This led to policies to attract foreign investment and develop the city-state into a financial centre. To achieve these goals, the PAP implemented strong property-rights protections, alongside harsh penalties for corruption, thereby dampening the need for personal relations to conduct business transactions. These efforts succeeded admirably. According to Transparency International's Corruption Perceptions Index for 2011, Singapore's level of corruption is the lowest in the world (equal with Denmark and New Zealand). The World Bank's Governance Indicators also indicate strong performance along each of its dimensions except Voice and Accountability, which may be seen as another indication of the extent of institutionalized trust.[8]

At the same time, interpersonal trust is quite low. According to the World Values Survey conducted in 1999/2000 over 66 countries, Singapore ranks 48th.[9] The survey question was 'Generally speaking, would you say that most people can be trusted or that you need to be very careful in dealing with people?' Three contributing factors likely produce this low score: (1) the high degree of ethnic, linguistic, and cultural heterogeneity, (2) the high level of income inequality (42.5 according to the United Nations Development Programme 2011; higher than the USA and about the same as Hong Kong), and (3) the relatively large non-resident population. According to the 2010 census, Singapore's total population is 5.07 million; 25 per cent were non-residents (usually those on work permits from other Asian countries). Of the resident population, approximately 75 per cent are ethnically Chinese, 14 per cent Malay, 9 per cent Indian, and 2 per cent Eurasians and others. With regard to religious affiliations, 33 are Buddhist, 18 per cent Christian, 17 per cent unaffiliated, 15 per cent Islam, 11 per cent Taoist, 5 per cent Hindu, and 1 per cent affiliated with other religions. The Singapore government also recognizes four official languages: English, Malay, Chinese (Mandarin), and Tamil.

At the same time, interpersonal relations among family owners as well as among civil servants remain important, especially in such a small country. The historical development of Chinese firms still pervades business practice, with personal relations, or *guanxi*, continuing to play an important role. The importance of interlocking directorates among firms belonging to a family group as well as among GLCs illustrates its contemporary relevance.

## Institutional Complementarities

Institutional complementarities encourage actors to focus more on the long term or short term. Of the dimensions examined here, the predominance of concentrated corporate ownership leads business owners—both families and state—to focus more on the long term. While the stock market is relatively large in relation to GDP, and minority shareholder protections are one of the strongest in the region, ownership and control remain firmly in the hands of families or the state. As a result, owners and their managers do not feel the pressure to meet quarterly earnings expectations in the same way that managers of US firms do.

However, this long-term orientation contrasts with the short-term incentives produced by the remaining institutions: internal firm structure, employment relations, education and skills training, inter-firm relations, and social capital. Specifically, internal firm structure concentrates decision-making power in the hands of owners and top executives, which gives them more hire-and-fire power; highly mobile employees, changing jobs frequently, complement the educational and skills training systems which foster general skills and knowledge; inter-firm relations tend to be arm's-length; and trust is highly institutionalized. These arrangements mirror those of Anglo-Saxon economies such as the US and UK.

An important implication of these institutional arrangements for high-income countries regards innovation. Innovation is a top priority for the Singapore government. Prime Minister Lee Hsien Loong opened his 2006 Budget Statement with the need for Singapore to become a knowledge hub in Asia, and that its future growth should be fuelled by research and development in niche areas. Hu and Shin (2002: 303) explain that Singapore has reached a point where higher-end capabilities securely based in its territory will increasingly become the determinant of its future growth. As Singapore inches closer to the technological frontier, an innovation strategy built around multinational corporations becomes less sufficient for catching up, as the 'core R&D capability is the last thing that multinational corporations will transfer to local subsidiaries'. The critical problem is thus the lack of innovation on the part of Singapore-owned firms. Although the government has implemented numerous initiatives, such as assisting start-ups, setting up research councils and educational programmes, and mobilizing vast resources to this end (see Khong and Koh 2002: 25 and Wong et al. 2006: 93–119 for details of various government policy initiatives and programmes), they have so far yielded disproportionately weak results (Patel 2006; Wyatt 2006).

Many ascribe this failure to a culture of risk aversion and a lack of creativity. The standard advice is to beef up local firms' awareness of technology, encourage risk-taking and creativity, foster closer inter-firm partnerships, cultivate more ambitious CEOs and self-driven managers and workers, create an innovation-friendly culture, and so on (Wyatt 2006). However, the cultural argument has been refuted by Black and Gilson (1998: 271) in their observation of successful immigrant entrepreneurs in high-technology ventures (Russians in Israel and Asians in the USA) where the right institutional infrastructure is present.

An alternative explanation emerges by considering the incentives to innovate created as a result of the city-state's institutional arrangements (Carney and Loh 2009). Innovation generally occurs in one of two ways: via incremental or small-scale improvements to existing products or via radical innovations which involve substantial shifts in product lines or the development of entirely new goods. An example of incremental innovation is the continuous improvements to cars since they were first invented in the late nineteenth century. Germany and Japan excel at such innovation. Examples of radical innovations include the internet and biotechnology, which the US excels at. Why the difference? Essentially, it is because the structure of a country's capitalist institutions generates incentives that foster different types of innovation. Incremental innovations occur most often when companies focus on the long term. The key institutional arrangements include employee job stability, stable inter-firm relationships and concentrated corporate ownership. Incremental innovation requires cumulative learning, where long-tenured workers acquire firm-specific skills. Firms will invest in the specialized training of their employees when they are sure other firms will not poach their employees, and when skilled workers are likely to stay and contribute. Likewise, for firms to invest in specific physical assets, they have to be confident of their long-term arrangements with major suppliers and clients. An environment that promotes long-lasting and intimate inter-firm relationships is crucial to incremental improvements. Such arrangements foster the cultivation of trust, certainty, and camaraderie throughout the value chain. This enables the costs, benefits (via knowledge spillovers), and risks of R&D to be spread among the parties (Tylecote and Conesa 1999: 28). Incremental innovation is also aided when firms have dominant owners. They can be shielded from short-run capital market pressures, greatly reducing the threat of being taken over. And by being held accountable to a dominant owner, managers will opt for low-risk strategies and continuous improvements of established products, and focus on incremental innovations to build a competitive edge.

Radical innovations occur when firms cultivate a short-term focus. The ongoing hit-and-miss of new product lines is an essential part of such businesses. Firms hope that one blockbuster product can yield rewards that recover the costs of all the other unprofitable endeavours. A flexible labour market is essential for such firms, enabling them to hire employees with the requisite skills, with the knowledge that they can be dismissed if the project does not materialize. Arm's-length relationships also enable such firms to quickly acquire new capabilities by poaching the employees of other firms, licensing a new product or simply buying out another firm with the requisite technology. In fast-evolving sectors, speed and flexibility are the keys to survival; commitment to a strong inter-firm relationship can be a liability. The nimbleness they require mandates that decision-making power in such firms be concentrated at the top. Managers of such firms must be able to formulate and implement a new plan, switch production lines, or reallocate resources rapidly throughout the enterprise without the need to seek the approval of workers or owners. Managers tend to wield greater power when ownership is dispersed, as in the USA. Moreover, compared to bank or state financing, a liquid and vibrant equity market is better at coping with novelty and catering to investors with heterogeneous risk appetites. A deep and vibrant stock market enables the development of a thriving venture-capital market, which is important to the success of technology districts such as Silicon Valley (Black and Gilson 1998). A vibrant stock market permits venture capitalists to exit through an initial public offering. Studies of Silicon Valley point also to the importance of employees moving between firms and start-ups in contributing to waves of radical innovation (Saxenian 1994; Gilson 1999). The constant flux of knowledge spillovers enables a high-tech cluster to continually renew itself through the formation of new firms and new R&D competencies (Koh, Koh and Tschang 2003: 12).

Singapore combines elements of both the incremental and radical approaches, which creates conflicting innovation incentives, and ultimately undermines innovative activity. In Singapore, employees are mobile, with job tenure generally short-lived. Poaching of employees by other firms is common and firms deal with one another at arm's length. These arrangements tend to be more compatible with radical innovations, as in the USA. However, corporate ownership tends to be highly concentrated, encouraging management to focus on low-risk strategies and pursue incremental innovation, as in Germany and Japan. Singaporean managers and employees may be exceptionally creative, but because the city-state's institutions foster conflicting innovation styles, their efforts do not easily yield sustainable innovative activity of either type (Carney and Loh 2009).

## CONCLUSIONS

A variety of implications can be highlighted, including theoretical implications for the policy arena, and managerial implications. Each is discussed in turn.

Recent work in the Varieties of Capitalism research stream has specifically pointed to the need for incorporating a distinct role for the state (e.g. Hancké, Rhodes, and Thatcher 2007). While France stands out among countries conventionally examined for state influence, and likewise for its mixed market economy, Singapore is an even more dramatic case of state intervention and hybrid institutions. The similarities between these two cases in terms of the existence of a strong state and hybrid outcomes may be more than coincidence; that is, hybrid forms may be more likely to arise in the presence of a strong state (where the state has motives independent of social and economic actors' interests). Analysis of other Asian states will be helpful in this regard.

Further, when institutional arrangements emerge from bargains struck among domestic economic and social interests, are they more likely to be part of a broad, coherent institutional bargain, and thus more likely to exist in democratic settings? For example, Cusack, Iversen, and Soskice (2007) argue that proportional representation has helped to preserve institutional arrangements of coordinated market economies, because it grants political power to numerous economic actors with mutual interests in sustaining the coordinated economic system. But in non-democratic settings, institutions may be designed more as a result of elites' interests, which may differ from social and economic interests. This can grant greater scope for the existence of non-complementary institutions, so long as such arrangements achieve some desired objective on the part of the elites. By restricting the focus to democratic states, prior studies on national innovativeness and varieties of capitalism may not pick up a discernible impact on innovation. This suggests that research on varieties of capitalism must be expanded not only to incorporate a role for the state, but also to account for the level of democracy.

With regard to policy implications, policy-makers in a young country may pick and modify different best practices from different successful countries, and expect the end product to be at least as good as the summation of its components. But institutions in different spheres interact with each other. This synergy of complementary institutions is often overlooked. The total will exceed the summation of its parts if their incentives complement; if they contradict, the total will be less. Institutional arrangements are foundational, as they shape and give rise to systemic incentives throughout the economy. Thus, in addressing the structure and outcomes of business systems, policy-makers should examine the institutions in place and their interaction.

Finally, with respect to managerial implications, managers of domestic firms need to recognize the broader institutional constraints within which their firm operates, and pursue business strategies that correspond to them. Indeed, the Singapore case illustrates the difficulties of spurring innovation when institutional incentives conflict. The lessons are most appropriate for managers working in high-technology sectors, and particularly in newly industrialized economies, where such technological comparative advantage arising from institutional arrangements may not yet be fully recognized (e.g. Singapore, Hong Kong, Taiwan, and South Korea). Understanding the institutional constraints gives managers a better understanding of what types of R&D to engage in, depending on the country context.

## Notes

1. The author gratefully acknowledges comments on an earlier draft from Michael A. Witt.
2. This includes five years, from 2007 to 2011. Singapore is ranked #3 for ease of doing business, according to the Global Competitiveness Report 2010–2011 issued by the World Economic Forum. It is the highest in Asia, with Switzerland and Sweden at #1 and #2.

3. World Development Indicators database; Singapore is ranked 3/183 according to the IMF's World Economic Outlook Database for 2010 (IMF 2010).

4. Banks offering non-domestic financial services fall into three categories—restricted banks, offshore banks, and merchant banks, each of which is subject to rigid guidelines with respect to the domestic banking market (Giap and Kang 1999). At the same time, local banks are required to maintain a capital adequacy ratio of between 6.5 and 10 per cent as of 2013, despite their relatively limited international dealings and although the Basel III agreement has set a minimum guideline of 4.5 to 8 per cent as of 2015. This has put Singapore banks among the strongest worldwide (Curran and Lee 2011).

5. The Stock Exchange of Singapore was established in June 1973; a secondary board, catering to smaller, newer firms, was established in 1987.

6. For example, the Tadano group service training centre, China Healthcare's Econ Careskill and KBA Training.

7. Basic Education for Skills Training enables workers to acquire basic proficiency in English; Worker Improvement Through Secondary Education prepares trainees for examinations in English; the Modular Skills Training Initiative offers part-time training to acquire new or upgrade existing skills; the Adult Cooperative Training Scheme is directed at unskilled adults under 40; the Training Initiative for Mature Employees is directed at those over 40; and the Reskilling for a New Economy programme promotes lifelong employability.

8. The dimensions include Voice and Accountability, Political Stability and Lack of Violence/Terrorism, Government Effectiveness, Regulatory Quality, Rule of Law, and Control of Corruption.

9. Denmark and Sweden ranked first and second.

## REFERENCES

Acharya, A. and M. Ramesh (1993). 'Economic Foundations of Singapore's Security: From Globalism to Regionalism?' In G. Rodan, Ed., *Singapore Changes Guard*: 135–152. New York, St. Martin's Press.

Alagappa, M. (1995). *Political Legitimacy in Southeast Asia: the Quest for Moral Authority*. Stanford, Stanford University Press.

Beck, T., A. Demirguc-Kunt, and R. Levine (2000). 'A New Database on Financial Development and Structure'. *World Bank Economic Review* 14: 597–605.

Bhaskaran, M. (2003). *Re-inventing the Asian Model: The Case of Singapore*. Singapore, Institute of Policy Studies.

Black, B. S. and R. J. Gilson (1998). 'Venture Capital and the Structure of Capital Markets: Banks versus Stock Markets'. *Journal of Financial Economics* 47: 243–277.

Brown, R. A. (2000). *Chinese Big Business and the Wealth of Asian Nations*. New York, Palgrave.

Brown, P. and H. Lauder (2001). 'The Future of Skill Formation in Singapore', *Asia Pacific Business Review* 7(3): 113–138.

Bryan, K. (2007). 'Rule of Law in Singapore: Independence of the Judiciary and the Legal Profession in Singapore'. Retrieved 14 April 2011 from <http://yoursdp.org/index.php/perspective/special-feature/325-lrwcs-report-on-singapores-judiciary-and-legal-profession>.

Carney, R. and Y.-Z. Loh (2009). 'Institutional (Dis)Incentives to Innovate: An Explanation for Singapore's Innovation Gap'. *Journal of East Asian Studies* 9(2): 291–319.

—— and T. B. Child (2013). 'Changes to the Ownership and Control of East Asian Corporations between 1996 and 2008: The Primacy of Politics'. *Journal of Financial Economics* 107(2): 494–513.

Chiu, S. W. K., K. C. Ho, and T.-L. Lui (1997). *City-States in the Global Economy: Industrial Restructuring in Hong Kong and Singapore.* Boulder, Westview.

Chua, H. B. (2006). *Singapore: A Dual Economy?* Singapore, Citigroup Global Markets Singapore.

Claessens, S., S. Djankov, and L. Lang (2000). 'The Separation of Ownership and Control in East Asian Corporations'. *Journal of Financial Economics* 58: 81–112.

CLSA Emerging Markets and ACGA (2010). 'CG Watch: Stray not into Perdition: Asia's CG Momentum Slows'. Report. Retrieved 14 April 2011 from <http://www.acga-asia.org/public/files/CG_Watch_2010_Extract.pdf>.

Coe, N. M. and P. F. Kelly (2000). 'Distance and Disclosure in the Local Labour Market: The Case of Singapore'. *Area* 32(4): 413–422.

Curran, J. and Y. Lee (2011). 'OCBC World's Strongest Bank in Singapore as Canadians Dominate'. *Bloomberg Markets Magazine*, May 11. Retrieved 14 April 2011 from <http://www.bloomberg.com/news/2011-05-09/ocbc-world-s-strongest-bank-in-singapore-with-canadians-dominating-ranking.html>.

Cusack, T., T. Iversen, and D. Soskice (2007). 'Economic Interests and the Origins of Electoral Systems'. *American Political Science Review* 101(3): 373–391.

Department of Statistics (2011). Yearbook of Statistics Singapore. Retrieved 17 April 2011 from <http://www.singstat.gov.sg>.

Deyo, F. (1981). *Dependent Development and Industrial Order: An Asian Case Study*, New York, Praeger.

*Economist* (2007). 'Family Capitalism: Our Company Right or Wrong', 15 March. Retrieved 18 April 2011 from <http://www.economist.com/node/8848426>.

Economist Intelligence Unit (2006). 'Country report: Singapore'. Retrieved 9 April 2011 from <http://www.eiu.com/index.asp?layout=displayIssue&publication_id=1870000987>.

—— (2010) '2010 Democracy Index'. Retrieved 9 April 2011 from <http://www.eiu.com/public/thankyou_download.aspx?activity=download&campaignid=demo2010>.

*Financial Times* (2003). 'Singapore Cracks down on Airline Pilots' Union', 2 December, 4.

—— (2007). 'Brussels Threat to Reform Take-over Laws', 27 February, 8.

Fukuyama, F. (1995). *Trust: The Social Virtues and the Creation of Prosperity.* New York, Free Press.

Giap, T. K. and C. Kang (1999). 'Singapore's Dichotomized Financial System'. In Asian Development Bank, Ed., *Rising to the Challenge in Asia: A Study of Financial Markets*, Vol. 3: 81–140. Manila, Asian Development Bank.

Gilson, R. J. (1999). 'The Legal Infrastructure of High Technology of Industrial Districts: Silicon Valley, Route 128, and Covenants Not To Compete'. *New York University Law Review* 74(3): 575–629.

Goldstein, A. and P. Pananond (2008). 'Singapore Inc. Goes Shopping Abroad: Profits and Pitfalls'. *Journal of Contemporary Asia* 38(3): 417–438.

Gopinathan, S. (2007). 'Globalisation, the Singapore Developmental State and Education Policy: A Thesis Revisited'. *Globalisation, Societies, and Education* 5(1): 53–70.

Hamilton, G. G. (1997). 'Organization and Market Processes in Taiwan's Capitalist Economy'. In M. Orru, N. W. Biggart, and C. C. Hamilton, Eds., *The Economic Organization of East Asian Capitalism*: 237–296. Thousand Oaks, Sage.

Hancké, B., M. Rhodes, and M. Thatcher (2007). *Beyond Varieties of Capitalism: Conflict, Contradictions, and Complementarities in the European Economy*. New York, Oxford University Press.

Hu, A. G. and J.-S. Shin (2002). 'Climbing the Technology Ladder: Challenges facing Singapore in a Globalized World'. In A. T. Koh, Ed., *Singapore Economy in the 21st Century*: 300–320. Singapore, McGraw Hill.

Huang, G. Z. D., M. H. Roy, U. A. Zafar, J. S. T. Heng, and J. H. M. Lim (2002). 'Benchmarking the Human Capital Strategies of MNCs in Singapore'. *Benchmarking* 9(4): 357–373.

IMF (2004). *Singapore: Financial System Stability Assessment*, IMF Country Report 04/104, Washington, DC, IMF.

—— (2010). 'World Economic Outlook Database'. Retrieved 16 April 2011 from <http://www.imf.org/external/pubs/ft/weo/2010/02/weodata/index.aspx>.

Katzenstein, P. (1984). *Corporatism and Change: Austria, Switzerland, and the Politics of Industry*. Ithaca, Cornell University Press.

Khong, C. (1995). 'Singapore: Political Legitimacy through Managing Conformity'. In M. Alagappa, Ed., *Political Legitimacy in Southeast Asia: The Quest for Moral Authority*: 108–135. Stanford, Stanford University Press.

—— and W. T. H. Koh (2002). 'Venture Capital and Economic Growth: An Industry Overview and Singapore's Experience', *SMU Economic & Statistics Working Paper 21-2002*. Retrieved 21 May 2011 from <http://www.research.smu.edu.sg/faculty/edge/entrep_fin/papers/SER-VCandGrowth_WP_dec_2002.pdf>.

Koh, F. C. C., W. T. H. Koh, and F.T. Tschang (2003). 'An Analytical Framework for Science Parks and Technology Districts with an Application to Singapore', *SMU Economics & Statistics Working Paper 18-2003*. Retrieved 21 May 2011 from <http://www.research.smu.edu.sg/faculty/edge/entrep_fin/papers/Koh_koh_tschang.pdf>.

La Porta, R., F. Lopez-de-Silanes, and A. Shleifer (1999). 'Corporate Ownership around the World'. *Journal of Finance* 14(2): 471–517.

Lee, K. Y. (2000). *From Third World to First: The Singapore Story, 1965–2000—Memoirs of Lee Kuan Yew*. Singapore, Times Editions.

Leggett, C. (2007). 'From "Industrial Relations" to "Manpower Planning": the Transformations of Singapore's Industrial Relations', *International Journal of Human Resource Management* 18(4): 642–665.

—— (2011). 'Labour Markets in Singapore: Flexibility in Adversity'. In J. Benson and Y. Zhu, Eds., *The Dynamics of Asian Labour Markets*: 83–106. London, Routledge.

Lopez-Claros, A., M. E. Porter, X. Sala-i-Martin, and K. Schwab (2006). *Global Competitiveness Report 2006–2007: Creating an Improved Business Environment*. New York, Palgrave Macmillan.

Low, L. (2006). *The Political Economy of a City-State Revisited*. Singapore, Marshall Cavendish Academic.

Mauzy, D. K. and R. S. Milne (2002). *Singapore Politics under the People's Action Party*. London, Routledge.

Ministry of Finance (2006). Budget Statement 2006. Retrieved 11 April 2011 from <http://www.mof.gov.sg/budget_2006/index.html>.

Ministry of Manpower (2003, 2004). *Annual Report*. Singapore: Singapore National Printers.

Monetary Authority of Singapore (2011). 'MAS Strengthens Capital Requirements for Singapore-incorporated Banks'. Retrieved 28 June 2011 from <http://www.mas.gov.sg/news_room/press_releases/2011/MAS_Strengthens_Capital_Requirements_for_Singapore_incorporated_Banks.html>.

Osman-Gani, A. M. (2004). 'Human Capital Development in Singapore: An Analysis of National Policy Perspectives'. *Advances in Developing Human Resources* 6(3): 276–287.

—— and W. L. Tan (2010). 'International Briefing 7: Training and Development in Singapore'. *International Journal of Training and Development* 4(4): 305–323.

Patel, H. (2006). 'The State of Innovation in Singapore: Study Presentation'. In M. Bhaskaran, Ed., *The Fifth Singapore Economic Roundtable*: 62–69. Singapore, SNP Reference for Institute of Policy Studies.

Redding, S. G. (1990). *The Spirit of Chinese Capitalism*. Berlin, de Gruyter.

—— and M. Hsiao (1990). 'An Empirical Study of Overseas Chinese Managerial Ideology'. *International Journal of Psychology* 3(6): 629–641.

Rodan, G. (2006). 'Singapore: Globalisation, the State and Politics'. In G. Rodan, K. Hewison, and R. Robison, Eds., *The Political Economy of Southeast Asia: Markets, Power and Contestation*, 3rd ed.: 137–169. Oxford, Oxford University Press.

Saxenian, A. (1994). *Regional Advantage: Culture and Competition in Silicon Valley and Route 128*. Cambridge, Harvard University Press.

*Straits Times* (1985). 'Speculative Attacks on the Singapore Dollar', 19 September: 12.

—— (2004). 'Why amend Act? Alpa-S Saga shows Workers' Interests not protected', 21 April: 4.

—— (2007). 'A Singapore Secret That Cannot Be Easily Copied', 25 January: 35.

Tan, J. Q. and K. S. Jomo (2001). *Comet in our Sky: Lim Chin Siong in History*. Selangor Darul Ehsan, Insan.

Tan, T. M., K. S. Leong, and Y. H. Pang (1999). 'Business Education in Singapore: the Past, the Present and the Future'. *Review of Pacific Basin Financial Markets and Policies* 2(4): 527–554.

Tong, C. K. and P. K. Yong (1998). 'Guanxi, xinyong and Chinese Business Networks', *British Journal of Sociology* 49(1): 75–96.

Tsui-Auch, L. S. (2004). 'The Professionally Managed Family-ruled Enterprise: Ethnic Chinese Business in Singapore'. *Journal of Management Studies* 41(4): 693–723.

—— and T. Yoshikawa (2010). 'Business Groups in Singapore'. In A. M. Colpan, T. Hikino, and J. Lincoln, Eds., *Oxford Handbook of Business Groups*: 267–293. New York, Oxford University Press.

Tylecote, A. and E. Conesa (1999). 'Corporate Governance, Innovation Systems, and Industrial Performance'. *Industry and Innovation* 6(1): 25–50.

Whitley, R. (1992). *Business Systems in East Asia*. London and Newbury Park, Sage.

Witt, M. A. (2011). 'Corporate Governance and Initial Public Offerings in Singapore'. In A. Zattoni and W. Judge, Eds., *Global Perspectives on Corporate Governance and Initial Public Offerings*: 378–396. Cambridge, Cambridge University Press.

Wong, P.-K., L. Lee, Y.-P. Ho, and F. Wong (2006). *Global Entrepreneurship Monitor 2005: Singapore Report*, National University of Singapore, NUS Entrepreneurship Centre.

Wong, S.-L. (1985). 'The Chinese Family Firm'. *British Journal of Sociology* 36: 58–72.

Woo-Cumings, M., Ed. (1999). *The Developmental State*. Ithaca, Cornell University Press.

World Values Survey (2009) 1981–2008 Official Aggregate v.20090901. World Values Survey Association (www.worldvaluessurvey.org). Aggregate File Producer, Madrid, ASEP/JDS.

Wu, J. (2009). 'Information Note: The Development of Government Bond Market in Singapore', Hong Kong, Legislative Council Secretariat. Retrieved 14 April 2011 from http://www.legco.gov.hk/yr08-09/english/sec/library/0809in19-e.pdf.

Wyatt, S. (2006). 'State of Innovation in Singapore: Some Findings of the IPS-Monitor Innovation Survey'. In Lai Ah Eng, Ed., *Singapore Perspectives 2006*: 137–152. Singapore, Marshall Cavendish Academic.

Yeung, H. W.-C. (2006). *Handbook of Research on Asian Business*. Cheltenham, Edward Elgar.

# CHAPTER 11

..................................................................................

# SOUTH KOREA

*Plutocratic State-Led
Capitalism Reconfiguring*

..................................................................................

## MICHAEL A. WITT

South Korea—formally the Republic of Korea, and in this chapter simply Korea—is one of Asia's four 'Tiger' economies.[1] Korea's 'miracle of the Han River'[2] took the nation from among the world's poorest in the early 1960s to OECD membership in 1996. Korean per capita GDP at purchasing-power parity has since surpassed that of the Southern European economies and is now within striking range of Korea's developmental policy model and arch-rival, Japan.

The take-off of modern economic growth in Korea is widely seen as the result of massive institutional change in 1961 following a military coup, as we will discuss in more detail. The state-led type of business system that emerged (Whitley 1999) survived in general outline until the Asian Financial Crisis of 1997/8, which drew the country and a number of its leading firms into bankruptcy. The impact on the Korean business system of this external shock, known in Korea as the 'IMF Crisis' because much of the pain was blamed on the International Monetary Fund's restructuring plan, has since been subject to considerable debate.

This chapter presents a portrait of the Korean business system some fifteen years after the crisis. Like all country chapters in this handbook, it emphasizes the current shape of affairs over historical developments and explores the role of the state, the financial system, ownership and corporate governance, firm-internal dynamics, employment relations, education and training systems, inter-firm relations, and social capital. It further identifies institutional complementarities in the present-day system and outlines the main dynamics of institutional change present in Korea. As will become apparent, post-crisis Korea has reconfigured in ways that are quite different from what many early observers had expected.

# ROLE OF THE STATE

There is considerable agreement in the literature about the types of state Korea represented in the past. Korea under its first president, Syngman Rhee (1948–1960), is generally described as a predatory state, in which high levels of corruption enabled political and business leaders to enrich themselves at the expense of the general public (Amsden 1989; Eckert et al. 1990; Song 2003). While Korea lacks the abundant natural resources that are typical of predatory states, a functional substitute existed in the form of US aid money, which was intended to shore up South Korea as a bulwark against communism. Rhee used these resources to buy the loyalty of key actors in the political and economic arena. Economic performance during this period was poor, save for a brief outburst of growth following the end of the Korean War (1950–1953). Following a popular uprising in 1960, Rhee left for exile in Hawaii.

After a one-year interregnum, the rules of the game changed fundamentally in 1961. Through a military coup on 16 May 1961, Major General Park Chung-hee became president, and the military took over the reins of the state. Concerned that public disorder and weak economic performance threatened the prospects of Korea's survival as a nation, Park's government constructed a developmental state on the Japanese model (Amsden 1989). From 1963 onward, this developmental state began to produce high levels of growth, taking Korea from one of the world's poorest countries in 1961 to OECD membership in 1996. Tempered from the 1980s by various efforts at liberalization, it survived in its general form until the 1997/8 Asian Crisis.

The characteristics of the Korean developmental path are well explored in the literature (Amsden 1989; Wade 1990; Kim, E. M. 1997; Woo-Cumings 1999). Broadly speaking, the goal of Korean developmental policies was to develop the country by using administrative means to accelerate the progress of Korean industries from labour-intensive to capital-intensive, and ultimately to technology-intensive industries. Central planning of which industries and firms to promote fell under the auspices of the Korean Development Board, which reported directly to Park. Firms in targeted industries received preferential and subsidized access to finance, a scarce resource, and various other forms of help, including the licences needed to expand. Capital controls prevented firms from squirrelling capital abroad, and barriers on imports and inward foreign direct investment prevented established international competition from driving budding Korean firms out of the market. At the same time, firms were required to meet ever-increasing export quotas if they wanted to stay in business. These export quotas were useful: not only did they earn foreign currency for their country, they also helped expose Korean companies to international competition, pushing them to improve their products, and provided a selection criterion by which government could establish which firms were well run and thus worthy of further promotion.

While the Korean model was Japanese inspired, there were noteworthy differences from the post-war Japanese model. First, the Korean developmental state was much more top down, especially in its early days. Business was not a partner, as in Japan, but a subservient tool. While general corruption levels in Korea remained (and remain) higher than in Japan (Transparency International 2012), enforcement of key economic policies was strict. Second, Korean strategy was built around the establishment of large family-led conglomerates, an organizational form that had been abolished in Japan by the Allied occupation. The Korean word for such conglomerates, *chaebol*, represents the Korean reading of the same Chinese characters used for the Japanese term, *zaibatsu*. Third, banks in Korea were state owned, which gave the Korean state more direct influence over the allocation of capital.

While the role of the Korean state historically is thus fairly unambiguous, there is little agreement on what type of state Korea represents today. Following the Asian Crisis of 1997/8, the Korean state moved to deregulate the economy, leading some scholars to argue that Korea has transformed into a liberal regulatory state (Hundt 2005; Pirie 2005). Indeed, from 1998 to 2008, the OECD product-market regulation index dropped considerably. However, it remains above the OECD average and is far higher than that in regulatory states such as the United Kingdom or the United States. This implies that a full regulatory state has not (yet?) emerged.

Others have pointed to the expanding role of social insurance in Korea to suggest the emergence, at least temporarily, of a welfare state—though in the form of a 'developmental welfare state' that tends to be state driven in a top-down manner (Mishra et al. 2004; Kwon and Holliday 2007; Lee and Ku 2007; Kim, E. M. 2010). OECD statistics (OECD 2012b) show that Korean public spending on social welfare indeed rose from 3.2 per cent of GDP in 1995 to 7.6 per cent in 2007 (latest year available). However, this was still far below the OECD average of 19.2 per cent, and in the OECD, only Mexico spent less (7.2%). At the same time, the Gini coefficient in Korea has been trending up since the 1990s, as has relative poverty, which is the seventh highest in the OECD (OECD 2012a). This would suggest that, for now, Korea is at best a welfare state in the making.

Given the absence of a strong shift to another state type, and taking into account the constraining effect of path dependence, the most plausible categorization of the Korean state today is thus that it probably represents a reconfiguring developmental state (cf. Chu 2009; Kim, E. M. 2010). Certainly with the election of Lee Myung-bak to the presidency in 2007, growth re-emerged as a policy priority. This was evident, for instance, in Lee's 7–4–7 plan, so called because it envisioned 7 per cent average growth during his presidency, so as to reach US$40,000 per capita GDP and make Korea the seventh largest economy in the world. Economic and budgetary planning, functions that had been separated in 1998, were reunited in the new Ministry of Strategy and Finance. While many of the original control structures, such as directed lending facilities, have been dismantled, functional equivalents seem to have developed. For instance, as we will note in the next section, long-term finance on preferential terms is still available to *chaebol* through the non-bank financial organizations they own. To the extent that the Korean state does not actively create structures benefiting the *chaebol*, it at least condones their presence. Whether this will change in the aftermath of the 2012 presidential elections, in which all candidates propose to enhance the welfare state, partially in response to a rapidly ageing population, and curb the power of the *chaebol*, remains to be seen.

Despite democratization from the 1980s onward, decision-making has remained top down and centred on the president, with the large conglomerates representing the major non-state actor in economic policy-making. As a result of limited consultation and consensus-building, political strike actions are relatively common. Implementation of policies is generally good, with the World Bank rating government effectiveness as on a par with Taiwan and only surpassed among the economies in this handbook by Singapore, Hong Kong, and Japan (World Bank 2012b).

# FINANCIAL SYSTEM

While the Korean financial system has undergone significant changes in recent years, it remains dominated by indirect finance (Tsutsumi, Jones, and Cargill 2010). In the heyday of Korean industrial policy, banks were state-owned vehicles for funnelling capital to targeted conglomerates. Banks operated in a system that would keep firms supplied with preferential loans—and more generally, alive—as long as they met industrial policy targets or, in later years, if they were well connected or 'too big to fail'. The long-term availability of cheap debt, paired with a desire by *chaebol* owners not to dilute their controlling stakes, led conglomerates to expand on leverage, rather than by raising equity. This general pattern survived liberalization and privatization in the banking sector in the 1980s, not least because the liberalization process opened the door to *chaebol* ownership of non-bank financial institutions such as insurance and securities houses. These non-bank financial institutions grew to contribute about half of all loans in the economy prior to the 1997/98 Asian financial crisis (Hahm 2008). By the time of the crisis, the average debt/equity ratio of the *chaebol* was about 450 per cent for all conglomerates (Lim 2012) and 600 per cent for the top thirty conglomerates (Hao, Hunter, and Yang 2001). The average debt/equity ratio for listed non-conglomerates was about 300 per cent (Lim 2012).

The Asian financial crisis necessitated a re-nationalization and restructuring of banks. While some banks still remain in state hands, most were re-privatized in the following years, often through sales to foreign investors. The Korean government further required the *chaebol* to reduce their dependence on bank loans by capping debt/equity ratios at 200 per cent (Lee, Park, and Shin 2009).

While these changes, egged on by the International Monetary Fund (IMF), could have led to a shift towards a more market-oriented and equity-based system, indirect finance continues to dominate. Between 1988 and 2009, the ratio of bank credit to the private sector over GDP expanded from about 0.45 to 1.1. During the same period, the ratio of stock market valuation over GDP increased from about 0.15 to about 0.6 (Bank for International Settlements 2010). These are about the same levels as for Japan, a bank-led system with respective 2009 levels at 1.05 and 0.55.

Helpful for the ability of the *chaebol* to obtain loans is their continued ownership of non-bank financial institutions, which by 2005 were estimated to account for about 30 per cent of loans in the entire economy (Hahm 2008). Given their ownership control by *chaebol*, it is likely that non-bank financial institutions are the main source of loans for the *chaebol*, and that the loans received are on preferential terms and patient in nature. In addition, as the next section will show, the state of corporate governance in Korea is such that impatient capital—in essence, minority shareholders—has limited influence on managerial decision-making.

# OWNERSHIP AND CORPORATE GOVERNANCE

Family ownership and control have been key characteristics of the Korean business landscape. Of the 200 largest listed firms in Korea in 2008, 159 published sufficient data to trace ultimate ownership. Of these, between 35.8 and 54.5 per cent (depending on the threshold applied for ultimate control) were family-controlled[3] (Carney and Child 2012). These levels represent a marked increase from 1996 levels of between 26.3 and 51.8 per cent (Carney and Child 2012).

A common tool for maintaining family control of listed firms is pyramidal share ownership. In this pattern, the largest shareholder holds a controlling share in one firm, which in turn holds a controlling stake in another. This makes it possible for the largest shareholder to retain control of the latter firm without possessing a majority ownership stake. Of the 159 firms already mentioned, 50.6 per cent were part of pyramids in 2008, up from 36.1 per cent in 1996, with cross-shareholdings in these pyramids exceeding 5 per cent (Carney and Child 2012). As a result, 'the typical large control holder has ten ultimate votes for each 7.8 shares held' (Carney and Child 2012: 30).

The same patterns apply for the country's leading conglomerates, the *chaebol*, but in more pronounced form. Family control is the norm among this group, even though consolidated ownership stakes are considerably below controlling levels. For instance, for a group of forty-seven *chaebol* with on average twenty-three member firms, the 'owner family' on average held only 21 per cent of the cash-flow rights during the period 1998–2004 but retained up to 68 per cent of voting rights through measures such as pyramids (Almeida et al. 2011). The Korea Fair Trade Commission reported for 2008, the latest year for which it published such data, that the controlling families of the twenty-eight leading privately owned conglomerates held on average 14.2 per cent of the stock but had 49.3 per cent of the voting rights (Korea Fair Trade Commission 2008). The most extreme case was the SK *chaebol*, with the controlling family holding 2.2 per cent of stock, while retaining 37.3 per cent of the voting rights.

This divergence between ownership and control creates enormous potential for abuse by the controlling family. Well documented (e.g. Bae, Kang, and Kim 2002; Claessens and Fan 2002; Baek, Kang, and Lee 2006; Kim and Yi 2006) is a phenomenon known as 'tunnelling', which involves the transfer of funds from firms in which the controlling shareholder has low cash-flow rights to firms in which that shareholder has high rights. This can be accomplished through a multitude of mechanisms, including transfer-pricing, preferential purchasing within the conglomerate, acquisitions, private-securities offerings, or the provision of loans or loan guarantees.

Despite years of government efforts to improve the corporate governance system, the quality of corporate governance in Korea continues to be a serious concern. Seven of the leaders of Korea's ten largest *chaebol*, including the chairmen of Samsung, Hyundai Motors, and SK, have been convicted of crimes such as breach of trust, corruption, embezzlement, and large-scale accounting fraud (Power 2012). In 2010, the Asian Corporate Governance Association (Gill, Allen, and Powell 2010) rated Korean corporate governance ninth among eleven countries, a drop of three places compared with 2007. Only Indonesia and the Philippines scored worse, while China and India, hardly paragons of corporate governance, scored better. Of various factors affecting the overall score, only accounting and auditing practices were seen to be close to world-class standards. By contrast, the report identified enforcement as the weakest link in the corporate governance system, scoring 28 out of 100 points—52 points below the world-class benchmark. While government reforms may have improved the formal institutions of Korean corporate governance in recent years, lax enforcement seems to enable considerable deviations in actual practice (Lee and Lee 2008). A number of reasons may be in play. One is the generally pro-*chaebol* stance of the current president, Lee Myung-bak, himself a former *chaebol* executive. Another may be genuine fear that full enforcement of corporate governance reforms may weaken the competitive power of the *chaebol*; given their importance to the economy—Samsung alone is said to account for about 20 per cent of Korean exports—it seems plausible that prosecutors and politicians will try to avoid the risk of blame for weakening Korea's industrial powerhouses.

Perhaps the most powerful check on the *chaebol* is the force of public opinion, with a considerable part of Korea's population being generally critical of the power and business practices of the *chaebol*. For instance, in a 2012 opinion poll, 74 per cent of respondents indicated that they considered the *chaebol* 'immoral' (Kim and Park 2012). At the same time, research in the first half of the 2000s found that Korean top executives regarded charity and contributing to the development of the South Korean economy as important (Witt and Redding 2012a). The same executives identified employees and society as major stakeholders alongside shareholders (Witt and Redding 2012b). It seems likely that a need to respond to the hostility of labour unions and public opinion were major considerations in shaping executives' views. The overall picture is thus one of owner families checked, not by the force of law or activism of international shareholders, but by a need to maintain social licence by appeasing employees and society as a whole.

# INTERNAL STRUCTURE OF THE FIRM

The post-war Korean management system has been described as authoritarian and top down in nature, personalistic and paternalistic, with high supervisory control, and key decisions made by top managers, especially the chairman. In a *chaebol*, the chairman was a member of the controlling family (Janelli and Yim 1995; Whitley 1999; Lee, Roehl, and Choe 2000). To implement control over the conglomerate, the chairman would maintain a central staffing office (also known as the chairman's office) of up to several hundred dedicated staff, and direct matters such as staffing, auditing, planning, and finances in member firms of the *chaebol* (Whitley 1999). This control could be extensive, as illustrated by the report that the founder of Samsung, Lee Byung-chull, participated personally in all hiring interviews between 1957 and 1986, a total of over 100,000 interviews (Whitley 1999). Promotion and pay under this system were predominantly a function of seniority (Whitley 1999; Bae, Chen, and Rowley 2011), that is, the number of years of service with the firm.

In the 1990s, globalization and the 1997/8 Asian financial crisis combined to bring considerable pressure for change to bear on this system (Bae, Chen, and Rowley 2011; Lee and Kang 2012). However, on the evidence available today, it seems that the changes have been considerably less pronounced than expected immediately after the crisis. Korean management continues to be top down, authoritarian, and paternalistic (Park and Lee 2008; Bae, Chen, and Rowley 2011; Chang 2012). The willingness to delegate in Korea scores 3.6 out of 7, par with Thailand; in this handbook, only Vietnam scores lower (Schwab 2011). For Samsung Electronics, a paragon of Korean industry, a 2009 survey revealed that respondents denied that decision-making had become less authoritarian and top down, that there were now fewer layers in the hierarchy, and that leadership was less paternalistic (Chang 2012). A time-series study of Korean human-resource practices shows that the influence of employees on the running of the firm, if anything, declined somewhat between 1996 and 2004/5 (Bae, Chen, and Rowley 2011). Despite repeated proposals to outlaw the chairman's office, the practice of centralized control by the chairman and his staff continues (Park and Lee 2008).

Change seems likewise to have been limited in the area of hiring, promotions, and pay. While hiring at lower levels seems to have become more merit-based (Chang 2012), often through the use of standardized tests, the propensity to select top management from among family and loyal friends seems to persist (Chang 2012). Counter to expectations that pay and promotions would move towards a performance-related system, seniority-based wages remain dominant, and performance-related elements seem to be more of an admixture than a main component. This is clearly visible in the tenure–wage profile, which looked almost exactly the same in 2010 as 2000 (OECD 2012a). As tenure lengths have increased during that period (again counter to expectations; see next section), the age–wage profile has become considerably more pronounced, with workers in the age group 40–49 earning almost 2.75 times more than those below 20 years of age in 2010, as compared with a multiple of about 2.2 in 2000 (OECD 2012a). Survey data further show that in 2008, 52.2 per cent of firms still retained a purely seniority-based base pay system (another 39.4% used a mixture including seniority), and on average only one-sixth of the overall bonuses paid were variable (Park and Park 2011). To the extent that performance has become more emphasized in determining pay and promotions, this seems mostly the case for management (Rowley, Benson, and Warner 2004; Lee and

Kang 2012). Interestingly, this seniority system coexists with relatively short employment tenures (see next section), which is possible because seniority is no longer defined in terms of time with the company, but in terms of working experience.

# EMPLOYMENT RELATIONS

The Park government effectively suppressed the labour-union movement. Although unions existed, with the Federation of Korean Trade Unions (FKTU) as their peak association, they were tools of government policy rather than independent representatives of labour interests. Accordingly, wage increases during the early days of Korean modern economic development lagged behind overall economic growth (Amsden 1989). The union movement re-asserted itself in the 1980s, when it became a key driver of the democratization process (Lee, Y. 2011). Helped by the formation of alternative unions, such as the Korean Confederation of Trade Unions (KCTU), which emerged in 1990 (Han, Jang, and Kim 2010), unionization rates reached 19.8 per cent in 1989, the year following the first democratic presidential elections after Park (Ministry of Employment and Labor 2011).

While overall membership numbers have since stabilized around the 1995 figures of about 1.6 million, a growing labour-force has meant that by 2010, the unionization rate had fallen to 9.8 per cent (Ministry of Employment and Labor 2011). Structural shifts in the economy towards the service sector, which is traditionally lightly unionized, are a major reason for this change.

There is considerable variation in union strength by sector and company size (Ministry of Employment and Labor 2011). In the private sector, the unionization rate in 2010 was 8.6 per cent. By contrast, 18.9 per cent of teachers and 58.0 per cent of government workers were unionized in the same year. Unionization rates in companies ranged from 0.1 per cent for establishments with up to 29 employees to 43.4 per cent for firms with more than 300 employees. The implication is that in the *chaebol*, whose member firms tend to be large, on average almost half of the workforce is unionized.

The organization principle of Korean unions has been in transition from company to industrial unions since the 1990s (Yoon 2010). In 2010, Korea had 346 industrial unions with 888,437 members, equivalent to 54.1 per cent of all unionized workers, while the remaining 45.9 per cent were organized in 4,074 company unions (Ministry of Employment and Labor 2011). Since 2003, industrial-union membership has increased by 83.4 per cent from 484,400 members (31.1% of the total), while consolidation has led to a decline in industrial-union numbers from 469 to 346 (Ministry of Employment and Labor 2011).

Most unions are members of one of two umbrella organizations, the FKTU or KCTU. As of 2010, the FKTU was larger, with 728,649 members in 2,292 unions, while the KCTU organized 580,064 workers in 432 unions (Ministry of Employment and Labor 2011). However, the KCTU is likely to gain in relative strength over time, as 79.5 per cent of its members are in industrial unions, while the FKTU has 58.4 per cent of its members in company unions (Ministry of Employment and Labor 2011). The balance of 334,400 unionized workers were members of 1,696 independent unions (Ministry of Employment and Labor 2011).

Korean unions are notorious for militancy. However, strike activity has been in marked decline in recent years. The number of strikes in 2010 was 74, down from a post-crisis peak of 462 in 2004 (Lee, S-H. 2011). The number of working days lost to strikes in 2010 was 422,000, less than a quarter of the post-crisis high of 1.893 million days registered in 2000 (Lee, S-H. 2011).

Since 1998, Korea has officially had a tripartite industrial-relations system built around the Korea Tripartite Commission (KTC) (Han, Jang, and Kim 2010). There is considerable disagreement over its effectiveness in balancing the interests of capital and labour, with some authors seeing most benefits accruing to capital (Han, Jang, and Kim 2010), while others take a more balanced view (Yoon 2010). There is agreement, however, that Korean-style tripartism would be considered dysfunctional by European standards (Han, Jang, and Kim 2010; Kim, Y.-S. 2010; Yoon 2010). In particular, the KCTU withdrew from the KTC in 1998 and again in 1999 and has since remained outside the frame (Han, Jang, and Kim 2010; Kim, Y.-S. 2010). In addition, Korean unions continue to be highly decentralized, and even where industry-level bargaining occurs, the most important issues are still addressed in 'supplementary bargaining' at company level (Yoon 2010). Employers have generally resisted industry-level bargaining (Lee, S.-H. 2011).

Korean companies, especially *chaebol*, used to offer a form of lifetime employment, though on looser lines than its Japanese counterpart, in that mass dismissals did occasionally occur (Lee, Roehl, and Choe 2000). The model was effectively abrogated in the context of the 1997/8 Asian financial crisis, as bankruptcies and restructurings of *chaebol* led to a high number of involuntary separations. Today, Korea features short- to medium-term average employment tenure—for companies with 5 or more employees, 6.2 years in 2010 (Ministry of Employment and Labor 2012). This is far shorter than for Japanese companies (Witt 2014) and only slightly longer than the median[4] tenure of 4.4 years for US firms in 2010 (United States Department of Labor 2010). Job-hopping is common (Park and Lee 2008). Unlike the Japanese case, there is also considerable variation by firm size. Average tenure for small firms employing 5 to 9 employees was 4.5 years in 2010, while for large firms with more than 500 employees it was 9 years. While average tenure has become longer for firms with up to 500 employees between 2003 and 2010, it has actually fallen from 9.3 years to 9 years for firms with more than 500 employees.

This tendency towards short- to medium-term employment is visible despite relatively high levels of employment protection. The OECD (2012b) rated formal employment protection for regular employees in 2008 at 2.37, higher than that of Japan (1.87) and the Anglo-Saxon countries, but a bit lower than Northern European countries as well as China, India, and Indonesia.[5] The extent to which these regulations represent an actual (rather than merely formal) constraint is evident in data from *The Global*

*Competitiveness Report* (Schwab 2011), which indicate the ease of hiring and firing on a scale from 1 to 7 (1 = impeded by regulations, 7 = flexibly determined by employers). Korea scores 3.3, which is lower than all other Asian nations except Japan (3.0), and in Western Europe would rank between the Netherlands (3.1) and Luxembourg (3.4). The difficulty of dismissal seems to be a function not only of legal regulations, but also of union strength (OECD 2012a).

One consequence of employment protection for regular workers is a pronounced labour-market dualism. In response to the difficulty of laying off regular employees, firms hire non-regular employees, such as temporary, part-time, and dispatched workers (OECD 2012a). In 2011, non-regular workers were 34.2 per cent of all wage workers, an increase from 26.8 per cent in 2001 (Han, Jang, and Kim 2010), and considerably higher than before the Asian financial crisis of 1997/8 (Lee and Lee 2007). The growth in non-regular employment to current levels was facilitated by a loosening of employment protection for temporary employment, from 2.25 up to 1997 to 1.69 from 1998 to 2007 and to 1.44 from 2008 onward (Lee and Lee 2007; OECD 2012b). The non-regular category includes relatively more workers who are 'older, female, less educated, engaged in elementary work and employed in small and medium-sized enterprises' (OECD 2012a: 49). In 2011, these workers earned on average 13 per cent less per hour after controlling for individual characteristics such as age and education (OECD 2012a), a relatively moderate gap that is consistent with the notion that firms are seeking flexibility, rather than large savings in wages. Given strong public opposition to the proliferation of non-regular employment and increasing union attention, it remains to be seen whether current levels are sustainable.

## EDUCATION AND SKILLS FORMATION

The present education system was put in place after World War II on the basis of the US model. Students go through six years of primary school, three years of junior high school, and three years of high school, before moving on to two-year or four-year college, which in turn may be followed by graduate-degree programmes. Schooling is essentially universal through high school, and Korea's 2010 secondary gross enrolment rate of 97 per cent was the third-highest in Asia, after Brunei and Japan (World Bank 2012a). The proportion of students attending college is even higher, with a 2010 tertiary gross enrolment rate of 103 per cent, the highest in the world (World Bank 2012a). Of all high-school graduates, 72 per cent advance to tertiary education, down from a previous peak of 84 per cent (OECD 2012a). This level is so high that even the OECD, which usually emphasizes the need for tertiary education, has diagnosed an 'over-emphasis on tertiary education' (OECD 2012a: 73).

The output of this system is generally good. In the 2011 UNDP education attainment index, which presents a composite score of mean years of schooling of adults and expected years of schooling of children (United Nations Development Programme

2011), Korea scores 0.934. Among the nations of the world, this places Korea sixth, approximately par with the Netherlands and United States and ahead of all Asian economies. In comparative studies of student attainment, Korea similarly tends to perform well. In the 2009 PISA studies (OECD 2010) comparing students' ability in reading, mathematics, and sciences, Korea is overall placed fourth of sixty-five economies, bettered only by Hong Kong, Finland, and Singapore. In the 2007 Trends in Mathematics and Science Study (National Center for Education Statistics 2009), Korea ranked third among thirty-six economies, behind Taiwan and Singapore.

By contrast, vocational training schemes are relatively weak and weakening. The share of vocational high-school students fell from 42 per cent in 1995 to 24 per cent in 2010 (OECD 2012a), and in 2010, only 6.4 per cent of parents of middle-school students indicated an intention to send their children to a vocational high school (OECD 2012a). Technical colleges are similarly undergoing decline (Chang, Jung, and Oh 2009). Reasons behind these developments include the almost universal availability of generalist tertiary education—the country has about 180 universities (OECD 2012a)—paired with a social stigma attached to vocational training, as a path for under-achievers (Chang, Jung, and Oh 2009; OECD 2012a). In addition, wages for technical-college graduates vary little from those offered to high-school graduates (Chang, Jung, and Oh 2009), in part because of the skills mismatch between curricula and real-world needs (OECD 2012a). Accordingly, the total number of graduates from vocational and technical programmes at the upper secondary level fell from 306,713 in 1998, the beginning of the time series, to 151,975 in 2009 (OECD 2012b). The 2009 numbers for Germany and Japan were 441,522 and 279,434, respectively (OECD 2012b), so adjusting for population size, Korea produces more vocational training graduates than Japan, but considerably fewer than Germany. Whether recent government policy aimed at strengthening vocational training, such as the introduction of twenty-eight 'Meister' schools from 2010 onward (OECD 2012a), will help change the trend remains to be seen.

As in most other East Asian nations, entrance examinations are an integral part of the education system. Most colleges have such exams, and competition at top schools is stiff. These examinations, which have their origins in the Confucian examination system for civil servants, give the system in principle a strong meritocratic element. However, family wealth seems to be an important component in how well students fare in this system. In 2008, almost 30 per cent of total spending of households in Korea went on education—excluding private after-school tutoring—and Korean universities are the most expensive in the world after those of the United States and Israel (OECD 2012a). In addition, 73.6 per cent of Korean children attended private after-school tutoring in cram schools (hagwon) in 2010, costing on average 10.7 per cent of household income, equivalent to 1.8 per cent of GDP (OECD 2012a). Such spending increases with household income (OECD 2012a). As a result, Koreans identify education costs as the most important discouragement to having children (OECD 2012a), a highly relevant fact, given the impending shrinking of Korea's population.

Even if the influence of money leaves some room for meritocracy, the examination system has several drawbacks. Pressure on students is tremendous, and it is common for school, cram school, and homework to keep students busy until the late evening hours. Rote rehearsal and recall are emphasized over application and creativity. And all else being equal, the fact that graduation is virtually assured once students have passed their entrance examinations is unlikely to be a strong motivating force for hard study.

The combined effect of weak vocational training and an over-emphasis on university degrees with limited practical applicability creates a large skills gap in the economy (Chang, Jung, and Oh 2009; OECD 2012a). A 2004 survey by the Federation of Korean Industries found that firms needed to invest '23 months of general management work and 30 months of technical work' to imbue inexperienced workers with the skills firms required (Park 2007: 420). Another indicator is that within the OECD, Korea has by far the highest proportion of inactive youth, that is, those not in employment, education, or training ('NEETs'). In 2009, approximately 17 per cent of youths in the age group 15–29 fell into this category (OECD 2012a). For those with tertiary education, the proportion was even higher, at about 22 per cent, or around three times the OECD average (OECD 2012a). In 2007, only 51.9 per cent of university graduates secured regular jobs within a year of graduation, and only about 60 per cent of natural and social-science university graduates find jobs in their fields of study (OECD 2012a). Returns on education in terms of employment rates and salaries are low by OECD standards (OECD 2012a).

To the extent that skills training does occur, it tends to happen inside firms (OECD 2012a). In 2005, only 12.8 per cent of waged workers participated in training, compared with an OECD average of 37.1 per cent, and firms generally spend little on training employees (Chang, Jung, and Oh 2009), preferring instead to hire people with the requisite experience and skills (Park 2007; Chang, Jung, and Oh 2009). Training intensity increases with firm size, and regular workers receive more training than non-regular workers (Park 2007; Chang, Jung, and Oh 2009). This is consistent with employment tenure patterns: regular employees tend to remain on the payroll longer than non-regular ones, and as discussed, larger firms tend to have longer average tenures than small firms. Willingness to train thus seems to be linked to the expectation that firms can reap some benefit from investing in their employees. Where training occurs, most of it takes the form of classroom training (67.1%); on-the-job training (OJT) is relatively rare (12.2%) (Chang, Jung, and Oh 2009).

# INTER-FIRM RELATIONS

The dominant form of inter-firm relations in Korea is the business group, in the form of the *chaebol*. As already discussed, these conglomerates play a dominant role in the Korean economy, and centralized control by the chairman facilitates a degree of coordination and resource-sharing among member firms (cf. the discussion on tunnelling, above). The business association of the *chaebol* is the Federation of Korean Industries (FKI). However, the FKI seems to serve mostly a coordinating function with respect to politics. At the business level, rivalry rather than cooperation seems the norm.

Supplier networks exist in the shape of long-term sourcing arrangements, especially between *chaebol* and SME suppliers. For instance, Hyundai Motors in 2008 had about 2,400 SME suppliers (just-auto.com 2008). These networks seem to be qualitatively different from Japan's supplier networks, with trust levels in Korea much lower than in Japan (and indeed lower than in the United States) (Dyer and Chu 2000). This may be linked to a sense of dependence of SMEs on the *chaebol* and the resultant potential for abuse (Dyer and Chu 2000).

Korea has numerous business associations at various levels. The Korea Chamber of Commerce and Industry (KCCI) has approximately 135,000 members from various industries (Korea Chamber of Commerce and Industry 2012). At the industry level, Korea created Japanese-style control associations to help implement developmental policies (cf. Park 1987; Witt 2006; Park 2009). While industry associations have since shed their function as instruments of control, their presence does not seem to have fostered the emergence of strong intra-industry cooperation. For instance, only a minority of 39.2 per cent of SMEs with fewer than 300 employees reported seeing a need for cooperation with other SMEs (Kim, S-B. 2011). Similarly, cooperation levels within R&D consortia in Korea seem to have been at considerably lower levels than those observed in Japan (Sakakibara and Cho 2002).

Informal networks matter to some extent. Members of *chaebol* families seem to mingle socially, and intermarriage occurs. Similarly, *chaebol* leaders often enjoy good personal access to politicians and bureaucrats. The incumbent[6] president, Lee Myung-bak, while not a member of any *chaebol* family, is connected to the *chaebol* world through his former position as CEO of Hyundai Engineering and Construction.

# SOCIAL CAPITAL

Korean society has a tradition of relatively high interpersonal trust, with such trust being based mostly on family membership or shared collective experiences (Whitley 1999). Accordingly, 2005 data suggest that Koreans, like most Asian societies, place high levels of trust in their families, with 87.2 per cent of them indicating such trust to be complete (average of other Asian societies for which data are available: 85.8%) (World Values Survey 2009). By contrast, only 14.9 per cent of Koreans reported trusting, at least a little, people they meet for the first time (other Asian nations: 19.1%) (World Values Survey 2009).

It is not clear how Korean interpersonal trust levels have developed in the immediate past. However, there has been strong growth in voluntary non-government organizations, from virtually non-existent until the 1980s, to intermediate levels by the mid-2000s, and probably strengthening further since (Joo, Lee, and Jo 2006; Kim, H-R. 2012). Such NGOs have been shown to foster interpersonal trust in other contexts (Anheier and Kendall 2002), and should this mechanism hold for Korea as well, inter-personal trust levels, especially those bridging different groups in society, may well have risen in recent years.

Institutionalized-trust levels are fairly high. In the 2011 Corruption Perception Index (Transparency International 2012), Korea scored 5.4 on a scale from 0 (completely cor-rupt) to 10 (completely clean), ranking forty-third among 182 territories. This puts it behind most Western nations, with the exception of Italy and Greece, but ahead of all other economies in this handbook other than Singapore, Hong Kong, Japan, and Taiwan. This implies that overall, the rule of law tends to apply. In addition, Korea's 2010 governance indicators for government effectiveness, regulatory quality, and rule of law fall between the 75th and 90th percentile, and the indicators for voice and accountabil-ity, political stability, and control of corruption lie between the 50th and 75th percentile among 213 economies in the world (World Bank 2012b). Looking at the average of all indicators, most Anglo-Saxon and northern European nations score higher, as do Japan, Hong Kong, Singapore, and Taiwan in Asia from India eastwards. To the extent that these statistics are indicative of institutionalized trust, they suggest a relatively high level compared with most of Asia, though relatively low by advanced industrialized-country standards. Holding back further development on this dimension may be the tendency of the Korean state to pardon *chaebol* leaders convicted of various crimes, effectively putting some parts of society above the law. Accordingly, public trust in government is generally low (Kim, S. 2010).

# INSTITUTIONAL COMPLEMENTARITIES

The Korean business system features a range of institutional complementarities. Focusing on those relevant to the *chaebol* as the most significant type of Korean firm, the main complementarities among the elements laid out earlier can be summarized as follows:

1. Indirect finance and long-term availability of financial capital to *chaebol* are linked. As noted before, *chaebol* can cover part of their capital requirements through non-bank financial organizations that they own. Given their own-ership control over the lending entities, it is unlikely that these entities will recall loans.
2. Indirect finance, in part provided by captive lenders, is connected to weak corporate governance, in the sense of weak shareholder control over the fate of the company. Korean companies remain firmly under the control of con-trolling families, who can afford to pay little attention to the interests of other

shareholders, because the low dependence on capital markets deprives shareholders of an important source of leverage.

3. Weak corporate governance is linked to cross-shareholdings, pyramidal shareholdings, and the prevalence of conglomerates more generally. These structures help controlling families remain in control of large numbers of firms even though they own, on average, only a small minority of shares. They further help insulate controlling families from shareholder pressure in the form of the threat of selling to the highest bidder in the context of a hostile takeover.

4. The presence of a controlling (but not really owning) shareholding dampens long-term employment, which should in principle be facilitated by the combination of indirect finance and weak corporate governance. Given historical experiences such as disproportionately slow wage growth in the 1970s and mass dismissals in the late 1990s, the track record suggests that controlling family interests supersede those of employees. As a result, employee loyalty is relatively low, and tenure lengths are accordingly below those seen in Japan.

5. Average durations of employment are linked to training. Small Korean firms have relatively high staff turnover and consequently make little effort at training. Large firms have average tenures of around nine years, which seems to provide sufficient time to recoup investments on training and is thus related to higher levels of training.

6. Strong family control and the attendant top-down centralized decision-making are connected to disharmonious labour relations. Top-down decision-making means that there is little transparency inside the firm about the circumstances of particular corporate policies. The resulting opacity prevents labour from verifying whether claims about the state of the company made by management—for example in the context of pay reductions or dismissals—are credible. Given the inherent possibility that controlling families may be maximizing their own benefits at the expense of their employees, Korean labour tends to exhibit relatively militant behaviour.

7. The inherent conflict between controlling families and employees is related to relatively low levels of institutionalized trust and delegation in Korean firms. Delegation means entrusting a task to someone in the confidence that the task will be done as the delegating party him/herself would have executed it. In the Korean context, there is a risk that empowering lower echelons to make decisions on behalf of the chairperson could lead to a greater emphasis on employee interests. Levels of institutional trust, which would entail confidence that a company will act appropriately and fairly toward its employees, seem to be too low to mitigate this effect (and it stands to reason that sufficiently high levels of institutionalized trust in Korea in general would imply a legal system that would put an end to the eminence of the controlling families).

Overall, the Korean business system and this set of complementarities seem to be conducive to fast-follower business strategies (cf. Redding and Witt 2007). *Chaebol* are quick to move into promising markets and can leverage patient finance as well as profits from other businesses in the conglomerate (and, in the background, a supportive developmental state) to finance their forays. Suitable employees can be hired from other firms, given the absence of true long-term employment, or from other firms inside the *chaebol*.

## EVOLUTIONARY DYNAMICS

Institutional change in the Korean business system seems to be driven predominantly by the state. It was clearly a major force, and also the object of institutional change itself, in the creation of the developmental state under Park. In the aftermath of the 1997/8 Asian Financial Crisis, the state was the major instigator of institutional changes aimed at reforming the *chaebol*, albeit egged on by powerful external actors such as the IMF and the United States as well as foreign investors (cf. Kim, Kang, and Kim 2012). That these reforms were ultimately less far-reaching than expected is perhaps as much a testament to the resilience of the *chaebol* as it is of the unwillingness of the Korean state to push the envelope on *chaebol* reform for fear of damaging Korea's leading businesses, and thus the foundations of the country's economic prosperity.

The top-down structure of institutional change in Korea is subject to the usual array of known constraints and flaws, such as creating policies without full information about relevant circumstances or due deliberation (cf. Witt and Lewin 2007). In addition, top-down decision-making invites political strikes, as the public usually does not get asked what it wants when the state makes decisions. For instance, in the context of the 2008 Free Trade Agreement negotiations with the United States, tens of thousands of Koreans protested against part of the agreement that called for the resumption of beef imports from the United States, because of concern over the prevalence of BSE in US cattle. By contrast, positive demonstrations, in the sense of those demanding changes (such as the introduction of democracy) rather than those seeking to prevent them, seem to have become relatively rare.

## CONCLUSION

In summary, in the absence of clear shifts to another state model and given continued emphasis on growth and industry promotion, the Korean state is probably best classified as a reconfiguring developmental state. The financial system is indirect, with non-bank financial institutions having special importance for the *chaebol*. Corporate governance continues to be among the weakest in Asia, with so-called 'owner' families retaining control over the *chaebol* despite low levels of overall shareholdings. Internal dynamics are top down with limited delegation, and promotion mostly based on seniority and, at the very top, family ties. Employment relations are characterized by a fragmented but militant union landscape, short- to medium-term average tenures that vary greatly with firm size, and a pronounced labour-market duality between regular and non-regular workers. The education system performs well in international comparisons, but fails to produce workers with needed skills, in part because vocational training is very weak. Firm-based training is present mostly in large firms such as the *chaebol*. Networking among firms occurs predominantly among members of the same *chaebol*. Social capital is high on an interpersonal level and reasonably well developed in terms of institutionalized trust, though the latter does not seem to extend strongly to the corporate realm. A series of institutional complementarities are present, and institutional change is mostly a top-down process driven by the state.

Interpreted in the context of the Hall and Soskice (2001) model, Korea falls somewhere between the opposite poles of coordinated and liberal market economies (CMEs and LMEs). Developments over the past fifteen years seem to have pushed the system somewhat closer towards the Anglo-Saxon LME model though, as we have seen, actual practice is far from what one would expect of an LME. Indeed, the closest relatives of the Korean business system in the West might well be the Southern European 'mixed' or 'state-led' economies, as also suggested in earlier analysis (Whitley 1999; Kang 2010).

As this chapter has illustrated, the Korean business system has changed less than expected since the 1997 financial crisis. This highlights the importance of structural inertia in institutional change, especially in response to sudden external shocks. By contrast, major internally generated institutional changes seem possible and even likely in the coming decades, especially with respect to the role of the state and the pre-eminence of the *chaebol*. Affecting the former is rapid societal ageing and attendant shrinking of the working population. In response, Korea will probably need to construct a much stronger social welfare system and in effect become a welfare state, ideally avoiding the pitfalls of the European experience. As regards the *chaebol*, we have discussed how the Korean industrial landscape is highly concentrated on a few conglomerates, whose controlling families have often seemed above the law. Public disquiet in both these areas is leading to growing pressure for change, supported at least rhetorically by major politicians across the political spectrum. While one should not underestimate the ability of the *chaebol* to resist, as the past decade has shown, eradicating these issues from the political agenda without major concessions will be difficult. For students of institutional change, Korea promises to be an interesting case to watch.

# ACKNOWLEDGEMENTS

I thank Ji Hee Yeo for very valuable research assistance and Nahee Kang and Eun Mee Kim for very helpful comments. Any remaining errors are my sole responsibility.

## NOTES

1. The others being Hong Kong, Singapore, and Taiwan.
2. The Han is the largest river of Seoul, the Korean capital.
3. Controlled does not necessarily mean owned, as will become clear below.
4. The United States does not publish average (mean) tenure data, while Japan and Korea do not publish median tenure data.
5. Other Asian countries not rated.
6. As of late fall 2012, when this chapter was finalized.

## REFERENCES

Almeida, H., S. Y. Park, M. G. Subrahmanyam, and D. Wolfenzon (2011). 'The Structure and Formation of Business Groups: Evidence from Korean Chaebols'. *Journal of Financial Economics* 99(2): 447–475.

Amsden, A. H. (1989). *Asia's Next Giant: South Korea and Late Industrialization*. Oxford, Oxford University Press.

Anheier, H. and J. Kendall (2002). 'Interpersonal Trust and Voluntary Associations: Examining Three Approaches'. *British Journal of Sociology* 53(3): 343–362.

Bae, J., S.-J. Chen and C. Rowley (2011). 'From a Paternalistic Model Towards What? HRM Trends in Korea and Taiwan'. *Personnel Review* 4(6): 700–722.

Bae, K. H., J.-K. Kang, and J. M. Kim (2002). 'Tunneling or Value Added? Evidence from Mergers by Korean Business Groups'. *Journal of Finance* 57(6): 2695–2740.

Baek, J-S., J.-K. Kang, and I. Lee (2006). 'Business Groups and Tunneling: Evidence from Private Securities Offerings by Korean Chaebols'. *Journal of Finance* 61(5): 2415–2449.

Bank for International Settlements (2010). *Long-Term Issues in International Banking*. Basel, Bank for International Settlements.

Carney, R. W. and T. B. Child (2012). 'Changes to Ownership and Control of East Asian Corporations between 1996 and 2008: The Primacy of Politics'. *Journal of Financial Economics*. doi: 10.1016/j.jfineco.2012.08.013

Chang, H-G., S-G. Jung and H-S. Oh (2009). 숙련개발체제와 노사관계 – 한국, 일본, 독일의 사례 [*Skill Development Regimes and Industrial Relations: The Cases of South Korea, Japan, and Germany*]. Seoul, Korea Labor Institute.

Chang, S.-I. (2012). 'Study on Human Resource Management in Korea's Chaebol Enterprise: A Case Study of Samsung Electronics'. *International Journal of Labour Research* 23(7): 1436–1461.

Chu, Y. (2009). 'Eclipse or Reconfigured? South Korea's Developmental State and Challenges of the Global Knowledge Economy'. *Economy and Society* 38(2): 278–303.

Claessens, S. and J. P. H. Fan (2002). 'Corporate Governance in Asia: A Survey'. *International Review of Finance* 3(2): 71–103.

Dyer, J. H. and W. Chu (2000). 'The Determinants of Trust in Supplier-Automaker Relationships in the US, Japan, and Korea'. *Journal of International Business Studies* 31(2): 259–285.

Eckert, C. J., K.-B. Lee, Y. I. Lew, M. Robinson, and E. W. Wagner (1990). *Korea Old and New: A History*. Cambridge, Harvard University Press.

Gill, A., J. Allen, and S. Powell (2010). 'CG Watch 2010: Corporate Governance in Asia'. Retrieved 1 September 2012 from <http://www.clsa.com/assets/files/reports/CLSA-CG-Watch-2010.pdf?disclaimer=on&accept=+Yes%2C+I+Agree>.

Hahm, J. (2008). 'Ten Years after the Crisis: Financial System in Transition in Korea'. In M. Karasulu and D.Y. Yang, Eds., *Ten Years after the Korean Crisis: Crisis, Adjustment and Long-run Economy Growth*: 65–99. Seoul, Korea Institute for International Economy Policy.

Hall, P. A. and D. Soskice (2001). 'An Introduction to Varieties of Capitalism'. In P. A. Hall and D. Soskice, Eds., *Varieties of Capitalism: The Institutional Foundations of Comparative Advantage*: 1–68. Oxford, Oxford University Press.

Han, C., J. Jang, and S. Kim (2010). 'Social Dialogue and Industrial Relations in South Korea: Has the Tripartite Commission Been Successful?' *Asia Pacific Viewpoint* 51(3): 288–303.

Hao, J., W. C. Hunter, and W. K. Yang (2001). 'Deregulation and Efficiency: The Case of Private Korean Banks'. *Journal of Economics and Business* 53: 237–254.

Hundt, D. (2005). 'Legitimate Paradox: Neo-Liberal Reform and the Return of the State in Korea'. *Journal of Development Studies* 41(2): 242–260.

Janelli, R. L. and D. Yim (1995). *Making Capitalism: The Social and Cultural Construction of a South Korean Conglomerate*. Stanford, Stanford University Press.

Joo, S., S. Lee, and Y. Jo (2006). *The Exploring of CSOs and Citizen Participation: An Assessment of Civil Society in South Korea 2004: Civicus Civil Society Index Report for South Korea*. Seoul, Hanyang University.

just-auto.com (2008). 'South Korea: Hyundai Signs "Pact" with Suppliers'. Retrieved 21 July 2012 from <http://www.just-auto.com/news/hyundai-signs-pact-with-suppliers_id95967.aspx>.

Kang, N. (2010). 'Globalisation and Institutional Change in the State-Led Model: The Case of Corporate Governance in South Korea'. *New Political Economy* 15(4): 519–542.

Kim, E. M. (1997). *Big Business, Strong State: Collusion and Conflict in South Korean Development, 1960–1990*. Albany, State University of New York Press.

—— (2010). 'Limits of the Authoritarian Developmental State of South Korea'. In O. Edigheji, Ed., *Constructing a Democratic Developmental State in South Africa: Potential and Challenges*: 97–125. Cape Town, HSRC Press.

—— N. Kang, and J. H. Kim (2012). 'The Role of Foreign (Direct) Investment in Corporate Governance Reform in South Korea'. In B.-K. Kim, E. M. Kim, and J. C. Oi, Eds., *Adapt, Fragment, and Transform: Corporate Restructuring and System Reform in South Korea*: 201–231. The Walter H, Storenstein Asia Pacific Center, Stanford University Press.

Kim, H.-R. (2012). *State-Centric to Contested Social Governance in South Korea: Shifting Power*. London, Routledge.

Kim, J. and J.-M. Park (2012). 'Analysis: South Korea's Unloved Chaebol'. *Thomson Reuters* Retrieved 13 April 2012 from <http://uk.reuters.com/assets/print?aid=UKBRE83405V20120405>.

Kim, J. B. and C. H. Yi (2006). 'Ownership Structure, Business Group Affiliation, Listing Status, and Earnings Management: Evidence from Korea'. *Contemporary Accounting Research* 23(2): 427–464.

Kim, S. (2010). 'Public Trust in Government in Japan and South Korea: Does the Rise of Critical Citizens Matter?' *Public Administration Review* 70(5): 801–810.

Kim, S.-B. (2011). 'SME Competitiveness: The Power of Cooperation Network'. Retrieved 21 July 2012 from <http://www.seriworld.org/08/wldPrint.html?p=k>.

Kim, Y.-S. (2010). 'Institutions of Interest Representation and the Welfare State in Post-Democratization Korea'. *Asian Perspective* 34(1): 159–189.

Korea Chamber of Commerce and Industry (2012). 'About KCCI'. Retrieved 21 July 2012 from <http://english.korcham.net/sub05/sub05_6.asp>.

Korea Fair Trade Commission (2008). '2008 소유지분구조_붙임 [2008 Owner Share Structure]', Korea Fair Trade Commission. Retrieved 4 May 2012 from <http://www.index.go.kr/egams/stts/jsp/potal/stts/PO_STTS_IdxMain.jsp?idx_cd=1176>.

Kwon, S. and I. Holliday (2007). 'The Korean Welfare State: A Paradox of Expansion in an Era of Globalisation and Economic Crisis'. *International Journal of Social Welfare 16*(3): 242–248.

Lee, B.-H. and H.-Y. Kang (2012). 'Hybridisation of Employment Relations in the Era of Globalization? A Comparative Case Study of the Automotive and Banking Industries in South Korea'. *International Journal of Labour Research 23*(10): 2034–2050.

—— and S. Lee (2007). 'Minding the Gaps: Non-Regular Employment and Labour Market Segmentation in the Republic of Korea'. *Conditions of Work and Employment Series*. Geneva, International Labour Office.

Lee, J., T. W. Roehl, and S. Choe (2000). 'What Makes Management Style Similar and Distinct across Borders? Growth, Experience and Culture in Korean and Japanese Firms'. *Journal of International Business Studies 31*(4): 631–652.

Lee, K. and C. H. Lee (2008). 'The Miracle to Crisis and the Mirage of the Post-crisis Reform in Korea: Assessment after Ten Years'. *Journal of Asian Economics 19*(5–6): 425–437.

Lee, S., K. Park, and H.-H. Shin (2009). 'Disappearing Internal Capital Markets: Evidence from Diversified Business Groups in Korea'. *Journal of Banking & Finance 33*(2): 326–334.

Lee, S.-H. (2011). 'Labor-Management Relations: 2010 Review and 2011 Outlook'. *Monthly Labor Review*. Seoul, Korea Labor Institute.

Lee, Y. (2011). *Militants or Partisans: Labor Unions and Democratic Politics in Korea and Taiwan*. Stanford, Stanford University Press.

Lee, Y.-J. and Y.-W. Ku (2007). 'East Asian Welfare Regimes: Testing the Hypothesis of the Developmental Welfare State'. *Social Policy & Administration 41*(2): 197–212.

Lim, K.-M. (2012). 'Structural Fundamentals of Korean Corporations: This Time Was Different'. In M. Obstfeld, D. Cho, and A. Mason, Eds., *Global Economic Crisis: Impacts, Transmission and Recovery*: 250–272. Cheltenham, Edward Elgar.

Ministry of Employment and Labor (2011). '2010년 노동조합 조직현황 주요 내용 [2010 Labor Union Structure Overview]'. Seoul, Ministry of Employment and Labor.

Ministry of Employment and Labor (2012). '규모,학력,연령계층,성별 임금 및 근로조건 [Salary and Working Conditions by Company Size, Education, Age, Gender]'. Seoul, Korean Statistical Information Service.

Mishra, R., S. Kuhnle, N. Gilbert, and K. Chung, Eds. (2004). *Toward the Productive Welfare Model*. New Brunswick, Transaction.

National Center for Education Statistics (2009). *Highlights from TIMMS 2007: Mathematics and Science Achievement of US Fourth- and Eighth-Grade Students in an International Context*. Washington, DC, National Center for Education Statistics.

OECD (2010). *PISA 2009 Results: What Students Know and Can Do—Student Performance in Reading, Mathematics and Science* (Volume I). Paris, OECD.

—— (2012a). *OECD Economic Surveys: Korea*. Paris, OECD.

—— (2012b). '*OECD.Stat*'. Paris, OECD.

Park, I. (2007). 'The Labour Market, Skill Formation and Training in the 'Post-Developmental' State: The Example of South Korea'. *Journal of Education and Work 20*(5): 417–435.

Park, J.-S. and E. K. Park (2011). *Pay in Korea: An Introductory Guide*. Seoul, Korea Labor Institute.

Park, M. K. (1987). 'Interest Representation in South Korea: The Limits of Corporatist Control'. *Asian Survey 27*(8): 903–917.

Park, S. (2009). 'Cooperation between Business Associations and the Government in the Korean Cotton Industry, 1950–70'. *Business History 51*(6): 835–853.

Park, W.-W. and S.-M. Lee (2008). 'Korean Cultural Heritage and Its Influence on Implementing Empowerment and Self-Directed Teams'. 경영논집 *[Journal of Management]* 42: 125–152.

Pirie, I. (2005). *The Korean Developmental State: From Dirigisme to Neo-Liberalism*. London, Routledge.

Power, J. (2012). 'Is Korea Soft on White-Collar Crime?' *The Korea Herald*. 5 March 2012.

Redding, G. and M. A. Witt (2007). *The Future of Chinese Capitalism: Choices and Chances*. Oxford, Oxford University Press.

Rowley, C., J. Benson, and M. Warner (2004). 'Towards an Asian Model of Human Resource Management? A Comparative Analysis of China, Japan and South Korea'. *International Journal of Labour Research 14*(4–5): 917–933.

Sakakibara, M. and D.-S. Cho (2002). 'Cooperative R&D in Japan and Korea: A Comparison of Industrial Policy'. *Research Policy 31*(2002): 673–692.

Schwab, K., Ed. (2011). *The Global Competitiveness Report 2011–2012*. Geneva, World Economic Forum.

Song, B-N. (2003). *The Rise of the Korean Economy*. Oxford, Oxford University Press.

Transparency International (2012). 'Corruption Perception Index 2011'. Retrieved 21 July 2012 from <http://www.transparency.org/policy_research/surveys_indices/cpi/2011/results>.

Tsutsumi, M., R. S. Jones, and T. F. Cargill (2010). *The Korean Financial System: Overcoming the Global Financial Crisis and Addressing Remaining Problems*. OECD Economics Department Working Paper 796. Paris, OECD.

United Nations Development Programme (2011). 'Education Index'. Retrieved 20 July 2012 from <http://hdrstats.undp.org/en/indicators/103706.html>.

United States Department of Labor (2010). 'Employment Tenure Summary'. Washington, DC, United States Department of Labor. Retrieved 6 May 2012 from <http://www.bls.gov/news.release/tenure.nro.htm>.

Wade, R. (1990). *Governing the Market: Economic Theory and the Role of Government in East Asian Industrialization*. Princeton, Princeton University Press.

Whitley, R. (1999). *Divergent Capitalisms: The Social Structuring and Change of Business Systems*: 98–120. Oxford, Oxford University Press.

Witt, M. A. (2006). *Changing Japanese Capitalism: Societal Coordination and Institutional Adjustment*. Cambridge, Cambridge University Press.

—— (2014). 'Japan: Coordinated Capitalism Between Institutional Change and Structural Inertia'. In M. A. Witt and G. Redding, Eds., *The Oxford Handbook of Asian Business Systems*: 100–122. Oxford, Oxford University Press.

—— and A. Y. Lewin (2007). 'Outward Foreign Direct Investment as Escape Response to Home-Country Institutional Constraints'. *Journal of International Business Studies 38*(4): 579–594.

—— and G. Redding (2012a). 'The Spirits of CSR: Senior Executive Perceptions of the Role of the Firm in Society in Germany, Hong Kong, Japan, South Korea, and the United States'. *Socio-Economic Review 10*(1): 109–134.

—— (2012b). *The Spirits of East Asian Capitalism: Hong Kong and South Korean Senior Executive Perceptions of Why Firms Exist*. INSEAD Working Paper. Fontainebleau, INSEAD.

Woo-Cumings, M., Ed. (1999). *The Developmental State*. Ithaca, Cornell University Press.

World Bank (2012a). 'World Development Indicators', World Bank. Retrieved 20 July 2012 from <http://data.worldbank.org/indicator/all>.

—— (2012b). 'Worldwide Governance Indicators'. Washington, DC, World Bank. Retrieved 21 July 2012 from <http://info.worldbank.org/governance/wgi/>.

World Values Survey (2009). 'World Values Survey 2005 Official Data File V. 20090901'. Madrid, World Values Association.

Yoon, J. H. (2010). 'The Asian Crisis of 1997–98: The Case of the Republic of Korea'. International Journal of Labour Research 2(1): 43–60.

# CHAPTER 12

........................................................................................

# TAIWAN

## *SME-Oriented Capitalism in Transition*

........................................................................................

## ZONG-RONG LEE AND HSIN-HUANG MICHAEL HSIAO

## INTRODUCTION

INDUSTRIALIZATION in Taiwan started in the late 1950s when the government provided tax incentives to attract foreign investment. The emphasis in economic policy shifted from imports to exports; restrictions on the establishment of companies were removed in the early 1960s, and it was then that Taiwanese entrepreneurs began to flourish and establish their foothold. The market then went through decades of rapid growth, with local businesses booming, diversifying, and becoming pivotal within the global economy, marking Taiwan out as one of the most successful late-developing capitalist nations. Previous studies have tended to point out that high levels of education, the shifting nature of cross-sectoral investments, and the prominence of family-owned small enterprises have been trademarks of the Taiwanese economy (Hamilton and Biggart 1988; Wade 1990).

As regards the present, however, the whole industrial structure has been changed, to the extent that old stereotypes may not be easy to recapture. In the early period of industrialization, the business system in Taiwan resembled the corporatist structure of oligopolistic cartels, only on a smaller scale, where state enterprises played an important role and overall integration was relatively high. After a transitional period in the late 1980s, the influence of state enterprises in the economy declined enormously, mainly because of the private sector's continuous growth and a series of deregulations of economic policies that loosened control on private businesses' horizontal expansion (Lee, Z. 2009). Since then, local Taiwanese companies have started to grow and consolidate as well as follow the path of globalization and export their mobile but close-knit production networks. In this chapter, we aim to highlight key ingredients inherent in this robust business system and outline the historical contours of its transformation.

# THE ROLE OF THE STATE

Scholars concerned with the development of East Asian economies emphasize the importance of competent state capacities in integrating and governing market forces for successful economic development, and Taiwan has long been recognized by scholars as an archetype of such a model (Johnson 1982; Amsden 1985; Wade 1990; Evans 1995; Fields 1995). Taiwan was a Japanese colony from 1895 to 1945, when it was handed back to the Chinese government. After this Retrocession in 1945, the Chinese Nationalist Party (Kuomintang, KMT) government confiscated all Japanese-owned industrial assets and turned them into state-owned enterprises. The KMT state not only controlled basic industries, such as petroleum, steel, and aluminium, but also consolidated control over the financial system. By the early 1950s, state-owned enterprises accounted for 56 per cent of Taiwan's industrial output (Amsden 1979), making it one of the largest public-enterprise sectors outside the communist bloc and Sub-Saharan Africa (Wade 1990: 176). The dominance of the public sector over private businesses in Taiwan has continued through more than four decades of economic development (Hsiao 1995). An unofficial estimate suggests that with the KMT-owned enterprises, the complex party/state-controlled economy may have had an annual turnover accounting for up to 30 per cent of Taiwan's GNP by 1990 (Chen et al. 1991).

The power of the KMT government over the islands was curtailed, however, by the Nationalist regime's dependence on the United States for economic and military assistance, as well as political support, in the early 1950s. In the Cold War environment, the United States, needing a model of successful capitalist development as an alternative to Russian-backed communist China, guided and helped the Nationalists in this effort. One condition for aid was the promotion of a private sector. Beginning in the 1950s, Taiwan was pressured to create a climate conducive to private-capital investment and to divest itself of some of its enterprises in the light industrial sectors (Gold 1988: 184). The United States provided the framework for potentially more profitable private business investments and played a critical role in helping to reverse the former Nationalist government policy of extensive state control (Simon 1988: 19). Nevertheless, the KMT government ensured that the emerging bourgeoisie would be dependent on it and would be active only in certain sectors. As upstream producers, state-owned enterprises and big businesses supplied intermediate products for tens of thousands of small and medium-sized firms, and the crucial factor for their growth stemmed from the demand for intermediate goods and services from small or medium-sized firms that were mostly export-oriented (Hamilton 1997; Hsieh 2011).

The state continued to dominate the market until the late 1980s, when the political system was democratized following the lifting of martial law in 1987, which triggered the liberalization and globalization of the economy and enabled a 'great transformation' to take place (Hsiao 1995). The importance of the role of state power in the economy has since declined rapidly, and the whole course of the Taiwanese economy since can be roughly described as progress away from the ideal model of the developmental state

(Lee, Z. 2009; Wong 2011), with the capacity of state bureaucrats to direct the private sector diminishing. One salient feature was that interest politics replaced regime autonomy as commonplace, and electoral competition has been leading politicians away from developmentalism (Wu 2007). With the economic policies of liberalization initiated in the early 1990s, monopolized industries were deregulated and state enterprises privatized, along with large-scale reductions in important controls and tariffs, as well as liberalization for foreign investment and bank interest rates, etc. Such measures forced the state to put a considerable number of shares in state-owned businesses on to the market and release previously state-owned industries into the hands of private businesses. Globalization, moreover, has pushed ODM-based (Original Design Manufacturer) Taiwanese manufacturing companies to become more mobile across Asian regions in order to break even in the face of global competition (Saxenian 2006; Hsiao, Kung, and Wang 2010). By 2009, state-owned enterprises accounted for 8.73 per cent of fixed assets, 11.6 per cent of operating margin, and only 3.8 per cent of total GNP (Executive Yuan 2010). In the meantime, according to the Economic Freedom Index Survey 2010, conducted by the Heritage Foundation, Taiwan's overall score for economic freedom was 70.8 in 2011, placing it seventh among Asia-Pacific countries (after Hong Kong, Singapore, Australia, New Zealand, Macau, and Japan) and twenty-fifth in the world. The index has also shown a steady decline of market regulatory activities, from 5.32 in 1980 to 6.96 in 2008.

As its capacity declined, the state became more and more regulatory in nature, less capable of direct intervention, and less predictable in the quality of implementation (Wong 2011). As a result, decision-making has been changing gradually from a top-down statist fashion to one that is increasingly more likely to be captured by emerging powerful business interests. Amid the liberalization of the 1990s, the government deregulated several industries through articulated licensing and pricing policies in order to limit competition and the number of new entrants, and thus had the newly deregulated industries under its control (Amsden and Chu 2003). Through regulatory measures, the state in Taiwan still seemed to have more of a say on market configuration than states in most advanced economies; although the consequences of such measures were far from successful. The grand finale of this long series of events in economic liberalization was the government-initiated policy of the Second Financial Reform in the early 2000s, when the Financial Institutions Merger Act and Financial Holding Company Act were enacted.

Since then, a wave of bank M&As have been incited in the market. By the end of 2006, fourteen financial holding companies had emerged in Taiwan, almost all of them family controlled. Ironically, the consequences of such a policy were not as positive as policy-makers had expected. No cost efficiencies were found within three years after the mergers for either state-owned entities or their private-sector counterparts (Wu 2008). Similarly, a study of eighteen privatized companies also found no direct evidence of improved operating or long-term investment performance (Yang, Ku, and Yao 2005). Moreover, such state-initiated policy reform was tarnished by a corruption scandal that broke out in 2008. The corruption case was in part against former president Chen Shui-bian and his family, but also highlighted the donations made by the business-owners of major financial holding groups. Detailed statements in the indictment and in the ruling exposed influence peddling by the patriarchs of Taiwan's family conglomerates and the astronomical sums that frequently change hands in these policy-changing contexts.

# FINANCIAL SYSTEM

During the long post-war decades of political domination of the whole economy, the KMT nationalists also took over the Japanese-established banking system. This, together with its own banks brought over from the mainland, enabled the KMT government to control virtually all the financial resources it needed to govern the economy (Cheng 1993). Prior to the financial deregulation of the late 1980s, virtually all the banks and major financial institutions in Taiwan were government owned, and only a few private financial institutions—whose owners usually had close political allegiance with the government—were allowed to set up. It was only when the New Banking Law was passed in 1990 that private banking was no longer prohibited and genuine private bankers began to emerge.

One of the key features to emerge from a financial system so tightly controlled for so long is a credit system that consistently favours public and big private businesses. Small and medium-sized firms (SMEs), which account for more than 95 per cent of the total number of firms in Taiwan, often experience difficulty accessing the formal domestic credit market. State-owned businesses not only have easier access to bank credit, but also tend to borrow larger amounts than private firms. Researchers have found, moreover, that more than three-quarters of all loans for large amounts have gone to big enterprises, which account for less than 5 per cent of the total number of firms, and the amount of money borrowed by big corporations has been two to five times higher than that by small and medium-sized firms between 1965 and 1982 (Wu 1992: 200). Taiwan's credit system is primarily a two-tiered market where public and big businesses have more ready access to bank credit with lower interest rates, while small and medium-sized firms are forced to seek financial resources in fringe credit markets at substantially higher costs. Among private businesses, moreover, the smaller their scale, the larger the proportion of their loans that come from informal credit markets (Tang 1995). According to Shea, Kuo, and Huang (1995), informal financing accounted for around 50 per cent of the total financing by private enterprises in the 1960s, and the ratio declined to around 40 per cent in the mid-1980s, and to 25 per cent in the early 1990s. Since the financial liberalization, the composition of business-sector financing sources provided by informal financial sectors has decreased continually (Chuang and Hoelscher 2008). The institutional disadvantage of SMEs in the financial market, however, seems either to remain constant or worsen as the market becomes liberalized. For one thing, the importance of SMEs declined rapidly and a number were forced out of the market as a result of fierce competition. The proportion of total sales for which SMEs accounted in Taiwan dropped from 40.2 per cent in 1986 to 29.5 per cent in 2002. In the meantime, the proportion of money that SMEs borrowed from banks dropped from 41.1 per cent in 1991 to 20.6 per cent in 2002 and 19.8 per cent in 2009 (SMEA 2010).

According to estimates from Taiwan's central bank, private corporate borrowing over the past two decades has broken down roughly as 60 per cent from external finance, and about 40 per cent from internal finance. Among the external finance, about 70 per cent was made up of corporate loans from financial institutions in 2003, declining to about 66 per cent in 2009. As the major part of the external funds of private corporate funds in Taiwan are from financial institutions, it is suggested that Taiwan's financial structure is much like a bank-based financial system, combining allocation based on relationships with long-term availability of credit. Scholars generally agree that the system is moving slowly from a regulated credit-rationing system to a market-oriented system gradually linked to global markets (Patrick and Park 1994; Shen and Wang 2005; Brookfield 2010).

As can be expected, the role of the stock market as a source of finance has become more important. In the mid-1980s, equity shares accounted for only 9.2 per cent of external finance for private businesses in Taiwan, a proportion that increased to 14 per cent by 1993 and has maintained a constant level of about 20 per cent during the past decade. Such an increase can be attributed mainly to the lifting of heavy financial regulations, as the criteria for being listed on the stock market have been relaxed by the government during the process of financial liberalization. In the early 1980s, the number of companies listed on the Taiwan Stock Exchange was less than 100, while by 2010 it was more than 784, with US$848,490 million as its total domestic market capitalization, ranking it twentieth in the world.

The financial system in Taiwan is in many ways pretty well developed nowadays, and yet Taiwan has the most fragmented banking market in East Asia and the market share accounted for by large Taiwanese banks is not great. Until 2007, none of the nation's fourteen financial holding companies had a market share above 10 per cent, and the total assets of the top ten companies accounted for only 55 per cent of the whole banking industry, while those of the top three accounted for only 24 per cent, a much lower ratio than those of neighbouring East Asian countries. Moreover, about half of the total assets in Taiwan's banking system are still controlled by the government.

## OWNERSHIP AND GOVERNANCE

The prevalence of family businesses in Taiwan has been consistently documented by scholars of different academic disciplines, and the prominence of family firms in the market has marked Taiwan as a typical case of 'family capitalism' (Hamilton 1997). It was found that 87 of 97 business groups in 1983 were owned by members of particular families (Hamilton 1997: 148). Family dominance of business did not seem to wane even after the market boom in the age of globalization. Among major listed companies in the Taiwan Exchange Market, between 76 and 85 per cent were consistently found to be family owned (Yeh, Lee, and Woidtke 2001; Lee, Z. 2010). Current data show that, in the year 2006, of the top 100 business groups in Taiwan, 62 were identifiably family owned or controlled, and the total revenue of these 62 groups constituted 89.1 per cent of Taiwan's GNP (China Credit Information Service 2008).

The emphasis on family ownership represents the high value placed on the growth of family wealth, rather than the firm, as a public corporation, and such a practice has engendered consequences that define the typical features of the corporate governance practices of Taiwanese firms. For one thing, ownership-based vertical integration is low, as most firms are rarely self-sufficient, and horizontal integration and diversification are usually high. Moreover, a common pattern of expansion is to establish a dominant or mostly 'quasi-monopolistic' presence in sectors supplying export-oriented firms, following the establishment of unrelated businesses run by the patriarch's sons and other male relatives. The diversification is informal, personal, and linked by common ownership and family management (Hamilton 1997; Whitley 1999).

As most firms in Taiwan are family controlled, major companies are managed and governed in ways that contrast sharply with those of other industrialized economies. Until the late 1990s, there was still an absence of effective audit committees in publicly listed companies in Taiwan and very low levels of institutional ownership (Yeh, Lee, and Woidtke 2001). In the early 1990s, ownership by financial institutions was only 4–5 per cent, and takeovers via financial markets were not yet widely seen. As a market for corporate control had yet to be fully developed, a push for revolution and reform from the market side at this point was unlikely. This was a typical family-dominated market, in strong contrast to its Japanese counterpart which had historically been controlled by major financial institutions, in which the market for corporate control has started to pick up momentum in recent years (Witt 2014).

In a market where firms are mainly controlled by families, it is probably not surprising to see that management structure in Taiwan is also a typical case of family capitalism. It is estimated that the management structure in 80 per cent of Taiwanese listed firms is family controlled (Claessens and Fan 2002; see also Lee Z. 2009). Survey evidence also indicates that in Taiwanese-listed companies 65 per cent of directors are still selected by family members (Solomon et al. 2003). Although earlier studies indicate that family dominance is typical only among SMEs, a study by Yeh, Lee, and Woidtke (2001) has revealed a very different updated picture. According to their adjusted calculations on critical levels of control (i.e. the minimum percentage of shareholding in order to control a firm effectively) in Taiwan, families usually only need a shareholding of 15 per cent to control a firm effectively, and among the major 208 listed companies in the mid-1990s, 76 per cent of firms exceeded that critical level. This indicates that more than three-quarters of the major listed companies in Taiwan are under de facto family control. Their study also finds that the critical level of control is inversely related to firm size, consistent with the view that families can easily gain control over large companies where shareholders are generally widely dispersed.

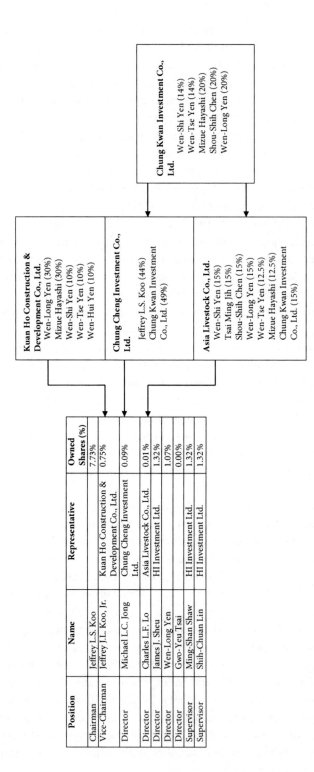

| Position | Name | Representative | Owned Shares (%) |
|---|---|---|---|
| Chairman | Jeffrey L.S. Koo | | 7.73% |
| Vice-Chairman | Jeffrey J.L. Koo, Jr. | Kuan Ho Construction & Development Co., Ltd. | 0.75% |
| Director | Michael L.C. Jong | Chung Cheng Investment Ltd. | 0.09% |
| Director | Charles L.F. Lo | Asia Livestock Co., Ltd. | 0.01% |
| Director | James J. Sheu | HI Investment Ltd. | 1.32% |
| Director | Wen-Long Yen | | 1.07% |
| Director | Gwo-Yeu Tsai | | 0.00% |
| Supervisor | Ming-Shan Shaw | HI Investment Ltd. | 1.32% |
| Supervisor | Shih-Chuan Lin | HI Investment Ltd. | 1.32% |

**Kuan Ho Construction & Development Co., Ltd.**
Wen-Long Yen (30%)
Mizue Hayashi (30%)
Wen-Shi Yen (10%)
Wen-Tse Yen (10%)
Wen-Hui Yen (10%)

**Chung Cheng Investment Co., Ltd.**
Jeffrey L.S. Koo (44%)
Chung Kwan Investment Co., Ltd. (49%)

**Asia Livestock Co., Ltd.**
Wen-Shi Yen (15%)
Tsai Ming Jih (15%)
Shou-Shih Chen (15%)
Wen-Long Yen (15%)
Wen-Tse Yen (12.5%)
Mizue Hayashi (12.5%)
Chung Kwan Investment Co., Ltd. (15%)

**Chung Kwan Investment Co., Ltd.**
Wen-Shi Yen (14%)
Wen-Tse Yen (14%)
Mizue Hayashi (20%)
Shou-Shih Chen (20%)
Wen-Long Yen (20%)

FIGURE 12.1 The shareholdings and the relationships between the board of directors of Chinatrust Financial Holding Co., Ltd.

*Note:* Jeffrey J. L. Koo, Jr is the eldest son of Jeffrey L. S. Koo. Mizue Hayashi is Jeffrey L. S. Koo's wife. Jeffrey L. S. Koo is the cousin of Wen-Shi Yen, Wen-Tse Yen, Wen-Long Yen, and Wen-Hui Yen. Shou-Shih Chen is the brother-in-law of Jeffrey L. S. Koo.

*Source:* 2004 Annual Report of Chinatrust Financial Holding Co., Ltd.

Such an institutional phenomenon creates a gap which shrewd business owners can manipulate to their own advantage. Current studies have revealed that family firms in Taiwan tend to exercise control through a pyramid structure or a cross-holding pattern; more often than not, investment companies or legal entities are mobilized by controlling families in order to secure control in the focal firm. Externally-associated investment companies are strategically arranged by family members to acquire shares within the focal firm, even though their personal share within the firm may appear to be low (Yeh, Lee, and Woidtke 2001; Lee Z. 2010). In some cases, philanthropic organizations such as hospitals, foundations, and universities are also found to be instrumental in such strategic measures adopted by prominent family groups. Pyramidal ownership structures involving, in some instances, organizations within the non-profit sector, where information concerning ownership is not within the public domain and is not well regulated, could thus generate concerned-agency implications too. As major family groups tend to have wider kinship connections and better political resources, they are more likely to exercise complicated pyramid ownership and use chains of networks that involve distant family members and retired government officials (Lee, Z. 2010). As the Securities and Futures Bureau in Taiwan only requires family board members within two degrees of kinship to be disclosed, distant family members sitting on boards of directors, or on external associated investment companies, can be hard to trace by members of the public unfamiliar with the family history of board members. As a result, investigation of corporate ownership through only listed companies and publicly available information can underestimate the true extent of family control.

Figure 12.1 illustrates such patterns of ownership control networks for one major family-controlled financial business group in Taiwan. Typical of most local groups, the China Trust Financial Holding Group is composed of several listed and unlisted companies. In the illustrated graph, the flagship company, the China Trust Company, which is listed on the Taiwan Security Exchange, has disclosed its founder Jeffrey Koo and his elder son Jeffrey Koo Jr. as board members. Michael Jong, a retired government official, was also on the board. While other board members may not have clear family connections to Koo, the externally associated investment companies are all members of the Koo family. From the list of board members we are able to identify the family members mobilized to secure the seats of control: they include the founder's wife, Mizue Hayashi, as well as his distant cousins, the Yen family. All members from the Yen family are within four degrees of kinship from the founder, Jeffrey Koo. None of these associated investment companies were listed on the exchange market, nor was their ownership information immediately available to the public.

# INTERNAL STRUCTURE

By definition, the salient feature of the family firm is its business ownership structure, which is effectively controlled and passed on to family members. In such a setting, a patriarchic head and his core family members usually make all the important decisions.

There is also a low degree of delegation of authority, as ethnic Chinese businessmen are reluctant to share information with subordinates. Essentially, Chinese business-owners tend to keep power within the hands of specific close relatives whom they trust. The low degree of delegation is also evident from a recent empirical survey. As suggested in the chapter by Witt (2014), executives from northern European countries tend to delegate within firms, in stark contrast to their Asian counterparts. When asked, in a survey for the World Competitiveness Report (Schwab 2010), the extent of delegation within firms in their specific national contexts, executives from northern European countries report an average score of 5.31 out of 7 (with 7 being highest). Taiwan reported an average score of 3.90, ranking 46th among 139 countries, higher than China (3.6), but lower than Japan (4.8), Singapore (4.5), and Hong Kong (4.1).

Organization scholars have found that firms in Taiwanese business groups also tend to share a distinctive management structure known as an 'inner circle' (Hamilton 1997). Within firms there is usually a person who formally occupies the position of manager, whereas the owner assumes the positions of both director of the board and general manager. Here management tends to be formal and localized, whereas control and ownership tends to be informal and span the entire group of family-owned firms. This duplication of hierarchies and managerial separation in firms leads to the multiplication of several specific positions that key people in a group collectively hold. The overlapping hierarchies around the core group of people in these business groups form an 'inner circle' whom the owners trust and in whom they have confidence. The members of the inner circle may be direct family members, distant relatives, or trusted partners with whom the family has a long-established relationship. This has led Taiwanese businesses to create horizontal linkages for inter-family networks or '*guanxi* ownership' (Hamilton 1997: 270).

By means of comparison to Korean *chaebol* and Japanese *keiretsu*, the inner-circle system of Taiwanese *jituanqiye* (business group) characteristics has been revealed. According to Chung's (2003) study on the inner circle of Taiwanese business groups, group leaders occupied overlapping positions at director level more than twice as often as at manager level. Moreover, inner-circle management has hinged on the social ties among the members, rather than on the group president, as in the case of the Korean *chaebol*, or the norms of corporate community as in Japanese *keiretsu*. A less formal relationship among members in the inner circle shows that key offices in Taiwanese businesses provide more linkages, but less hierarchy. As a result, the dynamics in decision-making and management practices are affected by the composition of the core leaders and the social relationships among them (Chung 2003). Empirical evidence, however, shows that the percentage of family members' representation in Taiwanese business groups has decreased over time. Family members accounted for 60 per cent of the inner circle in 1973 and 1986, and about 53 per cent in 1994 and 1998 (Chung and Mahmood 2010). The percentage of business partners and long-term employees has, by contrast, been increasing respectively from 29 per cent and 9 per cent in 1973, to 13 per cent and 37 per cent in 1994. Along with this transition in the late 1980s, business groups introduced more outsiders into their inner circles (Chung 2003: 58). A recent study has also found signs of change within the organizational structure, especially when the inheriting second-generation leaders are involved. Chung and Luo (2008) found that second-generation key leaders of Taiwanese business groups are in general less likely to keep family members in the inner circle after market transition, and, moreover, key leaders with a US management education are also less likely to use family members than those locally educated. Such changes imply that market-oriented transition and institutional change have enabled proactive leaders to break up the structural constraints inherent in traditional cultural practices.

## EMPLOYMENT RELATIONS

In Taiwan, small and medium-sized enterprises are the quintessential norm in business. Most Taiwanese firms are family-owned or otherwise influenced by the strong cultural norm of Chinese familism, and this has several implications for the employment system. For one thing, as Whitley (1999) has pointed out, both the general cultural preferences of personal business ownership over employment, and the unwillingness of employers to trust non-family subordinates, limit the scope and length of employer–employee commitments in the Chinese family business (Whitley 1999: 151). Earlier studies have more often than not documented long-term commitments as tending to be reserved for workers with strong personal ties to the owner, and many skilled workers without personal ties to the owner prefer to leave and start their own business once they acquire the capital and skills to do so (Greenhalgh 1988; Redding and Hsiao 1990; Shieh 1992; Hamilton 1997). Moreover, many SMEs are short-lived ventures and workers are usually paid less in SMEs than in large companies. Although this may explain the high self-employment rate within the labour market and also the robust spirit of entrepreneurship, it also implies a high turnover rate within the firm and the unlikelihood of cultivating the technology and professionalism needed to help grow the corporation. According to the statistics from the *Report on the Manpower Utilization Survey* conducted by the government, average employment tenure in the early 2000s was 7.7 years, and 8.8 years in 2011 (Directorate General of Budget, Accounting and Statistics 2011b).

Earlier studies on Chinese family businesses have noted the importance of personal relationships and the existence of patriarchic authority in Chinese family businesses (Redding and Hsiao 1990). As patriarchal leaders, bosses who enjoy the greatest amount of power in the company usually give flexible employment tenures, and their employees regard their companies as families. Along with the formal tool of contractual relationships, such a pseudo-family culture helps enhance the solidarity of employees and the stability of enterprises (Redding and Hsiao 1990).

Labour unions are another aspect of employment relations strongly influenced by political context and traditional culture. Trades unions in Taiwan are regulated by the Labour Union Law, first enacted by the KMT in mainland China in 1929 and last

amended in 1975. A union can be organized along two principles: either craft/occupa-
tion, or on industrial lines when there is a minimum of thirty workers in a firm. Only
one union is permitted per plant, and membership is mandatory. Here the industrial
unions are organized at the enterprise level and can be regarded as company or corporate unions, and craft/occupation unions are city-wide or county-wide. Craft or occupational unions usually have a higher membership than industrial unions. Usually, an
industrial or company union is for big corporations and the unionization rate is lower.
Most employees in SMEs go with a craft or occupational union, but mainly for insurance
purposes, because the Taiwanese government requires citizens to register as a member
of a union to obtain labour insurance.

For the majority of labourers who do not have stable employment in a big company,
a craft union is the only option. As a result, craft unions are not militant and rarely take
industrial action. Nonetheless, their membership is large, accounting for about 83.6 per
cent of all unionized workers; industrial unions only accounted for 16.3 per cent in 2009.
The unionization rate for industrial unions decreased from 30.7 per cent in 1987 to 20.9
per cent in 2000 and 15.4 per cent in 2009, whereas for craft unions the rate increased
from 36.3 per cent in 1987 to a peak of 61.2 per cent in 1993, before dropping to 49.2
per cent in 2000 and 52.5 per cent in 2009 (Council of Labour Affairs 2010). Until the
late 1980s, labour–management relations were relatively peaceful, and workers were not
militant, due to the dominant culture of Confucianism, which emphasizes deference to
authority and social harmony, an attitude nurtured by the KMT (Whitley 1999; Chen,
Ko, and Lawler 2003; see also Lee Y. 2011).

Historically, the KMT has exercised a strong hand in controlling unions in Taiwan.
This policy included actively developing its own political organizations (social work
committees) at the plant level to absorb and co-opt union members, while enforcing the
Labour Union Law to regulate workers' activities, such as strikes. Both measures paved
the way for state-controlled and employer-sponsored unions, as well as relatively peaceful labour–management relations. The situation changed, however, amid broader political change since the late 1980s, and the number of labour disputes, strikes, and general
union activism has been on the rise since the mid-1980s (Chen, Ko, and Lawler 2003).
The relatively non-militant nature of labour activism in Taiwan can also be attributed
to the inherent organizational structure of indigenous businesses. As most businesses
in Taiwan are family-owned SMEs, non-family members are passively alienated and
excluded from advancement opportunities, which results in high turnover rates within
the firm and makes it harder for unions to organize and take root.

Compared to their counterparts in state-owned enterprises, unions in the private
sector have tended to be less militant. Especially in the past decade, large-scale lay-offs
due to the relocation of local manufacturing companies to China and relatively higher
unemployment rates since the Asian financial crisis may have resulted in the formation of less militant labour movements (Chen, Ko, and Lawler 2003). Furthermore, the
1984 Labour Standards Act (LSA) has often served as a substitute for trade unions in
collective bargaining and has become a form of protection for workers in much of the
private sector. This may negate the necessity for militant union activities. According to

the Global Competitiveness Report (Schwab 2010), Taiwan scores 4.5 for ease of hiring and firing, on a scale from 1 to 7 (where 1 = impeded by regulations, 7 = flexibly determined by employers), higher than China and the UK, and it ranks twenty-sixth among 139 countries.

In Taiwan, the government generally does not directly intervene in private-sector wage bargaining, but only provides a legal framework of negotiation by stipulating a minimum wage for labour. Moreover, as SOEs in Taiwan constitute the backbone of the union movement, there has been a political element to any government involvement in the wage-bargaining process; and yet the involvement is by nature indirect (Lee, Y. 2009). The SOE wage policy is determined by the Ministry of Economic Affairs (MOEA), though it is frequently influenced by partisan forces on the budget and economic committees of the Legislative Yuan. Unions are able to play a role, mobilizing legislators and putting pressure on MOEA officials for wage settlements. On the other hand, unions in non-SOEs, having fewer resources and less political leverage, rely only on piecemeal and informal wage negotiations. For this reason, unions in Taiwan are less radical and militant in wage negotiations than, for example, those in Korea, and as a result, Taiwanese wage increases have been less dramatic than those in Korea (Lee, Y. 2009: 59; 2011).

## EDUCATION AND SKILLS FORMATION

There has generally been considered to be a high level of correlation between education planning in Taiwan and the nation's extraordinary economic growth in the post-war era, a successful experience similar to those enjoyed by Taiwan's East Asian neighbours, Japan and Korea (Woo 1991; Lin 2003; Greene 2008). Taiwan's education system comprises three levels: primary, secondary, and higher. The primary level is for young children. The secondary level comprises three years of junior high school and three years of senior high school/senior vocational school. After that, there is a unified university entrance exam for four years of university, or a two- or three-year junior college entrance exam.

The development of higher education in Taiwan was planned in accordance with the manpower resources available for economic development. In terms of age participation rate, Taiwan's higher education system is comparable to those of the United States and Japan. Net enrolment of students aged 18–21 for tertiary education in 1996 was 35.4 per cent in Taiwan, 45.2 per cent in Japan, 40.7 per cent in Korea, and 34.6 per cent in the United States (Wang 2003). After the political democratization of the 1990s, there was a rapid expansion in the university and college sectors as a result of deregulation of higher education. Between 1986 and 2000, the number of universities and colleges rose from 28 to 127, while the number of junior colleges declined from 77 to 23. By 2004, gross enrolment for students aged 18–21 was 78.11 per cent, reaching 83.77 per cent in 2010 (Ministry of Education 2011).

Such expansion in higher education has nevertheless resulted in the inflation of educational qualifications (Wang 2003). For decades, large numbers of Taiwanese graduates have gone to the United States for advanced study. The annual number of students returning to Taiwan with a master's degree or doctorate rose from 2,863 in 1990 to 3,264 in 1991, then to 5,157 in 1992, and 6,172 in 1993 (EID 1994). An indicator evidencing the inflation of educational qualifications is the higher unemployment rate among university or college graduates. In 2011, the unemployment rates for people educated to junior high and high school levels stood at 3.54 per cent and 4.67 per cent respectively, whereas for those educated to university level it was 5.31 per cent (Directorate General of Budget, Accounting, and Statistics 2011a). The performance of the Taiwanese education system has been relatively satisfactory, especially in science and technology, which in the later stages of Taiwan's economic development turned out to be crucial in accommodating the booming demand of high-tech industry. In the 2009 PISA study of students' abilities, Taiwan ranked fifth in mathematics and twelfth in science (OECD 2010). In the 2007 Trends in Mathematics and Science Study, Taiwan ranked second only behind Singapore among thirty-six countries (Martin, Mullis, and Foy 2008).

Skills formation in Taiwan, however, relies more on the general support of the educational system than on internal training by firms. Compared to neighbouring countries such as Japan, skills acquisition in Taiwan is usually not as systematic and efficient. Vocational schooling used to be important, but has declined over the past two decades as a result of the education reforms that led to the expansion of university education. On-the-job training and private initiatives are in general weak, except in high-tech industries, especially those located in industrial parks.

## INTER-COMPANY RELATIONS

Taiwan's industrial structure has been noted by many scholars to be based on prominent production networks nested in the large number of SMEs. In particular, Taiwanese business networks are highly segmented and show little evidence of vertical integration, unlike the large Japanese and Korean conglomerates (Hamilton and Feenstra 1995; Wang 2010). One important reflection of such a structure is the prominence of business groups within the Taiwanese economy. The history of Taiwan's economic development tells a story of the growth of the family business group. The majority of these groups had already begun to take form in the 1950s, reaping the benefits of the protectionist government policies of that era. In these early years, business groups were known to ordinary people as *guanxi* enterprises, yet their legal position remained ambiguous. It was only in 1997 that the Affiliated Enterprises Chapter of Taiwan's Company Law was promulgated and that the position of such business groups was clarified from a legal perspective, and financial disclosure became obligatory, allowing the public a deeper glance into the reality of business groups.

To the present day, the large business groups that branched out into different industries have continued to expand, becoming the backbone of Taiwan's economy. The
reality, of a market captured by large groups, strikes a stark contrast with traditional
stereotypes of an earlier Taiwanese economic development model led by SMEs. In the
1970s and 1980s, the total operating income of Taiwan's 100 largest groups comprised
only 30 per cent of GNP, but by the 1990s it had already reached 70 per cent, and by 2007
it comprised 137 per cent of GNP. During the same period, government revenue made
up just 17.4 per cent of GNP (Chu and Hong 2002; China Credit Information Service
2008; Lee Z. 2010). The number of member firms in the top 100 business groups also
increased steadily from 1973 to 1998 and jumped between 2002 and 2006. The standard
deviation of the number of member firms ranged between four and eight between 1973
and 1998, but was respectively forty-two and sixty-one in 2002 and 2006. The centralization of the Taiwanese economy by large business groups during the 1990s and 2000s
can also be seen from the fact that only about 5 per cent of the active labour force was
employed by large business groups before 1994, while the proportion grew to 7.9 per cent
in 1998, 9.5 per cent in 2002, and 24 per cent in 2006 (Chung and Mahmood 2010: 189).

For Taiwan's largest business groups, *guanxi* networks were a crucial source of investment capital and also served as a means to organize production, and a tie between firms
conducting business. In a sample of Taiwan's largest ninety-six business groups in 1983,
Gary Hamilton identified nearly 2,500 co-owners listed for the 743 firms, who were close
family members, friends, co-workers, and distant relatives (Hamilton 1997). Ownership
was predominantly held within the family circle, and analysis indicated that the ownership of firms was concentrated within business groups and not shared across groups,
indicating low-level ties among such business families. The low level of interlocking
between groups, together with the comparative high level *within* groups, revealed that
the ownership of Taiwan's largest firms is clustered within groups of key families and
their *guanxi* networks (Hamilton 1997: 283).

For business groups, kinship ties may not only serve as an intra-group mediating
buffer, but also as a form of external alliance when consolidating ownership and control, which is essential during times of market turbulence. Recent studies have identified
inter-family kinship networks as a salient feature, especially among large and prominent business owners, which are part of a major *kinecon group* integrating prestigious
political and social-elite families (Lee Z. 2010). Statistical analysis also shows that business groups that have experience in oligopolistic positions or in regulated industries
such as finance and banking are more likely to have higher inter-group kinship ties (Lee
Z. 2011). Current empirical findings show that the major component formed by the close
kinship network contained the fourteen most important financial-holding families and
other prominent business groups in Taiwan. The size of this interconnected kinship network component is so large it incorporates seventy-seven major business groups. The
total assets of these seventy-seven groups are twice that of the government of Taiwan,
and the sales generated by them amount to as much as 30 per cent of GNP (Lee Z. 2010).
This study also found that when the business group, structurally bound by inter-group
kinship networks, came up against fierce competition in shareholding wars, business

families with kinship ties were often mobilized as strong allies to secure ownership and leadership. Also, when a business group was branching out into new business territory, assistance in the form of resources drawn from other connected groups was also crucial.

The prominence and mobilization of kinship ties indicates a market heavily conditioned by an institutional legacy of strong ties. Empirical analysis on interlocking directorates of major Taiwanese listed firms from 1962 to 2003 shows that corporate networks in Taiwan have a much higher proportion of multiple ties (more than 30 per cent) than Western markets, even after the market was deregulated and globalized (Lee Z. 2009; see also Brookfield 2010). Such findings seem to suggest that Taiwanese businesses prefer to interact with specific business partners whom they trust deeply. Under the national ideology of 'picking winners', the government's policy is tolerant of the tacit and collusive connections among major big businesses, which has historically engendered an enormous amount of inter-company ties among competitors. An earlier study by Yang (1987) indicated that 40 per cent of director networks were among firms within the same industry. As there is virtually no anti-trust legal tradition in Taiwan, ties among competitors for securing privileged market positions seem to be a natural development. A study on data from the year 2000 revealed 116 ties among competitors, accounting for as much as 25.6 per cent of the total of 454 interlocking directorates among 191 firms; and of sixteen industries included in the analyses, nine had a higher percentage of intra-industry ties than predictable by mere chance (Brookfield 2010: 272).

# SOCIAL CAPITAL

Studies on Taiwan have found frequent mobilization of *guanxi* networks in economic life, in which strong kinship ties and privileged political connections are often found to be instrumental and effective (Numazaki 1986; Hsiao 1992; Chung 2005). Although familism may be considered a different kind of social capital, one which restricts particular trust to a close circle of family members, *guanxi* and *generalized trust* may also be considered as *antipodes*, or differing in function, as a 'bond and bridge', as Putnam's framework of social capital has suggested (Putnam 2000). The question is how they may complement each other and coexist for so long in a vibrant economy buttressed by a large number of family-owned SMEs.

Studies on the impact of family and primordial social relationships on corporate performance may represent other opportunities to investigate the effect of 'bonding' social capital. With a longitudinal analysis of business groups across two decades, Luo and Chung (2005) found that institutional transition increased the contribution of family and prior social ties to group performance. They propose that family relationships in the inner circle provided informal norms such as unconditional trust, and further contributed to the identification of opportunities for exchanges based on credible information resources. Yet the impact may not be described by a clear linear relation, as crowded family relationships may slow down the restructuring process. The more family members occupying the inner circle, the less likely the group may be to engage in strategic restructuring, which may result in poorer organizational performance (Luo and Chung 2005).

One study has found that, with rapid social change, the trust placed by the public in Taiwanese public institutions has undergone a steady decline between 1990 and 2003, whereas trust in people persists (Chang and Tam 2005). Participation in voluntary associations has continued to decline as well (Hsung, Chang, and Lin 2010). A recent study found that the East Asian cluster (i.e. Hong Kong, China, Taiwan, Korea, and Japan) gravitate together with similar strong tendencies towards familism and equally low scores in various aggregated measures concerning political trust and institutional confidence (Lee and Hsiao 2011). A distinct pattern confirms a long-standing empirical observation of the persistent influence of this cultural norm across the region. The Civicus Civil Society Survey (Civicus 2006) identified a fair level of trust in Taiwanese society, with a score of 2.0 (out of 3, with higher scores indicating greater trust). The World Value Survey (2010) showed that 78.8 per cent of Taiwanese could not trust people they met for the first time, revealing a lower tendency of generalized trust as compared to Western countries such as Germany (73.9%), Sweden (30.5%), Canada (49.1%), and the United States (59.5%), but a little bit higher than in its neighbouring cousin, China (88.8%).

In the 2010 Corruption Perception Index (Transparency International 2011), Taiwan scored a fair 5.8, ranking thirty-third out of 178 nations (with the UK 7.6, USA 7.1, and South Korea 5.4). A recent survey conducted by the World Bank painted a similar picture in that Taiwan's governance indicators in 2009 (for voice and accountability, government effectiveness, regulatory quality, rule of law, and control of corruption) all fall between the 50th and 75th percentile and 75th and 90th percentile among 213 economies in the world (World Bank 2011).

## INSTITUTIONAL CHANGE

Taiwan has gone through decades of rapid economic growth as well as drastic institutional changes. As the shaping of the business system in Taiwan bears the salient mark of strong institutional authority and the resilient societal forces of familism and *guanxi* networks, the dynamic development of the Taiwanese business system has become an ideal setting in which to study how pristine institutional and social structures may change in the face of ever more globalized and market-oriented competition (Lee Z. 2009). A pertinent question regarding the current system is to what extent such forces still demonstrate impacts upon an ever-changing and maturing market.

One highly prominent feature of the market is the dwindling influence of the state. The economic liberation was accelerated by the lifting of martial law in the late 1980s and a period of great transition followed. After more than two decades of transformation, the state has only the marginal forces of state-owned enterprises, and limited policy leverage in controlling or directing the private sector. Not only has the state's immediate involvement in the market declined, but also its once strong and coherent bureaucratic capacity has weakened. Within the overall network structure, the embeddedness between state and private sector has rapidly disintegrated since the early 1990s and the central position that the public sector used to occupy appears to be ever more marginalized (Lee Z. 2009).

As the resources controlled by the state decrease, the *guanxi* economy may become less vigorous. As business groups have accumulated resources over time and institutions have developed, the significance of *guanxi* and political ties has gradually decreased in the strategic planning and growth paths of the business groups (Chung 2005). And yet the role played by the societal forces of familism or *guanxi* may not be as clear cut, and its evolutionary direction may still be ambivalent. For one thing, the majority of the private sector in Taiwan is still under family control. The percentage of major listed firms that are family-controlled remains as high as 80 per cent (Lee Z. 2009). Moreover, as mentioned earlier, the liberalization of deregulated industry after the 1990s has engendered the consolidation and not the disintegration of family groups, especially in the financial sector. Even in high-tech and electronics groups, where destructive innovation may be most likely, as many as 74 per cent of the groups still have family members visible in the governing structure (Lee Z. 2011).

Another important dimension from which to examine the inherent continuity of the Taiwanese business system is the growth and operation of Taiwanese transnational business. Taiwanese transnational business (*taishang*) emerged in the mid-1980s, especially in the areas of South East Asia and southern China. Because of the increasing cost of domestic labour and land in Taiwan, *taishang* resorted to overseas investment as a strategy to decrease cost pressure from global buyers, and such investments often turned out to help Taiwanese enterprises step towards globalizing their business (Saxenian 2006). Studies have found that *taishang* presented a form of transnational capital with Chinese cultural traits, as well as heavily relying on the tactic of cultivation of institutional assistance (Hsing 1998; Wang and Lee 2007; Chen, Jou, and Hsiao 2008; Hsiao, Kung, and Wang 2010). The mobilization of ethnic Chinese all over Asia assisted *taishang* in supporting cross-regional production networks and consolidating competition. Most *taishang* recruited ethnic Chinese as employees from other countries, such as China, Malaysia, or Singapore. Local ethnic Chinese with connections to Taiwan were easy to hire and local ethnic Chinese have been indispensable, often occupying better positions in companies than other local workers (Hsiao, Kung, and Wang 2010). Authors of *taishang* studies frequently observe that *taishang* business structures and networks cannot be easily displaced in the global production market (Chen, Jou, and Hsiao 2008). This seems to suggest that although the changing route of the Taiwanese business system may converge with patterns in the major industrialized economies, the Taiwanese market may still hold a strong local flavour of its own.

# CONCLUSION

The dominant institutional influences on the Taiwanese business system are a combination of features from the traditional cultural norm of familism and strong political forces in the post-war period. Such characteristics reflect the process of industrialization and institutional influences, which were highly associated with the political and social organizations of the time (Whitley 1999). The big capitalists and small and medium businessmen alike could be considered products of the state's leadership in executing the consequent industrialization strategies (Hsiao 1995). Moreover, the business system in Taiwan has also been greatly influenced by the cultural practice of Chinese familism since the initial years of its emergence until the consolidation of family-controlled business empires today. Although the power of the state over the market has declined significantly in the past two decades, with its direct ownership in the market having decreased and its capacity to direct policies having waned, the legacy of the strong state still seems to hang over the market it helped create. The labour unions weakened under long repressive years of KMT rule, the persistent mobilization of *guanxi* networks, the generally low level of social capital, and the increasing weaving of kinship ties among the family groups, bear the historical mark and lasting consequences of a resilient traditional legacy.

## References

Amsden, A. H. (1979). 'Taiwan's Economic History'. *Modern China* 5: 341–380.

—— (1985). 'The State and Taiwan's Economic Development'. In P. B. Evans, T. Skocpol, and D. Rueschemeyer, Eds., *Bringing the State Back In*: 78–106. Cambridge, Cambridge University Press.

—— and W. W. Chu (2003). *Beyond Late Development: Taiwan's Upgrading Policies*. Cambridge, MIT Press.

Brookfield, J. (2010). 'The Network Structure of Big Business in Taiwan'. *Asia Pacific Journal of Management* 27: 257–279.

Chang, L. Y. and T. Tam (2005). 'Discovering the Trends and Structures of Institutional Trust: The Pooled Ordinal Ratings Approach'. *Taiwanese Sociology* 35: 75–126 (in Chinese).

Chen, D. S., S. C. Jou, and H. H. M. Hsiao (2008). 'Transforming Guanxi Networks: Taiwanese Enterprises' Production Networks in Thailand and Vietnam'. In R. S. K. Wong, Ed., *Chinese Enterpreneurship in a Global Era*: 149–165. London and New York, Routledge.

Chen, S. M., C. C. Lin, C. Y. Chu, J. J. Shih, and J. T. Liu (1991). *Disintegrating KMT-State Capitalism*. Taipei, Taipei Society (in Chinese).

Chen, S. J., J. J. R. Ko, and J. Lawler (2003). 'Changing Patterns of Industrial Relations in Taiwan.' *Industrial Relation* 42(3): 315–340.

Cheng, T. J. (1993). 'Guarding the Commanding Heights: The State as Banker in Taiwan'. In S. Haggard, Ed., *The Politics of Finance in Developing Countries*: 55–92. Ithaca, Cornell University Press.

China Credit Information Service (2008). *2008 Business Groups in Taiwan*. Taipei, China Credit Information Service (in Chinese).

Chu, W. W. and C. Y. Hong (2002). 'Business Groups in Taiwan's Post-Liberalization Economy'. *Taiwan: A Radical Quarterly in Social Studies* 47: 33–79 (in Chinese).

Chuang, D. H. and J. Hoelscher (2008). 'The Changing Financial System in Taiwan'. In R. W. McGee, Ed., *Accounting Reform in Transition and Developing Economies*: 215–233. New York, Springer.

Chung, C. N. (2003). 'Managerial Structure of Business Groups in Taiwan: The Inner Circle System and its Social Organization'. *Developing Economies* 41(1): 37–64.

—— (2005). 'Beyond Guanxi: Network Contingencies in Taiwanese Business Groups'. *Organization Studies* 27(4): 461–489.

—— and X. W. Luo (2008). 'Human Agents, Contexts, and Institutional Change: The Decline of Family in the Leadership of Business Groups'. *Organization Science* 19(1): 124–142.

—— and I. P. Mahmood (2010). 'Business Groups in Taiwan'. In A. M. Colpan, T. Hikino, and J. R. Lincoln, Eds., *The Oxford Handbook of Business Groups*: 180–209. New York, Oxford University Press.

Civicus (2006*). Civil Society Survey*. Retrieved 4 October 2012 from <https://civicus.org/csi/>.

Claessens, S. and J. P. H. Fan (2002). 'Corporate Governance in Asia: A Survey'. *International Review of Finance* 3: 71–103.

Council of Labour Affairs (2010). *Yearbook of Labour Statistics 2010*. Taipei, Council of Labour Affairs, Executive Yuan.

Directorate General of Budget, Accounting and Statistics (2011a). *Key Economic and Social Indicators*. Republic of China, Executive Yuan. Retrieved 4 October 2012 from <http://eng.stat.gov.tw/lp.asp?CtNode=2191&CtUnit=1050&BaseDSD=7&mp=5>.

—— (2011b). *Report on the Manpower Utilization Survey*. Taipei, Executive Yuan, Republic of China. Retrieved 4 October 2012 from <http://www.dgbas.gov.tw/ct.asp?xItem=18844&ctNode=4943&mp=1>.

EID (1994). *Education Information Digest* 193: 36–39 (in Chinese).

Evans, P. B. (1995). *Embedded Autonomy*. Princeton, Princeton University Press.

Executive Yuan (2010). *Performance Report of State-Owned Enterprises 2009*. Executive Yuan, Republic of China (in Chinese). Retrieved 4 October 2012 from <http://www.rdec.gov.tw/public/Data/01111522171.pdf>.

Fields, K. J. (1995). *Enterprise and the State in Korea and Taiwan*. Ithaca, Cornell University Press.

Gold, T. B. (1988). 'Entrepreneurs, Multinationals, and the State'. In E. A. Winckler and S. Greenhalgh, *Contending Approaches to the Political Economy of Taiwan*: 175–205. Armonk, M. E. Sharpe.

Greene, J. M. (2008). *The Origins of the Developmental State in Taiwan: Science Policy and the Quest for Modernization*. Cambridge, MA and London, Harvard University Press.

Greenhalgh, S. (1988). 'Families and Networks in Taiwan's Economic Development'. In E. A. Winckler and S. Greenhalgh, Eds., *Contending Approaches to the Political Economy of Taiwan*. Armonk, M. E. Sharpe.

Hamilton, G. G. (1997). 'Organization and Market Processes in Taiwan's Capitalist Economy'. In M. Orru, N. W. Biggart, and G. G. Hamilton, Eds., *The Economic Organization of East Asian Capitalism*: 237–295. Thousands Oaks, Sage.

—— and N. W. Biggart (1988). 'Market, Culture, and Authority: A Comparative Analysis of Management and Organization in the Far East'. *American Journal of Sociology* 94: S52–S94.

—— and R. Feenstra (1995). 'Varieties of Hierarchies and Markets'. *Industrial and Corporate Change* 4(1): 51–92.

Hsiao, H. H. M. (1992). 'The Entrepreneurial Process of Taiwan's Small-Medium and Big Businessmen'. *Chinese Journal of Sociology* (16): 139–167 (in Chinese).

—— (1995). 'The State and Business Relations in Taiwan'. In R. Fitzgerald, Ed., *The State and Economic Development: Lessons from the Far East*: 76–97. London, Frank Cass.

—— I. C. Kung and H. Z. Wang (2010). '*Taishang*: A Different Kind of Ethnic Chinese Business in Southeast Asia'. In Y. W. Chu, Ed., *Emergence and Political Implications*: 156–175. New York, Palgrave Macmillan.

Hsing, Y. T. (1998). *Making Capitalism in China: The Taiwan Connection*. New York and Oxford, Oxford University Press.

Hsieh, M. F. (2011) 'Similar Opportunities, Different Responses'. *International Sociology 26*: 364–391.

Hsung, R. M., F. B. Chang, and Y. F. Lin (2010). 'Changes in Participation in Post-Martial Law Voluntary Associations: Effects and Implications of Period and Cohort'. *Taiwanese Journal of Sociology 44*: 55–105 (in Chinese).

Johnson, C. A. (1982). *MITI and the Japanese Miracle: the Growth of Industrial Policy, 1925–1975*. Stanford, Stanford University Press.

Lee, Y. (2009). 'Divergent Outcomes of Labor Reform Politics in Democratized Korea and Taiwan'. *Studies in Comparative International Development 44*: 47–70.

—— (2011). *Militants or Partisans: Labor Unions and Democratic Politics in Korea and Taiwan*. Stanford, Stanford University Press.

Lee, Z. R. (2009). 'Institutional Transition and Market Networks: An Historical Investigation of Interlocking Directorates of Big Businesses in Taiwan, 1962–2003'. *Taiwanese Sociology 17*: 101–160 (in Chinese).

—— (2010). 'An Exploratory Analysis of Kinship Networks among Business Groups in Taiwan'. In T. Watanabe and T. Asamoto, Eds., *The Taiwan Economy Reader*: 95–130. Tokyo, Keiso Shobo (in Japanese).

—— (2011). 'The Determinants of Kinship Networks in Taiwanese Business Groups'. *Taiwanese Journal of Sociology 46*: 115–166 (in Chinese).

—— and H. H. M. Hsiao (2011). *Familism, Social Capital and Civic Culture*. Paper presented at Annual Meeting of Association of Asian Studies, Honolulu, Hawaii, USA, Association of Asian Studies.

Lin, T. C. (2003). 'Education, Technical Progress, and Economic Growth: The Case of Taiwan'. *Economics of Education Review 22*(2): 213–220.

Luo, X. W. and C. N. Chung (2005). 'Keeping it all in the Family: The Role of Particularistic Relationships in Business Group Performance during Institutional Transition'. *Administrative Science Quarterly 50*: 404–439.

Martin, M. O., I. V. S. Mullis, and P. Foy (2008). *TIMSS 2007 International Science Report*, Chestnut Hill, MA., Boston College, TIMSS and PIRLS International Study Center.

Ministry of Education (2011). *2010 Education Statistical Indicator*. Taipei, Ministry of Education.

Numazaki, I. (1986). 'Networks of Taiwanese Big Business: a Preliminary Analysis'. *Modern China 12*: 487–534.

OECD (2010). '*Pisa 2009 Results: What Students Know and Can Do: Student Performance in Reading, Mathematics and Science*' (Volume I). Paris, OECD.

Patrick, H. and Y. C. Park (1994). *The Financial Development of Japan, Korea and Taiwan*. New York, Oxford University Press.

Putnam, R. D. (2000). *Bowling Alone: The Collapse and Revival of American Community*. New York, Simon & Schuster.

Redding, S. G. and M. Hsiao (1990). 'An Empirical Study of Overseas Chinese Managerial Ideology'. *International Journal of Psychology 25*: 629–641.

Saxenian, A. (2006*). The New Argonauts: Regional Advantage in a Global Economy*. Cambridge, MA., Harvard University Press.

Schwab, K., Ed. (2010). *The Global Competitiveness Report 2010–2011*. Geneva, World Economic Forum.

Shea, J. D., P. S. Kuo, and C. T. Huang (1995). 'The Share of Informal Financing of Private Enterprises'. *Academia Economic Papers 23*: 265–297.

Shen, C. H. and C. A. Wang (2005). 'Does Bank Relationship Matter for a Firm's Investment and Financial Constraints? The Case of Taiwan'. *Pacific-Basin Finance Journal* 13: 163–184.

Shieh, G. S. (1992). *"Boss" Island: The Subcontracting Network and Micro- Entrepreneurship in Taiwan's Development*. New York, Peter Lang.

Simon, D. F. (1988). 'External Incorporation and Internal Reform'. In E. A. Winckler and S. Greenhalgh, Eds., *Contending Approaches to the Political Economy of Taiwan*: 138–150. Armonk, M. E. Sharpe.

SMEA (2010). *White Paper on Small and Medium Enterprises in Taiwan, 2010*. Taipei, Small and Medium Enterprise Administration, Ministry of Economic Affairs.

Solomon, J. F., S. W. Lin, S. D. Norton, and A. Solomon (2003). 'Corporate Governance in Taiwan: Empirical Evidence from Taiwanese Company Directors'. *Corporate Governance* 11(3): 235–248.

Tang, S. Y. (1995). 'Informal Credit Markets and Economic Development in Taiwan'. *World Development* 23(5): 845–855.

Transparency International (2011). Corruption Perception Index 2010. Retrieved 4 October 2012 from <http://www.transparency.org/cpi2010/>.

Wade, R. (1990). *Governing the Market*. Princeton, Princeton University Press.

Wang, J. H. (2010). *The Limits of Fast Followers: Taiwan's Economic Transition and Innovation*. Taipei, Jyu-liu (in Chinese).

—— and C. K. Lee (2007). 'Global Production Networks and Local Institutional Building: The Development of the Information Technology Industry in Suzhou, China'. *Environment and Planning A* 39(8): 1873–1888.

Wang, R. J. (2003). 'From Elitism to Mass Higher Education in Taiwan: The Problems Faced'. *Higher Education* 46(3): 261–287.

Whitley, R. (1999). *Divergent Capitalisms: The Social Structuring and Change of Business Systems*. New York, Oxford University Press.

Witt, M. A. (2014). Japan: Coordinated Capitalism Between Institutional Change and Structural Inertia. In M. A. Witt and G. Redding, Eds., *The Oxford Handbook of Asian Business Systems*: 100–122. Oxford, Oxford University Press.

Wong, J. (2011). *Betting on Biotech: Innovation and the Limits of Asia's Development State*. Ithaca, Cornell University Press.

Woo, J. H. (1991). 'Education and Economic Growth in Taiwan: A Case of Successful Planning'. *World Development* 19(8): 1029–1044.

World Bank (2011). *Worldwide Governance Indicators*. Retrieved 4 October 2012 from <http://data.worldbank.org/data-catalog/worldwide-governance-indicators>.

World Value Survey (2010). *World Value Survey*. Retrieved 4 October 2012 from <http://www.worldvaluessurvey.org/>.

Wu, C. Y. (1992). 'The Politics of Financial Development in Taiwan'. Ph.D. Dissertation. University of Pennsylvania Dept. of Sociology.

Wu, W. H. (2008). 'The Second Financial Reform and the Development of Financial Industry in Taiwan'. *Review of Pacific Basin Financial Markets and Policies* 11(1): 75–97

Wu, Y. S. (2007). 'Taiwan's Developmental State: After the Economic and Political Turmoil'. *Asian Survey* 47(6): 977–1001.

Yang, F. J., K. P. Ku, and A. Yao (2005). 'The Long-Term Performance Evaluation of Listed Privatized Firms in Taiwan'. *Journal of Accounting and Corporate Finance* 2(2): 47–78 (in Chinese).

Yang, Z. J. (1987). 'Strategic Organizational Affiliations and Financial Returns: Comparative Analysis of Patterns of Interlocking Directorates among Big Businesses'. Unpublished Ph.D. dissertation, National Cheng-chi University (in Chinese).

Yeh, Y. H., T. S. Lee, and T. Woidtke (2001). 'Family Control and Corporate Governance: Evidence from Taiwan'. *International Review of Finance* 2: 21–48.

CHAPTER 13

...........................................................................................

# THAILAND

*Post-Developmentalist*
*Capitalism*

...........................................................................................

AKIRA SUEHIRO AND NATENAPHA
WAILERDSAK YABUSHITA

THAILAND is one of the late-industrializing countries that have attempted to catch up with the developed countries by striving to create economic growth and alleviate poverty. In 2011, the World Bank announced that Thailand's income categorization had been upgraded from a lower-middle-income to an upper-middle-income economy (a country with per capita GNI between US$3,976 and 12,276). The upgrade recognized Thailand's economic achievements in the previous two decades, during which per capita GNI (gross national income) had almost doubled, while poverty was significantly reduced. The country has been prudent in sound macroeconomic management with a strong fiscal stance, and has low unemployment and inflation (World Bank 2011). Thailand has a friendly business environment and has been successful in attracting foreign direct investment (FDI) and achieving greater diversification in manufacturing production in terms of both higher value-added production and expansion into new emerging export markets.

To sustain its growth, Thailand needs to focus on raising productivity through technological and organizational change.[1] Higher levels of education and skills, as well as creativity, innovation, and international competitiveness, will be necessary to tackle the so-called 'middle-income trap'.[2] At the same time, Thailand must overcome a variety of new social problems accruing to middle-income countries, which include expanding domestic income/asset gaps, an insufficient social security system for the elderly as well as for farmers and workers in the informal sector, and an inadequate response to rapid changes in the traditional family system (Phongpaichit and Baker 2009; Suehiro 2009).

More importantly, businesses are the driving force for the economy and can help to promote sustainable economic growth and reduce poverty. It is generally acknowledged that as globalization evolves, the private sector and entrepreneurship are emerging as critical factors in development. However, in recent years, the comparative business system approach, mainly inspired by Richard Whitley (1992, 1999), has shown that the internal institutional capacities of groups of firms and entire industries in single countries affect economic outcomes to a large extent. The aim of this chapter is to apply the comparative business system approach to examining how Thailand's business system, the most significant factor contributing to its economic growth, has evolved during the past two decades, in particular after the economic boom started in 1988. We pay attention to the role of contemporary institutions to define the characteristics of economic coordination, control systems, and patterns of private-sector development in Thailand.

# BACKGROUND

Since the 1970s, as a late-industrializing country located in a strategic position in South East Asia, Thailand has maintained an open, market-oriented economy dominated by the private sector, together with government leadership in facilitating trade policies centred around import substitution and export promotion, and industrial policies aiming at the protection and fostering of domestic industries.[3] In particular, since the end of the 1980s, the government has intentionally shifted its economic policies from 'protection' to 'liberalization' in both the financial and industrial (oil-refining, cement, textiles, automobiles, petrochemicals, etc.) sectors, which in turn produced an unprecedented economic boom from 1988 to 1993, in association with massive inflows of foreign capital. However, this economic boom developed into a bubble economy in which stock prices and land prices soared to levels far above economic sustainability, which finally resulted in the 1997 Asian currency/financial crisis (Phongpaichit and Baker 1998; Suehiro 2009).

Owing to the success of diversification in both exportable products and trade partners, the Thai economy recovered from three years of recession and has enjoyed high export performance, with two-digit annual growth rates during the 2000s (except 2009, the year following the 2008 global financial crisis).[4] Thailand has been highly successful in inserting itself into the regional and global supply chains of large multinational companies (MNCs) in the electronic and electrical and automotive sectors, resulting in large inflows of FDI and rising production, employment, and trade.

# ROLE OF THE STATE

Thailand is a mixture of predatory and developmental state. The state has significant predatory or corrupt aspects, to the extent that there are elites using the system for personal enrichment; but there has also been give-and-take, with bribes being paid in exchange for policy measures required for business to prosper. The outcome of economic development in the last four decades suggests that the Thai state has been controlled by a ruling elite, comprising the military, vested-interest groups (mostly ethnic Chinese), and bureaucrats, who seem to plunder without providing their citizens with adequate welfare. Furthermore, the serious shortage of infrastructure since the mid-1980s has created an opportunity for elected politicians to carry out big government-sponsored projects. Economic rents (commissions, permits, licences, etc.) have been repeatedly appropriated by bribery or other corrupt means (Funston 2009; Chachavalpongpun 2010).

When viewed through the lens of the developmental state, or Japanese-inspired industrial policy tools, the Thai government is able and willing to protect its people from the negative consequences of foreign corporate exploitation. Thailand continued to protect its economy during the 1980s and 1990s, despite the large inflows of FDI it had attracted to support its import-substitution and export-oriented industrialization policies. Thai bureaucrats insisted on regulations such as demanding a certain percentage of domestic content in goods manufactured by MNCs in Thailand, and the 51 per cent shareholding rule, under which an MNC starting operations in Thailand must form a joint venture with a Thai company, the idea being that a company with 51 per cent Thai control is better able to keep jobs and profits in the country.

In addition, economic successes accompanying sound macroeconomic management have been sustained by cooperation between the four core agencies in economic policy-making—the National Economic and Social Development Board (NESDB), the Fiscal Policy Office (FPO) of the Ministry of Finance, the Bureau of the Budget (BOB) of the Prime Minister's Office, and the Bank of Thailand (BOT). The NESDB principally screened the bottom-up investment plans of each ministry with reference to the targets of the Five-Year Plans, while the BOB investigated revenue aspects. The FPO proposed possible government expenditure in accordance with the BOT's monetary policy (Muscat 1994; Warr and Nidhiprabha 1996).

In addition to these four core agencies, the Prem Tinsulanonda Government (1980–1988) introduced three new institutions to stabilize the national economy, the National Public Debt Committee, chaired by the finance minister; the Economic Ministers Meetings, which exclusively discussed economic matters; and the Joint Public and Private-Sector Consultative Committees (JPPCC), to discuss economic problems.

The Thaksin Shinawatra Government (2001–2006), however, completely changed this system and transformed policy-making from a bureaucrat-led mechanism into a politician-led or prime-minister-led one (the so-called 'Thaksinocracy'). Thaksin placed importance on the Prime Minister's Office, the Screening Committees chaired by the Deputy Prime Ministers, and the economic-policy committee members in his political party (Thai Rak Thai Party), rather than the traditional four core agencies. He also replaced the Economic Ministers Meetings by the Strategic Committee, consisting of military, police, professionals, and businessmen, and attempted to enhance cooperation between the pubic and the private, not through the existing Joint Public and Private-Sector Consultative Committees (JPPCC), but through direct dialogue with business leaders (Phongpaichit and Baker 2004; Suehiro 2009: Chapter 5). However, his ambitious reforms of bureaucracy were abruptly suspended by a military coup in September 2006. After that, the initiative of policy-making returned to economic technocrats in the four core agencies. This seems to have helped the restoration of sound management of the macro-economy, but hinders the strong leadership of the government in actually solving the problems facing contemporary Thailand.

Despite its economic recovery from the crises of 1997 and 2008, Thailand could find itself trapped in three key areas: the income-gap, corruption, and lower productivity growth, that is, the so-called 'middle-income traps'. First, despite its steady growth, Thailand has faced problems of income inequality. Those living in rural communities experience shortfalls in education, healthcare, and infrastructure. Young workers are needed to work in the city. Rural families now tend to consist of only elderly people and children. Parents cannot transfer knowledge and integrity to the younger generation, conferring vulnerability on families and rural communities (NESDB 2005a), so that inevitably rural populations rely more on government aid and are susceptible to populist politicians.

Second, the corruption trap causes weak government and lack of fairness in doing business. Politicians and bureaucrats receive bribes, which in turn lowers public trust in the government as well as raising the cost of doing business (see also the section 'Social Capital'). In Thailand, democracy and vote-buying are intimately related, examples of the dynamic of social capital and corruption. Decision-making is structurally statist, following the 2006 coup, and implementation is patchy, as seen in Thailand's Corruption Perception Index (CPI) rating, which in 2012 was 37 (from a possible 100), ranking Thailand eighty-eighth of 176 countries around the world, and thirteenth among the 28 countries in the Asia Pacific region; countries scoring similarly to Thailand included Malawi, Morocco, Suriname, Swaziland, and Zambia (Transparency International 2012).

Last, the middle-income trap, with low rates of R&D investment, innovation, and productivity growth, means that the Thai economy has been unable to continue to grow sufficiently.[5] Relatively low rates of economic growth (3–5% per year) during the past decade hardly improved well-being for the majority of people living outside the Bangkok Metropolis Area. In particular, economic growth is highly concentrated in certain types of businesses. While big business has become increasingly profitable, small businesses have not been able to develop or compete fairly, and consumers have had to pay higher prices for monopolistic goods and services, as the enforcement of Thai competition law, since its promulgation in 1999, has been undermined by political intervention. It is clear that big business has an almost complete stranglehold on Thai trade competition, either directly, through its representation on the Trade Competition Commission, or indirectly, by political lobbying and conflicts of interest among cabinet members who are also big-business tycoons (Nikomborirak and Tawankul 2006).

The question that arises is how the Thai economy can step up to the next level, or escape the middle-income trap. Until now, the technology upon which high-tech exports are based has not been home-grown, but imported (Intarakumnerd 2009). The clusters of supporting industries that have emerged are primarily logistical (i.e. reducing transaction costs in production) rather than technological (capitalizing on R&D spillovers between different players in the supply chain). To transform from an economy based on cheap labour to one of highly skilled and technologically sophisticated production (Porter 2003), Thailand requires two major improvements, (1) innovation development, and (2) educational upgrade in the context of its labour market needs.

# FINANCIAL SYSTEM

Commercial banks have been at the apex of Thailand's capitalist business structure since World War II. Banking capitalists, most notably Chinese-Thai families, emerged to lead large financial and industrial conglomerates, which became powerful in the protected environment of the 1960s and 1970s. The Commercial Banking Act of 1962 protected this group by restricting foreign banking and making the establishment of new local banks difficult. Bank licences for foreigners were strictly limited, as was their range of activities, which in effect restricted the share of foreign banks in Thailand's financial assets to 5 per cent. These business leaders also maintained close relations with powerful political figures (Hewison 1989; Suehiro 1989).

Before the Asian financial crisis of 1997, these banking families still controlled the financial sector, including thirteen of the sixteen commercial banks, and ranked amongst the wealthiest groups in the country. Corporate lending was the major activity for commercial banks, and bank loans were the major supply source of domestic investment funds.[6] Because companies did not have to worry about the effect of ownership dilution, which may occur with equity financing and in industries like finance and insurance, banks were at the centre of business groups and used their capital to finance all the firms in the group (Wailerdsak 2008a).

However, the heavy devaluation of the Thai Baht in July 1997 turned into a fully-fledged financial crisis within a few months. The exchange rate and stock-market collapsed, one-third of non-banking financial institutions were closed, and virtually all financial institutions had to be recapitalized. The government took over four struggling banks. By the end of 1998, only five commercial banks remained in majority Thai ownership, and just three of these (Bangkok Bank, Kasikornthai Bank, and Bank of Ayudhaya) were controlled by the previously dominant families (the Sophonpanich, Lamsam, and Rattanarak families, respectively). Each had foreign shareholdings of 40–49 per cent (Suehiro 2006: Chapter 7).

In addition, the fallout from the Asian crisis in the form of non-performing loans (NPLs) and foreclosed assets had made banks more cautious in their lending decisions.[7] In an attempt by the authorities to enhance the stability of the financial system, capital adequacy requirements became more stringent and enforcement more effective. Increasing competition from multinationals and capital markets also squeezed local bank profits. In response to declining lending growth and declining lending profits, leading local banks have been changing their strategies, diversifying their customer base and scope of activities; individuals and small- and medium-sized enterprises are among their fastest-growing customer segments.

In parallel with the reorganization of the banking sector, companies have embarked on a diversification of their capital structure. Faced with more stringent bank-lending conditions, and seeking to reduce their debt loads, larger firms have been turning to capital markets as part of an effort to diversify their sources of funding. Companies with a good reputation can acquire fresh funds by issuing debt securities. The corporate bond market, taking advantage of low interest rates, is experiencing unprecedented growth, due largely to the government's efforts to foster the bond market. Large privatization moves by utilities and other state-owned enterprises are expected to contribute to the revival of the equity market.

Figure 13.1 indicates how Thai firms have diversified their sources of financing since 1997, as reflected in the rise in the share of equities and domestic bonds from 14.7 per cent (1,133 billion baht) and 7.1 per cent (547 billion baht) respectively in 1997, to 33.2 per cent (8,408 billion baht) and 28.8 per cent (7,327 billion baht) respectively in 2011. The share of bank lending, short-term and long-term, on the other hand, has declined from 78.2 per cent (6,037 billion baht) in 1997 to 37.9 per cent (9,612 billion baht) in 2011 (Thai Bond Market Association 2012).

After the implementation of the Financial Sector Master Plan Phase I in January 2004, which provided only two types of banking licences—commercial and retail—a mixture of family (eight banks), government (four banks), and foreign (six banks) ownership has become the new image of the Thai banking sector (Wailerdsak and Suehiro 2010). Foreign investors have made significant inroads into the sector. Foreign owners and minority shareholders have changed patterns of doing business, suggesting the end of the bank-based conglomerates that were so central to development from the late 1950s. The banks that have survived, avoiding state takeover and maintaining majority Thai ownership and control, all had significant levels of foreign investment and relationships with overseas institutions. With the exception of the Bank of Ayudhaya, each also had significant international or regional operations.

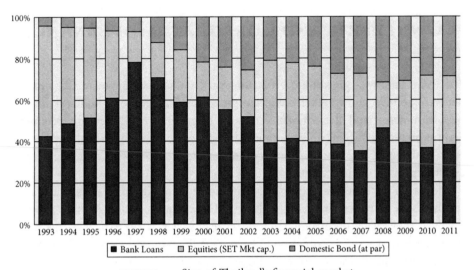

FIGURE 13.1 Size of Thailand's financial market

*Source*: Thai Bond Market Association 2012

The majority of Thailand's leading companies in all major sectors, including export, industrial, agriculture, and services, have relied on bank loans. The long-term relationship between large banks and their customers has played an important role in supporting Thai business. On the other hand, since the Asian crisis, small firms have been relying on credits from commercial banks and specialized financial institutions (SFIs) such as the Small and Medium Enterprise Development Bank of Thailand (or SME Bank, established in December 2002). Lower-income households rely mainly on government SFIs such as the Government Savings Bank (GSB) and Bank for Agriculture and Agricultural Cooperatives (BAAC) or, otherwise, informal financial intermediaries.

There are many forms of informal microfinance resources around the country, including saving groups, locally known as 'share groups',[8] which exist in almost every social group and include vendors' credit at almost every gold vendor and local coffee shop, operating like private pawnshops, as well as private moneylenders (Townsend 2011). Some illegal lending operations provide shark loans with interest rates as high as 2 per cent per day. Most loans to rural households are provided without any tangible assets as collateral. Conventional collateral is rarely used in rural credit markets. Lenders can enforce collateral-free loans through third-party guarantees and borrower–lender relationships, but also through reducing loan size, reducing duration, or increasing the interest rate.

The Stock Exchange of Thailand (SET) has become the main source of funds for large and medium firms, particularly financial institutions, property developers, telecommunications, and energy companies. To accelerate development in the capital market, the Capital Market Master Plan I (2002–2005) and Plan II (2006–2010) were proposed (World Bank 2011), aiming to make the Thai capital market an efficient channel for fundraising as well as a good saving choice, thereby helping to increase overall market capitalization and improve stock price stability.

## OWNERSHIP AND CORPORATE GOVERNANCE

The Thai economy is quite unique. If we look back, it was clear that no matter what happened in politics, and whether the government was democratic or military-run, business, commerce, and the national economy, in general, could develop persistently. Serious problems, such as military coups and economic crises, had short-term impacts only. Thai people and business appear quite flexible in response to changing domestic and international environments.

The reason for this is that the business community contains three levels. The first level involves basic activities, such as agriculture and small trades. Although many people are involved, they earn little, but enough to survive; however, at this basic level, the government needs to pay special attention to encourage them to persevere. At the next level, medium to large businesses have developed and collapsed continuously, but have not been definitively affected by political changes. Governments rarely interfere with this group, as it is the major group of the Thai business community. The last level is big busi-nesses, including those in joint ventures with foreign capital, those with state conces-sions, and those listed on the SET. Their investments are usually large and longstanding, require a peaceful and predictable political environment, and the patronage of political leaders—some have been forced to close due to military coup or change of government. However, as there are few such large businesses, there is limited risk of exposure to polit-ical changes.

We examine listed companies here, using the World Bank's classification concerning ultimate owners, including family, government, corporate (domestic and foreign firms), financial institution (domestic and foreign firms), and various widely held groups with no ultimate owners (Suehiro 2001b).[9] Generally speaking, major movements can be seen in the ownership structure of listed companies during the 2000s: a decline in family- and financial institution-owned (due to the impact of the 1997 Asian crisis) and an increase in government-linked companies (GLC) and corporate-owned companies (due to the active advance of foreign firms and the listing of giant state enterprises such as the Petroleum Authority of Thailand (PTT) and its associated companies).[10]

Our earlier research (Suehiro and Wailerdsak 2004; Wailerdsak 2008a), however, pre-sented data suggesting that, even after the 1997 Asian financial crisis, families continued to be the dominant form of ownership of Thai businesses, at least in terms of the num-ber of listed companies (not in terms of market capitalization). The crisis was widely believed to have financially weakened Thailand's business families, leaving many firms vulnerable to foreign investors, but the majority of these families survived and new fam-ilies listed their companies on the stock market in the process of restoration after the crisis. Using data for companies listed on the SET in three benchmark years of 1996, 2000, and 2006, we find that even though the percentage of family-owned firms (using the 20% cut-off rule) dipped in the year 2000 (42.3% of the total listed companies) com-pared with 1996 (48.2%), by 2006 it was higher than it had been before the crisis (50.4%).

Family-based capitalism in Thailand has been highly concentrated. Indeed, family-based control, and the desire to retain it, may be one reason why Thai companies relied heavily on debt to expand in the 1980s and 1990s. Family members were often insiders, meaning they were major shareholders, members of the board of directors, and managers. Outside director roles per se are minimal: usually just two or three people are nominated to the board committee, simply to meet SET requirements (Wailerdsak 2008b).

Two major channels that families used to maintain both ownership and control were holding shares directly in their names and through a pyramidal structure, in which the family held a majority of shares in a holding/investment (parent) company that, in turn, held a majority of shares in an operating company/subsidiaries (Suehiro 2006; Wailerdsak and Suehiro 2010). The ownership of holding/investment companies was highly concentrated, while the ownership of their operating companies became pro-gressively more diffused among outside shareholders. At the same time, control of oper-ating companies was exercised by those families who controlled the parent company (Wailerdsak 2006).

The corporate governance[11] reforms initiated by the SET and Office of the Securities and Exchange Commission (SEC) resulted from strong pressure from international financial institutions (IMF and World Bank) in the wake of the 1997 financial crisis (Suehiro 2001a). In 1998, the SET issued requirements for all listed companies to have an audit committee (comprising at least three independent directors) and a guideline, the 'Code of Best Practices for Directors of Listed Companies'. The Thai Institute of Directors Association (IOD) was established in December 1999 with the mission of developing and supporting company directors in their efforts to implement good corporate governance.

In 2002, when the Thai government set up the National Corporate Governance Committee (NCGC), chaired by the Prime Minister, the SET aggressively followed the government's lead in designating 2002 as the 'Compass for Good Corporate Governance' and proposed fifteen principles for listed companies to implement from the accounting period ending 21 December 2002. In the same year, the SET established a Corporate Governance Centre to advise listed companies on developing their corporate governance system (Montreevet 2006).

Two years later, the SET issued an updated version of the fifteen principles, in accordance with the five criteria of the OECD's Principles of Corporate Governance (2004), which included the rights of shareholders, equitable treatment of shareholders, roles of stakeholders, disclosure and transparency, and responsibilities of the board of directors. These criteria also followed World Bank Reports on the Observance of Standards and Codes (CG-ROSC).

Since then, Thai accounting and auditing systems have been improved in accordance with international standards, securities regulations have been enhanced, and corporate governance has been given high priority. Listed companies have taken the lead. The SET 50 companies, those with the largest capitalization, started applying International Financial Reporting Standards (IFRS) in their financial reports for the first quarter of 2011, followed by the SET 100 companies in 2013. By 2015, the IFRSs will be mandatory for all companies listed on the SET and the Market for Alternative Investment (MAI).

In the area of transparency, the SEC initiative—to introduce incentives for companies to improve their corporate governance practices voluntarily, including the introduction of a 'governance rating system' among listed companies by the Thai Rating and Information Service (TRIS) and the establishment of an independent association of minority shareholders (e.g. Thai Investors Association, Institutional Investors Club, Association of Asset Management Companies), and the introduction of the 'Corporate Governance Report project' by the IOD are commendable. In addition, there are several awards to honour companies for outstanding improvements in corporate governance practices, such as the SEC's 'Disclosure Award', the SET and IOD's 'Board of the Year Award', and the 'SET Award', by the SET and editorial board of *Warasan Kan Ngoen lae Thanakharn* (Journal of Money and Banking).

Although Thailand's rules and principles in the area of corporate governance are not inferior to those of other countries, it has received low ratings in corporate governance surveys and rankings conducted by such organizations as the Asian Corporate

Governance Association (ACGA), Credit Lyonnais Securities Asia's Regional CG Survey, and the International Institute for Management Development (IMD). The problem lies in enforcement and business ethics and practices. Claessens, Djankov, and Lang (1999) have argued that part of the reason was the high and persistent levels of ownership concentration by individuals and families, which contributed to excessive diversification, accumulation of bad debts, and poor corporate performance.

As the governance problem largely derives from the coupling of ownership and control, the relationship between firm performance and major (family) shareholders' ownership in Thailand has been the subject of empirical investigation. Suehiro (2001b) found that the relationship between ownership concentration and firm value, measured by ROE and ROA (representing the quality of corporate governance), depends on who the large shareholders are. The empirical evidence showed that ownership via family and foreign firms positively affects firm performance, while ownership by widely held firms is negatively associated with firm performance. More data suggest that some family-owned listed companies carry good corporate governance far beyond the national average. Family-owned companies such as Banpu, a mining company, and Thai Union Frozen Products, a tuna exporter, have been outstanding, winning several national and regional awards and recognition for good corporate governance.

It was found that listed companies with large market capitalization tend to practise the fifteen principles of corporate governance more comprehensively than their smaller counterparts, thanks to the larger companies' ability to access more financial and human resources. Institutional investors tend to pay more attention to these large companies, urging them to build investor confidence through the effective implementation of good corporate governance principles. Moreover, companies in the energy, petrochemicals, and mining sectors are leading the way, followed by the communications and finance and securities sectors. By contrast, companies in less prominent sectors, such as pulp and paper, printing, and publishing, are least successful in implementation (SET 2009).

At the same time, there is growing awareness that corporate social responsibility (CSR) will benefit a company, as it can help promote a company's reputation, and thereby improve its financial performance. Although CSR is distinct from good corporate governance, they are closely linked. Resource-based industries like mining (Banpu), cement (Siam Cement), and petrochemicals (Petroleum Authority of Thailand or PTT) especially need companies to behave in a socially and environmentally responsible way. The benefits of good corporate governance and good corporate social responsibility are more pronounced for companies in these industries than for those in other industries.

# INTERNAL STRUCTURE OF THE FIRM

Suehiro and Wailerdsak (2004) and Wailerdsak (2005) examined the composition of boards of directors and management committees, and type of managers, with reference to ownership (owner-manager), internal promotion, and invitation from the outside. The evidence suggests that a modern managerial structure, in terms of the employment of professional and salaried managers, is widely observed among government-linked companies (GLC) and reformed family businesses, particularly in industrial and banking groups. Nevertheless, in those family businesses that survived the 1997 financial crisis we still observe a strong influence of owner-family members over both board members and top management.

Concentrated control means that decision-making in the firm is centralized, often through a patriarchal owner at the top of the organization. Family members almost always maintain a controlling interest in the firm regardless of the percentages of their shareholdings. Thus, it is often the case that firms seek to place family members in positions of responsibility. Non-family members are not commonly admitted to top management ranks, and delegation of power is frequently limited to a part of the decision-making process, ultimate management control remaining in the hands of owner-family members. In addition, the firm may operate through a network of businesses in the form of a pyramidal structure that is difficult for outsiders to grasp, but easy for the founding family to control (Wailerdsak 2008b).

For non-family managers and employees, to be eligible for promotion, an employee must possess the qualifications required of the position, which are a combination of years of service, experience in related work at the lower level, and educational background. Sometimes, other job requirements and criteria, such as special training (Off-JT) or an advanced educational degree in a specific field, as well as certain personal characteristics, are additionally considered appropriate (Wailerdsak 2005).

# Employment Relations

## Overview of Changes in the Labour Force

Taking three benchmark years (1980, 1995, and 2010), workforce totals were 22.5 million in 1980, 30.8 million in 1995, and 38.1 million in 2010. Thanks to stable economic growth and a demographic 'bonus', the total number of employees has constantly increased for the past three decades. Of these totals, the distribution of employees by work status was as follows: government employees 5.3, 7.9, and 9.0 per cent, respectively; private-sector employees 16.5, 32.2 and 34.5 per cent; self-employed workers, including farmers, 30.1, 31.3, and 32.0 per cent; and unpaid family workers 46.8, 25.8, and 21.4 per cent. The most prominent changes occurred during the economic boom period (1988–1995), in which the private sector attracted a large number of unpaid family workers in addition to the fresh labour force (Suehiro 2008: Chapter 11). The latest workforce survey (39.3 million persons in 2011) indicates no notable changes for the past fifteen years, at 9.4 per cent for government employees, 32.7 per cent private-sector employees, 31.8 per cent self-employed workers, and 23.6 per cent unpaid family workers (NSO 2011).

Trade unions in Thailand have played a less important role in industrial relations. While there were 1,229 registered trade unions in the private sector in 2008, including 449 company-based unions, 750 industry-based unions, and 50 managerial-class unions, organized labour in the private sector is estimated at less than 10 per cent. According to the latest figures in 2011 (Ministry of Labour 2011), there were 44 trade unions with 179,000 members in public enterprises and 1,329 trade unions (366 in Bangkok Metropolitan Area) with 379,000 members in private enterprises. Labour disputes in the past decade have been relatively few, between 53 and 154 cases per annum, including 1–4 strikes (see Table 13.1). Management committees (representatives of employers and employees) have played a more important role in maintaining industrial relations. In 2011, there were four summit organizations—the State Enterprises Workers Relations Confederation (SERC) (1980: 43 enterprises and 150,000 members), Labour Congress of Thailand (LCT) (1978: 1,084 firms and 25,000 members), Thai Trade Union Congress (TTUC) (1983: 83 firms and 25,000 members), and National Congress of Private Industrial Employees (NCPE) (15,000 members) (Ministry of Labour 2011). In January 2008, these four organizations jointly set up the ITUC-Thai Council, but it has very limited bargaining power against the government and employers' associations.

**Table 13.1 Unemployment, trade unions, and labour disputes in Thailand, 2000–2010**

| Year | Unemployment (%) | Trade Unions | Labour Disputes | | Strikes | |
|---|---|---|---|---|---|---|
| | | Number | Cases | Employees involved | Cases | Employees involved |
| 2000 | 3.6 | 1,084 | 140 | 50,768 | 3 | 2,165 |
| 2001 | 3.2 | 1,123 | 154 | 47,759 | 4 | 449 |
| 2002 | 2.4 | 1,160 | 110 | 41,717 | 4 | 1,396 |
| 2003 | 2.2 | 1,239 | 97 | 43,801 | 1 | 1,700 |
| 2004 | 2.0 | 1,340 | 123 | 76,210 | 1 | 93 |
| 2005 | 1.8 | 1,369 | 87 | 29,111 | 3 | 348 |
| 2006 | 1.5 | 1,313 | 80 | 32,807 | 2 | 900 |
| 2007 | 1.4 | 1,243 | 100 | 48,069 | 2 | 183 |
| 2008 | 1.4 | 1,229 | 53 | 58,387 | 4 | 1,423 |
| 2009 | 1.5 | n/a | 81 | 50,075 | 2 | 456 |
| 2010 | 1.0 | n/a | 66 | 55,362 | 1 | 464 |

Sources: Ministry of Labour, *Yearbook of Labour Statistics*, various issues; Ministry of Labour and Welfare, *Yearbook of Labour Protection and Welfare Statistics*, various issues.

## Industrial Relations and Internal Labour Markets

Success in introducing and promoting outside (non-family) management can prove detrimental in a fast-growth industry. Wailerdsak (2005) examined the career paths of 4,190 executives of listed companies in Thailand, finding that almost all the listed companies were prepared to conduct management reforms, which would mean including non-family members on the board, hiring non-family members, and promoting them to senior management positions. Interestingly, 43.5 per cent of executives in the executive committees had been with their companies for fifteen to twenty years, while 31.3 per cent were hired directly as executives from outside. The remainder consisted of family members and representatives of other major shareholders. However, as already noted, such sizeable proportions of non-family members in top management do not necessarily imply the transformation of family-owned firms into managerial enterprises.

Managerial careers in Thailand tend to develop in association with an occupational ladder and be confined to a single employer or a few employers. Staffing based on occupation and developing occupation-specific skills makes it possible to create managers within a short period of time, minimizing training costs by focusing on specific expertise, and maximizing returns on investment. In addition, large companies have devoted themselves to establishing their internal labour markets to prepare manager pools for their business expansion and to train them for international business practices in order to gain legitimacy among potential investors.

However, the recent surge of business investment, coupled with a lack of skilled workers, creates a highly competitive market for employees. It is generally accepted that skilled employees are key assets, and the loss of such employees is unacceptable for most organizations. Currently, many Thai companies have adopted talent management, succession planning, and employee engagement strategies in order to attract and retain skilled employees and thus discourage the prevalent trend of job-hopping (Siengthai, Dechawatanapaisal, and Wailerdsak 2009). On the other hand, employees give numerous reasons for being dissatisfied with a firm, such as long working hours, poor supervisor, or general disorganization. As noted, good interpersonal relations and respect are vital to the retention of employees. In today's fiercely competitive market, companies must find an appropriate combination of both financial and social appeasement.

## Policies for Foreign Workers

A serious problem affecting Thailand's labour market is a shortage of production or unskilled workers. A 2011 survey on textile/garment industries in Thailand reported a labour shortage of 100,000 persons (NESDB 2011). Similar problems occur in industries requiring hard and dirty work, such as construction, fisheries, natural rubber (tapping), oil-palm (harvesting), and food-processing. For this reason, foreign workers are expected to play an important role in the unskilled labour market.

Thailand changed its policy concerning foreign workers from neighbouring countries such as Cambodia, Laos, and Myanmar (CLM) when the Chatichai government (1988–1991) adopted a new policy for CLM and Vietnam, employing a slogan of shifting 'from the Battlefield to the Trade Market'. Before the Chatichai government, the employment of foreign workers was strictly regulated by the 1978 Working of Aliens Act (Chalamwong 2004). In 1992, the government for the first time granted Burmese workers work permits in ten prefectures near Myanmar, and by 1995 the number of Burmese workers had increased to 400,000. In August 2000, the government further deregulated migrant-worker policies and extended the internal geographical and industrial scope to thirty-seven prefectures and eighteen industries. To overcome the chronic shortage of unskilled workers, the Thaksin government (2001–2006) liberalized the employment of foreign workers across the whole country.

In 2008, the 1978 Working of Aliens Act was completely revised in order to meet the changing circumstances. Under this act, employers were principally permitted to employ foreign workers for two years, excepting skilled workers and professionals (Article 8). At the end of 2009, foreign workers numbered 1,300,000, including Burmese (1,080,000), Cambodians (125,000), and Laotians (111,000). If illegal workers are included, the total foreign workforce is estimated to comprise around 2 million individuals, equivalent to 5 per cent of Thailand's working population (Otomo 2010).

# EDUCATION AND SKILLS FORMATION

## Educational System and Enrolment Ratios

Thailand is one of East Asia's most active countries in educational development. In terms of public education expenditure as a proportion of GDP, in 2007 Thailand ranked second (4.0%), after Malaysia (6.0%)—more than China (3.9%), Japan (3.8%), Korea (3.1%) and Singapore (3.1%) (Marginson, Kaur, and Sawir 2011). Gross enrolment in elementary education (aged 6–11) reached 100 per cent during the 1980s and that of lower secondary education (12–15) exceeded 90 per cent in the mid-2000s. As of 2008, the gross enrolment ratios were 105 per cent for elementary, 97 per cent for lower secondary, 69 per cent for upper secondary, and 48 per cent for tertiary education, including open universities (NSO 2010).

Thailand's education system is characterized by a combination of ordinary and vocational tracks, divided at the stage of upper secondary education. Owing to the spread of standard education to the masses, the percentage of students in vocational schools dropped from 44 per cent in 1990 to 35 per cent in 2008. The most prominent development has been the rapid increase of university students (203,000 in 1990, 1,134,000 in 2000, and 1,772,000 in 2007). In 2007, there were 145 universities, including 78 public (1,513,000 students, 85%) and 67 private universities (259,000 students, 15%). The gender proportion was 44 per cent male and 56 per cent female (NSO

2010). Public universities include two open universities (Ramkhamhaeng University and Sukhothai Thammathirat University) and forty Rajabhat Universities (reorganized teachers' colleges outside Bangkok Metropolis). According to the latest figures (2010), higher education covers 2,100,000 students taking bachelor courses, 156,000 students taking master courses and 16,000 students taking doctoral courses (Ministry of Education 2010).

## Problems Facing Higher Education

Despite the fact that the government has constantly pursued the promotion of higher educational reform through the implementation of the First 15-year Educational Development Plan (1990–2004) and the enactment of the 1999 Education Act, Thailand's educational system still has problems, including low student quality, low academic credentials among teachers, and a mismatch between education and the labour market.[12]

There is no adequate statistical data on the quality of students in universities. Here we use the PISA (Programme for International Student Assessment), which provides an international ranking of high-school student performance in three fields of reading, mathematics, and science. According to the 2009 PISA results, Thailand was ranked as low as fiftieth in total scores (fiftieth in reading, forty-ninth in mathematics, and fiftieth in science) (OECD 2010). By referring to the PISA results, the Commission of Higher Education emphasized the need to improve curricula in undergraduate courses in the Second 15-year Educational Development Plan (2008–2022).

Another problem is the low academic credentials of teachers. The 1999 Education Act obliged all teachers to obtain at least a bachelor's degree. By this policy, the academic credentials for teachers in universities were 30 per cent holding a bachelor degree, 60 per cent a master degree and 10 per cent a doctoral degree. The Second 15-year Plan aims to increase teachers with doctoral qualifications from 10 to 15 per cent (Matichon 2012).

The third problem is the most serious one for Thailand, now it has entered the upper-middle-income group of countries. Public universities in Thailand have traditionally focused on skills needed by the bureaucracy (political science, law, education), rather than skills needed by private corporations (finance, business administration, sciences). This mismatch of graduate profiles and skills required in the labour market was revealed in the 1997 Asian financial crisis (Phongpaichit and Baker 1998; Jestin 2009). This 'over-qualified and under-skilled' problem (OECD 2011:Chapter 4) is expressed in an imbalance in academic fields at universities (67% humanities and social sciences, 33% natural sciences in 2010). To improve this situation, the Second 15-year Plan aims to increase the proportion of natural sciences to 50 per cent by 2022 (Matichon 2012).

To meet the needs of the labour market, private institutions and corporations themselves have launched new types of higher educational institution. For instance, the Technology Promotion Association (TPA) opened the Thai-Nichi Institute of Technology (TNI) in July 2007 in cooperation with the Japanese Chamber of Commerce in Bangkok. TNI focuses on practical knowledge and production technology in the automotive and electronics industries, as well as the science of industrial management, while Japanese firms provide scholarship and internship services for students. The CP Group, one of the largest industrial conglomerates, with a strong stake in mainland China, also opened its own university (Panyapiwat Institute of Management, PIM) to educate professionals in management, including business practices in China. PIM invites Chinese students from abroad and in turn delegates Thai students to China, Japan, and Europe. Similarly, PTT, the largest petrochemical complex listed on the stock market, set up its own institution to educate engineers specializing in the petrochemical industry.[13] All these have emerged to resolve a massive under-supply from standard educational institutions of engineers and professionals specializing in such growing industries as automotive, electronics, petrochemicals, and modern retail business. These efforts are designed to help companies grow a workforce for business expansion.

With regard to skills formation, the activities available to employees on joining an organization include orientation, training, and development programmes. Orientation is usually provided to new employees, who are later expected to be acculturated into the company through on-the-job training. For training and development, most firms invest more in their human capital. Many management associations have been a catalyst for these changes in practice which, to a large extent, were due to the more competitive environment in both the domestic and international markets. Formal training programmes are generally provided at supervisory level or higher. Large organizations, such as Siam Cement and PTT, have their own training centres and provide in-house formal training programmes. These large organizations also provide in-house executive development programmes, as well as sending their executives abroad for short-term training (Siengthai, Dechawatanapaisal, and Wailerdsak 2009). However, most small and medium-sized enterprises do not have such systematic training and development programmes.

# INTER-FIRM RELATIONS

In his chapter on Japan, Witt (2014) introduces four different types of group in inter-company relations: business groups or horizontal *keiretsu* (*zaibatsu*-type and bank-led groups), production networks or vertical *keiretsu*, R&D consortia, and a government–association–industry nexus. In Thailand before the 1997 Asian crisis, the most popular types of inter-company relations were business groups (*glum thurakit*), which included *zaibatsu*-type groups, in which a particular family exclusively controlled both the ownership and the management of companies in a group, and bank-led groups, in which family-owned giant commercial banks served as core firms (Suehiro 1989, 2006).

During the economic crises and corporate reforms, these two types of inter-company group have changed their ownership structures as well as management strategy. The *zaibatsu*-type groups have reorganized their diversified (and unrelated) business activities into selected industries, in line with the new strategy of selection and concentration,[14] while bank-led groups have strategically shifted their capital and human resources from non-bank sectors to the bank sector to survive increasing competition with foreign competitors (Suehiro 2006: Chapters 3 and 7).

A new movement is the development of production networks or vertical *keiretsu*. This can be widely observed in the automobile industry, which has impressively organized close relations between foreign assemblers and local parts-suppliers in particular industrial cities and clusters (neighbouring areas, such as Banpakong and Ayudhya). Unlike Taiwanese electronic firms, which have developed an ODM (own-design manufacturing) system, Thai local firms have yet to find a place in global value chains in the electronics industry. This is partially due to the strong stake of MNCs in Thailand and partially because of the poor capacity of local firms to develop indigenous technology and new markets.

In contrast to the development of business groups and production networks, R&D consortia and the government-association–industry nexus are very poor (Intarakumnerd 2009; IMD 2010). In January 2001, the government set up the National Science and Technology Policy Commission (NSTPC) to design a national innovation system. In April 2002, the Government and the National Science and Technology Development Agency (NASDA), opened a 'Science Park' in the Rangsit area (near Donmuang Airport), and planned to promote three major sectors of computers and electronics (NECTEC), bio-technology (BIOTEC), and metal material technology (MTEC) in conjunction with successful foreign firms, in an attempt to seed new industrial clusters. At the same time, the NASDA also planned to combine government-sponsored agencies, private innovative firms (incubators), and universities. However, these attempts have not as yet produced significant products.

# Social Capital

## Institutional Trust and Social Values in East Asia

According to the World Economic Forum's Global Competitiveness Report 2010/2011, Thailand ranked thirty-eighth among 139 surveyed countries in overall score. However, it indicated a disgraceful status in both 'public trust in politicians' (eighty-third) and 'irregular payments and bribes' (seventieth), considerably lower than Singapore (first and third, respectively), Taiwan (thirty-sixth and thirty-seventh), and Malaysia (thirty-fifth and fifty-fifth) (World Economic Forum 2010). Thai and other East Asian peoples tend to show confidence in family and relatives, and weak confidence in social groups such as political parties, trade unions, and workplaces. Moreover, the mostly Buddhist Thais place less importance on religious associations (35%), compared to Islamic countries such as Indonesia (72%) and Malaysia (59%) (Inoguchi et al. 2006). These surveys on public trust and social values suggest what kinds of social capital are important to Thai people.

In 2003, the Thaksin government set up four strategic committees to tackle nation-wide problems: the National Poverty Reduction Committee, National Competitiveness Committee, National Committee for Sustainable Development, and National Committee for Social Capital Development. The last was tasked with examining the type of institutions (*sathaban*) that are social capital for Thailand and the kind of social capital that is useful in a context of social development for the country. After a year of discussions, the members concluded that the most important social capital was family institutions, followed by religious (Buddhism) and community institutions (*chumchon*) (NESDB 2005b). This political selection seems to reflect the inclinations of institutional trust among Thai people, as expressed in the Asia Barometer Survey (Inoguchi et al. 2006).

Thai people have traditionally placed special priority on family and kinship. Such social values of attaching importance to interpersonal relationships have frequently been reproduced in company or government offices, in which Thai people have tended to prefer a homely working environment to a competitive one. For this reason, when Prime Minister Thaksin severely criticized a diffusion of familialism in the government offices, and attempted to introduce strict doctrines of competition and performance appraisal, most government officers resisted his policy (Suehiro 2009: Chapter 5).

A family is a fundamental unit. However, Thailand seems to have experienced a crisis in the family system. According to a NESDB report (NESDB 2007), marriages per 1,000 households decreased from 37 in 1981 to 19 in 2006, while divorces per 1000 households increased from 2.4 in 1988 to 4.9 in 2006. The same report also warned that the number of persons aged 60 and over had increased from 3.6 million in 1988 to 7.5 million in 2006. In May 2004, the Ministry of Social Development and Human Security issued a ten-year plan for the 'Comprehensive Development of Family System 2004–2013', focusing on domestic violence and improved communication among family members (NESDB 2005a).

A typical case may be observed in the government's campaign on 'How family members can share a nice week'. In this campaign, the government recommended that parents and children share dinner, teach cooking, and take part in outside leisure activities during holidays. The government is beginning to intervene, not just in the market economy, but in family life. The decline of the family system inevitably affects stable industrial relations in companies as well as social stability. The idea of a sufficiency economy (*setthakit phophiang*), proposed by King Bhumibol Adulyadej in 1997, focused on three major principles of harmony, security, and sustainability, seemingly to counter such instability in both social values and the family system (UNDP 2007: 20–35; Suehiro 2009: Chapter 4).

## Buddhism

According to the 2010 census, most people in Thailand are Buddhist (93.6%), followed by Muslims (4.9%), Christians (1.2%), and Hindus (0.1%). Monks in temples have constantly supported people alienated from government policies, such as the disabled, orphans, elderly, and HIV/AIDS sufferers. Under conditions of inadequate public assistance, temples are important institutions in sustaining social safety-nets, and in the long run social stability, in Thailand. Although Thai people place top priority on family, rather than religion, they still have strong confidence in Buddhism and attach high respect to the social role of monks in a community.

## Community (*chumchon*)

Communities consist of two types: natural and artificial. Rural villages (74,000 in 2010) belong to the former category, while urban communities (4,000) the latter. The government has always supported the development of communities for the purposes of reducing rural poverty and creating national unity. The 1997 Constitution for the first time gave the status of 'juridical person' to a community (*chumchon*), officially recognizing communities as important agents for promoting decentralization in politics, rural development in economic fields, and social security in livelihoods. In this context, the autonomy of a community is crucial to the future of Thai society (Reynolds 2009). Since companies intending to enter the Thai economy are requested to invest in areas outside the Bangkok Metropolis Area, the autonomous development of a community is closely related to foreign investors' strategy.

## CONCLUSION

A big challenge for Thailand is to sustain the momentum of growth in the longer term and to avoid becoming stuck in the 'middle-income trap'. As of 1966, Thailand moved from a low-income country to a lower middle-income country, and further to an upper middle-income country in 2010, as a result of a sound growth in per capita income during that period. Its exports have also moved from primarily resource-based and labour-intensive to high-tech and capital-intensive. This was the result of many factors, including export-oriented policies, the opening-up of the industrial sector to FDI, and the exploitation of its abundant cheap labour, as well as accumulating capital. However, in recent years, real GDP growth has decelerated and so has per capita income growth, dropping Thailand below other emerging East Asian countries such as China, Indonesia, and Vietnam. Thailand faces a real challenge in sustaining higher growth and transitioning to a high-income country.

The development strategies that economies such as Thailand needed to make the transition from low-income to middle-income were different from those that are now needed to move up to high-income status. To effect this transition, the business system must pay attention to total factor productivity growth, rather than growth in input of capital and labour, through specialization in selected sectors and areas with significant potential for economies of scale and technological leadership.

Such specialization requires, for example, substantial increases in the proportion of people with tertiary education and specialized skills in favour of the labour market, transformation from an economy that largely absorbs knowledge from abroad (e.g. through FDI) to one that is also a source of innovation, the development of deep financial systems providing a diverse range of services, including support for innovation, and the movement of much of the population into liveable and well-organized cities with efficient and highly competitive clusters, including more medium-sized cities so that the country itself can become better integrated and growth benefits are better shared.

There is clear evidence that Thailand is beginning to move into areas that have significant scale-economies and potential for technological leadership, such as the automotive and electronics sectors. There is also potential in services such as the tourism and medical services sectors, as well as IT, logistics, and 'farm-to-table' agriculture. The government and private sector are indeed exploring these possibilities, but perhaps too slowly, allowing Thailand to fall behind.

## Notes

1. As stated by Prasarn Trairatvorakul, Governor of the Bank of Thailand in July 2012 (Trairatvorakul 2012).
2. For the concept and empirical studies concerning the 'middle-income trap', see Gill and Kharas (2007), Doner (2009), Yusuf and Nabeshima (2009), and Asian Development Bank (2011).
3. For analyses of economic policies and industrial changes in Thailand from the 1960s, see Suehiro (1989), Muscat (1994), Siamwalla et al. (1997), and Phongpaichit and Baker (1998).
4. The annual growth rates of exports in terms of US dollars are 20.5% for the period 1987–1996 and 10.9% for 2000–2009.
5. Total productivity growth between 1990 and 2008 in Thailand was just 0.7%, much lower than China (4.7%), Korea (1.6%), and Taiwan (1.3%). (Asian Productivity Organization 2011).
6. The leverage ratio (bank loans to equity capital ratio) of listed companies in Thailand increased from 1.60 in 1988 to 2.36 in 1996, lower than Korea (3.55), but higher than Singapore (1.05), Malaysia (1.18), and Indonesia (1.88) (Suehiro 2008: 87).
7. The percentages of NPLs in Thailand in July 1999 were 41% for private commercial banks and 70% for state-owned banks; these figures had dropped to 18 and 6%, respectively, by July 2001, due to bad-loans restructuring (Suehiro 2006: 268).
8. See <http://www.gdrc.org/icm/sher.html> (accessed 29 June 2013) for features of Thailand's share game.
9. The World Bank classification for listed companies in terms of ownership structure was defined by Claessens, Djankov, and Lang (1999).
10. According to the authors' survey of 461 listed companies in 2011, PTT and its five associated companies combined to account for 43% of total sales, 13% of total assets and 33% of profits. These figures suggest the revival of government-linked companies in the stock market.
11. The term 'corporate governance' is translated in Thai as *bansat-piban*, a Buddhist rule for a corporation. The difference in interpretation of 'good governance' between the Western concept and the Thai context is implicit in the term 'state governance' (*thammarat*). Tejapira (2009) provides insightful consideration of this problem.

12. For educational reform in Thailand since the 1990s, see Funatsu (2008), Jestin (2009) and Pimpa (2011).
13. All information concerning TNI, CP Group, and PTT was obtained from authors' interview research in Bangkok, August 2011.
14. A typical case is the CP Group, which restructured from thirteen widely diverse types of industrial activity into three—agro-industry, telecommunications, and modern retail business (Suehiro 2006: Chapter 6).

## References

Asian Development Bank (2011). *Asia 2050: Realizing the Asian Century*. Manila, Asian Development Bank.

Asian Productivity Organization (2011). *APO Productivity Databook 2011*. Tokyo, Keio University Press.

Chachavalpongpun, P. (2010). *Reinventing Thailand: Thaksin and His Foreign Policy*. Singapore, ISEAS.

Chalamwong, Y. (2004). 'Government Policies on International Migration: Illegal Workers in Thailand'. In A. Ananta and E. N. Arifin, Eds., *International Migration in Southeast Asia: International Politics and the Reordering of State Power*: 352–373. Singapore, ISEAS.

Claessens, S., S. Djankov, and L. H. Lang (1999). *Who Controls East Asian Corporations?* World Bank Policy Research Working Paper No.2054. Washington DC, World Bank.

Doner, R. F. (2009). *The Politics of Uneven Development: Thailand's Economic Growth in Comparative Perspective*. Cambridge, Cambridge University Press.

Funatsu, T. (2008). 'Educational Reforms'. In Y. Tamada and T.Funatsu, Eds., *Thailand in Motion: Political and Administrative Changes 1991–2006*: 159–201. Tokyo, Institute of Developing Economies (in Japanese).

Funston, J., Ed. (2009). *Divided Over Thaksin: Thailand's Coup and Problematic Transition*. Singapore, ISEAS.

Gill, I. and H. Kharas (2007). *An East Asian Renaissance: Ideas for Economic Growth*. Washington, DC, World Bank.

Hewison, K. (1989). *Bankers and Bureaucrats: Capital and State in Thailand*. Southeast Asian Monograph 34. New Haven, Yale University.

IMD (2010). *World Competitiveness Yearbook 2010*. Switzerland, IMD.

Inoguchi, T., A. Tanaka, S. Sonoda, and T. Dadabaey, Eds. (2006). *Human Belief and Values in Striding Asia*. Tokyo, Akashi Shoten.

Intarakumnerd, P. (2009). 'Catching Up or Falling Behind: Thailand's Industrial Development from the National Innovation System Perspective'. In P. Intarakumnerd and Y. Lecler, Eds., *Sustainability of Thailand's Competitiveness*: 52–77. Singapore, ISEAS.

Jestin, B. (2009). 'Industrial Upgrading and Educational Upgrading: Two Critical Issues for Thailand'. In P. Intarakumnerd and Y. Lecler, Eds., *Sustainability of Thailand's Competitiveness*: 78–125. Singapore, ISEAS.

Marginson, S., S. Kaur, and E. Sawir (2011). 'Global, Local, National in the Asia-Pacific'. In S. Marginson, S. Kaur, and E. Sawir, Eds., *Higher Education in the Asia-Pacific: Strategic Responses to Globalization*: 3–34. London, Springer.

Matichon (2012). 'Reforms of Higher Education'. *Matichon Weekly Magazine*, 24 January (in Thai).

Ministry of Education (2010). 'Statistics on Education B.E. 2553 (2010)'. Retrieved 20 March 2012 from <http://www.moe.go.th/data_sat/> (available only in Thai).

Ministry of Labour (2011). *Yearbook of Labour Protection and Welfare Statistics 2011*. Bangkok, Ministry of Labour.

Montreevet, S., Ed. (2006). *Corporate Governance in Thailand*. Singapore, ISEAS.

Muscat, R. J. (1994). *The Fifth Tiger: A Study of Thai Development Policy*. Helsinki, UN University Press.

NESDB (National Economic and Social Development Board) (2005a). *Policies and Strategy for Comprehensive Development of Family System*. Bangkok, NESDB (in Thai).

—— (2005b) *Construction of Social Capital for Resilient Communities*. Bangkok, NESDB (in Thai).

—— (2007). *Happiness of Thai Society on the Basis of Quietness*. Bangkok, NESDB (in Thai).

—— (2011). 'Social Report, Third Quarter 2011'. Bangkok, NESDB (in Thai).

Nikomborirak, D. and S. Tawankul (2006). 'Monopolies and Politics'. Paper presented at TDRI Academic Conference, 9–10 December 2006, Chonburi, Thailand.

NSO (National Statistical Office) (2010). *Statistical Yearbook Thailand (SYT)*. Bangkok, NSO.

—— (2011). 'People & Society: Labour. 2011 Labour Force Survey'. Retrieved 20 March 2012 from <http://web.nso.go.th/en/survey/lfs/lfs2011.htm>.

OECD (2004). *OECD Principles of Corporate Governance*, Paris, OECD.

—— (2010). *PISA 2009 Results: Executive Summary*. Paris, OECD.

—— (2011). *OECD Employment Outlook 2011*. Paris, OECD.

Otomo, N. (2010). 'Government Policies on Foreign Workers in Thailand'. *Gaikoku no Rippo* 246, December: 125–138 (in Japanese).

Phongpaichit, P. and C. Baker (1998). *Thailand Boom and Bust*. Chiangmai, Silkworm Books.

—— (2004). *Thaksin: The Business of Politics in Thailand*, Chiangmai, Silkworm Books.

—— (2009). *Thaksin* (2nd ed.), Chiangmai, Silkworm Books.

Pimpa, N. (2011). 'Strategies for Higher Education Reform in Thailand'. In S. Marginson, S. Kaur, and E. Sawir, Eds., *Higher Education in the Asia-Pacific: Strategic Responses to Globalization*: 273–289. London, Springer.

Porter, M. E. (2003). *Thailand's Competitiveness: Creating the Foundations for Higher Productivity*. Bangkok, NESDB.

Reynolds, C. J. (2009). 'Chumchon: Community in Thailand'. In C. Gluck and A. L. Tsing, Eds., *Words in Motion*: 286–305. London, Duke University Press.

SET (2009). *Corporate Governance Report of Thai Listed Companies 2009*. Bangkok, Stock Exchange of Thailand.

Siamwalla, A., P. Vichyanond, and S. Christensen (1997). *Thailand's Boom and Bust*. Bangkok, Thailand Development Research Institute.

Siengthai, S., D. Dechawatanapaisal, and N. Wailerdsak (2009). 'Human Resource Management: Future Trends'. In T. G. Andrews and S. Siengthai, Eds., *The Changing Face of Management in Thailand*: 115–145. London and New York, Routledge.

Suehiro, A. (1989). *Capital Accumulation in Thailand 1855–1985*. Tokyo, UNESCO and Centre for East Asian Cultural Studies.

—— (2001a). 'Asian Corporate Governance: Disclosure-Based Screening System and Family-Business Restructuring in Thailand'. *Shakai Kagaku Kenkyu*, 52(5): 55–98.

—— (2001b). *Family Business Gone Wrong? Ownership Patterns and Corporate Performance in Thailand*. ADB Institute Working Paper No.19. Tokyo, ADB Institute.

—— (2006). *A Study of Family Business: Agents of Late Industrialization*. Nagoya, Nagoya University Press (in Japanese).

—— (2008). *Catch-up Industrialization: The Trajectory and Prospects of East Asian Economies*. Singapore, National University of Singapore Press.

—— (2009). *Thailand: Challenge of Middle Income Country*. Tokyo, Iwanami (in Japanese).

—— and N. Wailerdsak (2004). 'Family Business in Thailand: Its Management, Governance and Future Challenges'. *ASEAN Economic Bulletin 21*(1): 81–93.

Tejapira, K. (2009). 'Thammarat: Good Governance in Globalizing Thailand'. In C. Gluck and A.L. Tsing, Eds., *Words in Motion*: 306–326. London, Duke University Press.

Thai Bond Market Association (2012). *Annual Report*. Bangkok, Thai BMA.

Townsend, R. M. (2011). *Financial Systems in Developing Economies: Growth, Inequality, and Policy Evaluation in Thailand*. London and New York, Oxford University Press.

Trairatvorakul, P. (2012). 'Financial Crises and the Future of Global and Asian Banking'. Statement at Sasin Bangkok Forum 2012, 9 July. Retrieved 18 October 2012 from <http://www.bis.org/review/r120719a.pdf>.

Transparency International (2012). 'Results of the 2012 Corruption Perceptions Index'. Retrieved 15 July 2013 from <http://cpi.transparency.org/cpi2012/results>.

UNDP (2007). *Thailand Human Development Report 2007: Sufficiency Economy and Human Development*. Washington, DC., UNDP.

Wailerdsak, N. (2005). *Managerial Careers in Thailand and Japan*. Chiangmai, Silkworm Books.

—— (2006). *Business Groups and Family Business in Thailand Before and After the 1997 Crisis*. Bangkok, BrandAge (in Thai).

—— (2008a). 'Companies in Crisis'. In P. Phongpaichit and C. Baker, Eds., *Thai Capital After the 1997 Crisis*: 17–57. Chiangmai, Silkworm Books.

—— (2008b). 'Family Business in Thailand: Ownership Structure and Stock Market'. In V. Gupta, N. Levenburg, T. Schwarz, and L. Moore, Eds., *Culturally-Sensitive Models of Family Business in Southern Asia*: 108–133. Hyderabad, ICFAI University Press.

—— and A. Suehiro (2010). 'Business Groups in Thailand'. In A. M. Colpan, T. Hikino, and J. R. Lincoln, Eds., *Oxford Handbook of Business Groups*: 239–266. London and New York, Oxford University Press.

Warr, P. and P. Nidhiprabha (1996). *Thailand's Macroeconomic Miracle: Stable Adjustment and Sustainable Growth*. Kuala Lumpur, Oxford University Press.

Whitley, R. D. (1992). *Business Systems in East Asia*. Thousand Oaks, Sage.

—— (1999). *Divergent Capitalisms*. London and New York, Oxford University Press.

Witt, M. A. (2014). 'Japan: Coordinated Capitalism Between Institutional Change and Structural Inertia'. In M. A. Witt and G. Redding, Eds., *The Oxford Handbook of Asian Business Systems*: 100–122. Oxford, Oxford University Press.

World Bank (2011). *Thailand Economic Monitor April 2011*. Bangkok, World Bank.

World Economic Forum (2010). *Global Competitiveness Report 2010/2011*. Geneva, WEF.

Yusuf, S. and K. Nabeshima (2009). *Tiger Economies under Threat: A Comparative Analysis of Malaysia's Industrial Prospects and Policy Options*. Washington, DC, World Bank.

## CHAPTER 14

·······················································································

# VIETNAM

## *Post-State Capitalism*

·······················································································

## QUANG TRUONG AND CHRIS ROWLEY

## INTRODUCTION

DURING 1991–2010, Vietnam achieved a steady annual gross domestic product (GDP) growth of 7.7 per cent, which gradually increased its average income per capita from a scant US$98 to US$1174 (Ohno 2009; Schwab 2011) and reduced the poverty level from over 58 per cent to 10 per cent (Asian Development Bank 2011). This was achieved by a combination of stimulants, such as an inflow of foreign direct investment (FDI), exports of low-value-added products, and private-sector development. With a GDP of US$890 per head in 2008, Vietnam effectively became a 'middle-income country' (following the World Bank's classification of GDP per capita between US$976 and US$3855) (Ohno 2009; Tran 2012).

Notwithstanding the growing interest in Vietnam as an emerging economy, little has been written on its business system. This gap requires an examination of the socio-economic and political system to help understand how the economy is structured at macro (country) as well as micro (enterprise) levels, and how the economy's actors relate, interact, and operate within the framework of the socialist–capitalist dichotomy. The business system encompasses state-owned enterprises (SOEs), private-owned enterprises (POEs), foreign-invested enterprises (FIEs), foreign-owned enterprises (FOEs), from small- and medium-sized enterprises (SMEs) to large enterprises.

## ROLE OF THE STATE

Vietnam remains a one-party state system under the sole leadership of the Communist Party of Vietnam (CPV). Party dominance and socialist principles, channelled through its controlled network of mass organizations, including trade unions, influence all business activities (Rowley and Truong 2009a). This provides privileges and monopolies to organizations under CPV control, especially SOEs. Socialist tenets such as 'democratic centralism' (*dan chu tap trung*) and 'collective leadership and responsibility' (*lanh dao tap the*), in the form of 'resolutions' (*nghi quyet*), are common practices in decision-making. The CPV leadership holds absolute power in deliberating strategic issues at country and enterprise level, leaving little room for bottom-up participation and grass-roots contributions.

The level of party/state control and involvement in the economy has been evolutionary and conditioned to the socio-economic challenges facing the country at the time. Thus, prior to 1986 the state followed the Soviet model, characterized by centralized planning, forced agricultural collectivization, and nationalization of industry. The economy performed disastrously after unification in 1976.

The economic reform (*doi moi*) programme in 1986 was a reaction to save the country from near-bankruptcy in the wake of the collapse of the Soviet Union and the abrupt cessation of all aid from the communist bloc, followed by an imminent embargo from the West. Despite the fact that economic policies were still highly *dirigiste*, this marked a dramatic shift towards becoming a more developmental/welfare state (Masina 2006), with priority targets in economic growth and welfare.

Following World Trade Organization (WTO) membership in 2007, the state continued integration into the global economy and set the highly ambitious goal of forging an industrialized country by 2020 (Communist Party of Vietnam 2010). Efforts focused on further reducing the role of the state and encouraging private-sector development, although SOEs continued to be 'flagships' of the economy. This mixture makes Vietnam more like a neo-liberalist (Masina 2010) or neo-capitalist (Le 2011) state than a genuine free-market economy.

In the late 1990s the state launched a comprehensive reform programme to reorganize itself into a development administration, shifting emphasis from bureaucracy-oriented to citizen- and market-oriented provider of public services (Do and Truong 2009). The 2001–2010 Public Administration Reform (PAR) campaign focused on developing a more complete regulatory framework by means of a decentralization programme (*phan cap quan ly*) to delegate decision-making authority from central to local government (e.g. the FDI license approval process). The state also attempted to reduce state subsidies by promoting the development of POEs and involving related stakeholders (businesses and communities) in providing social services (especially in education, health, and culture) through a 'socialization' process (*xa hoi hoa*). The continued reform of SOEs further pushed ownership rights, allowing more autonomy in operations (Do and Truong 2009).

These efforts to build a more effective and accountable state apparatus have not materialized. One explanation is that while the party–state–business monolithic system may be an effective mechanism to push policy through quickly, it does not guarantee smooth and successful implementation. As decision-making is based on consensus, checks and balances occur horizontally (across ministries and departments), vertically (between central and local governments), and geographically (North, South, Middle, and remote areas) (Ohno 2009). Hence, any important decision requires lengthy negotiations, extensive compromises, and networks to satisfy the vested interests of stakeholders. On the other hand, coordination among different central government agencies and provincial authorities is low (Masina 2010), typical of a decentralized, quasi-federalist structure (Redding and Witt 2007).

The need for accelerating the development and integration process led to greater 'autonomization', in which the state is forced to gradually yield more latitude to local authorities and thus forms of 'para-state' entities have emerged (Painter 2008). Under these circumstances, decentralization has given rise to localism (Nguyen 2008) and cronyism (Roberts 2010), notably the practice of 'favour distribution' ('*co che xin cho*' or 'application-approval') (Tran 2010). Vertical delegation (from central to local authorities) has delivered examples of effective urban planning (e.g. Da Nang City) and industrial development (e.g. Binh Duong and Dong Nai Provinces). In contrast, horizontal delegation (from ministries to SOEs) seems to be reversing after the bailout of the shipbuilding group Vinashin in 2010 (Business Insider 2011a). An example of localism can be seen in the race among provinces/cities for 'prestige' infrastructure projects. Many local CPV leaders also sit on the Party's Central Committee, the National Assembly, or key ministerial positions in the cabinet. The result of this 'political lobby' is a proliferation of airports, seaports, industrial/special economic zones, universities, etc. (Dat Viet 2011). Many of these costly facilities are close to each other in neighbouring provinces and often left idle or under-used. Unfocused and uncoordinated delegation/decentralization also allows corruption in the public sector, such as 'under-the-table payments' (or '*van hoa phong bi*', 'envelope culture') (e.g. Le et al. 2006; Nguyen 2010; Papin and Passicousset 2010).

Despite the state's continued commitment to build a more responsive and clean development administration and to create a more equitable business environment for all participants in the economy, problems continue. The World Economic Forum ranked Vietnam 65th out of 142 countries in 2011 (a drop of six places from 2010), with a special remark that corruption is considered frequent and pervasive (ranked 104th) (Schwab 2011). The Transparency International Index ranks Vietnam 116th out of 178 countries, the lowest of ASEAN countries, except for the Philippines (134th) (Transparency International 2010). The 'Ease of Doing Business' Report puts Vietnam at 78th out of 183 economies, highlighting that administrative procedures remain the main barriers for investors. For example, it still averages 9 procedures and 44 days to get licenses to start a business in Vietnam, compared to 7.8 procedures and 39 days in East Asian and Pacific countries and 5.6 procedures and 13.8 days in OECD countries (IFC/WB 2011).

## FINANCIAL SYSTEM

In many respects, the financial system is typically centralized and heavily dependent on state-owned banks (SOBs) to provide access to finance. The financial sector has undergone a series of structural changes post 1986, the US–Vietnam Bilateral Trade Agreement in 2000 and WTO membership in 2007. The main challenges comprise restructuring the SOB sector, stabilizing the currency and stock exchange, managing the debt market (Massmann and Rowley 2009), and creating a more level playing field between state and privately controlled financial institutions (Kovsted et al. 2003).

The banking system was substantially restructured in 1990, separating the central bank, the State Bank of Vietnam (SBV), from commercial banks and allowing private banks to participate in the financial market. The SBV became an independent bank charged with executing monetary policy and supervising the sector. The banking and finance sector has diversified relatively rapidly in terms of participants and activities. The new regulations also put subsidiaries of foreign-owned banks on an equal basis to local banks, allowing them, for example, to take unlimited local currency deposits from corporate borrowers and issue credit cards (*Business Times* 2010).

There are four main types of credit institutions: commercial banks, policy-lending institutions, credit funds, and financial companies. The ongoing equitization process (the Vietnamese version of privatization) reduced the total number of state-owned commercial banks (SOCBs) and the state's shareholding to 51 per cent by 2010, while limiting total foreign holding to a maximum of 30 per cent. There are five SOCBs, controlling about 70 per cent of banking sector assets and 70 per cent of total bank loans. Another 37 joint stock banks (JSBs), mainly small in size, control about 15 per cent, with the remaining 15 per cent spread among 37 foreign bank (FB) branches and five joint-venture banks (JVBs). Banks with foreign capital, whose clients are predominantly FIEs, account for about 10 per cent of bank loans (Kovsted et al. 2003; Harvard Business School 2008; Leung 2008; Bland 2012).

Stock exchanges opened in Ho Chi Minh City (HoSE) in 2000 and Hanoi (HNX) in 2005 and helped manage the inflow of foreign currency and FDI and facilitate SOE equitization. After a slow acceptance, the stock market developed from late 2006. The total number of listed companies, most of them small joint stock companies from former SOEs, increased to 193 (of which 87 were JSCs) by early 2007, six times the 2005 figure, due to tax incentives for listing by the deadline of 31 December 2006. However, only 4 per cent of more than 3,000 SOEs equitized by the end of 2006 listed on the stock market, as they preferred not to disclose company information, and/or because of under-valuation at equitization (Thai and Biallas 2007). By mid-2010 there were 258 listed companies on the HoSE and 328 on the HNX (Chu 2010), with a total market capitalization value of about VND740.433 trillion (about US\$37 billion) or 45 per cent of the country's GDP (Stockbiz 2011), compared to less than US\$1 billion at the end of 2005 (World Bank 2007). However, only 60 per cent of stock value can be traded freely, because the state continues to hold controlling stakes in large enterprises (Chu 2010). The HoSE's stock market index (VN-Index) is generally seen as a relatively reliable barometer of Vietnam's financial market, while the HNX is less developed, accounting for only about one-third of total market capitalization (IMF 2007).

The purpose of the financial reforms was to lessen persistent and indirect state control through the creation of a more market-oriented autonomous sector. However, there are risks for both the financial sector and economy (Kovsted et al.

2003; Leung 2009), given the discriminatory capital allocation. POEs often have difficulties accessing official financing sources, while SOCBs continue to give preferential treatment for loss-making SOEs, many of which are close to bankruptcy with heavy non-performing loans (NPLs). In 2009 the total debts of 81 of the 91 centrally controlled SOE groups soared to VND813.4 billion (about US$38.7 billion) from VND31.935 (about US$2 billion), equivalent to 49 per cent of the country's GDP. Many NPLs lack files and evidence for a complete audit (Bui 2006). For example, the debt share of the Vietnam Shipbuilding Industry Group (Vinashin) alone was VND86 trillion (about US$4.1 billion) (VietNam News 2011) or about 5 per cent of GDP in 2009 (Business Insider 2011a).

The need for more complete and effective regulation was apparent when the post-2008 global financial crisis hit. In 2011 the VN-Index lost 6 per cent of its total market capitalization value of VND643.395 trillion (about US$32 billion) from three months earlier, after already having lost 8.1 per cent of its trade value in 2010. The finance market became extremely difficult to access for POEs due to increasingly high interest rates (16–20 per cent p.a. during 2010) and conditions for loan applications (Thecurrencynewshound 2011). POEs commonly resorted to alternative sources of capital, such as the 'underground' sector with exorbitant interest rates (Vuong 2011). This informal market makes up as much as 20 per cent of GDP (Kotkin 2011), or about US$20.8 billion in 2010 GDP value.

The shortage of finance has been compensated for by the inflow of remittances from the Vietnamese diaspora overseas, who in 2011 alone sent home US$9 billion or about 7.8 per cent of the country's GDP (Nguyen 2011b; Deutsch Presse-Agentur 2012). Large amounts of these transactions are via informal channels (Pham 2010a) that help Vietnam to balance its payments.

In sum, under strong state intervention (SBV), Vietnam's finance tends to be indirect, with a large state-supported network of banks (SOCBs) providing soft loans to SOEs (the pillars of the socialist economy); many of these big borrowers (e.g. Vinashin, EVN, and Petrolimex) are unable to repay their loans. Meanwhile, the private sector often fails to meet the complex conditions for capital acquisition and hence has to turn to friends, families, and the informal market (loan sharks) for start-up and operations capital. Both banking system and capital market need further comprehensive reforms to meet international standards and sustain economic growth (Bland 2011a, 2011b, 2012).

# OWNERSHIP AND CORPORATE GOVERNANCE

Officially there are five main categories of ownership: SOEs, FOEs, collective enterprises, household enterprises, and POEs. Joint-venture enterprises (JVEs) are the preferred entry mode in the early phases of establishing enterprises that will eventually become FOEs once foreign partners, SMEs as well as multinational companies (MNCs), have sufficient access to local markets (Truong 1998). Through SOEs, the state retains a significant role in the economy. It is estimated SOEs account for approximately 40 per cent of total GDP, with 42 per cent from the non-state sector (household enterprises and POEs), and 18 per cent from FOEs in 2009 (GSO 2010; Vietnam News 2011).

As 'pillars' of the economy, SOEs enjoy favourable operating conditions and privileges, such as preferred access to credit, land use, and markets. There were about 12,500 SOEs in 1990, declining to 5,600 in 2001 and 2,100 in 2006 as a result of restructuring and equitization. About 950 more SOEs were planned to be equitized in 2010, leaving 554 SOEs, including 26 large-scale economic groups and corporations (Do and Truong 2009). However, equitization did not proceed according to plan. By 2010 there were still about 1,473 SOEs. Also, the state continues its influence by holding majority shares in equitized enterprises (Brown 2011), many of them reappearing in the form of joint-stock enterprises (JSEs).

SOEs can be characterized as bureaucratic, with many layers, duplicated functions, and excessive staffing, especially the ten groups or corporations (in energy, banking, transport, shipbuilding, telecommunications, oil, coal, etc.) operating on the South Korean *chaebol* model (Do and Truong 2009). The majority of SOEs lose money, with heavy debts and poor governance as a result of corruption and nepotism and mismanagement (Wright and Nguyen 2000). FOEs are seen to operate more effectively. In a recently published report on the VNR500 list of Vietnam's biggest firms, FOEs were ranked the most effective with return-on-assets (ROA) of over 13 per cent, but while more than double that of SOEs (5.2 %), it was also more than quadruple that of POEs (2.5 %) (VietNamNet 2010).

POEs are considered the engines of growth for the economy, despite unfavourable tax and regulations. Since the introduction of the first Enterprise Law in 2000, POEs increased quickly, from 49,000 in 1999 to 254,000 in 2006 and 520,000 in 2010 (Pham 2010c). Their contribution to the economy continued to grow from 2004, and by 2009 accounted for 41.1 per cent of GDP, about 5 per cent more than SOEs and 20 per cent more than FOEs (Business Insider 2011b). About two-thirds of listed companies and a substantial number of POEs are family-run or start-up businesses often lacking the necessary capital and managerial skills to be competitive in domestic and international markets. More than 80 per cent of POEs have capital under VND5 billion (about US$250,000) and 87 per cent have fewer than 50 employees (Le 2010). Nevertheless, POEs can be resilient (Harvie 2004), with self-motivated and young entrepreneurs who can be more receptive towards adopting technologies in production and innovative management methods.

Domestic and foreign investors have the right to operate businesses under various forms, such as limited-liability companies (LLCs), shareholding companies, proprietors, private enterprises, partnerships, cooperatives, and joint ventures. In particular, both the Company Law and the Law on Private Enterprises in 1990 followed corporate legal principles from Anglo-American jurisdictions. In preparation for WTO member-ship, the 2005 Enterprise Law added new dimensions to the existing legal framework and in effect formed the foundation of the Vietnamese corporate governance system.

Under the Enterprise Law, LLCs are classified into two forms: (i) two or more share-holders, and (ii) single member. The law provides different internal governance struc-tures for LLCs, defining different tasks between the Council of Members (CM, *hoi dong thanh vien*), CEO (*giam doc or tong giam doc*), and board of supervisors (BS, *ban kiem soat*). However, the law does not state the owner as a corporate decision-making body in the governance structure, which may result in the potential interference of the owner, especially the government agency as the sole owner of SOEs, in company management (Bui and Nunoi 2008). In addition, the law does not provide any rules for supervision mechanisms, which makes company internal governance structures lack flexibility, effi-ciency, and accountability (Bui and Nunoi 2008).

In effect, equitization did not result in much change in corporate governance; while a part of ownership (in the form of shares) was transferred to employees and manage-ment, the state retained a substantial share, with practically no change in new manage-ment teams or participation of strategic investors (Sjoholm 2006). For example, at its peak in 2004 the number of equitized enterprises grew to 715 from 123 in 1998, but state ownership stakes of equal and over 50 per cent in these new JSEs also increased from 12 to 42 per cent (Masina 2010).

Generally, corporate governance remains a new concept, alien to many in Vietnam. In a survey of 85 large local enterprises, fewer than 25 per cent of executives believed that business people in Vietnam understood the basic concepts and principles of corporate governance. The executives also revealed that there was still confusion over the differ-ence between corporate governance and operational governance (Vietnam Chamber of Commerce and Industry 2005). Companies need to improve corporate governance to ensure market transparency, investor protection, and effective management in order to ensure better development of the securities market (Le and Walker 2008).

## INTERNAL STRUCTURE OF THE FIRM

Organizations typically tend to be hierarchical in structure and patriarchal in operation (Truong and Nguyen 2002) and have task specialization. Being deeply rooted in the cen-trally planned system for many decades, firms still bear characteristics of 'mechanistic' organizations, with centralized decision-making, complex structures with many layers and departments, task duplication, and cumbersome procedures. In general, the gov-ernance structures and management of SOEs appear more bulky and less effective than those of FOEs and POEs of the same size and business coverage (Bui 2006).

Many large SOEs and centrally managed corporations opt for matrix structures, while small POEs are organized around functions and focused markets. Functions deemed strategically sensitive, such as finance and human resource management (HRM), are centralized and/or dealt with directly by top management. FOEs often pattern their branch organizations after corporate matrix/hybrid structures on a smaller scale, depending on line of business, often centralized at the top (Ren 2010).

Decisions are usually generated at the top and communication flows one way, down through organizational levels. Participation, especially in strategic matters, is often not encouraged or practised, although discussions and ideas are sometimes allowed in the implementation phase. Nevertheless, even SOEs are becoming more 'organic' to respond more quickly to market conditions.

Status is important in the business community (reflecting societal values), and respect is given to superiors and senior colleagues (Communicaid 2009). Status is obtained with age and education and in many cases relationships and connections. Titles are particularly important and are often used as a practical way of 'favour distribution' among 'followers'. However, abuse of this practice can make organizations difficult to manage. In SOEs, where 'mentor–protégé' relationships are common, executives and managers are appointed from among CPV members for fixed five-year terms, making them loyal to their mentors rather than their organizations. This 'patronage politics' is displacing the previous, more consensual, system (Bland 2011a). In POEs the owner is, in many cases, also the CEO and appointments and promotions can be based more on merit and the qualities of candidates, although nepotism also occurs, especially in family-owned companies.

As well as the Confucian heritage, there is strong Western influence in the management and leadership styles of organizations as a consequence of long foreign intervention (Truong 2006). On a comparative basis, Vietnamese organizations are seemingly more centralized at the top and managers are often reluctant to delegate authority down the line, typical characteristics of a socialist system and family-owned SMEs. One survey found that FOEs and joint ventures (many of them having SOE business partners) were more 'bureaucratic' and 'conservative' than POEs, while POEs ranked higher in 'participative' and 'entrepreneurial' aspects of management (Truong and Nguyen 2002). Types of enterprises also differed widely in leadership style. In particular, SOEs and JVs were higher in 'close supervision' and lower on 'giving freedom to subordinates', 'consulting subordinates' opinions' and 'delegation of authority to subordinates', as compared to POEs (Truong and Nguyen 2002). In this regard, the 2010–2012 World Economic Forum report ranks Vietnam 95th out of 142 countries on 'willingness to delegate authority', compared to Malaysia (14th), Singapore (21st), Indonesia (56th), Philippines (33rd), Thailand (77th), and China (54th). Hence, it is understandable that most important decisions concerning strategic planning, financial management, and HRM (including resourcing and development) are the prerogative of top management (Schwab 2011).

# Employment Relations

To deal with the new conditions post-*doi moi* reform, the Trade Union Law was adopted in 1990. This foresaw a tripartite relationship of the three key actors (state, trade union, employers' organizations) to resolve industrial disputes. A Labour Code was introduced in 1994 on key issues of employment practice, labour standards, and working conditions (ILO 2010).

The Vietnam General Confederation of Labour (VGCL, *Tong lien doan lao dong Viet Nam*) is the sole trade union, entrusted with the task of protecting the interests of the working class and general public (Clark and Pringle 2011). Officially, the basic functions of the VGCL are to defend the legitimate rights of workers, provide training and education to members, and help settle disputes. However, it is under the direct leadership of the CPV, with its chair often a member of the CPV's Central Committee. Union branches are expected to play a crucial role in the operations of organizations, together with the CPV's cell and representatives of other mass organizations, such as the Youth and Women's Unions (Truong et al. 2008).

Despite the formal 'closed shop' character, only about 20 per cent of enterprises are unionized and total membership density has fallen from nearly 86 per cent in 2000 to 67 per cent in 2005 (Truong et al. 2008). VGCL representation has been declining, partly due to failure to deliver in industrial disputes and because collective bargaining is not a practice used as an official device to regulate employment relations. FOEs often opt for works councils to deal directly with emerging issues, without union intervention.

In reality the tripartite consultation mechanism (represented by the National Labour Relations Committee) has failed to deliver on collective bargaining and industrial conflicts (Yoon 2009), for two reasons. First, the Vietnam Cooperative Alliance (VCA, *Lien hiep Hop tac xa Vietnam*) and Vietnam Chamber of Commerce and Industry (VCCI, *Phong Thuong mai va Cong nghiep Viet Nam*), which represent the employers' organizations, are semi-state organs affiliated with the Vietnam Father Front, a liaison body between the mass organizations and CPV (Cornell University ILR School 2002). Second, the representational gap between union and rank-and-file workers has also contributed. Basic union tasks are often taken over by enterprise human-resource managers, producing an emerging informal system to which employees resort when they feel that formal channels are not representing them. This growth of informality has led to employee turnover and labour shortages as workers react to poor pay and working conditions and the absence of a means to improve them (United Nations Vietnam 2010).

Industrial disputes, especially in the form of wildcat strikes, have been increasing. During 2000–2010, about 5,000 unofficial strikes without the VGCL's involvement were reported (ILO 2010), mainly over inappropriate wages, unpaid bonuses/allowances for special occasions, unfulfilled contributions to social insurance, and working conditions (Truong et al 2008; Tran and Coleman 2010). Full employment, a typical 'iron rice bowl' socialist practice, has been almost dismantled in all types of enterprises (Le et al. 2006), except SOEs. The minimum wage of VND830,000 (about US$47) to VND 1,270,000 (about US$65), recently fixed by the government to make it competitive to foreign investors, actually only covers 60–65 per cent of basic living costs, depending on location (Asian News Network 2010).

In many aspects Vietnam does not follow market rules on prices and wages and lacks a complete and consistent wage policy (Pham 2010a). The Labour Code and Trade Union

Law has failed to meet employment relations changes. Typical deficiencies in the system include low understanding of employment relations, lack of collective bargaining (especially in POEs and FOEs) (Luu 2011), and failure to protect workers' interests. Only a few enterprises have collective bargaining agreements, since the VGCL's ability to effectively bargain with management is handicapped by the fact that at many enterprises, union representatives are also human resource staff.

In anticipation of potential problems from an FDI surge, Vietnam introduced new mechanisms in 1994 for the resolution of collective disputes under the Labour Code, which provides for the use of strikes as a last resort. In reality the VGCL often fails in its role as workers' champion, especially when workers go on strike in difficult times (Clark 2006). The growth of strikes has led unions to pay increasing attention to employment relations issues, but responses are often slow and inconsistent. Unions show little inclination or ability to stand up to employers on behalf of their members, while workers show a preference for direct action (Clark et al. 2007). As an alternative to its traditional task, it is suggested that the VGCL mobilize its pro-labour press to play a mediating role among state agencies, union branches, and management (Tran 2007).

# EDUCATION AND SKILLS FORMATION

With a Confucian heritage and high expectations for the future, there is a strong commitment to education and human resource development (HRD). The country is rich in terms of people, having a large and young population of 87 million (in 2009), with 47 per cent between 15 and 34 years old and an adult literacy rate of 90.3 per cent (UNDP 2009). The Human Development Index Trends 1980–2010 includes Vietnam in the 'Medium Human Development' category (ranked 113th out of 169 countries), with a human development index (HDI) value of 0.572, compared to 0.407 in 1990 (UNDP 2010). In 2008 education accounted for approximately 20 per cent of total state budget expenditure and 5.5 per cent of GDP (Runckel 2009). However, the quality of output remains doubtful and the dearth of skilled labour remains acute, despite expenditure of about 6 per cent of the 2006 national budget on vocational and professional training (Hong 2008).

In quantitative terms, Vietnam has been relatively successful in widening the educational system from one reserved for the elite (World Bank 2008). In 2010 there were 409 higher education institutions (universities and colleges), 307 of which were established post 2000. Some 40 provinces (of 58 provinces and five centrally governed cities) now have a university and 60 provinces and cities have a college (VuVan 2010). However, many were established without proper infrastructure, faculty, or system quality control (Vu 2008). Official targets aim at 573 higher education institutions and 400 students per 10,000 (up from 195 in 2010) in 2020 (Nguyen 2011).

In the 2009–10 academic year there were 15 million students at all levels; 7.4 million female (49 percent), 6.9 million in primary education (46 per cent), and 8.1 million in high-school education (54 per cent). There were over 1.9 million students in higher education, compared with just 162,000 (49.9 per cent of them female) in 1993 (World Bank 2008; MOET 2011). About one-quarter (25.4 per cent) received some professional training in 2006 (Hong 2008). The drop-out ratio is high, especially at middle-education level. In 2006, only around 55 per cent finished high school (Hong 2008).

Overall, the education and training system is facing several issues, such as outdated curricula, neglect of vocational training, and lack of linkage with teaching and research activities. Labour force quality remains low and many have to be retrained to fit job requirements (Truong et al. 2010). About 60 per cent of young college graduates needed to be retrained for at least 6–12 months after recruitment (NUFFIC 2010). According to WEF criteria, the Vietnam's low competitiveness in 2011 (65th of 142 countries) is a combination of several related factors, such as quality of educational system (ranked 69th), availability of latest technologies (133rd), firm-level technology absorption (88th), capacity for innovation (58th), quality of scientific research institutions (74th), university–industry collaboration in R&D (82nd), and availability of scientists and engineers (66th) (Schwab 2011).

Attempts have been made to develop skills. For instance, a comprehensive HRD strategy concentrated on enhancing the skills of three groups: public servants and policy-makers, entrepreneurs, and workers (Ministry of Labour, Invalids, and Social Affairs 2006). Nevertheless, there remains a serious input–output mismatch between what education and training institutions offer (curricula) and what industry needs (requirements).

The training programmes and forms provided vary among enterprises, depending on their understanding of the role of human capital to their success and the strategic role of HRM departments in organizations (Truong and Hoang 1998; Le and Truong 2005a, 2005b; Zhu et al. 2008). In relation to this, the WEF score on 'extent of staff training' in Vietnam (107th of 142 countries) is surprisingly low compared with ASEAN counterparts such as Singapore (4th), Malaysia (9th), Philippines (34th), Indonesia (52nd), Thailand (56th) and even Cambodia (97th).

Local enterprises are focusing on improving competitiveness by investing more in HRD (Le and Truong 2005b; Zhu et al. 2008). Large MNCs are also driving demand for a more skilled workforce. The service sector has great potential, especially in information and communication technology, tourism, logistics management, finance, and banking, but 10–15,000 skilled people need to be trained in these fields annually, though at current training capacity, only 40–60 per cent of this demand can be met (NUFFIC 2010).

Foreign workers have been used to fill skills gaps. Their number has risen from 12,602 in 2004 to 21,117 in 2005 and 34,000 in 2007. Only 41.2 per cent filled managerial and professional positions, while half were from Asia and 14 per cent from Europe (Hong 2008). The intellectual resources of overseas Vietnamese professionals—about 300,000 of a total 3.6 million spread over 90 countries, many qualified in technology and management—could be tapped (Truong et al. 2010; Deutsch Presse-Agentur 2012).

The private sector is active, with increasing numbers of new higher-education institutions and professional training centres. In the 2009–2010 academic year, the number of private higher-education institutions increased to 76, 20 per cent of the total (MOET

2011). Cooperation programmes with foreign institutions (especially at postgraduate levels) have been approved and foreign universities encouraged to participate (e.g. RMIT from Australia, British University Vietnam, Vietnamese-German University). However, quality control and affordability, as well as the inherent bureaucracy of the system, are key issues in the operation of these institutions.

At the micro-level, HRD is considered necessary (Le and Truong 2005b). Yet the business community has divergent views and practices regarding the effectiveness of training. While FOCs see HRD as a motivational tool to make employees capable of meeting performance standards and as a high and quick return on investment, SOEs and POEs still consider HRD as an expense and hence tend to keep budgets small (Truong et al. 2008). A survey (of 166 enterprises across various sectors) also found that on-the-job methods of training were adopted equally by different types of enterprises, while off-the-job methods were less preferred by FOEs than by SOEs (Le and Truong 2005b). Furthermore, due to budget constraints, most SMEs relied only on informal training, whereas, compared with FOEs, SOEs and POEs rarely sent people abroad, financed self-study, or rotated jobs (Truong and Le 2004).

## INTER-COMPANY RELATIONS

Transfer of technology and management from FIEs to local partners and self-improvement by local organizations to improve productivity and quality of products and services is possible. There are associations organized around professions (e.g. Human Resources Professionals, Vietnam Young Entrepreneurs) and industries (e.g. Shrimp Farmers, Footwear, Garments, Coffee), but these exist more in formality than substance, with no concrete activities to foster inter-company relations among local enterprises.

In the early phase of economic development, because the level of technology and management was low, domestic organizations were eager to learn from practical experience and best practices from foreign counterparts. Domestic organizations gradually developed and spread success stories within their own organizations and among the local business community.

However, the propensity of the learning and applying process varies between organizational types. The influx of foreign firms has brought managerial expertise and Western HRM practices. In 1992 the first wave of restructured SOEs led to a new genre of mixed-ownership companies, in the hope that they would prosper after the ownership change through improved management (Le and Truong 2005b).

Changes have not occurred in many organizations, due to their fear of losing their own identity and competitive advantages. The state also insists that models should be 'typically Vietnamese', reflecting genuine Vietnamese characteristics (Le et al. 2006). At the micro-level, 'first-mover' enterprises are fearful of their creative/innovative ideas and products being imitated or duplicated by competitors in the absence of effective protection mechanisms for intellectual property and copyright (Huong 2011).

A culture favouring 'right relationships' (*quan he*) can evolve and develop into not only corruption as a result of nepotism, cronyism, and camaraderie (Le et al. 2006; Pei 2012), but also self-protection and isolation. These traits could prevent enterprises from forming strategic alliances with counterparts. SOEs prefer business-to-business (B2B), making optimal benefits from the 'quota distribution' system, while POEs are more in favour of business-to-customer (B2C) marketing methods to directly engage target markets. On the other hand, a supply value-chain system built on a cooperative and synergetic partnership between key players (e.g. producers, suppliers, and distributors) is yet to develop among local enterprises to help them compete internationally under a unified 'made-in-Vietnam' brand umbrella and to prevent such blunders as 'dumping' cases (e.g. catfish, footwear, and gas lighters in the USA and EU) due to lack of knowledge of foreign markets (Vietnam Business 2011).

In fact, supply-chain management is still in the early phase of development (Dinh 2011). In this regard, Vietnam scores relatively low on 'value-chain breadth' (101st of 142 countries) compared to Singapore (10th), Malaysia (23rd), Indonesia (29th), Thailand (36th), Philippines (67th), and China (45th) in the WEF Global Competitiveness Report (Schwab 2011). The importance of developing integrated supply-chain networks has been made (Vo 2011; Dinh 2011) and several professional institutions (e.g. Vietnam Supply Chain) and journals (e.g. *Tap Chi Chuoi Cung Ung Viet Nam*) have been set up to assist local enterprises in this respect.

# SOCIAL CAPITAL

Vietnam is a relationship-based society where trust is key in business culture and practice, albeit not fully institutionalized. The level of interpersonal trust is fairly high. For example, 41 per cent of local people say they trust their fellow citizens (Norlund 2006). There is a relatively conservative attitude towards foreigners, as the Vietnamese may see Westerners' individual assertiveness and directness as arrogant and tactless (Ashwill and Thai 2004).

In business a trust-testing approach is followed to gauge the amount of trust to put in a person, especially foreigners. Therefore, expectations for effective shortcuts to employee involvement and empowerment can be deemed naïve (Le et al. 2006). Compared to their ASEAN counterparts, Vietnamese managers give equal weight to personal qualities (dependable, trustworthy, honest, responsible) as to managerial behaviours (strategic vision, logical problem-solving, consistent decision-making), with a higher emphasis on being 'honest' in business relationships (Truong et al. 1998). In business, these networks are a matter of 'social security' and even of survival, hence 'sponsorship' is important in opening up a point of entry and building a viable business partnership (Ashwill and Thai 2004).

Yet, while *quan he* might work out positively, especially in harnessing long-term mutual benefits and cultivating trust and personal relationships (Yeung and Tung 1996), it can also develop into corruption (as a result of nepotism and cronyism) in the absence of an effective legal system and social control norms (Vuong 2005, Le et al. 2006). Lack of institutionalized trust may lead to 'collective responsibility' (*trach nhiem tap the*), in which individuals feel safer and are not concerned about personal accountability.

Business relationships are yet to be institutionalized, as business is still relatively formal and it usually takes time to build lasting trust. People prefer doing business based on personal relationships and through informal, rather than formal, talks (HR Solutions Vietnam 2010). This is visible, for instance, in the tendency to spend much time on trust-building with new business partners, especially foreigners, before transactions go ahead (Communicaid 2009).

As competition has intensified, trust among business partners needs to be further institutionalized, together with a competent arbitration mechanism to resolve conflicts. Fewer than a half of companies believe the court system is fair or impartial (World Bank 2010), as it was corrupt with political interference, the main reason preventing use of the courts to resolve business disputes (Global Integrity 2009; Malesky 2010). On average it takes 34 procedures and 295 days, at a cost of 28.5 per cent of the claim, to enforce a contract through the courts (World Bank 2011). Nevertheless, a recent survey supports the general assumption that trust can be intentionally developed to facilitate inter-firm relationships, especially in the private sector (Nguyen and Jerman 2009).

# Institutional Complementarities

Vietnam is a country of contradictions and compromises, given the complexities of its political and economic system. Some complementarities, which need to be further institutionalized, are summarized.

1. The party, state (government) and business (SOEs) alliance, characterized by CPV dominance, concentration at the top and collective responsibility, are linked to quick decision-making, but also negatively affect the quality of implementation, such as with favouritism, cronyism, red tape, and corruption.
2. The informal and 'underground' economy has functioned as an alternative for capital resources, especially to POEs.
3. FOEs have provided effective business models, with some limited transference of state-of-the art operations to local enterprises (SOEs and POEs alike).
4. The need for a skilled workforce has been partly resolved by a 'brain gain' policy to exploit the capital resources of overseas Vietnamese.

5. The involvement of foreign institutions in development and delivery has contributed to improving the overall quality of education and training and the demand for managers and professionals.

6. In employment relations, the use of the media as a temporary solution has partly helped relieve workers' grievances in the face of labour disputes in which unions have failed to act.

# EVOLUTIONARY DYNAMICS

After two decades of steady growth, Vietnam is at a crossroads, given the context of the post-2008 global economic crisis and overheating economy. Growth has been slowing and critical fundamentals for a sustainable economy are yet to be developed. Corruption as a result of 'capitalist cronyism' (Roberts 2010) or 'crony compitalism' (Pei 2012) and related vested interests is rampant, especially in SOEs; the debt-to-GDP ratio and living conditions have worsened due to soaring inflation underpinning a lack of consistent monetary policies and poor governance (Pham 2010b; Economist Intelligence Unit 2011). In 2009–2011 Vietnam led the region in having the highest inflation rate, a growing budget deficit and the weakest currency and sovereign risk rating (Koh 2011; Le 2011).

The next phase of development involves several issues. To begin with, the 'market economy with socialist orientation' (*kinh te thi truong dinh huong xa hoi chu nghia*) model (To and Hoang 2007) seems to be losing momentum (Quynh 2010; Vu 2010a; Nguyen 2011a). Second, SOEs have failed to perform as 'pillars of the economy', while POEs are growing (Sjoholm 2006; Vu 2009; Fuller 2011). Third, efforts to integrate into the global economy with comparatively moderate capacity based mainly on low-cost, low-tech manufacturing (with low local content and value-added), reliance on external resources, especially technology and R&D and exports (with huge trade deficits, mainly with China), and a poor global supply chain (Tencati et al. 2010), have not paid off (Truong et al. 2010). Fourth, to continue the projected strong growth for the next decade, it is imperative that Vietnam works to raise labour productivity (Breu et al 2012). Fifth, the focus on achieving fast growth (quantitative) has become an impediment to achieving more sustainable development (qualitative) (Tran 2008).

Vietnam remains an excellent economic prospect (Bremmer 2010; Brown 2011), recognized as one of the promising emerging economies of the CIVETS (Colombia, Indonesia, Vietnam, Egypt, Turkey, and South Africa) club, and benchmarked with the MIT (Malaysia, Indonesia, and Thailand) group in Asia for its resilience in the post-2008 financial crisis. In 2010 Vietnam was ranked among the ten most improved economies in terms of ease of doing business (78th of 183 countries) (IFC/WB 2011). Nevertheless, the gap with neighbours remains. The WEF Competitiveness Index 2010–12 Report ranked Vietnam 65th of 142 countries, a much lower position compared to

MIT countries (Malaysia 21st, Indonesia 46th, Thailand 39th), especially in such critical areas as 'Innovation and Business Sophistication' (Schwab 2011).

To a large extent, the future of Vietnam's state capitalism will greatly depend on its capacity to respond to challenges as noted and to build good governance and human capital (Rowley and Truong 2009b; Vu 2010). As such, Vietnam needs to also focus on 'institutional development' rather than just 'organizational development' in the form of adding and adjusting laws, restructuring SOEs, fighting corruption, etc. The drive towards more sustainable development will require a clearer ideological stand on the ambivalence of the 'socialism-capitalism' cohabitation, a long-term, clear-cut and realizable vision and a consistent implementation roadmap, not the 'amateurish' (Bremmer 2010) 'poor' government (Koh 2011) with a 'muddled approach' (Du Venage 2011), or the 'damage control mode' (Cain 2012) of current practice.

The experience gained in the last few decades has brought a new realism and greater economic resilience and maturity that could help Vietnam. The CPV recognizes the need for political restructuring (Le 2011) to foster sustainable economic growth (e.g. to combat rising inequality and corruption), but will never 'waver' from its socialist system.

# CONCLUSION

This chapter has examined the development and operation of the business system in Vietnam. After more than two decades of experimentation, Vietnam's economy still seems to be more a 'coordinated market economy' than a 'liberal market economy', according to the Hall and Soskice definition (2001). It remains to be seen whether the Vietnamese development model ('the Vietnamese miracle') will succeed (Cain 2012).

As described here, Vietnam's state capitalism is at a turning point. The challenges ahead involve both structural and strategic change. Structural change (immediate and short term) requires an overhaul of capacity at the national level (e.g. financial system and governance), a redefinition of internal (e.g. between organizations) and external (e.g. employment relations) factors, and above all a comprehensive HRD plan to improve competitiveness. The strategic transformation (long term) is more difficult to realize, as it would mean a departure of the CPV from its socialist perspective. More critically, civil society has to be equally developed in socio-cultural and educational terms to catch up with economic advances.

A developed and self-functioning civil society (*xa hoi dan su*) in tandem with good governance in the context of a state of rule of law (*nha nuoc phap quyen*) at the macro-level and effective management at the micro-level could help Vietnam overcome key structural challenges to more sustainable development. As the CPV will need economic success to justify its political legitimacy (Thayer 2009), it does not matter much whether it is labelled a 'socialist-oriented market economy', 'market socialism', or a 'market economy with Vietnamese character', provided that the new and adjusted model, a kind of 'grassroots capitalism' (Kotkin 2011), helps the country achieve the status of 'an industrialized country' as promised by the end of this decade.

## REFERENCES

Asian Development Bank (2011). *Viet Nam's Poverty Reduction, Development: A Regional Success Story*. Manila, Asian Development Bank.

Asian News Network (2010). 'Proposed Minimum Wage in Viet Nam too low'. Retrieved 20 September 2010 from <http://www.asianewsnet.net/home/news.php?id=14415&sec=2>.

Ashwill, M. A. and N. D. Thai (2004). *Vietnam Today: A Guide to a Nation at a Crossroads*. Boston, International Press.

Bland, B. (2011a). 'Vietnam: Grappling with Change'. *Financial Times*. Retrieved 24 November 2011 from <http://blogs.ft.com/beyond-brics/2011/11/24/vietnam-grappling-with-change/#axzz1eeXRUeWr>.

—— (2011b). 'Vietnam embarks on Banking Reform'. *Financial Times*. Retrieved 7 December 2011 from <http://blogs.ft.com/beyond-brics/2011/12/07/vietnam-embarks-on-banking-reform/#axzz22OmrQ7sl>.

—— (2012). 'Vietnam outlines Banking System Overhaul'. *Financial Times*. Retrieved 5 March 2012 from <http://www.ft.com/intl/cms/s/0/f91a89e0-66b5-11e1-9d4e-00144feabdc0.html#axzz22OoFBBA6>.

Bremmer, I. (2010). 'The Rise of Vietnam'. *EurAsia*, 25 February. Retrieved 6 August 2012 from http://eurasia.foreignpolicy.com/category/topic/development.

Breu, M., R. Dobbs, J. Remes, D. Skilling, and K. Jinwook (2012). *Sustaining Vietnam's Growth: the Productivity Challenge*. Washington, DC, McKinsey Global Institute.

Brown, D. (2011). 'Vietnam Change Courses', *Asian Times*, 12 April. Retrieved 8 December 2011 from www.atimes.com/atimes/ . . . Asia/MD12Ae01.html.

Bui, X. H. (2006). 'Vietnam Company Law: The Development of Corporate Governance Issues'. *Bond Law Review 18*(1): 22–44.

—— and C. Nunoi (2008). 'Corporate Governance in Vietnam: a System in Transition'. *Hitotsubashi Journal of Commerce and Management 42*(1): 45–65.

Business Insider (2011a). 'Will the Default of a Vietnamese State-Owned Company be the Black Swan of 2011?' Retrieved 4 January 2011 from <http://articles.businessinsider.com/2011-01-04/markets/30053505_1_bad-debts-crisis-hard-landing>.

—— (2011b). 'The Development of Small and Medium Enterprises in Vietnam'. Retrieved 26 January 2011 from <http://businessinsides.com/development-vietnam-small-medium-enterprises.html>.

*Business Times* (2010). 'Foreign Banks in Vietnam Compete Silently but Fiercely'. Retrieved 11 August 2010 from <http://businesstimes.com.vn/foreign-banks-in-vietnam-compete-silently-but-fiercely>.

Cain, G. (2012). 'The End of the Vietnamese Miracle: So much for the next Asian Success Story'. *Foreign Policy*. Retrieved 11 July 2012 from <http://www.foreignpolicy.com/articles/2012/07/11/the_end_of_the_vietnamese_miracle>.

Chu, K. (2010). 'Vietnam's Stock Market has come far in its first 10 Years', *USA Today*. Retrieved 23 August 2010 from <http://www.usatoday.com/money/markets/2010-08-22-vietnam-stocks_N.htm>.

Clark, S. (2006). 'The Changing Character of Strikes in Vietnam'. *Post-Communist Economies* *18*(3): 345–361.

—— and T. Pringle (2011). *Trade Unions in Russia, China, and Vietnam*. London, Palgrave Macmillan.

—— C. H. Lee and Q. C. Do (2007). 'From Rights to Interests: the Challenge of Industrial Relations in Vietnam'. *Journal of Industrial Relations 49*(4): 545–568.

Communicaid (2009). 'Doing Business in Vietnam: Vietnam Social and Business Culture'. Retrieved 26 July 2011 from <http://www.communicaid.com/access/pdf/library/culture/doing-business-in/Doing%20Business%20in20%Vietnam.pdf>.

Communist Party of Vietnam (2010). 'Vietnam's Development Goals, 2011-2020'. Retrieved 5 October 2011 from <http://www.cpv.org.vn/cpv/Modules/News_English/News_Detail_E.aspx?CN_ID=396692&CO_ID=30113>.

Cornell University ILR School (2002). *Foreign Labor Trends: Vietnam*. Federal Publications Paper 112. Washington DC, US Bureau of International Affairs.

*Dat Viet* (2011) 'Giam tang truong de cuu nen kinh te' (Reduce Economic Growth to save the Economy). Retrieved 24 September 2011 from <http://baodatviet.vn/Home/kinhte/Giam-tang-truong-de-cuu-nen-kinh-te/20119/169314.datviet>.

Deutsch Presse-Agentur (2012). 'Overseas Remittances to Vietnam rise 11 Percent in 2011'. Retrieved 2 January 2012 from <http://news.monstersandcritics.com/business/news/article_1683523.php/Overseas-remittances-to-Vietnam-rise-11-per-cent-in-2011>.

Dinh, T. P. (2011). 'Tan vo chuoi cung ung: tu huyet cua nen kinh te' (Disintegration of Supply Chain: the Death of the Economy). *Dien dan kinh te Viet Nam*, 18 July. Retrieved 6 August 2012 from <http://vef.vn/2011-07-17-tan-vo-chuoi-cung-ung-tu-huyet-cua-nen-kinh-te>.

Do, X. T. and Q. Truong (2009). 'The Changing Face of Public-sector Management in Vietnam'. In C. Rowley and Q. Truong, Eds., *The Changing Face of Vietnamese Management*: 187–220. London, Routledge.

Du Venage, G. (2011). 'Hasty Vietnam in a Hurry to catch up with its Neighbours', *The National*. Retrieved 13 April 2011 from <http://www.thenational.ae/thenationalconversation/industry-insights/economics/hasty-vietnam-in-a-hurry-to-catch-up-with-its-neighbours>.

Economist Intelligence Unit (2011). *Country Report: Vietnam*. London, Economic Intelligence Unit Ltd.

Fuller, T. (2011). 'Vietnam Confronts Economic Quagmire'. *New York Times*. Retrieved 9 February 2011 from <http://www.nytimes.com/2011/01/10/business/global/10iht-viet10.html?pagewanted=all>.

Global Integrity (2009). 'Global Integrity Report'. Retrieved 10 October 2011 from <http://report.globalintegrity.org/globalindex/results.cfm>.

GSO (General Statistics Office of Vietnam) (2010). 'Statistical Data'. Retrieved 13 August 2010 from <www.gso.gov.vn>.

Hall, P. A. and D. Soskice (2001). *Varieties of Capitalism*. New York, Oxford University Press.

Harvard Business School (2008). *Surviving a Crisis, Returning to Reform*. Policy Discussion Paper No. 2. Cambridge/Ho Chi Minh City: Fulbright Economic Teaching Programme.

Harvie, C. (2004). 'The Contribution of SMEs in the Economic Transition of Vietnam'. *Journal of International Business and Entrepreneurship Development 2*(2): 1–16.

Hong, L.T. (2008). 'Lao dong co ky nang: Lo hong nghiem trong trong phat trien o Viet Nam' (Skilled Labour: the Critical Hole in the Development of Vietnam). *Thoi dai moi* 13. Retrieved 5 January 2012 from <http://www.tapchithoidai.org/ThoiDai13/200813_HongLeTho_2.htm>.

HR Solutions Vietnam (2010). *HR Survival Guide for Foreign Managers in Vietnam*. Hanoi, HRSolutions-Vietnam.

Huong, X. (2011). 'Firms Encouraged to Apply Intellectual Property Rights', *VietNamNews*. Retrieved 7 May 2010 from <http://vietnamnews.vnagency.com.vn/in-bai/211039/firms-encouraged-to-apply-intellectual-property-rights.html>.

IFC/World Bank (2011). 'Doing Business: Measuring Business Regulations'. Retrieved 5 October 2011 from <http://www.doingbusiness.org/rankings>.

ILO (International Labour Organisation) (2010). 'Vietnam Commits to Strengthening Legal Frameworks for Employer-Worker Negotiations'. Retrieved 6 October 2011 from http://www.ilo.org/asia/info/public/pr/lang--eng/WCMS_125649/index.htm.

IMF (2007). 'Vietnam: Selected Issues'. IMF Country Report No. 07/385. Retrieved 18 February 2009 from <http://www.imf.org/external/pubs/ft/scr/2007/cr07385.pdf>.

Koh, D. (2011). 'Vietnam's Poor Government'. Retrieved 14 March 2011 from http://web1.iseas.edu.sg/?p=2786.

Kotkin, J. (2011). 'Hanoi's Underground Capitalism', *Forbes*. Retrieved 29 March 2011 from <http://www.forbes.com/sites/megacities/2011/03/29/hanois-underground-capitalism/>.

Kovsted, J., J. Rand, F. Tarp, D. T. Nguyen, V. H. Nguyen, and M. T. Ta (2003). *Financial Sector Reforms in Vietnam: Selected Issues and Problems*. Discussion Paper No. 0301. Hanoi, Central Institute for Economic Management/Nordic Institute of Asian Studies.

Le, C. T. and Q. Truong (2005a). 'Antecedents and Consequences of Dimensions of Human Resource Management Practices in Vietnam'. *International Journal of Human Resource Management*, 16: 1830–1846.

—— and Q. Truong (2005b). 'Human Resource Management Practices in a Transitional Economy: A Comparative Study of Enterprise Ownership Forms in Vietnam'. *Asian Pacific Business Review* 11(1): 25–47.

—— C. Rowley, Q. Truong and M. Warner (2006). 'To What Extent can Management Practices be Transferred between Countries: The Case of Human Resource Management in Vietnam'. *Journal of World Business 42*(1): 113–127.

Le, D. B. (2010). *Quick Review of Private Quality through Ten Years Implementation of the Enterprise Law*. Taskforce Report. Hanoi, CIEM.

Le, M. T. and G. Walker (2008). 'Corporate Governance of Listed Companies in Vietnam'. *Bond Law Review 20*(2): 1–80.

Le, S. L. (2011). 'Vietnam's State Capitalism and the Rise of Southeast Asia'. Bauer Global Studies. Retrieved 16 February 2011 from <http://www.bauerglobalstudies.org/archives/vietnam%E2%80%99s-state-capitalism-and-the-rise-of-southeast-asia>.

Leung, S. (2008). 'Vietnam's Banks under Scrutiny'. *East Asia Forum*. Retrieved 24 November 2011 from <http://www.eastasiaforum.org/2008/11/24/vietnams-banking-system-under-scrutiny>.

—— (2009). 'Banking and Financial Sector Reforms in Vietnam'. *ASEAN Economic Bulletin* 26(1): 44–57.

Luu, H. (2011). 'Collective Employment Agreement: Universal Application needed', *Vietnam Business Forum*. Retrieved 5 August 2011 from <http://www.vccinews.com/news_detail.asp?news_id=23852>.

Malesky, E., Ed. (2010). *The Vietnam Provincial Competitiveness Index 2010: Promoting Economic Governance & Sustainable Investment*. USAID/VNCI Policy Paper 5, Hanoi, USAID.

Massmann, O. and C. Rowley (2009). 'The Changing Face of Financial Market Management in Vietnam'. In C. Rowley and Q. Truong, Eds., *The Changing Face of Vietnamese Management*: 93–127. London, Routledge.

Masina, P. (2006). *Vietnam's Development Strategies*. Oxford, Routledge.

—— (2010). *Vietnam between Developmental State and Neoliberalism: the Case of the Industrial Sector*. Working Paper 1007, Department of Social Sciences, University of Naples.

Ministry of Labour, Invalids, and Social Affairs (2006). 'Labour and Social Issues emerging from Vietnam's Accession to the WTO'. Retrieved 10 November 2006 from http://www.worldbank.org/INTRANETTRADE/Resources/WBI-Training/Viet-labor_trao.pdf.

MOET (Ministry of Education and Training) (2011). 'So lieu thong ke giao duc dai hoc 2009–2010' (Statistics of Higher Education). Retrieved 29 June 2011 from <http://www.moet.gov.vn>.

Nguyen, D. C. (2008). *Corporate Governance in Vietnam: Regulations, Practices, and Problems*. Hanoi, CIEM/GTZ.

Nguyen, M. S. (2010). 'Van hoa phong bi' (The Envelope Culture), *Sai Gon Tiep thi*. Retrieved 15 November 2010 from http://sgtt.vn/Doi-the-ma-vui/132886/Van-hoa-phong-bi.html.

Nguyen, M. T. (2011). 'Nhung chuyen cot tu cua giao duc dai hoc' (Critical Issues of Higher Education). *VietNamNet*. Retrieved 26 October 2011 from <http://vietnamnet.vn/vn/giao-duc/45498/nhung-chuyen-cot-tu-cua-giao-duc-dai-hoc--p-2-.html>.

Nguyen, N. T., Q. Truong, and D. Buyens (2011). 'Training and Firm Performance in Economies in Transition: a Comparison between Vietnam and China'. *Asia Pacific Business Review 17*(1): 103–119.

Nguyen, Q. A. (2011b). 'Ky luc kieu hoi—mung va lo' (Record of Overseas Remittances—Happy and Worried), *Bee.Net.VN*. Retrieved 4 January 2011 from http://bee.net.vn/channel/4461/201101/Ky-luc-kieu-hoi-mung-va-lo-1785274.

Nguyen, T. (2011a). 'Doi moi mo hinh tang truong cua Viet Nam: van mo ho?' (Re-inventing the Growth Model of Vietnam: Still vague?), *VnEconomy*. Retrieved 14 March 2011 from <http://www.baomoi.com/Home/KinhTe/vneconomy.vn/Doi-moi-mo-hinh-tang-truong-cua-Viet-Nam-Van-mo-ho/5868291.epi>.

Nguyen, V. T. and R. Jerman (2009). 'Building Trust: Evidence from Vietnamese Entrepreneurs'. *Journal of Business Venturing 24*(2): 165–182.

Norlund, E., Ed. (2006). *An Initial Assessment of Civil Society Index*. Hanoi, Vietnam Institute of Development Studies.

NUFFIC (2010). *Trends in Vietnamese Education Reform*. Retrieved 25 August 2011 from <http://www.nesovietnam.com/dutch-organizations/general-market-information/trends-in-vietnamese-education-reform>.

Ohno, K. (2009). *Avoiding the Middle-income Trap: Renovating Industrial Policy Formulation in Vietnam*. Singapore, Institute of Southeast Asian Studies.

Painter, M. (2008). 'From Command Economy to Hollow State? Decentralization in Vietnam and China'. *Australian Journal of Public Administration 67*(1): 79–88.

Papin, P. and L. Passicousset (2010). *Vivre avec les Vietnamiens*. Paris, Editeur l'Archipel.

Pei, M. X. (2012). 'Remembering Deng in our Era of Crony Compitalism'. *Financial Times*. Retrieved 23 January 2012 from <http://www.ft.com/cms/s/0/98bba018-4386-11e1-adda-00144feab49a.html#axzz22m6qmiLX>.

Pham, A. T. (2010a). *The Returning Diaspora: Analyzing Overseas Vietnamese (Viet Kieu) Contribution Toward Vietnam's Economic Growth*. DEPOCEN Working Paper Series. London, London School of Economics.

Pham, H. (2010b). 'Viet Nam tranh rap khuon ve kinh te sang tao. (Vietnam should avoid Copy of Innovative Economy). *Dien dan Kinh te Viet Nam*. Retrieved 26 March 2011 from <http://vef.vn/2011-03-25-viet-nam-tranh-rap-khuon-ve-kinh-te-sang-tao>.

Pham, L. H. (2010c). *Signs of Industrial Relations Crisis in Vietnam: Poor Wage Bargaining, Labour Shortages and Strikes*. Report by National Labour Relations Committee, April 1-2. Hanoi, Central Institute for Economic Management.

Quynh, C. (2010). 'Vietnam Faces Challenges in Implementing Development Strategies', *Vietnam Business Forum*. Retrieved 23 September 2010 from <http://www.vccinews.com/news_detail.asp?news_id=21688>.

Redding, G. and M. A. Witt (2007). *The Future of Chinese Capitalism: Choices and Chances*. Oxford, Oxford University Press.

Ren, Y. (2010). 'Organisational Hierarchies and Decision-Making Process of Chinese Multinational Enterprises in Vietnam'. *Chinese Geographical Science* 20(1): 43–50.

Roberts, J. M. (2010). 'Cronyism: Undermining Economic Freedom and Prosperity around the World'. *Backgrounder* 2447, 9 August. Washington, DC, Heritage Foundation.

Rowley, C. and Q. Truong (2009a). 'Setting the Scene for the Changing Face of Management in Vietnam'. In C. Rowley and Q. Truong, Eds., *The Changing Face of Vietnamese Management*: 1–23. London, Routledge.

—— (2009b). 'The Changing Face of Vietnamese Management Revisited'. In C. Rowley and Q. Truong, Eds., *The Changing Face of Vietnamese Management*: 251–259. London, Routledge.

Runckel, C. (2009). 'Education in Vietnam'. Retrieved 8 August 2011 from <http://www.business-in-asia.com/vietnam/education_system_in_vietnam.html>.

Schwab, K., Ed. (2011). *The Global Competitiveness Report 2011-2012*. Geneva, World Economic Forum.

Sjoholm, F. (2006). *State-Owned Enterprises and Equitization in Vietnam*. EIJS Working Paper No. 228. Stockholm, European Institute of Japanese Studies/Stockholm School of Economics.

Stockbiz (2011) 'Vietnam's Stock Market Capitalization Value falls nearly 44tr dong in Three Months'. Retrieved 20 June 2011 from http://en.stockbiz.vn/News/2011/6/20/219276/vietnam-s-stock-market-capitalization-value-falls-nearly-44tr-dong-in-three-months.aspx.

Tencati, A., A. Russo, and V. Quaglia (2010). 'Sustainability along the Global Supply Chain: the Case of Vietnam'. *Social Responsibility Journal* 6(1): 1–17.

Thai, T. H. and M. O. Biallas (2007). *Vietnam: Capital Market Diagnostic Review*. Hanoi, IFC/MPDF.

Thayer, A.C. (2009). 'Political Legitimacy of Vietnam's One Party-State: Challenges and Responses'. *Journal of Current Southeast Asian Affairs* 28(4): 47–70.

Thecurrencynewshound (2011). 'Vietnam: Interest Rate Major Issue for 2011'. Retrieved 6 January 2011 from http://thecurrencynewshound.com/2011/01/06/vietnam-interest-rate-major-issue-for-2011.

To, X. D. and N. X. Hoang (2007). 'Nen kinh te thi truong dinh huong xa hoi chu nghia cua Viet Nam' (The Market Economy with Socialist Orientation of Vietnam), *Tap chi Cong san*. Retrieved 22 January 2007 from <http://www.tapchicongsan.org.vn/Home/kinh-te-thi-truong-XHCN/2007/2092/Nen-kinh-te-thi-truong-dinh-huong-xa-hoi-chu-nghia.aspx>.

Tran, A. N. (2007). 'The Third Sleeve: Emerging Labor Newspapers and the Response of the Labor Unions and the State to Workers' Resistance in Vietnam'. *Labor Studies Journal* 32(3): 257–279.

Tran, P. (2010). 'Ban ve co che xin-cho' (About the 'application-approval' Practice). *VnEconomy*. Retrieved 18 January 2010 from <http://www.baomoi.com/Ban-ve-co-che-xin--cho/108/3758555.epi>.

Tran, S. V. and B. Coleman (2010). 'Strikes and Resolutions to Strike Under Vietnamese Labour Law'. *International Trade Law 18*(2): 49–57.

Tran, V. T. (2008). 'Tu cai cach tiem tien den xay dung co che chat luong cao. Dieu kien de phat trien ben vung o Viet Nam' (From Gradual Reform to Building a High-quality Mechanism). *Thoi dai moi* 14. Retrieved 5 January 2012 from <http://www.tapchithoidai.org/ThoiDai14/200814_TranVanTho.htm>.

—— (2012). 'Bay thu nhap trung binh nhin tu cac nuoc ASEAN' (The Income Trap from the ASEAN Perspective), *Thoi Dai Moi, 24*(3): 48–78.

Transparency International (2010). 'Corruption Perceptions Index 2010 Results'. Retrieved 5 October 2011 from <http://www.transparency.org/policy_research/surveys_indices/cpi/2010/results>.

Truong, Q. (1998). 'A Case of Joint Ventures Failure: Procter & Gamble vs Phuong Dong in Vietnam'. *Journal of Euro-Asian Management 4*(2): 83–100.

—— (2006). 'Human Resource Management in Vietnam'. In S. Nankervis, S. Chatterjee and J. Coffrey, Eds., *Perspectives of Human Resource Management in Asia Pacific*: 231–252. Sydney, Pearson Education Australia.

—— and K. D. Hoang (1998). 'Human Resource Development in State-owned Enterprises in Vietnam'. *Research and Practice in Human Resource Management 6*(1): 85–103.

—— F. W. Swierczek and T. K. C. Dan (1998). 'Effective Leadership in Joint-ventures in Vietnam: A Cross-cultural Perspective'. *Journal of Organizational Change Management 11*(4): 357–372.

—— and T. V. Nguyen (2002). 'Management Styles and Organizational Effectiveness in Vietnam'. *Research and Practice in Human Resource Management 10*(2): 36–55.

—— C. T. Le (2004). 'HRM in Vietnam'. In P. Budhwar, Ed., *Managing Human Resources in Asia-Pacific*: 173–199. London, Routledge.

Truong, Q., C. T. Le, and C. Rowley (2008). 'The Changing Face of Human Resources in Vietnam'. In C. Rowley and S. Abdul-Rahman, Eds., *The Changing Face of Management in Southeast Asia*: 185–220. London, Routledge.

—— and B. I. J. M. van der Heijden (2009). 'The Changing Face of Human Resource Management in Vietnam'. In C. Rowley and Q. Truong, Eds., *The Changing Face of Vietnamese Management*: 24–49. London, Routledge.

—— and C. Rowley (2010). 'Globalisation, Competitiveness, and Human Resource Management in a Transitional Economy: The Case of Vietnam'. *International Journal of Business Studies 18*(1): 75–100.

UNDP (2009). 'Human Development Report'. Retrieved 2 August 2011 from <http://hdr.undp.org/en/media/HDR_2009_EN_Summary.pdf>.

—— (2010). *Human Development Report 2010: The Real Wealth of Nations, Pathways to Human Development*. New York, United Nations Development Programme.

United Nations Vietnam (2010). *Vietnam Moves Towards a New Industrial System*. Hanoi, United Nations in Vietnam.

Vietnam Business (2011). 'Catfish Export Target to go down due to US Tax Levy'. Retrieved 15 February 2011 from http://vietnambusiness.dztimes.net/2011/02/catfish-export-target-to-go-down-due-to.html.

Vietnam Chamber of Commerce and Industry (2005). 'Good Corporate Governance: a Prerequisite for Sustainable Business' *Business Issues Bulletin 10*(13): 1.

Vietnam News (2011). 'Leading SOEs Make Up 40 percent of GNP?' Retrieved 28 February 2011 from http://www.lookatvietnam.com/2011/02/leading-soes-make-up-40-percent-of-gdp.html.

VietNamNet Bridge (2011). 'Government Debt, a Big Concern'. Retrieved 7 September 2011 from <http://english.vietnamnet.vn/en/special-report/12334/government-debt--a-big-concern. html>.

Vo, T. X. (2011). 'Nghien cuu ung dung chuoi gia tri san xuat va tieu thu nong san' (Application of Value Chain in Production and Consumption of Agricultural Products). *Tia Sang.* Retrieved 22 June 2011 from <http://tiasang.com.vn/Default.aspx?tabid=62&News=4146& CategoryID=7>.

Vu, M. K. (2010). 'Positioning Vietnam: Today determines Tomorrow'. *East Asia Forum.* Retrieved 16 June 2010 from <http://www.eastasiaforum.org/2010/06/16/positioning-vietnam-to day-determines-tomorrow>.

Vu, Q. V. (2008). 'Giao duc Viet Nam: nguyen nhan cua su xuong cap va cac caci cach can thiet' (Education of Vietnam: Reasons for Degradation and Needed Reforms). *Thoi dai moi* 13. Retrieved 5 December 2011 from <http://www.tapchithoidai.org/ThoiDai13/200813_ VuQuangViet_1.htm>.

—— (2009). 'Vietnam's Economic Crisis: Policy Follies and the Role of State-owned Conglomerates'. *Southeast Asian Affairs* 2009: 389–417.

Vuong, H. (2005). '10 Co quant ham nhung pho bien nhat' (10 Organizations that are most Corrupted). *Dan Tri Online.* Retrieved 30 November 2005 from <http://dantri.com.vn/c21/ s20-90860/10-co-quan-tham-nhung-pho-bien-nhat.htm>.

Vuong, H. Q. (2011). 'Vietnam's Underground Economy: Where "Sharks" were Food'. *Stratford Global Intelligence.* Retrieved 6 July 2011 from <http://www.stratfor.com/other_voices/201 10706-vietnams-underground-economy-where-sharks-were-food>.

Vu Van (2010). '40 tinh, thanh da co truong dai hoc' (40 provinces and cities already have universities). *Ha Noi moi.* Retrieved 7 April 2010 from http://hanoimoi.com.vn/newsdetail/ Giao-duc/319788/40-tinh-thanh-da-co-truong-dai-hoc.htm.

World Bank (2007). 'Taking Stock: An Update on Vietnam's Economic Developments. Retrieved 18 February 2009 from <http://www.worldbank.org>.

—— (2008). *Higher Education and Skills for Growth.* Washington, DC, World Bank.

—— (2010). *Doing Business 2011: Making a Difference for Entrepreneurs.* Washington, DC, International Bank for Reconstruction and Development.

—— (2011). 'Enterprise Surveys: Vietnam 2009'. Retrieved 10 October 2011 from http://www. entreprisesurveys.org/ExploreEconomies/?economyid=202&year=2009.

Wright, C. P. and V. V. Nguyen (2000). 'State-owned enterprises (SOEs) in Vietnam: Perceptions of Strategic Direction for a Society in Transition'. *International Journal of Public Sector Management* 13(2): 169–177.

Yeung, Y. M. I. and R. L. Tung (1996). 'Achieving Business Success in Confucian Societies: The Importance of *guanxi*'. *Organizational Dynamics* 25(2): 54–65.

Yoon, Y. (2009). *A Comparative Study on Industrial Relations and Collective Bargaining in East Asian Countries,* ILO Working Paper No. 8. Geneva, ILO.

Zhu, Y., N. Collins, M. Weber, and J. Benson (2008). 'New Forms of Ownership and Human Resource Practices in Vietnam'. *Human Resource Management* 47(1): 157–175.

# PART II

THEMES IN COMPARATIVE
PERSPECTIVE

# CHAPTER 15

# BUSINESS GROUPS IN ASIA

## *An Institutional Perspective*

### MICHAEL CARNEY

How do improvements in market-supporting institutions affect the socio-economic value of business groups (BGs)? Received theory tells us that BGs are the product of weak institutions (Khanna and Yafeh 2007), but we know comparatively little about BGs and the effects of institutional change. Economic, sociological, and political economy theories of BGs define institutions in different ways and make different assumptions about how institutions and firms interact. Economic perspectives suggest BGs emerge and flourish in the context of missing institutions (Khanna and Palepu 1999). Sociological perspectives identify the stabilizing effects of cognitive, regulative, and normative institutions on continued existence (Granovetter 2005). Political economy theories emphasize the state's role in providing resources to BGs as a means of encouraging economic development (Amsden and Hikino 1994; Schneider 2010). With the specification of different forms of institution and causal mechanism, there is little theoretical consensus about how BGs will change over time.

Theories also differ over whether BGs create or destroy socio-economic value. Strategic management perspectives envisage BGs as quasi-internal markets that enable legally independent firms to enjoy benefits of scale and scope efficiencies (Chang and Hong 2000). Corporate governance perspectives point to the value-destroying effects of opaque BG corporate structures that enable majority owners to pilfer resources from minority investors (Claessens et al. 2002). Both perspectives have ample empirical evidence to support their position (Carney, Gedajlovic, and Yang 2009). Disagreement about the socio-economic value of BGs is evident in their characterizations as paragons and parasites (Khanna and Yafeh 2007), heroes and villains (Claessens, Djankov, and Lang 2000), and red barons and robber barons (Perotti and Gelfer 2001). Whether or not BGs create or destroy socio-economic value is a billion-dollar question, because BGs dominate the economic landscape of many Asian states. As scholars are deeply divided about their value, they offer conflicting policy recommendations. Starkly contrasting positions are found in the views that groups should be dismantled (Almeida and Wolfenzon 2006), actively nurtured (Amsden 2009), or left alone to cope with market forces (Khanna and Palepu 1999).

A BG is 'a collection of firms bound together in some formal and/or informal ways' (Granovetter 2005) and they have played a key role in Asia's industrialization by organizing export-oriented firms and helping firms acquire advanced technology (Guillen 2000). In recent years, affiliates of Asia's leading BGs have also become pioneers of foreign direct investment, becoming emerging-market multinationals (Mathews 2006; Yiu 2011).

Asian BGs are not a homogeneous population. They contain extremes of technological capability, ranging from highly sophisticated Japanese BGs (*keiretsu*) to the mercantile conglomerates of South East Asia. The affiliates of some groups are located on the technology frontier of their industries, while others are simply vehicles for trading or proprietors of government-granted monopolies. Few are driven by the logic of shareholder capitalism: China's and Singapore's state-owned groups pursue a politically determined mission. Most Asian groups are family owned and controlled, characterized by strong central, often personalistic, control and intimately embedded in kinship- and patronage-based networks. Examples are the Korean *chaebol*, dynastic Taiwanese groups such as Formosa Plastics, Hong Kong conglomerates such as Cheung Kong, and regional groups such as Kerry, Hong Leong, or Salim.

Asia's economic landscape is visibly changing, and a discussion of the role of BGs in Asia's business systems entails consideration of how their strategies co-evolve with the institutions making up the wider business system (Carney and Gedajlovic 2002). Granovetter (2005: 445) encourages BG researchers 'to look closely at how BGs have responded to changes in the economies they inhabit...and...address the question of how we understand their capacities and the way they change over time'. In this chapter, I respond to Granovetter's imperative and (1) review leading economic, sociological, and political economy accounts of the rationale for BG structure and performance, (2) review the prediction that each theory makes about the interaction between BGs and institutional change, and (3) present meta-analytical data on how BG profitability and prevalence (the percentage of a country's largest firms affiliated with a BG) changes over time. To guide future research, (4) I provide a theoretically grounded framework of competing propositions about the effect of institutional change on BG profitability and prevalence.

# ECONOMIC PERSPECTIVES ON BUSINESS GROUPS AND INSTITUTIONAL CHANGE

Transaction cost theory (TCT) (Williamson 1985) and agency theory (Jensen and Meckling 1976) are economic theories which have motivated distinct streams of BG research (Morck, Wolfenzon, and Yeung 2005; Khanna and Yafeh 2007). Both theories endow actors with a high level of rationality and capacity for strategic choice, but they differ in their analysis of BG value. TCT provides an efficiency explanation for BGs under conditions of resource privation and institutional underdevelopment (Fisman and Khanna 2004). The main thrust of agency theory research focuses upon BGs' potential for value destruction in the absence of legal protection for creditors and minority shareholders (Morck, Wolfenzon, and Yeung 2005; Claessens, Fan, and Lang 2006).

TCT represents a 'market failure' account of BG formation. In this respect, TCT takes the absence of market-supporting institutions as a starting point. Without clear rules protecting creditors from default, banks will be unwilling to supply credit on reasonable terms to independent firms that are unknown to them (Leff 1978). The formation and growth of independent firms will be stunted in these circumstances, since they cannot gain ready access to affordable capital. To solve their credit difficulties, entrepreneurs organize themselves into groups to internalize transactions in a quasi-internal market of loosely-associated affiliates (Strachan 1976). Goto (1982) extended the idea that BGs emerge to solve capital market failures, proposing that they can also solve market failures for other factors such as physical resources, know-how, and human capital. In what has now become known as the institutional voids hypothesis, Khanna and Palepu (1997) propose that BGs represent a 'safe haven' where property rights are respected and permit group affiliates to confidently trade with one another under conditions of poor commercial law. However, quasi-internal markets also have attendant costs arising from politics and the potential misallocation of capital (Scharfstein and Stein 2000). In some cases, costs can outweigh benefits, resulting in some firms paying a net penalty for their affiliation (Kim, Hoskisson, and Wan 2004).

Although not always explicitly articulated, TCT distinguishes between two types of institution: the first is concerned with regulatory institutions consisting of the prevailing property rights regime, the quality of rule of law, and the existence of efficient contract enforcement underpinning anonymous or arm's-length market transactions (Khanna and Palepu 1997). The second type of institution consists of a soft infrastructure of intermediary organizations, such as executive search firms, financial institutions, consumer watchdogs, market research firms, and technical standards committees, which facilitate economic specialization and market efficiency (Khanna and Palepu 1997). The distinction is important, since the establishment of the first type of institutions, e.g. rule of law, may take many years to fully develop, whereas soft market infrastructure is a function of economic development and may materialize very quickly (Carney, Shapiro, and Tang 2009). BGs can compensate for both types of voids and the differing rates at which voids are filled will determine the range of transactions in which BGs can efficiently deploy their competitive advantage.

There are at least two corollaries to the argument that BGs arise in response to missing institutions. The first is that once market-supporting institutions are established, BGs will lose their competitive advantage and we should expect that relative to independent firms, BG affiliation premiums should erode (Khanna and Palepu 2000a). Indeed, if there are costs associated with belonging to a BG, then we might expect BGs to underperform compared with independent firms. The second corollary suggests that as their competitive advantages erode, BGs may restructure to become more focused and eventually disappear as a common organizational form (Lee, Peng, and Lee 2008). Khanna and Palepu (1999: 126) build their policy advice on the expectation that BGs will fade away, in suggesting that 'governments in developing countries must focus on building up those market institutions in the long term. The dismantling of BGs will, we believe, follow naturally once these institutions are in place'. Similarly, Chang (2003: 238) says Korean *chaebols* 'are the creatures of market imperfections and government intervention ... as these forces diminish, *chaebols* will decline in the longer run'.

Agency theory accounts of BGs emphasize the potential for conflict between majority and minority owners, or principal–principal conflicts (Young et al. 2008). In this literature, majority shareholders adopt complex ownership pyramids and opaque governance structures that facilitate exploitation of minority investors. Using mechanisms such as tunnelling and related-party transactions, controlling owners transfer assets into peak firms where they own large cash-flow rights (Bertrand, Mehta, and Mullainathan 2002). Complex corporate structures also allow controlling owners to entrench under performing management. Rational minority investors anticipate these risks and discount the value of BG equity, which raises the group's cost of capital and generally depresses performance over the long run (Claessens et al. 2002).

To remedy this conflict, advocates of this perspective prescribe the implementation of protective institutions that explicitly curb controlling owners' ability to expropriate outside investors. Prescribed remedies include the establishment of anti-self-dealing rules (Djankov et al. 2008) and creditor protection (La Porta et al. 1998), as well as good governance constraints on rent extraction by public officials (Kaufmann, Kraay, and Mastruzzi 2009). Whether or not public officials and powerful corporate owners actually uphold 'best-practice' corporate governance standards remains an open question, because there are impediments to the enforcement of good governance institutions (Chen, Li, and Shapiro 2011). One school of thought suggests that the benefits to be gained from adopting best-practice corporate governance are relatively minor and there are few incentives to abandon existing practice (Almeida and Wolfenzon 2006). Other agency theorists suggest that best-practice corporate governance is detrimental to the interests of large powerful incumbent groups, who are capable of entrenching their positions and suppressing institutional changes that threaten their interests (Morck, Wolfenzon, and Yeung 2005). Both scenarios point to a 'locked-in' equilibrium consisting of second-best institutions, which diverge sharply from best practice (Rodrik 2008).

# SOCIOLOGICAL PERSPECTIVES ON BUSINESS GROUPS AND INSTITUTIONAL CHANGE

Sociologists are critical of economic theories of organization for their Western-centric assumptions about the role of efficient property rights as a means of securing transactions. These authors point to alternative exchange mechanisms that entrepreneurs in Asia have developed to solve their contracting problems and which cannot be understood from the TCT or agency perspectives (Biggart and Hamilton 1992). Comparative sociological studies of Asian organizations emphasize the role of family, inheritance norms, traditional authority, communal networks, and the historical role of the state to explain differences in organizational structure (Orru, Biggart, and Hamilton 1997). Prominent sociological perspectives include social exchange and institutional theories of organization, and both have been fruitfully applied to describe essential characteristics of BGs in Japan (Lincoln and Gerlach 2004), China (Keister 2000), Korea (Biggart 1998), and Taiwan (Chung 2001).

Social exchange theories stress the effects of trust, status, social capital, kinship, and relationships on actors' preferences for managing economic exchanges. In this view, individuals and firms are embedded in socially constructed patterns of exchange that shape exchange norms and institutionalize mutual expectations about appropriate business behaviour. Institutional theory identifies cognitive, normative, and regulative institutions that coordinate and stabilize exchange. Cognitive and normative rules generate taken-for-granted and prescribed behavioural patterns that limit embedded actors' ability to envisage and enact strategic choices. The mechanisms shaping exchange outcomes include isomorphism and imitation of culturally acceptable business practice. These mechanisms tend to make BG structures similar in particular jurisdictions, as actors adopt particular organizing modes not because they are efficient, but because they are legitimate. More generally, sociological theories are less concerned with organizational efficiency or financial performance than with the reproduction and persistence of stable organizational structures and exchange practices.

In a large body of work, Keister (1998, 2000, 2001) applies exchange theory to explain the development of China's BGs in the period following the dismantling of centralized economic planning. In her account of the origins of BGs, pre-existing social relationships played a critical role in the formation of long-lasting economic ties. China's BGs emerged as a response to prevailing institutional conditions at the time of reform, rather than from a purely economic rationale. Factors such as the legacy of a strong state, the importance of social connections within the state bureaucracy, and continuing uncertainty about the availability of scarce resources encouraged newly autonomous firms to seek stable inter-firm linkages as a response to risk. While these relationships had several functional benefits during the transitional period, such as assuring access to scarce resources, Keister finds that relationships persist long after the turbulent period of transition has passed. Hence, when alternative and more efficient resource suppliers and trading partners appear on the market, long-standing ties among firms persist and exert an increasingly negative influence over a firm's economic performance. 'Decisions that firms made early in reform about lending and trade ties will affect China's economic structure for decades, because these ties quickly began to solidify into stable inter-firm alliances' (Keister 2001 336).

In an institutional account of the emergence of BGs in Taiwan, Chung (2001) shows how regulative institutions, in this case ephemeral tax rules, stimulated group formation by encouraging entrepreneurs to form new independent businesses rather than expand existing businesses. Chung explains that because export-tax incentive programmes during the early 1960s were applied to investments in new firms, but not to new investments in existing firms, they encouraged entrepreneurs to form multiple independent companies rather than establish diversified multidivisional firms. However, long after export-tax incentives were repealed, BGs persisted because they were consistent with other institutional elements of Taiwanese society, specifically the Taiwanese social norms of equal inheritance in families that accommodated the succession of multiple sons (and sometimes daughters) to different businesses.

Maman (2002) and Biggart (1998) provide institutional explanations for the emergence of family-oriented and patrimonial BGs in Korea that underscore the role of elite preferences and state ideology. Maman argues that following Korea's independence from colonial rule, political elites held a developmental ideology with a strong desire for greater economic and military self-sufficiency and had little interest in the role of market forces—indeed, elites actively suppressed competition and provided support for the development of national champions. In Biggart's account, post-colonial period leaders embarked upon an economic development project without an indigenous capitalist class to lead the industrialization project. The government decided to channel resources towards a very small number of successful entrepreneurs and imitated Japan's *zaibatsu* corporate model, which was familiar to them from their colonial era. Biggart describes Korea's emergent capitalism as patrimonial in character, in which a political elite pragmatically developed capitalist institutions that built on the heritage of Korean society. Just as in the political domain, where power is held by a patriarch who rules over a household administered by a loyal personal staff, so modern *chaebol* reflect a patrimonial organizing model, albeit with some modern elements. As the Korean economy modernized, professional managers were integrated into the upper echelons of power, but patrimonial family control continued to characterize *chaebol* well into the 1990s (Biggart 1998).

Given the primary focus on institutional stability and reproduction of organizational forms, it is not surprising that sociological theories offer conservative accounts of institutional change. The main prediction of exchange theory suggests that dominant BGs are likely to occupy centrally located 'elite' positions within economic networks, where they are typically sheltered from pressures to change (Keister 2001). Elite organizations are more likely than newcomers to benefit from existing institutional structures and have a vested interest in preserving the status quo. In a series of studies of liberalization and restructuring in Taiwan, Chung and Luo (2008a) find that, compared with foreign-owned firms, family-controlled BGs were slow to either exit or enter new industries. They attribute BG inertia to institutionalized family practices of equal inheritance, which inhibit restructuring processes. In another study, Chung and Luo (2008b) find that despite growing competitive pressure and a growing functional need for professional managers, institutionalized norms of nepotism continue to prevail in the recruitment of senior personnel. The rare exception to nepotism is found only among second-generation family managers with management degrees from US universities.

Chung and Luo explain that these managers are cognitively less embedded in traditional norms and were more likely to appoint professional managers to the inner circle of top management. Chung and Luo (2008b) conclude that a powerful confluence of regulatory, competitive, and cognitive forces are needed to empower change agents to escape the structural constraints of family ties. Granovetter (2005) concludes that BGs have substantial staying power and that they have 'typically defied predictions of their imminent demise, surviving both conscious attempts by politicians to break them up and the impact of financial crisis'. This is because BGs can be deeply embedded in informal kinship networks, thereby forming a complex social unit in which economic and kinship interests are inextricably intertwined. Granovetter speculates that older, more established, BGs are especially resilient, and some, like India's Tata with its origins in the 19th century, show few signs of break-up.

Nevertheless, globalization represents continuing pressure for evolutionary incremental change in national institutional structures (Djelic and Quack 2003) and institutional theory has become more interested in understanding the process of institutional change. A growing body of work focuses upon the concept of institutional entrepreneurship (Battilana, Leca, and Boxenbaum 2009). One hypothesis emerging from this line of research suggests that centrally located organizations may become exposed to multiple influences that sharpen their awareness of the value of institutional change (Greenwood and Suddaby 2006). A related conjecture suggests that the internationalization of Asian BGs exposes these firms to multiple organizational fields (Kostova, Roth, and Dacin 2009), where they become exposed to alternative corporate governance practices. Just as in an earlier era, when BGs motivated economic catch-up by learning and diffusing advanced technological processes to affiliates, so may BGs become institutional entrepreneurs by diffusing new governance practices among their affiliates.

# POLITICAL ECONOMY PERSPECTIVES ON BUSINESS GROUPS AND INSTITUTIONAL CHANGE

Prominent political economy theories of BGs include a developmental state perspective (Amsden 1989; Wade 1990) and a 'varieties of capitalism' theory of competitive advantage (Hall and Soskice 2001; Schneider 2010). Developmental-state approaches emphasize the directive role of national states and policy processes that promote the accumulation of capital and the construction of firms with sufficient scale and scope to lead the process of industrial catch-up. The 'varieties of capitalism' approach focuses on the question of how states organize big business to build industrial capacity (Schneider 2010). In contrast with sociological perspectives, which view institutions as constraints, political economy perspectives view institutions as resources that firms can leverage to improve their competitive position in world markets (Hall and Thelen 2009).

Studies of the developmental state describe several models of state-led industrialization (Perkins 1994). The general focus is upon political institutions and specific policy choices, such as selective protectionism, the development or suppression of private capital markets, promotion of main bank or state capital allocation, promotion of or restrictions on FDI, and joint-venture rules requiring substantial technology transfer as a condition of market entry (Guillen 2000). By authoritatively coordinating these policy instruments, a strong and autonomous state overseeing a disciplined public bureaucracy can channel resources to high-performing firms (Ritchie 2009). Studies in this tradition describe organizational learning processes (Hobday 1995) and the acquisition and sharing of technology and project management skills that facilitate serial entry into new industries (Amsden 1989; Amsden and Hikino 1994).

In the developmental state perspective, BGs are 'policy-induced' by deliberative policy and the provision of state incentives (Schneider 2009a), but there are important differences in state capacities and variations in state-group relationships that produce divergent development paths and culminate in different economic outcomes. Where the state is powerful, autonomous, and immune to interest-group pressure, it may co-opt and direct entrepreneurial elites towards favourable economic outcomes (Evans 1995). However, policy-induced groups can also emerge in the context of crony capitalism, where, due to private rent seeking or public avarice, policy instruments are mishandled or combined in ways that impede firms from developing sustainable competitive advantages (Kang 2003). The underdevelopment of BG capabilities under crony capitalism is evident in patrimonial regimes where powerful politicians and parties, such as the People's Action Party in Malaysia (Gomez 2009) or Suharto in Indonesia (Dieleman and Sachs 2008), dominate politics for long periods. Under crony capitalism, BG scope is determined by the allocation of concessions to connected families and political supporters. Government policies restrict trade and foreign competition, but fail to monitor the technological and market achievements of domestic firms benefiting from protection. In these circumstances, the logic of BG diversification is driven by policy-generated rents rather than financial and technological achievements.

The 'varieties of capitalism' approach defines institutions as 'sets of regularized practices with a rule-like quality, in the sense that the actors expect the practices to be observed; and which in some but not all cases are supported by formal sanctions' (Hall and Thelen 2009: 9). While this definition is apparently similar to sociological conceptualizations, the 'varieties of capitalism' perspective sees institutions as potential resources rather than constraints on action. Political economy environments consist of 'entrepreneurial actors seeking to advance their interests as they construe them' (Hall and Thelen 2009: 9–10). Institutions can serve as resources available for firms to widen and strengthen the bases of their competitive advantage. Competitive advantages accrue to firms shaping their strategies to benefit from prevailing supportive institutions within a jurisdiction. For example, the availability of patient capital allows firms to retain skilled workers, who in turn are more likely to make long-term investments in firm-related skills and knowledge. Contrarily, firms that eschew institutional resources are likely to under perform. The most important institutions are those that facilitate knowledge acquisition, skill-building and technical capability. For example, as the Korean state gradually opened up its economy and exposed its *chaebol* to international competition, a small number of focused and technologically advanced groups such as Hyundai-Kia, Samsung, and LG established themselves as powerful international competitors. At the same time, the developmental trajectories of other groups stalled, and some BGs have failed (Hoskisson et al. 2005).

Scholars studying Asian capitalism have also identified new hybrid forms of capitalism, driven by novel organizational forms and new forms of cooperation not theorized in the original models. In his depiction of hierarchical varieties of capitalism, Schneider (2009b) proposes that hierarchical coordination of the economy by the state is transmitted into other institutional spheres through a process of institutional isomorphism. In this process, states' hierarchical coordination, born of state-led industrialization, is emulated by private-sector firms, where concentrated owners centralize strategic decision-making in family enterprises and determine the allocation of capital with little regard to capital markets. Similarly, in the wake of economic liberalization, hierarchical multinational enterprises (MNEs) enter the economy and acquire *de facto* control of firms that might otherwise be independent in other types of capitalism. The centrality of BGs and MNEs in these economies reinforces hierarchical coordination: since both substitute for external sources of capital, they impede the development of external capital markets. Strategic coordination and inter-firm cooperation is thwarted, since BGs are often highly diversified and there is little inter-group or even inter-firm cooperation, and MNEs are typically not well embedded in local business associations or have little interest in local strategic coordination. Hierarchical coordination is also evident in patriarchal labour–management relations that disenfranchises unions and institutionalizes hierarchy in the sphere of industrial relations. Hierarchical varieties of capitalism are also prone to developing low skill equilibria in which workers lack incentives to invest in training and skill development, because neither MNEs nor BGs demand it. Hierarchical market economies also coexist in Asia with a large informal economy which provides complementarities with weak enforcement of formal laws.

An alternative variety of capitalism that resonates in Asia is 'dependent market capitalism' (Nolte and Vliegenthart 2009). The idea suggests that economies can become permanently dependent upon foreign actors and institutions and reflects the growing importance of globalization and the growing market power of MNEs over domestic firms in emerging markets. As Asian economies have liberalized their trade and investment regimes over the past two decades, MNEs have increasingly penetrated their markets. Many emerging national champions are relatively small compared with their multinational rivals. When they are listed on their underdeveloped domestic stock exchanges, they can be highly undervalued and represent low-cost targets for foreign rivals who may easily assimilate them into their organizations. Because many other domestic firms develop only generic skills, they can be subordinated by MNEs into subsidiary roles as contract manufacturers in international global commodity value chains (Gereffi 2001). Dependent market capitalism is especially prone to develop under conditions of crony capitalism, because local BGs are heavily protected or sate themselves with local rent-generating monopolies, but otherwise fail to develop profound technological capabilities. If the affiliates of BGs struggle to attain international competitiveness, they develop complementarities based on a division of labour between MNEs, who provide technology, innovation, process production, and knowledge transfer, and local partners, who provide commercial infrastructure and disciplined labour. The precarious comparative advantage of firms located in dependent market capitalism is constantly threatened by countries further down the development-chain, who compete for foreign investment. Because MNEs require flexible and low-cost labour they are unwilling to accept costly institutions such as comprehensive collective agreements or cumbersome procedures for lay-offs; consequently, labour is reluctant to invest, resulting in a low-skills trap. Institutional development in dependent market capitalism is driven by MNEs whose mobile and impatient capital offers a strong bargaining position. Foreign capital and BGs favour law and order, but otherwise exert little pressure for property rights, e.g. for minority investors.

These perspectives also identify the potential for institutional inertia. Many middle- and low-income countries have been in an emerging condition for many years and show few signs of catching up with more advanced economies. The development-state literature now points to the problem of 'government failure' and the growing risk of economies becoming enmeshed in a middle-income trap (Wade 2010). Schneider's (2009b) hierarchical varieties of capitalism perspective holds that state-led industrialization in many middle-income countries may settle into solid institutional foundations on its own terms, rather than as some form of transitional capitalism in formation. Capitalism in these emerging or transitional economies may have already settled into permanent institutional foundations rather than transitioning to some other type of capitalism. If this is indeed the case, then a premature institutional stability represents a political problem, because institutional stability inhibits continued development of institutions capable of supporting more complex market transactions. In this case, Hall and Thelen (2009: 12) call for the creation of 'meta-institutions' capable of deliberation and diagnosis of stalled economic development that can reset and re-equilibriate cooperative endeavours. How to reignite the developmental process in stalled middle-income economies remains an open question on this agenda.

# EMPIRICAL PATTERNS

Empirical research on BGs has accelerated over the past decade. In a recent meta-analysis we found 141 studies covering 28 countries, including 12 Asian countries, published between 1994 and 2009. Each study contains at least one estimate of the value of group affiliation relative to independent firms (Carney et al. 2011). In this section I briefly report some of the main findings of this study, as well as preliminary findings from ongoing work using meta-analytical data.

With regard to the Asian countries in our sample, we find that in the aggregate, and for all time periods, the effect of group membership on firm performance was significantly positive in Hong Kong and Indonesia, but significantly negative in Japan, Pakistan, and South Korea, and that there was no significant overall effect in China, India, Malaysia, the Philippines, Singapore, Taiwan, and Thailand. However, our data point to several findings regarding BG strategy and institutional development that indicate new directions for future research.

With regard to strategy, we use meta-analysis structural equation modelling to examine the mediating effects of strategy choices about diversification, internationalization, and capital structure on the affiliation-performance relationship. We find that group affiliates are less internationalized than independent firms, but are more diversified and leveraged, and that these choices are always associated with lower performance. As both high levels of debt and diversification are suggestive of pyramiding and tunnelling behaviour, these findings point to the inefficient allocation of resources and are broadly supportive of agency theory perspectives that emphasize the negative effects of group affiliation.

Our meta-analysis also permitted examination of the performance effects of group-level scale and scope strategy choices. Received theory suggests that larger groups are more able to profit from economies of scale, because they can more effectively perform intermediation functions for capital and high-quality labour (Khanna and Palepu 2000b) and because large-scale groups command greater market power in their domestic markets (Khanna and Yafeh 2007). Contrarily, other theories predict that widely diversified groups are more likely to bear higher coordination and bureaucratic costs associated with managing greater complexity (Hoskisson et al. 2005).

Tests of these competing hypotheses are rare, because of difficulties in assembling large-scale data sets, so empirical research has little to say about the effects of group-level strategy on aggregate group performance. However, because meta-analysis can aggregate data from multiple countries, we are able to distinguish between scale and scope effects and find support for both the group-level scale and scope hypotheses. We find that large scale strongly and positively improves group performance relative to independent firms, while more widely diversified BGs are associated with comparative underperformance. These findings highlight the importance of strategy variables in BG research, but we also note the general scarcity of strategy variables in the main body of primary studies. This is a significant gap and presents an opportunity for future research to explore neglected dimensions of group- and firm-level strategy in areas such as internationalization, innovation, and restructuring.

With regard to institution effects, there is much agreement that BGs emerge as a response to institutional voids, but there is much less agreement about the relative importance of different types of institutional void. Agency theory emphasizes the importance of protective institutions, such as protection for minority investors (Djankov et al. 2008), while TCT is concerned with absent enabling institutions, such as the availability of external capital and highly qualified labour (Khanna and Palepu 1997). Conceptually, the existence of institutional voids can be understood as moderating variables affecting the relationship between group affiliation and performance. Theory predicts that voids exert stronger negative effects on stand-alone firms due to their inability to compensate for legal, capital, and labour-market deficiencies. In our meta-analysis we are able to unpack the concept of institutions to distinguish among voids in different institutional domains, including external capital markets, markets for highly qualified labour, and rule of law. In support of the institutional voids hypothesis, we found that financial and labour-market developments negatively moderate the group affiliation effect, suggesting that groups assist affiliates by providing capital or labour when these resources are scarce. However, we found no support for the hypothesis that BGs compensate for weaknesses in the legal environment, as measured by the rule of law index, as legal development positively moderates the affiliation effect.

While several scholars predict that the value of group affiliation will decline when robust institutions appear, few scholars specify the timeframe over which the value of group affiliation may be expected to persist. Campbell (2004) suggests fully functional capitalist institutions take many years to develop, because of the complex adjustment required by an interrelated matrix of formal laws and informal culture-specific normative modes of thinking. For example, states may pass 'parchment laws' affirming commitment to rule of law, but full compliance may take longer to achieve, as underlying behaviours continue to follow more deeply ingrained cognitive and normative imperatives. As predicted by institutional theories, BG practices may persist long after the reform of regulatory institutions.

Based upon available studies of BGs, using value estimates from different years, we are able to estimate the value of BG affiliation in seven Asian countries over several decades. Figure 15.1 describes a polynomial regression that shows a non-linear relationship between the mean values of group affiliation in multiple studies and the corresponding date of the estimate.

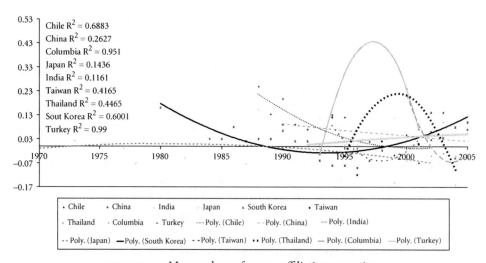

FIGURE 15.1 Mean values of group affiliation over time

(a)

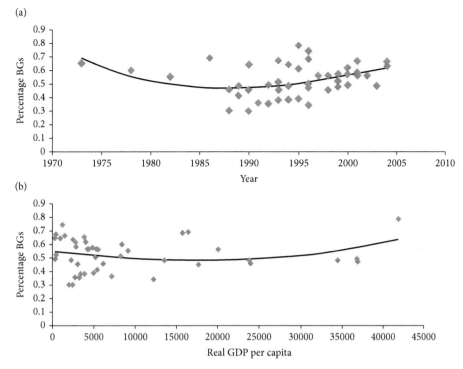

(b)

FIGURE 15.2  Business group prevalence in nine Asian economies

Figure 15.1 shows that the earliest estimates of the value of group affiliation were made in Japan during the early 1960s. Except for a period between 1975 and 1985 when affiliation was marginally positive, the mean value of affiliation in Japan has been negative. The estimates for two other East Asian countries—South Korea and Taiwan—depict a different trajectory. The first estimates of group affiliation in South Korea and Taiwan occurred in 1980 and 1994; in both cases, the value of group affiliation begins positively, but falls into negative territory around the time of the Asian financial crisis, and in both cases the value of affiliation recovers to positive levels after 2000. In the case of China and Indonesia, the value of affiliation falls consistently over time. In Thailand, the value rises and then falls rapidly. India provides an exception—the value of affiliation in Indian BGs shows continuous positive improvement.

Figure 15.2 sheds light on the aggregate prevalence of BGs in Asia. Prevalence is typically measured as the percentage of the top 100 publicly listed firms in the country that are group-affiliated (Claessens et al. 2000). We collected available estimates of BG prevalence for nine Asian countries. The figure shows estimates of BG prevalence over time and relative to *per capita* gross domestic product. These data lend support to anecdotal observations that BGs do not disappear or decline, but tend to persist even in economically advanced countries. Indeed, Figure 15.2 suggests that BGs become relatively more important in wealthy economies and offers support for sociological theories of BGs that emphasize their persistence and stability. Scholars are perplexed by observations that

BGs continue to be prominent in many countries such as Japan, Korea, Singapore, and Taiwan, which have now developed high-quality legal and contract-enforcement institutions. Morck (2010) finds that the persistence of BGs in highly developed economies is a 'riddle'. Khanna and Yafeh are equally perplexed by the persistence of BGs in developed economies when they say 'Can BGs ever die peacefully? We are not sure!' (2007: 369).

# Contingent Effects of Business Group Strategy and Institutional Conditions

Meta-analytical data showing different national trajectories of value creation and destruction among BGs, combined with an aggregate tendency towards persistence, suggest that any single theory is unlikely to do justice to the dynamics of the relationship between BG value and institutional change. Rather, the findings point to the possibilities that BG strategies and their relationship to the institutional environment are more varied and contingent than current theory allows. To guide future research, I outline a framework showing how divergent theoretical perspectives might be usefully combined to provide rival and competing propositions. Figure 15.3 juxtaposes BG value attributes and institutional change dimensions to provide competing hypotheses about the effects of institutional change on BG outcomes.

The vertical dimension of Figure 15.3 distinguishes between BG attributes in terms of their potential for socio-economic value creation or destruction under initial conditions: that is, the extent to which BGs generate net positive or negative social economic outcomes at the time of their founding. The horizontal dimension distinguishes between protective or enabling institutions. Protective institutions include rule of law (Haggard, MacIntyre, and Tiede 2008), labour-market regulation (Botero et al. 2004), and anti-self-dealing laws (Djankov et al. 2008). Strong protective institutions restrict the capacity of powerful economic and political actors from abusing their position through opportunistic behaviour against weaker or less organized stakeholders. For example, anti-self-dealing rules curb powerful owners' ability to exploit minority investors. It is commonly assumed that without such mechanisms in institutional protection, stakeholders will be deterred from investing in productive assets. Enabling institutions include agencies and intermediaries such as stock exchanges, credit-rating agencies, efficient government bureaucracy, and high-quality education and training and skills formation providers (Fisman and Khanna 2004). The development of enabling institutions allows independent firms to acquire the specialized resources needed to sustain productive business activities, and may undermine the competitive advantages of firms affiliated with a BG.

It is commonly assumed that the development of protective and enabling institutions will be highly correlated. For example, corporate governance theories predict that the provision of protection for minority shareholders will increase the depth and liquidity of

| Quadrant I | Quadrant II |
|---|---|
| Outcome 1a: BGs more profitable as positive effects of concentrated ownership prevail. | Outcome: BG affiliates' profit withers. BGs either re-focus or disappear |
| Mechanism 1a: Stronger protective institutions inhibit negative effects of concentrated ownership | Mechanism: Enabling institutions provide resources to independent firms, value of BGs' internal markets decline, costs of group affiliation outweigh benefits |
| Outcome 1b: BGs prone to fail with more constraints on corruption and public servants | |
| Mechanism 1b: BGs no longer have exclusive access to resources and opportunities | |
| **Quadrant III** | **Quadrant IV** |
| Outcome: No impact on BG functioning or performance | Outcome: BG increase in scope |
| Mechanism: Stronger protective institutions complement or are redundant to BG operations. BGs persist for non-economic reasons | Mechanism: Enabling institutions provide resources necessary for greater diversification, Market liberalization facilitates BG entry into new markets |

(Left axis, top: Group strategy destroys value; bottom: Group strategy creates value)

Development of protective institutions      Development of enabling institutions

FIGURE 15.3 Contingent outcomes of group strategy and institutional development

equity markets (Djankov et al. 2008) and improved rule of law will reduce public corruption and improve the quality of public administration. However, protective and enabling institutions are much less correlated than generally believed (Haggard, MacIntyre, and Tiede 2008). For example, both China and Taiwan provide very little formal protection for minority investors, yet both countries have developed very large equity markets relative to the size of their economies. Perhaps most anomalous is that East Asian economies have enjoyed relatively good government in the absence of formal checks upon the state; for example, the prevalence of public corruption and the absence of government accountability has not deterred private investment (Haggard, MacIntyre, and Tiede 2008). In other cases, extensive formal institutional development has not produced the desired results; for example, in many Asian jurisdictions, states have made legal provisions to support investment risk finance, but have failed to induce a substantial venture-capital sector (Bruton, Ahlstrom, and Yeh 2004). Accordingly, specific provisions for the development of either protective or enabling institutions (or both) represent different policy agendas for governments. The combination of the two dimensions is depicted in Figure 15.3, where each quadrant of the 2 × 2 matrix provides divergent propositions about BG outcomes.

Quadrant I represents two scenarios. In the first case, concentrated owners of BGs destroy socio-economic value by constructing opaque governance structures that allow the expropriation of minority investors or entrench incompetent management. Proposition 1a derives from corporate governance/agency theory perspectives that suggest the concentrated ownership typically found in Asia's large family-owned and controlled BGs can bring both benefits and costs (Claessens et al. 2002). While dominant owners may destroy value, e.g. by expropriating minority shareholders, they also have strong incentives and are well positioned to monitor affiliates and intervene if affiliate managers underperform; such oversight improves firm performance (Ma, Yao, and Xi 2006). Dominant owners can also create value through their ability to engage in relational contracting, which brings improved access to resources (Gilson, 2007). Whether the positive or negative tendencies prevail may depend crucially upon the quality of institutions. The logic of Proposition 1a suggests that the development of protective institutions, such as greater protection for minority shareholders, will curb dominant owners' capacity to expropriate and entrench, but should leave intact their value-creating monitoring and oversight incentives. The combination of external constraints, that ensure dominant owners respect their obligations towards minority investors, protects creditors from default, and internal incentives tend to have a net positive effect on profitability (Anderson and Reeb 2003).

> **Proposition 1a:** BGs controlled by concentrated owners will become more profitable with the development of protective institutions.

The second scenario in Quadrant II concerns the politics of crony capitalism, documented by developmental-state scholars (Kang 2003). Initial conditions favoured groups that grew to prominence due to their close relationships with authoritarian governments, who provided lucrative opportunities and scarce resources. Favoured groups privately profit from their political connections, but impose significant socio-economic costs on society. In these cases, efforts to improve protective institutions such as the rule of law and more accountable government should reduce corruption, curb crony capitalism, and undermine the viability of groups who profit from it. However, cronyism between public officials and business owners has highly contingent value (Siegel 2007) that can quickly decline with the growth of protective institutions such as rule of law and checks on corruption. For example, following Suharto's overthrow in the wake of the Asian financial crisis, Indonesia's new reformist government introduced a raft of anti-corruption policies and sought to seize the assets of Suharto-linked companies (Dieleman and Sachs 2008). In Korea, Siegel (2007) found that groups closely linked to the regime in power enjoyed significantly better access to profitable cross-border strategic alliance opportunities, but with the growth of democracy, changes in the political regime converted BGs' political assets into liabilities. Schneider (2010) describes numerous 'Icarus groups' whose fortunes rapidly rise and fall along with the fate of their political patrons.

> **Proposition 1b:** Rent-seeking BGs become prone to failure with the development of protective institutions

The proposition and mechanism described in Quadrant II derive from transaction-cost theories of BGs. As noted above, groups can create value by filling institutional voids, but group affiliation also imposes costs arising from bureaucratic costs and complexities of broad organizational scope (Hoskisson et al. 2005). Broadly diversified small-scale groups are especially prone to incurring these costs, because they lack the scale to provide centralized services to affiliates (Khanna and Palepu 2000b). These latter groups represent initial conditions where group affiliation is associated with value destruction. In a scenario of improved enabling institutions, independent firms have better access to resources such as equity and high-quality labour, and increasingly outcompete the bureaucratically encumbered BG affiliates, whose profits begin to erode. The prescribed strategy for a BG in more munificent resource environments is to refocus, loosen affiliation with its members and ultimately unravel as a group (Hoskisson et al. 2005). This theory predicts that failing to refocus will damage the profitability of BG affiliates as affiliation premia turn into discounts (Lee, Peng, and Lee 2008).

> **Proposition 2:** The development of resource-enabling institutions increases the cost of group affiliation. BG value is expected to decline further and groups will unravel and disappear.

Quadrant III represents the case where BGs create value in an environment where protective institutions are improving. In this scenario, BG value arises from the ability to serve as safe havens for property rights, and the positive effects of concentrated ownership and group affiliation are evident. The development of more effective protective institutions such as rule of law and protection for minority shareholders is likely to have at best a complementary effect upon BG functioning and will have little effect upon their profitability or scope.

The idea that BG functioning is unaffected by improvements in formal protection for stakeholders is consistent with institutional theories of BGs that suggest BGs persist because their behavioural logics are embedded in more tenacious normative and cognitive institutions, such as those governing the role of the family, traditional inheritance norms, and the historical role of the state in society (Biggart 1998).

> **Proposition 3:** The development of protective institutions will have no impact upon BG value or prevalence.

Quadrant IV represents the case where a BG creates value in an environment where enabling institutions are improving. Developmental-state perspectives view BGs as a valuable developmental tool, due to their capacity to acquire valuable know-how and technologies and diffuse them among their affiliates (Amsden and Hikino 1994). In this perspective, BGs progressively develop more complex organizational capabilities and climb the value-added curve with more differentiated and high-value added products (Kock and Guillén 2001). Siegel and Choudhury (2010) suggest that BGs typically support or 'prop' their affiliates. In a study of Indian BGs they find that groups 'tower above' independent firms and on average BGs invest 42 per cent more in marketing activities and fully 70 per cent more in R&D than independent firms. If BGs enjoy a competitive advantage in realizing scale and scope economies, they should grow as enabling institutions develop. For example, growing inflows of foreign portfolio investment increased the liquidity of Asian equity markets over the last decade and the region's largest BGs were the principal beneficiaries of these capital flows (Pepinsky 2012). The growing availability of equity enables well-established BGs to take advantage of a wider range of opportunities (Siegel and Choudhury 2010). For example, improved access to equity financing has facilitated the rapid international expansion of Indian and Chinese BGs (Ramamurti and Singh 2009; Yiu 2011). Similarly, liberal market policies of privatization and deregulation enable entry into previously restricted market segments. Accordingly, because of their superior ability to organize scale and scope economies, improvements in enabling institutions provide the freedom and resources for BGs to further expand the scope of their activities.

**Proposition 4:** BGs will become more profitable and more diversified as enabling institutions develop.

# CONCLUSION

In this chapter I have identified several problems with the application of institutional analysis to BGs, including a lack of consensus about actors' motivation and their capacities to perceive and realize their interests, the multidimensional nature of institutions and non-correlation of institutional components, and unspecified timeframe for institutional effects. Most studies surveyed in this chapter employ a single theoretical approach, such as agency or institutional theory. Individually, each offers useful insights into the impact of institutions and BG outcomes, but none is sufficiently comprehensive to fully account for the evident variation and complexity of this ubiquitous organizational form.

In future research, theoretical frameworks used to understand group behaviour will need to become more nuanced and varied. Both business systems and varieties of capitalism perspectives offer much potential in this regard, since they are more accommodating of the idiosyncratic effects of history and context. Both allow for more varied assumptions about the variable nature of institutional constraints, as well as the importance of proactive strategic choices. Each provides a multi-level framework for understanding the aggregate effects of goal-oriented collective action (Carney, Gedajlovic and Yang 2009). In particular, the varieties of capitalism perspective incorporates 'realist' assumptions about politics and power, generally absent from both sociological and economic theories, and the extent to which individual action can render institutions stable or subject to change.

A recurring criticism of business systems and varieties of capitalism perspectives is that they implicitly assume that a single organizational form or emblematic firm prevails within a given form of capitalism. In this respect it is easy to assume that BGs represent the emblematic form of Asian forms of capitalism. But this is not the case. BGs coexist with freestanding single-business firms throughout Asia. What explains the relative prevalence of each form in each national context is a question best jointly addressed by both BG and varieties of capitalism scholars. Moreover, an important challenge facing business-system theories of Asian capitalism is how to accommodate the evident variation in BGs' organizational capabilities, capital accumulation, and value-creation models. How diverse organizations become isomorphic and develop complementarities with a system of national institutions is not readily explained. Finally, BGs span multiple sectors of the economy and internalize many resource-allocation and regulatory functions that are performed by external institutions in other forms of capitalism. Because BGs blur sectorial distinctions and levels of analysis, they present difficulties to a body of scholarship that purports to provide a macro institutional account of the microeconomics of the firm's competitive advantage.

## REFERENCES

Almeida, H. and D. Wolfenzon (2006). 'Should Business Groups Be Dismantled? The Equilibrium Costs of Efficient Internal Capital Markets'. *Journal of Financial Economics 79*: 99–144.

Amsden, A. H. (1989). *Asia's Next Giant: South Korea and Late Industrialization*. New York, Oxford University Press.

—— (2009). 'Does Firm Ownership Matter? Poes and Foes in the Developing World'. In R. Ramamurti and J. V. Singh, Eds., *Emerging Multinationals in Emerging Markets*: 64–77. Cambridge, Cambridge University Press.

—— and T. Hikino (1994). 'Project Execution Capability, Organizational Know-How and Conglomerate Corporate Growth in Late Industrialization'. *Industrial and Corporate Change 3*: 111–147.

Anderson, R. C. and D. M. Reeb (2003). 'Founding Family Ownership, Corporate Diversification and Firm Leverage'. *Journal of Law and Economics 58*(3): 653–684.

Battilana, J., B. Leca, and E. Boxenbaum (2009). 'How Actors Change Institutions: Towards a Theory of Institutional Entrepreneurship'. *Academy of Management Annals 3*(1): 65–107.

Bertrand, M., P. Mehta, and S. Mullainathan (2002). 'Ferreting out Tunnelling: An Application to Indian Business Groups'. *Quarterly Journal of Economics 117*(1): 121–148.

Biggart, N. W. (1998). 'Deep Finance: The Organizational Bases of South Korea's Financial Collapse'. *Journal of Management Inquiry 7*(4): 311–320.

—— and G. G. Hamilton (1992). 'On the Limits of a Firm-Based Theory to Explain Business Networks: The Western Bias of Neoclassical Economics'. In N. Nohria and R. G. Eccles, Eds., *Networks and Organizations: Structure, Form and Action*: 471–490. Boston: Harvard Business School Press.

Botero, J. C., S. Djankov, R. L. Porta, F. Lopez-de-Silanes and A. Shleifer (2004). 'The Regulation of Labor'. *Quarterly Journal of Economics 119*(4):1339–1382.

Bruton, G., D. Ahlstrom, and K. S. Yeh (2004). 'Understanding Venture Capital in East Asia: The Impact of Institutions on the Industry Today and Tomorrow'. *Journal of World Business 39*(1): 72–88.

Campbell, J. L. (2004). *Institutional Change and Globalization*. Princeton, Princeton University Press.

Carney, M. and E. Gedajlovic (2002). 'The Co-Evolution of Institutional Environments and Organizational Strategies: The Rise of Family Business Groups in the ASEAN Region'. *Organization Studies 23*(1): 1–31.

—— E. Gedajlovic and X. Yang (2009). 'Varieties of Asian Capitalism: Toward an Institutional Theory of Asian Enterprise'. *Asia Pacific Journal of Management 26*(3): 361–380.

—— E. R. Gedajlovic, P. P. M. A. R. Heugens, M. Van Essen, and J. H. Van Oosterhout (2011). 'Business Group Affiliation, Performance, Context, and Strategy: A Meta-Analysis'. *Academy of Management Journal 54*(3): 437–460.

—— D. Shapiro, and Y. Tang (2009). 'Business Group Performance in China: Ownership and Temporal Considerations'. *Management and Organization Review 5*(2): 167–193.

Chang, S. J. (2003). 'Ownership Structure, Expropriation, and Performance of Group-Affiliated Companies in Korea'. *Academy of Management Journal 46*(2): 238–253.

—— and J. Hong (2000). 'Economic Performance of Group-Affiliated Companies in Korea: Intragroup Resource Sharing and Internal Business Transactions'. *Academy of Management Journal 43*(3): 429–448.

Chen, V., J. Li, and D. Shapiro (2011). 'Are OECD-Prescribed "Good Corporate Governance Practices" really good in an Emerging Economy?'. *Asia Pacific Journal of Management 28*(1): 115–138.

Chung, C. N. (2001). 'Markets, Culture and Institutions: The Emergence of Large Business Groups in Taiwan, 1950–1970'. *Journal of Management Studies 38*(5): 719–745.

—— and X. Luo (2008a). 'Institutional Logics or Agency Costs: The Influence of Corporate Governance Models on Business Group Restructuring in Emerging Economies'. *Organization Science 19*(5): 776–784.

—— (2008b). 'Human Agents, Contexts, and Institutional Change: The Decline of Family in the Leadership of Business Groups'. *Organization Science 19*(1): 124–142.

—— J. P. H. Fan, and L. H. P. Lang (2002). 'Disentangling the Incentive and Entrenchment Effects of Large Shareholdings'. *Journal of Finance 57*(6): 2741–2771.

Claessens, S., S. Djankov, and L. H. P. Lang (2000). *East Asian Corporations: Heroes or Villains?* World Bank discussion paper 409. Washington, DC, World Bank.

Claessens, S., Djankov, S., Fan, J. P., & Lang, L. H. (2002). Disentangling the incentive and entrenchment effects of large shareholdings. *The Journal of Finance, 57*(6), 2741–2771.

Claessens, S., J. P. H. Fan, and L. H. P. Lang (2006). 'The Benefits and Costs of Group Affiliation: Evidence from East Asia'. *Emerging Markets Review 7*(1): 1–26.

Dieleman, M. and W. M. Sachs (2008). 'Coevolution of Institutions and Corporations in Emerging Economies: How the Salim Group Morphed into an Institution of Suharto's Crony Regime'. *Journal of Management Studies 45*(7): 1274–1300.

Djankov, S., R. La Porta, F. Lopez-de-Silanes, and A. Shleifer (2008). 'The Law and Economics of Self-Dealing'. *Journal of Financial Economics 88*(3): 430–465.

Djelic, M.-L. and S. Quack (2003). 'Globalization as a Double Process of Institutional Change and Institution Building'. In M-L. Djelic and S. Quack, Eds., *Globalization and Institutions: Redefining the Rules of the Economic Game*: 302–333. Cheltenham, Edward Elgar.

Evans, P. (1995). *Embedded Autonomy: States and Industrial Transformation*. Princeton, Princeton University Press.

Fisman, R. and T. Khanna (2004). 'Facilitating Development: The Role of Business Groups'. *World Development 32*(4): 609–628.

Gereffi, G. (2001). 'Shifting Governance Structures in Global Commodity Chains, with Special Reference to the Internet'. *The American Behavioural Scientist* 44(10): 1616–1637.

Gilson, R. (2007). 'Controlling Family Shareholders in Developing Countries: Anchoring Relational Exchange'. *Stanford Law Review* 60(2): 633–655.

Gomez, E. T. (2009). 'The Rise and Fall of Capital: Corporate Malaysia in Historical Perspective'. *Journal of Contemporary Asia* 39(3): 345–381.

Goto, A. (1982). 'Business Groups in a Market Economy'. *European Economic Review* 19: 53–70.

Granovetter, M. (2005). 'Business Groups and Social Organization'. In N. J. Smelser and R. Swedburg, Eds., *Handbook of Economic Sociology*: 429–450. Princeton, Princeton University Press.

Greenwood, R. and R. O. Y. Suddaby (2006). 'Institutional Entrepreneurship in Mature Fields: The Big Five Accounting Firms'. *Academy of Management Journal* 49(1): 27–48.

Guillen, M. F. (2000). 'Business Groups in Emerging Economies: A Resource-based View'. *Academy of Management Journal* 43(3): 362–380.

Haggard, S., A. MacIntyre, and L. Tiede (2008). 'The Rule of Law and Economic Development'. *Annual Review of Political Science* 11(1): 205–234.

Hall, P. and D. Soskice (2001). *Varieties of Capitalism: The Institutional Foundations of Comparative Advantage*. Oxford, Oxford University Press.

Hall, P. A. and K. Thelen (2009). 'Institutional Change in Varieties of Capitalism'. *Socio-Economic Review* 7: 7–34.

Hobday, M. (1995). 'East Asian Latecomer Firms: Learning the Technology of Electronics'. *World Development* 23: 1171–1193.

Hoskisson, R. E., R. A. Johnson, L. Tihanyi, and R. White (2005). 'Diversified Business Groups and Corporate Refocusing in Emerging Economies'. *Journal of Management* 31(6): 941–965.

Jensen, M. C. and W. H. Meckling (1976). 'Theory of the Firm: Managerial Behaviour, Agency Costs and Ownership Structure'. *Journal of Financial Economics* 3: 305–360.

Kang, D. (2003). *Crony Capitalism: Corruption and Development in South Korea and the Philippines*. Cambridge, Cambridge University Press.

Kaufmann, D., A. Kraay, and M. Mastruzzi (2009). 'Governance Matters VIII: Aggregate and Individual Governance Indicators, 1996-2008'. World Bank Policy Research Working Paper No. 4978. Retrieved 10 October 2012 from <http://ssrn.com/abstract=1424591>.

Keister, L. A. (1998). 'Engineering Growth: Business Groups Structure and Firm Performance in China's Transition Economy'. *American Journal of Sociology* 104(3): 404–440.

—— (2000). *Chinese Business Groups: The Structure and Impact of Inter-firm Relations during Economic Development*. New York, Oxford University Press.

—— (2001). 'Exchange Structures in Transition: Lending and Trade Relations in Chinese Business Groups'. *American Sociological Review* 66(3): 336–360.

Khanna, T. and K. Palepu (1997). ' Why Focused Strategies May Be Wrong for Emerging Markets'. *Harvard Business Review* 75(4): 41–51.

—— (1999). 'The Right Way to Restructure Conglomerates in Emerging Markets'. *Harvard Business Review* 77(July–August): 125–134.

—— (2000a). 'The Future of Business Groups in Emerging Markets: Long-run Evidence from Chile'. *Academy of Management Journal* 43(3): 268–285.

—— (2000b). 'Is Group Affiliation Profitable in Emerging Markets? An Analysis of Diversified Indian Business Groups'. *Journal of Finance* 55(2): 867–891.

Khanna, T. and Y. Yafeh (2007). 'Business Groups in Emerging Markets: Paragons or Parasites?' *Journal of Economic Literature* 45(2): 331–372.

Kim, H., R. E. Hoskisson, and W. P. Wan (2004). 'Power Dependence, Diversification Strategy, and Performance in *keiretsu* Member Firms'. *Strategic Management Journal* 25(7): 613–636.

Kock, C. J. and M. F. Guillén (2001). 'Strategy and Structure in Developing Countries: Business Groups as an Evolutionary Response to Opportunities for Unrelated Diversification'. *Industrial and Corporate Change* 10: 77–113.

Kostova, T., K. Roth, and M. T. Dacin (2009). 'Theorizing on MNCs: A Promise for Institutional Theory'. *Academy of Management Review* 34(1): 171–173.

La Porta, R., F. Lopez de Silanes, A. Shleifer, and R. W. Vishny (1998). 'Law and Finance'. *Journal of Political Economy* 106(6): 1113–1155.

Lee, K., M. W. Peng, and K. Lee (2008). 'From Diversification Premium to Diversification Discount During Institutional Transitions'. *Journal of World Business* 43(1): 47–65.

Leff, N. H. (1978). 'Industrial Organization and Enterpreneurship in Developing Countries: The Economic Groups'. *Economic Development and Cultural Change* 26: 661–675.

Lincoln, J., R. and M. L. Gerlach (2004). *Japan's Network Economy: Structure, Persistence, and Change*. Cambridge, Cambridge University Press.

Ma, X., X. Yao, and Y. Xi (2006). 'Business Group Affiliation and Performance in the Transition Economy: A Focus on Ownership Voids'. *Asia-Pacific Journal of Management* 23(4): 467–484.

Maman, D. (2002). 'The Emergence of Business Groups: Israel and South Korea Compared'. *Organization Studies* 23(5): 737–758.

Mathews, J. A. (2006). 'Dragon Multinationals: New Players in 21st Century Globalization'. *Asia-Pacific Journal of Management*, 23(1): 5–27.

Morck, R. (2010). 'The Riddle of the Great Pyramids'. In A. M. Colpan, T. Hikino, and J. R. Lincoln, Eds., *Oxford Handbook of Business Groups*: 602–628. Oxford, Oxford University Press.

Morck, R. K., D. Wolfenzon, and B. Yeung (2005). 'Corporate Governance, Economic Entrenchment, and Growth'. *Journal of Economic Literature* 43(3): 655–720.

Nolte, A. and A. Vliegenthart (2009). 'Enlarging the Varieties of Capitalism: The Emergence of Dependent Market Economies in East Central Europe'. *World Politics* 61(4): 670–702.

Orru, M., N. W. Biggart, and G. G. Hamilton (1997). *The Economic Organization of East Asian Capitalism*. Thousand Oaks, Sage.

Pepinsky, T. B. (2012). 'The Political Economy of Financial Development in Southeast Asia'. In A. Walter and X. Zhang, Eds., *East Asian Capitalism: Diversity, Continuity, Change*: 179–200. New York, Oxford University Press.

Perkins, D. H. (1994). 'There are at least Three Models of East Asian Development'. *World Development* 22(4): 655–661.

Perotti, E. C. and S. Gelfer (2001). 'Red Barons or Robber Barons? Governance and Investment in Russian Financial-Industrial Groups'. *European Economic Review* 9: 1601–1617.

Ramamurti, R. and J. V. Singh (2009). 'Indian Multinationals: Generic Internationalization Strategies'. In R. Ramamurti and J. V. Singh, Eds., *Emerging Multinationals in Emerging Markets*: 110–166. Cambridge, Cambridge University Press.

Ritchie, B. K. (2009). 'Economic Upgrading in a State-Coordinated Liberal Market Economy'. *Asia-Pacific Journal of Management*, 26(3): 435–458.

Rodrik, D. (2008). 'Second-Best Institutions'. *American Economic Review* 98: 100–104.

Scharfstein, D. S. and J. C. Stein (2000). 'The Dark Side of Internal Capital Markets: Divisional Rent-Seeking and Inefficient Investment'. *Journal of Finance* 55(6): 2537–2564.

Schneider, B. R. (2009a). 'A Comparative Political Economy of Diversified Business Groups, or How States Organize Big Business'. *Review of International Political Economy* 16(2): 178–201.

—— (2009b). 'Hierarchical Market Economies and Varieties of Capitalism in Latin America'. *Journal of Latin American Studies 41*: 553–575.

—— (2010). 'Business Groups and the State: The Politics of Expansion Restructuring and Collapse'. In A. M. Colpan, T. Hikino, and J. R. Lincoln, Eds., *Oxford Handbook of Business Groups*: 650–669. Oxford, Oxford University Press.

Siegel, J. (2007). 'Contingent Political Capital and International Alliances: Evidence from South Korea'. *Administrative Science Quarterly 52*(4): 621–666.

Siegel, J. I. and P. Choudhury (2010). 'A Re-examination of Tunnelling and Business Groups: New Data and New Methods'. *Review of Financial Studies 25*(6): 1763–1798.

Strachan, H. W. (1976). *Family and Other Business Groups in Economic Development: The Case of Nicaragua*. New York, Praeger.

Wade, R. (1990). *Governing the Market: Economic Theory and the Role of Government in East Asian Industrialization*. Princeton, Princeton University Press.

—— (2010). 'After the Crisis: Industrial Policy and the Developmental State in Low-Income Countries'. *Global Policy 1*(2): 150–161.

Williamson, O. E. (1985). *The Economic Institutions of Capitalism: Firms, Markets, Relational Contracting*. New York, Free Press.

Yiu, D. W. (2011). 'Multinational Advantages of Chinese Business Groups: A Theoretical Exploration'. *Management and Organization Review 7*(2): 249–277.

Young, M. N., M. W. Peng, D. Ahlstrom, G. D. Bruton, and Y. Jiang (2008). 'Corporate Governance in Emerging Economies: A Review of the Principal-Principal Perspective'. *Journal of Management Studies 45*(1): 196–220.

# CHAPTER 16

..............................................................................................................

# CORPORATE GOVERNANCE AND BUSINESS SYSTEMS IN ASIA

..............................................................................................................

## CHRISTINA L. AHMADJIAN

## INTRODUCTION

..............................................................................................................

CORPORATE governance is a fundamental pillar of any business system, whose institutions interact with other sets of institutions—industrial relations, education and training systems, and inter-firm relations—to shape systems of capitalism (Hall and Soskice 2001). Corporate governance itself is the product of complex interrelationships between institutions, such as financial markets, legal systems, and shareholder protection, as well as taken-for-granted notions of the role of the firm in society (Vitols 2001b).

Business-systems literature has tended to focus on corporate governance in certain developed countries, with particular interest shown in the contrast between the relationally centred systems of Germany and Japan and the market-based systems of the US and UK (Hall and Soskice 2001; Streeck 2001). Broader comparisons of corporate governance in emerging and recently developed economies are rare (but see Millar et al. 2005; Aguilera et al. 2012; Claessens and Yurtoglu 2012). Asia presents a particularly interesting setting for comparative corporate-governance research, being highly diverse in terms of stages of development, legal traditions, cultural heritage, financial systems, and political regimes.

This chapter examines corporate governance in the thirteen Asian countries in this handbook. The business-systems perspective provides a starting point to evaluate corporate governance on five dimensions: the nature of the financial system, ownership structure, boards of directors and top management, employee representation, and purpose of the firm. The comparison confirms that corporate governance consists of a set of intertwined and complementary institutions. Comparisons that rely on single dimensions, such as ownership or board composition, provide an incomplete picture, and apparently single-dimensional systems may diverge greatly when the entire picture is considered. Similarly, systems that diverge in terms of legal system or ownership concentration may have considerable similarities when all attributes are taken into consideration. This chapter suggests that there is no 'typical' Asian type of corporate governance; each of the countries here has its own distinctive combination of governance attributes, rooted in unique histories, sets of actors and interests, legal and political systems, and cultures.

This overview suggests ways in which the business-systems perspective can be further developed to better understand emerging and late-developing economies, for example through more attention to the gap between formal and informal systems and practices that has always existed, but has widened with the introduction of new regulations such as mandated independent directors. The comparison also suggests the need for an expanded understanding of globalization, to include product and labour markets, the influence of non-Western economies, and the rise of state capitalism in the form of direct state ownership and sovereign-wealth funds.

This chapter begins by briefly reviewing the comparative corporate-governance literature. This is followed by a discussion of corporate governance in the thirteen countries, and a section highlighting themes and observations raised thereby relating to the business-systems perspective and corporate-governance theory. Strengths of the business-systems approach are identified, as well as areas where other perspectives can provide a more nuanced understanding.

# COMPARATIVE CORPORATE GOVERNANCE FROM BUSINESS SYSTEMS AND OTHER PERSPECTIVES

In the business-systems perspective, corporate governance is not only a central component of the interrelated and complementary institutions that form a business system, but is itself the product of interrelated and complementary institutions (Vitols 2001b; Aguilera et al. 2008; Goyer 2010; Filatotchev, Jackson, and Nakajima 2012). Thus, corporate governance cannot be described by a single measure or indicator, but must be evaluated and understood across a range of dimensions, including formal institutions such as legal system and board composition, as well as informal ones such as concepts of the purpose of a firm and who is to control it.

Corporate-governance systems have a profound effect on national economies, determining the nature of capital and funding of firms and affecting the degree to which corporate information is a public good in which it is embedded in private relationships (Hall and Soskice 2001). Corporate-governance systems determine the order of priority by which a firm assigns importance to stakeholders. They constrain or liberate managers (Whitley 1999), and influence and shape business systems with a conception of appropriateness in firm role and behaviour (Whitley 1999; Redding and Witt 2007). A corporate-governance system shapes a firm's investment horizons, affecting long- or short-term perspectives, and corporate-governance systems combined with other institutions determine the source of a country's competitive advantage (Hall and Soskice 2001).

The business-systems perspective tends to focus on the relationship of corporate governance with other institutions, and the existence of complementarities with these institutions (Hall and Soskice 2001). There is also an emphasis on categorization and grouping, often in dichotomous categories, including bank or market systems, share-holder or stakeholder systems, insider or outsider systems, or diffuse or concentrated ownership systems.

The focus of business-systems literature thus tends towards corporate governance in its relationship to entire business systems, rather than issues of origin. However, this question of the emergence of corporate-governance systems has been substantially addressed in a range of other disciplines, based on very different models of human behaviour, the role of law and politics, and the importance of history. As long as we do not assume a single 'correct' theory, and acknowledge how the diversity of theory reflects complexity and multi-causality in the emergence of corporate-governance systems, this set of studies can richly complement business-systems literature.

Several theoretical perspectives on corporate governance have particularly helped to provide a more nuanced view of national systems of corporate governance in Asia or elsewhere. Perhaps the most extensively developed is the law and finance perspective (La Porta et al. 1998), in which legal systems determine corporate governance, specifically through the mechanism of protecting minority-shareholder rights. The degree to which minority-shareholder rights are protected is associated with the development of equity markets (La Porta et al. 1998), as well as with concentration of ownership (Shleifer and Vishny 1997), and degree of separation of ownership and control (Claessens, Djankov, and Lang 2000). Common law, it is argued, offers better protection for minority-shareholder rights and encourages diffuse ownership, separation of ownership and control, vibrant equity markets, and therefore superior economic outcomes compared to civil-law or other systems.

This literature contrasts with the business-systems perspective, in that it asserts a 'best way' of corporate governance that solves the agency problem. Without protection of minority-shareholder rights, firms and owners may take advantage of information asymmetries, constructing pyramidal ownership, for example, and loosening the relationship between control rights and cash-flow rights (Shleifer and Vishny 1997; Claessens, Djankov, and Lang 2000). Scholars from the law and finance perspective have taken particular interest in Asia (Claessens, Djankov, and Lang 2000), especially since the Asian Financial Crisis of 1997, and attribute this crisis to the failure to protect minority shareholders from the predatory behaviour of controlling, usually family, shareholders (Johnson et al. 2000; Hanazaki and Liu 2003).

The law and finance perspective has been criticized on several grounds—for a relatively narrow emphasis on a tight link between legal heritage and corporate governance, for use of indicators of corporate governance on a national level that have not stood up well to closer looks at coding, and for a large number of national systems that seem not to fit (see, e.g. Aguilera and Williams 2009). Yet this perspective has been one of the few research streams to make a concentrated effort to develop indicators and international comparisons enabling the large-scale comparison of governance systems.

Another perspective on corporate governance attributes cross-national variation to politics and power. Roe (1994) argues that the US market-centred system of finance, with its strong regulation that reduced the power of banks and kept them at arm's length from management of firms was due to a process of evolution shaped by populist politics and anti-bank sentiment, and was not a natural product of the legal system or economic rationality. Hoshi and Kashyap (2001), in a similar vein, trace the development of the Japanese system of corporate governance to politics, political and bureaucratic interactions, and development policies, as well as the post-war US occupation and the aftermath of defeat.

Other political perspectives on corporate governance provide more explicit models of the interactions that lead to different systems. Gourevitch and Shinn (2005) see corporate-governance systems as the product of interaction between management, capital, and labour, and argue that the political system affects the nature of this interaction, and the specific alignment of actors. Aguilera and Jackson (2003) also model corporate-governance systems as the result of interactions between actors, but posit that the interests of these actors are highly influenced by, and embedded in, context.

Context not only determines actors' interests, but can also shape their fundamental conceptions as to the purpose of the firm, its obligations to various stakeholders, and its role in society. A number of scholars, writing in a sociological tradition, have argued that corporate-governance practices are related to institutional logics—generally held notions of the appropriate way to conduct business, or organize a system (Friedland and Alford 1991; Thornton and Ocasio 1999). One type of institutional logic is a conception of control. Research on the US has shown a shift in the conception of control from managerial to financial, in which managers are beholden to the financial markets and shareholders (Fligstein 1990; Zajac and Westphal 2004; Davis 2009). The notion that a company exists to maximize shareholder value has spread across borders and business systems, driven by foreign investors and managers educated and socialized in the US system (Fiss and Zajac 2004; Ahmadjian and Robbins 2005).

When different institutional logics and interests of actors around corporate governance come into conflict, firms may resolve the gap through de-coupling, that is, by adopting a practice in appearance but not substance (Westphal and Zajac 1998). This tendency seems particularly common in corporate governance, where a gap exists between the interests of principals and agents, and studies have shown how managers have adopted certain governance practices in name only (Fiss and Zajac 2004). This suggests that it may be misleading to study corporate governance only through observation of espoused practices, and it is important to examine both adoption and actual implementation.

Which perspective on comparative corporate governance best explains variation and similarities in corporate governance around the world? Perhaps the most useful conclusion is that they all have value in explaining different aspects of the intertwined sets of institutions that contribute to national variations. The following sections will present a comparative examination of practices in the countries in this handbook, and will draw from the business-systems, law and finance, political, and sociological perspectives, to provide a broader and deeper understanding of varieties of corporate governance than any one perspective or indicator can offer.

# COMPARATIVE CORPORATE GOVERNANCE IN ASIA

How does corporate governance in Asia vary? Is there a distinctive Asian system? Do corporate-governance practices in Asian countries cluster in any obvious way? To what extent does theory developed from studies of Western industrialized countries and Japan apply to Asia? This section reviews governance systems in three countries, based on five dimensions used in both the business-systems and law and finance literature to compare corporate governance. It draws in particular on the categories used by Whitley (1992) and Vitols (2001b). The five dimensions are financial systems, ownership structure, boards of directors and top management, employee representation, and the nature of the firm. Rather than provide a detailed description of each country on each dimension, the objective here is to give a sense of points of diversity and similarity, in particular for the largest and most influential countries in the region.

This section draws from the country chapters in this handbook. To support the more qualitative information in the country chapters, several tables present comparative statistics, drawn from a number of publicly available sources, on various aspects relating to corporate governance in Asia. Information on ownership and ownership change over time comes largely from Carney and Child (2012).

# THE NATURE OF FINANCIAL SYSTEMS

The essence of corporate governance is the relationship between providers of capital and firms (Vitols 2001b). Thus, the source of capital is a fundamental attribute of a business system (Amable 2003). The distinction between bank-based and equity-market-based systems has long been a mainstay of literature on comparative capitalism (Zysman 1983; Allen and Gale 2000; Vitols 2001a). The question of whether firms obtain capital through banks or through equity or debt markets has important implications for firms. The source of capital, and whether it is long term, in the form of bank debt, or from equity-holders with a short-term perspective, is likely to affect strategy (Hall and Soskice 2001). The source of funds, market or bank, is likely to affect the degree of openness of information-sharing and the relationship between providers and receivers of funds (Hall and Soskice 2001).

Where does capital come from in Asia? Table 16.1 shows the ratio of stock-market capitalization to GDP and the ratio between stock trading and stock-market capitalization for twelve of the thirteen Asian countries. These data give a sense of the degree of stock-market development in each country. It is clear that considerable variation exists in the size and activity of Asian stock markets. Hong Kong has the highest ratio of stock-market capitalization to GDP, and Singapore the second. Malaysia, Japan, and Taiwan are closely tied for third place, with Korea in fourth place. The common-law economies, with the exception of India, have larger stock markets, yet so do the civil-law economies (Japan, Taiwan, and Korea). In terms of trading activity, we see that the East Asian economies of Japan, Taiwan, Korea, and China are most active as regards stock-market capitalization.

Table 16.2 shows data for key finance sources in 1995 and 2010 in selected Asian countries. It is clear that for a substantial number of countries, bank financing is still very important, accounting for one-half to one-third of finance. Bank finance has, however,

### Table 16.1 Stock markets in Asia

| Country | Stock-market capitalization (billions of US$) 2010 | Stock-market cap. /GDP 2010 | Ratio of stock trading to stock-market cap. 2010 |
|---|---|---|---|
| Japan | 4099.59 | 0.95 | 104.4% |
| South Korea | 1089.21 | 0.74 | 149.4% |
| Taiwan | 804.10 | 0.98 | 111.0% |
| Hong Kong | 1079.60 | 8.39 | 148.0% |
| Singapore | 370.09 | 1.27 | 76.3% |
| Philippines | 157.32 | 0.45 | 17.0% |
| Indonesia | 360.39 | 0.35 | 36.0% |
| Malaysia | 410.53 | 0.99 | 22.0% |
| India | 1615.86 | 0.40 | 65.4% |
| Vietnam | 20.39 | 0.07 | 84.6% |
| Thailand | 277.73 | 0.48 | 78.5% |
| Laos | n/a | n/a | n/a |
| China | 4762.84 | 0.48 | 168.6% |

Source: World Bank 2012a, 2012b; IMF 2012; USCB 2012.

**Table 16.2 Methods of financing in 2010 and 1995 (change from 1995 in parentheses)**

| Country | Bank loans | Bonds | Stock |
|---|---|---|---|
| Japan | 48.4 (+11.5%) | 39.5 (+21.9%) | 12.1 (−50.0%) |
| South Korea | 34.1 (−40.8%) | 35.1 (+48.7%) | 30.9 (+63.5%) |
| Taiwan | n/a | n/a | n/a |
| Hong Kong | 14.2 (−62.9%) | 5.1 (−1.9%) | 80.6 (+42.7%) |
| Singapore | 19.0 (−29.4%) | 15.8 (+64.6%) | 65.2 (+2.7%) |
| Philippines | 21.3 (−40.0%) | 28.2 (+41.7%) | 50.5 (+13.2%) |
| Indonesia | 34.8 (−43.5%) | 16.7 (+882.4%) | 48.6 (+32.4%) |
| Malaysia | 35.1 (+14.3%) | 25.2 (+60.5%) | 39.7 (−25.9%) |
| India | n/a | n/a | n/a |
| Vietnam | n/a | n/a | n/a |
| Thailand | 48.5 (−20.4%) | 23.4 (+485.0%) | 28.2 (−19.7%) |
| Laos | n/a | n/a | n/a |
| China | 56.1 (−34.4%) | 20.0 (+124.7%) | 23.9 (+326.8%) |

*Source*: Japan Research Institute 2011.

been reduced considerably, replaced by a substantial increase in bond financing. There has been a move to market financing, but to debt rather than equity markets.

The chapters on Singapore (Carney 2014) and Hong Kong (Redding et al. 2014) also suggest that while both economies have very large stock-market capitalizations and a high dependence on equity finance, these measures, taken on their own, can be misleading, and a closer look indicates that at the domestic-firm level, reliance on bank loans is high. For example, while the ratio of market capitalization to GDP in Singapore is comparatively high, when compared to bank assets it falls between the US and Germany, a bank-centred economy (see Carney 2014) (Table 16.2). When non-Singaporean firms are removed, Singapore moves even closer towards a bank-centred economy. Similarly, while Hong Kong has a large and well-developed equity market, the representation of foreign firms is relatively high. Furthermore, representation of mainland Chinese firms is approximately 57 per cent of Hong Kong's market capitalization (Redding 1993; Redding et al. 2014).

The country chapters show wide diversity in the nature of bank-based systems, and suggest that distinguishing countries by bank-based or equity-based is insufficient in identifying the true extent of variation. First, the identity, ownership, and objectives of banks differ considerably. In China (Witt and Redding 2014b), for example, banks are state owned, lending preferentially to state-owned firms for state-sponsored and approved projects. These loans are basically state guaranteed, and policy achievement and promotion is a more important criterion for credit than solvency and ability to repay. In other economies, like the Philippines (Kondo 2014) and Thailand (Suehiro and Wailerdsak 2014), many banks are owned by family-business groups and provide financing for business-group activities. In Taiwan (Lee and Hsiao 2014), the banking sector is small and fragmented, while in Hong Kong (Redding et al. 2014) it is dominated by global powerhouses such as HSBC and Standard Chartered. In a single economy it is common to see a mix of banks, group-owned banks and state-owned banks, each lending to its own sector.

Even in countries with bank-based financial systems, access to bank loans can be uneven. As these country chapters show, in economies dominated by state or business group-owned banks, state-owned or business-group firms have access to loans, while others are reliant on internal funding or an informal financial sector. This results in an economy of 'haves and have-nots' when it comes to finance, and this phenomenon seems particularly apparent in the developing economies. It also appears that banks have become more risk-averse since the Asian financial crisis, at least in the hardest-hit countries, making bank loans even more difficult to obtain, and, it seems, increasing state influence and participation in finance (Carney and Child 2012).

Another source of variance is the mix of bank and equity finance by sector and firm type. India (Saez 2014) has the world's ninth and tenth largest stock markets, and yet banks remain the largest source of funds, and for many firms even access to bank loans is impossible. In Japan, large and financially sound firms have increasingly gone to international capital markets for funding, leaving smaller, more domestic, and less-sound firms reliant on bank finance (Hoshi and Kashyap 2001).

Stock markets also vary considerably in their purpose and use. In Malaysia, stock markets serve as convenient ways for business groups to reconfigure their assets and buy and sell businesses for relatively short-term gains (Carney and Andriesse 2014). In Singapore (Carney 2014) and Hong Kong (Redding et al. 2014), stock markets are truly global, and serve foreign companies to a larger extent than domestic ones, which are more likely to go to banks.

Asian firms seem largely dependent on banks for finance. If Asian countries have to be put in one category or another, it would have to be in bank, rather than market-based, finance. Yet this simple dichotomy obscures considerable variation. There are many types of banks, with different interests, depending in particular on the nature of their ownership, and the nature of the banking system inevitably affects access to loans, time horizons, and decision-making. Stock markets too differ, not only in size, but also in how they are used, and what sort of firms they attract. Furthermore, there is considerable diversity within countries, in terms of access to and sources of finance.

## Ownership Structure

The ownership structure of corporations varies significantly around the world, and is a key determinant of corporate-governance systems (Shleifer and Vishny 1997; La Porta et al. 1998). Researchers have identified a number of dimensions of ownership: identities of owners, degree of concentration of ownership, and the degree to which ownership ties link firms through cross-holding, pyramids, or other configuration (Claessens, Djankov, and Lang 2000; Khanna and Palepu 2004; Lincoln and Gerlach 2004).

Who owns the firms of Asia? Table 16.3 presents some data on ownership structure, drawn from the work of Carney and Child (2012). As elsewhere, prominent among owners are family and state (Claessens, Djankov, and Lang 2000; Carney and Child 2012); exceptions to the rule of high family-ownership are Japan and Taiwan. The state as owner is particularly important in Hong Kong, Singapore, and Malaysia. While the statistics are not available from Carney and Child's research, state ownership is also high in China, Vietnam, Laos, and India.

In most Asian countries, concentration of shareholding is high and a tight link exists between ownership and control (Carney and Child 2012). In many countries, there is a divergence between control and cash-flow rights, suggesting pyramidal structures in which owners can control other business-group firms through sequential and linked investments (La Porta et al. 1998; Claessens, Djankov, and Lang 2000). Table 16.3 shows that in all the Asian economies studied by Carney and Child (2012), there is a divergence between control and cash-flow rights, suggesting the existence of pyramids of ownership, where owners can exert control with lower degrees of ownership. The nature of ownership

**Table 16.3 Ownership structure in 2008 and 1996 (change from 1996 in parentheses)**

| Country | Family | State | Ratio of cash flow rights to control rights |
|---|---|---|---|
| Japan | 9.6 (2.8) | 6.3 (3.8) | 0.92 (0.21) |
| South Korea | 54.5 (2.8) | 6.9 (0.2) | 0.79 (-0.1) |
| Taiwan | 13.8 (51.8) | 9.2 (6.2) | 0.9 (0.09) |
| Hong Kong | 60.6 (-4.9) | 28.0 (24.0) | 0.89 (0.00) |
| Singapore | 60.2 (6.9) | 20.5 (-1.3) | 0.82 (0.09) |
| Philippines | 78.5 (36.4) | 5.2 (1.6) | 0.83 (-0.05) |
| Indonesia | 57.3 (-11.3) | 14.1 (3.9) | 0.85 (0.09) |
| Malaysia | 51.5 (-5.4) | 39.7 (20.3) | 0.81 (-0.02) |
| India | n/a | n/a | n/a |
| Vietnam | n/a | n/a | n/a |
| Thailand | 37.8 (-18.7) | 12.8 (5.3) | 0.82 (-0.13) |
| Laos | n/a | n/a | n/a |
| China | n/a | n/a | n/a |

Source: Carney and Child (2012), pp. 40, 56.

and concentration leads to what is largely referred to as a principal-principal agency relationship, in which one set of principals are in opposition to another (Globerman, Peng, and Shapiro 2011). Thus, the agency problem differs from what is commonly considered in corporate-governance theory. This principal-principal problem is not distinctive to Asia, but to anywhere with concentrated ownership—that is, much of the world.

A closer look at these countries suggests further that simple indicators of concentration or ownership proportion by different categories of owner obscures considerable variation. In Japan, for example, though the measure of concentration of shareholding is low, cross-shareholdings result in control and influence within business groups (Lincoln and Gerlach 2004). Low concentration is to a large extent the result of history and law: a regulation capping bank ownership of a firm's shares at 5 per cent, and the break-up of family-owned *zaibatsu* groups in the aftermath of the Second World War. In Korea, relatively low levels of concentration are due to the fact that *chaebol* owners control groups through complex pathways of small stakes (Chang 2003; Witt 2014b).

Furthermore, while it is possible to measure variation in ownership by different categories, for example state or family, the actual interests of these different categories vary substantially across economies. For example, the interests of family-owners differ across Asian economies. Quite a few are dominated by Chinese family groups, in which family interests such as long-term sustainability, stability, promotion prospects for family members, reputation, and patriarch honour may take precedence over shareholder value (Redding 1993). In other countries, such as Malaysia (Carney and Andriesse 2014) and Indonesia (Rosser 2014), business groups have arisen around individuals close to powerful politicians and their families, and because of the transience of these relationships, their interests appear to be more around short-term profit-seeking.

The effect of foreign ownership has been felt to different degrees across Asia. In some countries affected by the Asian Financial Crisis, foreign ownership decreased, scared off by unfamiliar corporate-governance practices and disastrous financial results (Carney and Child 2012). In other economies, the effect of foreign investors has become more pronounced. In Japan and Korea, foreign investment funds, in particular asset-management companies from the US and UK (liberal-market economies in the Varieties of Capitalism terminology), have increased their participation, and in both countries have called for reforms in corporate governance more consistent with practices with which they are familiar (Ahmadjian 2007). However, the origin of foreign portfolio investors is increasingly diverse, especially with the emergence of sovereign wealth funds, many of which are from Asia.

Simple indicators of foreign ownership mask not only the origins of these foreign investors, but also the distinction between foreign portfolio investors and foreign direct investment. In particular, in South East Asia there is a long history of ownership by foreign multinationals, and foreign multinationals, whose governance and management differs greatly from other categories, such as family-owned firms, make up an important sector of the economy. While historically foreign direct investment came from the Western industrialized countries and Japan, it increasingly comes from within Asia. Of particular note are Chinese and Thai investments in the Mekong River area, as well as direct investment in other parts of Asia by Japanese and Korean companies. These strategic owners are likely to have very different interests from foreign portfolio investors.

Particularly interesting are the role and interests of the state. The country chapters show that state interests and the ways that the state can wield its influence vary widely. Depending on country, the state can be a majority-owner and in full control of companies, or a minority investor through sovereign-wealth funds. The January 2012 edition of *The Economist* devoted a significant section to 'state capitalism', suggesting that the Chinese economy, with its dominant state ownership, might be a new model for development (Wooldridge 2012). 'State capitalism', however, is not limited to China. State-owned companies feature prominently in Malaysia, India, and other Asian economies. While privatization has been a feature in some economies—as in the selling of state-owned banks in Korea in the aftermath of the Asian Financial Crisis—in many others, state ownership has actually increased (Carney and Child 2012), in some cases to replace investment lost during the Financial Crisis.

One of the most interesting phenomena in Asia is the emergence of sovereign-wealth funds, which invest both within their own countries and internationally. Sovereign-wealth funds, such as Temasek and GIC in Singapore, hold stakes in domestic and foreign firms. While the image of the state-owned firm has often been one of inertia and bureaucracy, with privatization seen as the best alternative, there is emerging evidence that minority-ownership stakes by the state can benefit companies in the developing world (Lazzarini and Musacchio 2011). The Chinese investment funds SAFE Investment Company and China Investment Company manage US$568 billion and $410 billion (Wooldridge 2012), while Temasek controls about Singapore$200 billion. Sovereign-wealth funds are also important in Malaysia, Indonesia, and around Asia.

Research on these funds is still undeveloped, and it is unclear if they will introduce governance principles from their own countries or behave similarly to Anglo-American funds. But it is clear that state interests differ vastly. The interests of a Singaporean sovereign-wealth fund, for example, are likely to be very different from those of the Chinese government investing in a Chinese state-owned enterprise. The interests of the state in India, which owns 25 per cent of paid-up capital (Saez 2014), are likely to be very different from those in the Philippines, with its long history of inter-penetration between the state and elite family-controlled business groups (Kondo 2014).

In summary, firms in Asia tend to be owned by family or state. There is high concentration and low separation of ownership and control in most countries. Japan is an outlier on all these points, with diffuse ownership and low levels of family and state ownership. Yet despite the similarities in the big picture, there are very distinct differences in the nature and interests of these investors.

## Boards of Directors and Top Management

The composition and behaviour of the board of directors is a critical component of corporate governance (Monks and Minow 2001). In most of Asia, boards of directors were originally dominated by insiders, and represented the interests of majority-owners. As in many other aspects of corporate governance, Japanese boards differed from those in other Asian countries: directors tended to represent management, with some participation from banks, the government, or important business partners (Ahmadjian and Okumura 2011). Yet Japanese boards also followed the general Asian pattern of being dominated by insiders, and not considering the interests of minority shareholders.

Boards of directors in most Asian countries have changed substantially in the aftermath of the Asian Financial Crisis. In some cases, change was due to requirements imposed by the IMF. More generally, Asian economies have been influenced by the global diffusion of Anglo-American corporate governance, which has been pushed by investors, US-trained educated executives, popular business-school professors, and the mass media (Bradley et al. 1999; Coffee 2000; Fiss and Zajac 2004). There have also been domestic movements to reform governance, by business elites such as the Corporate Governance Forum of Japan, or non-governmental organizations such as the People's Solidarity for Participatory Democracy (PSPD) in Korea. A key aspect of Anglo-American corporate governance is independent directors, whose job is to monitor management and ensure that the voice of minority shareholders is heard. In most Asian countries, company law or listing requirements were revised to require firms to have a certain proportion of independent directors.

Table 16.4 summarizes the requirements for independent directors in most of the countries covered in this handbook. Most Asian economies require at least two independent directors, and recommend more. An exception is Japan, where companies have successfully resisted requirements for outside directors (Witt 2014a).

It is by no means clear, however, how effective these requirements have been in transforming corporate governance (Witt 2014a). For example, in China, regulations requiring independent directors coexist with strong Communist Party influence in management. And in many countries dominated by concentrated family ownership, it is not at all clear how much influence these outsiders can actually have. Corporate-governance activists argue that despite revisions in law and regulations, corporate governance in Asia remains far behind that of Western industrialized countries. For example, an annual corporate-governance ranking by GMI, a corporate-governance consulting firm (Governance Metrics International 2010), puts Australia, the US, and the UK at the top; Asian countries tend to be nearer the bottom, with Singapore and Hong Kong performing well. The Asian Corporate Governance Association also ranks the corporate-governance level of various Asian countries (see Table 16.4, and Gill, Allen, and Powell 2010). AGCA claims that Asian economies' governance stands at 70–80 per cent of their idea of a global standard at best, due to a poorly developed 'corporate-governance culture'. In other words, despite regulations on paper, actual implementation and even desire of companies to implement reform is low (Gill, Allen, and Powell 2010).

The country chapters in this handbook suggest that despite attempts to reform boards of directors, management practice remains relatively unchanged. In fact, management style seems to be one aspect where there is quite a bit of similarity. Most country

**Table 16.4 Requirements for outside directors and corporate governance ratings**

| Country | # of outside directors required | CLSA CG Watch market score, 2010, out of 100 |
|---|---|---|
| Japan | At least 1 independent director or 1 independent statutory auditor. | 57 |
| South Korea | At least 25% of the board must be outside directors. However, certain companies determined by Presidential Decree must have 3 or more. | 45 |
| Taiwan | No mandatory requirement for listed companies, but newly-listed firms must have at least 2 independent directors and 1 independent supervisor. Authorities have the right to require certain types of companies to appoint at least 2 independent directors. | 55 |
| Hong Kong | At least 3. | 65 |
| Singapore | At least 2 independent directors. | 67 |
| Philippines | At least 2 independent directors or at least 20% of the board, whichever is lower, to minimum of 2. | 37 |
| Indonesia | The board of commissioners of a newly listed company must have at least 30% independent commissioners. The board of directors must have at least 1 unaffiliated director. The number of independent commissioners must be in proportion to the number of shares owned by non-controlling shareholders, but at least 30%. | 40 |
| Malaysia | At least 2 independent directors or 1/3 of the board, whichever is higher. | 52 |
| India | At least 1/3 of directors should be independent if the chairman is a non-executive director. If he or she is an executive chairman, or non-executive chairman linked to the promoter (i.e. controlling shareholder), then 50% of directors should be independent. | 49 |
| Vietnam | At least 1/3 of board. | n/a |
| Thailand | At least 1/3 of the board and no fewer than 3 independent directors. | 58 |
| Laos | n/a | n/a |
| China | At least 1/3 of board. | 49 |

*Sources*: Asian Corporate Governance Association 2012; Gill, Allen, and Powell 2010.

chapters report the nature of management and managerial authority as top-down and highly authoritarian, with a low propensity to delegation. Family-controlled companies exert an emphasis on keeping key managerial positions within the family, and place high reliance on the patriarch, although there is a move to more professional management in Singapore (Carney 2014) and Hong Kong (Redding et al. 2014). The one country in which this pattern is less apparent is Japan (Witt 2014a), where there is more delegation of decision-making downwards, to middle-management level (Nonaka 1988).

The country chapters paint a picture for most of Asia in which autocratic top-down management is combined with relatively new requirements for independent directors. Assessments of organizations promoting corporate governance, such as the Asian Corporate Governance Association, suggest that top management does not completely accept the new role of independent directors nor the idea of corporate governance protecting minority-shareholder rights. In some places, in particular Hong Kong (Redding et al. 2014) and Singapore (Carney 2014), there has been a concurrent move to more professional management and independent boards. Japan (Witt 2014a) is an outlier on both, with greater resistance to independent directors and greater delegation of decision-making, as well as complete reliance on non-family management in most publicly listed companies.

## Employee Representation

The business-systems perspective has been attentive to the role of labour in corporate governance. The Varieties of Capitalism perspective, for example, gives a central role to the German co-determination system in constraining the management of large firms (Hall and Soskice 2001). Studies of Japanese corporate governance show that the strong presence of employees, whose influence is less through formal institutions than through a system in which all members of a corporation view themselves as a community (Dore 1973; Jacoby 2005), is a key component of corporate governance. What is striking in a review of corporate governance across Asia is the minimal role of labour, formal or informal, in corporate governance.

In China, in the words of Witt and Redding (2014b), there are the 'trappings of northern European social democracies'. The Communist Party, which has a strong hand in the personnel decisions of firms as well as in ownership and control through the state, represents labour, at least formally. Yet labour representation is fragmented, and as firm-owners, the interests of the Party and state often conflict with labour interests.

In India, labour relations are fragmented and dysfunctional, and even if labour relations were formalized and effective, they would still miss the huge percentage of employees in the informal sector (Saez 2014). In Indonesia and other countries there are restrictions on labour unions, and discouragement of union activity (Rosser 2014) . Singapore (Carney 2014) has a tripartite system, but a weak labour voice in the face of an authoritarian state. In Malaysia, an attempt to replicate Japanese labour relations, as part of the 'Look East' policy, has resulted in paternalistic labour relations rather than a real voice for labour (Carney and Andriesse 2014).

This review suggests that only in Japan does labour play a strong role, and not one that is mandated by law along the lines of co-determination, but rather is related both to legal difficulties in laying off workers, and to a strong sense of community and shared destiny among employees and management.

## Purpose of the Firm

Research in the sociology of corporate governance highlights that corporate governance is not necessarily an arrangement between rational and self-interested agents; rather, it is affected by what actors themselves think is important, and by widely held and taken-for-granted notions of the purpose of the firm and its role in society (Fligstein and Freeland 1995; Davis 2009). Researchers have referred to these notions as 'institutional logics' or 'conceptions of control', and have shown how they have a powerful influence on the behaviour of management, capital, and the state, and how they vary over time and place (Fligstein 1990; Thornton and Ocasio 1999; Fiss and Zajac 2004; Davis 2009).

Researchers in Japanese corporate governance have highlighted the institutional logic dominating much of Japanese business, in which a firm is a community embracing managers and employees as well as buyers, suppliers, and the wider community, while keeping shareholders at a distance (Dore 2000).

Witt and Redding (2012), comparing managerial attitudes towards CSR, suggest that managers in different Asian countries see the purpose of the firm very differently. In Hong Kong, charity is important, but only after the building of wealth. In Japan, a firm should contribute to society and managers should work for the firm's sustainability and continued existence. In South Korea, the notion of a firm having an important role in national development was once strong, but appears to be fading, and the idea that a firm has an obligation to maintain employment is much weaker than in Hong Kong or Japan. Thus, even when firms pay attention to community, they define this community, as well as the priority between profits, shareholders, and employees, in different ways.

A Chinese family-business group is likely to have very different interests and concerns from a socialist state. Foreign owners are likely to have very different notions of the purpose of a firm than local owners. The finding that ownership structures have not changed dramatically in Asian firms (Carney and Child 2012) suggests that notions of the purpose of a firm have not been changing rapidly in Asia.

## IMPLICATIONS FOR BUSINESS-SYSTEMS LITERATURE

This section returns to literature on corporate governance from business systems and other perspectives. It draws from the previous discussion of corporate governance in

Asia to identify several themes with implications for further development and enrichment of the business-systems perspective.

## Corporate Governance as a System of Complementary Institutions

The above comparison of Asian corporate-governance systems shows the value of a business-systems approach to corporate governance. Single-dimension comparisons such as ownership, though valuable, will not provide a complete picture of the system of institutions and practices, formal and informal, regulatory and cognitive, which go into a corporate-governance system. However, it also suggests that corporate-governance systems are very much embedded in local context—in history, politics, identities, and interests of actors—and defy the simple typologies that are a central focus of the business-systems perspective.

One clear conclusion is that there is no typical 'Asian' corporate governance. There is nothing new about this: it has been drawn by researchers in broader comparisons of Asian business systems, as well as this handbook's editors (Whitley 1992; Orru, Biggart, and Hamilton 1997; Witt and Redding 2014a). Furthermore, it is difficult to find similarities across regions or areas of cultural similarity, for example, the Confucian cultures of Japan, China, Taiwan, and Korea. While some scholars have argued that a similar Confucian heritage shapes business practices (Dore 1987), it is difficult to identify this influence shaping similar corporate governance patterns.

It is also difficult to classify corporate governance in Asia in the simple categories of common vs. civil law that are central to the law and finance literature. While common-law countries do seem to have larger equity markets in terms of relative size, the variation between Hong Kong, Singapore, Malaysia, and India seems greater than their similarities, and related far more to history, government, and stage of development than to legal heritage.

The dichotomies often used by corporate-governance researchers to categorize systems such as bank vs. market systems, concentrated or diffuse ownership, or stakeholder vs. shareholder systems, also seem to have limited value except as a starting point. Japan is the only system in Asia that can truly be described as a stakeholder system, in which firm management balances the interests of a set of stakeholders. In other systems, the firm's objective seems more clearly centred on shareholder value (though value to majority shareholders is prioritized over minority shareholders), enrichment of family and friends, or national interests. Categories such as concentrated vs. diffuse ownership cannot identify important differences in countries that appear quite similar at first glance: for example, the distinction between cross-holding in Japanese *keiretsu* and pyramidal shareholding in Korean *chaebol*. While categories of bank vs. market-based finance offers insight into one dimension on which systems diverge, a comparison between bank systems suggests considerable variation within bank systems themselves.

## Within-Country Diversity and Hybrids

The comparative examination of corporate governance in the thirteen Asian countries indicates another reason why it is difficult to assign countries to discrete categories of governance: considerable diversity in governance subsists *within* countries and between large and small firms. One emerging pattern in several countries is that the largest firms have access to market capital, smaller firms rely on bank capital, and the smallest can only rely on informal capital markets. In a number of countries, governance practices vary by the ethnic background of a firm's managers and owners. In India (Saez 2014) and the Philippines (Kondo 2014), there is a difference in governance between firms involved in global outsourcing operations and those more domestically focused (Khanna and Palepu 2004).

A review of corporate governance across Asia also suggests the existence of hybrid forms. Researchers on comparative corporate governance see hybrids as the result of interaction between global capital and local systems (Jackson 2002; Jackson 2005; Jackson and Moerke 2005; Aoki, Jackson, and Miyajima 2006), and this can be seen in Asia. For example, many large Chinese firms mix state ownership and Communist Party influence with Anglo-American-influenced governance practices (Witt and Redding 2014b). Korean *chaebol* mix firms with private and public ownership (Chang 2003). Many successful global Hong Kong and Singaporean firms mix family ownership and control with access to global capital markets (Carney 2014; Redding et al. 2014).

Within-country diversity and hybrids call into question the use of national-level measures or indices. These can only be averages or representatives of a specific subset of firms. This may be enough for foreign investors seeking to invest in the largest listed firms, but may not provide a complete picture of a country's system of corporate governance. Within-country diversity also suggests that more research must be done on the nature of complementary institutions: in business-systems literature, institutions are usually studied at the national level. If different sectors, ethnic groups, firm size, or other subsets differ in their corporate governance, does this mean that there are sector-specific complementarities, or that the general notion of complementarities needs to be relaxed or revised?

## Actors and Interests

While the business-systems literature was once criticized for paying insufficient attention to actors and agency (Deeg and Jackson 2007; Deeg and Jackson 2008; Jackson 2010), the notion that business systems are products of interactions between actors with very different interests is now widely accepted. One area of debate is the degree to which the interests of actors are generalizable across national contexts and determined by their category and the degree to which these interests are embedded in the local context (Aguilera and Jackson 2003).

The comparison of corporate-governance systems in Asia shows how much context determines the interests of actors (Aguilera and Jackson 2003). To take one example, the interests of majority owners differ greatly across national (also sectoral, ethnic, and other) lines. The interests of a member of an ethnic Chinese business group who is entrusted with the legacy and future of the family (Redding 1993) are likely to be very different from the interests of a manager of a Malaysian business group, which may be more oriented to short-term profit and political influence (Carney and Andriesse 2014). Interests of banks vary, depending on ownership, and regulation of finance. State-owned banks, for example, tend to support state enterprises and projects consistent with the state's development strategy. Group-owned banks, similarly, support their own business groups. More global banks, with widely diffused global ownership, follow a profit-maximization course. Thus, while corporate-governance systems in Asia are the product of interactions between management, capital, labour, and the state, it is difficult to explain the variation completely as different alliances between categories of actors. Interests are specific and local.

One actor that merits more attention is the state. In Asia, the state is not only active in corporate governance in setting and enforcing rules, but is also an important owner, in direct ownership of state-owned enterprise and also through sovereign-wealth funds. What does it mean for the state to take on a role as investor as well as regulator? What are the interests of a state investment fund in a non-market economy, and what does this mean for minority owners?

## Formal and Informal, Real and Symbolic

Corporate governance in Asia shows a gap between formal and informal practices, and the real and the symbolic. It is often difficult to tell exactly where the gap is, which practices are actually implemented and which are there for show. It appears that Asia is rife with cases of de-coupling of corporate-governance practices from actual implementation, a phenomenon apparent around the world (Westphal and Zajac 1998; Fiss and Zajac 2004).

It is not easy to identify exactly whether a practice is de-coupled, or to find a measure of de-coupling. However, the rapid spread of requirements for independent directors, combined with slow changes in ownership structure and management styles, suggest that this is an area of de-coupling. Another area in which there seems to be a gap between formal and informal, or espoused and actual, practice is labour regulation. Reasons for this include poor enforcement, favouritism of business elites, or, in the case of China in particular, a conflict of interest within the state over its stated ideology to support workers and its national strategy of economic development.

The gap between espoused and implemented practices cautions corporate-governance researchers to look beyond practices on paper and evaluate practices in actuality. It also suggests interesting research questions. Does adoption of requirements for independent directors simply reflect symbolic behaviour and de-coupling and have few substantive effects on governance? Or does it signal the first step in real change—as independent directors and management through proximity and familiarity gradually develop new roles and ways of working together? Research suggests that the degree of de-coupling of a practice may depend on the firm as well as the stage of diffusion of the practice (Kennedy and Fiss 2009; Ansari, Fiss, and Zajac 2010). It may be that the degree to which governance practices are actually implemented varies by firm, sector, or timing of adoption.

## Convergence, Change, and Globalization

A key concern of the business-systems perspective is understanding change. The notion that a business system consists of a set of complementary institutions helps to explain why extreme change is difficult and often inadvisable. Change in one aspect of the system will disturb the complementarities, leading to an inferior outcome.

A critical question in the business-systems literature, and more generally in corporate-governance literature, has been around 'convergence'. Generally, the convergence debate refers to whether corporate-governance systems around the world will all move towards Anglo-American practices, whether they will remain locally distinct, or whether each system will develop various forms of hybrid (Hansmann and Kraakman 2000; Aoki, Jackson, and Miyajima 2006; Yoshikawa and Rasheed 2009). Proponents of the convergence hypothesis argue that convergence will occur, because Anglo-American corporate governance is superior. Others have argued that whether one system is better or not, the globalization of US and UK investment funds, MBA programmes, and corporate-governance advocates promoting Anglo-American practices are likely to promote greater convergence. Globalization of labour and trade is also likely to drive convergence, at least in firms strongly linked to the global economy (Khanna and Palepu 2004). Proponents of the business-systems perspective, on the other hand, caution against simplistic assumptions of convergence, because there is no single 'best way', and because change in complementary and intertwined institutions is difficult and fraught with risk.

An examination of corporate governance in Asia offers some evidence of convergence towards 'global' or Anglo-American corporate governance, but far less than anticipated by convergence advocates. Ownership patterns have not changed much—families and the state still dominate in most countries (Carney and Child 2012). Business groups remain strong. Many countries have adopted regulations to protect minority shareholders, and independent directors are required in most countries, but it is unclear how much these regulations are enforced or implemented.

The 'state capitalism' model, seen in somewhat different variants in China and Singapore, seems to offer an alternative to free-market capitalism (Wooldridge 2012). In fact, the comparison of Asian economies suggests that 'globalization' cannot be defined as simply the spread of influence by Anglo-American capital and ideologies—in Asia, globalization is also the spread of Chinese (and other Asian) investment and engagement with a new model of economic organization that diverges from the liberal and coordinated market economy and other categories of the business-systems approach.

Chinese investment and models are just one example of new global influences: as international investment by Korean, Thai, and Japanese companies increases, there is greater interaction between models of governance, types of employment relations, managerial authority, and notions of the purpose of the firm. The effect of this sort of globalization, or regionalization, merits further research.

A comparison of Asian countries suggests also that change comes not only from outside, but also from within, and internal politics determines how and when new practices are adopted. For example, Carney and Child (2012) suggest that ownership patterns have changed most in Asian countries that have experienced political transition. Internal politics may result in an uneven back-and-forth process of change, as in Korea, where different political regimes have adopted very different stances on governance reforms and *chaebol* groups.

## Corporate Governance and Development

Is there one 'best type' of governance? According to the business-systems literature, the answer is strongly 'no'. One of the motivations of this perspective has been to demonstrate that there is no single 'best way', that neither the Western industrialized economies, nor the liberal market economies, have the single recipe for success. Outcomes may be different, but different systems have different strengths and weaknesses. In contrast, the law and finance literature takes a strong stance on the superiority of Anglo-American governance.

One reason why the business-systems literature has been able to argue that there is no single path to good governance is that it has generally considered successful developed economies. The study of Asian corporate governance requires us to consider a far wider range of outcomes: both successful developed economies and economies on the lower end of the development scale. There are countries stuck in the inertia of the 'middle-income' trap, such as Malaysia (Carney and Andriesse 2014), and others that have lagged further and further behind the rapid-developers, such as the Philippines (Kondo 2014) . Moreover, any study of corporate governance in Asia must consider the Asian Financial Crisis, widely blamed on poor corporate governance (Johnson et al. 2000; Hanazaki and Liu 2003).

In many Asian countries, the question is not only development of the country as a whole, but of allocation of the returns to development. The situation in India, with its huge informal economy, is particularly stark. In many of Asia's developing countries, access to capital is nearly impossible for large segments of the population. One key question regarding corporate-governance systems is how they affect inequality and privilege, or disenfranchise specific groups. This includes minority shareholders, but clearly goes further, to how business systems allocate capital (as well as education and other resources) to their members.

Clearly, not all systems lead to the best possible outcome. More research from a business-systems perspective is necessary to elucidate the link between corporate governance and under-development. The country chapters provide ample evidence of dysfunctional practices related to corporate governance: for example, preferential lending to state-owned or same-group enterprises, authoritarian management unchecked by independent boards, and cronyism between the state and elite families. What is the appropriate corporate-governance system for the Philippines, or Vietnam, or Laos? Can the business-systems perspective evolve to provide a useful alternative model for development to that offered by the law and finance perspective?

# CONCLUSION

This journey across corporate governance in Asia has shown the value of applying the business-systems perspective to the study of comparative corporate governance. It demonstrates that corporate governance in Asia, like anywhere in the world, cannot be evaluated solely on a single dimension such as ownership or legal heritage, though these elements are important. Corporate governance is a set of intertwined institutions, regulatory and cognitive, formal and informal, symbolic and real.

Corporate-governance systems are the result of interaction between a set of actors, management, labour, capital, and the state, but the outcomes are very different, and depend on the interests of these actors, which are very much tied to context (Aguilera and Jackson 2003). Moreover, while corporate governance is the result of a set of intertwined institutions, it cannot be completely captured through national-level indicators—considerable variation may exist within the same country across firm size, sector, and ownership.

While corporate governance in Asia is changing, there is no clear convergence towards the Anglo-American system. Equity markets are getting bigger and more important, but firms remain reliant on banks, or in the case of smaller firms, informal means of finance. Foreign ownership has increased in some countries, but ownership by family and state remain dominant. Most countries in Asia have attempted to introduce elements of Anglo-American corporate governance, in particular, outside directors, through law, listing regulations, or voluntary codes. But as the country chapters show, these changes are not necessarily accompanied by changes in ownership structures, basic attitudes of management, or existing networks of relationships.

Perhaps the biggest challenge of the business-systems approach in Asia and throughout the developing world is to consider the question of development and inequality. The law and finance perspective has clear prescriptions for governance reforms, and many of these were implemented (whether in fact or simply appearance) in Asian countries following the Asian Financial Crisis. Yet it is not clear if these prescriptions have been successful, or even if they have been completely implemented. Even if these reforms were successful in mitigating the crisis in investor confidence, it is not at all clear whether they are necessary for development—Japan, Korea, and Taiwan developed under governance systems that would be considered dysfunctional in the law and finance literature.

The business-systems perspective, on the other hand, has been able to explain why developed economies have been successful with very different systems. In general, however, writers in this perspective have shied away from the question of which system, or systems, is superior. Consequently, the business-systems perspective has not really touched the question of the relationship between corporate governance and development. Future research should do more to consider the question of under-development, how corporate governance contributes to the problem, and how it can be part of a solution.

# References

Aguilera, R., I. Filatotchev, H. Gospel, and G. Jackson (2008). 'An Organizational Approach to Comparative Corporate Governance: Costs, Contingencies, and Complementarities'. *Organization Science* 19(3): 475–492.

Aguilera, R. V. and G. Jackson (2003). 'The Cross-National Diversity of Corporate Governance'. *Academy of Management Review* 28(3): 447–465.

—— and C. A. Williams (2009). '"Law and Finance": Inaccurate, Incomplete, and Important'. *Brigham Young University Law Review* 2009/6: 1413–1434.

—— L. R. Kabbach-Castro, J. H. Lee, and J. You (2012). 'Corporate Governance in Emerging Markets'. In G. Morgan and R. Whitley, Eds., *Capitalisms and Capitalism in the 21st Century*: 319–344, Oxford, Oxford University Press.

Ahmadjian, C. L. (2007). 'Foreign Investors and Corporate-Governance Reform in Japan'. In M. Aoki, G. Jackson, and H. Miyajima, Eds., *Corporate Governance in Japan*: 125–150. Oxford, Oxford University Press.

—— and A. Okumura (2011). 'Corporate Governance in Japan'. In C. Mallin, Ed., *Handbook on International Corporate Governance* (2nd ed.): 247–268. Cheltenham, Edward Elgar.

—— and G. E Robbins (2005). 'A Clash of Capitalisms: Foreign Ownership and Restructuring in 1990s Japan'. *American Sociological Review* 70(2): 451–471.

Allen, F. and D. Gale (2000). *Comparing Financial Systems*. Cambridge, MIT Press.

Amable, B. (2003). *The Diversity of Modern Capitalism*. Oxford, Oxford University Press.

Ansari, S. M., P. C. Fiss, and E. J. Zajac (2010). 'Made to Fit: How Practices Vary as they Diffuse'. *Academy of Management Review* 35(1): 67–92.

Aoki, M., G. Jackson, and H. Miyajima, Eds. (2006). *Corporate Governance in Japan: Institutional Change and Organizational Diversity*. Oxford, Oxford University Press.

Asian Corporate Governance Association (2012). 'Rules & Recommendations on the Number of Independent Directors in Asia'. Retrieved 22 August 2012 from <http://www.acga-asia.org/public/files/Rules%20on%20Number%20of%20Independent%20Directors%20in%20Asia%20(ACGA%202010).pdf>.

Bradley, M., C. Schipani, A. K. Sundaram, and J. P. Walsh (1999). *Corporate Governance in a Comparative Setting: The United States, Germany, and Japan*. Durham, Duke University.

Carney, M. and E. Andriesse (2014). 'Malaysia: Personal Capitalism'. In M. A. Witt and G. Redding, Eds., *The Oxford Handbook of Asian Business Systems*: 144–168. Oxford, Oxford University Press.

Carney, R. W. (2014). 'Singapore: Open State-Led Capitalism'. In M. A. Witt and G. Redding, Eds., *The Oxford Handbook of Asian Business Systems*: 192–215. Oxford, Oxford University Press.

—— and T. B. Child (2012). 'Changes to Ownership and Control of East Asian Corporations between 1996 and 2008: The Primacy of Politics'. *Journal of Financial Economics*. DOI: 10.1016/j.jfineco.2012.08.013.

Chang, S. J. (2003). *Financial Crisis and Transformation of Korean Business Groups: the Rise and Fall of Chaebols*. Cambridge, Cambridge University Press.

Claessens, S., S. Djankov, and L. H. P. Lang. (2000). 'The Separation of Ownership and Control in East Asian Corporations'. *Journal of Financial Economics* 58(1–2): 81–112.

—— B. B. Yurtoglu (2012). 'Corporate Governance in Emerging Markets: A Survey'. Retrieved 27 September 2010 from <http://ssrn.com/abstract=1988880> and <http://dx.doi.org/10.2139/ssrn.1988880>.

Coffee, C. J., Jr (2000). 'The Future as History: The Prospects for Global Convergence in Corporate Governance and its Implications'. *Northwestern University Law Review* 93: 641–708.

Davis, G. F. (2009). *Managed by the Markets: How Finance Re-Shaped America*. Oxford, Oxford University Press.

Deeg, R. and G. Jackson (2007). 'Towards a More Dynamic Theory of Capitalist Variety'. *Socio-Economic Review* 5(1): 149–179.

—— (2008). 'How Many Varieties of Capitalism? From Institutional Diversity to the Politics of Change'. *Review of International Political Economy* 15(Oct.): 679–708.

Dore, R. (1973). *British Factory, Japanese Factory: The Origins of National Diversity in Industrial Relations*. Berkeley, University of California Press.

—— (1987). *Taking Japan Seriously: A Confucian Perspective on Leading Economic Issues*. Stanford, Stanford University Press.

—— (2000). *Stock Market Capitalism: Welfare Capitalism: Japan and Germany Versus the Anglo-Saxons*. Oxford, UK, Oxford University Press.

Filatotchev, I., G. Jackson, and C. Nakajima (2012). 'Corporate Governance and National Institutions: A Review and Emerging Research Agenda'. *Asia Pacific Journal of Management*. DOI: 10.1007/s10490-012-9293-9.

Fiss, P. C. and E. J. Zajac (2004). 'The Diffusion of Ideas over Contested Terrain: The (non) Adoption of a Shareholder-Value Orientation among German Firms'. *Administrative Science Quarterly* 49(4): 501–534.

Fligstein, N. (1990). *The Transformation of Corporate Control*. Cambridge, Harvard University Press.

—— and R. Freeland (1995). 'Theoretical and Comparative Perspectives on Corporate Organization'. *Annual Review of Sociology* 21: 21–43.

Friedland, R. and R. R. Alford (1991). 'Bringing Society back in'. In W.W. Powell and P. J. DiMaggio, Eds., *The New Institutionalism in Organizational Analysis*: 232–263. Chicago, University of Chicago Press.

Gill, A., J. Allen, and S. Powell (2010). *CG Watch 2010: Corporate Governance in Asia*. Hong Kong, CLSA.

Globerman, S., M. W. Peng, and D. M. Shapiro (2011). 'Corporate Governance and Asian Companies'. *Asia Pacific Journal of Management* 28(1): 1–14.

Gourevitch, P. A. and J. J. Shinn (2005). *Political Power and Corporate Control: The New Global Politics of Corporate Governance*. New Jersey, Princeton University Press.

Governance Metrics International (2010). 'Country Ratings'. Retrieved 27 September 2010 from <http://www.gmiratings.com/Images/GMI_Country_Rankings_as_of_10_27_2010.pdf>.

Goyer, M. (2010). 'Corporate Governance'. In G. Morgan, J. L. Campbell, C. Crouch, and O. K. Pedersen, Eds., *The Oxford Handbook of Comparative Institutional Analysis*: 423–452. Oxford, Oxford University Press.

Hall, P. A. and D. Soskice (2001). 'An Introduction to Varieties of Capitalism'. In P. A. Hall and D. Soskice, Eds., *Varieties of Capitalism*: 1–70. New York: Oxford University Press.

Hanazaki, M., and Q. Liu (2003). *The Asian Crisis and Corporate Governance: Ownership Structure, Debt Financing, and Corporate Diversification.* CEI Working Paper Series No. 2003-18. Tokyo, Center for Economic Institutions, Hitotsubashi University.

Hansmann, H. and R. Kraakman (2000). *The End of History for Corporate Law.* Yale Law School Working Paper 235. Harvard, Yale Law School.

Hoshi, T. and A. Kashyap (2001). *Corporate Financing and Governance in Japan.* Cambridge, MIT Press.

IMF (2012). 'World Economic Outlook Databases'. Retrieved 2 October 2012 from <http://www.imf.org/external/ns/cs.aspx?id=28>.

Jackson, G. (2002). 'Corporate Governance in Germany and Japan: Liberalization Pressures and Responses'. In W. Streeck and K. Yamamura, Eds., *The End of Diversity? Prospects of German and Japanese Capitalism*: 261–305. Ithaca, Cornell University Press.

—— (2005). *Contested Boundaries: Ambiguity and Creativity in the Evolution of German Co-determination.* New York, Oxford University Press.

—— (2010). 'Actors and Institutions'. In G. Morgan, J. L. Campbell, C. Crouch, O. K. Pedersen, and R. Whitley, Eds., *Oxford Handbook of Comparative Institutional Analysis*: 63–86. Oxford, Oxford University Press.

—— and A. Moerke (2005). 'Continuity and Change in Corporate Governance: Comparing Germany and Japan'. *Corporate Governance* 13(3): 351–361.

Jacoby, S. M. (2005). *The Embedded Corporation.* New Jersey, Princeton University Press.

Japan Research Institute (2011). なぜアジア債券市場を整備しなければならないのか ('Why should Asian Bond Market be Improved?'). *RIM Kantaiheiyo Business Joho* 11(43).

Johnson, S., P. Boone, A. Breach, and E. Friedman (2000). 'Corporate Governance in the Asian Financial Crisis'. *Journal of Financial Economics* 58(1/2): 141–186.

Kennedy, M. T. and P. C. Fiss (2009). 'Looking Good and Doing Better: Rethinking Motivations for Opting Innovations'. *Academy of Management Journal* 52(5): 897–918.

Khanna, T. and K. G. Palepu (2004). 'Globalization and Convergence in Corporate Governance: Evidence from Infosys and the Indian Software Industry'. *Journal of International Business Studies* 35(6): 484–507.

Kondo, M. (2014). 'The Philippines: Inequality-Trapped Capitalism'. In M. A. Witt and G. Redding, Eds., *The Oxford Handbook of Asian Business Systems*: 169–190. Oxford, Oxford University Press.

La Porta, R., F. Lopez-de-Silanes, A. Shleifer, and R. W. Vishny (1998). 'Law and Finance'. *Journal of Political Economy* 106(6): 1113–1155.

Lazzarini, S. G. and A. Musacchio (2011). *Leviathan as a Minority Shareholder: A Study of Equity Purchases by the Brazilian National Development Bank, (BNDES)1995–2003.* Boston, Harvard Business School.

Lee, Z. R. and H. H. M. Hsiao (2014). 'Taiwan: SME-Oriented Capitalism in Transition'. In M. A. Witt and G. Redding, Eds., *The Oxford Handbook of Asian Business Systems*: 238–259. Oxford, Oxford University Press.

Lincoln, J. and M. Gerlach (2004). *Japan's Network Economy.* Cambridge, Cambridge University Press.

Millar, C. J. M, T. I. Eldomiaty, C. J. Choi, and B. J. Hilton (2005). 'Corporate Governance and Institutional Transparency in Emerging Markets'. *Journal of Business Ethics* 59: 163–174.

Monks, R. A. G. and N. Minow (2001). *Corporate Governance*. Oxford, Blackwell.

Nonaka, I. (1988). 'Toward Middle-Up-Down Management: Accelerating Information Creation'. *Sloan Management Review 29*(3): 57–73.

Orru, M., N. W. Biggart, and G. G. Hamilton (1997). *The Economic Organization of East Asian Capitalism*. Thousand Oaks, Sage.

Redding, G. (1993). *The Spirit of Chinese Capitalism*. New York, de Gruyter.

—— G. Y. Y. Wong, and W. K. W. Leung (2014). 'Hong Kong: Hybrid Capitalism as Catalyst'. In M. A. Witt and G. Redding, Eds., *The Oxford Handbook of Asian Business Systems*: 33–54. Oxford, Oxford University Press.

—— and M. A. Witt (2007). *The Future of Chinese Capitalism: Choices and Chances*. Oxford, Oxford University Press.

Roe, M. J. (1994). *Strong Managers, Weak Owners*. Princeton, Princeton University Press.

Rosser, A. (2014). 'Indonesia: Oligarchic Capitalism'. In M. A. Witt and G. Redding, Eds., *The Oxford Handbook of Asian Business Systems*: 79–99. Oxford, Oxford University Press.

Saez, L. (2014). 'India: From Failed Developmental State Towards Hybrid Market Capitalism'. In M. A. Witt and G. Redding, Eds., *The Oxford Handbook of Asian Business Systems*: 55–78. Oxford, Oxford University Press.

Shleifer, A. and R. Vishny (1997). 'A Survey of Corporate Governance'. *Journal of Finance* 52(2): 737–783.

Streeck, W. (2001). 'Introduction: Explorations into the Origins of Non-liberal Capitalism in Germany and Japan'. In W. Streeck and K. Yamamura, Eds., *The Origins of Non-liberal Capitalism*: 1–38. Ithaca, Cornell University Press.

Suehiro, A. and N. Wailerdsak (2014). 'Thailand: Post-Developmentalist Capitalism'. In M. A. Witt and G. Redding, Eds., *The Oxford Handbook of Asian Business Systems*: 260–282 Oxford, Oxford University Press.

Thornton, P. H. and W. Ocasio (1999). 'Institutional Logics and the Historical Contingency of Power in Organizations: Executive Succession in the Higher-Education Publishing Industry, 1958–1990'. *American Journal of Sociology 105*(3): 801–843.

USCB (United States Census Bureau) (2012). 'International Statistics'. Retrieved 3 July 2012 from <http://www.census.gov/compendia/statab/2012/tables/12s1397.pdf>.

Vitols, S. (2001a). 'The Origins of Bank-Based and Market-Based Financial Systems: Germany, Japan, and the United States'. In W. Streeck and K. Yamamura, Eds., *The Origins of Non-liberal Capitalism*: 171–199. Ithaca, Cornell University Press.

—— (2001b). 'Varieties of Corporate Governance: Comparing Germany and the UK'. In P. A. Hall and D. Soskice, Eds., *Varieties of Capitalism*: 337–360. Oxford, Oxford University Press.

Westphal, J. D. and E. J. Zajac (1998). 'The Symbolic Management of Stockholders: Corporate-Governance Reforms and Shareholder Reactions'. *Administrative Science Quarterly 43*: 127–153.

Whitley, R. (1992). *Business Systems in East Asia*. London, Sage.

—— (1999). *Divergent Capitalisms*. New York, Oxford University Press.

Witt, M. A. (2014a). 'Japan: Coordinated Capitalism Between Institutional Change and Structural Inertia'. In M. A. Witt and G. Redding, Eds., *The Oxford Handbook of Asian Business Systems*: 100–122. Oxford, Oxford University Press.

Witt, M. A. (2014b). 'South Korea: Plutocratic State-Led Capitalism Reconfiguring'. In M. A. Witt and G. Redding, Eds., *The Oxford Handbook of Asian Business Systems*: 216–237. Oxford, Oxford University Press.

—— and G. Redding (2012). 'The Spirits of Corporate Social Responsibility: Senior Executive Perceptions of the Role of the Firm in Society in Germany, Hong Kong, Japan, South Korea and the USA'. *Socio-Economic Review 10*(1): 109–134.

—— (2014a). 'Asian Business Systems: Implications and Perspectives for Comparative Business Systems and Varieties of Capitalism Research'. In M. A. Witt and G. Redding, Eds., *The Oxford Handbook of Asian Business Systems*: 667–697. Oxford, Oxford University Press.

—— (2014b). 'China: Authoritarian Capitalism'. In M. A. Witt and G. Redding, Eds., *The Oxford Handbook of Asian Business Systems*: 11–32. Oxford, Oxford University Press.

Wooldridge, A. (2012). 'The Rise of State Capitalism'. *The Economist*, 21 January. Retrieved 27 August 2012 from <http://www.economist.com/node/21543160>.

World Bank (2012a). 'Financial Sector Indicators'. Retrieved 2 October 2012 from <http://data.worldbank.org/topic/financial-sector>.

—— (2012b). 'Data'. Retrieved 2 October 2012 from <http://data.worldbank.org/indicator/NY.GDP.MKTP.CD/countries>.

Yoshikawa, T. and A. A. Rasheed (2009). 'Convergence of Corporate Governance'. *Corporate Governance 17*(3): 388–404.

Zajac, E. J. and J. D. Westphal (2004). 'The Social Construction of Market Value: Institutionalization and Learning Perspectives on Stock Market Reactions'. *American Sociological Review 69*(June): 433–457.

Zysman, J. (1983). *Governments, Markets, and Growth*. Ithaca, Cornell University Press.

# CHAPTER 17

# CULTURE AND THE BUSINESS SYSTEMS OF ASIA

## GORDON REDDING, MICHAEL HARRIS BOND, AND MICHAEL A. WITT

THE business-systems literature is essentially an exercise in exploring and categorizing institutional variations across societies, determining their impact on various outcome variables such as social equality or comparative advantage, and understanding processes of institutional change. Culture rarely enters the picture (exceptions include Redding 2005; Redding and Witt 2007; Witt and Redding 2009). This is peculiar in that the impact of cultural variations is widely accepted and taken for granted in some social-science disciplines, including business (Kirkman, Lowe, and Gibson 2006). Likewise, seminal works in the business-systems and varieties of capitalism literature suggest that the origins and evolution of institutions cannot be divorced from underlying cultural factors. Hall and Soskice (2001: 13) noted that in addition to formal institutions,

> something else is needed to lead the actors to coordinate on a specific equilibrium and…what leads the actors to a specific equilibrium is a set of shared understandings about what other actors are likely to do, often rooted in a sense of what it is appropriate to do in such circumstances.

Their conception of culture is of 'a set of shared understandings and available "strategies for action"' (Hall and Soskice 2001: 13), acquired over time through experience in a given environment.

Whitley's (1999) account of the emergence of six major business-system types likewise incorporates the role of culture, in the form of shared beliefs about authority, trust, and communitarian ideals. While he underlines that institutions mediate both trust and authority, the narratives included in his work illustrate how cultural and historical forces lead to the emergence of some institutions.

A similar concern with culture can be seen in the related social sciences. Fligstein (2001), for instance, presented a theory of organized social spaces, or 'fields', in which collective actors such as corporate boards produce a system of dominance through local culture that so defines social relations as to legitimate the power structure. This results in a 'conception of control' deriving from the cognitive elements within that culture that give meaning to action and define social relations. As a consequence,

> ideas of market orders are embedded within a particular society and a government and reflect the society's peculiar history. The dominance of different groups in society means that those rules tend to reflect one set of interests over another...there are national styles of ownership and regulation. (Fligstein 2001: 16)

Similarly, Guillén (1994) pointed to 'elite mentalities' as a central ingredient in organizational paradigms. These mentalities are enduring interpretations of how the world works that dispose groups to prefer some kinds of organizational solutions to others. Elite mentalities are distinct from ideology, which serves more to legitimize positions of power (cf. Mannheim 1936), though the two are connected in practice.

Despite culture being a taboo topic in much of the social sciences today (cf. Landes 1998), there is considerable reason to believe that culture must play a role in explaining the shape and evolution of business systems.

The influence of culture on systems of economic coordination and control is subtle and complex. We therefore begin by taking a position on what culture is, what it does, and how it does it. We will point to related theoretical problems and examine data from principal cross-cultural studies as they illuminate the world of practice. Finally, we will summarize the implications in a series of vignettes for the clusters of countries we propose. Given space constraints, we will stay at a brief introductory level.

# WHAT CULTURE IS

Children of the species *homo sapiens* take a comparatively long time to learn adulthood (Konner 2010). What the child and adolescent learns is culture. General agreement can be assumed on culture having three main components within a society and its language: the shared understanding of what is, of the significance of what is, and the consequent understanding of what behaviours are needed to make life liveable and worthy.

A society contains people who share much of the same learning. Other societies work by different learning systems developed out of their distinctive heritages and, although there is much overlap stemming from the genetic inheritance of the species, in instincts such as sociability, curiosity, and pair-bonding there are nevertheless differences in interpretation and practice. These differences are typically addressed in research as differences in systems of meaning, in other words the interpretations of reality, society by society. At the base level of this acculturation process lies the question of what *is*, or 'the social construction of reality' (Berger and Luckmann 1966).

Especially potent here are questions about the *cosmos*. Looking at the night sky and seeing the universe can lead to deep curiosity as well as awe, uncertainty, and fear. To answer these puzzlings, early societies tended to create a way of explaining the encountered world, a *nomos*, that included unseen forces to be taken on trust and originating in their cosmos, usually gods or a single god, or alternative influences like fate, chance, or extended cosmic order.

# What Culture Does

These shared explanations became the 'sacred canopies' (Berger 1967) and eventually the axial religions under which people could shelter. Religions over time have also taken a major part in the evolving of societal order, having often been incorporated into political systems to legitimate authority and its enactments. This tendency to seek and accept an overarching explanation for the mysteries of life may itself be part of the human genetic inheritance (Schloss and Murray 2009).

The child will absorb that worldview along with the 'primary socialization' needed to make sense of the surroundings of his or her upbringing. This primary learning will cover immediate relationships, structures of authority and discipline, and the identification in language of the key features in the social system that matter and why. Later, the child will acquire 'secondary socialization' into more specialized domains of meaning found in different occupations and age-specific roles like parenting, or into such advanced sub-unit conformity as membership in a profession or trade, or a family role other than child.

Socialization both defines and interprets the meaning of social behaviour, adding value judgement in the process. The norms then get interpreted into guidelines for action according to espoused understandings. These guidelines are what Leung and Bond (2004) call 'social axioms'—propositions that say 'this is how the world works'. (See also Bond et al. 2004, and Leung and Bond 2009). Another term is 'rationale', or the set of reasons adopted by a culture or sub-culture for behaving in a certain way, as we shall describe for executives in different countries.

# How Culture Influences Human Life

Two caveats are in order here. The first is that societies and their cultures are not necessarily as tidy and homogeneous as this introductory account suggests (Archer 1996, Gelfand et al. 2011). The second is that as a society becomes more complex, and especially as its economy moves into a highly diffracted modern form, then much of its members' behaviour takes place inside discrete provinces of meaning, bounded by particular spheres of action (Sorge 2005; Redding 2008): lawyers, accountants, plumbers, all adopt their own meanings, priorities, operations, and norms. Sub-cultures then emerge, but the society defends itself from break-up by the work of the social axioms that penetrate all, or at least most, of the different semantic spaces, creating overarching umbrellas of agreed sharedness.

Culture inspires a first-stage implied contract of conformity to what is collectively seen as 'right and proper'. People accept this because they are instinctively gregarious and dependent on membership. Conformity has a cost worth paying. The second stage is to take such definitions and create a form of stable order to express them. When norms are embedded into regular patterns of behaviour, such as a business executive always wearing a suit, then when seen altogether the society has created a layer of *institutions*. These are not culture, but translations of cultural ideals into stable forms of action—situation-specific expressions of meaning in action.

Such conformity to what is right and proper extends to the economic realm and is thus relevant to understanding business systems. Prior research has indicated, for instance, that company leaders in different types of capitalism espouse fundamentally different views of such fundamental questions as why firms exist (Witt and Redding 2010; Redding and Witt 2012). In this research, US executives considered the pursuit of shareholder value to lie at the heart of their firms' existence, while German executives emphasized the importance of production for the sake of society as well as the provision of benefits to stakeholders, employees, and shareholders in particular. In Asia, Hong Kong executives pursued family wealth and status, Japanese executives focused on serving their employees and society at large, and South Korean executives saw a need to balance the demands of shareholders, employees, and society at large, the latter mainly through charity, but also through a residual commitment to economic development of the nation. At the heart of this diversity in views are societally contingent values as to the right and proper role of firms in the social fabric. Related work (Witt and Redding 2012) has found that the conceptions of corporate social responsibility held by executives in these societies vary considerably. Evidence suggests that these variations in values matter, at times predicting institutional outcomes in societies better than inside and outside experts (Witt and Redding 2009; Redding and Witt 2012).

The realms of culture and institutions are in constant mutual interaction, shaping each other and evolving together as the society attempts to deal with the emerging challenges of progress (Witt and Redding 2009) which, seen in the context of economic progress (Mokyr 2009), reduce to two essentials: the universal needs to demonstrate (1) high levels of cooperativeness in economic action and (2) high levels of innovativeness. The way these key challenges are met differs greatly between societies. As noted earlier, historians and comparativists have regularly concluded that explaining success and failure by societies needs to include a place for culture because of its significance in the shaping of institutions (Weber 1968; Landes 1998; Biggart and Delbridge 2004; North 2005; Greif 2006; McCloskey 2006; Beinhocker 2007; Nowak 2011).

Culture fits inside such models as a contributor to observable societal outcomes (Redding 2005; Beinhocker 2007). The forces of economic rationality and resource availability are seen to work alongside cultural influences that, through the medium of institutions, affect the availability (or otherwise) to society of forms of cooperativeness and innovativeness. Alternative societal formulae are differently effective in terms of per capita prosperity. Some societies are still not organized fully to release beneficial effects, and the Asian region contains the full range of options on display.

# THE VARIETY OF ASIAN CULTURES

This region contains immense cultural variety. Language and ethnicity illustrate the flows of ancient peoples generally moving from west to east and south-east, often pushed and then overrun by newer arrivals. This flow of populations has led to all the world's axial religions being represented. They are dispersed across the region and nowhere is there a tidy overlap of one country and one religion. Except for Islam, the norm is for people to adopt several religions and blend them into their daily lives as need be.

Three aspects of religion tend to intervene in the process of affecting societal behaviour. Some religions are more constraining than others, some more 'worldly', some import an external worldview. This last effect is now strengthened under the information flows that come with globalization and new technology.

Of the religions that are constraining, the foremost is Islam (Gelfand et al. 2011). In a study of thirty-five, the highest scores for tightness in Asia were in Pakistan and Malaysia. Here, extensive domains of life, especially public life, follow prescribed forms. Indonesia, the world's most populous Islamic state, has been secular since its founding in 1949 and practises a 'soft' form of Islam (Hefner 2010). Malaysia, by contrast, is a consciously Islamic state and, though less purist than its Middle Eastern counterparts, nevertheless fosters a strongly institutionalized role for religion in society, including laws informing company management.

On worldliness, it is commonly observed that Buddhism is 'unworldly', whereas Confucianism is the opposite and non-spiritual. Buddhism is humanist, egalitarian, and focused on individual salvation; its relevance for community and state is indirect (Tambiah 1970). Confucianism is not strictly speaking a religion, as it does not recognize a supreme being, nor does it provide an account of the cosmos. Nor does it have an organized 'church' structure. Instead, it is a very powerful system of social norms that perpetuate the stability of a family-based society and provide a strong sense of hierarchy (King and Bond 1985). Although it has always contained definitions of the ideal person as socially responsible, its focus has been less on society than on the family units upon which society's stability depends. Its practices result in a high level of self-sustaining and self-perpetuating order that at the same time is resilient against pressures. However, its family focus arguably inhibits a true sense of wider community and wider cooperativeness, restricting identity to the concentric circles around family units (Hsu 1963;

Fei 1992) and producing an outcome of 'utilitarianistic familism' (Lau 1982; Redding 1990; Lemos 2012).

Islam, respected for its intended tolerance, still controls the conduct of life in a mercantile world through, for instance, rules for usury. Inheritance and ownership are prescribed in ways that many current observers see as ancient and retrogressive. So too is there a core tension between identity with the mosque or *umma* and identity with the secular nation-state, with all that implies for 'modernization' (Kuran 2004).

The external ideas that have flowed into the region were first carried by colonial powers and the accompanying Christianity. Their legacies remain, some beneficent, many not. As far as culture is concerned, the principle imported idea-set was that of the rational pursuit of progress—in its latest guise, the 'Washington Consensus' (Serra and Stiglitz 2008), borne along with development aid. Historically, the same logics of market discipline, efficiency, cost control, and rationality were part of the trading, plantation, and extractive interests of the colonial powers. The adoption of these influences has led to varying degrees of hybridization.

# REVIEWING THE EVIDENCE ABOUT CULTURAL SIMILARITY

The clustering of countries into sets with some similarity is proposed in line with their economic prosperity, a key differentiator identified by Georgas and Berry (1995) for clustering prior to comparison. Culture will be examined from four perspectives, each illuminating an aspect of its complexity.

- First, we will look at the wide perspective of the eco-social (non-psychological) context of national cultures. This provides an account of the main alternative determinants of societal features alongside which culture must be placed in a full account.
- Second, we will note the data on national variations in espoused values. Included here will be the widely acknowledged studies of Hofstede, Schwartz, the ongoing World Values Survey, and the GLOBE study of the contexts of leadership behaviour.
- Third, we will turn our attention to patterns of societal behaviour by examining social axioms. These reflect how people normally behave within a particular culture.
- Fourth, we will describe findings on child socialization that reveal the early shaping of core societal ideals in different cultures.

# THE ECO-SOCIAL ORGANIZATION OF
# SOCIETAL CULTURES

We have noted that, in addition to its culture, there are many other things about a nation that need to be considered when analysing behaviour within it. Georgas and Berry (1995) presented a response to these challenges by arguing for the use of a battery of objective measures applying to nations, for use in cluster analysis. These measures define two main contexts: the *ecological* (geography and demography) and the *socio-political* (economic, political, judicial, religious, educational, and communications-based). Of the seventeen clusters they report in which our sample nations are represented, the same clustering as we have proposed occurs in fifteen. The point of this exercise is to displace the notion of culture as the *prime* cause of behaviour and instead explain links between operational aspects of culture and behaviour in, and comparatively between, societal contexts pre-understood to be different on other objective measures.

The twenty-five indicators derived by Georgas and Berry were subsequently simplified by factor analysis into a single umbrella factor called 'affluence', that is, the utility of the material and social-resource base out of which a society currently functions. We represent this as GDP per capita. By this measure it is possible to build in the influences on societies that stem from their stage of economic development, a crucial first determinant of differences in organizational and economic exchange behaviour.

In GDP per capita terms for 2011 expressed in international dollars (IMF), our clusters are as shown in Table 17.1.

We see here countries at different points on a long continuum, and longitudinal data show them moving at different speeds. As societies evolve they take distinct paths, but all come up against certain universal transitions and political achievements if they are to progress. As seen by Fukuyama (2011) in an analysis of such historical patterns, the initial stage of societal evolution is essentially tribal, and kinship or sub-group identity dominates social and societal structures. To make the transition beyond this, it is necessary for state administration to emerge and be seen as legitimate. The key to this legitimacy is normally adoption of the rule of law. For instance, Europe made an early exit from kinship with the catalyst of canon law under Christianity (Fukuyama 2011: 231). A much earlier equivalent in China was the use of Confucian ideals to produce a class of intellectual administrators to create the first 'modern' state able to claim an escape from tribalism, but here the rule of law remained essentially a matter of hierarchical control rather than the protection of rights (Fukuyama 2011). Under canon law in Europe, two significant basic institutions crystallized out: individual choice over social and property relations, and political rule limited by transparent and predictable law. From then on, both in Europe and elsewhere, the story is one of global experimentation over centuries to achieve a balance of three elements: having a state seen as legitimate; all being

Table 17.1 GDP per capita of clusters, 2011

| Cluster | Country | GDP |
| --- | --- | --- |
| Advanced cities | Singapore | 59,722 |
| | Hong Kong | 49,137 |
| Japan | | 34,740 |
| Advanced North-East | Taiwan | 37,720 |
| | Korea | 31,714 |
| Emerging SE Asian | Malaysia | 15,568 |
| | Thailand | 9,396 |
| | Indonesia | 4,666 |
| | Philippines | 4,073 |
| Post-Socialist | China | 8,382 |
| | India | 3,694 |
| | Vietnam | 3,359 |
| | Laos | 2,659 |

Source: IMF World Economic Outlook Database Dec. 2012.

subject to law; and a government accountable for its actions. As Fukuyama (2011: 16) observes: 'The fact that there are countries capable of achieving this balance constitutes the miracle of modern politics, since it is not obvious that they can be combined.' The region contains the full spectrum of such attempts.

The great cultural macro variables, such as the Traditional versus Secular-Rational in the World Values Survey (see below), reflect the positions of societies dealing with this challenge. The essence of the transition so far has been the replacement of personalism as a prime determinant of decisions by (1) calculative rationality and (2) principle conceived in the abstract. These latter two serve to slowly dismantle the instinct for traditional hierarchy. In essence, as seen by Kant (1784), it is a matter of societies becoming mature, and hence full of people able to use their own understanding without guidance from another.

Within such an ecological approach, a number of scholars have explored specific outcomes of interest. For example, Gelfand et al. (2011) set out to understand the degree of behavioural constraint experienced across a standard set of social situations by citizens of thirty-three nations. They aimed to distinguish 'tight' from 'loose' nations, contrasting those having many strong norms and a low tolerance of deviant behaviour from those having weak social norms and a high tolerance of deviant behaviour. From tight to loose, the Asian countries are: tight—Pakistan, Malaysia, India, Singapore, South Korea; relatively tight—Japan, China; relatively loose—Hong Kong.

# THE CLASSIC COMPARATIVE STUDIES
## OF VALUES

The contentions over epistemology that surround comparative surveys of values are well summarized in Lowe, Magala, and Huang (2012) for social psychology, and in Drew and Kriz (2012) for institutional theory. The essence of the problem in both fields is the absence of agreed general theory. Put simply, what is needed is 'the identification of dimensions across which cultures may be compared and along which they may be ordered with respect to one another' (Bond 2012: 11). The problem is partly an outcome of intellectual parochialism, as a result of which commentary can become aggressive and dysfunctional. Three over-riding questions are pointed to in commentary, namely:

1. The risk that data based on national aggregates of individual contributions may lead to misleading reifications.
2. These may include a danger of bias such as that of unconscious Western Cartesian cognition rooted in a distinct ontological individualism.
3. The search for theoretic universals is derailed by discipline parochialism and can only be progressed with intellectual collaboration.

In the interest of encouraging such progress, we present now some of the main empirical data in the field, but will also fold in parallel attempts to acknowledge and deal with the deeper challenges just defined, an example of which lies in the work of Gelfand et al. (2011) discussed above.

The first major comparative study of societal values to enter the world of management was that of Hofstede (1980). This revealed clearly the existence of three principal dimensions (presented as four by dividing one) to account for the majority of variance among the eventual foundation sample of 117,000 across fifty countries in one industry. Extension and replication studies have since proliferated, the primary outcome of which was the addition of a fifth dimension that helped illuminate 'Confucian dynamism', also labelled 'long-term orientation' (Bond and Hofstede 1990). As the Hofstede work is one of the most widely cited in social science, it is necessary only to summarize it here.

The original dimensions were: Power Distance, or the extent of a sense of hierarchy or its opposite, egalitarianism; Individualism–Collectivism, or the perceived focus of identity, either as self or as member of a specific social group such as family; Masculinity–Femininity, or the extent of a shared sense of nurturing or otherwise; and Uncertainty Avoidance, or a society's urge for specificity and control. The weighting of the dimensions gave strong prominence to the first two, and we see them as first-stage indicators of the universal societal challenges of producing institutional order in two dimensions, the horizontal and the vertical. Scores for high Power Distance and Collectivism are clustered together in Asia, compared with the opposite for many Western countries, especially the Anglo-Saxon sub-group. The Asian scores are high for supporting hierarchy as a principle in social ordering, although Japan is an exception and the principle is also less strongly endorsed in Korea and Taiwan. This suggests the possibility of a correlation with prosperity and democracy; other longitudinal data (Inglehart and Baker 2000) support this.

For the dimensions of Uncertainty Avoidance and Masculinity–Femininity, there is also clustering. Japan is again an outlier within Asia, with a very high score on Masculinity. The Singapore and Hong Kong cluster is another outlier, with low scores on Uncertainty Avoidance. This variable marks the sense of being threatened by uncertainty and it is possible that the success, relative stability, and prosperity of these two city-states have reduced the need for this response to be part of local psychology. It is especially marked for Singapore, arguably the most stable Asian country in recent history and now the world's second richest in GDP per capita terms. Hong Kong's relationship with China is not nearly so assuring of stability and may explain the somewhat lower score.

The fifth dimension, varyingly referred to as Confucian Dynamism or Long-Term Orientation, revealed linkages between values not conceived earlier in the Western frame of reference. It also suggested that in Chinese thinking there may be constant reciprocal interplays (*yin* and *yang*), whereby linkages exist outside the range of the many external actors' perceptions. This issue of alternative cognitive structures has been noted earlier (Nakamura 1964; Capra 1975; Redding 1980) and more recently analysed by Nisbett (2003), among others. It is also folded into the analysis of trust in Li and Redding (2014).

A recent study (Minkov and Hofstede 2012) has tested the universality of this fifth dimension by using the large database of the World Values Survey, and has concluded that Chinese and Western research instruments can produce a similar dimension of culture. Confucian Dynamism as a universal dimension with distinctly Asian scores has relevance for the world of business in the region. Its poles have been labelled long-term and short-term orientation, with the following components:

| Long-term | Short-term |
| --- | --- |
| Persistence/perseverance | Personal steadiness and stability |
| Order by status | Protecting 'face' |
| Thrift | Respect for tradition |
| Having a sense of shame | Having a sense of reciprocity |

Among scores on this for twenty-three countries, eight of the top (i.e. most long-term) nine are Asian, led by China, Hong Kong, Taiwan, Japan, and Korea, all in the highest quartile. By contrast, Sweden, Poland, Germany, Australia, New Zealand, USA, Britain, and Canada all score in the bottom third. In the extension study (Minkov and Hofstede 2012), the scores (on a 0–100 scale) were Korea 100, Japan 99, China 91, Singapore 75,

Vietnam 75, Indonesia 67, India 66, Pakistan 54, Philippines 42. There is in the Asian Confucian cluster a sense of lessons learned, interpreted into norms, and passed on from times of deprivation, and with strong vertical order. In all the societies in this set, contributing to four of our clusters, it would be easy to trace family histories and folklore embedded across the economy that speak of hardship, risk of insecurity, and a driving work ethic that supports the aim of achieving respect for the different collectivities: in Japan the work-group, in Korea the nation, in China the family (Redding 1990).

The Hofstede studies pointed clearly to the existence of cultural clusters and thus a cultural effect. There is, however, such complexity in values analysis that such one-dimensional descriptions may be accidentally obscuring.

To consider that, we turn to the work of Schwartz, which has tended to focus on ways in which values themselves interconnect as integrated structures. One would see that, for instance, 'if one cultural group gives greater importance to power values than a second group, the second will tend to give greater importance to benevolence values than the first' (Schwartz 1992: 56).

Schwartz takes an alternative position to Hofstede in alerting us to these complex interconnections, and the two studies end up equally powerful but different in the way they relate to societal theory. As Gouveia and Ros (2000: 25) suggest, Hofstede's model 'is better explained by macro-economic variables, while the Schwartz model is better accounted for by macro-social variables'. For Hofstede, Individualism is counterbalanced by Power Distance. For Schwartz, Autonomy is counterbalanced by Conservation, but only Individualism and Autonomy are strongly correlated across the two models. Hofstede's opposing pair relate to wealth. Schwartz's pair relate to the distribution of wealth. Citing Triandis (1995) Gouveia and Ros suggest that Hofstede's Collectivism may relate more to the vertical emphasis on obligation and obedience to authority, whereas Schwartz's equivalent may be more related to the horizontal emphasis on cooperation, harmony, and equality. This is relevant, because clusters of societal meanings surround the broad notion of collectivism, and become visible in Japanese *keiretsu*, or Korean *chaebol*, Chinese family business, or the state-owned business groups of Singapore, all such forms of coordination having played a key role in societal progress. The complexities attached to collectivism are also such that there are as many negative effects as positive, as suggested in the work of Fan, Jian, and Yeh (2009), which reveals that among the Chinese family conglomerates that reach the scale of stock market listing in Hong Kong and Singapore there is an average 57 per cent loss of capital value over the five-year period of generational transition, a finding supported also by Gomez (2009) in Malaysia (see Carney and Andriesse 2014).

Variations within Asia and also between Asia and the West are shown in Table 17.2.

*Conservation* is found in societies based on interdependent social relations where security, conformity, and tradition are priorities. It is strongly affirmed in the Chinese societies of Taiwan, Singapore, Hong Kong, and Shanghai. It is also strongly affirmed in Malaysia and Thailand (where ethnic Chinese influence is strong). The lowest regional score is for Guangzhou, and the China average is lower than that for overseas Chinese territories. The China result may well reflect the commonly observed ideological

**Table 17.2 Asian and comparative scores on the Schwartz (1994) dimensions of national values**

| Country | Conservation | Affective Autonomy | Intellectual Autonomy | Hierarchy | Mastery | Egalitarian Commitment | Harmony |
|---|---|---|---|---|---|---|---|
| Taiwan | 4.31 | 3.21 | 3.93 | 2.85 | 4.11 | 4.68 | 4.17 |
| Singapore | 4.38 | 3.04 | 3.68 | 2.75 | 3.93 | 4.79 | 3.72 |
| Hong Kong | 4.04 | 3.11 | 4.08 | 2.83 | 4.18 | 4.85 | 3.34 |
| Shanghai | 4.10 | 3.09 | 4.25 | 3.36 | 4.57 | 4.65 | 3.63 |
| Guangzhou | 3.75 | 3.45 | 4.58 | 3.78 | 4.84 | 4.35 | 3.83 |
| China (comb.) | 3.97 | 3.32 | 4.27 | 3.7 | 4.73 | 4.49 | 3.71 |
| Japan | 3.87 | 3.54 | 4.68 | 2.86 | 4.27 | 4.69 | 4.07 |
| Malaysia | 4.46 | 3.16 | 4.07 | 2.43 | 4.34 | 4.66 | 3.50 |
| Thailand | 4.22 | 3.62 | 4.08 | 3.32 | 3.99 | 4.34 | 3.93 |
| USA | 3.90 | 3.65 | 4.2 | 2.39 | 4.34 | 5.03 | 3.70 |
| Netherlands | 3.68 | 3.51 | 4.44 | 2.26 | 3.98 | 5.39 | 3.98 |
| Denmark | 3.64 | 4.01 | 4.58 | 1.86 | 3.97 | 5.52 | 4.16 |
| Australia | 4.06 | 3.50 | 4.12 | 2.36 | 4.09 | 4.98 | 4.05 |
| France | 3.35 | 4.41 | 5.15 | 2.16 | 3.89 | 5.45 | 4.31 |

weakness affecting Chinese society as it struggles with the discrepancies and contradictions of (1) declining Communist dogma, (2) powerful Party control, and (3) the successful market-driven logics of entrepreneurial capitalism.

*Affective Autonomy* is the opposite pole of collectivism. It receives only mild affirmation consistently across the region and is less strongly supported than in the West, where high scores on individualism would encourage its salience.

*Intellectual Autonomy* is a value that relates to an individual's freedom to think independently. It receives strong affirmation everywhere except (tellingly) in Singapore, where government efforts to sponsor its growth have been quite public. However, its affirmation in Western countries, most notably France, is even stronger than in Asia.

*Hierarchy* is only supported at all within this sample in China and then not strongly. The Western view of it is not at all positive.

*Mastery (in some accounts Competency)* is a value that supports behaviour to dominate surroundings and the legitimacy of changing the status quo. It is universally affirmed in Asia and especially in China, with the exception of a somewhat weaker response in Thailand. The China response may well be an outcome of a context of opportunism and risk-taking that has accompanied the economic explosion (Guthrie 2006). Minkov (2012) has also reported from his readings of the World Values Survey (see below) that East Asian cultures emphasize individual self-reliance in economic matters rather than dependence on help from others. For the special case of Thailand, there is literature suggesting higher levels of fatalism in Buddhist societies (Lawler and Atmiyanandana 2003) and this may well weaken values about mastery of circumstances.

*Egalitarian Compromise* is typical of societies that share a concern for the well-being of others, seen broadly. In collectivist societies, welfare is displaced into the collectivities, and this makes the wider concern to some degree redundant. The correlation of this value with Individualism suggests that it would not be strongly asserted in Asia. It is in fact asserted consistently in all cases, but at lower levels than in the West.

*Harmony* is essentially about the fit with nature and the protection of the environment. It is universally affirmed, but slightly more strongly in the West. Asian exceptions are high scores for Japan and Taiwan, where much cultural influence has been shared historically and where Japan's Buddhist heritage may be at work via the sacralization of nature that went with it (Eisenstadt 1996: 234).

## THE WORLD VALUES SURVEY

The World Values Survey, initiated, extended, and publicized academically under the guidance of Ronald Inglehart (Inglehart 1997, 2000; Norris and Inglehart 2004; Inglehart and Welzel 2005), has fostered the growth of a massive and growing global databank, as well as deep analyses of modernization, economic development, cultural change, and the role of religion (World Values Survey 2009). Analyses of its data across many of its waves of collection have revealed, as have other studies, that among the variety of values visible around the world lie two predominant and reciprocally balanced dimensions: (1) Survival versus Self Expression; (2) Traditional versus Secular-Rational.

The cultural map of the world in these terms is given in Figure 17.1. Here the Asian societies fall into two clusters. A secular-rational culture is at the top, with a wide separation within it between our two clusters, Japan and Advanced North-Eastern. The second broad grouping is biased more towards the traditional and includes Vietnam, India, Indonesia, and the Philippines. All the Asian societies reported are relatively neutral on the dimension of Survival versus Self Expression, and this suggests a possible counter-balanced combination of (1) escape from a condition of subsistence and the consequent opening of new opportunity spaces and (2) a collectivist rather than individualist ideal that subdues self-expression as a norm.

## THE GLOBE STUDIES ON LEADERSHIP

Another large-scale global study of cultural differences has been conducted under the research programme known as Global Leadership and Organizational Behaviour Effectiveness (GLOBE), initiated and led by the late Robert House. This study was

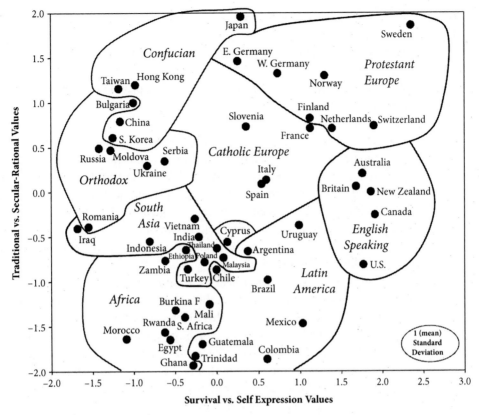

**FIGURE 17.1** Locations of 53 societies on global cultural map in 2005–2007

*Source*: Ronald Inglehart and Christian Welzel, 'Changing Mass Priorities: The Link between Modernization and Democracy', 2010, Perspectives on Politics, 8(2): 551–567.

designed to prepare American executives for work in other countries and bring them to terms with the cultural variety in managerial contexts arising from globalization (Javidan et al. 2006; Javidan, Steers, and Hitt 2007). One category within which findings were placed was termed 'societal cultural practices', and we shall concentrate on the distinctions revealed under that heading.

They were seen in two ways, 'What is?' and 'What should be?', in the context of organizational and leadership behaviour. Over ten years, 17,000 managers were studied in 62 countries by 170 researchers. Cultures were ranked on nine dimensions (derived from Hofstede 1980, 2001; Trompenaars and Hampden-Turner 1998; and Kluckhohn and Strodtbeck 1961).

In broad terms connecting culture and societal effectiveness, the GLOBE study concluded that Performance Orientation, Future Orientation, and Uncertainty Avoidance are 'positively and significantly related to most measures of economic health' (Javidan, House, and Dorfman 2004: 37). They also noted that Institutional Collectivism is positively and significantly correlated with three out of five measures of economic health, whereas In-Group Collectivism is negatively and significantly related to economic health (see Li and Redding 2014).

The key conclusions for our purposes can be summarized as follows:

1. The pattern of uncertainty tolerance follows that depicted by Hofstede, but here is seen against consistently higher levels of wishes for what should be. Only Singapore is an exception, with a higher actual tolerance of uncertainty than is seen as ideal. Elsewhere in the region, people aspire to greater flexibility.
2. Future orientation (or Confucian Dynamism) is confirmed, but there are strikingly strong aspirations for what should be. This is universal except for China, which shows an opposite result. The gap is especially wide in the countries of our Emerging South East Asian cluster and is arguably a reflection of their being outpaced by their more purely Confucian neighbours.
3. Both forms of collectivism—in-group and institutional—are generally seen as being in reality close to the ideal.
4. The humane orientation does not match the espoused ideal in China, Singapore, Hong Kong, Korea, Taiwan, or Japan, although it does so quite clearly in the Emerging South East Asian cluster. This difference in the perception of applied humanism may well find its explanation in the pragmatic responses to social order and hierarchy often attributed to Confucian forms of society and in contrast with Islam, Buddhism, and Animism. Another opposite to Confucian pragmatism is in the Philippines, with an unusually high score on humane orientation.
5. There is universal affirmation that hierarchy is a fact of life, but there is equally widespread strong rejection of it as an ideal. The only exceptions here are Thailand and Taiwan, where the scores for 'as is' and 'as should be' are high and fairly close together.
6. Assertiveness in managerial behaviour is moderately affirmed across the region as normal, but is judged very differently. In the Post-Socialist cluster, the Emerging South East Asian cluster (except in Thailand), and in Japan, more assertion is seen as an ideal. This is however rejected in the Advanced Cities and Advanced North-East. It may well be that the achievement of economic success in these societies has come at the cost of hardening relationships in the economy and that a reaction to favour a more sensitive style of behaviour is now apparent.
7. Performance orientation is confirmed throughout, especially in the Advanced Cities, Advanced North-East, and Japan. Aspiration to higher levels of this is universally high, although somewhat less so in the Post-Socialist cluster of China and India.

## Distinctions Across National Cultures Using Social Axioms

The classic studies of values have compared nations in terms of what their citizens deem to be *important*; recent work on social axioms has compared nations in terms of what their citizens deem to be *true*. Leung and Bond (2008) define social axioms as worldviews, assessments about how the physical, social, and spiritual worlds operate. Individuals in more than forty nations have been shown to organize these worldviews along five dimensions: Social Cynicism, Social Complexity, Reward for Application, Fate Control, and Religiosity.

Nations may be characterized by their citizens' typical profile on these axiom dimensions. Leung and Bond (2004) provide a cluster analysis of these national profiles that show the proximity of a nation's profile to that of 39 other national groups. The first striking thing is the variation between societies in strength of affirmation of axioms, with notably stronger responses in Hong Kong, Korea, Taiwan (and in the West, Germany as opposed to France). Countries where affirmation of axioms is relatively weak are China, Indonesia, Malaysia (and in the West, UK and France). This suggests an important point about culture noted earlier, but rarely surfaced: there are 'strong' and 'weak' cultures (Archer 1996). Arguably, this is affected by four forces: the strength and continuing clarity of the historical cultural legacy; cultural homogeneity within the demographic make-up of the society now; the impact of perceived societal success or failure on cultural affirmation; and possible close connections of norms to the basic integrity of the social unit around which life, and in recent memory survival, rests. In Asia the clarity, power, and success of the Confucian legacy is suggested in the clear beliefs reflected in certain societies.

Social Cynicism is a negative view about people and social institutions. A low sense of religiosity and high sense of social cynicism support the recognized pragmatism and 'utilitarianistic familism' (Lau 1982) of the Confucian world. So too does the high sense of reward for application resonate with the economic success of Korea, Taiwan, Hong Kong, and Singapore. Lower scores in China, Indonesia, Japan, and Malaysia on social cynicism suggest that people are not so resigned as elsewhere to that pragmatism.

The role of religion is predictably higher in India than elsewhere, and in China predictably very low. So too are there low scores for Japan and the Philippines. But Hong Kong, Singapore, and Taiwan score high on this element, something that suggests the persistence of both spirituality and ancestor veneration, attributed by observers to the grass-roots nature of much traditional Chinese religious observance (Weller 2010). It is also noteworthy that Fate Control is high for Confucian countries, and it is evident that religious practice as conducted in those societies remains associated for many with beliefs about fortune-telling, astrology, numerology, and *feng shui*.

# CITIZEN-MAKING: NATIONAL DIFFERENCES IN SOCIALIZING CHILDREN

As with earlier work by Minkov (2008), Bond and Lun (2012) have analysed ten goals for socializing children presented to respondents in Wave 5 of the World Values Survey, with responses from over 75,000 respondents in fifty-five countries (see Figure 17.2). Their results may be used to array nations across a two-dimensional structure. The first dimension, Self-Directedness versus Other-Directedness, contrasts a socialization emphasis on self-management, like independence and feeling of responsibility, versus an emphasis on being tractable by others, as in being obedient and showing religious faith; the second dimension, Civility versus Practicality, contrasts a socialization emphasis on public decency, as in being unselfish and showing respect and tolerance for other people, versus attention to material concerns, as in conserving resources and working hard.

The location of countries on this map of socialization emphases reveals again the clustering of countries into the same sets as already proposed. Japan is an outlier and so too are the Post-Socialist pair of India and China. Taiwan and Korea again converge and so too the Emerging South East Asian group of Malaysia, Thailand, and Indonesia. Only Vietnam varies from the earlier cluster pattern of Post-Socialist membership, being here close to the Emerging South East Asian group.

The Japanese findings on socialization reveal a tendency to approach—doubtless in principle rather than by copying specific practices—Western ideals of combining self-directedness and responsibility with the sense of duty to the public good seen in the variables of civility, public decency, tolerance, and unselfishness. This idea-set is strongly associated with societies that have achieved high levels of social capital and so trust of strangers (see Li and Redding 2014). Such an achievement is also associated with societal wealth, and general views of that broad phenomenon attribute it varyingly to 'bourgeois virtues' (McCloskey 2006), interpretations of Enlightenment values (Himmelfarb 2004), the social capital provided by religion (Berger and Redding 2010), and the dynamics of free-market capitalism when practised with 'decency' (ILO 2011; Nowak 2011).

The Confucian world, represented here by two success stories, Taiwan and Korea, shows again a clearer emphasis on pragmatism and less of a commitment to the public good as opposed to that of the inner social circle. The South East Asian group affirms practicality rather than communal idealism, but takes a middle position on passivity versus activism. China and India show the opposite of the self-directed ideals associated with individualism and so confirm the collectivism noted earlier. They also display strong ideals about community, perhaps reflecting the heritage of their recent political past, especially in the case of India.

These commonalities reflect the eco-social condition of their nations, described earlier. So for example, affluent nations endorse a profile of socialization goals emphasizing both Civility and Self-Directedness. These socialization goals may be regarded as promoting both typical citizen responses as well as national characteristics. For example, both Civility and Self-Directedness are associated with egalitarian values, less belief in Fate Control, and greater life satisfaction among a nation's citizens. Both Civility and Self-Directedness are associated with preferences for the national goal of providing individual voice as opposed to governmental control, as well as the judgement of that nation as being freer of corruption in its business practices. Thus, we can detect in nascent form a model for national development that moves from eco-social features,

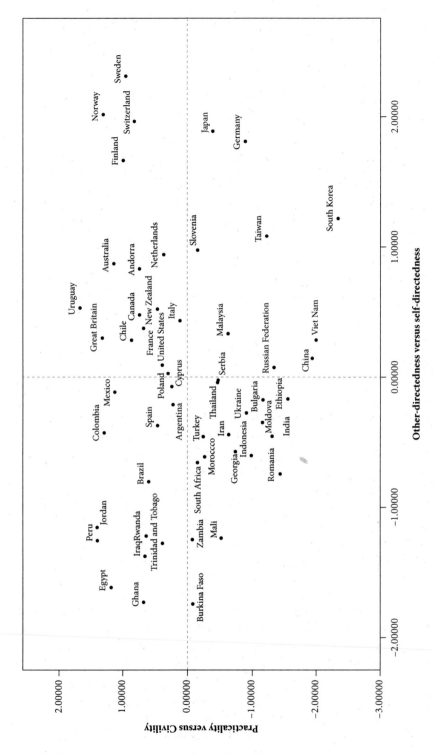

**Other-directedness versus self-directedness**

FIGURE 17.2  Goals for socializing children

*Source:* Bond and Lun 2012.

through socialization goals for its children, into national outcomes, both for individual and national characteristics. Citizen-making appears to work through culture to deliver appropriate behaviour.

# CULTURE AND BUSINESS SYSTEMS IN ASIA

We will conclude with a summary of findings, as a means of supporting the opening proposition that culture matters in the business systems of Asia, and by implication elsewhere.

There are three perspectives for consideration when looking at the interplay between the region's culture and business systems—how the structures of vertical order come to be shaped, how the structures of horizontal order come to be shaped, and how the societal ideals for a good society come to be reflected in its institutions. To consider these, we will retain the clusters, while acknowledging their approximate nature. For the question of societal ideals, we have earlier noted the variations in the meaning structures of executives in different societies.

## The Advanced Cities

The simple fact of prosperity in Singapore and Hong Kong has made them quite distinct as societies and has allowed them to construct institutions capable of world leadership. They are very different in detail, especially in the power of government in the economy, where they differ philosophically and in practice. They are also each culturally Chinese, but have also embraced a great deal of external influence now absorbed in their societal systems. They were in a sense always hybrid societies. So what does Chineseness bring to the hybrid?

In terms of vertical order, the Confucian heritage is one of the world's clearest and most robust. Founded on a moral order that sponsors the exchange of duty and protection, it induces a discipline that underlies virtually all relations. This clear sense of compliance presents the world of organizing with people already pre-formed to fit in.

In terms of horizontal order, the identity of Chinese people with family overwhelms all other alternatives. It similarly affects the business arena by being a primary source of organizational ownership, but also a provider of motivation and obligation for the owner to succeed. This means that the society is psychologically made up of discrete family units, each competing with the rest over scarce resources. This is visible in high Social Cynicism and Self-Reliance. The perception in Singapore that In-Group Collectivism is less than ideal may reveal the breaking of traditional identities attendant on modern levels of prosperity and social re-ordering. The wider sense of communal belonging is weaker than in many other societies and has been the target of much effort in Singapore as it blends in two other sub-cultures, Malay and Indian, to achieve racial harmony.

In both societies, the traditional Confucian societal design of the strong state with moral leadership, judged according to the delivery of peace and prosperity, is interpreted in two forms, neither of them democratic in a full sense, but each constructed to include extensive consultation, especially at grass-roots level. There is arguably a fertile connection between this basically stable order and the opportunities that flow from free-market capitalism. This latter is also here a hybrid that engages both (a) a very long Chinese tradition of mercantile behaviour and commerce and (b) an externally derived set of economic logics and institutions. Access to global markets has in both cases been especially relevant as an influence beyond culture.

# Japan

Japan is a cultural outlier in Asia and, despite early Confucian and Buddhist imports, has remained distinct in the evolution of its social psychology. It forms its own cluster. It has also achieved what no other Asian society has yet done: a very high level of advanced industrial power based on its own industrial formula, competing in world markets. The cultural inputs to this were arguably formed in earlier centuries of isolation and were quite radically re-interpreted in two waves of modernization, first in the late nineteenth century and second after World War II. Two main features distinguish the Japanese interpretation of both vertical and horizontal order from that of the Chinese.

Vertical order in Japan is also founded in Confucianism, but in a form based on the re-interpretation of that ideology by Tokugawa, the founder of the dynasty that controlled the country between 1601 and 1868. In this, power was allocated to local leaders, but only held as long as peace was maintained in that domain. This required the building-in of extensive processes of local consultation. Autocracy (and power-building) was consequently slowly eliminated. Along with this went the growth of an administrative class of intellectuals that (as in China) controlled from the centre and maintained orderly conduct without corruption. The two forces of (a) the consensus ideal and (b) the high sense of administrative calling, were then added to the mixture of influences that made modern Japan twice over, post-1868 and post-1945. Collectivism had earlier coalesced around the work-group (*ie*) and was carried forward into the new organizations, where it remains. The combination of Confucian pragmatism and administrative tradition contribute to the very high levels of secular-rational belief, the high Masculinity scores, and the high intolerance of uncertainty. At the same time, high social sensitivities reduce assertiveness, induce harmony as an ideal, and moderate self-directedness to include a sense of communal duty. This unique configuration of features is arguably conducive to the stable coordination of large-scale enterprises as well as their smaller equivalents.

# The Advanced North-East

Both Korea and Taiwan were under Japanese control during much of the first half of the twentieth century and Japan imposed on them its own version of state-directed industrialization, itself consistent with Confucian ideals. The post-war re-assertion of autonomy (including in the case of Taiwan a strong sense of asserted Chineseness) did not entirely eliminate the Japanese legacy, despite resentment of it, especially in Korea. Economic prosperity has been added to the mix of elements, and in achieving this it must be acknowledged that heavy influence came from the United States in both cases, especially in the field of technology and the societal ideals surrounding democracy.

Both societies display a mixture of the old and the new. There is, for instance, high Conservation and high Secular-Rationalism. The common Asian finding of high Collectivism and high Power Distance is found here and also the patrimonial view of power. Confucian dynamism is accompanied by high Self-Reliance and high Social Cynicism. The Pragmatism commonly found in Confucian societies is also high. In Korea there is reservation about institutional collectivism, which is seen as higher than the ideal, possibly revealing a negative response to the organizational militarism that can take over large companies. In Taiwan, there is notably high religiosity and concern with harmony, as well as the acknowledgement of high social interdependencies. This latter may be reflected in the tendency of Taiwan companies to be smaller in scale and more personalistically managed than in modern Korea.

## Emerging South East Asian

A wider spectrum may be expected here, as much of each economy is under ethnic Chinese control, while employing people of local cultures. So too is there a wide range of religious traditions and colonial experiences. Even so, common denominators are visible in high Power Distance, high Collectivism, tolerance of uncertainty, and traditional humanism. Another shared feature is non-assertion of Confucian Dynamism or performance orientation.

Indonesia, with its soft form of Islam, is nevertheless a society of relatively tight cultural constraints. Thailand under Buddhism displays low mastery. The Philippines displays unusually high humanism, but also social cynicism.

## Post-Socialist Economies

There are no obviously common cultural ideals that stretch across India and China, except for the sharing of Buddhism among many citizens and the tradition of hierarchy. India is mainly Hindu, traditionalist, with tight social constraints, high social cynicism, and a form of vertically-defined collectivism redolent of much earlier Confucian hierarchies. China is anti-traditionalist, high on secularity and rationalism, and stressing self-reliance.

Despite some overlaps, the essence of their current dissimilarity lies in their opposite responses to post-socialist existence. In India the path was that of democracy, free markets, and accountable government. In China it was state control and managed markets, with a constrained entrepreneurial sector. The instinct for hierarchy is exercised in contrasting ways.

In summary, the cultural clusters are visible and the role of this influence is arguable in the wider explanations. Stable forms of order have emerged and they vary following the same pattern. Rather than leave culture out of the account because it is untidy, we suggest its inclusion as one of the significant shapers of business systems.

## REFERENCES

Archer, M. (1996). *Culture and Agency: The Place of Culture in Social Theory* (2nd ed.). Cambridge, Cambridge University Press.

Beinhocker, E. (2007). *The Origins of Wealth*. London, Century.

Berger, P. L. (1967). *The Sacred Canopy: Elements of a Sociological Theory of Religion*. New York, Anchor.

—— and T. Luckmann (1966). *The Social Construction of Reality*. London, Penguin.

—— and G. Redding, Eds. (2010). *The Hidden Form of Capital: Spiritual Influences in Societal Progress*. London, Anthem Press.

Biggart, N. W. and R. Delbridge (2004). 'Systems of Exchange'. *Academy of Management Review* 29(1): 28–49.

Bond, M. H. (2012). 'How I am Constructing Culture-Inclusive Theories of Social-Psychological Process in Our Age of Globalization'. Paper presented at Conference on New Perspectives in East Asian Studies, Institute for Advanced Studies in Humanities and Social Sciences, National Taiwan University, Taipei, June 1.

—— and G. Hofstede (1990). 'The Cash Value of Confucian Values'. In S. R. Clegg and G. Redding, Eds., *Capitalism in Contrasting Cultures*: 383–390. New York, de Gruyter.

—— K. Leung, A. au, K-K Tong, S. R. de Carrasquel, F. Murakami, and J. R. Lewis (2004). 'Culture-level Dimensions of Social Axioms and Their Correlates Across 41 Cultures'. *Journal of Cross-Cultural Psychology* 35(5): 548–570.

—— and V. Lun (2012). *Socialisation Goals as Indicators of National Culture*. Department of Management Working Paper, Hong Kong Polytechnic University.

Capra, F. (1975). *The Tao of Physics*. New York, Bantam.

Carney, M. and E. Andriesse (2014). 'Malaysia: Personal Capitalism'. In M. A. Witt and G. Redding, Eds., *The Oxford Handbook of Asian Business Systems*: 144–168. Oxford, Oxford University Press.

Drew, A. J. and A. P. Kriz (2012). 'Towards a Theoretical Framework for Examining Societal-level Institutional Change'. In L. Tihanyi, T. M. Devinney and T. Pedersen, Eds., *Institutional Theory in International Business and Management*. Advances in International Management Series, Vol. 25: 65–98. Bingley, Emerald.

Eisenstadt, S. N. (1996). *Japanese Civilisation*. Chicago, University of Chicago Press.

Fan, J., M. Jian, and Y. Yeh (2009). *Succession: The Roles of Specialized Assets and Transfer Costs*. IEF Working Paper. Hong Kong, Chinese University of Hong Kong.

Fei, X. (1992). *From the Soil: The Foundations of Chinese Society* (trans. G. G. Hamilton and Z. Wang). Berkeley, University of California Press.

Fligstein, N. (2001). *The Architecture of Markets: An Economic Sociology of Twenty-First-Century Capitalist Societies*. Princeton, Princeton University Press.

Fukuyama, F. (2011). *The Origins of Political Order*. London, Profile.

Gelfand, M. J., J. L. Raver, L. Nishii, L. M. Leslie, J. Lun, B. C. Lim, S. Yamaguchi (2011). 'Differences between Tight and Loose Cultures: A 33-Nation Study'. *Science* 332: 1100–1104.

Georgas, J. and J. W. Berry (1995). 'An Ecocultural Taxonomy for Cross-Cultural Psychology'. *Cross-Cultural Research* 29(2): 121–157.

Gomez, E. T. (2009). 'The Rise and Fall of Capital: Corporate Malaysia in Historical Perspective'. *Journal of Contemporary Asia* 39(3): 345–381.

Gouveia, V. V. and M. Ros (2000). 'Hofstede and Schwartz's Models for Classifying Individualism at the Cultural Level: Their Relation to Macro-Social and Macro-Economic Variables'. *Psicothema* 12(Supl.): 25–33.

Greif, A. (2006). *Institutions and the Path to the Modern Economy*. Cambridge, Cambridge University Press.

Guillén, M. F. (1994). *Models of Management: Work, Authority, and Organization in a Comparative Perspective*. Chicago, University of Chicago Press.

Guthrie, D. (2006). *China and Globalization*. New York, Routledge.

Hall, P. A. and D. Soskice (2001). 'An Introduction to Varieties of Capitalism'. In P. A. Hall and D. Soskice, Eds., *Varieties of Capitalism*: 1–70. New York: Oxford University Press.

Hefner, R. W. (2010). 'Islam and Spiritual Capital: An Indonesian Case Study'. In P. L. Berger and G. Redding, Eds., *The Hidden Form of Capital: Spiritual Influences in Societal Progress*: 191–212. London, Anthem Press.

Himmelfarb, G. (2004). *The Roads to Modernity*. New York, Alfred A. Knopf.

Hofstede, G. (1980). *Culture's Consequences*. London, Sage.

—— (2001). *Culture's Consequences: Comparing Values, Behaviors, Institutions, and Organizations Across Nations* (2nd ed.). Thousand Oaks, Sage.

Hsu, F. L. K. (1963). *Clan, Caste and Club*. New York, Van Nostrand.

ILO (2011). *Regulating for Decent Work: New Directions in Labour Market Regulation*. Advances in Labour Studies Series. Geneva, International Labour Office.

Inglehart, R. (1997). *Modernization and Postmodernization: Cultural, Economic, and Political Change in 43 Societies*. Princeton, Princeton University Press.

—— (2000). In L. E. Harrison and S. Huntington, Eds., *Culture Matters*: 80–97. New York, Basic Books.

—— and W. E. Baker (2000). 'Modernization, Cultural Change, and the Persistence of Traditional Values'. *American Sociological Review* 65(1): 19–51.

—— and C. Welzel (2005). *Modernization, Cultural Change, and Democracy*. Cambridge, Cambridge University Press.

—— (2010). 'Changing Mass Priorities: The Link between Modernization and Democracy'. *Perspectives on Politics* 8(2): 555–567.

Javidan, M., P. W. Dorman, M. S. de Luque, and R. J. House (2006). 'In the Eye of the Beholder: Cross-Cultural Lessons in Leadership from Project GLOBE'. *Academy of Management Perspectives* 20(1): 67–90.

—— R. J. House, and P. W. Dorfman (2004). 'A Non-Technical Summary of GLOBE Findings'. In R. J. House, P. J. Hanges, M. Javidan, P. W. Dorfman, and V. Gupta, Eds., *Culture, Leadership and Organizations: The GLOBE Study of 62 Societies*: 29–48. London, Sage.

—— R. M. Steers, and M. A. Hitt (2007). *The Global Mindset*. Oxford, Elsevier JAI.

Kant, I. (1784/2000) 'What is Enlightenment?' In S. S. Schweder, Ed., *In the Shadow of the Bomb*: 28–41. Princeton, Princeton University Press.

King, A. Y. C. and M. H. Bond (1985). 'The Confucian Paradigm of Man: A Sociological View'. In W. S. Tseng and D. Y. H. Wu, Eds., *Chinese Culture and Mental Health*: 29–45. Orlando, Academic Press.

Kirkman, B. L., K. B. Lowe, and C. B. Gibson (2006). 'A Quarter Century of Culture's Consequences: A Review of Empirical Research Incorporating Hofstede's Cultural Values Framework'. *Journal of International Business Studies* 37(3): 285–320.

Kluckhohn, F. R. and F. L. Strodtbeck (1961). *Variations in Value Orientations*. New York, Harper and Row.

Konner, M. (2010). *The Evolution of Childhood*. Cambridge, MA, Belknap Press.

Kuran, T. (2004). *Islam and Mammon: The Economic Predicaments of Islamism*. Princeton, Princeton University Press.

Landes, D. (1998). *The Wealth and Poverty of Nations*. New York, Norton.

Lau, S. K. (1982). *Society and Politics in Hong Kong*. Hong Kong, Chinese University Press.

Lawler, J. and V. Atmiyanandana (2003). 'HRM in Thailand: A Post-1997 Update'. *Asia Pacific Business Review* 9(4): 165–185.

Lemos, G. (2012). *The End of the Chinese Dream: Why Chinese People Fear the Future*. New Haven, Yale University Press.

Leung, K. and M. H. Bond (2004). 'Social Axioms: A Model for Social Beliefs in Multi-cultural Perspective'. In M. P. Zanna, Ed., *Advances in Experimental Social Psychology* 36: 119–197. San Diego, Elvesier.

—— (2008). 'Psycho-Logic and Eco-Logic: Insights From Social Axiom Dimensions'. In F. J. R. van de Vijver, D. A. van Hemert and Y. H. Poortinga, Eds., *Multilevel Analysis of Individuals and Cultures*: 199–221. New York, Lawrence Erlbaum Associates.

—— Eds. (2009). *Psychological Aspects of Social Axioms: Understanding Global Belief Systems*. New York, Springer SBM.

Li, P. and G. Redding (2014). 'Social Capital in Asia: Its Dual Nature and Function'. In M. A. Witt and G. Redding, Eds., *The Oxford Handbook of Asian Business Systems*: 513–537. Oxford, Oxford University Press.

Lowe, S., S. Magala, and K.-S. Huang (2012). 'All We Are Saying is Give Theoretical Pluralism a Chance'. *Journal of Organizational Change Management* 25(5): 752–774.

McCloskey, D. N. (2006). *The Bourgeois Virtues: Ethics for an Age of Commerce*. Chicago, University of Chicago Press.

Mannheim, K. (1936). *Ideology and Utopia: An Introduction to the Sociology of Knowledge*. New York, Harcourt, Brace, & World.

Minkov, M. (2008). 'Self-enhancement and Self-Stability Predict School Achievement at the National Level'. *Cross-Cultural Research* 42(2): 172–196.

—— (2012, forthcoming). 'The Cultural Setting'. In M. Warner, Ed., *Managing Across Diverse Cultures in East Asia: Issues and Challenges in a Changing Globalized World: TBC*. London, Routledge.

—— and G. Hofstede (2012). 'Hofstede's Fifth Dimension: New Evidence from the World Values Survey'. *Journal of Cross-Cultural Psychology* 43(1): 3–14.

Mokyr, J. (2009). *The Enlightened Economy: An Economic History of Britain 1700–1850*. New Haven, Yale University Press.

Nakamura, H. (1964). *Ways of Thinking of Eastern Peoples*. Honolulu, East-West Center Press.

Nisbett, R. (2003). *The Geography of Thought*. New York, Free Press.

Norris, P. and R. Inglehart (2004). *Sacred and Secular: Religion and Politics Worldwide*. Cambridge, Cambridge University Press.

North, D. C. (2005). *Understanding the Process of Economic Change*. Princeton, Princeton University Press.

Nowak, M. A. (2011). *Super-Cooperators: Altruism, Evolution and Why We Need Each Other to Succeed*. New York, Free Press.

Redding, G. (1980). 'Cognition as an Aspect of Culture and its Relation to Management Processes: An Exploratory View of the Chinese Case'. *Journal of Management Studies* 17(2): 127–148.

—— (1990). *The Spirit of Chinese Capitalism*. New York, de Gruyter.

—— (2005). 'The Thick Description and Comparison of Societal Systems of Capitalism'. *Journal of International Business Studies* 36(2): 123–155.

—— (2008). 'Separating Culture from Institutions: The Use of Semantic Spaces as a Conceptual Domain and the Case of China'. *Management and Organization Review* 4(2): 257–290.

—— and M. A. Witt (2007). *The Future of Chinese Capitalism: Choices and Chances*. Oxford, Oxford University Press.

—— (2012). *West Meets East: Making Sense of Asian Business*. INSEAD Working Paper Series. Fontainebleau, INSEAD.

Schloss, J. P. and M. Murray, Eds. (2009). *The Believing Primate*. New York, Oxford University Press.

Schwartz, S. H. (1992). 'Universals in the Content and Structure of Values: Theoretical Advances and Empirical Tests in 20 Countries'. In M. P. Zanna, Ed., *Advances in Experimental Social Psychology*, 25: 1–65. New York, Academic Press.

—— (1994) 'Are there universal aspects in the structure and contents of human values'. *Journal of Social Issues* 50(4): 19–45.

Serra, N. and J. E. Stiglitz, Eds. (2008). *The Washington Consensus Reconsidered: Towards a New Global Governance*. New York, Oxford University Press.

Sorge, A. (2005). *The Global and the Local: Understanding the Dialectics of Business Systems*. Oxford, Oxford University Press.

Tambiah, S. J. (1970). *World Conqueror and World Renouncer: A Study of Buddhism and Polity in Thailand against a Historical Background*. Cambridge, Cambridge University Press.

Triandis, H. C. (1995). *Individualism and Collectivism*. Boulder, Westview Press.

Trompenaars, F. and C. Hampden-Turner (1998). *Riding the Waves of Culture*. New York, McGraw-Hill.

Weber, M. (1968/1930). *The Protestant Ethic and the Spirit of Capitalism* (Trans. T. Parsons). London, Unwin.

Weller, R. P. (2010). 'The Possibilities and Limitations of Spiritual Capital in Chinese Societies'. In P. L. Berger and G. Redding, Eds., *The Hidden Form of Capital: Spiritual Influences in Societal Progress*: 41–60. London, Anthem Press.

Whitley, R. (1999). *Divergent Capitalisms*. Oxford. Oxford University Press.

Witt, M. A. and G. Redding (2009). 'Culture, Meaning, and Institutions: Executive Rationale in Germany and Japan'. *Journal of International Business Studies* 40: 859–885.

—— (2010). *The Spirits of Capitalism: German, Japanese, and US Senior Executive Perceptions of Why Firms Exist*. INSEAD Working Paper No. 2010/94/EPS/EFE. Fontainebleau, INSEAD.

—— (2012). 'The Spirits of Corporate Social Responsibility: Senior Executive Perspectives of the Role of the Firm in Society in Germany, Hong Kong, Japan, South Korea and the USA'. *Socio-Economic Review* 10(1): 109–134.

World Values Survey (2009). '*World Values Survey 2005 Official Data File V. 20090901*'. Madrid, World Values Association.

## CHAPTER 18

# EMPLOYMENT RELATIONS AND HUMAN RESOURCE MANAGEMENT IN ASIA

*Explaining Patterns in Asian Societies*

### STEPHEN J. FRENKEL AND KYOUNG-HEE YU

## INTRODUCTION

IN this chapter we examine employment relations in most of the Asian countries included in this handbook. The term 'employment relations' (ER) refers to key features of relations between employers, workers' organizations (usually trade unions), and the state, commonly referred to as industrial relations. In addition, ER refers to relations between management and employees within the enterprise, or what is often referred to as Human Resource Management (HRM). In practice, industrial relations and HRM are interconnected: collectivized and institutionalized industrial relations regulate individual contracts within the enterprise, while their absence encourages workers to interpret individual contracts and relations with management from the perspective of informal rules developed by work groups. Nevertheless, it is analytically useful to distinguish these relations. Our focus is on patterns of relationships above and within the enterprise rather than ER outcomes, because it is difficult to distinguish these effects from the impact of other political-economic factors. The period of concern is 2005–2012.

Pursuing an inductive approach, we search for ER patterns by examining a set of comparable indicators across twelve countries.[1] Our main findings are three-fold. First, at the most abstract level, there is broad similarity in national ER patterns in Asia; however, the region's distinctiveness depends on systematic comparisons with other regions, for example North America or Northern Europe, an enterprise that is beyond the scope of this chapter. Second, at a lower level of abstraction, while a substantial minority of countries—China, Vietnam, India, Malaysia, and to a large extent, the Philippines—share a common ER pattern, the remaining seven countries reveal distinctive patterns, defying separate clustering based on available measures. Third, ER patterns in some countries are nevertheless more dissimilar to most others and accordingly merit further analysis. Singapore, and to a lesser extent Japan, fit this description. An important implication of our analysis is that if national ER patterns reflect the type of society in which they are embedded, as argued in the Varieties of Capitalism (VoC) and business systems tradition, then Asia is likely to be characterized by several types of society rather than a single form of capitalism, except perhaps at a higher, more abstract, regional level. Moreover, *contra* the VOC/business systems' line of argument, we shall show that there exist global tendencies that encourage convergence in ER patterns in spite of dissimilarities in national political economies.

The chapter proceeds as follows. We begin with a critique of relevant theory followed by an outline of our approach and methods. We then examine ER patterns in the twelve Asian countries. This is followed by a more detailed profile of ER in eight countries, selected on the basis of their approximation to the majority pattern (China, Vietnam, India, and the Philippines) or their distinctiveness (Thailand, Japan, South Korea, and Singapore). We then discuss factors potentially explaining similarities and differences across the region, concluding with suggestions for future research and noting limitations of our analysis.

# RELEVANT THEORY

We briefly consider several literatures—VoC and Business Systems, the regulation school and related theory, and industrial relations—with specific reference to ER in Asia. These are disparate in theoretical orientation, because ER is mainly treated as part of a wider issue, that is, as a sub-system which fulfils certain functions relative to the extant type of societal system in that country. Where this is not the case, as in industrial relations, the evidence has proved difficult to explain, so that frameworks rather than more detailed theories prevail.

## VoC and Business Systems

The VoC framework shows how innovation and economic development can be achieved through different institutional arrangements in advanced industrialized countries (Hall and Soskice 2001; Thelen 2004; Hall and Thelen 2009). Institutions, rather than the proverbial 'invisible hand', are viewed as dominant influences on market structures, and are thereby chosen as the focus of study in explaining the international diversity of capitalist forms. Institutions are presumed to evolve in such a way as to preserve complementarity with one another and provide institutional coherence (Morgan 2007: 134). Particular institutions—such as centralized collective bargaining and inter-organizational skills development programmes—reinforce each other, operating more efficiently as inter-dependent entities, and are therefore likely to persist as societies evolve. Because institutions in a mature society are complementary, the overall institutional configuration is resistant to change. Societies become 'path-dependent' because it is difficult to change one type of institution without reforming all institutions. This argument explains why VoC predicts that national differences will persist in the face of globalization (Thelen 2001).

The VoC framework has been extensively critiqued (Amable 2003; Jackson and Deeg 2008; Wilkins et al. 2010), but not specifically from an 'ER in Asia' viewpoint. From the latter perspective, three observations are particularly relevant. First, despite acknowledging that various economic systems are outcomes of political processes, the VoC framework does not directly analyse power in society (Thelen 2001). The discussion of 'political coalitions' implicitly assumes that there are no systemic inequalities between interest groups (Cusack, Iversen, and Soskice 2007; Soskice 2007). This plainly contradicts long-standing status and power differences between social actors in many Asian and other countries. Second, and related to the above, there is no theory and empirical analysis of the state's role. Interested mostly in co-ordination through firms and market institutions, the VoC literature neglects the state's role in shaping markets and outcomes. However, recent VoC scholarship does acknowledge the state's role in explaining how actors' strategies are influenced to varying degrees by state policy (Martin and Thelen 2007; Schmidt 2007), an anomaly unaccounted for by the two forms of advanced capitalism described by Hall and Soskice (2001). These studies are more relevant to addressing Asian capitalisms, where the state has been a major actor. A third observation is that industrial relations in the VoC framework is viewed as serving a functional, co-ordinating role in the economy. This restricted perspective fails to acknowledge that labour and management may pursue different interests, which may disrupt economic co-ordination, and whose resolution may contribute to social change rather than preserving social and economic stability.

The business systems literature developed in parallel with VoC analysis and shares with it certain common features (Berger and Dore 1996; Boyer and Drache 1996; Crouch and Streeck 1997; Hollingsworth and Boyer 1997; Amable 2003). Given our specific interest in ER in Asia, we focus on Whitley's (1992) business systems theory as applied to Asia. His framework, like the VoC approach, asserts the presence of institutional configurations—particularly the relationship between business owners and management as represented by corporate governance mechanisms—which he argues is key to explaining different forms of capitalism. According to Morgan (2007: 131), Whitley's typology allows for more variety in societies because it depends on a wider range of institutional pairings instead of focusing primarily on modes of co-ordination that result in one of two types of capitalism: Liberal-Market Economies (LMEs) or Co-ordinated Market Economies (CMEs). Whitley's (1992) characterization of Asian capitalisms is based on a historical examination of the origins of pre-industrial institutions that subsequently influenced industrialization. He therefore accorded importance to the role of the state and the family structure in explaining how work is organized in Asian enterprises. Thus, unlike VoC literature, the business systems approach avoids Eurocentricism and is cognisant of the importance of the state. Recent developments in this tradition have moved away from typologies of societies to understanding practices and processes of multinational businesses operating across and within business systems (Kristensen and Zeitlin 2005; Geppert and Mayer 2006).

## The Regulation School and Related Theory

The Regulation School originated in the 1970s out of intellectual efforts to account for Europe's destabilization as a result of stagflation. These efforts culminated in an updating of Marxist theory to understand systemic change (Boyer 1990). Since then, the school has contributed to the study of development as a dynamic process of contention between societal groups, particularly in the Asian context, as expressed in the work of Deyo (1987, 1989, 2012), who has emphasized the 'strategic capacity' of the Asian state in co-ordinating economic policy through peak economic organizations such as trade associations and national-level unions. Deyo (1989) argued that several characteristics of Asian economic development contributed to a weak labour movement. These included Export-Oriented Industrialization (EOI) development strategies that encouraged state control of unions and suppression of industrial conflict, industrialization based on light industry and a young female workforce, concentration of the workforce in geographically segregated and often government-controlled areas, weak elites (including the middle class) unable to challenge the state, and external regime support from Western powers. Thus, whilst privileging selected economic actors, the Asian developmental states took preventive measures to ensure that interest groups did not become *politically* powerful (Deyo 1987: 236–237). Consequently, the labour movement in Asia is marked by very limited union power, reflected in the low level of industrial conflict during the development process and low union density, coupled with an authoritarian workplace culture (Deyo 1989). The state is the main co-ordinating mechanism, organizing markets and fostering investment to further capital accumulation, while presiding over the workforce and society more generally in a repressive paternalistic fashion (Koo 2001). Recent conceptualizations depict the Asian state as less authoritarian and repressive, acknowledging the growth of interest groups and the need to facilitate negotiated compromise (see Deyo 2012).

## Industrial Relations

Industrial relations scholars have been interested in the question of convergence of ER patterns across nations. Kerr et al. (1964) argued that convergence would occur as similar experiences of technological change and industrialization led to similar problems which could only be resolved through the development of industrial rule-making institutions, of which collective bargaining was held to be superior. Lacking evidence for this view, alternative theories have been offered. According to Locke, Kochan, and Piore (1995), ER systems are diverging even as national institutions lose their influence in an international economy dominated by MNCs. This is because of different emphases placed on innovation and variations in the extent of innovation diffusion. Katz and Derbishire (2000) disagree, arguing that national institutions continue to shape ER patterns; however, they see a growing trend towards diversity within national systems, so that it is possible to speak of convergent divergences. Batt, Holman, and Holtgrewe (2009) also pursue the theme of convergent divergences in a seventeen-country comparative study of various labour relations issues relating to call centres. Key findings include a mix of convergent and divergent tendencies depending on exposure of particular IR aspects to international and national influence. For example, work-flow design and work practices tend to be similar, based on internationally available technology, while pay and conditions tend to vary according to legal frameworks and the related strength of employee representation. Of particular note is the authors' observation that industrial relations in call centres in emerging-market countries (including India and South Korea) are not homogeneous, especially in their institutional labour-relations arrangements, and therefore cannot be distinguished as a type from LMEs and CMEs. Yet call centres in these countries were characterized by decentralized bargaining structures, wage dispersion, low union density, and relatively high performance monitoring, characteristics more similar to call centres in LMEs than CMEs. Batt and her co-authors concluded that more research was needed to see if emerging-market economies could be integrated into a VoC framework.

Focusing specifically on four Asian societies (Singapore, Malaysia, the Philippines, and India), Kuruvilla (1996) showed that the type of government industrialization strategy influences ER goals. Import-Substitution Industrialization (ISI) was found to be associated with ER policy goals of pluralism and stability, while low-cost EOI strategy was associated with cost containment and union suppression. In countries that moved from a low-cost export-oriented strategy to a higher value-added export-oriented strategy, the focus of ER goals changed from cost containment to workforce flexibility and skills development. Divergent ER patterns resulted from the way these different strategic choices influenced the development of specific institutions to meet emerging goals and on account of different institutional industrial relations histories. An extension of this approach is the development of a 'logics of action' approach to explaining ER patterns. Frenkel and Kuruvilla (2002) argue that the interplay among three different logics of action—the logic of competition, the logic of industrial peace, and the logic of employment-income protection—determines the ER patterns in any given nation. The strengths of the logics themselves are influenced by five often related factors: economic development strategy, globalization intensity, union strength, labour-market features, and government responsiveness to workers. The authors' analysis of ER in four Asian countries (India, China, Philippines, and Malaysia) supports their view that ER patterns reflect different combinations of logic strengths. Militating against long-term convergence in ER are national variations in the combinations of logic strengths, and changes in logic strengths over time. Other studies have found that over time, the primary role of Asian ER systems have shifted from providing industrial peace and stability during the early phase of their development towards an institutional mechanism that facilitates flexibility. Kuruvilla and Erickson (2002) review changes in ER in seven Asian countries (Japan, Korea, Malaysia, China, India, Singapore, and the Philippines) and document that while all of them have adopted flexibility as a goal, they differed according to the emphasis placed on numerical (e.g. cost-cutting) or functional (e.g. adaptive production systems) flexibility. Citing Deyo (1997), the authors argue that a country (or particular sector in a country) is likely to prioritize numerical flexibility to the extent that it is highly exposed to competitive pressure. On the other hand, functional flexibility will be sought as a strategy where national institutions favour long-term human capital development through training and investment in R&D.

Given the relative paucity of detailed empirical studies in the VoC and business systems literatures that focus on ER in Asian countries and the lack of consensus in the IR literature on whether trends in ER are converging or diverging, we adopt an inductive approach to examining patterns in ER/HR for the countries in this handbook.

## Methods

In order to systematically compare ER across most of the countries in this handbook, we begin by profiling ER in each country, using appropriate contemporary data based on reliable secondary sources (see Table 18.1 for annotated sources). Although data on ER indicators are limited in various ways, they permit presentation of country ER profiles and provide a foundation for a deeper analysis.[2] We examine union characteristics, including density (number of union members relative to the formal-sector workforce) and the existence of tripartite processes that provide unions and employer organizations with opportunities to influence public policy. In addition, we note the extent of collective bargaining indicated by the proportion of the formal workforce covered by collective agreements and the extent to which pay decisions are centralized (at industry or national level) or decentralized (at or below the firm level). Two important workplace-level ER characteristics are the extent of labour–management cooperation and employment flexibility (the obverse of employment protection), that is, the ease with which employees can be employed or dismissed. Responses to these two indicators represent the views of management, since they are based on management surveys.

We manually coded the indicators, ordering the countries according to the extent to which their ER/HR systems are 'flexible' (giving wide latitude to employers vis-à-vis labour) or 'protective' (limiting employer discretion to direct employees). Following the simple statistical rule that standard deviation is a reliable measure of distance from the mean (Goldberg 1983) and noting its application in other cross-country comparison studies (e.g. Fernandez et al. 1997), we coded countries based on distance from the sample mean. Countries were coded as 'flexible' (light grey in Table 18.1) or 'protective' (dark grey in Table 18.1) if they scored one standard deviation below or above the mean in the relevant indicator, depending on the nature of the indicator. Countries were coded as

# Table 18.1 Dimensions of macro and micro ER indicators, 2005–2012, selected Asian countries

| | Hong Kong | Thailand | China | Vietnam | India | Malaysia | Philippines | Indonesia | Taiwan | Japan | Korea | Singapore |
|---|---|---|---|---|---|---|---|---|---|---|---|---|
| Union density[b] (0 to 100) | 22.5[i] | 2.1[5£] | 22[4£] | 10[w] | 5 | 10.19[*] | 10.6[3£] | 7[zz] | 36.1[6w] | 18.2[9<] | 10.1[7+] | 18.7[5£] |
| Extent of tripartism[d] (1 none, 4 full consultation) | 2 | 1 | 2 | 2 | 2 | 2 | 2 | 1 | 3 | 2 | 2 | 3 |
| Collective bargaining coverage[e] | <5 | 1.4[5£] | <5 | <5 | <5 | 2.45[£] (private sector) | 2.2[9£] | 1.4[8£] | 0.5[?11] | 15est | 11.5[li] | 17.3[5£] |
| Level of pay determination[f] (1 centralized, 7 decentralized) | 6.1 | 4.7 | 5.3 | 5.7 | 5.2 | 5.5 | 4.5 | 4.3 | 5.6 | 5.8 | 5.3 | 6 |
| Labour-employer co-operation[g] (1 confront, 7 co-operate) | 5.4 | 4.8 | 4.5 | 4.5 | 4.6 | 5.4 | 4.5 | 4.3 | 5.2 | 5.7 | 3.2 | 6.1 |
| Employment flexibility[j] (1 low, 7 high) | 5.7 | 4.4 | 4.3 | 4.3 | 4 | 4.5 | 4 | 4.2 | 3.8 | 2.8 | 3.3 | 5.8 |

Flexible   Protective   Moderate

*Note:* See text regarding bolded figures for union density in India and employment flexibility in the Philippines;
See Appendix for details on measures and sources of indicators.

'moderate' (grey in Table 18.1) if their score was in between. In two cases, we adjusted the statistics where the numbers belied a bias reflecting their source and were inconsistent with reliable secondary sources. Specifically, we coded India's union density as 'moderate', despite its high score (33%), to account for the especially large and important informal sector, which would bring actual union density in the workforce to approximately 5 per cent. We coded the Philippines employment flexibility as higher than provided by the data source (3.3), which was mainly MNCs whose average levels of protection would be relatively high.

Based on ER patterns revealed by these data, we chose eight countries that highlight both the similarities and substantial differences within Asian ER systems. These summaries, based on reliable secondary sources, provide sufficient detail for the reader to appreciate the nuances of these ER systems, how they are changing, and the factors that might account for convergence in some ER aspects and divergence in others.

# FINDINGS

## An Asian Employment Relations Pattern?

Table 18.1 shows the ordering of the twelve countries based on a qualitative interpretation of the distance of their score from the sample mean for each indicator. This suggests that Hong Kong and Thailand are the most flexible systems. China, Vietnam, India, and Malaysia follow, with the Philippines not very different from this group except for a relatively high level of pay determination. Flexibility–protection assessment becomes more complicated when examining the remaining five countries because of various score combinations across the indicators, the most intriguing being Singapore, which combines a relatively protective macro-institutional environment with flexible firm-level practices.

Before we try and answer the question of whether a common Asian ER pattern exists, it is useful to examine whether there are indicators in Table 18.1 for which most or least similarity can be found across the twelve countries. The average country similarity across the six indicators is 8. In other words, on average, at least eight of the twelve countries share similar scores (i.e. within one standard deviation of the average). They are most similar on low union density and a reasonably high degree of labour–employer cooperation, and least similar on collective bargaining coverage and level of pay determination, where seven of the twelve countries are similar and five are different.

What then does our cross-country analysis suggest regarding ER patterning? It shows the presence of an ER pattern that is common to a large minority—five of the twelve countries, if we include the Philippines—and the existence of some similarities among a minority of the seven remaining countries. In other words, there is no evidence of a common Asian pattern of ER, and considerable diversity exists between countries in the region. The pattern common to China, Vietnam, India, Malaysia, and the Philippines can be characterized by unilateral control by either management or state-sponsored parties. It comprises very weak collective representation (low union density, limited tripartism, low collective bargaining coverage) and management discretion to encourage or impose control over employees through decentralized pay determination and high employment flexibility. A feature of the pattern is considerable labour–employer cooperation. Traditional practices based on custom buttressed by strong social norms are likely to support rather than challenge prevailing authority systems (Deyo 1989), although rising education levels and the growth of transnational social media make this cultural form of support less reliable.

Beyond the presence of the pattern described above, what ER similarities exist among the remaining seven countries? Inspection of Table 18.1 suggests few discernible similarities. Only with regard to union density do four of the countries—Hong Kong, Korea, Indonesia, and Japan—share similar low scores with the five countries referred to above. And in regard to bargaining coverage, three of the seven countries—Indonesia, Japan, and Singapore—have relatively high coverage, compared with the twelve-country average.

Hong Kong is relatively decentralized in determining pay and has higher employment flexibility (i.e. lower employment protection), both reflecting the unilateral power of employers. It is the economy with the most flexible ER indicator scores. Thailand is also relatively flexible, being below the mean on three measures of collective relations: union density, tripartism, and collective bargaining coverage, and average on the other indicators. Indonesia is relatively low on tripartism, but has relatively high collective bargaining coverage with pay determination relatively centralized compared to the mean for the twelve countries, though the country score (4.3) is around the midpoint of the seven-point scale. Bargaining expanded with ILO guidance, possibly explaining why more workers are covered than are union members (Caraway 2009). Taiwan is different again. It has relatively high union density and tripartite consultation, but relatively low collective bargaining coverage. This seemingly anomalous set of arrangements becomes clear with additional information. Taiwanese unions administer health insurance, so that workers and self-employed contractors join unions in order to participate in this statutory scheme (Caraway 2009). While the government, especially Democratic Party administrations to which the unions are allied, favour tripartite consultation on a range of development and labour issues, employers prefer to retain unilateral control over labour within the enterprise, and so oppose collective bargaining (Chen, Ko, and Lawler 2003). Finally, Japan and Korea share relatively low levels of employment flexibility, but differ on levels of labour–management cooperation. Japan has relatively high collective bargaining coverage, together with comparatively cooperative labour–employer relations, but relatively low employment flexibility. This picture speaks to the formal ER system where enterprise unionism together with a commitment to long-term employment facilitate labour–employer cooperation, but limit employment or numerical flexibility (Sako 2006). On the other hand, as our vignette shows, Japanese employers are increasingly using non-standard labour to avoid the rigidities of the established ER system. Korea has limited cooperation between management and labour and relatively low employment flexibility. Its scores point to the threat of worker militancy and the existence of laws and norms limiting employer discretion.

Singapore is the outlier in Asian ER. As Table 18.1 shows, on five out of six indicators, Singapore's score is either one or more standard deviations above or below the mean. As described in our vignette, Singapore combines strong collective relations—tripartism and government-guided collective bargaining through corporatist unions—with decentralized, cooperative and flexible employment arrangements within the enterprise.

In summary, we have highlighted both similarities and differences in ER patterns. While a substantial minority of countries share a similar pattern, there is no dominant configuration. There is considerable diversity, which suggests the limited presence of regional or global factors that account for similarity or convergence over time, and the need to understand the development and characteristics of each national ER system. With this in mind, we have selected eight countries to examine in more detail.

## Employment Relations Patterns in Eight Asian Countries: A Closer Look

We have selected the following countries for further examination: Thailand, China, Vietnam, India, Philippines, Japan, Korea, and Singapore. Our selection criteria were three-fold. First, comprehensiveness, in the sense of covering both the substantial minority for which similar ER patterns were observed, and some of the variations, including the least similar country, Singapore. Second, type of society, including national historical trajectory. For example, across the six countries characterized by a pattern of unilateral control, we distinguish between Thailand, China, and Vietnam, and India and the Philippines. Thailand was not colonized and is dominated by business elites. The country's ER pattern is characterized by weak ER institutions resulting in very limited employee protection beyond that provided by customary values and norms. China and Vietnam are single-party (Communist) states where unions are under party control and collective bargaining has until recently been impossible to implement. This contrasts with India and the Philippines, whose ER reflects the early imprint of democratic colonial powers—the UK in the case of India and the USA in regard to the Philippines—and whose nationalist movements introduced laws that permitted autonomous unions and collective bargaining. A third criterion is geopolitical importance: we included China and India for this reason and excluded Hong Kong and Taiwan on the same grounds. Indonesia met this criterion, but limitations of space meant that we could not exceed eight vignettes. For ease of exposition, we have paired some of the countries where there is a rationale for doing so.

## Employment Relations in Thailand

The Thai economy has grown at a modest rate—around 5 per cent per year over the past decade—and unemployment has averaged less than 2.5 per cent (Suehiro and Wailerdsak 2014). Shortages of semi-skilled and unskilled labour and managers have become acute, and unskilled shortages have been filled mainly by immigrants from Burma, Cambodia, and Laos (Suehiro and Wailerdsak 2014). Thailand switched from an ISI development strategy to EOI in the early 1970s. ISI had enabled manufacturing industries to grow and a relatively stable urban working class to emerge. It was these workers who engaged in the mass activism and strikes that led to the highly significant institutionalization of industrial conflict in the guise of the 1975 Labour Relations Act. This landmark legislation enabled employees to join unions and for unions to engage in collective bargaining (Brown 2007). Further legislation in 1998 encouraged substantive improvements in employee welfare by restricting working hours and hazardous work, stipulating overtime rates and holiday entitlements, and regulating youth employment, bringing Thailand into line with ILO standards. However, implementation of labour laws is problematic, with many cases of reported violations (Caraway 2010).

Meanwhile, EOI encouraged industrial restructuring, which led to changes in labour-force composition that were unfavourable to trade unionism. Thailand began to specialize in light-industry exports, especially textiles, clothing, footwear, and plastics, subsequently moving rapidly into production of higher-technology electronics and computers, and supply of parts to the computer and auto industries. Women became a majority in the manufacturing workforce, rising from 50 per cent in 1995 to 53 per cent in 2009 (Deyo 2012). Growth in manufacturing was significant, although halted temporarily by the 1997–1998 financial crisis. By 2005, manufacturing and construction accounted for nearly 22 per cent of employed persons, while services accounted for nearly 36 per cent and agriculture accounted for most of the remainder, at 38.5 per cent (Siengthai 2007). A further barrier to union organizing in Thailand is that 42 per cent of the working population is employed in the informal sector (Deyo 2012: 108).

Thailand's politics have been relatively unstable, punctuated by a series of coups and periods of democratic government (Brown 2004). Politics are less about policies than about leader and factional loyalties. Until very recently, when both major parties have been attempting to attract voters with populist policies, two common factors have been a commitment to EOI, including encouraging both foreign and domestic investment, and policies that are broadly supportive of large Thai business interests, which are largely family-based (Suehiro and Wailerdsak 2014). Although protective legislation, especially regarding severance pay, exists (Caraway 2009), workers in the large informal sector are excluded (Brown 2004). In addition, in pursuing cost-reduction strategies, firms have been hiring contract rather than regular workers. The former are often excluded from labour legislation (Deyo 2012). There has also been a significant lack of enforcement of labour legislation, particularly in regard to workers' health and safety, as indicated by a 19.3 per cent rise in occupational injuries and diseases between 2000 and 2005, including a more than doubling of work-related deaths (Siengthai 2007).

Unions play a very limited role in protecting and advancing the interests of Thai workers. Table 18.1 shows that few workers are union members. The main exception is in the state enterprise sector, comprising around 1 per cent of employees, where unions do bargain effectively over pay and conditions, but are not permitted to strike. Unions in Thailand are enterprise based, small, and lacking in funds (Napathorn and Chanprateep 2011; Suehiro and Wailerdsak 2014). Despite the intent of the 1975 legislation, tripartism is also limited, partly by the structure of unions, and partly by the lack of desire by governments and business to consult regularly. Weak unions mean that collective bargaining is virtually absent, although some gains have been made by unions linking up with NGOs in the form of a social movement (Brown 2004; Deyo 2012: 152–153, 237–238). There are a few collective agreements in the auto, state enterprise, oil and chemicals, food and beverage, garments and textiles, and finance and banking industries. Collective agreements appear to benefit both employers and employees—disputes and strikes are rare (Napathorn and Chanprateep 2011; Suehiro and Wailerdsak 2014). This explains a cooperative labour relations climate, as indicated by a score of 4.4 out of 7 in Table 18.1.

## Human Resource Management in Thailand

In the absence of collective relations above the enterprise level, we focus on HRM. Lawler, Siengthai, and Atmiyanandana's (2007) four-fold characterization is useful in this regard. *Thai-owned firms* are family based, and many are ethnically Chinese (many include Sino-Thai owners). HR strategy is emergent and informal, recruitment is internal, and ascriptive criteria are important. Compensation is low, but there is more emphasis on job security. However, permanent job security appears to be restricted to family members. Training and development is limited. Larger *Thai-owned corporations* tend to develop formal HR strategies, recruit mainly internally, employ more transparent procedures, and provide more plentiful career opportunities. Compensation is higher, but less than in Western subsidiaries. There is an emphasis on job security and training, and development is systematic and broad. *Western foreign-owned subsidiaries*, like their Thai counterparts, usually have an HR strategy linked to business objectives. Less attention is paid to socializing employees into the firm and there is more reliance on external recruitment compared to large Thai firms. Western companies provide the most generous pay and benefits, but offer limited job security. Training and development is planned, but varies in extent. Finally, *Japanese foreign-owned subsidiaries* pursue HR strategies similar to other large firms; however, internal recruitment is emphasized, and there is extensive socialization and use of non-transparent procedures. Japanese subsidiaries tend to pay less than other large firms, but provide generous benefits, job security, and more extensive training and development opportunities. Japanese subsidiaries employ a larger proportion of expatriates than other foreign firms and attempt to import some Japanese work practices into Thailand.[3]

Returning to Table 18.1, pay determination is decentralized and employment flexibility relatively high (4.4). Employers, using contract labour and sub-contracting to informal workers, have sought to reduce unit costs mainly through numerical flexibility (Napathorn and Chanprateep 2011; Deyo 2012). Lacking a strongly enforced and reasonable minimum wage, this approach, and the low productivity of the service sector, contributed to a decline in average real wages in the private sector between 1999 and 2004 (Siengthai 2007). In addition, cost-based restructuring limits Thailand's capacity to overcome 'the middle-income trap' (Suehiro and Wailerdsak 2014).

## Employment Relations in China and Vietnam

These two countries share several ER features. First, the party-state remains the dominant actor: the state (at all levels) is a large employer, employing nearly 18 and 24 per cent of the respective workforces in the two countries (Tran 2009; NBSC 2011). The central government is responsible for relevant legislation, while implementation is in the hands of local administrations. Both countries reformed their labour legislation in the mid-1990s in order to facilitate the transformation from planned to market-based, export-oriented economies. In China, the Labour Law of 1994 guaranteed the ACFTU's union monopoly (Warner 2008). Further legislation, for example the Trade Union Law of 2001, prevented any other union from challenging the ACFTU, which is controlled by the Communist Party (Warner 2008). The same is true of the Vietnamese General Confederation of Labour (VGCL). With assistance from the ILO, subsequent legislation in the 2000s in both countries resulted in the development of ER systems that provided for collective and individual employment contracts, including fairness norms and dispute-resolution institutions and procedures.

Unions are organized under the central official organizations of the ACFTU in China and VGCL in Vietnam. Unions in both countries are structured along industrial and locality lines; however, in Vietnam occupational unions are permitted and present in the private sector (Edwards and Phan 2008). Table 18.1 shows union density in China to be around 22 per cent and Vietnam 10 per cent; however, these figures are not very meaningful, as unions in these countries are only beginning to represent workers in collective bargaining. Their main function is to assist the government in economic development by implementing government policy (e.g. regarding social benefits). Protecting workers' interests is a subsidiary function. This function enables employee representation in negotiations with management, a process that is increasing in both countries as worker protests remain at a high level and the number of disputes submitted to arbitration exceeds the capacity of existing institutions.[4] Unions are expected by the government to assist in resolving disputes. This is made possible on some occasions by locality-based unions acting more flexibly in representing workers' interests. It is noteworthy that compared to China, Vietnamese law permits workers slightly more latitude to strike, although such action remains severely circumscribed (Vo 2009; Cooke 2012).

While the government consults with the union federations at central and local levels, particularly concerning labour legislation, tripartism is weak, because the government dominates the process. In addition, as Table 18.1 shows, collective bargaining coverage is very limited. In most cases in both countries, bargaining is nothing more than an agreement between management and the union, often without member consultation, containing an addition to the minimum local wage, together with conditions and/or benefits unilaterally determined by management (Edwards and Phan 2008; Vo 2009; Cooke 2012: 134–135). Nevertheless, there are opportunities for future bargaining, particularly as NGOs (in China) and labour media (in Vietnam) provide useful information and advice on dealing with workers' grievances.

The limited collective regulation of pay and employment conditions is reflected in the substantial gap between legally prescribed rights, both substantive (e.g. limits on overtime hours) and procedural (workplace consultation), and actual practice. This reflects the low priority given by central and local governments to workers' interests, insufficient resourcing, and lack of motivation and bargaining skills by union officials who are keen to conform to Party policy in order to pursue their career interests. An exception to this are legally prescribed area pay rates, determined from time to time by local authorities in consultation with the central government and sometimes under pressure from striking workers. Limited legal enforcement, referred to above, gives employers considerable unilateral power over employees, a topic we address in more detail below.

## Human Resource Management in China and Vietnam

In China, a more strategic orientation has been adopted regarding employees, including rapid adoption of western HRM techniques (Wang, Bruning, and Peng 2007). This is most evident in foreign-invested firms and especially Western MNCs, but the trend is growing in private Chinese enterprises (Cooke 2010). It is least evident in state-owned enterprises, which contribute a diminishing proportion of economic output (Ngo, Lau, and Foley 2008). However, the differences between adoption of these practices among different ownership types are declining (Cooke 2012), especially since the central government also promotes particular HRM practices such as overseas recruitment fairs, occupational training and certification initiatives for HR professionals, and management development programmes (Cooke 2012). Other practices used by MNCs and favoured by large private Chinese companies include on-the-job training, coaching and mentoring, performance management (including 360-degree appraisals); market-based pay surveys; broad-band payment systems, employee assistance programmes, and pursuit of international labour standards. These HRM practices apply mainly to white-collar and professional employees in capital and knowledge-intensive sectors. Manual employees, including most migrant workers employed in labour-intensive sectors where competition is based on cost rather than quality, are managed in a more authoritarian traditional manner (Taylor 2001). A final caveat regarding convergence on Western HRM practices is that, owing to cultural differences, implementation of some practices (e.g. reward systems strongly biased in favour of individual rather than group performance) in China may not have the intended results. Consequently, indigenous practices may need to be extended or created (e.g. leadership based on morality and care). Nevertheless, as indicated by a score of 4.5 for employee cooperation in Table 18.1, Chinese employees are generally regarded as cooperative. At the same time, the regulations permit more employment flexibility than is indicated by a score of 4.3. This is facilitated by the employment of workers on an informal basis (i.e. without labour contracts) and on short-term contracts, either directly or through labour hire agencies (Park and Cai 2011).

Vietnam's scores on the above two criteria are similar to their Chinese counterparts. This is in spite of Western HRM practices being less widely practised, largely because the *DoiMoi* policy of opening up to foreign investment occurred some ten years later than in China. In addition, much of the investment has been in oil and gas, and labour-intensive, low value-added products like textiles, clothing, and footwear. In these sectors, advanced HR policies are the exception rather than the rule (Quang, Thang, and Rowley 2008). Four observations can be made about HRM in Vietnam (Quang, Thang, and Rowley 2008; Zhu, Collins et al. 2008; Vo 2009). First, state-owned companies have been slow to adapt. They have retained internal promotion and emphasis on personal recommendation, although external advertising is becoming more common. Second, more generally, there has been a gradual transition from politically oriented, bureaucratic performance management to merit-based systems. The government remains influential in setting guidelines for pay, but wage differentials have been allowed to widen. Third, training remains unsystematic, and fourth, there has been little reform of ER practices despite substantial legal changes.

According to Zhu, Collins et al. (2008), most private firms and joint ventures have adopted what they term a Personnel Management model, while MNCs have embraced an HRM model. The former represents a hybrid, combining some features of the traditional state-owned enterprise with modern HRM practices, including employment of both permanent and fixed-contract employees; recruitment and job allocation based on internal centralized decision-making; and pay according to team performance. More traditional features refer to collective contracts regulating pay and employment conditions, and unions advancing government rather than workers' interests. Private Vietnamese firms claim to act more like MNCs with regard to training; however, according to Quang, Thang, and Rowley (2008: 198), 'most SOEs [state-owned enterprises] and PCs [privately-owned companies] still consider employee development as an expense and hence tend to keep allocated budgets for this activity as small as possible'.

In summary, China appears to have charted a course that Vietnam is following, albeit at a slower pace. This includes adoption of Western HRM practices that acknowledge the importance of hiring, developing, and retaining skilled employees, while relying on numerical flexibility to manage semi-skilled and unskilled labour.

## Employment Relations in India and the Philippines

India and the Philippines are both pluralist democracies whose labour laws reflect the imprint of colonialism. India's constitution, introduced in 1948, gave workers the right to join or not join autonomous unions, and with the exception of public enterprises, unions were legally permitted to engage in collective bargaining. Later, extensive legislation concerning employment protection and dispute resolution was introduced (Venkataratnam and Verma 2011). Legislation is the responsibility of both the central and state governments, making legal complexity a feature of Indian labour relations. On the other hand, enforcement is weak and union strength varies considerably across states. Economic liberalization, which began in the early 1990s, has had limited impact on Indian unions, largely because successive central governments and many state governments have lacked motivation or sufficient power to alter existing legal arrangements.

In the Philippines, the key law is the Industrial Peace Act of 1953, which encouraged unions and collective bargaining. The law also provides for conciliation and mediation services and there is a National Labour Relations Commission which promotes compulsory arbitration to settle disputes (Rowley and Abdul-Rahman 2008). In 1972 the Marcos regime introduced changes that reduced union power, including the banning of strikes and the restructuring of unions along industrial lines. Subsequent governments removed some of these restrictions, the emphasis being on EOI, based on low wage costs and numerical flexibility. In both India and the Philippines, politics and the law became the preferred means of influencing labour relations. Employers in both countries have responded by avoiding collaborative relationships with unions.

Indian unions developed as part of a nationalist movement towards independence, leaving a legacy of political alignment—mainly but not exclusively to the Congress Party—and a tendency for unions to seek political influence (and appropriate legislation) to advance their interests. A related second characteristic is that Indian unions are fragmented. When parties split, so do unions (Venkataratnam and Verma 2011). There are seventeen central federations and around 66,000 registered unions (Sundar 2008) structured along industrial and enterprise-union lines. Union density is nearly one-third of the formal-sector workforce. However, taking into account that the informal sector (self-employed and casual workers) accounts for around 85 per cent of the workforce (Harriss-White 2003), union density declines to around 5 per cent (Sundar 2008), as indicated in Table 18.1. Consequently, the official figure overstates the power of unions in India, which tend to be concentrated in traditional industries and the public sector, including financial services, communications (e.g. railways and ports), and power. Although most unions are affiliated to central federations, there has been a growing trend towards non-affiliated, non-politically aligned, workplace unions (Bhattacherjee and D'Souza 2011).

Like their Indian counterparts, Philippine unions are fragmented—nearly 9,000 unions divided into over 170 federations affiliated with around ten labour centres—often with different political views and in competition with one another (Erickson et al. 2003). Unions are structured mainly along enterprise lines. As seen in Table 18.1, union density is 10.6 per cent of the formal workforce, bearing in mind that around half the workforce is employed in the informal sector. This 2008 figure has probably declined for two reasons: employers have sought numerical flexibility through union avoidance and the use of non-regular workers, and regional governors and export-zone administrators have promoted union-free environments in order to attract foreign investment (Erickson et al. 2003).[5] Meanwhile, unions have lost political influence and have failed to cooperate with one another around an agreed set of issues.

Tripartism in India refers to the role of the central or state governments in developing labour legislation through consultative institutions such as the Indian Labour

Conference and similar bodies at state level. The largest five national union centres and at least seven other national-level unions (Venkataratnam and Verma 2011) and two or three of the largest employer organizations are usually represented. In the Philippines, industrial relations are largely decentralized to the workplace level. However, regional statutory minimum wages are set by tripartite representatives (Ofreneo 2008). Reflecting the declining power of unions, strikes have been declining in recent years (see Kondo 2014; Anant et al. 2006).

Collective bargaining in India is limited to national/sectoral agreements in the coal, steel, ports, and financial services industries, and there is workplace-level bargaining in other private-sector areas. Workers usually enjoy rights to employment security, the right to strike, bonuses, and social security. Workplace-level bargaining is preferred by other employers whose employees are represented by unions. While there is a trend towards decentralized bargaining (Sundar 2008), there is a stronger tendency towards union avoidance by employers in modern sectors where unions are weak (software and business process engineering). New workplaces are established in rural areas where unions are absent and by outsourcing or subcontracting to the informal sector (Harriss-White 2003). According to Bhattacherjee and D'Souza (2011), while net employment in manufacturing declined between the early 1990s and 2004, contract jobs increased across all firm sizes, contributing to a declining share of labour costs to value-added, from 36 to 29 per cent. Contract work increased to nearly one-quarter of total formal manufacturing employment by 2004. Union avoidance has been encouraged by management perceptions of unions as strike-prone, which may have some basis in the experience of particular sectors, despite the declining overall trend noted above.

Table 1 shows that collective bargaining in the Philippines is very limited, covering 2.2 per cent of the total workforce, and declining. Workers are formally protected by substantial legislation which provides for minimum wages on a regional basis and limits employer discretion in the case of dismissals and wage reductions (Kondo 2014). However, legal amendments and avoidance encouraged by international competition has contradicted the progressive intentions of the law (Deyo 2012). Restructuring and the transformation of regular work into temporary contracts and casual work has increased in the Philippines, encouraging more than 10 per cent of the formal workforce to find jobs overseas, and leaving local workers little to fall back on apart from family relationships (Beerepoot 2008; Deyo 2012).

## Human Resource Management in India and the Philippines

At workplace level in the Indian formal sector, relations between management and employees vary between the relatively highly unionized state sector, private enterprises in the traditional industrial sector (steel, vehicles, railways, and textiles), and the non-union private sector. This includes IT and business process operations (BPO), which have grown significantly, hence India's characterization as 'the back-office of the world' (Bhattacherjee and D'Souza 2011: 169). India's traditional and state-owned industries are highly bureaucratized and unionized, giving rise to their reputation as conflict-prone and inflexible (Bhattacherjee and D'Souza 2011). However, as shown in

Table 18.1, a score of 4.6 and 4 for labour–management cooperation and employment flexibility, respectively, provides a more balanced picture that is further confirmed in recent research. According to Budhwar and Varma (2011), recent changes in Indian HR, especially in the IT and BPO sectors, include HR departments playing a stronger change-agent role in large organizations, and more emphasis on employee training and development and performance-based pay and promotions. A particular concern has been recruitment and retention in the context of skill shortages attendant on an economy growing at around 6.6 per cent a year, an inadequate education and training infrastructure, and a largely disengaged workforce managed by relatively few effective leaders.

Based on interviews with CEOs and other data from one hundred of India's largest and most effective publicly listed companies, Cappelli et al. (2010) identified four characteristics of modern Indian management, three of which are related to HRM. First, management's mission is social rather than shareholder (profit)-oriented. The authors claim that this motivates employees by making work more meaningful. Second, these companies invest in their employees, promoting internally and encouraging identification through empowerment and associated work arrangements. Third, the existence of a committed workforce facilitates *jugaad*, a persistent trial and error problem-solving process. The fourth characteristic concerns business strategy: a focus on improvements internal to the business and the firm's value chain rather than on competitors' behaviour. Illustrative evidence regarding the second point comes from Sasken, an Indian MNC employing around 3,500 employees in India. The company supplies network and related equipment to India's telecom industry. Where possible, Sasken hires internally through an internal referral programme and emphasizes needs-based training delivered by mentors and management education provided by leading international business schools (Cappelli et al. 2010: 16).

While advanced HR practices may be expected at the knowledge-worker end of the Indian labour market, this is not the case for less skilled employees. A summary of Flextronics' HR practices provides an example (Cividep 2010). Flextronics is a Singapore-based manufacturer of components to the Indian mobile phone industry. The company employs over 200,000 persons in thirty countries, including 1,600 persons in its own industrial park in Chennai. The workforce comprises 60 per cent men and 40 per cent women and is divided into skilled and unskilled categories. A minority (40%) of mainly skilled workers are permanent employees; the remainder are contract workers supplied mainly by four contractors. These workers can be laid off with one day's notice; permanent employees, by mutual agreement, receive between one and two months' notice. In 2009, unskilled workers' standard pay was 4.2 per cent above the State of Tamil Nadu minimum wage. Skilled workers received around 15 per cent higher pay than unskilled employees. Wage revisions are linked to the cost of living and are automatic rather than performance related. Employees usually work 48 hours a week, which is legally permitted, and receive annual and other leave above the legal minimum. There is no union, although procedures are available to employees for airing views and grievances. In addition, there is a safety committee and a recreational committee on which employees are represented (Cividep 2010). In sum, HR practices relating to less skilled jobs in the Indian modern hi-tech sector are much less favourable than their high-end counterparts, but nevertheless are superior to those offered in other parts of the formal sector, where under-employment, low pay, and inferior working conditions are common (Harriss-White 2003).

Table 18.1 indicates that labour–management relations in the Philippines are mainly cooperative (4.5), and an adjusted score of 4 (from 3.3) for labour flexibility is nevertheless low, given the lack of union protection for workers, the presence of a large informal sector, and high unemployment. Two reasons may account for this: strong social norms and informal networks that make it difficult to dismiss workers in times of recession in the absence of an official safety-net; and there may be difficulties in hiring skilled workers, which in turn reflects an inadequate education and training infrastructure. Evidence regarding HR in the Philippines comes mainly from Erickson et al. (2003), who conducted sixteen case studies of firms across six industries. Despite variation, there appear to be two dominant models. The first is a core-periphery model characterized by preferential treatment provided to a core of skilled, technical, and professional employees who are selectively recruited, trained, and developed using modern HR techniques. The peripheral workforce comprises semi-skilled and unskilled workers, who are increasingly hired as temporary workers or self-employed sub-contractors. An example of the core-periphery model is Jollibee, a highly successful fast-food chain and among the sixty largest companies in the Philippines. According to Ofreneo (2008), the company is very careful in selecting its employees, converting most of them from probationary to regular workers. However, the company relies on a large part-time temporary labour force comprised of college students. In this way it resembles the dominant numerical flexibility model that extends temporary work to all but a small minority of manager-owners and is found mainly in smaller and medium-sized labour-intensive sectors such as clothing and low-end electronics.

## Employment Relations in Japan and South Korea

Japan and Korea have successfully pursued EOI strategies (Deyo 1989). Japan industrialized in the late 1880s, eighty years earlier than Korea, where successive governments suppressed autonomous unions until the Great Labour Struggle that accompanied the 1987 democratization movement. Both countries are significant exporters of advanced manufacturing products, whose parts are increasingly produced in China and other low-cost Asian countries (Benson and Zhu 2011). Japan occupied Korea between 1910 and 1945 and thereafter has influenced Korean business and ER practices through contacts between Korean and Japanese managers. Both countries, Korea more than Japan, adhere to Confucian cultural values, which laid the foundation for a community-enterprise concept that included long-term employment, internal labour markets, and enterprise unionism. Both countries were influenced by the US in policy-making and drafting of initial ER legislation. However, a significant difference was that Japan's ER system, which combined the 'enterprise community' notion with collective bargaining, developed under the initial tutelage of the US occupation, whereas in Korea successive authoritarian governments directed economic development, changing the 1953 law to prevent autonomous unions, and outlawing strikes until 1987. Popular demands for democratization in Korea ushered in a new era of employment relations characterized by union militancy and large pay rises. This era of labour militancy eventually dissipated with concessions that permitted more labour flexibility (Lee 2011).

Trade unions in Japan continue to be organized mainly along enterprise lines. Unions cover employees of all types of jobs, but rarely include the hugely expanded number of 'non-regular workers' (i.e. part-time, self-employed, and temporary, including agency workers and family workers). Enterprise unions are often members of more than 100 industrial federations, which are usually affiliated to one of the three most prominent confederations, of which Rengo is the largest. Table 18.1 shows Japanese union density at 18.2 per cent of the formal workforce, which comprises an estimated 85 per cent of the total workforce. Union density declined from a high of 34 per cent in 1975, attributable mainly to lower worker commitment to unions and a shift of employment from large-scale, more highly unionized manufacturing towards smaller-scale service-sector firms with low levels of unionization (Suzuki and Kubo 2011). Of particular significance is the continuing trend towards non-regular employment. According to Benson (2011), non-regular employees (as defined above) in 2007 comprised 42.9 per cent of the total formal workforce, higher for women (50.8%) than for men (30.4%).

In 1980, Korean unions were legally required to be structured along enterprise lines. Until 1987, the majority of unions were members of the conservative Federation of Korean Trade Unions (FKTU). Industrial and occupational unions were permitted as part of legislative changes in the aftermath of the 1987 movement. Many new unions emerged and joined the left-leaning Korean Council of Trade Unions (KCTU), which gained legal recognition in 2000 (Rowley and Abdul-Rahman 2008). Amidst a high level of strikes, union density climbed to its highest point of 18.6 per cent in 1989, which contrasts with the 2009 figure of 10.1 per cent shown in Table 18.1, the decline reflecting off-shoring of significant numbers of manufacturing jobs to China and a growing number of non-regular workers. The KCTU has been gaining ground relative to the FKTU, accounting for 19.4 per cent of unions and 40.2 per cent of union members in 2008, compared to the FKTU's 58.2 per cent of unions and 48.4 per cent of union members (Lee 2011). There has been a growth of enterprise unions and some occupational unions independent of the two union federations. The KCTU has successfully pursued a strategy of industrial unionism: an estimated 80 per cent of unions affiliated to the KCTU in 2007, compared to only 20 per cent of FKTU affiliates that are members of industrial unions. Members of industrial unions currently account for 45 per cent of total union members. Meanwhile, the employers' side is represented by three national organizations. Most important among the three is the Korean Employers' Federation, representing over 3,000 firms in the manufacturing and service sectors (Lee 2011). Of note are 2012 labour-law reforms that have abolished the one-enterprise-one-union clause, opening the way for inter-union competition and the possibility of temporary workers' unions challenging existing unions.

The Japanese ER system has decentralized further in recent years. Tripartism exists as an informal feature, with representatives of the two main central federations consulting with employers represented by a central business organization (Nihon Keidanren) and government officials on key labour issues (Benson and Zhu 2011). The processes of co-ordinating bargaining claims and employer responses at the annual *Shunto* negotiations are less significant, as global competition has encouraged firms to make their own ER decisions. Enterprise-level collective bargaining remains important, although, as shown in Table 18.1, coverage is only around 15 per cent of the formal workforce. Workforce coverage is likely to erode as structural change continues in the direction of the service sector, where small-scale enterprises predominate. In addition, most enterprise unions continue to exclude non-regular workers from membership. In any case, temporary workers are not allowed to work in the manufacturing sector for more than three years (Suzuki and Kubo 2011). On the other hand, the line between regular, lifetime jobs and non-regular jobs is becoming blurred as income and job security are no longer guaranteed and retirement age and final salary are progressively lowered for all workers alike (Sako 2006).

In comparison with Japan, Korean ER has witnessed significant government involvement, from authoritarian control prior to 1987 to the promotion of bilateral collective bargaining in the early 1990s. The government ignored union opposition and in 1996 introduced major changes intended to increase labour-market flexibility. In response to the economic crisis in 1997–1998, consensus was sought through a recently established Tripartite Commission. A substantial package comprising flexibility, worker protection, and union facilitation measures was agreed. However, the KCTU later withdrew from the agreement in response to membership opposition to legislation permitting dismissal of redundant workers (Lee 2011). A second round of tripartite proceedings led to agreements on health insurance and union representation of teachers. However, the KCTU withdrew from the Commission in 1999, undermining the representativeness of the Tripartite Commission. After the financial crisis, the government introduced legislation that aimed to protect employees from unfair dismissals, introducing unemployment insurance and subsidies for re-hiring unemployed workers and providing training assistance, while seeking to improve corporate governance and protect the environment (Benson and Zhu 2011). As indicated in Table 18.1, collective bargaining coverage is estimated at 11.5 per cent of the formal workforce. Over three-quarters of agreements are with enterprise unions; the remainder are between employer organizations and industrial and occupational unions (Rowley and Abdul-Rahman 2008). As in Japan, international competition, structural change, and expansion of the non-standard workforce are tending to reduce bargaining coverage and limit strike activity.[6] Meanwhile, industrial unions have had limited success in developing multi-tier bargaining.

## Human Resource Management in Japan and South Korea

As noted above, the impact of global competition encouraged employers to concentrate on cost-reduction and flexibility, this tendency intensifying in the wake of the

2008–2009 global financial crisis. Efforts to retain ER decision-making within the firm in both countries have increased. Japanese management has been more successful, as suggested by the summary scores for level of pay determination in Table 18.1: 5.8 for Japan and 5.3 for Korea. Other similar HRM trends are evident, such as soliciting maximum performance from employees, thereby containing labour costs while attempting to retain key elements of long-term employment for a smaller core of employees. In Japan, Benson (2011) has noted experimentation based on rewards for individual performance. More intensive appraisal systems have resulted in differentiated promotion practices that enable high-potential employees to be identified earlier. Career opportunities have been expanded and multi-track promotion systems for generalists and specialists have been introduced.

Korean HR underwent significant change since the mid-1990s as globalization and increasing competitiveness encouraged management to develop more flexible and efficient practices. These pressures intensified in response to the 1997–1998 financial crisis, which hit Korea particularly hard. IMF loans were accompanied by conditions, including a more flexible labour market, and resulted in legal changes aimed at eliminating lifetime employment (Kim and Bae 2004). Management introduced new HR policies designed to increase employee productivity and flexibility. The seniority-based lifetime employment system came under major attack by new performance-based systems that give more recognition to individual achievement.

Regarding recruitment, interview procedures were reviewed to make more use of 'blind' interviews and recruitment specialists. Equal opportunity for women became more common, though problems still exist. Performance-management systems were amended to include multiple raters and appraisal feedback designed to develop employees. Remuneration became more geared to performance than seniority. Grade, pay, and position came to be separated, so that it was no longer assumed that a promotion would automatically lead to a particular grade that determined a specific pay rate. Dual job-grade systems that separated production and non-production employees were replaced by single systems allowing more career opportunities for production workers. Promotion systems were made more accessible by not requiring incremental progression.

HR management played a major role in encouraging various kinds of flexibility. There were substantial increases in numerical flexibility via increased retirements, dismissals of regular workers, recruitment of temporary workers, and changes in working hours. Functional flexibility was achieved by redeploying regular employees to different positions as required. Finally, labour costs were contained by limiting increases in base pay, bonuses and fringe benefits, and by outsourcing non-essential functions, including some HR activities such as education and training and outplacement of ex-employees. In some firms, these changes were introduced through consultation rather than by unilateral decision-making. Growth in labour–management councils has been observed since a 1997 amendment to the relevant Act lowered the threshold for introducing a council from establishments with more than fifty workers to those with a minimum of thirty workers. The number of councils doubled between 1996 and 2001 and further increased by 36.4 per cent between 2001 and 2006 (Lee 2011).

In summary, ER in Japan and Korea has changed appreciably over the past twenty years. In Japan, modification to the enterprise-community system has been more gradual, but nonetheless profound, while in Korea external economic shocks, including international political influences mainly via the IMF, have encouraged the government to intervene more forcefully in the labour market. Management in both countries has prioritized financial and numerical flexibility. The principle of seniority has been giving way to individual performance as a basis for remuneration and promotion, while numerical flexibility has been achieved mainly by replacing permanent workers with non-regular employees.

## Employment Relations in Singapore

Singapore stands alone in its emphasis on human resources as a basis for economic development. It is also unique in the way an authoritarian, partially democratic state served by an efficient bureaucracy has guided this process over an extended period (Carney 2014). Following independence as a city-state in 1965, Singapore's leading party, the People's Action Party, embarked on an EOI strategy that included the involvement of trade unions in policy decisions. Industrial peace was achieved by legislating longer durations for collective agreements and limiting the scope of issues that could be bargained. This was part of the strategy to encourage investment by MNCs (Leggett 2007). It was about this time that the peak union body, the National Trades Union Congress (NTUC), began to adopt a corporatist role, partnering in policy decision-making and assisting in policy implementation. Its role has been prominent in the peaceful resolution of industrial disputes and helping to ensure a strong connection between wage increases and productivity. In 1972 the government introduced the tripartite National Wage Council (NWC), which fixed wages and employer and employee superannuation contributions centrally through the Central Provident Fund. The NWC became a key instrument in the government's strategy to switch from labour-intensive EOI to high-technology development that continued to rely on attracting MNCs to Singapore. Wages were increased between 1979 and 1981 in order to encourage investment in technology upgrading that would substitute capital for labour. In the early 1980s, the NTUC embarked on a strategy of emulating Japan and transformed nine industrial unions into hundreds of enterprise unions.

Singapore weathered occasional recessions and maintained a high growth rate of around 8 per cent per year between 1990 and 1997. Growth declined to minus 2.2 per cent in 1998 as a result of the Asian financial crisis, and resumed at over 5 per cent a year until 2001, when it decelerated again by 1.2 per cent (see <http://knoema.com/tbocwag#Singapore>, accessed 19 July 2012). Perceived vulnerability to global crises led the government to develop the current 'Intelligent Nation 2015' action plan, disseminated in 2006. This blueprint emphasizes science and technology and the appropriation of knowledge, skills, and creativity as bases for future economic development. In this context, the NTUC plays a vital role as the largest vocational education and skills provider in the country. It offers 550 courses that include programmes for executives and professionals (NTUC 2012). The action plan is also a cultural strategy carried out by government-controlled media for transcending public fear about economic uncertainty and national security. In short, a knowledge-based economy has become a development strategy that is invoked as a collective identity and solution to major anticipated problems (Hornidge 2010).

The knowledge-economy concept is supported by tripartite employment-relations strategies focusing on skills development, more efficient allocation of employees to jobs, and improvements in HR practices. Non-conflictual ER and employment flexibility remain unstated objectives. Unsurprisingly, Table 18.1 shows that Singapore scores high on tripartism, and with nearly a fifth of workers unionized, union density in Singapore is relatively high. Unions continue to be encouraged by the government, but are not enthusiastically supported by employees, who perceive their objectives to be significantly compromised by relations with the state. Employers are also strongly institutionalized through membership in the Singapore National Employers' Association. Collective bargaining coverage is relatively high, but falls substantially short of the number of workers in unions. This suggests that while public-sector employment is regulated by collective agreements, the same is not true for many private-sector employers, who prefer individual contracts.

### Human Resource Management in Singapore

HRM in Singapore has several distinguishing features. First, as shown in Table 18.1, centralized wage-fixing has been replaced by decentralized pay determination. Second, labour-employer relations are noted for highly cooperative interaction similar to that of Hong Kong. Third, Singapore ranks highest for employment flexibility. A fourth feature, not included in the table, is the encouragement and support given to education and training, which makes Singaporean employees attractive to MNCs (Ministry of Finance 2008; Carney 2014). However, Stanton and Nankervis (2011) concluded that performance management systems in Singapore fall short of their objectives and that managers and employees lack training in these systems. More generally, while MNCs mainly use HR systems that derive from their home countries, Choo (2007) has argued that Singaporean organizations are control-oriented, highly bureaucratic, and strongly aligned with government requirements. Finally, it is noteworthy that although the government has provided strong tax incentives for innovative, science-based firms, the benefits have so far been limited, perhaps because the hegemonic culture is not conducive to innovation, despite its effectiveness in ensuring industrial order.

# DISCUSSION

Several observations can be made about the empirical patterns revealed in our analysis. First, it is possible to discern a number of similar ER features and pressures for convergence among these countries. Second, and importantly, despite pressures for convergence, there remain striking differences across the majority of countries surveyed. Third, the data suggest that the conventional argument for variation across Asian capitalisms—based on levels of economic development and changing societal norms—overlooks key exceptions that might be better explained with reference to political contestation between elites and interest groups, including actors' strategic choices based on particular logics of action.

Similarities across the twelve countries can be summarized by reference to Table 18.1. These include relatively weak unions, as shown in low union densities and limited collective bargaining coverage, bearing in mind the level of economic development of these countries. The second feature is the extent of control exercised by management, seen in the final three rows of the table. Pay determination is decentralized, which means that decisions are made by management of economic units rather than by collective bargaining at industry or national level. A possible exception to this is Indonesia, with a score of 4.3, which testifies to the influence of legislation introduced in 2003 that increased severance pay and limited outsourcing (Caraway 2010). The data on labour–employer cooperation indicate that order is regularly maintained, the only exception being Korea, where forceful union demands, sometimes backed by militancy, occur. Finally, management is able to hire and fire employees with little legal impediment, as indicated by country scores for employment flexibility. Exceptions include Japan (2.8) and Korea (3.3) and some sectors in India and the Philippines (not shown in Table 18.1). In the case of Japan, we noted that the lifetime employment system remains in place, but is limited to a shrinking core of male employees. The same is true of Korea, although substitution of the performance criterion for the seniority principle and employment of non-standard workers has been more rapid and extensive than in Japan (Kuruvilla and Chung 2012).

Four types of pressures for convergence exist for the countries surveyed. Three of the factors are associated with globalization, while the fourth is endogenous, though influenced by trade and inward investment. The first factor is international economic competition, which has encouraged manufacturing firms in particular to pursue improvements in productivity and cost containment in order to export successfully (Caraway 2009, 2010). Competitive striving encourages an emphasis on labour flexibility, particularly financial and numerical flexibility. This tendency has been accentuated in recent years as financialization has encouraged investors to pursue short-term gains. Second, the international institutional context fosters openness in trade, but also acknowledges the need to protect workers. This places pressure on governments to appear as just rulers in the eyes of their people and the international community. Most significant here are foreign governments, particularly the US (see Frenkel 2006) and the EU, and international agencies, for example the World Bank, which has favoured flexible labour markets, although in recent years the Bank has also supported poverty reduction schemes and active labour market policies (Caraway 2010). The ILO has played an especially significant role in advocating and advising governments on adherence to international labour standards through promulgation of international conventions, the pursuit of a 'decent work' strategy, and tripartite consultation (ILO 2012). A third factor fostering ER convergence is MNC ER practices, particularly by companies with international brand images, such as Nike and Apple. Keen to maintain brand reputation by appearing to pursue policies that exceed international labour standards, and to ensure product quality, MNCs either implement common HR practices in their subsidiaries in different countries or ensure that similar principles are upheld, so that employees are treated relatively favourably. MNC policies extend to first-tier suppliers in global value chains where supplier selection, regular external monitoring, and assistance with practice upgrading are commonly available, though not always successful (Locke, Qin, and Brause 2007; Seidman 2007; Frenkel and Sydow 2011). The fourth and final factor is structural change, which may to some extent be induced by external trade and investment linkages, but which is in any case linked to economic maturity. Structural change includes an expansion of employment in smaller-scale service-sector units and adoption of more advanced technology requiring fewer manual workers and more technical employees. Both processes are less conducive to union organizing and more suited to individualized employee relations (smaller service workplaces) or sophisticated HR systems (advanced technical work units).

A significant finding of our study is the striking divergence across the Asian countries in macro and micro levels of ER. Singapore embodies the epitome of this divergence, with highly centralized union representation and bargaining, yet extremely high levels of employment flexibility, labour–management cooperation, and decentralized wage-setting. Taiwan is similar, though not as extreme: it has the highest level of union density among all twelve countries surveyed and yet the lowest level of collective bargaining coverage. Pay is determined at workplace level and labour–management relations are not adversarial. By contrast, Thailand has the weakest levels of union representation, collective bargaining coverage, and tripartite consultation at the national level, yet has only moderate levels of employment flexibility and labour–management cooperation. Korea is similar, showing only moderate levels of protection at the macro level, yet, together with Japan, manifesting low levels of employment flexibility at the enterprise level. Korea is distinctive on the basis of its relatively adversarial labour–management relations.

Our findings challenge modernization theorists who argue that changes in societal norms and consequent institutional evolution occur as a result of economic development (Inglehart and Welzel 2005). This thesis informs the thinking of some regulation school (Deyo 1989) and IR scholars (Sharma 1985), who have argued that Asian societies can be categorized according to their level of development, and that in the early stages of industrialization, the state, with military backing, was the dominant force organizing production and markets. Preferring EOI, political elites emphasized the logics of competition and industrial peace respectively, so that unions and strikes were outlawed during the less-developed and developing-country stages. Later, as industrialization proceeded to the newly industrializing country stage, where economic competition relied less on cost than on quality and innovation, demands for representation emerged among entrepreneurs, managers, professionals, and more educated workers. Economic and social power became more dispersed, and as a result institutions changed, including the emergence of rights to union membership and representation through collective bargaining. In short, the logic of employment and income protection favoured by workers came to exist alongside, and sometimes transcend, the logics of competition and industrial peace.

The modernization argument suggests that countries at similar levels of economic development will be characterized by similar ER patterns. Our findings indicate that this is not so. For example, compare Singapore and Japan; and Indonesia and Thailand. ER patterns differ. Moreover, the modernization argument does not explain why in Taiwan and Korea, union power peaked during industrialization and is receding at a time of economic and societal maturity. In addition, we observe stark differences in the level of centralized consultation and firm-level employment flexibility among the more developed countries we surveyed, that is, Hong Kong, Singapore, Japan, and Korea.

A potential explanation for the above-mentioned variations may be found in the dynamic competition among conflicting interests, their respective power (Hyman 1975; Boyer 2005; Harvey 2005; Deyo 2012), and strategic choices (Kochan, McKersie, and Cappelli 1984; Hall and Thelen 2009). Two important institutions of power in Asian societies are the state and societal interest groups, including producer groups and large firms (Carney, Gedajlovic, and Yang 2009). According to the regulation school, societal change is the product of contestation between elites and 'subordinated groups' (Deyo 2012: 19, 1987). Traditionally, the state–business nexus has constituted the dominant elite in these countries. Therefore, in exchange for cooperation from businesses in pursuing state-guided policies, selected large businesses were given easier access to bank credit and wage controls in their sectors (Johnson 1987). While this may have been a reasonable characterization of the elite in some Asian societies in earlier decades, and while some states, such as Singapore, remain strong, this is not universally the case today. In an era of globalization, most states are weaker and more accountable. The elite now include varied groups such as foreign-owned businesses, while the views of international governance organizations are taken seriously. Furthermore, the distinction between foreign and domestic ownership and that between MNCs and local practices is becoming increasingly blurred. Similarly, there is a diversity of societal interests that place claims on the political process; labour is but one of those groups that must assert the importance of employment, job quality, and social welfare above the concerns of other groups pursuing security, trade, environmental, and other concerns. While institutional arrangements at the time of the adoption of labour laws provide a template on which to build ER systems, key events such as economic crises and milestones in democratic progress, including actors' strategic reactions to these events, appear to have shaped contemporary ER patterns.

# Conclusion

In conclusion, our findings suggest that in spite of globalizing forces encouraging convergence of ER patterns in Asia, particularly in regard to declining union power and increased wage and numerical labour flexibility, countries in the region are character-ized by diversity, even at similar levels of economic development. Since ER patterns are a product of labour-market and wider political institutions, our findings point to a multiplicity of societal types in Asia. This implies that the VoC typology is too restric-tive, and, as argued earlier, some of this literature's key assumptions—parity of powers among actors, synchronic developments across institutions at the macro and micro lev-els, an essentially functional understanding of ER—are unrealistic. Additional research is required, taking each Asian nation as the main but not sole unit of analysis, and exam-ining how actors' strategies and deployment of resources at a variety of levels—global, regional, national, industry, and firm—shape labour-market institutions and influence patterns of ER relations over time. From a sociological point of view, it will be important to examine the relative autonomy of these institutions vis-à-vis the economy, and hence their capacity to change independently of other institutions, and their consequences for economic development and employee well-being. For example, we have pointed to pressures from global markets, international standards institutions, and transnational NGOs that diminish national actors' capacities for independent strategic action. Only then will it be feasible to develop a stronger theory of Asian employment relations that is perhaps suggestive of varieties of Asian capitalism.

Our analysis is not without limitations. First, because of the wide country-coverage of our study, our data were restricted to basic ER characteristics. A more comprehensive study would include changes in ER patterns over time. Second, we used available indica-tors to build a taxonomy to describe national ER patterns. These measures are inevita-bly limited in range and reliability, but are nevertheless widely understood and used in public policy debates. Third, obtaining exactly comparable data across twelve countries has been a challenge, hence some unevenness in our empirical descriptions. Fourth and finally, in the space available it was not possible to undertake a detailed comparative analysis of ER within and between countries and between regions in order to refine or modify our ideas. This is a task for the future.

# Acknowledgements

We thank Sarah Minotti and Chongxin Yu for excellent research assistance. We also thank Michael A. Witt, Gordon Redding, Fred Deyo, and David Finegold for comments on an earlier draft of the chapter.

## Notes

1. Hong Kong is a territory of China rather than a separate country; however, its institutions reflect a history of development relatively independent of China. Bearing this in mind, we include Hong Kong as one of the twelve countries.

2.  Problems include absence of comparable data for some countries, data not being exactly comparable because of different dates of collection; different ways of calculating ratios in some countries; and reliance on single-source surveys for estimates of particular characteristics. In some cases we have adjusted the figures where secondary sources consistently point to the estimate being incorrect. See notes to Table 18.1.

3.  Shibata (2008) showed that three Japanese work practices—use of trouble-shooting skills by production workers, production support by supervisors, and broad roles (including design and development work) occupied by manufacturing engineers—did not transfer effectively. This was attributed to differences in plant requirements in Thailand; lack of familiarity of the Japanese advisors with operational details in the Thai plants; low wages paid to Thai workers who either lacked the ability or the necessary incentives to learn new skills; and finally, the orientation of Thai managers and workers, who retained a more rigid view of what their jobs comprised than was implied by the imported practices.

4.  Regarding China, see Cooke (2012: 151), Pringle (2011), and https://chinastrikes.crowdmap.com/. According to Vo (2009), in the period 1995 to mid-2002 there were 472 strikes in Vietnam, of which 262 occurred in foreign-invested companies, i.e. 55.5%. Strikes have been concentrated in firms owned by Taiwanese, Hong Kong, and Korean companies operating in labour-intensive industries. According to the Spice Digest (Fall 2009) (http://spice.stanford.edu, accessed 10 June 2010), fluctuating wages and below-minimum payment in the slow season have contributed to many recent strikes in foreign-invested firms, which spread to other industries and in 2009 encouraged the government to raise the minimum wage level to 20% above the 2008 level.

5.  According to Kondo (2014), of 38.9 million employees, only 1.7 million workers, i.e. 4.4%, were unionized.

6.  The annual average of working days lost per employee in Korea declined from 106.3 for the period 1999–2003 to 59.4 for the subsequent five-year period 2004–2008. Calculated from International Labour Office database <http://laboursta.ilo.org/STP/guest>, accessed 28 August 2012.

# References

Amable, B. (2003). *The Diversity of Modern Capitalism*. Oxford; New York, Oxford University Press.

Anant, T., R. Hasan, P. Mohapatra, R. Nagaraj, and S. K. Sasikumar (2006). 'Labour Markets in India: Issues and Perspectives'. In J. Felipe and R. Hasan, Eds., *Labour Markets in Asia: Issues and Perspectives*: 205–296. Basingstoke, Palgrave Macmillan.

Batt, R., D. Holman and U. Holtgrewe (2009). 'The Globalization of Service Work: Comparative Institutional Perspectives on Call Centres'. *Industrial & Labor Relations Review* 62(4): 453–488.

Beerepoot, N. (2008). 'Asian Informal Workers: Global Risk, Local Protection'. *Development and Change* 39(2): 340–341.

Benson, J. (2011). 'Labour Markets in Japan: Change and Continuity'. In J. Benson and Y. Zhu, Eds., *The Dynamics of Asian Labour Markets: Balancing Control and Flexibility*: 33–60. London & New York, Taylor & Francis.

—— and Y. Zhu (2011). *The Dynamics of Asian Labour Markets*, London & New York, Taylor & Francis.

Berger, S. and R. P. Dore (1996). *National Diversity and Global Capitalism*. Ithaca, Cornell University Press.

Bhattacherjee, D. and E. D'Souza (2011). 'Labour Markets in India: Informality and Inequality'. In J. Benson and Y. Zhu, Eds., *The Dynamics of Asian Labour Markets*: 157–176. London & New York, Taylor & Francis.

Boyer, R. (1990). *The Regulation School: A Critical Introduction*. New York, Columbia University Press.

—— (2005). 'How and Why Capitalisms Differ'. *Economy and Society* 34(4): 509–557.

—— and D. Drache (1996). *States against Markets: The Limits of Globalization*. London & New York, Routledge.

Brown, A. (2004). *Labour, Politics and the State in Industrializing Thailand*. London, Routledge Curzon.

—— (2007). 'Labour and Modes of Participation in Thailand'. *Democratization* 14(5): 816–833.

Budhwar, P. and A.Varma (2011) 'Emerging HR Management Trends in India and the Way Forward'. *Organizational Dynamics* 40: 317–325.

Cappelli, P., H. Singh, J. Singh, and M. Useem (2010). 'The India Way: Lessons for the US'. *Academy of Management Perspectives* 24(2): 6–24.

Caraway, T. L. (2009). 'Labour Rights in Asia: Progress or Regress?' *Journal of Asian Studies* 9(2): 153–186.

—— (2010). 'Labour Standards and Labour Market Flexibility in Asia'. *Studies in Comparative International Development* 45(2): 225–249.

Carney, M., E. Gedajlovic, and X. H. Yang (2009). 'Varieties of Asian Capitalism: Toward an Institutional Theory of Asian Enterprise'. *Asia Pacific Journal of Management* 26(3): 361–380.

Carney, R. (2014) 'Singapore: Open State-Led Capitalism'. In M. A. Witt and G. Redding, Eds., *The Oxford Handbook of Asian Business Systems*: 192–215. Oxford, Oxford University Press.

Chen, S.-J., R. Ko, and J. Lawler (2003). 'Changing Patterns of Industrial Relations in Taiwan'. *Industrial Relations* 42(3): 315–340.

Choo, S. (2007). 'Managing the Entrepreneurial Culture in Singapore'. In S. Chatterjee and A. Nankervis, Eds., *Asian Management in Transition: Emerging Themes*: 239–272. Basingstoke, Palgrave Macmillan.

Cividep (2010). *Changing Industrial Relations in India's Mobile Phone Manufacturing Industry*. Amsterdam, Stiching Onderzoek Multinationale Ondernemingen.

Cooke, F. L. (2010). 'Women's Participation in Employment in Asia: A Comparative Analysis of China, India, Japan and South Korea'. *International Journal of Human Resource Management* 21(12): 2249–2270.

—— (2012). 'Employment Relations in China and India'. In M. Barry and A. Wilkinson, Eds., *Edward Elgar Handbook of Comparative Employment Relations*: 184–213. Cheltenham, Edward Elgar.

Crouch, C. and W. Streeck (1997). *Political Economy of Modern Capitalism: Mapping Convergence and Diversity*. Thousand Oaks, Sage.

Cusack, T. R., T. Iversen, and D. Soskice (2007). 'Economic Interests and the Origins of Electoral Systems'. *American Political Science Review* 101(3): 373–391.

Deyo, F. C. (1987). *The Political Economy of the New Asian Industrialism*. Ithaca, Cornell University Press.

—— (1989). *Beneath the Miracle: Labour Subordination in the New Asian Industrialism*. Berkeley, University of California Press.

—— (1997). 'Labor and Post-Fordist Industrial Restructuring in East and Southeast Asia'. *Work and Occupations* 24(1): 97–118.

—— (2012). *Reforming Asian Labour Systems: Economic Tensions and Worker Dissent*. Ithaca, Cornell University Press.

Edwards, V. and A. Phan (2008). 'Trade Unions in Vietnam: From Socialism to Market Socialism'. In J. Benson and Y. Zhu, Eds., *Trade Unions in Asia: An Economic and Sociological Analysis*: 199–215, New York, Routledge.

Erickson, C. L., S. Kuruvilla, R. E. Ofreneo and M. A. Ortiz (2003). 'From Core to Periphery? Recent Developments in Employment Relations in the Philippines'. *Industrial Relations* 42(3): 368–395.

Fernandez, D. R., D. S. Carlson, L. P. Stepina, and J. D. Nicholson (1997). 'Hofstede's Country Classification 25 Years Later'. *Journal of Social Psychology 137*: 43.

Frenkel, S. (2006). 'Towards a Theory of Dominant Interests, Globalization, and Work'. In M. Korczynski, R. Hodson, and P. K. Edwards, Eds., *Social Theory at Work*: 388–423. Oxford & New York, Oxford University Press.

—— and S. Kuruvilla (2002). 'Logics of Action, Globalization, and Changing Employment Relations in China, India, Malaysia, and the Philippines'. *Industrial & Labour Relations Review* 55(3): 387–412.

—— and J. Sydow (2011). 'Institutional Conditions for Organizing Decent Work in Global Production Networks: The Case of China'. In P. Sheldon, S. Kim, Y. Li, and M. Warner, Eds., *China's Changing Workplace: Dynamism, Diversity and Disparity*: 241–258. London, Routledge.

Geppert, M. and M. Mayer (2006). *Global, National, and Local Practices in Multinational Companies*. Basingstoke, Palgrave Macmillan.

Goldberg, S. (1983). *Probability in Social Science: Seven Expository Units Illustrating the Use of Probability Methods and Models*. Boston, Birkhäuser.

Hall, P. A. and D. W. Soskice (2001). *Varieties of Capitalism*. Oxford, Oxford University Press.

—— and K. Thelen (2009). 'Institutional Change in Varieties of Capitalism'. *Socio-Economic Review 7*(1): 7–34.

Harriss-White, B. (2003). *India Working: Essays on Society and Economy*. Cambridge, Cambridge University Press.

Harvey, D. (2005). *A Brief History of Neoliberalism*. Oxford, Oxford University Press.

Hayter, S. and Stoevska, V. (2010) *Social Dialogue Indicators. Trade Union Density and Collective Bargaining Coverage. International Statistical Inquiry 2008-09. Technical Brief*. Geneva: ILO.

Hollingsworth, J. R. and R. Boyer (1997). *Contemporary Capitalism: The Embeddedness of Institutions*. Cambridge, Cambridge University Press.

Hornidge, A. K. (2010). 'An Uncertain Future: Singapore's Search for a New Focal Point of Collective Identity and Its Drive Towards "Knowledge Society"'. *Asian Journal of Social Science 38*(5): 785–818.

Hyman, R. (1975). *Industrial Relations: A Marxist Introduction*. London, Macmillan.

ILO (2012). 'International Labour Organization World of Work Report 2012: Better Jobs for a Better Economy'. Retrieved 12 July 2012 from <http://www.ilo.org/global/research/global-reports/world-of-work/lang--en/index.htm>.

Inglehart, R. and C. Welzel (2005). *Modernization, Cultural Change, and Democracy: The Human Development Sequence*. Cambridge, Cambridge University Press.

Isaac, J. and S. Sitalaksmi (2008). 'Trade Unions in Indonesia: From State Incorporation to Market Orientation'. In J. Benson and Y. Zhu, Eds., *Trade Unions in Asia: An Economic and Sociological Analysis*: 121–139. New York, Routledge.

Ishikawa, J. and S. Lawrence (2005). *Social Dialogue Indicators, Trade Union Membership and Collective Bargaining Coverage: Statistical Concepts, Methods and Findings*. Working paper No. 59. Geneva: International Labour Office.

Jackson, G. and R. Deeg (2008). 'From Comparing Capitalisms to the Politics of Institutional Change'. *Review of International Political Economy* 15(4): 680–709.

Johnson, C. (1987). 'Political Institutions and Economic Performance: The Government-Business Relationship in Japan, South Korea, and Taiwan'. In F. C. Deyo, Ed., *The Political Economy of the New Asian Industrialism*: 136–164. Ithaca, Cornell University Press.

Katz, H. C. and O. Derbishire (2000). *Convergent Divergences: Worldwide Changes in Employment Systems*. Ithaca, ILR/ Cornell University Press.

Kerr, C., J. Dunlop, F. Harbison, and C. Myers (1964). *Industrialism and Industrial Man*. New York, Oxford University Press.

Kim, D. and J. Bae (2004). *Employment Relations and HRM in South Korea*. London, Ashgate.

Kochan, T. A., R. B. McKersie, and P. Cappelli (1984). 'Strategic Choice and Industrial-Relations Theory'. *Industrial Relations* 23(1): 16–39.

Kondo, M. (2014). 'The Business System of the Philippines'. In M. A. Witt and G. Redding, Eds., *The Oxford Handbook of Asian Business Systems*: 169–191. Oxford, Oxford University Press.

Koo, H. (2001). *Korean Workers: The Culture and Politics of Class Formation*. Ithaca, Cornell University Press.

Kristensen, P. H. and J. Zeitlin (2005). *Local Players in Global Games: The Strategic Constitution of a Multinational Corporation*. Oxford, Oxford University Press.

Kuruvilla, S. (1996). 'Linkages between Industrialization Strategies and Industrial Relations/ Human Resource Policies: Singapore, Malaysia, the Philippines, and India'. *Industrial and Labour Relations Review* 49(4): 635–657.

—— and S. Chung (2012). 'HRM Strategies, Informality and Re-Regulation in Asian Employment Relations'. In M. Warner, Ed., *Managing across Diverse Cultures in East Asia: Issues and Challenges in a Changing Globalized World*: 211–231. London: Routledge.

—— and C. L. Erickson (2002). 'Change and Transformation in Asian Industrial Relations'. *Industrial Relations: A Journal of Economy and Society* 41(2): 171–227.

Lawler, J., S. Siengthai, and V. Atmiyanandana (1997). 'HRM in Thailand: Eroding Traditions'. *Asia Pacific Business Review* 3(4): 170–196.

Lee, B. (2011). 'Employment Relation in South Korea'. In G. J. Bamber, R. D. Lansbury, and N. Wailes, Eds., *International and Comparative Employment Relations: Globalisation and Change*: 281–306. Crows Nest, NSW, Allen & Unwin.

Leggett, C. (2007). 'From Industrial Relations to Manpower Planning: The Transformations of Singapore's Industrial Relations'. *International Journal of Human Resource Management* 18: 642–664.

Locke, R., F. Qin, and A. Brause (2007). 'Does Monitoring Improve Labour Standards? Lessons from Nike'. *Industrial and Labour Relations Review* 61(1): 3–31.

—— T. Kochan, and M. Piore    (1995). 'Reconceptualizing Comparative Industrial-Relations – Lessons from International Research'. *International Labour Review* 134(2): 139–161.

Martin, C. J. and K. Thelen (2007). 'The State and Coordinated Capitalism: Contributions of the Public Sector to Social Solidarity in Postindustrial Societies'. *World Politics* 60(1): 1–36.

Ministry of Finance (2008). 'Performance Management in Singapore's Public Service'. Workshop session, Ministry of Finance, APEC 2008 meeting, Taipei, Taiwan.

Morgan, G. (2007). 'National Business Systems Research: Progress and Prospects'. *Scandinavian Journal of Management* 23(2): 127–145.

Napathorn, C. and S. Chanprateep (2011). 'Recent Labour Relations and Collective Bargaining Issues in Thailand'. *Interdisciplinary Journal of Research in Business* 1(6): 66–81.

NBSC (National Bureau of Statistics of China) (2011). *China Statistics Yearbook*. Beijing, China Statistics Press.

Ngo, H-Y., C-M. Lau, and S. Foley (2008). 'Strategic Human Resource Management, Firm Performance, and Employee Relations Climate in China'. *Human Resource Management* 47(1): 73–90.

NTUC (National Trades Union Congress) (2012). Retrieved 15 January 2012 from <http://www.ntuclearninghub.com/home>.

Ofreneo, R. E. (2008). 'The Changing Face of Human Resource Management in Philippines'. In C. Rowley and S. Abdul-Rahman, Eds., *The Changing Face of Management in South Asia*: 185–214. New York, Routledge.

Park, A. and F. Cai (2011). 'The Informalization of the Chinese Labour Market in Kuruvilla'. In S. Kuruvilla, C. K. Lee, and M. E. Gallagher, Eds., *From Iron Rice Bowl to Informalization: Markets, Workers, and the State in a Changing China*: 17–35. Ithaca, Cornell University Press.

Pringle, T. (2011). *Trade Unions in China: The Challenge of Labour Unrest*: 87–113. New York, Routledge.

Quang, T., L. Thang, C., and C. Rowley (2008). 'The Changing Face of Human Resource Management in Vietnam'. In C. Rowley and S. Abdul-Rahman, Eds., *The Changing Face of Management in South Asia*: 185–214. New York, Routledge.

Rowley, C. and S. Abdul-Rahman (2008). *The Changing Face of Management in South Asia*. New York, Routledge.

Sako, M. (2006). *Shifting Boundaries of the Firm: Japanese Company – Japanese Labour*, New York, Oxford University Press.

Schmidt, V. A. (2007). 'Bringing the State Back into the Varieties of Capitalism and Discourse Back into the Explanation of Change', CES Working Papers Series 152. Retrieved 2 February 2012 from <http://aei.pitt.edu/9281/>.

Schwab, K., Ed. (2012). *Global Competitiveness Report 2011–2012*. World Economic Forum, retrieved 10 July 2012 from <http://www3.weforum.org/docs/WEF_GCR_Report_2011-12.pdf>.

Seidman, G. (2007). *Beyond the Boycott: Labour Rights, Human Rights, and Transnational Activism*. New York, Russell Sage Foundation.

Sharma, B. (1985). *Aspects of Industrial Relations in Asean*. Singapore, Institute of South Asian Studies.

Shibata, H. (2008). 'The Transfer of Japanese Work Practices to Plants in Thailand'. *International Journal of Human Resource Management* 19(2): 314–329.

Siengthai, S. (2007). 'Globalization and Changes in Employment Conditions in Thailand'. Paper presented at international workshop organized by the Korea Labour Institute/International Labour Organization on Changes in Employment Conditions in Asia and the Pacific. Seoul, Korea Labour Institute.

Soskice, D. (2007). 'Macroeconomics and Varieties of Capitalism'. In B. Hancké, M. Rhodes, and M. Thatcher, Eds., *Beyond Varieties of Capitalism: Conflict, Contradiction, and Complementarities in the European Economy*: 89–121. Oxford, Oxford University Press.

Stanton, P. and A. Nankervis (2011). 'Linking Strategic HRM, Performance Management and Organizational Effectiveness: Perceptions of Managers in Singapore'. *Asia Pacific Business Review* 17(1): 67–84.

Suehiro, A. and N. Wailerdsak (2014). 'Thailand: Post-Developmentalist Capitalism'. In M. A. Witt and G. Redding, Eds., *The Oxford Handbook of Asian Business Systems*: 260–282. Oxford, Oxford University Press.

Sundar, K. R. S. (2008). 'Trade Unions in India: From Politics of Fragmentation to Politics of Expansion and Integration?'. In J. Benson and Y. Zhu, Eds., *Trade Unions in Asia: An Economic and Sociological Analysis*: 157–176. New York, Routledge.

Suzuki, H. and K. Kubo (2011). 'Employment Relation in Japan'. In G. J. Bamber, R. D. Lansbury, and N. Wailes, Eds., *International and Comparative Employment Relations: Globalisation and Change*: 252–280. Crows Nest, NSW, Allen & Unwin.

Taylor, B. (2001). 'The Management of Labour in Japanese Manufacturing Plants in China'. *International Journal of Human Resource Management* 12(4): 601–620.

Thelen, K. (2001). 'Varieties of Labour Politics in the Developed Democracies'. In P. A. Hall and D. W. Soskice, Eds., *Varieties of Capitalism: The Institutional Foundations of Comparative Advantage*: 71–103. Oxford & New York, Oxford University Press.

—— (2004). 'How Institutions Evolve: The Political Economy of Skills'. In J. Mahoney and D. Rueschemeyer, Eds., *Comparative-Historical Perspective*: 208–240. New York, Cambridge University Press.

Tran, A. N. (2009). 'Vietnamese Labour-Management Relations: Restructuring and Coping with the Global Economic Crisis'. Retrieved 12 July 2012 from <http://spice.stanford.edu>.

Venkataratnam, C. S. and A. Verma (2011). 'Employment Relations in India'. In G. J. Bamber, R. D. Lansbury, and N. Wailes, Eds., *International and Comparative Employment Relations: Globalisation and Change*: 330–352. Crows Nest, NSW, Allen & Unwin.

Vo, A.N. (2009). *The Transformation of Human Resource Management and Industrial Relations in Vietnam*. New Delhi, Chandos.

Wang, X., N. S. Bruning and S. Peng (2007). 'Western High-Performance HR Practices in China: A Comparison among Public-Owned, Private and Foreign-Invested Enterprises'. *International Journal of Human Resource Management* 18(4): 684–701.

Warner, M. (2008). 'Trade Unions in China: In Search of a New Role in the "Harmonious Society"'. In J. Benson and Y. Zhu, Eds., *Trade Unions in Asia: An Economic and Sociological Analysis*: 140–156. New York, Routledge.

Whitley, R. (1992). *Business Systems in Asia: Firms, Markets and Societies*. London, Sage.

Wilkins, M., K. Thelen, R. Whitley, R. M. Miller, C. J. Martin, V. R. Berghahn, M. J. Iversen, G. Herrigel, and J. Zeitlin (2010). 'Varieties of Capitalism: Roundtable'. *Business History Review* 84(4): 637–674.

Zhu, C. J., B. Cooper, H. De Cieri, S. B. Thomson, and S. M. Zhao (2008). 'Devolvement of HR Practices in Transitional Economies: Evidence from China'. *International Journal of Human Resource Management* 19(5): 840–855.

Zhu, Y., N. Collins, M. Webber, and J. Benson (2008). 'New Forms of Ownership and Human Resource Practices in Vietnam'. *Human Resource Management* 47(1): 157–175.

## APPENDIX

# MEASURES AND SOURCES OF DATA FOR TABLE 18.1

[yy] Edwards and Phan (2008)

[zz] Isaac and Sitalaksmi 2008.

[a] Based on qualitative analysis saved under *right to strike and tripartism by country. Jan 31*

[b] Trade-union density corresponds to the ratio of wage and salary earners that are trade-union members, divided by the total number of wage and salary earners (OECD *Labour Force Statistics*). Density is calculated using survey data, wherever possible, and administrative data adjusted for non-active and self-employed members otherwise.

[d] Based on qualitative analysis saved under *right to strike and tripartism by country. Jan 31.*

[e] Measured as total per cent (%). Indicates the extent to which the terms of workers' employment are influenced by collective negotiation (OECD Definition).

[f] How are wages generally set in your country? [1 = by a centralized bargaining process; 7 = up to each individual company] 2010–2011 weighted average. Schwab (2012: 471).

[g] How would you characterize labour-employer relations in your country? [1 = generally confrontational; 7 = generally cooperative] 2010–2011 weighted average. Schwab (2012: 470).

[h] In your country, who holds senior management positions? [1 = usually relatives or friends without regard to merit; 7 = mostly professional managers chosen for merit and qualifications] 2010–2011 weighted average. Schwab (2012: 476).

[i] How would you characterize the hiring and firing of workers in your country? [1 = impeded by regulations; 7 = flexibly determined by employers] 2010–2011 weighted average. Schwab (2012: 473).

[4*] This figure for China taken from Deyo 2012: 143, rather than from ILO based on the China Labour Statistical Yearbook. Retrieved 27 November 2011 from Laboursta <http://laboursta.ilo.org/>.

[9] Statistic published in the Yearbook of Labour Statistics. Retrieved 27 November 2011 from Laboursta <http://laboursta.ilo.org/>.

[^] Statistic published in the Report of the Commissioner for Labour. Retrieved 27 November 2011 from Laboursta <http://laboursta.ilo.org/>.

[7+] + Statistic published in the Korea Statistical Yearbook. Retrieved 27 November 2011 from Laboursta <http://laboursta.ilo.org/>.

[5£] Hayter and Stoevska (2010). 2007 data.

[6=] Statistic published in the Yearbook of Labour Statistics, Taiwan Area. Retrieved 27 November 2011 from Laboursta <http://laboursta.ilo.org/>.

[9<] Statistic calculated by ILO based on the Japan Statistical Yearbook. Retrieved 27 November 2011 from Laboursta <http://laboursta.ilo.org/>.

[£] Hayter and Stoevska (2010).

[9£] Hayter and Stoevska (2010).
[1!] Ishikawa and Lawrence (2005).
[8£] Hayter and Stoevska (2010). 2005 data.
[11!] Ishikawa and Lawrence (2005).

# CHAPTER 19

## FINANCIAL SYSTEMS IN ASIA

### *Where Politics Meets Development*

LESLIE YOUNG

FINANCE provides a useful perspective on the varieties of capitalism and business systems. The contrast between security markets and banks as ways to mediate financial flows encapsulates the contrast between Liberal Market Economies (LME) and Coordinated Market Economies (CME), the archetypal Varieties of Capitalism (VoC) in developed economies. Most Asian economies, however, fit neither category, for important financial flows are coordinated by the state and by informal transactions. However, Asian economies could fit into Whitley's (1992, 1999) broader taxonomy of the systems used to coordinate a nation's business, as well as Redding's (2005) analysis of 'institutions'—both formal and informal—as the link between a business system and its cultural base.

To check how well Asia fits these schemas, the next section reviews data on the roles of banks and security markets, and on the quality of financial institutions, confirming the importance of the state and informal finance. Also, the quality of an economy's institutions turns out to correlate strongly with its concentration of wealth, and even with population size. This suggests that Asian business systems depend, not just on the cultural legacies emphasized by Whitley and Redding, but also on economic and political factors. Such is the theme of our review of how economic development has shaped Asian financial systems. This will suggest ways to augment the above analyses of business systems.

In the West, finance is governed by institutions of law, accounting, and financial regulation. In line with Redding (2005), we find the roots of such institutions in a culture that prioritizes individuals, assumes their inherent equality, and therefore concedes a great deal of state-level authority to formal frameworks governed by professionals who ensure a level playing-field. However, Asian cultures prioritize the group, whose members are differentiated vertically by status, while being linked horizontally by long-term relationships, leaving state authority to an elite that has institutionalized its claim to virtue (Whitley 1992). Therefore, formal financial institutions in Asia tend to be undercut by informal relationships, leaving more finance to flow within personal networks and opaque corporate groups. This can amplify initial discrepancies in power, wealth, and connections, allowing an elite to prey upon the rest—hence the importance of political and economic factors in shaping Asian financial systems.

East Asian economies have nevertheless grown fast, especially when led by an elite that was acculturated to demonstrate its virtue, and now seeks to do so by promoting economic development. But when a business system grows too complex for hands-on coordination, will that elite stand aside for market forces and allow a level playing-field governed by fair, transparent institutions? This is the critical question for Asian financial and business systems. While culture affects the outcome, so too do economic and political factors, as indicated by the evidence below.

# EMPIRICAL EVIDENCE

Pioneering VoC research (Hall and Soskice 2001) looked mostly within the OECD club of high-income economies. LMEs favoured short-term, arm's-length relationships driven by ongoing competition from alternative counter-parties; CMEs favoured longer-term cooperative relationships. This dichotomy showed up in finance—LMEs relied more on security markets, CMEs on banks. This contrast between securities and banks also drove the comparisons of financial systems by Allen and Gale (2000), Rajan and Zingales (2002), and Deeg (2010). What is the evidence on this contrast in Asia?

For selected countries, Table 19.1 displays total deposits at depository institutions, stock-market capitalization, and the value of corporate bonds as a percentage of GDP, as well as ratios of these numbers. The 'securities/deposits ratio' is the ratio of stocks plus corporate bonds to deposits at depository institutions. This is much higher than 1 for the US and much lower than 1 in Germany and Japan, confirming their respective classifications as LME and CME, at least in finance.

East Asia's post-war surge was led by the 'Newly-Industrializing Economies' (NIE). The international financial centres of Hong Kong and Singapore have high securities/deposits ratios, but these reflect the requirements of international investors, as well as of domestic business. These ratios are low for South Korea and Taiwan, which argues for their classification as CMEs, consistent with the accounts of their business styles elsewhere in this handbook. East Asia's surge was carried forward by the 'ASEAN4': Indonesia, Philippines, Thailand, and Malaysia. All except Thailand have high securities/deposits ratios. Yet can we conclude that they are LMEs? One caution is their very low ratios of corporate bonds to deposits, which indicate institutional environments ill-suited to arm's-length financing. Another is their low scores in Table 19.2's Economic Freedom Index (EFI), which summarizes measures of the rule of law, limited government regulatory efficiency, and open markets. As the EFI was devised by the Heritage Foundation, which promotes liberal-market

## Table 19.1  Securities versus deposits

|  | Deposits % GDP | Stocks % GDP | Bonds % GDP | Stocks/ deposits | Bonds/ deposits | Securities/ deposits |
|---|---|---|---|---|---|---|
| US | 106.30 | 91.40 | 95.90 | 0.86 | 0.90 | 1.76 |
| Germany | 132.00 | 43.92 | 37.06 | 0.33 | 0.28 | 0.62 |
| Japan | 323.60 | 37.00 | 38.50 | 0.11 | 0.12 | 0.23 |
| **NIE** | | | | | | |
| Hong Kong | 703.10 | 1,198.0 | 34.20 | 1.70 | 0.05 | 1.75 |
| Singapore | 287.00 | 270.90 | 31.90 | 0.94 | 0.11 | 1.06 |
| Korea, Rep. | 169.90 | 98.10 | 63.10 | 0.58 | 0.37 | 0.95 |
| Taiwan | 287.20 | 174.90 | 25.90 | 0.61 | 0.09 | 0.70 |
| **ASEAN4** | | | | | | |
| Indonesia | 34.40 | 50.60 | 1.80 | 1.47 | 0.05 | 1.52 |
| Philippines | 84.90 | 104.10 | 4.10 | 1.23 | 0.05 | 1.27 |
| Malaysia | 202.30 | 166.50 | 40.40 | 0.82 | 0.20 | 1.02 |
| Thailand | 150.50 | 82.50 | 12.40 | 0.55 | 0.08 | 0.63 |
| **GIANTS** | | | | | | |
| China | 229.80 | 45.00 | 10.70 | 0.20 | 0.05 | 0.24 |
| India | 98.00 | 97.90 | 11.10 | 1.00 | 0.11 | 1.11 |

Deposits%GDP: Value of deposits at depository institutions as % of GDP
Stocks%GDP: Stock-market Capitalization as % of GDP
Bonds%GDP: Value of corporate bonds as a % of GDP
Data based on 2010 values in Park (2011, Table 19.2), except German 2010 data, retrieved 19 November 2012 from <http://data.worldbank.org/topic/financial-sector>.

economics, it seems unlikely that economies with low EFI are LMEs, whatever their securities/deposits ratios. The discrepancy can be resolved by noting the ASEAN4's low Financial Access scores in Table 19.2, which indicate that many citizens cannot access either banks or security markets. Their only recourse is informal finance.

All transactions involving securities or banks are 'formal', that is, recorded in contracts that can be enforced in a law court. Personal relationships are involved, especially in CMEs, but the persons act as representatives of legal entities. In Table 19.2, a low EFI is associated with poor financial institutions and poor access to formal finance. In this situation, many financial transactions must be 'informal', that is, based on relationships between parties acting in a personal capacity, not as representatives of legal entities. Economies that rely heavily upon informal finance, hence on ongoing relationships, cannot be classified as LMEs. Thus, the low scores of Indonesia and the Philippines for Financial Access and Financial Institutions refute their classification as LMEs, despite

## Table 19.2 Development indices

| | Economic Freedom | Financial Develop't | Financial Institutions | Banking Services | Financial Markets | Financial Access | Population (Millions) |
|---|---|---|---|---|---|---|---|
| USA | 76.30 | 5.15 | 5.59 | 4.19 | 5.65 | 4.82 | 314 |
| Germany | 71.00 | 4.33 | 5.67 | 4.38 | 3.83 | 3.48 | 82 |
| Japan | 71.60 | 4.71 | 5.53 | 5.31 | 4.56 | 3.55 | 126 |
| **NIE** | | | | | | | |
| Hong Kong | 89.90 | 5.15 | 5.70 | 5.43 | 4.42 | 5.29 | 7 |
| Singapore | 87.50 | 4.97 | 6.14 | 4.40 | 5.04 | 4.41 | 5 |
| Korea, Rep. | 69.90 | 4.13 | 4.06 | 4.21 | 3.34 | 2.83 | 50 |
| Taiwan | 71.90 | | | | | | 23 |
| **ASEAN4** | | | | | | | |
| Indonesia | 56.40 | 2.92 | 3.43 | 2.69 | 1.45 | 2.59 | 238 |
| Philippines | 57.10 | 3.13 | 3.73 | 3.41 | 2.04 | 2.66 | 92 |
| Malaysia | 66.40 | 4.24 | 5.16 | 4.49 | 2.67 | 3.80 | 29 |
| Thailand | 64.90 | 3.32 | 4.16 | 3.70 | 1.76 | 3.11 | 65 |
| **GIANTS** | | | | | | | |
| China | 51.20 | 4.12 | 4.21 | 4.29 | 2.41 | 3.52 | 1347 |
| India | 54.60 | 3.29 | 3.13 | 3.12 | 2.35 | 2.80 | 1210 |
| Population/ Rank Correlation | −0.98 | −0.78 | −0.88 | −0.45 | −0.70 | −0.70 | 1 |

*Note*: Compiled from Economic Freedom Index 2011 (For constituent indices, see <http://www.heritage.org/index/book/methodology>) and World Economic Forum, Financial Development Report 2011 (See <http://www.weforum.org/reports/financial-development-report-2011>)
*Population/Rank Correlation* is the Spearman rank correlation between the populations of developing economies in Asia and their indices in the corresponding column.

their high securities/deposits ratios. Yet they should not be classified as CMEs, either, since ongoing relationships between persons acting in their personal capacity cannot provide the large-scale coordination that would be achieved if they acted on behalf of organizations.

Widespread recourse to informal finance indicates weak formal institutions, left by the wayside as the state drove economic development forward. The Asian Financial Crisis of 1997–1998 set back East Asia's state-led model of development and highlighted its weak institutions. Most studies of this crisis have focused on corporate governance, which lies outside the scope of this chapter, but we note the finding of Claessens, Jankov, and Lang (1999: 24) that institutional quality in East Asian nations is strongly correlated with the concentration of wealth, as measured by the share of the stock market controlled by the top fifteen families.[1] This suggests that many East Asian elites entrenched themselves by blocking/subverting independent institutions.

The scale of the economy could also affect institutional development: in Table 19.2, the EFI of developing Asian nations (i.e. excluding Japan) exhibits an almost perfect negative (rank order) correlation with population (−0.98), i.e. the larger the nation, the less the economic freedom. There is also a strong negative (rank order) correlation (−0.88) between population and the quality of financial institutions. We shall discuss these striking correlations after reviewing Asia's financial systems.

# JAPAN

Bombardment by Commodore Perry's 'Black Ships' in 1853 brought home to Japan the need for rapid modernization, which required the state to set up and coordinate a wide range of enterprises. This anticipated the Soviet effort by several decades, but was beset by all the problems that were to become notorious there: of information, incentives, and soft budget constraints. Lacking the USSR's ideological commitment to state enterprises, Japan responded to the resulting large fiscal deficits with mass privatization. Buyers included the business families of Mitsui, Sumitomo, Mitsubishi, and Nissan, who expanded into related industries (Morck and Nakamura 2007). Mines transferred from the state provided them with cash cows. Fledgling stock markets provided more capital, but threatened the controlling family's control, so the family stacked companies into a corporate pyramid or *zaibatsu*: the family directly controlled the companies in the top tier, which held controlling blocks of shares in the next tier, which held controlling blocks in the next tier, etc. The controlling family moved surpluses around their pyramid to fund new investment opportunities, while more funds came from the *zaibatsu*'s 'main bank'.

Japan's post-war resurgence replayed its earlier rise from a feudal society to an industrial power. Both incarnations benefited from a land reform whose surpluses the state captured through an agricultural tax. Both incarnations were coordinated by elite bureaucrats and business conglomerates in a partnership that blurred the distinction between private and state interests: large industrial conglomerates got favours from the state, but had to subordinate business decisions to a national development plan. The Ministry of International Trade and Industry coordinated industrial development by 'overloaning', channelling government credit to industry via banks (Johnson 1982). The Postal Savings Bank channelled private savings to industry and infrastructure via state-controlled financial institutions like the Development Bank of Japan. The Fiscal Investment and Loan Plan commingled private and public funds to develop national resources and infrastructure.

The *zaibatsu* were dismantled by the US Occupation and replaced by *keiretsu* with the same names, but a quite different structure of ownership and control: networks knit together by cross-holdings. This reflected their dominance by a network of managers, rather than by one family. Like the *zaibatsu*, the *keiretsu* coordinated the development of related industries and recycled the surpluses of one company into investment by another. Shareholders played little role in governance, but were pacified by stable dividends. Meanwhile, banks monitored corporate managers effectively, as they had direct information about company performance and could force changes on management by withholding funds. They organized 'soft' takeovers of less successful firms.

These informal relationships coped well with middling shocks, like the failure of one corporation or one bank. But the 'big bang' of financial deregulation in 1996 was a different matter. As large corporate customers moved to bond finance, banks sought new borrowers, whom they were ill-equipped to monitor. The result was a real-estate bubble whose collapse left many banks insolvent (Ueda 2000). Meanwhile, corporations used their surpluses to play finance games (*zaitech*). The Ministry of Finance suddenly had to process a mass of new complex highly codified information. This was beyond the capacity of its senior officials, who had risen through skill in interpreting uncodified information and managing complex relationships. Multiple layers of opacity in the relationship between banks and corporations masked vast indebtedness, indeed insolvency, in the financial system (Caballero, Hoshi, and Kashyap 2008). Private debts were shifted onto national balance sheets with massive, useless infrastructure projects. Japan was trapped in a balance-sheet recession (Koo 2009).

# NIE Financial Systems

South Korea's rapid growth began in 1961 with the coup by Park Chung Hee. South Korea suffered obvious disadvantages: the devastation of the Korean War and an acute shortage of business skills after generations as a colony of Japan. Its advantages were less obvious: compact geography, ethnic homogeneity, respect for education, effective bureaucracy, and early land reform. It also had exceptionally high motivation to build a strong economy: a military threat from North Korea, plus the bitter memory of colonization by Japan, which had recovered from defeat in the Second World War and was now entering its high-growth decades.

President Park's development plan took account of both strengths and weaknesses. He identified a few effective business leaders and leveraged their skills with finance from state banks and from abroad. The corporate pyramids that emerged as *chaebol* were closer to Japan's pre-war *zaibatsu* than to the contemporary *keiretsu*. In contrast to both these formations, the *chaebol* did not include a bank, which left them vulnerable to state pressure. The Asian Financial Crisis brought the collapse of eleven of the thirty largest *chaebol* and exposed their financial and accounting manipulations. The reforms mandated by the IMF reduced the size and reach of the *chaebol* and installed more professional managers, but their basic structure remained intact, for it allowed economies of scale and scope deemed crucial for South Korea's export growth. So *chaebol* continue to dominate the domestic economy, given their privileged access to finance, both from internal sources and, since they had more collateral to offer than smaller rivals, from banks. However, the *chaebol* are now more exposed to the external scrutiny of regulators, shareholders, and the press (Kim 2012).

Taiwan shared most of the advantages and disadvantages of South Korea, but differed in two critical respects. First, when the Guomindang regime fled the mainland to Taiwan in 1949, it carried along many businessmen fearful of the victorious Communists. These businessmen needed only finance to restart. Many businesses were funded from the informal 'kerb market', but they turned to bank loans as they expanded (Smith 2000: 67). Some local Taiwanese secured the capital to start businesses using the commodities certificates and stock in state-owned industries that they received as compensation for what they lost in the land reforms of the 1950s. So Taiwan evolved a financial system that operated at arm's length from business enterprises and the state, indicating that along the LME-CME spectrum, it is closer to an LME than South Korea.

The second difference from South Korea was that the Taiwan government was dominated, not by the military, but by a political party—the Guomindang—which appropriated the companies left by the defeated Japanese and expanded them by leveraging its government links. In fact, the Taiwan economy in 1980 and China's economy in 2000 looked curiously alike. Both featured a swarm of private entrepreneurs independent of the state, which was controlled by a party that also controlled a business empire. The Guomindang's electoral loss in 1996 set the stage for the separation of business, politics, and finance. It helped that Taiwan was exceptionally open to US influence through strategic dependence and to US intellectual currents through the US higher education that many in its elite had received.

As a stand-alone city-state, Singapore has been aggressive in attracting international investors in commodity funds, futures index, and wealth management products. A distinctive feature of its internal financial system is the Central Provident Fund, a state pension fund managed by the Government Investment Corporation, and reported to hold US$247.5 billion in 2012 (just over Singapore's 2011 GDP); another US$157.5 billion is controlled by Temasek, an investment company wholly owned by the Ministry of Finance.[2] These funds comprise a vast corporate empire controlled by a state that is in turn dominated by one political party. So the financial/political evolution of Singapore is the reverse of China's, which moved from central planning to a corporate empire controlled by the Party-State and which is now using that corporate empire to fund its pensions.[3]

Hong Kong is caught in an awkward political, but lucrative economic, relationship with China. It has long served as a roundabout for Chinese corporations seeking to exploit the tax advantages enjoyed by 'foreign' corporations in China, as an offshore haven for murky Chinese money, and as a stepping-stone for funds seeking secure property rights in overseas jurisdictions. More recently, the China connection propelled Hong Kong to become the largest market for IPOs in 2009, 2010, and 2011; it is now handling the bulk of China's international trade settlement in yuan (currently 10% of China trade) and external bank deposits of yuan (678 billion yuan in 2011), which are now being tapped by issuers of yuan-denominated bonds (Ng 2012).

# Culture vs. Politics and Economics in Shaping Business Systems

The above account of North-East Asia's financial systems challenges Whitley's (1992) analysis of the business systems of Japan, South Korea, and Taiwan/Hong Kong. Whitley argues that their reliance upon clan-like networks, patrimonial pyramids, and extended families respectively reflect how political and personal authority were exercised in pre-modern times. True, Japan's *keiretsu* use less hierarchical authority than the business systems of the other economies, but its pre-war *zaibatsu* were pyramidal structures just like Korea's *chaebol* (indeed, the two concepts are denoted by the same Chinese characters). In this respect, Japan after the Meiji Restoration and South Korea after the Korean War had enough in common to over-ride differences in their pre-modern social orders. In both cases, the state had to jump-start development by directing finance to the few persons or families who had demonstrated the requisite talent. In both cases, those parties then leveraged their skills via corporate pyramids.

Why did the *zaibatsu* have more autonomy in pre-war Japan than the *chaebol* in Korea? Not just because Japan's political heritage was more pluralistic, as Whitley noted, but also because the Meiji government had little leverage over Japan's established business families, whereas Park Chung Hee controlled both government and army, and could keep the *chaebol* on a tight leash by legislating to keep banks out of their hands. While Japan's post-war *keiretsu* indeed look like the clan networks of Tokugawa Japan, the key to their displacement of the *zaibatsu* was surely the US-mandated law barring corporate pyramids. Pre-modern patterns of authority turned out to be consistent with both the pre-war and post-war business systems.

Whitley (1992) links the dominant role of extended families in the business systems of Taiwan and Hong Kong to the social order of pre-modern China, where the state monopolized political power and left extended families as the only basis for large-scale organization. He contrasts this with the role of aristocratic families in pre-modern Korea, which finds echoes in the pyramidal structure of the *chaebol*. However, the contrast in corporate structures has a simpler explanation: managerial talent was scarce in South Korea, but plentiful in Taiwan and Hong Kong, given the exit of businessmen from the Chinese mainland after the Communist victory there. Of course, the success of both types of corporate structure required suitable patterns of authority and cooperation, as noted by Whitley.

# ASEAN4 Financial Systems

The contrasts between the NIEs and ASEAN4 are sharpest for the largest ASEAN4 economy, Indonesia. Unlike the NIEs, Indonesia is resource-rich, but ethnically and geographically fragmented: the population has comparatively low levels of education, its civil service tradition is weak, and it faces no geopolitical challenges. Hence, the state faces little pressure to build an industrial economy, which would require a strong financial system. The rising value of resources makes control of the state a valuable prize for competing oligarchs.

The Suharto era saw an alliance between the military and overseas Chinese corporate groups, which were given franchises to exploit the resources. The financial system served to raise funds, but the sophisticated legal system left by the Dutch had long been dismantled, and regulation of banks and security markets remained weak (see Indonesia's rock-bottom scores in Table 19.2's indices of economic freedom, institutional quality, and financial access). This allows powerful corporate groups to exploit minority shareholders with related-party transactions, and to exploit bank depositors and shareholders with related-party loans and strategic bankruptcies (Backman 1999).

The avarice of Suharto's adult children had antagonized his oligarchic allies by the time the Asian Financial Crisis struck in 1997, so they abandoned him to popular anger. An electoral democracy followed, which merely shifted power to competing oligarchs astride patron-client networks. They bought enough legislators to stall the financial reforms demanded by the IMF. Then the rising value of resources liberated Indonesia from its balance of payments problems, and from IMF sermons about its financial system.

In the Philippines, concentrated landholdings blocked modernization and growth, as this concentration left political leadership in the hands of a few wealthy families, each capable of funding private armies, buying judges, and ensuring parliamentary representation through control of rural votes. This is confirmed by the Philippines' low scores in EFI and institutional quality. The financial system was simply a manifestation of oligarchic dominance, a way to turn political and economic power into cash. Corporate pyramids included banks that made related-party loans on a spectacular scale (Backman 1999).

The Asian Financial Crisis did not destabilize the Philippine economy, but increased IMF scrutiny of regional economies did lead to significant financial and banking reforms. Today, the formal financial system is better regulated; banks are profitable and have few non-performing loans—they do well simply by mediating the cashflow from overseas workers to fund the government deficit. Low-income consumers and small businesses, however, have little access to this formal financial system (see the low score for financial access); instead, they must borrow informally at very high interest rates.

Thailand was the epicentre of the Asian Financial Crisis, which inflicted great suffering. The close attention of the IMF brought major reforms to its financial system, including better supervision of banks and the stock market. This shows up in the indices of institutional quality in Table 19.2, which generally exceed those of Indonesia and the Philippines. However, further progress has been limited by ongoing political tension between prospering cities and an impoverished countryside where, in contrast to the Philippines, the urban business elite lacks a power base. This tension was long held in check by the King and his Privy Council, but it now dominates Thai politics, following the premiership of Taksin Shinawatra, a populist businessman who favoured the coun-tryside. A relentless struggle between 'Redshirts' and 'Yellowshirts' now blocks coherent economic and financial policies.

Malaysia has much better financial institutions and access than other ASEAN4 economies (see Table 19.2). The reasons are ironic: the external challenge of the well-managed city-state of Singapore (ejected from the Malaysian Federation in 1965) and the internal challenge of the Chinese, who comprise about one-quarter of the population. Chinese economic success led to policies favouring Malay access to education and mandating roles for Malays in business. These policies generated a Malay elite deriving rents from ties to the state, so it acquiesced in the financial reforms that swept the region after the Asian Financial Crisis, even though Prime Minister Mahathir had aggressively rejected IMF intervention at the time. Political support from poorer Malays was secured with financial schemes to aid farmers and small businesses, while Islamic Finance was promoted for the sake of cultural soli-darity. Today, Islamic financial instruments account for 24.2 per cent of banking assets, 65 per cent of equities and 9 per cent of insurance assets (Reuters 2012). They play a significant role in household savings and small-business loans, even amongst non-Muslims. This success indicates that, in an Islamic society, moral/religious teach-ings provide a sound basis for finance.

# CHINA

China's modernization exhibits illuminating parallels and contrasts with Japan's. China also began with state enterprises with soft budget constraints, but achieved greater suc-cess. Its growth was also seeded by the expropriation of landowners and capitalists. Whereas Japan's land reforms enabled the state to capture some of the increase in farm income that landlords would have enjoyed, China's expropriation, then commercializa-tion, of land enabled the state to capture the capital gains from growth that landlords would have enjoyed. As in Japan, the state helped finance large corporate groups by sell-ing them state assets at favourable prices and by commingling corporate savings and public funding from state banks. As in Japan, these large corporate groups developed rational incentive structures for managers, disciplined each other through competi-tion, and tapped private savings through the stock market, but retained control through pyramiding. In China, these groups were initially controlled by a hierarchy of local gov-ernments, rather than the wealthy families that had controlled Japan's *zaibatsu*. Today, however, China's 'revolutionary families' have taken control of entire corporate groups.

China's state enterprises were more successful than Japan's, as they were built on Soviet experience and organizational structures: a Leninist party hierarchy that controlled both workers and managers, plus a central plan that encompassed the entire economy, prescribing wages and prices that ensured profits to fund the state. State domination of the economy ended, not because of a fiscal crisis, as in Japan, but because of the political crisis of the Cultural Revolution. This cracked the Party structure and undermined its legitimacy. To restore legitimacy required growth.

Then began a decentralized search for new structures of ownership and control that would promote growth while preserving Party control. First came agricultural reform via individual leases of state land. Then, Township and Village Enterprises were launched using local state resources, foreign enterprises brought their own capital into China, and private businesses were financed informally with loans from relatives, friends, and related businesses (Allen et al. 2009) Thereby, a dynamic sector grew up with little recourse to state banks. On the contrary, this sector accumulated cash surpluses that the state banks used to fund the reform of state enterprises.

China's state plan had funded capital investment by manipulating prices and wages to yield profits that were recycled into state enterprises, which held China's industrial assets. The gradual commercialization of this state sector is thus key to the financial system that emerged. For example, the financial pressures resulting from the deficits of state enterprises helped launch the stock and bond markets. These two markets were the most familiar to outside observers and so attracted most attention, but for most of the reform era, both were quite small relative to GDP; most of China's early growth was financed either informally or by monetizing state assets, especially land.

Outside observers tended to neglect informal finance because of data difficulties; they tended to neglect the state sector because they saw dinosaurs, kept alive only by state support. Nonetheless, this sector became profitable following Premier Zhu's reforms, which placed them under the ownership and control of holding companies linked to national and local governments. The ambiguous status of this key sector requires us to discuss the financial system as part of the fiscal system, corporate governance as part of political governance, and monetary policy and bank regulation as part of fiscal policy.

The People's Bank of China (PBC) began as a Soviet-type monobank. It served as a centralized accounting system that tracked the performance of state enterprises in the state plan. State enterprises kept their 'money' in accounts at the PBC; transactions between state enterprises were recorded as monetary transfers between those accounts. If the central plan required one state enterprise to purchase certain goods from another, but it lacked the funds, then the PBC simply added more to its account. This money of account, however, could not be converted into the medium of exchange that citizens used for daily transactions; the supply of the latter was strictly controlled, which kept inflation low throughout the state-planning era (Rana 2012).

The PBC spun off four state banks to be run on commercial lines, retaining only the classic central-bank functions of bank supervision and monetary control. Meanwhile, state enterprises gradually disengaged from central planning and acquired discretion over their own funds. Yet the attitudes and practices carried over from the central-planning era led state banks to lend to state enterprises without worrying much about repayment. After all, if they could not repay, then the only recourse was for the bank to take ownership, but it lacked the capacity to manage the assets. Nor were there private shareholders to pressurize bank managers to avoid losses from poor lending decisions.

As central planners no longer controlled the prices and wages of state enterprises, many started making losses, especially given their social-welfare burdens that private competitors did not have to carry. Many state enterprises were kept afloat only by bank loans that they had no hope of repaying. This required continual recapitalization of the state banks from the late 1990s. By 2005, the bill totalled US$4 trillion (Ma 2006). About 15 per cent of this was effectively borne by foreign financial institutions that took equity stakes prior to their listing. The rest came from the PBC and Ministry of Finance, which got bank shares in return. They held their shares via a limited-liability company, Central Huijin, which was 'to represent the PRC government in exercising its investor rights and obligations' as a bank shareholder and 'implement and execute PRC government policy arrangements in relation to the reform of state-owned financial institutions' (<www.huijin-inv.cn/hjen/aboutus/aboutus_2008.html>), retrieved 20 December 2012). The PBC's Huijin shares were held through the State Administration of Foreign Exchange, which later transferred them to the China Investment Corporation, the sovereign-wealth fund controlled by the Ministry of Finance (Lardy 2012).

The loss of state enterprises as a revenue source led to fiscal problems, requiring the issue of bonds. Some were simply assigned to profitable state enterprises and wealthy citizens; their attempts to sell off their involuntary holdings created an informal bond market. Another way of reducing the fiscal burden of state enterprises was to pay workers in enterprise shares; their attempts to sell off these shares created an informal share market. So China's bond and stock markets arose from the shut-down of state enterprises—the reverse of how these markets usually arise to fund enterprise start-ups.

The nascent stock market featured poor regulation, short-term trading dominated by speculation on rumour, front running, insider trading, and other abuses. Naïve investors pushed the Shanghai Index to a peak of 6251.5 in October 2007, but this fell to a low of 1800 in Autumn 2008 as investors wised up. Equities now account for about 10 per cent of urban household wealth, bank deposits for 42 per cent, real estate for 40 per cent and bonds for 1 per cent (Wang 2011). Attempts to resuscitate the market by attracting foreign investors and permitting margin trading have got nowhere. Meantime, enterprises were encouraged to list abroad, but a number of accounting scandals have resulted (Norris 2012).

Even as hopeless state enterprises were sold off, merged, or put under new management, local governments were launching new enterprises by monetizing their assets, especially land. China's investment-driven growth was turbo-charged by the gradual commercialization of land, which had appreciated as the economy grew. Thus, a lot of industrialization was financed without the funds passing through a formal financial system at all. This permitted enormous rates of investment, even as China ran a current account surplus. It helped that until 2007, state-linked enterprises paid no dividends, although they did pay profit tax. So they either reinvested their profits or saved them, providing more funding for investment that again bypassed the formal financial system (Lardy 2012).

Most state-linked enterprises are now profitable (Lardy 2012), admittedly due to entrenchment of monopolies and hidden subsidies, but due also to the incentive contracts offered to enterprise managers and the closer supervision of the local governments that own the surpluses they produce. Higher tiers of government are motivated to grow their local economies by their claim on the resulting increases in tax revenue, and by the prospect of promotion for top officials who manage localities that grow fast (Li and Zhou 2005). Moreover, all state-linked enterprises are controlled through Party committees of senior managers, so they are integrated into the personnel management system of the Party. For state banks, Pistor (2012) relates how these Party committees overshadow the formal authority of the management boards.

To cushion China from the global financial crisis of 2008, the central government unleashed investment by local governments. They set up over 8,000 investment vehicles that used land as collateral for bank loans to fund investment. In 2011, China's State Auditor estimated that local governments had piled up 10.7 trillion yuan of debt, but Moody's found another 3.5 trillion yuan of potential loans (Reuters 2011). The total of 14.2 trillion yuan was about 31 per cent of GDP. Thus, local governments exploited formal financial mechanisms to appropriate state resources, some to benefit corrupt officials.

Since state banks offer most of their loans to state enterprises, a wide range of shadowy companies and unregulated products have grown up to bridge the wide gap between the low regulated rates that bank depositors can earn and the high-interest rates that private entrepreneurs are willing to pay, for example for real-estate development and speculation. Examples include the 'Wealth Management Products' set up by state and commercial banks, the 'Entrusted Loans' between businesses that are arranged by banks, loans from trusts and underground banks, and peer-to-peer loans arranged online. Estimates of the size of China's shadow banking industry range from 2 trillion yuan (State Information Centre) to almost 18 trillion yuan (China Union Pay) (Borst 2011). This shadow banking arguably promoted economic efficiency by shifting funds towards higher-return activities, but led to inequity, uncertainty, and high interest rates for private businesses, over-investment by state-linked corporations, and system fragility.

# CHINA VS. JAPAN

In return for state resources, the state-linked conglomerates of Japan and China accepted guidance from elite bureaucrats. Yet once the alliance of businessmen, bureaucrats, and politicians had set the economy on a convincing growth path that legitimized their dominance, non-accountable power tempted them into cronyism and rent-seeking. This was easy when business transactions remained based on relationships rather than rules. Indeed, this was also true of 'transactions' between businesses and bureaucrats: businesses built long-term relationships with supervising ministries, relationships consummated by the transfer of personnel.

Growth nevertheless surged for several decades, because the cronyism was restrained by a sophisticated political and technocratic leadership, organized into a hierarchy of power and responsibility that allocated resources and rents in a way that allowed individual initiative, connected reward to opportunity, and commanded broad acceptance. As their economies modernized, these ruling hierarchies comprised so many key roles that political stability and long-term economic success could no longer be upheld by personal relationships. Relationships had to be formalized into rules; exercise of power had to be limited by rules that ensured enough predictability to decentralize the business initiatives required for economic dynamism.

What happens when a complex political economy so organized seeks to develop the decentralized, rule-governed financial system necessary for a sophisticated economy that must interface with a global economy whose rules and institutions were set in the West? The ruling hierarchy is already using a complex mixture of rules and tacit relationships, so the mechanisms and mindsets are already in place to complicate and subvert moves towards a rule-governed financial system.

Building a relationship requires considerable investment of personal time, so it is not easy to shift key transactions from one party to another. A long period of steady growth therefore channelled key transactions along networks of stable relationships, such as those governing flows of money, personal favours, and information in their financial systems. We now consider the causes and effects of the structural differences between the elite networks of Japan and China.

The US occupation of Japan imposed a democratic government that had formal authority over the bureaucracy, which had formal authority over business. The three elites coordinated Japan's export-led re-industrialization, developing deep personal networks. Still, each elite maintained its own career structure from recruitment to retirement. Information and pay-offs flowed around this 'iron triangle': financial contributions from businesses to politicians helped them win elections by handing out gifts to voters; politicians pressured the bureaucracy to offer contracts to friendly corporations; ministry officials favoured corporations that would give them jobs when they retired some years later. Japan's independent legal system and free press ensured that there were few direct exchanges of favours that would have concentrated personal wealth. The circulation of favours around the 'iron triangle' instead served to keep it atop Japan's political economy (Hagström 2000).

The flow of favours brought large-scale inefficiencies in the allocation of capital: see Japan's concreted hillsides and riverbeds, bridges, and bullet trains to nowhere. In finance, the key consequence was the long delay in cleaning up the real-estate boom-and-bust, as regulatory forbearance countenanced an enormous range of accounting tricks: bad debts were shunted off balance sheets in complicated 'shell games' just ahead of bank examiners; zombie companies and financial institutions piled up further debt.

By contrast, China's unitary elite moved back and forth between state-linked corporations and government. Without democratic checks and balances and the oversight of independent professionals, this ruling hierarchy could quietly negotiate massive wealth transfers via the one-on-one financial transactions that became possible when the centrally planned economy opened up. This was first seen during the liberalization of state banks, which were looted by sweetheart deals between managers of bank branches and state enterprises, negotiated behind closed doors. It was seen again when naïve stock-market investors were victimized by insider trading and the proceeds of stock-market listings were siphoned off for real-estate speculation by related-party transactions.

This corruption is restrained by the Party's Organization Department and the Central Discipline and Inspection Commission, which seek to maintain Party legitimacy. It is also limited by the practice of promoting senior officials for growing their jurisdictions, which ensures a personal return to local leaders from limiting corruption that would restrict growth. The upshot is that the safest way for the elite to extract value from the system is to generate so much as to mask their personal siphoning. Thus, the difference in the network structures governing finance in Japan and China helps explain why Japan suffered a low growth rate but maintained a low Gini coefficient in the last two decades, while the reverse was true in China.

We next consider the implications of elite network structure for the quality and continuity of the flow of information required to regulate a sophisticated financial system. Japan featured a one-way flow of personnel amongst elite groups: senior bureaucrats often join the firms they used to supervise, but business managers cannot join the bureaucracy. This injects deep knowledge of official procedures, attitudes, and plans into the business community, but the bureaucracy has little knowledge of recent developments in business. For example, the rapid development of *zaitech* amongst business corporations was little understood in the Ministry of Finance, which failed to check it. By contrast, there is a two-way flow of personnel between Chinese firms and their supervising ministries, for example, between the top managers of state banks and financial market regulators. This has ensured that financial regulators have sophisticated knowledge and hands-on experience.

In Japan, democracy allows abrupt changes in power that disrupt relationships between politicians and bureaucrats, hence the bureaucracy's capacity to deal with the more complex issues raised by a more sophisticated financial system. Amyx (2004: 33) has argued that the system proved unable to undertake the drastic action required because electoral defeat ruptured the personal links between the Liberal Democratic Party and the Ministry of Finance that had built up over Japan's high-growth era. Having lost its political protector, the Ministry of Finance focused on institutional survival, which required obfuscation of the financial debacle. That was why Japan's financial crisis lasted for decades.

Amyx (2004: 21) further argues that the breakdown in key links through democratic turnover was particularly damaging because Japan's elite networks are 'aristocratic', that is, key transactions tend to pass through a small number of privileged links (Buchanan 2002). Such a network structure is likely to emerge in a culture that carefully differentiates by status: high-status individuals network mainly with each other, while their subordinates network with each other only via their superiors. This is also true in China, but its elite networks seem less fragile, because membership is steadily renegotiated within the elite, and horizontal linkages amongst senior persons of similar status seem sufficiently robust to safeguard key information flows. In finance, these linkages are depicted in Figures 1–4 of Pistor (2012).

Japanese sensitivity to status differences is coupled with a reluctance to assume clear leadership. This created additional difficulties in dealing with a financial crisis that was severe, but not catastrophic. Chinese seem less reluctant to lead, so a strong personality can impose bold decisions after building a consensus. Top-down leadership drove the reform of the entire structure of financial supervision and management of state financial institutions. This started in 1998, led by Premier Zhu Rongji and implemented by the State Council's Central Financial Work Commission under Vice Premier Wen Jiabao (Pistor 2012).

In China, a rising problem is that key policy-makers are entangled in the economic interests of the factional and family empires that have grown up under their protection. As personal relationships dominate rules, even decisions promulgated by the State Council are difficult to enforce, being steadily eroded by renegotiation. Thus, Premier Wen has publicly criticized the monopoly power of state banks, but has made little progress in opening them to competition from the private sector, or narrowing the interest margins that pad their profits and the profits of state-linked enterprises. Another example is the Ministry of Finance's difficulties in extracting dividends from state enterprises, even though the state is their majority shareholder through the State-Owned Assets and Supervision Commission (SASAC) and the Party appoints all key personnel through its Organization Department. In 2007, the State Council required state enterprises to pay dividends to the Ministry of Finance at rates of 15, 10, and 5 per cent. These rates were first negotiated downward for a transition period, then the dividends were held in the State Capital Management Budget (SCMB), which recycled them to other SASAC enterprises (Lardy 2012: 150). Even when SCMB finally disgorged the dividends, it kept some back for competitive bidding by SASAC enterprises.

# India, by Comparison with China and Japan

India's stock market capitalization as a ratio of GDP and as a ratio of deposits is higher than the US, and its derivatives markets are sophisticated. India's growth has nevertheless lagged behind that of China and many smaller East Asian economies with less extensive and sophisticated financial markets. This indicates their secondary role in mobilizing capital for development, compared to state funds, state banks, recycled corporate profits, and informal finance.

India's land reform distributed land widely to individuals, so the state could not turbocharge finance with land and state assets. The capital gains on the land accrued to lucky private landowners who today hold up infrastructure and private investment for years on end as they haggle over the use of their land. In China, the capital gains are available to local governments to fund infrastructure and industrialization.

India sought both growth and redistribution via taxes, subsidies, and licences. This reduced the efficiency of resource allocation and became a potent source of rents and rent-seeking as local bureaucrats extracted bribes to bypass these interventions. Such interventions were less necessary in China, because Liberation saw a drastic redistribution of income and wealth through outright expropriation. Recently, a massive build-out of rural infrastructure is redressing rural–urban inequities more effectively than any of India's market interventions, but this is possible only because of China's stronger fiscal position (Anderlini 2012).

Over the years, India's state enterprises have received plenty of sweetheart loans from state banks, but they have never been a dynamic force in the economy, given their management by low-salaried bureaucrats. China has achieved greater success, if less equity, by directing funds from state banks to state-linked enterprises managed by a political/business hierarchy strongly motivated by the opportunity to make big profits, some to be recycled for reinvestment, the rest to be siphoned off for family and factional enrichment.

India's tax collection was weakened by corruption, yet it allocated a great deal of revenue to redressing social inequities, leaving little to fund infrastructure and industrialization. In China, tax collection efforts in the early days of reforms yielded ample funds because they were decentralized to provincial and local governments that were motivated by their share of revenue, as defined by fiscal contracts (Shirk 1993). Also, huge transfers went indirectly to state-linked corporations. The key example is the large margin between deposit and loan rates, which imposes a large implicit tax on bank depositors. Some of this helps fund welfare payments to state workers, some shows up in the profits of state enterprises and is reinvested to create more state-linked capital, some returns to the state as corporate tax payments, and some is siphoned off in corruption.

Allen et al. (2009) document the importance of informal finance for both China and India. This was because the state took an important role allocating finance, but the limited reach of financial regulation and corrupt demands by local officials left many inefficiencies, which informal finance has bridged. India's use of state policy to advance social groups conferred local monopolies on a variety of financial institutions. Krishnan (2011: 26) notes that 'A license to operate in a certain area of Indian finance is, all too often, a safe sinecure with stable profits and a near-zero probability of death. There is therefore little incentive to innovate to remain competitive. This is not unlike firms in the real economy before 1992.' Interventions proliferated as interest groups 'traded' political funding and vote-banks to democratic politicians in return for economic rents. All this served to divert economic activity into less productive channels.

In China, the key trades of power for money took place within the Party hierarchy, and top leaders tried to reduce local monopoly rents while spreading the benefits of the monopoly power of the largest state enterprises, especially the banks. These benefits are best characterized, not as 'rent-seeking' but as 'profit-seeking', insofar as value is captured, not by the restriction of economic activity, but by its expansion. Thereby, under-priced land and bank loans yielded profits for state-linked corporations. These profits (minus corrupt siphoning) were deposited in state banks and lent out again for industrial projects in a virtuous circle. Moreover, the firms paid taxes on their profits, which helped China's fiscal position. Thus, the use of state power to entrench monopolies and state assets to generate profits helps to explain why China has high rates of investment and saving, and a small fiscal deficit.

India's high tax rates have generated a 'black economy' of tax avoidance. Once income has been hidden from tax inspectors, it must circulate in cash within the black economy to avoid their attention. Illicit activities then arise to convert cash into legitimate bank deposits, often abroad. All this diverts resources into unproductive activities. China avoids this, because personal tax rates are low for most people, an advantage traceable to its expropriation of private land and capital in 1949: these have become ongoing sources of state revenue.

It is also useful to compare India with Japan, since both have been formal democracies since 1947, but remained effectively one-party states for a critical period. When genuine multi-party competition arrived, India boomed, but Japan stagnated. This contrast can be traced to the contrasting roles of finance in their economic development. Over 1955–1993, Japanese politics was dominated by the Liberal Democratic Party, which allied with bureaucrats and big business to lead Japan into high growth. Then the financial crisis brought other political parties to power. We have seen how this disrupted coherent financial policy, thereby turning crisis into stagnation. Over 1947–1977, Indian politics was dominated by the Congress Party, whose Fabian socialism slowed growth as it targeted inequality and large business groups. Then competitive elections broke the grip of socialist ideology and the License Raj. India's economy became more dynamic and more complex; its rule-based governance handled this by devolving more coordination to market forces. Highly professional, independent financial regulators kept India safe from a banking crisis. However, India's boom has faded as corruption scandals made the bureaucracy afraid of contact with large companies and paralyzed economic policy. Policy paralysis is now driving business abroad, as in Japan.

# BUSINESS INSTITUTIONS, EAST AND WEST

The above account of how Asia's financial institutions evolved suggests that in Asia caution is required in using the concept of 'institutions', which plays a key role in both the VoC and business-system literatures. Thus, in Redding's (2005) scheme, institutions arise from a nation's cultural base to frame its business system. His scheme works well for advanced Western economies: they embarked on capitalism so long ago that each national economy is today dominated by one suite of institutions. Moreover, the passage of time has attenuated the impact of the nation's 'initial conditions'—the distributions of wealth, power, and skills that obtained when capitalism arose. These impact on how its business system functions today only via their impact on its institutions.

Outside Japan, Asia's modernization is so recent that initial conditions still have a direct effect on how a business system functions. Examples noted in this chapter include how the financial systems of China and India differ today because the state took owner-ship of all assets in China, but few in India; how the financial systems of South Korea and Taiwan differ today because South Korea started with few entrepreneurs, while Taiwan started with many; and how the financial systems of the ASEAN4 differ today because of Indonesia's rich resources and diversity, the Philippines' entrenched landowning oli-garchy, the lack of rural roots of Thailand's urban elite, and Malaysia's ethnic divide. In the West, classifying a nation in terms of its institutional structure reveals a great deal about how capitalism functions there. It reveals less in Asia, given the impact of initial conditions.

There is a deeper problem with defining an Asian business system in terms of its suite of institutions. Institutions are frameworks/rules upheld by social practices and/or state power. We can identify such 'institutions' in all stable complex societies, but the West tended to build key institutions on a transcendental conception of society. Thus, the Church was built on the Judeo-Christian conception of history as purposeful and divinely ordered; the Soviet state was built on its secular counterpart, Dialectical Materialism; Western legal systems were built on a transcendental conception of the rule of law; the American Republic was built on a transcendental conception of democracy as an association of free individuals, as enunciated in the Declaration of Independence.

By contrast, China never sought to order society in terms of a preconceived tran-scendental framework. Taoism saw society as self-ordering, so it could hardly provide such a framework. Confucius' analogy between the state and the family became useful in ordering society, so it was institutionalized by selecting an elite through examina-tions in his writings. Only much later, through incorporating the abstract thought of Buddhism, did Neo-Confucianism arrive at an abstract conception of the state. Given this cultural heritage, East Asian states approached economic development pragmati-cally, without any preconception of an appropriate framework for an economy and soci-ety, such as that promoted by the World Bank, IMF, or Washington Consensus. While Communist China began with the grand preconceptions of Marxism-Leninism, these were discredited by the Cultural Revolution, so China returned to pragmatism under Deng Xiaoping. Thus, formal institutions are less salient in how business functions in East Asia today.

This is not to denigrate their importance for the future. There is a grave difficulty with East Asia's pragmatic approach to development: without a widely shared conception of how society and the economy ought to function, the political/bureaucratic/business elite that spearheads development can easily entrench and enrich itself by blocking/sub-verting independent institutions of law, accounting, and financial regulation. Striking empirical evidence has been presented above that larger nations in developing Asia have enjoyed less economic freedom because of weaker institutions. Why?

Like Japan, China and India are such massive distinctive societies that each conceptu-alized itself as a 'civilization', not merely a state, so each aspired to build a full-spectrum industrial economy. This required mobilizing a mass of capital and coordinating its use across many industries, hence the collaboration of a political/bureaucratic/business elite spanning the economy and polity. This tended to crystallize into a rent/profit-seeking oligarchy so comprehensive that it could be disrupted only by external shocks. The massive economies of China and India, like that of Japan, could withstand massive external economic shocks: their distinctive cultures ensured distinctive interpretations of external intellectual influences. This was less true of Indonesia and South Korea; it was even less so of smaller Asian economies, which tended to focus on export niches, so the elites that spearheaded their development were more vulnerable to external economic shocks and more open to Western concepts.

How can larger inward-looking Asian nations check predatory oligarchies? Imperial China provides a compelling antecedent: it braced the rule of Confucian scholar-officials by institutionalizing procedures to contain corruption. This is imperative for larger Asian economies today. Each Western business system comprises a wide range of institutions. Subjecting economic players to a multitude of rules, these institutions themselves constitute a strong check against corruption. For the cultural and historical reasons noted above, Asian business institutions are fewer and weaker, yet Asian government and business elites are typically entangled more deeply, especially in larger economies.

Thus, the future of Asian capitalism depends critically on whether formal institutions to contain corruption directly can arise from the collective self-interest of a self-selected elite, and on whether these institutions can keep pace with the rising complexity of Asian economies. We have seen how Japan's financial regulators failed to develop the independence and sophistication to cope with the rising complexity of their economy and financial system: decades of stagnation were the result. China's financial regulators have kept pace so far, but may falter as their political economy grows even more complex with the rise of families that both dominate large sectors of the economy and send scions to the highest levels of government.

While this chapter has emphasized the impact of the initial economic conditions and distribution of power on today's Asian financial systems, those systems now need strong institutions that transcend such economic and political factors. That is, the VoC and business systems focus on institutional structure ought to become the dominant theme of future accounts of Asian financial systems, not for the sake of scholarly tidiness, but for the sake of Asian development.

## NOTES

1. They used 1996 data that omitted China and India. 'The correlations between the share of the largest 15 families in total market capitalization, on the one hand, and the efficiency of the judicial system, the rule of law, and corruption are very strong...The Pearson correlation coefficients are −0.807, −0.834, and −0.841 respectively'.

2. See the Sovereign Wealth Fund Website, <http://www.swfinstitute.org/fund-rankings/>, retrieved 26 November 2012.

3. 10% of all IPO proceeds go into the state pension fund (Impavido et al. 2009).

# References

Allen F. A. and D. Gale (2000). *Comparing Financial Systems*. Cambridge, MA, MIT Press.

Allen, F., R. J. Chakrabarti, S. De, J. Qian, and M. Qian (2009). 'The Financial System Capacities of China and India'. Retrieved 18 November 2012 from <http://papers.ssrn.com/sol3/papers.cfm?abstract_id=1361708>.

Amyx, J. A. (2004). *Japan's Financial Crisis*. Princeton, Princeton University Press.

Anderlini, J. (2012). 'Rural Investment Pays Off in China'. *Financial Times*, 11 September. Retrieved 18 November 2012 from <http://www.ft.com/intl/cms/s/0/8a576f22-fbd0-11e1-af33-00144feabdc0.html>.

Backman, M. (1999). *Asian Eclipse: Exposing the Dark Side of Business in Asia*. Singapore, John Wiley.

Borst, N. (2011). 'China Shadow Banking Primer', *China Economic Watch*, Peterson Institute for International Economics. Retrieved 18 November 2012 from <http://www.piie.com/blogs/china/?p=587>.

Buchanan, M. (2002). *Small Worlds and the Groundbreaking Science of Networks*. New York, W. W. Norton.

Caballero, R. J., T. Hoshi, and A. K. Kashyap (2008). 'Zombie Lending and Depressed Restructuring in Japan'. *American Economic Review* 98(5): 1943–1977.

Claessens, S., S. Djankov, and L. H. P. Lang (1999). *Who Controls East Asian Corporations?* Policy Research Working Paper 2054. Washington DC, World Bank.

Deeg, R. (2010). 'Institutional Change in Financial Systems'. In G. Morgan, J. Campbell, C. Crouch, O. K. Pedersen, and R. Whitley, Eds., *The Oxford Handbook of Comparative Institutional Analysis*: 309–334. Oxford, Oxford University Press.

Hagström, L. (2000) *Diverging Accounts of Japanese Policymaking*. Working Paper 102. Stockholm, European Institute of Japanese Studies.

Hall, P. A. and D. W. Soskice (2001). *Varieties of Capitalism: The Institutional Foundations of Comparative Advantage*. Oxford, Oxford University Press.

Impavido, G., Y. W. Hu, and X. Li (2009). *Governance and Fund Management in the Chinese Pension System*. IMF Working Paper WP/09/246. Washington, DC, International Monetary Fund.

Johnson, C. (1982). *MITI and the Japanese Miracle: The Growth of Industrial Policy 1925–1975*. Stanford, Stanford University Press.

Kim, R. (2012). 'Yale Grad Fights Families Who Rule Samsung to Hyundai', *Bloomberg Businessweek*, 29 August. Retrieved 18 November 2012 from <http://www.bloomberg.com/news/2012-08-28/yale-graduate-fights-korean-families-who-rule-samsung-to-hyundai.html>.

Koo, R. (2009). *The Holy Grail of Macroeconomics: Lessons from Japan's Great Recession*. New York, John Wiley.

Krishnan, K. P. (2011). *Financial Development in Emerging Markets: The Indian Experience*. Working Paper No. 276. Tokyo, Asia Development Bank.

Lardy, N. R. (2012). *Sustaining China's Economic Growth after the Global Financial Crisis*. Washington, DC, Peter G. Peterson Institute for International Economics.

Li, H. B. and L. A. Zhou (2005). 'Political Turnover and Economic Performance: The Incentive Role of Personnel Control in China'. *Journal of Public Economics* 89(9): 1743–1762.

Ma, G. (2006). *Who Pays China's Bank Restructuring Bill?* CEPII Working Paper 2006–4. Paris, Centre d'Études Prospective et d'Informations Internationales.

Morck, R. and M. Nakamura (2007). 'Business Groups and the Big Push: Meiji Japan's Mass Privatization and Subsequent Growth'. *Enterprise and Society 8*(3): 543–601.

Ng, E. (2012). 'More Exports Can Be In Yuan'. *South China Morning Post*, 13 November. Retrieved 18 November 2012 from <http://www.scmp.com/business/money/investment-products/article/1081143/more-exports-can-be-yuan-says-economist>.

Norris, F. (2012). 'In China, Little Urge to Audit the Auditors'. *New York Times*, 13 July. Retrieved 18 November 2012 from <http://www.nytimes.com/2012/07/13/business/in-china-inspecting-the-inspectors.html?pagewanted=all>.

Park, C. Y. (2011). *Asian Financial Systems: Development and Challenges*. Working Paper 285. Tokyo, Asian Development Bank Institute.

Pistor, K. (2012). 'The Governance of China's Finance'. In J. Fan and R. Morck, Eds., *Capitalizing China*: 35–62. Chicago, University of Chicago Press.

Rajan, R. G. and L. Zingales (2002). 'Banks and Markets: The Changing Character of European Finance'. Discussion paper No. 3868. London, CEPR.

Rana, S. (2012). 'The Emergence of the New Chinese Banking System: Implications for Global Politics and the Future of Financial Reform'. *Maryland Journal of International Law* 27: 215–234

Redding, G. (2005). 'The Thick Description and Comparison of Societal Systems of Capitalism'. *Journal of International Business Studies 36*(2): 123–155.

Reuters (2011). 'Chinese Local Debt Understated by $540 Billion: Moody's'. Retrieved 18 November 2012 from <http://www.reuters.com/article/2011/07/05/us-china-debt-moodys-idUSTRE7640EN20110705>.

—— (2012). 'Islamic Banks' Market Share Grows in Malaysia'. Retrieved 18 November 2012 from <http://www.reuters.com/article/2012/09/28/us-malaysia-banks-idUSBRE88R0DL20120928>.

Shirk, S. L. (1993). *The Political Logic of Economic Reform in China*. Berkeley, University of California Press.

Smith, H. (2000). *Industry Policy in Taiwan and Korea in the 1980s*. Cheltenham, Edward Elgar.

Ueda, K. (2000). 'Causes of Japan's Banking Problems in the 1990s'. In T. Hoshi and H. Patrick, Eds., *Crisis and Change in the Japanese Financial System*: 59–81. Boston, Kluwer Academic.

Wang, T. (2011). 'Bubble or No Bubble? The Great Chinese Property Debate'. *UBS Investment Research 25*. Retrieved 18 November 2012 from <http://www.nuhc.cn/ENNewsShow.aspx?NewsID=2>.

Whitley, R. (1992). *Business Systems in East Asia*. London and Newbury Park, Sage.

—— (1999). *Divergent Capitalisms: The Social Structuring and Change of Business Systems*. London, Oxford University Press.

..............................................................................................................

# CHAPTER 20

# MNEs IN ASIAN BUSINESS SYSTEMS

..............................................................................................................

## AXÈLE GIROUD

## INTRODUCTION

.............................................................................................................

THIS chapter explores ways in which multinational enterprises (MNEs) impact upon and shape local business systems in Asian countries, focusing particularly on countries that are major recipients of FDI. Using business-systems theoretical considerations, we review existing studies on MNE activities, knowledge transfers and linkages, development, and economic areas of relevance to FDI spillovers, to provide an overview of how MNEs may influence the business systems of host economies.

The international business literature has long accepted that MNE activities are affected by and impact upon different institutional regimes (Jackson and Deeg 2008). Some studies investigate the means by which host institutions shape the strategies adopted by MNEs, for instance by attracting FDI, or influencing the entry mode that firms adopt; other studies explore more generally how the institutional distance between the home country (in which the MNE has its headquarters) and host countries (in which subsidiaries operate) leads to variations in strategic and managerial decisions (Kostova 1999; Mudambi and Navarra 2002). Another stream of literature on MNE impacts in host countries has suggested that institutional variations can influence potential benefits from the presence and activities of MNEs, as well as shown how MNEs, in turn, influence the institutional setting of the host economy (Dunning and Lundan 2008a).

From a business-systems perspective, numerous studies focus on varieties of capitalism (Morgan and Whitley 2013), though none specifically distinguishes the activities of MNEs and how they influence local business systems. The fundamental insight is that firm organization, strategy, and structure is shaped by the national institutional context in which it exists (Redding 2005; Morgan 2012). In this context, this leads to the presence of two institutional logics: that of the MNE itself and that of the host economy in which it operates. This in turn leads to two expected outcomes: first, the MNE or its subsidiary will adapt some of their practices to reflect the country in which they operate, and second, the MNE will alter the host institutional context. When MNE subsidiaries adapt their own practices, this has been termed the micro-politics of the MNE; when the MNE alters the host institutional context, it is macro-politics (Dörrenbächer and Geppert 2011). Both are potentially important in countries where FDI plays an important role in the economic development process, and yet, to date, there remains a gap in the literature addressing the processes by which MNEs can shape local business environments, especially in Asia.

This chapter focuses on the macro-politics of the MNE, exploring how MNEs alter local business systems across Asian countries through significant levels of inward FDI. In line with Jackson and Deeg (2008: 552), it is suggested that particular types and interactions of home- and host-country institutions influence the form and effectiveness of MNE strategies (such as agglomeration or export of practices, adaptation, and arbitrage) and impact on host economies.

In the next section, theoretical considerations from the business systems and international business literatures are developed, followed by a review of FDI inflows in key Asian recipient economies, together with key government policies that have facilitated the activities of MNEs across the region. This is followed by an exploration of MNE impacts, linking spillovers, linkages, and other impacts to variations in Asian business systems. The final section concludes and provides suggestions for theoretical development.

# MNEs AND HOST ECONOMIES AS BUSINESS SYSTEMS

## MNEs, Home and Host Business Systems

The business systems literature suggests that a firm's strategies and structures reflect its home institutional environment. Institutions can be classified into labour system (forms of employment regulations, protection, wage-bargaining, skills and training regime, union system, and participation), capital system (means of capital provision, banks, types of loans, shares or bonds), inter-firm relationships system (degree of formal and informal rules, and how this influences opportunism exercised in relationships), and political system. 'These institutions set the framework within which firms put together key resources of capital, labour and supply inputs, and within which forms of competition and cooperation evolve' (Morgan 2012: 19). In other words, institutional features affect firm characteristics (Whitley 2010: 468). These conditions help to explain firms' competitive advantages, and why certain types of firm, such as family firms, are more prevalent in some environments than others. Social contexts and experiential learning are important, and therefore specific interest groups play a role in the structuring of economic relations as well as the organization of local systems (Redding 2005).

Of course, many of these institutions in a single-country setting are interrelated. Business systems have complex determinants, and the context therefore matters (Redding and Witt 2006: 96). For instance, societies with strong states play a dominant role in coordinating economic development, and where the state shares risks with the private sector, strong intermediary associations tend not to be developed. However, low levels of state risk-sharing and economic coordination are often combined with capital market-based financial systems in what might be termed arm's-length or differentiated business environments.

Whitley (2010) describes various competition models, following a radical–incremental distinction, with speed and scale of innovation and production as dominant factors. Each model leads to variation in firms' competences and capabilities within their national contexts. The distinction matters because it explains how and why firms may move from an export-led strategy to overseas strategies with operations in favourable locations, and to multinationality (Jackson and Deeg 2008).

With the increase in FDI over the past few decades, scholars have questioned whether being exposed to different institutional contexts means that MNEs have become significantly different from non-multinational firms. It is clear that we now have a view of the MNE as consisting of different types of social actors with different interests and power derived from their distinctive institutional origins (Morgan 2011: 415). Home institutions influence MNE activities in various ways (Whitley 2010). Firms from liberal market economies are used to short-term, highly specific relationships with workers and suppliers, whilst firms from coordinated forms of capitalism favour a long-term approach, asset specificity, cooperation, and trust with business partners. Depending on the MNE's origin, it will be accustomed to specific ways of managing its workforce, organizing supply chains, and implementing strategies. A high degree of coordination in the home market also means that MNEs from one coordinated market may not necessarily have an advantage when investing in another coordinated market; this is because local contexts are highly specific. In contrast, firms from liberal market economies are expected to find it easier to operate in another free-market economy.

From the MNE perspective, a number of issues must therefore be addressed when analysing their activities and impact upon local business systems. First, the MNE's situation as originating from a specific business system which will have shaped its strategies and practices is to be taken into consideration. This implies a degree of global standardization in the firm, in terms of key policies and practices applied in different locations. This does not preclude that individuals may exert a degree of power or that some divergence in practices may occur in specific host-country contexts.

Reversely, MNEs learn from the local business system of the host economy in which they are operating (though MNEs from some countries, such as Japan, seem to try and minimize the absorption of new practices into overseas subsidiaries; Whitley et al. 2003). Overall, with a move towards MNEs as integrated business networks (Bartlett and Ghoshal 1998; Buckley 2009), managers develop complex new internal systems to facilitate and even encourage cross-border learning.

By operating in a foreign country, an MNE can create institutional complementarity, that is, the presence of one institution increases the efficiency of another. The emphasis lies on *how* and *why* institutions differ, with underlying strengths and weaknesses for different kinds of economic activity. The inclusion of business-systems considerations is essential, because it means a broad set of institutional resources needs to be employed to explain how firms compete. Therefore, a focus on the rule of law to explain firms' behaviour is insufficient (Allen and Aldred 2012: 383).

Morgan (2011, 2012) has recently initiated such a combination and suggests that the macro-politics between firms and the institutions of the national business system implies that MNEs seek to change institutions as part of their strategy. Morgan (2012: 32–35) builds upon Dunning's identification of three broad strategies pursued by MNEs (Dunning and Lundan 2008a), namely efficiency-seeking, market-seeking, and strategic asset-seeking. In efficiency-seeking strategies, MNEs wish to minimize costs in the value chain by accessing cheaper factors of production and producing on a larger scale. In this context, MNEs exert power inasmuch as FDI may decline if local institutions do not reinforce their efficiency-seeking objectives. When engaging in market-seeking strategies, the micro-politics of acquiring knowledge assets are prevalent, and MNEs will try and favour the establishment of free trade. This can be substantial in coordinated-market environments where large parts of economic activity are closed to market forces. In this case, MNEs push for changes in the business system that will enable them to operate, expand, and develop. If adopting asset-seeking strategies, MNEs focus on securing access to raw materials and commodities. When activities require a high level of technological expertise and large capital investment, the MNE may require close political connections, and may become explicitly politicized. Other concepts to be considered when analysing the macro-economics of MNEs include, first, the size of FDI in the country and numbers of foreign affiliates, and, second, the country's dependence on MNEs for economic growth. In such contexts, establishing an environment which supports MNEs may lead to institutional changes, sometimes to the detriment of existing forms of local embeddedness (Morgan 2011: 425).

This argument is useful, as it combines MNEs' strategic considerations with ways through which they influence or operate in various systems. It is however, not sufficient to fully encompass the wide-ranging impact that MNEs have on host economies. In this chapter, I argue that, whilst MNE activities do indeed lead to changes in local business systems, such changes do not solely occur from the *intentional* actions of the MNEs. International business and international economics studies have long analysed the impact of MNEs on host economies. By combining these insights, we can provide a more holistic view of the role played by MNEs in shaping local business systems.

In addressing this specific research agenda, this chapter reinforces the notion that 'the comparative capitalism approach has examined how institutions shape the supply of inputs collectively available to firms and the legitimate forms of coordination or governance that determine their usage .... The comparative capitalism approach may benefit by drawing on IB to better understand how MNEs engage in institutional arbitrage and diffusion, strategically manage their global value chains, and thereby create regime competition that may trigger institutional change' (Jackson and Deeg 2008: 541).

In the next section, we look further into international business considerations and existing literature on FDI impact to better understand the macro-politics of MNEs in Asian countries.

## MNEs, Institutions, and International Business

Studies have demonstrated that institutional differences and levels of economic development lead to varying degrees of spillover (Meyer and Sinani 2009), and in general exploring institutions is a useful route to advance understanding of the contemporary MNE, since it considers both formal and informal institutions and tries to bridge both macro and micro levels of analysis (Dunning and Lundan 2008b). For instance, in transition economies, investors have responded positively to encouragement by government policy promoting both the exploitation and expansion of own-resources and capabilities (Meyer and Peng 2005). Thus, country-specific institutions influence firms' objectives and behaviours, because firms may organize transactions differently, depending upon various combinations of transactions, resources, and patterns of governance. As a result, multiple embeddedness of multinationals results from the fact that institutions (i.e. national business systems) vary internationally (Whitley 2010; Meyer, Mudambi, and Narula 2011).

Institutional distance and differences between the home and host countries are often used as predictors for the level of difficulty faced by a foreign investor in understanding and responding to a new environment. Institutional differences may enhance the liability of foreignness and the lack of familiarity with the foreign environment in which the MNE has entered operations, creating relational hazards (Eden and Miller 2004). Institutional distance provides an alternative explanation for MNE behaviour (Xu and Shenkar 2002). It has been linked to two aspects of MNE operations, namely (1) the establishment of legitimacy in the host country (Kostova and Zaheer 1999) and (2) the transfer of strategic orientations and organizational practices from parent firm to foreign subsidiary (Kostova 1999). This is why institutional differences between countries also have an impact on MNE strategy and performance (Peng, Wang, and Jiang 2008).

To date, scholars examining emerging-country FDI in Asia have noted that little is known about the means through which institutional environments shape the patterns of international expansion by MNEs (Li and Yao 2010), although in the specific context of least-developed countries, Cuervo-Cazurra and Genc (2008) suggest that developing-country MNEs are more prevalent in environments with worse institutional conditions, because, given their prior home-country experience, managers can more easily understand and adapt. This is often the case in developing countries, which can exhibit 'institutional voids' (Giroud, Mirza, and We 2012). These voids offer opportunities for institutional entrepreneurship and co-evolution. MNEs are welcome in part because they introduce institutional elements absent in the local environment (Meyer 2004; Peng, Wang, and Jiang 2008). In such dynamic environments, MNEs are more likely to be seen as legitimate if they contribute to a transformational process that is already ongoing. New practices introduced by MNEs can become part of a wider process of changing values and institutional structures in the host country (Cantwell, Dunning, and Lundan 2010: 578).

Given that the contemporary network MNE is best considered as a coordinator of a global system of value-added activities that it controls and manages, institutions play an important part in providing the underpinning 'rules of the game', which help determine the complementarity or substitutability of different modes of coordination (Dunning and Lundan 2008a: 588).

When considering the issue of MNE technology transfer in the host country, cross-border knowledge and technology exchanges must be considered, as such internal cross-border transfers are themselves the result of the need to implement and adapt technology to the specificity of the host environment, and can be supported by the development of complementary institutions. MNEs will have already developed their own routines (Kogut and Zander 1993), so it is easier for an MNE to extend these practices into the host-country environment than to turn to non-ownership modes of transfer (Teece 1977; UNCTAD 2011). The MNE gains, because in the process of technology adaptation it extends its own range of competences and innovation (Cantwell 1989). For the subsidiary in the host economy, the evolution of its competences is inter-dependent with the dynamism of the local environment—it gains from it, but also contributes to its dynamism (Cantwell and Mudambi 2005). Cantwell, Dunning, and Lundan (2010) identified several mechanisms for institutional diffusion, with a focus on mimetic isomorphic pressures, as these illustrate how MNE affiliates seek to gain legitimacy, both in the eyes of their parent companies, and within the context of the institutions of the host countries in which they operate (Kostova and Zaheer 1999).

# MNE Impact: Knowledge Transfer, Spillovers, and Linkages

The international business and international economics literatures have developed concepts to assess means through which MNEs impact upon host economies. Omitting macro-economic considerations on balance of payments or government tax revenues, foreign firms may have an impact on local business systems through FDI spillovers and linkages. Spillovers are the externalities created by foreign firms, positive or negative, leading to changes in the competitive environment and in indigenous firms (Castellani and Zanfei 2006; Giroud 2012). Indirect FDI spillovers (otherwise known as horizontal spillovers) are the result of demonstration effects, labour turnover, and enhanced competition, with an impact upon strategies, activities, and performance of local firms in the host economy. Direct spillovers, by contrast, are the result of direct relationships between MNEs and local firms, through linkages leading to an increase in local firms' production and sales and/or potential knowledge technology-sharing, including training of local employees. These are referred to in the literature as vertical spillovers, either backward with local suppliers, or forward with local buyers. Studies on linkages emphasize the fact that MNEs also create links with local research institutions, universities, or other government bodies, thereby also having an impact on non-business entities in the host economy (Santangelo 2009).

To further assess how spillovers affect the local business environment, one must also consider FDI linkages and how, why, and when indigenous firms' development occurs (Giroud and Scott-Kennel 2009). Linkages act as mechanisms for spillovers. Spillover studies focus mainly on net FDI country-wide or industry-wide effects, while linkage studies focus on the activities of individual multinational enterprises and their relationships with local businesses (Giroud 2012). In both cases, it is essential to link MNE activities with technology and knowledge diffusion to local indigenous firms.

Literature suggests that it is through such diffusion that MNEs provide the greatest potential for development (Lall 1980; Kugler 2006; Giroud 2012), because MNEs possess superior knowledge compared to local firms in host economies (Caves 1996; Dunning and Lundan 2008a). This is partly because they operate complex knowledge systems and are able to benefit from resources acquired in multiple local contexts, therefore engaging in knowledge exchange internally across borders and externally within each location (Foss and Dos Santos 2011). Through spillovers and linkages, MNEs engage in voluntary and involuntary knowledge transfer, and it is often through this process that local firms are able to improve and upgrade their own competencies (Lorentzen, Mollgard, and Rojec 2003).

Scholars have pointed to the notion that MNE impact will vary depending on a number of firm-level heterogeneities at the level of the MNE (Jindra, Giroud, and Scott-Kennel 2009) or local business partners (Gentile-Lüdecke and Giroud 2012), as well as a number of country-level factors, such as government policies, local institutional environment, level of economic development, or position of the host country, for example proximity to large globalized economies or membership of regional groupings that might affect MNE strategies and behaviours.

To summarize, it is widely accepted that local institutions impact upon MNE activities, on their FDI levels, entry modes, or location. In return, however, through their activities, MNEs will also have an impact upon local business contexts, either through indirect mechanisms or direct interaction with local businesses or institutions. Whilst the pecuniary effect may be substantial, the impact on employees and local businesses is also significant. Through interacting with companies adopting foreign business practices and technology, local firms and employees are also led to modify their own behaviour and practices.

Now that the core theoretical considerations drawing upon the business-systems and international business literature have been developed, it is time to review existing empirical studies conducted in East Asian environments to draw an initial map enabling us to understand the macro-politics of MNEs in this part of the world.

# Foreign Direct Investment In East Asia

## World FDI and Asia

FDI to East and South East Asia has increased since the 1970s, at different paces depending on country. World inward FDI flows increased dramatically until the financial crisis in 2008 and despite a slow-down since, levels remain very high at US$1.2 trillion in 2010 (Table 20.1a). Flows to developing countries (note that the United Nations still includes South Korea, Taiwan, Singapore, and Hong Kong within the developing countries classification) have been rising steadily over the past two decades, reaching 46 per cent of inflows in 2010. More than half of this (28.8% of world flows) was directed at developing Asia, with 15 per cent towards East Asia and 6.4 per cent towards South East Asia. FDI stocks to the region have grown continuously, to over US$1.8 trillion in 2010 for East Asia and US$79.4 million for South East Asia.

Like many other countries across the world, East Asian economies have progressively relaxed government policies towards FDI over the past few decades. Not all countries embarked upon FDI liberalization at the same time, nor have they done so with the same orientation. Nevertheless, a common feature that can be observed in East Asia is that FDI-friendly policies proliferated in the 1990s (Lall and Narula 2004). It is generally accepted that Hong Kong, Singapore, and Malaysia have been most open to FDI, while China, the Philippines, Indonesia, Thailand, and Vietnam have concentrated on actively attracting FDI. Korea liberalized FDI policies later, mostly following the Asian crisis in the late 1990s, having previously demonstrated a cautious and conservative approach. Taiwan has encouraged outward rather than inward FDI. Partly as a result of these policies, by 2010, the main recipients of inward FDI across developing East and South East Asia were China, Hong Kong, Singapore, Indonesia, Malaysia, Vietnam, Korea, Thailand, and Taiwan (Table 20.1b).

There exist noticeable differences amongst the main recipients of inward FDI across the region in terms of reliance on FDI as an engine for economic growth. Hong Kong and Singapore have been the two most liberalized, and for these two countries, the share of inward FDI in terms of GFCF, GDP, and trade (particularly in merchandise) is the highest in the region, closely followed by Vietnam, Indonesia, Malaysia, and Thailand, where the influence has also been (with changes over time) above world averages (see Tables, 20.2, 20.3, 20.4, and 20.5). By contrast, for Korea and Taiwan, both of which have adopted different development policies, inward FDI is less prominent in local investment, GDP, and trade. The role of FDI in China has changed noticeably over the past decade, and the role played by MNEs in its overall economic performance is not as prominent nowadays compared to the early 2000s.

The rise of outward FDI from Asian countries is worth noting, as this region accounts for a rising share of world FDI since 2008. The main countries hosting MNEs in the

**Table 20.1a  Inward and outward FDI in the world, developing economies, and developing Asia, 1970–2010 (in million US$, percentages)**

| | 1990 | | 1995 | | 2000 | | 2005 | | 2010 | |
|---|---|---|---|---|---|---|---|---|---|---|
| | US$ | % | US$ | % | US$ | % | US$ | % | US$ | % |
| *Inward FDI Flows* | | | | | | | | | | |
| World | 207,455 | 100.0 | 342,391 | 100.0 | 1,402,680 | 100.0 | 982,593 | 100.0 | 1,243,671 | 100.0 |
| Developing economies | 34,853 | 16.8 | 115,801 | 33.8 | 257,625 | 18.4 | 332,307 | 33.8 | 573,568 | 46.1 |
| Of which: Asia | 22,628 | 10.9 | 80,082 | 23.4 | 148,747 | 10.6 | 215,834 | 22.0 | 357,846 | 28.8 |
| East Asia | 8,791 | 4.2 | 46,575 | 13.6 | 116,641 | 8.3 | 116,189 | 11.8 | 188,291 | 15.1 |
| South East Asia | 12,821 | 6.2 | 28,225 | 8.2 | 23,656 | 1.7 | 40,737 | 4.1 | 79,408 | 6.4 |
| *Inward FDI Stocks* | | | | | | | | | | |
| World | 2,081,299 | 100.0 | 3,392,763 | 100.0 | 7,445,637 | 100.0 | 11,539,452 | 100.0 | 19,140,603 | 100.0 |
| Developing economies | 517,322 | 24.9 | 847,707 | 25.0 | 1,731,604 | 23.3 | 2,700,998 | 23.4 | 5,951,203 | 31.1 |
| Of which Asia | 342,937 | 16.5 | 568,027 | 16.7 | 1,072,694 | 14.4 | 1,618,468 | 14.0 | 3,662,985 | 19.1 |
| East Asia | 240,645 | 11.6 | 357,419 | 10.5 | 716,103 | 9.6 | 950,570 | 8.2 | 1,888,390 | 9.9 |
| South East Asia | 64,303 | 3.1 | 152,403 | 4.5 | 266,292 | 2.6 | 404,062 | 3.5 | 938,401 | 4.9 |

*Source*: Data extracted 24 May 2012 from <http://www.unctad.org>.

### Table 20.1b  FDI Inflows by country (in million US$, selected years)

|                       | 1970   | 1980   | 1990    | 2000      | 2005    | 2010      | 2011      |
|-----------------------|--------|--------|---------|-----------|---------|-----------|-----------|
| China                 | n/a    | 57     | 3,487   | 40,715    | 72,406  | 114,734   | 123,985   |
| Hong Kong SAR, China  | 50     | 710    | 3,275   | 61,938    | 33,625  | 71,069    | 83,156    |
| Taiwan                | 62     | 166    | 1,330   | 4,928     | 1,625   | 2,492     | −1,962    |
| India                 | 45     | 79     | 237     | 3,588     | 7,622   | 24,159    | 31,554    |
| Indonesia             | n/a    | n/a    | n/a     | n/a       | 8,336   | 13,771    | 18,906    |
| Japan                 | 94     | 278    | 1,806   | 8,323     | 2,775   | −1,252    | −1,758    |
| Korea, Republic of    | 66     | 17     | 759     | 9,004     | 7,055   | 8,511     | 4,661     |
| Lao PDR               | 0      | 0      | 6       | 34        | 28      | 333       | 450       |
| Malaysia              | 94     | 934    | 2,611   | 3,788     | 4,065   | 9,103     | 11,966    |
| Philippines           | −1     | 114    | 550     | 2,240     | 1,854   | 1,298     | 1,262     |
| Singapore             | 93     | 1,236  | 5,575   | 15,515    | 18,090  | 48,637    | 64,003    |
| Thailand              | 43     | 189    | 2,575   | 3,410     | 8,067   | 9,733     | 9,572     |
| Vietnam               | 0      | 2      | 180     | 1,298     | 1,954   | 8,000     | 7,430     |
| WORLD                 | 13,346 | 54,078 | 207,455 | 1,400,541 | 980,727 | 1,309,001 | 1,524,422 |

*Source*: Data extracted 14 Sept. 2012 from <http://www.unctad.org>.

developing East and South East Asia region are Hong Kong, China, Singapore, Korea, and Malaysia (see Table 20.6). Of these, two types of MNE are attracting attention, namely Sovereign Wealth Funds (SWFs) and State-Owned MNEs. Key SWFs in Asia originate mostly from China and Singapore, with five of the top twelve large FDI deals by SWFs in 2010 conducted by three SWFs from these two countries (namely China Investment Corp., Temasek Holdings Pte Ltd., and GIC Real Estate Pte Ltd.). Worldwide, there were 653 state-owned MNEs in 2010, with over 8,500 subsidiaries. Of these, fifty were from China (representing 7.7% of all Chinese MNEs), forty-five from Malaysia (6.9% of Malaysian MNEs) and nine from Singapore (1.4% of Singaporean MNEs). The vast majority of these firms operate in services (UNCTAD 2011).

## Government Policies, FDI Flows and Economic Impact

Overall, countries try and attract FDI by liberalizing the conditions for the admission and establishment of MNEs, or by engaging in FDI promotion generally or selectively, focusing on activities, technologies, or investors. As discussed in the previous section, despite differences in the use of FDI in individual countries' economic

**Table 20.2 Share of inward FDI in gross fixed capital formation (by country, selected years, percentages)**

| % | 1970 | 1980 | 1990 | 2000 | 2005 | 2010 |
|---|---|---|---|---|---|---|
| China | n/a | 0.1 | 3.5 | 10.0 | 8.0 | 4.3 |
| Hong Kong SAR, China | 6.6 | 7.6 | 16.3 | 138.9 | 90.4 | 147.4 |
| Taiwan | 5.0 | 1.3 | 3.4 | 6.1 | 2.0 | 2.7 |
| India | 0.5 | 0.2 | 0.3 | 3.3 | 2.9 | 4.5 |
| Indonesia | n/a | n/a | n/a | n/a | 12.3 | 6.1 |
| Japan | 0.1 | 0.1 | 0.2 | 0.7 | 0.3 | −0.1 |
| Korea, Republic of | 2.9 | 0.1 | 0.8 | 5.6 | 2.9 | 2.9 |
| Lao PDR | 1.2 | 0.0 | 6.1 | 7.3 | 2.9 | 13.8 |
| Malaysia | 16.5 | 11.9 | 17.5 | 16.0 | 14.4 | 18.8 |
| Philippines | −0.1 | 1.1 | 4.4 | 12.5 | 9.0 | 3.2 |
| Singapore | 15.1 | 26.0 | 46.1 | 54.3 | 68.3 | 87.4 |
| Thailand | 2.3 | 2.1 | 7.5 | 12.6 | 15.8 | 12.3 |
| Vietnam | 0.0 | 0.6 | 21.2 | 15.1 | 11.2 | 21.7 |
| WORLD | 1.8 | 1.9 | 4.1 | 20.1 | 9.9 | 9.5 |

*Source*: Data extracted 14 Sept. 2012 from <http://www.unctad.org>.

development path, all countries in the region have established strong independent investment-promotion agencies, which work with the government to improve the investment environment, conduct international marketing, and facilitate investment (Giroud 2007). Governments have also had an influence on the strategies and types of activities conducted by MNEs. In China, strict ownership requirements applied in many sectors until recently. Key policies are either mandatory measures aimed at enhancing the impact of foreign affiliates in host countries, or non-mandatory measures focusing on raising MNEs' contribution by targeting selected strategies and activities. In Singapore, the government has encouraged MNEs to relocate their HQs there with a favourable tax regime. Malaysia has actively encouraged the establishment of high value-added activities, such as R&D centres.

Over the past two decades, East Asian economies have also promoted a competitive environment (Uchida and Cook 2005), by encouraging competition and inter-firm relationships between MNEs and local businesses. These policies are part of mixed strategies adopted by governments, often with the aim of enhancing the competitiveness and technological competencies of local firms. For instance, most governments have established special industrial zones. Singapore (Pereira 2005) and Hong Kong pioneered

**Table 20.3 Share of inward FDI in gross domestic product (by country, selected years)**

| % | 1970 | 1980 | 1990 | 2000 | 2005 | 2010 | 2011 |
|---|------|------|------|------|------|------|------|
| China | n/a | 0.0 | 0.9 | 3.4 | 3.2 | 2.0 | 1.8 |
| Hong Kong SAR, China | 1.3 | 2.5 | 4.3 | 36.6 | 18.9 | 31.7 | 34.1 |
| Taiwan | 1.1 | 0.4 | 0.8 | 1.5 | 0.4 | 0.6 | −0.4 |
| India | 0.1 | 0.0 | 0.1 | 0.8 | 0.9 | 1.4 | 1.6 |
| Indonesia | n/a | n/a | n/a | n/a | 2.9 | 1.9 | 2.2 |
| Japan | 0.0 | 0.0 | 0.1 | 0.2 | 0.1 | 0.0 | 0.0 |
| Korea, Republic of | 0.7 | 0.0 | 0.3 | 1.7 | 0.8 | 0.8 | 0.4 |
| Lao PDR | 0.1 | 0.0 | 0.7 | 2.0 | 1.0 | 5.1 | 5.8 |
| Malaysia | 2.6 | 3.7 | 5.7 | 4.0 | 2.9 | 3.8 | 4.3 |
| Philippines | 0.0 | 0.3 | 1.1 | 2.8 | 1.8 | 0.7 | 0.6 |
| Singapore | 4.8 | 10.3 | 14.4 | 16.5 | 14.4 | 21.8 | 25.1 |
| Thailand | 0.6 | 0.6 | 3.0 | 2.8 | 4.6 | 3.1 | 2.8 |
| Vietnam | 0.0 | 0.1 | 2.8 | 4.2 | 3.7 | 7.7 | 6.2 |
| WORLD | 0.4 | 0.5 | 0.9 | 4.3 | 2.1 | 2.1 | 2.2 |

*Source*: Data extracted 14 Sept. 2012 from <http://www.unctad.org>.

these in the 1960s, followed by Malaysia, Indonesia, and Thailand. Recently, China and Vietnam have initiated special zones providing favourable conditions for foreign and local investors.

While these policies have resulted in the fast growth of manufactured exports and export-led growth, especially in Malaysia, Thailand, and China, with enhanced levels of economic development, countries such as Singapore and Hong Kong are now attracting more investment in the services sector, leading to changes in the role played by MNEs. In less-developed economies, critics are concerned with the minimal impact of MNEs, even if they contribute significantly to exports. As the host economy develops, the jobs that MNEs create involve more skills, and the transfer of technology rises. Again, governments across Asia have developed unique policies to enhance inter-firm relations, for instance by encouraging training.

Governments also play a role in inter-firm relations by targeting specific industries and sectors. Countries in South East Asia have facilitated activities by firms in the textile and garments, as well as electronics, industries. Through its Industrial Master Plans, Malaysia has supported the development of clusters, some with more advanced technologies, such as the Multi-Media Super-Corridor. While the effectiveness of such policies

Table 20.4  Share of inward FDI in merchandise trade (by country, selected years)

| % | 1970 | 1980 | 1990 | 2000 | 2005 | 2010 | 2011 |
|---|---|---|---|---|---|---|---|
| China | n/a | 0.3 | 5.6 | 16.3 | 9.5 | 7.3 | 6.5 |
| Hong Kong SAR, China | 2.0 | 3.6 | 4.0 | 30.7 | 11.6 | 18.2 | 19.4 |
| Taiwan | 4.3 | 0.8 | 2.0 | 3.3 | 0.8 | 0.9 | −0.6 |
| India | 2.2 | 0.9 | 1.3 | 8.5 | 7.7 | 10.9 | 10.6 |
| Indonesia | n/a | n/a | n/a | n/a | 9.7 | 8.7 | 9.4 |
| Japan | 0.5 | 0.2 | 0.6 | 1.7 | 0.5 | −0.2 | −0.2 |
| Korea, Republic of | 7.9 | 0.1 | 1.2 | 5.2 | 2.5 | 1.8 | 0.8 |
| Lao PDR | 1.4 | 0.0 | 7.6 | 10.3 | 5.0 | 19.0 | 18.8 |
| Malaysia | 5.6 | 7.2 | 8.9 | 3.9 | 2.9 | 4.6 | 5.2 |
| Philippines | −0.1 | 2.0 | 6.8 | 5.6 | 4.6 | 2.5 | 2.6 |
| Singapore | 6.0 | 6.4 | 10.6 | 11.3 | 7.9 | 13.8 | 15.6 |
| Thailand | 6.0 | 2.9 | 11.2 | 4.9 | 7.3 | 5.0 | 4.2 |
| Vietnam | 0.9 | 0.5 | 7.5 | 9.0 | 6.0 | 11.2 | 7.9 |
| WORLD | 4.5 | 2.8 | 6.0 | 21.5 | 9.4 | 8.3 | 8.1 |

Source: Data extracted 14 Sept. 2012 from <http://www.unctad.org>.

has not been demonstrated, they do, in part, contribute to the facilitation of inter-firm relationships between MNEs and local businesses.

Finally, governments contribute indirectly to outward FDI policies. For instance, in Singapore, International Enterprise is a unique endeavour to support outward investment projects by firms located in the city-state, whether local or foreign-owned.

# MNE INFLUENCES ON ASIAN BUSINESS SYSTEMS: REVIEW OF STUDIES AND EMPIRICAL EVIDENCE

The previous section discussed the importance of institutional change through liberalization, particularly when considering trade, capital flows, FDI, and business regulations. In this section, we explore in more detail how MNEs have led to changes in selected Asian business systems through their activities and strategies.

## Table 20.5 Share of inward FDI in trade of merchandise and services

| % | 1970 | 1980 | 1990 | 2000 | 2005 | 2010 | 2011 |
|---|------|------|------|------|------|------|------|
| China | n/a | 0.3 | 5.1 | 14.6 | 8.7 | 6.6 | 6.0 |
| Hong Kong SAR, China | 2.0 | 2.8 | 3.3 | 25.6 | 9.5 | 14.3 | 15.1 |
| Taiwan | 4.3 | 0.8 | 1.8 | 2.9 | 0.7 | 0.8 | −0.6 |
| India | 2.2 | 0.7 | 1.0 | 6.1 | 5.0 | 7.0 | 7.3 |
| Indonesia | n/a | n/a | n/a | n/a | 8.4 | 7.9 | 8.5 |
| Japan | 0.5 | 0.2 | 0.5 | 1.5 | 0.4 | −0.1 | −0.2 |
| Korea, Republic of | 7.9 | 0.1 | 1.0 | 4.4 | 2.1 | 1.5 | 0.7 |
| Lao PDR | 1.4 | 0.0 | 5.9 | 6.7 | 3.7 | 14.7 | 15.1 |
| Malaysia | 5.6 | 6.6 | 7.8 | 3.4 | 2.5 | 3.9 | 4.5 |
| Philippines | −0.1 | 1.6 | 4.8 | 5.2 | 4.2 | 2.0 | 2.0 |
| Singapore | 6.0 | 5.1 | 8.5 | 9.3 | 6.3 | 10.5 | 11.9 |
| Thailand | 6.0 | 2.4 | 8.7 | 4.1 | 6.2 | 4.2 | 3.6 |
| Vietnam | 0.9 | 0.4 | 7.0 | 7.6 | 5.3 | 10.1 | 7.2 |
| WORLD | 4.5 | 2.3 | 4.8 | 17.4 | 7.6 | 6.6 | 6.6 |

*Source*: Data extracted 14 Sept. 2012 from <http://www.unctad.org>.

# MNEs, Business Networks and Infrastructure

First, let us consider Asia and global production networks. MNEs have had a significant influence upon the economic specialization of East and South East Asian economies and their integration within global value chains. Trade and investment flows have intensified steadily across the region since Japan, Korea, Taiwan, Hong Kong, and Singapore emerged in the 1960s and 1970s, followed successively by other economies in the region, and more recently the emergence of China and Vietnam. Countries are more integrated, with a division that matches a hierarchical arrangement (in Akamatsu's terms; Ozawa 2005). This is illustrated on Japanese MNEs' investments in the electronics and automobile industries in the region, such as Mitsubishi's goal to build an Asian car. There is no doubt that economic integration across the region, activities of local firms, and the need to adapt to international standards has changed business perceptions and attitudes. Some authors go so far as to suggest that China will become the 'leader of the flock' (Palacios 2008).

If we focus on durable goods, the region is very much perceived nowadays as the world's factory, inasmuch as Asia's share in world durable goods exports has grown from 35 per cent in 2000 to 42 per cent in 2007 (ADB 2012b). Of these durables, the electronics industry constitutes a substantial share of the total (more than 50% of total exports of

**Table 20.6 FDI outflows by country (in million US$, selected years)**

| | 1970 | 1980 | 1990 | 2000 | 2005 | 2010 | 2011 |
|---|---|---|---|---|---|---|---|
| China | n/a | n/a | 830 | 916 | 12,261 | 68,811 | 65,117 |
| Hong Kong SAR, China | 0 | 82 | 2,448 | 59,374 | 27,196 | 95,396 | 81,607 |
| Taiwan | 1 | 42 | 5,243 | 6,701 | 6,028 | 11,574 | 12,766 |
| India | 0 | 4 | 6 | 514 | 2,985 | 13,151 | 14,752 |
| Indonesia | n/a | n/a | n/a | n/a | 3,065 | 2,664 | 7,771 |
| Japan | 355 | 2,385 | 50,775 | 31,557 | 45,781 | 56,263 | 114,353 |
| Korea, Republic of | n/a | 26 | 1,052 | 4,233 | 6,366 | 23,278 | 20,355 |
| Lao PDR | 0 | 0 | 0.2 | 9.9 | −0.1 | 5.7 | 7 |
| Malaysia | 0 | 201 | 129 | 2,026 | 3,076 | 13,329 | 15,258 |
| Philippines | n/a | 86 | 22 | 125 | 189 | 616 | 9 |
| Singapore | 0 | 98 | 2,034 | 6,650 | 11,589 | 21,215 | 25,227 |
| Thailand | n/a | 3 | 154 | −20 | 529 | 5,415 | 10,634 |
| Vietnam | 0 | 0 | 0 | 0 | 65 | 900 | 950 |
| WORLD | 14,151 | 51,590 | 241,498 | 1,226,633 | 888,561 | 1,451,365 | 1,694,396 |

*Source*: Data extracted 14 Sept. 2012 from <http://www.unctad.org>.

durables in 2007 in each country except Vietnam, Indonesia, and Japan). It is therefore noticeable that economies have specialized, predominantly under the spur of economic activities conducted by MNEs along global value chains (see Figure 20.1).

Integration in these value chains has implications in terms of government changes in local rules and regulations, its involvement in developing appropriate technological and logistic infrastructure, the activities local firms are engaged in within countries, the level of skills required, and their resources and competencies.

Second, we ought to consider regional institutional changes. Linked to value-chain activities and links created by MNEs across various subsidiaries located in countries in relation to comparative advantages, the case of ASEAN is worth presenting. Numerous MNEs have slowly taken the benefit of successive liberalization programmes and stages of economic development (Ozawa 2005) in this region, and they have steadily established a complex region-wide network of interdependent activities (Borrus, Ernst, and Stephan 2000; Staples 2008). Subsidiaries are inter-dependent, with complementary activities in the form of regional production networks, found particularly in the automotive and electronics industries. Such MNE strategies have prompted governments in the region to improve the institutional framework that would facilitate such regional networks. Resulting ASEAN economic integration schemes devised to encourage these

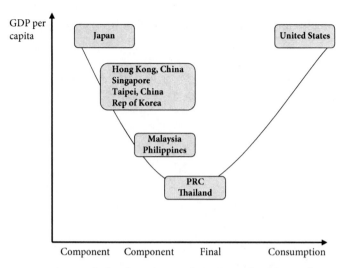

FIGURE 20.1 Stylized structure of GVCs in durable goods

Source: ADB, *Asian Development Outlook* 2012a: 21.

include the ASEAN Investment Area (AIA) (which came to further support the ASEAN Free Trade Area (AFTA) and the ASEAN Industrial Cooperation (AICO) schemes).

Third, local infrastructure does matter. Other actions taken by governments to facilitate region-wide value chains have occurred within countries. In China, the government is engaged in rapidly developing its infrastructure, such as by addressing congestion problems in Shanghai and Shenzhen ports—it is suggested that bottlenecks arise at the border between Shenzhen and Hong Kong, with repeated customs clearances needed because of inconsistent provincial regulations. Boyson and Han (2008: 54) suggest that as a result of integration in global supply chains, China needs to address concerns related to (1) complexity of local laws, regulation, and business practices, (2) poor enforcement, (3) lower environmental, labour, and health and safety standards, (4) governance issues, including lack of accountability, transparency, disclosure, and corruption, (5) insufficient network and transport infrastructure, and (6) technology and awareness gaps. By contrast, Singapore has invested significantly in digital commerce infrastructure, and resorts to technology and advanced management practices. These opposite examples demonstrate how much has changed in Singapore, as against how much remains to be done within China.

In other cases, governments have changed the local infrastructure specifically to facilitate MNE activities. The China–Singapore Suzhou Industrial Park was created in 1994 for a variety of reasons, one of which was to facilitate business activities by Singapore-based MNEs within China. The park nowadays is host to many MNEs, from various countries of origin, and hosts the first Sino-British university (http://www.sipac.gov.cn). The advantage of Suzhou Industrial Park was that many officials could be trained in Singapore, where the cultural divide was not so large. Singaporean firms benefited by setting up much of the infrastructure, and subsequently investing there.

# MNES: FDI and Spillovers

There are many studies on FDI spillovers in Asian emerging markets, with a predominance on China and Indonesia. Studies point to a generally positive spillover effect on local firms' productivity, with variations depending on regional disparities, ownership share of the foreign investor, and horizontal or vertical effects. In the case of China, the nature of FDI has changed with time and liberalization efforts. Spillovers tend to be small when the technology gap between local and foreign firms is too high, or when local firms do not possess sufficient absorptive capacity (Takii 2005).

Once mainly found in the manufacturing sector, MNEs now operate increasingly in more technology-driven activities and engage in R&D. As a result, there has been a significant increase in local firms' productivity, horizontally through an increase in competitive pressures, and vertically, with reallocation of resources such as capital and labour. In fact, most studies find positive spillover effects on local firms (Buckley, Clegg, and Chengqi 2002; Wei and Liu 2006; Liu and Buck 2007; Wang and Kafouros 2009), but it is essential to understand channels or sources of FDI technology spillovers. Tian (2007) finds that while MNE technology spillovers on domestic firms through capital are positive, they do not arise through products and employment. An additional distinction is made by Wang and Li (2007), inasmuch as spillovers do not occur linearly in labour-intensive industries.

One major drawback of MNE activities lies in market-stealing effects, or the confinement of local firms to specific sectors. For instance, in China, some authors suggest that MNEs draw demand away from local firms or confine them to less profitable segments of industry, through the introduction of new differentiated products and of process innovation with improved quality control. There is now empirical evidence suggesting that spillovers will therefore only be positive up to a point, after which the performance of local firms starts to suffer (Buckley, Clegg, and Wang 2007; Wang and Li 2007); the pace at which MNEs invest also matters (Wang and Kafouros 2009).

Variation in spillover is also related to employee experience and the notion that knowledge diffusion is facilitated through human mobility across national borders. Filatotchev et al. (2011) focus on Chinese returnee entrepreneurs, and demonstrate that rather than worrying about brain-drain, the positive effects of Chinese nationals with experience overseas is many-fold. In particular, returnees with advanced technological knowledge have helped to enhance the technological base of Chinese high-tech industries, and they have even had a positive effect on the innovation performance of non-returnee SMEs.

Studies have also explored the ownership patterns of foreign firms. Wei and Liu (2006) state that there are two main types of investors in China, namely overseas Chinese investors from Hong Kong, Macao, and Taiwan (HMT), and others (mostly from OECD countries). They suggest that OECD firms possess superior resources in product and innovation and in technological development, which is why they generate greater inter-industry spillovers, whilst intra-industry spillovers are similar for both types of MNE. They argue, however, that the type of spillover is likely to differ, with HMT firms being more instrumental to the development of indigenous Chinese firms, as their projects are more labour-intensive and more compatible with local Chinese firms' resource endowments. Buckley, Clegg, and Wang (2007) also found that FDI spillovers on Chinese domestic industry depend on the nationality of investors, emphasizing the curvilinearity effect for HMT investors in low-technology sectors. They suggest that decreasing spillover effects result from market stealing, and from the low-technology nature of the industries, combined with the low technological contribution of HMT firms.

## MNEs: Inter-Firm Linkages with Local Firms

Numerous studies have explored inter-firm relations and linkages in various Asian countries. A study by Giroud and Mirza (2010) compared MNE linkages in both the electronics and textile and garment sectors across ASEAN countries, finding that linkages remain low in Malaysia and Thailand, yet higher than in Vietnam and Cambodia. In Malaysia and Thailand, however, MNEs have established clear programmes, including training programmes to enhance the quality and competences of local suppliers.

MNEs show a variety of governance structures, and to explore how they influence local businesses, one needs to consider both the intra- and inter-firm practices and preferences of MNEs. In particular, it is important to understand how formalized the network can be, whether it has defined rules and common business practices, and whether there are shared information practices. In close networks, one expects that an MNE will rely on the skills and knowledge of local business partners, and therefore will also be more inclined to share knowledge. Looking at innovation helps in understanding how changes may occur. MNEs are increasingly decentralizing their R&D and innovation centres. In chip design, there are rising clusters led by MNEs across Asia, such as in Hsinchu and Tainan in Taiwan, the Yangtse River Delta, Beijing, Shenzhen, the Pearl River Delta, and Xían in China (Ernst 2008: 69).

Focusing on electronics companies in Johor and Penang (Malaysia), Oyelaran-Oyeyinka and Rasiah (2009: 91) demonstrate that without sufficient formal support by the local government, the region will remain confined to low value-added activities such as printed-circuit boards, monitor assembly, and the manufacture of ink cartridges and printers. Yet MNEs can only truly impact upon local businesses if real upgrading occurs among the latter. One interpretation of why none of the firms manufactured original brands is that foreign MNEs offshore few high value-added activities, and local firms lack their own competences and the institutional support to expand into R&D activities. Although China benefits from a small number of internationally competitive firms, similarities can be seen. Both Duanmu and Fai (2007) and Ivarsson and Alvstam (2005) suggest that for inter-firm linkages to fully benefit local firms in China, much rests on local firms acquiring sufficient levels of competency.

In the case of the computer industry, Kraemer et al. (2008) describe how focal firms have not only enhanced their own IT systems, but have also extended these applications to suppliers of the contractors, and to the suppliers of their suppliers further up the value chain in both Taiwan and China. In Taiwan, local industry associations and governments have also been proactive in encouraging their members to upgrade their IT systems. The Taiwan government created two plans to create electronic information linkages using the RosettaNet system and XML between PC-makers and ADMs on the one hand (Plan A) and between ODMs and their suppliers on the other hand (Plan B) (Kraemer et al. 2008: 94). IBM, HP, and Compaq participated in Plan A, and overall both plans involved 4000 participants (Kraemer et al. 2008: 102). The RosettaNet was extended to China with the backing of China's Ministry of Science and Technology. Despite such improvements, however, there is no doubt that the structure of information and communications technology (ICT) in the notebook supply-chain remains asymmetric.

Interaction between Western MNEs and Taiwanese and Chinese suppliers has also meant adaptation in terms of perceptions of social relationships. Local business partners favour personal relationships and face-to-face communications. As a compromise, therefore, the network is connected to branded PC-makers through Western-style business transactions, including formal contracts and heavy use of ICT. In the Taiwanese network, however, there is much heavier reliance on personal and informal relationships, or *guanxi*, to coordinate production, logistics, development, and other activities (Kraemer et al. 2008: 110). The notebook example demonstrates how local business partners within the value chain adapt their own business attitudes and methods, not solely Western MNEs. This is further demonstrated by the example of Victor Fung, a Hong Kong clothing and textile executive, who describes himself as being in the supply-chain management business (as opposed to mentioning he works in the textile and clothing industry) (Dee 2008: 233).

Linkage studies have demonstrated that MNEs contribute to capabilities enhancement in local business partners through close business relationships and knowledge exchange, and they also contribute by taking an active part in labour skilling improvements. One such example comes from the PSDC (Penang Skills Development Centre). The centre was established in 1989 and was the first tripartite industry-led skills training and education centre in Malaysia (www.psdc.org.my), involving the CEOs of Motorola, Intel, and Hewlett-Packard. This initiative has now spread to other states in Malaysia, where similar skills-development centres have emerged. Another way through which MNEs impact upon skill levels lies in demand, which can have a profound effect on Asian countries as providers of highly skilled labour. For instance, China now graduates almost four times as many engineers as the US; South Korea, with one-sixth of the population and one-twentieth of the GDP, graduates nearly the same number (Ernst 2008: 63).

# Conclusions, Ways Forward, and Suggestions for Further Theory Development

This chapter is novel in its topic, inasmuch as few, if any, studies have explored the impact of MNEs on Asian business systems. There exist, however, as demonstrated, numerous studies from various disciplines, analysing the impact of MNEs, either on economic development, on local competitive conditions, or specifically in terms of inter-firm relationships across Asian economies. We have highlighted a variety of influences exerted by foreign MNEs, not only on government activities, but also on related institutional environments for local firms to operate in. We have also detailed direct and indirect effects of MNE activities on local businesses and skills across the region.

In reviewing MNE impact, positive aspects have been emphasized, but we also acknowledge that there are concerns that MNE activities may not be sufficient for real prospects of long-term growth, and the short-term benefits may not translate into upgrades of host-country industry to higher value-added and more knowledge-intensive activities (Ernst 2008: 78). Similarly, not all changes related to MNEs are positive: in some cases, they can lead to profound changes in the industrial structure. We therefore suggest caution when examining the means through which MNEs impact upon Asian local business systems.

This chapter does not claim to provide an exhaustive presentation of the macro-politics of MNEs. Rather, it provides a review of all aspects that ought to be considered. First, MNEs are embedded in a variety of business systems, each influencing MNE strategies and activities. Thus, MNEs influence and are influenced by the local environments in which they operate. Second, the literature examining the macro-politics of MNEs is dispersed. There are numerous studies grounded in the business-systems, international business, or international economics literatures. Hence, numerous macro- and micro-economic concepts have been discussed in this chapter. The vast majority of the literature focuses on activities conducted by MNEs from outside the region, though recent studies (as in the case of HMS firms' activities in China) point to the need to also focus on intra-regional multinational activity in Asia. There exist distinct business systems across the regions, and with rising outward FDI from Asian economies—a large share of which is directed towards neighbouring countries—more is to be understood about the intra-regional effect of MNEs on regional business systems. Third, the evidence presented remains somewhat anecdotal and linked to more general impacts of MNEs in terms of integrating Asian economies within Global Value Chains, FDI spillovers, or MNE linkages across and within countries. These studies do not focus specifically on resulting changes in business systems.

This draws our attention to a key gap in the theoretical discourse on MNEs and business systems. There is increasing acknowledgement that MNEs differ from other firms because of the nature and spread of their cross-border activities; they therefore deserve more attention within the business-systems literature. This review has also identified a key gap within the international business literature, as it mostly explores the effect of institutional settings upon MNEs themselves, and little attention is given to how MNEs also impact upon institutions and business systems in individual countries.

To conclude, we suggest that more theoretical development is needed to better understand how MNEs affect (i.e. not just how they are affected by) business systems in countries where they operate.

## REFERENCES

ADB (2012a). *Asian Development Outlook 2012: Confronting Rising Inequality in Asia*. Manila, Asian Development Bank.

—— (2012b). *How Can Asia Respond to Global Economic Crisis and Transformation?* Manila, Asian Development Bank.

Allen, M. and M. L. Aldred (2012). 'Internationalization, Institutions and Economic Growth: A Fuzzy-Set Analysis of the New EU Member States'. In G. Wood and M. Demirbag, Eds., *Handbook of Institutional Approaches to International Business*: 382–407. Cheltenham, Edward Elgar.

Bartlett, C. A. and S. Ghoshal (1998). *Managing across Borders: The Transnational Solution*. Boston, Harvard Business School Press.

Borrus, M., D. Ernst, and H. Stephan, Eds. (2000). *International Production Networks in Asia: Rivalry or Riches?* London & New York, Routledge.

Boyson, S. and C. Han (2008). 'Eras of Enterprise Globalisation: From Vertical Integration to Virtualisation and Beyond'. In J. J. Palacios, Ed., *Multinational Corporations and the Emerging Network Economy in Asia and the Pacific*: 26–57. Abingdon, Routledge.

Buckley, P. J. (2009). 'The Impact of the Global Factory on Economic Development'. *Journal of World Business* 44(2): 131.

—— J. Clegg, and W. Chengqi (2002). 'The Impact of Inward FDI on the Performance of Chinese Manufacturing Firms'. *Journal of International Business Studies* 33(4): 637–55.

—— and C. Wang (2007). 'Is the Relationship between Inward FDI and Spillover Effects Linear? An Empirical Examination of the Case of China'. *Journal of International Business Studies* 38: 447–459.

Cantwell, J. (1989). *Technological Innovation and Multinational Corporations*. Oxford, Basil Blackwell.

—— H. Dunning and S. M. Lundan (2010). 'An Evolutionary Approach to Understanding International Business Activity: The Co-Evolution of MNEs and the Institutional Environment'. *Journal of International Business Studies* 41(4): 567–586.

Cantwell, J. and R. Mudambi (2005). 'MNE Competence-Creating Subsidiary Mandates'. *Strategic Management Journal* 26: 1109–1128.

Castellani, D. and A. Zanfei (2006). *Multinational Firms, Innovation and Productivity*. Cheltenham, Edward Elgar.

Caves, R. E. (1996). *Multinational Enterprise and Economic Analysis*, 2nd ed. Cambridge, Cambridge University Press.

Cuervo-Cazurra, A. and M. Genc (2008). 'Transforming Disadvantages into Advantages: Developing-Country MNEs in the Least Developed Countries'. *Journal of International Business Studies* 39(6): 957–979.

Dee, P. (2008). 'Multinational Corporations and Pacific Regionalism'. In J. J. Palacios, Ed., *Multinational Corporations and the Emerging Network Economy in Asia and the Pacific*: 232–266. Abingdon, Routledge.

Dörrenbächer, C. and M. Geppert, Eds. (2011). *Politics and Power in the Multinational Corporation: The Role of Institutions, Interests and Identities*. Cambridge, Cambridge University Press.

Duanmu, J.-L. and F. M. Fai (2007). 'A Processual Analysis of Knowledge Transfer: From Foreign MNEs to Chinese Suppliers'. *International Business Review* 16(4): 449–473.

Dunning, J. and S. Lundan (2008a). *Multinational Enterprises and the Global Economy*. Cheltenham, Edward Elgar.

—— (2008b). 'Institutions and the OLI Paradigm of the Multinational Enterprise'. *Asia-Pacific Journal of Management* 25(4): 573–593.

Eden, L. and S. R. Miller (2004). 'Distance Matters: Liability of Foreignness, Institutional Distance and Ownership Strategy'. In M. A. Hitt and J. Cheng, Eds., *Advances in International Management*: 187–221. New York, Elsevier.

Ernst, D. (2008). 'Innovation Offshoring: Root Causes of Asia's Rise and Policy Implications'. In J. J. Palacios, Ed., *Multinational Corporations and the Emerging Network Economy in Asia and the Pacific*: 58–88. Abingdon, Routledge.

Filatotchev, I., X. Liu, J. Lu, and M. Wright (2011). 'Knowledge Spillovers through Human Mobility across National Borders: Evidence from Zhongguancun Science Park in China'. *Research Policy* 40(3): 453–462.

Foss, N. J. and J. F. P. Dos Santos (2011). 'A Knowledge System Approach to the Multinational Company: Conceptual Grounding and Implications for Research'. In C. G. Asmussen, T. Pedersen, T. M. Devinney and L. Tohanyi, Eds., *Dynamics of Globalization: Location-Specific Advantages or Liabilities of Foreignness?*: 425–454. Bingley, Emerald Group.

Gentile-Lüdecke, S. and A. Giroud (2012). 'Knowledge Transfer from TNCs and Upgrading of Domestic Firms: The Polish Automotive Sector'. *World Development* 40(4): 796.

Giroud, A. (2007). 'Government Policies towards FDI across East and Southeast Asia: A Comparative Review of Business Policies Encouraging Inter-Firm Relationships between MNEs and Local Firms'. In H. W-C. Yeung, Ed., *Handbook on Research in Asian Business*: 266–284. Cheltenham, Edward Elgar.

—— (2012). 'Mind the Gap: How Linkages Strengthen Understanding of Spillovers'. *European Journal of Development Research* 24(1): 20–25.

—— H. Mirza, (2010). 'MNEs' Linkages in Southeast Asia'. In P. Gugler and J. Chaisse, Eds., *Competitiveness of the ASEAN Countries: Corporate and Regulatory Drivers*: 82–102. Cheltenham, Edward Elgar.

—— H. Mirza, and K. H. We (2012). 'South-South Foreign Direct Investment: Key Role of Institutions and Future Prospects'. In G. Wood and M. Demirbag, Eds., *Handbook of Institutional Approaches to International Business*: 365–381. Cheltenham, Edward Elgar.

Giroud, A. and J. Scott-Kennel (2009). 'MNE Linkages in International Business: A Framework for Analysis'. *International Business Review* 18(6): 555–566.

Ivarsson, I. and C. G. Alvstam (2005). 'Technology Transfer from TNCs to Local Suppliers in Developing Countries: A Study of AB Volvo's Truck and Bus Plants in Brazil, China, India, and Mexico'. *World Development* 33(8): 1325–1344.

Jackson, G. and R. Deeg (2008). 'Comparing Capitalisms: Understanding Institutional Diversity and its Implications for International Business'. *Journal of International Business Studies* 39(4): 540–561.

Jindra, B., A. Giroud, and J. Scott-Kennel (2009). 'Subsidiary Roles, Vertical Linkages and Economic Development: Lessons from Transition Economies'. *Journal of World Business* 44(2): 167–179.

Kogut, B. and U. Zander (1993). 'Knowledge of the Firm and the Evolutionary Theory of the Multinational Operation'. *Journal of International Business Studies* 24: 625–645.

Kostova, T. (1999). 'Transnational Transfer of Strategic Organizational Practices: A Contextual Perspective'. *Academy of Management Review* 24: 308–324.

—— and S. Zaheer (1999). 'Organizational Legitimacy under Conditions of Complexity: The Case of the Multinational Enterprise'. *Academy of Management. The Academy of Management Review* 24(1): 64–81.

Kraemer, K. L., J. Dedrick, W. Foster and Z. Cheng (2008). 'Information and Communication Technologies and Inter-Corporate Production Networks: Global Information Technology and Local Guanxi in the Taiwanese Personal Computer Industry'. In J. J. Palacios, Ed., *Multinational Corporations and the Emerging Network Economy in Asia and the Pacific*: 89–113. Abingdon, Routledge.

Kugler, M. (2006). 'Spillovers from Foreign Direct Investment: Within or Between Industries?'. *Journal of Development Economics* 80(2): 444–477.

Lall, S. (1980). 'Vertical Inter-firm Linkages in LDCs: An Empirical Study'. *Oxford Bulletin of Economics and Statistics* 42: 203–226.

—— and R. Narula (2004). 'Foreign Direct Investment and Its Role in Economic Development: Do We Need a New Research Agenda'. *European Journal of Development Research* 16(3): 445–462.

Li, J. and F. K. Yao (2010). 'The Role of Reference Groups in International Investment Decisions by Firms from Emerging Economies'. *Journal of International Management* 16(2): 143–153.

Liu, X. and T. Buck (2007). 'Innovation Performance and Channels for International Technology Spillovers: Evidence from Chinese High-Tech Industries'. *Research Policy* 36(3): 355–366.

Lorentzen, J., P. Mollgard, and M. Rojec (2003). 'Host Country Absorption of Technology: Evidence from Automotive Supply Networks in Eastern Europe'. *Industry and Innovation* 10(4): 415–432.

Meyer, K. E. (2004). 'Perspectives on Multinational Enterprises in Emerging Economies'. *Journal of International Business Studies* 35(4): 259–276.

—— R. Mudambi, and R. Narula (2011). 'Multinational Enterprises and Local Contexts: The Opportunities and Challenges of Multiple Embeddedness'. *Journal of Management Studies* 48(2): 235–252.

—— and M. W. Peng (2005). 'Probing Theoretically into Central and Eastern Europe: Transactions, Resources, and Institutions'. *Journal of International Business Studies* 36(6): 600–621.

—— and E. Sinani (2009). 'When and Where Does Foreign Direct Investment Generate Positive Spillovers? A Meta-Analysis'. *Journal of International Business Studies* 40(7): 1075–1094.

Morgan, G. (2011). 'Reflections on the Macro-Politics of Micro-Politics'. In C. Dörrenbächer and M. Geppert, Eds., *Politics and Power in the Multinational Corporation: The Role of Institutions, Interests and Identities*: 415–436. Cambridge, Cambridge University Press.

—— (2012). 'International Business, Multinationals and National Business Systems'. In G. Wood and M. Demirbag, Eds., *Handbook of Institutional Approaches to International Business*: 18–40. Cheltenham, Edward Elgar.

—— and R. Whitley (2013). *Capitalisms and Capitalism in the 21st Century*. Oxford, Oxford University Press.

Mudambi, R. and P. Navarra (2002). 'Institutions and International Business: A Theoretical Overview'. *International Business Review* 11(6): 635–646.

Oyelaran-Oyeyinka, B. and R. Rasiah (2009). *Uneven Paths of Development: Innovation and Learning in Asia and Africa*. Cheltenham, Edward Elgar.

Ozawa, T. (2005). *Institutions, Industrial Upgrading, and Economic Performance in Japan: the 'Flying-Geese' Paradigm of Catch-up Growth*. Cheltenham, Edward Elgar.

Palacios, J. J., Ed. (2008). *Multinational Corporations and the Emerging Network Economy in Asia and the Pacific*. Abingdon, Routledge.

Peng, M. W., D. Y. Wang, and Y. Jiang (2008). 'An Institution-Based View of International Business Strategy: A Focus on Emerging Economies'. *Journal of International Business Studies* 39(5): 920–936.

Pereira, A. (2005). 'Singapore's Regionalization Strategy'. *Journal of Asia-Pacific Economy* 10(3): 380.

Redding, G. (2005). 'The Thick Description and Comparison of Societal Systems of Capitalism'. *Journal of International Business Studies* 36(2): 123–155.

—— and M. A. Witt (2006). 'The 'Tray of Loose Sand': A Thick Description of the State-Owned Enterprise Sector of China Seen as a Business System'. *Asian Business and Management* 5(1): 87–112.

Santangelo, G. D. (2009). 'MNCs and Linkages Creation: Evidence from a Peripheral Area'. *Journal of World Business* 44(2): 192–205.

Staples, A. (2008). *Responses to Regionalism in East Asia: Japanese Production Networks in the Automotive Sector* Basingstoke, Palgrave Macmillan.

Takii, S. (2005). 'Productivity Spillovers and Characteristics of Foreign Multinational Plants in Indonesian Manufacturing 1990–1995'. *Journal of Development Economics* 76(2): 521–542.

Teece, D.J. (1977). 'Technology Transfer by Multinational Firms: The Resource Cost of Transferring Technological Know-how'. *Economic Journal 87*: 242–261.

Tian, X. (2007). 'Accounting for Sources of FDI Technology Spillovers: Evidence from China'. *Journal of International Business Studies* 38(1): 147–159.

Uchida, Y. and P. Cook (2005). 'The Transformation of Competitive Advantage in East Asia: An Analysis of Technological and Trade Specialization'. *World Development* 33(5): 701–728.

UNCTAD (2011). *World Investment Report 2011: Non-Equity Modes of International Production and Development*. New York, United Nations.

Wang, C. and Y. Li (2007). 'Do Spillover Benefits Grow with Rising Foreign Direct Investment? An Empirical Examination of the Case of China'. *Applied Economics* 39(3): 397–405.

Wang, C. and M. I. Kafouros (2009). 'What Factors Determine Innovation Performance in Emerging Economies? Evidence from China'. *International Business Review* 18(6): 606–616.

Wei, Y. and X. Liu (2006). 'Productivity Spillovers from R&D, Exports and FDI in China's Manufacturing Sector'. *Journal of International Business Studies* 37: 544–557.

Whitley, R. (2010). 'The Institutional Construction of Firms'. In G. Morgan, J. L. Campbell, C. Crouch, O. K. Pedersen, and R. Whitley, Eds., *The Oxford Handbook of Comparative Institutional Analysis*: 453–495. Oxford, Oxford University Press.

—— G. Morgan, W. Kelly, and D. Sharpe (2003). 'The Changing Japanese MNC'. *Journal of Management Studies 40*: 639–668.

Xu, D. and O. Shenkar (2002). 'Institutional Distance and the Multinational Enterprise'. *Academy of Management Review* 27(4): 608–618.

# CHAPTER 21

# NATIONAL R&D SYSTEMS AND TECHNOLOGY DEVELOPMENT IN ASIA

### ARNOUD DE MEYER

## INTRODUCTION

THROUGHOUT Asia there has been a significant commitment to investment in research and development, though mainly in the fields of the traditional science and technology (S&T). In many of the multi-year plans developed by governments in China, East, and South East Asia it is considered essential to invest in S&T to grow the economy. These good intentions are not always followed through in practice, but there is undeniably an intention to use S&T as a lever to enhance productivity and create wealth.

The translation of investment to real industrial progress is not guaranteed, however, and seems to lag in Asia compared to what has been observed in typical OECD countries in Europe or the USA. This may well be due to countries' inability to absorb the results of their S&T investment. As well as typical difficulties and institutional hurdles in the different societies of Asia, such inability may be the consequence of a lack of institutional support and alignment, and an ill-conceived model of innovation—ill-conceived, because it is rooted in a relatively linear model where science is supposed to precede technological development and later application (be it commercialization or translation into policies). The lack of absorption may well be the consequence of specific difficulties in the region or its cultures, for example the inappropriateness of institutions (and in particular their coordination mechanisms), a lack of market information, a lack of respect for intangibles, the shortage of specific skills, or the hierarchical culture.

Another reason for the lower return on investment in S&T may be the low investment in social sciences, perhaps because they are not seen as very relevant for a developing society. In some instances they may even be considered dangerous to central authority, as they may question political traditions. Innovation requires investment in R&D

in S&T, but also investments in business models, design, etc. The lack of social-science research in Asia leaves industrial development often quite skewed.

In the following pages some characteristics of Asian R&D investment will be reviewed, and some specific opportunities and challenges indicated. We will examine how the impact of investment in R&D and innovation can be improved, leading to suggestions for further research.

# Literature Review and Observations

## Investing in R&D to Stimulate Growth

Investment in R&D, in particular in S&T, is anchored in a strong conviction that such investment will lead to productivity improvements and later to economic growth. Early work by Mansfield (1972) concluded that investment in R&D and the creation of R&D capital had led to output growth in a variety of industries in the USA and Japan. Similar observations have been made for other OECD countries, for example Australia, France, and Germany (Nadiri 1993; Link and Spiegel 2003).

The need to invest in R&D has also been supported by much of the work on the 'middle-income trap', that is, the observation that countries can grow to a middle-income level by adding capital to human resources, but that to go beyond this level of development, they need to invest in innovation. This was illustrated in the recent World Bank's report on China 2030 (World Bank 2012), and the concept has been used by many governments to justify the allocation of resources to R&D.

In Singapore, work on the relationship between R&D and productivity was reproduced and tested by Ho, Wong, and Toh (2009). They found that in Asia, R&D investment had a significant impact on total factor productivity (TFP). Specifically for Singapore they found, on the basis of a database covering the period 1978–2001, that a 1 per cent increase in the stock of R&D capital led to a 1.33 per cent increase in TFP. Over the long run, a 1 per cent increase in R&D stock led to an 8.14 per cent increase in TFP. The mean lag between investment and impact on GDP was about 5.12 years for Singapore.

These observations compare negatively to the long-run elasticities of 17.1 per cent (for public R&D), and a mean lag of 4.55 years for sixteen OECD countries, as estimated by Guellec and Van Pottelsberghe (2001). They also contrast with the results of Madden, Savage, and Bloxham (2001), who found for six Asian countries that the impact of domestic R&D stock accumulation was higher in a bloc of Asian countries than in two groups of advanced industrialized nations. These numbers were, however, doubtless distorted by the inclusion of the Republic of Korea (hereafter Korea), with its very high R&D intensity and GDP level.

The exact returns for Singapore are probably not that relevant, but it is interesting to note that the productivity impact of R&D investment seems be lower for young economies, compared to established economies (Birdsall and Rhee 1993). Ho, Wong, and Toh (2009) argue that this lower performance may be due to a relatively lower level of private R&D investment in Asia, compared to older industrialized nations. Elsewhere I have argued that translating the results of R&D into innovation (which will lead to productivity improvement and growth) is more difficult in Asia because of an industrial organization and institutional framework which is not well suited to creativity and innovation (De Meyer and Garg 2005).

Assumptions about translation may be poorly guided by a linear model of how R&D results translate into market or policy applications. The current model in most countries in Asia has been inspired by the US model of research universities, the role played by the National Science Foundation, and the apparently easy interfaces between research institutions and business. This has led to a somewhat simplistic view that governments only need to invest in upstream research, and somehow the research outcomes will automatically translate to private business and state-owned enterprises, which will use those results of outcomes to improve productivity and create new products and processes. This has proved idealistic. First of all, the process is clearly not linear, but rather a concurrent development of science and technology and business or policy application. Second, this concurrent development and mutual nurturing requires organizations to act as intermediaries, something often lacking in the different countries in Asia.

## Institutional Influence on R&D Systems

Investments in R&D and S&T across Asia are no doubt also influenced by the different institutional contexts. Hall and Soskice (2001) argue that the difference between countries where coordination between industrial actors happens through liberal markets or through non-market coordination provides countries with a comparative advantage in developing either radical innovation (in the case of coordination through markets), or incremental innovation (in the case of non-market coordination). They illustrated this with some evidence from the European Patent Office, comparing the USA and Germany. Obviously the question arises whether this hypothesis applies in Asia.

Over the last decade there have been several thorough empirical tests of this proposition, with rather disappointing results. Most scholars remain respectful of the original model and hypothesis formulated by Hall and Soskice, as illustrated by the fact that several of these studies actually accept the original classification of OECD countries as liberal or coordinated market economies. But Schneider and Paunescu (2012) point out that this classification may not be correct, and that, at least for smaller countries, classification as one or the other may evolve over time. Even when adhering to the original classification, Taylor (2004) shows through an extensive analysis of US patents and science citations that predictions based on Hall and Soskice are not supported when the USA is excluded from the analysis. Taylor argues that the USA is so different from other countries that results from any analysis that includes the USA become highly skewed. Akkermans, Castaldi, and Los (2009) also had to largely reject the original hypothesis, except for the fact that economies that coordinate though markets actually have more patents that cite earlier patents from a higher variety of sectors. Hermann and Peine (2011) focused on the pharmaceutical sector in Germany, Italy, and the UK, and came to the conclusion that radical innovation indeed requires scientists and employees with more generalist skills (as one would find in economies coordinated through markets), while incremental product innovation requires employees and scientists with specific skills. Yet they do not find significant differences between these three countries in the number of companies pursuing radical or incremental innovation. While they do not provide a strong argument why this is the case, we can hypothesize that pharmaceutical companies are highly internationalized, such that home-country institutions play a less important role than in other industries.

There is no doubt that innovation and innovation policies will be determined by the institutions in each country. However, the original Hall and Soskice hypothesis may suffer from simplification about the process of innovation. Taylor (2004: 628) argues that the original 'varieties of capitalism' hypothesis is 'perhaps not wrong, but innovation is special because states play such an important role.... Bringing the firms to the centre stage is not wrong, but perhaps more than for other firm's activities, the state plays an important role as a market maker'.

A further simplification may well be that the original hypothesis recognized only two forms of capitalism. Schneider and Paunescu (2012) cluster four different groups: the original liberal and coordinated markets, plus a hybrid form (to which Japan and Korea belong) and a group of state-dominated economies. One can wonder where most Asian economies would figure. For example, it is fair to assume that both China and India would fall into the category of state-dominated economies (with respect to innovation at least), while Singapore, Malaysia, and Indonesia may well be in the hybrid category, following the example set by Japan and Korea.

Carney, Gedajlovic, and Yang (2009) also formulate three significant limitations to the 'varieties of capitalism' hypothesis when applied to Asia—they do not see an emblematic Asian firm. They speculate that there are more than two types of capitalism in Asia, and argue that in Asia institutions are often weak and evolving. Therefore, it seems more interesting to them to understand how firms and institutions co-evolve and how companies influence institutions. They also raise the question of how traditional diversified and family-controlled firms in Asia partly align themselves with national institutions, but also try to escape to a transnational space in order to become less dependent on the institutional whims of their local government (Witt and Lewin 2007).

From the perspective of a scholar of innovation management, the original 'varieties of capitalism' hypothesis also has limitations. It does not take into account that over the last ten years innovation has become much more global, combining technological and market inputs from all over the world (Doz, Santos, and Williamson 2001). This will be discussed in the next section. Second, it focuses mainly on the behaviour of the workforce, while innovation is also built on cumulative organizational knowledge and the active management of this organizational knowledge (Nonaka and Takeuchi 1995). The distinction between incremental and radical innovation and medium- and high-tech industries is, at the level of the firm, also less relevant. Radical innovations often require a large variety of incremental innovations in production, distribution, or business models to become successful in the market. The definition of incremental or radical is for the individual firm a very relative concept: what is incremental for one firm may be radical for another.

It thus appears that when we analyse R&D systems in Asia, we see that these systems will be influenced by existing or developing institutions, but that it is not straightforward to apply the original hypothesis about innovation as formulated by Hall and Soskice (2001). The systems are determined by the administrative heritage of each of the Asian countries. The former colonial regimes, be they Great Britain for Singapore, India or Malaysia, the Netherlands for Indonesia, or Japan for Korea and Taiwan, have left administrative systems for education and applied research that may still influence R&D systems today. The influence of allies, such as the Soviet Union for both China and India, has equally determined today's R&D systems. These systems and institutions were, however, often weak and have evolved over recent decades under the influence of strong companies and political institutions.

Both Taylor (2004) and Akkermans, Castaldi, and Los (2009) offer interesting additional but speculative hypotheses. Taylor mentions, on the basis of his empirical analysis, that the most innovative countries are those that have the strongest military and economic ties with the USA, that is, international relations with the USA are an important factor in explaining innovation. Akkermans, Castaldi, and Los speculate that specialization (and the comparative advantage of a country with respect to innovation) may well be the result of the cumulative nature of knowledge. This last hypothesis is very much aligned with the innovation management literature.

## Other Changes in the Global and Asian R&D Environment

The conceptual and linear model that leads governments to invest in local R&D in S&T, in the expectation that this will somehow translate to more applications and entrepreneurial activities, is further complicated by an evolution in the global landscape for R&D and innovation. Asia plays a particular and crucial role in this evolution. There are at least three major shifts:

a. *A clear shift in sources of innovation*: Thirty years ago, management scholars worked with a rather simple but effective 'international product lifecycle' model that argued that most innovations would be initiated in the USA, would then be rolled out in middle-income countries in Europe (and Japan), followed by a gradual diffusion in developing countries (Vernon 1966; Hill 2007). Its basic premise was that innovations would start in a limited number of places. For all practical purposes, this was correct: most sophisticated lead customers were concentrated in certain places (mainly the USA), and technological developments were also limited to a few places: Boston, Silicon Valley, or Texas for semiconductor development, Basel and a few places in the UK, Germany, and the USA for pharmaceuticals, etc. This model has been revolutionized. Sources of innovation (whether technological or market-driven) have been diffused. For example, in a recent projection reported by the European Institute for Strategic Studies (ISS 2012) in Paris, spectacular growth was predicted in the middle classes in the coming twenty years. But this growth would be uneven: decline in the USA and Europe, modest growth in Latin America and Africa, but strong growth in Asia, where the current middle class of about 525 million is expected to grow to 1,740 million in 2020 and 3,225 million in 2030. These consumers will express their consumer preferences, and thus Asia has the potential to become a dominant force in defining needs, fashions, and consumer trends. R&D institutes in Asia, which nowadays have to cater to expressed or unexpressed needs far away, will see the source of information about markets move closer. At the same time, Asian investment in R&D multiplies sources of technology. Producing research output is no longer the oligopoly of a few top-quality institutions in the USA and Europe: there are now pockets of excellence in Asia in, for example, biotechnology (Korea, Singapore), agricultural technology (Thailand), or semiconductors and electronics (Singapore, Malaysia, Taiwan). A bibliometric analysis of ASEAN research strengths (Hassan et al. 2011) provides a very good insight into the respective strengths of ASEAN research institutions compared with the EU, Japan, Korea, or China and supports the observation that we are witnessing a gradual dispersion of technological resources.

b. *Technological developments now happen more in networks or ecosystems than in centralized R&D departments or institutes*: Private R&D was until recently one of the last bastions of centralization. R&D was closely guarded and protected, and its location often close to headquarters (De Meyer and Mizushima 1989). In the last decade, however, we have seen private investors reducing their investment in R&D. Wanting a higher return on their investment, they have either moved R&D to environments where it can be done faster (Williamson and Zeng 2007) or cheaper, or have outsourced R&D. Innovation and R&D are now performed in networks or eco-systems (Williamson and De Meyer 2012) with many geographically distributed partners. It is not the place here to dwell on the difficulties of implementing such eco-systems, but it is clear that this trend offers opportunities for companies and research institutes in Asia. It is no wonder that we see a gradual increase in the number of MNC research laboratories in India and China (Nadjou and Prabhu 2012). Many of these laboratories have a complex set of functions: low-cost development, tapping into local markets of ideas, or just developing new ideas more efficiently. Different countries in Asia have different competitive advantages in attracting or creating such laboratories. The biggest challenge in turning opportunity into reality is the ability of these laboratories to integrate themselves into global networks. One consequence of the dispersion of sources and capabilities is that the development of products, process, and services is often scattered and fragmented. Narrow research ideas and technological developments from different sources need to be integrated, and one single laboratory can rarely develop a full product or process (Doz, Santos, and Williamson 2001). International collaboration in ecosystems that combine private and public institutions becomes a real imperative in order to be effective. Our section on empirical observations will mainly focus on national differences, but we need to recognize that because of the internationally linked nature of R&D, an analysis based on national differences is only one lens through which to observe the development of R&D systems.

c. *Real innovation is shifting from products or processes towards business-model innovation*: There are many reasons for such a shift. It may be the increasing sophistication of consumers wanting solutions for their problems, rather than products. It may be the decreasing willingness of business to invest in fixed assets that are not core to the business, and desire to lease the assets with services included. This is the consequence of a dramatic shift in the availability of resources: we come out of a world with a relative abundance of raw materials and energy and scarcity of information, and we have moved towards a world with an increasing scarcity of raw materials and energy and a sudden abundance (if not overload) of information. This has led among other consequences to a consumerisation of information technology and systems (Moschella et al. 2004), and an increased importance placed on the combination of products/processes with the intelligent use of information. This has two major effects for R&D in Asian countries. First, information flows do not stop at geographical borders or organizational boundaries, and an R&D lab in a remote area with access to a good broadband connection may be as well placed as a lab in the capital of an industrialized country to tap into the latest ideas for business models. Second, business models are always influenced by local laws and regulations and cultural traditions. This may provide an early lead to the application of new business-model insights to operators in emerging countries. The example of telecom operators in the Philippines, for example Globe or Smart, is often cited to illustrate how they could use the technological advances made elsewhere to their advantage in their own institutional and regulatory framework in the development of early mobile-payment systems or the growth in SMS usage (De Meyer and Garg 2005).

For R&D and technology systems in Asia, these trends provide a growing advantage and challenge: advantage in the sense that they are developing at the geographical heart of a source of ideas that is growing in importance and relevance; challenge in the sense that it forces them to re-invent a new model of innovation, one where research, technology development, and application in business or government need to develop in parallel and in networks with different degrees of strength in ties. As suggested by Carney, Gedajlovic, and Yang (2009), it will require companies and other actors in the political economy to redefine and develop the institutions that enable this new type of innovation.

# Empirical Observations

## Some Comparative Statistics

In Table 21.1, I have brought together some key indicators on the R&D intensity of selected Asian countries. While this enables us to look at some comparative data, it goes almost without saying that we have very different countries with very different systems. Between the two largest countries and a city-state like Singapore there are huge differences in terms of volume. Countries are also at very different stages of development. Korea, Japan, and Singapore are industrialized nations, while China, Indonesia, and India are in different stages of industrial development and thus have quite different R&D systems. We should also recognize that these countries have a very different administrative heritage: Singapore and Malaysia build on British traditions, Indonesia's universities and research institutions go back to the Dutch, China borrowed the Soviet Union's system of Academies of Sciences, India combines a British administrative framework with influence from the Soviet Union, etc.

Let us start with some general comments. Global Expenditure on Research and Development (GERD) varies strongly from one country to another. It may be interesting to keep in mind that one of the EU's goals for 2020 is to have 3 per cent of its GDP

### Table 21.1 Some key figures for 2008 on R&D in selected countries

| Country | Public expenditure on education (% of GDP) | Total R&D personnel (2008) | Researchers per million inhabitants | GERD (2008) as % of GDP | Applied research (%) | Basic research (%) |
|---|---|---|---|---|---|---|
| China | n/a | 1,965,357 | 1199 | 1.47 | 12.5 | 4.8 |
| Hong Kong | 4.5 | 22,053 | 2663 | 0.73 | | |
| Singapore | 3.0 | 33,165 | 5833 | 2.66 | 25.3 | 17.0 |
| Republic of Korea | 4.2 | 294,439 | 4946 | 3.36 | 19.6 | 16.1 |
| Japan | 3.5 | 882,739 | 5189 | 3.45 | 21.7 | 11.4 |
| Indonesia | 2.8 | 21,272 | 89 | 0.08 | | |
| Malaysia | 4.1 | 13,415 | 364 | 0.63 | 45.1 | 11.3 |
| India | 3.1 | 391,149 | 136 | 0.77 | 25.1 | 18.1 |

Source: UNIDO 2012.

put towards R&D. Table 21.1 shows Indonesia spends a very small percentage of GDP on R&D, while both Korea and Japan spend more than 3 per cent. Singapore and China are somewhere in the middle (though we will see later that Singapore is moving up fast), while the other countries spend less than 1 per cent. Also, China has been increasing its spending and between 2005 and 2008 increased its R&D spend from 1.32 to 1.47 per cent of its GDP.

The last two columns indicate how the spending is allocated. I only looked at the distinction between basic and applied research (excluding others as well as military spending). Relatively speaking, India, Singapore, and Korea spend more on basic research. In the case of India, this reflects the strengths of some of the top research laboratories and IITs, whose research has traditionally been quite focused on basic research. In the case of Singapore and Korea, this is aligned with the emphasis of both countries on developing a set of top-class universities.

Japan and Malaysia focus, again in relative terms, more on applied research. Indeed, Japanese universities have a strong research tradition, but the strength of Japan's research is in its application in industry (OECD 2011). The low percentage for both basic and applied research in China probably suggests strong spending on military research.

Financial resources are important, but in R&D we also need to understand the deployment of personnel. Ideas are created by people. The table confirms what we all know: the sheer size of the Chinese R&D workforce. With 1.965 million people working in R&D, it beats the capacity of any other country. Of these 1.965 million, 1.396 million (71%) are deployed in business enterprises (though this includes SOEs, State-Owned Enterprises). Similar percentages of around 70 per cent of personnel employed in business enterprises can also be observed for Japan and Korea. In Singapore this drops to 59 per cent (about 19,703 of the 33,165), indicating the government's stronger role in Singapore R&D.

Interesting also is the number of R&D personnel per million inhabitants. Singapore and Japan lead clearly the pack, with more than 5,000 researchers per million; Korea is a close follower, with more than 4,900 researchers per million. Behind them we see a quick drop to mid-two thousand for Hong Kong, slightly more than 1,000 in China, and then a significant drop for the other selected countries. India, with a similar population to China, is clearly lagging in its number of researchers, and has one-fiftieth the capacity (in relative terms) of Singapore or Japan, and only about one-tenth the capacity of China.

The country showing the biggest change over the last five years is China, where R&D personnel per million inhabitants grew from 855 in 2005 to 1,198 in 2008.

These figures confirm some traditional views on the different countries. Singapore and Korea are both investing heavily in developing their capacity to execute basic research, and have the ambition to transform their universities into world-class institutions. Japan's industry is strong in driving R&D towards application. In light of the speculative hypothesis formulated by Taylor (2004), it is interesting to observe that these three economies are among the closest allies of the USA.

India traditionally has strengths in basic research, concentrated in a few top-class institutions, but its overall R&D capacity is limited. This may be a reflection of the weakness of national institutions. China's sheer size in R&D beats everybody else, and is rapidly increasing in capacity, most of which is still oriented towards military-related applications.

# SELECTED COUNTRY CASES[1]

The following sections offer a short and somewhat biased view of the R&D system in a few typical countries.

## Singapore

The city-state of Singapore has invested heavily in R&D in order to make the transition from a manufacturing-based to a service and knowledge economy. The government has set an ambitious target to raise R&D expenditure to 3.5 per cent of GDP by 2015. In the current five-year plan, announced by the Ministry of Trade and Industry in September 2010, S$13.55bn was earmarked for government-sponsored R&D.

As R&D priorities, the government has opted to focus on what it feels are its national requirements, for example the development of a biotechnology hub, alternative and renewable energy (to counter its lack of resources), ICT, and electronics. These priorities change over time. For example, research in electronics engineering accounted for half of spending in 2008, but a year later had dropped to only 33 per cent.

Oversight on R&D investment is shared by several ministries. The Ministry for Education is in charge of funding R&D at the four research universities (National University of Singapore, Singapore Management University, Nanyang Technological University, and Singapore University for Technology and Design). The Ministry for Technology and Industry (MTI) oversees A*STAR, and the Ministry of Health oversees medical research centres. The National Research Foundation reports directly to the Cabinet.

Two institutions are of particular importance. A*STAR is an agency of MTI that combines the role of developing Singapore's research strategy with a significant proportion of the actual research. In combining these, it stands out: in many OECD countries the role of setting and executing government strategy would probably be separate. However, this mixing of roles is characteristic of other Singapore institutions.

A*STAR has two research councils (biomedical and engineering science), and has invested in efforts to commercialize R&D results. One particular characteristic of A*STAR (and the universities) is openness to foreign talent. Of its research staff, more than half are from overseas, and it has succeeded in attracting some global leaders, particularly in biosciences and nanotechnology.

The second institution is the National Research Foundation, whose major achievements to date are investments in Research Centres of Excellence at local universities and the establishment of CREATE, a campus that welcomes several overseas research institutions, from Switzerland, Israel, Germany, UK, and USA (most in collaboration with research teams from local universities). This is an interesting experiment, because it is probably the first time that researchers from many different institutions are co-located on one campus and on such a scale.

Next to these government-driven agencies and initiatives, Singapore's government has also created an industrial infrastructure to support R&D for local and international business. Two hubs were created: Biopolis (a biomedical hub) and Fusionopolis (a technology hub, with a strong ICT and media concentration). Both were created as integrated units where work and living are combined. These concepts were based on earlier less successful experiences with research parks.

Singapore's R&D investments are similar to many of its other policies: it is driven by the government, in strong alignment with the country's priorities, open to foreign institutions, researchers, and investment, and with a business-like approach. There was initially a heavy emphasis on basic research, but currently there is increased debate over the need to translate research results into value creation for the overall economy.

One of the relative weaknesses of Singapore's R&D strategy is the low emphasis on social-science research. Most investments have gone into 'hard' science and technology, and little attention has been paid to research that can serve the service sector, or that enquires into the impact of scientific and technological developments on society.

# Indonesia

Indonesia, a giant in terms of population, is at the other end of the spectrum to Singapore in terms of investment in R&D. As we can see from the indicators above, investment in R&D, number of researchers, and even number of patents are low. This is actually a relative reduction compared to the situation before the global financial crisis of 2007–2009 when Minister (later President) Habibie was known for focused and bold projects, investing in areas such as satellite communication, aeronautics, and some specific investments in the energy sector.

Indonesia has always paid lip service to the role of R&D in its economic development, but even in 2010 it still allocated a relatively small sum to R&D, compared to its size and GDP. Current President Yudhoyono has indicated several times that this should be raised to an adequate level, without really indicating objectives.

Responsibility for investment in R&D and S&T is the State Ministry of Science and Technology (RISTEK), and it has adopted the concept of a National Innovation System with the objective of creating a 'solid system of innovation for increasing global competitive ability'. Recent five-year plans for Indonesia have objectives such as: (SEA-EU-NET 2012b: 12)

- 'To sharpen R&D priorities in S&T to be oriented towards the demands of the private sector and the needs of society, following a clear roadmap;
- Enhance S&T capacity and capability by strengthening S&T institutions, resources, and networks at central and regional levels;

- Create a suitable innovation climate with an effective incentive scheme to foster industrial restructuring;
- implant and foster an S&T culture in order to enhance Indonesia's civil development.'

Similar to Singapore (and other countries in the region), Indonesia's R&D priorities are focused on national needs, such as food security, renewable energy, transportation, ICT, medicine, and defence, and—specifically for a country prone to earthquakes, tsunamis, and other natural disasters—disaster risk reduction.

The challenge for Indonesia's R&D investment is the fragmentation of its S&T policy and organization. Several ministries other than RISTEK are involved in policy-setting and some agencies report directly to the President. In addition to coordinating agencies such as the Agency for the Assessment and Application of Technology, there are several research institutes, of which some of the most important are the Indonesian Institute of Sciences (LIPI) and the Eijkman Institute of Molecular Biology.

In 2002 a National Research Council was established to better coordinate the different agencies, institutions, and programmers. The NRC is an advisory body and acts as an intermediary between the national research agenda and industry needs. This Council has a number of regional councils charged with coordinating regional policies on R&D.

Indonesia is no doubt a complex society and a big country, with important regions. There is clearly a need for a relatively complex set of organizations and infrastructure to support R&D investment. Current R&D and S&T policies, however, suffer from a lack of coordination, the absence of a real innovation agenda and policy, and relatively poor basic hard-, soft-, and orgware. This last item, building capacity among institutional actors when new technology is being adapted, is particularly important. The education system still needs significant improvements (and investment), the physical infrastructure is lacking (with some notable exceptions), and the regulatory and legal framework for protecting and enforcing intellectual property is still underdeveloped.

# China

The development of R&D investment in China is quite different from Indonesia. For more than twenty years there has been constantly growing investment towards improving higher education and the research environment.

For any observer, the commitment of the Chinese government to higher education is striking. There are over 2,000 universities and colleges in China, and enrolment in higher education has boomed: in 2006, fresh enrolment in universities stood at 5.46 million.

Of course, not all universities are of high quality and carry out research, but the nearly-100 universities that report to the education or other ministry are gradually performing to international levels. They are building on the capabilities of returning talent and investing heavily in improving PhD education. Many universities are now looking for joint PhD supervision with quality universities overseas, rather than relying solely on returning PhDs and existing faculty. They use the networks of faculty from overseas to increase rapidly the quality of their own tertiary education.

The indicators and more detailed numbers provided above indicate that the Chinese government is stepping up its investment in R&D in general. In 2008, R&D expenses were 1.47 per cent of GDP, from only 0.57 per cent in 1996. Given the fast pace of economic growth, this is a remarkable rate, often of more than 20 per cent per year.

The returns on these investments are not always clear. There are some success stories of research-based companies, like Huawei in the telecom sector or Lenovo in PCs, and this is illustrated by the expansion of high-tech exports. Some more critical observers, however, will note that a high percentage of export products are produced by subsidiaries of foreign firms and are often assemblies of imported high-tech components.

Investment by Chinese firms and the government in basic research is low, as indicated in Table 21.1, and actually lower in percentage terms than at the beginning of the 2000s. In consequence, the Chinese economy has not yet built a strong capabilities base that allows Chinese companies to compete on a global scale in high-tech products and solutions. There is no doubt that China has become a sophisticated manufacturing base for the world, but this may become more a curse than a blessing if it cannot develop its R&D competencies to develop the breakthrough products that will help it escape the middle-income trap.

Notwithstanding the apparent weakness in basic research, there are more positive indicators. In a recent issue of the *McKinsey Quarterly*, dedicated to 'Innovation in China', Orr and Roth (2012) argued that China could rapidly become a hotbed for innovation, not only in industries often appearing in the popular press (e.g. wind turbines, solar power), but also by exploiting domestically oriented consumer electronics, instant messaging, and online gaming. They state that the strength of the Chinese innovation system is the government's emphasis on indigenous innovation and the role of the government as a sophisticated buyer, but they also recognize the weaknesses: a lack of analytical understanding in consumers, corporate cultures that do not support risk-taking, scarcity of internal collaboration, and a huge difficulty in retaining talent. In my own empirical observations I have noted that Chinese companies have a real advantage in what I have called the 'spiral model' of innovation (Dutta, De Meyer, and Srivastawa 2001), that is, gradually improving the product or process based on constant feedback from customers and suppliers, but we have yet to see a lot of disruptive or conceptual innovations coming out of China. Williamson and Zeng (2007) have described in detail how this spiral approach has been refined and honed into cost-efficient innovation.

In their impressive research on the Chinese innovation system, Breznitz and Murphree (2011) describe in detail how the innovation and R&D system in China is not homogeneous: there are significant differences in institutions and culture between Beijing, Shanghai, and Guangzhou. Beijing is more driven by government investment, Shanghai is the city of large corporations and big laboratories, and Guangzhou is an entrepreneurial hotbed. It would be interesting to investigate how these differences appear in cities like Chengdu and Wuhan. They also qualify their work by arguing that their analysis cannot be limited to China: the industry is now typified by global linkages, and in particular in China one sees companies compensating for weakness in fundamental research with linkages abroad. Therefore, even for a large country like China, one cannot limit the analysis of R&D and innovation to a purely national level.

As one would expect for a country like China, there is no single approach to R&D development. The government is pumping money into education and research, and spends apparently a significant amount on defence research. However, the provinces have their own input, and the different regions have developed in their own idiosyncratic ways. The strength of the R&D and S&T system is the growing quality of the educational system, the speed and flexibility of innovation, and the gradually growing openness to foreign and returning talent. The big question-mark is to what extent China will be able to claim its fair share of basic research and the ensuing scientific breakthroughs.

## Malaysia

Malaysia is an interesting case because it shows some of the characteristics of Singapore and Indonesia. It early declared that R&D would be important for its industrial development. It has succeeded in transforming itself from an exporter of agricultural commodities to a leading assembler and producer in electronic and IT-based products, processes, and services. Based on its agricultural heritage, it has also developed some interesting inroads into agro- and pharma- biotech.

Malaysia's government loves five-year plans. In successive plans since the beginning of the 1990s, the central importance of knowledge for national development has been emphasized. At the same time, one can witness in more recent times an emphasis on regional development, such as the creation of development corridors in the East, the South, close to Singapore (Iskandar), and the Sarawak Corridor for renewable energy.

Compared to other nations in ASEAN (except Singapore), Malaysia has invested relatively more in R&D and in education. Its investment in universities may not have followed the same pattern as Singapore, but there have been significant improvements, and the country has been able to attract some decent overseas universities from the UK and Australia.

The Malaysian government created in 1986 a centralized grant scheme for research projects. This has evolved over the years and has been complemented with initiatives like the Science Fund, to stimulate investment in ICT, biotechnology, industrial applications, etc., and a Techno Fund to help in pre-commercialization and the acquisition of IP.

Like Singapore, Malaysia wants to attract more international talent (in particular by incentivizing overseas Malaysians to return or to contribute to the local economy), and it encourages inward technology transfer. It has also developed some excellent infrastructure to support innovative companies, in particular in the corridors mentioned above.

Policies are mostly formulated by the Ministry of Science, Technology and Innovation (MOSTI). There is a National Council for Research and Development that has an advisory and coordination role, and which has representatives from universities and public research institutes.

Malaysia is an interesting case for students of innovation policies, because the country runs a real risk of the middle-income trap. It has successfully industrialized and invested a reasonable amount of resources and energy in R&D on S&T. It has also adapted quite well its R&D policies to its federalized organization and politics. It has better coordination than, for example, Indonesia. The real question is whether its investments are sufficient to escape the middle-income trap and whether its policies provide enough incentives for its excellent scientific diaspora to return.

## South Korea

An OECD report on Korea's innovation system (OECD 2009) mentions that the country seeks to move from a catch-up to a creative innovation system, as formulated in its 2004 National Implementation plan for the Innovation System. The catch-up model concentrated on large-scale strategic development, with government-affiliated research institutes and large global conglomerates (*chaebol*) taking a leading role. This, however, has not led to many creative start-ups, technology transfer, or the creation of real research capabilities. The creative model relies on strongly increased spending on R&D and on attempts to improve knowledge flows across the system.

Korea has suffered in the past from poor coordination between the different agencies and ministries in charge of innovation. Successive governments have put in place elaborate mechanisms to deal with these issues and now two super-ministries have the greatest influence on innovation policy: MEST, responsible for the public science base and education, and MKE, responsible for industrial technology R&D and cluster policy.

The OECD report observes that the objective of moving towards a more creative innovation system is in fact not new (and had been the goal in earlier plans), but that the institutions have problems: difficulty escaping the strong influence of *chaebol*, an emphasis on short-term industrially oriented research, a weakly developed university research capacity, an under-utilization of women in the workforce, and a relatively weak internationalization of domestic research. The OECD made a number of interesting recommendations to overcome these problems. They argue, among other things, for better inter-ministerial coordination, and broadening of areas of specialization, a change in research performance indicators, promotion of innovation in the business sector, more mobility in the workforce, and better integration of women in S&T.

## Taking Stock

Having made brief reference to some statistics and detailed cases, we can draw some preliminary conclusions:

a. All countries in Asia share a similar goal to invest in R&D as a core strategy for economic growth. However, we can see that while Singapore is indeed applying

the conceptual script to invest in research, then development, followed by application, China focuses on development and pays relatively less attention to basic
research, while others, such as Indonesia, seem only to pay lip-service to the
whole process of R&D in S&T.

b. The overall result of these diverse efforts has been in fact positive. Asia's research
capability and output has been growing rapidly: investments, patent applications, publications in scientific journals, and number of research institutions are
rapidly rising (Hassan et al. 2011; Huang 2010).

c. There are huge differences in levels of investment across the different countries.
Some of these differences have to do with the stage of development and absorption capacity of the country, but there may also be more conscious choice behind
the levels of investment in people and infrastructure, based on the objectives of
the country. Moreover, there is certainly strong influence from existing institutions, many of which are rooted in colonial history or close relationships with
allies. It would be interesting, in particular, to test further the hypothesis that
close military and economic linkages with the USA renders R&D systems more
effective.

d. One of the biggest challenges in national R&D systems is coordination
among different institutions. Some countries are better at coordinating the
efforts put into R&D. The political organization and structure of the respective countries are mirrored in the organization of R&D investment. Yet as
the case of Korea suggests, it is not sufficient to have better coordination as a
goal. It requires a lot of political investment to render a change in institutions
possible.

e. There is an interesting question looming: how much must be spent to escape the
middle-income trap? What is going on in South East and East Asia is an almost
perfect quasi-experiment for this.

f. All countries, whether investing a high amount in R&D on S&T or not, wrestle
with a similar issue: how does investment in R&D translate into a contribution
to GDP growth through the intermediary of innovation? This is what will be
discussed in the next section.

## The Challenge of Innovation[2]

We have referred to Ho, Wong, and Toh (2009), who indicated that return on investment in R&D was lower in Singapore than in traditional industrialized countries, and
that the lag time was higher. Since there are no indications that R&D as practiced by
Asian research institutes is inherently more difficult than it is in Europe or the USA,
I would suggest that the reason for this slower and lower leveraging of R&D investments
can be partly explained by the lower absorptive capacity of industrial networks in Asia.
This raises an issue of whether it is more difficult to innovate in Asia than in the USA or
Europe.

At first sight there should not be much difference. Good innovation management is similar all over the world. It requires good leadership, a willingness to listen to users, excellent capabilities in project management under uncertain conditions, intelligent knowledge management, stimulating imagination and creativity, an ability to manage risks, a significant effort to protect intellectual property, an integrated organization, and often luck. These eight good principles apply equally well in Asia.

From our own case-studies and observations over ten years, however, we have learned that innovators in Asia have to confront four additional management challenges (De Meyer and Garg 2005), as described below.

## Asian Organizations Need to Adapt

Asian organizations struggle with three structural challenges:

- Many companies in Asia, particularly in countries with a significant overseas Chinese population, are family businesses. As such, they are controlled by a relatively small group of family members who need to be involved in most decisions. This often leads to slow decision-making, in particular for strategic decisions concerning innovation.
- The prevailing culture in many Asian organizations (be it in the Confucian cultures of East Asia, or the Hindu culture of India) is one of respect for hierarchy and elders. This often helps in rapid implementation of operational issues, but does not allow for creativity at the bottom to bubble up to higher levels, a process which may challenge the strategic top of the organization. Imagination and creativity may exist in the organization, but often cannot express itself well.
- The organization was often created to be a 'server' for a principal agent somewhere in Japan or the United States. Therefore, organizations do not have the capability to work outside the home country, or to effectively capture market signals from elsewhere.

These challenges should not be insurmountable, but they do require Asian-based organizations to unlearn some lessons from the past on how to be successful, and to rebuild themselves. From case-based research we learn that the more successful innovators were companies and institutions that had attracted top talent with significant experience in the USA, Australia, or Europe, either as students or through work experience. The Taiwanese semiconductor industry is an interesting example. It was basically built with capable managers who had studied and worked in the USA with companies like IBM, Motorola, or Texas Instruments. They brought the organizational structure and international openness to Taiwan and built what is probably one of the most formidable set of companies in the semiconductor industry (De Meyer and Garg 2005).

## Many Asian Organizations Cannot Handle Intangibles, In Particular Intellectual Property

There are many stories circulating about how Chinese or Indian companies blatantly copy products from the West and bring them out at a much lower price. Often this is described as a lack of respect for intellectual property laws, and it is true that such laws are either only available in crude form or are difficult to enforce.

We have however observed that there is more than a lack of respect for IPR. In our case studies, we found that Asian entrepreneurs have little feeling for, or concept of, the value of intangibles such as brands or know-how. Brands are often simply equated with logos and few entrepreneurs seem to realize that it is much more about values and how the company expresses those values. If it is not tangible, that is, raw materials, land, or hard products, it does not seem to invoke value for many Asian individuals. In such a managerial culture it is difficult to manage IPR effectively.

Governments in Asia are working hard to encourage innovators to accept and implement respect for IP. Singapore has invested heavily in both legislation and education on IP. The Chinese government is promoting IP: it recently organized an IP week, and published proudly that in 2011 nearly 60,000 intellectual property cases were filed in courts of first instance, an increase of 40 per cent in the number of IP-related court cases since 2010 (China Daily 2012). In other countries, though, implementation of IP legislation is little more than lip-service.

### A Need for a Different Kind of Market Research

Asia is notorious for its lack of good market research. Many would even say that available statistics and market research have to be taken with pinches of salt. There are several reasons for this. First of all, the whole market-research sector is underdeveloped and often not very professional. But there are more important underlying reasons. Most research techniques have been developed for an American and Western European culture, where generally speaking individualism is accepted and where governments are democratic and accountable. There are of course nuances between countries, but these characteristics mean that consumers are prepared to talk about their needs and wishes, and can do so without the risk of being singled out by an autocratic government that may not like their opinion. These characteristics, however, are not present in all Asian countries. Democracy and government accountability is in most places progressing and we can expect that future consumers and citizens will be prepared to voice their opinion, but individualism is not part of Asian culture, and that will not change soon.

### Develop Design Capabilities

One consequence of the rapid development in Asia's growth economies, and the difficulty in appreciating the value of intangibles, is that the resources to make innovation happen are in short supply: there are shortages of engineers, marketers, financial specialists, and most importantly designers. China and India annually produce in absolute terms a lot of engineers, but many of these are needed simply to run the operations of factories, telecoms, transport, and other infrastructure. Few go into development and even fewer become sophisticated innovators.

The most challenging shortage, however, is in designers, individuals who can take a concept for a product or service and translate it into an attractive value proposition for the customer. There are few schools for such training, even fewer for its development. Recently there have been some efforts in Singapore to create appropriate design courses: one of its newest university's is called 'Singapore University of Technology and Design'.

This shortage of designers may well be the biggest challenge for innovation in Asia. It is not that there is no design creativity, but there is no real grooming of such creativity into design capabilities.

# AVENUES FOR FURTHER RESEARCH

Based on the previous paragraphs I see several opportunities for research:

a. Innovation and R&D systems are not independent of the institutional framework in which they operate. But the hypothesis as formulated by Hall and Soskice (2001) needs drastic reformulation, in particular for Asia.
b. In many Asian countries, institutions are still weak and in development. It would be interesting to understand how the behaviour of Asian and international firms operating in Asia is influencing the development of institutions.
c. In the short case studies I have tried to show that each country has a very different approach to R&D investment. It is worth analysing how much this is a consequence of the stage of development, or a result of administrative heritage and colonial regime (or ally in the case of China and India).
d. I have discussed above how R&D is not an exclusively national activity, but consists of international dependencies. Companies operate across borders and may even want to escape the national framework in order to gain independence from national institutions. These international interdependencies are outside the scope of this chapter, but deserve further analysis of how national systems interact with international private and public networks of innovation and R&D.
e. There is little case-based knowledge on the role of R&D investment in creating a middle-income trap. Most high-quality research is econometric in nature and does not analyse innovation from a micro perspective. ASEAN is a quasi-experiment to test the role of different variables that determine this middle-income trap, and it would be worthwhile to develop a set of case studies to understand how each country is trying to overcome this problem.
f. I have argued that the lack of investment in social sciences has determined the lower absorptive capacity of industry and governments in Asia for the fruits of R&D investment. This is clearly a hypothesis that deserves more research.

g. I have indicated four more challenges for translating R&D into innovation. Each is based on clinical cases, and, again, deserves more in-depth empirical research on how to overcome them.

# Conclusion

We see enormous differences in how Asian countries have approached investment in R&D. Some of these differences have to do with the country's size, stage of development, and ambition. I also argue that there may be an influence on the organization of R&D systems from the country's administrative heritage and institutions.

My main observation is that all Asian countries suffer from a slower and less effective translation of research results into innovation, which is the 'holy grail' of investment in R&D: through innovation, one hopes to achieve productivity improvements and later on economic growth. Slower and less effective translation may be due to a lack of absorptive capacity, which is the consequence of a set of institutional, organizational, and managerial factors which render innovation more difficult in Asia.

## Notes

1. This section is based on a combination of my own personal observations and interactions, and analysis of websites of relevant ministries and departments. For South East Asia there is extensive information on the website of the SEA-EU-Net or the project to facilitate the bi-regional EU-ASEAN Science and Technology Dialogue (SEA-EU-NET 2012a) and summarized in Schüller et al. (2008). For OECD member countries (Japan, Korea) and China, the OECD has published many reports on National Innovation Systems.
2. This section is largely based on empirical research described in De Meyer and Garg (2005) and also De Meyer (2011).

## References

Akkermans, D., C. Castaldi, and B. Los (2009). 'Do "Liberal Market Economies" Really Innovate More Radically than "Coordinated Market Economies"?: Hall and Soskice Reconsidered'. *Research Policy 38*(1): 181–191.

Birdsall, N. and C. Rhee (1993). *Does Research and Development Contribute to Economic Growth in Developing Countries?* Policy Research Working Paper No.1221. Washington DC, World Bank.

Breznitz, D. and M. Murphree (2011). *Run of the Red Queen: Government, Innovation, Globalization, and Economic Growth in China*. New Haven, Yale University Press.

Carney, M., E. Gedajlovic, and X. Yang (2009). 'Varieties of Asian Capitalism: Toward an Institutional Theory of Asian Enterprise'. *Asia Pacific Journal of Management 26*: 361–380.

*China Daily* (2012). 'SIPO: Thirty Years of Growing Awareness, Yet More Needed'. *IP special*, 15 April: 17.

De Meyer, A. (2011). 'Diving Into the New Innovation Landscape'. *IESE Insights*. Retrieved 29 July 2012 from <http://www.ieseinsight.com/doc.aspx?id=1268&ar=16>.

—— and S. Garg (2005). *Inspire to Innovate: Management of Innovation in Asia*, London, Palgrave MacMillan.

—— and A. Mizushima (1989). 'Global R&D Management'. *R&D Management* 19(2): 135–146.

Doz, Y., J. Santos, and P. Williamson (2001). *From Global to Metanational: How Companies Win in the Knowledge Economy*. Cambridge, Harvard Business School Press.

Dutta, S., A. De Meyer, and S. Srivastawa (2001). *The Bright Stuff*. London, Prentice Hall.

Guellec, G. M. and B. van Pottelsberghe de la Potterie (2001). *R&D and Productivity Growth: Panel Data Analysis of 16 OECD countries*. STI Working Paper 2001/3. OECD Directorate for Science, Technology, and Industry, Paris.

Hall, P. A. and D. Soskice (2001). *Varieties of Capitalism: The Institutional Foundations of Comparative Advantage*. New York, Oxford University Press.

Hassan S., P. Haddawy, P. Kuinkel, A. Degelsegger, and C. Blasy (2011). 'A Bibliometric Study of Research Activity in ASEAN related to the EU in FP7 Priority Areas'. *Scientometrics* 91(3): 1035–1051.

Hermann, A. M. and A. Peine (2011). 'When "National Innovation System" Meets "Varieties of Capitalism" Arguments on Labour Qualifications: on the Skill Types and Scientific Knowledge Needed for Radical and Incremental Product Innovations'. *Research Policy* 40(5): 687–701.

Hill, C. W. L. (2007). *International Business: Competing in the Global Marketplace*. New York, McGraw-Hill.

Ho, Y. P., P. K. Wong, and M. H. Toh (2009). 'The Impact of R&D on the Singapore Economy: An Empirical Evaluation'. *Singapore Economic Review* 54(1): 1–20.

Huang, K. G. (2010). 'China's Innovation Landscape'. *Science* 329: 632–633.

ISS (Institute for Security Studies) (2012). 'Citizens in an Interconnected and Polycentric World'. Retrieved 29 July 2012 from <http://www.iss.europa.eu/uploads/media/ESPAS_report_01.pdf>.

Link, A. N. and D. S. Spiegel (2003). *Technological Change and Economic Performance*. New York, Routledge.

Madden, G., S. J. Savage, and P. Bloxham (2001). 'Asian and OECD International R&D Spillovers'. *Applied Economic Letters* 8: 431–435.

Mansfield, E. (1972). 'Contribution of Research and Development to Economic Growth of the United States'. Papers and Proceedings of a Colloquium on Research and Development and Economic Growth productivity. Washington, DC, National Science Foundation.

Moschella, D., D. Neal, J. Taylor, and P. Opperman (2004). 'Consumerization of Information Technology'. *Leading Edge Forum*. Retrieved 1 July 2012 from <http://lef.csc.com/projects/70>.

Nadiri, I. (1993). *Innovations and Technological Spillovers*. NBER Working Paper 4423. Cambridge, MA, National Bureau of Economic Research.

Nadjou, N. and Prabhu, J. (2012). 'Mobilizing for Growth in Emerging Markets: To Reach the 'Next Billion' Consumers, Multinational Companies Will Need to Move Beyond Value Chain Localization and Create New Networks of Local Partners'. *MIT Sloan Management Review* 53(3): 81–88.

Nonaka, I. and H. Takeuchi (1995). *The Knowledge Creating Company: How Japanese Companies Create the Dynamics of Innovation*, New York, Oxford University Press.

OECD (2009). *OECD Reviews of Innovation Policy:* Korea. Paris, OECD.

—— (2011). *OECD Science, Technology and Industry Scoreboard 2011: Innovation and Growth in Knowledge Economies.* Paris, OECD.

Orr, G. and E. Roth (2012). 'A CEO's Guide to Innovation in China'. *McKinsey Quarterly.* Retrieved 29 July 2012 from <http://www.mckinseyquarterly.com/A_CEOs_guide_to_innovation_in_China_2919>.

Schneider, M. R. and M. Paunescu (2012). 'Changing Varieties of Capitalism and Revealed Comparative Advantages from 1990 to 2005: A test of the Hall and Soskice claim'. *Socio-Economic Review 10*(4): 731–753.

Schüller, M., F. Gruber, R. Trienes, and D. Shim (2008). 'International Science and Technology Cooperation Policies of Southeast Asian Countries'. Consultation Paper for EU Commission on the Occasion of the First Bi-Regional Science & Technology Policy Dialogue, EU-ASEAN, 19–20 November 2008, Paris. Retrieved 29 August 2012 from <https://www.zsi.at/attach/ConsultationPaper.pdf>.

SEA-EU-NET (2012a). Retrieved 19 July 2013 from <http://sea-eu.net/facts/sea>.

—— (2012b). 'R&D Country Profile: Indonesia'. Retrieved 19 July 2013 from <http://sea-eu.net/facts/sea/indonesia>.

Taylor M. Z. (2004). 'Empirical Evidence against Varieties of Capitalism Theory of Technological Innovation'. *International Organization 58*: 601–631.

UNIDO (2012). Retrieved 26 February 2012 from <http://www.unido.org/index.php?id=1002110>.

Vernon, R. (1966). 'International Investment and International Trade in the Product Cycle'. *Quarterly Journal of Economics 80*: 190–207.

Williamson, P. and A. De Meyer (2012) 'Ecosystem Advantage: How to Boost your Success by Harnessing the Power of Partners'. *California Management Review 50*(1):24–42.

Williamson, P. J. and M. Zeng (2007). *Dragons at your Door: How Chinese Cost Innovation is Disrupting the Rules of Global Competition.* Boston, Harvard Business School Press.

Witt, M. and A. W. Lewin (2007). 'Outward Foreign Direct Investment as Escape Response to Home-Country Institutional Constraints' *Journal of International Business Studies 38*(4): 579–594.

World Bank (2012). 'China 2030: Building a Modern, Harmonious, and Creative High-Income Society'. Retrieved 23 November 2012 from <http://www.worldbank.org/en/news/2012/02/27/china-2030-executive-summary>.

# CHAPTER 22

# THE CO-EVOLUTION OF GLOBAL SOURCING OF BUSINESS SUPPORT FUNCTIONS AND THE ECONOMIC DEVELOPMENT OF ASIAN EMERGING ECONOMIES

ARIE Y. LEWIN AND XING ZHONG

## INTRODUCTION

COMPANIES in advanced economies are continuously experimenting with the use of advanced information and communication technology (ICT), new human resource (HR) management practices, and new forms of coordination and control in response to, or anticipation of, top-line growth from the fast-growing economies of Asia, Latin America, and Africa. As early as the 1960s, firms in advanced economies began to relocate production to foreign, mostly lower-cost, countries. The 1980s witnessed a significant increase in outsourcing the manufacture of both components and entire products for the domestic market (as distinct from capturing market in the country where the products were produced)—for example, the US doubled its imported inputs between 1975 and 1995 for all manufacturing (Campa and Goldberg 1997). A second outsourcing wave from the 1990s involved firms in developed economies relocating technical and administrative work[1] to low-cost economies (Beulen, van Fenema, and Currie 2005; Lewin and Peeters 2006; Sako 2006). By 2010, offshoring of dis-intermediate business processes, information technology (IT) applications, and back-office functions had become a mainstream business practice (UNCTAD 2005).

As Asian countries emerged as popular offshore destinations for manufacturing, they were increasingly integrated into global manufacturing value chains (Gereffi and Korzeniewicz 1994) through an export-oriented model of economic development first implemented by Japan and later by South Korea. Although Asian countries exhibit varying degrees of participation in manufacturing offshoring, factors explaining location attractiveness usually include geopolitical stability/risks, opportunities for exploiting labour arbitrage, and labour availability (Kearney 2007; Kotlarsky and Oshri 2008; Sudan et al. 2010). Surprisingly, few studies have explored to what extent the characteristics of host countries' configuration of national business systems affect or mediate the way they engage in global manufacturing value-chain networks. Many scholars have applied transaction-cost economics (Coase 1937; Williamson 1985) in studies of manufacturing companies' offshoring decisions. However, the varieties of capitalism/business systems (VoC/BS) literature has not directly addressed how different configurations of national business systems affect a country's attractiveness for outsourcing manufacturing and, therefore, the decisions of companies from high-wage economies to explore outsourcing in low-wage economies. This may be partly because the national business-system framework does not specifically accommodate considerations affecting economic development at the level of devising specific economic policy-development instruments, although the outcomes of these instruments are an outcome of interactions among institutional actors characterizing a business system.

Beyond transaction-cost explanations, the strategic management literature argues that firms should outsource only peripheral non-core activities (Schilling and Steensma 2001; Jacobides and Winter 2005). However, strategy scholars find it difficult to explain the global growth of sourcing higher value-added knowledge-intensive processes and the reorganization of innovation-sourcing processes. Herrigel and Zeitlin (2010: 542) note 'This shift in the strategic character of offshoring has initiated a dynamic process of capacity and know-how reallocation that appears to be radically redefining the division of labour between high- and low-wage regions.' In highlighting the dynamic aspect of the evolution of global sourcing, Manning, Massini, and Lewin (2008) have stressed companies' increasing recognition that labour arbitrage, the most important strategic driver underlying offshoring decisions, is being supplanted by other drivers, like the need to access pools of highly skilled talent and capture new markets for new top-line growth. Emerging economies have become attractive destinations, because they offer access to underutilized science, technology, engineering, and mathematics (STEM) talent. These economies not only have national cultures that value education, and higher-education systems that have the capacity to expand, but also have begun to implement national policies to attract global sourcing—especially higher value-added activities—as another lever of economic development. Consequently, global sourcing practices have been co-evolving with the emergence of local and global industries providing business services. A few years ago, no observer of global sourcing trends would have predicted that China and other emerging economies would adopt national strategies to attract and develop the domestic business-services outsourcing industry, especially science- and engineering-based service outsourcing, or that Indian providers such as Wipro, TCS, and Infosys would evolve into multinational enterprises spanning North Africa, Eastern Europe, and Latin America, and competing directly with Western providers on their turf.

The dynamic evolution of offshoring calls for a deeper understanding of how global sourcing is affecting the global organization of value-adding business processes within and across industries, and to what extent variances among business systems mediate the outcome of policy aspirations as well as the growth of service-provider industries in host countries, which in turn are crucial for gaining share in the global-sourcing space. This chapter examines the dynamic evolution of the offshoring phenomenon, with an emphasis on the interaction between the mechanisms affecting demand for and supply of these services. To highlight the co-evolution of global sourcing and offshoring, we pay particular attention to interactions between the growth of global sourcing/offshoring and labour markets in Asia, especially STEM talent, to further address an under-explored dimension in existing literature. We use India's experience as an illustration of business-services offshoring to anchor the development of a proposed framework for future research on the dynamics of how emerging economies might execute a national strategy for attracting business-services outsourcing as a lever for economic development. In particular, we focus on configuration of policy instruments and institutional changes when such economies are diversifying their growth strategies.

# THE PHENOMENON OF AND LITERATURE ON OFFSHORING

## Offshoring

Offshoring refers to the process of sourcing and coordinating tasks and business functions across national borders. Different authors have included different aspects of offshoring in their conceptualization (Farrell and McKinsey Global Institute 2006; Jahns, Hartmann, and Bals 2006), but in its broadest scope, offshoring encompasses two subsets of inter-firm relationships that, though related, developed relatively independently: (1) vertically disintegrated production; and (2) disintermediation of business processes and functions.

Literature on vertically disintegrated production (often referred to as offshoring manufacturing facilities and blue-collar jobs) dates back to the 1980s' discussions on the crisis facing 'Fordist' or 'Chandlerian' firms (Piore and Sabel 1984; Chandler and Hikino 1990). Empirical work showed that large manufacturing companies across a range of sectors had disintegrated since the 1970s (Essletzbichler 2003), and case studies from the apparel, consumer electronics, and automobile sectors (Gereffi and Korzeniewicz

1994; Borrus, Ernst, and Haggard 2000) have found that companies have become more effective in leveraging offshore cost differences in production. As companies grow and diversify their strategies for outsourcing manufacturing (components, sub-assemblies, and entire products) across multiple countries, they become sensitive to the capital costs of carrying inventories of 'goods in process'. Supply-chain management practices therefore serve to coordinate lean production (just-in-time delivery) of components to be assembled in the home country or intermediary locations, and specialists emerge, such as UPS, Maersk, FedEx, and DHL, competing on optimizing supply-chain management. Since the dynamic is mainly one of 'push' by Western companies (pushing out labour-intensive work to low-wage countries), literature on supply-side mechanisms is not well developed.

The VoC/BS literature has paid little attention to offshoring, nor to the attendant transnational effect of disintermediation of manufacturing. Companies from high-wage countries devise and evolve supply-chain management strategies independently of host-country business systems. Manufacturing firms have developed capabilities to 'unplug' production from one location and move elsewhere if production costs in the former location deteriorate. However, the source and availability of surplus labour that can be utilized in the manufacturing and higher value-added sectors of the economy affects companies' offshoring decisions, a reality overlooked in the VoC literature and various formulations of business-system arguments.

Another subset of offshoring practice, the disintermediation of business processes, only recently gained traction in academic research (Lewin and Volberda 2011). The beginning of the global business-services sourcing industry can be traced to the 1970s, when American Express outsourced its accounts-receivable processes to Tata Consultancy Services (TCS), which was founded in 1968 in Mumbai and opened its first international office in New York in 1979 to serve their client on-site (Lewin and Peeters 2006). Soon after, in the mid-1980s, Citibank, Texas Instruments, Motorola, and GE relocated some of their centres to India (Dossani 2007). In those early days, managerial intentionality played an important role in firm decisions to offshore business processes and services (Hutzschenreuter, Pedersen, and Volberda 2007), although Delios and Henisz (2003) have noted that some relocation decisions, such as those by GE and Motorola, were initiated to gain political favour (e.g. strategic decisions to establish captive-technology centres).

Initially, scholars assumed that companies would offshore tasks requiring rule-based logic or back-office activities needing relatively low levels of process knowledge (Youngdahl and Ramaswamy 2008; Tambe and Hitt 2012), However, research shows that companies began to offshore higher value-added innovation work as well. Advances in ICT and process innovations in the 1990s further enabled a wide range of tasks from users and service-providers to be seamlessly relocated to distant locations at ever-declining costs (Dalal 2007). Key enabling technologies and events include the introduction of broadband in 1990, which enabled rapid end-to-end communications for frequent interactions; enterprise resource-planning software, enabling the distribution of activities to multiple location-independent computers (released by SAP R/3 in 1992); and the

1996 deregulation of the US telecommunications industry, which unleashed worldwide improvements in data communication infrastructure (Hutzschenreuter, Lewin, and Ressler 2011). The burst of the dotcom bubble in early 2000 and subsequent recession further intensified the pressure on companies to offshore non-core activities to low-cost countries (Lewin and Peeters 2006; Nassimbeni and Sartor 2008). As codification and standardization evolves, competitive pressure drives late adopters to imitate (DiMaggio and Powell 1983). Advances in ICT have also greatly assisted firms in dis-intermediating and externalizing innovation processes through outsourcing and relocating R&D off-shore (Howells 1990). The dis-intermediation of business processes in general, and off-shoring of innovation functions in particular, create a dynamic context for research on internationalization and the emerging ecosystem of global innovation (Patel and Pavitt 1991; Kenney and Florida 1994; Cantwell 1995; Pearce 1999; Murtha 2004).

International business and operations management literature on offshoring focuses mainly on the demand side (firm-specific intentionality and capabilities), neglecting supply-side mechanisms in explaining the dynamic growth of global sourcing of business processes and functions that do not fall into the traditional category of foreign direct investment (FDI) (see Aharoni, Tihanyi, and Connelly 2011). However, it is important to recognize that the exponential growth of global sourcing of business processes and functions is a co-evolutionary process between demand-side and supply-side mechanisms (Lewin and Volberda 2011). The national business-system literature can provide some insights into how the competitive advantage of the service-provider industry in a host country can result from policies that reflect the configuration of specific national business systems. The trajectory of capability development of indigenous service-providers in host countries can dynamically shape how supply drives demand for offshored services. Analyzing inter-firm relationships between offshoring companies and offshored operations calls for a better understanding of how a national business system may influence the trajectory of capability development of business-services outsourcing in the host country.

# SUPPLY OF LOW-SKILLED AND HIGH-SKILLED LABOUR IN LOW-COST ECONOMIES

## Manufacturing Offshoring and Surplus Labour in Host Countries

One of the most salient mechanisms affecting the supply side is the availability of labour, which is an immediate input factor in manufacture offshoring. Manufacture offshoring does not directly affect organization and competition within local business systems in host countries, since such production does not compete with local manufacturers that produce directly for the local market. For this reason, supply-chain management practice does not necessarily interact with the 'rationality' and 'efficiency' of local managerial structures and practices, which constitute particular interests of the business system literature. Whitley (1999, 2005) concluded that business-system characteristics of host countries have not been significantly impacted by inward FDI and internationalization in the financial market. Although it is widely acknowledged that certain country-development agencies can devise infrastructure investments (e.g. transportation, telecommunications, and power) and tax regimes or other incentives to attract foreign investors/capital as a way of shaping competition in local markets (Lau 1996), the variation in the type and proliferation of specific policy instruments in general is not conditioned on differences among the configurations of specific national business systems.

Nonetheless, manufacturing can directly affect factor markets in host countries. Outsourcing of manufacturing offshore mostly involves low-cost labour-intensive work. The availability of labour is an outcome of the host country's institutional configuration, which in reality shapes the creation of surplus labour for employment opportunities in the manufacturing sector. However, the policy choices that have the potential to create the surplus labour necessary for attracting manufacture offshoring are not addressed in the VoC/BS literature, perhaps because such literature does not address the relationship between the manufacturing/industrial sector and agricultural sector, which is particularly salient in transition economies. The missing link is the mechanisms of the underlying supply of labour and its relationship to manufacturing outsourcing, and how it can be accommodated in the business-system framework for creating surplus labour and shifting these resources from agriculture to industry.

The VoC framework has highlighted that strong institutional complementarities across various institutional arenas (industrial relations, finance, training, corporate governance) characterize the dynamics of reproduction of a national model (Hall and Soskice 2001; Hancké, Rhodes, and Thatcher 2007). BS literature has further focused on how such stability and coherence among social-economic institutions resulting from institutional complementarities play a significant role in shaping the strategies of economic organizations, configuring distinctive business-system characteristics, and formalizing specific feedback mechanisms that sustain distinctive trajectories of development (Whitley 2005). Although both approaches are deeply attuned to the impact of institutions, the analyses are anchored on economic actors—specifically, firms in the industrial sector. The economic organization of the agricultural sector has not been integrated into VoC or BS models. Not surprisingly, the configuration of institutional arrangements linking the transfer of sectoral resources between agricultural and industrial sectors in transitional economies is not addressed. Comparative institutional analysis has explored the political dynamics or policy-based resource shifts underlying institutional changes (Aoki, Kim, and Okuno-Fujiwara 1996; Thelen 2010). Teranishi (1996) stressed that industrializing economies should pay more attention to balancing growth between agriculture and industry, since the transfer of agricultural surplus labour has been identified as one measure for mobilizing resources for industrialization. In comparing Latin America and East Asia, Teranishi found that the structural characteristics of an agricultural economy have a significant impact on the level of market-based resource transfer as well as the strategies adopted by economic organizations in the agricultural sector: structural differences, such as an agricultural sector mostly composed of small farmers[2] in Asia versus the dominance of large farmers in Latin America (Otsuka, Chuma, and Hayami 1992), are fundamental in explaining the degree of resource shift from agriculture, and the link between policy-based resource shift and macro-economic stability.

When companies first began to relocate manufacturing to Asia, most of the destination economies were predominantly agricultural societies. The varying degrees of intensity in shifts from agriculture to industry have affected countries' attractiveness for manufacturing outsourcing. One form of resource shift from agriculture to industry is the creation of surplus labour in the agricultural sector to drive industrialization. The transition period, when agricultural employment undergoes major adjustments (Williamson 1985; Lucas 2004) has various effects on output and factor markets. Researchers have shown that privatization of farm assets and removal of constraints to factor allocation increase the flow of surplus labour from food-production activities to various labour-intensive industrial sectors. Moreover, the dynamics of country-specific labour adjustments vary with institutional reforms such as privatization, farm restructuring, and price and trade policy reforms (Lin and Yao 2001; Swinnen, Dries, and Macours 2005). Forms of land ownership can also affect a country's ability to release surplus labour in food production to the industrial sector. Teranishi (1996) showed that large landowners and small farmers react differently to incentives targeted at increasing land productivity and consequently releasing surplus labour for manufacturing outsourcing. In the past few decades, countries in Asia that attracted manufacture offshoring have experienced a decreasing percentage of rural population, and the percentage of agricultural land under cultivation has been increasing during the same period. Between the 1970s and 2008, the percentage of rural population in countries such as China, Indonesia, and the Philippines as a proportion of the agrarian population has decreased by over 25 per cent (from about 85%), while at the same time cultivation of agricultural land increased (from 10 to 20%). However, this trend is significantly less salient in Vietnam. India has not experienced the population shift from agrarian to industrial economy, and as a result manufacture offshoring to India is low (World Development Indicators 1970–2011). These empirical trends reinforce our view that appropriate agricultural policies are important for releasing surplus labour for industrial production.

In the process of creating surplus labour and managing the shift to industry, it is important to consider how institutional legacy (e.g. land ownership) shapes the conditions for productivity growth in agriculture and for shifting surplus labour to the industrial sector. The state can play a pivotal role, given the authority relationships and agrarian and industrial structure (Griffin 2001; Kay 2002). However, the mix of policy instruments will necessarily vary by country because of variation in mechanisms such as taxation and manipulation of terms of trade, as well as in organizing and mobilizing peasantry.

# Global Sourcing of Business Processes: Talent Supply in Home and Host Countries

The seemingly unlimited availability of STEM talent in emerging economies, particularly Asia, has been perceived as an answer to the increasing challenges firms face in finding such talent in advanced economies. According to *Science and Engineering Indicators 2012*, in 2008, Asian universities graduated 2.4 million science and engineering students (approximately 50% of the world total). In engineering alone, over 1 million degrees were awarded in Asia, compared to 1.2 million across Europe (including Eastern Europe and Russia) and 700,000 in North and Central America. In terms of advanced degrees, 'about 194,000 [science and engineering] doctoral degrees were earned worldwide in 2008: The United States awarded 33,000, followed by China (about 28,000), Russia (15,000), Germany (11,000), and the United Kingdom (9,500)' (National Science Board 2012: 2–34).

However, the employability of this growing pool of science and engineering graduates is falling short in terms of the technical and scientific quality of the education. According to the McKinsey Global Institute's interviews in 2005 with eighty-three HR managers for multinationals, only 10 and 25 per cent of graduates in China and India, respectively, were deemed suitable to work for the multinationals interviewed. The McKinsey report stated, 'In India the quality of the educational system—top university apart—handicaps graduates, and a lack of strong English language skills is the most pressing issue for Brazil and China.' Other reasons involve large variation in the quality of education, over-emphasis on theory at the expense of practical knowledge, and a lack of cultural fit (e.g. interpersonal skills, and attitudes towards teamwork and flexible work). A further complicating factor is the expectation that a fast-growing domestic economy, like China and India's, will easily absorb most of the available qualified supply (Farrell and McKinsey Global Institute 2006: 15). As these countries become increasingly important in global innovation, it is highly likely that the most acute shortage will be felt in the supply of science and engineering talent with advanced degrees. If developing economies continue to be attractive destinations for sourcing business services in general and innovation activities specifically, these countries will face the challenge of developing and implementing policies that increase the supply of 'employable' STEM graduates in the short and, more importantly, long run.

# Inter-Firm Interface/Relationship: In-house Captive versus Outsource to Service Providers

As relocating business-support functions (including engineering and R&D) offshore becomes mainstream practice, the institutional differences between the offshoring home country and the offshore destination moderates options for governance mode

(Hennart 1988; Safizadeh, Field, and Ritzman 2008). The FDI literature (Anderson and Gatignon 1986; Kogut and Singh 1988; Agarwal and Ramaswami 1992) and the OLI model or eclectic paradigm (Dunning 1988) in most cases are insufficient to address why firms select captive versus outsource (make or buy) operations. Business-system features, such as efficiency of host-country institutions (Henisz and Delios 2001; Bevan, Estrin, and Meyer 2004) or 'the rules of the game' (North 1990), can shape the choice of governance mode for offshoring firms (Delios and Beamish 1999; Oxley 1999) and consequently the inter-firm relationship in terms of knowledge/information flow (Kshetri 2007; Liu, Feils, and Scholnick 2011).

The difference between captive versus outsource has important implications for the organization of value-creation and the configuration of firm boundary, and therefore for how capability may develop on the supply side (Quinn and Hilmer 1994; Leiblein, Reuer, and Dalsace 2002). Manning et al. (2012) report that initial firm governance decisions are strongly influenced by process commoditization, external availability of services from providers, and strategic objectives. However, subsequent governance decisions are primarily affected by path dependency and experience with sourcing decisions and emerging—internal and/or external—sourcing capabilities.

In the long term, sourcing of increasingly sophisticated activities in emerging economies, particularly when the outsourced mode becomes more prevalent, gives rise to a rapidly growing global service-provider industry with a growing capacity to provide full services or specialized innovation services (Lewin et al. 2009). Nonetheless, the literature is still in its infancy in exploring the dynamics of the growth in global sourcing of services from the perspective of how supply drives demand for ever-more sophisticated capabilities as a consequence of competition among service providers, and how it contributes to economic development in emerging economies. In particular, it is not well understood how these dynamics give birth to firms from developing economies that become credible rivals of firms such as IBM and HP (e.g. Lahiri and Kedia 2011); with one exception (Athreye 2005), there have been no established efforts to collect data on the evolution of service-provider capabilities.

## The Role of Knowledge Clusters

The mechanism underlying the emergence of knowledge clusters has contributed significantly to the growth momentum of global business-service sourcing. This new form of science and engineering functional clusters in emerging economies is especially notable in India (Bangalore), China (Shanghai) (Chaminade and Vang 2008), Russia (Moscow and St Petersburg), and Israel (Herzelia). The literature on industrial districts (Marshall 1920) has long discussed the importance of clusters for the competitive advantages of firms, and identifies that the externality effect of knowledge spillovers is one of the main mechanisms of a specialized knowledge cluster in creating positive feedback mechanisms and sustaining growth in demand (Porter 1990; Bell 2005). The literature on vertically disintegrated production with studies on industrial districts further enriches such insights with comparative studies on different business systems (Herrigel and Zeitlin 2010). However, traditional industrial-district studies on flexible production-systems have mainly examined industry clusters in advanced economies and manufacturing processes. Knowledge-based service clusters in emerging economies are relatively new (Apte and Mason 1995; Metters and Verma 2008; Manning et al. 2010). These specialized-knowledge clusters provide technical talent and knowledge-intensive upstream business-service capabilities for a particular segment of the global market (Chaminade and Vang 2008).

Nonetheless, the tradition of comparative institutional analysis acknowledges that national or regional innovation systems play a crucial role in shaping firms' innovative capabilities (Lundvall 1992; Nelson 1993), and that the comparative advantages of specialized clusters are embedded within the nation's broader business systems. It is unsurprising to find that government incentives and policies, particularly at local level, are crucial for the emergence and development in developing countries of specialized-knowledge clusters serving national goals of moving higher on the value chain (Porter 2000; Arora and Gambardella 2005). The propensity of a specialized cluster to move up the global value chain is shaped (Lundvall, Intarakumnerd, and Vang-Lauridsen 2006) by system-level characteristics at regional level, such as the provision of regional research infrastructure, technology-transfer agencies, specialized training systems, policies for physical infrastructure, and investment attraction (Cooke, Uranga, and Etxebarria 1997; Asheim and Coenen 2005). Government public procurement policies can become central for compensating for a lack of lead customers, and complementary macro-policies are needed for promoting local entrepreneurship, particularly in conjunction with the presence of specialized knowledge (often functional knowledge) within the region. Still, collaboration with central government is crucial for designing and evaluating policy instruments targeted at global positioning and competitiveness in the service-provider industry. For example, strategic policy decisions by the Indian government in the 1980s promoted the development of software-industry clusters and attracted technology-oriented foreign investment (Patibandla and Petersen 2002; Dossani and Kenney 2007). As gains from knowledge activities become increasingly important (Dunning 2000), the choice of offshore location becomes more sensitive to potential knowledge spillover opportunities (Feinberg and Gupta 2004), Another externality crucial to positive feedback for cluster growth is the availability of supporting industries offering inputs, such as firms providing laboratory equipment, maintenance services, or specialized laboratory testing services. On the one hand, the engagement of pioneering Western MNEs functioned as a catalyst for clustering, fuelling the development of local service capabilities and the attraction of further foreign investment (Patibandla and Petersen 2002). On the other hand, the availability of local high-quality education institutions supports the accumulation of human capital, and even serves as a provider of R&D in some cases. Dossani and Kenney (2009) show that, in India's case, a combination of indigenous firms, MNEs, and entrepreneurs has been responsible for learning and building capabilities in the knowledge clusters. Developing countries, nevertheless, tend to be characterized by a low degree of institutional thickness and thus weak interactive learning, which may explain why relatively few well-functioning regional systems are found in developing countries (Chaminade and Vang 2008). What is clear, though, is that the co-location of a number of high-quality educational and research institutions with the services-provider industry has given rise to specialized knowledge hubs which feed back to the capability development of indigenous firms in developing economies.

# Empirical Patterns and Trend

## Overall Trend

Although offshoring has been in practice for a few decades, there is still no consensus on how to define and measure the phenomenon. A lack of official records suggests that indirect measures should be considered (Ricart 2011).[3] At industry level, 'Asia's five leading electronics-exporting countries (China, Republic of Korea, Taiwan province of China, Singapore, and Malaysia) account for roughly one-third of world electronics manufacturing output' (Ernst 2008: 552). The apparel industry is another pillar of manufacture offshoring. Clothing assembly processes have been offshored throughout the Asia-Pacific region; China, as the top exporter, has seen its share of global apparel exports increase from 22 per cent in 1995 to 41 per cent in 2009, and Bangladesh, India, Vietnam, and Indonesia are among the top ten exporters, all gaining global market-share since the 1990s (Fernandez-Stark, Bamber, and Gereffi 2011). Asia is less significant a player for the export of auto-parts manufacture. The rapid evolution of Asia's auto industry has created opportunities for parts producers to expand production for both local assembly and export, particularly in Thailand (International Trade Association 2011).

The global sourcing of business services, on the other hand, has by all accounts experienced astronomical growth in recent years. India, China, and the Philippines have become major business-services offshoring destinations, given their scalable talent pools (see Figure 22.1). There is no consensus on the market size of global sourcing of business services. Advisory firms vary greatly in their estimates. In 2010, the estimated market size ranged between $448.6bn (Gartner 2011) and $800bn (Dunn, Harris, and Blatman 2011); in 2005 the market was estimated between $46.6bn (BCG 2007) and $81.4bn (OECD 2008). This translates to an annual compound rate of growth ranging from 40.7 to 57.9 per cent for the period 2005–2011. The great variation in estimates is largely due to the inclusion or exclusion of certain factors, such as significant governmental or commercial contracts (with or without management-services contracts or the huge market for spillover projects). In addition, estimates from governmental agencies tend to use aggregate revenues identified by sectors or enterprises, while private advisory companies tend to use aggregated executed contract values in calculating market size.

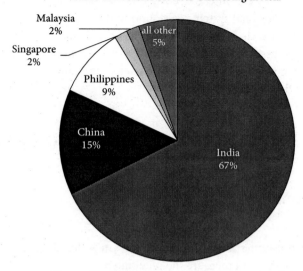

**Share of Business Services Offshoring in Asia**

FIGURE 22.1  Share of business services offshoring in Asia by 2010

*Source*: Duke Offshoring Research Network Corporate Client Survey (2004–2011).

Global sourcing of business services has become an important part of global trade in services and intangibles and has been perceived by many developing economies as a new lever of economic development. A value-chain model proposes that the development of business-service sourcing is a process of climbing the value chain: a country usually begins by offering standardized services in IT, followed by more complex back-office business services, and then gradually upgrades its capabilities to export knowledge processes and high value-added services across different industry segments (Fernandez-Stark, Bamber, and Gereffi 2011). An examination of the most successful case, India, yields an analytical framework that identifies actors and mechanisms shaping the attractiveness of host countries and defining the scope of economic development potential derived from business-services offshoring.

## The Dynamic Growth of Business-Services Offshoring in India

Business-services offshoring has become one of the most significant growth catalysts for the Indian economy. An early study using 2002 data estimated that, for every dollar of US offshore spending, India gained 33 cents in the form of government taxes, wages paid by US companies, and revenues earned by Indian vendors of business-process services and their suppliers (Agrawal and Farrell 2003). This study downplays more indirect economic measures. Between 1998 and 2010 the industry grew 15-fold in revenue, and its contribution to GDP grew from 1.2 to 6.4 per cent; export share generated by this industry relative to total Indian exports increased from 4 to 26 per cent over the same period; industry revenue per capita increased from $17,202 in 2005 to $35,240 in 2010 (NASSCOM 2011); and direct employment by the service-provider industry increased more than eight-fold between 2000 and 2009 (from 284,000 to 2.2 million), making it one of the largest employers in the private sector. Much of this growth in employment (58%) occurred in second- and third-tier cities; 31 per cent of the employees are women, 74 per cent less than 30 years old, and 5 per cent come from economically backward classes (NASSCOM 2011).

A differentiating characteristic of the global business-services sourcing industry is the sector's potential to enhance human capital and advance innovation in emerging economies. The development of the service-provider industry has created opportunities for individuals to attain a much higher socio-economic status by a significant income shift. An Indian employee switching from the informal sector to an entry-level software engineer position sees a more than ten-fold increase in annual wage. With experience, the same individual can expect at least an eighteen-fold increase over the minimum wage. This scale of income shift not only becomes life-changing at personal and community level, but also has a huge impact on the national or regional economy. In 2005, production from knowledge-intensive services in India was about $26.7bn (UNESCO 2010), mostly in revenue from IT and business-process outsourcing.

# Learning from India's 'Natural Experiment' to Inform National Economic Development

It is one thing to observe India's experience, but an entirely different challenge to fully explicate India's case and draw country-specific implications on how another country can develop this industry as a new lever of economic development. In contrast to the development success of countries such as South Korea and Singapore in transforming their economies from low- to high-endowment economies through top-down transformations, India's economy evolved mainly through an unplanned natural experiment. The evolution has several key characteristics. First, it benefited from institutional changes introduced by the central government involving the decision to invest in computer science and technology education. The National Conference on Electronics in 1970 recommended launching specialized masters-level programmes at Indian Institutes of Technology (IITs) and other major institutions. Proficiency in computer programming became mandatory for all IIT undergraduates and science postgraduates at all India's major universities (Indian Electronics Commission 1975). The Computer Manpower Development Programme, launched in 1983, is supported by the Department of Electronics in both financial grants and curriculum development (Kumar 2001), and also by the government, which has permitted private investment in IT training since the early 1980s. In the meantime, the Department of Electronics has intervened to provide accreditation and control over the quality and standardization of courses. Government procurement contracts for projects like automating railway reservations and bank orders also helped the software industry develop (Heeks 1996). Second, it benefited from central government decisions to liberalize the economy in the early 1990s in the context of India's 1991 fiscal crisis and the impetus from the IMF to shift from centralized to sector-targeted industrial policy. Third, and also totally unplanned, the 'Y2K' trigger serendipitously put India on the world map for IT outsourcing as the service-provider industry co-evolved with a demand for services and ready utilization of the available computer science and technology talent pool, without a full understanding of the individual dynamics at work. In sum, the Indian government, without clear foresight, had made foundational national investments in science, engineering, and technology education as early as the 1970s (World Bank 1992).

Separately and independently of exploiting under-utilized IT software skills, IT software start-up companies were able to exploit opportunities to present themselves as competent and reliable business partners for business services. Initially, these outsourcing activities were co-located in the US alongside their customers' captive or shared service operations. Competition with their clients' captive operations was an important element in the rapid rise in the maturity level and management effectiveness of the Indian business-service providers. India's service providers also became known for quality as they self-imposed high operating standards, such as Six Sigma, CMM level 5,[4] and ISO9000 (Schaaf 2005), which became the core competences of Indian service providers. Infosys, for example, now has more than 141,000 employees of thirty-eight nationalities in twenty-eight countries (Infosys 2011). In recent years, India-based service providers have taken on higher value-added services and are aggressively engaging in the production of knowledge-intensive services (Lewin et al. 2010).

Intentional replication of the success and comparative advantage of India's experience by other countries is a complex and daunting national challenge. Chile has experienced some success in building a services-outsourcing dimension for its economy; its economic development agency, CORFO, launched an initiative in 2001 to promote Chile as a destination for business-services outsourcing. Over an eight-year period, Chile expanded its industry fourfold to $1bn, but the workforce accounts for approximately 1 per cent of India's, and inhibits Chile in areas where employee scale is important, such as call-centres. CORFO realized that Chile needed to become a destination for higher value-added sourcing of services such as engineering services, application development, and software maintenance (Fernandez-Stark, Bamber, and Gereffi 2010).

The Chile example highlights the fact that not all countries aspiring to attract the sourcing of business services as a lever of economic development will be able to attain India's level of momentum. However, China's quest to leapfrog India's service-provider industry is particularly notable. China's Ministry of Commerce launched the '1000-100-10' project in 2006, accompanied by a set of policy instruments that mainly targeted cost incentives for potential clients of the global business-services sourcing industry; however, the absence of seeking complementarities between policy intiatives resulted in competition for resources with other ministries, with conflicting interests and constituencies. However, in 2009, the national aspiration to jump-start the service-provider industry became an initiative of the State Council, thereby command-ing attention from all levels of government. Given that local governments enjoy great autonomy in incentivizing and regulating China's local economy, the State Council des-ignated twenty-one 'Service Outsourcing Model Cities' to compete in promoting and developing the local service-outsourcing industry as well as attracting international service providers and corporate captive operations. A more comprehensive agenda out-lined increased efforts to train science and engineering students, as well as creating local competition to speed up the maturity of local service providers. By 2011, many of these designated model cities had shown significant growth, as measured by executed con-tract value, ranging from 35 to 81.8 per cent annual increases (CCIIP 2011). Although it remains to be seen to what extent the national policy instruments devised will impact economic development, comparative country studies of different policy configurations and changes in job creation, revenue, and profitability of the emerging business-services outsourcing industry are required for a systematic understanding of how complementa-rities at the level of promulgating and implementing bundles of policy instruments can trigger a positive-feedback mechanism spurring industry growth and maturity.

# An Analytical Framework for Attracting Global Sourcing of Services to an Aspiring Host Country

To better analyse the dynamics underlying this industry's growth and the implications for economic development, we propose to identify and group the growth mechanisms of the service-provider industry in order to relate them to economic development. The framework consists of factors that contribute to a country's attractiveness for harness-ing global sourcing of business-services capabilities, such as policy instruments, human capital, and provider-industry maturity level, where complementarities among them are essential (see Figure 22.2). In other words, at the national economy level, top-down policy design and bottom-up self-organizational involvement of local actors' capability development would be mediated by another set of mechanisms managing interdepend-encies (i.e. complementarities) serving to integrate such dynamics.

It is particularly important to achieve complementarities within the configuration of policy instruments when orchestrating efforts at national level. That is, the effectiveness of disparate policy instruments is a function of achieving complementarities among piecemeal policies originating from different ministries, independent policy-making agencies, etc. Piecemeal adoption of policy instruments by countless quasi-independent governmental bodies without overarching coordinating and consensus-building mech-anisms cannot realize the full potential benefits, and are more likely to result in dysfunc-tional outcomes. For example, China is investing in university research quite early in the economic development process, which has a significant impact on the process of human

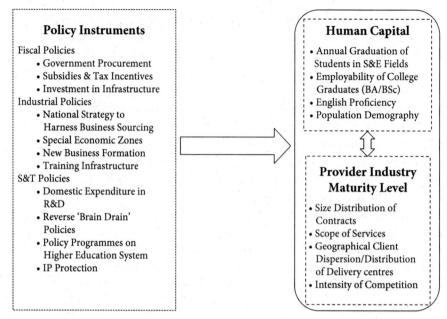

**Policy Instruments**

Fiscal Policies
  • Government Procurement
  • Subsidies & Tax Incentives
  • Investment in Infrastructure
Industrial Policies
  • National Strategy to
    Harness Business Sourcing
  • Special Economic Zones
  • New Business Formation
  • Training Infrastructure
S&T Policies
  • Domestic Expenditure in
    R&D
  • Reverse 'Brain Drain'
    Policies
  • Policy Programmes on
    Higher Education System
  • IP Protection

**Human Capital**

  • Annual Graduation of
    Students in S&E Fields
  • Employability of College
    Graduates (BA/BSc)
  • English Proficiency
  • Population Demography

**Provider Industry
Maturity Level**

  • Size Distribution of
    Contracts
  • Scope of Services
  • Geographical Client
    Dispersion/Distribution
    of Delivery centres
  • Intensity of Competition

FIGURE 22.2 Model of country attractiveness for sourcing business services

capital accumulation (Kenney, Zhang, and Patton 2012), and such policy effort could also contribute to complementary outcomes in both human capital accumulation and industry maturity. However, in parallel, other policy efforts are required to also target complementary outcomes involving developing and incentivizing the maturity level of the business services outsourcing industry.

# Conclusion and Avenues
## for Future Research

This chapter has provided a broad review of the dynamic growth of the global sourcing phenomenon and has highlighted the potential for VoC/BS literature to incorporate country differences involving development of human capital at a more micro level in order to account for issues of supply chains and offshoring/outsourcing and economic development of countries, especially emerging economies. The VoC/BS literature would benefit from a deeper understanding of underlying explanatory temporal mechanisms with a co-evolutionary perspective and with a focus on the extent to which emerging economies can harness the global sourcing of business services as a deliberate lever of economic development. The chapter advances an analytical framework for framing research efforts to trace country capability development for realizing aspirations to attract the business-services outsourcing industry as another lever of economic development. Additional research themes are proposed below to gain a more nuanced understanding of how such dynamic processes unfold.

## Human Capital Policy and Diaspora Network

Despite the apparent availability of STEM graduates in the emerging economies, large populations of highly skilled expatriates from developing countries are found in developed countries, because of the rapidly expanding migration of international students from developing to developed countries in pursuit of advanced degrees (National Science Board 2012). These talent pools constitute a globally dispersed diaspora of talent with the potential to contribute to their home countries' economic development (Lewin and Zhong 2012). However, the effect of the diaspora phenomenon is not well understood. A few studies have illustrated the role of the Indian diaspora in jump-starting the dynamic growth of the Indian outsourcing industry and diminishing the institutional distance between firms in two countries (Saxenian 2002; Vang and Overby 2006). This suggests that potential home-country opportunities, as well as the industry's growth potential, can positively contribute to the active engagement of overseas talent (IFC 2011).

## Internationalization of Innovation and Open-Source Innovation Networks

The dynamic growth of global sourcing of innovation is indicative of the evolving ecology of global innovation that is expected to usher in significant changes in firms, industries, and organizations of talent around the globe (Lewin and Zhong 2012). New contexts arise as companies structure new forms of collaboration and coordination: firms are learning to take advantage of web-based collaboration platforms, as web-based collaborative technologies increasingly become powerful tools for organizing the workflow and products of scientists and R&D collaborators in offshore locations on a daily basis. Agerfalk and Fitzgerald (2008) discuss cases of open-sourcing as a global sourcing strategy and have documented that implementing open-sourcing organizational capabilities provides ample opportunity for companies to headhunt STEM development, and hence move from outsourcing to a largely unknown workforce towards recruitment of STEM talent from a global open-source community whose talents have become known through open-sourcing experience. How trends in open-source innovation affect the competitive advantages of firms and the role of business systems warrants further research.

# APPENDIX

# ORN Survey Data

The annual Offshoring Research Network (ORN) survey, initiated in 2004 at Duke University Centre for International Business Education and Research, Fuqua School of Business, tracks offshoring activities in more than 1,500 companies around the world, as well as companies that are considering or have rejected such ideas. Instead of surveying the general experience of companies with offshoring practices, the ORN survey identifies every specific function that a company has offshored in a particular location by the year it was launched (see Table 22.1, top). At the same time, for a number of business

### Table 22.1 Descriptive statistics on buy-side database

|  | N | Percentage |
|---|---|---|
| **Company Level** | | |
| *Size of Companies* | | |
| Large | 256 | 16.89 |
| Midsize | 513 | 33.84 |
| Small | 747 | 49.27 |
| *Offshoring Status* | | |
| Currently offshoring | 731 | 45.89 |
| Considering offshoring | 288 | 18.08 |
| Decided not to offshore | 574 | 36.03 |
| *Headquarters of Companies* | | |
| US | 493 | 31.1 |
| Western Europe | 913 | 57.6 |
| Asia-Pacific | 159 | 10 |
| Other region | 20 | 1.3 |
| **Implementation Level** | | |
| *Function Type of Offshored Implementations* | | |
| Application Development and Maintenance | 435 | 10.67 |
| Contact Centre | 614 | 15.06 |
| Design Services | 179 | 4.39 |
| Engineering Services | 336 | 8.24 |
| Finance and Accounting | 408 | 10.01 |
| Human Resources | 218 | 5.35 |
| IT Infrastructure | 805 | 19.74 |

*(Continued)*

**Table 22.1  Continued**

|  | N | Percentage |
|---|---|---|
| Knowledge/Analytical Services | 195 | 4.78 |
| Legal Services | 65 | 1.59 |
| Marketing & Sales | 222 | 5.45 |
| Other | 79 | 1.94 |
| Supply Chain & Facilities | 267 | 6.55 |
| Research & Development | 254 | 6.23 |
| *Location of Offshored Implementations* | | |
| Africa | 59 | 1.94 |
| Asia | 1,778 | 58.51 |
| Australia | 41 | 1.35 |
| Eastern Europe | 286 | 9.41 |
| Latin America | 353 | 11.62 |
| Middle East | 39 | 1.28 |
| US | 140 | 4.61 |
| Western Europe | 343 | 11.29 |

*Source*: Offshoring Research Network survey, 2004.

**Table 22.2  Descriptive statistics on service provider database**

|  | N | Percentage |
|---|---|---|
| *Size of Companies* | | |
| Large | 133 | 21.49 |
| Midsize | 185 | 29.89 |
| Small | 301 | 48.63 |
| *Provider Headquarters Region* | | |
| US | 228 | 34.03 |
| Western Europe | 149 | 22.24 |
| India | 114 | 17.01 |
| China | 32 | 4.78 |
| Other Asia | 53 | 7.91 |
| Eastern Europe | 44 | 6.57 |
| Latin America | 39 | 5.82 |
| Other region | 11 | 1.64 |

*Source*: Offshoring Research Network survey, 2004.

functions, the entire process has been relocated in their offshoring implementations (see Table 22.1, bottom).

Since 2007, the annual ORN survey of corporate (buy side) is complemented by an annual ORN Service Provider Survey to collect data on the supply of offshore services. The rapid growth of the global business-services industry is not just a story of demand (buy side), but is also driven by the emergence and rapid rise of a global and highly competitive business-services provider industry (supply-side). The provider survey tracks service providers in the key dimensions of service offering and implementation, contract and client relationships, and operation risks, as well as future plans and expectations. Over 800 providers are in the ORN service provider database (Table 22.2). With both the buy-side and service-provider survey, ORN surveys provide researchers with empirical observations on the dynamic growth of the service-sourcing industry.

## NOTES

1. Including IT infrastructure, software and application development and maintenance, finance and accounting, HR, engineering and R&D, and knowledge and analytical services.
2. Teranishi (1996) noted that after World War II, large farmers were eliminated by land reform (Korea and Taiwan), substituted by state ownership (Indonesia), or suppressed by anti-Chinese policy (Malaysia).
3. The OECD (2008) report attempted an exhaustive list of direct and indirect measures of offshoring with proposed direct indicators of offshoring, primarily with data on production, FDI, and exports and imports.
4. CMM, 'Capability Maturity Model', developed at the Software and Engineering Institute of Carnegie Mellon University, describes and appraises methods and processes involved in software development. For the transition from an 'immature' to 'mature' software development organization, CMM defines five levels—Level 5 is the highest rating that a software company can attain.

## REFERENCES

Agarwal, S. and S. N. Ramaswami (1992). 'Choice of Foreign-Market Entry Mode: Impact of Ownership, Location and Internationalization Factors'. *Journal of International Business Studies* 23(1): 1–27.

Agerfalk, P. J. and B. Fitzgerald (2008). 'Outsourcing to an Unknown Workforce: Exploring Open-Sourcing as a Global Sourcing Strategy'. *MIS Quarterly* 32(2): 385–409.

Agrawal, V. and D. Farrell (2003). 'Who Wins in Offshoring?' *McKinsey Quarterly* 4 (Special Edition: Global Directions): 37–43.

Aharoni, Y., L. Tihanyi, and B. L. Connelly (2011). 'Managerial Decision-Making in International Business: A 45-Year Retrospective'. *Journal of World Business* 46(2): 135–142.

Anderson, E. and H. Gatignon (1986). 'Modes of Foreign Entry: A Transaction Cost Analysis and Propositions'. *Journal of International Business Studies* 17(3): 1–26.

Aoki, M., H.-K. Kim, and M. Okuno-Fujiwara, Eds. (1996). *The Role of Government in East Asian Economic Development*. New York, Oxford University Press.

Apte, U. M. and R. O. Mason (1995). 'Global Disaggregation of Information-Intensive Services'. *Management Science* 41(7): 1250–1262.

Arora, A. and A. Gambardella, Eds. (2005). *From Underdogs to Tigers: The Rise and Growth of the Software Industry in Brazil, China, India, Ireland, and Israel*. Oxford, Oxford University Press.

Asheim, B.T. and L. Coenen (2005). 'Knowledge Bases and Regional Innovation Systems: Comparing Nordic Clusters'. *Research Policy* 34(8): 1173–1190.

Athreye, S. S. (2005). 'The Indian Software Industry and its Evolving Service Capability'. *Industrial and Corporate Change* 14(3): 393–418.

BCG (2007). *Estudios de Competitividad en Clusters de la Economía Chilena: Documento de Referencia Offshoring*. Boston, Boston Consulting Group.

Bell, G. G. (2005). 'Clusters, Networks, and Firm Innovativeness'. *Strategic Management Journal* 26(3): 287–295.

Beulen, E., P. van Fenema, and W. Currie (2005). 'From Application Outsourcing to Infrastructure Management: Extending the Offshore Outsourcing Service Portfolio'. *European Management Journal* 23(2): 133–144.

Bevan, A., S. Estrin, and K. Meyer (2004). 'Foreign Investment Location and Institutional Development in Transition Economies'. *International Business Review* 13(1): 43–64.

Borrus, M., D. Ernst, and S. Haggard, Eds. (2000). *International Production Networks in Asia: Rivalry or Riches?* London, Routledge.

Campa, J. and L. Goldberg (1997). 'The Evolving External Orientation of Manufacturing Industries'. NBER Working Paper. New York, Federal Reserve Bank.

Cantwell, J. (1995). 'The Globalisation of Technology: What Remains of the Product-Cycle Model?' *Cambridge Journal of Economics* 19(1): 155–174.

CCIIP (2011). *China Outsourcing Newsletter 15*. Beijing, China Council for International Investment Promotion.

Chaminade, C. and J. Vang (2008). 'Globalisation of Knowledge Production and Regional Innovation Policy: Supporting Specialized Hubs in the Bangalore Software Industry'. *Research Policy* 37(10): 1684–1696.

Chandler, A. D. and T. Hikino (1990). *Scale and Scope: The Dynamics of Industrial Capitalism*. Cambridge, Belknap Press.

Coase, R. H. (1937). 'The Nature of the Firm'. *Economica*, New Series 4(16): 386–405.

Cooke, P., M. G. Uranga, and G. Etxebarria (1997). 'Regional Innovation Systems: Institutional and Organisational Dimensions'. *Research Policy* 26(4–5): 475–491.

Dalal, J. (2007). 'Tipping Point for Offshore BPO'. *Siliconindia* 10(5): 28–29.

Delios, A. and P. W. Beamish (1999). 'Ownership Strategy of Japanese Firms: Transactional, Institutional, and Experience Influences'. *Strategic Management Journal* 20(10): 915–933.

—— and W. J. Henisz (2003). 'Policy Uncertainty and the Sequence of Entry by Japanese Firms 1980–1998'. *Journal of International Business Studies* 34(3): 227–241.

DiMaggio, P. J. and W. W. Powell (1983). 'The Iron Cage Revisited: Institutional Isomorphism and Collective Rationality in Organizational Fields'. *American Sociological Review* 48(2): 147–160.

Dossani, R. (2007). 'Entrepreneurship: The True Story Behind Indian IT'. In H. Rowen, M. G. Hancock, and W. F. Miller, Eds., *Making IT: The Rise of Asia in High Tech*. Stanford, Stanford University Press.

—— and M. Kenney (2007). 'The Next Wave of Globalization: Relocating Service Provision to India'. *World Development* 35(5): 772–791.

—— (2009). 'Service Provision for the Global Economy: The Evolving Indian Experience'. *Review of Policy Research* 26(1-2): 77–104.

Dunn, S., H. Harris, and P. Blatman (2011) 'Beyond the Contract: Driving Value from the Renegotiation Process'. *Deloitte Review*. Retrieved 27 November 2012 from <http://www.deloitte.com/view/en_US/us/Insights/Browse-by-Content-Type/deloitte-review/af2a881dc918d210VgnVCM2000001b56f00aRCRD.htm>.

Dunning, J. H. (1988). 'The Eclectic Paradigm of International Production: A Restatement and Some Possible Extensions'. *Journal of International Business Studies* 19(1): 1–31.

—— (2000). *Regions, Globalization, and the Knowledge-Based Economy*. Oxford, Oxford University Press.

Ernst, D. (2008). 'Innovation Offshoring and Asia's Electronics Industry'. *International Journal of Technological Learning, Innovation and Development* 1(4): 551–576.

Essletzbichler, J. (2003). 'From Mass Production to Flexible Specialization: The Sectoral and Geographical Extent of Contract Work in US Manufacturing 1963–1997'. *Regional Studies* 37(8): 753–771.

Farrell, D. and McKinsey Global Institute (2006). *Offshoring: Understanding the Emerging Global Labour Market*. Boston, Harvard Business School Press.

Feinberg, S. E. and A. K. Gupta (2004). 'Knowledge Spillovers and the Assignment of R&D Responsibilities to Foreign Subsidiaries'. *Strategic Management Journal* 25(8–9): 823–845.

Fernandez-Stark, K., P. Bamber, and G. Gereffi (2010). *Workforce Development in Chile's Offshore Services Value Chain*. Report prepared for Chilean Agency for Economic Development. Durham, NC, Duke University.

—— (2011). 'The Offshore Services Value Chain: Upgrading Trajectories in Developing Countries'. *International Journal of Technological Learning, Innovation and Development* 4(1–2–3): 206–234.

Gartner (2011). 'Global BPO/ITO Revenue 2010'. Retrieved 25 July 2011 from <http://coreadvisor.com/globalwise/2010/03/03/numb3rs-global-bpoito-revenue-2010/>.

Gereffi, G. and M. Korzeniewicz, Eds. (1994). *Commodity Chains and Global Capitalism*. Westport, Greenwood Press.

Griffin, K. (2001). 'Poverty and Land Distribution: Cases of Land Reform in Asia'. In H. R. Morales Jr, J. Putzel, F. Lara Jr, E. Quitoriano, and A. Miclat-Teves, Eds., *Power in the Village: Agrarian Reform, Rural Politics, Institutional Change and Globalization* 17–37. Quezon City, University of the Philippines Press.

Hall, P. A. and D. W. Soskice, Eds. (2001). *Varieties of Capitalism*. Oxford, Oxford University Press.

Hancké, B., M. Rhodes, and M. Thatcher (2007). 'Introduction: Beyond Varieties of Capitalism'. *Beyond Varieties of Capitalism: Conflict, Contradictions, and Complementarities in the European Economy*. Oxford, Oxford University Press.

Heeks, R. (1996). *India's Software Industry*. Thousand Oaks, Sage.

Henisz, W. J. and A. Delios (2001). 'Uncertainty, Imitation, and Plant Location: Japanese Multinational Corporations 1990–1996'. *Administrative Science Quarterly* 46(3): 443–475.

Hennart, J. F. (1988). 'A Transaction Costs Theory of Equity Joint Ventures'. *Strategic Management Journal* 9(4): 361–374.

Herrigel, G. and J. Zeitlin. (2010). 'Inter-Firm Relations in Global Manufacturing: Disintegrated Production and Its Globalization'. In G. Morgan, J. Campbell, C. Crouch, O. K. Pedersen, and R. Whitley, Eds., *The Oxford Handbook of Comparative Institutional Analysis*: 527–564. New York, Oxford University Press.

Howells, J. (1990). 'The Location and Organization of Research and Development: New Horizons'. *Research Policy* 19(2): 133–146.

Hutzschenreuter, T., A. Y. Lewin, and W. Ressler (2011). 'The Growth of White-Collar Offshoring: Germany and the US from 1980 to 2006'. *European Management Journal* 29(4): 245–259.

—— T. Pedersen, and H. W. Volberda (2007). 'The Role of Path Dependency and Managerial Intentionality'. *Journal of International Business Studies* 38(7): 1055–1068.

Indian Electronics Commission (1975). *Perspective Report on Electronics in India*. New Delhi, Electronics Commission.

IFC (2011). 'Investing Across Borders 2010: Indicators of Foreign Direct Investment in 87 Economies'. Retrieved 25 July 2011 from <http://iab.worldbank.org/~/media/FPDKM/IAB/Documents/IAB-report.pdf>

Infosys (2011). Company Website. Retrieved 2 October 2012 from <http://www.infosys.com/about/Pages/index.aspx>

International Trade Administration, US Dept of Commerce (2011). 'US Automotive Parts Industry Annual Assessment'. Retrieved 25 July 2011 from <http://www.trade.gov/mas/manufacturing/oaai/build/groups/public/@tg_oaai/documents/webcontent/tg_oaai_003660.pdf>.

Jacobides, M. G. and S. G. Winter (2005). 'The Co-Evolution of Capabilities and Transaction Costs: Explaining the Institutional Structure of Production'. *Strategic Management Journal* 26(5): 395–413.

Jahns, C., E. Hartmann, and L. Bals (2006). 'Offshoring: Dimensions and Diffusion of a New Business Concept'. *Journal of Purchasing and Supply Management* 12(4): 218–231.

Kay, C. (2002). 'Why East Asia Overtook Latin America: Agrarian Reform, Industrialisation and Development'. *Third World Quarterly* 23(6): 1073–1102.

Kearney, A. T. (2007). *Making Offshore Decisions: Offshoring for Long-Term Advantage: The A.T. Kearney Global Services Location Index*. Chicago, A.T. Kearney.

Kenney, M. and R. Florida (1994). 'The Organization and Geography of Japanese R&D: Results from a Survey of Japanese Electronics and Biotechnology Firms'. *Research Policy* 23(3): 305–323.

Kenney, M., H. Zhang, and D. Patton (2012). 'Building Global-Class Universities: An Assessment of Chinese Government Policy'. Unpublished manuscript.

Kogut, B. and H. Singh (1988). 'The Effect of National Culture on the Choice of Entry Mode'. *Journal of International Business Studies* 19(3): 411–432.

Kotlarsky, J. and I. Oshri (2008). 'Country Attractiveness for Offshoring and Offshore Outsourcing: Additional Considerations'. *Journal of Information Technology* 23(4): 228–231.

Kshetri, N. (2007). 'Institutional Factors Affecting Offshore Business Process and Information Technology Outsourcing'. *Journal of International Management* 13(1): 38–56.

Kumar, N. (2001). 'National Innovation Systems and the Indian Software Industry Development'. World Industrial Development Report 2001, Vienna, UNIDO.

Lahiri, S. and B. Kedia (2011). 'Co-Evolution of Institutional and Organizational Factors in Explaining Offshore Outsourcing'. *International Business Review* 20(3): 252–263.

Lau, L. J. (1996). 'The Role of Government in Economic Development: Some Observations from the Experience of China, Hong Kong, and Taiwan'. In M. Aoki, H.-K. Kim, and M. Okuno-Fujiwara, Eds., *The Role of Government in East Asian Economic Development*: 41–73. New York, Oxford University Press.

Leiblein, M. J., J. J. Reuer, and F. Dalsace (2002). 'Do Make-or-Buy Decisions Matter? The Influence of Organizational Governance on Technological Performance'. *Strategic Management Journal* 23(9): 817–833.

Lewin, A. Y. and C. Peeters (2006). 'Offshoring Work: Business Hype or the Onset of Fundamental Transformation?' *Long Range Planning* 39(3): 221–239.

Lewin, A. Y., N. Perm-Ajchariyawong, D. Sappenfield, and C. Aird (2009). 'Is the Global Outsourcing Industry in for a No-Holds-Barred Competition?'. 2009 ORN Service Provider Survey Report. Durham, CIBER/PricewaterhouseCoopers.

—— (2010). 'The Ever-Changing Global Service-Provider Industry'. 2010 ORN Service-Provider Survey Report. Durham, CIBER/PricewaterhouseCoopers.

—— and H. W. Volberda (2011). 'Co-Evolution of Global Sourcing: The Need to Understand the Underlying Mechanisms of Firm Decisions to Offshore'. *International Business Review* 20(3): 241–251.

—— and X. Zhong. (2012). 'Institutional Entrepreneurship: Learning From the Emerging Service Provider Industry'. Working paper. Durham, NC, Duke University.

Lin, J. Y. and Y. Yao (2001) 'Chinese Rural Industrialization in the Context of the East Asian Miracle.' In J. E. Stiglitz and S. Yusuf, Eds., *Rethinking the East Asia Miracle*: 143–196. New York, Oxford University Press.

Liu, R. J., D. J. Feils, and B. Scholnick (2011). 'Why Are Different Services Outsourced to Different Countries?' *Journal of International Business Studies* 42(4): 558–571.

Lucas, R. E. (2004). 'Life Earnings and Rural-Urban Migration'. *Journal of Political Economy* 112(1): S29–S59.

Lundvall, B.-Å., Ed. (1992). *National Systems of Innovation: Towards a Theory of Innovation and Interactive Learning*. London, Pinter.

—— P. Intarakumnerd, and J. Vang-Lauridsen (2006). *Asia's Innovation Systems in Transition*. Cheltenham, Edward Elgar.

Manning, S., S. Massini, and A. Y. Lewin (2008). 'A Dynamic Perspective on Next-Generation Offshoring: The Global Sourcing of Science and Engineering Talent'. *Academy of Management Perspectives* 22(3): 35–54.

—— S. Massini, C. Peeters, and A. Y. Lewin (2012). 'Global Co-evolution of Firm Boundaries: Process Commoditization, Capabilities Development, and Path Dependencies'. Unpublished MS.

—— J. E. Ricart, M. S. Rosatti Rique, and A. Y. Lewin (2010). 'From Blind Spots to Hotspots: How Knowledge Services Clusters Develop and Attract Foreign Investment'. *Journal of International Management* 16(4): 369–382.

Marshall, A. (1920). *Principles of Economics*. London, Macmillan.

Metters, R. and R. Verma (2008). 'History of Offshoring Knowledge Services'. *Journal of Operations Management* 26(2): 141–147.

Murtha, T. P. (2004). 'The Metanational Firm in Context: Competition in Knowledge-Driven Industries'. In M. A. Hitt and J. L. C. Cheng, Eds., *Theories of the Multinational Enterprise*: 101–136. Bingley, Emerald Group.

NASSCOM (2011). 'The IT BPO Sector in India—Strategic Review 2011'. Retrieved September 3, 2012 from http://www.nasscom.org/it-bpo-sector-indiastrategic-review-2011.

Nassimbeni, G. and M. Sartor (2008). *Sourcing in India: Strategies and Experiences in the Land of Service Offshoring*. Basingstoke, Palgrave Macmillan.

National Science Board (2012). *Science and Engineering Indicators: 2012*. Arlington, National Science Foundation.

Nelson, R. R. (1993). *National Innovation Systems: A Comparative Analysis*. New York, Oxford University Press.

North, D. C. (1990). *Institutions, Institutional Change and Economic Performance*. Cambridge, Cambridge University Press.

OECD (2008). *Regional Investment Strategy: Key Findings of the Sector-Specific Study*. Sarajevo, OECD.

Otsuka, K., H. Chuma, and Y. Hayami (1992). 'Land and Labour Contracts in Agrarian Economies: Theories and Facts'. *Journal of Economic Literature* 30(4): 1965–2018.

Oxley, J. E. (1999). 'Institutional Environment and the Mechanisms of Governance: The Impact of Intellectual Property Protection on the Structure of Inter-Firm Alliances'. *Journal of Economic Behaviour & Organization* 38(3): 283–309.

Patel, P. and K. Pavitt (1991). 'Large Firms in the Production of the World's Technology: An Important Case of Non-Globalisation'. *Journal of International Business Studies* 22(1): 1–21.

Patibandla, M. and B. Petersen (2002). 'Role of Transnational Corporations in the Evolution of a High-Tech Industry: The Case of India's Software Industry'. *World Development* 30(9): 1561–1577.

Pearce, R. D. (1999). 'Decentralised R&D and Strategic Competitiveness: Globalised Approaches to Generation and Use of Technology in Multinational Enterprises (MNEs)'. *Research Policy* 28(2–3): 157–178.

Piore, M. J. and C. F. Sabel (1984). *The Second Industrial Divide: Possibilities for Prosperity*. New York, Basic Books.

Porter, M. E. (1990). 'The Competitive Advantage of Nations'. *Harvard Business Review* 68(2): 73–93.

—— (2000). 'Location, Competition, and Economic Development: Local Clusters in a Global Economy'. *Economic Development Quarterly* 14(1): 15–34.

Quinn, J. B. and F. G. Hilmer (1994). 'Strategic Outsourcing'. *Sloan Management Review* 35(4): 43–55.

Ricart, J. E. (2011). *Offshoring in the Global Economy: Management Practices and Welfare Implications*. Bilbao, Fundacion BBVA.

Safizadeh, M. H., J. M. Field, and L. P. Ritzman (2008). 'Sourcing Practices and Boundaries of the Firm in the Financial Services Industry'. *Strategic Management Journal* 29(1): 79–91.

Sako, M. (2006). 'Outsourcing and Offshoring: Implications for Productivity of Business Services'. *Oxford Review of Economic Policy* 22(4): 499–512.

Saxenian, A. (2002). 'Silicon Valley's New Immigrant High-Growth Entrepreneurs'. *Economic Development Quarterly* 16(1): 20–31.

Schaaf, J. (2005). *Outsourcing to India: Crouching Tiger Set to Pounce*. Frankfurt, Deutsche Bank Research.

Schilling, M. A. and H. K. Steensma (2001). 'The Use of Modular Organizational Forms'. *Academy of Management Journal* 44(6): 1149–1168.

Sudan, R., S. Ayers, P. Dongier, A. Muente-Kunigami, and C.Z-W. Qiang (2010). *The Global Opportunity in IT-Based Services: Assessing and Enhancing Country Competitiveness*. Washington, DC, World Bank.

Swinnen, J. F. M., L. Dries, and K. Macours (2005). 'Transition and Agricultural Labour'. *Agricultural Economics* 32(1): 15–34.

Tambe, P. and L. M. Hitt (2012). 'Now it's Personal: Offshoring and the Shifting Skill Composition of the US Information Technology Workforce'. *Management Science* 58(4): 678–695.

Teranishi, J. (1996). 'Sectoral Resource Transfer, Conflict, and Macrostability in Economic Development'. In M. Aoki, H-K. Kim, and M. Okuno-Fujiwara, Eds., *The Role of Government in East Asian Economic Development*: 279–322. New York, Oxford University Press.

Thelen, K. (2010). 'Beyond Comparative Statistics: Historical Institutional Approaches to Stability and Change in the Political Economy of Labour'. In G. Morgan, C. Campbell, C. Crouch, O. K. Pedersen, and R. Whitley, Eds., *The Oxford Handbook of Comparative Institutional Analysis*: 41–62. New York, Oxford University Press.

UNCTAD (2005). *Prospects for Foreign Direct Investment and the Strategies of Transnational Corporations 2005–2008*. Geneva, UNCTAD.

UNESCO (2010). *Science Report 2010: The Current Status of Science around the World*. Paris, UNESCO.

Vang, J. and M. Overby (2006). 'Transnational Communities, TNCs and Development: The Case of the Indian IT Services Industry'. In B.-Å. Lundvall, P. Intarakumnerd, and J. Vang-Lauridsen, Eds., *Asia's Innovation Systems in Transition*: 54–74. Cheltenham, Edward Elgar.

Whitley, R. (1999). *Divergent Capitalisms*. Oxford, Oxford University Press.

—— (2005). 'How National Are Business Systems? The Role of States and Complementary Institutions in Standardising Systems of Economic Co-ordination and Control at the National Level'. In G. Morgan, R. Whitley, and E. Moen, Eds., *Changing Capitalisms? Internationalization, Institutional Change, and Systems of Economic Organization*: 190–234. Oxford, Oxford University Press.

Williamson, O. E. (1985). *The Economic Institutions of Capitalism*. New York, Free Press.

World Bank (1992). *India: An Information Technology Development Strategy*. Washington, DC, World Bank.

World Development Indicators (1970–2011). Retrieved 3 December 2012 from <http://data.worldbank.org/data-catalog/world-development-indicators>.

Youngdahl, W. and K. Ramaswamy (2008). 'Offshoring Knowledge and Service Work: A Conceptual Model and Research Agenda'. *Journal of Operations Management* 26(2): 212–221.

# CHAPTER 23

# SOCIAL CAPITAL IN ASIA

## *Its Dual Nature and Function*

### PETER PING LI AND GORDON REDDING

## INTRODUCTION

SOCIAL capital, when it exists, can be possessed by both individuals and societies. A simple word for it is 'trust'. Having it leads to a proclivity to cooperate. Such cooperation might be between individuals, as for instance in an 'old-boy network', between organizations, as in a Japanese *keiretsu,* or between both and the surrounding infrastructure of the society, as for instance in willingness to pay taxes and to be law-abiding. When it is present, its value for business lies in its capacity to stimulate economic growth by reducing transaction costs and competitive risk as well as by enhancing transaction value and cooperative opportunities (Li 1998, 2007a). It also fosters an increase in the total volume of transactions. In Fukuyama's (1995) classic treatment of the subject it is a social virtue, a theme echoed more recently in a rising number of scholarly treatments of human cooperativeness (e.g. McCloskey 2006; Mokyr 2009; Wrangham 2009; Seabright 2010; Nowak 2011; Acemoglu and Robinson 2012; Pagel 2012). It is normally seen as operating in two ways: *relational capital* between individuals and organizations where ties of reciprocity evolve; and *system capital* between individuals, organizations, and the surrounding institutional order of the society, where reciprocity is not so much involved, but where confidence in the surrounding institutions reduces perceived risk. The working of social capital varies between societies both in intensity and in the processes and institutions related to trust that have evolved.

A century ago, Sun Yat Sen was accustomed to asking why China was like a tray of loose sand, with each grain being an individual family, while Japan was like a piece of solid granite. That metaphor stands for the central question in this chapter. Understanding it for a highly varied region requires an account that looks at recent international research, but also takes note of Asian theorizing about society and cooperation. We will conclude that the phenomenon has many dimensions as well as many determinants, including history, socio-cultural traditions, the political structuring of institutions, and often influences brought in from the outside world.

# Basic Understandings about Social Capital

Esser (2008) has identified six types of resources and benefits in play in social capital transactions. The first three apply mainly to relational capital, and the second three mainly to system capital:

1. *Positional-based.* Access to information and a certain kind of social life through relationships.
2. *Trust-based.* Readiness of actors to become trustfully involved in risky ventures with other actors.
3. *Obligation-based.* The production of support, help, and solidarity.
4. *System Control.* The availability of social control and a certain level of attention to the fate and action of other members of an entire social network, as in a family or a business network.
5. *System trust.* A climate of trust in the network.
6. *System morality.* The validity of norms, values, and morality within a group, organization, or society.

Esser summarizes conditions for the effective working of such capital in an economy, as follows. Effective relational capital, working through individuals, will benefit from personal skills in the management of such relationships. These include (a) the building of an extensive portfolio of weak and non-redundant ties, (b) reliable and visible commitments with a selected number of strong ties, (c) doing favours to accumulate credits and obligations. The effective working of system capital rests on (d) the speed and completeness of information flow, (e) experiencing the performance of the system, and (f) system morality visible in the attitudes and orientations of the members. Systemic capital will also be influenced by the system's own density, closure, and stability, as well as members' dependence on the system's performance.

In a parallel defining of social capital, Lin (2008) places it within a theory of networking, in that it is a bundle of resources embedded in a person's social networks and accessed through ties. The sources of social capital (of the relational kind) that then determine the amount available for use are the strength of a person's position, their position in the network, and the purposes of any specific action. This does not mean that networks in themselves equate to social capital. Whether they are open or closed, what kinds of resources are involved, what the aims of the transactions are, and the intensity and reciprocity of relations, will all influence the eventual workings of the process.

A crucial component in understanding the workings of social capital is contained in what Ahn and Ostrom (2008) refer to as *trustworthiness*. This feature receives attention in what they term second-generation theories of social action. In these, the sparse logics of economics are enriched with the addition of psycho-social factors. Uslaner (2008) has also proposed the notion of *moralistic trust,* arguing that this is necessary if trust is to extend beyond cooperation with known people, and on into civic engagement with unknown people. Another useful contribution here is his clarification of trust in institutions: faith in institutions such as law is more accurately *confidence*, as such institutions are inanimate and cannot reciprocate. An ideal end result is a society in which there is enough moralistic trust for people to believe that most others are trustworthy, honest, and cooperative, and there is enough reinforcement through experience of the institutional system for people to extend cooperativeness to strangers. It is the barrier of trusting strangers that guards access to the world of intensive and extensive economic exchange, and so to societal progress. Surmounting it is essentially a political question and one of daunting difficulty.

# Social Capital and Societal Progress

There is strong evidence that high amounts of social capital are correlated with societal success in economic progress (Fukuyama 1995; Inglehart and Baker 2000). The GLOBE study of differences across sixty-two societies among 17,000 respondents analysed the two main forms of cooperativeness, which they termed *Institutional Collectivism* (i.e. system capital) and *In-Group Collectivism* (i.e. relational capital), and found that the former correlated significantly positively with national economic health and the latter significantly negatively (Javidan, House, and Dorfman 2004).

Cooperativeness was identified by Mokyr (2009), along with inventiveness, as key in explaining the success of the first Industrial Revolution—in nineteenth-century Britain. This effect can follow from either relational or system capital, or both. There is recognition that in societal progress towards higher per capita prosperity, a point of transition is reached where reliance on relational capital gives way to an increasing reliance on system capital. If this transition cannot be achieved, the society stops growing. This barrier is not yet fully theorized, but is showing in the literature as 'the middle-income trap' (World Bank 2010; Eichengreen, Park, and Shin 2011; Zhang et al. 2012). It is a contention of this chapter that successful transitions will always see the addition of system capital to a *compatible form* of relational capital.

# CONCEPTUAL DEBATES ABOUT
# SOCIAL CAPITAL

The theory of social capital remains work-in-progress, as its nature, functioning, and sources are both complex and varied between societies (cf. Portes 1998; Lin 2001; Adler and Kwon 2002). So too do its effects range across a wide spectrum of positives and negatives. For example, it is unclear how social capital is related to the concepts of social ties and trust at either ego-centric or communal level (Li 2007a). Further, it seems that social capital in different cultures tends to derive from different sources, but all with both positive (e.g. sharing tacit knowledge) and negative (e.g. corruption) effects within diverse institutional contexts. For instance, social capital in Chinese culture tends to derive mostly from *guanxi*, a special form of personalized social tie in the context of weak institutions, in contrast to the commonly described depersonalized ties in the West in the context of strong institutions (Li 2007a).

As the notion of social capital is complex, ambiguous, and elusive, it is somewhat controversial. Its identification as a social feature lies in the work of Bourdieu (1980, 1986) and Coleman (1988) who, building on Mauss (1954) on gift exchange, were interested in explaining the effects of social relations. Both saw social capital as a special resource for individuals. For Coleman, the concept provided a middle way between theories based on rational self-interest, and theories based on the impact of social norms. For Bourdieu (1986), it was part of a theory in which economic, social, and cultural capital are what individuals and groups use to transfer resources across generations. Some later accounts have also seen social capital as a property of organizations, whereby managers build networks for organizational purposes. In this section, we outline some current theoretical controversies around the nature of social capital.

We begin with the conceptual controversy over the *nature* of social capital, especially its link with social ties and trust. In particular, we focus on addressing both similar and different sources of social capital in Asia. Second, we consider the *function* of social capital, especially its positive and negative effects across Asia's diverse contexts. In particular, we focus on the complex interplay between informal and formal institutions in Asia as both complementary and conflicting. We see here the balanced coming together of alternative and possibly opposing features. We consequently adopt a cognitive framework designed for such complexity and interplay—the Chinese cognitive frame of *yin-yang* balancing—to capture the holistic and dynamic interplay between two opposite elements in a duality (Li 2008).

The use of a frame of reference based in an Asian epistemology is deliberate here, as Eastern and Western ways of thinking do not necessarily overlap, and one perspective may benefit from the revealing of another (Tsui, Nifakdar, and Ou 2007; March 2005). We analyse social capital in a non-Cartesian framework of balanced interdependent forces (Chen and Miller 2011; Li 2012). A significant reason for this approach is that Asian policy-makers and business actors are likely to be thinking through the evolutions of their societies using cognitive frameworks of their own (Nakamura 1964; Maruyama 1980; Hsu 1981; Nisbett 2003; Li 2012).

## Unclear Definitions

We have noted that there is little consensus on the link between social capital and socially available resources, as well as between social capital and social ties, or trust (Portes 1998; Lin 2001). This especially applies for organization-level social capital (Nahapiet and Ghoshal 1998; Adler and Kwon 2002; Kostova and Roth 2003). Some define social capital as privileged access to rare resources (Portes 1998; Adler and Kwon 2002), whereas others define it as privileged access plus accessible resources (Bourdieu 1986; Lin 2001). However, among these definitions is no explicit statement regarding the distinction and link between social capital and social ties or trust. There is a common but unexplored assumption that social capital is equivalent to social ties and social trust.

## Informal and/or Formal

There is a related debate on whether social capital is primarily instrumental in nature via weak social ties or trust (Portes 1998; Burt 2001; Adler and Kwon 2002), or both instrumental and sentimental via strong social ties or trust (Bourdieu 1986; Bian 1997; Lin 2001). In addition, there is little consensus on an appropriate level of analysis (Woolcock 1998; Portes 2000; Lin 2001). Some analyse social capital at the level of a social network as either large communities (Fukuyama 1995; Putnam 1993) or small groups (Bourdieu 1986; Coleman 1990; Portes 1998; Burt 2001), others at both dyadic and ego-centric network level (Bian 1997; Lin 2001). Nor is there agreement on the 'proper' structure of social networks for social capital (Burt 2001). Some regard strong ties in closely knit local groups as most effective for social capital (Coleman 1990; Bian 1997), while others regard an open diverse global network as better (Granovetter 1983; Burt 2001). All debates hinge on one quintessential issue—the personalized uniqueness of informal elements in contrast to formal ones. This has been comparatively neglected, even though it is central to the conceptualization of social capital and its links with social ties and social trust (see Li 2006, 2007a, 2007b).

The nature of social capital vis-à-vis social ties and social trust can be captured by the dimensions of (a) *substance* (e.g. informal access to others' resources and sentimental sources rooted in tie strength) and (b) *structure* (e.g. social ties and network formation rooted in network configuration) (Portes 1998; Lin 2001; Wellman and Frank 2001; Adler and Kwon 2002; Kostova and Roth 2003; cf. Nahapiet and Ghoshal 1998; Tsai and Ghoshal 1998; Flap and Boxman 2001). These two core dimensions of social capital are related to the duality of social embeddedness (Granovetter 1992) with its relational and structural dimensions. We argue that the core of the substance dimension is *social trust,* or committed goodwill as the key source of privileged access to others' resources on a 'free-rental' basis at the interpersonal level. The core of the structure dimension is *social option*, or accessibility to diverse resource choices at the ego-centric and communal levels (Li 2006, 2007a).

## Yin–Yang Balancing

The Chinese cognitive frame of yin–yang has the special capability to disentangle the balance between two opposite elements working as a duality (Li 2008, 2012). It has three core tenets: (1) holistic (interdependent components within a multidimensional and comprehensive 'spatial' substance); (2) dynamic (interactive components in a multi-phase and non-linear temporal process), and (3) duality (paired dialectical components as opposites-in-unity with both complementary synergy and conflicting trade-off). Readers of complexity theory will find echoes of similar principles evoked by Beinhocker (2005) and Kauffman (1995), as well as parallels with quantum physics (Capra 1975).

As the holistic and dynamic tenets are opposites in unity, the duality tenet holds them in place reciprocally (Li 2008). In general, all trade-offs, dilemmas, dichotomies, dualisms, or paradoxes can be reframed as dualities to achieve the holistic and dynamic balances. As two sides of the same coin, the relative or partial nature of duality is where the frame of *yin–yang* balance differs from 'either/or' logic as well as the dialectical 'both/or' (Li 2008, 2012).

Applying the frame of *yin–yang* balancing to research on social capital helps to explain both its nature and function (see Figure 23.1). First, we can frame social capital as informal compared to other types of capital (e.g. financial or physical), but the formal and informal capitals often interact so much with each other that each contains some element of the other, and they are thus never mutually exclusive. As proposed by Li (2006, 2007a), *informality* refers to the nature of social ties and events (e.g. subjective, affective, people-oriented, and sentimental), while *formality* refers to that which is explicitly prescribed and external (e.g. objective, cognitive, task-oriented, and instrumental). In a similar way we can frame social capital as both similar to and different from social tie or trust. Further, social capital can be treated as related to, but also differentiated from, socially available resources.

## A Special Enabler

As an informal access to others' resources, social capital is not itself a typical *resource* as such, even though it is related to it, nor, as an informal means of access via social tie or trust, is it either the *tie* or *trust* itself. Social trust is a core component of the social tie, but not the tie itself. In other words, social capital is best regarded as a *special enabler for social cooperation*. It is the proclivity shared by people, either familiar with or strange to each other, to behave cooperatively, either interpersonally, or with the types of formal institutions the society has framed. The overall effect of informal–formal interaction and balance will be a context-specific social order (Li 2007a; Redding and Rowley 2013).

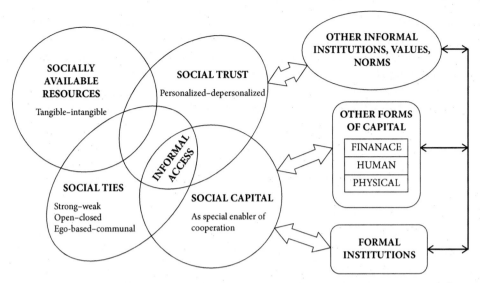

FIGURE 23.1 A holistic model of Yin–Yang relationship balancing, within Chinese cognition

## Strong and Weak

It is useful to further differentiate social capital into stronger and weaker forms, using the dimension of *tie strength* as the core substance of social capital (Granovetter 1983). *Strong* social capital refers to personalized access to others' resources based on sentimental ties in an ego-centric network, thus relationship-specific social capital (Lin 2001); while *weak* social capital refers to depersonalized access to others' resources, based on instrumental ties in a communal network, thus community-generic social capital (Putnam 1993). On the specific dimension of tie strength, Asia's typical form of social capital tends to differ from that in Europe and North America. In general, in Asia, social capital takes the strong form, while the normal form of social capital in the West is weak (Li 2006, 2008). The definition of strong/weak does not imply performance, as there can be strong organizations with weak ties (Granovetter 1973). One final consideration is *tie configuration* in terms of closed or open networks and ego-centric or communal networks (Li 2007a).

# INFORMAL KINDS OF SOCIAL TIE IN PRACTICE

In most societies where the contribution to societal order by formal institutions is weak, people rely on their own networking to establish a basis for reliable conduct. This is a natural response and standard condition for most of the world's population. It is usually accompanied by the spontaneous evolution of supportive norms, especially those influencing the practice of reciprocity (Mauss 1954; Foster 1967). Such norms often stabilize as institutions and are widely adopted, but with different labels and subtle variations in interpretation from one society to another.

Examples of such norms and institutions at work in the context of economic exchange are *guanxi* for Chinese culture, *wasta* in the Middle East, *jeitinho* in Brazil, *svyazi* in Russia, and *pulling strings/old boy networks* in Britain. In a study with 718 subjects across five cultures, Smith et al. (2012) analysed the workings of these indigenous forms of informal influence. (It should be noted here that *guanxi* was studied in both Singapore and China with almost identical results.) They concluded as follows: although these influence processes are widely disseminated, they occur more frequently in societal contexts with (a) high self-enhancement values, (b) low self-transcendence values, and (c) high endorsement of business corruptibility. High self-enhancement is associated with strong needs for achievement and sensitivity to hierarchy. Low self-transcendence is associated with particularism and the absence of concern with wider public good. The endorsement of business corruptibility suggests a pragmatic realism and perhaps fatalism. All three patterns are typical in most Asian cultures (see Redding, Bond, and Witt 2014). We may therefore expect to see informal ties playing a big part throughout this region.

We now turn to examine, by way of example, one of the most widely acknowledged of these responses, the Chinese institution of *guanxi,* seeing it through Chinese eyes.

## GUANXI AS THE UNIQUE SOCIAL TIE IN GREATER CHINA

To elaborate on the conceptual distinction between the East and West, we now compare the Western construct of social tie with that of *guanxi* as a Chinese construct (Li 2006; Luo 2011). First, *guanxi* regards the substantive attributes of personal tie as the essence of social interaction (King 1991; Yang 1999), while the Western notion of social tie tends to focus on the structural attributes of social networks, such as centrality, density, and shared social identity (Coleman 1990; Burt 1992). From the perspective of *guanxi*, the quality of personal tie is of paramount importance, not only in interpersonal, but also inter-firm exchange. However, the dyad-specific attributes of personal tie tend to receive limited attention in Western research (Nahapiet and Ghoshal 1998; Moran 2005). Second, pre-existing *guanxi* ties are salient determinants of social interaction and new *guanxi* development in China (Jacobs 1982; Tsui and Farh 1997), while impersonal social identities, such as race, gender, and age, are salient social categories that affect social networking in the West (e.g. Ibarra 1992, 1997). Third, *guanxi*, either at the dyadic or network level, tends to be more hierarchically based on position and age than the Western social tie (Chua, Morris, and Ingram 2009). Fourth, *guanxi* users emphasize the utility of strong and close *guanxi* to gain influence and cooperation, while in Western theorizing, networkers often leverage weak and distant social ties to gain access to diverse information and other benefits (Bian 1997; Xiao and Tsui 2007).

In addition to the above four distinctions between *guanxi* and the Western notion of social tie, there are two more critical distinctions. In terms of content, *guanxi* is more holistic, with parties caring about the psychological, social, and economic welfare of each other by engaging in all types of resource-sharing across formal and informal ties (e.g. Chen, Chen, and Portnoy 2009; Luo 2011), while Western parties tend to compartmentalize their social ties by separating work from family, profession from friendship, and instrumental exchange from sentimental exchange (Morris, Podolny, and Sullivan 2008). In other words, while the relational dimension in the West is a continuum, with most social ties falling towards the two ends, denoted as weak and strong (with tie strength related to tie nature, i.e. instrumental and sentimental; Granovetter 1973), *guanxi* focuses on a third, more central, position along the weak–strong continuum, with a mix of both instrumental and sentimental elements (Hwang 1987; Li 2006; Luo 2005; Yang 1993). Specifically, in building and utilizing *guanxi*, the Chinese tend to extend the model of familial ties to non-family ties so as to turn them into family-like ties with a mix of instrumental and sentimental elements, while Westerners adopt either a model of organizational and professional ties or a model of private friendship (Hwang 1987; Li 2006; Morris, Podolny, and Sullivan 2008; Chua, Morris, and Ingram 2009). It is these mixed features that delineate *guanxi* as uniquely indigenous to the Chinese. They also reflect the Chinese frame of *yin–yang* balancing by integrating opposite forces into a unified system as the duality of opposites-in-unity (e.g. *guanxi* as a balanced mix of weak and strong elements as well as instrumental and sentimental elements), thus making *guanxi* holistic, dynamic, and dual in its substance, structure, antecedents, and outcomes (Li 1998, 2008; Luo 2011).

Finally, in terms of quantitative structure, *guanxi* has a unique set of different associations, which consist of multiple layers or rings of *guanxi* around a focal person (Fei 1992). Different moral standards and exchange rules apply for various layers, which have different psychological distances to the focal person (Hwang 1987; Yang 1993). Each layer symbolizes a specific mix of instrumental and sentimental elements, including the three categories of layers along the weak–strong continuum: family, familiar, and stranger ties (Yang 1993; also see Hwang 1987). Consistent with the frame of *yin–yang* balancing (Li 1998, 2008, 2012), the category of familiar ties is the core of *guanxi* in China. *Guanxi* structure is, then, an ego-centric network without clear boundaries, thus adaptive for specific actions via the balancing mechanism of flexibly coupling and decoupling various ties within and across various layers of differentiated associations. In contrast, the Western network tends to consist of people with equal status as stable association members, but with specified boundaries between different associations. The Chinese often call an ego-network a 'circle' (Luo and Yeh 2012). Because circles are simulated 'families' with paternalistic leadership, the Chinese way of organizing small groups is 'clan' as the basic form of association, in contrast to 'club' as the Western form (Hsu 1963).

In sum, this unique Chinese form of social capital relies on the strongest social ties, with a balance of both highly sentimental and highly instrumental elements as its substance. It also works with both highly closed and highly open patterns as its structure. Its effect is widely visible as a distinctly powerful means of stabilizing interpersonal cooperation. However, such interpersonal cooperation may not necessarily bring the best results at the societal level when the usually invisible connections become fertile ground for widespread cronyism, corruption, and vested-interest protection, all of which are evident both in China and some other Asian countries (Li and Chang 2000; Li 2005, 2009).

We now turn to the indicators of societal trustworthiness as backdrop to a regional review of social capital.

# INDICATORS OF SOCIETAL
# TRUSTWORTHINESS

We have proposed that the *relational* form of social capital may well hold a society in a state of cooperativeness adequate for it to reach the 'middle-income gap', but that transcending that gap into higher levels of cooperativeness and national economic performance rests upon the folding-in of *system* capital. Only then can an economy be based on exchange relations between relative strangers, and reach a condition of unrestricted growth. International comparative data are suggestive of this logic without being able to illuminate the inner workings of the processes that may enable it.

The scores for relational or interpersonal trust in column 2 of Table 23.1 are weighted sample averages from a combination of World Values Survey and East Asian barometer data. They are 100 plus when responses are positive to generally trusting others, and 100 minus when people are not so trusted. It is necessary to note that these research questions are imperfect as probes into the different salience in a society of relational and system trust. For that reason we add other measures relating to system trust, such as perceptions of the rule of law and of trust in politicians. Comparing the columns leads to the conclusion (as far as such data allow) that high relational trust occurs, probably as a necessity, in conditions where system trust is weak.

We noted earlier the correlation between trust and economic growth, and we now probe that further. Countries where corruption is perceived to be high are not surprisingly also countries with the highest levels of out-group mistrust. They are also the least developed. Table 23.1 shows that the prosperous countries of the region, that is, those that have escaped the middle-income trap, also have the least corrupt public sectors, and lowest levels of mistrust in out-groups. It should be noted that in Western countries such as Australia, France, Scandinavia, and the US, out-group trust scores turn from negative to positive.

**Table 23.1 Social capital indicators in Asia**

| | World Bank GNI per capita @ PPP US$[1] | Index of inter-personal trust[2] | Perceived level of public-sector corruption 0–1, higher = cleaner[3] | Irregular payments and bribes 1–7 very common to never[4] | Diversion of public funds 1–7 common to never[5] | Public trust in politicians 1 very low 7 very high[6] | Dealing with construction permits. Cost as % of income per capita[7] | Rule of law, percentile rank[8] | Control of corruption, percentile rank[9] |
|---|---|---|---|---|---|---|---|---|---|
| Singapore | 59,790 | 59.8 | 9.2 | 6.6 | 6.2 | 6.3 | 18.1 | 93.43 | 96 |
| Hong Kong | 51,490 | 82.4 | 8.4 | 6.1 | 5.7 | 4.1 | 17.8 | 90.61 | 94 |
| Japan | 35,510 | 79.6 | 8.0 | 6.2 | 5.3 | 3.1 | n/a | 86.85 | 91 |
| Taiwan | n/a | 70.0 | 6.1 | 5.1 | 4.6 | 4.3 | 41.9 | 82.63 | 78 |
| Korea | 30,290 | 56.9 | 5.4 | 4.4 | 3.5 | 2.1 | n/a | 80.75 | 70 |
| Malaysia | 15,190 | 17.7 | 4.3 | 4.7 | 4.2 | 4.4 | 7.1 | 66.20 | 58 |
| China | 8,430 | 120.9 | 3.6 | 4.0 | 3.7 | 4.1 | 444.0 | 40.38 | 29 |
| Thailand | 8,390 | 83.1 | 3.4 | 3.7 | 3.0 | 2.2 | 9.5 | 48.36 | 45 |
| India | 3,620 | 52.5 | 3.1 | 3.4 | 2.8 | 2.2 | n/a | 52.58 | 35 |
| Indonesia | 4,530 | 16.9 | 3.0 | 3.2 | 3.4 | 3.0 | 105.3 | 30.99 | 27 |
| Vietnam | 3,260 | 104.1 | 2.9 | 3.1 | 3.3 | 3.4 | 109.0 | 38.00 | 30 |

(Continued)

**Table 23.1 Continued**

| | World Bank GNI per capita @ PPP US$[1] | Index of inter-personal trust[2] | Perceived level of public-sector corruption 0–1, higher = cleaner[3] | Irregular payments and bribes 1–7 very common to never[4] | Diversion of public funds 1–7 common to never[5] | Public trust in politicians 1 very low 7 very high[6] | Dealing with construction permits. Cost as % of income per capita[7] | Rule of law, percentile rank[8] | Control of corruption, percentile rank[9] |
|---|---|---|---|---|---|---|---|---|---|
| Philippines | 4,160 | 20.1 | 2.6 | 3.2 | 2.8 | 2.4 | 110.0 | 34.74 | 23 |
| Laos | 2,600 | n/a | 2.2 | n/a | n/a | n/a | 52.4 | 18.31 | 14 |
| Cambodia | 2,260 | 15.6 | 2.1 | 3.2 | 3.4 | 3.7 | 40.6 | 15.49 | 13 |
| Burma | n/a | n/a | 1.5 | n/a | n/a | n/a | n/a | 4.23 | 0 |

[1]World Bank. GNI per capita, PPP (current international $), 2007–2011. <http://data.worldbank.org/indicator/NY.GNP.PCAP.PP.CD> (accessed 8 July 2012).
[2]ASEP/JDS. Interpersonal Trust Data Series, 1995–2009. <http://www.jdsurvey.net/jds/jdsurveyActualidad.jsp?Idioma=I&SeccionTexto=0404&NOID=104> (accessed 8 July 2013).
[3]Transparency International. Corruption Perception Index 2011. Berlin. <http://cpi.transparency.org/cpi2011/results/> (accessed 8 July 2013).
[4]World Economic Forum (2012). Global Competitiveness Report 2012–2013, Irregular payments and bribes, p. 392.
[5]World Economic Forum (2012). Global Competitiveness Report 2012–2013. Diversion of public funds, p. 390.
[6]World Economic Forum (2012). Global Competitiveness Report 2012–2013. Public trust in politicians, p. 391.
[7]The World Bank/IFC (2012). Doing Business 2012: East Asia and the Pacific. Washington, DC, International Bank for Reconstruction and Development/The World Bank.
[8]Kaufmann, D., A. Kraay, and M. Mastruzzi (2011). The Worldwide Governance Indicators Project. <http://info.worldbank.org/governance/wgi/index.asp> (accessed 8 July 2013).
[9]Kaufmann, D., A. Kraay, and M. Mastruzzi (2011). The Worldwide Governance Indicators Project. <http://info.worldbank.org/governance/wgi/index.asp> (accessed 8 July 2013).

Why such associations occur has been the subject of a study by Rothstein and Stolle (2008) to examine an institutional theory of generalized trust. Taking a wide array of data across forty-eight countries from the World Values Survey, they study the way in which social capital is embedded in and linked to formal political and legal institutions. They conclude that, although generalized interpersonal trust (i.e. towards strangers) is the most important part of social capital, its contribution is greatly enhanced by 'effective, impartial, and fair street-level bureaucracies' (2008: 3). As noted earlier, given that the system cannot reciprocate, it is confidence in the system rather than trust per se that builds systemic social capital. The workings of this process are seen in terms of four influences: an individual's perception of their security; an individual's confidence that those guarding the public interest can be trusted; the shaping of observable behaviour that acts as a model; and the direct experience of interaction with formal institutions. They find that institutions that are essentially political in nature, and so affected by choices of ideology, do not influence generalized trust. On the other hand, confidence in institutions designed to provide order is clearly correlated with generalized trust. Two further influences are indicated: long-term experience of democratic institutions, and equality of outcomes. In order of the strength of correlation with generalized trust, the context variables measured were as follows:

| | |
|---|---|
| Length of democracy | 0.6591 |
| Institutional impartiality | 0.6457 |
| Institutional efficiency | 0.6455 |
| GDP | 0.5964 |
| Secondary-school enrolment | 0.4730 |

To understand how a society accumulates its particular degree of cooperativeness and particular social architecture for trust, we believe it necessary to acknowledge the influence of early social structures that have remained influential. We have in mind two deep-seated factors in particular, the fundamental responses to the challenge of stabilizing vertical and horizontal order. How did authority come to be legitimated? How did identity come to be formed? For this, we now analyse the very different Japan and China. We also consider the relatively stagnant condition of the Philippines, in both social capital and economic progress. We will conclude with a brief regional review. The three cases will allow insight into Japan scoring 8 out of 10 for clean administration, China scoring 3.6, and the Philippines scoring 2.6. Their scores for trust are not strictly comparable on data currently available, but between Japan and the Philippines they are, Japan scoring 40 and the Philippines 9 on the World Values Survey of social trust. So too between China and the Philippines on the Asian Monitor data where (on a scale of 1 low to 4 high) China's overall trust score is 2.49, with 2.0 for strangers and 3.0 for family, whereas the Philippines scores 2.92 overall, with 2.4 for strangers and 3.41 for family. Japan data are affected by a 'precipitous drop in trust' in government as it struggles with a long series of political challenges and crises (including nuclear meltdown), with responses seen as weak (Edelman 2012: 2).

The narratives provide some indication of the variety of origins and responses that characterize the region. They also illustrate some of the intervening variables that come into play between social capital and beneficial societal outcomes. That there is such a connection is suggested strongly in a macro study by Ozcan and Bjornskov (2011), who document a strong and robust effect of social trust on the speed with which human development improves, especially in non-democratic countries.

# Formative Societal Influences on Social Capital

## Japan

One of the great puzzles in the study of Asia is the enormous contrast between China and Japan, despite much shared heritage. Nowhere is the contrast more stark than over the question of trust; the 'tray of loose sand' and the 'piece of solid granite'. The contrast stems from different histories and philosophies.

Japan has an especially high level of perceived public-sector honesty and responsible citizenship behaviour, and arguably has had for centuries (Okazaki 2001). Its scores for public probity are among the world's highest (see Table 23.1). It is also manifestly a very advanced, efficient, and prosperous industrial society.

Seen sociologically by Eisenstadt (1996: 370) in a major study of Japanese civilization,

> the conceptions of self as embedded in social nexus and the obligations pursuant on these conceptions are strongly emphasized through the processes of symbolizing and extending trust, which are played out often very openly. The pinnacle of such extensions is—or at least used to be—the symbolism of the emperor as the focus of the overarching trust and solidarity of the national community... the meta-language of group is continually promulgated and reinforced.

In a reflection of what was said earlier about the Chinese dualistic perception of trust, Eisenstadt also refers to the Japanese equivalent emphasis on

> the movement between contexts of interaction defined in dualistic terms of *tatemae* and *honne*, *uchi* and *soto*, and *omote* and *ura*. Such reconstruction makes the extension of trust seem to flow naturally from one context to another; trust is conceived as embedded in such settings, not as conditional on adherence to principles that are beyond these settings. It is... self-referential. This reconstruction of trust recalls the strong emphasis on finding transcendence in the rules of form—an emphasis that

at the same time allows considerable scope for innovation in contents. (Eisenstadt 1996: 372)

The psycho-social fabric of high trust extends through social conformity, predictable behaviour, and suppressed individualism. To prevent regressive conservatism, innovations are presented in terms of continuity, and individual contributions as belonging to the group. Trust then comes to be extended through both (a) regulation and control, and (b) interaction and exchange. But one extra feature marks out Japan as distinct, and Eisenstadt (1996: 372) describes it as 'the crucial key for understanding the dynamics of social interaction in Japanese society'. This is a 'continuous kinship-family symbolism with its strong maternal components'. He notes 'the fact that the modes of regulation employed by the elites and influentials are very similar to those prevalent within families', but—highly important for the contrast with China—the trading of coercion and societal interests between elites and the broader sectors of the society in Japan is in continual interaction. Consultation is sacred here. It allows the up and down and sideways flow of influences, creation of new social spaces, bringing-in of external influences, and incorporation of change, as long, that is, as a second force—that of conservatism—is there to counterbalance the potential disequilibrium. This Japanese form of duality has the forces of change enmeshed with the forces of stability, the latter of a deep and subtle kind. As noted by Eisenstadt (1996: 374), new themes and orientations have been unable to break through the relative hegemony of the 'contextual settings defined in some combination of primordial, social, and natural terms'.

Eisenstadt defines the major aspects of the Japanese historical experience as (a) great openness to change and external influence, (b) distinctive modes of social interaction, (c) continuous Japanization of the impact of Axial civilizations, (d) consultative response to change and protest, and (e) achievement of an equilibrium between high regulation and high innovativeness. He attributes these high societal achievements to two deep elements: the willingness of elites to consult lower ranks, and the constant expandability of 'generalized particularistic trust'. It is as if, under the overarching umbrella of the nation, it became possible to fuse relational and system trust, to produce an infinite capacity to recreate community through an ongoing past.

How did Japan evolve with these very rare capacities when China did not? The matter is too complex for extensive discussion here, but is nevertheless significant for comparisons with other societies, and so will be summarized. Four key historical features are commonly brought into accounts of the special nature of Japanese society: its unity, and its resilience.

1. *Escape from dominance by an Axial civilization.* Japan is both geographically separate from mainland Asia and an ethnically homogenous entity itself, containing almost no sub-groups of strong identity or size. It was not invaded. Although new ideas filtered in, ideological principled struggles did not disturb the Japanese process of constant regional shifts and adaptations in the feudal era. The society then evolved with a high degree of stable consistency.

2. *Divided, balanced power.* In the normally crucial transition away from a clan-based order, societies can be exposed to the influence of autonomous centres of power, as with the Church in Europe. China resisted such by extending its Axial Confucian justification for tight central control and it has never fundamentally changed. Japan, by contrast, divided power in the late seventh-century Taika reforms, and also did not change, maintaining the balanced tension until 1868, and to a degree thereafter. The Emperor, elevated at the apex, represented the *authority* of the collective identity and this was almost never challenged. If it was, the response was to stamp out the contender, as with the early seventeenth-century control of Buddhism and banning of Christianity. The other axis—that of the aristocratic groups led by the *shogun*—held the *power* to deal with the economy. This duality—authority and power, Emperor and *shogun*—left the components distinct but integrated. It left the state stable for a very long period.

3. *Primogeniture and ie.* The ability to retain assets within a corporation for very long periods is largely dependent on the ability to transmit them intact between generations. This response developed in Japan as it emerged from feudalism in the thirteenth century. It was reinforced by evolution of the *ie* as the core unit of identity, and hence an *iemoto* (work-group-based) society (Murakami 1985). It is 'kinship-like', implying hierarchy and security, and is the essence of Japanese social structure (Nakane 1971). The stability and reliability of such forms—including many large corporations—have a bearing on the overall culture of high trust.

4. *Tokugawa administration.* In his re-interpretation of Confucianism in the early seventeenth century, the *shogun* Tokugawa used the respected rules of conduct to fix roles, duties, and order in the interests of stability. This entailed new and rigorous centralization, accompanied by rationally organized delegation, all of which was managed by an elite administrative class, the *samurai*. This class was noteworthy for its diligence, competence, and honesty. It served to found an ideal of high-quality public service. The retention of power by subordinate regional chiefs was conditional on their delivering local peace and prosperity, or they would lose their lands. To achieve this, they were required to use extensive consultation with the people in their charge. For three centuries up to the late nineteenth century, Japan's people experienced 'the Tokugawa peace', a period of relative stability, prosperity, honest government, and a measure of empowerment (Arnason 1988). Historical legacies affecting social capital have consequently been a long experience of participation and empowerment, impartial institutions for order, efficient institutions, equality of outcomes, education, and prosperity.

# China

We contend that China depends heavily on relational capital, that it has in recent years seen its small stock of system capital weakened by corruption and autocracy, and that it may well find it extremely difficult to escape the middle-income trap when it reaches it (in about ten years). To pass the barrier would require substantial social, administrative, and political change—not impossible, but currently not discernible. Not escaping the trap will hamper wider and deeper cooperativeness and this in turn may induce an era of slowing innovativeness and weaker productive and allocative efficiency. How did China come to this position, and where does the recent miracle fit in history?

China, unlike Japan, was an Axial civilization, and it vested its transcendental vision in a uniquely long-lasting territorial, political, and cultural continuity centred in a fundamentally unchanging political structure. In 1949, millennia of imperial control transitioned to the Party-state without fundamental redesign of the power structure. The legitimating authority of the mandate of heaven is now the mantle of the Politburo, whose most sacred duty is the maintenance of order. In the earlier imperial form, the proper performance of duties made the secular sacred and connected daily life with the maintenance of cosmic harmony. Yet, as Eisenstadt has observed (1996: 415), this long-established and deeply socialized pattern of vertical conformity had 'in comparison with those which developed in other post-Axial civilizations and especially in the great monotheistic civilizations, relatively limited institutional effects'. This is not to say that China was unchanging, but that there have never been far-reaching changes to the core institutional fabric. China was the only Axial civilization in which no secondary breakthrough took place to compare with Christianity within Judaism, Islam within Christianity or Judaism, or Buddhism within Hinduism. Such new interpretations were always hemmed in by the hegemony of the Chinese elite, and arguably still are.

The significant consequence for our interest in comparisons of social capital is that, in contrast with Japan, China remains highly resistant to sharing power between the elite and the masses. Centres of influence have always emerged, but never with autonomous access to the centre. There is currently much decentralization of economic decision-making and local development initiatives, but always with tight eventual control by the Party. The state has always had strong institutions capable of politicizing alternative collectivities, whereby any such collectivities were themselves always institutionally weak. This is currently visible in the extension of political control into the economy. The strength of the state was also buttressed by its control of ideology, and the tying of ideology to its institutions.

In these circumstances, the society's response has been to rely on relational trust, with all its strengths and limitations, and to remain fundamentally mistrustful of the wider system that the average citizen takes such little part in influencing. Many societies have emerged from such constraint, led by a body of people who have acquired both independence resulting from prosperity and common feeling through shared social ideals. Such *bourgeoisies* have been instrumental in the evolution of system capital, not just in many Western countries, but also in Japan and Korea. One of their routes to influence is political engagement. Another is the building of civil-society institutions to act as autonomous enablers of spontaneous order, as for instance with the rise of professions. In China now, as Bergere (2007) has observed from studies of Chinese business evolution, the Party co-opts new agents of change. The state is attempting to create a form of capitalism without capitalists.

# The Philippines

The countries of South East Asia share a number of features that we do not have space to analyse in detail from the standpoint of social capital. To focus on why they share dilemmas in achieving widespread cooperativeness, we analyse now the case of one of them. What happened here happened also in varying ways, and to different extents, under the Dutch in Indonesia, the British in Malaya, the French in Vietnam, and the Japanese in Korea, Manchuria, and Taiwan.

Social capital in the Philippines is weak, and the economy has until very recently been growing only slowly. Its score of 2.6 out of 10 for clean administration places it alongside Laos, Cambodia, and Vietnam, all deeply scarred by more recent wars. Its score for trust is the fifth lowest out of eighty-six countries (Ozcan and Bjornskov 2011). To understand the dilemma of cooperativeness in this country of 95 million people, we will explore themes of weak integrating ideology and social fragmentation.

## Absence of Integrating Ideology

Filipinos themselves will readily explain their lack of an integrating societal ideal: 'If you had spent four hundred years in a convent, and fifty years in Hollywood, you would be screwed up too' is a common saying. But this omits the earlier and later part of the historical account. Before Spanish colonization, it was an agrarian society of local settlements under indigenous forms of headship, but not a nation-state as such. There is in many traditional institutions, practices, and language, the fading memory of this lost age of protective paternalism and imagined social harmony. The subsequent overlay of Catholicism added ritual and formal structure, but did not supplant the old traditions. As reported from a study of the question by Alegre (1994: xii):

> The people in these islands continue to use their pre-Spanish languages, they have the same mores and customs, and basically the same belief system....We came culturally intact through centuries of uninvited intervention. We are still Pinoy. And that is no mean triumph.

The interpretation by Fernandez (1989) of this earlier culture is that it was based in small rural communities, close to subsistence level. It emphasized mutual help, respect for ancestors and for others, caring leadership, and the sharing of land and responsibilities. It is carried forward today in norms such as *pakikisama* (conformity), *hiya* (sense of propriety), and *utang na loob* (reciprocity). Such ideals are consistent with those of other subsistence-level communities across the world (Foster 1967). These old traditions are all examples of relational trust.

As described by Slater (2010), the native social order that the Spanish incorporated into their regime from the 1600s on had at the top a chiefly class (*datu*), one of whose members would rule a rural community (*barangay*). The chief oversaw the agricultural calendar, was custodian of village lands, military leader, and dispenser of justice. Below the *datu* were freemen, and below them debt peons. Class divisions and social mobility were both quite open. When the Spanish arrived, this structure was co-opted into the colonial framework. From the sixteenth century onwards, it became oligarchical and controlled by regional bosses.

Two events eventually precipitated the breakdown of the trust that had been residual from the pre-colonial paternalism. The shared access to land was gradually replaced with a system of land ownership, leading to the effective loss of land access by most of the people. Instead, land fell under the ownership of the privileged *datu* class, the Catholic Church, and Spanish colonists. Most people were left as low-paid labourers. The old values began to waste away.

The second crucial change was the wider dispersion of Chinese traders out of their long-established port Chinatowns, to create a new Sino-Filipino *mestizo* class. Through the course of the nineteenth century, this class would eventually include the 'sugar barons' who would join the Spanish as predators. As largely absentee landlords interested in extracting surplus, they would break the remaining traditional social bonds between landlord and tenant. Political co-option of this class strengthened its hold. Under the American regime of the early twentieth century, rather than dealing with the polarizing agrarian problems directly, the treatment meted out was the application of profit-driven rationality. The legacy has been that

> The extremes of inequality which were a product of the consolidation of a Filipino upper class, the domination of *caciquism*[1] and the crucial role of this class as an intermediary between the external power and the local population, have remained a dominant feature of Philippine society. (Slater 2010: 88)

After the Americans left, the initial ideals of democracy were undermined by the Marcos years of crony capitalism and his bankrupting of the country by the mid-1980s. Since then, the political scene has been turbulent, but the vested interests of earlier times have proved both deeply resilient and politically resourceful. In the meantime, though recently improving, corruption levels have remained disturbingly high.

## Social Fragmentation and Corruption

Without consistent legitimate sources of societal ideals, and starting without a unified historical national identity, the norms of a highly diffracted subsistence-level society based on personalized relations will inevitably be strained in the encounter with modernity. The main stress on the old social structure has been severe inequality, dating back to the destruction of the old system of land-sharing and subsistence farming. Thus, the separation of people by wealth has become extreme. The diffraction of the old paternalism under modern business rationality has also broken ties, especially of obligation to protect the disadvantaged. Catholicism was never deeply shared and the Philippines score for religiosity is the second lowest in the region after China (Leung and Bond 2004). The 'American Dream' was abandoned when they departed, leaving its nightmare component of a legal jungle.

There remains a 'generalized nostalgia for patron-client relations' (Sidel 1995: 143). The lost idealized harmony and reciprocal protection implicit in the role of *compadre*[2] is now replaced for many by a new role for patronage: that of extraction and predation. This is an unintended consequence of the arrival of a modern bureaucratic state into a society where the institutions of order are spread too thinly to allow the bureaucracy to function with the necessary built-in protection. Extortion over such matters as licensing becomes predictable when bureaucracy is weak or absent.

Commentaries on the plight of the Philippines in this regard are often savage. Hutchcroft (1991) talked of law as a means of manipulation, compilation, stratagem, and violence, by which those with power and influence further their interests. Sidel (1995: 146) saw the society 'dominated neither by personal loyalties nor formal institutions but, rather, by money, violence, and a predatory state.. with a widespread sense of loss, betrayal, decline, disillusionment with *pulitika*'. Licences are instruments for petty-rentiers. The *tong* is a fixed bribe. *Lagay* is grease money. The 'milk cows' are land, concessions, government loans, contracts, franchises. Oligarchs and cronies abound. The Philippines is ranked the third most corrupt of fourteen regional countries (see Table 23.1). More recent, cleaner administrations face a very long uphill struggle.

## Social Capital in the Philippines

We have here a classic case of a wounded society, where both relational trust and the once-possible system trust have been largely destroyed. The relational trust of the early agrarian period was badly affected by the land deprivation suffered by the majority of people, which at the same time removed the logics behind the earlier paternalist ethics of the traditional elite. Catholicism, while doubtless providing some form of order, also became complicit in the extraction. The final reduction of the majority of people to selling their labour in the open market would have ended most of any residual legitimacy for the authority structure. The break-up of the traditional social fabric of the villages would have left most people alienated and necessarily self-reliant. With twenty-eight main sub-ethnic groups, the variety of languages and local traditions would have hindered achievement of a clear and shared set of cultural meanings.

System capital, as we have noted, requires heavy accompanying administrative infrastructure, and agrarian societies anywhere in the region are not normally in a position to supply that. When the system of licensing is then left unguarded, and when opportunities to abuse it are rife, predators move in and the system cannot meet the requirement of public confidence in its workings. Trust is badly broken, in both relational and system forms, and social capital at a very low ebb, along with overall societal prosperity.

# CONCLUSIONS FOR THE REGION

We began by pointing out that societal progress rests largely on the degree to which a society has achieved a proclivity for widespread cooperation within it. We argued in addition that higher levels of economic success require the implementation of system capital to supplement available relational capital. We outlined certain conditions, or enablers, that affect the processes in play in these complex interplays.

Japan stands out as an example of a society with high levels of both relational and system capital. We argue that their nature is influenced by their historical origins and that such nature also influences the specific forms of cooperation now seen in the Japanese business system.

China and Vietnam suffer in this context from an imbalance, whereby their traditional reliance on relational capital remains, without having been reinforced by the benevolent effects of well-functioning system capital. This latter is not available to societies in which empowerment remains stunted. The necessary confidence in the administrative superstructure becomes psychologically hampered, no matter how well control appears to be exercised.

Korea and Taiwan, as societies that have made successful transitions to the empowering of their populations, are now displaying the advantages of the support to transaction efficiency that is possible in conditions of higher general trust. In these two cases the original Confucian heritage has been brought forward for use in both the relational and system domains of trust. A high level of administrative quality in the public domain and private sector works in tandem with a high level of interpersonal trust founded in their own fully endorsed civilizational ideals.

The city-states of Hong Kong and Singapore also display very high social capital in two modes and are coincidentally equally prosperous. In these cases, the origins vary slightly, and so too the formulae of application vary substantially today. But the common denominators are a capacity to hybridize in societal design, in the interests of similar aims, and the use of traditional Chinese ideals of order and reciprocity, combined with imported rational bureaucracy using either market-based competitive order, or 'strong-state' development strategy.

The countries of South East Asia vary greatly in their historical legacies and cannot be detailed here. But they all tread a similar path from a largely agrarian past to a future that attempts to blend in new means of cooperation. They all equally face the challenge of not destroying the older ideals that underpin in all cases the trust between individuals, and in some cases underpin much of the trust at the larger system level.

## NOTES

1. The rule of local chiefs or 'bosses'.
2. The boss who looks after you because he accepts a symbolic link to your family.

## REFERENCES

Acemoglu, D. and J. A. Robinson (2012). *Why Nations Fail: The Origins of Power, Prosperity and Poverty*. London, Profile.

Adler, P. S. and S. Kwon (2002). 'Social Capital: Prospects for a New Concept'. *Academy of Management Review 27*: 17–40.

Ahn, T. K. and E. Ostrom (2008). 'Social Capital and Collective Action'. In D. Castiglione, J. W. van Deth, and G. Wolleb, Eds., *The Handbook of Social Capital*: 70–100. Oxford, Oxford University Press.

Alegre, E. N. (1994). *Pinoy na Pinoy: Essays on National Culture*. Manila, Anvil.

Arnason, J. P. (1988). 'Paths to Modernity: The Peculiaritities of Japanese Feudalism'. In G. McCormack and Y. Sugimoto, Eds., *The Japanese Trajectory*: 235–263. Cambridge, Cambridge University Press.

Beinhocker, E. D. (2005). *The Origin of Wealth*. London: Random House.

Bergere, M.-C. (2007). *Capitalisme et Capitalistes en Chine des Origines à nos Jours*. Paris, Perrin.

Bian, Y. (1997). 'Bringing Strong Ties Back In: Indirect Ties, Network Bridges, and Job Searches in China'. *American Behavioural Review* 62(3): 366–385.

Bourdieu, P. (1980). 'Le Capital Social'. *Actes de la Recherche en Sciences Sociales* 31(2–3).

—— (1986). 'The Forms of Capital'. In J. G. Richardson Ed., *Handbook of Theory and Research for the Sociology of Education*: 241–258. New York, Greenwood Press.

Burt, R. S. (1992). *Structural Holes: The Social Structure of Competition*. Cambridge, Harvard University Press.

—— (2001). 'Structural Holes versus Network Closure as Social Capital'. In N. Lin, K. Cook, and R. S. Burt, Eds., *Social Capital*: 31–56. New York, de Gruyter.

Capra, F. (1975). *The Tao of Physics*. New York, Bantam.

Chen, M. J. and D. Miller (2011). 'The relational perspective as a business mindset: managerial implications for East and West', *Academy of Management Perspectives* 25(3): 6–18.

Chen, Y., X. P. Chen, and R. Portnoy (2009). 'To Whom do Positive Norm and Negative Norms of Reciprocity Apply? Effects of Inequitable Offer, Relationship, and Relational Self-Orientation'. *Journal of Experimental Social Psychology* 45: 24–34.

Chua, R. Y. J., M. W. Morris, and P. Ingram (2009). 'Guanxi vs. Networking: Distinctive Configurations of Affect- and Cognition-based Trust in the Networks of Chinese vs. American Managers'. *Journal of International Business Studies* 40(3): 490–508.

Coleman, J. S (1988). 'Social Capital in the Creation of Human Capital'. *American Journal of Sociology* 94: S95–S120.

—— (1990). *Foundations of Social Theory*. Cambridge, Harvard University Press.

Edelman (2012). 2012 Edelman Trust Barometer Survey Executive Summary. Retrieved 3 September 2012 from <http://trust.edelman.com>.

Eichengreen, B., D. Park, and K. Shin (2011). *When Fast-Growing Economies Slow Down: International Evidence and Implications for China*. National Bureau of Economic Research Working Paper 16919. Cambridge, NBER.

Eisenstadt, S. N. (1996). *Japanese Civilisation*. Chicago, University of Chicago Press.

Esser, H. (2008). 'The Two Meanings of Social Capital'. In D. Castiglione, J. W. van Deth, and G. Wolleb, Eds., *The Handbook of Social Capital*: 22–49. Oxford, Oxford University Press.

Fei, X. (1992). *From the Soil: The Foundations of Chinese Society* (Trans. G. G. Hamilton and Z. Wang). Berkeley, University of California Press.

Fernandez, D. G. (1989). 'Mass Culture and Cultural Policy: The Philippine Experience'. *Philippine Studies* 37: 488–502.

Flap, H. and E. Boxman (2001). 'Getting Started: The Influence of Social Capital on the Start of the Occupational Career'. In N. Lin, K. Cook, and R. S. Burt, Eds., *Social Capital*: 159–181. New York, de Gruyter.

Foster, G. M. (1967). 'Peasant Society and the Image of Limited Good'. In J. M. Potter, M. N. Diaz and G. M. Foster, Eds., *Peasant Society*. 31–50. Boston, Little Brown.

Fukuyama, F. (1995). *Trust: The Social Virtues and the Creation of Prosperity*. New York, Free Press.

Granovetter, M. (1973). 'The Strength of Weak Ties'. *American Journal of Sociology 78*: 1360–1380.

—— (1983). 'The Strength of Weak Ties: A Network Theory Revisited'. *Sociological Theory 1*: 201–233.

—— (1992). 'Problems of Explanation in Economic Sociology'. In N. Nohria and R. C. Eccles, Eds., *Networks and Organizations*: 25–56. Boston, Harvard Business School.

Hsu, F. L. K. (1963). *Clan, Caste and Club*. New York, Van Nostrand.

—— (1981). *Americans and Chinese: Passage to Differences*. Honolulu, University of Hawaii Press.

Hutchcroft, P. D. (1991). 'Oligarchs and Cronies in the Philippine State: The Politics of Patrimonial Plunder'. *World Politics 43*(3): 413–450.

Hwang, K. K. (1987). 'Face and Favor: The Chinese Power Game'. *American Journal of Sociology 92*(4): 944–974.

Ibarra, H. (1992). 'Homophily and Differential Returns: Sex Differences in Network Structure and Access in an Advertising Firm'. *Administrative Science Quarterly 37*: 422–447.

—— (1997). 'Paving an Alternative Route: Gender Differences in Managerial Networks'. *Social Psychology Quarterly 60*: 91–102.

Inglehart, R. and W. E. Baker (2000). 'Modernization, Cultural Change, and the Persistence of Traditional Values'. *American Sociological Review 65*(1): 19–51.

Jacobs, J. B. (1982). 'The Concept of Guanxi and Local Politics in a Rural Chinese Cultural Setting'. In S. L. Greenblatt, R. W. Wilson, and A. A. Wilson, Eds., *Social Interaction in Chinese Society*: 209–236. New York, Praeger.

Javidan, M., R. J. House, and P. W. Dorfman (2004). 'A Non-Technical Summary of GLOBE Findings'. In R. J. House, P. J. Hanges, M. Javidan, P. W. Dorfman, and V. Gupta, Eds., *Culture, Leadership and Organizations: The GLOBE Study of 62 Societies*: 29–48. London, Sage.

Kauffman, S. (1995). *At Home in the Universe*. New York, Oxford University Press.

King, A. Y. (1991). 'Kuan-hsi and Network Building: A Sociological Interpretation'. *Daedalus 120*: 63–84.

Kostova, T. and K. Roth (2003). 'Social Capital in Multinational Corporations and a Micro-Macro Model of its Formation'. *Academy of Management Review 28*(2): 297–317.

Leung, K. and M. H. Bond (2004). 'Social Axioms: A Model for Social Beliefs in Multi-cultural Perspective'. In M. P. Zanna, Ed., *Advances in Experimental Social Psychology 36*: 119–197. San Diego, Elsevier.

—— Eds. (2009). *Psychological Aspects of Social Axioms*. New York, Springer.

Li, P. P. (1998). 'Towards a Geocentric Framework of Organizational Form: A Holistic, Dynamic and Paradoxical Approach'. *Organizational Studies 19*(5): 829–861.

—— (2005). 'The Puzzle of China's Township-Village Enterprises: The Paradox of Local Corporatism in a Dual-track Economic Transition'. *Management and Organization Review 1*(2): 197–224.

—— (2006). 'Guanxi as the Chinese Norm for Personalized Social Capital: Toward an Integrated Duality Framework of Informal Exchange'. In H. W. Yeung, Ed., *Handbook of Research on Asian Business*: 62–83. London: Edward Elgar.

—— (2007a). 'Social Tie, Social Capital, and Social Behavior: Toward an Integrated Framework of Organized Exchange'. *Asia Pacific Journal of Management 24*(2): 227–246.

—— (2007b). 'Towards Inter-disciplinary Dimensions and Delineations of Trust: A Diversity-in-Unity Approach'. *Management and Organization Review 3*(3): 421–445.

—— (2008). 'Toward a Geocentric Framework of Trust: An Application of Organizational Trust'. *Management and Organization Review* 4(3): 413–439.

—— (2009). 'The Duality of Crony Corruption in Economic Transition: Toward an Integrated Framework'. *Journal of Business Ethics* 85: 41–55.

—— (2012). 'Toward an Integrative Framework of Indigenous Research: The Geocentric Implications of Yin-Yang Balance'. *Asia Pacific Journal of Management* 29(4): 849–872.

—— and T. Chang (2000). 'The Asian Paradox of Miracle and Debacle'. *International Finance Review* 1: 429–453.

Lin, N. (2001). *Social Capital*. New York, Cambridge University Press.

—— (2008). 'A Network Theory of Social Capital'. In D. Castiglione, J. W. van Deth, and G. Wolleb, Eds., *The Handbook of Social Capital*: 50–69. Oxford, Oxford University Press.

Luo, J.-D. (2005). 'Particularistic Trust and General Trust: A Network Analysis in Chinese Organizations'. *Management and Organization Review* 3: 437–458.

—— (2011). 'Guanxi Revisited: An Exploratory Study of Familiar Ties in a Chinese Workplace'. *Management and Organization Review* 7(2): 329–351.

—— and K. Yeh (2012). 'Neither Collectivism nor Individualism: Trust in the Chinese Circles'. *Journal of Trust Research* 2(1): 53–70.

McCloskey, D. N. (2006). *The Bourgeois Virtues: Ethics for an Age of Commerce*. Chicago, University of Chicago Press

March, J. G. (2005). 'Parochialism in the Evolution of a Research Community: The Case of Organization Studies'. *Management and Organization Review* 1(1): 5–22.

Maruyama, M. (1980). 'Paradigmatology and its Application to Cross-disciplinary, Cross-Professional, and Cross-Cultural Communication'. *Dialectica* 29(3–4): 135–196.

Mauss, M. (1954). *The Gift*. London, Cohen and West.

Mokyr, J. (2009). *The Enlightened Economy: Britain and the Industrial Revolution 1700–1850*. London, Penguin.

Moran, P. (2005). 'Structural vs. Relational Embeddedness: Social Capital and Managerial Performance'. *Strategic Management Journal* 26(12): 1129–1151.

Morris, M. W., J. Podolny, and B. N. Sullivan (2008). 'Culture and Co-worker Relations: Interpersonal Patterns in American, Chinese, German, and Spanish Divisions of a Global Retail Bank'. *Organization Science* 19(4): 517–532.

Murakami, Y. (1985). 'Ie Society as a Pattern of Civilization: Response to Criticism'. *Journal of Japanese Studies* 11(2): 401–421.

Nahapiet, J. and S. Ghoshal (1998). 'Social Capital, Intellectual Capital and the Organizational Advantage'. *Academy of Management Review* 23: 242–266.

Nakamura, H. (1964). *Ways of Thinking of Eastern Peoples*. Honolulu, East–West Centre.

Nakane, C. (1971). *Japanese Society*. London, Weidenfeld and Nicholson.

Nisbett, R. E. (2003). *The Geography of Thought*. New York, Free Press.

Nowak, M. A. (2011). *Super-Cooperators*. New York, Free Press.

Okazaki, T. (2001). *The Role of the Merchant Coalition in Pre-Modern Japanese Economic Development*. Working Paper, Faculty of Economics, University of Tokyo.

Ozcan, B. and C. Bjornskov (2011). 'Social Trust and Human Development'. *Journal of Socio-Economics* 40(6): 753–762.

Pagel, M. (2012). *Wired for Culture: The Natural History of Human Cooperation*. London. Allen Lane.

Portes, A. (1998). 'Social Capital: Its Origins and Applications in Modern Sociology'. *Annual Review of Sociology* 22: 1–24.

—— (2000). 'The Two Meanings of Social Capital'. *Sociological Forum* 15: 1–12.

Putnam, R. D. (1993). *Making Democracy Work: Civic Traditions in Modern Italy*. Princeton, Princeton University Press.

Redding, G., M. H. Bond, and M. A. Witt (2014). 'Culture and the Business Systems of Asia'. In M. A. Witt and G. Redding, Eds., *The Oxford Handbook of Asian Business Systems*: 358–382. Oxford, Oxford University Press.

—— and C. Rowley (2013). 'Methodology Challenges in the Study of Social Capital in Asia'. In D. D. Bergh, D. J. Ketchen, and C. L. Wang, Eds., *West meets East: Building Theoretical Bridges: 265–287*. London, Emerald.

Rothstein, B. and D. Stolle (2008). 'The State and Social Capital: An Institutional Theory of Generalized Trust'. *Comparative Politics* 40(4): 441–459.

Seabright, P. (2010). *The Company of Strangers*. Princeton, Princeton University Press.

Sidel, J. T. (1995). 'The Philippines: The Languages of Legitimation'. In M. Alagappa, Ed., *Political Legitimacy in Southeast Asia*: 136–169. Stanford, Stanford University Press.

Slater, D. (2010). *Ordering Power: Contentious Politics and Authoritarian Leviathans in Southeast Asia*. Cambridge, Cambridge University Press.

Smith, P. B., C. Torres, C.-H. Leong, P. Budhwar, M. Achoui, and N. Lebedeva (2012). 'Are Indigenous Approaches to Achieving Influence in Business Organizations Distinctive? A Comparative Study of Guanxi, Wasta, Jeitinho, Svyazi, and Pulling Strings'. *International Journal of Human Resource Management* 23(2): 333–348.

Tsai, W. and S. Ghoshal (1998). 'Social Capital and Value Creation: The Role of Intra-Firm Networks'. *Academy of Management Journal* 41: 464–476.

Tsui, A. S. and J.-L. Farh (1997). 'Where Guanxi Matters'. *Work and Occupations* 24(1): 56–79.

—— S. S. Nifakdar, and A. Y. Ou (2007). 'Cross-National, Cross-Cultural Organizational Behaviour Research'. *Journal of Management* 33(3): 426–478.

Uslaner, E. M. (2008). 'Trust as a Moral Value'. In D. Castiglione, J. W. van Deth, and G. Wolleb, Eds., *The Handbook of Social Capital*: 101–121. Oxford, Oxford University Press.

Wellman, B. and K. A. Frank (2001). 'Network Capital in a Multi-Level World: Getting Support from Personal Communities'. In N. Lin, K. Cook, and R. S. Burt, Eds., *Social Capital*: 233–273. New York, de Gruyter.

Woolcock, M. (1998). 'Social Capital and Economic Development: Toward a Theoretical Synthesis and Policy Framework'. *Theory and Society* 27: 151–208.

World Bank (2010). 'Robust Recovery, Rising Risks'. *East Asia and Pacific Economic Update 2010* 2: 27–43.

Wrangham, R. (2009). *Catching Fire*. London, Profile.

Xiao, Z. and A. S. Tsui (2007). 'When Brokers May Not Work: The Cultural Contingency of Social Capital in Chinese High-Tech Firms'. *Administrative Science Quarterly* 52: 1–31.

Yang, C.-F. (1999). 'Conceptualization of Interpersonal Guanxi and Interpersonal Affect'. *Indigenous Psychological Research* 12: 105–179. (in Chinese)

Yang, K. S. (1993). 'Chinese Social Orientation: An Integrative Analysis'. In L. Y. Cheng, F. M. C. Cheung, and C. N. Chen, Eds., *Psychotherapy for the Chinese*: Selected Papers, 1st International Conference (9–11 Nov. 1992): 19–55. Hong Kong, Chinese University of Hong Kong.

Zhang, L., H. Yi, R. Luo, C. Liu, and S. Rozelle (2012). 'The Human Capital Roots of the Middle-Income Trap: The Case of China'. Annual Conference, International Association of Agricultural Economists, Rio de Janeiro. 18 Aug. 2012. Retrieved 20 November, 2012 from <http://purl.umn.edu/131119>.

# CHAPTER 24

# THE ROLE OF THE STATE IN ASIAN BUSINESS SYSTEMS

RICHARD W. CARNEY AND MICHAEL A. WITT[1]

THE original formulation of the 'varieties of capitalism' argument (Hall and Soskice 2001) attracted considerable criticism. Not all of this was altogether fair or on the mark (for a review, and criticism of the criticism, see Hancké, Rhodes, and Thatcher 2007). However, one point that has stood the test of time is that the theory underplayed the importance of politics and the state. A large and growing range of theoretical and empirical contributions have since emphasized that understanding the formation, maintenance, and evolution of business systems requires accounting for the role of the state in the economy.

Taking its cue from this body of work, this chapter seeks to shed light on the role of the state in Asian business systems. It begins by reviewing existing theory about the role of the state in the political economy, both from the social-sciences literature more generally and from the business-systems literature in particular. It then explores the utility of existing frameworks for the Asian context. We conclude that existing business-systems theory needs further refinement in accounting for the varying roles of the state, and we propose remedies.

## EXISTING THEORY

The first notable role of government with regard to its influence on the structure of business systems emerges from its efforts to foster rapid economic growth. Gerschenkron's (1962) analysis of late development in Germany is a notable early articulation of the state-led development thesis. A variant of this approach was utilized in analysing the modernization of developed economies following World War II (Shonfield 1965). The principal challenge was to shake out pre-war patterns and instil more modern business practices in order to secure high rates of national growth. Critical to this endeavour, in the view of many, was the state's control over the allocation of credit, mirroring Gerschenkron's emphasis on German banking in the late nineteenth century (Cohen 1977; Zysman 1983). National governments were categorized as either 'strong' or 'weak' (Katzenstein 1985; Skocpol and Amenta 1985), with the strong states of France and Japan as models of success, while Britain's weak state was regarded as a laggard (Shonfield 1965; Johnson 1982).

The economic disruptions of the 1970s led to a stronger focus on how effectively government could negotiate durable bargains between capital and labour. This neo-corporatism literature examines the capacity of the state to generate durable bargains with employers and labour unions with regard to wages, employment conditions, and social or economic policy (Schmitter and Lehmbruch 1979; Berger 1981; Goldthorpe 1984; Alvarez, Garrett, and Lange 1991). A nation's neo-corporatist model depended on whether its trade unions were more encompassing and could more successfully internalize the economic effects (such as inflation) of their wage settlements (Cameron 1984; Calmfors and Driffill 1988; Golden 1993). For many, such bargains were the result of a clear political exchange in which the outcome was due to the government's capacity to offer inducements, as well as the disciplinary power unions held over their members (Pizzorno 1978; Przeworski and Wallerstein 1982). In this literature, governments were categorized according to the organizational strength of the national trade union movement, with the small, open economies of northern Europe being models of success.

In the context of these advanced industrialized countries, there has also been considerable interest in the welfare state and variations in its structures. The welfare state is defined in the *Oxford English Dictionary* as a country with 'a system whereby the state undertakes to protect the health and well-being of its citizens, especially those in financial or social need, by means of grants, pensions, and other benefits'. In the seminal work of this literature, Esping-Andersen (1990) identified three types of welfare state: liberal, which emphasizes private provision and usually provides only a rudimentary social safety net (e.g. USA); Christian-democratic, which relies mostly on social insurance schemes to respond to needs (e.g. Germany); and social-democratic, which gives universal access to benefits (e.g. Sweden). Japan was the only Asian country to be included by Esping-Andersen, who classified it as 'liberal'. Recent years have seen increased interest and discussion in Asia in the welfare state, not least in the context of a rapidly ageing population in many of the more advanced industrialized nations in the region, such as Singapore, South Korea, and Taiwan (e.g. Witt 2014b).

The expansion of globalization has led to the retreat of government in its involvement with industry, and its role in economic governance has become more restricted. Increasingly mobile capital has forced the state to attempt to create an attractive investment environment for transnational capital via low taxes, easy labour laws, and a generally permissive regulatory system. In this way, the global economy produced a 'constraining effect' on states' macroeconomic policies by inducing increased budgetary pressure. This led to several streams of literature examining how the state's economic role was being restricted or reconstituted by market forces.

Several of these have focused on how business and society organize systems of production that are largely independent of government oversight, including sectoral governance, national innovation systems, and flexible production regimes. These works are influenced by the French regulation school and emphasize the movement of firms away from mass production towards new production regimes as a result of technological change, and depend on collective institutions at the regional, sectoral, or national level (Streeck and Schmitter 1985; Dore 1986; Piore and Sabel 1986; Boyer 1990; Herrigel 1996; Hollingsworth and Boyer 1997; Whitley 1999). In comparison to the modernization, neocorporatism, and welfare-state literatures, these works encompass a wider range of institutions and stress the ways in which institutions generate trust or enhance learning within economic communities, without an explicit role for the state. As a result, regional production networks are often emphasized over national categories.

While this literature focused on phenomena associated with the withdrawal of the state as a 'direct' producer of goods and services, or privatization, this decline in direct state intervention was matched by an increase in the state's indirect influence via a growth in the regulatory apparatus. The nature of these regulatory changes nevertheless conformed to existing institutional traditions that have tended to preserve power for the status quo. What are these existing institutional traditions, and how have policy-makers implemented rules that enhance, rather than hinder, competitiveness?

Hall and Soskice (2001) propose a framework that yields two contrasting outcomes. For some countries, regulatory changes that enhance competitiveness do so by improving the functioning of markets. For other countries, however, the regulatory apparatus achieves improved outcomes by enhancing the sharing of information, improving actors' ability to make credible commitments, and altering actors' expectations about what others will do. The first type of system, in which coordination is secured primarily through market mechanisms, is labelled a liberal market economy (LME), while policies that reinforce the capacities of actors for non-market coordination occur in coordinated market economies (CMEs).

Because of the nature of non-market coordination, policy-making in CMEs encounters higher levels of information asymmetries, transaction costs, and time-inconsistency problems. To resolve these issues, governments of these economies work closely with business associations, trade unions, and other para-public organizations. Policies get effectively implemented because these organizations are independent of the government and accountable to their members. Hence, these members trust them with private information to bargain for and administer the chosen policies. These associations can effectively work with the government to implement these policies at lower transaction costs, because they possess the authority to monitor and sanction members. At the same time, the capacity to implement effective long-term coordination policies depends on the credibility of the government to abide by its commitment. This credibility varies across political regimes.

Scholars observe a clustering of coordinated market economies with consensus political systems, and liberal market economies with majoritarian political systems. In CMEs, skills are viewed as co-specific assets that are invested in and utilized by multiple actors, such as business, labour, and handwork organizations covering many different sectors of the economy. These actors, however, will only be prepared to invest in such specialized skills if they have political representation, both directly, via bureaucratic appointments (corporatism), and indirectly, via political parties. To achieve this, proportional representation of different parties in legislative institutions, especially parliamentary committees, is necessary.

Conversely, majoritarian institutions undermine the incentives of multiple actors to commit to co-specific assets. In such systems, plurality electoral rules enable a large block of opinion to be defeated by a narrow majority. As a result, these political systems have greater policy variance than do consensus systems. Because long-term bargains among multiple actors are difficult to sustain, firms seek flexibility, the ability to hire and fire, and the ability to quickly change according to shifting market conditions. In essence, LMEs yield support for policies that privilege non-specific assets.

The key mechanism is due to the capacity of consensus institutions to generate credible commitments among multiple actors. 'Credible commitment' indicates the probability that partners think the other side will hold to an agreement. Consensus institutions increase the probability, because actors wield more power to veto a bargain they dislike (Tsebelis 2002). Their consent to change is needed; thus, they can enter an agreement with greater confidence that the bargain will hold. This process then becomes self-enforcing. Participants make decisions based on the degree of stability of policy, and then seek to preserve that system.

Critical to determining the strength of credible commitments is the electoral system. PR permits the election of numerous political parties, thereby expanding the number of actors and veto points. Plurality systems tend to yield fewer political parties, thereby reducing the number of veto points. This view of government removes any purposeful activist role for it. The government is seen as a complex of political institutions mediating strategic interactions among economic and social actors, thereby sustaining particular institutional equilibria.

Many, however, argue that a more prominent role for the state is needed. Amable (2003), in his analysis of the diversity of modern capitalism, introduces a grouping of countries in which the state plays a determining role—the European-integration/public social system of innovation and production (SSIP)—alongside three other European SSIPs (market-based, meso-corporatist, and social-democratic) and goes on to propose five international models of capitalism: market-based, social-democratic, Asian, continental European, and south European. These categories mirror those analysed in the Regulation School more broadly, except for the addition of the Asian model (Boyer 2005).

Schmidt (2002) creates her own typology of capitalist models, separating 'state capitalism' (France) from 'managed' and 'market capitalisms' (Germany and Britain, respectively). For her, ideas and national discourses matter for their capacity to generate and legitimize changes in policies and practices (Schmidt 2009). Hancké, Rhodes, and Thatcher (2007) propose a classical two-by-two matrix with the type of state–economy relations and interest organization as dimensions. They distinguish *étatisme* (close relations, fragmented interests, e.g. France), LMEs (arm's-length relations, fragmented interests, e.g. UK), compensating states (close relations, organized interests, e.g. Italy), and CMEs (arm's-length relations, organized interests, e.g. Germany). Both of these extensions allow for a wider range of state responses and dynamics of neo-liberal reform in national political economies.

But even these models that grant a larger role for the state fail to adequately account for its varying roles in the East Asian context. In the developmental states of East Asia, government officials direct lending to industries considered of strategic importance to lifting the nation up the rungs of the development ladder via export-oriented industrialization (Johnson 1982, 1987; Amsden 1989; Wade 1990; Evans 1995). However, given the prevailing theoretical assumptions about government failure coming from neoclassical economists, accompanied by the lack of success for industrial policies in other parts of the world, debates have occurred on why such policies seem to work in these particular countries.

One set of arguments focused on the state's use of the financial system. Wade (1990) argued that government intervention increased the capital available for spurring industrial development by heightened savings rates and by holding savings within the country for use by domestic investors. Amsden (1989) showed that subsidies directed towards bolstering the supply of capital not only spurred investment, but also helped to overcome two key costs associated with export-oriented industrialization: currency devaluation in an import-dependent economy and the high degree of uncertainty associated with entering foreign markets.

A second set of arguments in response to the neoclassical position attempted to show how the broader institutional and political environment contributed to relatively efficient outcomes. Johnson (1982) pointed to the autonomy of technocrats from political interference, and their interactive relationship with business in targeting and implementing market-conforming development policies. Haggard (1990) emphasized the role of the state in solving collective-action problems associated with economic policy reform, including through the exercise of authoritarian power. Along these lines, Wade (1990) argued that the one-party state was crucial for Taiwan's development, and Amsden's (1989) study of Korea referred to the power of the state to 'discipline' the private sector.

In further refinements, the developmental state was seen as effective because of bureaucrats' autonomy from political pressure, while also retrieving information from the private sector via trade associations to make decisions. This 'embedded autonomy' (Evans 1995) kept it from capture on the one hand and predation on the other. In other words, to be effective, the developmental state needs not just an independent sense of purpose; it also needs access to and information from the economic actors it seeks to influence. These dual needs become increasingly important as development becomes less certain and more complex. In other words, the increasingly sophisticated and complicated nature of industrial production and greater reliance on innovation as a nation's income status rises reinforces the need for autonomy and reliable information (Amsden and Chu 2003; Wade 1990; Amsden and Chu 2003). As a result, the developmental state's ability to 'impose' its decisions is of diminishing relevance to its capacity to institute a continuing conversation with economic actors about the opportunities for innovation and the obstacles to be overcome in the context of a performance-based incentives structure that disciplines its beneficiaries.

The developmental state as an ideal type needs to be juxtaposed to its opposite, the predatory state. Much of South East Asia, with the exceptions of Singapore and India, has historically fallen at least partially into this category (Evans 1995; Doner, Ritchie, and Slater 2005). Predatory states 'extract such large amounts of otherwise investable surplus while providing so little in the way of "collective goods" in return that they impede economic transformation' (Evans 1995: 44). Typical of this form of state is a high concentration of economic benefits in a relatively small group whose members are usually intimately connected to top political leaders on the basis of family or kinship ties. With politics representing predominantly a tool for self-enrichment, corruption is common, with attendant results for the rule of law and government effectiveness. Compared with developmental states, economic performance is usually poor (Evans 1995). At the same time, growth rates may, at least for some time, exceed those in advanced industrialized countries, for reasons that include population growth (higher population growth usually means faster gross domestic product (GDP) growth) and low base effect (a small economy needs to grow much less in absolute terms to produce a high growth rate than a large one).

But what political prerequisites led to the adoption of developmental or predatory strategies in Asia? Doner, Ritchie, and Slater (2005) point to three key variables that, together, offer necessary and sufficient conditions for the existence of a developmental state. First, a lack of resources tends to push states towards developing a modern economy based on manufacturing and services. By contrast, resource-abundant economies such as those of South East Asia—Indonesia having an abundance of oil, Malaysia rubber and tin, the Philippines sugar, and Thailand rice—lend themselves to more predatory orientations.

Second, the severity of an external threat to a nation's survival tends to be associated with developmental strategies, though as the case of Pakistan illustrates, it is certainly not a sufficient condition. Such threats were and are clear and real in North-East Asia, first during the Cold War and presently given the state of affairs between the two Koreas, between China and Taiwan, and between China and Japan. It was also acutely felt in Singapore, with both Malaysia and Indonesia initially attempting to absorb it. Threat levels in South East Asia have arguably been lower in recent decades. The Vietnam War proved the major exception to the rule and helped spur economic reforms in the region at the time.

Third, political leaders' reliance on an encompassing coalition is associated with developmental policies. While leaders' political survival depends on the maintenance of a minimum winning coalition, pressure to enlarge it can arise due to the threat of domestic elite conflict or disruptive mass mobilization. To retain power, side-payments are often made to popular sectors, but these can be difficult to sustain in the presence of severe security threats, which siphon revenues to the defence sector. Revenue may be further constrained by resource limitations, thereby leading to the reconciliation of coa-litional, geopolitical, and fiscal constraints via the widening of the coalition. Building and holding it together, however, can only occur by continuously expanding the national pie through sustained growth and jettisoning a cheap-labour strategy that could alien-ate coalition members. The presence of these three variables therefore leads to the pur-suit of a higher-skill, quality-based export trajectory, rather than a low-wage-based export-growth model. Sustaining such a broad coalition over the long run requires the ability to export high value-added goods by continuous upgrading. Only strong states have the capacity to implement these policies; states with weak institutions lack the capacity to overcome these political-economic challenges.

While this development strategy may foster certain institutional patterns, important differences often remain. For example, Singapore's institutional arrangements differ in important ways from those of Japan and both of these differ from China, as case studies clearly demonstrate. Hence, a nation's particular business-system arrangements cannot be explained solely by its development strategy.

In the context of North-East Asia, Whitley (2005) argues that the state plays a critical role in determining the characteristics of the business system and how employers behave associationally. He also argues that where the state adopts an active role in economic development (the developmental state) by directly intervening in certain sectors of the economy, the result is greater diversity in employment policies, bargaining procedures, corporate governance, systems of skills formation, etc., between firms of different size within the same sector. In this analysis of potential business system outcomes, Whitley identifies four types of state: arm's-length, dominant developmental (Korea: paternal-istic), business-corporatist (Japan after the Second World War: state agencies, banking system, and large companies), and inclusive-corporatist (Germany).

In contrast to Whitley's focus on developmental states, Tipton (2009) argues that the 'strong' states of South East Asia owe their features to their heritage of colonialism and reactive nationalism. Of critical importance is the political dominance of a narrow elite, which gets reflected in the top-down management style of business. Yet often these strong states are ineffective in generating high levels of growth compared to their devel-opmental counterparts, for reasons pointed to by Doner, Ritchie, and Slater (2005).

While elite political influence is predominant among these states, it is nevertheless tempered by the structure of national political institutions, as shown by their responses to the Asian Financial Crisis. MacIntyre (2001) explains that the distribution of veto authority can account for differences in investment reversals. Countries with many veto points exhibit more rigid policy responses, while those with very few display greater policy volatility. Both extremes are bad for investors; a balance between the two is pref-erable. Thus, there is a U-shaped relationship between the number of veto players and policy risk for investors. While MacIntyre's analysis is directed towards explaining for-eign investment, the mapping of veto points onto political regimes that extend beyond the advanced democracies traditionally examined in the varieties of capitalism litera-ture offers a potentially useful way to apply the relationship between electoral systems and the varieties of capitalism framework to the East Asia setting.

Seeking to develop a general explanation for business systems that can span North and South East Asia, Tipton (2009) points to state capacity and state direction as indicators for whether governments fit the liberal or coordinated approach to business systems. Together, these attributes refer to the state's ability to make and implement policies that effectively achieve the government's goals, as well as the extent of state involvement and resources used to do so. Countries with high levels of state direction and state capacity are CMEs; countries that are low on both dimensions are LMEs.

In the most recent contribution to the topic, Walter and Zhang (2012) apply a framework resembling that of Hancké, Rhodes, and Thatcher (2007) (summarized earlier) to the Asian context. They present a fourfold typology in which the organization of social groups is characterized as strong or weak (Hancké et al.: organized or fragmented) and state organization of the economy is extensive or modest (Hancké et al.: close or arm's-length). Capitalist institutions reflect the interaction of these two dimensions, yielding co-governed (Republic of Korea (ROK), Taiwan), state-led (China, Malaysia), networked (Japan), and personalized (Indonesia, Philippines, Thailand) state systems. Hong Kong and Singapore, two important cases with economies larger than Malaysia or the Philippines, are not classified.

As with the framework proposed by Hancké, Rhodes, and Thatcher (2007), the benefit of this approach lies in its applicability to varying regime types and degrees of social coordination. However, Walter and Zhang (2012) argue that the combination of weak or modest state organization of the economy, paired with weak coordination of economic action, produces personal capitalism (i.e. predatory states) in Asia, while Hancké, Rhodes, and Thatcher (2007) see essentially the same combination as leading to liberal market economies in the West. The presence of different outcomes despite similar characteristics suggests that there are missing variables that need to be accounted for and that further theoretical development concerning the state's role in the context of Asia is required.

# MAPPING STATE THEORIES ON TO BUSINESS SYSTEM OUTCOMES

To make sense of how the government influences contemporary business systems, we consider two different approaches. The first examines how conventional political-economy categorizations of the state influence the various dimensions of a business system. These categories include the regulatory, welfare, developmental, and predatory state. Britain and several of its former colonies, such as the USA, Canada, Australia, New Zealand, and Hong Kong are generally regarded as regulatory states; most of the West European states fit into the welfare-state category; the East Asian Tigers—Japan, South Korea, Taiwan, and Singapore—fall into the developmental category; and most South East Asian, Sub-Saharan African, and Latin American states fall into the predatory-state group. Japan is often categorized as either a developmental or a welfare state.

There are a couple of drawbacks to this approach. First, it was never intended to explain the institutional arrangements of business systems, although inferences can be drawn with regard to them. Second, states that were once seen as falling into a particular category may no longer clearly belong there, such as the developmental states. Moreover, and as with any typology, some states, such as Japan, could be placed into more than one category. But bearing in mind these potential drawbacks, the benefit of this approach is that these political-economy typologies of the state are widely accepted and understood. Hence the exercise of drawing implications for business-system structures could offer generally acceptable insights about the government's influence on them.

## Regulatory State

A regulatory state governs the economy mainly through regulatory agencies that are empowered to enforce a variety of standards of behaviour to protect the public against market failures of various sorts, including monopolistic pricing, predation, and other abuses of market power, and by providing collective goods (such as national defence or public education) that otherwise would be under-supplied by the market (Levi-Faur 2012).

Although the idea of the regulatory state was not intended to explain business systems, by virtue of its emphasis on the USA, several of the features of a Liberal Market Economy have come to be associated with it (Majone 1997). Hence, modern regulatory states, which have given rise to regulatory capitalism (Levi-Faur 2005), tend to be equated with strong financial markets and corporate ownership, and governance arrangements that offer strong protections to shareholders. By virtue of this, managers tend to have more power, although this is an implication that derives from stronger regulatory power and not from theories of the regulatory state. Such states tend to have relatively basic protections for workers, especially when compared to the welfare state. As a result, employee turnover tends to be higher, and by implication, general educational skills and training are favoured. With regard to inter-firm relations, theories of the regulatory state are mute. Finally, because of the emphasis on providing institutions that protect the integrity of a market economy, there is a tendency towards strong institutionalized trust.

Table 24.1 displays the ranking of states according to proxy measures for each of the four state types. The measures used do not precisely capture the characteristics of each state category, but offer a reasonable and objective method of comparing and ranking them. Among the economies of Asia, Hong Kong most clearly fits the regulatory state model, though not quite perfectly. First, the regulatory state is normally associated with fully functioning democracies, which Hong Kong is not. Second, strong protections for minority shareholders, and therefore a tendency for the dilution of concentrated ownership, is expected, yet Hong Kong's enterprises are dominated by family ownership. Finally, and partially due to the importance of these family groups, interpersonal trust

# Table 24.1 State type rankings

| Regulatory State Indicator | | Welfare State Indicator | | | Developmental State Indicator | | Predatory State Indicator | |
| --- | --- | --- | --- | --- | --- | --- | --- | --- |
| Economic Freedom Index 2012[c] | | Social Protection Index 2011[a] | OECD Public Social Expenditure as % of GDP, 2007 | | Government Effectiveness 2011[b] | | Control of Corruption 2011[b] | |
| Hong Kong | 89.9 | Japan 0.54 | 18.7 | Singapore | Singapore | 2.16 | Laos | −1.06 |
| Singapore | 87.5 | South Korea 0.28 | 07.6 | Sweden | Sweden | 1.96 | Philippines | −0.78 |
| US | 76.3 | Malaysia 0.15 | | Hong Kong | Hong Kong | 1.70 | Indonesia | −0.68 |
| UK | 74.1 | China 0.14 | | UK | UK | 1.55 | China | −0.67 |
| Taiwan | 71.9 | India 0.11 | | Germany | Germany | 1.53 | Vietnam | −0.63 |
| Sweden | 71.7 | Vietnam 0.09 | | US | US | 1.41 | India | −0.56 |
| Japan | 71.6 | Indonesia 0.06 | | France | France | 1.36 | Thailand | −0.37 |
| Germany | 71.0 | Philippines 0.06 | | Japan | Japan | 1.35 | Malaysia | 0.00 |
| South Korea | 69.9 | Laos 0.02 | | South Korea | South Korea | 1.23 | South Korea | 0.45 |
| Malaysia | 66.4 | | | Taiwan | Taiwan | 1.17 | Taiwan | 0.90 |
| Thailand | 64.9 | | | Malaysia | Malaysia | 1.00 | US | 1.25 |
| France | 63.2 | | | China | China | 0.12 | Japan | 1.50 |
| Philippines | 57.1 | | 28.4 | Thailand | Thailand | 0.10 | France | 1.51 |
| Indonesia | 56.4 | | 27.3 | Philippines | Philippines | 0.00 | UK | 1.54 |
| India | 54.6 | | 25.2 | India | India | −0.03 | Germany | 1.69 |
| Vietnam | 51.3 | | | Indonesia | Indonesia | −0.24 | Hong Kong | 1.84 |
| China | 51.2 | | 20.5 | Vietnam | Vietnam | −0.28 | Singapore | 2.12 |
| Laos | 50.0 | | 16.2 | Laos | Laos | −0.91 | Sweden | 2.22 |

[a] Asian Development Bank 2011

[b] Worldwide Governance Indicators, World Bank 2011

[c] Heritage Foundation 2012

*Note*: Higher values on the Economic Freedom Index denote higher economic freedom. For government effectiveness and control of corruption, higher values indicate greater effectiveness or better control.

plays a more important role in Hong Kong than in the ideal-typical regulatory state. Also of note is Singapore's high placement in this category, though it is often regarded as belonging to the developmental state category.

## Welfare State

As discussed earlier, a welfare state is a concept of government in which the state plays a key role in the protection and promotion of the economic and social well-being of its citizens, primarily through the redistribution of funds by the state.

With regard to implications for the business system, financial systems tend to be more reliant on banking than stock markets (van Kersbergen 1995). This is partly due to the greater social protections granted to employees, which disfavour the use of hostile mergers and acquisitions that could lead to layoffs. Correspondingly, concentrated corporate ownership prevails. The representation of numerous interests in government likewise translates into a number of actors having influence on a key management decisions such as hiring and firing, as well as wages (Esping-Andersen 1990). This tendency towards greater employment stability likewise facilitates more specialized education and training (Hall and Soskice 2001). In addition to the generally more cooperative relationships between owners, managers, and employees, these firms also coordinate their behaviour with each other. Together, these more coordinated forms of market interaction support more enduring forms of interpersonal trust.

In the context of Asia, Japan most clearly fits the welfare-state model, though its classification in the liberal sub-type, alongside the USA and Canada, indicates that it does not display key features associated with this category. For example, employee welfare is conducted more heavily at firm level rather than by the state, and mainly among large firms. Moreover, the form of blockholding prevalent in Japan is due to cross-shareholdings among member firms of the business group or long-term shareholdings by friendly firms rather than by a single family owner. Japan also uses a proportional representation electoral system for less than half of its legislative seats, the system commonly used in Continental Europe, which some would regard as partially responsible for observed deviations from the ideal-typical welfare state. Table 24.1 shows that South Korea would be next, and if data were available, Taiwan would probably also be in the mix.

## Developmental State

In this model, the state has more independent, or autonomous, political power, as well as more control over the economy. The argument from this perspective is that a government ministry can have the freedom to plan the economy and look to long-term national interests without having its economic policies disrupted by either corporate-class or working-class short-term or narrow interests (Doner, Ritchie, and Slater 2005). This autonomy from the political process is easier to accomplish in a non-democratic state, and Taiwan, South Korea, and Singapore all went through the majority of their developmental phases with such political regimes. However, Japan illustrates that such developmental states may also exist in democracies. Moreover, although Taiwan and South Korea have democratized, important features of the developmental state persist.

As for implications for the business system, there is an expectation that the financial system will be heavily reliant on banking, since over-borrowing and over-lending tend to be a crucial mechanism by which strategic industries are rapidly developed (Wade 1990; Hoshi and Kashyap 2004). As a consequence of the underdevelopment of the stock market as a source of external financing, corporate ownership will tend to remain concentrated, although this may be in the hands of families, the state, or through cross-shareholdings that form part of a business group, as with Japan's *keiretsu*. There are no hard-and-fast rules about the internal decision-making structure of firms: Japanese firms have engaged in consensual decision-making, while Korean, Taiwanese, and PRC firms have displayed more top-down processes (Whitley 1992). These internal decision-making dynamics are reflected in the structure of industrial relations, which exhibited stronger informal protections for workers in the case of Japan, compared with their Taiwanese, People's Republic of China (PRC), and Korean counterparts. The more inclusive political arrangements in Japan likewise corresponded to relatively strong education and training (both public and private) programmes, more tepid support in Korea and Taiwan, and relatively little in PRC. The prevailing importance of business groups to organizing economic activity contributes to a greater likelihood for inter-firm relations to occur exclusively among these firms, and social capital is likely to have stronger interpersonal trust attributes.

One of the drawbacks of this model is that there are several different kinds of political regime that fall within its remit. Moreover, two of the countries, Korea and Taiwan, switched regimes near the end of their developmental phases, leading to stronger protections for workers. Hence, it is a little difficult to draw clear implications for the business system from this model. For many, the PRC would also fall into this category with regard to its large state-owned enterprises, but much of the rest of the Chinese economy would not. Additionally, the PRC has a high level of income inequality, which differs from the other developmental states.

Many countries categorized as developmental do not fully belong in this category any longer, as they have largely completed their development phase, although institutional inertia means that many of the institutional arrangements persist. Generally, these countries rely on strong interpersonal trust to enable rapid development, but Singapore exhibits strong institutionalized-trust characteristics. Overall, there are many inconsistencies in business systems among the variety of countries placed into this category.

Table 24.1 uses government effectiveness as a measure for the developmental state, since this is regarded as a crucial feature. Asian economies line up in a way that is broadly consistent with the developmental-state typology (though Hong Kong is placed highly, but is more generally regarded as a regulatory state, as the government did not play an active role in guiding the development of the economy). As the high scores of the European nations indicate, this measure loses its discriminant power as GDP per capita levels increase. It is, however, a useful measure for distinguishing developmental from predatory states at lower levels of economic development. Detailed country analyses show that the state in China, Malaysia, and Thailand has played a developmental role, though perhaps less clearly so than in the other North-East Asian states (Carney and Andriesse 2014; Suehiro and Wailerdsak 2014; Witt and Redding 2014a). The same cannot be said about the lower-ranking Asian economies.

## Predatory State

Predatory states are characterized as being governed by elites who monopolize power through the use of opaque decision-making procedures, weak institutions, and a lack of market competition, so as to generate profits that benefit them rather than society at large (Robinson 1999). With regard to expectations about the structure of the business system, the financial system is expected to be heavily banking oriented, because the legal system is too weak to allow for a well-performing stock market to develop (Evans 1989). Corporate ownership is concentrated in the hands of families or the state, which is used for the benefit of a clientelist group. With few checks in place to prevent abuse, state ownership provides state officials with ample opportunities for rent-seeking. Mirroring the broader hierarchical structure of society, the internal structure of the firm is top-down, with no protections for employees. Likewise, there are few education-and-skills training opportunities. Inter-firm relations are likely to occur only between firms from the same family group, and social capital is strongly oriented towards interpersonal trust.

There is considerable variation in how closely these states conform to type, as seen by their rankings in the control of corruption and government effectiveness in Table 24.1. India, Indonesia, the Philippines, Laos, and Vietnam generally exhibit business-system characteristics indicative of predatory states, while China, Malaysia, and Thailand combine predatory elements with developmental aspects. Variation also occurs with regard to the control of each country's largest corporations. For example, Vietnam, Laos, and Malaysia exhibit high levels of state ownership, while Indonesia, the Philippines, and Thailand have more family ownership; Thailand has seen an increase in widely held ownership since the 1997 Asian Financial Crisis. There are also important differences in political regimes. Vietnam and Laos retain strict state control due to the continuing political dominance of the Communist Party. The Malaysian state exhibits slightly weaker, but still strong, centralized control, but with more market-oriented economic policies. Thailand, Indonesia, and the Philippines have more democratic governance, but are not yet mature and well-functioning, and patronage politics continues to play a vital role in economic policy-making. In summary, predatory states display considerable variation, which makes it problematic to ascribe uniform business-system characteristics to countries in this category.

# ASSESSING BUSINESS SYSTEMS THEORIES

The second approach to evaluating how the state influences business systems is to examine the utility of existing business-systems theories. We focus on the framework of Hancké, Rhodes, and Thatcher (2007), which is mirrored in Walter and Zhang (2012). While other frameworks exist, as reviewed earlier, this framework is the most elaborate model aiming for universal applicability.

The key dimension for understanding the state in this model is the extent of state intervention. Conceptually, such state intervention can occur in several ways: through the regulatory framework, through direct state activity, and informally through processes such as 'administrative guidance' in Japan (cf. Witt 2014a).

While informal processes are difficult to measure, reasonable proxies of the other two dimensions are available. The Index of Economic Freedom (Heritage Foundation 2012) measures predominantly the extent of economic regulations, but also accounts for the level of direct state activity in the economy as evident in government spending and associated taxes. In addition, states may be directly involved in the economy through ownership of productive assets. As a proxy measure, we use the percentage of state-controlled enterprises among the top 200 listed firms in each economy. This is an imperfect measure, as it reports ownership only for firms that are at least partially listed. However, it is the best available, as no comparative statistics on total state ownership are available. Carney and Child (2012) report state ownership among the top-200 listed firms for nine Asian economies. For the remaining four—China, India, Laos, and Vietnam—we know from empirical analyses (Andriesse 2014; Saez 2014; Truong and Rowley 2014; Witt and Redding 2014a) that state ownership levels among major firms are high. To enable a meaningful comparison, we further report the respective values of these variables for five Western advanced industrialized economies: France, Germany, Sweden, the UK, and the USA (Christiansen 2011).

Table 24.2 shows the results for each measure in rank order. To reconcile the different rankings, we calculate a weighted average rank order, giving twice the weight to the Economic Freedom Index, as it is more encompassing than the ownership measure. Building on prior classifications (Schmidt 2002; Hancké, Rhodes, and Thatcher 2007), we use the weighted average rank order of France as the threshold for high levels of state intervention. Five Asian economies thus have relatively low levels of state intervention: Hong Kong, Singapore, Taiwan, Japan, and South Korea. The remaining eight nations have high levels.

The second dimension of the framework relates to societal organization with respect to the economy. While this dimension is, strictly speaking, not related to the state as such, it is still worth exploring so as to gain a fuller sense of the validity of the framework.

Measuring societal organization is difficult. We assume that there are two key societal forces, employees and employers. With some reservations, union membership can serve as a proxy for the organizational strength of the former. A concern here is that

## Table 24.2 Measures of state intervention in rank orders

| Economic Freedom Index 2012[a] | | State Ownership among Top 200 Companies[b, *] | | Weighted Average Ranking | |
|---|---|---|---|---|---|
| Economy | Index | Economy | Ownership, % | Economy | Ranking |
| Hong Kong | 89.9 | US | 1.0 | US | 2.3 |
| Singapore | 87.5 | UK | 1.0 | UK | 3.3 |
| US | 76.3 | Germany | 1.5 | Sweden | 5.0 |
| UK | 74.1 | Sweden | 1.5 | Hong Kong | 5.0 |
| Taiwan | 71.9 | Philippines | 5.2 | Singapore | 5.3 |
| Sweden | 71.7 | France | 5.5 | Germany | 6.3 |
| Japan | 71.6 | Japan | 6.3 | Taiwan | 6.3 |
| Germany | 71.0 | S. Korea | 6.9 | Japan | 7.0 |
| S. Korea | 69.9 | Taiwan | 9.2 | S. Korea | 8.7 |
| Malaysia | 66.4 | Thailand | 12.8 | France | 10.0 |
| Thailand | 64.9 | Indonesia | 14.1 | Philippines | 10.3 |
| France | 63.2 | Singapore | 20.5 | Thailand | 10.7 |
| Philippines | 57.1 | Hong Kong | 28.0 | Malaysia | 11.3 |
| Indonesia | 56.4 | Malaysia | 39.7 | Indonesia | 13.0 |
| India | 54.6 | India | (high) | India | 15.0 |
| Vietnam | 51.3 | China | (high) | Vietnam | 16.3 |
| China | 51.2 | Vietnam | (high) | China | 16.7 |
| Laos | 50.0 | Laos | (high) | Laos | 18.0 |

[a] Heritage Foundation 2012
[b] Christiansen 2011; Carney and Child 2012; Andriesse 2014; Saez 2014; Truong and Rowley 2014; Witt and Redding 2014a.
* The high score for Hong Kong reflects the large number of mainland-Chinese SOEs listed on the exchange, rather than HK state-owned firms.

high or low levels of membership do not necessarily translate into low or high levels of influence, because existing institutions may amplify or attenuate strength in numbers—German unions, for instance, are more powerful than their membership numbers suggest, because they can leverage entrenched legal rights. Unfortunately, comparative statistics of union rights are not available for most of Asia.

To our knowledge, there are no comparative statistics for Asia that measure employer organization. However, qualitatively viewed, organization levels of employers seem to be consistent with those of employees (cf. country chapters in Witt and Redding 2014b). That does not mean that employers and employees are equally influential. Employers in most Asian countries wield considerable influence on government through a range of measures, such as personal connections or bribery (Faccio 2006). However, that form of influence is usually not organized and thus unrelated to societal organization as a dimension.

We consequently use union densities as a proxy for social organization levels. Table 24.3 shows union densities for our sample in rank order. We take Japanese density levels, which are low by CME standards (though the same as for Germany), to be the threshold for high levels of organization. The results suggest that by this measure, there are four economies with high levels of societal organization: Hong Kong, Japan, Taiwan, and Vietnam. However, we know that in Vietnam, as in all Asian economies with governing Communist Parties, unions are a branch of the party and thus not a means of labour organization, but part of the state apparatus (Truong and Rowley 2014; Witt and Redding 2014a). The same logic applies to Laos, for which unionization rates are not available (Andriesse 2014). Furthermore, we know that unions in Hong Kong exist mostly in the context of a few public enterprises and are virtually absent from the private sector (Redding, Wong, and Leung 2014). On the other hand, while unionization rates

**Table 24.3 Union densities in rank order**

| Economy | Union Density, % | Notes |
| --- | --- | --- |
| Sweden | 68.4 | |
| Vietnam | 67.0 (2005) | Union branch of the Communist Party |
| Taiwan | 37.3 | |
| UK | 26.5 | |
| HK | 23.2 | Unions focused on few large public enterprises |
| Japan | 18.5 | |
| Germany | 18.5 | |
| Singapore | 17.7 (2009) | Union effectively part of government |
| China | 16.1 (2007) | Union branch of the Communist Party |
| US | 11.4 | |
| Philippines | 11.2 (2007) | |
| Malaysia | 10.2 (2007) | |
| S. Korea | 10.0 (2009) | Close to 50% unionization in *chaebol* |
| Thailand | 10.0 | |
| France | 7.6 (2008) | |
| India | 6.9 (2008) | |
| Indonesia | 5.0 (2007) | |
| Laos | n/a | Union branch of the Communist Party |

*Note*: Numbers are 2010 or latest available.
*Sources*: OECD 2012; Witt and Redding 2013.

in Korea in general are low, about half of the employees of the most important companies—those belonging to the *chaebol*—are unionized (Witt 2014b). Singapore, while
close to Japanese levels, has effectively made unions part of the government (Carney
2014). Taking these points into account, three economies remain with a high level of
societal organization on the labour side: Japan, Korea, and Taiwan.

The overall result is summarized in Figure 24.1. It is reasonably consistent with the
labels proposed by Hancké, Rhodes, and Thatcher (2007). Hong Kong and Singapore
are arguably LMEs, and it is well accepted that Japan is a CME. Most observers would
probably also agree with the placement of the states identified as generally *étatist*.
Problematic are Korea and Taiwan, which the framework suggests to be CMEs, a classification not borne out by detailed business-systems analysis (Lee and Hsiao 2014; Witt
2014b).

The result is much less consistent with the empirical results and proposed labelling
by Walter and Zhang (2012). In terms of empirics, they classify South Korea and Taiwan
as having high levels of state intervention. While one can argue about the South Korean
case—perhaps Korea rather than France should be the threshold—Taiwan is clearly in
the low-intervention camp, having a higher rank than Japan, which Walter and Zhang
accept as having low intervention. It is also inconsistent with respect to Indonesia, the
Philippines, and Thailand, which Walter and Zhang classify as having low state intervention. In terms of labelling, Hong Kong and Singapore in their scheme would be classified
as having 'personalized' forms of business systems—read, predatory. This is clearly not
the case according to the indicators.

|  |  | State Intervention | |
|---|---|---|---|
|  |  | **low** | **high** |
| *Social Organization* | **high** | *'CME'/'networked'*<br>Japan<br>Korea<br>Taiwan | *'compensating'/*<br>*co-governed'*<br>n/a |
|  | **low** | *'LME'/'personalized'*<br>Hong Kong<br>Singapore | *'étatist'/'state-led'*<br>China<br>India<br>Indonesia<br>Laos<br>Malaysia<br>Philippines<br>Thailand<br>Vietnam |

FIGURE 24.1 Placement of Asian economies using existing frameworks

*Note:* Terms in quotation marks are labels proposed by Hancké, Rhodes, and Thatcher (2007) and Walter and
Zhang (2012) respectively.

In terms of the overall utility of the 2 × 2 matrix, two points stand out. First, one of the quadrants remains empty. The data suggest that co-governed or compensating states do not exist in Asia unless one reclassifies Korea as a case of high government intervention, as discussed earlier. Second, one might question whether it is sensible to lump together relatively well-performing economies such as China or Malaysia with problem cases such as Laos or the Philippines. As the weighted-average rank order shows, the level of state intervention is not a useful discriminant for this question.

# IMPLICATIONS FOR THEORY AND CONCLUSION

Our analysis suggests that existing business-systems theories that address the role of the state are in need of further development. Given the presence of considerable empirical challenges to the Walter and Zhang (2012) model, we propose to build on the model by Hancké, Rhodes, and Thatcher (2007). If we accept that compensating states do not (yet) exist in Asia, two key challenges to this model remain. First, Korea and Taiwan were classified as CMEs, even though detailed analysis suggest otherwise. This could suggest a fundamental flaw in the system. However, it might also be the result of institutional inertia. Both Korea and Taiwan have undergone relatively recent transformations to democracy, allowing for a stronger role of organized societal interests. While the

| | | State Intervention | | | | | |
|---|---|---|---|---|---|---|---|
| | | **low** | **high** | | | | |
| *Social Organization* | high | *CME* Japan Korea Taiwan Germany Sweden | *compensating* Italy Spain | | | | |
| | low | *LME* Hong Kong Singapore UK US | *étatist, advanced* France | | | | *high income* |
| | | | *étatist, developmental* Malaysia China India | Thailand | *étatist, predatory* Philippines Vietnam Indonesia | Laos | *low or medium income* |
| | | | **high state capacity** | | **low state capacity** | | |

FIGURE 24.2 Placement of Asian and major European economies using proposed framework

current political configuration may thus have newly come to resemble that associated with CMEs, the institutional structure of their business systems may not reflect these new realities yet. If the framework is correct, one would consequently predict these business systems to become more Northern European in institutional structure over time.

Second, the *étatist* category mixes, to borrow terminology from the more general models, predatory and developmental states; that is, polities with very different business and political dynamics. In our view, it may be possible to address this issue by adducing a third dimension for cases with high levels of state intervention: state capacity, as expressed by government effectiveness and its control of corruption. This is in line with prior work that has argued that state capacity, in the sense of state ability to get things done, may distinguish developmental from predatory states (Evans 1995). Given that developmental and predatory states tend to be relatively poor countries in terms of per capita GDP, we expect this dimension to have discriminatory power only for lower-income economies. We remain agnostic about the question of whether states combining low state capacity with high per capita GDP represent a meaningful analytical category. Some oil-rich countries, such as Equatorial Guinea, may fit these criteria. We leave this question for future research to explore.

The resultant refinement to the *étatist*/state-led quadrant is presented in Figure 24.2. We present the Asian *étatist* economies from most developmental (left) to most predatory (right), using the average of the World Bank's government effectiveness and control of corruption measures, discussed earlier, as a proxy. Four rough clusters emerge, indicated by the columns. Within each column, states cited higher are relatively more developmental than those below them. Although this proposed model adds some complexity to the existing framework, we think it is a necessary step in order to distinguish among different types of *étatist* states, consistent with empirical facts for Asia and Europe.

Identifying systematic differences among these *étatist* states provokes questions about their origins and the long-term effects they have on business systems as well as other dimensions of the political economy. For example, Iversen and Soskice (2009) find that electoral systems not only exhibit strong correspondence to capitalist arrangements among OECD countries (particularly those related to industrial relations), but also to income inequality and the extent of redistribution. Systematic differences among *étatist* states in Asia may lead to similarly clear institutional and related economic outcomes. For instance, developmental and predatory states may develop distinct sectoral patterns of comparative advantage that resemble those proposed by Hall and Soskice (2001), i.e. of CMEs being more competitive in areas with incremental innovation, and LMEs with radical innovation. Developmental states would present an interesting object of exploration with regard to how such advantages develop over time. For most predatory states, on the other hand, sectoral advantages are likely to be heavily skewed towards resources and related low-technology industries.

A further challenge to theory is the lack of democracy among many Asian countries. Current theories about the political origins of OECD business systems point to a persistent relationship with the electoral system. How might the political institutions of non-democratic states be differentiated, and does their non-democratic apparatus impede the possibility to predict future trajectories? Moreover, to what extent, and in what ways, do informal institutions generate and preserve business-systems arrangements? Whitley (1992) has pioneered work in this area, primarily among North-East Asia's developmental states, and found considerable variation among them. It would be useful to see this work extended to cover predatory states.

## Notes

1. Richard Carney is the lead author of this chapter and contributed about two-thirds of the total length. Michael A. Witt contributed the remaining third.

## References

Asian Development Bank (2011). 'Social Protection Index'. Retrieved 13 November 2012 from http://www.adb.org/sectors/social-protection/main.

Alvarez, R. M., G. Garrett and P. Lange (1991). 'Government Partisanship, Labor Organization, and Macroeconomic Performance'. *American Political Science Review* 85(2): 539–556.

Amable, B. (2003). *The Diversity of Modern Capitalism*. Oxford, Oxford University Press.

Amsden, A. H. (1989). *Asia's Next Giant: South Korea and Late Industrialization*. Oxford, Oxford University Press.

—— and W. Chu (2003). *Beyond Late Development: Taiwan's Upgrading Policies*. Cambridge, MIT Press.

Andriesse, E. (2014). 'Laos: Frontier Capitalism'. In M. A. Witt and G. Redding, Eds., *The Oxford Handbook of Asian Business Systems*: 123–143. Oxford, Oxford University Press.

Berger, S. (1981). *Organizing Interest in Western Europe: Pluralism, Corporatism and the Transformation of Politics*. Cambridge, Cambridge University Press.

Boyer, R. (1990). *The Regulation School: A Critical Introduction*. New York, Columbia University Press.

—— (2005). 'How and Why Capitalisms Differ'. *Economy and Society* 34(4): 509–557.

Calmfors, L. and J. Driffill (1988). 'Centralization of Wage Bargaining and Macroeconomic Performance'. *Economic Policy* 6(April): 13–61.

Cameron, D. R. (1984). 'Social Democracy, Corporatism, Labour Quiescence, and the Representation of Economic Interest in Advanced Capitalist Society'. In J. H. Goldthorpe, Ed., *Order and Conflict in Contemporary Capitalism*: 143–178. Oxford, Clarendon Press.

Carney, M. and E. Andriesse (2014) 'Malaysia: Personal Capitalism'. In M. A. Witt and G. Redding, Eds., *The Oxford Handbook of Asian Business Systems*: 144–168. Oxford, Oxford University Press.

Carney, R. W. (2014). 'Singapore: Open State-Led Capitalism'. In M. A. Witt and G. Redding, Eds. *The Oxford Handbook of Asian Business Systems*: 192–215. Oxford, Oxford University Press.

—— and T. B. Child (2012). 'Changes to Ownership and Control of East Asian Corporations between 1996 and 2008: The Primacy of Politics'. *Journal of Financial Economics*. DOI:10.1016/j.jfineco.2012.08.013.

Christiansen, H. (2011). *The Size and Composition of the SOE Sector in OECD Countries*. OECD Corporate Governance Working Paper No. 5. Paris, OECD.

Cohen, S. S. (1977). *Modern Capitalist Planning: The French Model*. Berkeley, University of California Press.

Doner, R. F., B. K. Ritchie, and D. Slater (2005). 'Systemic Vulnerability and the Origins of Developmental States: Northeast and Southeast Asia in Comparative Perspective'. *International Organization* 59(2): 327–361.

Dore, R. (1986). *Flexible Rigidities: Industrial Policy and Structural Adjustment in the Japanese Economy, 1970–1980*. Stanford, Stanford University Press.

Esping-Andersen, G. (1990). *The Three Worlds of Welfare Capitalism*. Cambridge, Polity Press.

Evans, P. B. (1989). 'Predatory, Developmental, and Other Apparatuses: A Comparative Political Economy Perspective on the Third World State'. *Sociological Forum* 4(4): 561–587.

—— (1995). *Embedded Autonomy: States and Industrial Transformation*. Princeton, Princeton University Press.

Faccio, M. (2006). 'Politically Connected Firms'. *American Economic Review* 96(1): 369–386.

Gerschenkron, A. (1962). *Economic Backwardness in Historical Perspective: A Book of Essays*. Cambridge, MA, Belknap Press.

Golden, M. (1993). 'The Dynamics of Trade Unionism and National Economic Performance'. *American Political Science Review* 87(2): 437–454.

Goldthorpe, J. H. (1984). *Order and Conflict in Contemporary Capitalism*. Oxford, Clarendon Press.

Haggard, S. (1990). *Pathways from the Periphery: The Politics of Growth in the Newly Industrializing Countries*. Ithaca, Cornell University Press.

Hall, P. A. and D. Soskice (2001). 'An Introduction to Varieties of Capitalism'. In P. A. Hall and D. Soskice, Eds., *Varieties of Capitalism: The Institutional Foundations of Comparative Advantage*: 1–68. Oxford, Oxford University Press.

Hancké, B., M. Rhodes, and M. Thatcher (2007). 'Introduction: Beyond Varieties of Capitalism'. In B. Hancké, M. Rhodes, and M. Thatcher, Eds., *Beyond Varieties of Capitalism: Conflict, Contradictions, and Complementarities in the European Economy*: 3–38. Oxford, Oxford University Press.

Heritage Foundation (2012). '2012 Index of Economic Freedom'. Retrieved 13 November 2012 from <http://www.heritage.org/index/>.

Herrigel, G. (1996). *Industrial Constructions: The Social Foundations of German Industrial Power*. Cambridge, Cambridge University Press.

Hollingsworth, R. and R. Boyer (1997). *How and Why Do Social Systems of Production Change*. New York, Cambridge: Cambridge University Press.

Hoshi, T. and A. Kashyap (2004). *Corporate Financing and Governance in Japan: The Road to the Future*. Cambridge, MA, MIT Press.

Iversen, T. and D. Soskice (2009). 'Distribution and Redistribution: The Shadow of the Nineteenth Century'. *World Politics* 61(3): 438–486.

Johnson, C. (1982). *MITI and the Japanese Miracle: The Growth of Industrial Policy 1925–1975*. Stanford, Stanford University Press.

—— (1987). 'How to Think About Economic Competition from Japan'. *Journal of Japanese Studies* 13(2): 415–427.

Katzenstein, P. J. (1985). *Small States in World Markets: Industrial Policy in Europe*. Ithaca, Cornell University Press.

Lee, Z. R. and M. Hsiao (2014). 'Taiwan: SME-Oriented Capitalism in Transition'. In M. A. Witt and G. Redding, Eds., *The Oxford Handbook of Asian Business Systems*: 238–259. Oxford, Oxford University Press.

Levi-Faur, D. (2005). 'The Global Diffusion of Regulatory Capitalism'. *Annals of the American Academy of Political and Social Science* 598(1): 12–32.

—— (2012). *Handbook on the Politics of Regulation*. Cheltenham, Edward Elgar.

MacIntyre, A. (2001). 'Institutions and Investors: The Politics of the Economic Crisis in Southeast Asia'. *International Organization* 55(1): 81–122.

Majone, G. (1997). 'From the Positive to the Regulatory State: Causes and Consequences of Changes in the Mode of Governance'. *Journal of Public Policy* 17(2): 139–167.

OECD (2012). 'OECD.Stat'. Retrieved 11 November 2012 from <http://stats.oecd.org>.

Piore, M. and C. Sabel (1986). *The Second Industrial Divide: Possibilities for Prosperity*. New York, Basic Books.

Pizzorno, A. (1978). 'Political Exchange and Collective Identity in Industrial Conflict'. In C. Crouch and A. Pizzorno, Eds., *The Resurgence of Class Conflict in Western Europe since 1968*: 277–298. Basingstoke, Macmillan.

Przeworski, A. and M. Wallerstein (1982). 'The Structure of Class Conflict in Democratic Capitalist Societies'. *American Political Science Review* 76(2): 215–238.

Redding, G., G. Wong, and W. Leung (2014). 'Hong Kong: Hybrid Capitalism as Catalyst'. In M. A. Witt and G. Redding, Eds., *The Oxford Handbook of Asian Business Systems*: 33–54. Oxford, Oxford University Press.

Robinson, J. A. (1999). 'When Is a State Predatory?' Harvard University. CESifo Working Paper Series No. 178. Available at SSRN: <http://ssrn.com/abstract=273022>.

Saez, L. (2014). 'India: From Failed Developmental State Towards Hybrid Market Capitalism'. In M. A. Witt and G. Redding, Eds., *The Oxford Handbook of Asian Business Systems:* 55–78. Oxford, Oxford University Press.

Schmidt, V. A. (2002). *The Futures of European Capitalism*. Oxford, Oxford University Press.

—— (2009). 'Putting the Political Back into Political Economy by Bringing the State Back in yet Again'. *World Politics* 61(3): 516–546.

Schmitter, P. C. and G. Lehmbruch (1979). *Trends toward Corporatist Intermediation*. Beverly Hills, Sage.

Shonfield, A. (1965). *Modern Capitalism; the Changing Balance of Public and Private Power*. London & New York, Oxford University Press.

Skocpol, T. and E. Amenta (1985). 'Did Capitalists Shape Social Security?'. *American Sociological Review* 50(4): 572–575.

Streeck, W. and P. C. Schmitter (1985). *Private Interest Government*. London, Sage.

Suehiro, A. and N. Wailerdsak (2014). 'Thailand: Post-Developmentalist Capitalism'. In M. A. Witt and G. Redding, Eds., *The Oxford Handbook of Asian Business Systems:* 260–282. Oxford, Oxford University Press.

Tipton, F. B. (2009). 'Southeast Asian Capitalism: History, Institutions, States, and Firms'. *Asia Pacific Journal of Management* 26(3): 401–434.

Truong, Q. and C. Rowley (2014). 'Vietnam: Post-State Capitalism'. In M. A. Witt and G. Redding, Eds., *The Oxford Handbook of Asian Business Systems:* 283–305. Oxford, Oxford University Press.

Tsebelis, G. (2002). 'Veto Players and Institutional Analysis'. *Governance* 13(4): 441–474.

van Kersbergen, K. (1995). *Social Capitalism: A Study of Christian Democracy and the Welfare State*. London, Routledge.

Wade, R. (1990). *Governing the Market: The Role of Government in East Asian Industrialization*. Princeton, Princeton University Press.

Walter, A. and X. Zhang (2012). 'Understanding Variations and Changes in East Asian Capitalism'. In A. Walter and X. Zhang, Eds., *East Asian Capitalism: Diversity, Continuity, and Change*: 247–280. Oxford, Oxford University Press.

Whitley, R. (1992). *Business Systems in East Asia: Firms, Markets and Societies*. London, Sage.

—— (1999). *Divergent Capitalisms: The Social Structuring and Change of Business Systems*. Oxford, Oxford University Press.

—— (2005). 'How National Are Business Systems? The Role of States and Complementary Institutions in Standardizing Systems of Economic Coordination and Control at the National Level'. In G. Morgan, R. Whitley, and E. Moen, Eds., *Changing Capitalisms? Internationalization, Institutional Change, and Systems of Economic Organization*: 190–231. New York, Oxford University Press.

Witt, M. A. (2014a). 'Japan: Coordinated Capitalism between Institutional Change and Structural Inertia'. In M. A. Witt and G. Redding, Eds., *The Oxford Handbook of Asian Business Systems*: 100–122. Oxford, Oxford University Press.

—— (2014b). 'South Korea: Plutocratic State-Led Capitalism'. In M. A. Witt and G. Redding, Eds., *The Oxford Handbook of Asian Business Systems*: 216–237. Oxford, Oxford University Press.

—— and G. Redding (2013). Asian Business Systems: Institutional Comparison, Clusters, and Implications for Varieties of Capitalism and Business Systems Theory. *Socio-Economic Review* 11(2): 265–300.

—— (2014a). 'China: Authoritarian Capitalism'. In M. A. Witt and G. Redding, Eds., *The Oxford Handbook of Asian Business Systems*: 11–32. Oxford, Oxford University Press.

—— Eds. (2014b). *The Oxford Handbook of Asian Business Systems*. Oxford, Oxford University Press.

World Bank (2011). 'Worldwide Governance Indicators'. Retrieved 13 November 2012 from <http://info.worldbank.org/governance/wgi/index.asp>.

Zysman, J. (1983). *Governments, Markets, and Growth: Financial Systems and the Politics of Industrial Change*. Ithaca, Cornell University Press.

..............................................................................................

# CHAPTER 25

# A SURVEY OF STRATEGIC BEHAVIOUR AND FIRM PERFORMANCE IN ASIA

..............................................................................................

SHIGE MAKINO AND DAPHNE W. YIU

## INTRODUCTION

..............................................................................................

EXTANT literature has accepted the view that business environments are not monolithic across Asia. However, strategic behaviours and performance outcomes, and in particular the extent to which indigenous firms pursue similar or dissimilar strategic behaviours, and how these behaviours lead to successful or unsuccessful performance in the region, are issues that remain unknown. The focus on why firm strategies and performance differ in different countries and regions, and how a country's institutions shape firm strategy and performance have given rise to an institution-based view of firm strategy with an emphasis on institution-firm linkage. Taking the perspective of varieties of capitalism (VoC) as an institutional theory of firm strategy, Carney, Gedajlovic, and Yang (2009) highlight that Asian economies are at various stages of emergence and transition that shape firm strategies, while firms also collectively and intentionally feed back to shape institutions. This chapter aims to provide systematic empirical evidence on how heterogeneous business systems and institutional environments across economies affect strategic behaviours and performance in indigenous firms in Asia.

Asia consists of diverse but distinctive economic systems: it has one of the largest advanced economies (Japan), economies with the highest per capita GDP (Brunei, Hong Kong, and Singapore, Hong Kong), the world's two largest emerging economies (China and India), and many less developed economies. To conceptualize such societal variations of capitalism, business systems theory views business systems as societally distinct modes of coordinating economic action, in which a mix of institutional structures, formal and informal in nature, provides the stability and predictability needed for economic exchange (Whitley 1992, 1999; Dore 2000; Hall and

Soskice 2001; Redding 2005). Due to institutional multiplicities and complementarities (Carney, Gedajlovic, and Yang 2009; Witt and Redding 2013), each country produces distinctive organizational forms, and firms adopt strategies for leveraging resources and opportunities given by the institutional mix. The business systems or VoC perspective has laid an institutional foundation accounting for the origins of firms' competitive advantages. In other words, the institutional elements of a country confer comparative institutional advantage to those firms that can align themselves with their environment. Because of unique historical, cultural, and location-specific factors that affect the composition of local industry, and domestic and foreign investors that influence firm behaviour and performance (Yeung 2007), a comparison of strategic behaviour and performance across economies is unlikely to provide a causal estimate of the impact of the economies on strategic behaviour and performance. We therefore focus mainly on outlining unique characteristics of strategic behaviours and patterns in performance distribution among firms that vary across Asian economies, rather than on explaining the sources of such variations.

In the following section, we first provide a synopsis of business systems in Asia by closely examining institutional environments in the region. We then identify distinctive strategic behaviours of Asian firms, based on a systematic longitudinal review and content analysis of published articles in mainstream strategic management and international business journals. The four most-researched Asian strategic behaviours are highlighted: internationalization strategies, network-based strategies, diversification and acquisition strategies, and ownership and strategy. Next, we present evidence on the performance of indigenous firms in Asia. We measure firm performance in several ways, including sales growth, mean and variation of profitability (return on sales, or ROS), and skewness in performance (ROS) distribution among firms in each country. Our evidence clearly shows that all the measures of firm performance, that is, ROS growth, mean and standard deviation, and skewness, vary noticeably across Asia. We also find a positive association between risk (ROS standard deviation) and return (ROS mean), and a negative association between return and skewness, and observe that the negative side of skewness in performance distribution has tended to widen during periods of economic downturn and crisis. Finally, we close the chapter by discussing the implications of business-systems theory on Asian firm strategy and performance, as well as providing avenues for future research. To conclude, this chapter provides a synopsis about salient strategic behaviours and firm performance across countries in Asia.

# AN OVERVIEW OF STRATEGIC BEHAVIOURS OF ASIAN FIRMS

Although studies of Asian firm strategy have been carried out for decades and the trend continues, it is surprising that little effort has been made to systematically review studies of Asian firm strategy. In this section, we aim to shed light on state-of-the-art empirical findings of strategic behaviours of Asian firms. As firms are embedded in the environment, we begin with a critical review of the business systems theory of firm competitiveness, with a focus on the distinctive business systems of Asian countries. This is followed by the results of a content analysis of Asian firm strategy research published in mainstream management journals.

# BUSINESS SYSTEMS IN ASIA

Business environments are not monolithic across countries in Asia. To account for institutional variations, researchers have proposed theories and models of comparative institutional analysis, such as business systems theory (Whitley 1999; Witt and Redding 2013) and the varieties of capitalism approach (Hall and Soskice 2001). Business systems are defined as 'distinctive configurations of hierarchy-market relations which become institutionalized as relatively successful ways of organizing economic activities in different institutional environments' (Whitley 1992: 13). Business systems tend to be enduring and stable over time, because they are bounded by historical legacies, institutional embeddedness, and social cohesiveness (Yeung 2007). The basic proposition of business systems theory is that societal systems of capitalism constitute structures that stabilize coordination and control among parties in an economic exchange (Redding 2005). Also, variations in countries' institutional features have resulted in a variability of competitive business systems and dependence on societal contexts (Whitley 1991).

Past studies have identified key institutional dimensions characterizing a country's business system, including education and skills formation, employment relations, financial system, inter-firm networks, internal dynamics of the firm, corporate governance and ownership, product markets, social capital and trust, social protection, the role of the state, and the role of civil society (Whitley 1999; Hall and Soskice 2001; Amable 2003; Redding 2005; Witt and Redding 2013). To unpack the institutional frameworks of Asian countries, we follow North's (1990) and Redding's (2005) dichotomy of institutions by examining the formal and informal dimensions of institutional frameworks in Asia. Formal institutions refer to the use of formal written rules to govern behaviour. They include political and judicial rules, economic rules, and contracts (North 1990). Countries in Asia differ in their development and enforcement of formal institutions. To a large extent, such variations in the development of formal institutions are concerned with the organization of the polity (Mantzavinos 2001), because it is the polities that define and enforce the economic rules of the game (North 1990). Countries like Hong Kong and Singapore have adopted more state-free capitalism, and their governments have aimed at regulating firm behaviour by formulating an institutional structure based on more developed formal institutions, such as secure property rights and economic institutions. On the other hand, formal institutions in many Asian emerging and transition economies are still underdeveloped, with political institutions characterized by strong government intervention, cronyism and corruption, legal institutions characterized by ineffective enforcement of laws and inefficient judiciary system, and economic institutions with a lack of transparency and financial intermediaries (Khanna and Palepu 1997; La Porta, Lopes-de-Silanes, and Shleifer 1999). Because of these institutional voids (Khanna and Palepu 2000), firms in Asia formulate various coping strategies.

Informal institutions refer to the norms of behaviour, conventions, and self-imposed codes of conduct that regulate economic exchanges in a society (North 1990). North (1990) pointed out that informal institutions come into place when formal institutions are under-developed. In the absence of well-developed formal institutions, the business systems of Asia are highly characterized by extensive networks based on trust and long-term relationships, which serve to govern business transactions more effectively. The prominence of informal institutions in Asian business systems is also highly related to the history and culture of Asian societies, which emphasize patrimonial authority, family solidarity, kinship groups, subordination to collective interests, norms of reciprocity, and mutual trust and dependence (Whitley 1991). The analysis of strategic behaviours of Asian firms cannot be complete without taking social and cultural institutions into consideration. For example, *guanxi*, inter-firm networks, and business groups are identified as important social institutions that engender business transactions among related parties in Asia (Yeung 2007). Peng and Heath (1996) also highlighted how the blurring of boundaries through extensive networking with firms and governments has become the dominant logic (Prahalad and Bettis 1986) for firms in Asia.

Formal and informal institutions are also developed in cross-national relations. Makino and Tsang (2011) studied three major historical factors affecting cross-country ties with Vietnam—namely, Chinese occupation and conflict, French colonization, and socialist ideology—and examined the ways in which these historical ties influenced FDI. They found that firms from Hong Kong, Taiwan, France, and former and current socialist countries tended to be early-movers in Vietnam, whereas firms from mainland China tended to be late-movers, and suggested that historical ties can provide additional explanatory power regarding the strategic behaviour of Asian firms, such as FDI decisions, beyond the conventional country-specific factors.

To conclude, Asian business systems in general are characterized by strong intervention of the state in business, heavy reliance on personal relationships in business transactions, and extensive formation of inter-firm networks (Yeung 2000), and are shaped by formal and informal institutions uniquely developed within and between countries (Whitley 1991; Redding 2005; Makino and Tsang 2011).

A similar phenomenon, differentiated pluralism in business systems, can also be observed in Asia. Reflecting different historical patterns of authority, trust, and loyalty, Whitley (1991) identified three distinctive forms of business systems, namely the Japanese specialized clan or *kaisha*, the Korean patrimonial bureaucracy, and the Chinese family business (Redding 1990; Whitley 1990). In a recent study based on systematic and detailed comparative data across thirteen Asian countries, Witt and Redding (2013) identified five major clusters of Asian business systems, namely (post-)

socialist economies (e.g. China and India), advanced capitalist economies (Hong Kong and Singapore), emerging South East Asian economies (e.g. Indonesia and Malaysia), advanced North-East Asian economies (Korea and Taiwan), and Japan. Therefore, although Asian business systems tend to be substantially different from those in Western societies, there are also variations among Asian countries. It is important to examine how the institutional features and internal dynamics of Asian business systems shape firms' strategic behaviours and the resulting competitiveness and performance outcomes.

# Business Systems, Firm Strategy, and Competitiveness

Strategies are about making choices under institutional constraints (North 1990). Given such an intricate relationship between firm strategy and institutional environment, it is important to comprehend the distinctive characteristics of a country's business system and understand how strategic behaviours and firm competitiveness will be shaped. Hall and Soskice (2001) formulated the 'varieties of capitalism' approach to account for how national variations in the institutions of political economy affect economic performance. They distinguish capitalist economies as either liberal market economies (LMEs), where relations between firms and other actors are coordinated primarily by competitive markets, and coordinated market economies (CMEs), where firms typically engage in more strategic interaction with trade unions, suppliers of finance, and other actors. The VoC approach contends that whether a firm coordinates its endeavours through market relations or strategic interactions depends on the institutional setting. In institutional settings where the market is imperfect and there is substantial institutional support for the formation of credible commitments, firms are expected to rely more extensively on strategic coordination. The VoC approach also predicts that variations among political economies give rise to comparative institutional advantages, national responses to globalization, and public policies, as well as firm strategies. For example, LMEs are supportive of radical innovations, while CMEs are better at spurring incremental innovations.

To understand more about the strategic behaviours and firm competitiveness of Asian firms, Carney, Gedajlovic, and Yang (2009) have also called for a closer look at the varieties of Asian capitalism. They maintain that specific attention has to be paid to how Asian firms collectively and intentionally behave to cope with, and even shape, institutional structures. For example, Asian firms adopt strategies to fill institutional voids. The emergence of business groups is to internalize market transactions due to institutional deficiencies (Khanna and Palepu 2000). Another adaptation strategy is institutional escape (Carney, Gedajlovic, and Yang 2009): closed and heavily protected economies may give rise to the use of political connection strategies, while firms without such context-specific assets are forced to escape from home countries by engaging in more outward FDI (Witt and Lewin 2007).

In summary, given that firms are embedded in the institutional environment, Asian firm strategic behaviours are best understood as an outcome of interactions between firms and their institutional environment. The unique configuration of Asian business systems exerts a long-term impact on the strategy formulation and performance outcomes of firms in the region.

The next section offers a systematic review of strategic behaviours of Asian firms in the literature.

# LITERATURE REVIEW OF ASIAN STRATEGY RESEARCH

We selected eight management journals that have high citation impacts (according to the Social Science Citation Index in Management), are common on established journal lists such as the *Financial Times* and University of Texas-Dallas (UTD), have been included in a review of Asian management research (Bruton and Lau 2008), and focus on strategic management research. The eight journals are *Academy of Management Journal (AMJ), Academy of Management Review (AMR), Administrative Science Quarterly (ASQ), Journal of International Business Studies (JIBS), Journal of Management (JOM), Journal of Management Studies (JMS), Organization Science (OS), and Strategic Management Journal (SMJ)*. It should be noted that a substantial number of studies on Asian firm strategy can be found in journals like *Asian Business and Management, Asian Journal of Business Management Studies, Asia Pacific Journal of Management,* and *Journal of World Business,* but these are not included in the current literature review. We used both ABI/INFORM Global and Google Scholar to search for articles on Asian strategy research published in the above eight journals. Two researchers used an identical list of keywords to identify relevant research. The articles selected needed to have a focus on a strategic management topic and include an Asian nation in their sample, or for conceptual pieces to focus on a topic. We identified a total of 228 articles published between 1980 and 2011.

The earliest piece was by Suzuki in SMJ in 1980, examining the strategy and structure of the top 100 industrial companies in Japan between 1950 and 1970. Among the eight journals, JIBS and SMJ published 71 per cent of research on Asian firm strategy, with ninety-four and sixty-nine articles respectively; they were followed by JMS (19), AMJ (18), and OS (18), AMR (4) and ASQ (4), and JOM (2). It is interesting to find that publications on Asian strategy research hit several peaks: in 1999, 2001–2002, 2004, and 2008–2009, probably reflecting the economic fluctuations in the region.

With regard to country focus, among the twelve South East Asian countries, Japan is ranked first as the focal sample in Asian strategy research, with ninety-eight articles accounting for almost 40 per cent of the published total. China ranked second, with seventy-six articles (31%). Taken together, Japan and China accounted for seventy-one per cent of the Asian country samples. This, again, may be due to the political and economic power of the countries in focus, attracting more attention from researchers, practitioners, and policy-makers. Studies on Korea, Taiwan, and India are increasing, with seventeen, thirteen, and thirteen articles respectively, followed by Singapore (9) and Hong Kong (7). Other articles adopted samples from Indonesia (4), Malaysia (3), Thailand (3), the Philippines (2), and Vietnam (2).

Finally, we classified the literature search by strategic management topics. Based on the abstracts of articles, which are supposed to convey the main message of the research, we performed two analyses—(1) classification into a strategic management topic by two researchers using the article abstracts, and (2) a content analysis counting the frequency of words appearing in the abstracts. Our content-analysed findings reveal four salient patterns of strategic behaviour of Asian firms, summarized below.

# PATTERNS OF STRATEGIC BEHAVIOURS IN ASIA

*International strategies*: From our content analysis, the majority of Asian strategy research is related to the international strategy domain, ranging from outward FDI topics such as internationalization motives, entry mode, entry timing, and subsidiary performance, to inward FDI topics such as location choices of foreign partners, inter-partner relationships, and knowledge spillovers. Early research on the internationalization of Asian firms tended to adopt an asset-exploitation view, such as the OLI model (Dunning 1980), to explain how firms expand internationally in order to leverage their home-grown ownership, location, and internalization advantages. For example, Kimura (1989) found that Japanese FDIs are mostly driven by firms' technological lead and domestic size. The home region-bound firm-specific advantages are found to constrain the ability of Japanese MNEs to implement internationalization strategies (Collinson and Rugman 2008). However, with the rise of emerging multinationals from less developed countries in Asia, researchers began to develop new theories, such as asset-seeking, organizational learning, and springboard perspectives, to account for the newer internationalization pattern of emerging Asian countries entering developed economies to acquire resources and strategic assets unavailable at home, and to reduce institutional and market constraints at home (e.g. Makino, Lau, and Yeh 2002; Luo and Tung 2007). Other newly proposed internationalization motives include facilitation by home-country networks (Yiu, Lau, and Bruton 2007), following clients (Qian and Delios 2008), enhancing firm flexibility and hedging risks (Lee and Makhija 2009), and leveraging entrepreneurial dynamics of learning from early internationalization (Zhou, Barnes, and Lu 2010). Researchers also found that economic crises are detrimental for subsidiaries with stronger within-country orientations, but advantageous to those with stronger across-country orientations (Chung et al. 2010).

Another unique pattern is sequential foreign entry. Extensive findings show that Japanese and Korean firms pursue international expansion sequentially, with initial entry in the form of a joint venture, aiming to reduce uncertainty and gather local market information, develop market legitimacy, and imitate location choices and entry/ exit decisions made by their home-country counterparts (e.g. Chang 1995; Greve 2000; Henisz and Delios 2001; Song 2002; Delios and Henisz 2003; Guillen 2003; Chan, Makino, and Isobe 2006; Goerzen and Makino 2007; Delios, Gaur, and Makino 2008). These studies adopted arguments from the literature of mimetic isomorphism, mutual forbearance, capability-building and learning, information-based theory, and competitive rivalry theory.

The flux of studies on foreign entry mode choice and subsidiary ownership strategy has been facilitated by the availability of foreign subsidiary data for Japanese firms. Over the past two decades, researchers have identified a comprehensive set of firm-, industry-, and country- determinants of entry mode, and subsidiary ownership choice, based on various theoretical perspectives, such as transaction-cost theory, institutional theory, national culture, knowledge transfer, resource complementarity, and corporate governance (e.g. Hennart and Larimo 1998; Brouthers and Brouthers 2000; Lu 2002; Yiu and Makino 2002; Filatotchev, Strange, and Piesse 2007). Recently, researchers began to adopt multi-level perspectives and integration of institution-based and resource-based views to comprehend the analysis of foreign entry mode (Mani, Antia, and Rindfleisch 2007; Meyer et al. 2009).

The entry mode that has received most attention is the joint venture, both as an entry mode to expand to foreign countries and as an organizational form that had not existed before inward FDI was allowed in Asian countries such as China. Studies on joint ventures have examined issues like ownership structure (e.g. Makino and Beamish 1998), joint-venture stability and exit (e.g. Inkpen 1997; Makino et al. 2007), control and performance (e.g. Luo, Shenkar, and Nyaw 2001), knowledge acquisition and learning (e.g. Shenkar and Li 1999; Tsang 2002), and opportunism and governance (e.g. Luo 2007). Using a flexibility perspective, Belderbos and Zou (2007) found that a joint venture, relative to a wholly-owned subsidiary, is less flexible in responding to changing environmental conditions such as the Asian financial crisis. It is also found that the decline of joint ventures coincided with the growth of M&A as a competing entry mode in China (Xia, Tan, and Tan 2008).

*Network-based strategies*: Network-based strategy is regarded as the dominant logic of Asian firms. The business group, defined as a collection of legally independent firms linked by multiple ties, including ownership, economic, and/or social (family, kinship, friendship) ties through which they coordinate to achieve mutual objectives (Khanna and Rivkin 2001; Yiu et al. 2007), is a prevalent organizational form that accounts for significant economic contributions in many Asian countries. Business groups carry different labels in different countries, such as qiye jituan in China (Keister 2000), business houses in India (Encarnation 1989), chaebol in South Korea (Chang and Choi 1988), keiretsu in Japan (Gerlach 1992), and *guanxi qiye* in Taiwan (Numazaki 1986).

There is a consensus in the literature that business groups play a very important role in Asian countries. The dominant view of the emergence of business groups lies in the institutional economics and transaction-cost perspective: that the diversified nature of the group generates a more efficient internal market that substitutes for institutional voids in external markets (Khanna and Palepu 2000; Chang and Hong 2002). The socio-logical view, on the other hand, proposes that the sustainability of business groups is closely related to particularistic ties such as family and social ties, and the cultural her-itage of the society (Granovetter 1994; Luo and Chung 2005). In countries like China and Korea, business groups enjoy privileges from the state, such as government subsidy, exclusive rights for import and export, and local monopoly (Keister 2000). Business group formation is also regarded as part of privatization and corporatization in China (Yiu, Bruton, and Lu 2005). Despite the value creation of business groups, researchers have found that the value of group affiliation can be negative due to power dependence (Kim, Hoskisson, and Wan 2004), contingent on the economic transition of the country (Khanna and Palepu 2000), and varies across institutional contexts (Khanna and Rivkin 2001). Business group affiliation has also been found to be critical in enhancing the per-formance of international joint ventures (Lu and Ma 2008), and a significant moderator in the relationship between international diversification and firm performance (Kim, Kim, and Hoskisson 2010).

In addition to business groups, Asian strategy research highlights the importance of different types of network. In Japan, buyer-supplier relationships constitute a stable ver-tical network in the automobile sector. Martin, Mitchell, and Swaminathan (1995) found that Japanese automobile firms recreated almost 60 per cent of their links with tradi-tional buyers in North America. Banerji and Sambharya (1996) also found that Japanese automobile ancillary firms followed their major automakers in setting up production facilities in the USA. Network is also considered a source of knowledge creation (Kogut 2000). Networks of interlocking directorates serve as important sources of information exchange and relational governance (Gerlach 1992). Research on Chinese firm strat-egy always highlights the importance of *guanxi* as a substitute for formal institutions (Xin and Pearce 1996). Managers' business and political ties are found to improve firm performance (Peng and Luo 2000). Luo (2003) found that the value of managerial net-working with other stakeholders increases when uncertainty and competition increase. The value of networks is further extended to internationalization and new ventures. Network linkage is found to be a critical determinant of location choice for Taiwanese FDI (Chen and Chen 1998), and new venture performance is subject to political ties (Li and Zhang 2007) and external networks (Lee, Lee, and Pennings 2001; Issa and Chacar 2009).

*Diversification and acquisition strategies*: In Asia, diversification strategy is a domi-nant strategy that leads to positive firm performance, as evidenced by the predomi-nance of diversified conglomerates in the region. The formation of internal markets through diversification substitutes for less developed external markets in some Asian countries. Chakrabarti, Singh, and Mahmood (2007) found that diversification is nega-tively related to firm performance in more developed institutional environments, while such relationship is positive in the least-developed environments. Besides, Lim, Das, and Das (2009) found that Singapore firms pursuing unrelated product diversification take on less debt financing in stable environments than in dynamic environments, and there is a reciprocal relationship between a firm's diversification strategy and its levels of debt financing. Chung and Luo (2008) found that family-controlled business groups in Taiwan are less likely to divest unrelated businesses.

The pursuit of acquisition strategy by Asian firms also demonstrates unique characteristics. Cross-border acquisitions are often regarded as a quick and efficient means to acquire resources and capabilities (e.g. Chen 2008). Using a real option logic, Xu, Zhou, and Phan (2010) found that the acquisition strategy of Chinese firms is sequential due to severe information disadvantages. However, the performance implications of acquisition strategy are rather mixed in the literature: it has been found that acquisition is positively related to firm performance during an environmental jolt or during low market cycles, using samples from Hong Kong and Singapore (Pangarkar and Lie 2004; Wan and Yiu 2009).

*Ownership and strategy:* Studies have found that different ownership groups exert different preferences on firms' diversification and investment strategies (Ramaswamy, Li, and Veliyath 2002; Colpan et al. 2011). For example, ownership by banks and financial owners is positively associated with an unrelated diversification strategy, while ownership by mutual fund and foreign owners is negatively associated with unrelated diversification (Ramaswamy, Li, and Veliyath 2002). In China, state-owned and privately-owned enterprises tend to adopt defender and prospector strategies respectively, while collectively-owned and foreign-owned enterprises tend to adopt analyser strategy (Peng, Tan, and Tong 2004). Zou and Adams (2008) found that firms with more state ownership tend to experience lower stock returns, while firms with more legal-person' shares have higher stock returns. In Japan, cross-shareholding between banks and client firms is a prominent feature. However, using social exchange and role theories, Wan and his colleagues (2008) found that cross-shareholding is positively related to bank performance during economic expansion, but negatively related to bank performance during economic contraction. Finally, family ownership is also a typical phenomenon in Asian firms. Korean family-controlled business groups prefer using product diversification to diversify risks (Chang 2003). Filatotchev, Strange, and Piesse (2007) found that high family ownership in a parent company tends towards a lower commitment mode in entering emerging markets, to minimize potential adverse selection problems and hold-up costs.

To conclude, due to the intricate relationship between institutions and firm strategy, one has to incorporate the features of business systems in Asia in order to fully comprehend Asian firms' strategic behaviours. Our review has identified four salient strategies of Asian firms that may differ from global counterparts due to differences in history, culture, and political economy. In the following section, we will examine the performance implications of these strategies.

# ASIAN FIRM PERFORMANCE

This section provides evidence of firm performance across major Asian countries. Specifically, it examines a longitudinal comparison of sales growth and the average and variation of profitability of indigenous firms across Asian countries. Our analysis reveals that patterns in growth path and performance distribution vary conspicuously.

## Methodology

A comparison of firm performance across economies is unlikely to provide a causal estimate of the impact of economies on performance, since economies are likely to possess unique location-specific factors that affect the composition of local industry, and domestic and foreign investors influencing firm performance. We therefore focus mainly on outlining patterns of growth and performance distributions that vary across economies, rather than explaining the sources of such variations. To examine growth and performance distribution, we used the Compustat Global database, which covers the core financial information of indigenous firms in major countries across years. We selected eleven countries for the analysis: China, Hong Kong, India, Indonesia, Korea, Japan, Malaysia, the Philippines, Singapore, Taiwan, and Thailand. Other countries in Asia were not included, due to either lack of data or significant missing information. The data used in the analysis consists of a balanced panel over fourteen years, from 1997 to 2010. We selected the firms for their survival over the observation period, that is, firms established after 1997 or that exited before 2010, and those firms for which information is missing over the period 1997–2010, were excluded. We used return on sales (ROS) as a primary performance indicator, measured by earnings before interest and tax (EBITA) divided by net sales. We also used annual sales growth, the standard deviation of ROS, skewness, and kurtosis of the ROS distribution for the analysis of the data.

## Analysis

Asia provides diverse business environments. Figure 25.1 provides a scatter plot of GDP and GDP per capita across twenty-two countries in Asia.

Figure 25.1 indicates that most countries in Asia are emerging economies with GDP per capita of US$10,000 or less. The belief that emerging economies provide a low-cost production base and large potential market opportunities has led many MNCs to undertake major investments in these economies. By the year 2010, FDI in Asian countries accounted for 32 per cent of the world's FDI flow (in terms of greenfield investments) and has grown rapidly at a rate of over 30 per cent through the last decade. This section aims to examine how heterogeneous environments across economies affect firm performance. We first show the pattern of sales growth of firms across countries, and then how much firm performance, on average (or ROS mean), varies across countries. Our second analysis shows how much the variation of firm performance (or ROS standard deviation) among indigenous firms varies across countries. In a general term, the former performance measure represents the 'return' and the latter the 'risk' of business operations in a country. The two measures together show patterns of distribution of firm

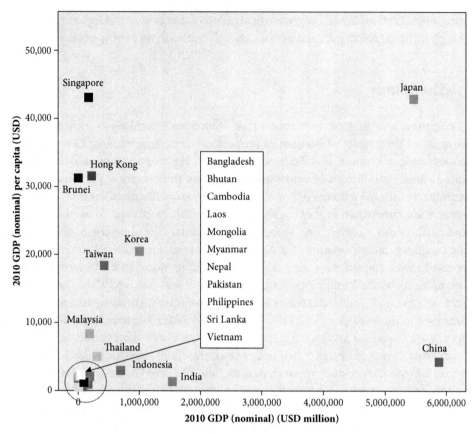

FIGURE 25.1  GDP and GDP capita by country

performance across countries. We then examine the skewness of performance distribution among the firms across countries.

# FINDINGS

## Performance: Growth, Risk, and Return

Figure 25.2 shows the matrix of the average annual growth rate of total sales. The amount of sales was set to 1, at 1997 levels. The chart indicates that large emerging economies such as China, India, and Indonesia had the highest growth rate throughout the period 1997–2010. These countries grew by six to eight times after 1997. In contrast, advanced economies had a much lower growth rate; Japan, with almost no growth over the period, had the lowest. Korea, Malaysia, and Singapore had a slightly higher rate than Japan, but relatively low compared to the emerging economies. This evidence confirms a rapid

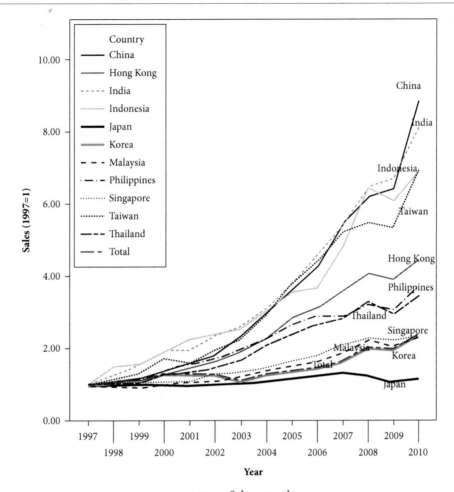

FIGURE 25.2  Sales growth

growth of firm size in emerging economies and somewhat stagnant growth in advanced economies.

Figure 25.3 shows asset turnover measured by net sales divided by total assets. This is a measure of a firm's efficiency in using its assets to generate revenue. Indonesia, Thailand, and Taiwan had an asset turnover of two or greater in 2010, meaning that firms in these countries had achieved significant improvements in operational efficiency over the previous fourteen years. By contrast, the advanced economies of Japan and Korea showed almost no improvement in asset turnover. While this evidence does not suggest that firms in emerging economies are more efficient than those in advanced economies, as the initial level differs, it clearly indicates that they have been catching up rapidly with those in advanced economies.

ROS was highest in Hong Kong (0.094), China (0.091), and the Philippines (0.090), and lowest in Japan (0.033). However, the standard deviation of ROS significantly varies across countries, ranging from 0.08 (Japan) to 0.28 (Hong Kong). Figure 25.4 shows the scatter plot of ROS mean and standard deviation over the period 1997–2010. There

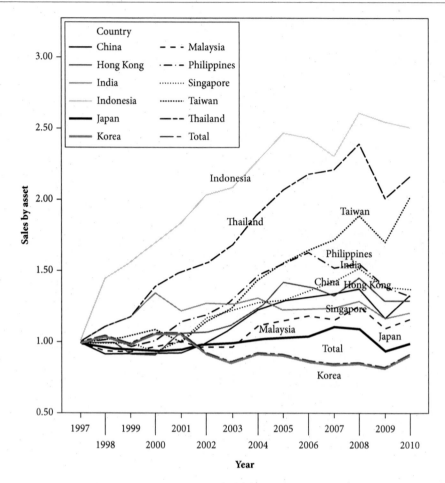

FIGURE 25.3 Asset turnover

is a relatively strong positive association between ROS mean and standard deviation ($R2 = 0.459$), suggesting a trade-off between risk (ROS standard deviation) and return (ROS mean). If a general term of the 'risk-return' analogy is used, Hong Kong and the Philippines can be classified as 'high-risk and high-return' economies, and Japan and Korea as 'low-risk and low-return' economies. The other economies are positioned somewhere between the two. Two large emerging economies, China and India, show an interesting contrast. While both countries have almost the same level of standard deviation, China has a much higher level of ROS than India. Firms in China seem to have better prospects than those in India. While Japan and Korea seem to provide relatively stable business environments, firms in these countries seem to have weaker performance prospects compared to firms in the rest of Asia.

It is often said that growth and profitability trade off. Firms pursuing expansion often sacrifice profit margins, as earning tends to be reinvested for further expansion. Firms pursuing improvement in profit margins tend to pursue focus strategy, concentrating on

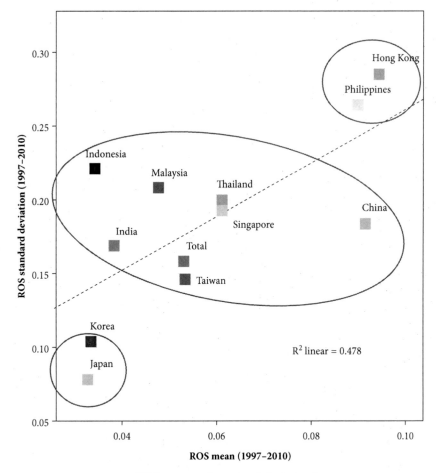

FIGURE 25.4 ROS mean and standard deviation by country

the core business generating stable and superior profits, although this may not always be the case in emerging economies (Khanna and Palepu 1997). Figure 25.5 shows the scatter plot of ROS mean and sales growth. The pattern that appears in Figure 25.5 is similar to that in Figure 25.2, suggesting that high (low) growth firms tend to have high (low) ROS standard deviation. The exceptions are Indonesia, India, and China, which have high growth rates relative to the position in Figure 25.2. This evidence suggests that firms in these countries have achieved relatively low risks despite their high growth rates. Figure 25.5 shows that China has achieved the highest growth rate and the second-highest ROS mean. In contrast, Japan has achieved both the lowest growth rate and the lowest ROS mean.

The above observations show some noticeable patterns. First, firms in relatively large advanced economies, such as Japan and Korea, tend to have low-risk, low-return operations. Japan also has the lowest growth rate. Second, firms in two large emerging economies, China and India, have contrasting performance patterns. While both countries

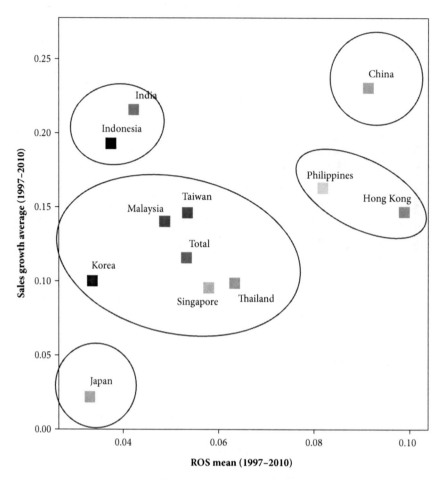

FIGURE 25.5 ROS mean and sales growth by country

have almost the same level of risk (or ROS standard deviation) and growth rate, returns (or ROS mean) differ significantly between them: China has the highest return, while India has the lowest. It is interesting to see if India will follow the trajectory of China's growth and develop better performance prospects in the process of future economic development. Third, most small- to medium-size emerging economies except Hong Kong—namely, Taiwan, Singapore, Thailand, and Malaysia—have similar performance patterns in terms of growth, risk, and return. Hong Kong follows the performance pattern of China, perhaps due to the fact that Hong Kong's economy is deeply integrated in and highly dependent on China's economy.

## Skewness in Performance Distribution

Skewness is a measure of asymmetry in a distribution. In our study, a zero value indicates that the observed values of ROS are evenly distributed on both sides of the mean.

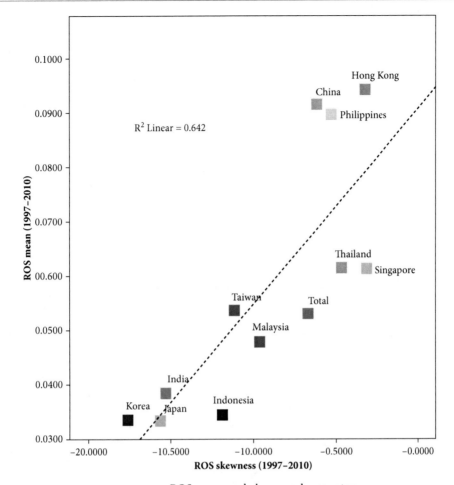

FIGURE 25.6 ROS mean and skewness by country

A negative (positive) skew indicates that the distribution of the data is skewed to the left (right). All the countries have negative skew values, with the range of lower ROS being greater than that of higher ROS. A negative skew value is greatest in two advanced economies, Korea and Japan, and two large emerging economies, India and Indonesia. The other two large emerging economies, China and the Philippines, have the smallest negative skewness. Similar to the case in the growth and mean association, Hong Kong has a similar level of skew value to China.

Does skewness affect ROS mean? Figure 25.6 illustrates the relationship between ROS mean and skewness. A strong positive association appears between the two, with r = 0.62. This suggests that countries with low (high) ROS mean are more likely to have a greater (smaller) number of under performing firms relative to well-performing firms. In other words, countries will have low ROS mean either when they have environments that allow indigenous firms to innovate and expand their business and hence become more productive, or when they allow under performing firms to stay in the market. The

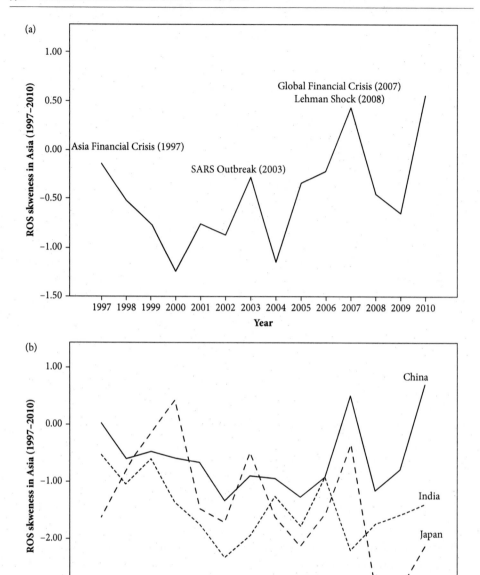

FIGURE 25.7 Skewness (1997–2010): (a) total, (b)

evidence suggests that skewness of ROS significantly varies across countries and has a strong positive association with ROS mean. In our sample, China has a high skewness value and high mean, whereas Japan has a low skewness value and low mean.

Why does the impact of skewness on ROS vary across countries? One possible answer would be that countries have different abilities or attributes to buffer the negative impact of external pressures on firm performance. Figure 25.7 shows a longitudinal trend of skewness of ROS in Asia. It appears that the extent of skewness dropped significantly when economic crisis occurred. For example, the skewness value sharply fell three times over the period 1997–2010, coinciding with the 1997 Asian Financial Crisis, the 2003 SARS outbreak, and the 2007 global economic crisis, followed by the Lehman shock in 2008. These economic crises widened the range of negative ROS of the firms and hence lowered the mean ROS.

The impact of these economic shocks on skewness varies across countries. Figure 25.7 shows the longitudinal change in skewness in China, India, and Japan. It appears that China tended to be less impacted by these economic shocks and had on average a smaller negative skewness value than Japan and India throughout the observation period. A sharp drop in skewness in Japan in 2008 and 2009 partly shows the fact that Japan's economy, and hence firm performance, is highly integrated into the global economy. The impact of the global financial crisis rooted in the sub-prime mortgage crisis in the USA and the subsequent Lehman Shock seems to have had a more severe influence on the performance of Japanese indigenous firms than those firms in China whose economy is driven by powerful domestic demand and growth.

# SUMMARY

Using firm performance data for the period 1997–2010, we find that indigenous firm performance—growth, average and variation, and skewness—varies significantly across countries in Asia. Our evidence shows some contrasting patterns in performance distribution. For example, China achieved among the highest growth in sales, highest average ROS, and lowest skewness, whereas Japan came amongst the lowest growth, lowest ROS, and highest skewness. Other countries were positioned between these two extremes to a varying extent. We also found that ROS means were negatively associated with skewness during the period of economic turbulence such as the Asia financial crisis, SARS outbreak, and global economic crisis. Some countries, most typically China, were less vulnerable to the turbulence and hence maintained a high level of ROS. However, it should be noted that the result of the analysis is subject to the availability of longitudinal data of firm-level performance. A large number of firm cases were excluded from the analysis in this study due to a lack of data. Future study should develop a more comprehensive set of the data of firm performance and conduct systematic and longitudinal data analysis.

# CONCLUSION

Based on our findings of performance variations across countries in Asia, we can conclude that Asian firms' strategic behaviours tend to differ substantially from firms in Western societies, but differences can also be found among Asian countries themselves, resulting in variations of firm performance across countries in the region. Using the tripod of institutions, strategy, and performance, the Asian context is an ideal setting to examine how institutions shape the choice of strategic behaviours and how both affect the performance outcome of a firm. To move Asian strategy research forward, we offer some avenues for future research on Asian firm strategy and performance.

First, our longitudinal findings of performance patterns open up new thoughts and questions for extending the business systems perspective in the future. Our results show clear variations in performance across countries in Asia; however, the country clusters of performance may not match those developed by past studies in Asian business systems theory. This may imply equifinality of performance outcomes, even though countries fall into different types of business systems. Another future direction of research on business systems theory might be to explore the dynamics between types of business system. For instance, our findings demonstrated increasing convergence between China and Hong Kong, suggesting the importance of exploring the dynamics between business systems. Finally, our findings on the impacts of global and regional economic shocks show that some countries' business systems are more integrated into the global economy and therefore more affected by the global institutional environment. Future research might delve into the relationships between Asian business systems and global institutional dynamics over time.

Second, some researchers have argued that Asian management research should go beyond using the Asian context to test Western-developed theories, to pursue more context-specific or 'indigenous' research grounded in Asian realities and uniqueness (Meyer 2006; Bruton and Lau 2008). Due to institutional complementarities, business systems studies have highlighted the importance of exploring in greater depth issues of social capital, culture, informality, and multiplexity in Asian countries (Witt and Redding 2013). As demonstrated in our review and performance analysis of Asian firms, there is room to develop new theories and perspectives for Asian strategy and performance. For example, our review of the internationalization, network-based, and diversification and acquisition strategies of Asian firms reveals that there may be an Asian perspective on the scope of the firm that lies in the relationship between firm boundaries and institutions, as Asian firms tend to have blurred boundaries extending beyond the firm's legal entity and infused with ownership and relational ties. In addition, the historical background and evolution of Asian societies also provide rich insights in understanding strategic behaviours in Asian firms. A notable example is how tracing the history of Japanese *keiretsu* has given rise to numerous strategic management concepts, such as networks and business groups, relational governance, institution-based diversification and restructuring, and the tacit knowledge and knowledge-based view of the firm. Thus, instead of assuming convergence of global practices, researchers may find that some Asian strategic behaviours are home-grown and integrated with their unique institutional environment. Also, researchers are encouraged to take further steps to incorporate unique institutional attributes of Asian business systems and institutional innovations or creations (e.g. business groups and other unique organizational forms such as collectively owned enterprises) in theorizing strategic phenomena and their performance implications.

Third, the interwoven relationships among institutions, strategy, and performance indicate the need to adopt a multi-level perspective in Asian strategy and performance research. Our review of the literature of strategic behaviour and the descriptive analysis of firm performance in Asia clearly suggests that Asian countries provide unique institutional environments that influence the strategic behaviour and performance of indigenous firms in different ways. Traditional strategic management research tends to focus on industry structure and firm resources as the major determinants of strategic behaviour and performance in a firm, assuming that the effects of country-specific factors such as institutional environments are less important or constant (Makino et al. 2004; Chan, Isobe, and Makino 2008). In conducting research on Asian business systems, particularly strategic behaviour and performance in Asia, researchers need to separate country effects from the effects of industry and firm characteristics and examine how and why these country effects uniquely explain the variation in strategic behaviour and performance of indigenous firms. One promising avenue for future research is to bring history back to strategic management research (Jones and Khanna 2006; Makino and Tsang 2011). For better understanding of the unique institutional environments in Asia and their impact on strategy and performance, we should accumulate more studies on the historical background of institutional developments in Asian countries.

This chapter takes stock of Asian strategy research over the last three decades and presents the performance patterns of Asian firms over the years. We believe that attention to Asian business systems should bring more opportunities to understand the intricate relationships between the institutional environment and the strategic behaviours and performance outcomes of firms in Asia.

# ACKNOWLEDGEMENT

This chapter was supported by a grant from the Research Grants Council of the Hong Kong Special Administrative Region (Project No. CUHK 451010H).

## REFERENCES

Amable, B. (2003) 'The Diversity of Modern Capitalism. Oxford, Oxford University Press.
Banerji, K. and R. B. Sambharya (1996). 'Vertical keiretsu and International Market Entry: The Case of the Japanese Automobile Ancillary Industry'. Journal of International Business Studies 27(1): 89–113.

Belderbos, R. and J. Zou (2007). 'On the Growth of Foreign Affiliates: Multinational Plant Networks, Joint Ventures, and Flexibility'. *Journal of International Business Studies* 38(7): 1095–1112

Brouthers, K. D. and L. E. Brouthers (2000). 'Acquisition of Greenfield Start-up? Institutional, Cultural, and Transaction Cost influences'. *Strategic Management Journal* 21(1): 89–97.

Bruton, G. D. and C. M. Lau (2008). 'Asian Management Research: Status Today and Future Outlook'. *Journal of Management Studies* 45(3): 636–659.

Carney, M., E. Gedajlovic, and X. Yang. (2009). 'Varieties of Asian Capitalism: Toward an Institutional Theory of Asian Enterprise'. *Asia Pacific Journal of Management* 26(3): 361–380.

Chakrabarti, A., K. Singh, and I. Mahmood (2007). 'Diversification and Performance: Evidence from East Asian Firms'. *Strategic Management Journal* 28(2): 101–120.

Chan, C. M., Isobe, T., and Makino, S. (2008) 'Which Country Matters? Institutional Development and Foreign Affiliate Performance'. *Strategic Management Journal* 29: 1179–1205.

—— S. Makino, and T. Isobe (2006). 'Interdependent Behaviour in Foreign Direct Investment: The Multi-Level Effects of Prior Entry and Prior Exit on Foreign Market Entry'. *Journal of International Business Studies* 37(5): 642–665.

Chang, S. J. (1995). 'International Expansion Strategy of Japanese Firms: Capability'. *Academy of Management Journal* 38(2): 383–407.

—— (2003). 'Ownership Structure, Expropriation, and Performance of Group-Affiliated Companies in Korea'. *Academy of Management Journal* 46(2): 238–253.

—— and U. Choi (1988). 'Strategy, Structure, and Performance of Korean Business Groups: A Transactions-Cost Approach'. *Journal of Industrial Economics* 37(2): 141–158.

—— and J. Hong (2002). 'How Much does the Business Group Matter in Korea?' *Strategic Management Journal* 23(3): 265–274.

Chen, H. and T. Chen (1998). 'Network Linkages and Location Choice in Foreign Direct Investment'. *Journal of International Business Studies* 29(3): 445–467.

Chen, S. S. (2008). 'The Motives for International Acquisitions: Capability Procurements, Strategic Considerations, and the Role of Ownership Structures'. *Journal of International Business Studies* 39(3): 454–471.

Chung, C. C., S. Lee, P. W. Beamish, and T. Isobe (2010). 'Subsidiary Expansion/Contraction during Times of Economic Crisis'. *Journal of International Business Studies* 41(3): 500–516.

Chung, C.-N. and X. Luo (2008). 'Institutional Logics or Agency Costs: The influence of Corporate Governance Models on Business Group Restructuring in Emerging Economies'. *Organization Science* 19(5): 766–784.

Collinson, S. and A. Rugman (2008). 'The Regional Nature of Japanese Multinational Business'. *Journal of International Business Studies* 39(2): 215–230.

Colpan, A. M., T. Yoshikawa, T. Hikino, and E. B. Del Brio (2011). 'Shareholder Heterogeneity and Conflicting Goals: Strategic Investments in the Japanese Electronics Industry'. *Journal of Management Studies* 48(3): 591–618.

Delios, A., A. Gaur, and S. Makino (2008). 'The Timing of International Expansion: Information, Rivalry, and Imitation among Japanese Firms, 1980–2002'. *Journal of Management Studies* 45(1): 169–195.

—— and W. J. Henisz (2003). 'Policy Uncertainty and the Sequence of Entry by Japanese Firms, 1980–1998'. *Journal of International Business Studies* 34(3): 227–241.

Dore, R. P. (2000) *Stock Market Capitalism: Welfare Capitalism: Japan and Germany Versus the Anglo-Saxons*. Oxford, Oxford University Press.

Dunning, J. H. (1980). 'Towards an Eclectic Theory of International Production: Some Empirical Tests'. *Journal of International Business Studies* 11(1): 9–31.

Encarnation, D. J. (1989). *Dislodging Multinationals: India's Strategy in Comparative Perspective*. Ithaca, Cornell University Press.

Filatotchev, I., R. Strange, and J. Piesse (2007). 'FDI by Firms from Newly Industrialized Economies in Emerging Markets: Corporate Governance, Entry Mode, and Location'. *Journal of International Business Studies* 38(4): 556–572.

Gerlach, M. L. (1992). 'The Japanese Corporate Network: A Blockmodel Analysis'. *Administrative Science Quarterly* 37(1): 105–139.

Goerzen, A. and S. Makino (2007). 'Multinational Corporation Internationalization in the Service Sector: A Study of Japanese Trading Companies'. *Journal of International Business Studies* 38(7): 1149–1169.

Granovetter, M. (1994). 'Business Groups'. In N. J. Smelser and R. Swedborg, Eds., *Handbook of Economic Sociology*: 453–475. Princeton, Princeton University Press; New York, Russell Sage Foundation.

Greve, H. R. (2000). 'Market Niche Entry Decisions: Competition, Learning, and Strategy in Tokyo Banking, 1894–1936'. *Academy of Management Journal* 43(5): 816–836.

Guillen, M. F. (2003). 'Experience, Imitation, and the Sequence of Foreign Entry: Wholly-Owned and Joint-Venture Manufacturing by South Korean Firms and Business Groups in China, 1987–1995'. *Journal of International Business Studies* 34(2): 185–198.

Hall, P. A. and Soskice, D. (2001) 'An Introduction to Varieties of Capitalism'. In P. A Hall and D. Soskice, Eds., *Varieties of Capitalism*: 1–68. Oxford, Oxford University Press.

Henisz, W. and A. Delios (2001). 'Uncertainty, Imitation, and Plant Location: Japanese Multinational Corporations, 1990–1996'. *Administrative Science Quarterly* 46(3): 443–475.

Hennart, J. F. and J. Larimo (1998). 'The Impact of Culture on the Strategy of Multinational Enterprises: Does National Origin Affect Ownership Decisions?' *Journal of International Business Studies* 29(3): 515–538.

Inkpen, A. C. (1997). 'Knowledge, Bargaining Power, and the Instability of International Joint Ventures'. *Academy of Management Review* 22(1): 177–202.

Issa, B. and A. S. Chacar (2009). 'Leveraging Ties: The Contingent Value of Entrepreneurial Teams' External Advice Networks on Indian Software Venture Performance'. *Strategic Management Journal* 30(11): 1179–1192.

Jones, G. and T. Khanna (2006). 'Bringing History (back) into International Business'. *Journal of International Business Studies* 37(4): 453–468.

Keister, L. A. (2000). *Chinese Business Groups: The Structure and Impact of Inter-Firm Relations during Economic Development*. New York, Oxford University Press.

Khanna, T. and K. Palepu (1997). 'Why Focused Strategies may be Wrong for Emerging Markets'. *Harvard Business Review* 75(4): 41–51.

—— (2000). 'The Future of Business Groups in Emerging Markets: Long-Run Evidence from Chile'. *Academy of Management Journal* 43(3): 268–285.

—— and J. W. Rivkin (2001). 'Estimating the Performance Effects of Business Groups in Emerging Markets'. *Strategic Management Journal* 22(1): 45–74.

Kim, H., R. E. Hoskisson, and W. P. Wan (2004). 'Power Dependence, Diversification Strategy, and Performance in keiretsu Member Firms'. *Strategic Management Journal* 25(7): 613–636.

—— H. Kim, and R. E. Hoskisson (2010). 'Does Market-Oriented Institutional Change in an Emerging Economy Make Business-Group-Affiliated Multinationals Perform Better?' *Journal of International Business Studies* 41(7): 1141–1160.

Kimura, Y. (1989). 'Firm-Specific Strategic Advantages and Foreign Direct Investment Behaviour of Firms: The Case of Japanese Semiconductor Firms'. *Journal of International Business Studies* 20(2): 296–314.

Kogut, B. (2000). 'The Network as Knowledge: Generative Rules and the Emergence of Structure'. *Strategic Management Journal* 21(3): 405–425.

La Porta, R., F. Lopez-de-Silanes, and A. Shleifer (1999). 'Corporate Ownership around the World'. *Journal of Finance* 54(2): 471–517.

Lee, C., K. Lee, and J. M. Pennings (2001). 'Internal Capabilities, External Networks, and Performance: A Study on Technology-Based Ventures'. *Strategic Management Journal* 22(6–7): 615–640.

Lee, S. and M. Makhija (2009). 'The Effect of Domestic Uncertainty on the Real Options Value of International Investments'. *Journal of International Business Studies* 40(3): 405–420.

Li, H. and Y. Zhang (2007). 'The Role of Managers' Political Networking and Functional Experience in New-Venture Performance: Evidence from China's Transition Economy'. *Strategic Management Journal* 28(8): 791–804.

Lim, E. N., S. S. Das, and A. Das (2009). 'Diversification Strategy, Capital Structure, and the Asian Financial Crisis (1997–1998): Evidence from Singapore Firms'. *Strategic Management Journal* 30(6): 577–594.

Lu, J. W. (2002). 'Intra- and Inter-Organizational Imitative Behaviour: Institutional Influences on Japanese Firms' Entry Mode Choice'. *Journal of International Business Studies* 33(1): 19–37.

—— and X. Ma (2008). 'The Contingent Value of Local Partners' Business-Group Affiliations'. *Academy of Management Journal* 51(2): 295–314.

Luo, X. and C.-N. Chung (2005). 'Keeping it All in the Family: The Role of Particularistic Relationships in Business Group Performance during Institutional Transition'. *Administrative Science Quarterly* 50(3): 404–439.

Luo, Y. (2003). 'Industrial Dynamics and Managerial Networking in an Emerging Market: The Case of China'. *Strategic Management Journal* 24(13): 1315–1327.

—— (2007). 'An Integrated Anti-Opportunism System in International Exchange'. *Journal of International Business Studies* 38(6): 855–877.

—— O. Shenkar, and M. K. Nyaw (2001). 'A Dual-Parent Perspective on Control and Performance in International Joint Ventures: Lessons from a Developing Economy'. *Journal of International Business Studies* 32(1): 41–58.

—— and R. Tung (2007). 'International Expansion of Emerging Market Enterprises: A Springboard Perspective'. *Journal of International Business Studies* 38(4): 481–498.

Makino, S. and P. Beamish (1998). 'Performance and Survival of Joint Ventures with Non-Conventional Ownership Structures'. *Journal of International Business Studies* 29(4): 797–818.

—— C. M. Chan, T. Isobe, and P. Beamish (2007). 'Intended and Unintended Termination of International Joint Ventures'. *Strategic Management Journal* 28(11): 1113–1132.

—— T. Isobe, and C. M. Chan (2004), Does country matter? *Strategic Management Journal*, 25: 1027–1043.

—— C. M. Lau, and R. Yeh (2002). 'Asset-Exploitation Versus Asset-Seeking: Implications for Location Choice of Foreign Direct Investment from Newly Industrialized Economies'. *Journal of International Business Studies* 33(3): 403–421.

—— and E. W. K. Tsang (2011). 'Historical Ties and Foreign Direct Investment'. *Journal of International Business Studies* 42(4): 545–557.

Mani, S., K. D. Antia, and A. Rindfleisch (2007). 'Entry Mode and Equity Level: A Multilevel Examination of Foreign Direct Investment Ownership Structure'. *Strategic Management Journal* 28(8): 857–866.

Mantzavinos, C. (2001). *Individuals, Institutions, and Markets*. Cambridge, Cambridge University Press.

Martin, X., W. Mitchell, and A. Swaminathan (1995). 'Recreating and Extending Japanese Automobile Buyer-supplier Links in North America'. *Strategic Management Journal* 16(8): 589–620.

Meyer, K. (2006). 'Asian Management Research Needs More Self-confidence'. *Asia Pacific Journal of Management* 23: 119–137.

—— S. Estrin, S. K. Bhaumik, and M. W. Peng (2009). 'Institutions, Resources, and Entry Strategies in Emerging Economies'. *Strategic Management Journal* 30(1): 61–80.

North, D. C. (1990). '*Institutions, Institutional Change and Economic Performance*'. Cambridge, University Press.

Numazaki, I. (1986). 'Networks of Taiwanese Big Business: A Preliminary Analysis'. *Modern China* 12(4): 487–534.

Pangarkar, N. and J. R. Lie (2004). 'The Impact of Market Cycle on the Performance of Singapore Acquirers'. *Strategic Management Journal* 25(12): 1209–1216.

Peng, M. W. and P. S. Heath (1996). 'The Growth of the Firm in Planned Economies in Transition: Institutions, Organizations, and Strategic Choice'. *Academy of Management Review* 21(2): 492–528.

—— and Y. Luo (2000). 'Managerial Ties and Firm Performance in a Transition Economy: The Nature of a Micro-Macro Link'. *Academy of Management Journal* 43(3): 486–501.

—— J. Tan, and T. W. Tong (2004). 'Ownership Types and Strategic Groups in an Emerging Economy'. *Journal of Management Studies* 41(7): 1105–1129.

Prahalad, C. K. and R. A. Bettis (1986). 'The Dominant Logic: A New Linkage Between Diversity and Performance'. *Strategic Management Journal* 7(6): 485–501.

Qian, L. and A. Delios (2008). 'Internalization and Experience: Japanese Banks' International Expansion, 1980–1998'. *Journal of International Business Studies* 39(2): 231–248.

Ramaswamy, K., M. Li, and R. Veliyath (2002). 'Variations in Ownership Behaviour and Propensity to Diversify: A Study of the Indian Corporate Context'. *Strategic Management Journal* 23(4): 345–358.

Redding, S. G. (1990). *The Spirit of Chinese Capitalism*. Berlin, de Gruyter.

Redding, G. (2005) 'The Thick Description and Comparison of Societal Systems of Capitalism', *Journal of International Business Studies* 36: 123–155.

Shenkar, O. and J. Li (1999). 'Knowledge Search in International Cooperative Ventures'. *Organization Science* 10(2): 134–143.

Song, J. (2002). 'Firm Capabilities and Technology Ladders: Sequential Foreign Direct Investments of Japanese Electronics Firms in East Asia'. *Strategic Management Journal* 23(3): 191–210.

Tsang, E. W. K. (2002). 'Acquiring Knowledge by Foreign Partners from International Joint Ventures in a Transition Economy: Learning-by-Doing and Learning Myopia'. *Strategic Management Journal* 23(9): 835–854.

Wan, W. P. and D. W. Yiu (2009). 'From Crisis to Opportunity: Environmental Jolt, Corporate Acquisitions, and Firm Performance'. *Strategic Management Journal* 30(7): 791–801.

—— R. E. Hoskisson, and H. Kim (2008). 'The Performance Implications of Relationship Banking during Macroeconomic Expansion and Contraction: A Study of Japanese Banks'

Social Relationships and Overseas Expansion'. *Journal of International Business Studies* 39(3): 406–427.

Whitley, R. D. (1990). 'Eastern Asian Enterprise Structures and the Comparative Analysis of Forms of Business Organization'. *Organization Studies* 11(1): 47–54.

—— (1991). 'The Social Construction of Business Systems in East Asia'. *Organization Studies* 12(1): 1–28.

—— (1992). *Business Systems in East Asia: Firms, Markets, and Societies*. London, Sage.

—— (1999). *Divergent Capitalisms: The Social Structuring and Change of Business Systems*, Oxford, Oxford University Press.

Witt, M. A. and A. Y. Lewin (2007). 'Outward Foreign Direct Investment as Escape Response to Home-Country Institutional Constraints'. *Journal of International Business Studies* 389(4): 579–594.

—— and Redding, G. (2013). 'Asian Business Systems: Institutional Comparison, Clusters, and Implications for Varieties of Capitalism and Business Systems Theory'. *Socio-Economic Review* 11(2): 265–300.

Xia, J., J. Tan, and D. Tan (2008). 'Mimetic Entry and Bandwagon Effect: The Rise and Decline of International Equity Joint Venture in China'. *Strategic Management Journal* 29(2): 195–217.

Xin, K. and J. Pearce (1996). 'Guanxi: Connections as Substitutes for Formal Institutional Support'. *Academy of Management Journal* 39(6): 1641–1658.

Xu, D., C. Zhou, and P. Phan (2010). 'A Real Options Perspective on Sequential Acquisitions in China'. *Journal of International Business Studies* 41(1): 166–174.

Yeung, H. W. (2000). 'The Dynamics of Asian Business Systems in a Globalizing Era'. *Review of International Political Economy* 7(3): 399–433.

—— (2007). 'Unpacking the Business of Asian Business'. In H. Y. C. Yeung, Ed., *Handbook of Research on Asian Business*: 1–16. Cheltenham, Edward Elgar.

Yiu, D. W., G. D. Bruton, and Y. Lu (2005). 'Understanding Business Group Performance in an Emerging Economy: Acquiring Resources and Capabilities in Order to Prosper'. *Journal of Management Studies* 42(1): 183–206.

—— C. M. Lau, and G. D. Bruton (2007). 'International Venturing by Emerging-Economy Firms: The Effects of Firm Capabilities, Home Country Networks, and Corporate Entrepreneurship'. *Journal of International Business Studies* 38(4), 519–540.

—— Y. Lu, G. D. Bruton, and R. E. Hoskisson (2007). 'Business Groups: An Integrated Model to Focus Future Research'. *Journal of Management Studies* 44(8): 1551–1579.

—— and S. Makino (2002). 'The Choice between Joint Venture and Wholly-Owned Subsidiary: An Institutional Perspective'. *Organization Science* 13(6): 667–683.

Zhou, L., B. R. Barnes, and Y. Lu (2010). 'Entrepreneurial Proclivity, Capability Upgrading and Performance Advantage of Newness among International New Ventures'. *Journal of International Business Studies* 41(5): 882–905.

Zou, H. and M. B. Adams (2008). 'Corporate Ownership, Equity Risk and Returns in the People's Republic of China'. *Journal of International Business Studies* 39(7): 1149–1168.

# PART III

## EVOLUTIONARY TRAJECTORIES

CHAPTER 26

........................................................................................................

# PICTURES OF THE PAST

*Historical Influences in Contemporary
Asian Business Systems*

........................................................................................................

REGINA M. ABRAMI

# INTRODUCTION

........................................................................................................

FEW would argue that the past is irrelevant. Understanding how historical forces shape the present, however, is far more complex. For the non-historian especially, it means taking a view of history as more than static legacy. We have to ask instead how something in the past can be the basis both of continuity and change. Nowhere perhaps is such inquiry more necessary than in Asia. Today, the region is distinguished by differences in levels of economic growth, industrial specialization, ethnic diversity, political regime types, forms of corporate governance, and global economic integration. At the same time, Asia is a place where a shared cluster of factors often takes centre stage in explanations of how business systems emerge and change.

In this chapter, I focus on three distinct explanations of how the present—in this case, varieties of contemporary Asian capitalism—arose from initial conditions.[1] These explanations view initial conditions as (a) destiny, (b) strategic choice, or (c) 'switchmen' that put people and places on a different track. We have, in other words, three distinct pictures of the past.

The first picture emphasizes outcomes as the result of historical institutional origins—social, cultural, and economic. In this view, change is constitutively path-dependent and typically evolves over long time horizons. The second picture emphasizes outcomes as the result of strategic choices arising from the structural context in which decision-making occurs. Change thus is no longer constitutively path-dependent, as the structural conditions under which strategic interests emerge can only partially determine resulting resolutions to competition over scarce goods. The 'switchmen' approach, in contrast, allows that exogenous forces may radically alter a country's path. Historical influences from this angle are thus less a matter of indigenous context than of transnational elements. Change, as such, is neither fully path-dependent nor fully unrestrained.

Before turning to this perspective on the origins of Asian varieties of capitalism, I consider examples from the other two approaches. As I hope will become clear, each hinges deeply on distinct theories of order and change driven by different motives and mechanisms. Thus, it bears noting from the start that above all else we have a 'varieties of the past' to contend with, upon which accounts of contemporary Asian capitalism have been built, and against which explanations of comparative advantage should be considered.

## GETTING HERE: THE PAST AS DESTINY

The importance of initial conditions in the evolution of a country's business system is a common theme in the literature on Asian capitalism. Institutions such as socio-cultural beliefs, rules for economic exchange and distribution, and the state itself have been invoked to explain (a) the rise of business groups (Leff 1978; Granovetter 1995; Carney and Gedajlovic 2003; Khanna and Yafeh 2005; Jones and Colpan 2010), (b) the role of the Chinese as business intermediaries (Skinner 1957; McVey 1992; Gomez and Xiao 2001), (c) the prevalence of family business throughout Asia (Carney and Gedajlovic 2002; Studwell 2007; Steier 2009), (d) patterns of industrial upgrading (Deyo 1987; Amsden 2001; Welsh 2002; Doner, Ritchie, and Slater 2005), (e) patterns of redistributive politics (Haggard and Low 2002; Welsh 2002; Benjamin et al. 2008; Jodhka 2010), (f) forms of corporate governance,[2] and (g) national economic performance (Doner 1991; Booth 1999; Kohli 1999).

This is an impressive array of evidence that history, and particularly the role of institutions, shapes economic opportunities and constraints. For Marx, this meant that making history was never simply how we might choose it to be. For Weber, the constraint came through authority relations and acts of sense-making. Either way, change was path-dependent; a view that has been emphasized especially with respect to the state's role in shaping Asia's various business systems.

Starting first with colonialism as a sub-type, it has been invoked to explain sharp differences in the development trajectories of South East and North-East Asia. Specifically, whereas Japanese colonialism arguably seeded impressive economic performance in North-East Asia's post-colonial era, Dutch, Spanish, and US colonialism is said to have done just the opposite for South East Asia (Cumings 1999; Welsh 2002; Booth 2007). The reasoning is several-fold, starting with the entrepreneurial class of actors who served colonial interests, but were subjected unevenly to discipline by the very same.

Hutchcroft (2011: 546), for example, studied the Philippines under US colonialism and found that American promises to grant the indigenous elite a governing role allowed this group to transform its political power into economic power. In Korea and

Taiwan, in contrast, Japanese colonialists set out to marginalize indigenous political elites (Peattie and Myers 1984). Japanese colonialism, in turn, transformed the Korean economy through Japanese-led industrialization (Cumings 1984), which helped create a disciplined Korean labour force dedicated to economic modernization (Deyo 1989; Park 1999; Hutchcroft 2011), and through strategic alliances between the Japanese colonial state and Korean entrepreneurs (Eckert 1991). While most businesses were Japanese owned, Korean entrepreneurship also continued to develop, leading Eckert (1991: 6) to describe this period as the 'first flowering' of Korean capitalism as we now know it.

Dutch and British colonialists were no less interested in reconfiguring the political economies newly under their control, but whereas Japanese colonialists arguably facilitated economic diversification through industrialization, Dutch and British colonialists in South East Asia favoured economic mono-specialization, which allowed the colonialists to extract ever greater amounts of primary export products (Post and Touwen-Bouwsma 1997). This came at the expense of local food self-sufficiency. By the 1930s, according to Booth (2007: 153), 'Indonesia, the Philippines, and British Malaya were all net importers of rice.' The problem was not lack of land or resources, but the direction of labour towards export-oriented plantations and, with this, increasingly dependent tenant-cultivators throughout pre-independence South East Asia (Booth 2007).

Reid (2001: 59) described this period as a time of great transformation in the wrong direction. 'As never before,' he wrote, 'Southeast Asians became a peasant people living in rural villages insulated by paternalistic officials and culturally distant traders.' The introduction of revenue farming—the granting of monopoly rights to collect taxes on behalf of those in power—also allowed these traders to expand their power in new ways. As Brown (1997: 4) notes, South East Asian rulers 'frequently favoured foreign merchants at the expense of their own subjects'. These outsiders attained commercial, and in some cases, political positions in South East Asian port capitals centuries before the arrival of Western colonialists. In other words, colonialism on its own did not create the privileged Chinese and Indian diaspora that operated in parts of South East Asia (Salmon 1981; Sandhu and Mani 1993; Markovits 2000; Tagliacozzo and Chang 2011).

Western colonialists also came to rely on these intermediaries for a steady stream of labour, exportable goods, and tax revenue. Revenue farmers, in turn, had every reason to guard European colonial borders to serve their own material interests (Trocki 2009). Revenue farming, in other words, not only aided Western colonial powers, it also put the Chinese on track to accumulate wealth as business intermediaries. These intermediaries, with their regional commercial networks and access to newly immigrant Chinese labour, had a great advantage over indigenous South East Asians (Trocki 2004). It does not seem, in other words, that either colonial or royal authorities deliberately stifled the economic potential of indigenous populations. It was rather that most home-grown entrepreneurs, lacking direct access to international markets and financial resources, had little ability to curry favour with those in power. Even in Thailand, which was never colonized, the business elite were and remain predominantly Chinese in origin (Skinner 1957; Cushman 1991; Hamilton 2006).

By the early twentieth century, the institution of revenue farming had all but disappeared. Colonial governments came to see it as an impediment to their own control over resources and that of Western businesses in the region (Brown 1997). The Chinese of South East Asia, in turn, sought financial gain in other ways, including their first foray into modern banking (Brown 1994). According to Brown (1997: 56), over fifteen Chinese banks were created in the Malay States and Straits Settlements between 1902 and 1932. Indeed, many of the great South East Asian Chinese family businesses had their start in this period (Rudolph 1998; Wan 2001).

Colonialism left its mark in other ways too, including differences in levels of industrialization, and in the educational, public health, and state bureaucratic systems of East and South East Asia (Welsh 2002; Booth 2007). Equally significant were 'ethnicized' divisions of labour that remain to this day. While colonialism gave the Chinese an advantage in the business system of South East Asia, it disadvantaged other minorities. In the cases of Koreans in Japan or minority populations in China or India, the histories that brought them to minority status have also disadvantaged them in each country's business system (Hicks 1997; Dirks 2001; Gladney 2004). Current parameters of redistributive politics in Asia reflect these colonial legacies. Malaysia's *Bumiputera* policies, seeking economic equity for non-Chinese citizens (Hashim 1998), and efforts to impose a government minority jobs quota in several Indian states (Yadav 2010) show the persistence of ethnic differences, despite a common discourse of post-liberation national unity. In Singapore, Lee Kwan Yew, facing significant pro-Communist opposition, had little choice but to build alliances with workers of every kind (Haggard and Low 2002: 308–309). In turn, he embarked on a plan that led to redistributive institutions that ultimately benefited all Singaporeans. This might never have happened had his position depended on winning over the entrepot's Chinese business elite alone.

In Singapore, as elsewhere in post-colonial Asia, the combined task of nation-building and industrialization made states and policies, rather than markets and prices, the primary force for economic development. There should be no surprise here. The backdrop of royal authority, warlords, and colonialism made clear that those in power, no matter their type, had vast influence over the economic well-being of all. Given this, turning full power over to free markets would have appeared an odd strategy to the region's post-independence political elite.

The task instead was 'coordination for change', to borrow Ha-Joon Chang's (1999: 192) phrase. That meant a centralized bureaucracy able to maintain a steady hand over the economy and business (Chang 1999). By deploying a mix of financial incentives, industry protections, and social-welfare policies, such administrators arguably did improve national economic performance (Johnson 1999). The absence of similar types of administrators in South and South East Asia is often considered a reason for their divergent development (Herring 1999; Searle 1999; Kang 2002). Despite these intra-regional differences, there have been some noteworthy parallels in post-war Asia, particularly the concentration of wealth within family-based conglomerates (Chang 2006; Studwell 2007; Colpan, Hikino, and Lincoln 2010) and the concurrent rise of state-owned enterprises, still found in Singapore, India, Taiwan, China, and Vietnam. Their persistence, despite campaigns of economic liberalization, belies any easy link between ownership forms, economic performance, and regime type.

At the same time, it seems implausible to claim that regime type is irrelevant to the making of a country's business system. In the Asian context, two relevant examples stand out. First, there is evidence of greater potential for weak states to emerge in newly democratic regimes. Cambodia is the paradigmatic example here. Second, state social-ism as a regime type deliberately aims to change, not only the ends of economic action, but also the property rights and other institutions thought necessary for market-based exchange. Such was the case for China and Vietnam.

Even now, decades after the introduction of market-oriented economic reforms in China and Vietnam, regime type continues to be cited as the origins of their con-temporary business systems. First, there is the vaulted position of state-affiliated and state-owned enterprises, resulting in preferential access to bank lending and exclu-sive rights to certain economic sectors (MKE 2002; Walter and Howie 2011). Second, township-and-village-owned enterprises in reform-era China are regarded as the out-come of insecure private property rights (Taube 2002; Huang 2008). Finally, the per-sistence of *guanxi* (social connections) in Chinese economic life has been depicted as a result of China's weak regulatory environment and the high uncertainty of eco-nomic transactions a legally insecure environment (Wank 1999; Gold, Guthrie, and Wank 2002).

Important differences in reform-era economic organization in Vietnam and China urge caution, however. Functionalist accounts of Chinese township-and-village-owned enterprises, for example, imply that the same form of organizational hedging ought to have emerged in Vietnam, but no such industrial engine emerged. Instead, industrial zones tailored to foreign investors and export markets form the boundaries of Vietnam's industrial boom. Each country's Communist Party also has adopted different positions regarding the political status of private entrepreneurs.

In China, against the historical backdrop of the term 'capitalist roader', deployed to censure unorthodox thinking, private entrepreneurs seem unlikely figures to be invited into the Communist Party. Nonetheless, this co-option policy has been under way for some time (Fewsmith 2003). The Vietnamese Communist Party made no such move, focusing instead on regulating the economic activities of its existing members, first asserting in 1996 that Party members and their relatives may not engage in private busi-ness, then saying in 2002 that they may at any scale.

These distinct patterns are rooted in historical differences in levels of informal com-mercial activities in the pre-reform era, which in Vietnam included Communist Party and non-Party members alike. To draw the contrast even more clearly, consider that more than half of retail sales volume in Vietnam was in private hands by the early 1980s, several years before the government had announced market-oriented economic reforms (GSO 1995; GSO 1999). The private sector's share of retail trade in China did not reach that amount for another two decades.

The contrast suggests that each country's business ecosystem at the onset of socialist transformation mattered deeply for the divergent patterns we see today. In Vietnam, the

French and the Chinese Vietnamese dominated the upper reaches of the economy; the latter still play an important economic role. In contrast, pre-revolutionary China had a well-developed indigenous business class.

Put a different way, the legacies of colonialism seem to have shaped each country's socialist transformation as much as Marxist ideology. In the early days of independence, for example, Vietnam's leaders could hold outsiders responsible for the people's economic troubles, but China's leadership could hardly ignore the country's long-standing domestic business class, resulting in harsher forms of political change from the start.

Path-dependent effects, however, are not only institutional in origin. The structural composition of an economy is also relevant, and arguably has second-round effects on the evolution of state institutional development and economic performance. Lack of natural resources, for example, is thought to have contributed to high levels of state-led intervention in post-World War II North-East Asia (Doner, Ritchie, and Slater 2005). In contrast, resource abundance in Indonesia, Malaysia, and other parts of South East Asia allowed for economic growth without economic upgrading (or industrialization). These endowments may also have encouraged the rent-seeking and bribery that continue to weaken state administrative capacity in the region (Gomez and Jomo 1997; Gomez 1999; Ross 2001; Kang 2002).

Looking back further, Booth (2007) rejects the idea that colonialism in South East Asia shuttered indigenous populations and broke their connections to the global economy. On the contrary, she finds that the structure of Chinese cross-border networks deepened the integration of indigenous agricultural producers into regional networks of exchange, sometimes raising their standard of living. Rooted in the great Asian port cities, these networks pre-date the advent of Western colonialism (Reid 1990; Kang 2010; Tagliacozzo and Chang 2011).

Perhaps the most famous example of the historical impact of structural factors is the 'Needham Puzzle', which asks why the Industrial Revolution never happened in China. According to Elvin's (1973) 'high-level equilibrium trap', China's increasingly unfavourable man-to-land ratio led to an oversupply of cheap labour which diminished structurally driven demand for labour-saving inventions, a claim later supported by Tang (1979) and Zhao (1986). For Needham himself, the greater problem was a bureaucracy which could not link the inventiveness of rural artisanal craftsman to the scholarly pursuits of the elite within the administrative system (Needham 1969). The latter's mission instead was the maintenance of a vast agricultural system. The organizational matrix associated with science and scientific experiment, in turn, never developed in China. For this reason, Needham said, Britain and others were able to leap ahead, while no scientific revolution in China occurred.

For economist Justin Yifu Lin (1995), the key factor was not state bureaucracy in general, but a specific institutional practice: the civil-service examination system and the perks that came with positions in the civil bureaucracy. These material interests, he claims, diverted the best and brightest from science, channelling them instead into mastery of Confucian classics, over decades if need be. Highly coveted positions in the bureaucratic system, after all, changed the fate of not just individuals, but entire families (He 1962).[3]

Even today, China's state bureaucracy powerfully shapes scientific development through incentives that reach across Chinese society, particularly the promotion criteria for state bureaucrats. In this, the Chinese state system differs somewhat from conventional depictions of 'developmental states', a category in which it is increasingly placed. The latter deploy incentives to direct economic enterprise towards activities that enhance national productivity. The Chinese state, in contrast, has used incentives foremost to direct its own members. A recent government campaign, for example, declares that China will become an 'innovative society' by 2020 (McGregor 2010; Hu 2011) and provides a roadmap for ambitious officials. For Jacques (2009) and Huntington (1996), among others, China's economic rise cannot be set apart from the cultural roots of its administrative system.

Before moving to the role of culture as a force of path-dependency, it is worth noting that all the aforementioned explanations of the Needham Puzzle are implicitly based on the distribution of human resources. They thus present a structural explanation for divergent economic and technological development, but whether it is ever possible to separate the ends of economic action from the cultures in which they are embedded remains a question.

Indeed, culture looms rather large in explanations of Asian business systems. Max Weber's typologies of rationalism have deservedly drawn the most attention (Buss 1987; Hamilton and Kao 1987). Later studies, inspired by Weber, both criticize and build upon 'culturalist' approaches to Asian economic development and the broader question of whether a given 'culture' helps or hinders economic growth. Weber himself saw little promise for India and China. Hinduism and Confucianism, he contended, could not spawn Western-style entrepreneurialism, because neither offered any means to evade social norms.

In effect, Weber presents a theory of order and change nested within distinct systems of understanding that give rise to varying kinds of authority relations and economic organization. Early applications of Weber's work, however, were less nuanced. Mid-twentieth-century theories of backwardness and modernization especially cast culture rather statically, implying convergence towards a unitary notion of modernity (Jacobs 1958; Lerner 1958; Bellah 1959).

In response, regional experts identified ways in which 'tradition' had, in fact, been the basis for economic growth and development. No business history of India, for example, can be written without recognition of the role of the Vaishaya, India's trading caste, in the evolution of indigenous industry and financial networks. Among them, the Marwari, for example, eased into a dominant place in private industry in post-colonial 1950s India (Timberg 1978; Kudaisya 2009). The Chettiars, in contrast, never attained the same level of wealth and prestige (Rudner 1994). In South East Asia, however, they had great influence in the post-World War II period, serving as middlemen between Chinese and non-Chinese communities, as well as bankers to some of the earliest Chinese South East Asia businesses (Sandhu 1969; Sandhu and Mani 1993; Kudaisya 2009).

Nevertheless, there is debate in the scholarly literature over the exact role of caste as opposed to region, religion, or other identities in shaping the evolution of Indian business networks (Subrahmanyam 1990). For researchers of India's lowest caste, the answer is clear (Jodhka 2010)—caste matters. Either way, the lesson is the same. Indian business networks are portrayed as the organizational outcome of social norms that over time have led to distinct economic roles within the business systems of India, South East Asia, and elsewhere (Subrahmanyam 1990; Sandhu and Mani 1993; Markovits 2000).

Emphasis upon social norms in shaping the form and persistence of networks is common to sociological and cultural approaches (Swedberg 2007). New institutional economic approaches, by contrast, focus on the functional aspects of networks, viewing them as solutions to the weakness or non-existence of such state institutions as laws of contract or property right. The underlying assumption, of course, is that these networks should disappear when no longer needed, but that has failed to materialize, further buttressing earlier studies on the role of tradition in economic development. (Greif 1993; Greif, Milgrom, and Weingast 1994; Heydemann 2008.)

Modernization theory also presumed the demise of tradition, leaving many observers to scratch their heads over Japan's economic take-off in the 1950s. To no one's surprise, the starting point had been an examination of Japanese traditions, seeking parallels with Weber's explanation of the 'capitalist spirit' in the West. Bellah (1959), most famously, identified the 'samurai ethic' as the normative agent of Japan's transformation. Collins (1997) situated these cultural forces even earlier in Japan's history.

Such explanations of Japan's success were not complimentary to China. Negative depictions of Confucian-bred patrimonialism, in turn, persisted, but quickly ran up against the economic dynamism of Taiwan, Hong Kong, and Korea in the 1960s. Later studies recast Confucianism more positively (Hofstede and Bond 1988; Chung, Shepard, and Dollinger 1989). In place of stasis, Hofstede and Bond, for example, identified a cluster of values that they defined as 'Confucian dynamism'. Rozman (1991) and Tu (1996) also set out to demonstrate, on a country-by-country basis, Confucianism's role in the creation of a distinct East Asian modernity.

Redding's study perhaps went the farthest, showing how Chinese executives embodied in word and deeds a set of values that had deep historical roots and shaped understandings of their situation and business decisions (Redding 1990). A key, if often overlooked, point in this study is that organizations do not determine their practice: cultures do. Redding (1990: 239) illustrates as much by suggesting that Chinese family businesses are distinct from what exists of family firms elsewhere. Redding's work also implies that the organization of economic life in its own right is hardly the basis of economic decision-making or of the past century's transformation in Asian business systems.

Other studies look cross-nationally to show how features of Confucianism, including its emphasis on patrimonialism, consensus, and social hierarchies, operate in practice, with important case differences (Hamilton and Biggart 1988; Greenhalgh 1994; Redding 1996; Biggart 1997). Kim's ethnography of Korea's Poongsan Corporation, for example, contrasts sharply with work on Japan's managerial system (Yoshino and Chandler 1968; Dore 1973; Kim 1992). Even so, these studies all show the working of group norms towards consensus. There is, as a result, strong path-dependency in studies emphasizing the cultural origins of Asian business systems. This approach does not, however, preclude the influence of other forces on economic and social change, which the next section explores.

# Getting Here: A Matter of Strategic Choice

Critics of cultural approaches have been quick to point to unspoken utilitarian logics in the practice of cultural traditions.[4] Greenhalgh (1994), for example, confronts the strong emphasis on 'Confucian familistic culture' in accounts of East Asian economic dynamism, suggesting that existing divisions of labour within the household are a reaction to demands of global capitalism, specifically its need for flexible labour. Traditional culture, as such, does little to explain Taiwan's family firms or the country's economic take-off. Janelli and Janelli (1993) take an equally forceful view, in their case pointing to 'tradition' as a managerial weapon used to instill control over Korean workers, ultimately driving the national economy in a more prosperous direction.

Even so, recognizing the strategic deployment of cultural tropes is not to deny that culture is a force shaping economic development and change. Wong (1996), for example, applies a strategic frame, but in his case to show how the Singaporean government invoked Confucianism, not entirely successfully, to facilitate economic development. Abrami (2002) shows how Vietnamese small-scale rural enterprise owners and traders deployed official constructions of the 'peasantry', based on norms rooted in both socialist and traditional Vietnamese moral culture, to advance their economic activities against state regulations.

There is also a growing body of work undercutting material-based constructions of strategic interest by demonstrating across disciplines that maximizing rationalities (or 'calculability'), much like notions of fairness or gender, are culturally embedded forms of reasoning (Callon 1998; Henrich 2000; Henrich et al. 2005; Herrera 2005; Maurer 2005; Stark 2009). Applying this approach to the evolution of modern Chinese business, Faure (2009) lists several traditional institutions that historically allowed Chinese businesspeople to render risk calculable in the absence of anything resembling the rule of law. The advent of company law in early twentieth-century China, as such, only rendered the risk of economic transactions calculable in new ways (Kirby 1995; Ruskola 2000).[5] My own work on the evolution of private business in China and Vietnam (Abrami n.d.) draws on Weber's claim of calculability as the foundation of capitalism's emergence, to show how differences in socialist-era constructions of political worth set forth a metric by which people learned to assess the marginal risks of engaging in private business, and ultimately to calibrate the credibility of each regime's commitment to economic liberalization.

While the above examples portray strategic interests as the outcome of socially situated knowledge, a different body of work views strategic interests as a structural outcome. In the Asian context, perhaps Marx himself was the earliest variant of this approach. His still-controversial concept of an Asiatic mode of production drew a connection between the nature of state power and class relations of production (Dunn 1982; Brook 1989). World-system theorists and others subsequently interpreted the evolution of Asian business systems, including China's economic take-off, as rooted in a global production system and shifting global patterns of labour exploitation (Deyo 1989; Greenhalgh 1994; Chan 2001; Abbott 2003; Arrighi 2007).

An alternative approach, inspired by game theory and new institutional economics, acknowledges how both economic and political structures shape understandings of strategic interest, but the focus is on individual self-interest, as opposed to that of economic classes. Using this approach to explain the political economies of Taiwan and Korea, Kang (1995: 579) identifies a key shortcoming in historical institutional approaches, finding that they are too focused on 'the origin of outcomes' rather than the 'origin of choices', and thus ignore the immediate importance of collective-action problems facing political and economic decision-makers.

Building off this framework, Haggard, Kang, and Moon (1997) deny that Japanese colonialism played a role in Korea's economic take-off. The Philippines is an equally important case here. At the time of its independence from the US, it had the right building blocks in place for economic development. With regard to access to primary and secondary education, it surpassed much of South East Asia, Taiwan, and Korea (Booth 2007). Along with Korea, Taiwan, and Malaysia, the Philippines also had lower infant mortality rates than Indonesia. By the mid-1950s, its per capita GDP was second only to colonial Malaya (Booth 2007). Nonetheless, the Philippines quickly fell behind its neighbours.

Such an economic turnaround raises the question of the role of leadership as opposed to legacy in explaining contemporary Asian business systems. Studies show that the personal traits of some of Asia's leading political figures profoundly affected their countries' trajectories (Celoza 1997; Barr 2000; Domínguez 2011; Hutchcroft 2011; Vogel 2011a; Vogel 2011b). Others present a more constrained view, showing how leaders' impacts are shaped by what is politically feasible (Doner, Ritchie, and Slater 2005).

Viewing the past as a matter of structural constraints overturns the tidy attribution of the 'Asian miracle' to state capacities. Noble (1998), for example, shows how differences in electoral systems influenced both the content and efficacy of industrial policy. Detailed industry-level and policy-focused studies make it harder even to speak of 'state autonomy' in the region any longer. Instead, it seems that the structural conditions under which political interests can achieve their ends matter greatly, even within seemingly omnipotent single-party regimes (Ritchie 2001; MacIntyre 2003; Malesky 2008; Shih 2008; Doner 2009). The economic stage of an industry can also affect a firm's ability to navigate bureaucratic constraints. Not surprisingly, more mature, globalized firms seem better able to do this, something we now also see in China, where the largest enterprises are increasingly able to bargain with the government over a wide range of matters.

Doner, Noble, and Ravenhill (2006) illustrate the importance of timing too, showing how economies of scale in Japan's auto sector were the result of the state's early support of coordination between assemblers and parts and materials firms. Government provision of testing and certification processes, in turn, led to a diffusion of skill formation and industry-wide product standardization. In contrast, the Korean government acceded to the insistence of entrenched auto assemblers that their suppliers not manufacture for competitors, such that technology diffusion was deferred. In Indonesia, government intentions to increase local content instead aided the protection of selected auto-industry businesses at the expense of industry-wide upgrading (Doner 1991: 145; Abbott 2003: 125–130).

The domestic context of strategic decision-making also influenced responses to the 1997 Asian financial crisis. In Japan and Korea, for example, not only were new financial regulations put in place to discourage cross-shareholdings, but considerable consolidation through mergers, acquisitions, and outright bankruptcy occurred (Ahmadjian 2006). Still, despite the ostensible rationalization of the financial sector across Asia, there remains poor governance in the region, including corruption in Korea (Chang 2006), persistent *rentier* capitalism in Indonesia (Brown 2006), limited reform capacity in Thailand (Wingfield 2002; Doner 2009), and on-going government protection of business allies in Malaysia (Gomez 2002).

In sum, strategic-choice explanations describe the evolution of Asian business systems as constrained adaptation to existing conditions. Change is thus utilitarian in origin, determined by resolutions to problems of collective action, and not by institutional forces per se. Actors within this approach also understand their material interests in objective-material rather than normative-cultural terms. The past, in other words, is just a backdrop against which actors aim to maintain or improve upon existing gains.

For us, it means that fundamentally different histories exist even when speaking of a similar outcome or event. For example, while earlier accounts of the rise of Asian developmental states focused on historical legacies, scholars favouring a strategic-choice approach are puzzled that developmental states emerge at all. To them, the collective-action problems associated with coordinating economic change suggest that fundamental transformation of any economic ecosystem should be rare. As such, emphasis is placed on the structural conditions under which cross-cutting shifts in the interests of government, business, and the masses are likely to emerge. According to Doner, Ritchie, and Slater (2005), the key is 'systemic vulnerability', a condition under which ruling elites perceive the political necessity to forge broad coalitions and abandon favouritism for redistributive policies that will support industrial upgrading. Among these policies, education, social welfare, inter-firm collaboration, and public-private partnerships have been identified as the best means to channel businesses towards greater productivity, while keeping a check on the worst forms of patronage (Campos and Root 1996; Doner, Ritchie, and Slater 2005; Ritchie 2009).

Exogenous political and economic shocks also have a role to play, but much like the impact of colonialism discussed earlier, outcomes nonetheless originate within national boundaries in strategic-choice approaches. Differences in business systems, thus, are understood as the result of existing conditions and the actors therein, who adapt, mutate, or reject what the world has brought them. A final approach rejects this view, arguing instead that exogenous forces are crucial in shaping national-level outcomes. With this perspective, history as an evolutionary force is no longer plausible. Instead, the past becomes a 'switchman'.

## GETTING HERE: SWITCHMEN EFFECTS

The force of Max Weber's 'switchmen' concept was its recognition of the ability of ideas to put people and places on a different track. Ideas, as such, mattered not so much for their content as for their consequences. Switchman-like forces may thus be extended to include such equally disruptive elements as new technologies and shifts in global demand, both of which have had a profound effect on business organization and practice throughout Asia. In a sense, switchman elements seem to be the game-changers of Asian history.

Starting first with the role of ideas as switchmen, few have been more transformative or transgressive than the idea of modernity itself. Competing ideas of modernity, in fact, remade the Asian region over the past two centuries. Japan and China, for example, looked to Germany to find answers to the enigma of industrial and military power, which subsequently influenced their education systems, administrative bureaucracies, and military organization (Pyle 1974; Kirby 1984; Anderson 1991; Grimmer-Solem 2005). In due course, Japanese corporatism drew the attention of regional neighbours (Pempel 1999). The rise of Soviet Communism influenced early twentieth-century intellectual circles in India, China, Indochina, and Japan. And, if those persistent portraits of Lenin and Stalin are any indication, Soviet Communism helped inspire state-socialist transition in Vietnam and China.

Viewed more broadly, ideas of 'best practice' have always been historically situated, but little attention has been paid to the relation between changes in capital flows and the diffusion of ideas across borders. To draw a few examples, US aid to Japan, Korea, and Taiwan increased the appeal of an 'export-oriented' industrialization model in those countries. Simultaneously, this developmental path had little attraction to India's policymakers, who steadily favoured import substitution and socialist inspiration. By the early 1990s, India's precipitous drop in national reserves and IMF bailout came with an embrace of more market-oriented policies. Price liberalization in Vietnam, some decades later, also had in its timing and scope far more to do with the sudden loss of Soviet aid than the appeal of capitalism per se. While the 2007 Asian financial crisis is commonly blamed on poor governance, it might as easily be blamed on the push from the IMF and World Bank for open capital markets (Lim 1998; Chang 2000).

Today, the idea of corporate social responsibility also seems global. Chinese state conglomerates, for example, sign up in droves to advance the UN Global Compact's support of human rights, though all the while heeding Chinese government commands against the free movement of information and labour at home. Institutional approaches would look to the past to make sense of this curious combination. Strategic-choice approaches would start with each actor's material interests and the configuration of veto players to explain this outcome. In both cases, emphasis is placed on domestic institutions to explain outcomes.

Hamilton (2006: 146–183) argues that a 'demand-side' view of the origins of comparative advantage better captures the varieties of capitalism in the region, as it links outcomes to fundamental features of global capitalism, such as inter-firm competition, changing prices, and consumer preferences. Cross-border networks among Chinese entrepreneurs, for example, were earlier portrayed as rooted within kinship and ethnic ties that happened to grant market advantage. Demand-side explanations place them within a broader system of global capitalism, subject to competitive pressures that may preserve or destroy them (Feenstra and Hamilton 2006). The expansion of corporate social responsibility across the globe might also be viewed as a 'demand-side' phenomenon, reflecting global buyer wishes, and thus having little to do with domestic institutions or beliefs.

Recent changes in global demand give further support to a demand-driven view of business-system development and change. Most notably, the 2008 global recession forced the Chinese government to institute a domestic pro-consumer stimulus package to balance declining demand in the US and elsewhere. It also sparked a wave of Chinese outward direct investment, including acquisitions of US and European assets. Either way, the story is not how domestic economic actors shape the impact of exogenous shocks, but how shock itself can change a country's economic system. Pepinsky (2008), for example, finds that the distributional consequences of the 1998 Asian financial crisis altered Malaysia's political coalitions, allowing state agents to implement policies that might otherwise have been resisted. Zheng and Abrami (2011) tell a similar story, but with regard to the origins of industrial concentration in China's petrochemical sector.

Switchmen may also bring forth new forms of inter-subjectivity, not just material interests per se. These have been as wide ranging as notions of trade fairness and human rights. It is worth noting too that the institutions associated with these ideas seem unable to command economic action alone. For example, the rise of the Multi-Fiber Arrangement (1974–2004), a system of quota-based access to preferential tariff rates, aided the global expansion of textile manufacturing. The resulting supply chain was predicted to come apart when the Arrangement ended, but technological innovations kept it together in ways that make a case for a demand-driven view of varieties of capitalism, as consumers beyond each nation's borders continued to hold influence.

Invention, however, is the ultimate switchman. Taking a demand-driven view of the past, the rise of automation, modular production, and RFID technology arguably remade the economic landscape of much of Asia. Put a different way, 'flying geese' without computers may have gone nowhere (Bernard and Ravenhill 1995; Kojima 2000).[6]

# CONCLUSION

This chapter set out to identify historical influences shaping variation in Asian business systems today, and found instead three distinct theories of order and change. It found no unified picture of the past to explain how history matters. Instead, we have ideas of the past as destiny, as creator of strategic choices, and as a switchman opening new paths of development, while cutting off the rest. Such a spectrum of explanations has broad implications for the varieties of capitalism approach.

To start with, it calls into question the origins of comparative advantage as an institutional phenomenon. We might want to consider instead how structural factors, as wide ranging as degrees of regional integration, a country or firm's location within global supply chains, an industry's age, or its share of national employment, matter. Each has a role to play in a nation or industry's capacity for adaptation and change, such that differences in domestic institutions ultimately may be less relevant to explanations of global competitiveness.

As the cases explored earlier suggest, we would also benefit from incorporating a temporal element in our analysis. Doing so makes clear that the comparative advantage of institutional arrangements is largely in relation to change and continuity within a global economic system. The Asian cases are especially instructive here if we consider how the highly coordinated socialist market economies were better able to weather global economic shocks owing to controls on their capital accounts, a feature lacking in their neighbours. Years earlier, open capital accounts had been the basis of attracting foreign investment, with the point being that forms of financial institutions in their own right have no intrinsic competitiveness.

Having said this, there are certain institutional features common to Asia that have served well over long periods, and about which the varieties of capitalism approach has little to say. Foremost among these are social norms of authority relations and obligation that elevate the role of informal social ties in economic life to a degree not seen elsewhere. These social ties trump formal organizational rules in many cases, thus making a focus on the latter insufficient for any accounting of economic preferences. They also, as earlier explored in the case of the Chinese diaspora, have aided economic performance at national and firm levels. As such, it is impossible to rule out culture as a force of global competitiveness.

Even so, the 'varieties of capitalism' approach is surprisingly silent on the role of culture in shaping distinct business systems and in establishing the credibility of associated institutions. Here too, the Asian region has much to offer, serving as a laboratory of sorts, where family businesses take different forms, where trust in the idea of 'rule of law' remains uneven, and clusters of religious and ethnic differences continue to influence economic life.

In sum, the 'varieties of capitalism' approach has contributed greatly to our understanding of divergent paths to economic prosperity. At the same time, the longer time horizon on which this chapter is based suggests that capacity for adaptation, rather than any fixed institutional form, may be the most distinguishing hallmark of national economic prosperity.

## NOTES

1. A comprehensive review of the vast literature on the relation of contemporary Asian capitalism to history is beyond the scope of this chapter. For helpful Asia-specific reviews, see Wilkinson (1996); Carney, Gedajlovic, and Yang (2009); Tipton (2009).
2. See Christina L. Ahmadjian's article titled 'Corporate Governance and Business Systems in Asia.'
3. The author's name also appears as Ping T. Ho.
4. Methodological criticisms can also be found, but are not discussed in the context of this article's emphasis on historical forces underpinning the development of Asian business systems.
5. These authors do not situate their work within Weber's discussion of calculability, but the evidence they present is illustrative of Weber's discussion.
6. Neither reference, however, gives much attention to the role of technology in shaping where the birds might be heading.

## REFERENCES

Abbott, J. (2003). *Developmentalism and Dependency in Southeast Asia: The Case of the Automotive Industry*. New York, RoutledgeCurzon.

Abrami, R. (n.d.). 'Naming Progress, Finding Vice: Class Labeling and the Making of Private Business in Vietnam and China' (Manuscript in Progress).

—— (2002). 'Just a Peasant: Economy and Legacy in Northern Vietnam'. In P. Leonard and D. Kaneff, Eds., *Post-Socialist Peasant? Rural and Urban Constructions of Identity in Eastern Europe, East Asia and the Former Soviet Union*: 94–116. New York, Palgrave.

Ahmadjian, C. (2006). 'Japanese Business Groups'. In S. J. Chang, Ed., Business Groups in *East Asia: Financial Crisis, Restructuring, and New Growth*: 29–51. New York, Oxford University Press.

—— (2014). 'Corporate Governance and Business Systems in Asia. In M. A. Witt and G. Redding, Eds., *The Oxford Handbook of Asian Business Systems*: 332–357. Oxford, Oxford University Press.

Amsden, A. H. (2001). *The Rise of 'the Rest': Challenges to the West from Late-Industrializing Economies*. New York, Oxford University Press.

Anderson, P. (1991). 'The Prussia of the East?' *Boundary 2* 18(3): 11–19.

Arrighi, G. (2007). *Adam Smith in Beijing: Lineages of the Twenty-First Century*. New York, Verso.

Barr, M. D. (2000). *Lee Kuan Yew*. Richmond, Curzon.

Bellah, R. N. (1959). *Tokugawa Religion: The Cultural Roots of Modern Japan*. London, Free Press.

Benjamin, D., L. Brandt, J. Giles, and S. Wang (2008). 'Income Inequality During China's Economic Transition'. In L. Brandt and T. G. Rawski, Eds., *China's Great Economic Transformation*: 729–775. Cambridge, Cambridge University Press.

Bernard, M. and J. Ravenhill (1995). 'Beyond Product Cycles and Flying Geese: Regionalization, Hierarchy, and the Industrialization of East Asia'. *World Politics* 47(2): 171–209.

Biggart, N. W. (1997). 'Institutionalized Patrimonialism in Korean Business'. In M. Orrú, N. W. Biggart, and G. G. Hamilton, Eds., *The Economic Organization of East Asian Capitalism*: 215–236. Thousand Oaks, Sage.

Booth, A. (1999). 'Initial Conditions and Miraculous Growth: Why Is Southeast Asia Different from Taiwan and South Korea?' *World Development* 27(2): 301–321.

—— (2007). *Colonial Legacies: Economic and Social Development in East and Southeast Asia.* Honolulu, University of Hawaii Press.

Brook, T. (1989). *The Asiatic Mode of Production in China.* Armonk, M. E. Sharpe.

Brown, I. (1997). *Economic Change in South-East Asia, c.1830–1980.* New York, Oxford University Press.

Brown, R. A. (1994). *Capital and Entrepreneurship in Southeast Asia.* New York, Palgrave Macmillan.

—— (2006). *The Rise of the Corporate Economy in Southeast Asia.* New York, Routledge.

Buss, A. (1987). 'Introductory Comments on Max Weber's Essays on India and China'. *International Sociology* 2(3): 271–276.

Callon, M. (1998). *The Laws of the Markets.* Malden, MA, Blackwell Publishers/The Sociological Review.

Campos, J. E. L. and H. L. Root (1996). *The Key to the Asian Miracle: Making Shared Growth Credible.* Washington, DC, Brookings Institution.

Carney, M. and E. Gedajlovic (2002). 'The Co-Evolution of Institutional Environments and Organizational Strategies: The Rise of Family Business Groups in the ASEAN Region'. *Organization Studies* 23(1): 1–29.

—— and E. Gedajlovic (2003). 'Strategic Innovation and the Administrative Heritage of East Asian Family Business Groups'. *Asia Pacific Journal of Management* 20(1): 5–26.

—— and X. Yang (2009). 'Varieties of Asian Capitalism: Toward an Institutional Theory of Asian Enterprise'. *Asia Pacific Journal of Management* 26: 361–380.

Celoza, A. F. (1997). *Ferdinand Marcos and the Philippines.* Westport, Praeger.

Chan, A. (2001). *China's Workers under Assault: The Exploitation of Labor in a Globalizing Economy.* Armonk, NY, M. E. Sharpe.

Chang, H.-J. (1999). 'The Economic Theory of the Developmental State'. In M. Woo-Cumings, Ed., *The Developmental State*: 182–199. Ithaca, Cornell University Press.

—— (2000). 'The Hazard of Moral Hazard: Untangling the Asian Crisis'. *World Development* 28(4): 775–788.

—— (2006). *Business Groups in East Asia: Financial Crisis, Restructuring, and New Growth.* New York, Oxford University Press.

Chung, C. H., J. M. Shepard, and M. J. Dollinger (1989). 'Max Weber Revisited: Some Lessons from East Asian Capitalistic Development'. *Asia Pacific Journal of Management* 6(2): 307–321.

Collins, R. (1997). 'An Asian Route to Capitalism: Religious Economy and the Origins of Self-Transforming Growth in Japan'. *American Sociological Review* 62(6): 843–865.

Colpan, A. M., T. Hikino, and J. R. Lincoln (2010). *Oxford Handbook of Business Groups.* Oxford, Oxford University Press.

Cumings, B. (1984). 'The Legacy of Japanese Colonialism in Korea'. In M. R. Peattie and R. H. Myers, Eds., *The Japanese Colonial Empire, 1895–1945*: 478–496. Princeton, Princeton University Press.

—— (1999). 'Colonial Formations and Deformations: Korea, Taiwan, and Vietnam'. In B. Cumings, Ed., *Parallax Visions: Making Sense of American-East Asian Relations at the End of the Century*: 69–94. Durham, Duke University Press.

Cushman, J. W. (1991). *Family and State: The Formation of a Sino-Thai Tin-Mining Dynasty, 1797–1932*. Oxford, Oxford University Press.

Deyo, F. C. (1987). *The Political Economy of the New Asian Industrialism*. Ithaca, Cornell University Press.

—— (1989). *Beneath the Miracle: Labor Subordination in the New Asian Industrialism*. Berkeley, University of California Press.

Dirks, N. B. (2001). *Castes of Mind: Colonialism and the Making of Modern India*. Princeton, Princeton University Press.

Domínguez, J. I. (2011). 'The Perfect Dictatorship? South Korea Versus Argentina, Brazil, Chile, and Mexico'. In P. M. Kim and E. F. Vogel, Eds., *The Park Chung Hee Era: The Transformation of South Korea*: 573–602. Cambridge, Harvard University Press.

Doner, R. F. (1991). 'Approaches to the Politics of Economic Growth in Southeast Asia'. *Journal of Asian Studies* 50(4): 818–849.

—— (2009). *The Politics of Uneven Development: Thailand's Economic Growth in Comparative Perspective*. New York, Cambridge University Press.

—— G. W. Noble, and J. Ravenhill (2006). *Industrial Competitiveness of the Auto Parts Industries in Four Large Asian Countries: The Role of Government Policy in a Challenging International Environment*. World Bank Policy Research Working Paper 4106. Washington, DC, World Bank.

—— B. K. Ritchie and D. Slater (2005). 'Systemic Vulnerability and the Origins of Developmental States: Northeast and Southeast Asia in Comparative Perspective'. *International Organization* 59(02): 327–361.

Dore, R. P. (1973). *British Factory, Japanese Factory*. Berkeley, University of California Press.

Dunn, S. P. (1982). *The Fall and Rise of the Asiatic Mode of Production*. London, Routledge & Kegan Paul.

Eckert, C. J. (1991). *Offspring of Empire: The Koch'ang Kims and the Colonial Origins of Korean Capitalism, 1876–1945*. Seattle, University of Washington Press.

Elvin, M. (1973). *The Pattern of the Chinese Past*. Stanford, Stanford University Press.

Faure, D. (2009). 'Beyond Networking: An Institutional View of Chinese Business'. In M. M. Kudaisya and C. K. Ng, Eds., *Chinese and Indian Business: Historical Antecedents*: 31–60. Boston, Brill.

Feenstra, R. C. and G. G. Hamilton (2006). *Emergent Economies, Divergent Paths: Economic Organization and International Trade in South Korea and Taiwan*. New York, Cambridge University Press.

Fewsmith, J. (2003). 'Studying the Three Represents'. *China Leadership Monitor* 8(1): 1–11.

Gladney, D. C. (2004). *Dislocating China: Reflections on Muslims, Minorities, and Other Subaltern Subjects*. Chicago, University of Chicago Press.

Gold, T. B., D. Guthrie, and D. L. Wank (2002). *Social Connections in China*. New York, Cambridge University Press.

Gomez, E. T. (1999). *Chinese Business in Malaysia*. Honolulu, University of Hawaii Press.

—— (2002). 'Political Business in Malaysia: Party Factionalism, Corporate Development, and Economic Crisis'. In E. T. Gomez, Ed., *Political Business in East Asia*: 82–114. New York, Routledge.

—— and K. S. Jomo (1997). *Malaysia's Political Economy*. New York, Cambridge University Press.

—— and X. Xiao (2001). *Chinese Business in Southeast Asia: Contesting Cultural Explanations, Researching Entrepreneurship*. Richmond, Curzon.

Granovetter, M. (1995). 'Coase Revisited: Business Groups in the Modern Economy'. *Industrial and Corporate Change* 4(1): 93–130.

Greenhalgh, S. (1994). 'De-Orientalizing the Chinese Family Firm'. *American Ethnologist* 21(4): 746–775.

Greif, A. (1993). 'Contract Enforceability and Economic Institutions in Early Trade: The Maghribi Traders' Coalition'. *The American Economic Review* 83(3): 525–548.

—— P. Milgrom, and B. R. Weingast (1994). 'Coordination, Commitment, and Enforcement: The Case of the Merchant Guild'. *Journal of Political Economy* 102(4): 745–776.

Grimmer-Solem, E. (2005). 'German Social Science, Meiji Conservatism, and the Peculiarities of Japanese History'. *Journal of World History* 16(2): 187–222.

GSO (1995). *Statistical Yearbook 1994*. Hanoi, General Statistical Office 265.

—— *Vietnam Statistical Data in the 20th Century*: (espec. 647–648, 1484–1486). Hanoi, General Statistical Office.

Haggard, S., D. Kang, and C. I. Moon (1997). 'Japanese Colonialism and Korean Development'. *World Development* 25(6): 867–881.

—— and L. Low (2002). 'State, Politics, and Business in Singapore'. In E. T. Gomez, Ed., *Political Business in East Asia*: 301–323. New York, Routledge.

Hamilton, G. G. (2006). *Commerce and Capitalism in Chinese Societies*. New York, Routledge.

—— and N. W. Biggart (1988). 'Market, Culture, and Authority: A Comparative Analysis of Management and Organization in the Far East'. *American Journal of Sociology* 94: S52–S94.

—— and C-S. Kao (1987). 'Max Weber and the Analysis of East Asian Industrialisation'. *International Sociology* 2(3): 289–300.

Hashim, S. M. (1998). *Income Inequality and Poverty in Malaysia*. Lanham, Rowman & Littlefield.

He, B. (1962). *The Ladder of Success in Imperial China: Aspects of Social Mobility, 1368–1911*. New York, Columbia University Press.

Henrich, J. (2000). 'Does Culture Matter in Economic Behavior? Ultimatum Game Bargaining among the Machiguenga of the Peruvian Amazon'. *American Economic Review* 90(4): 973–979.

—— R. Boyd, S. Bowles, C. Camerer, E. Fehr, H. Gintis, R. McElreath, M. Alvard, A. Barr, J. Ensminger, N. S. Henrich, K. Hill, F. Gil-White, M. Gurven, F. W. Marlowe, J. Q. Patton, and D. Tracer (2005). '"Economic Man" in Cross-Cultural Perspective: Behavioral Experiments in 15 Small-Scale Societies'. *Behavioral and Brain Sciences* 28(6): 795–815.

Herrera, Y. M. (2005). *Imagined Economies: The Sources of Russian Regionalism*. New York, Cambridge University Press.

Herring, R. J. (1999). 'Embedded Particularism: India's Failed Developmental State'. In M. Woo-Cumings, Ed., *The Developmental State*: 306–334. Ithaca, Cornell University Press.

Heydemann, S. (2008). 'Institutions and Economic Performance: The Use and Abuse of Culture in New Institutional Economics'. *Studies in Comparative International Development* 43(1): 27–52.

Hicks, G. (1997). *Japan's Hidden Apartheid: The Korean Minority and the Japanese*. Brookfield, Ashgate.

Hofstede, G. and Bond, M. H. (1988). 'The Confucius Connection: From Cultural Roots to Economic Growth'. *Organizational Dynamics* 16(4): 5–21.

Hu, A. (2011). *China in 2020: A New Type of Superpower*. Washington, DC, Brookings Institution.

Huang, Y. (2008). *Capitalism with Chinese Characteristics*. New York, Cambridge University Press.

Huntington, S. P. (1996). *The Clash of Civilizations and the Remaking of World Order*. New York, Simon & Schuster.

Hutchcroft, P. D. (2011). 'Reflections on a Reverse Image: South Korea under Park Chung Hee and the Philippines under Ferdinand Marcos'. In P. M. Kim and E. F. Vogel, Eds., *The Park Chung Hee Era*: 542–572. Cambridge, Harvard University Press.

Jacobs, N. (1958). *The Origin of Modern Capitalism and Eastern Asia*. Hong Kong, Hong Kong University Press.

Jacques, M. (2009). *When China Rules the World: The End of the Western World and the Birth of a New Global Order*. New York, Penguin.

Janelli, R. L. and D. Y. Janelli (1993). *Making Capitalism: The Social and Cultural Construction of a South Korean Conglomerate*. Stanford, Stanford University Press.

Jodhka, S. S. (2010). 'Dalits in Business: Self-Employed Scheduled Castes in Northwest India'. Indian Institute of Dalit Studies, *Working Paper Series*, Volume IV, Number 2.

Johnson, C. (1999). 'The Developmental State: Odyssey of a Concept'. In M. Woo-Cumings, Ed., *The Developmental State*: 32–60. Ithaca, Cornell University Press.

Jones, G. and A. M. Colpan (2010). 'Business Groups in Historical Perspective'. In G. Jones, A. M. Colpan, T. Hikino, J. R. Lincoln, and T. Khanna, Eds., *Oxford Handbook of Business Groups*: 67–96. Oxford, Oxford University Press.

Kang, D. C. (1995). 'South Korean and Taiwanese Development and the New Institutional Economics'. *International Organization* 49(3): 555–587.

—— (2002). *Crony Capitalism: Corruption and Development in South Korea and the Philippines*. New York, Cambridge University Press.

—— (2010). *East Asia before the West*. New York, Columbia University Press.

Khanna, T. and Y. Yafeh (2005). 'Business Groups and Risk-Sharing around the World'. *Journal of Business* 78(1): 301–340.

Kim, C. S. (1992). *The Culture of Korean Industry: An Ethnography of Poongsan Corporation*. Tucson, University of Arizona Press.

Kirby, W. C. (1984). *Germany and Republican China*. Stanford, Stanford University Press.

—— (1995). 'China Unincorporated: Company Law and Business Enterprise in 20th-century China'. *Journal of Asian Studies* 54(1): 43–63.

Kohli, A. (1999). 'Where Do High-Growth Political Economies Come From? The Japanese Lineage of Korea's "Developmental State"'. In M. Woo-Cumings, Ed., *The Developmental State*: 93–136. Ithaca, Cornell University Press.

Kojima, K. (2000). 'The 'Flying Geese' Model of Asian Economic Development: Origin: Theoretical Extensions, and Regional Policy Implications.' *Journal of Asian Economics* 11(4): 375.

Kudaisya, M. M. (2009). 'Marwari and Chettiar Merchants, c.1850s–1950s'. In M. M. Kudaisya and C. K. Ng, Eds., *Chinese and Indian Business: Historical Antecedents*: 85–120. Boston, Brill.

Leff, N. H. (1978). 'Industrial Organization and Entrepreneurship in the Developing Countries: The Economic Groups'. *Economic Development and Cultural Change* 26(4): 661–675.

Lerner, D. (1958). *The Passing of Traditional Society: Modernizing the Middle East*. Glencoe, Free Press.

Lim, L. Y. C. (1998). 'Whose "Model" Failed? Implications of the Asian Economic'. *Washington Quarterly 21*(3): 25.

Lin, J. Y. (1995). 'The Needham Puzzle: Why the Industrial Revolution did not originate in China'. *Economic Development & Cultural Change 43*(2): 269.

McGregor, J. (2010). 'China's Drive for "Indigenous Innovation": A Web of Industrial Policies'. *Global Regulatory Cooperation Project*. Washington, DC, US Chamber of Commerce.

MacIntyre, A. J. (2003). *The Power of Institutions: Political Architecture and Governance*. Ithaca, Cornell University Press.

McVey, R. T. (1992). 'The Materialization of the Southeast Asian Entrepreneur'. In R. T. McVey, Ed., *Southeast Asian Capitalists*: 7–33. Ithaca, Cornell University.

Malesky, E. J. (2008). 'Straight Ahead on Red: How Foreign Direct Investment Empowers Subnational Leaders'. *Journal of Politics 70*(1): 97–119.

Markovits, C. (2000). *The Global World of Indian Merchants, 1750–1947*. New York, Cambridge University Press.

Maurer, B. (2005). *Mutual Life, Limited: Islamic Banking, Alternative Currencies, Lateral Reason*. Princeton, Princeton University Press.

MKE (2002). 'SOE Reform in Vietnam: Background Paper'. Retrieved 29 July 2013 from <http://s3.amazonaws.com/zanran_storage/www.mekongeconomics.com/ContentPages/43471220.pdf>

Needham, J. (1969). *The Grand Titration: Science and Society in East and West*. London, Allen & Unwin.

Noble, G. W. (1998). *Collective Action in East Asia*. Ithaca, Cornell University Press.

Park, S. W. (1999). 'Colonial Industrial Growth and the Emergence of the Korean Working Class'. In G. W. Shin and M. E. Robinson, Eds., *Colonial Modernity in Korea*. Cambridge, Harvard University Press.

Peattie, M. R. and R. H. Myers (1984). *The Japanese Colonial Empire, 1895–1945*. Princeton, Princeton University Press.

Pempel, T. J. (1999). 'The Enticement of Corporatism: Appeals of the "Japanese Model" in Developing Asia'. In D. L. McNamara, Ed., *Corporatism and Korean Capitalism*: 26–53. New York, Routledge.

Pepinsky, T. B. (2008). 'Capital Mobility and Coalitional Politics: Authoritarian Regimes and Economic Adjustment in Southeast Asia'. *World Politics 60*(3): 438–474.

Post, P. and E. Touwen-Bouwsma (1997). *Japan, Indonesia, and the War: Myths and Realities*. Leiden, KITLV.

Pyle, K. B. (1974). 'Advantages of Followership: German Economics and Japanese Bureaucrats, 1890–1925'. *Journal of Japanese Studies 1*(1): 127–164.

Redding, S. G. (1990). *The Spirit of Chinese Capitalism*. New York, de Gruyter.

—— (1996). 'Societal Transformation and the Contribution of Authority Relations and Cooperation Norms in Overseas Chinese Business'. In W. M. Tu, Ed., *Confucian Traditions in East Asian Modernity*: 310–327. Cambridge, Harvard University Press.

Reid, A. (1990). 'An "Age of Commerce" in Southeast Asian History'. *Modern Asian Studies 24*(1): 1–30.

—— (2001). 'Southeast Asian Population History and the Colonial Impact'. In C. Liu, Ed., *Asian Population History*: 45–62. New York, Oxford University Press.

Ritchie, B. K. (2001). 'Innovation Systems, Collective Dilemmas, and the Formation of Technical Intellectual Capital in Malaysia, Singapore, and Thailand'. *International Journal of Business and Society 2*(2): 21–48.

—— (2009). 'Economic Upgrading in a State-Coordinated, Liberal Market Economy'. *Asia Pacific Journal of Management* 26(3): 435–457.

Ross, M. L. (2001). *Timber Booms and Institutional Breakdown in Southeast Asia*. New York, Cambridge University Press.

Rozman, G. (1991). 'The East Asian Region in Comparative Perspective'. In G. Rozman, Ed., *The East Asian Region: Confucian Heritage and Its Modern Adaptation*: 3–42. Princeton, Princeton University Press.

Rudner, D. W. (1994). *Caste and Capitalism in Colonial India: The Nattukottai Chettiars*. Berkeley, University of California Press.

Rudolph, J. (1998). *Reconstructing Identities: A Social History of the Babas in Singapore*. Brookfield, Ashgate.

Ruskola, T. (2000). 'Conceptualizing Corporations and Kinship: Comparative Law and Development Theory in a Chinese Perspective'. *Stanford Law Review* 52(6): 1599–1729.

Salmon, C. (1981). 'The Contribution of the Chinese to the Development of Southeast Asia: A New Appraisal' *Journal of Southeast Asian Studies* 12(1): 260–275.

Sandhu, K. S. (1969). *Indians in Malaya*. London, Cambridge University Press.

—— and A. Mani (1993). *Indian Communities in Southeast Asia*. Singapore, Times Academic Press and Institute of Southeast Asian Studies.

Searle, P. (1999). *The Riddle of Malaysian Capitalism: Rent-Seekers or Real Capitalists?* Honolulu, Asian Studies Association of Australia/Allen & Unwin/University of Hawai'i Press.

Shih, V. C. (2008). *Factions and Finance in China: Elite Conflict and Inflation*. New York, Cambridge University Press.

Skinner, G. W. (1957). *Chinese Society in Thailand*. Ithaca, Cornell University Press.

Stark, D. (2009). *The Sense of Dissonance: Accounts of Worth in Economic Life*. Princeton, Princeton University Press.

Steier, L. P. (2009). 'Familial Capitalism in Global Institutional Contexts: Implications for Corporate Governance and Entrepreneurship in East Asia'. *Asia Pacific Journal of Management* 26(3): 513–535.

Studwell, J. (2007). *Asian Godfathers: Money and Power in Hong Kong and Southeast Asia*. New York, Atlantic Monthly Press.

Subrahmanyam, S. (1990). *The Political Economy of Commerce: Southern India, 1500–1650*. New York, Cambridge University Press.

Swedberg, R. (2007). *Principles of Economic Sociology*. Princeton, Princeton University Press.

Tagliacozzo, E. and W. C. Chang (2011). *Chinese Circulations: Capital, Commodities, and Networks in Southeast Asia*. Durham, Duke University Press.

Tang, A. M. (1979). 'China's Agricultural Legacy'. *Economic Development and Cultural Change* 28(1): 1–22.

Taube, M. (2002). 'Stability in Instability: China's TVEs and the Evolution of Property Rights'. *ASIEN 84*: S.59–66.

Timberg, T. A. (1978). *The Marwaris, from Traders to Industrialists*. New Delhi, Vikas.

Tipton, F. B. (2009). 'Southeast Asian Capitalism: History, Institutions, States, and Firms'. *Asia Pacific Journal of Management* 26(3): 401–434.

Trocki, C. A. (2004). 'The Internationalization of Chinese Revenue Farming Networks'. In N. Cooke and T. Li, Eds., *Water Frontier: Commerce and the Chinese in the Lower Mekong Region, 1750–1880*: 159–174. Lanham, Rowman & Littlefield.

—— (2009). 'Chinese Revenue Farms and Borders in Southeast Asia'. *Modern Asian Studies* 43(01): 335–362.

Tu, W.-M. (1996). *Confucian Traditions in East Asian Modernity*. Cambridge, Harvard University Press.

Vogel, E. F. (2011a). *Deng Xiaoping and the Transformation of China*. Cambridge, Belknap Press of Harvard University Press.

—— (2011b). 'Nation Rebuilders: Mustafa Kemal Atatürk, Lee Kuan Yew, Deng Xiaoping, and Park Chung Hee'. In P. M. Kim and E. F. Vogel, Eds., *The Park Chung Hee Era*: 513–541. Cambridge, Harvard University Press.

Walter, C. E. and F. J. T. Howie (2011). *Red Capitalism: The Fragile Financial Foundation of China's Extraordinary Rise*. Singapore, Wiley & Sons.

Wan, E. L. (2001). 'Straits-Born Chinese: The Peranakan Story'. Retrieved 10 June 2012 from <http://www.thingsasian.com/stories-photos/1742>.

Wank, D. L. (1999). *Commodifying Communism: Business, Trust, and Politics in a Chinese City*. New York, Cambridge University Press.

Welsh, B. (2002). 'Lessons from Southeast Asia: Growth, Equity and Vulnerability'. In E. Huber, Ed., *Models of Capitalism: Lessons for Latin America*: 237–276. University Park, Pennsylvania State University Press.

Wilkinson, B. (1996). 'Culture, Institutions and Business in East Asia'. *Organization Studies* 17(3): 421.

Wingfield, T. (2002). 'Democratization and Economic Crisis in Thailand: Political Business and the Changing Dynamic of the Thai State'. In E. T. Gomez, Ed., *Political Business in East Asia*: 250–300. New York, Routledge.

Wong, J. (1996). 'Promoting Confucianism for Socio-economic Development: The Singapore Experience'. In W. M. Tu, Ed., *Confucian Traditions in East Asian Modernity*: 277–294. Cambridge, Harvard University Press.

Yadav, S. (2010). 'Jobs: The Great Quota Race'. Retrieved 9 June 2012 from <http://indiatoday.intoday.in/story/Jobs:+The+great+quota+race/1/97382.html>.

Yoshino, M. Y. and A. D. Chandler (1968). *Japan's Managerial System*. Cambridge, MIT Press.

Zhao, G. (1986). *Man and Land in Chinese History*. Stanford, Stanford University Press.

Zheng, Y. and Abrami, R. (2011). 'The New Face of Chinese Industrial Policy: Making Sense of Anti-Dumping Cases in the Petrochemical and Steel Industries'. *Journal of East Asian Studies* 11(3): 373–406.

# CHAPTER 27

# BEYOND PRODUCTION

## *Changing Dynamics of Asian Business Groups*

### SOLEE I. SHIN AND GARY G. HAMILTON

## INTRODUCTION

LET's start with a theoretical question. Do capitalist economies converge over time? The question, of course, needs further specification, which we will supply shortly, but, as a first cut, we can say that there are a number of theories that would argue for and a number that would argue against convergence.

Among those that would argue for convergence are several associated with the discipline of economics. Most economic theories positing rational decision-making in pursuit of maximum efficiency and profits would be inclined to predict that firms facing similar problems would adopt similar optimal strategies for maximizing profit and efficiency. These theories would further predict that as firms from different economies become more integrated in the global economy, the likelihood of firms in the same industries and of economies with similar manufacturing and service profiles becoming more alike would increase.

This economic theory, applied to business groups, is particularly applicable here. Most influential economic theories of business groups hypothesize that business groups are a necessary feature of economies in the early stages of industrialization, because market failures of one kind or another are ubiquitous in developing economies (Khanna and Yafeh 2007). Creating a network of interlinked firms under some kind of common ownership or management system, which is the definition of a business group, is a rational solution to such market failures as inadequate financial institutions or lack of market information. Accordingly, these theories suggest that, as economies mature and such market failures are corrected, then business groups should, in theory, diminish in importance.

In contrast to theories favouring convergence, a number would argue against convergence. These theories are mostly associated with the disciplines of sociology and political science, in particular with the embeddedness approach (Granovetter 1985) and with institutional theories of capitalism, such as business systems (Whitley 1992, 1999; Morgan and Whitley 2012), varieties of capitalism (Hall and Soskice 2001), and developmental-state theories (Woo-Cumings 1999). These argue that economic activities, specifically those associated with capitalism, are shaped by other institutional spheres, such as the state and its regulatory framework, or the family and patterns of hereditary succession. They suggest that economic changes over time are 'path-dependent', meaning that developmental trajectories are directly influenced by social and political configurations in the initial stages of industrialization. These configurations become 'institutionalized', so ingrained in continuing economic activities that they influence the dynamics of development. Accordingly, these theories would not only predict no capitalist convergence, but might even suggest that divergence among economies might occur.

Although these theories seem far apart, even contradictory, we should recognize from the outset that many of the differences arise more from disciplinary differences than from the actual substance of the cases being examined. We can see the disciplinary divide very clearly: economists argue that many economic factors that are intrinsic to economic activities themselves lead firms and economies, as they develop and become more globally interconnected, to become more similar over time. Sociologists and political scientists equally argue that there are many social and political factors quite separate from the economy that still give firms and economies distinctive characteristics and that turn out to be advantageous or disadvantageous for continuing economic development. Both sets of disciplinary approaches make valid and significant contributions, as this chapter shows, but the problem with the disciplinary divide is exactly that it is a divide, that leaves a gap where a theory of economic change ought to be.

In this chapter, we will begin working on the gap by analysing economic changes in the three Asian economies in which post-World War II Asian industrialization was most prominent: Japan, South Korea, and Taiwan. The latter two, together with Hong Kong and Singapore, comprised the so-called Little Dragons. With Japan, they were the first Asian economies to rapidly industrialize after World War II. The Japanese economy, of course, reindustrialized after being largely destroyed during the war, but the others started from scratch. From poor, barely developed countries, they rapidly industrialized in the course of a generation. In this chapter, we will concentrate on Japan, South Korea, and Taiwan, largely because they represent national economies instead of city-state economies, which have very different and largely non-industrial trajectories of change.

The empirical focal points of this chapter are changes that have occurred in each of the domestic economies in the past two decades. These economies have gone from being primarily insulated manufacturing economies exhibiting distinctive organizational characteristics to multi-sectored economies deeply integrated in regional and global economies. The service and in particular the retail sectors of these economies are of particular concern. With continuing economic crises around the world and falling demand for consumer products in the USA and Europe, East Asian firms, as well as governments, have been trying to increase consumption in their local markets. This chapter primarily focuses on how these economies have gone through major economic events—recessions, depressions, and global economic crises—and have refocused on domestic consumer markets in Asia. Examining this issue tells us much about the ways firms and business groups integrate and structure the economies of which they are so much a part.

The first two sections of this chapter provide the background. In the first section, we briefly describe the organization of these economies in the period up to the Plaza Accord, from 1965 to 1985. This is the period when each economy developed its own distinctive domestic approach to export-oriented industrialization. In the second section, we describe the confluence of events that occurred roughly from 1985 through the Asian Financial Crisis in 1997, and the effects of these events on the three economies. In this period, firms in these economies began to internationalize aggressively through foreign direct investments (FDI). The ensuing patterns of development led to different economic outcomes.

In the third section and main body of the chapter, we document the changes in domestic consumer markets in East Asia occurring after the Asian Financial Crisis in 1997, the dot.com bust in 2000–2001, 9/11 disaster in 2001, and the global financial crisis beginning in 2007. This series of events have collectively and substantially changed the global economy. Over this period, which runs up to the present, the three economies have been deeply integrated in the Asian regional economy, which is now centred on China, and in the global economy, in which the Asian region plays an ever more prominent role. Despite becoming increasingly integrated in and dependent on regional and global economies, leading firms in these three national economies have also turned importantly towards their own consumer markets. Their strategies in doing so, however, remain distinct and quite differently organized. In this section, we pay special attention to domestic consumption and the development of local retailing. Then, in the final section, we reiterate the theoretical approach running through our chapter, an approach that offers a framework to answer the questions about global convergence with which we began.

# Building Domestic Manufacturing Networks for Export-Led Industrialization, 1965–1985

In a 1988 article, Hamilton and Biggart described organizational differences among the Japanese, Korean, and Taiwanese economies. This analysis, as well as their subsequent work on these three economies (Orrù, Biggart, and Hamilton 1997; Feenstra and Hamilton 2006), centres on the organizational configuration of business groups in relation to the overall economy, especially in the earliest period from 1965 to 1985. Although Japan had, during this period, an extremely large domestic economy, the rapid growth experienced by all three economies, particularly South Korea and Taiwan, is largely explained by the huge (relative to domestic consumption) production of consumer goods manufactured for export. The explicit theme of their analysis is that each of the three economies developed an integrated and distinctive organizational approach to export-led industrialization and that this organizational approach was directly related to underlying social institutions.

In Japan, a small number of large horizontal *keiretsu* dominated the manufacturing sectors of the economy (Lincoln and Gerlach 2004). *Keiretsu* are large business groups, some of which grew out of pre-World War II *zaibatsu* (e.g. Mitsui and Mitsubishi), while others began after the war and are a product of Japan's post-1950s industrialization (e.g. Sanwa and Fuyo). The characteristic features of these horizontal *keiretsu* are that they are not family-owned groups and are not centrally managed, both of which char-acterize Taiwanese and South Korean business groups. Instead, Japanese *keiretsu* (e.g. Mitsubishi) represent communitarian alliances of large clusters of cross-shareholding firms that are themselves vertically integrated in their respective industrial sector (Orrù, Biggart, and Hamilton 1997, Anchordoguy 2005). According to the best estimate made in the early 1980s (Dodwell 1984), the sixteen largest vertical and horizontal *keiretsu* directly owned and controlled over 1,000 firms and nearly 3 million workers and indi-rectly controlled many thousands more firms through their informal contracting systems. These firms and workers dominated all the leading manufacturing sectors sup-plying products for Japan's export-oriented economy.

In South Korea, by the 1980s, the largest business groups, called *chaebol*, dominated Korea's export-oriented economy in an even more pronounced way than Japan's busi-ness groups. In 1985, the top five *chaebol* controlled substantially more than 50 per cent of South Korea's exports, 45 per cent of all manufacturing sales in the country, and 66 per cent of all construction projects (Feenstra and Hamilton 2006: 269). Most of the *chaebol* are family-owned business groups led by patriarchal heads who manage the group's operation through controlling firm budgets and personnel. Family members (sons, daughters, and in-laws) and loyal friends (e.g. classmates) usually manage key firms in the group, and workers are often drawn from the owner's home region. In 1985, the top four *chaebol* (Hyundai, Samsung, Lucky Goldstar, and Daewoo) were all verti-cally integrated around the principal products being produced for export. Smaller *chae-bol* specialized in service and upstream industries, such as chemicals, construction, and food production.

Unlike Japan and South Korea, in Taiwan, most large family-owned business groups specialized in production of upstream products (e.g. plastics and chemicals) and services (e.g. shipping, insurance) and did not engage directly in manufacturing for export. In 1985, small and medium-sized firms manufactured the majority of all exports. The owners of these firms organized production networks that effectively and efficiently produced a vast array of goods, and their production networks depended on large upstream firms to supply the necessary inputs. Some of these upstream firms were state-owned (e.g. China Steel) and others privately owned (e.g. Formosa Plastics). The entire spectrum of privately owned firms was overwhelmingly family owned and centrally managed by a key individual (*laoban*) responsible for making key decisions.

Despite substantial differences among the three economies, in the early period they all shared several key characteristics. First, the export sector in each economy was deeply integrated in the larger domestic economy, and as industrialization progressed the entire economy (especially in Taiwan and South Korea) became increasingly organized around intermediary demand generated by what Gereffi (1994) calls the 'big buyers' (Hamilton, Petrovic, and Senauer 2011: 181–210). The big buyers arose as a consequence of the transformation of retailing in the USA and Europe, a transformation based on the development of shopping centres, malls, and chain stores (Feenstra and Hamilton 2006; Hamilton, Petrovic, and Senauer 2011). The evolving synergy between big buyers and Asian manufacturers was the key factor driving the process of industrialization in East Asia. Second, each economy, going from one success to another, developed an increasingly complex and increasingly distinctive economic system that integrated all aspects of producing goods for export. Third, in response to rising but differentiated orders from Western buyers, the evolving system of production in each country became increasingly attuned to the manufacture of a particular assortment of goods (Feenstra and Hamilton 2006: 212–298).

## THE PLAZA ACCORD, LEAN RETAILING, AND CRISES IN NATIONAL ECONOMIES, 1985–2001

The distinctive Asian business systems that were in the process of emerging before 1985 began to come apart after that date. There are two main reasons for this.

First, in 1985, the Reagan administration persuaded the governments of Japan, South Korea, and Taiwan to revalue their respective currencies. The resulting agreement, signed in the Plaza Hotel in New York City, is known as the Plaza Accord. In the course of a year, the three currencies increased in value relative to the US dollar by up to 40 per cent. Suddenly, successful people and firms in these countries became richer, property and company assets mushroomed, stock markets boomed, and people accustomed to making products quickly became consumers of all types of goods and services. The impression of success, however, was short-lived. Almost immediately after the Plaza Accord was signed, Asian manufacturers began to feel the pinch: labour costs and the price of inputs went up. More money could be made from property and stock-market speculation than from making products for export.

Second, throughout the 1980s, large retailers and brand-name merchandisers began to engage in what Abernathy et al. (1999) call 'lean retailing'. Lean retailing refers to the transformation of retailing that resulted from the adoption of industry-wide standards for computerized inventory systems. During the 1970s, supermarkets and food manufacturers developed Uniform Product Codes, barcodes, and point-of-sales scanning technology. In 1974, the first such item, a pack of Wrigley's gum, was scanned in a Columbus, Ohio, grocery store. By the early 1980s, Wal-Mart had put together the lean retailing package—bar codes on all products, point-of-sales scanning, computerized inventory system, just-in-time distribution, and a standardized language across all firms—and aggressively required all their suppliers to adopt lean-retailing techniques. K-Mart and other retailers followed suit. Fuelled by fierce competition among retailers and merchandisers, lean retailing soon diffused across all consumer-oriented markets and all products in those markets, and invigorated changes that were already under way in global logistics. By the early 1990s, containerized shipping by both land and sea and just-in-time deliveries had become standard practice for the retail industry worldwide.

Lean retailing forged a new relationship between retailers and manufacturers (Hamilton, Petrovic, and Senauer, 2011). Retailers organized supply chains and practised supply-chain management, and manufacturers became organizational extensions of retailers. Retailers and factory-less brand-name merchandisers gained leverage over manufacturers and, in competition with other retailers, could determine precise price points for their products by following anticipated demand for a product backward to the site of manufacturing. As manufacturers came under intense pressure to bow to the demands of retailers, more and more production went to contract manufacturers, and increasingly those contract manufacturers were in Asia.

The Plaza Accord and lean retailing combined to cause a comprehensive restructuring of East Asian economies. In East Asia, firms and business groups had to decide how to rearrange their production to meet the price points and manufacturing requirements of Western retailers, who by the 1990s had started to internationalize across Europe and North America.

In the decade after the Plaza Accord, once well-established industries in Japan, South Korea, and Taiwan had come apart as the key manufacturing firms in those countries began to relocate to other parts of Asia and beyond. Japanese automobile firms moved some of their factories to the USA and South East Asia. Some of Japan's leading consumer-electronics manufacturers moved to Malaysia, and a large assortment of Japanese firms started factories in Thailand. Japan's popular press filled with stories about the hollowing-out of the Japanese economy. In 1990, the Japanese stock and property markets collapsed, and continued to fall in an oscillating fashion for the next two decades, finally hitting their lowest point in twenty-seven years during the 2009 global financial crisis. By the mid-1990s, Japan's recession had become a depression, forming an economic trough that has lasted over twenty years and from which it has yet to fully emerge.

South Korean and Taiwanese stock and property markets also fell sharply, but neither economy collapsed. As in Japan, entire industries were disbanded locally and relocated, sometimes unsuccessfully, to other countries. South Korean light industries (e.g. textile, garments, footwear) moved mainly to South East Asia and Latin America. After some manufacturers experimented in South East Asia, Taiwanese light industries (e.g. footwear, garments, bicycles) ended up moving their factories to mainland China. For example, before 1985, footwear was the largest single export from both South Korea and

Taiwan. In the peak year, 1987, the combined export of shoes from the two countries accounted for over 50 per cent of all footwear imported into the USA, but by 1992 their combined total of footwear exports to the USA was under 5 per cent of the total: the footwear industry had left both countries (Hamilton 2006: 175–177). The same outcome occurred across all the light industries. The mainstay industries before the Plaza Accord were now collapsing and in disarray.

What saved these two economies and allowed them to grow further was the sudden worldwide expansion in demand for consumer electronics, especially personal computers. The rapid growth in manufacturing high-technology products began in the early 1980s, with Japanese firms being prominent players. But like the firms along Route 128 that Saxenian (1994) analysed, Japanese high-technology companies placed their bets on making work-stations and mainframes operating on proprietary software. Out of a crowded field of competitors in the late 1980s came, in the early 1990s, the nearly universal success of personal computers operating on a standardized hardware based on the Intel core processor, and standardized software based on the Microsoft operating system, an alliance often referred to as Wintel. This combination promoted standardization of component parts throughout high-technology industries, which in turn fuelled the rapid success of factory-less PC merchandisers, in particular Dell Computers and Gateway Computers, established respectively in 1984 and 1985. With the success of the Wintel architecture, Taiwanese firms quickly emerged as Asia's most prominent maker of PC components and peripherals, and by the mid-1990s they were the largest manufacturers of PCs, the majority of which were based on contract manufacturing. Losing out in a head-to-head competition with brand-name American computer-makers and distributors, Japanese firms instead supplied Taiwanese firms with some of the most sophisticated upstream component parts, such as monitors, flat-screen panels, and memory chips.

South Korean business groups took a different path. Rather than integrating themselves piecemeal into the flexible production networks steered by USA and European retailers and merchandisers, South Korean firms instead built on capital-intensive vertical integration existing within the top *chaebol*. These *chaebol* began self-conscious programmes to create self-branded products that could compete with Japanese brands in both consumer electronics and automobiles. In the late 1980s, Samsung, Hyundai, and LG (Lucky-Goldstar), South Korea's three largest *chaebol*, succeeded in creating brand-name recognition for their products through global advertising campaigns, constant product improvements, a domestic market sheltered from foreign competition, and building ties to global retailers. Also in competition with Japanese high-technology firms, all three of these *chaebol* invested heavily in hugely expensive state-of-the-art factories to build dedicated RAM memory chips, and largely succeeded in driving Japanese and USA competition out of the marketplace.

The successes experienced by the Taiwanese and South Korean economies during the 1990s, however, were relatively short lived, as successive shock waves rippled across East Asian economies. The first was the Asian Financial Crisis in 1997, which began in South East Asia in 1997 and moved across the rest of Asia in the following year. In the span of a year, over half of the top thirty and one of the top five *chaebol* either went bankrupt, were absorbed into another group, or otherwise ceased operation. Already in decline, Japan receded yet further as overseas investments lost value and overseas markets lost customers. Although Taiwan quickly devalued its currency against the US dollar, its economy continued to grow due to rising US demand for high-technology and consumer products, low bank debts, and the relatively stable political and economic environment that China provided for Taiwanese firms in the face of economic collapse throughout much of Asia (Hamilton 2006: 184–200).

As we come to the main section of our chapter, it is appropriate to return briefly to the questions we asked in the introduction. The Japanese, South Korean, and Taiwanese economies all industrialized in the period before the Asian Financial Crisis in 1997–1998, but they did not converge. Sharp differences divided the economies as a whole, as well as firms and business groups within the economies. In fact, by most measures (Feenstra and Hamilton 2006), the economies diverged as they successfully industrialized. Each moved along a different trajectory, a trajectory set in place by different economic organizations—different arrangements of firms and business groups and different social and political underpinning for those arrangements—that created systems of production operating in increasingly different ways.

# The New Crises and the New East Asian Economies, 1997–2012

The Asian Financial Crisis in 1997–1998 set the stage for the changes that would come in the next fifteen years. The economic shocks kept coming. Two years later, American and European stock markets fell abruptly with the collapse of what became known as the dot.com bubble. The high-technology boom stalled and the demand for personal computers dropped precipitously. The following year, the European and US economies entered mild recessions, further dampening demand. The global economy was shaken again in the wake of the 9/11 destruction of New York's World Trade Center in 2001. With the slump in global demand for all types of consumer products, the Taiwanese economy also retreated. Over five years, all Asian economies, except China, had entered into recessionary periods. Then, just over five years after this reassessment, in 2007, the Global Financial Crisis occurred, the Great Recession in the USA began, and the European Union entered its most serious crisis, pushing the euro-zone almost to the point of collapse. The question we now turn to is how firms and business groups in these three Asian economies reacted to these continuing shocks.

There are essentially two parts to this answer. The first, the reorganization of Asian production, is reasonably well known and discussed elsewhere in this handbook. We will simply summarize the production part of this answer by noting that the mainstay of Asia's export-oriented economies, the manufacture of consumer products, regionalized across the East Asian economies. The bulk of assembly factories that had been located in one of the three economies moved to mainland China. Included in this relocation were assembly factories for Taiwan's high-technology industries. This movement was accompanied by huge increases in FDI from these economies into China.

The second part of the answer—the re-entrenchment into the respective domestic economies—is less well known and is the focus of the remainder of our chapter. While a considerable portion of the production part of these economies moved to China and elsewhere, a set of favourable domestic factors in South Korea and Taiwan led businesses to look inward and focus on their domestic economies beyond production. The largest effort by far has been in expanding and formalizing retail operations. Although some retailers recognized the market potential of these domestic economies early on (Makro and Carrefour entered Taiwan in 1989 and Shinsegae started operating its hypermarket chain, E-mart, in 1993), after 1997 it became obvious to domestic and multinational firms alike that internal conditions in Asia were now ripe for large retail investments.

For the large *chaebol*, many of whom had been restructured, downsized, and split into sub-groups after 1997, domestic conditions provided opportunities to diversify operations beyond the already saturated production industries. Such diversifications were especially prominent among the newly formed *chaebol* sub-groups such as the Hyundai Department Store Group (a 1999 spin-off from Hyundai Group), Cheil Jedang and Shinsegae (launched in 1997 as spin-offs from Samsung Group), and GS (which split from LG group in 2005).

In Taiwan, although not as large scale a trend as among the Korean *chaebol*, a number of large Taiwanese business groups also started expanding into retail operations. Notable among them were the Ruentex Financial Group, which since 1996 has developed RT-Mart into one of the largest domestic hypermarket chains in Taiwan and mainland China; the Far Eastern Group, operating a number of department-store chains and the hypermarket chain *ai'mai* (Géant); and Uni-president, responsible for a number of retail operations including 7-Eleven, Carrefour, and Starbucks. However, most Taiwanese businesses did not deviate from their traditional sectors of export-oriented manufacturing, and for this reason, the development of Taiwan's domestic retail market has heavily depended on direct technology transfers through joint ventures with foreign multinationals. As a consequence, Taiwan's retail landscape is a segmented mix of large foreign retail chains often managed by Taiwanese business groups and small technologically underdeveloped family-run stores.

Finally, the Japanese retail landscape has also been experiencing dramatic changes since the mid-1990s. A number of retailers have risen to prominence, especially in the convenience-store and speciality-retailing sectors. Initially, the structurally stagnant *keiretsu* did not participate in these changes. For the most part, until recently, the horizontal *keiretsu* groups seemed unsuccessful in overcoming the problems posed by their traditional emphasis on multi-layered distribution networks linked to large production networks. However, after a host of new retailers entered the marketplace to successfully revolutionize supply chains, some *keiretsu* member firms, notably the *sogo shosha* or generalized trading companies, have started, belatedly, to participate in this effort.

In response to slumping and unpredictable demand for consumer goods in the USA and Europe, and in response to rising demand for consumer goods and services in Asia, how did the large business groups in the three economies reposition themselves within their domestic economies? As one might predict from earlier trajectories of development, concrete responses varied by location. We find that where the large business groups in these three economies headed and how they coped with the crises depended on their previous position in the overall economy. We will discuss these concrete responses for each economy in turn.

# JAPAN: RESTRUCTURING
## *KEIRETSU*-CONTROLLED RETAILING

Although many have argued that the *keiretsu* structure served as the engine of growth for the post-World War II Japanese economy, a number of recent studies show that after the 1990s the *keiretsu* structure may actually have slowed the economy down and made it resistant to restructuring (e.g. Lincoln and Gerlach 2004). Earlier writers emphasized that affiliation with a horizontal *keiretsu* brought firms '(1) access to stable-financing; (2) insulation from market pressures; (3) risk reduction; (4) monitoring benefits and reduction of information asymmetries; and (5) mutual assistance' (McGuire and Dow 2009: 335). However, since 1992, many of these benefits may have turned into inefficiencies retarding change in the Japanese economy (Hoshi and Kashyap 2004; Lincoln and Gerlach 2004). In fact, two decades into the decline, bank-oriented *keiretsu* groupings are still struggling to pull themselves out of debt. In the retail sector, these *keiretsu* inefficiencies are obvious.

Before the 1980s, the horizontal *keiretsu* controlled Japan's retail markets, but were unable to maintain this after the 1990s. From the beginning of the twentieth century up to the 1970s, department store chains such as Mitsukoshi, Takashimaya, Isetan, and Matsuzakaya dominated the urban Japanese retail landscape. They were the first modern retailers in an otherwise traditional sector of small family-owned retail stores. Most of these department stores operated as part of *keiretsu* groupings. These often century-old stores, many of which started as kimono retailers, co-evolved with the traditional Japanese distribution system, and 'developed their own system of purchasing and trade relationships with suppliers and customers, and adapted them to handle new goods' (Tatsuki 1995). They emphasized display and spectacle, educated potential customers on trends and aesthetics, and triggered desires to consume (Hatsuda 1993). In this regard, department stores have been credited for creating and contributing to a new culture of consumption (Creighton 1991).

While the efforts in marketing and store operations were extensive, department stores showed clear limitations as a modern retail format. They operated under a manufacturer-driven system in which retailers did not have active control over the distribution channels. The stores instead established long-lasting relationships with suppliers and operated through a consignment system in which suppliers and whole-salers were responsible for much of the actual retail operation (Sternquist et al. 2000). Suppliers had control over almost every aspect of the retail operation, including every-thing from control of sales space and sales staff to merchandise pricing (Larke and Causton 2005).

Despite a limited capacity to modernize, department stores still dominated the high-end retail sector and remained profitable until the 1990s. In the heyday of luxury and conspicuous consumption, consumers stockpiled the most expensive items from department stores, and foreign and domestic luxury retailers alike channelled energy into marketing to the public. However, as the 'bubble era' came to an end in the early 1990s, consumption of luxury goods declined, and department stores found their sales dwindling.

Their narrow focus on marketing and limited capacity for innovation opened the way for other groups of retailers, mostly supermarkets and convenience stores, which were unaffiliated with the bank-centred *keiretsu* networks. These retailers provided an alter-native to the uniformly high prices in both department stores and the small traditional 'mom-and-pop' stores that dotted Japan's retail landscape. They started to introduce previously untried retail formats copied from the West, combined with innovative dis-tribution strategies devised to capture and flexibly react to consumer demand. As these new retailers became successful, department stores and mom-and-pop stores began to decline.

As early as the 1930s, large manufacturers started to develop vertical-distribution *keiretsu* to ensure the widespread distribution of their products. Big manufactur-ers aligned with selected retailers, especially cosmetic shops and drugstores, to jointly organize 'a wholesale company [with existing wholesalers] and later appoint[ing] retail-ers as sole agents' (Tatsuki 1995: 74). The cosmetics company Shiseido and electron-ics company Matsushita are the best-known cases (Shimotani 1995). In the latter case, Matsushita built a distribution *keiretsu* by linking wholesalers and retailers to their network of manufacturing firms. 'Manufacturers ranked distributors hierarchically and, through incentives, encouraged exclusivity' (Shimotani 1995: 68). Manufacturers were thus able to avoid price competition and to control prices by emphasizing 'quality, technology and promotion' (Shimotani 1995: 68). Manufacturers also established a fran-chise system or direct sales channels, enabling them to exert even stricter controls over the market (Tatsuki 1995). The market integration strategy of the vertical-distribution *keiretsu*, though usually adopted by manufacturers of various speciality items, was consistent with the existing organizational structure of producer-driven distribution systems.

In the 1960s, however, large retailers (mostly supermarkets that sold an array of other goods as well) began to challenge department stores and producer-driven distribution networks for the first time. The largest of these retail chains (Daiei, Ito-Yokado, and Aeon/Jusco) appeared during this time. Daiei was the first of the three to aggressively cut costs and challenge the existing manufacturer-driven distribution system; the others

soon followed suit. All three companies had their roots in retailing as general merchandisers. Although some were involved in non-related sectors such as food processing
and finance, the majority of their profits derived, and continue to derive, from retailing (Dodwell 2001). Because they remained relatively independent of large manufacturers and were not affiliated with the existing distribution *keiretsu*, these supermarket
chains had sufficient autonomy to win control of their supply chains and pricing, and as
a consequence were able to develop their own form of distribution *keiretsu*. As shown in
Table 27.1, these large supermarket chains and associated networks became the highest
grossing retail format in Japan.

As the Japanese economy dipped into recession, the cost-cutting supermarket chains
gained at the expense of the department stores. In the last two decades, the same chains
further strengthened their hold on the Japanese retail sector by expanding and greatly
improving the convenience-store format. These convenience stores have provided by
far the most innovative recent changes in the Japanese retail market. When they first
appeared in the 1970s they were 'not competitors of superstores, but rather an alternative
means of expansion by superstore companies' (Bernstein 1997: 507). In 1973, Ito-Yokado
obtained a licence to operate 7-Eleven stores; Daiei established Lawson Daiei as a subsidiary in 1975; Uny imported Circle K in 1979, and Aeon and Saison started operations
of Ministop and FamilyMart in 1980.

Although convenience stores date from the 1970s, they expanded quickly and widely
only in the last two decades. The reason for this successful recent expansion is their
adoption of lean-retailing techniques, combining logistics and supply-chain management with state-of-the-art technology to manage everything from sales data to inventory. They developed joint distribution centres, drastically reduced channel length,
used bar-coding and point-of-sales scanning, just-in-time inventory management, and
standardized EDI (electronic data interchange) (Maruyama 2000). Convenience-store
retailers, such as 7-Eleven, extensively monitored demand and merchandised widely,
all of which led them to respond to consumer desires flexibly and rapidly. 'By the
mid-1990s, Seven-Eleven Japan was annually replacing between one-half and two-thirds
of the 6,000 products that it recommended to its stores' (Bernstein 1997: 516). Moreover,
7-Eleven also developed an array of own-label products that became huge successes.
As a consequence of their aggressive promotion of modern retailing techniques, these
now-large retail chains and their associated networks of firms are widely diversified
across Japan's retail landscape.

Recognizing their miscalculation, the large horizontal *keiretsu* have started to enter
the domestic consumer market, usually through the activities of their trading companies (*sogo shosha*). For example, in 1999 Itochu established ownership of FamilyMart,
and shortly thereafter Mitsubishi became the main shareholder of Lawson. These trading companies have also become shareholders of multiple previously unrelated retail
operations. Itochu has purchased shares in Seven-Eleven, Uny, and Millenium Retailing,
among others; Mitsubishi became the leading shareholder for Life Corporation, and
also owns shares in convenience-store retailers am/pm and Seicomart. In another example, Marubeni, a member of Fuyo group, took a significant share of Maruetsu and Daiei.

Table 27.1 The ten largest Japanese retailers ranked by sales (billion)

| Rank | 1960 | | 1972 | | 1980 | | 1993 | | 1999 | |
|---|---|---|---|---|---|---|---|---|---|---|
| | Company | Sales | C | S | C | S | C | S | C | S |
| 1 | Mitsukoshi | 45 | Daiei | 305 | Daiei | 1134 | Daiei | 2073 | Daiei | 2205 |
| 2 | Daimaru | 45 | Mitsukoshi | 292 | Ito-yokado | 688 | Ito-yokado | 1536 | Ito-yokado | 1509 |
| 3 | Takashimaya | 39 | Daimaru | 213 | Seiyu | 599 | Jusco | 1061 | Jusco | 1422 |
| 4 | Matsuzakaya | 37 | Takashimaya | 199 | Jusco | 554 | Seiyu | 1050 | Mycal | 1081 |
| 5 | Toyoko | 30 | Seiyu | 167 | Mitsukoshi | 546 | Nichii | 822 | Takashimaya | 1021 |
| 6 | Isetan | 23 | Seibu | 155 | Michii | 455 | Mitsukoshi | 801 | Seiyu | 875 |
| 7 | Hankyu | 21 | Jusco | 155 | Daimaru | 421 | Takashimaya | 724 | Uny | 774 |
| 8 | Seibu | 19 | Matsuzakaya | 149 | Takashimaya | 415 | Seibu | 681 | Mitsukoshi | 676 |
| 9 | Sogo | 15 | Nichii | 144 | Seibu | 375 | Uny | 577 | Seibu | 589 |
| 10 | Matsuya | 12 | Uny | 126 | Uny | 126 | Daimaru | 543 | Marui | 481 |

*Source:* Bernstein 1997; Nikkei Ryutsu Shimbun 2000.

After Daiei filed for bankruptcy, Marubeni took steps to become the controlling owners in 2006.

More notably, the *sogo shosha* have recently expanded into the distribution sector, most notably in the wholesaling of food (Larke and Davies 2007). In 1994, Marubeni started participating in Daiei's food-sourcing activities from China, and more recently teamed up with Aeon for joint distribution and purchasing. Other *sogo shosha*, including Mitsubishi, Itochu, and Mitsui, all established themselves in the ranks of the largest food wholesalers in Japan by the mid-2000s. Larke and Davies (2007) argue that these recent activities of the *sogo shosha* resulted in renewed organization of Japanese supply chains, linking their traditional ability in international procurement directly to internal sourcing within the domestic market. They have done this through heavily networking and collaborating with new companies that developed independently from the *keiretsu* structure, which initially challenged their dominance in retail.

# Taiwan: Retail Market Development through Multinational Expansion

For the most part, Taiwanese businesses, both large groups and SMEs, have not departed from their traditional focus on manufacturing. When Taiwan's manufacturers faced challenges of currency appreciation and rising labour costs in the late 1980s, many started relocating overseas, the majority to export-processing zones in southern China. Formerly, products made by these firms had entered Taiwan's local consumer markets, often illegally, through Taiwan's informal markets, mainly night markets and street stalls. After these factories moved to China, these low-cost and often pirated consumer goods were no longer so available.

This void in local markets was filled with a new wave of retailers. In 1986, the Taiwanese government deregulated the domestic retail sector in 1986, leading to the entry of a number of multinational retailers into the Taiwan market and the crowding-out of large department stores, along with traditional wet-food markets, mom-and-pops, and a small number of government and military-introduced supermarkets (provisional or PX stores) (Trappey and Lei 1997). One feature of the government's 1986 deregulation was 'the policy of limiting foreign investment in the service industry' to less than 50 per cent (Hitoshi 2003: 35). At the time, the largest multinational retailers, almost all European-owned, were starting to look beyond their already saturated domestic markets for expansion. Simultaneously, several large Taiwanese business groups were looking to diversify their operations beyond upstream manufacturing. At this opportune moment, multinational retailers and local business groups established a number of joint ventures that began rapidly to change retailing in the Taiwan market. This partnering proved beneficial for both sides: multinationals benefited from the local partner's insight into the domestic market, and local business groups benefited from the transfer of retail knowledge and technology, as well as from a vast assortment of already well-advertised brands that they sold elsewhere and that multinationals could now promote in Taiwan.

Local business groups had little experience in the rapidly changing organization that global retailing was then going through. They took up retail ventures as a vertical-integration strategy. As early as 1979, Uni-President group, the largest processed-food manufacturer in Taiwan, which had once struggled to gain control over its own distribution channels, solved its problems through entering a technology transfer agreement with Southland Corporation. This joint venture allowed Uni-President to establish 7-Eleven stores in Taiwan (Liu 1992). In a market with little competition, after a few years of trial and error, 7-Eleven saw tremendous growth and quickly positioned itself as the retail store posting the largest sales in Taiwan. In addition to managing stores, they also set up their own distribution centres as a way to bypass wholesalers, which controlled the distribution of consumer goods in most small retail stores throughout Taiwan. Uni-President group integrated their supply chains from manufacturing to distribution exceptionally early. However, soon afterwards, other manufacturers, such as Kuang Chuan group (FamilyMart and Hi-Life) and Taisun Group (FamilyMart), moved into the convenience-store sector in a similar manner (Chung 2008), quickly crowding the market.

As the first wave of retail joint ventures started making profit, a host of global hypermarket retailers also entered the Taiwanese market. Holland-based retail group Makro was the first to introduce the hypermarket format in 1989 through a tie-up with Holmsgreen Holdings. Soon afterwards, Carrefour entered as a joint venture with Uni-President Enterprise Corp. In 1993, French retailer Promodès teamed up with department-store retailer Far Eastern Group, and in 1997 Costco started a joint venture with the President Group. A number of local hypermarket chains started up, most notably Ruentex's RT-Mart in 1996. Although some hypermarket retailers like Makro and Tesco struggled to obtain satisfactory sales figures in the rapidly saturating market, most foreign retail chains, particularly Carrefour, saw solid growth. By 1993, only four years after entry, Carrefour's sales had already exceeded that of the largest department store group at the time, Pacific Sogo (Hitoshi 2003).

Since their introduction to the Taiwanese market, convenience-store and hypermarket retailers have combined innovative retail practices and strategic pricing with a large assortment of goods sourced through local and global channels, to aggressively expand and become integral parts of Taiwanese consumption. Hypermarket retailers have set up food-courts and various retail stores in the same complex in order to lure families hoping both to make a one-stop shopping trip and to entertain their children at the weekends. Convenience stores have opened on nearly every street corner in neighbourhoods and commercial districts (Taiwan has the highest convenience store-to-population density in the world!) to attract busy workers, students, and single women in need of 'quick bites', a few groceries, or assorted services, including cashing cheques, paying bills, mailing letters, and copying documents.

Some of the retailers behind these successful formats have more recently been work-ing to transfer their retail businesses into the larger Chinese market. The geographical and cultural proximity to the mainland has given an added advantage to such retailers as Sun Art Retail Group, a joint venture between Ruentex financial group and Auchan. Despite a later start than its competitors in 1998, the Sun Art Retail Group developed RT-Mart into China's largest hypermarket operator. The President Chain Store division of Uni-President group also started operating 7-Eleven stores in Shanghai, took part in several joint ventures to operate Starbucks and Mister Donut in Shanghai, and operates Coldstone Creamery as a wholly-owned venture.

Using lean-retailing techniques, large multinational retailers partnering with large Taiwanese business groups overcame the problems that had traditionally stymied Taiwan's retail sector. These global retailers set up centralized distribution channels and directly purchased from their local investment partners, who were often manufactur-ers already looking for more effective distribution strategies. Unlike Japan, where large retailers met with resistance from manufacturers and wholesalers, most local Taiwanese manufacturers did not have enough leverage to challenge the large foreign retail-ers trying to reverse the traditional power relationships embedded in supplier-driven channels. The multinationals also had the advantage of being able to utilize their already-established channels abroad to directly source Western products to their newly added outlets in Taiwan.

Successful retail modernization has also heightened the visibility of foreign branded products in the marketplace. The products that show up in the Taiwanese retail market often come through the same retail channels as Western-bound consumer goods. These goods are often manufactured in Taiwanese-owned factories. This high level of interna-tional connectivity among global retailers and Taiwanese manufacturers in China gives the Taiwanese consumer market a truly international flavour. By contrast, Japanese and Korean marketplaces are relatively insulated from Western-based retailers, and thus the products that show up in these markets often bear the names of various large and medium-sized domestic brand manufacturers, products that are actually manufactured overseas.

# Korea: Flexible Diversification of *Chaebol* and Retail Concentration

After the 1997 financial crisis, the Korean economy went through extensive restruc-turing. Half of the top thirty *chaebol* went bankrupt, and *chaebol* affiliates deemed 'non-viable' were liquidated. Pressured by the government, the largest *chaebols* also had to reform. The top groups reorganized through voluntary business-division swaps and were able to dispose of unprofitable and non-core businesses. This led to a number of *chaebol* spin-offs.

Of the top four *chaebol* in 1997, the Daewoo Group filed for bankruptcy in 1999, and the other three—Samsung, Hyundai, and LG—went through extensive reforms. The specific groupings of the new *chaebol* divisions changed over time, but many of the spin-off groups were still large enough after the restructuring to make it into the annual top-thirty *chaebol* list announced by the Fair Trade Commission a decade later. While the large groups of Hyundai Motors, Samsung, and LG mostly stayed in their concentrated core business lines in various manufacturing sectors, the newly formed groups have seen remarkable growths in the post-crisis years by looking beyond the traditional *chaebol* speciality of manufacturing. The most notable among the spin-offs are the Shinsegae, CJ, Hyundai Department Store, and GS groups. Lotte, a Korean-Japanese *chaebol* that managed to keep its group structure relatively intact through the crisis years, has also been successful in diversifying beyond their main business lines of food manufacturing, department-store, and hotel operations.

Modernizing the previously underdeveloped retail sector has been a new focus of these groups since the mid-1990s. Before that, with the exceptions of a small number of department stores, supermarkets, franchise food services, and convenience-store chains, the Korean retail sector had been largely inefficient and traditional. However, as the government announced plans to support development of the retail industry in 1993 by relaxing restrictions on store size and increasing the possible number of franchise locations, *chaebol* groups have sought ways to counter rising trade deficits and sluggish overseas sales.

The *chaebol* groups brought the most revolutionary changes—rapid concentration and modernization—into the food retailing sector. In 1993, Shinsegae opened Korea's first hypermarket, E-mart, introducing large-scale modern retailing. In the following year, Shinsegae launched a discounter, Price Club, through a technology tie-up with US retailer Costco. In 1998, Lotte started operating their hypermarket chain, Lotte Mart. These groups rapidly increased the number of hypermarket locations, drastically changing the market environment for food marketing and distribution.

The hypermarket sector became even more replete as the Korean government removed various restrictions on foreign retailers in 1996. Foreign retailers that used to participate in the Korean domestic market only indirectly through technological tie-ups began directly entering the market, either through acquisitions or through joint ventures with Korean companies: Makro, Carrefour, Wal-Mart, and Tesco entered the market between 1996 and 1998. Although a relatively new industry, the hypermarket sector's annual sales from 435 outlets nationwide reached almost 5 trillion *won* by the end of 2010.

The *chaebol* groups also started actively restructuring distribution channels and technologies. Starting with E-mart's first distribution centre in 1996, the top *chaebol* groups invested in establishing state-of-the-art distribution centres that not only functioned as points for efficient distribution (transfer, labelling, and sorting), but also played central roles of inventory control, stocking, and quality inspection. Some even added processing and production facilities for own-label products. Also, by directly working with suppliers and reducing their reliance on other regional and manufacturer-designated intermediaries, they reduced overall channel lengths, traditionally involving five to seven levels, to three to four levels.

E-mart, for example, operates five distribution centres nationwide (as of June 2012), and its newest and largest Yeoju facility processes 35,000 boxes of goods every hour and operates 1,400 trucks, supplying goods to ninety E-mart locations daily. Using EDI (Electronic Data Interchange), it coordinates with 1,020 supplier of dry food products and 660 suppliers of wet-food products. E-mart was the first in Korea to adopt a cold-chain system that automatically adjusts the storage temperature of food between 8° and 25°C throughout the supply chain. E-mart is also the developer of an EAN-14 container shipping code that, when combined with an automatic sorter, reduces time separating products by destination (Hanhwa Securities Research 2009). Altogether, these and other cutting-edge technologies helped cut costs by dramatically reducing out-of-stock rates (from 30% in 1996 to 5% by 1999), safety stock rates, and average store time (20 days in 1996 to 14.6 days in 1999). These measures also reduced the total number of personnel needed in labelling and quality-control processes by increasing automation.

Since 2000, the *chaebol* groups also started introducing various other retail formats, including non-store retailing (catalogue, TV, online, or mobile-commerce sales), consumer-food service, and category-killers. Using the same distribution networks established through hypermarket retailing, these groups started opening up smaller enterprise-class supermarkets (called Super-Supermarkets or SSM), chain-food retailers measuring between 1,000 and 3,000 square metres in neighbourhood corner locations and non-major commercial areas. They also expanded the range of own-label goods in hypermarkets and SSMs in the 2000s. In 2009, 22.6 per cent of E-mart's sales, 26 per cent of Homeplus's, and 19.2 per cent of LotteMart's derived from own-label sales (KOCA 2010). Although production of own-label goods began mainly to reduce costs and obtain higher profit-margins, *chaebol* groups are increasingly using it as a way to increase market power. Especially since the mid-2000s, instead of merely selling low-quality products sourced from SMEs, retailers are actively participating in the production processes of own-label products of various quality and price points, and using them to differentiate themselves from competitors in the market (*Hankook Ilbo* 2011).

In summary, *chaebol* expansion into retailing has led to a dramatic restructuring of the Korean consumer market since the financial crisis. The most dramatic change has been the rapid decline of traditional distributors, wholesalers, and marketplaces. During the single decade 2000–2010, traditional market sales halved, from approximately 40 trillion to 20 trillion *won* (*Hankyoreh* 2011), and the total number of traditional markets in Korea declined from 1,695 in 2003 to 1,517 in 2010 (*Hankyoreh* 2012).

*Chaebol* retailers also challenged the market power of manufacturers and brought changes to the distribution structure. Until the mid-1990s, retail-market intermediaries worked simply to push manufactured goods into consumer markets. By introducing lean-retailing techniques, the new *chaebol* retailers now guide production processes by sourcing own-label brands, often from SMEs, and by giving inputs to producers after monitoring consumer demand.

# CONCLUSION

Our survey of recent changes in domestic retailing in Japan, Taiwan, and South Korea helps to answer the questions posed at the beginning of this chapter. In the first place, as disciplinary theory from economics would suggest, all leading retail firms have converged in their adoption of lean-retailing techniques. These techniques greatly increase the efficiency and market leverage of retail firms and have transformed the nature of the global economy. More than ever before, retailing is the sector that drives the production of consumer goods worldwide.

Convergence in matters of technology and supply-chain management does not mean that firms and business groups, or economies for that matter, lose their distinctive characteristics. In each of the three cases, social and political factors remain important and decisive factors in how economic activities get organized. For example, the *chaebol*-led modernization of the retail market is based on the same organizational characteristics of the Korean economy that supported the rapid export-led development over the last half-century. These large *chaebol* dominate the entire retail structure. In this regard, *chaebol* control of retailing in South Korea contrasts sharply with the modest success that Japanese *keiretsu* have achieved in Japanese retailing. Firms in Japanese horizontal *keiretsu* have only loose ties with other firms in the same *keiretsu*. The horizontal *keiretsu* itself is without a clear central-authority structure. By contrast, the centralized-authority structure of the *chaebol* groups has enabled central planning of business lines, channeling of resources to new divisions, coordination between different subsidiaries and, hence, smooth large-scale diversification to previously underdeveloped industries. In Japan, independent firms have become the country's leading retailers.

A different set of factors is at play in Taiwan. Taiwanese business groups did not have the cross-sector capabilities of the vertically integrated Korean *chaebol*. However, the long history of Taiwanese business collaborations with Western retailers gave a few Taiwanese business groups with pre-existing ties to domestic retailing another advantage: the capacity to make supply-line deals with Western retailers. By entering into joint ventures with Western retailers and running and profiting from their firms in Taiwan, these Taiwanese-run Western firms, in a matter of a few years, have utterly changed Taiwan's retail landscape.

We can expect the dynamics of retail-market organization in the newly emerging economies to be likely to depend on the interplay between global economic trends and local patterns of organization and socio-political factors. China and India, the two largest emerging markets, would show variation in the role and significance that foreign multinational retailers play in retail expansion. China, being at the centre of global production networks of consumer goods, will see relative ease in coordination between multinational retailers' sourcing and distribution operations, with their already well-positioned manufacturing activities. For multinationals, competition against rapidly growing (and Chinese government-invested) local chains such as Lianhua and Nonggongshan is increasingly challenging, but opportunities for technological tie-ups or partial outsourcing in logistics and distribution are also plentiful, as seen in the examples of local supermarket chain Wu-Mei, which outsourced their distribution operations to a British multinational firm, Tibbett and Britten Logistics (Reardon and Gulati 2008).

By contrast, India, while having established a competitive advantage in the global market in IT and service-related operations, has been late to develop a manufacturing sector closely integrated into the structure of the global production economy as extensively as in China. The country's relatively underdeveloped supply-chain infrastructure has posed difficulties for global retailers from outsourcing products. Even with the gradual deregulation of the retail sector in progress since the mid-2000s, it is more likely that domestic retailers will be first to reorganize the retail market before successful large-scale penetration of global retailing into the Indian market. Many large domestic conglomerates have been actively entering the retail market, including Bharti enterprises, Mahindra group, Aditiya Birla group, and Tata group. Together, they are rapidly modernizing the still-traditional retail market.

The lesson to be learned from this chapter, then, is that the gap between disciplinary theories of capitalism is an artefact more of disciplines than of empirical fact. In the real world, local society and politics do create differences in how economies operate, and there is no reason to think that these differences will gradually disappear. In equal measure, however, regardless of how they are organized, in the global economy today, firms and business groups must be economically accountable, must compete successfully, must make money, or go out of business. Under these circumstances, standardization of techniques and diffusion of best practices must also occur. How these two trends combine—local social and political forces on one side, and global economic forces on the other—is a serious topic for future research.

# REFERENCES

Abernathy, F. H., J. T. Dunlop, J. H. Hammond, and D. Weil (1999). *A Stitch in Time: Lean Retailing and the Transformation of Manufacturing*. New York, Oxford University Press.

Anchordoguy, M. (2005). *Reprogramming Japan: The High-Tech Crisis Under Communitarian Capitalism*. Ithaca, Cornell University Press.

Bernstein, J. (1997). '7-Eleven in America and Japan'. In T. K. McCraw, Ed., *Creating Modern Capitalism*: 490–528. Cambridge, MA, Harvard University Press.

Chung, S.-L. (2008). 'Competitions and Characteristics among Taiwanese Higher-Rank Retailers'. *Ritsumeikan Business Journal* 2: 49–66.

Creighton, M. (1991). 'Maintaining Cultural Boundaries in Retailing'. *Modern Asian Studies* 25(4): 675–709.

Dodwell Marketing (1984, 2001). *Industrial Groupings in Japan*. Tokyo, Dodwell Marketing Consultants.

Feenstra, R. C. and G. G. Hamilton (2006). *Emergent Economies, Divergent Paths: Economic Organization and International Trade in South Korea and Taiwan*. Cambridge, Cambridge University Press.

Gereffi, G. (1994). 'The Organization of Buyer-Driven Global Commodity Chains: How US Retail Networks Shape Overseas Production Networks'. In G. Gereffi and M. Korzeniewicz, Eds., *Commodity Chains and Global Capitalism*: 95–122. Westport, Greenwood Press.

Granovetter, M. (1985). 'Economic Action and Social Structure: The Problem of Embeddedness'. *American Journal of Sociology* 91(3): 481–510.

Hall, P. A. and D. Soskice (2001). *Varieties of Capitalism: The Institutional Foundations of Comparative Advantage*. New York, Oxford University Press.

Hamilton. G. G. (2006). *Commerce and Capitalism in Chinese Societies*. London, Routledge.

—— and N. W. Biggart (1988). 'Market, Culture, and Authority: A Comparative Analysis of Management and Organization in the Far East', *American Journal of Sociology* 94 (Supplement): S52–S94.

—— M. Petrovic, and B. Senauer (2011). *The Market Makers: How Retailers Are Reshaping the Global Economy*. Oxford, Oxford University Press.

Hanhwa Securities Research (2009). *Industry Analysis: Distribution*. Retrieved 15 July 2012 from <http://www.koreastock.co.kr/research/main.html>.

Hankook Ilbo (2011). 'yu'tong insai't?: tae'hyŏngmat'? PB to'ip 10 nyŏn' ('Inside Distribution: 10 years of large retailer's PB products'), 3 March. Retrieved 17 July 2012 from <http://economy.hankooki.com/lpage/industry/201103/e2011030317075547670.htm>.

Hankyoreh (2011). '10 nyŏn sa'i jŏntongsijang maechul 'pant'omak'' ('Traditional market sales halve over last ten years'), 20 September. Retrieved 17 July 2012 from <http://m.hani.co.kr/arti/politics/politics_general/497097.html>.

—— (2012). 'j?ntongsijang 178 got sa'ra'jilttae SSM 632kot nŭlŏtta', ('While 178 traditional markets disappear, 632 SSMs added'), 25 January. Retrieved 17 July 2012 from <http://www.hani.co.kr/arti/economy/economy_general/516052.html>.

Hatsuda, T. (1993). *Hyakkaten no tanjo* ('The Birth of a Department Store'). Tokyo, Seisando.

Hitoshi, T. (2003). 'The Development of Foreign Retailing in Taiwan'. In J. Dawson, Ed., *The Internationalisation of Retailing in Asia*: 35–48. London, Routledge.

Hoshi, T. and A. Kashyap (2004). 'Japan's Financial Crisis and Economic Stagnation'. *Journal of Economic Perspectives* 18(1): 3–26.

Khanna, T. and Y. Yafeh (2007). 'Business Groups in Emerging Markets: Paragons or Parasites?' *Journal of Economic Literature* 45(June): 331–371.

KOCA (2010). *Yearbook of Retail Industry*. Seoul, Korea Chainstores Association.

Larke, R. and M. Causton (2005). *Japan: A Modern Retail Superpower*. Basingstoke, Palgrave Macmillan.

—— and K. Davies (2007). 'Recent Changes in the Japanese Wholesale System and the Importance of the Sogo Shosha'. *International Review of Retail, Distribution and Consumer Research* 17(4): 377–390.

Lincoln, J. and M. Gerlach (2004). *Japan's Network Economy: Structure, Persistence, and Change*. Cambridge, Cambridge University Press.

Liu, S.-S. (1992). '7-Eleven in Taiwan'. In N.-T. Wang, Ed., *Taiwan's Enterprises in Global Perspective*: 297–308. New York, M. E. Sharpe.

McGuire, J. and S. Dow (2009). 'Japanese Keiretsu: Past, Future, and Present'. *Asia Pacific Journal of Management* 26(2): 333–351.

Maruyama, M. (2000). 'Japanese Wholesale Distribution: Its Features and Future'. In M. Czinkota and M. Kotabe, Eds., *Japanese Distribution Strategy*: 19–32. London, Thomson.

Morgan, G. and R. Whitley, Eds. (2012). *Capitalisms and Capitalism in the Twenty-First Century*. Oxford, Oxford University Press.

Nikkei Ryutsu Shimbun (2000). *Ryutsu keizai no tebiki 2000* (2000 Handbook of the Economics of Distribution). Tokyo, Tokyo Keizai Shimbun.

Orrù, M., N. W. Biggart, and G. G. Hamilton (1997). *The Economic Organization of East Asian Capitalism*. Thousand Oaks, Sage.

Reardon, T. and A. Gulati (2008). *The Rise of Supermarkets and Their Development Implications: International Experience Relevant for India*, IFPRI Discussion Paper 00752, Washington, DC, International Food Policy Research Institute.

Saxenian, A. (1994). *Regional Advantage: Culture and Competition in Silicon Valley and Route 128*. Cambridge, MA, Harvard University Press.

Shimotani, M. (1995). 'The Formation of Distribution Keiretsu: The Case of Matsushita Electric'. In E. Abe and R. Fitzgerald, Eds., *The Origins of Japanese Industrial Power: Strategy, Institutions, and the Development of Organisational Capability*: 54–69. London, Routledge.

Sternquist, B., J. Chung, and T. Ogawa (2000). 'Japanese Department Stores: Does Size Matter in Supplier-Buyer Relationships?' In M. Czinkota and M. Kotabe, Eds., *Japanese Distribution Strategy*: 67–77. London, Thomson.

Tatsuki, M. (1995). 'The Rise of the Mass Market and Modern Retailers in Japan'. *Business History* 37(2): 70–88.

Trappey, C. and M. K. Lai (1997). 'Differences in Factors Attracting Consumers to Taiwan's Supermarkets and Traditional Wet Markets'. *Journal of Family and Economic Issues* 18(2): 211–224.

Whitley, R. (1992). *Business Systems in East Asia*. London, Sage.

—— (1999). *Divergent Capitalisms: The Social Structuring and Change of Business Systems*. New York, Oxford University Press.

Woo-Cumings, M. (1999). *The Developmental State*. Ithaca, Cornell University Press.

# CHAPTER 28

# CHANGE AND CONTINUITY IN EAST ASIAN BUSINESS SYSTEMS

RICHARD WHITLEY

## INTRODUCTION

THE international success of firms from Japan, and later South Korea, Taiwan, and elsewhere in Pacific-Asia in the 1960s and 1970s encouraged considerable academic and journalistic interest in the distinctive features of these companies and the socio-political environment in which they became competitive (e.g. Amsden 1989; Wade 1990; Calder 1993). A central part of the post-war environment in which these firms became successful was the strong 'developmental state' (Johnson 1982; Wu 2007; Weiss 2010) that coordinated and often directed investments and strategic choices in different technologies, industries, and markets. The role of the state in guiding socio-economic development has been crucial in structuring the kind of market economy and dominant firms that became established in Asian societies over the past half-century or so. However, relationships between political elites, senior civil servants in different part of the state bureaucracy, and major economic interest groups have varied greatly between Asian countries and over time, as have state policies towards steering industrialization and later development.

These differences have had significant influence on the prevailing patterns of economic coordination and control, or business systems, dominating Asian economies in the first three decades after 1945 and subsequent changes. Because the state has been so important in structuring the nature of dominant business systems in different national territories, especially in its strong developmental form, the comparative analysis of economic organization has tended to focus on national, rather than intra-national regional or sectoral, similarities and differences.

This was particularly so during the heyday of the Bretton Woods System (BWS) for managing international financial flows and imbalances, when national economies were more insulated from each other and governed by predominantly national institutions reflecting the choices of powerful, nationally organized groups. Consequently, many key institutions governing the constitution and behaviour of economic actors, including property-rights regimes and the organization of capital and labour markets, were nationally specific and variable between countries. Hence, the governance of leading companies, their dominant strategic goals and how they pursued these differed considerably between nationally distinct institutional regimes, thus generating different kinds of economic organization at national level. Most of the diverse systems of economic coordination and control established in the post-war period did so within nation states.

However, in practice, the homogenizing impact of national institutions has differed between countries and varied over time. Currently dominant ways of organizing economic activities in any given jurisdiction can be transformed through both internal conflicts and external pressures. In particular, the collapse of the BWS in the early 1970s, subsequent deregulation of many national capital markets, and expansion of the visible hand of managerial coordination and control across national borders through foreign direct investment by multinational companies have arguably reduced national specificities.

The national distinctiveness and homogeneity of post-war Asian business systems are, then, contingent and changeable. It is particularly in countries most successful in pursuing strong developmental policies that we might expect shifts in the dominant forms of economic organization, as successful firms attempt to increase their autonomy, and influential interest groups become more diverse and assertive. This is especially likely where an authoritarian state undergoes substantial democratization, as in South Korea (henceforth Korea) and Taiwan. The very success of these policies in generating or at least strongly contributing to high economic growth and the development of internationally competitive companies is likely to change the conditions that enabled them, as well as changes in the external political environment, reducing the viability of protectionist policies and autarchic economic strategies, as Gray (2011) has emphasized in Taiwan.

In this chapter, I explore the changing connections between dominant institutions and business systems through a comparative analysis of how significant institutional changes in Japan, Korea, and Taiwan and their environments have been associated with shifts in some characteristics of their nationally dominant business systems. While some changes could be considered complementary in the sense of reinforcing the impact of key institutions on leading firms and market structures, others have had mixed consequences for established patterns of economic organization. Initially, I summarize the characteristics of the East Asian business systems dominating these economies in the high-growth periods in terms of concepts developed previously (Whitley 1992, 1999), before comparing key institutional factors that helped to generate and reproduce them. In the following section I outline major changes in some of these institutional features after the collapse of the BWS and oil-price shocks of 1973 and 1979. In the final section, I consider how these changes seem to have altered the national homogeneity and dominance of these business systems and led to significant shifts in some characteristics.

# POST-WAR EAST ASIAN BUSINESS SYSTEMS

In Table 28.1, I contrast the eight major characteristics of the post-war business systems that became established in Japan, Korea, and Taiwan (Gerlach 1992; Whitley 1992; Fields 1995; Orrù, Biggart, and Hamilton 1997; Shin and Hamilton 2014). These summarize the prevalent patterns of coordination and control of economic activities that the strong complementarities of the major national institutions governing economic relationships and actions helped to ensure dominated each national political economy (Whitley 2005).

Considering first the degree of ownership-based coordination and control of economic activities, a major contrast between these three countries concerns the

## Table 28.1 Characteristics of dominant post-war business systems in East Asia

| Dominant Business System Characteristics | Japan | South Korea | Taiwan |
| --- | --- | --- | --- |
| Ownership-based coordination and control | | | |
| Owner-manager relationships | Committed | Direct | Direct |
| Vertical integration of dominant private firms | Medium | High | Low |
| Horizontal integration by dominant firms | Medium, but mostly in related industries | High | High |
| Alliance-based coordination and control | | | |
| Vertical alliance integration | Considerable | Low | Limited to short-term connections except for centre-satellite networks in some industries |
| Horizontal alliance integration | Considerable | Low | Limited to short-term partnerships |
| Competitor collaboration | Considerable | Low | Limited, predominantly short term |
| Organizational integration and commitment | | | |
| Employer–employee commitment | High for male workers in large firms | Limited, except for college-educated staff in large firms | Limited |
| Delegation to, and involvement in problem-solving of, the bulk of the regular workforce | Considerable | Low | Low |

involvement and control of investors in the management and strategic direction of dominant firms. As numerous analyses have attested, their role has been much less direct and decisive in Japan than in Korea and Taiwan, where owning families tend to dominate top management positions and decision-making (see, e.g. Aoki and Dore 1994; Fields 1995; Kim 1997; Orrù, Biggart, and Hamilton 1997). In many large Japanese companies, significant shareholdings were often owned by committed financial institutions and friendly members of the same business groups, who functioned more as business partners sharing risks, knowledge, and senior personnel than as strategic decision-makers or remote portfolio investors (Witt 2014a). In contrast, most Korean and Taiwanese companies were established and run as family enterprises dominated by the founding family, even when its own direct shareholding fell below 50 per cent.

The extent to which leading private companies owned their supply chains and integrated forward into distribution and retailing activities also differed considerably. Large Japanese firms sometimes integrated backwards, but usually preferred in the post-war period to hold less than 50 per cent, and often under 30 per cent, of suppliers' shares, to conserve capital outlays and save on personnel costs and commitments. Wholly owned vertical integration in Japan thus tended to be lower than in the USA amongst comparable firms, and considerably less than that common amongst the Korean *chaebol*, particularly in the heavy and chemical-industry sectors (Fields 1995; Kim 1997). In contrast, most private Taiwanese companies and business groups exhibited relatively limited degrees of vertical integration, especially in more capital-intensive industries, not least because of the state/KMT dominance of the upstream sectors (Hamilton and Kao 1990; Fields 1995; Orrù, Biggart, and Hamilton 1997; Hsieh 2011).

Ownership-based horizontal coordination and control varied considerably, with relatively few Japanese companies operating as highly diversified conglomerates, in contrast to Korea's *chaebol*, which were highly diversified across unrelated industries (Witt 2014b). Taiwanese family businesses also tended to diversify, especially those forming business groups, although these operated more as sets of related enterprises than wholly owned and centrally managed integrated firms like the *chaebol* (Fields 1995: 66–67).

As the title of Gerlach's (1992) book about the post-war Japanese economy, *Alliance Capitalism*, suggests, economic coordination through alliances between legally independent firms was a major, if not defining, feature of its dominant business system. Both vertically and horizontally, companies were enmeshed in wide-ranging networks of obligations and mutual assistance, from long-term customer-supplier connections to large ex-*zaibatsu* inter-market groups tied to large banks, and the often state-encouraged collaborations between competing firms to develop new technologies, manage declining demand in recessions, and deal with foreign competitors (Lincoln and Gerlach 2004). The Korean *chaebol*, in contrast, adopted a largely adversarial approach to suppliers and preferred to buy innovative SMEs rather than develop long-term obligational links to them. Company alliances have rarely been long lived in Korea.

While Taiwanese family firms often develop partnerships for new ventures, these tend to be fairly narrowly focused on particular activities and based on personal commitments rather than long-term organizational alliances (Fields 1995, 2012). Coordination through inter-firm networks may have been greater in Taiwan than Korea up to the 1980s, but partnerships were more changeable and project specific than in Japan (Lee and Hsiao 2014). As Numazaki suggests (2000: 159), 'Chinese partnership tends to be temporary in nature. This implies the temporary nature of family trade...a Chinese partnership is a coalition of autonomous entrepreneurs.' Economic activities, then, are quite highly coordinated through networks between firms in Japan and Taiwan, but these networks are more specific, changeable, and tied to personal relationships in Taiwan than in Japan.

Patterns of authoritative coordination and control of work activities also varied significantly between major firms in these countries. While the popular view of Japan's lifetime employment may have been overstated, the extent of mutual dependence and long-term commitments between employers and regular—usually male—employees in larger companies was clearly considerable, and often included manual workers in a process described as 'white-collarization' (Dore 1973; Koike 1987). Even smaller firms recognized the importance of maintaining skilled-worker commitment to organizational success, as in the Sakaki township machine-tool industry (Friedman 1988).

In contrast, employment commitments were much weaker in most Korean and Taiwanese enterprises, particularly for manual workers, although college-educated *chaebol* employees could reasonably expect long-term careers in these fast-growing conglomerates (Bae 1987; Kim 1992; Janelli 1993). Such expectations tended to be limited in Taiwan, not least because of the common preference for running one's own business on what Shieh (1992) has termed 'Boss Island' (Numazaki 1997). Long-term commitments tended to be restricted to family members, or employees who had established family-like ties to the owning family (Hamilton and Kao 1990; Lee and Hsiao 2014).

Allied to these differences was considerable variation in the degree of delegation of control over task performance and organization, and the extent to which staff were expected to contribute to problem-solving and organizational improvements. As numerous scholars have suggested, such involvement was considerable in many Japanese companies, and in particular the role of middle-management in developing initiatives was an important feature of decision-making (Rohlen 1974; Fruin 1992; Fujimoto 1999).

Such delegation and openness to suggestions from subordinates seem to have been much lower in Korea and Taiwan, where staff were expected to follow orders and anticipate supervisors' wishes (Silin 1976; Kim 1992; Janelli 1993). Management styles tended to be more authoritarian than participative, and rarely invited independent contributions. Strategic decision-making in particular was reserved to the owning family, and often to the individual patriarch, with little initiative expected of senior and middle management.

These considerable differences between the key characteristics of the dominant post-war business systems of Japan, Korea, and Taiwan highlight the diversity of ways in which market economies can be organized while experiencing high economic growth. This diversity resulted from significant differences in the nature of the societal institutions governing economic activities in the product, capital, and labour markets, as well as in the actions of the dominant domestic political-economic coalitions and major surrounding powers during the early post-war period. These institutions and coalitions were nationally distinct and relatively homogenous across sectors and regions within each society, thus encouraging the establishment of nationally distinctive business systems for several decades after the war.

I now turn to a summary of their key features that help to explain the diversity of dominant post-war business systems in East Asia, before considering changes in some that may have affected the national dominance of these systems and their major characteristics in recent years.

# Institutional Differences in Post-War Japan, Korea, and Taiwan

The key institutions affecting business-system characteristics can be summarized under four main headings: the state, the financial system, the labour system, and those institutions governing trust and authority relationships (Whitley 1999, 2007). Their major features in these three societies before and during their high-growth period are listed in Table 28.2.

For much of the post-war period, the role of the state can be characterized as developmentalist in all three countries, with respect to: (a) its relative autonomy from socio-economic interest groups, (b) the cohesion and integration of political and bureaucratic elites, and (c) their overwhelming commitment to achieving rapid economic growth (Johnson 1982; Evans 1995; Wu 2007). However, the extent of state dominance of the economic system, risk-sharing with private companies, and active promotion of particular sectors and firms differed considerably. In very broad terms, Japan's post-war democratic developmental state was less dominant and less directly involved in the direction of enterprises than its Korean counterpart after the 1961 military coup, as well as being more influenced by business associations in determining and implementing socio-economic policies. In general, the state here promoted its developmental policies more through reciprocal consent with major companies than through direct instruction (Samuels 1987; Whitley 1992; Calder 1993).

As elsewhere, a key instrument of the Japanese development state was its control of the financial system, especially during the high-growth period. The main bank system dominated corporate finance and governance until the 1980s and was managed by the Ministry of Finance and other parts of the bureaucracy to provide ample investment funding for growing companies and to support new developments (Aoki and Patrick 1994). Strong segmentation of financial markets, restriction of the corporate-bond market, and control over branch banking enabled the state to exercise considerable power over the major banks and the flow of credit to companies.

The critical role of major banks in financing expansion during the high-growth period and institutionalization of the main bank system as the central component of

## Table 28.2 Dominant institutions affecting post-war business systems in East Asia

|  | Japan | Korea | Taiwan |
|---|---|---|---|
| *The State* | | | |
| State cohesion and autonomy | Considerable | High | High |
| Dominant state-private coalitions | 'Iron triangle' of LDP leaders, bureaucratic elite, big business elite | Military-backed political elite, bureaucratic elite (especially EPB) and *chaebol* | KMT dominated political and bureaucratic elites, SOEs and a few Taiwanese businesses |
| State commitment to economic growth | High | High | High |
| State promotion of particular industries | Considerable | High, including favoured firms | Medium, but limited for most Taiwanese companies |
| Strength of intermediary organizations | Considerable | Low | Low |
| *Financial System* | | | |
| State ownership of banks | Low | High | High |
| State regulation and segmentation of financial markets | High | High | High |
| Firm dependence on bank finance | High | High | Low for most Taiwanese firms |
| *Labour system* | | | |
| State regulation of employment conditions | Considerable | High for larger firms | High, but not strongly enforced in SME sector |
| Strength of labour unions | Considerable in late 1940s, reduced thereafter | Low | Low |
| *Authority and trust relations* | | | |
| Prevalent authority patterns | Paternalist | Patriarchal | Patriarchal |
| Level of trust between strangers and in formal institutions | Considerable | Low | Low |

post-war corporate governance meant they became locked into the fate of their large customers and committed to their success (Aoki and Patrick 1994). These close bank–firm connections inhibited radical diversification into unrelated industries, as the main banks benefited from companies expanding existing competences and skills into related technologies and markets, rather than investing in unconnected and remote ones. Collaboration within sectors was additionally encouraged in the post-war period by state support for cooperation between firms, recession cartels, and relatively weak enforcement of anti-trust legislation (Matsuura et al. 2004).

In contrast, for most of the time before the mid-1980s, both the Korean and Taiwanese states, backed by military power, pursued top-down development policies as well as owning much of the banking system. However, they differed in the extent of their active steering of firms' strategies and direct involvement in industrial development, as well as in the level of state ownership of enterprises. The post-1961 Korean state systematically used its control of banks to allocate credit at subsidized rates to favoured firms and industries, and to withdraw such financing when companies failed to meet expectations and/or engaged in antagonistic political activities (Woo 1991; Kim 1997). Business dependence on the state, especially on personal relationships with political leaders, was considerable in post-war Korea, such that large firms were unable to develop the sort of autonomy and strategic independence enjoyed by Japanese counterparts (Witt 2014b). The combination of this dependence on the military-backed regime and ample supply of cheap debt to fund expansion into state-favoured industries encouraged firms to grow so fast that they became too big to fail, and to maintain high levels of personal and family control of the *chaebol*. As Woo (1991: 149) suggests: 'To join the hallowed chosen few, enterprises had to be big; but to remain chosen, they had to be gigantic. Size was an effective deterrent against default...big state and big business would have to sink or swim together.'

The post-1961 state's commitment to export-oriented industrialization and development of heavy industries encouraged *chaebol* to move rapidly into new sectors when supported by cheap credit and other incentives. Diversification into non-banking financial services was also a means of reducing dependence on state elites, as it increased financial flexibility and could facilitate access to loans. As a result, ownership-based coordination within and across industrial and service sectors has been high in Korea (Kim 1997: 68–70).

Competition for state favours, both before and after industrialization, inhibited horizontal collaboration between companies and other socio-economic actors in Korea. The dominant role of the central state and its reluctance to permit independent private accumulations of wealth and control over economic activities has meant that private firms often competed through the state as well as through the market, and establishing links with industry partners was subsidiary to seeking political allies and influence. Widespread state suspicion of private alliances that could threaten its dominant role inhibited the establishment of long-term inter-firm commitments, powerful trade associations, and private cartels.

Taiwan's post-war state was dominated by the nationalist Kuomintang (KMT) government from the mainland, which operated by martial law from 1947 to 1987. As an external occupying force, the KMT had few, if any, ties to existing Taiwanese elites, many of whom it had destroyed after the February 1947 uprising (Gold 1986), and was long able to monopolize the political executive, bureaucracy, and legislature (Fields 1995). This control extended to the commanding heights of the economy, especially the upstream capital-intensive sectors that became mostly state owned, and the KMT itself owned extensive economic assets (Matsumoto 2002). As Wade (1990: 176) puts it: 'From the early 1950s onward Taiwan has had one of the biggest public-enterprise sectors outside the communist bloc and sub-Saharan Africa'.

Similarly to Korea, a key instrument of state direction of economic development was its ownership of the major banks, which were not encouraged to lend large amounts to most Taiwanese firms (Gold 1986; Fields 1995: 66–92). Despite, then, the move to a more export-oriented economy in the 1960s, under considerable US pressure, and reliance on economic growth to legitimize its rule, the KMT remained largely aloof from the Taiwanese-dominated export sector and did not attempt to coordinate or steer the development of the SMEs that constituted the bulk of these firms (Gold 1986; Wade 1990). Thus, although overall private-business dependence on the state has been quite high, the willingness and ability of state agencies to steer private firms' strategic decisions have been much less than in Korea.

This dominant yet largely remote role of the state in most Taiwanese firms' development, especially with regard to bank finance, foreign technologies, and access to markets, reinforced traditional Chinese merchants' fear of the predatory state and preference for strong owner control and secrecy. Taiwanese entrepreneurs relied heavily on informal sources of finance in which personal networks of obligation and commitment were key, and on forming collaborative partnerships for undertaking new ventures based largely on personal ties between owning families (Numazaki 1997). New networks were usually based on cliques of family members to ensure trust, but later grew around other ascriptive attributes, such as shared native place, surnames, and even birth year (Fields 1995: 73; Numazaki 2000).

Turning to the institutions governing labour markets and their influence on employment policies, the radical reforms of land ownership and encouragement of labour unions by the US occupation forces in Japan between 1945 and 1952 achieved substantial changes by destroying much of the economic and political power of the landlord class and greatly increasing union membership from 381,000 in 1945 to 6,600,000 in 1949 (Fujimura 1997; Mosk 1995: 95–96). Even if membership declined in the 1950s after the 'red purge' and industry/craft based unions were increasingly replaced by enterprise unions (Garon 1997), the unions played an important role in institutionalizing seniority-based promotion, limiting flexible hire-and-fire employment policies, and encouraging long-term employer–employee commitments, especially in larger firms. In this they were supported from the late 1940s onwards by laws regulating employment conditions, dispute-resolution processes, and the supply and use of temporary workers (Sugeno and Suwa 1997; Inagami and Whittaker 2005). The combination of relatively long-term employment commitments, shortage of skilled workers during the high-growth period, and enterprise unions encouraged substantial delegation of control over task performance (though not necessarily work organization) to work-groups and a more facilitative style of management (Dore 1973: 231–242; Nakamura 1997; Clark 1979).

In contrast, Korea's authoritarian developmental state directly controlled and manipulated labour organizations in support of export-oriented industries and ensured that wages remained relatively low (Deyo 1989; Kim 1997: 120–123). Employers did not have to gain union cooperation or invest resources in gaining workers' commitment. Rapid urbanization and population growth maintained a labour surplus for many jobs and enabled the *chaebol* to rely on the external labour market to deal with changes in demand, especially for manual workers. Traditional patterns of authority, coupled with the dominant role of the military after 1961 and difficulty of establishing trust relations beyond kinship and other particularistic connections, limited delegation of authority and discretion in most *chaebol* (Bae 1987; Kim 1992; Janelli 1993). Additionally, traditional disdain for manual workers and less-educated employees tended to restrict longer-term employment commitments to college-educated white-collar staff, though this appeared less firm in Korea than in large Japanese firms (Bae 1987; Janelli 1993).

In Taiwan, the KMT-dominated state also exercised strong control over the labour movement, encouraging enterprise-based unions that could not bargain over wages and making the appointment of officials subject to the approval of local KMT committees (Deyo 1989: 117–118). These unions were more concerned with providing member services than representing workers' interests, and reinforced traditional employer paternalism. Additionally, many factory workers viewed employment as a temporary status before starting their own business and strongly preferred self-employment, not least because of the reluctance of most owner-managers to delegate decision-making (Shieh 1992; Fields 1995: 73–74; Numazaki 1997).

The combination of an authoritarian, ethnically distinct state apparatus, limited regulation of employment relations in the SME-dominated private sector, traditional reliance on family-like particularistic ties in trust relationships, and patrimonial patterns of authority has limited the development of credible commitments between employers and most employees in post-war Taiwan, as well as restricting the substantive decentralization of authority and task performance. Such restriction was reinforced by the traditional Confucian legitimation of power, which stressed the moral superiority of leaders, that continued to be important in Taiwan as the Nationalists relied extensively on the doctrines of Sun Yat-sen in their legitimating ideology, justifying the tutelary role of the state and the wide discretion allowed to senior officials in managing the economy (King 1996). As Wade (1990: 286) puts it: 'Those near the top of bureaucratic hierarchies are assumed to have reached their position by their superior knowledge and strength of moral character, which frees them from the constraints of formal law ... the imperial scholar-official tradition taught officials to feel superior to their business clients and to exercise leverage with them. Today's officials are descendants of that tradition'.

# Changes in Dominant Institutions in East Asia, 1980–2010

Some of these institutional features have altered considerably in the last thirty or so years, along with major shifts in the wider political and economic environment, and there has been much discussion about whether these developmental states are being reformed in a 'liberal' market economy direction (Weiss 2004; Beeson 2009; Fields 2012). Equally, the growth of transnational investment and trade flows, coupled with attempts to increase the amount and effectiveness of transnational economic governance (Braithwaite and Drahos 2000; Djelic and Quack 2003; Djelic and Sahlin-Andersson 2006), can be seen as weakening national institutions' influence on leading firms' structures and behaviour in East Asia, such that nationally specific business systems are becoming less homogenous and distinctive (Sako 2006; Lechevalier 2007). In this section, I compare major changes in dominant institutions in each of these societies (Table 28.3), as a prelude to considering how these have led to shifts in the dominant characteristics of the post-war business systems discussed above.

Perhaps the most significant shifts have taken place in the structure and policies of the developmental state, as the cohesion of political and bureaucratic alliances with big business, especially in Japan and Korea, weakened and economic growth became less overwhelming as the focus of public policy-making (Wu 2007; Fields 2012). The recent relative decline in the autonomy of the state and its pursuit of export-oriented industrialization in all three societies was accompanied by a variety of measures aimed at liberalizing product, capital, and labour markets as international competition intensified and geo-political alliances were reorganized (Thurbon and Weiss 2006; Gray 2011; Song 2012). However, these broad changes in dominant coalitions, institutions governing capital and labour markets, and public policies occurred in different ways and with varied consequences for business systems (e.g. Lee 2009; Zhang 2009, 2012; Fields 2012).

The most far-reaching and radical institutional changes occurred in Korea and Taiwan, where democratization, political competition, and the establishment of independent interest groups, especially organized labour, developed in the late 1980s and 1990s. Although policies fluctuated, especially with regard to the liberalization and reregulation of financial markets before and after the Asian financial crises of 1997–1998, both societies underwent political reforms that changed the make-up of dominant coalitions and of the policies pursued (Thurbon 2001; Fields 2012; Zhang 2012).

In Korea, the advent of electoral democracy after 1987 led to the formation of a conservative coalition that supported an expansion of bank-lending to farmers and SMEs at the same time as enabling the *chaebol* to maintain their dominant economic position and accessing the growing corporate-bond market for investment funds. Within the bureaucracy, the previously dominant Economic Planning Board was merged with the Ministry of Finance in 1995, and the new Ministry of Finance and Economy became more influenced by advocates of financial liberalization. While privatization

**Table 28.3  Major changes in dominant institutions in Japan, Korea, and Taiwan, 1980–2010**

|  | Japan | Korea | Taiwan |
|---|---|---|---|
| *The State* | | | |
| State cohesion and autonomy | Reduced | Reduced | Reduced |
| Dominant state-private coalitions | Weakening of 'iron triangle', limited inclusion of trade union federation | Some expansion to include SMEs, farmers and workers | Expansion to include Taiwanese-owned large business groups |
| Dominance of economic growth priorities | Reduced | Reduced, but still strong | Reduced, but still strong |
| State promotion of industries | Considerable, but more indirect | Considerable, but less dirigiste | Considerable in newer sectors |
| Strength of intermediary associations | Considerable | Increased, but still limited | Increased, especially in new ICT sectors |
| *Financial System* | | | |
| State ownership of banks | Low | Reduced, but chaebol ownership still restricted | Reduced, but still significant |
| Dependence of firms on bank finance | Reduced for larger successful firms, high for others | Reduced for largest chaebol, increased for SMEs | Increasing use of capital markets, but bank finance remains important |
| State regulation and segmentation of financial markets | Considerably reduced | Considerably reduced | Considerably reduced, but state regulation remains strong |
| *Labour system* | | | |
| State regulation of employment conditions | Reduced, but more than USA/UK | Reduced, but still significant | Reduced, but still significant in SOE sector |
| Union strength | Reduced, enterprise unions remain strong in large firms | Increased in late 1980s, reduced in 2000s | Considerable in SOE sector, low elsewhere |
| *Authority and trust* | | | |
| Prevalent authority patterns | Paternalist | Less authoritarian | Less authoritarian |
| Trust of strangers and in formal institutions | Declining trust of state agencies | Low | Low |

of state-owned banks and other SOEs remained slow, non-bank financial institutions (NBFIs) expanded fast, and supplied *chaebol* with relatively cheap credit. According to Thurbon (2001: 242), Korea's liberalization process in the 1990s was 'rapid, reckless and ill-designed...accompanied by the build-up of massive amounts of short-term foreign debt, over-investment in critical export industries and a debt-riddled banking sector'.

After the 1997–1998 financial crises, deregulation of both financial and labour markets became more wide ranging, partly at the behest of the IMF and other international agencies. However, equity markets remained relatively illiquid and unimportant in providing investment capital, compared to the expanding bond market and foreign investors (Zhang 2012). With the election of Kim Dae Jung in 1997, interest groups that had largely been excluded from policy considerations, particularly labour unions, gained in political influence as the new regime sought to restrict *chaebol* power more effectively, especially after some required state support. Bank lending to SMEs continued to grow substantially, while the NBFIs were reined in, and the central bank gained some independence, along with the newly established Financial Supervisory Commission. Despite the *chaebols'* reluctance to embrace equity financing if it meant a loss of control, the opening of capital markets to outsiders—albeit somewhat hesitant—led overseas investors to amass 40 per cent of issued shares on the Korean stock exchange in 2005, mostly in the largest listed companies and banks. The Capital Market Consolidation Act, passed in 2007, aimed to remove barriers between financial markets, but restrictions on industrial firms owning financial companies remain and in general Korea's financial markets are still dominated by the larger banks and their supervisors (Zhang 2012).

In the aftermath of democratization and lifting of some restrictions on labour organizations, union membership grew considerably and led to the establishment of the independent Korean Confederation of Trade Unions, although this only achieved official recognition after the 1997–1998 financial crises and Kim Dae Jung's election. As Lee (2009) emphasizes, while the unions were successful in gaining wage increases and reductions in the working week, at least in larger companies, after 1987 the state continued to repress independent unions and take an active role in managing labour disputes, which remained confrontational. After 1997–1998, however, the state more formally institutionalized semi-corporatist consultation processes and extended unions' legal rights as part of a trade-off for enabling redundancies in large firms (Kong 2006; Song 2012; Witt 2014b). Such forced reductions in the numbers of regular workers were dependent on significant enterprise restructuring, usually by selling off more peripheral subsidiaries to pay down debt, and substantial restrictions on dismissing such employees in major companies remain, as does strong and effective union resistance to such redundancies (Song 2012).

In Taiwan, in contrast, the lifting of martial law in 1987 and Taiwanization of the ruling KMT encouraged closer links between the state and private business groups, as policy-makers sought to play a more active role in promoting high-technology industries and gain popular support (Fields 2012). This included the encouragement of stronger business associations, especially in the newer sectors (Tung 2001), although some of the largest business groups preferred to deal with the state through direct personal contacts rather than to participate in the construction of effective collective associations (Zhang and Whitley 2012). Both the KMT and main opposition party, the Democratic Progressive Party (DPP), supported the expansion of capital markets and liberalization of the banking sector, but more cautiously and incrementally than in Korea (Thurbon 2001; Wu 2007). The Central Bank of China and Ministry of Finance gained influence and pushed through regulatory reforms to boost the Taipei Stock Exchange (TSE) and encourage institutional investment, leading to much larger TSE capitalization and liquidity than in its Korean counterpart (Zhang 2009, 2012), as well as allowing business groups to establish private banks and, eventually, financial holding companies.

Whereas the dominant role of the *chaebol* in Korea during the high-growth period and their close association with the military-backed authoritarian regime had led the opposition movement to remain antagonistic to them when it eventually succeeded in winning the presidency, the relatively low profile and detached nature of most Taiwanese business groups from the KMT party-state meant that the DPP developed quite close ties to many of them, initially at local level and then nationally. As a result, when the DPP won the presidency in 2000, government-business links did not weaken greatly, despite the opposition's previous support for labour-union interests. Indeed, if anything, the influence of some business groups on economic policies and priorities may well have increased, and some suggest that corruption intensified (Wu 2007; Copper 2009). The autonomy of the state and its capacity for pursuing developmental economic goals in opposition to the short-term interests of big business have, then, declined in Taiwan relative to its position in the 1960s and 1970s, as the economic bureaucracy became more controlled by elected politicians competing for support from major interest groups (Wu 2007: 986; Lee and Hsiao 2014).

As Lee (2009) makes clear, the political role of the independent unions was quite different in Taiwan from that in Korea. Because large enterprises were mostly state- or KMT-owned in Taiwan before democratization, and the KMT sought to incorporate the organized labour movement into the party-state regime, the bulk of the union membership worked in the state-owned and/or controlled-enterprise sector and was only weakly represented in SME-dominated industries. Despite being denied official recognition at the national level, the existence of elected administrations at local and regional levels enabled opposition groups to support independent union activities and ensured that unions could become political actors, at first locally, but eventually nationally (President Chen granted de facto recognition of the Taiwan Confederation of Trade Unions in 2000).

Since the unions were overwhelmingly represented in the state-dominated sector, they were able to use their political influence after electoral competition was established to obtain wage increases in ways that their Korean counterparts could not. However, their weakness in the private sector—and relatively low membership, at under 10 per cent once the craft unions of largely self-employed workers are excluded (Kong 2006: 370)—has limited wage increases since 1987. Similar political manoeuvrings in the late 1990s and 2000s enabled the unions to slow down, and sometimes prevent, the pace of privatizations of SOEs and to protect workers against sudden and large-scale redundancies. By 2002, Taiwan still had ninety-seven SOEs contributing 10.2 per cent of GDP, while Korea only had thirty-five, contributing 5.3 per cent of GDP (Lee 2009), although more have been privatized since then, albeit with quite strong union involvement.

While political democratization in both societies seems to have encouraged a more responsive pattern of leadership, at least for the major interest groups, it remains unclear whether prevalent authority patterns will become much more reciprocal for others and justified in more communitarian terms. As Lee and Hsiao (2014) and Witt (2014b) point out, trust in strangers and formal institutions remains limited in both Korea and Taiwan, despite political changes, and family-like patterns of commitment and trust continue to form the basis of major economic transactions.

Institutional change in Japan has been rather less dramatic, and may be more formal than realized in practice. While the 'iron triangle' of political, bureaucratic, and big-business elites has weakened, it would be misleading to claim that the developmental state has withered away, or that shifting dominant coalitions of politicians, bureaucrats, and business leaders no longer see the state playing a major—if not the central—role in coordinating and promoting economic growth (Witt 2014a). Few senior managers actively seek the abolition of state regulation of market behaviour and, as Fields (2012: 48) suggests, 'even as bureaucrats and capitalists have "remodelled" industrial policies and refashioned corporate strategies…the state's developmental orientation and substantive intervention and private capital's continued reliance on its corporate and bureaucratic networks have persisted'.

What does seem to have changed is the level of direct intervention and guidance of business strategies as product, capital, and labour markets have become more liberalized since the 1970s and the state has pursued more indirect ways of upgrading technologies and supporting new industries. The 1999 Industry Revitalization Law and its 2003 revisions, for example, provided state support for declining industries while encouraging private investment in growth sectors and joint ventures for innovative technologies (Fields 2012). While the reconstituted Ministry of Economy, Trade and Industry supported some neo-liberal reforms, it also played a significant role in boosting bottom-up strategic alliances and promoting collaboration between state agencies, firms, and universities to advance new technologies.

Substantial reforms to the financial system, culminating in the 'big bang' changes of 1996–2001, liberalized capital markets, gave the Bank of Japan formal independence, and removed barriers between financial markets, as well as permitting the formation of holding companies (Laurence 2001). Over time, they led to foreigners owning 26 per cent of issued shares on the Tokyo Stock Exchange in 2009, substantial mergers of banks, insurance companies, and other financial institutions, as well as some reduction in the level of cross-shareholdings between firms. Additionally, there has been a limited expansion of private equity and similar means of funding new companies, albeit from a very low baseline (Sako and Kotosaka 2012).

However, many bank and securities firms' mergers were more defensive than a radical break from the past, and bank-led finance continues to be significant for many Japanese firms, especially those unable to obtain funding from corporate bond markets. As Fields (2012) suggests, there remain substantial coalitions of interests willing and able to resist radical changes in a number of markets, including financial services, and these appear to have restricted the shift towards a more capital market-based system, despite the establishment of new stock exchanges, such as JASDAQ and MOTHERS, for start-ups, and some changes in prevalent forms of venture capital.

Changes in labour-market institutions in Japan have also supported some liberalization of regulations governing employment conditions and use of non-regular workers. In particular, the employment of agency workers and other temporary staff has become more widely permitted and such workers can be used across a wider range of tasks than was common before the 1990s. Non-regular workers increased from 20.2 per cent of the labour force in 1990 to 32.3 per cent in 2008, and 12.6 million people worked part-time in 2002 (Sako 2006: 210). However, much of the growth in non-regular employment seems to have occurred amongst the 25–34 age-group and women in part-time roles in the health and welfare service sectors, and so reflects an increased variability of employment conditions between different parts of the economy, rather than a qualitative shift in established patterns in longer-established industries (Witt 2014a).

Although the strength of labour unions overall may have declined, with union membership falling to 23.8 per cent of the workforce in 1995 and 18.7 per cent in 2005, and the *Shunto* spring offensive losing much of its coordinating role in national wage-bargaining (Sako 2006), enterprise unions retain significant influence over corporate decisions in most large companies, and the labour movement as a whole has become more unified and involved in policy discussions (Shinoda 1997; Walter and Zhang 2012). Furthermore, core workers in large firms seem to continue to benefit from regulatory restrictions on dismissal and relatively long-term employment commitments remain common, for this group at least (Jackson 2007; Song 2012). Equally, while performance-based pay has become more important at an earlier age in many companies, it remains limited to more senior staff, and seniority in general is still a significant component of wage increases (Keizer 2009, 2011).

Although recent scandals amongst politicians and bureaucrats may well have reduced the level of trust in state agencies, as witnessed perhaps by recent sizeable demonstrations against nuclear power stations, and possibly encouraged the rise of NGOs in Japan, overall willingness to trust strangers and formal institutions seems to remain quite high, especially compared with elsewhere in Asia (Witt 2014a). Japan continues to be a highly networked society in which both formal and informal reputations play a considerable role in policing behaviour, and communitarian justifications of authority seem to remain significant components of organizational cultures (Inagami and Whittaker 2005).

# East Asian Business Systems in the Twenty-first Century

Given these changes in many of the dominant institutions and interest groups governing economic activities in these societies, it would be surprising if at least some of the post-war characteristics discussed above have not also altered. However, not all recent

changes have been so mutually reinforcing that they can be expected to generate significant shifts in a particular direction, and in some countries they have stimulated
substantial and effective resistance from key interest groups. Consistent and systemic
changes in dominant business-system characteristics towards, for example, those seen
as emblematic of Anglo-American capitalism, are less evident than some have expected.

The gradual loosening of many restrictions on firm behaviour in capital and labour
markets in some states can, though, be expected to have encouraged greater strategic heterogeneity amongst leading companies, especially those encountering diverse
technological and market conditions in different parts of the world, and to have weakened the complementarity of major institutions in encouraging homogenous patterns of economic coordination and control across sectors and regions within national
boundaries. Given that the post-war dominance of state agencies and particular
political-bureaucratic elites in steering economic development has declined in the societies considered here (Wu 2007; Weiss 2010), an obvious question arises about the continued national specificity and distinctiveness of their post-war business systems and
the extent to which these continue to reflect the dominant ways of organizing economic
activities across the larger and more complex economies.

Has the standardizing role of the developmentalist state become so reduced in East
Asia as to permit the variety of firm-governance practices and strategic priorities found
in some liberal market economies, or would it be more accurate to discern, in the mixture of homogeneity and heterogeneity in economic coordination and control, patterns
seen across different industries and regions in some European societies (Schmidt 2002;
Boyer 2004)? Relatedly, to what extent has the growing internationalization of investment and operations of many Japanese, Korean, and Taiwanese firms, and somewhat
less widespread opening of these domestic economies to foreign portfolio and strategic
investments, so altered these patterns within national boundaries as to render the idea
of nationally distinct and dominant business systems in East Asia less convincing than
in the heyday of the developmental state?

While definitive answers to these sorts of questions require more sustained discussion
than feasible here, recent collections (e.g. Aoki, Jackson, and Miyajima 2007; Colpan,
Hikino, and Lincoln 2010; Walter and Zhang 2012), together with other analyses, permit
some tentative conclusions. In Table 28.4 I have suggested how the major post-war characteristics outlined above seem to have altered over the past three decades as a result of
institutional changes and more general shifts in the global business environment.

## Japan

In Japan, the considerable restructuring of post-war inter-market groups and banking
system that has taken place since 1991 has, together with the fluctuating growth of foreign shareholdings in some of the largest companies, further hastened the decline of the
main bank system for many of the more successful firms, especially regarding the effectiveness of the bank and *keiretsu* monitoring of corporate performance (Lincoln and

### Table 28.4 Changing East Asian business system characteristics, 1980–2010

| Dominant Business System Characteristics | Japan | Korea | Taiwan |
|---|---|---|---|
| *Ownership-based integration* | | | |
| Owner-manager relationships | Committed except for firms with large numbers of foreign shareholders | Direct | Direct |
| Vertical integration | Medium | High | Increased in some business groups, but still mostly limited |
| Horizontal integration | Medium | High for most chaebol, but less than in 1980s | High for most business groups |
| *Alliance-based Integration* | | | |
| Vertical integration | Reduced in large firms that have invested abroad and in some new industries | Low | Expansion of centre-satellite hierarchical alliances with state support |
| Horizontal integration | Weakened in restructured inter-market groups | Low | Limited, except for kinship-based alliances |
| Competitor collaboration | Considerable | Low | Increased, but mostly short-term except for kinship-based alliances |
| *Organizational integration and commitment* | | | |
| Employer-employee commitment | Reduced in some new sectors and MNCs, considerable in most large firms | Low | Limited |
| Delegation to, and involvement in problem solving of, the bulk of the regular workforce | Considerable in many large firms | Low | Low |
| Overall Homogeneity of Business-System Characteristics | Reduced, especially for newer firms and MNCs, but still considerable | Despite some restructuring of chaebol, still considerable | Increasing dominance of family-controlled business groups, with some differences between sectors |

Shimotani 2010). However, the decline in bank control and share ownership that accelerated in the late 1990s (Miyajima and Kuroki 2007) has not radically reshaped owner–manager relationships, as predicted by some. As Nakamura (2011) indicates, financial institutions as a whole, including trust funds run by many banks, still owned 32.4 per cent of shares listed on the Tokyo Stock Exchange in 2008, with a further 22.4 per cent owned by non-financial companies, and the latter figure represented an increase from earlier in the 2000s, as many companies sought to protect themselves against hostile takeovers. While, then, some of the largest Japanese firms that have been successful in export markets have attracted substantial foreign investment and secured much of their externally provided funding from the corporate-bond market over the past three decades, committed ownership still seems to constitute the dominant form of owner–manager relationships in the Japanese economy, with market-based forms remaining a limited phenomenon with little impact on firm behaviour (Jackson 2007).

Considering changes in ownership- and alliance-based coordination and integration of economic activities, the 'withering away' of some *keiretsu* discerned by Lincoln and Shimotani (2010) suggests an overall reduction in the degree of both vertical and horizontal coordination through alliance networks, as well as some—but not massive—increase in large-firm incorporation of supply-chain alliance partners into fully owned subsidiaries. However, as Kikutani, Itoh, and Hayashida's (2007) analysis of business-portfolio restructuring in the 1990s suggests, the degree of vertical specialization of large Japanese firms in general seems likely to remain considerable, and much greater than in Korean *chaebol* or their American counterparts.

In some industries, such as parts of the consumer-electronics sector, where technological modularization has increased, alliance-based vertical integration within Japan may have declined as the largest firms relocated some operations abroad and began to cultivate foreign suppliers. However, the continuing limited extent of backward integration through full ownership in many sectors and extensive commitment to supplier learning and capability improvement observed in vehicle production and other sectors (MacDuffie and Helper 2006; Sako 2006) suggest that relational contracting and vertical alliances remain significant characteristics of Japan's contemporary business system. Even in the modularized electronics industry, the outsourcing of some standardized, high-volume component production to Taiwanese and other suppliers on a more arm's-length basis has been accompanied by the formation of numerous alliances within Japan to develop new products and technologies and a number of joint factory investments from which it will be difficult to withdraw (Sturgeon 2006).

Equally, while Kikutani et al. (2007) describe considerable levels of industry exit and entry by large companies in the 1990s, this activity does not seem to have resulted in significant changes to the overall level of ownership-based horizontal integration, especially to the extent of market and technologically unrelated diversification, which remains relatively limited in an Asian context. There is also little evidence that the weakening and restructuring of post-war *keiretsu* relationships have significantly reduced the level of collaboration and cooperation between competing firms in most product markets, not least because the state has continued to promote such cooperation in declining industries, and for the development and diffusion of new technologies. As Nakamura (2011: 195) suggests, product-market competition remains relatively weak in Japan, and Amable (2003: 123) claims that 'Japan is also characterized by opacity and emphasis on outward-oriented policies, meaning that protection against competition is stronger than in other members of the cluster (Germany, France, Belgium)'.

In the light of changes in employment regulations intended to enhance flexibility and external mobility (Inagami and Whittaker 2005: 31–32), and the internationalization of some operations by Japanese firms, it might be expected that the three pillars of the post-war employment system—long-term employment, seniority-linked pay, and enterprise unions—would have undergone substantial changes after the collapse of the bubble economy. However, the evidence for widespread and significant restructuring of these pillars remains limited, and employer–employee commitments continue to be considerable, particularly for male workers over 30 in the larger firms (Inagami and Whittaker 2005; Keizer 2009, 2011). While this is partly because the regulatory environment remains quite restrictive despite the recent changes (Jackson 2007), it also reflects a widespread belief amongst Japanese employers, including many smaller ones, that long-term commitment to company success on the part of the core workforce represents a crucial component of a firm's competitiveness.

This is not to deny the considerable growth of 'non-regular' and part-time employment and performance-based pay, especially in some sectors and for some staff (Song 2012). However, the significance of these can be overstated and—like many of the heralded changes to corporate governance practices (Dore 2007)—may represent more an accretion of innovations to established practices than their overthrow (Witt 2014a). Performance-based pay, for instance, seems to be limited to senior staff and affects bonus payments rather than influencing promotion, which largely remain seniority-based for many grades (Keizer 2011).

There is, though, some evidence of increasing variability of employment practices, as indicated by a number of surveys in the early 2000s. While over 80 per cent of companies responding to a METI survey claimed to be committed to long-term employment for core workers, another survey, conducted by the Policy Research Institute of the Ministry of Finance, indicated that a number of firms are combining corporate governance characteristics with employment policies in novel ways, to constitute different kinds of hybrid companies (Jackson 2007; Jackson and Miyajima 2007).

The same Ministry of Finance survey suggested that employee involvement in strategic decision-making remained quite significant in many Japanese companies, particularly for issues concerning employment policies and practices (Miyajima and Kuroki 2007). About half the firms claimed that decisions about production and sales planning and profit indicators involved discussions with unions, while over half considered that employee stock-ownership proposals and corporate restructuring also required some explanation or agreement. In 63 per cent of cases, employment adjustment was thought to require union agreement. Such continued delegation to, and involvement of, core workers in problem-solving, task performance, and some corporate decisions remain a distinctive feature of many Japanese companies (Witt 2014a).

Overall, then, there is some evidence of a decline in the homogeneity of firm govern-ance and behaviour and in the extent to which the national economy is highly coor-dinated, following a reduction of state cohesion and autonomy and the weakening of *keiretsu* and the coordinating role of the *shunto* wage-bargaining system (Sako 2006; Lechevalier 2007). However, if some reduction in the high level of institutional com-plementarities has enabled firms to develop somewhat more diverse coordination and control patterns, it is remarkable how much of the post-war business system seems to remain widespread. Zero-sum arm's-length competition between isolated hierarchies is still unusual in many industries and there are few signs of an active market for corporate control developing. Firms remain dominated by insider interests and average employ-ment tenure-periods remain considerable. Given the contradictory nature of many institutional reforms, and the continued strength of interest groups opposing extensive liberalization of many markets, this is perhaps not too surprising.

# Korea

Considering the changes in dominant business-system characteristics in Korea, it is clear from recent analyses that family control remains considerable, if not indeed dominant, despite reductions in the direct shareholdings of top managers. This is typi-cally achieved through pyramidal structures and complex inter-firm share ownership. According to a recent Korean Free Trade Commission report, internal ownership (i.e. the combination of direct family with inter-corporate shareholdings) of the largest ten *chaebol* was over 50 per cent (Aguilera et al. 2012), and Almeida et al. (2009) have shown that the average level of family and associated firms' consistent voting rights in 1085 member companies of the top 47 *chaebol* between 1998 and 2004 was 68 per cent.

Furthermore, despite considerable reforms of the formal corporate governance sys-tem designed to encourage outside investors by increasing transparency and reducing the manipulation of subsidiary accounts following the 1997–1998 financial crisis and the election of Kim Dae Jung, widespread scepticism remains about their implemen-tation and enforcement (Walter and Zhang 2012; Witt 2014b). The increase in foreign share ownership to 16.3 per cent in 2009 and in direct financing of the *chaebol* from the corporate-bond market has not resulted in a general move to market-dominated investor–manager relationships.

Similarly, while post-crisis political pressures to reduce the degree of unrelated diver-sification pursued by many *chaebol* may have resulted in some reduction in the extent of horizontal ownership-based integration, it remains considerable, particularly as they expanded into non-bank financial services in the 1980s and 1990s (Kim et al. 2004; Choe and Roehl 2007; Zhang 2012). The average number of two-digit industries in the Korean SIC code in which member firms of the top thirty *chaebol* were active—exclud-ing the financial sector—rose from 9.9 in 1987 to 14.5 in 1997 and then declined to 10.0 in 2006 (Kim 2010). Vertical integration also remains high, even in modularized indus-tries such as consumer electronics, as exemplified by Samsung Electronics. It should be noted, though, that not all *chaebol* are equally diversified, as the comparison of how the Hyundai and LG *chaebol* responded to the 1997–1998 crisis revealed (Kim et al. 2004). After a long and bitter dispute between members of the family controlling the Hyundai *chaebol*, the Hyundai Motor group that emerged as a separate entity has followed a much more focused strategy than the LG group.

Attempts to boost the size and economic significance of SMEs as independent actors and counterweights to the *chaebol* seem to have had little effect on subcontractors' autonomy from their largest customers, and inter-firm networks in Korea tend to be *chaebol*-centred, vertical, and exclusive (Witt 2014b). Overall, the level of alliance-based coordination between large and small firms remains relatively low, as does inter-firm collaboration and cooperation (Hsieh 2011; Walter and Zhang 2012).

Considering the next changes in employment relations and managerial authority, the liberalization of some restrictions on external labour mobility for regular workers after the financial crisis enabled *chaebol* to make large-scale redundancies in the late 1990s in conjunction with significant restructuring of their sprawling empires, as well as introducing more individualized merit-based reward systems (Kim et al. 2004). According to Park and Kim (2008), over 70 per cent of listed manufacturing firms significantly reduced employee numbers in 1998 and average job tenure in Korean firms as a whole remains low, though increasing for workers in large companies (Song 2012; Witt 2014b).

Equally, many firms used the opportunities created by labour-market reforms to increase the use of non-regular and employment-agency workers considerably, thus reducing their core workforce, for whom organizational careers remained a realistic expectation. Particularly in more technologically advanced industries, many large firms combined increasing numerical flexibility with reinforced internal career hierarchies, to develop greater organizational commitment amongst skilled technical staff (Deyo 2012). In general, the two-tier labour market characteristic of the high-growth period has continued, and indeed become more intensified (Song 2012), but employment contingency is being extended to the growing ranks of skilled and technical labour in larger companies.

While there is still little evidence of democratization stimulating widespread change in the prevalent authoritarian management style, with most *chaebol* decision-making being highly centralized (Kim et al. 2004; Witt 2014b), a few case studies in the electronics and ICT industries suggest that some Korean companies are both capable and willing to involve employees in problem-solving and, in an Internet start-up, developing new products and services (Kim and Bae 2005; Lee, Rho, and Kim 2007). However, even when so-called high-performance work organization, involving considerable task-performance delegation to workers, has been adopted by large companies, it tends to be imposed top down, following the lean-production model, rather than developed collaboratively with employee representatives, especially where a firm, like Samsung, follows a doctrinaire non-union policy (Kim and Bae 2005).

Overall, then, it seems that the significant changes in the Korean business environment following democratization in 1987, violent labour disputes in the late 1980s, and the 1997–1998 financial crisis, as well as the weakening of the strong developmentalist state in the 1990s (Weiss 2004), and numerous political attempts to reorganize the *chaebol*, have failed to alter the dominant characteristics of the post-war business system to any great extent. In particular, the domestic economy remains dominated by very large, very diversified family-controlled conglomerates engaging in adversarial, zero-sum competition with other firms, and continuing to exploit their market power over SMEs. Extra-firm coordination of economic policies and development of collective competition goods continues to be limited, although employers' federations seem to have gained some autonomy, and employer–employee commitments are mostly short term. While this situation might be thought surprising given the extent of institutional change since 1980, it becomes more explicable by considering the following points.

First, the weakening of the developmental state and its move towards a more regulatory approach to economic coordination and steering were not accompanied by the mobilization of strong interest groups that could form a dominant coalition in opposition to the *chaebol*. The labour-union movement remains divided between two major federations and was neither strong enough to prevent the easing of restrictions on enforced redundancies in larger firms, nor to provide major support for government attempts to restructure the *chaebol*. It did, however, succeed in expanding the social safety-net for the unemployed and, more widely, the welfare state (Peng and Wong 2008).

Second, although the *chaebol* as a whole were weakened both economically and politically by the 1997–1998 financial crisis, those that survived seem to have successfully internationalized their activities with improved and innovative products. These conglomerates became stronger and more able to resist and/or circumvent many of the corporate-governance reforms, sometimes by invoking nationalist sentiments against foreign takeovers and entry into markets such as banking.

Third, the continuing weakness of most SMEs, and the tendency of many *chaebol* to absorb any that promise to be successful, has meant that policy-makers have had little choice but to work with the large conglomerates when seeking to upgrade the skills and capabilities of Korean firms and help them compete effectively in international markets and new industries. With the revival of state planning and coordination of economic development in the 2000s and chastening experiences from somewhat ill-thought-out and poorly implemented neo-liberal policies in the 1990s (Thurbon 2001), the dominant developmental state of the 1960–1980s is implementing a more collaborative form of industrial policy in which some *chaebol* remain key actors, thus limiting its ability to enforce their radical transformation (Weiss 2004, 2010).

## Taiwan

As Lee and Hsiao (2014) emphasize, ownership and control of most firms in Taiwan remains dominated by families, including the largest business groups, which have come to play the leading role in the economy since democratization (Chung 2004), with 62 of the largest 100 groups being family owned or controlled in 2006. Similarly, Chung and Mahmood (2010: 196–197) found that 'many of the ultimate owners of group affili-ates were in fact private holding companies and investment companies that were con-trolled by the family... The pyramid is a multiple-level ownership network constructed by chains of inter-organizational shareholding... Through this mechanism, the con-trolling family can control the whole group by maintaining sufficient equity only in the controlling centre' in much the same way as the Korean *chaebol*. Despite the liberal-ization of many financial markets and the formation of privately controlled financial holding-companies, institutional ownership of large firms' shares, while increasing, remains limited (Zhang 2009) and market-based arm's-length relationships between investors and firms are hardly visible.

Similarly, although the privatization of some state- and KMT-controlled enterprises in upstream sectors since 1990 has enabled some groups to integrate backwards (Chung 2006), the extent of ownership-based vertical coordination remains relatively limited, especially when contrasted with that of the larger Korean *chaebol*. Horizontal diversi-fication has, however, grown substantially, with the largest 100 business groups becom-ing active in 11.51 2-digit SIC industries in 2004, mostly through entering sectors that have become deregulated and where privatized firms became available for acquisition (Chung and Mahmood 2010).

It is worth noting here that the level of unrelated diversification has become more varied between these groups, with the standard deviation of the number of affiliates active in different 2-digit industries rising from 3.12 in 1981 to 7.42 in 2004, often because of differential access to information and support from politicians and senior bureau-crats (Chung 2006). It has also tended to be greater amongst groups with particularly high amounts of family ownership and control, principally because as they expanded into new sectors, they appeared more reluctant to leave declining ones (Chung and Mahmood 2010). There is some evidence that groups based mostly in the newer indus-tries of electronics and ICT tend to diversify into unrelated sectors rather less than longer-established groups originating in other industries, but overall ownership-based horizontal integration is still considerable (Lee and Hsiao 2014).

Alliance-based integration remains limited to relatively short-term partnerships, although the centre–satellite network structure of vertical alliances seems to have become more established with state encouragement (Guerrieri and Pietrobelli 2006; Lin and Chaney 2007). The growing importance of business groups seems to have intensi-fied ownership and directorship linkages within them, at the expense of those between groups (Brookfield 2010), but Lee and Hsiao (2014) indicate the importance of kinship connections between many of the financially dominated groups, and suggest that the groups active in recently deregulated industries, and those where substantial capital resources for new ventures are required, tend to form particularistic alliances cemented through family ties. At least in some areas of Taiwan's economy, then, highly personal alliance-based coordination is quite significant.

Equally, while much inter-firm collaboration and cooperation has been fairly short term and opportunistic in the SME sector (Schak 2000), it has become more for-mally organized in the newer high-technology industries, often with substantial state support and the active participation of business associations (Tung 2001; Guerrieri and Pietrobelli 2006; Tzeng, Beamish, and Chen 2011). Also, the weak anti-trust tradition has allowed a number of overlapping directorships and other forms of connecting firms' activities to become established between companies in the same industry in some sectors, notably plastics, textiles, electrical machinery, iron and steel, and shipping (Brookfield 2010), and oligopolistic structures seem to be more common since democratization. Overall, then, the increasingly dominant role of business groups in Taiwan appears to have led to a more interlinked network of alliances and collaborations, particularly between those based around financial holding-companies, and more formal arrangements for cooperation between companies involved in developing new technologies (Tung 2001; Zhang 2012; Zhang and Whitley 2013).

Turning finally to employment relationships and the organization of authority within firms, labour turnover has traditionally varied considerably between the predominantly Taiwanese-owned SME sector, where it was quite high with frequent job-hopping, and the more stable large-firm state-owned sectors. Since democratization, business-group growth, some SOE privatization, and regulatory reform have reduced these differences, but the relative strength of unions in the SOE sector and their ability to mobilize political support have both limited the extent of privatization compared to Korea and ensured that employment remains somewhat longer term than in the small-firm sector (Lee 2009). Overall, though, despite the expansion of business groups and average firm size, companies remain reluctant to institutionalize long-term organization-specific careers for staff without family or family-like connections with the owners, and employer–employee commitment in the bulk of the economy remains weak.

This relative lack of commitment to investing in, and developing, firm-specific knowledge and long-term careers with particular companies is partly explained by, and reinforces, the widespread centralization of decision-making by family and other members of the 'inner circle' dominating the management of most Taiwanese firms (Chung and Mahmood 2010; Lee and Hsiao 2014). This core group may extend beyond the immediate founder and members of his immediate family to more distant relatives and trusted partners as successful firms grow, and second- or third-generation family members take control (Chung and Luo 2008), but there is little evidence of such changes leading to more collegiate management practices and delegation of authority to middle-managers, let alone to trusting the bulk of the workforce with greater task autonomy and involvement in problem-solving.

This summary of the key characteristics of the dominant business system in contemporary Taiwan indicates that changes to the political and financial systems have resulted in the growth of private-sector coordination of economic activities through diversified business groups. However, continuing, if reduced, state influence over the financial system and ownership of some large enterprises, coupled with a more proactive state role in developing new industries in conjunction with private Taiwanese firms than was typical in the 1960–1970s, have limited the decline of the developmental state and led to an expansion of state–big business collaboration and coordination of industrial development, especially in high-technology sectors (Thurbon and Weiss 2006; Lee 2009; Fields 2012).

In fact, it is arguable that the previous dualist division of the political economy between the large-enterprise upstream sector dominated by state- and KMT-owned companies and the private Taiwanese-owned SME sectors has been superseded by a more integrated system in which business groups constitute the major economic actors, although differences exist between sectors in how much these groups coordinate activities (Zhang and Whitley 2013). However, these groups continue to be largely family owned and controlled, despite some growth in equity-based investment funding, with little evidence of significant change in authority relationships between owners, managers, and most employees, or in labour-turnover rates. The overall expansion of economic coordination within and between sectors represented by the growth of business groups in Taiwan, then, has not been accompanied by much change in prevalent patterns of corporate governance or employment practices.

# Concluding Remarks

This discussion of change and continuity in dominant institutions, geo-political contexts, and business-system characteristics in East Asia has highlighted four main points. First, despite the weakening of the strong developmental state, varied liberalization of capital and labour markets, and internationalization of many companies, there is little evidence that dominant business systems in these three political economies are becoming more similar to those in the Anglo-American world, or indeed to each other (Shin and Hamilton 2014). Both the broad system of governing institutions, dominant interest-groups, and patterns of political cooperation and competition on the one hand, and the prevalent form of economic coordination and control on the other hand, still display significant differences between Japan, Korea, and Taiwan, even as their economic interdependence grows. The semi-globalized (Ghemawat 2003) world economy, expansion of democratic politics, and growing influence of transnational governance (Djelic and Quack 2003; Djelic and Sahlin-Andersson 2006) have not resulted in the homogenization of either dominant institutions or business systems along Anglo-American lines, nor have these phenomena generated the same kinds of radical changes. Nationally specific changes in dominant coalitions, patterns of industrialization, and state–business relations in particular geo-political situations continue to exert major, if not dominant, influences on how institutional changes such as democratization take place and affect patterns of economic organization (Walter and Zhang 2012).

Second, while the decline in the cohesion and autonomy of strong developmental states and the reduction of institutional complementarities may in general be expected to reduce the homogeneity and standardization of dominant firm-type and competitive behaviour across sectors and regions as companies become less dependent on government loans and other forms of direct support, and less constrained to follow state priorities, this is unlikely to happen quickly, and often does not apply to all aspects of corporate governance and behaviour. In post-war Japan, for instance, the weakening of the 'iron triangle' between LDP, bureaucratic and big-business elites, and the restructuring of the banking system and many *keiretsu* in the 1990s and early 2000s may have led to some diversity of corporate governance and employment policies in different firms and sectors. However, the continuing close involvement of the state in coordinating responses to economic decline and promoting new industries, the continuing importance of business associations in developing and implementing policies and coordinating actions, and the continuing significance of banks in supporting many companies, together with less than radical deregulation of many markets and commitment of key interest groups to established ways of organizing economic activities (Zhang and Whitley 2013), have limited the extent of change to the networked alliance capitalism that remains Japan's prevalent mode of economic coordination and control.

Third, just as the deregulation of capital markets does not always, or even often, lead to an expansion of equity-financed investment, arm's-length relationships between investors and managers, and an active market for corporate control (as shown by these countries), so too the removal of some restrictions on hiring and firing, use of temporary and part-time staff, and similar deregulatory measures need not intensify adversarial employment relationships and a widespread decline in long-term employment commitments. Rather, such measures permit a greater variety of firm behaviours, especially between sectors, as seen in Japan, and can often be combined with considerable employer–employee commitment, albeit with a somewhat shrunken core workforce.

Fourth, as the considerable continuities in many aspects of corporate governance, inter-firm connections, and employment practices amongst leading firms in these political economies indicate, quite substantial changes in dominant institutions and geo-political contexts need not, and often do not, produce equally marked shifts in prevalent business-system characteristics in the short to medium term. This is especially so where other features of the business environment, such as the continuing limited levels of trust in formal institutions and willingness to trust people with whom one does not have family-like relationships in Korea and Taiwan, remain substantially the same. In these cases, such low trust seems to have inhibited owners from delegating more and relying less on personal knowledge and contacts to generate competitive advantages.

As Wong, Wan, and Hsiao (2011) suggest, democratization of political competition does not, per se, automatically lead to greater trust in political institutions and actors, particularly if it fails to reduce corruption and the political favouring of special interests. Indeed, it may increase awareness of such phenomena, as mass media become more independent of the state, and encourage firms to rely more on personal contacts and special favours than on formal rules and sanctions, as arguably has happened in Taiwan (Wu 2007; Copper 2009). Thus, while declining authoritarianism and state domination of the economy may well create opportunities for businesses to pursue a variety of strategies and behaviours, it won't necessarily encourage them to decentralize control and trust formal institutions to manage uncertainty and deviance if personal connections remain key to many sources of competitive advantage, especially in the short to medium term.

## REFERENCES

Aguilera, R., L. R. Kabbach de Castro, J. H. Lee, and J. You (2012). 'Corporate Governance in Emerging Markets'. In G. Morgan and R. Whitley, Eds., *Capitalisms and Capitalism in the Twenty-First Century*: 319–344. Oxford, Oxford University Press.

Almeida, H., S. Y. Park, M. Subrahmanyam, and D. Wolfenzen (2009). 'The Structure and Formation of Business Groups: Evidence from Korean Chaebols'. National Bureau of Economic Research Working Paper 14983, Cambridge, USA: National Bureau of Economic Research.

Amsden, A. H. (1989). *Asia's Next Giant*. Oxford, Oxford University Press.

Amable, B. (2003). *The Diversity of Modern Capitalism*. Oxford, Oxford University Press.

—— G. Jackson, and H. Miyajima, Eds. (2007). *Corporate Governance in Japan*. Oxford, Oxford University Press.

Aoki, M. and H. Patrick, Eds. (1994). *The Japanese Main Bank System*. Oxford, Clarendon.

—— and R. Dore, Eds. (1994). *The Japanese Firm*. Oxford, Oxford University Press.

Bae, K. (1987). *Automobile Workers in Korea*. Seoul, Seoul National University Press.

Beeson, M. (2009). 'Developmental States in East Asia: A Comparison of the Japanese and Chinese Experiences'. *Asian Perspective* 33(2): 5–39.

Boyer, R. (2004). 'New Growth Regimes, But Still Institutional Diversity'. *Socio-Economic Review* 2: 1–32.

Braithwaite, J. and P. Drahos (2000). *Global Business Regulation*. Cambridge, Cambridge University Press.

Brookfield, J. (2010). 'The Network Structure of Big Business in Taiwan'. *Asia-Pacific Journal of Management* 27: 257–279.

Calder, K. E. (1993). *Strategic Capitalism: Private Business and Public Purpose in Japanese Industrial Finance*. Princeton, Princeton University Press.

Choe, S. and T. Roehl (2007). 'What to Shed and What to Keep: Corporate Transformation in Korean Business Groups'. *Long Range Planning* 40: 465–487.

Chung, C.-N. (2004). 'Institutional Transition and Cultural Inheritance: Network Characteristics and Corporate Control of Business Groups in Taiwan, 1970s–1990s'. *International Sociology* 19: 25–50.

—— (2006). 'Beyond Guanxi: Network contingencies in Taiwanese business groups'. *Organization Studies* 27: 461–489.

—— and X. Luo (2008). 'Human Agents, Contexts and Institutional Change: The Decline of Family in the Leadership of Business Groups'. *Organization Science* 19: 124–142.

—— and I. Mahmood (2010). 'Business Groups in Taiwan'. In A. Colpan, T. Hikino, and J. Lincoln, Eds., *Oxford Handbook of Business Groups*: 180–209. Oxford, Oxford University Press.

Clark, R. (1979). *The Japanese Company*. New Haven, Yale University Press.

Colpan, A., T. Hikino, and J. Lincoln, Eds. (2010). *Oxford Handbook of Business Groups*. Oxford, Oxford University Press.

Copper, J. (2009). 'The Devolution of Taiwan's Democracy during the Chen Shui-bian Era'. *Journal of Contemporary China* 18: 463–478.

Deyo, F. C. (1989). *Beneath the Miracle: Labour Subordination in the New Asian Industrialism*. Berkeley: University of California Press.

—— (2012). 'Reform and Institutional Change in East Asian Labour Markets'. In A. Walter and X. Zhang, Eds., *East Asian Capitalism*: 91–109. Oxford: Oxford University Press.

Djelic, M.-L. and S. Quack, Eds. (2003). *Globalization and Institutions*. Cheltenham, Edward Elgar.

—— and K. Sahlin-Andersson, Eds. (2006). *Transnational Governance*. Cambridge, Cambridge University Press.

Dore, R. P. (1973). *British Factory, Japanese Factory*. London, Allen and Unwin.

—— (2007). 'Insider Management and Board Reform'. In M. Aoki, G. Jackson, and H. Miyajima, Eds., *Corporate Governance in Japan*: 370–395. Oxford, Oxford University Press.

Evans, P. (1995). *Embedded Autonomy*. Princeton, Princeton University Press.

Fields, K. (1995). *Enterprise and the State in Korea and Taiwan*. Ithaca, Cornell University Press.

—— (2012). 'Not of a Piece: Developmental States, Industrial Policy and Evolving Patterns of Capitalism in Japan, Korea, and Taiwan'. In A. Walter and X. Zhang, Eds., *East Asian Capitalism*: 46–67. Oxford: Oxford University Press

Friedman, D. (1988). *The Misunderstood Miracle*. Ithaca, Cornell University Press.

Fruin, M. (1992). *The Japanese Enterprise System*. Oxford, Oxford University Press.

Fujimoto, T. (1999). *The Evolution of a Manufacturing System at Toyota*. Oxford, Oxford University Press.

Fujimura, H. (1997). 'New Unionism: Beyond Enterprise Unionism?'. In M. Sako and H. Sato, Eds., *Japanese Labour and Management in Transition*: 296–314. London, Routledge and Kegan Paul.

Garon, S. (1997). *Molding Japanese Minds*. Princeton, Princeton University Press.

Gerlach, M. (1992). *Alliance Capitalism*. Berkeley, University of California Press.

Ghemawat, P. (2003). 'Semi-Globalization and International Business Strategy'. *Journal of International Business Studies 34*: 138–152.

Gold, T. B. (1986). *State and Society in the Taiwan Miracle*. Armonk, M. E. Sharpe.

Gray, K. (2011). 'Taiwan and the Politics of Late Development'. *Pacific Review 24*: 577–599.

Guerrieri, P. and C. Pietrobelli (2006). 'Old and New Forms of Clustering and Production Networks in Changing Technological Regimes: Contrasting Evidence from Taiwan and Italy'. *Science, Technology & Society 11*: 9–38.

Hamilton, G. and C.-S. Kao (1990). 'The Institutional Foundation of Chinese Business: The Family Firm in Taiwan'. *Comparative Social Research 12*: 95–112.

Hsieh, M. (2011). 'Similar Opportunities, Different Responses: Explaining the Divergent Patterns of Development between Taiwan and South Korea'. *International Sociology 26*: 364–391.

Inagami, T. and H. Whittaker (2005). *The New Community Firm: Employment, Governance and Management Reform in Japan*. Cambridge, Cambridge University Press.

Jackson, G. (2007). 'Employment Adjustmeunt and Distributional Conflict in Japanese Firms'. In M. Aoki, G. Jackson, and H. Miyajima, Eds., *Corporate Governance in Japan*: 282–309. Oxford, Oxford University Press.

—— and H. Miyajima (2007). 'Introduction: The Diversity and Change of Corporate Governance in Japan'. In M. Aoki, G. Jackson, and H. Miyajima, Eds., *Corporate Governance in Japan*: 1–47. Oxford, Oxford University Press.

Janelli, R. L. (1993) *Making Capitalism: The Social and Cultural Construction of a South Korean Conglomerate*. Stanford, Stanford University Press.

Johnson, C. (1982). *MITI and the Japanese Miracle*. Stanford, Stanford University Press.

Keizer, A. (2009). 'Transformations In and Outside the Internal Labour Market: Institutional Change and Continuity in Japanese Employment Practices'. *International Journal of Human Resource Management 20*: 1521–1535.

—— (2011). 'Flexibility in Japanese Internal Labour Markets'. *Asia-Pacific Journal of Management 28*: 573–594.

Kikutani, T., H. Itoh, and O. Hayashida (2007). 'Business Portfolio Restructuring of Japanese Firms in the 1990s'. In M. Aoki, G. Jackson, and H. Miyajima, Eds., *Corporate Governance in Japan*: 227–256. Oxford, Oxford University Press.

Kim, C. S. (1992). *The Culture of Korean Industry*. Tucson: University of Arizona Press.

Kim, D-O. and J. Bae (2005). 'Workplace Innovation, Employment Relations, and HRM: Two Electronics Companies in South Korea'. *International Journal of Human Resource Management 16*: 1277–1302.

Kim, E. M. (1997). *Big Business, Big State: Collusion and Conflict in South Korean Development 1960–1990*. Albany, State University of New York Press.

Kim, H. (2010). 'Business Groups in Korea'. In A. Colpan. T. Hikino, and J. Lincoln, Eds., *Oxford Handbook of Business Groups*: 157–179. Oxford, Oxford University Press.

—— R. Hoskisson, L. Tihanyi, and J. Hong (2004). 'The Evolution and Restructuring of Diversified Business Groups in Emerging Markets: The lessons from chaebol in Korea'. *Asia-Pacific Journal of Management 21*: 25–48.

King, A. Y. C. (1996). 'State Confucianism and its Transformation: The Restructuring of the State-Society Relation in Taiwan'. In W.-M. Tu, Ed., *Confucian Traditions in East-Asian Modernity*: 228–243. Cambridge: Harvard University Press.

Koike, K. (1987). 'Human Resource Development and Labour Management Relations'. In K. Yamamura and Y. Yasuba, Eds., *The Political Economy of Japan I*: 289–330. Stanford, Stanford University Press.

Kong, T. Y. (2006). 'Globalization and Labour-Market Reform: Patterns of Response in Northeast Asia'. *British Journal of Political Science 36*: 359–383.

Laurence, H. (2001). *Money Rules*. Ithaca, Cornell University Press.

Lechevalier, S. (2007). 'The Diversity of Capitalism and Heterogeneity of Firms: A Case Study of Japan during the Lost Decade'. *Evolutionary and Institutional Economic Review 4*: 113–142.

Lee, K., S. Rho, and S. Kim (2007). 'Creativity-Innovation Cycle for Organizational Exploration and Exploitation: Lessons from Neowitz, a Korean Internet Company'. *Long Range Planning 40*: 505–523.

Lee, Y. (2009). 'Divergent Outcomes of Labor-Reform Politics in Democratized Korea and Taiwan'. *Studies in Comparative International Development 44*: 47–70.

Lee, Z.-R. and H.-H. M. Hsiao (2014). 'Taiwan: SME-Oriented Capitalism in Transition'. In M. A. Witt and G. Redding, Eds., *Oxford Handbook of Asian Business Systems* 238–259. Oxford, Oxford University Press.

Lin, K.-H. and I. Chaney (2007). 'The Influence of Domestic Inter-Firm Networks on the Internationalization Process of Taiwanese SMEs'. *Asia-Pacific Business Review 13*: 565–583.

Lincoln, J. and M. Gerlach (2004). *Japan's Network Economy*. Cambridge, Cambridge University Press.

—— and M. Shimotani (2010). 'Business Networks in Post-War Japan: Whither the *Keiretsu?*' In A. Colpan, T. Hikino, and J. Lincoln, Eds., *Oxford Handbook of Business Groups*: 127–156. Oxford, Oxford University Press.

MacDuffie, J. P. and S. Helper (2006). 'Collaboration in Supply Chains: With and Without Trust'. In C. Heckscher and P. Adler, Eds., *The Firm as a Collaborative Community*: 417–466. Oxford, Oxford University Press.

Matsumoto, M. (2002). 'Political Democratization and KMT Party-Owned Enterprises in Taiwan'. *Developing Economies XL*: 359–380.

Matsuura, K., M. Pollitt, R. Takada, and S. Tanaka (2004). 'Institutional Restructuring in the Japanese Economy since 1985'. In J. Perraton and B. Clift, Eds., *Where Are National Capitalisms Now?* 133–153. Basingstoke: Palgrave Macmillan.

Miyajima, H. and F. Kuroki (2007). 'The Unwinding of Cross-shareholding in Japan'. In M. Aoki, G. Jackson, and H. Miyajima, Eds. *Corporate Governance in Japan*: 79–124. Oxford, Oxford University Press.

Mosk, C. (1995). *Competition and Cooperation in Japanese Labour Markets*. Basingstoke, Macmillan.

Nakamura, K. (1997). 'Worker Participation: Collective Bargaining and Joint Consultation'. In M. Sako and H. Sato, Eds., *Japanese Labour and Management in Transition*: 280–295. London, Routledge.

—— (2011). 'Adoption and Policy Implications of Japan's New Corporate Governance Practices after the Reform'. *Asia-Pacific Journal of Management 28*: 187–213.

Numazaki, I. (1997). 'The Laoban-Led Development of Business Enterprises in Taiwan: An Analysis of Chinese Entrepreneurship'. *Developing Economies XXXV*: 440–457.

—— (2000). 'Chinese Business Enterprise as Inter-Family Partnership: A Comparison with the Japanese Case'. In K. B. Chan, Ed., *Chinese Business Networks: State, Economy, and Culture*: 152–175. Singapore, Pearson Education Asia.

Orrù, M., N. Biggart, and G. Hamilton (1997). *The Economic Organization of East Asian Capitalism*. Thousand Oaks: Sage.

Park, C. and S. Kim (2008). 'Corporate Governance, Regulatory Changes, and Corporate Restructuring in Korea, 1933–2004'. *Journal of World Business 43*: 66–84.

Peng, I. and J. Wong (2008). 'Institutions and Institutional Purpose: Continuity and Change in East Asian Social Policy'. *Politics and Society 36*(1): 61–88.

Rohlen, T. P. (1974). *For Harmony and Strength*. Berkeley, University of California Press.

Sako, M. (2006). *Shifting Boundaries of the Firm*. Oxford, Oxford University Press.

—— and M. Kotosaka (2012). 'Continuity and Change in the Japanese Economy: Evidence of Institutional Interactions in Financial and Labour Markets'. In A. Walter and X. Zhang, Eds., *East Asian Capitalism*: 132. Oxford, Oxford University Press.

Samuels, R. J. (1987). *The Business of the Japanese State*. Ithaca, Cornell University Press.

Schak, D. (2000). 'Networks and Their Uses in Taiwanese Society'. In C. K. Bun, Ed., *Chinese Business Networks*: 112–128. Singapore, Prentice-Hall.

Schmidt, V. A. (2002). *The Futures of European Capitalism*. Oxford, Oxford University Press.

Shieh, G. S. (1992). *'Boss' Island: The Subcontracting Network and Micro-Entrepreneurship in Taiwan's Development*. New York, Peter Lang.

Shin, S. and G. Hamilton (2014). 'Beyond Production: Changing Dynamics of Asian Business Groups'. In M. A. Witt and G. Redding, Eds., *Oxford Handbook of Asian Business Systems*: 611–632. Oxford, Oxford University Press.

Shinoda, T. (1997). 'Rengo and Policy Participation: Japanese-Style Neo-Corporatism?'. In M. Sako and H. Sato, Eds., *Japanese Labour and Management in Transition*: 187–214. London, Routledge.

Silin, R. H. (1976). *Leadership and Values: The Organization of Large-Scale Taiwanese Enterprises*. Cambridge, Harvard University Press.

Song, J. (2012). 'Economic Distress, Labor-Market Reforms and Dualism in Japan and Korea'. *Governance 25*: 415–438.

Sturgeon, T. (2006). 'Modular Production's Impact on Japan's Electronics Industry'. In H. Whittaker and R. Cole, Eds., *Recovering from Success*: 47–69. Oxford, Oxford University Press.

Sugeno, K. and Y. Suwa (1997). 'Labour-Law Issues in a Changing Labour Market: In Search of a New Support System'. In M. Sako and H. Sato, Eds., *Japanese Labour and Management in Transition*: 53–78. London, Routledge.

Thurbon, E. (2001). 'Two Paths to Financial Liberalization: South Korea and Taiwan'. *Pacific Review* 14: 241–267.

—— and L. Weiss (2006). 'Investing in Openness: The Evolution of FDI Strategy in South Korea and Taiwan'. *New Political Economy* 11(1): 1–22.

Tung, A.-C. (2001). 'Taiwan's Semiconductor Industry'. *Review of Development Economics* 5: 266–288.

Tzeng, C.-H., P. Beamish, and S.-F. Chen (2011). 'Institutions and Entrepreneurship Development: High-Technology Indigenous Firms in China and Taiwan'. *Asia-Pacific Journal of Management* 28: 453–481.

Wade, R. (1990). *Governing the Market: Economic Theory and the Role of Government in East Asian Industrialization*. Princeton, Princeton University Press.

Walter, A. and X. Zhang, Eds. (2012). *East Asian Capitalism*. Oxford, Oxford University Press.

Weiss, L. (2004). 'Developmental States Before and After the Asian Crisis'. In J. Perraton and B. Clift, Eds., *Where are National Capitalisms Now?* 154–168. Basingstoke, Palgrave Macmillan.

—— (2010). 'The State in the Economy: Neo-Liberal or Neo-Activist?'. In G. Morgan, J. Campbell, C. Crouch, O. Pedersen, and R. Whitley, Eds., *Oxford Handbook of Comparative Institutional Analysis*: 183–210. Oxford, Oxford University Press.

Whitley, R. (1992). *Business Systems in East Asia*. Thousand Oaks, Sage.

—— (1999). *Divergent Capitalisms*. Oxford, Oxford University Press.

—— (2005). 'How National are Business Systems?'. In G. Morgan, R. Whitley, and E. Moen, Eds., *Changing Capitalisms?* 190–231. Oxford, Oxford University Press.

—— (2007). *Business Systems and Organizational Capabilities*. Oxford, Oxford University Press.

Witt, M. A. (2014a). 'Japan: Coordinated Capitalism Between Institutional Change and Structural Inertia'. In M. A. Witt and G. Redding, Eds., *Oxford Handbook of Asian Business Systems*: 100–122. Oxford, Oxford University Press.

—— (2014b). 'South Korea: Plutocratic State-Led Capitalism Reconfiguring'. In M. A. Witt and G. Redding, Eds., *Oxford Handbook of Asian Business Systems*: 216–237. Oxford, Oxford University Press.

Wong, T., P.-S. Wan, and H.-H. M. Hsiao (2011). 'The Bases of Political Trust in Six Asian Societies'. *International Political Science Review* 32: 263–281.

Woo, J.-E. (1991). *Race to the Swift*. New York, Columbia University Press.

Wu, Y. (2007). 'Taiwan's Developmental State'. *Asian Survey* 47: 977–1001.

Zhang, X. (2009). 'From Banks to Markets'. *Review of International Political Economy* 16: 382–408.

—— (2012). 'Dominant Coalitions and Capital-Market Changes in Northeast Asia'. In A. Walter and X. Zhang, Eds., *East Asian Capitalism*: 223–243. Oxford, Oxford University Press.

—— and R. Whitley (2013). 'Changing Macro-Structural Varieties of East Asian Capitalism'. *Socio-Economic Review* 11: 301–336.

# PART IV

## CONCLUSIONS

# CHAPTER 29

......................................................................................................

# ASIAN BUSINESS SYSTEMS

*Implications and Perspectives for
Comparative Business Systems and Varieties
of Capitalism Research*

......................................................................................................

## MICHAEL A. WITT AND GORDON REDDING

IN the introduction to this *Oxford Handbook,* we argued that despite the long tradition of research on Asian business systems, much remains to be done in terms of idiographic description and subsequent nomothetic theorizing. The twenty-eight chapters in Parts I to III of this handbook have responded to this challenge, predominantly in terms of describing the characteristics of Asian business systems today, but also in terms of deriving theoretical implications.

In this concluding chapter, it is our privilege as editors to distil an overall picture and conclusions from the wealth of information these chapters contain. Such an effort must by necessity be relatively high level, and while a higher vantage point has advantages in terms of identifying overall features of the landscape, the trade-off is that finer details begin to disappear. As such, this chapter complements, not substitutes for, the chapters it draws on.

Our main objective for this chapter is to present a summary of salient institutional characteristics across the region, to identify patterns, and to draw conclusions for business-systems theory. Accordingly, the chapter starts at the idiographic level by presenting a comprehensive comparison of the institutional structures of the thirteen major Asian business systems covered in this handbook—those of China, Hong Kong, India, Indonesia, Japan, Laos, Malaysia, the Philippines, Singapore, Korea, Taiwan, Thailand, and Vietnam—as well as those of five major Western states—France, Germany, Sweden, the UK, and the USA—as comparison points.

Using these data, the chapter identifies five major clusters of Asian business systems: (post-)socialist economies, advanced city economies, emerging South East Asian economies, advanced North-East Asian economies, and Japan. Comparison with leading exponents of Western business systems suggests that, excepting Japan, Asian business systems are fundamentally distinct from those of the West.

Based on these findings, the chapter argues that the Varieties of Capitalism dichotomy is not applicable to Asia; that none of the existing major frameworks capture all Asian types of capitalism; and that Asian business systems (except Japan) cannot be understood through categories identified in the West. It further draws on a number of patterns visible in the comparative data to suggest at the nomothetic level that business-systems theories need to incorporate and conceptualize social capital, culture, informality, and multiplexity.

The chapter concludes with a brief summary of some of the main points emerging from the chapters focused on factors influencing business systems, outcomes, and historical trajectories.

# Asian Business Systems: A Comparison of Institutional Characteristics

Any comparison of the Asian business systems surveyed here must rely largely on qualitative assessments. The underlying issue is that published comparative statistics, readily available for advanced industrialized economies, are often difficult or impossible to obtain for these economies.

One response to this might be not to study Asian business systems until solid comparable statistics become available. However, for much of Asia, we would then be waiting a very long time.

A second approach would be to work only with statistics that are available. Some studies have taken this approach (e.g. Amable 2003) and made great contributions. Such an approach is most likely to work where comparative statistics are plentiful, that is, for advanced industrialized countries, but even there, not all matters can be measured. As a result, existing theory, though derived mostly from OECD countries, relies extensively on constructs for which reliable comparative statistics do not exist. For instance, the notion of consensual decision-making in firms is as central to VoC theory (Hall and Soskice 2001) as it is impossible to measure reliably across all advanced industrialized nations.

The issue of construct validity of comparative statistics has not necessarily been fully recognized in the field. For instance, the proportion of stock-market capitalization over GDP is often used as an indicator whether a business system is market- or bank-based (e.g. Hall and Gingerich 2009; Schneider and Paunescu 2012). In fact, it is highly problematic without further qualitative judgement, considering fluctuations in valuations over time and by market (e.g. Japan has relatively high valuations, for no clear reason), foreign listings inflating market capitalization (e.g. Russian listings in the UK), and, especially for emerging markets, difficulties in obtaining accurate GDP figures. What we would need is a national measure of how much of the fresh money that companies receive from external sources in a given year comes from which sources. Even for advanced industrialized countries, this is next to impossible to get, with few exceptions (Witt 2006). Similar issues plague other widely-used measures, such as credit to the private sector over GDP, which does not distinguish between corporate and consumer loans, and graduation rates for vocational and tertiary education, which measure flow rather than stock and say nothing about the quality of such education.

As a result, much existing theory, including in the key foundational works by Whitley (1992, 1999) and Hall and Soskice (2001), is built on a third approach, qualitative comparative assessment. The methodological validity and utility of qualitative measures for the comparison of business systems has experienced extensive discussion and validation (Ragin 2000, 2008).

Our own approach consequently represents a mix of statistics and qualitative data. Where reliable comparable statistics with construct validity are available, we make use of them. Our main source, however, is the series of country chapters in Part I of this *Oxford Handbook* (Andriesse 2014; Carney and Andriesse 2014; Carney 2014; Kondo 2014; Lee and Hsiao 2014; Redding et al. 2014; Rosser 2014; Saez 2014; Suehiro and Wailerdsak 2014; Truong and Rowley 2014; Witt 2014a; Witt 2014b; Witt and Redding 2014b), supplemented by insights from Part II chapters. For each economy, these chapters present a comprehensive survey of the institutional dimensions identified in Chapter 1, leveraging a large diversity of the most recent available empirical research and statistics on the various aspects of each business system. Since most of these empirical bases are context-specific and thus not comparative in nature, we have translated them to qualitative assessments. Table 29.1 combines a summary of these findings with pertinent comparative statistics.

As Table 29.1 indicates, there is large variation in institutional structures across Asian economies. However, there are patterns, which we will now explore in some detail, drawing on insights and examples from the above works as appropriate, before identifying clusters of similarity. Several empirical regularities present have important implications for extending and elaborating extant business-systems theories, as we will argue later.

*Education and Skills Formation.* While universal education to decent levels can be assumed for the advanced industrialized nations of the West, the same cannot be said for Asia. As Table 29.1 indicates, there is considerable spread in educational attainment. Basic skills, such as the ability to read and write, cannot be taken for granted, as evident in adult literacy rates in Asia ranging from 61 per cent in India to full literacy in Japan. Except Japan, even the richer Asian economies of Hong Kong, Korea, Singapore, and Taiwan have not yet attained the 99 per cent literacy rates common in the West.

A similar picture emerges in the United Nation's education index, which measures the mean years of schooling received and the expected years of schooling for adults and children, respectively. The underlying assumption is that, *ceteris paribus*, more time spent in school will result in higher education levels and lower rates of illiteracy. Higher levels of the indicator express greater educational attainment in terms of schooling received. There is considerable variance on this measure, ranging from 0.432 in Laos to 0.934 in Korea. Within the full UNDP sample of 188 countries, Laos ranks 151st, Korea, 6th. The other economies in the sample run the gamut.

Table 29.1, Part 1 Comparison of the institutional characteristics of 13 Asian business systems

| Category | Measure | China | Hong Kong | India | Indonesia | Japan |
|---|---|---|---|---|---|---|
| Education and Skills | Adult Literacy | 0.922 | 0.969 | 0.61 | 0.904 | 0.99 |
| | Education Attainment Index (2010) | 0.623 | 0.837 | 0.45 | 0.584 | 0.883 |
| | Employment Tenure | short (private), long (state-owned) | short | short (private), long (state-owned) | unclear | long |
| | Skills Acquisition[1] | private | private | private, some corporate | private | OJT |
| Employment Relations | Union Density | 16.1% (2007) | 23.2% (2010) | 6.9% (2008) | 5.0% (2007) | 18.5% (2010) |
| | Organization Principle | party-controlled single union | industry | industry | company | company |
| | State Intervention in Wage Bargaining | high | low | low-medium | medium | low |
| | Coordination | 5 | 1 | 2 | 2 | 3 |
| | Belligerence: Days Lost to Strikes, Average 2000–2008 | n/a | n/a | 25,230,911 | n/a | 11,693 |
| Financial System | Main Source of External Capital | banks | banks | banks | banks | banks |
| | Allocation Criterion[1] | relationships, state | relationships | relationships, state | relationships | market, relationships |
| | Term | long | long | long | long | long |
| Inter-firm Relations | Presence of Business Groups | qituan qiye | hongs | business houses | yes | keiretsu |
| | Noteworthy Other Networks[1] | Communist Party, personal networks (guanxi) | investment networks, SME networks | caste or religion-based networks, industrial clusters (IT) | n/a | intra-industry loops with strong associations, R&D consortia, supplier and distribution networks |

(Continued)

**Table 29.1 Part 1  Continued**

| Category | Measure | China | Hong Kong | India | Indonesia | Japan |
|---|---|---|---|---|---|---|
| Internal Structure | Decision-making Structure | top-down | top-down | top-down | top-down | participatory |
|  | Extent of Delegation | low | some | low | low | medium-high |
|  | Main Basis of Promotion and Pay Raises[1] | relationships | relationships | relationships, seniority | relationships | seniority |
| Ownership and Governance | Main Ownership Form, Large Firms[1] | family, state | family | family, state | family | public |
|  | Main Controlling Owner[1] | family, state | family | family, state | family | firms |
|  | Investor Protection Index (out of 10) (2012) | 5.0 | 9.0 | 6.0 | 6.0 | 7.0 |
| Social Capital | Interpersonal Trust | high | high | high | high | high |
|  | Institutionalized Trust: Rule of Law | −0.35 | 1.56 | −0.06 | −0.63 | 1.31 |
| State | Type[1] | developmental and predatory | regulatory | predatory with developmental trend | predatory | residual developmental, welfare elements |
|  | Decision-making[1] | bottom-up and top-down | bottom-up and top-down | top-down, variation at state level | top-down | participatory through associations and committees |
|  | Voice and Accountability | −1.65 | 0.58 | 0.42 | −0.06 | 1.05 |
|  | Government Effectiveness | 0.12 | 1.74 | −0.01 | −0.20 | 1.40 |
|  | Regulatory Quality | −0.23 | 1.89 | −0.39 | −0.38 | 0.98 |

*Sources*: 13 chapters cited in the chapter, unless otherwise marked in Table 29.1 Part 3.

**Table 29.1 Part 2 Comparison of the Institutional Characteristics of 13 Asian Business Systems**

| Category | Measure | Korea | Laos | Malaysia | Philippines | Singapore |
|---|---|---|---|---|---|---|
| Education and Skills | Adult Literacy | 0.979 | 0.730 | 0.887 | 0.926 | 0.925 |
| | Education Attainment Index (2010) | 0.934 | 0.432 | 0.730 | 0.684 | 0.751 |
| | Employment Tenure | medium | short (private), long (state) | short | short | short |
| Employment Relations | Skills Acquisition[1] | OJT, private | private | private | private, some OJT | companies, private |
| | Union Density | 10.0% (2009) | n/a | 10.2% (2007) | 11.2% (2007) | 17.65% (2009) |
| | Organization Principle[1] | company | party-controlled single union | company | company | mix of company, craft, industry |
| | State Intervention in Wage Bargaining | medium | high | medium–high | medium | medium–high |
| | Coordination | 3 | 5 | n/a (low) | n/a (low) | 3 |
| | Belligerence: Days Lost to Strikes, Average 2000–2008 | 1,160,940 | n/a (strikes illegal) | n/a | 145,050 | 0 |
| Financial System | Main Source of External Capital | banks, non-bank financial institutions | banks | banks | banks | banks |
| | Allocation Criterion[1] | market, relationships | relationships, state | relationships, state | relationships (conglomerate owned) | relationships |
| Inter-firm Relations | Term | long | long | long | long | long |
| | Presence of Business Groups | chaebol | yes | yes | yes | yes |

(Continued)

**Table 29.1 Part 2 Continued**

| Category | Measure | Korea | Laos | Malaysia | Philippines | Singapore |
|---|---|---|---|---|---|---|
| | Noteworthy Other Networks[1] | n/a | Communist Party | personalistic, state-mediated | n/a | government (GLCs) |
| Internal Structure | Decision-making Structure | top-down | top-down | top-down | top-down | top-down |
| | Extent of Delegation | low | low | low | low | some |
| | Main Basis of Promotion and Pay Raises[1] | seniority | relationships | relationships | relationships | performance, relationships |
| Ownership and Governance | Main Ownership Form, Large Firms[1] | public | state | family, state | family | family, state |
| | Main Controlling Owner[1] | family | state | family, state | family | family, state |
| | Investor Protection Index (out of 10) (2012) | 6.0 | 1.7 | 8.7 | 4.3 | 9.3 |
| Social Capital | Interpersonal Trust | high | high | high | high | high |
| | Institutionalized Trust: Rule of Law | 0.99 | −0.90 | 0.51 | −0.54 | 1.69 |
| State | Type[1] | developmental | predatory | developmental, predatory | predatory | developmental, regulatory |
| | Decision-making | top-down | top-down | top-down | top-down | top-down |
| | Voice and Accountability | 0.71 | −1.63 | −0.53 | −0.09 | −0.29 |
| | Government Effectiveness | 1.19 | −0.94 | 1.10 | −0.10 | 2.25 |
| | Regulatory Quality | 0.91 | −1.03 | 0.58 | −0.26 | 1.80 |

Table 29.1 Part 3 Comparison of the institutional characteristics of 13 Asian business systems

| Category | Measure | Taiwan | Thailand | Vietnam | Sources |
|---|---|---|---|---|---|
| Education and Skills | Adult Literacy | 0.961 | 0.926 | 0.940 | CIA World Factbook |
|  | Education Attainment Index (2010) | 0.8 (own estimate) | 0.597 | 0.503 | <http://hdrstats.undp.org/en/indicators/103706.html> |
| Employment Relations | Employment Tenure | medium | short | long (SOEs), short (private) private |  |
|  | Skills Acquisition[1] | OJT, private | private | private |  |
|  | Union Density | 37.3% (2010) | <10% | 67% (2005, text) | http://www.uva-aias.net/208; ILO; chapters |
|  | Organization Principle | company | company, industry | party-controlled single union |  |
|  | State Intervention in Wage Bargaining | n/a | n/a | high | http://www.uva-aias.net/208 |
|  | Coordination | n/a | n/a | 5 | http://www.uva-aias.net/208 |
|  | Belligerence: Days Lost to Strikes, Average 2000–2008 | 55,234 (2008–11) | 45,217 | n/a (5,000 strikes from 2000 to 2010) | ILO; chapters |
| Financial System | Main Source of External Capital | banks | banks | banks |  |
| Inter-firm Relations | Allocation Criterion[1] | relationships | relationships | relationships, state |  |
|  | Term | long | long | long |  |
|  | Presence of Business Groups | qituan qiye | glum thurakit | hiep hoi doanh nghiep |  |
|  | Noteworthy Other Networks[1] | interlocks even among competitors, personal ties (guanxi) | supplier networks | personal ties, Communist Party |  |
| Internal Structure | Decision-making Structure | top-down | top-down | top-down |  |

(Continued)

**Table 29.1 Part 3 Continued**

| Category | Measure | Taiwan | Thailand | Vietnam | Sources |
|---|---|---|---|---|---|
| | Extent of Delegation | low | low | low | |
| | Main Basis of Promotion and Pay Raises[1] | relationships, seniority | relationships | relationships | |
| Ownership and Governance | Main Ownership Form, Large Firms[1] | family | family | family, state | |
| | Main Controlling Owner[1] | family | family | family, state | |
| | Investor Protection Index (out of 10) (2012) | 6.3 | 7.7 | 3.0 | http://www.doingbusiness.org/data/exploretopics/protecting-investors |
| Social Capital | Interpersonal Trust | high | high | high | |
| | Institutionalized Trust: Rule of Law | 1.01 | −0.20 | −0.48 | http://info.worldbank.org/governance/wgi |
| State | Type[1] | developmental | developmental, predatory | predatory with developmental trend | |
| | Decision-making | top-down | top-down | top-down | |
| | Voice and Accountability | 0.90 | −0.56 | −1.43 | http://info.worldbank.org/governance/wgi |
| | Government Effectiveness | 1.21 | 0.09 | −0.31 | http://info.worldbank.org/governance/wgi |
| | Regulatory Quality | 1.18 | 0.19 | −0.58 | http://info.worldbank.org/governance/wgi |

*Sources:* 13 chapters cited in the chapter unless otherwise marked.
[1] Given in alphabetical order unless relative order is indicated

In terms of acquiring skills for employment, we see a clear pattern. In a majority of Asian economies, the acquisition of professional skills is left to private initiative. In a number of countries, private employers try to provide at least some skills training, though usually at a low level. Public vocational-training systems are usually very weak. This may partially be related to a shared cultural notion that manual labour is a reflection of academic failure, with parents usually steering their children away from vocational training schools. In addition, the curricula of existing vocational-training programmes tend to be misaligned with the requirements of employers. Extensive on-the-job training (OJT) is essentially a Japanese phenomenon, though the practice is also evident, to a lesser degree, in Korea and Taiwan.

The reluctance of employers to provide extensive OJT is related to employment tenures, which tend to be short term across most countries in the region. While not all countries provide comparative statistics of employment tenures, the evidence on most countries reports frequent job-hopping and high employment turnover. As has been argued (e.g. Hall and Soskice 2001), this discourages the formation of firm-specific skills. Exceptions are Japan, Korea, and Taiwan, which is consistent with OJT in these countries. In addition, state-owned enterprises in China, India, Laos, and Vietnam maintain relatively long terms of employment. This should enable them to provide OJT to their employees. In practice, however, the absence of systematic human-resource development programmes and incentive structures encouraging the acquisition of valuable skills means that little such OJT occurs. In addition, relatively low levels of development in these latter economies and their associated industrial structures, with an emphasis on labour-intensive rather than skills-intensive production, are likely to work against the widespread implementation of OJT.

*Employment Relations.* All thirteen economies feature labour unions. Unionization rates for most run from about 5 per cent in Indonesia to about 23 per cent in Hong Kong (albeit focused on relatively few organizations). Vietnam emerges as an outlier, with unionization rates of about 67 per cent, comparable to Northern European nations.

The dominant organizational principle is the company union. Accordingly, the degree of coordination across these economies tends to be low to medium. Major exceptions to the rule are the nominally socialist economies of the region, that is, China, Laos, and Vietnam. These countries have party controlled unitary unions, such as the All China Federation of Trade Unions (ACFTU). Given high levels of centralization, the level of coordination in these economies is consequently high. However, this is not necessarily to the advantage of labour; for instance, in labour disputes, the ACFTU usually sides with employers. Party-controlled unions are essentially tools of state control rather than civil-society representatives of labour interests.

A relatively strong desire of states to remain in control of the economy is also visible in the extent of state intervention in wage bargaining. Such intervention is high in the socialist economies. Most of the other nations, to the extent that data are available, show considerable levels of state involvement, with only Hong Kong and Japan scoring low. The means of such involvement vary. In Korea, for instance, the government has created a tripartite commission. In Singapore, by contrast, the union movement has de facto been brought into the fold of government, with union leaders receiving cabinet-level posts.

Union belligerence likewise varies considerably, though statistics on this point are patchy. Some countries, especially socialist ones, outlaw strikes and do not report official statistics of strike activity. In the countries for which statistics are available, strike activity is generally moderate. This is sometimes the result of restrictions. For instance, in Singapore, the right to strike officially exists, but given the incorporation of unions in government, the last registered strike occurred in 1986. Wildcat strikes are discouraged by the fact that any group of five or more persons not registered with the authorities may constitute an unlawful assembly. On the other side of the spectrum, in Japan, high levels of alignment between workers and management and participatory decision-making keep the need to strike low. Korea and especially India stand out as high-strike countries, with 1.2 and 25 million strike days in an average year between 2000 and 2008. However, in both, the recent trend has been downwards.

*Financial System.* The main source of external financing is banks. A common pattern is that business groups maintain their own banks or similar financial institutions, which they can tap for long-term funding on preferential terms. For instance, the leading Korean conglomerates use non-bank financial institutions such as insurance companies that they own.[1] In most Asian markets, officially licensed lending coexists with an informal banking landscape serving firms usually excluded from access to banks or markets. For instance, China's informal banking sector is estimated at about 3–4 trillion *yuan*, about one-third of the size of the total financial system (Yao 2011). The importance of such informal finance for understanding economic activity can be considerable. In the Chinese case, informal finance is the main avenue of obtaining external funding for the private sector, which accounts for about two-thirds of Chinese GDP.

The main criteria for allocation of credit across the region are relationships and state direction. Relationships often involve joint ownership of lender and creditor, as in the Korean example above, but also long-standing business relationships akin to the German Hausbank model. In China, India, Laos, and Vietnam—all countries with a central planning background—state influence on capital allocation remains strong. There, the major banks remain in state hands and engage in policy-driven directed lending, with preference given to state-owned enterprises. The hand of the state is also visible in countries with developmental-state elements, such as Malaysia and Singapore, where industrial policy targets certain sectors or firms for further development.

Given the mix of bank-led finance and allocation based on relationships or state direction, capital is usually available for the long term for the recipients of such loans—that is, funds will tend not to be withdrawn quickly in response to adverse developments, as would typically be the case in Anglo-Saxon environments (Whitley 1999; Hall and Soskice 2001).

*Inter-firm Relations.* The key characteristic in this category is the presence of business groups across all Asian nations. These are usually defined as large conglomerates that are ultimately owned and/or controlled by the same party, typically a family or the state. Again Japan proves to be the exception, in that its business groups, or *keiretsu,* have no one ultimate owner or controlling party, an aberration based on anti-trust policies the US occupation enacted following World War II.

Absent from the picture, except for Japan, are the kinds of institutionalized long-term cooperative ties among different firms present in some of the continental European economies (Hall and Soskice 2001).

Other forms of cooperation across firms are based on party networks, especially in Communist countries where the party retains ownership and control of at least some firms and permeates the private sector through measures such as the mandatory unionization of employees under party-controlled unitary labour unions. Important are further personalistic ties, that is, personal relationships on an individual level. These networks enable, among other things, the finding of new business opportunities and occasional ad-hoc cooperation in production networks in which large orders are filled by distributing the work across several independent enterprises.

*Internal Structure.* Decision-making in Asian firms is usually hierarchical and top-down. Centralization is usually high, with major decisions resting in the hands of top management. Only Japan features a relatively participatory mode of decision-making cutting across levels and functions.

Accordingly, the degree of delegation in Asian firms is generally low. Management below the top level is usually a conduit of orders from the top, supervising whether instructions are properly executed. The main exception to this rule is Japan, as a participatory structure cannot work without some delegation. Hong Kong and Singapore similarly show some delegation. In general, the extent of delegation correlates positively with levels of institutionalized trust, as discussed later.

The key criteria for promotion are relationships and, less so, seniority. Relationships are important especially at top levels, which in private businesses are usually reserved for relatives of the owning family or their close and trusted friends. In state-owned enterprises, relationships with governing parties or powerful individuals are important. Seniority—the length of time spent working for the company—is a key component in Japan and Korea, but important also at lower levels of state-owned enterprises across the region.

*Ownership and Corporate Governance.* In most Asian economies, family ownership is dominant. This is true in particular for the business groups already noted. In nominally socialist economies, there is also an important element of state ownership, and where state-owned enterprises are listed on stock exchanges, the state usually retains a controlling stake. Only in Japan and Korea are the largest firms majority-publicly held.

In line with ownership patterns, management control of firms usually also rests with families or the state. Family ownership is partially a function of the relative youth of modern economic development in most of Asia, in the sense that many firms, even large ones, were founded relatively recently. It is also connected to the absence or relative recency of institutionalized trust, discussed later; this discourages not only delegation, but also the separation of ownership from control that is crucial for modern enterprises. Korea is unusual in that firms are majority publicly owned, but family-controlled, a trick accomplished through creative shareholding patterns such as pyramidal and circular shareholdings. Japan is again an outlier, in that firms essentially control themselves, a feat accomplished through a combination of high levels of friendly and disinterested long-term shareholders and fairly weak implementation of formally strong corporate governance rules.

Consistent with the importance of family and state control, corporate governance rules, intended to guard the interests especially of minority shareholders, are generally weak. Best of class are Singapore and Hong Kong, respectively, with both economies highly reliant on foreign investments and their stock markets attracting large volumes of foreign listings. On the other hand, Vietnam is only beginning to understand the concept of corporate governance, and Laos has only two firms listed on its recently founded stock exchange. In general, families usually retain a controlling stake in firms, even if they decide to list them. Where conglomerates are involved, pyramids and circular shareholdings as well as shares with multiple voting rights entrench family control and help owner families reap a disproportionate share of profits.

*Social Capital.* In keeping with Whitley (1999) and Redding (2005), we define social capital as trust (for a review article supporting this and the following conceptualizations of social capital, see Esser 2008). We follow these prior works in distinguishing two basic types of trust: (1) interpersonal (or relational) trust, that is, the kind of trust that exists between two persons on the basis of prior experience that suggests that the respective other will be honest and uphold debts of reciprocity (usually involving family and friends), and (2) institutionalized (or system) trust, based on the presence of a system that keeps others honest.

Across the board, Asian economies are rich in interpersonal trust, as expressed in extensive networks of reciprocal relationships between individuals, both inside the firm and outside. This is consistent with the well-established finding in the literature that individuals in Asian societies tend to build stronger interpersonal networks, both inside the family and with friends, than their Western counterparts, and to leverage them for business (cf. Li and Redding 2014).

By contrast, there is considerable variation in the presence of institutionalized trust. Institutionalized trust enables strangers to do business with each other without much fear of opportunism, because there is fair recourse in case of disputes. One proxy measure is the extent of the rule of law in a given economy. The range of institutionalized trust thus operationalized ranges from very low in Indonesia, Laos, and the Philippines to very high in Hong Kong and Singapore. Not captured in this measure are further dimensions of institutionalized trust for which no similar comparative measures exist, as we will discuss later. The reliance on relational trust is unsurprising in societies with weak system institutions to foster trust between strangers.

*The Role of the State.* Most states in the region fall into either the developmental or predatory state categories (cf. Johnson 1982; Evans 1995), with some of them representing hybrid cases. The clearest predatory states are Indonesia, Laos, and the Philippines. India arguably also best fits into this category, a point vividly illustrated by recent mobile-phone and coal corruption cases that cost the Indian treasury an estimated US$39bn and US$210bn in lost revenues, respectively. Others, such as China, combine predatory elements, in which top leaders and their families use the state to enrich themselves, with industrial policies modelled, with some licence, on the Japanese template. Developmental states include Korea, Singapore, and Taiwan, with some residual elements visible in Japan. Clear welfare-state elements are visible only in Japan. Regulatory states, defined as those aiming at creating regulatory frameworks enabling free and fair competition, include Hong Kong and, outside government-promoted sectors, Singapore.

Decision-making in most Asian states is statist. The exception is Japan, which tends towards corporatism, in the sense that policy formulation involves the participation of various sectors of society, notably industry associations, and is usually consensual. China and Hong Kong mix top-down statism with a strong bottom-up element. In Hong Kong, this occurs because many areas of economic activity are unregulated, allowing actors to evolve their own informal institutions. In China, local variations in institutions, often in breach of formal institutions, have been a central element in economic policy-making since the 1990s. Successful institutional innovations diffuse across different localities and inform national-level institutional changes (Xu 2011). In line with these variations, the extent of voice given to citizens and accountability of government to citizens varies widely, with China and Laos virtually tied at the lower end and fully-democratic Japan taking the top score.

In terms of outcomes, there is considerable variation expressed in government effectiveness and quality of institutions. Worst on both dimensions is Laos, best are Hong Kong and Singapore. Japan, Korea, Taiwan, and less so Malaysia occupy positions towards the top, with the remaining countries retaining considerable upside potential.

# TYPES OF ASIAN BUSINESS SYSTEMS IN COMPARATIVE PERSPECTIVE

To identify the different types of Asian business systems present in our sample, we submitted the data in Table 29.1 to hierarchical cluster analysis. For comparison with the West, we added five representatives of major forms of Western capitalism identified in the literature: France as an exemplar of 'mixed' or state capitalism; Germany as a case of continental coordinated capitalism; Sweden as an example of social-democratic capitalism; and the UK and USA as illustrations of liberal market capitalism (Whitley 1999; Hall and Soskice 2001; Schmidt 2002; Amable 2003; Hancké, Rhodes, and Thatcher 2007).

We recoded qualitative data in the form of dummy variables. For instance, differences in employment tenure were captured in three dummy variables, one for short-term, one for medium-term, and one for long-term employment. Variables with missing data had to be omitted. Since this would have left us with only one variable for employment relations, we imputed a union density of 0.5 for Laos; the actual value is unknown, and the value has no impact on the result for Laos, but lets us retain the variable. All measures were normalized to eliminate distortions arising from differences in numerical magnitude across variables.

We employed hierarchical cluster analysis as implemented in Stata 12 (StataCorp 2011b), using the Gower dissimilarity measure, which is suitable for mixed continuous and categorical variables as present in our data (StataCorp 2011a). Since there is no theoretical reason to prioritize one type of linkage over another, we ran multiple analyses using different linkage specifications. We found that the resultant clusters are robust across specifications.

Figure 29.1 shows the resultant clusters, and Table 29.2 presents the attendant pairwise dissimilarity measures, or 'institutional distances' (cf. Jackson and Deeg 2008). The main Asian clusters are, from left to right: the (post-)socialist countries of China, Vietnam, Laos, and India, the latter clustering here because its socialist heritage of central planning and state control of the economy remains strong; the advanced city economies of Hong Kong and Singapore; the remaining South East Asian nations; and the advanced North-East Asian economies of Korea and Taiwan.

The Western economies as well as Japan cluster separately from the Asian economies. They form two large branches, broadly consistent with the notion of coordinated and liberal market economies (Hall and Soskice 2001). Consistent with prior treatment in the literature of Japan as a case of coordinated capitalism (e.g. Hall and Soskice 2001; Redding and Witt 2007), Japan falls into the coordinated branch, between the two Germanic economies and France.

We ran an additional series of cluster analyses in which we separated Chinese and Indian private and state business. The rationale for this was that we wanted to see how the institutional structures of private business, which in both countries is the driving force of growth and accounts for about two-thirds of GDP (Saez 2014; Witt and Redding 2014b), fit into the overall picture. Figure 29.2 shows the results. As prior works have suggested (Redding and Witt 2007), Chinese private business broadly clusters with the poorer South East Asian economies, which tend to be dominated by ethnic Chinese businesses. Indian private business is on the same branch as Chinese private business and the poorer South East Asian nations, but splits off earlier into a branch of its own. State businesses in both countries cluster with one another and, at a higher level, with Laos and Vietnam, as one would expect.

This structural similarity of Chinese and Indian business may at first seem surprising. The most striking contrast between these nations is that India is socio-culturally highly diverse, while China is both different from India and homogeneous. A second obvious contrast is between the democracy of India and the autocracy of China.

Despite these differences, their business systems have many common features, as is readily apparent when one compares the institutional characteristics of the two economies in Table 29.1. Of these, perhaps the most significant are the inefficiency of the state institutions on which the economy depends, the vibrancy of the private sector, despite selectivity in capital allocation, the dominance of bank financing, the power of personally dominated large firms with crony-capitalist connections (in India business houses, in China local corporates), management-skill shortages and weak delegation, endemic

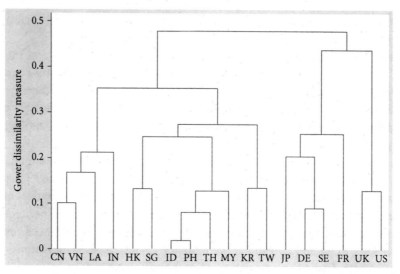

FIGURE 29.1 Dendrogram of clusters of Asian business systems in comparative perspective

corruption and predatory tendencies, dis-organized labour, weak educational quality, and debilitatingly weak institutional trust. They share a daunting future as they face the challenges of the expanded rationalisms of modernizing, and they do so being more similar than they may at first seem.

There are also important historical parallels. First, China and India share several formative decades of re-birth as states from the late 1940s, in each case with a Marxist political ideology, and with a continued legacy of very heavy government. Second, post-1980 they evolved out of this in parallel by adopting market discipline and the use of controlled influences from outside. Third, they have encouraged alliances of various mercantile forms between strongly entrepreneurial business initiatives and government-sourced funding and licensing.

Overall, our results are broadly consistent with the clusters of Asian capitalisms identified by Harada and Tohyama (2012), which to our knowledge represents the one prior work of this kind. However, the present results improve and extend on their work in a number of ways. First, geographical coverage is widened to include India and Vietnam, two important and fast-rising economies, as well as Laos. As a result, we know that China does not constitute a singular case, as concluded by Harada and Tohyama, but is part of a larger cluster of (post-)socialist economies. Second, the dimensions used to produce the present results are compatible with leading models of business-systems analysis. Third, the measures underlying the present analysis draw on the institutional structures in Asian business systems, not as published in official rules and regulations, but as actually practised, a point that is of great relevance in Asia, as we will discuss (cf. also Aoki 2007). Fourth, the clusters derived in this chapter emerge entirely from the data, and we refrain from reassigning economies to different clusters based on reinterpretations of the results. Fifth, representation using

Table 29.2 Pairwise gower dissimilarity matrix (institutional distances)

| | CN | HK | IN | ID | JP | KR | LA | MY | PH | SG | TW | TH | VN | FR | DE | SE | UK |
|---|---|---|---|---|---|---|---|---|---|---|---|---|---|---|---|---|---|
| Hong Kong | 0.406 | | | | | | | | | | | | | | | | |
| India | 0.170 | 0.420 | | | | | | | | | | | | | | | |
| Indonesia | 0.275 | 0.269 | 0.283 | | | | | | | | | | | | | | |
| Japan | 0.594 | 0.504 | 0.608 | 0.511 | | | | | | | | | | | | | |
| Korea | 0.457 | 0.346 | 0.466 | 0.315 | 0.255 | | | | | | | | | | | | |
| Laos | 0.207 | 0.499 | 0.271 | 0.299 | 0.582 | 0.502 | | | | | | | | | | | |
| Malaysia | 0.219 | 0.305 | 0.240 | 0.137 | 0.505 | 0.316 | 0.313 | | | | | | | | | | |
| Philippines | 0.268 | 0.263 | 0.297 | 0.019 | 0.505 | 0.310 | 0.300 | 0.134 | | | | | | | | | |
| Singapore | 0.395 | 0.133 | 0.367 | 0.261 | 0.469 | 0.311 | 0.492 | 0.185 | 0.255 | | | | | | | | |
| Taiwan | 0.407 | 0.287 | 0.421 | 0.216 | 0.369 | 0.134 | 0.487 | 0.214 | 0.210 | 0.251 | | | | | | | |
| Thailand | 0.272 | 0.251 | 0.242 | 0.080 | 0.498 | 0.309 | 0.368 | 0.114 | 0.085 | 0.186 | 0.208 | | | | | | |
| Vietnam | 0.100 | 0.440 | 0.195 | 0.249 | 0.578 | 0.443 | 0.127 | 0.208 | 0.245 | 0.382 | 0.375 | 0.257 | | | | | |
| France | 0.428 | 0.287 | 0.440 | 0.343 | 0.295 | 0.307 | 0.472 | 0.400 | 0.335 | 0.359 | 0.317 | 0.392 | 0.414 | | | | |
| Germany | 0.608 | 0.405 | 0.576 | 0.532 | 0.191 | 0.380 | 0.651 | 0.587 | 0.519 | 0.477 | 0.443 | 0.527 | 0.592 | 0.244 | | | |
| Sweden | 0.589 | 0.367 | 0.549 | 0.506 | 0.216 | 0.410 | 0.604 | 0.559 | 0.500 | 0.438 | 0.452 | 0.498 | 0.532 | 0.222 | 0.091 | | |
| UK | 0.660 | 0.296 | 0.647 | 0.469 | 0.452 | 0.329 | 0.587 | 0.510 | 0.463 | 0.368 | 0.370 | 0.478 | 0.637 | 0.353 | 0.415 | 0.428 | |
| USA | 0.604 | 0.249 | 0.588 | 0.463 | 0.498 | 0.419 | 0.594 | 0.502 | 0.457 | 0.375 | 0.485 | 0.473 | 0.644 | 0.397 | 0.465 | 0.493 | 0.129 |

dendrogram allows for a more fine-grained picture of similarities and differences to emerge. Among others, it becomes clear how different from the rest of Asia Japan really is (consistent with the oft-heard comment in Japan that its business system represents a kind of 'Galapagos'), while Harada and Tohyama paired it with Korea. We also see that Indonesia, Malaysia, the Philippines, and Thailand are part of one larger cluster. And finally, we are able to parcel out the institutional structures governing state-owned and private business in China and India, allowing us to generate a sense of how these driving forces of economic development in both countries compare with other Asian business systems.

# IMPLICATIONS FOR BUSINESS SYSTEMS THEORY

The data and analyses presented above have important implications for business-systems theory, which we spell out in this section. We commence by drawing conclusions from the results of the cluster analysis before turning to larger points.

The overall conclusion from the cluster analysis is that none of the existing business-systems typologies adequately categorizes the institutional variations visible in Asia and the West. This is most immediately obvious for what still remains the leading framework for classifying business systems, the Varieties of Capitalism (VoC) approach of Hall and Soskice (2001), distinguishing between coordinated market economies (CMEs) and liberal market economies (LMEs), and acknowledging the possibility of a third, Mediterranean, type overlapping with essentially agricultural economies and traditionalist administrations. The original geographic scope of the VoC framework was limited to the Western OECD countries and Japan, and our cluster analysis shows that despite all the arguments over the past decade about variations within the dichotomy, there is some justification in applying a dichotomous approach to the said set of OECD economies. Compared with the differences between the West and Asia, the variations inside the West seem minor.

When it comes to understanding Asia, however, the VoC framework clearly falls short. All Asian economies, except Japan, cluster on a completely different branch from the countries that the VoC framework identifies as CMEs or LMEs. To be fair, the framework was not designed for Asia, but that has not prevented people from trying to make it fit. Our findings suggest very strongly that such efforts to categorize Asian economies using the CME-LME dichotomy are misguided.

Viewed more broadly, the cluster analysis suggests that neither of the other major typologies—those by Amable (2003) and Whitley (1999)—are complete.[2] This is again a function of geographic scope. Amable's work focused on the West, so one would not expect it to apply to Asia. Whitley (1999) took into account the North-East Asian context, and arguably, three of the six types of capitalism he identifies (fragmented, state-organized, and collaborative) correspond roughly to the clusters on Chinese private business, Korea and Taiwan, and Japan in Figure 29.2. Missing from his account, then, would be the cases of the advanced city-states as well as those of the post-socialist economies (though one might respond, with some justice once private business is parcelled out, that the latter cannot be called 'capitalism').

Rather, our research brings the total number of known types of capitalism in Asia and the West to at least six and possibly as many as nine: four in Asia (post-socialist, advanced city-state, emerging South East Asian, advanced North-East Asian), plus some two to five in the West (including Japan), depending on the specific typology for the West one subscribes to. It stands to reason that further empirical work on other geographies, such as South America and the Middle East, will yield further types.

Our analysis further suggests that in search of these types, it may not be fruitful to attempt to generalize categories identified in one context to another. Schmidt (2009), for instance, applies a label derived in the European context, that of 'state-led market economies' (SMEs), to Korea and Taiwan. Our cluster analysis is inconsistent with this categorization, and as Table 29.2 shows, France is institutionally closer to Sweden, Germany, Hong Kong, and Japan (none of them 'SMEs') than to Korea or Taiwan. Even if one uses only the various state-related measures in Table 29.1 to cluster countries, France clusters with Germany, Japan, and Sweden, not with Korea or Taiwan. Rather, the cluster analysis suggests that Asia and the West are two very different beasts indeed, and trying to analyse one using a lens designed for the other is unlikely to lead to a full understanding.

The data presented in this chapter further open up a number of questions and suggestions for further refinement of business-systems theory. In particular, the evidence

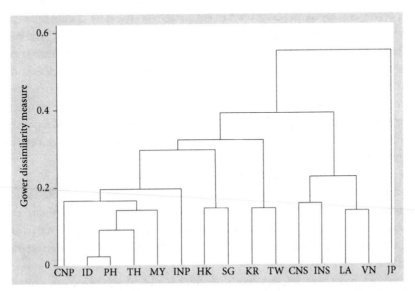

FIGURE 29.2 Dendrogram of clusters of Asian business systems; China and India split into private and state-owned business systems (XXP = Private, XXS = State-Owned)

underlines the need for business-systems analyses to incorporate social capital and cultural elements as well as the need to conceptualize variations in the extent of informality in a business system and its interplay with formal institutions. In addition, the coexistence of multiple dissimilar business systems within the same economies raises questions about our conceptualizations of institutional change and the larger question of institutional convergence.

*Social Capital.* As already stated, we define social capital as trust (Li and Redding 2014). Within that category, we distinguish between interpersonal (or relational) trust, based on knowledge of the honest disposition of the other, and institutionalized (or system) trust, based on confidence that the other will act honestly because a system exists that sanctions dishonesty (Whitley 1999; Redding 2005; Esser 2008). Our concern in this section is with the latter, for which the data suggest a great deal of variation across Asian economies (Table 29.1).

Seen as a collective good, institutionalized trust may be disaggregated into three components (Esser 2008):

- *System control.* The availability of social control and a certain level of attention to the fate and action of other members of an entire social network, e.g. a family, network or societal reputation.
- *System trust.* A climate of trust in the network, meaning that there is confidence in its working.
- *System morality.* The validity of norms, values, and morality within a group, organization, or society.

To understand the workings of institutionalized trust, an ideal starting checklist would include (1) the legal system, (2) systems of regulation, (3) the state of civil society, (4) the society's openness, and the quality and quantity of information, and (5) the reliability of credentials such as educational diplomas. A good comparative measure is available only for the first of these. While we have used this as a proxy measure of institutionalized trust in general (Table 29.1), we would like to underline the importance of understanding its other forms and expressions. Institutionalized trust in Japan, for instance, relies relatively little on its legal system and relatively much on reputational mechanisms that can be used to sanction offenders informally, which may be captured under the third component listed above (cf. Witt 2006).

Two of the major business systems models underlying this chapter—Whitley (1999) and Redding (2005), both developed with Asia in mind—have incorporated social capital in general and institutionalized trust specifically. Similarly, economists and legal scholars have recognized the relevance of institutionalized trust, usually narrowly interpreted as functioning legal systems, for explaining variations in economic outcomes (e.g. La Porta et al. 2000).

By contrast, most business-systems research has not. The tendency to exclude institutionalized trust in the field is understandable, given that most business-systems models were developed within the context of the Western advanced industrialized nations, plus Japan, to explain variations within this set of economies. There, however, institutionalized trust is essentially universally present. For instance, for the nineteen Western countries explored in Hall and Gingerich (2009), the mean score for the rule of law index is 1.62, with a standard deviation of 0.39. The lowest scoring country is Italy, at 0.38. All other countries score above 1.0, the highest score being 1.97 (Finland). As a result, this variable and the underlying concept do not afford much explanatory leverage for these countries, though it might be useful in conceptualizing the positioning of the Mediterranean countries against the rest of the sample (mean without France 0.87; mean with France 1.04; mean of fifteen other countries 1.78).

By contrast, in our Asian sample, the mean score is 0.30, with a standard deviation of 0.91 and a range from -0.63 (Laos) to 1.69 (Singapore). This has important implications for other elements of the business system, and we choose to emphasize two in this chapter. The first is the tendency for businesses to form business groups. This pattern is universal in Asia, though the Japanese post-war implementation is unusual, as explained earlier, and will be bracketed from this discussion. A leading explanation of the emergence of business groups is that they represent responses to the absence of a reliable legal framework that, among other things, can be used to enforce contracts (Khanna and Palepu 1997). As a result, firms prefer to internalize transactions that in Western markets would occur on an arm's-length basis, and form conglomerates.

The second is the high levels of family control of firms across the region. Only in Japan and Laos does this form of governance play no role in the major enterprises in the economy. Lack of institutionalized trust seems to underlie this phenomenon as well (Redding 1990). Without institutionalized trust, business leaders will fall back on delegating important tasks to people they trust as persons. These could in principle include long-term friends, but in general, nowhere is interpersonal trust as automatic and strong as within the family. Separating ownership from control, as is often the case in Northern European family-owned businesses in which professional managers run the company, is not seen as a viable option, because there are no reliable means of ensuring that third parties will act honestly.

It would seem odd to try to explain two constant outcomes with a factor that shows considerable variance. In particular, the question arises as to why environments with high institutionalized trust, such as Hong Kong and Singapore, retain business-group structures and family control. The apparent contradiction is resolved when we consider that Hong Kong and Singapore, and also Korea and Taiwan, had vastly lower degrees of institutionalized trust in the not-so-distant past. In the 1960s, for instance, Singapore was notorious for corruption, and as late as the 1980s, a government minister was prosecuted for this reason. The business groups extant today thus emerged in more unsettled times, and the general inertia inherent in any organization is likely to prevent their sudden disappearance. In addition, Hong Kong and Singaporean business groups have high levels of business activities in neighbouring countries with much lower levels of institutionalized trust, which is likely to reinforce inertial forces.

*Culture.* Culture is commonly defined as the 'social construction of reality' (Berger and Luckmann 1966) or the 'software of the mind' (Hofstede 1997). Culture is dangerous territory, and most social scientists prefer to stay away from it, not least because of its 'sulfuric odor of race and inheritance' (Landes 2000: 2). Yet there is growing evidence that culture *does* matter and can be conceptualized and handled in scientifically acceptable ways. Serious scholars such as Douglass North have incorporated it in their theories (North 2005). Others hint at a role for culture in business systems. For instance, Hall and Soskice (2001) suggest that institutional configurations are based on 'shared understandings', and Fligstein (2001) speaks of 'conceptions of control' for explaining corporate governance structures. Considerable effort has gone into identifying the key dimensions of culture and measuring them with rigour (e.g. Hofstede 1997; Bond et al. 2004; House et al. 2004), including how culture changes across time (Ralston et al. 1997).

Similar to social capital, the models by Whitley (1999) and Redding (2005) include cultural dimensions, though Whitley avoids the term 'culture'. By contrast, most business-systems literature stays away from culture, apart from hints as quoted above. In addition to the general aversion to culture in the social sciences, it is arguably again the case that within the context of the advanced industrialized Western nations, the explanatory leverage of cultural variables (at least those with published metrics) may be limited.

The chapter by Redding, Bond, and Witt (2014) lays out the various dimensions of culture present in Asia in considerable detail and proposes linkages to the shape of business systems in the region. By way of illustrating some of these possible linkages, Figure 29.3 shows a scatterplot locating the same nineteen Western nations as for our discussion of social capital and the thirteen Asian nations compared in this chapter along the two dimensions of culture that are essentially undisputed among scholars in that field: power distance, which is a measure of hierarchy, and individualism, which is a measure of the extent to which a society is group-based. Both measures are highly correlated, as group-based societies usually rely on hierarchy to establish order within groups. As is clearly visible, the advanced industrialized nations tend to cluster in the bottom-left quadrant, meaning they tend towards low hierarchy and high individualism. The Asian nations cluster in the upper-right quadrant, implying high hierarchy and greater importance of groups. Noteworthy again is that Southern European nations tend to fall in between.

The existence of relatively strong hierarchical values in Asia, and indeed in Southern Europe, is consistent with the prevalence of top-down decision-making in firms (again except Japan). While decision-making in Anglo-Saxon countries is interpreted as top-down as well (Whitley 1999; Hall and Soskice 2001), there are important differences in quality and degree. While Anglo-Saxon managers seek input from subordinates before reaching decisions, this is rarely the case in Asian contexts.

*Informality.* Not expressed in any single variable, but pervading all of Asia and influencing most if not all aspects of Table 29.1 is a strong element of informality, which we define as reliance on informal (uncodified) institutions such as unwritten norms, conventions, or codes of behaviour (cf. North 1990). In some cases, informal institutions simply supersede formal institutions, as in Chinese employment relations, which are *de jure* tripartites but de facto centralized under the Communist Party. In other cases,

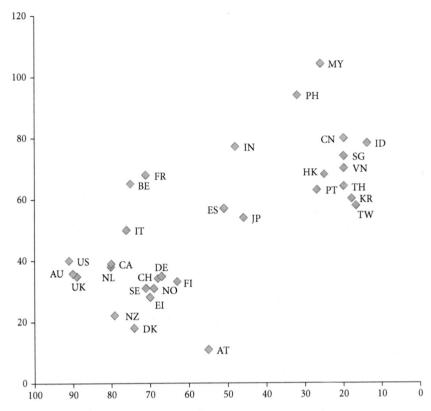

FIGURE 29.3 Power distance and individualism, Western and Asian economies.

*Notes*: Vertical axis is power distance, higher values mean stronger hierarchy. Horizontal axis is individualism, lower values mean stronger group orientation.

*Source*: <http://geert-hofstede.com/>, retrieved 1 June 2012.

institutions complement formal ones, as in the Japanese practices of long-term or life-time employment and the seniority principle, both of which are informal practices (and continue in practice, despite rhetoric to the contrary; cf. Witt 2014a). In some cases, these institutions support institutional change by necessitating or preparing institutional change (for the general mechanisms, cf. Witt 2006). For instance, deviation from formally codified laws and regulations paired with local variation in such deviations has been a key mechanism for formal institutional change in China and evolving information about the feasibility of formal institutional innovations (for a review, cf. Xu 2011). In other cases, they retard it, as in the circumvention of newly instituted corporate governance rules in Japan (cf. Dore 2007).

This dimension seems under-appreciated and under-theorized in the business-systems literature. Of the main models used in this chapter, none incorporates it. Similarly, the bulk of business-systems literature more generally has focused on formal institutions. For instance, Streeck and Thelen (2005) explicitly exclude informal institutions, and most of the edited volume by Aoki, Jackson, and Miyajima

(2007) explores changes in the formal structure of Japanese corporate governance. At some level, this emphasis on formal structure is justifiable, as the focus of most business-systems research has been on advanced industrialized countries, where economic actors generally play by the official rules of the game. However, once we move to Southern Europe or Japan, this alignment of practice and structure starts to deteriorate. For instance, Dore (2007) illustrates how the structural changes noted in other chapters of Aoki et al. (2007) were not necessarily followed by changes in actual practice. And once we leave the advanced industrialized world, correspondence between structure and practice tends to break down, as in the case of China. This suggests a need to acknowledge, in Aoki's words (2007: 434), that 'the law defines the formal rules, but [what] we should ultimately be concerned with are [sic] the "ways by which the game is actually played"'. The data in Table 29.1 represent an effort to do exactly this: reflect the actual workings of the respective business systems, regardless of whether they follow formal institutional structures.

The extent of informality is probably linked to the extent of institutionalized trust. In the absence of a reliable formal institutional structure, actors will evolve their own informal institutions as functional substitutes. Conversely, institutionalized trust is difficult to develop in the presence of embedded and entrenched informal institutions. There is also likely to be a linkage to culture, in that informal institutions are easier to sustain in group-based societies, which feature higher levels of group conformity pressures (Hofstede 1997). The experience of Asia suggests that these connections, and the role of informality more generally, need incorporating into business-systems theory.

*Multiplexity.* A final feature of Asian business systems worth underlining is that of multiplexity, which is the presence of multiple business systems within one economy. China and India, for instance, feature coexisting state-owned and private sectors following different rules of the game. While the state-owned business systems have been shrinking in both countries, current rates do not suggest that they will disappear anytime soon; indeed, recent years seem to have seen a renewed interest in China in preserving a hard core of state-owned enterprises.

Multiplexity is not part of any of the models on which this chapter draws, though Whitley's (1999) model probably permits for this in that it identifies two ideal types that are present within the national boundaries of Germany. In the literature more widely, the notion of rigid nationally based, punctuated equilibriums has slowly given way to theories of incremental institutional change, in which increasing heterogeneity in practices drives change (e.g. Aoki et al. 2007; Lechevalier 2007). If institutions are flexible (or weak) enough, however, to permit high levels of variance, one possible end result is the emergence of multiple punctuated equilibria, and thus multiple business systems, in an economy. Viewed from that perspective, the emergence of a sub-group of Japanese firms with the trappings of a more Western-style corporate governance regime (Jackson and Miyajima 2007), for instance, may not be the beginnings of systemic institutional change in Japan, but an adaptive response around a new equilibrium point by a select group of firms. A case in point is similarly the unintended rise of the Chinese private business system following the 1978 reforms, which in effect established a second business system in China.

The presence of multiplexity raises important questions. One is what preconditions allow the coexistence of multiple business systems in the same institutional space. High levels of institutionalized trust are likely to be inimical to it, unless different rules are written for different parts of the economy. Informality of institutions, on the other hand, may be conducive to it. Likewise, information codification and diffusion may play a role, as suggested for China by Boisot, Child, and Redding (2011).

A second question relates to the concept of institutional convergence. There is now general agreement in the business-systems literature that such convergence among advanced industrialized countries has been at best partial. However, if we allow for multiple equilibria within one national context, then the question of institutional convergence at the national level becomes moot, as firms subject to convergence pressures may create their own equilibrium points.

# Salient Points from Chapters Focused on Influences, Outcomes, and Evolutionary Trajectories

In addition to the chapters focused on analyzing institutional characteristics, this handbook contains a series of chapters about shaping influences on business systems, variations in outcomes, and evolutionary trajectories. This section very briefly reviews the main points developed by these contributions.

*Shaping Influences.* This category includes four topics: culture (Redding et al. 2014), the role of multinational enterprises (MNEs) (Giroud 2014), offshoring, outsourcing, and regional supply chains (Lewin and Zhong 2014), and the role of the state (Carney and Witt 2014). The preceding discussion has already subsumed the discussions on culture and the state.

The chapter on MNEs argues that these firms alter local business systems through their international strategies, business networks, spillovers, and linkages. The chapter concludes that despite fairly extensive coverage of these phenomena in the wider social-science literature, there is considerable development potential in the business-systems literature on this topic, especially in the Asian context. This would seem to represent a promising avenue for future research.

Similarly, the contribution on offshoring, outsourcing, and supply chains (Lewin and Zhong 2014) suggests that the business-systems literature has had relatively little to contribute to this topic, both theoretically and empirically. It highlights some of the avenues by which the offshoring of production may impact on local business systems—for instance, in the context of human capital development—and proposes a model of local attractiveness to service-sector offshoring. The authors challenge the field to explore how 'emerging economies can harness the global sourcing of business services as a deliberate lever of economic development', with the implication that offshoring, outsourcing, and global sourcing are driven by both firms and host countries.

*Outcomes.* This category comprises two main topics: national R&D systems (De Meyer 2014) and strategic and performance outcomes (Makino and Yiu 2014). The chapter on the former presents an overview of the R&D environment in Asia. It shows that despite strenuous efforts and large expenditures, R&D activities in Asia show relatively low productivity in terms of actual industrial results. The chapter proposes a number of possible reasons for this phenomenon and outlines avenues for further research. Given the interest of the business-systems literature in innovation and attendant outcomes (Hall and Soskice 2001; Whitley 2007), this chapter should provide fruitful grounds for further exploration.

The second chapter in this category represents a comprehensive overview of firm strategy and performance in Asia. It argues that there are distinctive strategic behaviours of Asian firms in four areas: internationalization, networks, diversification and acquisitions, and ownership. It further finds large variation in performance outcomes that do not match up well against prior or current categorizations of Asian business systems. This suggests a need for further research on the linkage between institutions and performance, and especially a need to adduce further variables to the analysis.

*Evolutionary Trajectories.* Last but not least, three chapters look at Asian business systems in a longitudinal perspective. The chapter by Abrami (2014) identifies three depictions of historical influences in Asia: the past as destiny, as strategic choice, or as 'switchman' effects. In doing so, it challenges the notion of institutional comparative advantage and points to a range of missing variables in business-systems theory, in particular with respect to culture.

The chapters by Shin and Hamilton (2014) as well as Whitley (2014) both explore the dynamics of institutional change in Asia. Shin and Hamilton approach this question by analysing retail markets in the region, an area of economic activity that is as important as under-researched in the field, while Whitley examines changes in organizational forms in North-East Asia. Both chapters conclude that institutional convergence has not occurred in the past decades, with important implications for the question of institutional convergence across business systems.

In summary, we conclude that studying Asian business systems adds variety to what is already in the extant typologies, and raises important questions about the incompleteness of theorizing if it is to be globally relevant. We conclude also that the act of comparing large systems yields much understanding, and—although adding complexity to explanation at a level some will be diffident about accepting—is justified by the simple fact that economies deserve to be seen as essentially complex. Encouraging this challenge to much single-discipline orthodoxy we find an overall tendency in social science to accept and deal with the question of complexity. Two major movements run parallel with our own interests, and encourage us. They are linked but still distinct.

The first of these newer forms of theorizing is complexity theory, producing much of value by way of the study of patterns in the way complexity works, and formulae to guide its study. Its extension into the social sciences is still tentative, doubtless hampered by the institutional inertia brought about by single discipline dominance of the academic world's work, and leading to too few foxes among the hedgehogs. Handbooks by their nature present an opportunity to encourage multiple perspectives for a field of study, then hopefully cross-fertilization, and in turn perhaps an enhancement of sophistication in future accounts.

The second theoretical stimulus is that of evolutionary theorizing, transferring forms of understanding from the world of nature to the social world. Still in infancy for the study of organizations in societies, it is nevertheless feasible that, in the future, handbooks such as this will open with a theory of the extended phenotype as a conceptual framework, and make it stick for societal comparative analysis. So too may much of what we see as important but 'informal' institutional structure be argued as traceable to the trajectories of the last fifty thousand years of the evolution of *homo sapiens*, and the genetic heritage.

Such thoughts simply remind us that our disciplines are alive and making progress. It causes us then to conclude that so too is our subject. We study living objects and we try to explain them in a way that conveys their momentum, but they will make their own fates, and they will make them on their own terms. If we have conveyed that simple idea in all its real-world complexity, then this collection of accounts will be justified.

# ACKNOWLEDGEMENT

Most of the text of this chapter was previously published in Witt and Redding (2013a). We thank Oxford University Press for permission to use it for this chapter.

## NOTES

1. Korean law forbids conglomerate ownership of banks.
2. Redding (2005) focuses on identifying dimensions of variation without developing a typology of outcomes.

## REFERENCES

Abrami, R. M. (2014). 'Pictures of the Past: Historical Influences in Contemporary Asian Business Systems'. In M. A. Witt and G. Redding, Eds., *The Oxford Handbook of Asian Business Systems*: 589–610. Oxford, Oxford University Press.

Amable, B. (2003). *The Diversity of Modern Capitalism*. Oxford, Oxford University Press.

Andriesse, E. (2014). 'Laos: Frontier Capitalism'. In M. A. Witt and G. Redding, Eds., *The Oxford Handbook of Asian Business Systems*: 123–143. Oxford, Oxford University Press.

Aoki, M. (2007). 'Conclusion: Whither Japan's Corporate Governance?'. In M. Aoki, G. Jackson, and H. Miyajima, Eds., *Corporate Governance in Japan: Institutional Change and Organizational Diversity*: 427–448. Oxford, Oxford University Press.

—— G. Jackson, and H. Miyajima, Eds. (2007). *Corporate Governance in Japan: Institutional Change and Organizational Diversity*. Oxford, Oxford University Press.

Berger, P. L. and T. Luckmann (1966). *The Social Construction of Reality: A Treatise in the Sociology of Knowledge*. Garden City, NY, Doubleday.

Boisot, M., J. Child, and G. Redding (2011). 'Working the System: Towards a Theory of Cultural and Institutional Competence'. *International Studies in Management and Organization* 41(1): 63–96.

Bond, M. H., K. Leung, A. Au, K-K. Tong, S. R. de Carrasquel, F. Murakami, S. Yamaguchi, G. Bierbrauer, and others (2004). 'Culture-Level Dimensions of Social Axioms and Their Correlates across 41 Countries'. *Journal of Cross-Cultural Psychology* 35(5): 548–570.

Carney, M. and E. Andriesse (2014). 'Malaysia: Personal Capitalism'. In M. A. Witt and G. Redding, Eds., *The Oxford Handbook of Asian Business Systems*: 144–168. Oxford, Oxford University Press.

Carney, R. (2014). 'Singapore: Open State-Led Capitalism'. In M. A. Witt and G. Redding, Eds., *The Oxford Handbook of Asian Business Systems*: 192–215. Oxford, Oxford University Press.

—— and M. A. Witt (2014). 'The Role of the State in Asian Business Systems'. In M. A. Witt and G. Redding, Eds., *The Oxford Handbook of Asian Business Systems*: 538–560. Oxford, Oxford University Press.

De Meyer, A. (2014). 'National R&D Systems and Technology Development in Asia'. In M. A. Witt and G. Redding, Eds., *The Oxford Handbook of Asian Business Systems*: 465–486. Oxford, Oxford University Press.

Dore, R. P. (2007). 'Insider Management and Board Reform: For Whose Benefit?' In M. Aoki, G. Jackson, and H. Miyajima, Eds., *Corporate Governance in Japan: Institutional Change and Organizational Diversity*: 370–398. Oxford, Oxford University Press.

Esser, H. (2008). 'The Two Meanings of Social Capital'. In D. Castiglione, J. W. van Deth, and G. Wolleb, Eds., *The Handbook of Social Capital*: 22–49. Oxford, Oxford University Press.

Evans, P. B. (1995). *Embedded Autonomy: States and Industrial Transformation*. Princeton, Princeton University Press.

Fligstein, N. (2001). *The Architecture of Markets: An Economic Sociology of Twenty-First Century Capitalist Societies*. Princeton, Princeton University Press.

Giroud, A. (2014). 'MNEs in Asian Business Systems'. In M. A. Witt and G. Redding, Eds., *The Oxford Handbook of Asian Business Systems*: 441–464. Oxford, Oxford University Press.

Hall, P. A. and D. W. Gingerich (2009). 'Varieties of Capitalism and Institutional Complementarities in the Political Economy: An Empirical Analysis'. *British Journal of Political Science* 39(3): 449–482.

—— and D. Soskice (2001). 'An Introduction to Varieties of Capitalism'. In P. A. Hall and D. Soskice, Eds., *Varieties of Capitalism: The Institutional Foundations of Comparative Advantage*: 1–68. Oxford, Oxford University Press.

Hancké, B., M. Rhodes, and M. Thatcher (2007). 'Introduction: Beyond Varieties of Capitalism'. In B. Hancké, M. Rhodes, and M. Thatcher, Eds., *Beyond Varieties of Capitalism: Conflict, Contradictions, and Complementarities in the European Economy*: 3–38. Oxford, Oxford University Press.

Harada, Y. and H. Tohyama (2012). 'Asian Capitalisms: Institutional Configurations and Firm Heterogeneity'. In R. Boyer, H. Uemura, and A. Isogai, Eds., *Diversity and Transformations of Asian Capitalisms*: 243–263. Abingdon, Routledge.

Hofstede, G. H. (1997). *Cultures and Organizations: Software of the Mind*. New York, McGraw-Hill.

House, R. J., P. J. Hanges, M. Javidan, P. W. Dorfman, and V. Gupta, Eds. (2004). *Culture, Leadership, and Organizations: The Globe Study of 62 Societies*. London, Sage.

Jackson, G. and R. Deeg (2008). 'Comparing Capitalisms: Understanding Institutional Diversity and Its Implications for International Business'. *Journal of International Business Studies 39*: 540–561.

—— and H. Miyajima (2007). 'Introduction: The Diversity and Change of Corporate Governance in Japan'. In M. Aoki, G. Jackson, and H. Miyajima, Eds., *Corporate Governance in Japan: Institutional Change and Organizational Diversity*: 1–47. Oxford, Oxford University Press.

Johnson, C. (1982). *MITI and the Japanese Miracle: The Growth of Industrial Policy 1925–1975*. Stanford, Stanford University Press.

Khanna, T. and K. Palepu (1997). 'Why Focused Strategies May Be Wrong for Emerging Markets'. *Harvard Business Review 75*(4): 41–51.

Kondo, M. (2014). 'Philippines: Inequality-Trapped Capitalism'. In M. A. Witt and G. Redding, Eds., *The Oxford Handbook of Asian Business Systems*: 169–191. Oxford, Oxford University Press.

Landes, D. (2000). 'Culture Makes Almost All the Difference'. In L. E. Harrison and S. P. Huntington, Eds. *Culture Matters: How Values Shape Human Progress*: 2–13. New York, Basic Books.

La Porta, R., F. Lopez-de-Silanes, A. Shleifer, and R. Vishny (2000). 'Investor Protection and Corporate Governance'. *Journal of Financial Economics 58*: 3–27.

Lechevalier, S. (2007). 'The Diversity of Capitalism and Heterogeneity of Firms: A Case Study of Japan During the Lost Decade'. *Evolutionary and Institutional Economics Review* 4(1): 113–142.

Lee, Z.-R. and M. Hsiao (2014). 'Taiwan: SME-Oriented Capitalism in Transition'. In M. A. Witt and G. Redding, Eds., *The Oxford Handbook of Asian Business Systems*: 238–259. Oxford, Oxford University Press.

Lewin, A. Y. and X. Zhong (2014). 'The Co-Evolution of Global Sourcing of Business Support Functions and the Economic Development of Asian Emerging Economies'. In M. A. Witt and G. Redding, Eds., *The Oxford Handbook of Asian Business Systems*: 487–512. Oxford, Oxford University Press.

Li, P. P. and G. Redding (2014). 'Social Capital in Asia: Its Dual Nature and Function'. In M. A. Witt and G. Redding, Eds., *The Oxford Handbook of Asian Business Systems*: 513–537. Oxford, Oxford University Press.

Makino, S. and D. W. Yiu (2014). 'A Survey of Strategic Behaviour and Firm Performance in Asia'. In M. A. Witt and G. Redding, Eds., *The Oxford Handbook of Asian Business Systems*: 563–586. Oxford, Oxford University Press.

North, D. C. (1990). *Institutions, Institutional Change and Economic Performance*. Cambridge, Cambridge University Press.

—— (2005). *Understanding the Process of Economic Change*. Princeton, Princeton University Press.

Ragin, C. C. (2000). *Fuzzy-Set Social Science*. Chicago, Chicago University Press.

—— (2008). *Configurational Comparative Methods: Qualitative Comparative Analysis (QCA) and Related Techniques*. London, Sage.

Ralston, D. A., D. H. Holt, R. H. Terpstra, and K.-C. Yu (1997). 'The Impact of National Culture and Economic Ideology on Managerial Work Values: A Study of the United States, Russia, Japan, and China'. *Journal of International Business Studies 28*(1): 177–207.

Redding, G. (2005). 'The Thick Description and Comparison of Societal Systems of Capitalism'. *Journal of International Business Studies* 36: 123–155

—— M. H. Bond and M. A. Witt (2014). 'Culture and the Business Systems of Asia'. In M. A. Witt and G. Redding, Eds., *The Oxford Handbook of Asian Business Systems*: 358–382. Oxford, Oxford University Press.

—— and M. A. Witt (2007). *The Future of Chinese Capitalism: Choices and Chances*. Oxford, Oxford University Press.

—— G. Wong, and W. Leung (2014). 'Hong Kong: Hybrid Capitalism as Catalyst'. In M.A. Witt and G. Redding, Eds., *The Oxford Handbook of Asian Business Systems*: 33–54. Oxford, Oxford University Press.

Redding, S. G. (1990). *The Spirit of Chinese Capitalism*. Berlin, Walter de Gruyter.

Rosser, A. (2014). 'Indonesia: Oligarchic Capitalism'. In M. A. Witt and G. Redding, Eds., *The Oxford Handbook of Asian Business Systems*: 79–99. Oxford, Oxford University Press.

Saez, L. (2014). 'India: From Failed Developmental State Towards Hybrid Market Capitalism'. In M. A. Witt and G. Redding, Eds., *The Oxford Handbook of Asian Business Systems*: 55–78. Oxford, Oxford University Press.

Schmidt, V. A. (2002). *The Futures of European Capitalism*. Oxford, Oxford University Press.

—— (2009). 'Putting the Political Back into Political Economy by Bringing the State Back in yet again'. *World Politics* 61(3): 516–546.

Schneider, M. R. and M. Paunescu (2012). 'Changing Varieties of Capitalism and Revealed Comparative Advantage: A Test of the Hall and Soskice Hypothesis'. *Socio-Economic Review* 10(4): 731–753.

Shin, S. and G. G. Hamilton (2014). 'Beyond Production: Changing Dynamics of Asian Business Groups'. In M. A. Witt and G. Redding, Eds., *The Oxford Handbook of Asian Business Systems*: 611–632. Oxford, Oxford University Press.

StataCorp (2011a). *Stata 12 Base Reference Manual*. College Station, TX, Stata Press.

—— (2011b). *Stata Statistical Software: Release 12*. College Station, TX, StataCorp LP.

Streeck, W. and K. Thelen (2005). 'Introduction: Institutional Change in Advanced Political Economies'. In W. Streeck and K. Thelen, Eds., *Beyond Continuity: Institutional Change in Advanced Political Economies*: 1–39. Oxford, Oxford University Press.

Suehiro, A. and N. Wailerdsak (2014). 'Thailand: Post-Developmentalist Capitalism'. In M. A. Witt and G. Redding, Eds., *The Oxford Handbook of Asian Business Systems*: 260–282. Oxford, Oxford University Press.

Truong, Q. and C. Rowley (2014). 'Vietnam: Post-State Capitalism'. In M. A. Witt and G. Redding, Eds., *The Oxford Handbook of Asian Business Systems*: 283–305. Oxford, Oxford University Press.

Whitley, R. (1992). *Business Systems in East Asia: Firms, Markets and Societies*. London, Sage.

—— (1999). *Divergent Capitalisms: The Social Structuring and Change of Business Systems*. Oxford, Oxford University Press.

—— (2007). *Business Systems and Organizational Capabilities*. Oxford, Oxford University Press.

—— (2014). 'Change and Continuity in East Asian Business Systems'. In M. A. Witt and G. Redding, Eds., *The Oxford Handbook of Asian Business Systems*: 633–664. Oxford, Oxford University Press.

Witt, M. A. (2006). *Changing Japanese Capitalism: Societal Coordination and Institutional Adjustment*. Cambridge, Cambridge University Press.

—— (2014a). 'Japan: Coordinated Capitalism between Institutional Change and Structural Inertia'. In M. A. Witt and G. Redding, Eds., *The Oxford Handbook of Asian Business Systems*: 100–122. Oxford, Oxford University Press.

—— (2014b). 'South Korea: Plutocratic State-Led Capitalism'. In M. A. Witt and G. Redding, Eds., *The Oxford Handbook of Asian Business Systems*: 216–237. Oxford, Oxford University Press.

—— and G. Redding (2013). 'Asian Business Systems: Institutional Comparison, Clusters, and Implications for Varieties of Capitalism and Business Systems Theory'. *Socio-Economic Review* 11(2): 265–300.

—— (2014). 'China: Authoritarian Capitalism'. In M. A. Witt and G. Redding, Eds., *The Oxford Handbook of Asian Business Systems*: 11–32. Oxford, Oxford University Press.

Xu, C. (2011). 'The Fundamental Institutions of China's Reforms and Development'. *Journal of Economic Literature* 49(4): 1076–1151.

Yao, W. (2011). *China's Shadow Banking Needs a Rescue*. Paris, Societé Generale.

# CHAPTER 30

# ASIAN BUSINESS SYSTEMS

## *Implications for Managerial Practice*

### GORDON REDDING AND MICHAEL A. WITT

THIS chapter addresses lessons for practitioners from the research-oriented remainder of the book. It takes as its theme the long-respected saying of Kurt Lewin that there is nothing so practical as a good theory. Hence, it works to make connections between theory and practice. Entrepreneurs and senior executives often become successful after working out a 'formula' of their own that gives them competitive power, and serves to reduce the complexity they deal with. As researchers go into greater detail, with new vocabularies battling for precedence, there is always the danger of separation of research jargon from everyday managerial language. This chapter attempts some bridging to show the interdependence of these mental worlds.

The size and complexity within the topic of Asian business systems is immense, as the many specialist chapters indicate. So too is there a great variety of perspectives among those likely to be seeking practical guidance: Western managers coming to the region for the first time, or after experience still coming to terms with the variety within it; Japanese managers running factories in South East Asia; foreign direct investors in China and their people on the ground; partner investors from different backgrounds; local managers taking firms into other environments; country-risk analysts; regional management consultants, etc. It is not possible to satisfy in specific terms all such interests in one chapter.

Nevertheless, it is possible to propose certain 'lessons worth learning' that in themselves might help untangle some of the knots encountered, and that would produce insights for wider application in the real world. The aim is to make the learning curves shorter and less steep. For that reason, this chapter is divided to cover the topics that seem most consistently hard to comprehend and the most dangerous to misunderstand, in that they will be traps for the unwary and may lead to business failure.

Behind this book's theories and technical language are stories that its writers encounter: the American firm that went to Japan to do financial dealing, only to discover after lost millions that the Japanese stockmarket does not work like Wall Street and there is no market for corporate control like some in the West; the Italian scooter manufacturer who built an assembly plant in China and wrote off 30 million euros after finding that its own workers had set up factories of their own to build the same machine with a different name and at a much lower price; the American car-factory CEO who had to expand a factory in Shanghai by double, but discovered that Chinese production engineers could not handle taking responsibility and initiative like the engineers he was used to back home, and had to ship in help or face a crisis; the firms comfortable with their relationships with the Jakarta government discovering that the ties had evaporated under democracy, had become dispersed all over the country, and had to be built all over again on much less certain ground.

This book, and particularly this chapter, is devoted to the reduction of laments along the lines of 'if only we had understood...'. To best achieve that requires reading the whole handbook, but that may be unrealistic for busy executives. Instead, therefore, this chapter contains summaries and pointers to where individual enquiries can be directed. Although it may sometimes make a broad general statement, it will resist offering advice for application equally in all countries, and will ask the reader to allow for the huge variety of business life on the ground in the region. It starts with a way of comprehending that variety as a contribution to good practice, and so will address the following issues:

1. *Understanding the context.* It is possible to come to a reasonably comprehensive understanding of what you are dealing with in a business environment that is new to you. This handbook and its underlying theories explain local practice.

2. *Regional organizing.* It is possible to divide the region into clusters that have some internal similarity and so may relate sensibly to the geographical allocation of corporate divisions.

3. *Same bed, different dreams.* The basic reasons behind economic behaviour differ, and have strong effects on business contracting, financing, strategic priorities, the assessment of risk, and the nature of partnering.

4. *Trust and mistrust.* The basic social architecture of trust varies a great deal and influences a large range of business behaviours, including principles of organization. The corruption question also arises here.

5. *The people dimension.* Employing people must take account of influential factors that can be known in advance, but that stem from societal variations in attitudes to authority, to education and learning, to focuses of loyalty, and to the acceptance of responsibility.

6. *How money works.* Access to, and use of, finance does not necessarily follow rules that work elsewhere.

7. *Government involvement.* The role of government in many Asian societies is much more intrusive and controlling than in many Western countries. This requires appropriate management responses.

8. *Modern and pre-modern societies.* Surrounding administrations vary between societies in their capacity to guarantee predictable, rational, and professional behaviour in processes of business. This uncertainty has costs and requires managerial responses.

# Understanding the Context

Consider the case of a country manager brought up in China and working for one of China's few successful global-brand companies, assigned to Germany, or an Italian executive assigned to manage the export of machine tools to India. They need to make decisions on many fronts and to make them with two background questions: What are the relevant local circumstances? How different are they from what I am used to back home? In other words, what might or might not apply here?

To deal with this mental challenge, an exercise in societal business system analysis can yield answers, but the analysis needs to be (a) comprehensive of what matters, (b) designed to show up contrasts between societal business systems, and (c) able to include any important changes that might affect the shelf-life of decisions. It would, for instance, be pointless to ignore the increasing effects in Indonesia of democratization, or—if considering labour skills—the likely effects of new education delivery systems by Internet.

This handbook focuses mostly on the institutional dimensions of the context—that is, differences in how things are done. Complementing this focus on institutions is the chapter on culture, which is related to societal values about what should be done and how.

Our recommendation for managers preparing for business in Asia is first to take a look at Table 30.1, which shows the extent of difference between leading Western economies and the thirteen Asian economies discussed in this handbook—what international business scholars call 'institutional distances'. These vary between 0 (no difference) and 1 (everything is different). There are obviously many more non-Asian countries than those listed in the table; the recommended approach is to identify the country that is closest to one's own system and use that value as a proxy. For example, for a German firm going to China, the value is 0.608. This is a relatively high value, and indeed only the UK is more dissimilar from China than Germany. One would consequently expect considerable management challenges.

The precise nature of these challenges will become evident by going through the eight institutional categories discussed in the chapter on the host country in Part I—here, China—and comparing the descriptions given there with how things are done in the home country—here, Germany.

The key challenges tend to arise in the categories in which the differences are greatest. For example, while Germany has high levels of highly skilled labour, China does not. For a German company with a business model and processes relying on a highly qualified workforce, that would represent a major challenge in the Chinese context.

In general, there are five generic responses to such differences:

1. *Adapt to local conditions in the host country*. In the concrete case, for instance, the German company may be able to revise processes so that they can be handled by unskilled labour. Usually, this involves breaking them down into smaller elements that are easily executed with minimal training.

**Table 30.1 Institutional distances**

| | CN | HK | IN | ID | JP | KR | LA | MY | PH | SG | TW | TH | VN | FR | DE | SE | UK |
|---|---|---|---|---|---|---|---|---|---|---|---|---|---|---|---|---|---|
| Hong Kong | 0.406 | | | | | | | | | | | | | | | | |
| India | 0.170 | 0.420 | | | | | | | | | | | | | | | |
| Indonesia | 0.275 | 0.269 | 0.283 | | | | | | | | | | | | | | |
| Japan | 0.594 | 0.504 | 0.608 | 0.511 | | | | | | | | | | | | | |
| Korea | 0.457 | 0.346 | 0.466 | 0.315 | 0.255 | | | | | | | | | | | | |
| Laos | 0.207 | 0.499 | 0.271 | 0.299 | 0.582 | 0.502 | | | | | | | | | | | |
| Malaysia | 0.219 | 0.305 | 0.240 | 0.137 | 0.505 | 0.316 | 0.313 | | | | | | | | | | |
| Philippines | 0.268 | 0.263 | 0.297 | 0.019 | 0.505 | 0.310 | 0.300 | 0.134 | | | | | | | | | |
| Singapore | 0.395 | 0.133 | 0.367 | 0.261 | 0.469 | 0.311 | 0.492 | 0.185 | 0.255 | | | | | | | | |
| Taiwan | 0.407 | 0.287 | 0.421 | 0.216 | 0.369 | 0.134 | 0.487 | 0.214 | 0.210 | 0.251 | | | | | | | |
| Thailand | 0.272 | 0.251 | 0.242 | 0.080 | 0.498 | 0.309 | 0.368 | 0.114 | 0.085 | 0.186 | 0.208 | | | | | | |
| Vietnam | 0.100 | 0.440 | 0.195 | 0.249 | 0.578 | 0.443 | 0.127 | 0.208 | 0.245 | 0.382 | 0.375 | 0.257 | | | | | |
| France | 0.428 | 0.287 | 0.440 | 0.343 | 0.295 | 0.307 | 0.472 | 0.400 | 0.335 | 0.359 | 0.317 | 0.392 | 0.414 | | | | |
| Germany | 0.608 | 0.405 | 0.576 | 0.532 | 0.191 | 0.380 | 0.651 | 0.581 | 0.519 | 0.477 | 0.443 | 0.527 | 0.592 | 0.244 | | | |
| Sweden | 0.589 | 0.367 | 0.549 | 0.506 | 0.216 | 0.410 | 0.604 | 0.559 | 0.500 | 0.438 | 0.452 | 0.498 | 0.532 | 0.222 | 0.091 | | |
| UK | 0.660 | 0.296 | 0.647 | 0.469 | 0.452 | 0.329 | 0.587 | 0.510 | 0.463 | 0.368 | 0.370 | 0.478 | 0.637 | 0.353 | 0.415 | 0.428 | |
| US | 0.604 | 0.249 | 0.588 | 0.463 | 0.498 | 0.419 | 0.594 | 0.502 | 0.457 | 0.375 | 0.485 | 0.473 | 0.644 | 0.397 | 0.465 | 0.493 | 0.129 |

2. *Look for exceptional cases*. The descriptions in this handbook usually focus on what is true on average. But around any average, there will be a distribution of cases. In our example, while there is generally a scarcity of skilled labour in China, it is not the case that there are no skilled workers at all. They are just relatively scarce. Our German company may thus try to work with this set of exceptional people. The drawback of this approach is that other companies usually fish in the same pond, which bids up prices.

3. *Change the host country*. This is fairly difficult, especially in large countries such as China. That said, it is sometimes possible to change conditions locally. For instance, our German firm may intentionally move to a relatively remote area in China with few foreign firms and then form an employers' cartel discouraging poaching of employees. This could then enable firms to invest in on-the-job training and build the requisite skills.

4. *Live with the differences*. This is an option usually only if the difference has no salient impact on operations. Otherwise, the company is setting itself up for failure.

5. *Stay home*. This is the residual option that remains if none of the above are possible.

# Regional Organizing

When organizations become large and complex, and stretch across different business environments, they struggle constantly to manage the variety. In essence, what they are trying to do is assign decision-making intelligence to those points where it can yield the highest returns to justify cost. In organizations where local conditions need to be given high weighting in the complex of decision elements, it is sensible for them to cultivate knowledge of such local conditions in their key decision-makers. This will vary by industry, as in some industries the level of standardization overrides local factors and most decisions can be handled centrally (e.g. in the Internet router industry). But the majority of multinational firms need at least some local sensitivity, and they increasingly rely on focusing key decisions at the regional level (e.g. in consumer goods marketing). Earlier responses based primarily on country-level control still occur, but have given way in many cases to regional control, because of the new ease and quality of communications.

If a regional headquarters is being established on the basis that its remit is regional understanding (and one would anticipate, within that, specific societal sensitivity within any such region), then a key question arises of defining a region or sub-region with some internal consistency, some minimum variety. The chances are then higher that decision-makers will achieve the required understanding.

Comparative analyses of the business systems of the region of the kind seen in this book suggest a clustering of business systems into the following sub-regions, given here broadly in order of per-capita prosperity:

1. *The Advanced Cities*: Hong Kong and Singapore share a British colonial heritage combined with a Chinese cultural tradition. Although they diverge now in the role of government and in the structure of their economic priorities, they keep pace with each other as world cities, with a magnetic attraction as centres of globally-connected industrial and financial action.

2. *Japan*: This is a major world economy with powerful industry, a strong and distinct culture, and a capacity for large-scale organization to world standards. Moreover, there is diminishing government–business interdependence.

3. *The Advanced North-East*: Korea and Taiwan have striven to follow in Japan's path as industrial powerhouses. They remain culturally distinct from Japan and from each other, and are very effective on the global stage. They are each now transiting from an earlier phase as government-guided developmental states.

4. *Emerging South East Asia*: Indonesia, Malaysia, Thailand, and the Philippines. Resource-rich and heavily populated (except Malaysia), these medium-wealth economies have a variety of colonial heritages (except Thailand) and religions (Islam, Buddhism, Catholicism, and Animism). They also have economically significant ethnic Chinese minorities. Crony capitalism varies, and social trust is generally low. Growth is now flowing from administrative improvements.

5. *Large post-socialist states*: China, India, Vietnam. These historically recent versions of Marxist states are now at varying stages of transition towards open societies and free-market competition. Government control, bureaucracy, and corruption counterbalance vibrant private sectors.

# SAME BED, DIFFERENT DREAMS

A common feature in international business practice is that the people who establish cross-cultural agreements such as joint ventures are the head-office lawyers and accountants who set up the arrangements. In doing so, they concentrate on their natural priorities in legal and financial contracts. The full exchange of 'meanings' understood by each side only appears later as the practitioners take over from the planners. At this point—often several trading seasons later—previously unexplained assumptions come to the surface, and people discover that the agreement did not penetrate to include the core purposes of the venture. The tensions that then arise lie behind the high failure rate, with the average joint venture experiencing 'joint venture decay' within about six years.

In negotiating such agreements, and especially where strategic decision-making power is shared, care needs to be taken to ensure the likelihood of 'same bed, same dreams'. At the heart of this negotiating challenge is understanding how each side makes sense for itself of the reasons for the existence of their firm. Even though such perceptions may be shared among their senior executives, this does not mean that they are openly discussed. They are usually just implicit. They are part of the firm's culture, and how people are programmed over years to behave towards their achievement; otherwise, they would not have got to where they are in the boardroom.

To provide an introductory insight into these differences, it is possible to take from research some simplified summary pictures of executive mindsets as they vary between business systems. They represent commonly expressed answers to the question, 'Why does your firm exist'?

*Japan.* The firm is a community, embracing managers, employees, buyers, suppliers, and the wider society it serves. The essential priority is to take care of employees. Shareholders are kept at some distance.

*Korea.* The large *chaebol* have emerged from a history of serving the nation's growth by achieving global success, with government sponsorship. They are now pursuing rational competitive performance as more independent actors, but are subject to contestation and suspicion from labour and society at large. Loyalty to employees is lower than in Japan. Family control remains typical.

*Regional ethnic Chinese.* Almost always family-owned, the aim of the firm is to accumulate family wealth and later bestow charity, which in turn bestows status. Secretiveness and pyramids of controlling shareholdings are common, as is the co-option of political support where necessary. Professionalism is usually subservient, and in most cases power is highly centralized and personalized.

*Anglo-Saxon.* Driven by shareholder value, the firm is rational and professional. It is also impersonal, with changing executives. Its challenges include surrounding personalism and uncertainty.

In practice in the region, government involvement in the economy is often strong and has an influence on firms' purposes, usually seeing them as instruments of national development. State capitalism is quite visible in China, Vietnam, Malaysia, Singapore, Laos, and India, with the widespread addition of cronyism and the temptations of predation; the latter is reaching very high levels, especially in Indonesia and the Philippines. The pattern of its expression varies: in China and Vietnam through state ownership and direct involvement, in Singapore through sovereign wealth funds and government-linked companies, in Hong Kong via co-opted oligopoly, in India via ownership and licensing. The free-market capitalism in which many external firms evolved in the West is not a universal condition, either in practice or in terms of ideals. This is a key lesson for new arrivals.

As a broad statement to practitioners engaging in negotiations, it is useful to come to terms with the fact that across the table in much of Asia are likely to sit interests of either family-wealth accumulation, or state backing, or both. These will add complexity to the core purposes shared among the team on the other side of the table and possibly will not be brought out into the open.

# TRUST AND MISTRUST

Arguably the most significant difference between the advanced economies of the West and both the advanced and advancing economies of Asia is the way trust is handled. Along with political participation (with which it is connected), high trust is the key to becoming a modern society. Achievement of modernity releases both innovative energy and reliable cooperation. Without trust and political empowerment, economic machines such as that of China eventually slow down. Their firms may resort to borrowing what is needed by incorporating it in various ways (alliancing, copying, leaving their home bases, active learning), or they may invent a new version of modernity. We shall see.

The key practical lesson here is that many Asian firms seek something out of alliances beyond the sharing of activity and the pooling of benefits. They need to acquire, and then protect as possessions, new sources of competence for their longer-term evolution, and they are often in societies where these are hard to find. In many cultures, their recent industrial histories have taught them to compete hard to survive, and to be responsible first to themselves in this process of acquisition. Although this is a universal basic rule of business, the intensity of its espousal tends to be higher when poverty remains recent in the memory.

Whatever the next few decades bring, it is unlikely that the rules of human nature will themselves change. The instincts and responses surrounding trust and cooperation are genetic. In essence, you do business with people you know, until a point comes when you have reason to trust others. The first stage rests on personalistic trust; the second stage on institutionalized trust. The second stage is reached slowly as society (through both top-down government imposition and bottom-up citizen initiatives) creates rules that work to govern behaviour and make it predictable. Once you can trust strangers, economic exchange knows no limits and growth explodes. All societies that are rich in per capita wealth have both forms of trust. Those societies still poor in per capita terms have only the first kind. Many are working on the challenge. The real dilemma for autocracies is that the sharing of power, even though necessary, is deeply resisted. Its key is that bottom-up contribution will not work without political empowerment, hence the dilemma of the post-Communist autocracies.

No other issue so divides business systems. It introduces severe challenges for organizations straddling the boundary. Managers need great elasticity in such circumstances, and organizations, too, need the tolerance of maturity and understanding.

The world of personalistic trust is one in which corporate ownership tends to be with a family, and power is normally concentrated in one big boss representing that family. In the long term, this is not a stable structure unless the culture has a way of handling transition of authority from one generation to another. The Japanese do, and consequently have the world's longest-lasting organizations. The Chinese do not, and their large organizations are notoriously likely to break up at the point of transition, often losing half their stock-market value.

Prior to that pitfall, however, the large Chinese and Korean family conglomerates of the region have overriding strengths in certain industries: they can make decisions fast, can aggregate large amounts of risk capital on their networks, can build stable alliances, and can make long-term strategic bets without too much shareholder pressure. The *chaebol* are also advancing fast towards modernity. Large ethnic firms often look to non-Asian firms in their alliance-building, but do not normally follow Western norms of behaviour in all regards when managing such alliances. Personalism is favoured over professionalism, the latter being seen as useful but subordinate. The realpolitik in many countries also makes this approach understandable, with government holding much power and often capital.

For outsiders used to the rational allocation of capital, full accountability, clear and open competition on level playing fields, and effective regulation, the world of personalism and high dependence on authority can be disturbing and hard to adjust to. It is more so when the local environment provides no alternative, in other words when the society is unable to fully control and regulate action, or oversee its effective self-regulation. The outsider is not unarmed in this struggle for influence: the foreign firm has bargaining power, often from its technology, managerial skills, global market access, and capacity to raise international capital. High skills are needed to play this game without losing the goodwill on which the relationship is likely to rest.

Here there comes into play a special effect. Most Asian executives are willing to treat most Western executives as honorary insiders, as long as the latter understand the rules and ethics of trust relations. Long-term stable reciprocity can be established without formal contracts, and the flowing together of the personal and the practical can be achieved. It also is a process founded in a strong ethically based Asian civilizational ideal, and must not be seen as anything other than an alternative, as it is not morally inferior. It does however take time, and the worst thing a Western firm can do is to constantly change senior executives and expect them to be able to function at this deep level. Relationships are the architecture of Asian economies. There is not (yet) anything else and there may never be.

The most persistent and problematic outcome of weak institutionalized trust is corruption. It is not a major issue in Singapore, Hong Kong, Japan, or Taiwan. It is moderate in Korea, Malaysia, and Thailand; serious in India, China, and Vietnam; and very serious in Indonesia, Philippines, Laos, and Cambodia. There is a clear correlation between societal wealth and absence of corruption. Although it is thus tied to poverty, and contributes to maintaining that poverty, corruption is only counteracted by heavy investment in societal infrastructure such as laws, regulations, and information access. Only rarely, as in Hong Kong's sudden introduction of the Independent Commission Against Corruption in 1974, does the disease receive an immediate cure.

What is a manager to do in the face of corruption? As the question is about ethics, it is not possible to be specific without appearing to preach. So instead three points of advice are offered that leave choices of action optional, but need careful consideration. First, it is useful to take on board the simple fact that corruption will damage the happiness of the majority of people in a country by restricting progress towards prosperity. Second, it is useful to make a distinction between (a) *facilitation*, which is paying people to accelerate their performance of a duty they are responsible for carrying out anyway (a form of tipping) and (b) *corruption*, which is paying people for doing something they are not supposed to do. It is ethically feasible to judge corruption negatively, while condoning facilitation as local tradition, even though perhaps distasteful or frustrating. Third, the conquering of corruption has usually been achieved by a coalition of forces, such as chambers of commerce, multinationals, government agencies, international bodies such as UN agencies, and business leaders as individuals. The work of an active *bourgeoisie* in making business practice honest and accountable serves as a facilitator of greater business exchange, but also as a demonstration of virtue being applied for the wider good. All managers have some form of access to the expression of such virtue and its promulgation in their host society.

# The People Dimension

Just as it is necessary to deal with people from different mental universes in boardrooms, it is necessary to do the same for employees more generally. Although the mixing of cultures occurs now at all organizational levels, practical issues for managers occur when a hierarchy in one culture sets conditions that apply to employees from another. A benevolent effect may also be available, however. As a broad background feature, it is commonly found that imported systems of management control are regularly welcomed by Asian employees, as they are usually founded in external ideals of empowerment and respect for the individual, whereas Asian managerial traditions (except in Japan) tend to rest on discipline, hierarchy, and autocracy. Still speaking broadly, the challenge for many outside firms is to wean employees away from the dependencies that hierarchy instils, and so release their fuller contributions.

The pattern of ways of employing people in Asia shows a cluster of countries with some shared features at the hierarchical end of the social system of authority. China, Vietnam, India, Malaysia, and to a degree the Philippines, all display five features, namely, (1) top-down control, (2) weak collective representation, (3) decentralized pay determination, (4) high labour flexibility, and (5) high levels of traditional cooperation between management and employees. Outside that set, the variety is such that national systems can only be seen as unique. This variety stems from the particular form of elite that emerged from the country's history, the strength of the institutions that have evolved to affect industrial relations, and the impact of imported ideals such as democracy.

Many firms naturally develop standardized employment systems as they expand globally, and the first practical challenge in regional HR management is the degree of flexibility that should be used in their application. The answer is not simple. Certain aspects of employment stem from workflow design and work practices, as in a factory with production lines. It would seem logical for technology to predominate here and for methods of managing to converge across the region. Other aspects may be heavily influenced by local factors over which the firm has no control, but cannot ignore. Consultation methods, wage negotiations, government labour policies, styles of communication, attitudes to discipline—all of these vary between societies and will influence how systems work. The lesson here is that many of the universalist systems of managing work processes can require extensive adjustment to local conditions. At the same time, it is necessary to acknowledge the sometimes deliberate importing of systems such as ISO 9000 as a means of changing local supervisory habits, and there are cases where the breaking-down of autocracy under such pressures has had productive effects.

# How Money Works

Money often gives the appearance of being used according to universal rules of conduct—that it is available for worthwhile investment; is released on grounds of rationally argued proposals; its price is knowable; and the results of using it are subject to scrutiny. The same goes for the instruments that surround its use—stocks, shares, bonds, audited accounts, and widespread public information. This does not deny other sources like retained earnings or private investments. Nor does it ignore the possibility of government funding. But it does suggest that many assumptions about the sourcing and use of capital that are taken as 'normal' are not normal in many financial contexts of Asia. The supposedly normal are products of Western logics of economic rationality. In turn, these rest on institutions such as level playing-fields, market forces, and transparent fairness that come from the societal philosophies of the Western Enlightenment. The first lesson for outsiders coming to terms with finance in Asia is that alternative rules are in play.

A simple stereotype of these contrasts is:

(a) *Western* law, accounting, and regulation are based on ideals of individualism, equality, and freedom, and the notion that the application of rationality to foster competition on a level playing-field will yield efficiency and progress for the common good. Rationality, being based essentially on measurement and calculation, will work best when firms are clearly defined and bounded, so that their performances are made comparable. This may be achieved by the combination of two forces inducing predictability and hence trust in 'the system', as well as in individuals. The two forces are government top-down pressure to regulate, and professional bottom-up pressure to self-regulate.

(b) *Asian* traditions and institutions often give priority to the group rather than the individual. So too do they emphasize status and relationships as bases for social order. States are often run by elites claiming legitimacy. Formality is often undercut by informality. Calculative rationality is often undercut by opaque organization structures and information weakness. There are often discrepancies in power, wealth, and connections, and they give rise to predatory temptations. There is of course a very wide range of expression of these features, with Hong Kong and Singapore setting world standards for modernity (while being elastic enough to include some of the others).

The responses in the region reflect distinct historical trajectories by society. At the same time, the globalization of capital markets and the penetration of multinationals have each carried deep influences into all Asian societies. This brings with it interfaces that must be straddled by individuals who operate in two worlds. It could be argued that their training in Western-biased formal and professional educational programmes may have left them only half-prepared.

Two practical implications are connected. First, the nature of the Asian alternatives must be understood for the way they are embedded in their societies' traditions and experience. Second, certain new behaviours and dispositions may need to be cultivated so that individuals are able to inhabit both universes. As encouragement, it needs to be added that the hybridizing of systems—as for instance in releasing access to Western capital for investment in Asian ventures, or in applying globally based techniques and experience to emergent Asian organizations—can be highly positive. But it does normally rest on a form of double familiarity. Its practice requires quite refined analytical and social skills.

As practices in this field are so very specific to circumstances, it is not possible to do more than alert the reader to the nature of the alternative contexts, and trust that comprehending them and adapting accordingly will then recommend itself. The main bases for difference are the ways capital is sourced and allocated, its term of temporal availability to firms, the role of government, the use of informal financing, and the quality of surrounding institutions. These features will directly and indirectly shape the behaviours of people using money in that society.

# GOVERNMENT INVOLVEMENT

One of the most crucial skills needed by senior executives in many Asian contexts is the capacity to co-opt political support. For many outsiders this is suspect: surely the job of government is to stand back and let the world of business get on with it? In practice, however, the economies of Asia are extensively shaped by their governments and, if they are not now, it was not long ago that that they were, and the influences subside slowly, often moving into the hands of provincial administrators. For several key countries—China, Vietnam, India, Singapore, Laos, and Cambodia—the government is the dominant influence on economic life and nothing substantial can happen without its involvement. If you consider regional or local government as an intermediary, you can add to the list Indonesia, Malaysia, and the Philippines. Japan, Korea, and Taiwan are now less constrained, but only Hong Kong can claim a government that stands back.

There are two manners in which this influence works. Positively, a government will help its country's development and will engage with outsiders in a form of partnership; the classic case of this is Singapore, but other notable achievers are Thailand, Malaysia, and Taiwan. Negatively, the relationship may be one of protectionism, and of hard-negotiated extraction via foreign direct investment. At worst, the situation descends into corruption.

Successful local firms have often built their wealth on their political skills, and these skills are bargaining chips in international deal-making. Many business heads spend a great deal of effort and money cultivating ministers and heads of state, not only in their own country. The reality of many Asian economies is that they reflect predatory behaviour, using alliances between political leaders and crony capitalists. This phenomenon can transmute over time into respectability, but it often also re-invents itself, as in the cases of China and Vietnam. The key to the problem's persistence is government use of licensing as a means of control, and it is in this regard that a foreign firm may find itself caught up in a web of permission-seeking and obligation-trading.

For an outsider it is necessary to build direct links with a host government in order to avoid dependence on local firms for access to influence. This can be done in two ways, depending on the society. One is to go direct and to make friends with key policy-makers, perhaps using behaviours no longer seen as strategic in the home base. If that is difficult—as when there are language barriers or when government decision-making is carried out in mysterious ways, as in China—then it is worth hiring a senior go-between to represent your interests and negotiate on your behalf. Such a role is well understood and respected in most Asian countries, and it fits logically into a social system in which relationships (rather than formal bureaucracy) are the primary glue holding together patterns of action.

# MODERN AND PRE-MODERN SOCIETIES

As societies evolve historically, most try to improve the lot of their people by increasing general prosperity and in turn the quality of life. The societies that have prospered most so far have followed one core principle and then seen that stimulate two significant consequences. The core principle is encouraging individuals to think for themselves as independent judges of their circumstances. The two significant consequences of that have been the exercise of deep human instincts (i) to exercise curiosity and to learn, and (ii) to cooperate voluntarily with others and over time on a large scale. These are the underlying dynamics of the world's political attempts to build societies and economies. The full spectrum of attempts is on display in Asia, from what is one of the world's richest societies in per-capita terms, Singapore, to the starving prison camp that is North Korea.

It is possible to suggest a point of transition where a society moving forward makes a kind of breakthrough, and changes from a condition of restrained to unrestrained progress. In the former condition, an equilibrium often stabilizes in which power is exercised by a non-elected elite, the mass of the people are sedated by some imposed ideology into accepting that, and elite members usually set about extracting the society's economic surplus for themselves. This has been the situation in China and Vietnam (except in sectors where private initiative came to be released) and Burma. It was for some decades (and in adjusted form still remains) the condition of Indonesia, the Philippines, and, some argue, India. It also occurs in pockets, such as certain industries, in other environments.

The modern condition achieved by prosperous societies works via a different equilibrium: a government widely seen as legitimate, an accepted ideal of balanced progress, and a rational and openly competitive economy favouring no interest group.

The contrasts between modern and pre-modern societies are more than just theoretically interesting. The growth of societies historically is essentially a story of varying ways of making the transition, and the region contains a wide range of living examples. At the level of the practising manager, they also define the two worlds in which he or she operates, and especially the two mental universes of the employees: the factory production line and the village house; the ISO guidebook and the *feng shui* consultant.

Two practical points of general applicability emerge when standing between the pre-modern and modern worlds. When local employees are brought across the threshold of a modern factory, they enter a different world. The gap across which they are stretching needs to be acknowledged, and their lifelong embeddedness in another social, technical, and political reality needs to be treated realistically. Second, the systems of a modern enterprise need to be flexible enough to make such a transition easier.

We will close with an anecdote from a factory once visited in Penang. It employed 800 workers, mainly young females from the region's villages. They did micro-welding for electronic components, using microscopes on production lines. Two weeks earlier, the factory had been the scene of a riot and had been wrecked by the workers, and it closed for a week for repairs. The cause had been one worker who screamed suddenly that there was an evil eye in the microscope and it was on her. Within a minute there were evil eyes all over the place and the factory floor was an uproar of flying microscopes and supervisors pinned to the floor under attacking staff. The company bussed them all home, and would do so regularly every weekend afterwards. They also held a ceremony to sacrifice a black he-goat at the corner of the factory. Things returned to normal. A local government report revealed there had been seventy-two such outbreaks in the area in the previous two years.

# INDEX